i.a.	inter alia / unter anderem	*st.ex.*	stock exchange / Börse
i.e.	that is / das heißt	*s.th.*	something / etwas
ind	industry / Industrie	*tax*	taxation / Steuerwesen
ins	insurance / Versicherungswesen	*tech*	technology / Technik
jur	jurisprudence, law / Rechtswesen	*transp*	transportation / Transportwesen
m	masculine / Maskulinum	*UK*	United Kingdom (of Great Britain and Northern Ireland) / Vereinigtes Königreich (von Großbritannien und Nordirland)
manuf	manufacturing / Produktion		
maths	mathematics / Mathematik		
min	mining / Bergbau	*USA*	United States of America / Vereinigte Staaten von Amerika
n	neuter / Neutrum		
obs	obsolete / veraltet	*jmd.*	jemand / someone
o.s.	oneself / sich (selbst, selber)	*jmds.*	jemandes / of someone
pl	plural / Plural	*jmdm.*	jemandem / to someone
plan	planning / Planungswesen	*jmdn.*	jemanden / someone *(Akkusativ/ accusative)*
pol	politics, political / Politik, politisch		
pol ec	political economy / Politische Ökonomie	*s.*	siehe / see
post	postal service / Postwesen	*s. a.*	siehe auch / see also
railw	railways / Eisenbahnwesen		
s.b.	somebody / jemand		
sg	singular / Singular		
s.o.	someone / jemand		
stats	statistics / Statistik		

Wirtschaftswörterbuch
Deutsch – Englisch

Economic Dictionary German – English

With about 50 000 terms

General Editor
Rengasamy Tharmalingam Murugiah

W

Verlag Die Wirtschaft GmbH Berlin · München

Wirtschaftswörterbuch
Deutsch – Englisch

Mit rund 50 000 Fachbegriffen

Herausgeber
Rengasamy Tharmalingam Murugiah

W

Verlag Die Wirtschaft GmbH Berlin · München

Autoren:
Dr. phil. Rengasamy Tharmalingam Murugiah
Prof. Dr. oec. habil. Hermann Linsel
Prof. Dr. oec. habil. Edwin Stiller
Prof. Dr. oec. habil. Manfred Engert

Herausgeber:
Dr. phil. Rengasamy Tharmalingam Murugiah

Gutachter:
Prof. Dr. oec. Heinz Joswig
John Tarver, M. A. (Oxon)
Dr. oec. Volker Wirth

Lektorin:
Gerlind Schmidt

Redaktionelle Mitarbeit:
Helga Jelitte
Ingeborg Benthin

Murugiah, Rengasamy Tharmalingam:
Wirtschaftswörterbuch Deutsch – Englisch /
Rengasamy Tharmalingam Murugiah. – 1. Aufl. – Berlin:
Verlag Die Wirtschaft GmbH Berlin · München 1993
604 Seiten

ISBN 3-349-00597-7

© Verlag Die Wirtschaft GmbH Berlin · München 1993
Am Friedrichshain 22, O-1055 Berlin
Joseph-Dollinger-Bogen 5, W-8000 München 40
Einbandentwurf: Marlies Hawemann
Typographie: Verlag Die Wirtschaft/Rolf Ortner
Printed in Germany
Satz, Druck und Buchbinderei:
INTERDRUCK Leipzig GmbH

Inhaltsverzeichnis

Contents

Vorwort	7	Preface	7
Benutzungshinweise	9	Directions for Use	9
Alphabetisches Wörterverzeichnis	13	Alphabetical Vocabulary	13

Vorwort

Mit dem freien Verkehr von Kapital und Arbeitskräften, dem freien Warenaustausch sowie der Harmonisierung der Rechtsgrundlagen und Institutionen, die für die Mitte der neunziger Jahre in der Europäischen Gemeinschaft vorgesehen sind, ist ein Wirtschaftswörterbuch, wie es hier vorgelegt wird, eine wertvolle Hilfe und ein wirtschaftlicher, sozialer und politischer Leitfaden. Diese Veröffentlichung erscheint in einer wichtigen Zeit der Umgestaltung der in der Europäischen Gemeinschaft integrierten Wirtschaftsformen. Die verzeichneten 50 000 deutschen Ausgangsbegriffe erstrecken sich auf einen weiten Bereich der Wirtschaft und angrenzender Gebiete wie Statistik, Mathematik, Datenverarbeitung und Rechtswesen. Es ist zu hoffen, daß dieses deutsch-englische Wirtschaftswörterbuch ein zuverlässiges Verständigungsmittel in der Hand des Wirtschaftspraktikers und -theoretikers, des Übersetzers, Dolmetschers und Wirtschaftshistorikers sowie des allgemein an deutscher Wirtschaftsliteratur interessierten Lesers wird. Ferner werden Benutzer des Wörterbuches es besonders in dieser Übergangsperiode nützlich finden, daß eine Reihe wirtschaftlicher Begriffe aus der ehemaligen DDR aufgenommen wurde.
Allgemeine deutsch-englische Wörterbücher können verständlicherweise bei der Übersetzung von Begriffen spezifisch wirtschaftlichen Charakters und Sinngehalts nur unvollkommene Hilfe leisten. Der Schwerpunkt unseres Wörterbuches liegt auf der wirtschaftlichen Bedeutung der Begriffe. Die allgemeine Bedeutung wird in den meisten Fällen vorausgesetzt, denn das Buch wurde mit der Absicht verfaßt, die englischen wirtschaftlichen Bedeutungen zu benennen oder, falls erforderlich, die Wirtschaftsbegriffe englisch zu erläutern. Abgesehen von unterschiedlichen Nebenbedeutungen können sich auch Abstufungen oder Nuancen im wirtschaftlichen Inhalt mancher Begriffe ergeben. In solchen Fällen wurden kurze Erläuterungen *in Kursivdruck* hinzugefügt.

Mein Dank gilt an erster Stelle Herrn Professor Linsel für seine gute Zusammenarbeit, ferner den Herren Professor Stiller und Professor Engert für ihre Unterstützung.

Besonderen Dank schulde ich Herrn Professor Heinz Joswig, der Mitte der sechziger Jahre, als mein alter Freund Diplom-Dolmetscher Horst Jaskorski und ich Material für ein Glossar zu Wirtschaftsbegriffen sammelten, die Vorbereitung des Kleinen Ökonomischen Wörterbuches Deutsch-Englisch tatkräftig voranbrachte. Darüber hinaus möchte ich ihm meinen Dank für seine wertvollen Ratschläge und seine Gutachtertätigkeit auch für das vorliegende Wörterbuch aussprechen. Dank gebührt auch Mr. John Tarver, M. A. (Oxon), und Herrn Dr. Volker Wirth, die ebenfalls als Konsultanten und Gutachter mitwirkten. Schließlich gehen Würdigung und Dank an Frau Gerlind Schmidt, Frau Helga Jelitte und Frau Ingeborg Benthin, Verlag Die Wirtschaft Berlin · München, die für die Druckreife des Manuskripts sorgten.

Hinweise und Vorschläge der Benutzer dieses Wörterbuches sind willkommen und werden mit Dank entgegengenommen.

Rengasamy Tharmalingam Murugiah
Herausgeber

Januar 1993

Preface

With the free flow of capital, labour and goods as well as the harmonization of laws and other institutions envisaged for the mid-nineties in the European Community, an economic dictionary such as this is a valuable aid and guide to economic, social and political relations. This publication appears at a crucial time during the transition period in the economies integrated in the European Community. The 50,000 German terms here encompass a broad area of economics as well as the related fields such as statistics, mathematics, data processing and law. It is hoped that this German-English economic dictionary will serve as a reliable tool for the economist, translator, interpreter and economic historian as well as the interested reader of German economic literature. Further, users of this dictionary will find the inclusion of some important economic terms used in the former GDR useful especially in the transition period.

The general German-English dictionaries, understandably, cannot be expected to be an all-round tool when it comes to translating terms with a specific economic connotation or meaning. In the main our dictionary has laid emphasis on the economic meaning, leaving out in most cases the general meaning since this dictionary has been compiled for the purpose of giving the equivalent or explaining the economic terms in English. Again, apart from differences in connotation, there may be distinctions or nuances in the economic content of some terms. In such cases and for the purpose of clarity a brief explanation has been given *in italics*.

My thanks go, in the first place, to Professor Linsel for his good co-operation and further, to Professor Stiller and Professor Engert for their assistance.

I owe a debt of gratitude to Professor Heinz Joswig who, at a time when my old friend Mr. Horst Jaskorski, Dipl. Dolm., and I were collecting terms for a glossary of economic terms in the mid-sixties, backed up the publication of the Concise Economic Dictionary German-English. Further, I wish to thank him for his advice and for acting as a consultant for this edition as well. Thanks are also due to Mr. John Tarver, M. A. (Oxon), and Dr. Volker Wirth for acting as consultants. Finally, my appreciation and thanks go to Ms. Gerlind Schmidt, Ms. Helga Jelitte and Ms. Ingeborg Benthin, Verlag Die Wirtschaft Berlin · München, for preparing the manuscripts for the printers.

Comments and suggestions from the users of this dictionary will be welcome and will be gratefully acknowledged.

Rengasamy Tharmalingam Murugiah
General Editor

January 1993

Benutzungshinweise

1. Alphabetische Ordnung
Die deutschen Stichwörter sind alphabetisch nach dem Substantiv-Nestprinzip geordnet:
- Grundwort
- mehrgliedrige verbale und präpositionale Ausdrücke
Sie erscheinen bei dem betreffenden Substantiv als Block (durch ◊ gekennzeichnet) und werden alphabetisch in natürlicher Wortfolge geordnet.
- Zusammensetzungen mit dem Grundwort
Sie sind in alphabetischer Reihenfolge angeordnet, wobei voranstehende Adjektive nachgestellt werden. (Die Umstellung wird durch Komma angezeigt.)
- Präpositionen und Artikel werden bei der Alphabetisierung berücksichtigt.
- Singulare und Plurale werden getrennt sortiert.

Beispiel:
Abgabe *f* ... ◊ **gegen ~ von** ...
~, außerordentliche ...
~ einer Verzichterklärung ...
~, ökonomisch begründete ...
Abgabebeschränkungen *fpl* ...
Abgabekurs *m* ...
Abgaben *fpl* ...

- Mit Bindestrich gekoppelte Begriffe werden wie ein zusammengeschriebenes Wort behandelt, unabhängig davon, ob es sich um gekoppelte Wörter, Wortteile oder Einzelbuchstaben handelt.
- Die Umlaute werden bei der Alphabetisierung nicht berücksichtigt.
- Hat ein allgemeines Wort in einem zusammengesetzten Begriff ökonomische Bedeutung, wird dieses Wort *ohne* Äquivalente mit Doppelpunkt versehen und nur der ökonomisch relevante Begriff wird mit Äquivalenten angeführt.

Beispiel:
Abhilfe *f* :
~, gesetzliche ...

- Verben oder Adjektive gelten immer als Einzelstichwörter. Nur wenn mit ihnen Redewendungen gebildet sind, werden sie zum Nestwort.

Beispiel:
begründen ... ◊ **eingehend ~** ...

2. Bedeutung der Zeichen

~ Innerhalb eines Nestes wird das Grundwort durch die *Tilde* wiederholt.
, Das *Komma* trennt echte Synonyme.
; Das *Semikolon* trennt nichtsynonyme bedeutungsähnliche Begriffe.

Beispiel:
sinken to sink, to go down; to fall, to drop ...

1. ...; Fortlaufend numeriert werden *Begriffe,*
2. ...; *die in keiner Beziehung zueinander stehen*
... (Homonyme).

Beispiel:
Emission *f* 1. issue *(bank notes, shares etc.)*; 2. emission *(noxious particles, fumes etc.)*

[ ] Der Begriff in *eckigen Klammern* ersetzt das vorstehende Wort bzw. die vorstehende Wortgruppe.

Beispiel:
Sofortmaßnahme *f* immediate [prompt, urgent] measure = immediate measure, prompt measure, urgent measure

( ) *Runde Klammern* enthalten fakultative Begriffe und mögliche Varianten, die ausgelassen werden können.

Beispiele:
Abschrift *f* transcript(ion) = transcript *oder* transcription
Abzahlungssystem *n* (system of) payment by instalments = system of payment by instalments *oder* payment by instalments

( ) *In runden Klammern kursiv gesetzte Stellen vor den englischen Äquivalenten* sind

Fachgebietsangaben, Angaben zu territorial, umgangssprachlich oder sozialökonomisch begrenzter Verwendung (*s.* Abkürzungsverzeichnis).

Beispiel:
Reaktion *f* reaction, response; *(pol)* reaction

Kursiv in runden Klammern nach den englischen Äquivalenten angeführt sind kurze Erläuterungen, Hinweise und Definitionen.

Beispiel:
Selbstentzündung *f (agric)* self-ignition during storage *(inflammable material etc.)*

Kursiv gesetzt (ohne Klammern) sind die Genusangaben und die Äquivalenzdarstellung von Begriffen, für die im Englischen kein entsprechender Terminus existiert, sondern eine Erläuterung gegeben werden muß.

3. Orthographie
Da in der englischsprachigen Literatur die Getrennt- oder Zusammenschreibung bzw. der Gebrauch des Kopplungsbindestriches bei ein- und derselben Zusammensetzung schwanken, ist in diesem Wörterbuch in der Regel nur eine Schreibvariante aufgeführt.

Arrangement of the dictionary

1. Alphabetical order
The German entries are arranged alphabetically according to key words (usually the noun):
- key word
- idiomatic expressions
  These appear after the appropriate noun as a block (marked ✧) and are arranged in normal alphabetical order.
- combinations with the key word
  These are alphabetically arranged with any preceding adjective following. (This is indicated by a comma.)
- Prepositions and articles with the key word are arranged alphabetically.

- Singulars and plurals are shown separately.
Example:
Abgabe *f* ... ✧ **gegen ~ von**
~, außerordentliche ...
~ einer Verzichterklärung ...
~, ökonomisch begründete ...
Abgabebeschränkungen *fpl* ...
Abgabekurs *m* ...
Abgaben *fpl* ...

- Hyphenated terms are treated like complete words regardless of whether they are compound words, parts of words or single letters.
- The German diaeresis, i.e. "Umlaut", has not been taken into account.
- If a general word has economic significance in a compound term, this word is indicated by a colon *without* an equivalent and only the economically relevant term is given an equivalent.

Example:
Abhilfe *f*:
~, gesetzliche ...

- Verbs and adjectives are always treated as single entries. They are key words only if they are used to form a standard expression.

Example:
begründen ... ✧ **eingehend ~**

2. Signs
~   Within a word group the key word is repeated by a *swung dash*.
,   The *comma* separates actual synonyms.
;   The *semicolon* separates related but not synonymous terms.

Example:
sinken to sink, to go down; to fall, to drop ...

1. ...;   *Unrelated terms* (homonyms) are listed
2. ...;   in numerical order.
...   *Example:*
Emission *f* 1. issue *(bank notes, shares etc.)*; 2. emission *(noxious particles, fumes etc.)*

[ ]   The term in *square brackets* can replace the previous word or word group.

Example:
Sofortmaßnahme *f* immediate [prompt, urgent] measure = immediate measure, prompt measure, urgent measure

( ) *Round brackets* contain optional terms and possible variants which may be omitted.

Example:
Abschrift *f* transcript(ion) = transcript *or* transcription
Abzahlungssystem *n* (system of) payment by instalments = system of payment by instalments *or* payment by instalments

( ) *Words in italics in round brackets* preceding the English equivalents indicate the subject, particular area or the areas of limited colloquial and socio-economic usage (*s.* Abbreviations).

Example:
Reaktion *f* reaction, response; *(pol)* reaction

Italics in round brackets after the English equivalents are brief explanations, hints and definitions.

Example:
Selbstentzündung *f* *(agric)* self-ignition during storage *(inflammable material etc.)*

Italics without any brackets are the generic entries and the equivalents of terms for which there are no appropriate terms in English but which require an explanation.

3. Orthography

Since the separation or hyphening of words is sometimes arbitrary in English, in this dictionary only one variant is given.

A

à at (the price of), at a price of; at a piece; per *(day etc.)*; ... each

A 1 *(erstklassig)* A 1, first quality, top grade *(product etc.)*, excellent

ab 1. effective, as of [from], with effect from; from *(time of departure etc.)*; 2. from that time forward [onward], henceforth; from there on; from that time; from now on; 3. ex, free out of *(warehouse etc.)*

abänderlich alterable; amendable *(parliamentary bill etc.)*; variable; *(jur)* commutable *(sentence)*

abändern to alter, to change; to amend *(parliamentary bill etc.)*; to correct, to rectify *(mistake etc.)*; to revise *(decision etc.)*; to vary; to improve; to modify; *(jur)* to commute *(sentence)*

Abänderung *f* alteration, changing; amendment *(parliamentary bill etc.)*; correction, rectification *(mistake etc.)*; revision *(decision etc.)*; variation; improvement; modification; *(jur)* commutation *(sentence)*

Abänderungsantrag *m* amendment tabled ⋄ **einen ~ einbringen [stellen]** to table an amendment

abänderungsfähig alterable; amendable *(parliamentary bill etc.)*; modifiable

Abänderungsklausel *f* reopening clause

Abänderungspatent *n* reissue patent

Abänderungsplan *m* plan for alterations *(to building etc.)*; proposal for amendment *(to bill etc.)*

Abänderungsvorschlag *m* amendment proposed [suggested]

Abandon *m (ins)* abandonment *(insured goods, ship etc.)*

Abandonerklärung *f* notice of abandonment

Abandonklausel *f* abandonment clause

abandonnieren to abandon *(insured goods, ship etc.)*; to relinquish *(possession, right etc.)*

Abarbeit *f* bonded labour

abarbeiten 1. to work off *(relief, debt etc.)*; 2. to complete (task); 3. to trim, to rough down, to rough-plane *(timber)*; to rough-dress, to scabble *(stone)*; 4. *(d.pr.)* to process, to handle *(instructions)*; to execute *(program)*; to service *(interrupt)*; to act on *(an input)*; **sich ~** to wear, to tire *(o.s. out)*, to exhaust *(o.s.)*

Abarbeiten *n* 1. working off *(relief, debt, etc.)*; 2. completion (of task)

Abarbeitssystem *n* system of bonded labour

Abarbeitung *f* execution, completion *(current instruction etc.)*

Abarbeitungszeit *f* execution time

Abbau *m* 1. reduction *(staff, prices etc.)*; lay off *(workers)*; elimination, removal *(customs barriers)*; lifting *(restrictions)*; 2. demolition, pulling down *(structure)*; dismantling, dismantlement *(machine, factory etc.)*; 3. exploitation, exploiting *(minerals)*

~ der Auftragspolster reducing [working off] the backlog of orders

~ der Zwangs(be)wirtschaft(ung) decontrol *(gradually)*

~ unter Tage *(min)* underground working

abbauen 1. to reduce *(staff, prices etc.)*; to lay off *(workers)*; to eliminate [remove] *(gradually)* *(customs barriers)*; to lift *(restrictions)*; 2. to demolish, to pull down *(structure)*; to dismantle *(machine, factory etc.)*; 3. to exploit, to work *(minerals)*

abbaufähig *(min)* workable, exploitable

Abbaufeld *n (agric)* fallow field

Abbaugebiet *n* mining area

Abbaugerechtigkeit *f* rights to mining

Abbaukoeffizient *m*:

~ der Vorräte coefficient of stock reduction

Abbauland *n* land for clearance *(for mining, construction, roads etc.)*

Abbauleistung *f (min)* working

Abbauplan *m* 1. retrenchment plan *(staff, personnel)*; reducing plan *(excess stocks, claims etc.)*; 2. dismantling plan *(machine, factory etc.)*

Abbauprogramm *n (manuf)* dismantling programme

Abbaurecht *n s.* **Abbaugerechtigkeit**

Abbauverlust *m* mining losses

abbauwürdig *s.* **abbaufähig**

Abbauzeit *f (d.pr.)* discharge time

abberufen to remove, to dismiss *(officials)*; to call home, to recall *(diplomats)*

Abberufung *f* dismissal *(officials)*; recall *(diplomats)*

Abberufungsschreiben *n* letter(s) of recall

abbestellen to countermand *(an order for s.th.)*; to cancel *(reservation etc.)*

Abbestellung *f* countermanding *(of an order for s.th.)*; cancellation *(reservation etc.)*

abbezahlen to pay off

Abbezahlung *f* paying off; payment on account; repayment *(debt)*

Abbildfunktion *f* reflecting function

~ **der Bilanzen und Modelle** reflecting function of balance sheets and models
abbrechen 1. to break off, to discontinue *(relations, negotiations etc.)*; to call off *(strike)*; to stop, to interrupt *(work)*; 2. to demolish, to pull down *(building)*; 3. *(d.pr.)* to terminate, to abort *(instruction etc.)*; to truncate
abbröckeln to crumble away, to drop, to ease off *(rates of exchange)*
Abbröck(e)lung *f* crumbling away, easing off *(rates of exchange)*
Abbruch *m* 1. breaking off, discontinuance *(relations, negotiations etc.)*; calling off *(strike)*; stopping, interrupting, interruption *(work)*; 2. demolition, pulling down *(building)*; 3. *(d.pr.)* termination, abortion *(instruction etc.)* ⋄ **auf ~ verkaufen** to sell as scrap [old material]; to sell at demolition value *(building etc.)*
Abbrucharbeit *f* demolition (work)
Abbruchkosten *pl* demolition costs, costs of demolition
abbruchreif due for demolition
abbuchen to debit (a sum to an account); to write off; *(bank)* to transfer
Abbuchung *f* debit; write-off; *(bank)* transfer ⋄ **durch ~ einziehen** to collect by cashless transfer *(taxes etc.)*
~ **fälliger Steuern und Abgaben** (cashless) transfer of taxes and levies due
Abbuchungsauftrag *m (bank)* transfer order
abdanken to resign office; to resign *(one's post)*; to abdicate *(monarch)*
Abdankung *f* resignation *(from one's office)*; abdication *(monarch)*
abdecken to cover *(overdraft etc.)*; to meet, to settle *(debt)*; to repay *(credit)*; to make up [good] *(deficit)*
Abdeckung *f* 1. settlement *(debt)*; repayment *(credit)*; making up [good] *(deficit)*; 2. (protective) covering
abdingen to haggle over terms of *(purchase)*; to hire *(s.th. from s.o.)*; to do a deal *(with s.o. for s.th.)*
Abdruckrecht *n* copyright
Abendkasse *f* box-office (for evening performance)
Abendkurs(us) *m* evening classes
Abendoberschule *f* evening school (of secondary standard)
Abendschule *f* evening school [classes]
Abendstudium *n* evening classes
abfahren to depart, to leave; to drive off *(car)*; to start, to move off, to pull out *(train)*
Abfahrt *f* departure, start *(train etc.)*
~, **planmäßige** scheduled departure
Abfahrtshafen *m* port of departure

Abfahrtszeit *f* time of departure
Abfall *m* 1. waste products *(production)*; scrap metal; chippings *(stone, metal)*; cuttings, shavings *(wood, metal)*; waste, refuse, garbage *(household, town)*; 2. *(d.pr.)* decrease, decay, drop; fall(-off); release *(relay)*; roll-off *(operational amplifier)*; tail *(pulse)*; decrease *(battery)*
~, **nicht verwertbarer** waste product that cannot be utilized
~, **unverwertbarer** *s.* ~, **nicht verwertbarer**
~, **verwendbarer** waste product that can be recycled
~, **verwertbarer** *s.* ~, **verwendbarer**
~, **wiederverwendungsfähiger** *s.* ~, **verwendbarer**
Abfallbrennstoff *m* waste [refuse] fuel
abfallen 1. to fall [drop] off; to fall away, to desert from *(a party etc.)*; 2. to decrease, to diminish; 3. to come off badly by comparison *(with s.o., s.th.)*; 4. to come off as waste; 5. *(d.pr.)* to decrease, to decay, to drop; to fall (off); to become de-energized; to be disabled *(relay)*; to open *(closed relay contact)*
Abfallindustrie *f* recycling industry
Abfallmaterial *n* waste material
Abfallprodukt *n* waste product
Abfallproduzent *m* producer of waste products
Abfallprozentsatz *m* percentage of waste products
Abfallstoff *m s.* **Abfallmaterial**
Abfallstoffaufbereitung *f* processing [preparing] of waste material
Abfallverwendung *f s.* **Abfallverwertung**
Abfallverwertung *f* utilization of waste (products), waste utilization
Abfallverwertungsanlage *f* waste utilization plant
Abfallwirtschaft *f* 1. utilization of waste products; 2. recycling industry
Abfallzeit *f (d.pr.)* fall time; (pulse) decay time
abfangen 1. to intercept *(news, letter etc.)*; 2. *(build)* to underpin; *(min)* to timber
abfassen to draw up, to make out, to write out *(agreement, report, letter)*; to make out *(contract)*; to draft *(minutes)*
Abfassung *f* drawing up, drafting *(agreement, report, letter etc.)*; wording, formulation *(contract etc.)*; drafting *(minutes)*
abfertigen to dispatch, to expedite *(goods)*; to serve, to attend to *(customers)*; *(cust)* to clear
Abfertigung *f* dispatching, expedition *(goods)*; serving, attending to *(customers)*; *(cust)* clearance
~, **binnenzollamtliche** *s.* ~, **zollamtliche**
~, **direkte** customs clearance while travelling *(in trains, on ships etc.)*
~, **zollamtliche** customs clearance

Abfertigungsbeschränkungen *fpl* forwarding restrictions
Abfertigungsgebühr *f* forwarding charges
Abfertigungshilfsstelle *f* branch dispatch office
Abfertigungsschein *m (com)* dispatch note; waybill; *(cust)* customs declaration (form)
Abfertigungsstelle *f* dispatch office
Abfertigungsunterlagen *fpl* clearance papers
Abfertigungsverfahren *n* procedure of clearance; *(cust)* clearance
Abfertigungsvorschriften *fpl* dispatch rules; customs regulations
Abfertigungszeit *f* dispatching [handling] time; *(cust)* clearance time; check-in time *(airport)*
abfinden to satisfy, to pay off, to compound with *(creditors)*; to make a settlement *(upon s.th.)*; to buy out [off] *(partners)*; to compensate, to indemnify
Abfindung *f* satisfaction, paying-off, composition *(creditors)*; settlement; buying out [off] *(partners)*; compensation, indemnification
~, **einmalige** lump sum [one-time payment] as compensation, single payment
Abfindungsbetrag *m s.* **Abfindungssumme**
Abfindungsleistung *f* payment of compensation
Abfindungsmenge *f s.* **Abfindungssumme**
Abfindungssumme *f* (sum of) indemnity [compensation]
Abfindungsvertrag *m* deed of settlement; deed of indemnification [compensation]
Abfindungszahlung *f s.* **Abfindungsleistung**
abflauen to slack(en) off *(business etc.)*; to drop, to weaken, to sag *(prices etc.)*
Abflauen *n* slack(en)ing off *(business etc.)*; sagging *(prices, rates etc.)*; *(st.ex.)* reaction
~ **der Kurse** *(st.ex.)* sagging of rates [prices]
~ **des Marktes** slack(en)ing of the market
abfließen to drain off *(capital, money)*; to flow out, to drain off *(waste water etc.)*
Abfluß *m* draining off, efflux *(capital, money)*; outflow, draining off *(waste water etc.)*
abfordern to demand, to require *(s.th. of/from s.o.)*; *(d.pr.)* to recall *(data)*; *(d.pr.)* to fetch *(from a storage)*
abfragen to question, to examine *(s.o. about s.th.)*; *(d.pr.)* to query, to inquire, to interrogate; to call; to sense; to sample; to scan *(storage area)*
Abfragezeit *f (d.pr.)* interrogation time
Abfuhr *f* removal *(refuse etc.)*; cartage
abführen to pay *(taxes, interest etc.)*
Abfuhrkosten *pl* transport charges; cartage
Abführung *f* payment *(taxes, interest etc.)*
~ **an den Betriebsfonds** payment to the enterprise fund
~ **an den Haushalt** *s.* **Abführungen, haushaltswirksame**

~ **überschüssiger Umlaufmittel** refund of excess capital *(to the budget)*
Abführungen *fpl*:
~, **betriebliche** payments of enterprise *(to the budget, higher organs etc.)*
~, **feste** fixed payments *(to the budget)*
~, **haushaltswirksame** effective payments to the budget
Abführungsnormativ *n* standard rate of payments *(to the budget)*
Abführungsverpflichtung *f* obligation to make payments *(to the budget)*
Abgabe *f* 1. *(fin)* tax, duty; levy; payment; 2. delivery *(letters, goods etc.)*; 3. sale, selling; 4. *(d.pr.)* output; delivery; release; read-out; 5. counter *(luggage etc.)* ◊ **gegen ~ von** upon delivery of
~, **außerordentliche** supplementary [additional] levy
~ **einer Einkommensteuererklärung** filing of an income tax return
~ **einer Erklärung** issue of a statement
~ **einer Verzichterklärung** signing of a waiver
~, **ökonomisch begründete** economically justified tax [duty, levy]
~, **produktgebundene** levy on highly-priced products
Abgabebeschränkungen *fpl* sales restrictions
Abgabedruck *m (st.ex.)* sales pressure
Abgabekurs *m (st.ex.)* issue price [rate]
Abgabematerial *n (st.ex.)* stock offered, offerings
Abgaben *fpl*:
◊ ~ **erheben** *s.* **mit ~ belegen; frei von ~** exempt from taxes, tax-free, duty-free; **mit ~ belegen** to impose taxes [levies]
~, **direkte** direct taxes
~, **erpreßte** exaction(s)
~, **fixe** fixed taxes [duties, levies]
~, **gewerbliche** industrial taxes [levies]
~, **innere** internal taxes [levies]
~, **öffentliche** rates and taxes
~, **rückständige** arrears in taxes [levies]
~, **soziale** social security contributions
~, **spezielle** special taxes and levies
~, **staatliche** *s.* ~, **öffentliche**
~, **städtische** town rates
Abgabenanalyse *f* analysis of state revenues
Abgabenbefreiung *f* exemption from payment of taxes
abgabenfrei exempt from taxes, tax-free, duty-free
Abgabenfreiheit *f s.* **Abgabenbefreiung**
Abgabenhoheit *f* authority [right] to collect taxes and levies
Abgabenkontrolle *f* checking of taxes and levies
Abgabenordnung *f* tax regulations

abgabenpflichtig taxable; rateable, assessable
Abgabenplanung *f* planning of taxes and levies
Abgabensatz *m* tax rate, rate of taxes [duties, levies]
Abgabenstrafrecht *n* criminal law of taxes and levies
Abgabensystem *n* system of taxes and levies
Abgabenverkürzung *f* tax-evasion
Abgabenverteilung *f* 1. allocation of revenue; 2. graduation of tax(ation)
Abgabenverwaltung *f* administration of taxes and levies
Abgabenwesen *n* system of taxes and levies
Abgabepreis *m* delivery price; issue price *(shares)*
Abgabetermin *m* (last) date of delivery
Abgang *m* 1. departure; start *(vehicle)*; sailing *(ship)*; dispatch *(mail etc.)*; 2. waste, wastage, loss; depreciation, loss in value *(owing to damage or waste)*; reduction, decrease, loss *(stocks)*; 3. leakage, escape *(liquid, gas)*
~ **an Beständen** reduction [decrease, loss] in stocks
~ **von Arbeitskräften** outflow [drain] of labour force [manpower]; decrease [reduction] of labour force [manpower]
~ **von Arbeitskräften, natürlicher** natural outflow of labour force [manpower] *(following retirement etc.)*
Abgänge *mpl* 1. losses *(balance sheet)*; 2. sales
~ **von Schülern und Studenten, vorzeitige** drop-outs
abgängig missing, deficient
Abgangsbahnhof *m* station of dispatch *(goods)*; station of departure
Abgangsentschädigung *f* severance pay
Abgangshafen *m* port of sailing
Abgangsvergütung *f s.* **Abgangsentschädigung**
Abgangswahrscheinlichkeit *f* probability of withdrawal *(from a statistical universe)*
Abgangszeit *f* time of departure *(train, vehicle)*; time of sailing *(ship)*; time of dispatch *(telegram)*
Abgas *n* exhaust gas; *(ind)* waste [flue] gas
abgeben 1. to deliver, to hand over *(letter, parcel etc.)*; 2. to pass, to transmit *(documents to other authorities etc.)*; 3. to give *(an expert opinion etc.)*; 4. to pay, to contribute *(tax etc.)*; 5. to draw (upon) *(bill etc.)*; to sell, to supply, to furnish *(goods etc.)*; to dispose of *(stock etc.)*; 6. to give up, to part with, to concede, to cede *(functions, office etc.)*; 7. to give off [out], to emit, to radiate *(heat etc.)*; 8. *(d.pr.)* to supply, to deliver, to issue
abgehen 1. to depart, to leave, to start; to sail away *(ship)*; to leave (station) *(train)*; 2. to be dispatched *(letter, message etc.)*; 3. to sell (readily), to find a ready sale; to be in great demand *(goods etc.)*; 4. to alter, to change *(one's opinion etc.)*; 5. to be deducted, to be taken off *(sum from the total)*
abgehoben cashed, collected *(money, dividends etc.)*
abgelagert matured *(wine etc.)*; seasoned *(wood etc.)*; deposited *(sediment etc.)*
abgelaufen expired, elapsed *(appointed period etc.)*; due, mature *(bill etc.)* ◇ **noch nicht ~** unexpired, not elapsed *(appointed period etc.)*; not due, still valid *(bill etc.)*
Abgeld *n* disagio, discount
abgelegen remote, distant, out-of-the-way *(place)*
abgelten to settle obligations in full; to make full payment *(for s.th.)*; to satisfy *(claim)*
Abgeltung *f* settlement of obligations; compensation; satisfaction *(claim)*
Abgeltungsbetrag *m* amount settled, compensation
Abgeltungsdarleh(e)n *n* redemption loan
abgenutzt worn out, used up
Abgeordnetenhaus *n* house of deputies; parliament; *(UK)* House of Commons; *(USA)* House of Representatives
Abgeordnetenkammer *f s.* **Abgeordnetenhaus**
Abgeordneter *m* member of parliament, deputy
abgerechnet settled (up) *(account)*; deducted, reduced ◇ **nicht ~** unsettled *(account)*; not deducted, not reduced
abgerundet in round figures
Abgesandter *m* delegate
abgeschätzt rated *(s.o.'s ability etc.)*; assessed *(value of property etc.)* ◇ **nicht ~** unvalued
abgeschlossen 1. settled, agreed *(contract etc.)*; completed *(work)*; 2. self-contained *(flat)*
abgeschrieben depreciated; written off
abgesichert secured; covered ◇ **finanziell ~** financially secured; **materiell ~** materially secured; materially covered *(loan etc.)*; **vertraglich ~** covered by contract
abgestimmt co-ordinated *(plan etc.)*; timed *(programme etc.)*
abgewirtschaftet run down *(business etc.)*
abgezeichnet initialled, signed
abgleichen to equalize, to adjust, to balance *(weights, values etc.)*
Abgleichung *f* equalization, adjustment, balancing *(weights, values etc.)*
abgleiten to slide down, to decline *(exchange rates etc.)*
abgrenzen 1. to delimit, to demarcate, to mark the boundaries of *(territory etc.)*, to mark out *(field etc.)*; 2. to define *(powers, rights, duties etc.)*, to circumscribe *(powers, field of action)*
Abgrenzung *f* 1. delimitation, demarcation, marking of the boundaries *(territory etc.)*,

marking out of *(field etc.)*; 2. definition *(powers, rights, duties etc.)*, circumscription *(powers, field of action)*
~ **der Hoheitsgewässer** demarcation [delimitation] of territorial waters
~, **zeitliche** chronological delimitation
Abgrenzungskonten *npl (acc)* accruels and deferrals
Abgrenzungsposten *mpl (acc)* items in deferrals and accruals
~, **antizipative** *(acc)* deferrals
~, **transitorische** *(acc)* transitory items
abhaken to tick [*(Am)* check] off *(list, items in list etc.)*, to tick *(name etc.)*, *(Am)* to check [mark] against *(name etc.)*
abhalten 1. to keep off *(person etc.)*; to restrain *(s.o. from doing s.th.)*; 2. to hold *(meeting, auction etc.)*; to celebrate *(event etc.)*
abhandeln 1. to handle *(business etc.)*; to discuss, to deal with, to treat *(subject etc.)*, to dissertate on; 2. to purchase *(s.th. from s.o.)*; to beat down, to knock off *(price of s.th.)*
Abhandlung *f* treatise; paper *(written discourse)*; dissertation *(non-doctorial thesis)*; (oral) discourse, discussion *(on/about/upon s.th.)*
abhängen to depend *(on/upon s.th.)*
abhängig dependent *(on/upon s.th.)*
Abhängigkeit *f* dependence *(on/upon s.th.)*
~, **direkte** direct dependence
~, **gegenseitige** interdependence
~, **indirekte** indirect dependence
~, **koloniale** colonial dependence
~, **lineare** *(maths)* linear dependence
~, **neokoloniale** neocolonial dependence
~, **ökonomische** economic dependence
~, **organisationsbedingte** dependence on organization *(production process etc.)*
~, **politische** political dependence
~, **stochastische** *(stats)* stochastic dependence
~, **strukturelle** structural dependence
~, **technologische** technological dependence, dependence in technology
~, **vollständige** total dependence
Abhängigkeitsverhältnisse *npl* dependent relationship(s), relationship(s) of dependence; conditions of dependence
abheben 1. *(fin)* to withdraw *(money from an account)*; to collect *(dividend)*; 2. to take off *(plane)*; 3. *(d.pr.)* to lift off
Abheben *n (d.pr.)* lift-off
Abhebung *f (fin)* withdrawal *(of money from an account)*; collection *(dividend)*
Abhebungen *fpl*:
~, **tägliche** *(fin)* day-to-day withdrawals
Abhebungsbefugnis *f (fin)* right of withdrawal
Abhebungsbeschränkungen *fpl (fin)* withdrawal restrictions

Abhebungserfordernisse *npl (fin)* withdrawal requirements
abheften to file (away)
Abhilfe *f* remedy, redress, relief; correction *(mistake)*
~, **gesetzliche** (legal) remedy, redress, relief
Abhilfemaßnahmen *fpl* remedial measures
Ab-Hof-Preis *m* ex-farm price
Abholausweis *m* identity card for collecting *(documents etc.)*
Abholdienst *m* pick-up service *(persons)*; collecting service *(mail etc.)*
abholen to fetch, to collect *(letter etc.)*; to pick up *(persons)* ◊ ~ **lassen** to send for *(s.o., s.th.)*
Abholung *f* collection *(goods)*; fetching, pick-up *(persons)*
Abitur *n* final examination *(equivalent to matriculation examination)*, 12-year comprehensive school leaving examination
Abiturklasse *f* matriculation class, final class of comprehensive school
abkaufen to buy, to purchase *(s.th. from s.o.)*
Abkäufer *m* buyer, purchaser
abkommen 1. to get away from, to get off *(one's route, subject etc.)*; to lose *(one's way)*; to get rid of *(idea, habit etc.)*; 2. to go out *(fashion etc.)*; to fall into disuse, to die out *(customs)*
Abkommen *n* agreement, convention, treaty; composition, settlement
~, **bilaterales** bilateral agreement
~, **finanzielles** financial agreement
~, **gültiges** valid agreement
~, **gütliches** amicable settlement
~, **internationales** international agreement [convention, treaty]
~, **laufendes** standing agreement
~, **multilaterales** multilateral agreement
~, **mündliches** oral agreement
~ **über technische Hilfe** agreement on technical assistance
~ **über wirtschaftliche Zusammenarbeit** agreement on economic co-operation
~, **unwiderrufliches** binding agreement
~, **vorläufiges** provisional agreement
~, **zeitweiliges** temporary agreement
~, **zweiseitiges** *s.* ~, **bilaterales**
Abkommensklausel *f* (agreement) clause
Abkommenskonto *n* account of trade agreement
Abkommensland *n* country party to an agreement, partner country
Abkommenslieferung *f* delivery according to contract [agreement]
Abkommenspartner *m* party [partner] to an agreement
Abkommensverlängerung *f* extension of an agreement

Abkommenswährung *f* agreed currency
Abkunft *f* origin
Abkupplung *f* disassociation *(from a group, institution etc.)*
Abladedokumente *npl* unloading papers
Abladefrist *f* time allowed for unloading [discharging] *(goods)*
Abladegebühr *f* handling charges
Abladegeschäft *n* unloading [shipping] business
Abladegewicht *n* shipping weight
Abladehafen *m* port of discharge
Abladeklausel *f* shipping clause
Abladekommando *n* team of dockers [unloading workers]
Abladekonnossement *n* shipped bill of lading
Abladekosten *pl* unloading [discharging] costs
abladen to unload, to discharge *(from a vehicle)*; to ship
Abladeplatz *m* 1. unloading platform [rack]; 2. port of discharge; 3. dumping ground *(refuse etc.)*
Ablader *m* shipper
Ablage *f* 1. depot, store, depository, repository; 2. filing (rack) *(papers, documents etc.)*; 3. cloak-room *(theatre, restaurant etc.)*
ablagern to mature *(wine etc.)*; to season *(wood etc.)*; to deposit *(sediments etc.)*
Ablagerung *f* sediment; deposit; layer
ablassen 1. to let *s.o.* have *s.th.*; *(com)* to sell *s.th.* to *s.o.*; 2. to give a discount, to make an allowance
Ablauf *m* 1. course *(of production)*; 2. expiration *(passport etc.)*; maturity *(bill)*; 3. *(d.pr.)* operation; execution, run *(program)*; process, procedure; flow; sequence *(operation)*; job *(computer system)* ◊ **bei ~** at the time of expiration; **nach ~ des Vertrages** on expiration of the contract; **nach ~ von** at the end of
~ der Amtsperiode expiration of the term of office
~ der Kündigungsfrist fulfillment of the period of notice
~ der Schutzrechte expiration of patent [property, protective] rights; expiration of trademark rights
~ einer Frist lapse of time
~ eines Patents expiry of a patent
~ eines Zeitraumes passage of a period
~, technologischer (course of) technological process
~, terminlicher flow [process] according to schedule
~, zeitlicher sequence flow over time *(work, production etc.)*
Ablaufdiagramm *n* flow diagram
ablaufen to expire, to run down [out]; to lapse *(time)*

Ablauffrist *f* period [date] of expiration *(agreement etc.)*; time of payment, (date of) maturity *(bill)*
Ablaufmodell *n* flow model
Ablauforganisation *f* organization of work [production] flow
Ablaufplan *m* timing schedule; working schedule; timetable
Ablaufplanung *f* planning of work [production] flow
Ablaufschema *n s.* **Ablaufdiagramm**
Ablauftermin *m s.* **Ablauffrist**
ablegen to (put on) file *(letters etc.)*; to pass *(examination)*; to render *(account)*; to take *(an oath)*
ablehnen to refuse, to reject, to decline *(responsibility, liability, obligation, commission)*; to turn down *(offer)*; *(jur)* to dismiss
Ablehnung *f* refusal, rejection, declining *(responsibility, liability, obligation, commission)*; non-acceptance, turning down *(offer)*; *(jur)* dismissal
~ einer Gerichtsbarkeit refusal to acknowledge a jurisdiction
Ablehnungsbereich *m (stats)* rejection region
Ablehn(ungs)grenze *f (stats)* lot tolerance fraction [per cent] defective
Ablehnungslinie *f (stats)* rejection line
Ablehnungszahl *f (stats)* rejection number
ableiten 1. to derive, to deduce, to educe *(information etc.)*; 2. *(d.pr.)* to drain; to dissipate; to remove
Ableitung *f* 1. derivation; *(d.pr.)* drainage *(of a charge)*; leakage; 3. derivative *(function)*
Ablieferer *m* bearer *(letters etc.)*; supplier, furnisher, purveyor *(goods etc.)*; *(com)* deliverer *(documents, stocks etc.)*
abliefern to deliver, to supply, to furnish, to hand over
Ablieferung *f* delivery, delivering, supply(ing), furnishing, handing over
Ablieferungsbescheid *m* delivery quota bill
Ablieferungsbuch *n* delivery book
Ablieferungsfrist *f* delivery date, period allowed for delivery
Ablieferungsgewicht *n* delivery weight
Ablieferungskontingent *n* delivery quota
Ablieferungspflicht *f* compulsory deliveries
Ablieferungsprämie *f* delivery bonus; bounty
Ablieferungsschein *m* delivery note, receipt [certificate] of delivery
Ablieferungssoll *n* delivery quota
Ablieferungstermin *m* date of delivery
Ablieferungszeit *f* time of delivery
ablösbar *(fin)* redeemable *(stock, annuity etc.)*
Ablösbarkeit *f (fin)* redeemability *(stock, annuity etc.)*

ablösen to discharge *(obligation, debt)*; to redeem *(annuity, pledge)*; to settle, to pay *(debt)*; to replace, to supersede; to dismiss *(staff)*
Ablösung *f* discharge *(obligation, debt)*; redemption *(annuity, pledge)*; settlement, payment *(debt)*; replacement, supersession; dismissal *(staff)*
Ablösungsanleihe *f* redemption loan
Ablösungsfinanzierung *f* financing of redemption
Ablösungsfonds *m* sinking [*(Am)* redemption] fund
Ablösungsschicht *f* oncoming shift
Ablösungssumme *f* amount of redemption, redemption amount
Ablösungswert *m* *(ins)* surrender value *(of policy)*
abmachen to arrange, to settle *(business etc.)*; to agree on *(price, course of action etc.)*; to conclude *(bargain etc.)*
Abmachung *f* arrangement, settlement *(business etc.)*; agreement *(price, course of action etc.)*; conclusion *(bargain etc.)*
~, **schriftliche** written agreement
abmelden to cancel, to call off *(visit, engagement etc.)*; to withdraw *(name from list of participants, candidates etc.)*; to notify *(authorities etc.)* of one's departure
Abmeldung *f* cancellation, calling off *(visit, engagement etc.)*; withdrawal *(from list of participants, candidates etc.)*; notification of departure *(authorities etc.)*
abmeßbar measurable, mensurable
Abmeßbarkeit *f* measurability, mensurability
abmessen to measure; to measure out *(corn, liquid etc.)*; to survey *(land)*; to measure (off) *(clothes etc.)*; (build) to level *(wall etc.)*
Abmessung *f* 1. measuring, measurement; surveying *(land)*; *(build)* levelling; 2. dimension, size
abmustern to pay off, to discharge *(ship's crew etc.)*
Abnahme *f* 1. purchase, buying, taking (delivery of) *(goods)*; 2. acceptance *(machine etc. after inspection)*; taking over *(machine, bridge etc.)*; 3. diminishing, decreasing, lessening; depreciation *(in value)*; declining *(strength, power etc.)*; dropping, falling away *(demand)*; shrinkage, dwindling *(resources etc.)* ◊ **die ~ verweigern** to refuse to accept (delivery of) *(goods)*; to dishonour *(bill, draft etc.)*
Abnahmebedingung *f* condition of acceptance
Abnahmebescheinigung *f* acknowledgement of receipt
Abnahmebestätigung *f* confirmation of acceptance
Abnahmefrist *f* (final) date of acceptance
Abnahmeklausel *f* acceptance clause

Abnahmekontrolle *f* (final) test before acceptance *(products, industrial plants etc.)*; quality control [inspection] *(manufactured goods etc.)*
Abnahmemenge *f* quantity of purchase
Abnahmepflicht *f* obligation to accept delivery *(goods etc.)*
Abnahmeprotokoll *n* report on [of] acceptance *(after checking quality and quantity of goods to be delivered)*
Abnahmeprüfung *f* acceptance inspection
~ **mittels qualitativer Merkmale** *(stats)* inspection by attribute
~ **mittels quantitativer Merkmale** *(stats)* variables inspection
~, **normale** normal inspection
Abnahmeschein *m* *(fin)* receipt *(shares etc.)*; *(com)* acceptance certificate
Abnahme- und Gütebestimmungen *fpl* (technical) quality specifications
Abnahmeuntersuchung *f s.* **Abnahmekontrolle**
Abnahmeverweigerung *f* non-acceptance; refusal to accept (delivery of) *(goods)*; dishonouring *(bill, draft etc.)*
Abnahmeverweigerungsrecht *n* right of rejection *(of articles not up to specification)*
Abnahmevorschrift *f* *(com)* specifications for acceptance, quality specifications
abnehmen 1. to purchase, to buy, to take (delivery of) *(goods)*; 2. to accept *(machine etc. after inspection)*; to take over *(machine, bridge etc.)*; 3. to diminish, to decrease, to lessen; to depreciate *(in value)*; to decline *(strength, power etc.)*; to drop, to fall away *(demand)*; to shrink, to dwindle *(resources etc.)*
Abnehmer *m* 1. buyer, purchaser, customer; user *(electricity etc.)*; consumer; 2. quality inspector
~, **gewerblicher** purchaser [customer] (in trade), wholesale purchaser [customer] *(for production etc.)*
~, **privater** private purchaser [customer, buyer]
Abnehmerbetrieb *m* receiving [purchasing] enterprise
Abnehmergruppe *f* group of purchasers [buyers, customers]; consumer group, consumers
Abnehmerkreis *m s.* **Abnehmergruppe**
Abnehmerland *n* importing [customer] country
abnutzen, sich to use up, to wear out (by use)
Abnutzung *f* wear and tear *(machinery etc.)*; abrasion *(coin)*; depreciation *(in value)*
Abnutzungserscheinung *f* sign of wear; sign [symptom] of attrition
Abnutzungsgröße *f* degree of wear
Abnutzungssatz *m* rate of depreciation *(machinery etc.)*; annual yield *(forest)*
Abonnement *n* subscription *(newspapers etc.)*
Abonnementsliste *f* list of subscribers

Abonnementspreis *m* subscription price [rate] *(newspapers etc.)*; reduced price *(for regular customers of restaurants etc.)*
Abonnent *m* subscriber *(newspapers etc.)*
abonnieren to subscribe *(to newspapers etc.)*
Abpackanlage *f* packing plant
abpacken to pack (up) *(goods etc.)*
Abprodukt *n* waste product
~, **absatzfähiges** saleable [marketable] waste product
~, **industrielles** industrial waste product
~, **wiederverwendungsfähiges** reusable waste product
abproduktarm low-waste *(technology etc.)*
abproduktfrei non-waste *(technology etc.)*
Abraum *m (min)* rubbish, dump-heap; overburden *(of a seam)*
Abraumarbeiter *m (min)* clearing pitman
abrechenbar calculable
abrechnen to settle (up) *(accounts)*; to deduct
Abrechnung *f* settlement, clearing *(accounts)*; accounting *(cash)*; deduction
~ **der Banken untereinander** bank clearing
~, **endgültige** final settlement
~, **erzeugnisbezogene** cost accounting of products
~, **innerbetriebliche** internal enterprise accounting
~, **monatliche** monthly accounting
~, **statistische** statistical accounting
Abrechnungsbestand *m* accounting stock
Abrechnungsblatt *n (acc)* summary sheet
Abrechnungsbogen *m s.* **Abrechnungsblatt**
Abrechnungseinheit *f* accounting unit
Abrechnungsergebnis *n* accounting result
Abrechnungsfrist *f* settling [settlement] period
Abrechnungsinformation *f* information on accounting
Abrechnungskonto *n* settlement [clearing] account
Abrechnungsmethode *f* accounting method, method of accounting
Abrechnungsperiode *f* accounting [settlement] period
Abrechnungsposten *m* item in an account
Abrechnungsstelle *f* clearing house [office]
Abrechnungssystem *n* accounting system, system of accounting
Abrechnungstag *m* settling day
abrechnungstechnisch from the aspect of accounting technique
Abrechnungsverfahren *n* accounting technique [procedure]; procedure of clearing
Abrechnungsverkehr *m* clearing (transactions)
Abrechnungszeitraum *m* settlement [accounting] period; reporting period, period under review

Abriß *m* 1. demolition *(buildings)*; 2. draft, summary, abstract *(document etc.)*; compendium *(science)*; digest *(legal problems etc.)*
Abruf *m* calling in *(of a sum advanced)*; request for delivery *(goods)*; recall *(diplomats etc.)* ⋄ **auf ~** at [on] call
Abrufauftrag *m* order for goods to be delivered on demand, order with provision for staggered deliveries, *(Am)* make-and-take order
abrufen to call up *(capital)*, to call in *(a sum advanced)*; to request delivery *(of goods)*; to recall *(diplomats etc.)*
abrunden to round (off)
Abrundung *f* rounding (off)
abrüsten 1. *(build)* to remove the scaffolding; *(ind)* to take down, to dismantle, to disassemble *(machine etc.)*; 2. to put out of commission *(ship)*; 3. to disarm
Abrüsten *n* 1. removal of the scaffolding; *(ind)* dismantling, disassembling *(machine etc.)*; 2. putting out of commission *(ship)*
Abrüstung *f* disarmament
absacken 1. to put *s.th.* into sacks, to pack *s.th.* in bags; 2. to sink down
Absackmaschine *f* bagging [sacking] machine
Absackwaage *f* bagging and weighing machine
Absage *f* cancellation, calling off *(meeting etc.)*; refusal, declining *(invitation)*
absagen to cancel, to call off *(meeting etc.)*; to refuse, to decline *(invitation)*
Absatz *m* 1. sale, disposal; 2. paragraph
Absatzabkommen *n* marketing agreement
Absatzabteilung *f* sales department, marketing division
Absatzanalyse *f* market analysis
Absatzaufgaben *fpl* tasks [aims] of marketing [sale(s)]
Absatzaufwand *m* marketing costs
Absatzaussichten *fpl* marketing [sales] prospects
absatzbedingt due to marketing
Absatzbereich *m* 1. sales department; 2. marketing [trading] area, outlet
Absatzbeziehungen *fpl* market(ing) relations
Absatzergebnis *n* proceeds from marketing [sales]
absatzfähig marketable, saleable
Absatzförderung *f* promotion of sale(s), sales promotion
Absatzfunktion *f* marketing function *(of an enterprise etc.)*
Absatzgebiet *n* market, marketing [trading] area, outlet
Absatzgenossenschaft *f* marketing co-operative
Absatzgröße *f* volume of sales
~, **optimale** optimal size [volume] of sales
Absatzkartei *f* sales card index
Absatzkette *f* distribution chain

Absatzkontor *n* sales office
Absatzkonzeption *f* marketing scheme
Absatzkosten *pl* marketing [selling, distribution] costs, costs of marketing
Absatzlage *f* market [sales] situation
Absatzlager *n* warehouse, store
Absatzleiter *m* head of the sales department, sales manager
Absatzleitung *f* sales management
Absatzlenkung *f* control(ling) of the market; sales control
Absatzmarkt *m* market(s), outlet
Absatzmethoden *fpl* marketing [selling, distribution] methods
Absatzmöglichkeit *f* market, outlet, opening (for sales/marketing)
Absatzmonopol *n* market [sales] monopoly
Absatzoperation *f* sale(s) transaction)
Absatzorganisation *f* 1. marketing organization; 2. organization of marketing *(as part of the sphere of circulation including the institutional set-up and marketing methods)*
~, innere home marketing organization *(for imported goods)*
Absatzperspektive *f s.* **Absatzaussichten**
Absatzplan *m* marketing [sales] plan
Absatzplanung *f* marketing [sales] planning
Absatzpolitik *f* marketing [sales] policy
Absatzprognose *f* marketing [sales] forecast
Absatzprogramm *n* marketing [sales] programme
Absatzprozeß *m* marketing [sales] process
Absatzreserve *f* reserve stocks for sale
Absatzrisiko *n* sales risk
absatzseitig from the aspect of marketing [sales]
Absatzsicherung *f* securing of markets [sales]
Absatzsortiment *n* range [assortment] of goods for sale [marketing]
Absatzstatistik *f* marketing [sales] statistics
Absatzsteigerung *f* sales increase
Absatzstockung *f* stagnation of the market; flagging [slowing down] of sales
Absatzstrategie *f* marketing [sales] strategy
Absatzstruktur *f* sales structure, kinds of goods sold
Absatzsystem *n* marketing [sales] system
Absatztätigkeit *f* marketing [sales] activities
Absatz- und Bezugsorganisation *f* sales and supplies organization; organization of sales and supplies
Absatz- und Lieferbeziehungen *fpl* sales and delivery relations
Absatzvereinbarung *f* sales agreement
Absatzvolumen *n* amount of sales, amount marketed
Absatzvorbereitung *f* preparatory activities for marketing

Absatzvorrat *m* stock for sales
Absatzwege *mpl* channels of distribution [marketing]; channels for trade
Absatzwerbung *f* (sales) advertising
absatzwirksam affecting [stimulating] sales
abschaffen to abolish, to do away with *(law, tax, office, institution etc.)*; to abrogate, to annul, to repeal, to rescind *(decree etc.)*
Abschaffung *f* abolition, doing away with *(law, tax, office, institution etc.)*; abrogation, annulment, repeal, rescission *(decree etc.)*
abschätzen to estimate *(value, weight, number etc.)*; to assess, to evaluate *(damages, capabilities etc.)*; to appraise *(goods, property etc.)*
Abschätzung *f* estimation *(value, weight, number etc.)*; assessment, evaluation *(damages, capabilities etc.)*; appraisal *(goods, property etc.)*
abschicken to send off, to dispatch; to post, to mail, to forward; to consign, to ship *(goods)*; to remit *(money)*
Abschied *m* 1. departure, farewell; 2. retirement; resignation (from office) ◇ **~ nehmen** 1. to take (one's) leave; 2. to retire; to resign (from office)
Abschiedsbesuch *m* farewell call, parting visit
Abschiedsbrief *m* 1. farewell letter; 2. letter of discharge [dismissal]
Abschiedsessen *n* farewell dinner; valedictory dinner
Abschiedsgesuch *n* request to be retired
Abschiedsrede *f* farewell speech; valedictory address
Abschlag *m* payment by instalments, partial payment *(wages)*; discount, reduction *(prices)* ◇ **auf ~** on account; **auf ~ bezahlen** to pay by instalments; **mit ~ verkaufen** to sell at a reduced price; **mit einem ~ von** at a discount of
abschließen 1. to end, to complete *(work, investigation etc.)*; 2. to sign, to conclude, to finalize *(agreement etc.)*; to contract *(loans)*; to make out *(insurance policy)*; 3. to balance *(accounts)*
Abschluß *m* 1. ending, completion *(work, investigation etc.)*; 2. signing, conclusion, finalization *(agreement etc.)*; contracting *(loans)*; taking out *(insurance policy)*; 3. balancing *(accounts)*
Abschlußbericht *m* closing statement
Abschlußbilanz *f* (annual) balance sheet
Abschlußbogen *m* *(bank)* settlement sheet
Abschlußbuchung *f* balancing entry
Abschlußdatum *n* *(acc)* date of settlement, closing date; date of signing *(contract etc.)*
Abschlußkosten *pl* *(ins)* initial expenses
Abschlußkurs *m* *(st.ex.)* closing price
Abschlußmeldung *f* final report
Abschlußmenge *f* amount agreed upon
Abschlußnota *f* contract note

Abschlußprämie f s. **Abschlußprovision**
Abschlußprovision f (sales) commission; (ins) final commission
Abschlußprüfer m (fin) auditor
Abschlußprüfung f 1. (fin) audit; 2. school leaving examination
Abschlußrechnung f balancing of accounts; final account
Abschlußstichtag m delivery date
Abschlußtabelle f settlement sheet
Abschlußtag m (st.ex.) settling day
Abschlußtermin m s. **Abschlußdatum**
Abschlußübersicht f final review (report); (acc) settlement sheet
Abschlußvergütung f (ins) final commission
Abschlußvertreter m agent, agency
Abschlußvollmacht f full power to conclude contracts
Abschlußvorschriften fpl (acc) rules of balancing
Abschlußwechsel m remittance to balance account
Abschlußzahlung f final payment; final instalment (hire-purchase)
Abschlußzeit(punkt m) f date of signing (contract), date of conclusion (deal, bargain); (acc) date of settlement
Abschnitt m 1. (manuf) production stage; 2. paragraph (contract etc.); part, section (regulations etc.); 3. counterfoil (cheque); 4. (maths) segment
abschnittsweise in sections [portions]
abschöpfen to absorb, to drain off (purchasing power); to skim [siphon] off (profits)
Abschöpfung f absorption, draining off (purchasing power); skimming [siphoning] off (profits); (import) levy (on a product of a third country in the EEC)
~ **von Devisenreserven** absorption of foreign exchange reserves
~ **von Kaufkraft** absorption of income [purchasing power]
Abschöpfungsanleihe f absorptive loan
Abschöpfungsbetrag m amount of purchasing power absorbed; price adjustment levy, (import) levy (on a product of a third country in the EEC)
abschreiben 1. to write off (capital); to cancel, to wipe out (debt); to deduct (sum from amount); to depreciate (value); 2. to copy, to transcribe
Abschreibeversicherung f transport booking insurance (automatically paid by transfer order)
Abschreibung f write-off (capital); cancellation, wiping out (debt); deduction (of a sum from an amount); depreciation (value); (sum allowed for) depreciation
~, **außerordentliche** extraordinary depreciation

~, **beschleunigte** accelerated depreciation
~, **buchmäßige** book-value depreciation
~, **degressive** degressive depreciation
~, **direkte** direct depreciation
~ **einer Kapitalanlage** depreciation on capital
~, **indirekte** indirect depreciation
~, **jährliche** annual depreciation
~, **kalkulatorische** fictitious rate of depreciation (to increase costs)
~, **leistungsbedingte** depreciation depending on probable performance
~, **lineare** linear (rate of) depreciation, straight-line (method of) depreciation
~, **normale** ordinary depreciation
~, **progressive** progressive depreciation
~, **proportionale** s. ~, **lineare**
~, **steuerliche** depreciation for taxation (purposes)
~, **übermäßige** excessive depreciation
~, **unmittelbare** s. ~, **direkte**
~, **verbrauchsbedingte** depreciation through wear and tear
~, **zeitabhängige** depreciation through age
Abschreibungsart f s. **Abschreibungsmethode**
Abschreibungsaufwand m s. **Abschreibungsbetrag**
Abschreibungsausgleich m adjustment of depreciation
Abschreibungsbasis f s. **Abschreibungsgrundlage**
Abschreibungsbetrag m (amount of) depreciation
Abschreibungsfonds m depreciation fund, fund for depreciation
Abschreibungsformel f depreciation formula
Abschreibungsgrundlage f basis of depreciation
Abschreibungskonto n depreciation account
Abschreibungskosten pl depreciation costs
Abschreibungsmethode f method of depreciation
Abschreibungsnorm f depreciation standard
abschreibungspflichtig liable to depreciation
Abschreibungsplan m system of depreciation
Abschreibungspolitik f depreciation policy
Abschreibungspraxis f s. **Abschreibungsmethode**
Abschreibungsquote f amount of depreciation (in absolute numbers)
Abschreibungsrate f rate of depreciation
Abschreibungsreserve f accrued depreciation, depreciation reserve fund
Abschreibungsreservekonto n depreciation reserve account
Abschreibungsrestwert m depreciated (residual) value
Abschreibungsrichtsatz m standard rate of depreciation

Abschreibungsrücklage f s. **Abschreibungsreserve**
Abschreibungsrückstellung f allowance for depreciation *(in balance sheet)*
Abschreibungssatz m s. **Abschreibungsrate**
Abschreibungsstichtag m depreciation date
Abschreibungssumme f s. **Abschreibungsbetrag**
Abschreibungsverfahren n depreciation procedure, procedure of depreciation
Abschreibungsvergünstigung f allowance for depreciation
Abschreibungsverhältnis n ratio of depreciation *(to the value of fixed assets)*
Abschreibungsverlust m loss through depreciation
Abschreibungswert m depreciation value
Abschreibungszeit f period of depreciation
Abschrift f copy *(letter, text etc.)*; transcript(ion) *(speech, notes etc.)*
~, **notariell beglaubigte** certified copy
~, **ordnungsgemäß beglaubigte** authentic copy
Abschwung m levelling off *(business cycle)*
Abschwungphase f recession [depression] stage *(business cycle)*
absenden to send (off), to dispatch, to forward, to consign; to ship; to post, to mail
Absender m sender, dispatcher, forwarder, consignor
Absenderangabe f return address
Absenderanweisung f consignor's instruction
Absendererklärung f consignor's customs declaration
Absenderhaftung f consignor's liability
Absenderverfügung f consignor's disposal
Absendervertrag m dispatch agreement *(long--term agreement between transport company and consignor for planning transport capacities needed)*
Absendestelle f forwarding point [station]; *(post)* office of dispatch, office of origin *(telegram)*
Absendetag m date of forwarding [dispatch, shipping, conveyance]
Absendung f sending (off), dispatch, forwarding, consigning, consignment; shipping; posting, mailing
absetzbar 1. saleable *(commodities etc.)*; marketable *(securities etc.)*; 2. depreciative, to be written off *(depreciation)*; 3. deductible *(sum)*; 4. removable *(item from list, staff members etc.)*; 5. dismissable *(staff members)*
Absetzbarkeit f 1. saleability *(commodities)*; *(st.ex.)* marketability *(securities)*; 2. deductibility *(sum)*
absetzen 1. to sell, to market *(commodities etc.)*; 2. to write off *(depreciation)*; 3. to deduct *(sum)*, to strike a sum of; 4. to strike out, to remove *(item from list)*; 5. to remove, to dismiss *(staff members)*
Absetzung f dismissal, removal *(staff members)*
~, **zeitweilige** suspension *(staff members)*
absichern to guard; to exclude *(risk etc.)*
Absicherung f covering *(loan, debt etc.)*
Absicht f intention, purpose, motive, design ✧
in böswilliger ~ with malice aforethought; **in gewinnsüchtiger** ~ for pecuniary reasons
~, **betrügerische** fraudulent intent
~, **böswillige** malicious intent
absichtlich intentional; deliberate *(omission etc.)*; wilful *(action etc.)*
absinken to sink down *(rates etc.)*; to drop *(prices, speed etc.)*
Absinken n decline, drop *(in prices etc.)*
absolut absolute
Absolutwert m absolute value
~ **einer Abweichung** *(stats)* absolute deviation
Absolvent m graduate
Absolventenbilanz f balance (sheet) of graduates and school-leavers *(balancing leavers of all educational levels and national economic demand)*
Absolventenförderungsvertrag m graduate development indenture *(special contract between a graduate entering an enterprise and the management for prospective promotion)*
absolvieren to complete *(task etc.)*; to pass *(examination, studies etc.)*
absondern to separate, to disjoin, to isolate; to put s.th. apart
Absonderung f separation; putting [setting] apart
Absonderungsanspruch m creditor's preferential claim
absonderungsberechtigt preferential
Absonderungsberechtigter m preferential [secured] creditor
Absonderungsrecht n preferential right
Absorption f absorption; absorbing
absorptionsfähig absorptive *(market for commodities etc.)*
Absorptionsfähigkeit f s. **Absorptionskraft**
Absorptionskraft f absorptive capacity [power] *(of market for commodities etc.)*
Absorptionsvermögen n s. **Absorptionskraft**
Absprache f (verbal) arrangement [agreement] ✧ **laut unserer** ~ in accordance with our agreement, as per arrangement
absprachegemäß s. **laut unserer Absprache**
absprechen 1. to discuss; 2. *(jur)* to deprive s. o. of s.th. ✧ **etwas mit jmdm.** ~ to discuss s.th. with s. o.; **sich mit jmdm.** ~ to come to terms with s. o.; to come to an agreement [arrangement] with s.o.
abstammen to stem from; to descend from; to be descendent from

24 Abstammung

Abstammung *f* descent, lineage, ancestry; origin; parentage
Abstand *m* distance *(from a given point)*; gap, clearance, interval; space ◊ **~ von einer Forderung nehmen** to relinquish [forego, abandon, waive] a claim; **~ von etwas nehmen** to refrain from doing s.th.; **im ~ von** at an interval of
~, verallgemeinerter *(stats)* D^2-statistic, Mahalanobis' generalized statistic
Abstandsgeld *n* 1. compensation, indemnification; 2. forfeit, penalty *(for not fulfilling contract etc.)*; 3. *(st.ex.)* option money; 4. key money *(paid by a person taking a flat)* ◊ **als ~ zahlen** to pay by way of compensation
Abstandsmaß *n*:
~, Mahalanobis' verallgemeinertes *(stats)* Mahalanobis's generalized distance
Abstandssumme *f s.* **Abstandsgeld**
Abstandstest *m* *(stats)* distance power test
~, gleichmäßig bester *(stats)* uniformly best distance power test, U.B.D.P. test
abstecken to demarcate, to mark out *(estate etc.)*
Abstellbahnhof *m* railway yard
abstellbar 1. that can be stopped [put out of action]; that can be switched off *(machine etc.)*; 2. reformable *(abuse etc.)*; redressable *(grievance etc.)*
abstellen 1. to stop, to put out of action *(machine etc.)*; 2. to remedy, to redress, to rectify *(mistake etc.)*
abstempeln to stamp *(document, passport, weights etc.)*; to hallmark *(metal objects)*
abstimmen 1. *(pol)* to vote; 2. *(acc)* to adjust, to check; 3. to co-ordinate *(plans etc.)* ◊ **geheim ~** to ballot
Abstimmung *f* 1. *(pol)* voting; 2. *(acc)* adjustment, check; 3. co-ordination *(plans etc.)*
~ des Messekalenders co-ordination of the fair calendar
~, territoriale regional co-ordination
Abstriche *mpl:*
~ am Haushalt cuts in the budget
Abteilung *f* department, division
~ **Abgaben** tax department
~ **Absatz** marketing [sales] department
~ **Allgemeine Verwaltung** department of general administration
~ **Arbeitsökonomie** department of labour economics *(mainly dealing with labour productivity)*
~ **Ausland** foreign department
~, bautechnische building department
~ **Betriebsorganisation** department of industrial organization
~ **Finanzen** finance department
~ **Forschung und Entwicklung** research and development department
~ **für Gütekontrolle** department of quality control [inspection]
~ **für Öffentlichkeitsarbeit** public relations department
~ **Investitionen** investment department
~ **Konstruktion** projection and drawing department [office]
~ **Märkte und Preise** department of market und price studies
~ **Materialwirtschaft** store department *(of enterprises and institutions concerned with planning, supply, storing etc. of material)*
~, nichtproduzierende non-producing section
~ **Planung** planning department
~, produzierende production department
~ **Statistik** statistical department
~, technische technical department
~ **technische Informationen** department of technical information
~ **Technologie** department of production engineering *(responsible for production engineering and technique, process planning etc.)*
~, wirtschaftspolitische economic policy department
~ **wissenschaftlich-technische Informationen** department of scientific and technical information
Abteilungen *fpl*:
~ **der gesellschaftlichen Produktion** departments of social production *(production of means of production – department I, and production of consumer goods – department II)*
~ **I und II der gesellschaftlichen Produktion** departments I and II of social production *(s.* **Abteilungen der gesellschaftlichen Produktion)**
~, produktionsvorbereitende production preparing departments *(research and development, design department, engineering department, materials department etc.)*
~, sonstige miscellaneous departments
~, sonstige produktionsbedingte miscellaneous departments involved in production *(enterprise departments involved in training, retraining, catering etc.)*
Abteilungsabrechnung *f* departmental cost accounting
Abteilungsaufgaben *fpl* departmental tasks
Abteilungsbericht *m* departmental report
Abteilungschef *m* head of the department, departmental head
Abteilungsfristenplan *m* departmental time schedule
Abteilungsgemeinkosten *pl* departmental overhead costs
Abteilungskalkulation *f* departmental (cost) calculation

Abteilungskosten *pl* departmental costs
Abteilungsleiter *m* head of department
Abteilungsleitungskosten *pl* departmental management costs
Abteilungsökonom *m* economist (in a production department)
Abteilungsplan *m* departmental plan
Abteilungs- und Betriebsgemeinkosten *pl* departmental and enterprise overhead costs
abtragen 1. to carry off, to remove; to excavate *(earth etc.)*; 2. to discharge, to settle, to wipe off, to pay *(debt etc.)*
abträglich detrimental
Abtragung *f* 1. removal; excavation *(earth etc)*; 2. discharge, settlement, payment *(debt etc.)*
Abtransport *m* transporting [carrying] away
abtransportieren to transport [carry] away
abtreiben 1. to drive away [off] *(cattle from pasture etc)*; 2. to drift away *(boat etc.)*; 3. to procure (an) abortion, to bring on a miscarriage
Abtreiben *n* 1. driving away [off] *(cattle from pasture ect.)*; 2. drifting away *(boat etc.)*
Abtreibung *f* abortion
abtrennbar separable; detachable *(coupons etc.)*
◊ nicht ~ non-detachable
abtrennen to separate; to detach; to sever *(relations, proceedings etc.)*
Abtrennung *f* separation; severance *(relations, proceedings etc.)*
abtretbar transferable *(claims)*; that can be ceded *(rights)*; assignable, conveyable *(estate etc.)*
Abtretbarkeit *f* transferability *(claims);* assignability *(estate etc.)*
abtreten *(jur)* to resign *(possession etc.)*; to give up *(s.th.)*, to yield *(right)*; to transfer, to assign, to surrender *(right, goods etc.)*; to convey *(estate etc.)*; to cede *(territory etc.)*; to abandon *(mortgaged estate)*
Abtretung *f (jur)* resignation, resigning *(possession etc.)*; transfer, assignation, assignment, surrender *(right, goods etc.)*; conveyance, conveying *(estate)*; cession *(territory etc.)*; abandonment, abandoning *(mortgaged estate)*
Abtretungsbrief *m* letter of assignment
Abtretungserklärung *f* declaration of assignment
abtretungsfähig *s.* abtretbar
Abtretungsrecht *n* right to assign
Abtretungsurkunde *f* deed of cession [assignment, conveyance]
Abtretungsvertrag *m* treaty of cession *(territory etc.)*
abverlangen to demand *(s.th. of/from s.o.)*; to require *(s.th. of s.o.)*
abvermieten to let off, to sublet *(room)*
abwählen to remove *s.o.* from office *(by a majority vote)*, to vote *s.o.* out of office

abwälzen to pass on *(the increase in cost, prices etc. to consumers)*; to shift *(responsibility to others)*
Abwälzung *f* passing on *(increase in costs, prices etc. to consumers)*; shifting *(of responsibility to others)*
abwandern to migrate
Abwanderung *f* migration
Abwärtsbewegung *f* downturn *(business cycle)*; downward movement *(prices)*; downward tendency [trend] *(rates etc.)*
Abwasser *n* waste water, sewage
Abwehrzoll *m* protective duty
abweichen to deviate, to diverge
Abweichung *f* deviation, divergence
~, äquivalente *(stats)* equivalent deviate [deviation]
~, aufsummierte *(stats)* accumulated deviation
~, durchschnittliche *(stats)* mean deviation
~, gleichsinnige *(stats)* concurrent deviation
~, kumulierte *s.* ~, aufsummierte
~, mittlere *(stats)* standard deviation
~, mittlere quadratische *(stats)* standard square deviation
~, normierte *(stats)* deviate
~, prozentuale mittlere *(stats)* percentage standard deviation
Abweichungsquadrat *n:*
~ vom jeweiligen Bezugspunkt, mittleres *(stats)* mean-square deviation
~ zwischen den Behandlungsarten, mittleres *(stats)* treatment-mean-square
abweisen to reject, to refuse, to dismiss
Abweisung *f* rejection, refusal, dismissal
abwerben to seduce *(s.o. to leave service)*, to entice *(s.o. from his job)*
Abwerbung *f* enticing, enticement *(of s.o. to leave his job)*; brain drain
~ von Arbeitskräften enticement of manpower
abwerfen *(com)* to bring in, to bear, to yield, to produce *(profit etc.)*
abwerten to devaluate, to devalue, to devalorize *(currency)*; to depreciate *(assets etc.)*
Abwertung *f* devaluation, devalorization *(currency);* depreciation *(assets etc.)*
~ von Grund- und Umlaufmitteln depreciation of fixed and working capital
abwickeln to settle *(matter, transaction etc.)*; to wind up, to liquidate *(business, company etc.)*
Abwicklung *f* settling, settlement *(matter, transaction etc.)*; winding-up, liquidation *(business, company etc.)*
~ eines Konkurses administration of a bankruptcy
Abwicklungsgeschäft *n* winding-up transaction
Abwicklungsverfahren *n* procedure of liquidation

abwracken to break up *(ship)*
Abwracken *n* breaking up *(ship)*
Abwracker *m* ship-breaker
Abwrackpreis *m* break-up price *(ship)*
Abwrackungsgeschäft *n* ship-breaking
abzahlbar payable in instalments
abzahlen to pay in [by] instalments
abzählen to count up, to enumerate, to number; to count over [out] *(money)*
Abzahlung *f* payment in [by] instalments ⋄ **auf ~ kaufen** to buy by instalments [on the instalment system, on hire-purchase]
Abzahlungsgeschäft *n* 1. hire purchase, sale on the instalment system; 2. hire-purchase firm
Abzahlungskauf *m* hire purchase
Abzahlungskonto *n* instalment account
Abzahlungskosten *pl* hire-purchase charges
Abzahlungskredit *m* consumer credit
Abzahlungsplan *m* hire-purchase plan; instalment schedule
Abzahlungspreis *m* instalment [hire-purchase] price
Abzahlungsrate *f* instalment
Abzahlungssystem *n* (system of) payment by instalments
Abzahlungsverpflichtungen *fpl* hire-purchase debts
Abzahlungsvertrag *m* hire-purchase agreement
abzeichnen 1. to draw, to sketch; to copy, to reproduce; 2. to initial, to sign
Abzeichnen *n* 1. drawing; copying; 2. initialling; signing
Abzeichnung *f* initialling; signing
abziehen 1. to draw off *(customers etc.)*; to alienate *(persons from a place)*; 2. to withdraw *(money, capital etc.)*; to deduct *(from the price)*; 3. to rack, to bottle *(wine etc.)*; 4. to mimeograph
Abziehen *n* 1. drawing off *(customers etc.)*; 2. withdrawal *(money, capital etc.)*; deduction *(from the price)*; 3. bottling *(wine etc.)*; 4. mimeographing
abzinsen to discount, to deduct unaccrued interest
Abzinsung *f* discount, deduction of unaccrued interest
Abzinsungsfaktor *m* discount factor
Abzug *m* withdrawal *(capital, money etc.)*; deduction *(from the price)*
abzüglich less, minus; deducted
abzugsfähig deductible, allowable
abzweigen 1. *(com)* to divert *(capital)*; to turn to other uses *(money etc.)*; 2. to fork *(road)*, to bifurcate; to branch, to tap *(gas, mains etc.)*
Abzweigen *n* 1. *(com)* diversion *(capital, money etc.)*; 2. forking *(road)*, bifurcation; branching, tapping *(gas, mains etc.)*

Abzweigung *f* 1. *(com)* diversion *(capital, money etc.)*; ramification, bifurcation; 2. *(trans)* road junction, fork; *(railw)* branch line
Achsengeld *n* money paid for carriage *(goods)*
Achsgebühr *f* carriage rate *(calculated according to axles needed for loading)*
Achskilometer *mpl* *(railw)* actual distance covered by carriage [waggon] in a given time; mileage covered
Achtstundentag *m* eight-hour working day
Acker *m* arable land, cultivated field
Ackerbau *m* agriculture, crop farming; soil culture [management] *(branch of agricultural sciences)*
Ackerbausystem *n* cropping system
Ackerbestellung *f* tillage, cultivation *(of the soil)*
Ackerfeld *n* tilled [ploughed] field; field in [under] cultivation, plough-land, ploughed land
Ackerfläche *f* land [fields] under cultivation, plough-land
Ackerflächenbewertung *f* land evaluation
Acker-Grünland-Verhältnis *n* ratio of arable to pasture land
Ackerklassifizierung *f* classification of (arable) land
Ackerland *n* arable land
Ackerschlag *m* field, plot
Acker- und Pflanzenbau *m* field farming, agronomy
a conto on account
addieren to add *(number)*; to add [total] up *(numbers)*, to cast up
Addition *f* addition; adding [totaling] up
~ von Zufallvariablen *(stats)* addition of variables
Additivität *f* additivity
~ von Mittelwerten *(stats)* additivity of means
Administration *f* administration
Adressant *m* sender *(letter)*; consignor *(goods)*; drawer *(bill)*
Adressat *m* addressee *(letter)*; consignee *(goods)*; drawee *(bill)*
Adreßbuch *n* directory
Adresse *f* 1. address *(of persons)*; direction, destination *(letter, consignment etc.)*; 2. *(formal)* address *(to assembly etc.)*
Adressennachweis *m* inquiry office
Adressenverzeichnis *n* list of addresses; directory
adressieren to address, to direct *(letter, parcel etc.)*; to label, to consign *(goods)*
Adressieren *n* addressing
Adreßprogrammierung *f* address programming
Adreßzettel *m* label, adhesive address label; tag
Ad-valorem-Zoll *m* ad-valorem duty
Agentur *f* agency

Agglomeration *f* agglomeration *(concentration of population, industries etc.)*; built-up area
Aggregat *n* set, unit *(machinery, electrical equipment etc.)*
Aggregation *f* aggregation
Aggregationsfähigkeit *f* aggregatability *(statistical or planning data)*
Aggregationsgrößen *fpl* aggregative magnitudes
~, **volkswirtschaftliche** national economic aggregation magnitudes *(productivity, labour input etc.)*
Aggregationsmethode *f* method of aggregation
Aggregattafel *f (ins)* aggregate table
Agio *n* agio, exchange premium
Agrarbank *f* agricultural bank
Agrarerzeugnisse *npl* agricultural products [produce], farm products
Agrarexport *m* agricultural [farm] export(s)
Agrarflug *m* farm aviation *(for spraying fertilizers etc.)*
Agrarforschung *f* agricultural research
Agrarfrage *f* agrarian question [issue]
Agrargebiet *n* agricultural region [district]
Agrargemeinde *f* agricultural community
Agrargeschichte *f* agrarian history
Agrargesetz *n* land act [law]
Agrargesetzgebung *f* agrarian legislation
Agrarier *m* landed proprietor
Agrarimport *m* agricultural [farm] import(s)
Agrar-Industrie-Betrieb *m* agro-industrial enterprise; agri-business
Agrar-Industrie-Gebiet *n* agricultural-industrial area
Agrar-Industrie-Kombinat *n* agro-industrial combine *(combining several farms along with a processing enterprise of the food industry, e. g., sugar refinery)*
Agrar-Industrie-Komplex *m* **(AIK):**
~, **volkswirtschaftlicher** national-economic complex of agro-industries
Agrarindustrieland *n* agricultural-industrial country
Agrar-Industrie-Vereinigung *f* agro-industrial association *(of co-operative and state-owned farms for specialized production)*
Agrarkredit *m* agricultural [farm] credit
Agrarkreis *m* agricultural district
Agrarkrise *f* agricultural crisis
Agrarland *n* agricultural [agrarian] country
Agrarmarkt *m* agricultural market
Agrarmarktordnung *f* system of state measures for agriculture
Agrarökonom *m* agricultural economist
Agrarökonomie *f* agricultural economics
Agrarplanung *f* agrarian planning
Agrarpolitik *f* agricultural policy
Agrarpreis *m* farm price

Agrarpreisniveau *n* farm price level
Agrarpreisreform *f* reform in farm prices, farm price reform
Agrarproduktion *f* agricultural [farm] production
Agrarprogramm *n* agrarian programme
Agrarprotektionismus *m* protectionism in agricultural products
Agrarreform *f* agrarian [land] reform
Agrarsektor *m* agricultural sector
Agrarsoziologie *f* rural sociology
Agrarstaat *m* agricultural [agrarian] country
Agrarstatistik *f* agricultural statistics
Agrarstruktur *f* agrarian structure
Agrartechnik *f* 1. agricultural technology [technique]; 2. agricultural [farm] machinery
Agrarunion *f* agricultural [agrarian] union
Agrarverfassung *f (approx.)* structure of agricultural land
Agrarwesen *n* agriculture
Agrarwirtschaft *f* agricultural [agrarian] economy
Agrarwissenschaft *f* agricultural science
Agrarzoll *m* agricultural tariff [customs, duty]
Agrikultur *f* agriculture
Agrikulturchemie *f* agricultural chemistry
agrochemisch agro-chemical
Agronom *m* agronomist
Agronomie *f* agronomy
agronomisch agronomic
Akkord *m* 1. accord, agreement; arrangement, settlement; 2. piecework *(form of wage payment)*
Akkordarbeit *f* piecework
Akkordlohn *m* piece(-rate) wage
Akkordprämie *f* piece-rate bonus
Akkordrichtsatz *m* job rate
Akkordschere *f* wage scissors
Akkordsystem *n* piece-price system
Akkordtarif *m* piece-wage rates
Akkordzettel *m* job ticket
Akkordzuschlag *m s.* **Akkordprämie**
akkreditieren 1. *(com)* to open a credit *(for s. b.)*; 2. to accredit *(an ambassador to a government)*
akkreditiert 1. *(com)* financed by a letter of credit; 2. accredited *(ambassador to a government)*
Akkreditiv *n* 1. *(com)* (letter of) credit (L/C); 2. credentials *(of representative)* ◇ **ein ~ eröffnen** to establish [open] a letter of credit; **ein ~ zurückziehen** to revoke a letter of credit
~, **bestätigtes** confirmed letter of credit
~, **einfaches** clean letter of credit
~, **revolvierendes** *s.* ~, **sich automatisch erneuerndes**
~, **sich automatisch erneuerndes** revolving letter of credit

~, **teilbares** packing [*(Am)* transferable] credit
~, **unbestätigtes** unconfirmed credit
~, **unwiderrufliches** irrevocable letter of credit
~, **widerrufliches** revocable letter of credit
Akkreditivbedingungen *fpl* L/C conditions
Akkreditivdokumente *npl* L/C documents
Akkreditivverfahren *n* (procedure of) payment by letter of credit
Akkumulation *f* accumulation
~, **betriebliche** accumulation (of funds) by an enterprise
~ **des Kapitals** accumulation of capital
~ **des Kapitals, ursprüngliche** primary [original] accumulation of capital
~ **für Konsumzwecke** accumulation for consumption purposes
~ **für Produktionszwecke** accumulation for production purposes
~, **nichtproduktive** non-productive accumulation
~, **produktive** productive accumulation
Akkumulationseffekt *m* efficiency of accumulation
Akkumulationsentscheidungen *fpl* decisions on accumulation (policy); investment decisions
Akkumulationsfaktor *m* accumulation factor
Akkumulationsfonds *m* accumulation fund, total accumulation
Akkumulationskraft *f* accumulation potentiality [capacity]
Akkumulationsmasse *f* total accumulation, volume of accumulation
~, **kritische** critical volume of accumulation
Akkumulationsmaßnahmen *fpl* accumulation policies [activities, measures]
Akkumulationsmittel *npl* accumulation funds, resources for accumulation
Akkumulationsprozeß *m* accumulation process
Akkumulationsquellen *fpl* sources of accumulation
Akkumulationsrate *f* rate of accumulation
~, **optimale** optimal rate of accumulation
Akkumulationsstruktur *f* structure of accumulation (*distribution of accumulation by economic sectors; economic composition of accumulation, i.e. fixed assets, working capital, stocks*)
Akkumulationsvolumen *n s.* **Akkumulationsmasse**
akkumulieren to accumulate
akkumulierend accumulative
Akontozahlung *f* payment on account; part payment
Akt *m* action, act, deed
Akte *f* file, record; document, instrument, deed
~, **notarielle** notarial document [deed], document [deed] executed and authenticated by a notary

Akten *fpl* files, records ⋄ **zu den ~** (z. d. A.) to be filed; **zu den ~ legen** to put on file
Aktenablage *f* 1. files; 2. filing system
Aktendeckel *m* folder
aktenmäßig authentic, documentary
Aktennotiz *f* memorandum, note
Aktenplan *m* filing system
Aktenvermerk *m s.* **Aktennotiz**
Aktenverzeichnis *n* filing list [catalogue, register]
Aktenzeichen *n* file [reference] number
Aktie *f* share, *(Am)* stock
~, **alte** original share [*(Am)* stock]
~, **amortisierte** redeemed share [*(Am)* stock]
~, **dividendenberechtigte** participating share [*(Am)* stock]
~, **eigene** own share, *(Am)* treasury stock
~, **eingezogene** recalled share [*(Am)* stock]
~, **gebundene** restricted share [*(Am)* stock]
~, **gezeichnete** subscribed share [*(Am)* stock]
~, **hinterlegte** deposited share [*(Am)* stock]
~, **junge** new share [*(Am)* stock]
~ **mit Nennwert** par value share [*(Am)* stock]
~, **nennwertlose** non-par(-value) share, *(Am)* no par stock
~, **nicht dividendenberechtigte** deferred stock
~, **stimmberechtigte** voting share [*(Am)* stock]
~, **stimmrechtlose** non-voting share [*(Am)* stock]
~, **unentgeltliche** bonus share [*(Am)* stock]
~, **vinkulierte** *s.* ~, **gebundene**
Aktien *fpl* shares, *(Am)* stocks ⋄ **~ besitzen** to hold shares [*(Am)* stocks]; **~ einziehen** to pay off shares [*(Am)* stocks]; **~ zeichnen** to apply [subscribe] for shares [*(Am)* stocks]; to take up shares [*(Am)* stocks]
~, **an der Börse notierte** officially quoted shares, *(Am)* listed stock
~, **ausgegebene** issued shares [*(Am)* stocks]
~, **börsenfähige** stocks negotiable
~, **eingebrachte** vendor's shares
~, **nicht ausgegebene** unissued shares [*(Am)* stocks]
~, **nicht börsenfähige** stocks non-negotiable
~, **nicht notierte** displaced shares, *(Am)* unlisted stocks
~, **notierte** shares quoted on the stock exchange, *(Am)* listed stocks
~, **voll eingezahlte** fully paid up shares, *(Am)* full-paid stocks
Aktienausgabe *f* issue of shares [*(Am)* stock]
Aktienbank *f* joint stock [*(Am)* incorporated] bank
Aktienbesitz *m* shareholdings, *(Am)* stockholdings
Aktienbesitzer *m* shareholder, *(Am)* stockholder
Aktienbörse *f* stock exchange
Aktienerwerb *m* purchase of shares [*(Am)* stock]

Aktiengesellschaft *f* joint stock company, *(Am)* incorporated company, stock corporation
Aktiengesetz *n* companies act, *(Am)* corporation law
Aktienhandel *m* dealing in shares, *(Am)* stock jobbing
Aktienindex *m* share (price) index
Aktienkapital *n* share capital, *(Am)* capital stock
Aktienkauf *m* purchase of shares [*(Am)* stock]
Aktienkontrollpaket *n* controlling block of shares, *(Am)* stock controlling majority
Aktienkurs *m* share [*(Am)* stock] price
Aktienmakler *m* sharebroker, stockbroker
Aktienmarkt *m* share [stock] market
Aktienmehrheit *f* majority stock ◊ **die ~ haben** to hold the controlling interest
Aktiennotierung *f* (share [*(Am)* stock]) quotation
Aktienpaket *n* block [parcel] of shares, *(Am)* block of stock
Aktienrecht *n* company [*(Am)* corporation] law
Aktienschein *m* share warrant, *(Am)* stock certificate
Aktienstreuung *f* dispersal of stock ownership
Aktienverkauf *m* selling of shares [*(Am)* stock]
Aktienzeichnung *f* subscription of shares [*(Am)* stock]
Aktienzertifikat *n s.* Aktienschein
Aktion *f* action, operation, drive, campaign
Aktionär *m s.* Aktienbesitzer
Aktionärsversammlung *f* general meeting of shareholders [*(Am)* stockholders]
Aktionsausschuß *m* executive committee
Aktionsbereich *m* scope [range, radius] of action
Aktionseinheit *f* unity in action
Aktionsprogramm *n* programme of action
Aktiva *pl* assets
~, **ständige** constant assets
~ **und Passiva** *pl* assets and liabilities
Aktivbestand *m* available assets
Aktivbilanz *f* favourable balance
Aktivgeschäft *n* credit transactions
aktivieren to activate; *(acc)* to carry as assets, to enter on the asset side
Aktivierung *f* activation; *(acc)* entry on the credit side; improvement of the balance; *(for tr)* achievement of an export surplus
~ **von Investitionen** carrying investments as assets
Aktivität *f* activity
~, **kritische** critical activity *(PERT)*
Aktivposten *m* (item among the) asset(s)
Aktivsaldo *m* credit balance
Aktivschulden *fpl* outstanding debts, book debts ranking as assets
Aktivseite *f* assets side, credit (side)
Aktivvermögen *n* assets

Aktivzinsen *mpl* interest receivable, outstanding interest
Akzeleration *f* acceleration
Akzept *n* acceptance *(bill)*; acceptance [accepted] bill ◊ **ein ~ decken** to provide for acceptance; **ein ~ einholen** to obtain [secure] an acceptance; **mangels Akzepts** for want [in default] of acceptance; **zum ~ vorlegen** to present (a bill) for acceptance
~, **allgemeines** clean [general] acceptance
~, **bedingtes** qualified acceptance
~, **bedingungsloses** unconditional acceptance
~, **erstklassiges** first-class bill
~, **formell gültiges** approved acceptance
~, **laufendes** outstanding acceptance
~, **reines** clean acceptance
~, **unbedingtes** unconditional acceptance
~, **vor Fälligkeit bezahltes** anticipated [*(Am)* rebated] acceptance
Akzeptant *m* acceptor, drawee (of a bill)
Akzeptation *f* acceptance
Akzeptaustausch *m* exchange of drafts
Akzeptbank *f* acceptance house
Akzeptbesorgung *f* procuring acceptance
Akzeptbestand *m* bill holdings
Akzeptdatum *n* date of acceptance
akzeptfähig bankable, negotiable
Akzeptfrist *f* term of acceptance
Akzeptgebühr *f* acceptance charge
Akzeptgeschäfte *npl* acceptance business, (bill-)broking, brokerage
akzeptieren to accept; to agree to, to acquiesce *(claims, proposals etc.)*; to honour *(bill)*
akzeptiert accepted, honoured *(bill)*
Akzeptkredit *m* acceptance credit
Akzeptobligobuch *n* bills-payable book, bill book
Akzeptprovision *f* acceptance commission
Akzeptverbindlichkeiten *fpl* bills [trade acceptances] receivable
Akzeptvermerk *m* endorsement on a bill
Akzeptverweigerung *f* non-acceptance *(bill)*
Akzessionsvertrag *m* treaty of accession
Akzise *f* excise (duty), indirect tax
Algorithmus *m* algorithm
Alienation *f* alienation
Alienationskoeffizient *m* *(stats)* coefficient of alienation
Alleinberechtigung *f* exclusive [sole] right
Alleinbesitz *m* exclusive possession
Alleinhersteller *m* sole manufacturer
Alleinverkauf *m* exclusive [monopoly in] sale
Alleinverkaufsrecht *n* exclusive right of sale, sole right to sell
Alleinvertreter *m* sole agent
Alleinvertretungsanspruch *m* claim to sole representation

alleinvertretungsberechtigt authorized to sole representation
Alleinvertrieb *m* sole [monopoly over] distribution, exclusive sale
Allgemeinbildung *f* general education
allgemeingültig universally valid
Allgemeingültigkeit *f* universal validity
allgemeinverbindlich generally binding *(law, contract etc.)*
al pari at par
Al-pari-Emission *f* at par issue
Altenheim *n s.* **Altersheim**
Altenteil *n* farm annuity
Altenwohnheim *n s.* **Altersheim**
Alter *n* age; old age
~, **arbeitsfähiges** working age
Alternativhypothese *f (stats)* alternative hypothesis
Altersaufbau *m* age structure
Altersbegrenzung *f* age limit [restriction]
Altersermäßigung *f* reduction for pensioners *(charges etc.)*
Altersgrenze *f* age limit; retirement age
Altersgruppe *f* age group
Altersheim *n* home for senior citizens [old-age pensioners]
Altersjahrgang *m* age group [cohort]
Altersklasse *f* age group [class]
Alterspyramide *f* age pyramid
Altersrente *f* old-age [retirement] pension
~, **durchschnittliche monatliche** average monthly old-age [retirement] pension
Altersrentner *m* old-age pensioner
Altersstruktur *f* age structure
~ **der Beschäftigten** age structure of persons employed [working people]
Altersversicherung *f* old-age insurance
Altersversorgung *f* old-age pension
~, **betriebliche** supplementary old-age pension paid by enterprises
Alterszulage *f* seniority allowance [bonus], superannuation
Alterszusammensetzung *f (stats)* age distribution
Altglas *n* broken bottles and glasses
Altgummi *m* scrap rubber
Altmaterial *n* scrap
~, **metallisches** metallic scrap
~, **nichtmetallisches** non-metallic scrap
Altmetall *n* scrap metal
Altöl *n* waste oil
Altölwirtschaft *f* recycling of waste oil
Altpapier *n* scrap paper
Altstoffe *mpl* waste material, worn-out goods
Altstofferfassung *f* collection [collecting] of waste material [worn-out goods] *(scrap, old newspapers etc.)*

Altstoffpreis *m* price of waste material [worn-out goods]
Alttextilien *pl* worn-out textiles
Amortisation *f* amortization; redemption *(loan, stocks, obligation)*; paying off, liquidation *(debt)*
Amortisationsabführung *f* payment of amortization (amounts)
Amortisationsabführungsnormativ *n* standard rate of [for] paying amortization (amounts) *(to higher organs)*
Amortisationsaufkommen *n* total amount of amortization
Amortisationsaufwandskoeffizient *m* coefficient of amortization input
Amortisationsbetrag *m* amount of amortization
Amortisationsfonds *m* amortization fund; sinking fund
Amortisationshypothek *f* amortizable mortgage
Amortisationskasse *f* sinking fund
Amortisationskennziffer *f* index [rate] of amortization
Amortisationsrate *f* rate of amortization
Amortisationsüberschuß *m* surplus [excess] amortization
Amortisationsverteilung *f* distribution (of the amount) of amortization
Amortisationsverwendung *f* utilization of (the amount of) amortization
Amortisationswert *m* amortized value
Amortisationszeit *f* period of amortization
amortisierbar amortizable
amortisieren to amortize; to redeem *(loan, stocks, obligation);* to pay off, to liquidate *(debt)*
Amplitude *f (stats)* amplitude
Amt *n* 1. office, bureau, board; 2. official position, public function, appointment, post, employment; 3. sphere of duty ◇ **ein ~ ausüben** to perform the duties of an office
amtieren to hold office, to be in charge ◇ **~ als** to act as
amtlich official
Amtsantritt *m* (upon) entering office, accession to office
Amtsbefugnis *f* authority, competence
Amtsdauer *f* tenure [term] of office
Amtseinführung *f* inauguration *(into an office)*
Amtsenthebung *f* dismissal [removal] from office
Amtsgeheimnis *n* official secret
Amtshandlung *f* official act
Amtsmißbrauch *m* undue use [misuse, abuse] of authority
Amtsperiode *f s.* **Amtsdauer**
Amtsvorgänger *m* predecessor in office
Amtsweg *m* official channels ◇ **auf dem ~** officially, through official channels

Amtszeit *f* 1. period [term] of office; 2. office hours
analog analogous; similar
Analogie *f* analogy
Analogie-Modell *n* analogy model, model of analogy
~, physikalisches physical analogy model
Analogie-Rechengerät *n s.* **Analogrechner**
Analogieschluß *m* reasoning by analogy, argument from example
Analogrechner *m* analog computer
Analyse *f* analysis
~ der wirtschaftlichen Tätigkeit analysis of economic performance
~, gesamtvolkswirtschaftliche analysis of the national economy
~, harmonische *(stats)* harmonic analysis
~, mehrdimensionale *(stats)* multivariate analysis
~, numerische numeric analysis
~, ökonometrische econometric analysis
~, ökonomische economic analysis
~, programmierte programmed analysis
~, rückschauende retrospective analysis
~, statistische statistical analysis
~, technologische analysis of technology
~, volkswirtschaftliche national economic analysis
~, vorausschauende prospective analysis
Analysemethode *f* method of analyzing
Analysetätigkeit *f* analyzing activity
analysieren to analyze
Analytiker *m* analyst
analytisch analytic(al)
Anarchie *f:*
~ der Produktion anarchy in production
anbahnen to pave [smooth] the way for *(relations, undertaking etc.)*; to prepare [clear] the ground for *(negotiations etc.)*; to negotiate *(business etc.)*; to make an opening for *(talks etc.)*
Anbau *m* 1. *(agric)* cultivation, culture, growing; tillage; 2. annex(e), extension *(building)*
anbauen 1. *(agric)* to cultivate, to grow; to till; 2. to build on, to add *(to building)*
anbaufähig arable
Anbaufläche *f* area under cultivation, arable land, agricultural production area
Anbaugebiet *n* cropping area; area under cultivation
Anbaumethode *f* cultivation method
Anbauplan *m* crop cultivation plan
Anbauprämie *f* cultivation bonus
Anbausystem *n* cultivation [cropping] system
Anbau- und Liefervertrag *m* cultivation and supply contract
Anbauverhältnis *n* proportion of different crops *(on a piece of arable land)*

Anbauzone *f* arable area *(zone for special cultures and/or under special climatic conditions)*
anberaumen to appoint, *(Am)* to schedule; to call *(meeting)*; to set, to fix *(date)*
anbieten to offer; to bid; to tender
Anbieter *m* offerer; bidder; tenderer
Anbietungspflicht *f:*
~ für Devisen obligation to offer foreign currency to the bank
An-Bord-Konnossement *n* on-board bill of lading
ändern to change; to alter; to modify; to vary
Änderung *f* change; alteration; modification; variation
Änderungsvertrag *m* amended contract
andienen to tender *(payment, documents, goods etc., in fulfilment of contract)*; to hand over *(foreign exchange etc., to the authorities)*; to notify *(s.o. of intended shipment)*
Andienung *f* tender *(of payment, documents, goods etc., in fulfilment of contract)*; handing over *(of foreign exchange etc., to the authorities)*; notification *(to s.o. of intended shipment)*
Andrang *m* rush, run *(customers etc.)*; press, crowd; dense mass *(traffic)*
aneignen, sich to acquire; to appropriate *(s.th. to o.s.)*; to seize, to usurp *(power etc.)*
Aneignung *f* acquisition; appropriation *(of s.th. to o.s.)*; seizure, usurpation *(power etc.)*
~ der Arbeitsergebnisse, gesellschaftliche social appropriation of the results of labour
~, gewaltsame forcible appropriation; annexation
~, private private appropriation
Aneignungsgesetz *n* law of appropriation
Aneignungsprozeß *m* process of appropriation
Aneignungsverhältnisse *npl* relations [conditions] of appropriation
anerkennen to acknowledge, to recognize *(right, claim, authority etc.)*
Anerkennung *f* acknowledgement, recognition *(right, claim, authority etc.)*
~, gerichtliche legalization
~, völkerrechtliche recognition under international law
Anerkennungsschreiben *n* letter of acknowledgement
Anerkennungsurkunde *f* act of ratification and acknowledgement
Anfangsbestand *m* opening stock *(storage)*; *(acc)* opening [initial] capital
Anfangsbestandsposition *f* item of opening [initial] capital
Anfangsgehalt *n* commencing [initial, starting] salary
Anfangskapital *n* initial [original] capital, capital to start with; original investment

Anfangskosten *pl* initial costs
Anfangskurs *m* opening price
Anfangsoperation *f* initial operation
Anfangsproduktion *f* initial production
Anfangsschwierigkeiten *fpl* teething troubles, initial difficulties
Anfangsstadium *n* initial [primary] stage
Anfangszustand *m* original state
anfechtbar contestable; questionable, disputable; *(jur)* voidable, defeasible
Anfechtbarkeit *f* contestableness; questionableness, disputability; *(jur)* voidableness, defeasibility
anfechten to contest; to bring *s.th.* in question, to dispute; *(jur)* to avoid, to challenge, to impugn
Anfechtung *f* contestation *(rights);* avoidance *(contract)*
Anfechtungsklage *f (jur)* action to invalidate a contract; opposition [interference] proceedings (against a patent); to set aside a will; petition for nullity *(marriage)*
anfertigen to manufacture, to produce *(goods),* to make *(goods, copy, draft, list etc.);* to prepare, to draw up *(document),* to draft *(agreement, deed)*
Anfertigung *f* manufacturing, producing *(goods),* making *(goods, copy, draft, list, etc.);* preparation, drawing up *(document),* drafting *(agreement, deed)*
Anfertigungskosten *pl* cost of making [production], manufacturing costs
anfordern to demand, to require, to claim; to request, to call for *(funds etc.);* to order, to request delivery of *(article)*
Anforderung *f* demand, requirement, claim; request, calling for *(funds etc.);* order, request for delivery of *(article)*
Anforderungsnorm *f* standard (job) requirements *(qualification etc., needed for a particular job)*
Anfrage *f* inquiry, question
anfragen to inquire, to ask
Anfuhr *f* cartage, transport, carriage; delivery
Angabe *f* 1. indication; information; 2. declaration, statement, assertion; 3. *(jur)* testimony, evidence, deposition; return ✧ **jmds. ~ gemäß** s. **nach jmds. ~;** **laut ~** according to statement; **mit ~ der Gehaltsansprüche** statement of salary expected; **nach jmds. ~** according to s.b.'s statement; according to what s.b. said; according to him; **ohne ~ von Gründen** without giving reasons; **unter ~ von** giving *(specifications etc.)*
Angaben *fpl* data; given information *(of a problem etc.);* instructions, directions, specifications ✧ **nach jmds. ~ angefertigt** made in accordance with s.b.'s instructions [directions], made to s.b.'s specifications
~, betrügerische s. **~, falsche**
~, falsche false [fraudulent] statements
~, technische technical data
~, vertrauliche confidential data
angeben 1. to indicate; to inform; to declare, to state, to assert; to give *(name, reasons etc.);* *(com)* to quote *(price etc.)*
Angebot *n* offer *(to buy or to sell);* bid *(at auction);* tender; supply *(goods);* quotation *(prices);* range of goods ✧ **das ~ erstreckt sich auf** the range of goods offered comprises; **das ~ reicht von ... bis ...** the offer ranges from ... to ...; **dieses ~ bleibt noch gültig bis** this offer is still firm till; **ein ~ unterbreiten** to make an offer; to offer [submit] a range of products
~, elastisches variable tender
~, erstes first bid
~, festes firm offer [bid]
~, freibleibendes unbinding [open, free] offer, offer without commitment
~, gleichbleibendes standing offer
~, großzügiges liberal offer
~, internationales international range of goods offered
~, kontinuierliches continuous supply *(goods)*
~, laufendes present [current] supply *(consumer goods etc.); (st.ex.)* floating supply
~, lückenloses s. **~, umfassendes**
~, mündliches verbal offer
~, reiches rich array of products
~, reichhaltiges abundant supply *(consumer goods etc.)*
~, reizvolles attractive offer
~, solides bona fide offer
~, tägliches daily supply [offer]
~, umfassendes comprehensive supply [offer]
~ und Nachfrage *f* supply and demand
~, unelastisches inelastic supply
~, unverbindliches offer subject to confirmation
~, ursprüngliches original offer
~, verbindliches binding offer *(goods and services)*
~, vernünftiges reasonable offer
~, wirksames effective offer
angeboten:
   ✧ **~ werden** to be on offer
Angebotsabgabe *f* making an offer
Angebotsannahme *f* acceptance of offer
Angebotsbestand *m* tender stock
Angebotselastizität *f* elasticity of supply, supply elasticity
Angebotsform *f* type of offer
Angebotskalkulation *f* calculation of offers
Angebotsknappheit *f* shortage of supplies

Angebotskollektion *f* assortment of supply, range of goods
~, **bedarfsgerechte** assortment of supply [range of goods] according to demand
Angebotslage *f* situation of supply
Angebotsmonopol *n* monopoly of supply [offer]
Angebotspflicht *f* obligation to offer
Angebotspreis *m* supply [asking] price; tender price
~, **verbindlicher** binding tender price
Angebotsprojekt *n* project offer *(by construction enterprise to prospective investor containing data on construction and technology)*
Angebotsreserve *f* reserve of supplies
Angebotsüberschuß *m* excess supply
Angebotsverzeichnis *n* list of offers
Angebotsvollmacht *f* authorization to submit an offer
Angelegenheit *f* matter, affair, business, concern; *(jur)* case
~, **dienstliche** official business
~, **dringende** pressing matter
~, **finanzielle** financial matter
~, **fragliche** matter in question [dispute]
~, **private** private [personal] matter
~, **schmutzige** sordid [dirty] business
~, **schwebende** pending question
~, **strittige** matter in dispute
Angelegenheiten *fpl* matters, affairs
~, **auswärtige** foreign affairs
~, **familiäre** family affairs
~, **geschäftliche** business matters [affairs]
~, **häusliche** domestic affairs
~, **innere** internal affairs
~, **öffentliche** public affairs [matters]
~, **persönliche** personal matters
angelegt invested *(capital etc.)* ⋄ **fest** ~ locked [tied] up *(capital etc.)*
angelernt semi-skilled
angemeldet registered *(birth etc.)*; booked *(trunk call etc.)*; put forward *(claim etc.)*; applied (for) *(membership etc.)*
angemessen reasonable, appropriate, adequate, adapted; suitable, suited; conformable; consistent; proper, fit(ting)
angenommen 1. accepted *(gift, proposal, offer etc.)*; taken *(employment etc.)*; taken up *(challenge etc.)*; adopted *(resolution, child etc.)*; 2. assumed, supposed, presumed *(fact, statement)*
angesammelt accumulated, earned; collected, hoarded [stored] up
angeschlossen affiliated; connected
angestellt employed
Angestellte *pl* (salaried) employees; office workers
Angestelltenverhältnis *n* employee status

Angestelltenversicherung *f* social insurance of salaried employees
Angestellter *m* (salaried) employee; clerk
angewandt applied *(sciences, research etc.)*; employed, used, exercised
angewiesen 1. dependent on; 2. remitted *(sum of money etc.)*; 3. instructed
ANG-Kosten *pl s.* **Kosten für technologisch bedingten Ausschuß, Nacharbeit und Garantieverpflichtungen**
Angleichung *f* approximation, matching up, assimilation, adjustment
~ **des ökonomischen Entwicklungsniveaus** approximation of the levels of economic development
angliedern to affiliate *(organization to another etc.)*; to integrate *(economy to another etc.)*; to annex *(territory by force)*
Angliederung *f* affiliation *(of an organization to another etc.)*; integration, incorporation *(of an economy to another etc.)*; annexation *(of a territory by force)*
Angstkauf *m* panic buying
Anhaltspunkt *m* guiding point, guide; guiding principle *(for comprehension, action)*; clue
Anhang *m* 1. appendix, supplement, annex; *(jur)* rider *(to document etc.)*; schedule *(to act)*; *(com)* allonge, rider *(to bill of exchange)*; slip; 2. followers, adherents, supporters *(cause, idea etc.)*; 3. near relatives; (family) encumbrances
Anhängeadresse *f* tie-on label, address tag
Anhänger *m* 1. adherent, supporter *(cause, idea, party etc.)*; follower, advocate, upholder *(custom etc.)*; *(pol)* backer; henchman; 2. *(transp)* trailer; 3. tie-on label, tag
anhängig *(jur)* pending, pendent; undecided
Anhängigkeit *f* *(jur)* pendency
anhäufen to accumulate *(wealth etc.)*; to hoard, to amass *(money etc.)*; to increase *(stocks etc.)*; to stockpile *(supplies etc.)*
Anhäufung *f* accumulation *(wealth etc.)*; hoard, hoarding *(money etc.)*; stockpiling *(supplies etc.)*
anheben 1. to lift *(s.th.)*; 2. to raise *(price etc.)*
Anhebung *f* rise, increase *(price etc.)*
anheuern to sign on, to engage, to hire *(seamen)*
Ankauf *m* buying, purchase; acquisition
ankaufen to buy, to purchase; to acquire
Ankäufer *m* buyer, purchaser; acquirer; *(jur)* vendee
Ankaufskurs *m* *(st.ex.)* buying rate
Ankaufspreis *m* purchase price
Ankaufssumme *f* purchase money
Ankaufstelle *f* buying agent *(1. gold, silver, coins for the mint; 2. second-hand books, antiquities etc., for a state or other trading organization)*
Ankaufszettel *m* purchase note
Anklage *f* accusation, charge, indictment

anklagen to accuse; to charge, to indict
anknüpfen 1. to enter into, to establish *(business relations etc.)*; 2. to refer to
ankommen to arrive at [in]
ankündigen to announce, to give notice of; to publish, to advertise *(in a newspaper etc.)*
Ankündigung *f* announcement, notification
Ankunft *f* arrival
Ankunftshafen *m* port of arrival
Ankunftsort *m* place of arrival
Ankunftstag *m* day of arrival
Ankunftszeit *f* time of arrival
ankurbeln to boost, to liven up, to give (the economy) a shot in the arm
Ankurbelung *f* boosting, livening up *(industry, economy etc.)*
Anlage *f* 1. construction, building, establishment; plant, works; installation, equipment, facility, unit; 2. layout, plan, disposition; 3. *(fin)* invested capital, investment, employment *(funds)*; 4. endowment, gift, faculty; 5. enclosure, attached letter; annex, appendix; 6. *(d.pr.)* hardware
~ in Pourtefeuille-Effekten portfolio investment
Anlageart *f* kind of investment
Anlagebedarf *m* investment requirements
Anlageberater *m* investment adviser
Anlageberatung *f* investment consultancy [advisory] service
Anlagefonds *m* fixed assets
Anlagegeschäft *n* investment banking
Anlagegesellschaft *f* investment company [trust]
Anlagegüter *npl* capital goods
Anlageinvestition *f* investment in assets
Anlagekapital *n* fixed [capital] assets; invested [fixed] capital
Anlagekonto *n* investment account
Anlagekosten *pl* fixed capital expenditure; cost of construction *(factory etc.)*; cost of installation *(plant etc.)*; promotion costs *(foundation of an enterprise)*
Anlagemarkt *m* investment market
Anlagemittel *npl s.* **Anlagefonds**
Anlagenart *f* kind [type] of assets
Anlagenbewertung *f* asset evaluation; investment rating *(securities)*
Anlage(n)buchführung *f* accounting of investments [fixed assets]
Anlagenbuchhaltung *f* 1. bookkeeping of investments; 2. bookkeeping department of investments
Anlagenerneuerung *f* replacement of assets
Anlagenerweiterung *f* extension of fixed assets; plant extension
Anlagenexport *m* export of industrial equipment [plants, units]

Anlagenfinanzierung *f* financing of fixed assets
Anlagenintensität *f* capital intensity
anlagenintensiv capital-intensive
Anlagenkomplex *m* plant complex
Anlagenkonto *n* investment ledger; investment account
Anlage(n)kredit *m* investment credit
Anlagenneubewertung *f* revaluation of assets
Anlagenpreis *m* price of complete equipment *(plants etc.)*
Anlagenseite *f* *(acc)* assets side
Anlagensphäre *f* investment field
Anlagepapiere *npl* investment papers [bills], securities
~, festverzinsliche investment bonds
Anlageplan *m* plan of site *(factory etc.)*
Anlagerichtlinien *fpl* investment directives [guidelines]
Anlagevermögen *n* fixed assets [capital]; invested capital
Anlagewerte *mpl s.* **Anlagepapiere**
Anlauf *m* launching, start *(production)*
anlaufen 1. to start *(production etc.)*; 2. to call at a port *(ship)*
Anlaufkosten *pl* launching [running-in] cost
Anlaufkredit *m* opening credit
Anlaufschwierigkeiten *fpl* initial difficulties
Anlaufzeit *f* initial [starting] period; set-up time; *(d.pr.)* acceleration [start, response] time
anlegen 1. *(com)* to invest *(money, capital etc.)*; to spend *(money on s.th.)*; 2. to establish, to found *(enterprise etc.)*; to build, to construct, to put up *(building, dam, railway etc.)*; 3. to berth *(ship)*; to moor *(boat etc.)*; 4. *(d.pr.)* to apply
Anleger *m* investor
Anleihe *f* loan *(of money)*, bond; advance ⋄ **eine ~ aufnehmen** to raise a loan
~, gemeinsame joint loan
~, gesicherte secured loan
~, hypothekarische mortgage loan
~, konsolidierte consolidated funds, consols
~, kurzfristige short-term loan
~, langfristige long-term loan
~, mittelfristige medium-term loan
~, nicht gesicherte unsecured loan
~, öffentliche public loan
Anleiheablösung *f* redemption of a loan
Anleiheausschreibung *f* invitation to subscribe for a loan
Anleiheemission *f* issue of a loan
Anleihekapital *n* loan capital, bonded debt
Anleihekonsortium *n* loan consortium *(a consortium underwriting a loan)*
Anleihemarkt *m* market in government [municipal] securities [bonds], bond market
Anleihepapiere *npl* government [municipal] securities [bonds], stocks, bonds

Anleiheschuld *f* funded [*(Am)* bonded] debt
Anleihestock *m* reserve fund
Anleihetilgung *f* redemption of a loan, loan redemption
Anleihezeichnung *f* loan subscription, subscription to a loan
anleiten to direct, to instruct, to guide; to control
Anleitung *f* direction, instruction, guidance; control
Anlernberuf *m* semi-skilled trade
anliefern to deliver, to supply
Anlieferung *f* delivery, supply
Anlieger *m* neighbours; *(jur)* abutter, abutting owner ◊ **frei für ~** for (local) residents only
Anliegerstaat *m* neighbouring state
Anliegerverkehr *m s.* **frei für Anlieger**
anlocken to attract, to allure, to draw, to entice *(customers)*
Anlockung *f* attraction, allurement, drawing of, enticement *(customers)*
Anmeldeformular *n* registration form; application form; entry form *(competition etc.)*
Anmeldefrist *f* period for registration; period for application; period for entry
Anmeldegebühr *f* registration fee; appplication fee; filing fee *(bankruptcy)*
anmelden to register *(trademark etc.)*; to declare *(goods)*; to notify *(an authority of s.th.)*; to lodge *(claim)*; to make an appointment; *(d.pr.)* to sign on
Anmeldenummer *f* number of registration; number of application; number of entry
Anmeldepflicht *f* compulsory registration, obligation to register *(with the police etc.)*
anmeldepflichtig notifiable
Anmeldestelle *f* registry office
Anmeldetermin *m* (last) date of registration; (last) date of application; (last) date of entry
Anmeldung *f* 1. announcement, notification; registration *(trademark etc.)*; application; declaration *(customs)*; lodging *(claim etc.)*; making of an appointment; 2. reception (desk) *(hotel etc.)*
Anmeldungs- *s.* **Anmelde-**
anmustern to enrol(l), to enlist
Anmusterung *f* enrol(l)ment, enlistment
annähern to bring [draw] *s.th.* nearer [closer], to come together; to approach *(models etc.)*; to approximate *(values etc.)*; to converge, to reconcile *(views, theories etc.)*
Annäherung *f* bringing [drawing] *s.th.* nearer [closer], coming together; approach *(models etc.)*; approximation *(values etc.)*; convergence, reconciliation *(views, theories etc.)*; rapprochement *(between countries, adversaries etc.)* ◊ **eine ~ herbeiführen** to bring about a reconciliation [rapprochement] *(between countries, adversaries etc.)*
~, soziale coming closer socially
~ zwischen Stadt und Land narrowing the gap between town and countryside
Annäherungswert *m* approximate value [figure], approximation
Annahme *f* 1. acceptance, accepting *(proposal, applicant etc.)*; receipt, receiving *(letter, luggage etc.)*; taking delivery of *(goods etc.)*; passsing *(bill, resolution etc.)*; adoption *(theory etc.)*; 2. assumption, supposition; 3. counter *(luggage office etc.)*
Annahmebedingung *f* condition of acceptance
Annahmebereich *m (stats)* acceptance region
Annahmebescheinigung *f* receipt
Annahmefrist *f* period of acceptance
Annahmegrenze *f (stats)* acceptance boundary
Annahmelinie *f (stats)* acceptance line
Annahmestelle *f* receiving office *(letters, parcels etc.)*; centre [shop, counter] buying scrap *(and other waste material)*
Annahmeuntersuchung *f (stats)* acceptance inspection
Annahmevermerk *m* (note of) acceptance
Annahmeverweigerung *f* non-acceptance, rejection (of acceptance) *(goods, bill)*; refusal to accept *(delivery of letter etc.)*
Annahmewahrscheinlichkeit *f (stats)* probability of acceptance
Annahmezahl *f (stats)* acceptance number
annehmbar acceptable; reasonable; fair *(price etc.)*
annehmen 1. to accept *(proposal, application etc.)*; to receive *(letter, luggage etc.)*; to take delivery of *(goods etc.)*; to pass *(bill, resolution etc.)*; to adopt *(theory etc.)*; 2. to assume, to suppose, to presume ◊ **einstimmig ~** to carry [agree] unanimously
Annehmer *m* acceptor; drawee *(bill of exchange)*
annektieren to annex
Annexion *f* annexation
Annonce *f* advertisement *(s.a.* **Anzeige***)* ◊ **eine ~ in die Zeitung setzen** to put an advertisement in the newspaper
annoncieren to advertise
Annuität *f* annuity
Annuitätenanleihe *f* instalment loan
Annuitätenhypothek *f* instalment mortgage
annullierbar annullable
annullieren to annul, to nullify, to declare null and void, to cancel *(order, contract etc.)*; to set aside *(judgement)*
Annullierung *f* annulment, cancellation
Annullierungskosten *pl* cost of annulment [cancellation]
Anomalität *f (stats)* abnormality

anordnen 1. to decree; to order, to instruct; to regulate, to direct *(procedure etc.)*; 2. to arrange, to lay out *(machinery etc.)*
Anordnung *f* 1. degree; order, instruction; regulation, direction *(procedure etc.)*; 2. arrangement, layout *(machinery etc.)*
~, **behördliche** administrative order
~, **einstweilige** restraining order
~, **gerichtliche** judicial writ, fiat
~, **ministerielle** ministerial order
~, **räumliche** configuration; spatial relationships *(parts of residential areas, buildings etc.)*
~, **zeitliche** arrangement according to time schedule
~, **zyklische** *(stats)* cyclical order
Anordnungsmaßzahl *f (stats)* order statistic
Anordnungsmeßzahl *f s.* **Anordnungsmaßzahl**
Anordnungsstatistik *f (stats)* order statistics
Anordnungswerte *mpl* (order of magnitude of) values
Anormalität *f s.* **Anomalität**
Anormalitätsindex *m (stats)* index of abnormality
anpassen to fit (on) *(garment etc.)*; to adjust, to conform *(s.th. to s.th.)*; to make *s.th.* suitable for *s.th.*; **sich ~** to adapt o.s. *(to situation etc.)*
Anpassung *f* adaptation, adjustment *(to situation etc.)*; conformity *(with standards etc.)*
~, **beste** *(stats)* best fit
~ der Preise adjustment of prices
Anpassungsfähigkeit *f* adaptability, flexibility
Anpassungsklausel *f* accomodating clause *(allowing for adjustment or invalidation of agreement, contract etc., by mutual consent)*
Anpassungsprozeß *m* process of adjustment
Anpassungstest *m* fitness [aptitude] test; *(stats)* smooth test
anpflanzen to plant, to cultivate
Anpflanzung *f* 1. plantation; 2. planting *(cultivation)*
anpreisen to (re)commend, to praise, to boost
Anpreisung *f* recommendation; praise, boost
Anrainer *m* neighbour; *(jur)* abutter, abutting owner
Anrainerstaat *m* neighbouring state
anrechnen 1. to credit *(a sum to s.o., s.o. with a sum)*; to charge *(s.o. a sum, a sum to s.o.)*; to apply *(payment to a debt etc.)*; 2. to count *(s.th. to s.o.'s credit)*, to appreciate *(s.o.'s help etc.)*
Anrechnung *f* crediting, charge, debiting
anrechnungsfähig countable
Anrecht *n* 1. claim, right, title; 2. season ticket *(theatre)*
Anreiz *m* incentive, stimulus; inducement
~, **materieller** material incentive
~, **moralischer** moral [non-material] incentive
Anreizfonds *m* incentive fund

Anreizsystem *n* system of incentives *(material and moral)*
ansammeln to collect, to gather *(information)*; to accumulate *(capital)*; to pile up *(stocks)*
Ansammlung *f* collection, gathering *(information)*; accumulation *(capital)*; piling up *(stocks)*
ansässig resident, domiciled ◊ **~ machen** to make (people) settle down (permanently); **~ werden** to settle; **sich ~ machen** to take up one's residence
Ansatz *m* estimate; appropriation, amount budgeted
Ansatzfehler *m (stats)* error in equations
anschaffen to buy, to purchase; to procure, to provide, to acquire
Anschaffung *f* buying, purchase; procurement, provision, acquisition
Anschaffungskosten *pl* purchase cost; procurement cost, cost of acquisition; original cost, price delivered
Anschaffungspreis *m* purchase price
Anschaffungswert *m* value of acquisition
Anschlag *m* 1. estimate, valuation *(costs, price)*; assessment *(tax)*; 2. notice, announcement; 3. placard, poster, bill ◊ **durch ~ bekanntmachen** to put up a notice; **einen ~ machen** to post [stick] a notice [bill]
anschlagen to post, to stick *(notice, bill etc.)*
Anschlagwerbung *f* advertizing by posters
Anschluß *m (pol)* annexation *(territory)*; joining *(party)*; connection *(train)*; supply *(electricity, gas etc.)*
anschreiben 1. to write *(to s.o.)*; 2. to debit *(s.th. to s.o.)*, to charge *(s.th. up to s.o.)*, to put *s.th.* on *s.o.'s* account ◊ **~ lassen** to buy *s.th.* on credit
Anschreiben *n* letter; circular; covering note
Anschrift *f* address
Anschriftenverzeichnis *n* directory
Ansicht *f* 1. view, prospect, outlook; 2. point of view, opinion, idea ◊ **zur ~** for inspection, on approval [approbation]
ansiedeln to settle (down); **sich ~** to settle; ◊ **sich wieder ~** to resettle, to relocate
Ansiedlung *f* settlement, colony
Ansiedlungsaufwand *m* settlement costs
Ansprechwiederholung *f (stats)* call-back
Anspruch *m* right, title; claim; demand ◊ **~ erheben** to raise a claim; **~ haben auf** to have right [title] to; to have a claim to; **einen ~ abtreten** to assign a claim; **einen ~ anerkennen** to admit [allow] a claim; **einen ~ anmelden** to notify [file] a claim *(bankruptcy)*; **einen ~ aufgeben** to waive [renounce] a claim; **einen ~ aufrechterhalten** to keep up a claim; **einen ~ befriedigen** to settle a claim; **einen ~ durchsetzen** to enforce a claim;

einen ~ feststellen to establish a claim;
einen ~ geltend machen to assert a claim;
seinen ~ auf dem ordentlichen Rechtsweg verfolgen to prosecute one's claim before the ordinary civil courts
~, älterer prior claim
~, anerkannter proved claim
~ auf Lohnrückforderung claim for repayment [for recovery] of wage(s)
~, befristeter deferred claim
~, begründeter sound claim
~, berechtigter rightful claim
~, bevorrechtigter preferential claim
~, gemeinschaftlicher joint right
~, gesetzlicher lawful claim
~, persönlicher personal right
~, rechtmäßiger legal claim
~, schuldrechtlicher debt claim
~, unberechtigter false claim
~, verfallener forfeited claim
~, verjährter claim barred by the statute of limitations
~, vermögensrechtlicher claim under the law of property
~, zusätzlicher additional [supplementary] claim
Anspruchsabtretung *f* assignment of an interest
Anspruchsbefriedigung *f* satisfaction of claim
anspruchsberechtigt eligible for, entitled to *(claim etc.)*; to have the legal right *(to file a claim)*
Anspruchsberechtigter *m* rightful claimant
Anspruchsverjährung *f* extinction of claim
Anstalt *f* institution, establishment
Anstaltsfürsorge *f* institutional care
Ansteckungsverteilung *f (stats)* contagious distribution
anstehen 1. to queue (up), *(Am)* to line up, to stand in line; 2. to be up for *(decision etc.)*
ansteigen to increase, to rise; to improve *(conditions, quality etc.)*
Ansteigen *n* increase, rise; improvement *(conditions, quality etc.)*
anstellen 1. to queue, *(Am)* to line up; 2. to give employment, to employ, to engage, to hire *(workmen etc.)*; 3. to switch on, to start *(machine)*; 4. to make, to carry out *(experiments etc.)*
Anstellung *f* employment, job
Anstellungsvertrag *m* contract of employment
Anstieg *m s.* Ansteigen
Anstoß *m* impact; impulse
anstrengen 1. to exert, to strain; 2. *(jur)* to initiate, to institute *(proceedings against s.o.)*; sich ~ to make an effort, to exert o.s., to endeavour *(to do s.th.)*
Anstrengung *f* 1. effort, strain; endeavour; 2. *(jur)* initiation *(of proceedings against s.o.)*

Ansturm *m* run, rush
Antagonismus *m* antagonism
antagonistisch antagonistic
Anteil *m* part, portion, share; interest; quota
~, bestimmter stated portion
~, gleicher aliquot portion
~, verhältnismäßiger comparative share; quota
anteilig proportional, sharing, in proportion to
anteilmäßig proportionate, proportional; pro rata
Anteilpapier *n* share certificate
anteilsberechtigt participating, to be entitled *(to a share in s.th.)*
Anteilschein *m* share certificate; share (of stock); coupon *(dividend)*
Anteilseigentum *n* share of ownership [property]
Anteilseigner *m* shareholder, *(Am)* stockholder
Anteilspacht *f* percentage lease
Anteilsübertragung *f* assignment of an interest
Anteilwirtschaft *f* half-share farming; share-crop system
Anteilzahl *f* contingent; numerical quota
Anteilziffer *f* share index
Antidumpingzoll *m* antidumping duty
Antifaschismus *m* antifascism
Antifaschist *m* antifascist
antifaschistisch antifascist
Antigewerkschaftsgesetze *npl* anti-trade-union laws
Antihavarietraining *n* training for emergencies *(fire, flood etc.)*
antiimperialistisch anti-imperialist(ic)
antiinflationär anti-inflationary
antiinflationistisch *s.* antiinflationär
antikapitalistisch anti-capitalist(ic)
antikolonial anti-colonial
Antikommunist *m* anti-communist
antikommunistisch anti-communist
antinational antinational
Antiquariat *n* second-hand bookshop; antiquarian bookshop
antiquarisch second-hand; antiquarian
Antiquität *f* antique
Antiquitätenhandel *m* antique trade, trade in antiques
Antiquitätenhändler *m* antique dealer; curio-dealer
Antiquitätenhandlung *f* antique shop; curio-shop
Antiquitätenladen *m s.* Antiquitätenhandlung
antirevolutionär anti-revolutionary
Antitrustgesetze *npl* anti-trust laws
Antrag *m* application; proposition; motion *(parliament)*
~ auf Beteiligung application to participate
Antragsformular *n* application form
Antragsteller *m* applicant; proponent; claimant; mover *(of motion in parliament etc.)*

Antwort *f* answer, reply, response ◊ **in Erwartung Ihrer ~** awaiting your reply
antworten to answer, to reply, to respond
Antwortkarte *f* reply card
Antwortschein *m* reply coupon
~, internationaler international reply coupon
Antwortschreiben *n* (written) answer [reply]; answering letter
An- und Verkauf *m* buying and selling of second-hand goods
An- und Verkaufsgeschäft *n* second-hand shop
anvertrauen to entrust *(s.o. with s.th.)*, to place *s.th.* in *s.o.'s* charge; *(jur)* to deliver *s.th.* to *s.o.* in trust; to confide *(s.th. to s.o.)*
anwachsen to (begin to) grow, to increase
Anwachsen *n* growth, increase
Anwalt *m* lawyer; solicitor; advocate, attorney; barrister, *(Am)* counselor-at-law *(for the defence)*; plaintiff's counsel *(for prosecution)*
Anwaltsbüro *n* lawyer's office
Anwaltsfirma *f* firm of lawyers
Anwaltsgebühr *f* lawyer's fee
Anwaltshonorar *n s.* **Anwaltsgebühr**
Anwaltskosten *pl* legal costs
Anwaltszwang *m* obligation to be legally represented in court
anweisen to direct, to instruct, to order *(s.o. to do s.th.)*, to give directions [instructions] *(to s.o.)*; to assign *(a place, a position etc., to s.o.)*; to allocate, to allot *(s.th. to s.o.)*; to remit *(money to s.o.)*; to transfer, to credit (a sum) to *(s.o.'s account)*
Anweisung *f* direction, instruction *(to s.o. to do s.th.)*; guidance *(on s.th. to s.o.)*; assignment, assignation *(of place, position etc., to s.o.)*; allocation, allotment *(of s.th. to s.o.)*; remittance *(of money to s.o.)*; transfer, transference, crediting (a sum) to *(s.o.'s account)*
anweisungsberechtigt authorized *(to give orders, instructions etc.)*
anwendbar applicable *(rule etc.)*, useable *(method etc.)*, employable *(force etc.)*
anwenden to apply *(rule etc.)*, to use *(method etc.)*, to employ, to resort to *(force etc.)*
Anwender *m* user
Anwenderberatung *f* technical advice *(to users of investment goods etc.)*
Anwenderbetrieb *m* industrial user *(of tools, machinery etc.)*
anwenderfreundlich user-friendly
Anwendernutzen *m* user's gain *(investment goods etc.)*
anwenderorientiert user-orient(at)ed
Anwenderprogramm *n (d.pr.)* user (application) program
anwenderprogrammierbar *(d.pr.)* field-programmable

Anwendersoftware *f (d.pr.)* application software
Anwendung *f* application *(rule etc.)*, use *(method etc.)*, employment, resort to *(force etc.)*
~ auf Produktionsebene application on the production floor
Anwendungsbereich *m* field [range, scope] of application [utilization]
Anwendungsforschung *f* applied research
Anwendungsparameter *m* parameter of application [utilization]
Anwohnerschutz *m* protective measures for residential areas, local environmental protection
Anzahl *f* number, quantity
~ in einer Klasse *(stats)* absolute frequency
anzahlen to pay on account; to make a down payment, to pay a first instalment *(hire-purchase)*
Anzahlung *f* payment on account; first instalment *(hire-purchase)* ◊ **eine ~ leisten** to pay (a sum) an account; to pay a first instalment
Anzeige *f* announcement, notice, advice; advertisement; *(ins)* disclosure; *(jur)* information, denunciation ◊ **~ erstatten** to give information; **eine ~ aufgeben** to advertise; **laut ~** per advice; **ohne weitere ~** without further notice; **zur ~ bringen** to give notice; to denounce, to inform
~, amtliche official announcement
~, gerichtliche legal notice
~, schriftliche notice in writing
~, telegrafische cable (message) *(from overseas)*, telegram *(inland)*
anzeigen to indicate, to announce, to advise; to record, to register; to advertise; *(ins)* to disclose
Anzeigenannahmestelle *f* advertising agency
Anzeigenpreis *m* advertising rate
Anzeigepflicht *f* duty to report *(to police etc.)*
anzeigepflichtig notifiable
anziehen 1. *(com)* to rise, to advance, to increase *(price etc.)*; to attract, to draw *(customers etc.)*; 2. to absorb, to take up *(moisture etc.)*
anziehend attractive; rising *(prices, market etc.)*
Appropriation *f* appropriation *(property etc.)*
Approximation *f* approximation
Äquivalent *n* equivalent
Äquivalentenaustausch *m* equivalent exchange
Äquivalentform *f* equivalent form
Äquivalentgröße *f (stats)* equivalent
Äquivalenz *f* equivalence
Äquivalenzbeziehungen *fpl* relations [relationships] of equivalence
Äquivalenzmethode *f* equivalence method *(for calculating similar goods)*
Äquivalenztheorie *f* theory of equivalence, equivalence theory

Äquivalenzwert *m* equivalent value
Äquivalenzziffer *f* equivalent rate
Äquivalenzziffernrechnung *f* calculation with equivalent rates
Arbeit *f* 1. work, labour; toil; 2. employment, occupation, job; task, assignment; 3. order in hand; 4. operation, activity; business, concern ◇ **eine ~ verrichten** to work [be working] on (s.th.)
~, **abstrakte** *(pol ec)* abstract labour *(labour capacity in general, irrespective of its concrete appearance and creating the value of a good)*
~, **analytisch-prognostische** long-term forecast
~, **ehrenamtliche** honorary work
~, **einfache** simple labour *(requiring no specialized skill)*
~, **gebrauchswertschaffende** *(pol ec)* use-value creating labour
~, **geistige** mental [intellectual] work
~, **geistig-schöpferische** mental [intellectual] creative work *(as opposed to mental routine work)*
~, **gelernte** skilled labour
~, **gemeinschaftliche** joint work, teamwork
~, **genossenschaftliche** co-operative work
~, **geschützte** light work (for the partially disabled)
~, **gesellschaftlich notwendige** *(pol ec)* socially necessary labour
~, **gesellschaftliche** public honorary work *(voluntary work for the good of the community)*
~, **gesundheitsgefährdende** labour involving hazards to health
~, **individuelle** *(pol ec)* individual labour
~, **industrielle** industrial labour
~, **kollektive** *(pol ec)* collective work, teamwork
~, **komplizierte** skilled [complicated, comprehensive] labour
~, **konkrete** *(pol ec)* concrete labour *(well-directed activity creating the use-value of goods)*
~, **körperlich schwere** heavy manual [bodily] labour [work]
~, **körperliche** physical [manual, bodily] labour
~, **lebendige** *(pol ec)* living labour *(expenditure of physical and mental capacity in work process)*
~, **leichte** light work
~, **manuelle** manual [bodily] work
~, **Mehrwert produzierende** *(pol ec)* labour creating surplus value
~, **multiplizierte einfache** *(pol ec)* multiplied simple labour *(equivalent to* **Arbeit, komplizierte***)*
~, **nichtproduktive** non-productive labour
~, **notwendige** *(pol ec)* necessary labour *(part of living labour necessary to produce goods for reproducing the working capacity of a worker and his family)*

~, **potenzierte einfache** s. **multiplizierte einfache**
~, **private** private labour
~, **produktive** productive labour; productive work
~, **qualifizierte** qualified labour *(labour with skills and other qualifications in connection with working process)*
~, **schöpferische** creative work
~, **unbezahlte** unpaid work
~, **unmittelbar gesellschaftliche** directly social labour
~, **unproduktive** s. **nichtproduktive**
~, **verantwortungsbewußte** responsible job, job with a sense of responsibility
~, **vergegenständlichte** *(pol ec)* materialized [dead] labour *(previously expended labour now materialized in machinery, material etc.)*
~, **warenproduzierende** *(pol ec)* commodity producing labour
Arbeiten *fpl*:
~, **durch Zeitstudien erfaßte** measured work
~, **durch Zeitstudien nicht erfaßte** uncontrolled work
~, **durch Zeitwerte erfaßte** controlled work
Arbeiter *m* worker, workman; operative, mechanic, operator; labourer *(usually unskilled)*
~, **angelernter** semiskilled worker
~, **ungelernter** unskilled worker
Arbeiteraristokratie *f* labour aristocracy
Arbeiterausschuß *m* workers' committee, shop council
Arbeiterberufsverkehr *m* workers' commuter service
Arbeiterbevölkerung *f* working population
Arbeiterbewegung *f* working class [workers', labour] movement
~, **internationale** international working class [workers', labour] movement
Arbeiterbildung *f* workers' education
Arbeiterfahrkarte *f* workman's ticket
Arbeiterfamilie *f* working-class family
Arbeiterklasse *f* working class
Arbeiterpartei *f* workers' party
Arbeiterrückfahrkarte *f* workman's return ticket
Arbeiterschaft *f* working people, workers, workmen
Arbeitersiedlung *f* worker's settlement, housing estate (for workers)
Arbeiterstamm *m* permanent workers *(particularly skilled workers)*
Arbeiterverband *m* workers' association
Arbeiterversorgung *f* employee supply system *(shopping and other facilities in enterprises)*
Arbeiterviertel *n* working-class quarter
Arbeiterwohnungen *fpl* workers' flats

Arbeiterwohnungsbaugenossenschaft *f* (AWG) workers' housing co-operative
Arbeitgeber *m* employer
Arbeitgeberanteil *m* employer's contribution *(to social insurance)*
Arbeitgeberverband *m* employers' association
Arbeitnehmer *m* worker, wage earner, employee
Arbeitnehmeranteil *m* employee's contribution *(to social insurance)*
Arbeitsablauf *m* flow of work [operations], process of operations, (flow) process
Arbeitsablaufplan *m* (flow) process chart
Arbeitsablaufstudie *f* work flow [operations process] analysis, (flow) process study
Arbeitsamt *n* labour exchange
Arbeitsanalyse *f* work [operation] analysis
Arbeitsanforderungen *fpl* job requirements *(knowledge, skills, physical attributes etc., needed for a particular job)*
Arbeitsanweisung *f* 1. job assignment; 2. job instructions
Arbeitsäquivalent *n* labour equivalent
Arbeitsästhetik *f* industrial aesthetics
Arbeitsatmosphäre *f* working atmosphere
Arbeitsaufgabe *f* job *(duties to be fulfilled according to the terms of the contract of employment)*
Arbeitsaufnahme *f* taking up a job; assumption of office
Arbeitsauftrag *m* job [work] order
Arbeitsauftragsschein *m* job-order form
Arbeitsaufwand *m* expenditure of labour, labour input
~, **betrieblich notwendiger** necessary expenditure [input] of labour at an enterprise
~, **direkter** direct expenditure [input] of labour
~, **gesellschaftlich notwendiger** socially necessary expenditure [input] of labour
~, **gesellschaftlicher** expenditure [input] of social labour
~, **indirekter** indirect expenditure [input] of labour
~, **individueller** individual expenditure [input] of labour
~, **voller** full expenditure [input] of labour
Arbeitsaufwandskoeffizient *m* coefficient of expenditure [input] of labour
Arbeitsaufwandsmodell *n* model of expenditure [input] of labour
Arbeitsaufwandsveränderung *f* change [alteration] of expenditure [input] of labour
arbeitsaufwendig labour-expensive
Arbeitsausfall *m* loss of working hours, man-days lost
Arbeitsausgleich *m* (agric) levelling work load *(to ensure an even work load throughout the year)*
Arbeitsbeanspruchung *f* occupational strain [stress], strain on the job

Arbeitsbedingungen *fpl* working conditions
~, **kulturvolle** attractive occupational environment
~, **materielle** physical [material] working conditions
~, **menschenwürdige** humane working conditions, working conditions commensurate with human dignity
~, **persönlichkeitsfördernde** working conditions promoting personality
~, **produktivitätsfördernde** productivity-promoting working conditions
arbeitsbefreit given leave from work *(due to illness etc.)*
Arbeitsbefreiung *f* leave from work *(sick leave etc.)*
Arbeitsbefreiungsbescheinigung *f* medical certificate *(for sick leave)*
Arbeitsbeginn *m* start [commencement, beginning] of work
Arbeitsbegleitkarte *f* job order card
Arbeitsbelastung *f* work load
Arbeitsberatung *f* (job) discussion session, (departmental) meeting
Arbeitsbereich *m* sphere [field] of work; scope *(administrative department etc.)*
Arbeitsbereitschaft *f* willingness [readiness] to work
Arbeitsbericht *m* report
Arbeitsbeschaffung *f* creation [providing, provision] of employment, creation of jobs, job creation
Arbeitsbeschaffungsmaßnahmen *fpl* measures to create employment [jobs]
Arbeitsbeschaffungsprogramm *n* employment programme [scheme]
Arbeitsbeschränkung *f* work [job] limitation
Arbeitsbeschreibung *f* work specification; job description
Arbeitsbewertung *f* job evaluation
~, **analytische** analytical job evaluation
~, **qualitative** *(obs)* qualitative job evaluation
~, **quantitative** *(obs)* quantitative job evaluation
Arbeitsbeziehungen *fpl* labour relations
Arbeitsbrigade *f* work team
Arbeitsbuch *n* employment book [record]
Arbeitscharakteristik *f* job description; description of a working cycle [operation]
Arbeitsdisziplin *f* work [job] discipline
Arbeitseffektivität *f* labour efficiency
Arbeitseinheit *f* (AE) work unit, basic man-day *(unit for measuring the work done by a member of a co-operative farm; basis for payment to members)*
Arbeitseinkommen *n* earned income
Arbeitseinsatz *m* voluntary work *(cultivation of gardens in residential areas etc.)*

Arbeitseinstellung f (personal) attitude to work
Arbeitsentgelt n pay; wage(s) *(workers)*; salary *(employees)*; remuneration *(co-operative members, liberal professions)*
Arbeitserfahrungen fpl job [vocational, occupational] experience
Arbeitserleichterungen fpl devices and facilities to enlighten work
Arbeitserschwernis f excessive work strain
Arbeitsersparnis f saving of labour
arbeitsfähig able-bodied, able to work, capable of work(ing), fit for employment [work, duty]
Arbeitsfähigkeit f ability to work, working capability, fitness for employment [work, duty]
Arbeitsfertigkeiten fpl skills, workmanship
Arbeitsfluß m flow of operations
Arbeitsfolge f sequence of operations
Arbeitsfortschrittsbild n *(stats)* Gantt progress chart
Arbeitsgang m work cycle, (working) operation [process]; pass
Arbeitsgegenstand m material, subject of work
Arbeitsgemeinschaft f team, working group
~, **überbetriebliche** inter-enterprise working group
Arbeitsgenauigkeit f accuracy (in work)
Arbeitsgericht n labour [industrial] court
Arbeitsgerichtsbarkeit f jurisdiction in labour disputes
Arbeitsgeschwindigkeit f working speed
Arbeitsgesetzbuch n labour code
Arbeitsgestaltung f job layout [design]
Arbeitsgrundlage f basis of work, working basis
Arbeitsgruppe f (work)team, group of workers, working group
Arbeitshaltung f 1. attitude to work; 2. working position
Arbeitshilfen fpl:
~, **technische** technical devices [aids]
Arbeitshygiene f factory hygiene [sanitation]
Arbeitsingenieur m industrial [production] engineer *(in charge of work organization, job and workplace layout etc.)*
Arbeitsinstruktion f job instruction
Arbeitsinstrumente npl instruments of labour
Arbeitsintensität f labour intensity
arbeitsintensiv labour-intensive, labour-consuming
Arbeitsjahre npl years of employment [service]
Arbeitskampagne f work campaign; seasonal work
Arbeitskampf m labour dispute, industrial struggle; strike
Arbeitskittel m s. **Arbeitskleidung**
Arbeitsklassifizierung f s. **Arbeitsbewertung**
Arbeitskleidung f overalls, work(ing) clothes
Arbeitsklima n s. **Arbeitsatmosphäre**

Arbeitskollektiv n work(ing) team, workteam
Arbeitskraft f 1. working power; capacity for work; 2. worker
Arbeitskräfte fpl labour (force), manpower; workers, personnel
~, **ausländische** foreign workers
~, **einsetzbare** employable labour force
Arbeitskräftebedarf m labour [manpower] demand [requirements]
Arbeitskräftebereitstellung f labour [manpower] supply
Arbeitskräftebestand m manpower stock, size of the labour force *(of an enterprise etc.)*
Arbeitskräftebilanz f labour force [manpower] balance (sheet)
Arbeitskräfteeinsatz m placement [use] of labour force [manpower]
Arbeitskräfteeinsparung f saving [economizing] of labour
Arbeitskräfteentwicklung f labour force [manpower] development
~, **territorial differenzierte** variable development of labour force according to regions
Arbeitskräftefluktuation f labour [manpower] turnover
Arbeitskräftelenkung f direction of labour force [manpower]
Arbeitskräftenormativ n manpower standard [norm] *(used to indicate the permissible number of personnel in enterprises)*
Arbeitskräftependler m commuter, commuting worker
Arbeitskräfteplan m manpower plan
Arbeitskräfteplanung f workforce [labour force, humanpower] planning
Arbeitskräfterechnung f manpower calculation(s)
Arbeitskräftereserven fpl labour force [manpower] reserves
Arbeitskräfteressourcen fpl labour (force) [manpower] resources [potential], human resources
Arbeitskräfteressourcenbilanz f balance (sheet) of labour (force) [manpower] resources [potential]
Arbeitskräftestatistik f labour force [manpower] statistics
Arbeitskräftestruktur f labour force [manpower] structure *(total number of employees broken down according to age, sex, educational level, training, occupation and other attributes)*
Arbeitskräfteüberschuß m labour force [manpower] surplus
Arbeitskräfteumsetzung f transfer of labour [manpower]
Arbeitskräfteverteilung f labour force [manpower] allocation

Arbeitskräftewerbung *f* labour [manpower] recruitment
Arbeitskreis *m* workteam, study group, committee
Arbeitskultur *f* (attractive) occupational environment
Arbeitskurve *f* performance curve
~, **physiologische** (physiological) performance curve
Arbeitsleistung *f* performance; amount of work done; output *(machine, factory etc.)*; efficiency *(personnel, machines etc.)*; power *(engines etc.)*
Arbeitslohn *m* pay; wage(s) *(workers)*; salary *(employees)*
arbeitslos unemployed
Arbeitslosenarmee *f* army of unemployed (workers)
Arbeitslosenheer *n s.* **Arbeitslosenarmee**
Arbeitslosenunterstützung *f* unemployment benefit(s) [pay], dole
Arbeitslosenversicherung *f* unemployment insurance
Arbeitsloser *m* unemployed person
Arbeitslosigkeit *f* unemployment
~, **chronische** chronic unemployment
~, **entwicklungsmäßig bedingte** technological unemployment
~, **fließende** temporary unemployment *(after losing a job)*
~, **latente** disguised unemployment
~, **saisonale** seasonal unemployment
~, **schwankende** fluctuating unemployment
~, **stockende** stagnating unemployment *(unemployment of workers who find jobs irregularly)*
~, **strukturelle** structural unemployment
~, **verschleierte** *s.* ~, **latente**
~, **vorübergehende** temporary unemployment
Arbeitsmangel *m* lack [shortage] of work [jobs]
Arbeitsmarkt *m* labour market
Arbeitsmethode *f* work(ing) method, method of work
Arbeitsmilieu *n* working environment [conditions]
Arbeitsmittel *npl* tools, means of work
~, **geringwertige und schnellverschleißende** tools and devices of low value and short service life
Arbeitsmittelbestand *m* stock [store] of tools *(machines etc.)*
Arbeitsmittelintensität *f* equipment-labour [equipment-manpower] ratio *(value of equipment divided by number of persons operating it)*
Arbeitsmittelproduktivität *f* productivity of tools *(machines etc.)*
Arbeitsmittelstudie *f* analysis of tools *(machines etc.)*
Arbeitsmoral *f* work morale

Arbeitsmotivation *f* work [job] motivation
Arbeitsnachweis(stelle *f***)** *m* labour exchange (office/agency), employment agency [bureau]
Arbeitsnorm *f* work standard
~, **technisch begründete (TAN)** technological work standard *(based on technical and economic data etc.)*
~, **vorläufige (VAN)** temporary work standard
Arbeitsnormung *f* fixing [setting] of work standards; work [labour] measurement
Arbeitsökonomie *f* labour economics
Arbeitsökonomik *f s.* **Arbeitsökonomie**
Arbeitsoperation *f* working operation
Arbeitsordnung *f* factory [shop] regulations
Arbeitsorganisation *f* work organization
~, **wissenschaftliche (WAO)** scientific work organization *(including time and motion studies, job classification, work standardization, job layout, working conditions etc.)*
Arbeitsort *m* place of work
Arbeitspapiere *npl* employment documents
Arbeitspause *f* interval, break
Arbeitspflichten *fpl* employment duties, duties under [arising from] the employment contract
Arbeitspflichtverletzung *f* violation of employment duties
Arbeitsphase *f* stage of processing [work]
Arbeitsplan *m* working plan; production schedule (of operations)
Arbeitsplanstammkarte *f* card for working plan [production schedule]
Arbeitsplanung *f* work planning; operations planning [scheduling]; production scheduling (of operations)
Arbeitsplatz *m* 1. job, employment, situation; 2. workplace, work bench
~, **geschützter** workplace for partially disabled
Arbeitsplatzanalyse *f* workplace study
Arbeitsplatzbewertung *f* workplace evaluation
Arbeitsplätze *mpl* jobs ◊ ~, **schaffen** to provide [create] jobs
Arbeitsplatzgestaltung *f* work(place) layout
Arbeitsplatzkartei *f* card index of workplaces
Arbeitsplatzmethode *f* workplace method *(for fixing manpower demand)*
Arbeitsplatzstammkarte *f* record card of workplace *(with details of machine, devices etc.)*
Arbeitsplatzstudie *f* workplace study
Arbeitsplatzversorgung *f* 1. supply at workplace *(material, tools etc.)*; 2. catering at workplace
Arbeitsplatzwechsel *m* change of job; change of workplace
Arbeitsprobit *n* *(stats)* working probit
Arbeitsproduktivität *f* labour productivity
Arbeitsproduktivitätsmessung *f* measurement of labour productivity

Arbeitsprozeß *m* work (process)
Arbeitspsychologie *f* industrial psychology
Arbeitsquantum *n* quota of work
Arbeitsrecht *n* labour law
~, **internationales** international labour law
Arbeitsrechtsfähigkeit *f* legal capacity under labour code
Arbeitsrechtssache *f* industrial [labour] case
Arbeitsrechtsstreitigkeiten *fpl* work [industrial] disputes
Arbeitsrechtsverhältnis *n* employment relationship
Arbeitsrente *f (hist)* labour rent *(a form of ground rent in feudalism)*
Arbeitsressourcen *fpl s.* **Arbeitskräfteressourcen**
Arbeitsrhythmus *m* work(ing) rhythm
Arbeitsrichter *m* arbitrator [judge] for labour affairs
Arbeitsrückstände *mpl* arrears in work
Arbeitsschutz *m* labour protection
Arbeitsschutzanordnung *f* labour protection rules
Arbeitsschutzaufsicht *f* supervision of labour protection
Arbeitsschutzbelehrung *f* instructions on safety rules
Arbeitsschutzingenieur *m* labour safety engineer, engineer in charge of labour protection
Arbeitsschutzinspektor *m* labour safety inspector
Arbeitsschutzinstruktionen *fpl* labour safety rules *(in an enterprise)*
Arbeitsschutzkleidung *f* (industrial) protective clothing
Arbeitsschutzkommission *f* labour protection committee
Arbeitsschutzkontrollbuch *n* labour protection record *(for registering accidents, instructions on labour protection and safety rules etc.)*
Arbeitsschutzobmann *m* union steward for labour protection
Arbeitsschutzorgane *npl* labour protection bodies
Arbeitsschutzvorschriften *fpl* labour protection rules
Arbeitssicherheit *f* labour safety
Arbeitssoziologie *f* labour sociology
arbeitssparend labour-saving
Arbeitssphäre *f* field of work [activity]
Arbeitsspitze *f* peak of work
Arbeitsstatistik *f* labour statistics
Arbeitsstätte *f s.* **Arbeitsstelle**
Arbeitsstättensystematik *f (obs)* classification of places of employment [work]
Arbeitsstelle *f* place of employment [work]

Arbeitsstreitigkeiten *fpl s.* **Arbeitsrechtsstreitigkeiten**
Arbeitsstudie *f* work study
Arbeitsstudium *n* work analysis
Arbeitsstufe *f* stage [phase] of manufacture
Arbeitsstunden *fpl* working hours; man-hours
Arbeitstag *m* working day, workday
Arbeitstagaufnahme *f* workday study [analysis] *(a form of work study analysing all activities during a workday or shift)*
Arbeitstakt *m* 1. (working) cycle time; 2. *(tech)* number of strokes (per cycle)
Arbeitstarifvertrag *m* agreed wage-rate, wage-rate contract, wage [industrial, *(Am)* collective] agreement
Arbeitstechnik *f* 1. working method, method of work; 2. *(agric)* machines and equipment specialized (according to division of labour)
Arbeitsteilung *f* division of labour
~, **allgemeine** general division of labour *(industry, agriculture, transport etc.)*
~, **arbeitskraftbezogene** division of labour in relation to manpower
~, **berufliche** occupational division of labour, division of labour according to occupation
~, **besondere** particular division of labour *(chemicals, metal manufacturing, electrical engineering etc.)*
~, **gesellschaftliche** social division of labour
~ **im einzelnen** individual division of labour *(in an enterprise)*
~, **innerbetriebliche** -work specialization, intra--works division of labour
~, **internationale** international division of labour
~, **intersystemare** inter-system division of labour *(between countries with different social orders)*
~, **intrasystemare** intra-system division of labour
~, **natürliche** natural division of labour
~, **qualifikationsmäßige** division of labour according to qualification [skills]
~, **technologische** technological division of labour, division of labour according to technology
~, **territoriale** regional division of labour
~ **zwischen Zentrum und Peripherie** division of labour between the centre and the periphery *(in development economic theory)*
Arbeitstempo *n* pace [tempo, speed] of work
Arbeitstherapie *f* occupational therapy
Arbeitstraining *n* work [on-the-job] training
Arbeitsumwelt *f* working [occupational] environment; working atmosphere
Arbeits- und Forschungsgemeinschaft *f* work and research team [group]

Arbeits- und Lebensbedingungen *fpl* working and living conditions
Arbeits- und Zeitstudium *n* time and motion study
arbeitsunfähig disabled, unable to [unfit for] work
Arbeitsunfähigkeit *f* disablement, inability to [unfitness for] work
~, **dauernde** permanent disablement [inability to work, unfitness for work]
~, **zeitweilige** temporary disablement [inability to work, unfitness for work]
Arbeitsunfall *m* industrial accident, accident at work
~, **meldepflichtiger** notifiable industrial accident
Arbeitsunterbrechung *f* interruption of work, work stoppage
Arbeitsunterweisung *f* job instruction
Arbeitsverfahren *n* working method; technique of operation
Arbeitsvergütung *f* payment, remuneration
~ **in den landwirtschaftlichen Produktionsgenossenschaften (LPG)** payment [remuneration] in co-operative farms
Arbeitsverhalten *n* behaviour at work; work habits
Arbeitsverhältnis *n s.* **Arbeitsrechtsverhältnis**
Arbeitsvermittlung *f* 1. supply [provision] of employment; 2. employment [labour] exchange
Arbeitsvermögen *n* capacity for work
~, **betriebliches** labour capacity of an enterprise
~, **genutztes** utilized capacity for work
~, **gesellschaftliches** 1. social capacity for work; 2. labour force [manpower] resources, labour force *(on the national level)*
~, **individuelles** individual capacity for work
~, **potentielles gesellschaftliches** potential social capacity for work
Arbeitsverrichtung *f* working operation
Arbeitsvertrag *m* contract of employment
Arbeitsvorbereitung *f* preparations for work; operations scheduling
Arbeitsvorgang *m* work process, operation
Arbeitsvorschrift *f* job instruction, working rule
Arbeitswechsel *m* change of job
Arbeitsweise *f* method [style] of work
Arbeitswert *m (pol ec)* labour value
Arbeitswerttheorie *f (pol ec)* labour theory of value
Arbeitswettbewerb *m* emulation drive
Arbeitswissenschaft *f* labour science(s)
Arbeitswoche *f* working week
~, **gleitende** continuous [uninterrupted] working week [time]
~, **rollende** *s.* ~, **gleitende**

Arbeitszeit *f* working time [hours], hours of work
~, **gesellschaftlich notwendige** socially necessary working time [hours] *(to produce a good under average conditions of production)*
~, **gesetzliche** legally fixed working time [hours]
~, **nominelle** nominal working time [hours]
Arbeitszeitaufwand *m* expenditure [consumption] of working time, working time consumption
Arbeitszeitausfall *m* loss of working time [hours]
Arbeitszeitausnutzung *f* utilization of working time [hours]
Arbeitszeitbedarf *m* required working time *(based on work standards and other technical and economic indicators)*
Arbeitszeitbegrenzung *f* limitation of working time [hours]
Arbeitszeitbilanz *f* balance (sheet) of working time
Arbeitszeiterfassung *f* registration [recording] of working time [hours]
Arbeitszeitermittlung *f* timing *(carried out by time studies for one or a sequence of operations)*
Arbeitszeitfonds *m* total working time [hours]
Arbeitszeitgliederung *f* classification [breakdown] of working time
Arbeitszeitnachweis *m* record of working time
Arbeitszeitplan *m* timetable, time schedule *(for all employees)*
Arbeitszeitregelung *f* working time regulations
Arbeitszeitregime *n s.* **Arbeitszeitregelung**
Arbeitszeitreserven *fpl* reserves in working time
Arbeitszeitstaffelung *f* staggered working hours
Arbeitszeitstatistik *f* statistics of working time
Arbeitszeitstruktur *f* structure of working time
Arbeitszeitverkürzung *f* reduction of working time, shortening of working hours
Arbeitszeitverlust *m* loss of working time; loss of man-hours
Arbeitszufriedenheit *f* work [job] satisfaction, contentment with work
Arbeitszurückhaltung *f* holdback in performance
Arbeitszwang *m* obligation to work
Arbitrage *f* 1. arbitrage, arbitration; 2. arbitration court
~, **direkte** direct arbitration
~, **indirekte** indirect [*(Am)* triangular] arbitration
~ **über mehrere Zwischenplätze** compound arbitrage
arbitragefähig able to be admitted for arbitration
Arbitragegeschäfte *npl* arbitrage dealings [transactions]
Arbitrageklausel *f* arbitration clause

Arbitragerechnung *f* arbitration of exchange *(in foreign exchange transactions)*
Arbitragewerte *mpl* arbitrage stocks
Architekt *m* architect
Architektenbüro *n* architect's office
Archiv *n* 1. archives, records *(documents etc.)*; 2. archives *(building, room)*
Archivar *m* keeper of public records, registrar, archivist
archivieren to keep public records, to register (documents) for the archives
Arcus-Sinus-Transformation *f* *(stats)* arc-sine transformation; inverse-sine transformation
Arcus-Sinus-Verteilung *f* *(stats)* arc-sine distribution
Arcus-Tangens-Transformation *f* *(stats)* inverse-tan transformation
Arcus-Tangens-Verteilung *f* *(stats)* arc-tan distribution
arm poor
Armenkasse *f* (poor) relief fund
Armenpflege *f* poor relief, public assistance
Armenpfleger *m* guardian of the poor
Armenrecht *n* right to legal aid; right to sue in forma pauperis
Armenviertel *n* slum; poor quarter
ärmlich poor; paltry, scanty, meagre
Armut *f* poverty; destitution, indigence, penury, distress ⋄ **in ~ leben** to live in poverty
Art *f* kind, sort *(products etc.)*; nature, class *(people etc.)*; manner, mode, way *(acting, speaking etc.)*; style *(artistic work etc.)*; species *(plants, animals etc.)*; type *(persons etc.)*; breed *(dogs, horses etc.)*; variety *(flowers etc.)*
Arten *fpl*:
~ von lateinischen Quadraten *(stats)* species of latin squares
Artikel *m* 1. article *(commodity etc.)*; 2. article, section *(law etc.)*; article *(press etc.)* ⋄ **einen ~ führen** to deal in an article
Arzt *m* doctor; physician ⋄ **als ~ zulassen** to licence to practise medicine
ärztlich medical
Arztwahl *f*:
~, freie right to choose a doctor *(freedom to choose or change medical practitioner)*
asozial antisocial
Asozialer *m* antisocial person
Asozialität *f* antisocial attitude [behaviour, character]
Aspirant *m* candidate
Aspirantur *f* postgraduate studies *(for doctoral thesis)*
~, außerplanmäßige postgraduate studies by correspondence course
~, planmäßige full-time postgraduate studies
Assekurant *m* insurer

Assekuranz *f* insurance
Assekuranzbrief *m* insurance policy
Assekuranzfonds *m* compensatory reserve fund
Assekuranzpolice *f* insurance policy
Assekurat *m* policy-holder, insured (person)
Assekurator *m* *s.* **Assekurant**
assortieren to assort *(goods of various kinds)*; to lay in stock *(goods)*
Assortiment *n* assortment, range of articles [goods]
Assoziation *f* 1. association, society; partnership; 2. *(stats)* association
~, partielle *(stats)* partial association
Assoziationskoeffizient *m* *(stats)* coefficient of association
Assoziationsrecht *n* right of association
assoziieren:
sich ~ to associate *(o. s.)*; to enter into a partnership ⋄ **sich mit jmdm. ~** to become associated with s. o.; to enter into partnership with s. o.
assoziiert associate(d)
Assoziierung *f* association
Asymmetrie *f* *(stats)* dissymmetry
Atemschutz *m* respiratory protection
Atomenergie *f* atomic [nuclear] energy
Atomenergiekommission *f* atomic energy commission
Attest *n* attestation, certificate
attestieren to attest, to certify
Attestierung *f* attestation
aufarbeiten 1. to work [clear] off *(backlog of work)*; 2. to renovate; to recondition
Aufarbeitung *f* 1. working [clearing] off *(backlog of work)*; 2. renovation; reconditioning
Aufarbeitungskosten *pl* costs of renovation; costs of reconditioning
Aufbau *m* 1. building up, construction, erection, organization *(new social order etc.)*; 2. structure, set-up, construction *(edifice, machine, organization etc.)*; 3. composition *(age group etc.)*; 4. assembling *(machines etc.)*
~ des Messegutes arrangement of the exhibits
~, organisatorischer organizational set-up
Aufbauarbeit *f* reconstruction (work)
aufbauen 1. to build up, to construct, to erect, to organize *(new social order etc.)*; to set up *(organization etc.)*; 2. to assemble *(machine etc.)*
Aufbaugebiet *n* reconstruction centre [area, site]
Aufbaugrundschuld *f* *s.* **Aufbauhypothek**
Aufbauhypothek *f* mortgage on land for construction purposes
Aufbau-Lebensversicherung *f* low-premium life insurance *(of long duration but can be shortened by payment of additional premium)*
Aufbauleitung *f* management of construction work

Aufbauprogramm *n* construction programme
Aufbauprozeß *m* process of construction [building up]
aufbereiten to prepare, to process *(raw material etc.)*; to dress, to prepare, to refine *(ore etc.)*
Aufbereitung *f* preparing, processing *(raw material etc.)*; dressing, preparing, refining *(ore etc.)*
~, **statistische** preparation and processing of statistical data
Aufbereitungsanlage *f (min)* preparing [dressing] plant
Aufbereitungsfehler *m* processing error
aufbessern to improve, to amend; to raise, to increase *(salary, wages etc.)*
Aufbesserung *f* improvement, amendment; rise, *(Am)* raise, increase *(salary, wages etc.)*
aufbewahren to store *(provisions, luggage, furniture etc.)*; to preserve *(documents, perishable goods etc.)*; to have custody of *(records etc.)*; to deposit for safe keeping *(in a bank)*; to hold *(securities)*
Aufbewahrung *f* storage *(provisions, luggage, furniture etc.)*; preservation *(documents, perishable goods etc.)*; custody *(records etc.)*; safe keeping *(in a bank)*; holding *(securities)*
Aufbewahrungsgebühr *f* charge(s) for storage; charge(s) for safe-deposit services
Aufbewahrungsort *m* depository, store
Aufbewahrungspflicht *f* obligation to preserve business records
Aufbewahrungsschein *m* safe-custody receipt; receipt for left luggage, *(Am)* baggage check
aufblähen to inflate *(currency)*
Aufblähung *f* inflation *(currency)*
aufbrauchen to use up, to exhaust, to consume
aufbringen to procure *(goods etc.)*; to raise *(money)*; to meet, to defray *(costs etc.)*
Aufbringung *f* defray; raising *(capital etc.)*
Aufbringungsklausel *f (ins)* contributory clause
aufbringungspflichtig *(ins)* contributory
Aufbringungspflichtiger *m (ins)* contributory
Aufbringungsschuld *f (ins)* contribution
Aufbringungsschuldner *m s.* **Aufbringungspflichtiger**
aufbürden to impose a burden *(on s. o.)*
Aufenthalt *m* stop, stay
Aufenthaltsbescheinigung *f* residence permit
Aufenthaltsbeschränkung *f* 1. limitation of residence *(period)*; 2. restriction of residence *(area)*
Aufenthaltsdauer *f* period [length] of stay; length of stop *(train, bus etc.)*
Aufenthaltserlaubnis *f* residence permit, permission to reside
Aufenthaltsgenehmigung *f s.* **Aufenthaltserlaubnis**
Aufenthaltsort *m* place of residence [domicile]

auffordern to invite, to ask, to request, to call (up)on *(s. o. to do s. th.)*; *(jur)* to summon *(s. o. to do s. th.)*
Aufforderung *f* invitation, request; call; demand; *(jur)* summons
~ **zur Einzahlung (von Kapital)** calling up of capital
~ **zur Zahlung** demand for payment
aufforsten to afforest, to retimber
Aufforstung *f* afforestation, retimbering
aufführen to enter, to book, to list *(items etc.)*; to specify
Aufführung *f* entry, booking, listing *(items etc.)*; specification
Aufgabe *f* 1. task, duty, job, function, mission; 2. *(post)* posting, *(Am)* mailing *(letter etc.)*; *(railw)* registering, registration, booking, *(Am)* checking *(luggage)*; 3. giving up, closing down *(business)*; abandonment *(position)*, retirement
Aufgabebahnhof *m* dispatching station
Aufgabenabgrenzung *f* definition of tasks
Aufgabenbereich *m* 1. field [scope] of duties [activities]; (extent of the) functions *(organization etc.)*; scope *(science etc.)*; 2. budgetary division
Aufgabengebiet *n* scope [field] of responsibility [duties]; scope of science; terms of reference *(committee of inquiry)*
Aufgabenstellung *f* task
~, **verbindliche** binding [obligatory] task
Aufgabenverteilung *f* allocation of tasks [duties]
Aufgabeschein *m* receipt, *(Am)* claim check
aufgeben 1. to set *(s. o. a task)*; 2. *(post)* to post, *(Am)* to mail *(letter etc.)*, to hand in *(telegram)*; *(railw)* to register, to book *(luggage)*, *(Am)* to check *(luggage)*; 3. to insert, to put *(advertisement)*; to give, to place, to send *(order)*; 4. to give up, to close down *(business)*; to abandon *(position)*, to retire *(from an office)*; to waive *(rights)*
aufgebraucht used up
Aufgeld *n* advance, earnest money; additional [extra] charge, premium, agio; *(st. ex.)* contango
aufgewertet revalued, revalorized
aufgliedern to classify *(information, material etc.)*; to process *(figures, statistical material etc.)*; to subdivide, to breakdown
Aufgliederung *f* classification *(information, material etc.)*; processing *(figures, statistical material etc.)*; subdivision, breakdown
aufheben 1. to take up, to pick up; to lift (up), to raise *(hand etc.)*; 2. to keep, to preserve; to store, to warehouse; 3. to stop; to remove, to cancel *(prohibition etc.)*; to call off *(strike etc.)*; to dissolve *(organization etc.)*; to break off [up]

(meeting etc.); to declare null and void, to annul *(contract, marriage etc.)*; 4. *(jur)* to repeal, to abrogate *(laws etc.)*; to quash, to reverse, to set aside *(findings)*; to withdraw *(confiscation etc.)*
Aufhebung *f* removal, lifting *(restrictions etc.)*; abolition; cancellation, nullification *(contracts etc.)*; annulment *(marriage etc.)*; dissolution *(organization etc.)*; breaking up *(meeting etc.)*; neutralization *(effects etc.)*; *(jur)* reversal *(findings)*; withdrawal (of an action), nonsuit
~ **der Rationierung** derationing
Aufhebungsvertrag *m* agreement to terminate employment by mutual consent
Aufkauf *m* buying up *(land etc.)*; (wholesale) purchase *(commodities etc.)*; cornering *(goods)*, forestalling *(market)*
aufkaufen to buy up *(land etc.)*; to purchase *(commodities etc.)*; to corner *(goods)*, to forestal *(market)*
Aufkäufer *m* wholesale buyer [purchaser]; forestaller
Aufkaufkontor *n* purchasing department
Aufkaufpreis *m* wholesale purchasing price
Aufkaufstelle *f* purchasing centre *(of a co-operative or state organization of horticultural produce of small-holders)*
Aufkaufvertrag *m* purchase contract
aufklären to clear up, to clarify *(situation, issue)*; to illuminate *(subject etc.)*; to explain *(s. th. to s. o.)*, to enlighten *(s. o. on s. th.)*; to instruct *(s. o. about s. th.)*, to inform *(s. o. on s. th.)*
Aufklärung *f* elucidation *(question etc.)*, clarification *(situation, issue etc.)*; illumination *(subject etc.)*; explanation, enlightenment *(fact etc.)*
aufkommen to pay, to defray *(costs, expenses etc.)*; to compensate for *(damages etc.)*, to make good *(loss)*
Aufkommen *n* revenue, yield *(tax)*; output; availabilities; uses *(indicator in foreign trade)*
Aufkommensanalyse *f* output analysis; analysis of budget revenues
Aufkommensanteil *m* share of output *(goods, material etc.)*
Aufkommensquellen *fpl*:
~, **natürliche** natural resources
Aufkommensseite *f* left-hand side of a balance (sheet), sources
Aufkommensvolumen *n* quantity of output *(goods, material etc.)*
aufkündbar subject to call; terminable *(contract etc.)*
aufkündigen to give notice, to terminate, to cancel, to annul, to rescind *(contract etc.)*
Aufladegebühr *f* loading charges
Auflage *f* direction, instruction, order, injunction *(official)*; *(plan)* target, task; impost *(tax)*

auflassen to abandon *(mine, factory etc.)*; *(jur)* to transfer, to assign, to convey *(property etc.)*
Auflassung *f* abandonment *(mine, factory etc.)*; *(jur)* transfer, assignation, assignment, conveyance *(property etc.)*
auflösen to dissolve *(assembly, partnership)*; to break up *(relations)*; to liquidate, to wind up *(business etc.)*; to annul, to cancel *(contract, agreement)*; to close *(account)*; to release *(reserves)*
Auflösung *f* dissolution *(assembly, partnership)*; break-up *(relations)*; liquidation, wind-up *(business etc.)*; annulment, cancellation *(contract, agreement)*; closing *(account)*; release *(reserves)*
Auflösungsantrag *m* petition for bankruptcy
Auflösungsbeschluß *m* dissolution [winding-up] order; resolution of surrender
Auflösungsbestimmungen *fpl* provisions for [regulations of] dissolution
aufmachen 1. to set up, to establish *(business)*; 2. to make out, to draw up *(invoice)*; 3. to make [get] up, to pack attractively *(goods)*
Aufmachung *f* 1. making out *(invoice)*; striking *(balance)*; *(ins)* average adjustment; 2. make-up, get-up, window-dressing *(goods)*
Aufnahme *f* 1. taking-up *(work, discussion etc.)*, starting *(production etc.)*; entering into, establishment *(negotiations, relations etc.)*; 2. integration, incorporation; insertion *(clause, paragraph etc.)*; inclusion; admission *(as member)*; 3. reception *(hotel etc.)*; accommodation; 4. raising, floatation *(loan)*; contraction *(debt)*; taking up, borrowing *(capital)*; 5. stocktaking, inventory; 6. drawing-up, recording *(protocol)*; 7. *(ins)* assessment *(damages)*
Aufnahmeantrag *m* application for membership
Aufnahmebedingungen *fpl* terms of admission
aufnahmefähig capable of absorbing, absorbable, capacious, active *(market)*
Aufnahmefähigkeit *f* capacity of absorption, absorptive capacity *(market)*
Aufnahmegebühr *f* admission [entry] fee
Aufnahmegesuch *n* application for admission
Aufnahmekapazität *f* absorptive capacity *(loans, market etc.)*; seating capacity
Aufnahmeprüfung *f* entrance examination
◊ **die ~ bestehen** to pass the entrance examination
aufnehmen 1. to take up *(work, discussion etc.)*, to start *(production etc.)*; to enter into, to establish *(negotiations, relations etc.)*; 2. to integrate, to incorporate; to insert *(clause, paragraph etc.)*; to include; to admit *(as member)*; 3. to accommodate *(in a hospital, hotel etc.)*; 4. to raise, to float *(loan)*; to contract *(debt)*; to take up, to borrow *(capital)*; 5. to draw up, to record *(protocol)*; 6. *(ins)* to assess *(damages)*

Aufpreis *m* additional price, surcharge; premium *(securities)*
Aufräumungsarbeiten *fpl* site clearing
aufrechnen to reckon up; to balance, to settle *(account)*; to set off, to offset; to compensate
Aufrechnung *f* balancing, settling, squaring *(accounts)*; set-off, offset; compensation
aufreißen 1. to rip open *(envelope etc.)*; 2. to tear up *(road surface etc.)*; to split; 3. to draw, to design
Aufruhrversicherung *f* civil commotion insurance
aufrunden to round (off)
Aufrundung *f* rounding(-off)
aufrüsten to rearm; to assemble *(machine etc.)*
Aufrüstung *f* (re)armament
aufschiebbar postponable
aufschieben to postpone, to put off, to adjourn *(visit, meeting etc.)*; to defer *(payment etc.)*; to delay; *(jur)* to stay, to suspend
aufschiebend suspensive
Aufschlag *m* advance, rise; additional charge *(for higher quality etc.)*; premium; surtax, additional duty *(tax)*; markup *(margin for trading and processing)*
aufschlagen to rise, to raise; to charge (additionally) *(for higher quality etc.)*
aufschließen to develop *(land etc.)*; to open up *(markets)*
Aufschließung *f* development *(land etc.)*; opening-up *(markets)*
Aufschließungskosten *pl* development costs *(land etc.)*; opening-up costs *(markets)*
Aufschluß *m* 1. explanation, information; 2. exposure *(area)*; *(min)* open lode
aufschlüsseln to subdivide, to break down *(sum etc.)*; to distribute, to allocate *(costs in a fixed ratio)*
Aufschlüsselung *f* subdivision, breakdown *(sum etc.)*; distribution, allocation *(of costs in a fixed ratio)*
Aufschrift *f* inscription; address *(letter etc.)*
Aufschub *m* postponement, postponing, adjournment *(visit, meeting etc.)*; deferring, deferment *(payment etc.)*; respite *(debt)*; delay; *(jur)* stay
Aufschwung *m* increase, growth; progress, rise, advance; improvement, recovery; impetus, stimulus; boom, *(Am)* upswing
~, **konjunktureller** economic [business] recovery
~, **wirtschaftlicher** boom, *(Am)* upswing; economic progress
Aufschwungphase *f* phase of prosperity, boom phase
Aufschwungtendenz *f* rising tendency
Aufseher *m* supervisor, inspector *(civil service)*; overseer, foreman *(factory etc.)*; guardian *(museum etc.)*; warder, *(Am)* guard *(jail)*

aufsetzen to draw up *(contract, statement etc.)*, to make out *(invoice etc.)*, to draft *(letter etc.)*
Aufsicht *f* supervision, inspection, control ◇ **die ~ führen** to supervise
~, **polizeiliche** surveillance
~, **vormundschaftliche** guardianship, tutorage
Aufsichtsamt *n* supervisory board
Aufsichtsbehörde *f* supervising authority
aufsichtsführend supervisory, supervising
Aufsichtsperson *f* supervisor, inspector
Aufsichtspersonal *n* supervising personnel
Aufsichtspflicht *f* supervising [supervisory] duty
Aufsichtsrat *m* *(approx.)* board of directors, supervisory board *(in FRG type of companies)*
Aufsichtsratsmitglied *n* *(approx.)* board member, member of the board of directors, member of the supervisory board *(in FRG type of companies)*
Aufsichtsratsposten *m* directorship
Aufsichtsratsvergütung *f* director's remuneration
Aufsichtsratsvorsitzender *m* chairman of the board of directors
Aufsichtstätigkeit *f* supervision, control ◇ **die ~ ausüben** to supervise, to control
aufspalten to split, to break up; *(stats)* to decompose
Aufspaltung *f* splitting, breaking up; *(stats)* decomposition
aufspeichern to store, to warehouse
Aufspeicherung *f* storage, warehousing
aufstellen 1. to set up, to instal *(machine etc.)*; 2. to make up *(balance)*, to make out *(list, invoice etc.)*; to specify, *(Am)* to itemize *(costs etc.)*; 3. to state *(rule etc.)*; 4. to put forward, to nominate *(candidates etc.)*
Aufstellung *f* 1. setting-up, installation *(machine etc.)*; 2. making-up, make-up *(balance)*, making out *(list, invoice etc.)*; 3. list; specification, *(Am)* itemization *(costs etc.)*; 4. nomination *(candidates etc.)* ◇ **eine ~ anfertigen** to draw up a list
~, **amtliche** (official) register
~ **der Kosten** statement of costs
~ **einer Tagesordnung** fixing of an agenda
~ **eines Programms** fixing of a programme
~, **statistische** statistical statement
~, **tabellarische** table
Aufstellungskosten *pl* installation costs
Aufstellungsmöglichkeit *f* possibility of erecting *(building etc.)*; possibility of arranging *(exhibits etc.)*
Aufstellungsort *m* place of erection
Aufstellungsplan *m* location plan
Aufstieg *m* rise, advancement, promotion
Aufstiegsmöglichkeit *f* opportunity for promotion

Aufwand 49

aufstocken to raise *(production)*; to increase *(capital etc.)*; to stockpile
Aufstockung *f* raise *(production)*; increase *(capital etc.)*; stockpiling
aufteilen to divide, to split up, to partition; to distribute, to apportion, to allot; to parcel out *(land etc.)*
Aufteilung *f* division, partition(ing); distribution, allotment
~, **bestmögliche** *(stats)* optimum allocation
~ **der Welt** division of the world *(according to spheres of influence etc.)*
~ **einer Stichprobe auf Schichten** *(stats)* allocation of a sample
~ **nach Industriegruppen** division according to industrial trade groups
~, **räumliche** spatial distribution
Aufteilungsverhältnis *n* proportion
~ **verfügbarer Fonds** proportion of available funds
Auftrag *m* task, charge; instruction, direction(s); mission; commission; order *(goods etc.)*; contract *(fixed order)*; *(jur)* contract of agency, mandate ⋄ **einen ~ ausführen** to execute [fill] an order; to do [carry out] a commission; **einen ~ erteilen** to place an order *(with s.o.)*, to entrust *s.o.* with *s.th.*, to ask *s.o.* to do *s.th.*, to give *s.o.* instructions to do *s.th.*; to appoint *s.o.* with a commission; **etwas in ~ geben** to order s.th.; to commission s.o. to do s.th.; **Ihrem ~ gemäß** in accordance with your instructions; **im ~ (i.A.)** on s.o.'s behalf, in s.o.'s name; by attorney, by procuration, per pro (p.p.), by order, *(Am)* per power of attorney (p.p.a.); **im ~ eines Dritten** by order of a third person [party]; **im ~ und auf Rechnung von** by order and for account of; **im ~ von** by order [on behalf] of; **in einem besonderen ~** on a special mission
~, **eiliger** rush order
~, **öffentlicher** official order; official contract
Auftraggeber *m* orderer; customer, client; *(jur)* mandator; *(st.ex.)* principal
Auftragnehmer *m* contractor, supplier, consignee; acceptor of an order [commission]
Auftragsabrechnung *f* order costing *(method of internal cost accounting in enterprises where costs are calculated according to orders received and fulfilled)*
Auftragsbearbeitung *f* dealing with [handling of] orders
Auftragsbestand *m* (number of) orders in hand, *(Am)* unfilled orders
Auftragsbestandsbuch *n* order book
Auftragsbestätigung *f* confirmation of order
Auftragsbuch *n s.* **Auftragsbestandsbuch**
Auftragsdatum *n* date of order

Auftragseingang *m* incoming orders, orders received
Auftragsentwicklung *f* trend of orders
Auftragserledigung *f* filling of orders
Auftragserneuerung *f* renewal of orders
Auftragserteilung *f* ordering, placing of order; award *(tender)* ⋄ **bei ~** when ordering
Auftragsfertigung *f* manufacture [production] to order
Auftragsformular *n* order form
Auftragsforschung *f* commissioned research, research work by order
auftragsgebunden bound by contract, contractually bound
auftragsgemäß as ordered, as per order, according to instructions
Auftragsgeschäft *n* commission business, business by order
Auftragsgröße *f* size of order
~, **optimale** optimum order [commission]
Auftragsgruppe *f* group of orders
Auftragshandel *m* commission business
Auftragslage *f* situation of (receiving) orders
Auftragslenkung *f* distribution of orders
auftragsmäßig *s.* **auftragsgemäß**
Auftragsnummer *f* (register) number of an order, order number
Auftragspapiere *npl* specification papers *(for machining operations)*
Auftragsplanung *f* production planning according to time schedule of orders *(part of operations scheduling)*
Auftragsprüfung *f* checking of orders
Auftragsrückgang *m* falling (off) of orders
Auftragsrückstand *m* backlog of orders, unfilled orders
Auftragsüberhang *m s.* **Auftragsrückstand**
Auftragsvergabe *f* placing of orders, allocation of contract *(by public institutions)*
Auftragsverhältnis *n* contractual relationship
Auftragsverlagerung *f* transferring of orders
auftragswidrig contrary to order [instruction]
Auftragszettel *m* order slip
Auftragszuweisung *f* awarding of contract *(by public institutions)*
Auftrieb *m* 1. impetus, stimulus; 2. driving of cattle to mountain pasture
Aufwand *m* costs, expenditure, expense, outlay, input
~ **an Geld** expenditure of money
~ **an Kraft** expenditure of energy
~ **an lebendiger Arbeit** *(pol ec)* expenditure of living labour *(s.* **Arbeit, lebendige***)*
~ **an vergegenständlichter Arbeit** *(pol ec)* expenditure of materialized [dead] labour *(s.* **Arbeit, vergegenständlichte***)*
~ **an Zeit** expenditure of time

~, **außergewöhnlicher** extraordinary expenditure [cost]
~, **direkter** direct expenditure [cost]
~, **einmaliger** non-recurrent expenditure [outlay]
~, **gebietswirtschaftlicher** regional overhead costs *(to build up and maintain infrastructure needed in a particular region)*
~, **indirekter** indirect expenditure [cost]
~, **laufender** current expenditure [cost]
~, **nationaler** inland [domestic] cost(s)
~, **periodenfremder** deferred [accrued] cost
~, **spezifischer** specific expenditure [cost]
~, **territorialer** *s.* ~, **gebietswirtschaftlicher**
~, **totaler** total expenditure [cost]
~, **unnützer** waste
~, **voller** *s.* ~, **totaler**
Aufwand-Nutzen-Analyse *f* cost-benefit analysis
Aufwand-Nutzen-Rechnung *f* cost-benefit calculation
Aufwandselement *n* expenditure [cost] item
Aufwandsentschädigung *f* expense allowance, repayment [reimbursement] of expenses
Aufwandsfaktoren *mpl* expense factors
Aufwandsfinanzierung *f* cost financing *(e. g. financing research projects to the extent of actual costs)*
Aufwandskennziffer *f* index of expenditure, cost index
Aufwandskoeffizient *m* input [expenditure] coefficient
Aufwandskonto *n* expense account
Aufwandsmatrix *f* input matrix
Aufwandsmessung *f* quantifying expenditure [cost]
Aufwandsminimum *n* minimum (of) expenditure [cost]
Aufwandsmodell *n* input model
Aufwandsnorm *f* standard (rate) of expenditure
Aufwandsnormierung *f* fixing the standard (rate) of expenditure
Aufwandsnormung *f s.* **Aufwandsnormierung**
Aufwandsposten *m* expense [cost] item
Aufwandspreis *m* (real) cost price
Aufwandsprinzip *n (tax)* sumptuary principle
Aufwandssenkung *f* decrease of expenditure [cost]
Aufwandssteuern *fpl* general tax on non-essentials *(dog licence, hunting licence etc.)*
Aufwandsstruktur *f* structure of expenditure [cost]
Aufwandssumme *f* total expenditure [cost]
Aufwandsteil *m* part of expenditure, cost ratio
Aufwands- und Ertragsrechnung *f* profit and loss accounting
Aufwandsvergleich *m* comparison of expenditure [cost]

aufwenden to spend, to expend
aufwendig expensive, costly
Aufwendungen *fpl* expenditures, expenses
~, **außerordentliche** extraordinary expenditures
~, **betriebsfremde** outside expenditures
~, **einmalige** non-recurrent expenditures [outlay]
~, **finanzielle** financial expenditure(s)
~, **laufende** current expenditures [costs]
~, **nichtabzugsfähige** non-deductible expenditures
~, **periodenfremde** deferred expenditure(s)
~, **produktive** expenditure(s) for productive purposes, productive expenditure(s)
~, **saisonbedingte** seasonal expenditure(s)
~, **soziale** social expenditure(s)
~, **tatsächliche** actual expenditure(s)
~, **unproduktive** expenditure(s) for non-productive purposes, non-productive expenditure(s)
Aufwendungsersatz *m* compensation of expenditure(s) *(labour, material etc.)*
aufwerten to revalue, to (re)valorize *(currency, debt etc.)*; to reassess *(land)*; to appreciate *(assets etc.)*
Aufwertung *f* revaluation, (re)valorization *(currency, debt etc.)*; reassessment *(land)*; appreciation *(assets etc.)*
Aufwertungsanleihe *f* stabilization loan
Aufwertungserlös *m* revaluation profit
aufzählen to enumerate *(reasons, events etc.)*; to recite, to detail *(facts etc.)*
Aufzählung *f* enumeration *(reasons, events etc.)*; recitation, detailing *(facts etc.)*
aufzeichnen 1. to draw, to sketch, to make a sketch [diagram]; 2. to write [note] down, to make a note; to record
Aufzeichnung *f* note; record
aufziehen 1. to pull, to draw (up); to hoist; 2. to rear, to raise *(animal etc.)*; to cultivate, to grow *(plant etc.)*; to bring up *(child)*; 3. to set up, to start *(enterprise etc.)*; to wind up *(business etc.)*; to plan, to arrange, to organize *(event etc.)*
Aufzins *m* interest *(paid on capital etc.)*
aufzinsen to pay interest *(on capital etc.)*
Aufzinsungsfaktor *m* rate of interest *(on capital etc.)*
Aufzucht *f* rearing, raising *(animal etc.)*
Auktion *f* (sale by) auction, public sale
~, **gerichtliche** sale by order of court, compulsory sale
Auktionator *m* auctioneer
auktionieren to sell by [*(Am)* at] auction; to auction (off)
Auktionsgebühren *fpl* auction fees
Auktionskatalog *m* auction list
Auktionsliste *f s.* **Auktionskatalog**
Auktionslokal *n* auction room, sale-room
Auktionsmakler *m* auction broker

Auktionspreis *m* auction price
Auktionsverfahren *n* auction
Ausbau *m* 1. completion *(building etc.)*; 2. extension *(knowledge, policy etc.)*; expansion *(railway network etc.)*, enlargement *(factory etc.)*; development *(institution etc.)*; elaboration *(theory etc.)*; strengthening *(trade relations etc.)*; consolidation *(power etc.)*
Ausbaubetrieb *m* construction enterprise [firm], building contractors
ausbauen 1. to complete, to finish *(building etc.)*; 2. to extend *(knowledge, policy etc.)*; to expand *(railway network etc.)*; to enlarge *(factory etc.)*; to develop *(institution etc.)*; to elaborate *(theory etc.)*; to strengthen *(trade relations etc.)*; to consolidate *(power etc.)*
ausbaufähig capable of being enlarged *(factory etc.)*; capable of being developed [expanded] *(railway network etc.)*; capable of development *(machine, trade relations etc.)*; with good prospects *(position)*
Ausbaufirma *f s.* **Ausbaubetrieb**
Ausbauleistungen *fpl* interior construction work *(carpentry, painting etc.)*
Ausbaustufe *f* investment phase, stage of (project) construction
ausbessern to repair *(building etc.)*; to correct *(piece of work etc.)*
Ausbesserung *f* repair *(building etc.)*; correction, rectification *(piece of work etc.)*
Ausbesserungsarbeit *f* repair work, repairs
ausbesserungsbedürftig in need of repair
ausbesserungsfähig repairable
Ausbesserungskosten *pl* repair costs
Ausbesserungswerk *n* *(railw)* repair shop
Ausbesserungswerkstatt *f* repair workshop
Ausbeute *f* yield, output *(mining)*; profit *(returns)*
ausbeuten to make use of, to utilize *(invention etc.)*; to exploit *(people, land, natural resources)*; to work *(mine)*
Ausbeuter *m* exploiter
Ausbeutergesellschaft *f* exploiting [exploitative] society
Ausbeutersystem *n* system of exploitation, sweating system
Ausbeutung *f* making use of, utilization *(invention etc.)*; exploitation *(people, land, natural resources)*; working *(mine)*
~, **extensive** extensive exploitation
~, **industrielle** industrial exploitation
~, **intensive** intensive exploitation
~, **sekundäre** indirect exploitation
ausbeutungsfähig exploitable
Ausbeutungsform *f* kind of exploitation
Ausbeutungsgrad *m* degree of explotation
Ausbeutungskosten *pl* exploitation costs
Ausbeutungsrate *f* rate of exploitation

Ausbeutungsrecht *n* right to exploit *(mines etc.)*
Ausbeutungstheorie *f* 1. theory of exploitation; 2. theory of surplus value
ausbezahlen to pay out
ausbezahlt paid out
ausbieten to offer; to bid; to tender; to put *s. th.* up for [to] auction
Ausbieter *m* auctioneer
ausbilden 1. to form, to develop; 2. to educate, to train, to instruct
Ausbilder *m* instructor
Ausbildung *f* 1. formation, development; 2. education, training, instruction
~, **abschnittsweise** training by stages, stage by stage training
~, **akademische** higher education
~, **berufliche** vocational training
~, **kaufmännische** commercial training
~, **künstlerische** education in the fine arts
~, **naturwissenschaftliche** education in science
~, **ökonomische** economic training
~, **polytechnische** polytechnical education
~, **praktische** practical training; on-the-job training
~, **technische** technical training
~, **theoretische** theoretical training
~ **von Führungskräften** training of managerial personnel
~, **wissenschaftliche** scientific education
~, **wissenschaftlich-praktische** scientific-technical education
Ausbildungsabschnitt *m* part of education and training
Ausbildungsbedürfnisse *npl* training needs
Ausbildungsbeihilfe *f* training [education(al)] grant
Ausbildungsberechtigung *f* instructor's certificate
Ausbildungsberuf *m* skilled trade *(requires training varying from $1^1/_2$ to 3 years)*
Ausbildungsbetrieb *m* training enterprise *(enterprise entitled to train apprentices)*
Ausbildungsdauer *f* period of education and training
Ausbildungsergebnis *n* result in education and training
Ausbildungsgang *m* educational background [qualification]
Ausbildungsgruppe *f* group of people to be trained
Ausbildungskapazität *f* training capacity
Ausbildungskosten *pl* education and training costs
Ausbildungskurs *m s.* **Ausbildungslehrgang**
Ausbildungslager *n* training camp
Ausbildungslehrgang *m* training course
Ausbildungsleiter *m* chief instructor

Ausbildungsmöglichkeiten *fpl* training facilities
Ausbildungsprogramm *n* training programme
Ausbildungsrichtung *f* field of training [study]
Ausbildungsstand *m* state of training; educational level
Ausbildungsstätte *f* training centre [institution]
Ausbildungsstufe *f* stage of education and training
Ausbildungsunterstützung *f s.* **Ausbildungsbeihilfe**
Ausbildungsvereinbarung *f* training agreement
Ausbildungsversicherung *f* education insurance
Ausbildungsvertrag *m* training contract
Ausbildungsvorschriften *fpl* training regulations
Ausbildungszeit *f* training period
Ausbildungsziel *n* purpose of training
ausbuchen to cancel, to get off the books; to transfer
Ausbuchung *f* cancellation; transfer
ausbürgern to deprive *s.o.* of citizenship, to expatriate
Ausbürgerung *f* deprival of citizenship, expatriation
ausdehnen to extend, to expand
Ausdehnung *f* extension, expansion
~ **des Geldvolumens** expansion of the money supply
~, **lineare** linear expansion
ausdehnungsfähig extendable, extensible, expandable, elastic *(material etc.)*; capable of expansion [extension, enlargement] *(towns etc.)*; tensile, ductile *(metal)*
Ausdehnungsfähigkeit *f* extensibility, expansibility, expansiveness, elasticity *(material etc.)*; tensility, ductility *(metal)*
Ausdehnungspolitik *f* policy of expansion
Ausdruck *m* expression; term; phrase, idiom
~, **analytischer** *(maths)* analytical expression
~, **logarithmischer** logarithmic expression
~, **mengenmäßiger** quantitative expression, expression in terms of quantity
~, **qualitativer** qualitative expression, expression in terms of quality
~, **wertmäßiger** value expression, expression in terms of value [in value terms]
~, **zahlenmäßiger** numerical expression, expression in terms of numbers
auseinandersetzen to set forth, to explain *(plan, reasons etc.)*; to state, to declare *(views, theories, reasons etc.)*; to thresh out *(a matter)*; **sich** ~ to have it out *(with s.o.)*; to argue *(with s.o.)*; to conduct a polemic *(with s.o.)*; to make an arrangement, to come to an agreement [understanding] with *(s.o.)*; to compound, to come to terms *(with one's creditors)*; to come [get] to grips with *(situation etc.)*

Auseinandersetzung *f* explanation, exposition *(views, theories etc.)*; argument; discussion; dispute, controversy; difference settlement *(with creditors etc.)* ◊ **eine harte ~ haben** to come to blows, to have a fierce argument with
~, **gerichtliche** legal [judicial] dispute
~, **lohnpolitische** wage dispute
~, **parlamentarische** parliamentary dispute
Auseinandersetzungsvertrag *m* settlement agreement, deed of partition [separation]
Ausfall *m* 1. failure, non-payment *(income, revenue)*; breakdown, stoppage *(plant, machine etc.)*; loss, deficit; cancellation; 2. result *(harvest etc.)*
Ausfallbetrag *m* deficiency
Ausfallbürge *m* surety, bail absolute
Ausfallbürgschaft *f* letter of indemnity, indemnity letter [*(Am)* bond] ◊ **eine ~ übernehmen** to give a letter of idemnity, *(Am)* to execute a bond
ausfallen 1. to fail (to be paid), not to be forthcoming *(income, revenue)*; to become unserviceable, to be out of action *(plant, machine etc.)*; to be cancelled, to be off, not to take place; to be omitted, to be left out; 2. to turn out *(well, badly)*
Ausfallmuster *n* outturn sample
Ausfallrate *f* frequency of breakdown [stoppage]
Ausfalltage *mpl* days of absence
Ausfallwahrscheinlichkeit *f* probability of breakdown
Ausfallzeit *f* dead time, downtime
~, **beeinflußbare** downtime that can be controlled
~, **unbeeinflußbare** downtime that cannot be controlled
ausfertigen to draw up, to draft *(report etc.)*; to make out, to write out *(document, cheque etc.)*; to issue *(passport etc.)*; *(jur)* to execute *(document)*
Ausfertigung *f* 1. drawing up, drafting *(report etc.)*; marking out, writing out *(document, cheque etc.)*; issuing *(passport etc.)*; *(jur)* execution *(document)*; 2. draft, copy ◊ **in doppelter** ~ in duplicate; **in dreifacher** ~ in triplicate; **in fünffacher** ~ in five copies; **in vierfacher** ~ in quadruplicate
Ausfertigungsdatum *n* date of issue *(passport etc.)*
Ausfertigungsgebühr *f* charges for issuing *(document, passport, visa etc.)*
Ausflugsverkehr *m* weekend [holiday] traffic
Ausfuhr *f* export(ation); export(s) *(s. a.* **Export**)
~, **direkte** direct export(s)
~, **indirekte** indirect export(s)
~, **unsichtbare** invisible export(s); invisibles
Ausfuhrabgabe *f* export tax [duty]

Ausgaben 53

Ausfuhragent *m* export agent
Ausfuhrartikel *m* export article
Ausfuhrbeschränkung *f* export restriction
Ausfuhrbewilligung *f* export permission; export licence [permit]
Ausfuhrbürgschaft *f* export guarantee
ausführen 1. to carry out *(s.th.)*; to implement, to realize *(plan etc.)*; to fulfil *(contract etc.)*, to perform *(operation etc.)*, to execute *(order etc.)*; 2. to export *(goods)*
Ausfuhrerklärung *f* export declaration
Ausfuhrerzeugnis *n* export product
Ausfuhrfinanzierung *f* financing of exports, export financing
Ausfuhrförderung *f* export promotion
Ausfuhrgarantie *f s.* Ausfuhrbürgschaft
Ausfuhrgenehmigung *f s.* Ausfuhrbewilligung
Ausfuhrgüter *npl* export goods
Ausfuhrhandel *m* export trade
Ausfuhrhändler *m* exporter, export dealer
Ausfuhrhändlervergütung *f* export dealer's commission
Ausfuhrkontingent *n* export quota
Ausfuhrkontrolle *f* export control
Ausfuhrkredit *m* export credit
Ausfuhrkreditversicherung *f* export credit insurance
Ausfuhrland *n* exporting country
Ausfuhrlizenz *f s.* Ausfuhrbewilligung
Ausfuhrmeldung *f* export declaration
Ausfuhrprämie *f* export bounty [premium]
Ausfuhrpreis *m* export price
Ausfuhrschein *m* export permit, certificate of clearance; preferential export licence
Ausführung *f* 1. carrying out *(s.th.)*; implementation, realization *(plan etc.)*; fulfilment *(contract etc.)*, performance *(operation etc.)*, execution *(order etc.)*; 2. construction; design; finish; type, model, version, pattern; 3. workmanship, quality; 4. (detailed) statement, account
Ausführungsbestimmungen *fpl* regulations, implementing provisions, *(Am)* executive orders
Ausführungsprojekt *n* project to be executed *(construction etc.)*
Ausführungsqualität *f* quality of performance
Ausführungsverfahren *n* technique used in a job
Ausfuhrverbot *n* ban on exports, export ban
Ausfuhrverfahren *n* export regulations
Ausfuhrvergütung *f* export premium; *(cust)* drawback *(on certain goods)*; tax rebate *(to exporters)*
Ausfuhrvolumen *n* volume of exports, total export
Ausfuhrware *f* export good [article]

Ausfuhrzoll *m* export duty
Ausgabe *f* 1. giving [handing] out; distribution, delivery *(mail etc.)*; issue, issuing *(tickets, passports etc.)*; emission *(paper money)*; 2. expense, expenditure; outlay, disbursement; cost; 3. counter *(luggage etc.)*; 4. *(d.pr.)* output, read out; 5. edition *(newspaper etc.)*
~ **von Obligationen** floating of bonds
Ausgabebank *f* bank of issue
Ausgabebedingungen *fpl* terms of issue
Ausgabebewilligung *f* budgetary appropriation
Ausgabedatum *n* date of issue
Ausgabedisposition *f* budgetary allocation
Ausgabeeinheit *f (d.pr.)* output unit
Ausgabegerät *n (d.pr.)* output device
Ausgabekurs *m* issue price, rate of issue
Ausgaben *fpl* expenditures, expenses; outlay
◇ **als ~ buchen** to enter as expenditures;
~ **decken** to cover expenditures [expenses];
~ **einschränken** to cut down [reduce] expenditures [expenses]; ~ **und Einnahmen ins Gleichgewicht bringen** to balance revenues [receipts] and payments
~, **abzugsfähige** deductible expenditures [expenses]
~, **angefallene** expenses incurred
~, **außerordentliche** extra-budgetary expenditures
~, **außerplanmäßige** non-planned expenditures [expenses]
~, **berufsbedingte** *(approx.)* expenses involved in certain professions
~ **der öffentlichen Hand** disbursements of public money, payments from state funds
~ **des Staates** budget expenditures [expenses]
~, **einmalige** non-recurrent expenditures [expenses]
~, **entstandene, aber noch nicht fällige** accrued expenses
~, **feste** fixed charges
~ **für den künftigen Abrechnungszeitraum** deferred expenditures [expenses]
~, **gelegentliche** occasional [casual] expenses
~, **gleichbleibende** expenses that remain constant
~, **laufende** current expenditures
~, **nichtabzugsfähige** non-deductible expenditures [expenses]
~, **notwendige** necessary expenditures [expenses]
~, **öffentliche** government expenditures
~, **ordentliche** ordinary expenditures [expenses]
~, **private** private expenses
~, **regelmäßig wiederkehrende** recurrent expenditures [expenses]
~, **tatsächliche** actual expenses
~, **unproduktive** non-productive expenditures [expenses]

Ausgaben

~, **unvorhergesehene** unforeseen expenditures [expenses]
Ausgabenabbau *m* reduction of expenditure
Ausgabenaufstellung *f* statement of expenditure
Ausgabenbeleg *m* voucher
Ausgabenbetrag *m* (sum of) expenditure
Ausgabenbuch *n* petty cash book
Ausgabendeckungsverfahren *n* method of covering expenditures [expenses]
Ausgabenelastizität *f* elasticity of expenditure
Ausgabengliederung *f* structure [composition] of expenditures [expenses]
Ausgabenhöhe *f* amount of expenditure [expenses]
Ausgabenkonto *n* expense account
Ausgabenkontrolle *f* control of expenditure
Ausgabenkürzung *f* curtailment of expenditure [expenses]
Ausgabenlimit *n* limit of expenditure
Ausgabenpolitik *f* policy of budget expenditures [expenses]
Ausgabenposition *f* item of budget expenditures [expenses]
Ausgabe(n)posten *m* expenditure item
Ausgabenrest *m* undistributed funds
Ausgabenseite *f* debit side
Ausgabenstruktur *f. s.* **Ausgabengliederung**
Ausgabenüberhang *m* deficit; excess of expenditure
Ausgabenverteilung *f* allocation of expenditure
Ausgabenverzeichnis *n* list of expenditure
Ausgabeposten *m* expense item
Ausgabepreis *m (st.ex.)* issue [issuing] price
Ausgabestelle *f* issuing office *(parcels etc.)*
Ausgang *m* 1. outcome, result *(decission etc.)*; 2. exit, way out; departure; 3. (short) leave
Ausgänge *mpl (fin)* outgoings
Ausgangsbasis *f* starting point
Ausgangsbedingungen *fpl* starting [initial] conditions
Ausgangsdaten *pl* primary [initial, original] data
Ausgangsgesamtheit *f (stats)* parent population
Ausgangsgewicht *n* base weight
Ausgangsgröße *f* base [basis] value; *(d.pr.)* output value
Ausgangsinformation *f* basis [basic] information [data]
Ausgangskapital *n* initial capital; original investment
Ausgangskennzahl *f* basis index
Ausgangsmaterial *n* primary [initial, original, starting] material
~, **statistisches** basic data
Ausgangsprodukt *n* primary product
Ausgangsrohstoff *m* primary [initial] raw material

Ausgangsstoff *m* primary [initial] material
Ausgangswert *m s.* **Basiswert**
Ausgangszoll *m* export duty
ausgeben 1. to give [hand] out; to distribute, to deliver *(mail etc.)*; to issue *(tickets, passports etc.)*; to emit *(paper money)*; 2. to spend, to expend
ausgebucht booked out *(plane, flight etc.)*
Ausgeglichenheit *f*:
~ **des Staatshaushalts** (favourable) balance [balancing] of the state [central] budget
ausgelastet working at full capacity *(machines)*; fully employed [occupied] *(persons)*
ausgestalten to arrange, to make the arrangements for *(celebration etc.)*; to lay out, to decorate
Ausgestaltung *f* arrangement; layout, decoration
ausgesteuert:
◊ ~ **sein** *(ins)* to be no longer in receipt of social [national] insurance benefits
Ausgleich *m* adjustment, equalization *(weights, values etc.)*; balance *(exports and imports, income and expenditure etc.)*; settlement *(account)*; *(acc)* compensation, offset; compromise *(opinion)* ◊ **zum ~ der Verluste** offsetting the losses
~ **von Preisdifferenzen** compensation for price differences
ausgleichen to adjust, to equalize *(weights, values etc.)*; to balance *(exports and imports, income and expenditure etc.)*; to settle *(account)*; *(acc)* to compensate, to offset
Ausgleichsabgabe *f* equalization levy
Ausgleichsanspruch *m* claim for compensation
Ausgleichsarbitrage *f* arbitration of exchange
Ausgleichsbestand *m* buffer stock
Ausgleichsbetrag *m* (amount of) compensation
Ausgleichsfinanzierung *f* compensatory financing
Ausgleichsfonds *m* compensation fund
Ausgleichsforderung *f* equalization claim
Ausgleichskapazität *f* balancing capacity
Ausgleichskasse *f* equalization fund
Ausgleichskonto *n* adjustments account
Ausgleichslager *n* buffer stock
Ausgleichsleistungen *fpl* compensation allowances
Ausgleichsrücklage *f* adjustment [equalization] reserve
Ausgleichssteuer *f* equalization tax
Ausgleichsverfahren *n* procedure for settlement of international debts; partial satisfaction of creditors
Ausgleichszahlung *f* equalization payment, *(Am)* co-ordination pay
Ausgleichszoll *m* compensatory [contingent, countervailing] duty

Ausgleichszuschlag m additional compensatory payment
Ausgleichung f adjustment, balancing, equalization *(weights, values etc.)*; balancing *(exports and imports)*; compensation *(loss)*; settlement *(debt)*
~ **nach Augenmaß, grafische** *(stats)* freehand method
ausgliedern to separate (out)
Ausgliederung f 1. *(stats)* grouping; 2. separation *(of work or stage of production for specialization etc.)*
ausgrenzen to exclude, to discriminate against *(people, organization etc.)*
Ausgrenzung f exclusion, discrimination *(people, organization etc.)*
aushandeln to negotiate; to bargain
aushändigen to hand out *(leaflets etc.)*; to hand over, to deliver *(goods etc.)*
Aushändigung f handing out *(leaflets etc.)*; handing over, delivery *(goods etc.)* ◊ **zahlbar gegen ~ der Verschiffungspapiere** payable against (surrender of) shipping documents
Aushilfe f 1. temporary help [assistance]; 2. temporary helper [assistant]
Aushilfsarbeit f temporary work; odd job
Aushilfsarbeiter m auxilliary worker, odd-job man, odd jobber
Aushilfskräfte fpl temporary workers
Aushilfstätigkeit f temporary [auxiliary, seasonal] job
ausklarieren to clear (outward-bound ship); *(cust)* to take out of bond
Auskunft f 1. information; 2. inquiry office, *(Am)* information desk
Auskunftsbüro n inquiry office, *(Am)* information bureau
Auskunftspflicht f *(ins)* obligation to give information
auskunftspflichtig *(ins)* obliged to give information
Auskunftsschalter m inquiries, inquiry desk [counter]
Auskunftsstelle f inquiry office
Ausladekosten pl unloading expenses, discharging costs
ausladen to unload, to discharge
Ausladeort m s. **Ausladeplatz**
Ausladeplatz m unloading place, unloading dock
Auslader m unloader
Ausladestelle f s. **Ausladeplatz**
Auslage f 1. outlay, disbursement, advance; expense(s); 2. display *(in a shop window)*
Auslagen fpl 1. expenditure(s), expenses; 2. (sales) display
Auslagerungsindustrialisierung f industrialization based on redeployment [the transfer of industries]
Auslagewerbung f window display; counter display
Ausland n foreign country; foreign countries ◊ **für das ~ bestimmt** outbound; **im ~ geboren** foreign-born; **im ~ hergestellt** foreign-made; **im ~ Leben** to live abroad; **im ~ wohnen** to reside abroad; **im ~ zahlbar** payable abroad; **ins ~ gehen** to go abroad; **ins ~ reisen** to travel abroad; **ins ~ schicken** to send abroad; **vom ~ kontrolliert werden** to be controlled by foreign interests
~, **befreundetes** friendly countries
~, **feindliches** enemy countries
~, **neutrales** neutral countries
Ausländer m foreigner; alien
Ausländerdienst m service for foreign visitors *(at a fair)*
ausländerfeindlich hostile to foreigners
Ausländerfeindlichkeit f hostility to foreigners
ausländerfreundlich friendly to foreigners
Ausländerfreundlichkeit f friendliness to foreigners
Ausländergesetzgebung f alien legislation
Ausländerklub m foreigners' club
Ausländerkonto n foreigner's account
Ausländerkonvertibilität f external [nonresidential] convertibility
Ausländertreffpunkt m foreign visitors' centre *(at a fair)*
Ausländervermögen n foreign-owned property; alien property
ausländisch foreign; alien
Auslandsabsatz m sales abroad
Auslandsabteilung f foreign department
Auslandsangebot n foreign offer
Auslandsanlage f foreign investment
Auslandsanleihe f foreign [external] loan
Auslandsanmeldung f foreign application
Auslandsanteil m share [proportion, percentage] of foreign participation *(in investments etc.)*
Auslandsaufenthalt m stay [residence] abroad
Auslandsauftrag m foreign order
Auslandsaufwand m expenditures [expenses] incurred abroad
Auslandsbank f foreign bank
Auslandsbesitz m assets held abroad, foreign holdings
Auslandsbeteiligung f foreign participation *(in investments etc.)*; foreign investments
Auslandsbevollmächtigter m foreign agent
Auslandsbeziehungen fpl relations with foreign countries
Auslandsbonds mpl foreign securities
Auslandsdienst m foreign service
Auslandseinkünfte pl s. **Auslandserlös**

Auslandserlös *m* export earnings [proceeds]
Auslandsfiliale *f* foreign branch
Auslandsgeschäft *n* foreign business [transaction]
Auslandsgläubiger *m* foreign creditor
Auslandsguthaben *n* deposits in foreign countries
Auslandshilfe *f* foreign aid
Auslandshilfsprogramm *n* foreign aid programme
Auslandsinteresse *n* foreign interest
Auslandsinvestitionen *fpl* investments abroad; foreign investments
~, **direkte** direct investments abroad; direct foreign investments
~, **indirekte** indirect investments abroad; indirect foreign investments
Auslandskapital *n* foreign capital
Auslandskonkurrenz *f* foreign competition
Auslandskonto *n* external account
Auslandskredit *m* external [foreign] credit
Auslandskunde *m* foreign customer
Auslandslieferung *f* delivery abroad; shipment abroad
Auslandsmarkt *m* foreign market
Auslandsmarktanalyse *f* analysis of foreign markets
Auslandsmesse *f* foreign fair
Auslandsmontage *f* assembling abroad
Auslandsniederlassung *f* external branch; overseas branch
Auslandsnotierung *f* quotation on a foreign market
Auslandspatentanmeldung *f* application of patent abroad
Auslandspost *f* foreign mail
Auslandspostverkehr *m* external mail service
Auslandspreis *m* international [foreign] price
Auslandspreisstatistik *f* international [foreign] price statistics
Auslandspresse *f* foreign press
Auslandsrechnung *f* export invoice; import invoice
Auslandsreise *f* journey [trip] abroad
Auslandsschuld *f* foreign [external] debt
auslandsseitig concerning external [international] conditions
Auslandstourismus *m* international tourism
Auslandsumsatz *m* (total) export, export business
Auslandsvaluta *f* foreign currency
Auslandsverbindlichkeiten *fpl* foreign liabilities
Auslandsverkauf *m s.* **Auslandsabsatz**
Auslandsverkehr *m* international traffic
Auslandsvermögen *n* external assets [property]
Auslandsverpflichtungen *fpl* foreign liabilities; obligation to foreign customers [countries]

Auslandsverschuldung *f* foreign debts [indebtedness]
Auslandsversicherung *f* foreign [external] insurance
Auslandsvertretung *f* official representation abroad
Auslandswährung *f s.* **Auslandsvaluta**
Auslandswaren *fpl* foreign goods; import goods
Auslandswerbung *f* foreign advertising
auslasten to work at full capacity, to employ fully
Auslastung *f* utilization at full capacity
Auslastungsgrad *m* degree of utilization at full capacity
Auslastungskoeffizient *m* coefficient of utilization; utilization coefficient
Auslastungsplan *m* utlization schedule *(machine etc.)*
auslaufen 1. to discontinue *(production)*; 2. to set sail, to leave port *(ship)*
Auslaufen *n*:
~ **der Produktion** discontinuation of production
Auslaufmodell *n* discontinued model
Auslaufzeit *f* running-out time *(production)*
auslegen 1. to lay out, to expose for sale, to display *(wares)*; 2. to interpret, to explain, to construe, to expound *(text etc.)*
Auslegung *f* interpretation, explanation, construction, exposition; commentary
~, **falsche** misinterpretation, misconstruction, wrong interpretation [construction]
Ausleihdienst *m* lending [hire] service
Ausleihe *f* 1. lending *(books etc.)*; 2. issuing counter [department] *(library)*
ausleihen to lend *(s.th.)*; to lend out ◇ **sich etwas** ~ to borrow s.th. *(from s.o.)*
Ausleihstation *f* hire service establishment
Auslese *f* 1. selection, choice, picking out *(fruit etc.)*; 2. pick *(vegetables, fruit etc.)*, selected leaf *(tobacco)*, choice [finest] fruit *(grapes etc.)*
auslesen to select, to choose, to pick out *(fruit etc.)*; to sort, to grade
ausliefern to deliver, to hand over, to supply *(goods)*; *(jur)* to extradite *(criminal)*
Auslieferung *f* delivery, supply *(goods)*; *(jur)* extradition *(criminal)*
Auslieferungsantrag *m (jur)* extradition warrant
Auslieferungsbedingungen *fpl* terms of delivery
Auslieferungsgebühr *f* delivery charge
Auslieferungslager *n* warehouse; store
Auslieferungsschein *m* delivery note
Auslieferungssperre *f* ban on delivery, suspension of delivery
Auslieferungstermin *m* delivery date, date of delivery
Auslieferungsvertrag *m (jur)* extradition treaty

Auslieferungszeit f period of delivery
auslöhnen to pay wages
Auslöhnung f payment of wages; pay
Auslösegeld n ransom ⋄ **gegen ein ~** on payment of a ransom
auslösen 1. to redeem *(pledge, goods, bills etc.)*; 2. to cause, to set up *(reaction)*; to spark off *(revolution)*
Auslosung f drawing lots *(for s.th.)*
Auslösung f 1. redemption *(pledge, goods, bills etc.)*; 2. additional pay for separation from the family
Auslosungsanleihe f prize [lottery] bonds
Auslosungsstichprobenverfahren n *(stats)* lottery sampling
Ausmaß n measure, degree, extent; scale, scope ⋄ **in geringem ~** to a slight degree [extent]; on a small scale; **in großem ~** on a large scale; **in größerem ~** to a higher degree [extent]; to a greater [wider] scale
ausmessen to measure, to take the measurement of
Ausmessung f measuring, measurement
ausmieten 1. to hire out; 2. *(agric)* to take out of the clamp [silo] *(potatoes etc.)*
Ausnahme f exception ⋄ **mit ~ von** with the exception of, except; **ohne ~** without exception
Ausnahmebedingungen fpl exceptional circumstances
Ausnahmebestimmung f saving clause
Ausnahmeerlaubnis f special permit
Ausnahmefall m special case
Ausnahmefrachtsätze mpl differential rates
Ausnahmetarif m special [exceptional] rate
Ausnahmezollsatz m differential customs rate
Ausnahmezustand m state of emergency
ausnutzen to exploit, to utilize, to use
Ausnutzung f exploitation, utilization, use ⋄ **die ~ eines Patents verhindern** to suppress a patent
~ der Produktionskapazität utilization of production capacity
~, zeitliche utilization over time
Ausnutzungsfaktor m utilization factor, commercial efficiency
Ausnutzungsgrad m degree [level] of utilization
Ausnutzungskennziffer f indicator of utilization *(equipment, plant etc.)*
Ausnutzungskoeffizient m coefficient of utilization
Ausnutzungsnorm f standard rate of utilization
Auspendler m commuter
ausprägen to mark, to stamp; to mint *(gold etc.)*; **sich ~** to be visible, to be well marked *(character etc.)*
Ausprägung f minting *(gold etc.)*

auspreisen to mark the prices, to price
Ausreise f departure, exit
Ausreisegenehmigung f exit permit
Ausreisevisum n exit visa
Ausreißer m *(stats)* maverick; outliers
ausrüsten to equip, to fit out
Ausrüstung f equipment, outfitting, fittings
Ausrüstungsanteil m share of equipment in total investment costs *(share of cost for buying, assembling and installing machines or equipment in the total outlay for investment)*
Ausrüstungsbedarf m requirement of [demand for] equipment
Ausrüstungsbilanz f balance sheet of equipment *(used in planning for balancing resources and uses of specific kinds of equipment)*
Ausrüstungsgegenstand m piece of equipment
Ausrüstungsgrad m level of equipment
Ausrüstungskosten pl equipment costs, costs of equipment; cost to equip *(factory etc.)*
Ausrüstungsquote f s. **Ausrüstungsanteil**
Ausrüstungsstruktur f layout [set-up] of equipment
Aussaat f 1. sowing; dissemination *(seed)*; 2. seed
aussäen to sow, to scatter *(seed)*
Aussage f statement; *(jur)* evidence, testimony ⋄ **die ~ verweigern** *(jur)* to refuse to give evidence; **eine ~ machen** to make a statement; *(jur)* to testify, to give evidence
~, eidliche *(jur)* sworn evidence, affidavit
~, handelspolitische economic policy statement [announcement]
Aussagekraft f impact of a statement
aussagen to state, to make a statement *(about s.th.)*; *(jur)* to give evidence [testimony]
ausschiffen to disembark, to land *(passengers)*; to unship, to unload, to discharge *(cargo)*
ausschließen to exclude, to expel; to disqualify
Ausschließungsfrist f time limit
Ausschließungspatent n exclusive patent
Ausschließungsverfahren n *(jur)* foreclosure proceedings
Ausschluß m exclusion, exception, expulsion, non-admission; disqualification ⋄ **bei ~ von** by excluding; **unter ~ der Öffentlichkeit** behind closed doors; *(jur)* in camera; **unter ~ des Rechtsweges** eliminating legal proceedings
ausschreiben to write out *(cheque)*, to make out *(bill)*; to invite tenders [*(Am)* bids]; to advertise *(post etc.)*
Ausschreibung f writing out *(cheque)*, making out *(bill)*; invitation of tenders [*(Am)* bids]; advertisement (of a vacancy)
Ausschuß m 1. committee, board, commission, panel; 2. waste, scrap; substandard goods;

rejects; ⋄ **einen ~ einsetzen** to appoint [set up] a committee; **einen ~ mit den Tatsachen bekannt machen** to lay the facts before a committee
~, **arbeitskraftbedingter** rejects due to [caused by] operator
~, **arbeitsmittelbedingter** rejects due to [caused by] tools
~, **beratender** advisory committee [board]
~, **eingeschränkt verwendungsfähiger** rejects with limited utility
~, **endgültiger** scrap
~, **engerer** select committee
~, **interparlamentarischer** interparliamentary committee
~, **materialbedingter** rejects due to [caused by] material
~, **reparaturfähiger** repairable rejects
~, **ständiger** standing committee
Ausschußabrechnung f scrap and rejects accounting
Ausschußanteil m proportion of substandard goods; (stats) fraction defective
~, **durchschnittlicher** (stats) process average fraction defect
~, **tolerierter** acceptable proportion of substandard goods; acceptable proportion of rejects
~, **zulässiger** permissible proportion of substandard goods; permissible proportion of rejects
Ausschußkosten pl cost of scrap; cost of rejects
Ausschußmitglied n member of a board [committee]
Ausschußquote f rate of rejects
Ausschußtoleranz f tolerance fraction [per cent] defective; (stats) lot tolerance
~ **für Lose, prozentuale** lot tolerance fraction [per cent] defective
Ausschußverlust m losses due to rejects
Ausschußzahl f (stats) number of defects
~, **tolerierte** (stats) tolerable number of defects
~, **zulässige** (stats) allowable defects; tolerable number of defects
ausschütten to distribute (dividends etc.)
Ausschüttung f distribution (dividends etc.)
Außenbezirk m suburb (town); outlying district
Außenbilanz f balance of payments
Außendienst m field service [work]; customer engineering (after-sales service)
Außenfinanzierung f financing from external [foreign] sources, external financing
Außenhandel m foreign trade
außenhandelsabhängig dependent on foreign trade
Außenhandelsabhängigkeit f dependence on foreign trade

Außenhandelsarbitrage f foreign trade arbitration
Außenhandelsausstellung f foreign trade exhibition
Außenhandelsbank f foreign trade bank
Außenhandelsbedingungen fpl foreign trade conditions [terms]
Außenhandelsbetrieb m foreign trade company
Außenhandelsbeziehungen fpl foreign trade relations
Außenhandelsbilanz f foreign trade balance (sheet)
Außenhandelsbilanzierung f balancing of foreign trade
Außenhandelsdiskriminierung f discrimination in foreign trade
Außenhandelsdokumente npl foreign trade documents
Außenhandelseffektivität f efficiency of foreign trade, foreign trade efficiency
Außenhandelsergebnis n foreign trade profit
Außenhandelserlös m foreign trade proceeds [earnings]
Außenhandelsfinanzierung f financing of foreign trade operations
Außenhandelsfonds mpl foreign trade funds (1. physical and financial funds of export and import including services; 2. fixed assets and working capital of foreign trade companies)
Außenhandelsförderung f promotion of foreign trade
Außenhandelsgeschäft n foreign trade business [deal]
Außenhandelsgesellschaft f foreign trade company
Außenhandelsgewinn m s. **Außenhandelsergebnis**
Außenhandelsintensität f high degree of dependence on foreign trade (expressed by indicators such as export quota, import quota etc.)
außenhandelsintensiv highly dependent on foreign trade
Außenhandelskalkulation f calculation in foreign trade
Außenhandelskaufmann m export sales manager [(Am) executive]
Außenhandelskaufvertrag m foreign trade sales contract
Außenhandelskennziffern fpl foreign trade indicators
Außenhandelskontingent n foreign trade quota
Außenhandelskontor n trading department of foreign trade company
Außenhandelskundendienstvertrag m external service contract
Außenhandelsliefervertrag m export-import [foreign trade] delivery contract

Außenhandelslizenz f export-import [foreign trade] licence
Außenhandelsmesse f trade fair
Außenhandelsmodell n foreign trade model
Außenhandelsmonopol n foreign trade monopoly
Außenhandelsmontagevertrag m contract for project assembling [erection] abroad
Außenhandelsniederlassung f foreign trade (branch) office
Außenhandelsnomenklatur f Standard International Trade Classification
Außenhandelsökonomik f economics of foreign trade, foreign trade economics; international economics
Außenhandelsoperation f foreign trade transaction
Außenhandelsoptimierung f optimization of foreign trade
Außenhandelsorgan n foreign trade organ
Außenhandelsplan m foreign trade plan
Außenhandelsplanung f planning of foreign trade
Außenhandelspolitik f foreign trade policy
Außenhandelspreis m export price; import price
Außenhandelspreisbildung f pricing of [price formation for] export and import goods, pricing in foreign trade
Außenhandelspreisindex m export price index; import price index
Außenhandelspreispolitik f foreign trade price policy
Außenhandelspreisstatistik f foreign trade price statistics
Außenhandelsprognose f foreign trade forecast
Außenhandelsquote f foreign trade ratio
Außenhandelsrentabilität f foreign trade profitability
Außenhandelsrestriktionen fpl restrictions on foreign trade
Außenhandelsrichtung f regional compositions of foreign trade
Außenhandelssaldo m foreign trade balance
Außenhandelsschiedsgericht n foreign trade arbitration court
Außenhandelsspanne f foreign trade margin
Außenhandelsstatistik f foreign trade statistics
Außenhandelsstruktur f foreign trade structure *(commodity composition of foreign trade)*
Außenhandelstätigkeit f foreign trade activities
Außenhandelsumsatz m foreign trade turnover
Außenhandelsunternehmen n s. **Außenhandelsbetrieb**
Außenhandelsverfahren n foreign trade procedure
Außenhandelsversicherung f export insurance; import insurance

Außenhandelsvertrag m 1. foreign trade agreement; 2. export contract; import contract
Außenhandelsvertretung f trade representation
Außenhandelsvolumen n volume of exports and imports
Außenhandelswaren fpl export and import goods [commodities]
Außenhandelswarenverzeichnis n list of export and import goods [commodities]
~, **internationales** international catalogue of export and import commodities, international trade classification
Außenhandelswerbegesellschaft f foreign trade advertising company
Außenhandelswerbung f sales promotion in foreign trade, advertising of export goods
Außenmarkt m foreign [export] market
Außenpolitik f foreign policy
Außenreede f outer roadstead
Außenstände mpl outstanding debts, *(Am)* accounts receivable
Außenstelle f branch office
Außenverkäufer m trade agent *(of a wholesale trading organization)*
Außenversicherung f external insurance *(covering articles housed elsewhere, taken on a journey etc.)*
Außenwerbung f outdoor advertising
Außenwirtschaft f external economy
Außenwirtschaftler m foreign trade economist
Außenwirtschaftsbeziehungen fpl foreign [external, international] economic relations
Außenwirtschaftsbilanzierung f balancing of foreign economic operations
Außenwirtschaftseffekt m efficiency of foreign [external] economic relations
Außenwirtschaftspolitik f foreign [external] economic policy
Außenwirtschaftsprognose f forecast of foreign economic relations
Außenwirtschaftsrecht n law of foreign economic relations [foreign trade]; law of international economic relations
Außenwirtschaftstätigkeit f external [international] economic activities
Außenwirtschaftstheorie f theory of external [foreign] economy, theory of international economics
Außenzoll(tarif) m external tariff
~, **gemeinsamer** common external tariff
außerbetrieblich external *(from the aspect of an enterprise)*
Außerbetriebsetzung f putting out of operation
Außerbilanzvorräte mpl extra stocks
außeretatmäßig extra-budgetary
Außer-Haus-Lieferung f home delivery *(e.g. of ready-to-serve meals)*

Außerkraftsetzung f repeal (law etc.); annulment (contract etc.); abrogation (treaty etc.); suspension (rights etc.)
außerökonomisch non-economic
außerplanmäßig extra, non-planned; outside the schedule
außervertraglich non-contractual
aussetzen 1. to suspend (payment); to stay (proceedings); to defer (negotiation); 2. to offer, to hold out (reward)
Aussetzung f 1. suspension (payment); stay (proceedings); deferment (negotiation); 2. offer (reward)
Aussicht f view; chance; outlook, prospect
⋄ **mit der ~ späterer Beteiligung** with the view to partnership
Aussichten fpl:
⋄ **gute ~ haben** to stand a good chance
~, **allgemeine** general outlook
~, **berufliche** job prospects
~, **günstige** favourable outlook, good prospects
~, **kurzfristige** short-term prospects
~, **schlechte** unfavourable outlook, poor prospects
~, **wirtschaftliche** outlook of the economy
aussiedeln to evacuate; to resettle
Aussiedler m evacuee; person resettled
Aussiedlung f evacuation; resettlement
aussondern to sort [single] out, to select; to discard (obsolete equipment)
Aussonderung f sorting out, selection; discarding (obsolete equipment)
~ **von Grundmitteln** discarding of fixed [capital] assets
Aussonderungsquote f rate [percentage] of discarding (obsolete equipment)
aussortieren to sort [single, pick] out
aussperren to lock out (workers)
Aussperrung f lockout (workers)
Ausstand m strike, (Am) walkout ⋄ **in den ~ treten** to go on strike, (Am) to walk out
ausstatten to provide, to supply; to furnish, to equip, to fit out
Ausstattung f provision, supply; equipment, outfit
~, **infrastrukturelle** provision with infrastructure
Ausstattungsarbeiten fpl work involved in equipping (factory etc.); work involved in furnishing (flat etc.)
Ausstattungsgrad m level of equipment
~ **der Haushalte** rate of households furnished with consumer durables
Ausstattungskosten pl costs involved in equipping (factory etc.); costs involved in furnishing (flat etc.)
Ausstattungsstandard m standard of equipping (factory etc.); standard of furnishing (flat etc.)

ausstehen to be outstanding (payment etc.); to be overdue (consignment etc.); to be still pending (decision); to be still expected (news)
ausstehend outstanding, receivable, owing, unpaid (payment etc.); overdue (consignment etc.), (still) pending (decision)
ausstellen 1. to show, to display, to exhibit (goods etc.); 2. to make out (document, certificate, bill etc.); to write out (cheque etc.); to issue (passport etc.)
Aussteller m 1. exhibitor, exhibiting firm (goods etc.); 2. writer (cheque etc.); issuer, issuing authority (passport etc.)
~, **branchenverwandter** exhibitor of related trade groups
~, **gemeinsamer** co-exhibitor
~, **langjähriger** exhibitor of long standing
~, **ständiger** regular [permanent] exhibitor
Ausstelleranmeldung f registration of exhibitors
Ausstellerausweis m exhibitor's pass [identity card]
Ausstellerbetrieb m exhibiting enterprise, exhibitor
Ausstellerfirma f exhibiting firm, exhibitor
Ausstellerland n exhibiting country
Ausstellerversicherung f insurance for exhibitors
Ausstellerverzeichnis n list of exhibitors
Ausstellung f 1. show, display, exhibition (goods etc.); 2. making out (document, certificate, bill etc.); writing out (cheque etc.); issue (passport etc.)
~, **einmalige** single exhibition
~, **internationale** international exhibition
~, **landwirtschaftliche** agricultural exhibition
~, **technische** engineering exhibition
Ausstellungsamt n bureau of exhibitions
Ausstellungsbedingungen fpl terms of participation (in an exhibition)
Ausstellungsbesucher m visitor to an exhibition
Ausstellungsdatum n date of issue (passport etc.)
Ausstellungsfläche f exhibition [display] area [space]
Ausstellungsführer m exhibitor's guide
Ausstellungsgebäude n exhibition building
Ausstellungsgegenstand m exhibit, exhibition article; display item (shop window)
Ausstellungsgelände n exhibition grounds [site]
Ausstellungsgüter npl exhibits, exhibition goods
Ausstellungshalle f exhibition hall [pavilion]
Ausstellungskiosk m exhibition kiosk
Ausstellungskosten pl exhibition costs
Ausstellungspavillon m exhibition pavilion
Ausstellungsraum m exhibition room, showroom
Ausstellungsschutz m protection of exhibits (s. **Ausstellungsversicherung**)

Ausstellungsstand *m* exhibition stand [booth]
Ausstellungsstück *n s.* **Ausstellungsgegenstand**
Ausstellungstag *m* day [date] of issue *(passport etc.)*
Ausstellungsversicherung *f* insurance of exhibits *(covering transport and period of exhibition)*
Ausstellungsvitrine *f* display showcase
Ausstellungsware *f* exhibit(s), exhibition good(s); display item(s)
Aussteuerung *f (ins)* expiry of s.o.'s claim to insurance benefits
Aussteuerversicherung *f* children's endowment insurance
Ausstoß *m* output, production
~, **jährlicher** annual output [production]
~, **monatlicher** monthly output [production]
~ **pro Arbeitsstunde** output per hour
~, **täglicher** daily output [production]
~, **vierteljährlicher** quarterly output [production]
Ausstoßbeschränkung *f* restriction of output [production]
ausstoßen to turn out, to produce
Ausstoßleistung *f* output, capacity
Ausstoßmenge *f* volume of output [production]
Ausstoßtermin *m* output date
Ausstoßvolumen *n s.* **Ausstoßmenge**
Austausch *m* exchange; barter *(goods against goods)*; interchange *(ideas etc.)*
~, **äquivalenter** equivalent exchange
~, **nichtäquivalenter** non-equivalent exchange
Austauschabkommen *n* barter agreement
Austauschakt *m* exchange
Austauschbarkeit *f* exchangeability, interchangeability
austauschen to exchange; to barter *(goods against goods)*; to interchange *(ideas etc.)*
Austauschprozeß *m* process of exchange
Austauschrelation *f* rate of exchange, exchange rate
Austauschsphäre *f* sphere of exchange
Austauschstoff *m* substitute (material)
Austauschverfahren *n* substituting technology
Austauschverhältnisse *npl (for tr)* terms of trade; relations of exchange; exchange relations
Austauschvolumen *n* quantity of exchange
Austauschware *f* substitute (commodity)
Austauschwerkstoff *m* alternative [substitute] material
austragen 1. to delete, to take out *(items, name from list etc.)*; *(acc)* to cancel; 2. *(post)* to deliver *(letters, newspapers)*
Austragung *f* deletion *(item, name from list etc.)*; *(acc)* cancellation

austreten to leave *(association etc.)*, to secede *(from federal union)*, to withdraw *(from society etc.)*; to resign
Austritt *m* leaving *(association etc.)*, secession *(from federal union)*, withdrawal *(from society)*; resignation
Austrittserklärung *f* declaration of withdrawal [secession]
Aus- und Weiterbildung *f* training and further [on-the-job] training
Ausverkauf *m* clearance sale, selling off [out]
ausverkaufen to clear, to sell off [out], *(Am)* to close out *(stock)*
Ausverkaufspreis *m* clearance sale price
ausverkauft sold out
Auswahl *f* choice, selection; assortment ◊ **eine ~ treffen** to make a selection; **zur ~** for selection
~, **bewußte** judgement sample; *(stats)* purposive sample
~, **große** wide choice [range]
~, **mehrstufige** *(stats)* stratified sample
~ **mit gleichen Wahrscheinlichkeiten** *(stats)* selection with equal probability
~ **mit größe-proportionalen Wahrscheinlichkeiten** *(stats)* selection with probabilities proportional to size
~ **mit willkürlich festgesetzten Wahrscheinlichkeiten** *(stats)* selection with arbitrary (variable) probability
~, **reiche** rich assortment
~, **repräsentative** *(stats)* controlled sampling
~, **zufällige** *(stats)* sample, random test
Auswahlabstand *m (stats)* sampling interval
Auswahlbefragung *f* selective inquiry
Auswahleinheit *f (stats)* sampling unit
~ **erster Stufe** *(stats)* first-stage unit (of sampling)
Auswahleinheiten *fpl*:
~, **überlappte** *(stats)* overlapping sampling units
auswählen to choose, to select
Auswahlgrundlage *f (stats)* frame
Auswahlmethode *f (stats)* sampling method
Auswahlprinzip *n* selection principle
Auswahlreihe *f (stats)* series of samples
Auswahlsatz *m (stats)* sampling fraction [ratio]
~, **einheitlicher** *(stats)* uniform sampling fraction [ratio]
Auswahlverfahren *n (stats)* patterned sampling
~, **systematisches** *(stats)* systematic sampling
Auswanderer *m* emigrant
auswandern to emigrate
Auswanderung *f* emigration
auswechselbar interchangeable, exchangeable; replaceable
Auswechselbarkeit *f* interchangeability, exchangeability; replaceability

auswechseln to change, to exchange; to replace
Auswechslung *f* change, interchange, exchange; replacement
Ausweichklausel *f* escape clause *(contract etc.)*
Ausweichlager *n* reserve store
Ausweis *m* identity [*(Am)* identification] card *(citizen)*; pass *(train etc.)*; membership card *(library etc.)*; statement, return *(account)*; certificate; proof, evidence
~ **der Staatsbank** state bank return
~, **kostenmäßiger** statement of costs
ausweisen 1. to prove, to show, to testify; to give account of; 2. to deport, to expel *(from country)*
Ausweiskarte *f* identity [*(Am)* identification] card; membership [admission] card
Ausweispapiere *npl* documents of identification, identification papers
Ausweisung *f* expelling, deportation *(from country)*
Ausweisungsbefehl *m* expulsion [deportation] order
ausweiten to expand, to extend, to enlarge, to widen
Ausweitung *f* expansion, extension, enlargement, widening
auswerten to evaluate, to analyse *(facts etc.)*, to interpret *(statistical data)*, to assess *(situation etc.)*; to exploit, to utilize *(patent, invention)*
Auswertung *f* evaluation, analysis *(facts etc.)*, interpretation *(statistical data)*, assessment *(situation etc.)*; exploitation, utilization *(patent, invention)*
~, **statistische** evaluation [interpretation] of (set of) statistics [statistical data]
~, **technische** technological utilization [exploitation]
auswirken, sich to have consequences, to have its effects ◊ **sich benachteiligend** ~ to be prejudicial; **sich günstig auf etwas** ~ to have a favourable effect on s.th.
Auswirkung *f* consequence, result, effect
Auswirkungen *fpl*:
~, **sozialpolitische** effects of social policy measures
auszahlen to pay (out) *(sum of money, wages etc.)*, to pay off; to disburse *(sum of money)* ◊ **in bar** ~ to pay cash down
auszählen to count
Auszahlung *f* payment *(money, wages etc.)*; disbursement *(money)* ◊ ~ **sperren** to stop payment; **zur** ~ **gelangen** to be paid out
~, **bevorrechtigte** preferred [preferential] payment
~ **in voller Höhe** full payment
~, **telegrafische** telegraphic [cable] transfer
~, **vollständige** payment in full

Auszählung *f* counting
Auszahlungen *fpl*:
~ **im Rahmen einer Anleihe** disbursements under a loan
Auszahlungsanordnung *f* rules of payment, payment rules
Auszahlungsbescheinigung *f* payment voucher
Auszahlungsdatum *n* date of payment
Auszahlungsmatrix *f (stats)* pay-off matrix
Auszahlungsschein *m* pay(ment) slip
auszeichnen 1. to price *(goods for sale)*; 2. to award *(s.o. a medal)*, to decorate *(s.o. with s.th.)*
Auszeichnung *f* 1. pricing *(goods for sale)*; 2. award, decoration *(order, medal)*
~, **staatliche** state award
Auszeichnungspflicht *f* obligation to price goods
Auszubildender *m* trainee
Auszug *m* extract *(book)*; statement, abstract *(account)*; excerpt *(documents)*
autark autarkic(al), self-supporting, self-sufficient, independent
Autarkie *f* autarky; national [economic] self-sufficiency
Auto *n*: ◊ **ein** ~ **zulassen** to register a car, to allow registration of a car
Autobahn *f* motorway, autobahn
~, **gebührenpflichtige** toll road [highway]
Autobahnbenutzungsgebühr *f* highway [autobahn] charges, motorway tolls
Auto-Kasko-Versicherung *f* comprehensive (vehicle) insurance
Autokorrelation *f (stats)* autocorrelation
Autokorrelationsfunktion *f (stats)* autocorrelation function
Autokorrelationskoeffizient *m (stats)* autocorrelation coefficient
Autokovarianz *f (stats)* autocovariance
Automat *m* automatic machine; *(home tr)* slot machine, automatic (selling) machine, vending machine
Automatenhandel *m (home tr)* automatic selling, machine business, sales by vending machines
Automatenverkauf *m* sale by vending machines
Automation *f s.* **Automatisierung**
automatisch automatic; automatically
automatisieren to automate
automatisiert automated
Automatisierung *f* automation
~, **komplexe** comprehensive automation *(of a whole plant including automation of managerial and planning activities)*
~, **volle** complete automation
Automatisierungseffekt *m* efficiency of automation
Automatisierungsgrad *m* level [degree] of automation

~ **auf Zeitbasis** level [degree] of automation related to working time
~ **der Produktion** level [degree] of automation of production
Automatisierungskoeffizient *m* automation coefficient *(ratio between goods manufactured automatically and total output)*
Automatisierungsmittel *npl* devices [instruments] of automation
Automatisierungsnutzen *m* benefit derived from automation
Automatisierungsstufe *f* stage [level] of automation
autonom autonomous
Autonomie *f* autonomy, self-government
Autoregression *f (stats)* autoregression
Autorenkontrolle *f* investment project control by drawing office *(in charge of the particular project)*
Aval *m* guarantee, surety *(for a bill)*
Avalbürgschaft *f s.* **Aval**
Avalgeber *m s.* **Avalist**
avalieren to guarantee, to back *(a bill)*, to stand security [surety] *(for a bill)*
Avalist *m* guarantor
Avalkonto *n* guarantee account
Avalkredit *m* surety credit, credit secured by a bank guarantee
Avis *m/n* advice, notice
avisieren to advise, to notify, to give notice *(of s.th.)*
Avisschreiben *n* letter of advice
a vista at sight
Avistawechsel *m* draft payable on presentation

B

Baby-bond *m* savings bond; share with low par--value, low par-value share
Bäcker *m* baker
Bäckerei *f* baker's [baking] trade; bakery; baker's shop
Bäckergewerbe *n s.* **Bäckerhandwerk**
Bäckerhandwerk *n* baker's trade, bakery
Backwaren *fpl* bakery goods, bread and biscuits, cakes, pastries
Bagatellbetrag *m* trifle, trifling sum
Bagatellbeträge *mpl* petty cash
Bagatelle *f (jur)* petty law-case
Bagatellgericht *n* court of summary jurisdiction
Bagatellklausel *f* trifle [bagatelle] clause
Bagatellprozeß *m (jur)* petty law-case; summary offence

Bagatellsache *f s.* **Bagatellprozeß**
Bagatellschaden *m (ins)* (case of) petty damage(s)
Bagatellschulden *fpl* petty debts
Bagatellstücke *npl (st.ex.)* small securities
Bahn *f* 1. railway, *(Am)* railroad; tramway, *(Am)* streetcar line; line, *(Am)* track; train; 2. carriageway, carriage-road; (traffic) lane; 3. runway *(airport)* ◊ **an der ~** at the station; **frei ~** free on rail (f.o.r.), *(Am)* free on board (f.o.b., F.O.B.) ◊ **mit der ~ fahren** to go [travel] by train; ◊ **mit der [per] ~ (ver)senden [befördern, verschicken]** to send [forward, dispatch] (goods) by [per] rail(way); **per ~ zum Versand bringen** to consign by rail
Bahnangestellter *m* railway employee
Bahnbeamter *m* railway official
Bahnbeförderung *f* railway carriage [transportation]
Bahnbegleitpapiere *npl (railw)* accompanying papers [documents]
Bahnbetrieb *m* operation of a railway line; railway undertaking
bahnbrechend pioneering *(research etc.)*, epoch--making *(discovery etc.)* ◊ **~ sein** to pioneer
Bahnbrecher *m* pioneer
Bahndienst *m* employment on the railway ◊ **im ~** working on the railway
Bahnfracht *f* railway carriage, rail transportation, *(Am)* rail(road) freight
Bahnfrachtbrief *m* bill of carriage
Bahnfrachtgut *n* railway parcels
Bahnfrachtsätze *mpl* rail transport rates, *(Am)* railroad rates
Bahnhof *m* (railway [*(Am)* railroad]) station
Bahnhofsanlagen *fpl* station premises
Bahnhofsbuchhandlung *f* station bookstall
Bahnhofssendung *f* railway mail
Bahnhofsvorsteher *m* stationmaster
Bahnhofswirtschaft *f* refreshment room; station restaurant
Bahnknotenpunkt *m* railway junction
bahnlagernd to be collected from the station
Bahnlieferung *f* consignment by rail
Bahnpolizei *f* railway police
Bahnpost *f* railway postal service
Bahnpostamt *n* railway post-office
bahnpostlagernd to be colleced from the railway post-office
Bahnspediteur *m* rail forwarding agent
Bahnspedition *f* forwarding of goods by rail; rail forwarding agency
Bahnstation *f* railway station ◊ **frei ~ liefern** to deliver free (railway) station
Bahnsteig *m* platform
Bahnsteigkarte *f* platform ticket

Bahntransport *m* transport by rail, rail transport
Bahntransportversicherung *f* rail transport insurance
Bahnverbindung *f* train connection
Bahnverkehr *m* railway [*(Am)* railroad] traffic
Bahnversand *m* rail dispatch, forwarding [*(Am)* shipping] by rail
Bahnvorschriften *fpl* railway regulations
Bahnzustellung *f* rail delivery
Baisse *f* *(st.ex.)* decline [fall, drop, slump] in prices; depression *(on the market, on the exchange)* ✧ **auf ~ spekulieren** to speculate on a fall; to sell [go] a bear, to bear [sell] short; **erwartete ~ im voraus berücksichtigen** to underdiscount the (stock) market; **im Zeichen der ~ stehen** bearish, to be marked by a decline [fall] in prices; **in der ~ verkaufen** to go a bear, to sell (shares) short, to sell [short] (shares) in anticipation of a fall; **sich in einer ~ eindecken** to raid the bears; **während der ~ kaufen** to buy on a fall
~, konjunkturelle cyclical depression
Baisseangriff *m* *(st.ex.)* hammering (of) the market ✧ **einen ~ machen** *(st.ex.)* to hammer the market
Baissegerücht *n* *(st.ex.)* bear rumour
Baissegeschäft *n* *(st.ex.)* bear transaction
Baissehaltung *f* *(st.ex.)* bearish attitude
Baisseklausel *f* *(st.ex.)* slump clause
Baissekonto *n* *(st.ex.)* bear account
Baissemarkt *m* *(st.ex.)* bear(ish) [sagging] market, *(Am)* falling [short] market
Baissespekulant *m* *(st.ex.)* speculator for a fall; bear
Baissespekulation *f* *(st.ex.)* bear speculation, speculation for a fall [decline]
Baissestimmung *f s.* **Baissetendenz**
Baisseströmung *f s.* **Baissetendenz**
Baissetendenz *f* *(st.ex.)* bear tone, downward tendency (of prices); bearish [falling, declining] tendency [trend]
Baissier *m* *(st.ex.)* bear
Ballast *m* ballast ✧ **~ abwerfen** to discharge ballast; **~ aufnehmen** to take in ballast; **mit ~ beladen** to ballast; **nur mit ~** in ballast
ballasten to ballast *(ship)*
Ballastfracht *f* dead freight, ballast
Ballastladung *f s.* **Ballastfracht**
Ballastreise *f* ballast passage
Ballastschiff *n* ballast lighter
Ballen *m* bale
Ballengüter *npl* bale-goods
Ballenwaren *fpl s.* **Ballengüter**
ballenweise in bales, by the bale
Ballenzeichen *n* bale mark
Ballot *n* small bale
Ballotage *f* *(pol)* voting by ballot, balloting

ballotieren *(pol)* to (vote by) ballot
Ballung *f* *(stats)* concentration; congestion *(traffic)*
Ballungsgebiet *n* congested area
Band *n* 1. band; tape; belt; 2. bond, tie, link
Bandangabenwähler *m* *(d.pr.)* tape data selector
Bandanlauf *m* *(d.pr.)* tape start
Bandanzeiger *m* *(d.pr.)* tape indicator
Bandblock *m* *(d.pr.)* tape block
Bandbreite *f* 1. *(fin, stats)* spread; *(st.ex.)* range of variation *(exchange rates etc.)*; 2. *(d.pr.)* band width
Banddatei *f* *(d.pr.)* tape file
Bandeingabe *f* *(d.pr.)* tape input
Bandeinheit *f* *(d.pr.)* tape drive [unit]
Banderole *f* *(fin)* revenue stamp
Banderolensteuer *f* *(fin)* stamp duty
Bandfabrikation *f s.* **Bandfertigung**
Bandfehler *m* *(d.pr.)* tape error
Bandfertigung *f* mass production (on the assembly line), (moving-)belt production
Bandförderung *f s.* **Bandtransport**
Bandgeschwindigkeit *f* *(manuf)* speed of the assembly line; *(d.pr.)* tape speed
bandgesteuert *(d.pr.)* tape-operated
Bandrolle *f* *(d.pr.)* spool
Bandspeicher *m* *(d.pr.)* tape store
Bandspule *f* *(d.pr.)* reel of tape
Bandsteuerung *f* *(d.pr.)* tape control
Bandtransport *m* *(d.pr.)* tape transport
Bandzuführung *f* *(d.pr.)* tape feed
Bank *f* bank, banking house [establishment] ✧ **bei der ~ im Debet sein** to be overdrawn at the bank; **bei einer ~ arbeiten** to be employed in a bank; **bei einer ~ einzahlen** to pay in [deposit] at a bank; **bei einer ~ zahlbar** payable at a bank; **durch eine ~ überweisen** to remit through a bank; **in der ~ sein** to lie at the bank *(bonds, shares etc.)*; **ungenutzt in einer ~ liegen** to lie idle in a bank
~, abwickelnde transacting bank
~, als Hinterlegungsstelle fungierende deposit [*(Am)* depository] bank
~, anweisende ordering bank
~, ausführende *s.* **~, abwickelnde**
~, auswärtige 1. out-of-town bank; 2. foreign bank
~, auszahlende paying bank
~, barzahlende cash-paying [specie-paying] bank
~, beauftragte bank assigned *(to execute s.th.)*
~, bekannte reputable [well-known] bank
~, bezogene drawee bank
~, dem Abrechnungsverkehr angeschlossene clearing bank
~, diskontierende accepting [discounting] bank
~, Effektenemissionsgeschäfte betreibende investment bank *(issuing and selling shares)*

~, **einziehende** collecting bank
~, **führende** leading bank
~ **für Überseehandel** overseas bank
~, **konsortialführende** leading member bank of a syndicate
~, **kontenführende** accounting bank
~, **konzessionierte** chartered bank
~, **korrespondierende** co-operating [corresponding] bank
~, **landwirtschaftliche** agricultural bank
~, **öffentliche** public bank
~, **öffentlich-rechtliche** bank under public law
~, **örtliche** local bank
~, **seriöse** sound bank
~, **überweisende** remitting bank
~, **zahlungsfähige** solvent bank
~, **zahlungsunfähige** insolvent bank, bank in failing condition
Bankabhebung *f* bank withdrawal
Bankabrechnungsbuch *n* bank book
Bankabschluß *m* bank balance; bank return [statement]
Bankabteilung *f* banking department, department of a bank
Bankagent *m* exchange [bank] broker
Bankagentur *f* bank agency [broker]; branch of a bank
Bankagio *n* bank agio
Bankakkreditiv *n* letter of credit
Bankakt *m* bank(ing) operation
Bankaktie *f* bank share [*(Am)* stock]
Bankaktionär *m* bank shareholder, *(Am)* holder of bank stock
Bankaktiva *pl* bank assets
Bankakzept *n* bank acceptance [*(Am)* bill]
~, **erstklassiges** fine bank [*(Am)* prime banker's] acceptance
Bankangestellter *m* bank clerk
Bankanleihe *f* bank loan
Bankanstalt *f* banking house, bank
Bankanteil *m* bank share [*(Am)* stock]; bank quota
Bankanteilschein *m s.* **Bankaktie**
Bankanteilseigner *m* shareholder [*(Am)* stockholder] in a bank
Bankanweisung *f* order for payment, (bank) check ◊ **durch ~ bezahlt** paid by cheque [*(Am)* check]
Bankaufgeld *n s.* **Bankagio**
Bankauftrag *m* banker's order
Bankauskunft *f* banker's reference, credit information
Bankausweis *m* bank return [*(Am)* statement]
~, **wöchentlicher** weekly bank return [*(Am)* statement]
Bankauszug *m* statement of account
Bankaval *m s.* **Bankgarantie**

Bankavis *n* bank advice
Bankbeamter *m* bank official
Bankbedingungen *fpl* bank conditions
Bankbeleg *m* bank receipt
Bankbericht *m* bank(ing) report
Bankberichterstattung *f* reporting on bank affairs
Bankbeteiligung *f* bank participation
Bankbetrieb *m* bank; banking business
Bankbilanz *f* balance sheet of a bank, bank report [return, statement]
Bankbote *m* bank-messenger
Bankbuch *n* bank book, pass-book
Bankbuchhaltung *f* bank accounting
Bankbürgschaft *f* bank security [surety]
Bankdarleh(e)n *n* bank loan [credit]
Bankdebitor *m s.* **Bankschuldner**
Bankdeckung *f* backing of a bank, bank backing; note cover (by bankable securities)
Bankdepositen *pl* bank deposits
Bankdepotgesetz *n* safe custody law
Bankdirektor *m* bank manager
Bankdirektorium *n* board of directors of a bank
Bankdiskont *m* bank discount
Bankdiskontsatz *m* bank [discount] rate
Bankdisponent *m* dealer
Bankeinbruchsversicherung *f* bank burglary insurance
Bankeinlage *f* bank deposit
Bankeinzahlung *f* payment to the bank
Bankenabkommen *n* banking agreement, agreement between banks
Bankenabrechnung *f* bank clearing
Bankenabrechnungsstelle *f* (interbank) clearing house, clearing centre
Bankenaufgabe *f* banking function
Bank(en)aufsicht *f* supervision of bank(s)
Bankenaufsichtsbehörde *f* supervising authority of banks
Bankenausschuß *m* banking committee
Bank(en)berechtigung *f s.* **Bankvollmacht**
Bankenbesteuerung *f* taxation of banks
Bankenbonifikation *f* underwriting fee
Bankendezentralisation *f* decentralization in banking; decentralization of (large) banks
Bankendezentralisierung *f s.* **Bankendezentralisation**
Bank(en)fusion *f* bank merger [consolidation]
Bankengesetz *n* bank act
Bankengesetzgebung *f* banking legislation
Bankengruppe *f* group of banks
Bank(en)inkasso *n* encashment by bank(s)
Bankenintervention *f (st.ex.)* bank intervention, banking support
Bank(en)kartell *n* bank cartel
Bankenkonsortium *n* banking syndicate
~, **ausländisches** foreign banking syndicate

Bankenkonzentration *f* concentration of banks
Bank(en)konzern *m* banking concern
Bank(en)krach *m* bank crash [failure]
Bank(en)kredit *m* bank credit [loan] ✧ **einen ~ aufnehmen** to obtain a loan from a bank
Bankenkrise *f* bank crisis
Bankenliquidität *f* bank liquidity, liquidity of a bank
Bankenmarkt *f* market for bank shares [*(Am)* stocks]; banking market
Bankenorganisation *f* banking organization
Bankenpfandrecht *n* banker's lien
Bankenprivileg *n* bank charter (with special privileges)
Bank(en)ring *m* bank cartel [trust]
Bankenrun *m* bank run
Bankenstimmrecht *n* bank's right to vote
Bankensystem *n* system of banks
Bankenvereinbarung *f* agreement on banking co-operation
Bankenverrechnung *f* clearing
Bankenzentrum *n* banking centre
Bankfach *n* 1. banking business; 2. bank safe
Bankfachmann *m* banking expert
bankfähig bankable, negotiable *(securities etc.)* ✧ **nicht ~** unbankable, non-negotiable *(securities etc.)*
Bankfähigkeit *f* bankability, negotiability *(securities etc.)*
Bankfazilitäten *fpl* banking facilities
Bankfeiertag *m* bank holiday
Bankferien *pl* bank holidays
Bankfiliale *f* branch (bank)
Bankfirma *f s.* **Bankhaus**
Bankgarantie *f* bank(er's) guarantee
Bankgebäude *n* bank building
Bankgebühren *fpl* bank charges, banker's commission
Bankgeheimnis *n* bank secrecy, banking secret
Bankgeld *n* bank money [funds]
Bankgeschäft *n* 1. banking business; 2. banking transaction [operation]
~, kaufmännisches commercial banking
Bankgeschäfte *npl*:
 ✧ **sämtliche ~ ausführen** to transact all kinds of banking
~, alle complete banking facilities
~ in Anlagenwerten investment banking
Bankgesetzgebung *f* banking legislation
Bankgewerbe *n* banking (business)
Bankgewinn *m* bank profit
bankgiriert endorsed by a bank
Bankgiro *f* endorsement of a bank
Bankgläubiger *m* bank creditor
Bankguthaben *n* bank deposits [balance], sum at the bank; *(acc)* cash at bank
Bankhaus *n* banking house, bank

Bankier *m* banker
Bankindossament *n* bank endorsement
Bankingtheorie *f* banking theory
Bankinhaber *m* proprietor of a bank, banker
Bankinstitut *n* banking institution, bank establishment, bank
Bankkapital *n* banking capital, bank stock [funds, assets]
Bankkassierer *m* cashier of a bank, bank cashier
Bankkaufmann *m* bank clerk
Bankkommanditist *m* partner of a bank with limited liabilities
Bankkompensation *f* bank compensation
Bankkonditionen *fpl* banking terms [conditions]
Bankkonkurs *m s.* **Bank(en)krach**
Bankkonteninhaber *m* bank depositor
Bankkonto *n* bank account (**s. a. Konto**) ✧ **ein ~ eröffnen** to open a bank account; **ein ~ haben bei** to have a bank account with; **ein ~ überziehen** to make an overdraft, to overdraw one's account
~, überzogenes overdrawn bank account
Bankkontokorrent *n* current bank account
Bankkontor *n* banking office
Bankkontrolle *f* auditing by banks
Bankkorrespondent *m s.* **Bank, korrespondierende**
Bankkreise *mpl* bank experts, banking circles, bankers
Bankkunde *m* customer of a bank
Bankkundschaft *f* customers of a bank
Bankkuratorium *n* board of bank trustees
Bankleitzahl *f* bank code (number)
Bankliquidität *f* bank liquidity
~, echte genuine bank liquidity
~, geborgte indirect bank liquidity
bankmäßig bankable, negotiable *(securities etc.)*; banking; through the bank
Bankmonopol *n* banking monopoly
Banknebenstelle *f* branch (bank)
Bankniederlassung *f s.* **Bankfiliale**
Banknote *f* bank note
~, als gesetzliches Zahlungsmittel geltende legal tender (note)
~, ausländische foreign note
~, beschädigte damaged bank note
~, echte good bank note
~, einlösbare *s.* **~, konvertierbare**
~, falsche *s.* **~, gefälschte**
~, gefälschte counterfeit [bogus] note
~, konvertible *s.* **~, konvertierbare**
~, konvertierbare convertible bank note
~, nicht einlösbare inconvertible bank note
Banknoten *fpl*:
 ✧ **~ aus dem Verkehr ziehen** to withdraw bank notes (from circulation); **~ ausgeben** to

issue (bank) notes; ~ **einziehen** to withdraw bank notes
~ **mit kleinem Nennwert** money of small denominations
Banknotenausgabe *f* issue [emission] of bank notes, note issue
Banknotenfälscher *m* note forger, forger [counterfeiter] of bank notes
Banknotenfälschung *f* counterfeiting of bank notes
Banknotenkurs *m* rate of exchange of bank notes
Banknotenmonopol *n* note-issuing monopoly
Banknotenprivileg *n* right to issue bank notes
Banknotenumlauf *m* (bank) note circulation, bank notes in circulation
Banknotenvorrat *m* reserve of bank notes
Banknotenzähler *m* teller
Banknotenzirkulation *f s.* **Banknotenumlauf**
Bankobligationen *fpl* bank bonds
Bankoperationen *fpl* banking transactions [operations]
Bankorder *f* bank(ing) order
Bankorganisation *f* organization of banking operations
Bankpapiere *npl* bank papers; banker's notes; banking shares [*(Am)* stocks]
Bankpapiergeld *n s.* **Banknote**
Bankpassiva *pl* bank liabilities
Bankplatz *m s.* **Bankenzentrum**
Bankpolitik *f* bank(ing) policy
bankpolitisch of banking policy
Bankpraxis *f* banking practice
Bankprofit *m* banker's profit, profit of the bank
Bankprokura *f s.* **Bankvollmacht**
Bankprovision *f* bank charges, banker's commission
Bankprüfung *f* bank audit *(by higher authorities)*
Bankquittung *f* bank receipt
Bankrate *f* bank rate
Bankraub *m* bank robbery
Bankrechnung *f* bank invoice
Bankreferenz *f* banker's reference
Bankrembours *m* revolving (commercial) bank credit
Bankreserven *fpl* bank's reserves
~, **gesetzliche** minimum reserve(s)
Bankrestriktion *f* bank restriction
Bankrevisor *m* bank auditor
bankrott bankrupt, insolvent ◊ **jmdn. für** ~ **erklären** to adjudicate [adjudge] *(s.o.)* bankrupt
Bankrott *m* bankruptcy, insolvency ◊ **den** ~ **erklären** to declare bankruptcy; **seinen** ~ **anmelden** to file a petition in bankruptcy
~, **betrügerischer** fraudulent bankruptcy
~, **böswilliger** *s.* ~, **betrügerischer**

~, **einfacher** simple bankruptcy
~, **politischer** political bankruptcy
~, **strafbarer** *s.* ~, **betrügerischer**
~, **wirtschaftlicher** commercial failure
Bankrotterklärung *f* declaration of bankruptcy
Bankrotteur *m* bankrupt
Bankrücklage *f* bank reserves
Banksaldo *m* bank balance
Banksammelverrechnung *f* collective bank clearing
Banksatz *m* bank rate
Bankscheck *m* bank cheque [*(Am)* check]
Bankschließfach *n* bank safe
Bankschuldenkonto *n* bank credit account
Bankschuldner *m* debtor of a bank
Bankspesen *pl s.* **Bankgebühren**
Bankstatus *m* 1. bank status; 2. financial condition (of a bank)
Bankstelle *f s.* **Bankfiliale**
Bankstellennetz *n* network of branch banks
Banksteuer *f* bank tax
Bankstimmrecht *n* bank voting rights
Banktag *m* bank-return day
Banktechnik *f* 1. banking methods; 2. equipment of banks
Banktransaktion *f s.* **Bankoperationen**
Banktratte *f* bank(er's) draft
Banktresor *m* (bank) strong-room, vault
Banküberweisung *f* bank transfer
Banküberziehung *f* overdraft
Bankunternehmen *n* banking firm, bank
Bankverbindung *f* 1. bank account *(customers)*; 2. corresponding banks
Bankverkehr *m* banking (business), business of banking
Bankvermögen *n* bank assets
Bankverschuldung *f* bank indebtedness
Bankvollmacht *f* power of attorney (to transact banking business), bank procuration
Bankvorstand *m* board of management of a bank; bank management
Bankwechsel *m* banker's draft, bank-bill
Bankwelt *f* the banks, banking world
Bankwerte *mpl s.* **Bankpapiere**
Bankwesen *n* banking (system), banks
Bankwoche *f* bank-return week
Bankzahlung *f* bank payment
Bankziehung *f* bank draft
Bankzins *m* bank interest
Bankzinssatz *m* bank rate
Bankzusammenbruch *m s.* **Bank(en)krach**
bar 1. devoid of, lacking, without; 2. pure *(gold etc.)*; 3. *(com)* (in) cash ◊ ~ **bezahlen** to pay (in) cash, to pay ready money; ~ **gegen 5 Prozent Diskont** cash less 5 per cent discount; ~ **ohne Abzug** in cash without deduction; **gegen** ~ for cash, cash down, on cash

terms; **gegen ~ kaufen** to buy for cash [ready money]; **gegen ~ verkaufen** to sell for cash; **in ~** in cash; **in ~ bezahlen** s. **bar bezahlen**; **in ~ übersenden** to remit [make remittance] in cash; **nur gegen ~** cash sales only [down only, only]
Barabdeckung *f* settlement in cash
Barabfindung *f* cash settlement [indemnity], compensation in cash
Barabhebung *f* cash withdrawal, withdrawal in cash
Barablösung *f s.* **Barabdeckung**
Barablösungswert *m* cash value
Barabschluß *m* cash transaction
Barabwicklung *f* settlement in cash *(debts etc.)*
Barakkreditiv *n* letter of credit *(for travellers)*
Baranforderung *f* cash requirements
Baranschaffung *f s.* **Barkauf**
Barartikel *m* ready money article
Baraufwand *m* cash outlay [expenditure(s)]
Barausgänge *mpl* cash outlays [payments, disbursements]; cash withdrawals *(from an account)*
Barauslagen *fpl* cash outlays [expenditure(s)], out-of-pocket expense(s)
Barauszahlung *f* disbursement of cash (money)
Barbestand *m* cash in hand [(*Am*) (cash) holdings]
Barbetrag *m* amount in cash
Barbezüge *mpl* remuneration in cash
Bardarleh(e)n *n* cash loan, advance in cash
Bardeckung *f* cash cover, cash available for cover; cash reimbursement
Bardepot *n* cash deposit
Bardepotpflicht *f* compulsory cash deposit
Bardevisen *fpl* foreign currency (in cash), spot exchange
Bardiskont *m* cash discount
Bardividende *f* cash dividend, dividend in cash
Bareingänge *mpl* cash receipts
Bareinkauf *m s.* **Barkauf**
Bareinkommen *n s.* **Bareinnahme(n)**
Bareinlage *f* cash deposit
Bareinnahme(n) *f(pl)* cash receipt(s)
Bareinzahlung *f* paying in cash
Barentnahme *f* withdrawal of cash
Barerlös *m* cash proceeds [takings]
Barertrag *m s.* **Barerlös**
Bargeld *n* cash, ready money, money in hand ✧ **~ einbringen** to put up cash; **knapp an ~ sein** to be short of cash
Bargeldabfluß *m* outflow of cash, cash outflow
Bargeldanforderung *f* demand for cash (money)
Bargeldanleger *m* cash investor
Bargeldausgaben *fpl* expenses [expenditures] in cash

Bargeldbedarf *m* requirements in cash (money)
Bargeldbestand *m s.* **Barbestand**
Bargeldbetrag *m s.* **Barbetrag**
Bargelddisposition *f* planning of the use of ready money
Bargeldeingang *m* cash entry
Bargeldeinkommen *n s.* **Bareinnahme(n)**
Bargeldeinlage *f s.* **Bareinlage**
Bargeldeinnahme(n) *f(pl) s.* **Bareinnahme(n)**
Bargeldemission *f* issue of cash money
Bargeldfluß *m* cash flow, flow of cash money
Bargeldgeschäft *n s.* **Bargeschäft**
Bargeldguthaben *n s.* **Barguthaben**
Bargeldhortung *f* hoarding of cash money
Bargeldinkasso *n s.* **Barinkasso**
Bargeldkontrolle *f* cash money audit
Bargeldlimit *n* limit of cash in hand
bargeldlos without ready money [cash], cashless
Bargeldplan *m* cash money plan
Bargeldplanung *f* planning of cash money, cash money planning
Bargeldplanungspflicht *f* obligation to plan cash money
bargeldplanungspflichtig obliged to plan cash money
Bargeldprämie *f* cash bonus
Bargeldquote *f* cash proportion [ratio]
Bargeldreserve *f* cash (money) reserve(s), reserve(s) in cash
Bargeldstrom *m s.* **Bargeldfluß**
Bargeldüberweisung *f* remittance; transfer of cash (money)
Bargeldumlauf *m* cash (money) circulation, circulation of cash (money)
Bargeldumlaufplan *m* plan of cash (money) circulation
Bargeldumlaufplanung *f* planning of cash (money) circulation
Bargeldumsatz *m* cash (money) turnover
Bargeldumsatzplan *m* plan of cash transactions
Bargeldumsatzplanung *f* planning of cash transactions
Bargeldumsatzregulierung *f* regulation of cash (money) turnover
Bargeldverkehr *m* cash transactions
Bargeldvermögen *n* fortune (in cash)
Bargeldvolumen *n* total amount of cash in circulation
Bargeldzufluß *m* inflow of cash, cash inflow
Bargeschäft *n* cash transaction
Bargeschenk *n* cash gift
Barguthaben *n* cash balance
Barhinterlegung *f s.* **Bardepot**
Barinkasso *n* encashment, collection of cash (money) ✧ **zum ~** for encashment
Barkapital *n* cash capital
Barkauf *m* cash purchase

Barkaution f security in cash; (jur) bail in cash
Barkredit m cash credit [loan]
Barleistung f s. **Barzahlung**
Barleistungen fpl payments in cash
Barlohn m money wage
Barmittel pl cash ◇ **mangels Barmitteln** for lack of ready money [cash]
Barposition f cash item
Barpreis m cash price
Barpreisbedingungen fpl cash terms
Barrabatt m cash discount
Barrabattsatz m rate of cash discount
Barregulierung f cash adjustment
Barren m bar, ingot (gold, tin etc.); bullion (gold, silver)
Barrengold n bar gold, gold in ingots, gold bullion
Barreserve f cash in hand, minimum cash reserve(s) (banks)
Barsaldo m s. **Barguthaben**
Barschaft f cash, ready money
Barscheck m open [uncrossed, cash] cheque, (Am) open [uncrossed] check
Barsendung f cash remittance, remittance in cash
Barüberweisung f s. **Barsendung**
Barvergütung f cash refund, (ins) cash bonus
Barverkauf m cash sale, sale for cash
Barverkehr m business on cash terms; cash trade
Barverlust m clear loss
Barvermögen n cash assets
Barvorrat m cash in hand
Barvorschuß m cash advance
Barwert m cash [current] value
Barzahlung f cash payment, (Am) spot cash ◇ **nur gegen ~** for cash only
~, **sofortige** immediate down payment
Barzahlungsbasis f cash basis
Barzahlungsnachlaß m discount on cash payment, discount for cash
Barzahlungspreis m s. **Barpreis**
Barzahlungsrabatt m s. **Barrabatt**
Barzahlungssystem n (system of) cash payments, (Am) cash-and-carry system
Barzeichnung f subscription in cash
Basis f 1. basis, foundation; base; 2. (maths) base (triangle etc.); root, radix (logarithm); 3. (d.pr.) base (transistor); (number) base, radix (of a number representation); base line; substrate ◇ **auf gesunder ~** on a sound basis; **auf gleicher ~** on equal terms
~, **experimentelle** experimental basis
~, **gesetzliche** statutory basis
~, **jährliche** yearly basis
~, **materiell-technische** material and technological basis (the material and technological conditions as well as natural resources necessary and available for the existence and development of a society)
~, **metallurgische** metallurgical basis
~, **monatliche** monthly basis
~, **ökonomische** economic basis
~, **soziale** social basis
~, **sozialökonomische** socio-economic basis
~, **tägliche** daily basis
~, **technische** technological basis; technical basis
~, **wöchentliche** weekly basis
~ **zur Aufgliederung der indirekten Kosten** overhead base
Basisdaten pl:
~, **mitlaufende** (d.pr.) on-line base data
Basiseinheit f base unit
Basisfrachtrate f basic [normal] freight rate
Basisgewicht n base weight
Basisgruppe f (stats) base group
Basiskosten pl base costs (calculated for the planned production on the basis of the cost level of a fixed base period)
Basisladung f main loading [lading]
Basislohn m basic wage(s)
Basispreis m base [standard] price
Basisselbstkosten pl cost in base year
Basiswert m base [basis] value
Basiszeitraum m base period
Bau m building, construction, erection; structure; manufacture ◇ **auf dem ~ arbeiten** to be in the building trade; **einen ~ stillegen** to stop construction; **im ~ begriffen** under construction, in the course of construction
~, **gesellschaftlicher** s. ~, **öffentlicher**
~, **öffentlicher** public building
~ **von Eigenheimen** construction of private-owned [owner-occupied] houses
~, **wilder** illegal construction, construction without (local) government permission
Bauabgabe f 1. building tax; 2. delivery of building [construction]
Bauabgabepreis m building [construction] delivery price
Bauablaufplan m construction schedule
Bauabnahme f taking over of a new building (by the investor or owner)
Bauabschnitt m 1. stage [phase] in the construction (building, road etc.); 2. part of structure (of building under construction)
Bauakkord m construction work on contract
Bauaktien fpl building issues [shares, (Am) stocks]
Bauamt n (local) building authority
Bauanschlag m builder's estimate
Bauanteil m investment share expended on construction

Bauarbeiten *fpl* building operations, construction work
Bauarbeiter *m* building [construction] worker
Bauart *f* design, type; model; version
Bauaufseher *m* building supervisor
Bauaufsicht *f*:
~, **staatliche** department of building supervision *(of a central or local authority)*
Bauauftraggeber *m* person [institution, investor, agent] who places an order for construction *(of s.th.)*
Bauauftragnehmer *m* building contractor
Bauaufwand *m* building cost; expenditure on construction
Bauausführender *m* construction enterprise, builder
Bauausschreibung *f* invitation to tender for building construction
Baubedarf *m* building supplies *(materials etc.)*
Baubedarfsträger *m* investing enterprise [institution, person]
Baubehörde *f* building authority
Baubeschränkungen *fpl* building restrictions
Baubeschreibung *f* construction specification
Baubestimmungen *fpl* building regulations
Baubetrieb *m* building enterprise [firm]
Baubewilligung *f s.* **Baugenehmigung**
Baubilanz *f* construction balance sheet *(of required and currently operating capacity)*
~ **für Baureparaturen** *s.* **Baureparaturbilanz**
~, **zusammengefaßte** summary construction balance sheet *(s.* **Baubilanz***)*
Bauchladenverkäufer *m* vendor
Baudarleh(e)n *n* building loan
Baueinheit *f* (standard) component, (basic) unit, building block; constructional unit
Bauelement *n* component device; (structural) element
bauen to build, to construct *(houses, roads, ships etc.)*, to manufacture, to assemble *(TV sets etc.)*
Bauer *m* farmer, peasant
~, **landarmer** peasant (with a small plot of land), small farmer [peasant]
~, **landloser** landless peasant
Bauerlaubnis *f s.* **Baugenehmigung**
bäuerlich rural
Bauernbank *f* agricultural [rural, farmers] bank
Bauernbefreiung *f* rural emancipation; *(hist)* abolition of serfdom, liberation of peasants
Bauernbevölkerung *f* farming population
Bauerneigentum *n* farmer's property
Bauernfrage *f* agrarian issue
Bauerngemeinde *f* farming community; rural community
Bauerngut *n* farmer's [peasant's] holdings
Bauernhaus *n* farm-house
Bauernhof *m* farm(stead)

Bauernklasse *f* class of farmers; class of peasants, peasantry
Bauernkrieg *m* peasants' war
~, **Großer Deutscher** *(hist)* Peasants' War *(in 1525 in Germany)*
Bauernland *n* farm-land
Bauernlegen *n* dispossession [expropriation] of peasants *(in feudalism)*
Bauernmarkt *m* farmers' [peasants'] market
Bauernmarktpreis *m* farmers' market price
Bauernschaft *f* peasantry, farmers
Bauernschutzgesetz *n* law protecting peasants
Bauernschutzgesetzgebung *f* legislation protecting peasants
Bauernstand *m s.* **Bauernschaft**
Bauerntum *n s.* **Bauernschaft**
Bauernverband *m* farmers' union
Bauernverein *m* farmers' association
Bauernwirtschaft *f* peasant farming
Baufach *n* building trade
baufällig beyond repair, dilapidated, ramshackle, tumble-down, derelict
Baufälligkeit *f* state of being beyond repair, dilapidated [ruinous] state (of building), dilapidation
Baufehler *m* structural fault *(building, machine etc.)*
Baufertigungsprinzipien *npl* methods of construction
Baufinanzierung *f* financing of construction
Baufirma *f* building [construction] firm, building contractor
Baufonds *m* physical and financial resources for building [construction]
Bauforschung *f* construction [building] research
Baufreiheit *f* construction-site clearance *(for unhindered access to construction site by construction workers)*
Bauführer *m* overseer of building works, (building) site overseer
Baugelände *n* building site [land]
Baugeld *n* building capital
Baugelder *npl* financial resources for building [construction]
~, **bereitgestellte** money allocated for building [construction]
Baugeldervertrag *m* agreement on financing building [construction]
Baugeldkredit *m* construction [building] loan
Baugenehmigung *f* building permit [licence]
Baugenossenschaft *f* co-operative building society
Baugeschäft *n* building contractor
Baugesellschaft *f* building society; housing association
Baugesetz *n* building law [act]
Baugewerbe *n* building trade(s)

Baugewerkschaft *f* building [construction] trade union(s), construction union(s)
Baugrund *m s.* **Baugelände**
Baugrundstück *n* building plot, plot (of land for building)
Baugruppe *f* assembly group; module
Baugruppenabrechnung *f* accounting of assembly groups
Baugruppeneingabe *f* input of assembly groups
Baugruppenersatzverfahren *n* method of assembly [module] replacement
Baugruppenfristenplan *m* time schedule of assembly groups
Baugruppenkooperation *f* co-operation in the production of assembly groups [construction units]; co-operation in module production
Baugruppenmontage *f* assembling of construction units; assembling of modules
Baugruppennorm *f* material input norm per assembly group
Baugruppenpreis *m* assembly-group price, price of an assembly group; module price, price of module
Baugruppenspezialisierung *f* specialization in the production of assembly groups [construction units]
Bauhandwerk *n* building trade
Bauhandwerker *m* building craftsman, skilled worker in the building trade, building [construction] worker
Bauhandwerksbetrieb *m* building trade enterprise
~, privater private building trade enterprise
Bauhandwerksgenossenschaft *f* co-operative building trade society
Bauhauptgewerbe *n* main building trade(s)
Bauhauptleistungen *fpl* erection of outer structure of building
Bauhauptvertrag *m* main building contract
Bauherr *m* builder-owner
Bauhof *m* contractor's yard
Bauhypothek *f* building mortgage
Bauindex *m* indicator of building and construction, building and construction indicator
Bauindustrie *f* building industry
Bauingenieur *m* civil engineer
Bauinvestitionen *fpl* investments in building and construction
Baujahr *n* year in which s.th. was built; date of a building; year of construction *(ship etc.)*, year of manufacture *(machine, car etc.)*
**~ 19.. ** 19.. model *(car etc.)*
Baukalkulation *f* calculation of building costs
Baukapazität *f* building capacity
Baukapital *n* building capital
Baukastenmethode *f* modular [unit] method of construction, unit construction method

Baukastenprinzip *n* modular-design [unit assembly] principle
Baukastensystem *n* modular [unit] construction system
Baukommission *f* building commission *(advisory body of local councils)*
Baukomplex *m* building complex
Baukonjunktur *f* boom in building trade
Baukonsens *m s.* **Baugenehmigung**
Baukontingent *n* building quota
Baukonto *n* construction account
Baukontrakt *m s.* **Bauleistungsvertrag**
Baukonzession *f s.* **Baugenehmigung**
Baukosten *pl* construction [building] costs
Baukostenanschlag *m* (detailed) building cost estimate, builder's (detailed) estimate
Baukostenanteil *m* share of construction costs *(in total investment costs)*
Baukostenindex *m* index of building costs, building cost index
Baukostenplanung *f* planning [budgeting] of building costs
Baukostenüberschlag *m* (general) building cost estimate, builder's (general) estimate
Baukostenzuschuß *m* subsidy for building costs
Baukredit *m* building loan
Baukreditvertrag *m* building loan contract
Baukunst *f* architecture
baukünstlerisch architectural
Bauland *n* building land [ground]
Baulandbeschaffung *f* acquisition of building land
Baulandsteuer *f* building land tax, tax on building land
Bauleistungen *fpl* building work [performance(s)]
Bauleistungspreis *m* building [construction] price
Bauleistungsvertrag *m* building contract
Bauleiter *m* (building) site engineer [supervisor]
Bauleitung *f* construction site management [supervision]
Baulimit *n s.* **Bauanteil**
Baumaschinenindustrie *f* construction machinery industry
Baumaterial *n s.* **Baustoff**
Baumaterialhandel *m s.* **Baustoffhandel**
Baumaterialindustrie *f s.* **Baustoffindustrie**
Baumbestand *m* stock of trees
Baumechanisierung *f* mechanization of construction [building]
Baumeister *m* master builder; architect
Baumuster *n* model, type
Baumwollbörse *f* cotton exchange
Baumwollgewebe *n* cotton fabric [cloth]
Baumwollkämmerei *f* cotton combing
Baumwollspinnerei *f* cotton-mill

Baumwollwaren *fpl* cotton textiles
Baunebengewerbe *n* allied building trades
Baunormen *fpl* building [construction] standards
Bauobligationen *fpl* construction bonds
Bauordnung *f* building regulations
Bauparzelle *f s.* **Baugrundstück**
Bauplanung *f* planning of construction
Bauplatz *m s.* **Baustelle**
Baupolizei *f* building control department
Baupreis *m* construction cost(s)
Bauprogramm *n* building programme; housing programme; construction schedule
Baurecht *n* 1. building law; 2. right to build
baureif ready for erection *(after groundwork)*; ready for construction *(after completion of construction plan)*
Baureparaturen *fpl* building repairs
Baurisikoversicherung *f* builder's risk insurance
Bauschema *n (manuf)* construction schedule
Bauschhandel *m* trade in bulk goods
Bauschkauf *m* bulk purchase
Bauschutt *m* rubble, debris (on building site)
Bauschverkauf *m* bulk sale
Bausparen *n* saving in a building and loan society
Bausparer *m* investor in a building and loan society
Bausparkasse *f* building and loan society
Bausperre *f* ban on (further) building and construction
Bausperrgebiet *n* restricted area (for construction)
Baustadium *n* stage of construction
Baustelle *f* building [construction] site
Baustellen(vor)fertigung *f* on-site precasting
Baustoff *m* building material
Baustoffhandel *m* building material trade
Baustoffhandlung *f* building material shop
Baustoffindustrie *f* building material(s) industry
Baustoffpreis *m* price of building material
Bausubstanz *f* buildings *(general term for all buildings of an area or of an industry etc.)*
Bautätigkeit *f* building activity
Bautechnik *f* construction technique; constructional engineering
Bautechniker *m* constructional engineer
Bautechnologie *f* building [construction] technology
Bauten *pl* buildings
~, öffentliche public buildings
Bautischler *m* joiner
Bauträger *m* builder
Bauunternehmen *n* building contractor, builders
Bauunternehmer *m* building contractor
Bauverbot *n* ban on building

Bauvertrag *m s.* **Bauleistungsvertrag**
Bauvolumen *n* (total) amount of construction work *(of a period under review)*
Bauvorhaben *n* building project
Bauvorschriften *fpl* building regulations
Bauweise *f* method of construction
~, industrielle industrial type [method] of construction
Bauwerk *n* structure, building, edifice
Bauwert *m* value of building, building value
Bauwesen *n* building industry *(covers architectural work, building materials industry, construction enterprises, building ministry and other building institutions)*
~, kommunales local building industry
~, ländliches rural construction
Bauwirtschaft *f* construction enterprises; construction trade
Bauzeit *f* construction time [period]
Bauzyklogramm *n* cyclic building schedule [diagram]
Beamtenapparat *m* civil service machinery
Beamtenlaufbahn *f* civil service career
Beamtenschaft *f* civil servants
Beamter *m* official, officer, *(Am)* executive
beanspruchen to claim, to demand, to call for *(attention etc.)*, to take, to require *(time etc.)*, to make use of *(aid, service etc.)*
Beanspruchung *f* claim, demand *(attention etc.)*, taking up, requiring *(time etc.)*, making use of *(aid, service etc.)*
beanstanden to object to, to raise objections to *(s.th.)*, to take exception to, to complain of *(s.th.)*; to demur to [at] *(claim etc.)*; to question, to contest, to oppose *(a point, right etc.)*; to reject *(services etc.)*
Beanstandung *f* objection, raising objection, taking exception to, complaint of; demurring *(claim etc.)*; questioning, contesting, opposing *(a point, right etc.)*; rejection *(services etc.)* ✧ **keinen Anlaß zur ~ geben** to offer no reason for objections; **ohne ~ annehmen** to accept without dissent
~, berechtigte legitimate [justified] complaint
beantragen to apply for, to make an application for *(s.th.)*, to put in a claim for *(s.th.)*; to bring forward, to move *(a motion for s.th. etc.)*
Beantragung *f* application, claim; bringing forward *(a motion for s.th.)*, moving *(an amendment)*
~ einer einstweiligen Verfügung *(jur)* filing of an application for an injunction
beantworten to answer, to reply to *(letter etc.)*; to respond to *(call etc.)*
Beantwortung *f* answer, reply; response ✧ **in ~ Ihres Briefes** in reply to your letter
~, schriftliche written answer

bearbeiten 1. to work on, to deal with, to treat *(subject, matter)*; 2. *(manuf)* to process *(raw material)*, to work *(wood, iron etc.)*, to dress *(timber, leather etc.)*, to machine *(tool)*; 3. *(agric)* to cultivate *(soil)*; 4. *(com)* to canvass *(customers etc.)*
Bearbeitung *f* 1. working on, dealing with, treatment *(subject, matter etc.)*; 2. *(manuf)* processing *(raw material)*, working *(wood, iron, clay etc.)*, dressing *(timber, leather etc.)*, machining *(tool)*; 3. *(agric)* cultivation *(soil)*; 4. *(com)* canvassing *(customers etc.)*
~, **manuelle** manual operation
~, **maschinelle** machining operation
Bearbeitungsdauer *f* 1. *(manuf)* processing time; 2. time for dealing with [handling] *(case, application etc.)*
Bearbeitungskosten *pl* 1. tooling costs; 2. administrative charges [fees]
Bearbeitungsplan *m* operation plan
Bearbeitungsverfahren *n* 1. method of dealing with *(matter etc.)*; 2. *(manuf)* tooling method
beauflagen to order *(s.o to do s.th.)*; to charge *(s.o.)* with *(s.th.)*
Beauflagung *f* order *(to s.o. to do s.th.)*, charging *(s.o. with s.th.)*
beauftragen to charge, to entrust *(s.o. with s.th.)*; to direct, to instruct, to order *(s.o. to do s.th.)*; to put *(s.o.)* in charge of *(s.th.)*; to appoint *(s.o.)*; to authorize, to empower, to commission; *(jur)* to retain
Beauftragter *m* representative, agent, authorized person
~ **für (den) Datenschutz** person authorized to protect confidential data
Beauftragung *f* charging, entrusting *(s.o. with s.th.)*; directing, instructing, ordering *(s.o. to do s.th.)*; putting *(s.o.)* in charge of *(s.th.)*; appointing, authorizing, empowering, commissioning; *(jur)* retention
bebaubar cultivable, tillable
bebauen 1. *(agric)* to cultivate, to till, to farm; 2. *(ind)* to build upon
Bebauung *f* 1. *(agric)* cultivation, tilling, farming; 2. *(ind)* building upon
Bebauungsplan *m* housing plan; master plan; layout *(town)*
Bedarf *m* demand; need, want, requirement *(money, food etc.)*; ⋄ ~ **haben an** to need, to want, to require; **bei** ~ if [when, as may be] required, if need(s) be, on request; **den** ~ **befriedigen** to meet the demand; to cover the need of, to meet one's requirements; **den** ~ **decken** to meet [supply] the demand; to satisfy the needs; **den** ~ **übersteigen** to outstrip [exceed] demand; **einen** ~ **schaffen** to create a demand; to create a need; **einen** ~

wecken *s.* **einen** ~ **schaffen**; **für den sofortigen** ~ for immediate needs [requirements]; **nach** ~ *s.* **bei** ~; **nur für den eigenen** ~ **erzeugen** to produce only for one's own requirements
~, **akuter** burning needs
~, **angenommener** *s.* **Bedarfsvorwegnahme**
~, **aperiodischer** non-periodic demand
~, **atypischer** untypical demand
~, **aufgestauter** pent-up [backlog of] demand, deferred demand
~, **befriedigter** demand covered; needs covered
~, **einmaliger** onetime demand
~, **elastischer** elastic demand
~, **ermittelter** derived demand
~, **erwarteter** expected [anticipated] demand
~, **gehobener** demand for higher quality goods
~, **geplanter** planned demand
~, **geringer** not much demand
~, **gesellschaftlich notwendiger** socially necessary needs
~, **gesellschaftlicher** social needs
~, **gesteigerter** increased demand
~, **inländischer** domestic [inland] demand
~, **konsumtiver** demand for consumer goods and service
~, **ländlicher** rural demand
~, **landwirtschaftlicher** needs [requirements] of agriculture, agricultural needs [requirements]
~, **laufender** current demand
~, **lebenswichtiger** vital needs
~, **möglicher** potential demand
~, **notwendiger** necessary requirements
~, **öffentlicher** public demand; public needs [requirements]
~, **örtlicher** local demand
~, **periodenfremder** demand untypical of the season
~, **periodischer** periodic demand [needs]
~, **persönlicher** personal wants
~, **perspektivischer** demand in the long run, prospective demand
~, **potentieller** *s.* ~, **möglicher**
~, **privater** private demand; personal need(s) [requirement(s)]
~, **produktiver** productive demand, demand for investment goods, materials etc. *(for production)*
~, **saisonbedingter** seasonal demand
~, **spezifischer** selective demand
~, **ständiger** permanent demand
~, **täglicher** daily needs, everyday requirements
~, **unbefriedigter** *s.* ~, **ungedeckter**
~, **unelastischer** inelastic demand
~, **unerwarteter** unexpected demand
~, **ungedeckter** unsaturated demand
~, **volkswirtschaftlicher** national economic needs

Bedarf

~, **voraussichtlicher** probable demand
~, **vordringlicher** urgent needs; priority needs
~, **vorgegebener** given demand
~, **wirklicher** real demand
~, **wirksamer** effective demand
~, **zurückgestellter** deferred demand
~, **zusammengefaßter** aggregate demand
~, **zusätzlicher** additional demand
Bedarfsabnahme *f* reduced [decreasing] demand
Bedarfsanalyse *f* analysis of demand
Bedarfsartikel *m* article of consumption; requisite
Bedarfsäußerung *f* expression of demand
Bedarfsbeeinflussung *f* controlling demand; controlling consumption
Bedarfsbefriedigung *f s.* **Bedarfsdeckung**
Bedarfsbegründung *f* substantiation of requirements
Bedarfsberechnung *f* calculation of requirements
Bedarfsdeckung *f* satisfaction of demand [needs], meeting demand [needs]
Bedarfseinschätzung *f* estimate of demand
Bedarfselastizität *f* demand elasticity
Bedarfsentwicklung *f* growth [increase] of demand
Bedarfsermittlung *f* calculation of requirements [demand], derivation of demand
Bedarfsfaktor *m* demand factor
Bedarfsfall *m*:
 ◊ im ~ if [when, as may be] required, if need(s) be, on request
Bedarfsflugverkehr *m* charter (air) service
Bedarfsforschung *f* market research, demand analysis
~, **handelsseitige** research on demand carried out by trading enterprises
~, **komplexe** complex research on demand
~, **lieferseitige** research on demand carried out by producing enterprises
Bedarfsforschungsverfahren *n* methods of research on demand
Bedarfsfunktion *f* function of demand, demand function
Bedarfsgegenstand *m s.* **Bedarfsartikel**
bedarfsgerecht according to (consumer) demand [needs] ◊ ~ **strukturiert** having an output [production] structure according to demand [needs]
Bedarfsgüter *npl* consumer goods
Bedarfsgüterfonds *m* (stock of) essential consumer goods
Bedarfsgüterindustrie *f* consumer goods industry
Bedarfskategorie *f* category of demand
Bedarfskoeffizient *m* coefficient of demand
Bedarfskomplex *m* complex of requirements [needs]

Bedarfslage *f* state of demand
Bedarfslenkung *f* consumer guidance; control of consumption
Bedarfsliste *f* list of requirements [needs]
Bedarfsmanipulation *f* manipulation of demand
bedarfsmindernd reducing the demand
Bedarfsprognose *f* forecast of demand
Bedarfsreserve *f* backlog of orders
Bedarfssättigung *f* saturation (of the market); satisfaction of needs [requirements]
Bedarfsspanne *f* margin of demand
Bedarfsstruktur *f* structure [composition] of demand [requirements]
Bedarfsträger *m* user, consumer
~, **gesellschaftlicher** public [non-private] consumer
Bedarfsumfang *m* extent of requirements [needs]
Bedarfs- und Marktforschung *f* research on demand and market, (demand and) market research
Bedarfs- und Marktforschungskartei *f* card--index of (demand and) market research
Bedarfsveränderungen *fpl* changes in demand
Bedarfsverschiebung *f* shift in consumption
Bedarfsvorwegnahme *f* anticipated demand
Bedarfsweckung *f* stimulation of new demand, creation of demand
Bedarfszunahme *f* increase in demand
Bedenkfrist *f s.* **Bedenkzeit**
Bedenkzeit *f* time to think s.th. over, time to consider; respite
bedienen to serve, to attend (to) *(customers etc.)*; to operate *(machine)*
Bedienkosten *pl* operating costs
Bedienung *f* service, attention *(customers etc.)*; operation *(machine)*
Bedienungsanleitung *f* operating instructions, directions for use
Bedienungsaufschlag *m (cat)* service charges
Bedienungsbereich *m s.* **Bedienungszone**
Bedienungselement *n* control [operative] element
Bedienungsgeld *n* service charge
Bedienungskosten *pl* service costs
Bedienungskraft *f* servant; waiter *m*, waitress *f*; operator
Bedienungskräfte *fpl s.* **Bedienungspersonal**
Bedienungsnorm *f* standard of service
Bedienungspersonal *n* service personnel; operating personnel *(machine, plant etc.)*
Bedienungssystem *n* serving system; *(cat)* system of serving (customers); *(manuf)* control system *(machines, automized processes etc.)*
Bedienungsverkauf *m* over-the-counter sale *(as opposed to self-service)*
Bedienungsvorschrift *f s.* **Bedienungsanleitung**

Bedürfnisse 75

Bedienungszone *f* service area *(part of the sales area in self-service shops where customers are served by personnel)*
Bedingung *f* condition; prerequisite; requirement; condition; reservation; qualification; stipulation; proviso ⋄ **unter der ~, daß** on condition that; **unter der ~ einer Gegenleistung** on reciprocal terms; **unter dieser ~** with this reservation, subject to one qualification; **unter einer ~** subject to one condition
~, **vorläufige** preliminary condition
Bedingungen *fpl* conditions; prerequisites; requirements; *(com)* terms; stipulations ⋄ **jmds. ~ vorbehaltlos annehmen** to accept s.o.'s conditions without reservation; **~ einhalten** to adhere to the terms; **~ festlegen** to stipulate [lay down] terms [conditions]; **~ nicht einhalten** to fail to comply with the terms; **bestimmte ~ annehmen** to agree upon certain conditions; **bestimmte ~ erfüllen** to comply with [fulfil] certain conditions; **entsprechend den ~ der Klausel** under the terms of the clause; **jmdm. ~ auferlegen** to impose [lay down] conditions on s.o.; **jmdm. vorteilhafte ~ gewähren** to grant favourable terms to s.o.; **seine ~ nennen** to state one's terms [conditions]; **seine ~ stellen** *s.* **seine ~ nennen; sich den ~ unterwerfen** to submit to the terms [conditions]; **unter Druck auf die ~ eingehen** to yield to the conditions [accept the terms] under pressure; **unter günstigen ~** under favourable conditions; **unter normalen ~** under normal conditions; **unter ungünstigen ~** under unfavourable conditions; **vorteilhafte ~ erhalten** to obtain favourable terms [conditions]; **zu gegenseitig vorteilhaftesten ~** on mutually most favourable terms [conditions]; **zu gleichen ~** on equal terms; **zu günstigen ~** on easy terms; **zu leichten ~** *s.* **zu günstigen ~**; **zu ungünstigen ~** on unfavourable terms
~, **ähnliche** similar terms
~, **allgemeine** general terms *(sale etc.)*
~, **angenommene** terms agreed upon
~, **annehmbare** acceptable [accommodating] conditions [terms]
~, **aufschiebende** *(jur)* suspensory conditions
~, **äußerste** best terms; worst terms
~, **besondere** special [exceptional] conditions
~, **eindeutige** clear [unambiguous] terms
~, **einschränkende** restrictive conditions
~, **festgesetzte** fixed terms [conditions]
~, **gegenständliche** *s.* ~, **materielle**
~, **gesellschaftliche** social conditions
~, **gleichartige** same kind of conditions [terms]
~, **günstige** favourable terms [conditions]
~, **hinreichende** adequate conditions

~, **in einem Vertrag festgelegte** conditions [terms] set forth [stipulated] in a contract
~, **knechtende** enslaving conditions
~, **kommerzielle** commercial terms
~, **kulante** liberal terms
~, **materielle** material [physical] conditions
~, **menschliche** conditions fit for human beings
~, **natürliche** natural conditions
~, **notwendige** essential [necessary] conditions
~, **objektive** objective conditions
~, **ökonomische** economic conditions
~, **präzise** unambiguous [well-defined] terms [conditions]
~, **sachliche** material conditions; realistic terms [conditions]
~, **scharfe** hard conditions
~, **schwere** onerous conditions [terms]
~, **subjektive** subjective conditions
~, **technische** technical conditions
~, **übliche** usual terms
~, **unerläßliche** indispensable conditions
~, **ungünstige** unfavourable terms [conditions]
~, **unveränderte** same [unchanged] terms
~, **unvorteilhafte** *s.* ~, **ungünstige**
~, **veränderte** changed terms
~, **vertragsgemäße** terms [conditions] of contract
~, **zufriedenstellende** satisfactory terms
bedingungslos unconditional, without reservation [qualification]
bedürfen to need, to want, to require, to be in need of
Bedürfnis *n* need, want, requirement, necessity ⋄ **einem ~ abhelfen** to supply a want
Bedürfnisarten *fpl* kinds of needs [wants, requirements]
Bedürfnisbefriedigung *f* satisfaction of needs, meeting of requirements
Bedürfnisgattung *f s.* **Bedürfnisarten**
Bedürfniskategorie *f* category of needs [wants, requirements]
Bedürfniskomplex *m* complex of needs
Bedürfnisprognose *f* forecast of needs [requirements]
Bedürfnisprüfung *f* examining of needs [wants]; checking of requirements
Bedürfnisschätzung *f* estimate of needs [wants, requirements]
Bedürfnisse *npl*:
⋄ **befriedigen** to satisfy *(s.o.'s)* needs, to meet *(s.o.'s)* requirements
~ **des Lebens, die dringendsten** the bare necessities
~, **geistige** intellectual [mental] needs
~, **geistig-kulturelle** intellectual and cultural needs
~, **gesamtgesellschaftliche** general social needs

Bedürfnisse

~, **gesellschaftliche** social needs
~, **individuelle** individual needs
~, **materielle** material needs
~, **öffentliche** public needs
~, **private** personal [private] needs
~, **soziale** social needs [requirements]
~, **staatliche** needs of the state, state requirements
~, **unmittelbar gesellschaftliche** directly social [*(Am)* communal] needs
Bedürfnisstrategie *f* strategy of creating and satisfying needs
~, **profitorientierte** profit-oriented strategy of creating demand
Bedürfnisstruktur *f* structure of needs [wants, requirements]
bedürftig needy, poor, indigent
Bedürftigkeit *f* need(iness), indigence, destitution
beeid(ig)en to declare *(s.th.)* on oath, to take one's oath, to affirm by oath
Beeid(ig)ung *f* declaring *(s.th.)* on oath, taking one's oath, affirmation by oath
Beeinflussung *f* influence, influencing
~ **durch die Verbraucher** consumer power
beeinträchtigen to be detrimental to, to be prejudicial to, to detract from, to prejudice *(s.o.'s rights etc.)*, to derogate from *(quality, right etc.)*, to damage, to be injurious to, to be hurtful to *(s.o's rights etc.)*, to impair *(authority etc.)*
Beeinträchtigung *f* detriment, prejudice, detraction, derogation, damage, injury, impairment
beend(ig)en to end, to complete, to conclude, to terminate *(work etc.)*
Beend(ig)ung *f* end, completion, conclusion, termination *(work etc.)*
befähigen to enable *(s.o. to do s.th.)*, to qualify *(s.o. for doing s.th.)*
befähigt fit (for), capable (of), qualified (for)
Befähigung *f* fitness, capability; qualification; aptitude; skill; competence ◊ **seine ~ nachweisen** to qualify; to prove one's qualification
~, **erforderliche** necessary qualification
~, **juristische** legal qualification
~, **rechtliche** (legal) competence
Befähigungsnachweis *m* certificate of qualification [competence]
befahrbar passable, practicable *(for verhicles)*, navigable *(river)*
Befehl *m (d.pr.)* command, instruction, order, simple statement
Befehle *mpl:*
◊ ~ **einstellen** *(d.pr.)* to set up instructions
befehlen *(d.pr.)* to command, to instruct, to order; to make a simple statement
Befehlsadresse *f (d.pr.)* instruction address, location of order

Befehlsänderung *f (d.pr.)* instruction modification
Befehlsblock *m (d.pr.)* block of instructions
Befehlskode *m (d.pr.)* instruction code
Befehls-Dekodierschaltung *f (d.pr.)* instruction decoder
Befehlseinheit *f (d.pr.)* instruction processing unit
Befehlsfolge *f (d.pr.)* control [instruction] sequence
Befehlsfolgeregister *n (d.pr.)* instruction [program] register
Befehlskontrollsignal *n (d.pr.)* instruction check indicator
Befehlsliste *f (d.pr.)* instruction code
Befehlsstreifen *m (d.pr.)* instruction tape
Befehlsverteilkanal *m (d.pr.)* instruction distribution channel
Befehlsvorrat *m (d.pr.)* instruction [repertoire] set
Befehlswort *n (d.pr.)* order word
Befehlszähler *m (d.pr.)* instruction (location) counter
Befischungsrechte *npl* right of fishing
~, **vorrangige** privilege of fishing
Beförderer *m* carrier, conveyer; shipper
befördern 1. to transport, to carry, to convey *(goods by rail etc.)*; to dispatch, to forward *(parcels etc., by post)*, to mail *(letters etc.)*; to ship *(goods by sea)*; 2. to promote, to further *(cause, person in employment etc.)*
Beförderung *f* 1. transport(ation), carriage, carrying, conveyance *(goods by rail etc.)*; dispatch, forwarding *(parcels etc., by post)*, mailing *(letters etc.)*; shipping, shipment *(goods by sea)*; 2. promotion, furtherance *(cause, person in employment etc.)* *(s.a.* **Transport***)*
~ **auf dem Seewege** sea transport
~, **durchgehende** through transport(ation)
~, **gegenläufige** two-way transport(ation)
~ **in der Linienschiffahrt** liner transport(ation)
~ **mit Fuhrwerken** transport by carriage
~, **multimodale** multi-modal transport(ation)
~ **per Bahn** transport(ation) by rail
~ **per Bus** transport(ation) by bus
~ **per Schiene** *s.* ~ **per Bahn**
~ **über kurze Entfernung** short-distance transport
Beförderungsart *f* mode of conveyance [transportation, shipment]
Beförderungsausgaben *fpl s.* **Beförderungskosten**
Beförderungsauslagen *fpl* transport outlay
Beförderungsbedarf *m* transport requirements, required transport capacity
Beförderungsbedingungen *fpl* terms of transport(ation)

Begebungsvertrag 77

~, **Allgemeine** General Terms [Conditions] of Transport
Beförderungsbestimmungen *fpl* transport regulations
Beförderungsdienst *m* transport service
Beförderungsdurchschnittsleistung *f* average transport performance
Beförderungseinheit *f* transport unit
beförderungsfähig transportable, ready [fit] for transport
Beförderungsfähigkeit *f* capacity to transport
Beförderungsgebühr *f* 1. *(post)* postage, postal charges; 2. transport charges
Beförderungsgenehmigung *f* transport authorization; transport permit
Beförderungsgeschäft *n* transport business; transport firm
Beförderungskapazität *f* capacity of transport(ation)
Beförderungskosten *pl* transport charges; carriage; railway [*(Am)* railroad] charges
Beförderungsleistung *f* transport performance *(in terms of load or persons and distance)*
Beförderungsmittel *npl* means of transport(ation)
Beförderungspapiere *npl* transport documents
Beförderungspflicht *f* obligation to transport
Beförderungspreis *m* transport(ation) rate [charge]
Beförderungsselbstkosten *pl* prime cost of transport
Beförderungsstruktur *f* transport structure *(usually passengers)*
Beförderungstarif *m* transport rates
Beförderungsumfang *m s.* **Beförderungsvolumen**
Beförderungsvertrag *m* transport contract
Beförderungsvolumen *n* extent of transportation
Beförderungsweg *m* transport route
Beförderungszeit *f* forwarding [transporting] time
befrachten to load *(vehicle)*; to freight, to charter and load *(ship)*
Befrachter *m* consignor; freighter, charterer *(of ships)*, shipper
Befrachtung *f* loading; charterage, affreightment
Befrachtungstarif *m* charter rates
Befrachtungsumfang *m* extent of loading [charterage, affreightment] *(sea transport)*
Befrachtungsvolumen *n s.* **Befrachtungsumfang**
Befrachtungszeit *f* time used for loading [charterage, affreightment]; *(ship)* loading time
Befragter *m* respondent
Befragung *f* 1. poll; survey; 2. examination, hearing *(witness)*

~, **mündliche** *(stats)* interview
~, **nachfassende** *(stats)* follow-up (survey)
~, **nachgehende** *s.* ~, **nachfassende**
~, **repräsentative** *(stats)* representative (public) poll
~, **stichprobenweise** *(stats)* (public) sample poll
Befragungsaktion *f* inquiry [survey] by the method of questionnaires
Befragungsbericht *m* interview report, report of the interview
Befragungsbogen *m* questionnaire, inquiry form
Befragungskarte *f s.* **Befragungsbogen**
Befragungstest *m* opinion poll
befreien 1. to liberate *(nation etc.)*; 2. to exempt *(from payment of taxes etc.)*
Befreiung *f* 1. liberation *(nation etc.)*; 2. exemption *(from payment of taxes etc.)* ◊ ~ **bewilligen** to grant an exemption
Befreiungsbewegung *f* liberation movement
~, **nationale** national liberation movement
befriedigen to satisfy *(person etc.)*; to meet, to cover *(demand etc.)*
Befriedigung *f* satisfaction *(person etc.)*; meeting *(demand etc.)*
befristen to set a date for the beginning/ending of *(contract etc.)*, to limit the duration of *(agreement etc.)*, to set a time-limit [deadline] to
befristet limited as to time; for a fixed period; temporary
Befristung *f* setting a time limit [deadline]
Befugnisse *fpl* authority, authorization, power; warrant; right ◊ **außerhalb seiner ~ handeln** to act beyond one's authority; ~ **festlegen** to prescribe powers *(to s.o.)*; to authorize *(s.o.)*; **seine ~ überschreiten** to act in excess of one's authority, to act ultra vires
Befund *m* result *(technical test etc.)*, findings *(investigation etc.)*
~, **zollamtlicher** customs report
Befundbuch *n* inventory
befürworten to recommend, to support *(application etc.)*; to advocate *(cause etc.)*
Befürwortung *f* recommendation, support *(application etc.)*; advocacy *(cause etc.)*
begebbar negotiable; transferable; *(st.ex.)* marketable
Begebbarkeit *f* negotiability; transferability; *(st.ex.)* marketability
begeben to issue *(bonds etc.)*; to float *(loan etc.)*; to negotiate *(bills etc.)*
Begebung *f* issue *(bonds etc.)*; floating *(loan etc.)*; negotiation *(bill of exchange etc.)*
Begebungskurs *m* rate of issue
Begebungsvermerk *m* endorsement
Begebungsvertrag *m* issuing agreement [contract]

beglaubigen 1. to attest, to certify, to authenticate *(document etc.)*, to legalize *(copy etc.)*; 2. to accredit *(an ambassador to a government)* ◊ **amtlich ~** to legalize
beglaubigt 1. certified, attested; witnessed; attested by seal [notary public]; 2. accredited *(ambassador)* ◊ **nicht ~** 1. uncertified, not attested *(by notary public)*; 2. unaccredited *(ambassador)*
Beglaubigung *f* 1. attestation, certification, authentication *(document etc.)*, legalization *(copy etc.)*; 2. accreditation *(of an ambassador to a government)* ◊ **zur ~ der Echtheit** in pledge of good faith
Beglaubigungsbescheinigung *f* certificate of authentication
Beglaubigungsformel *f* attestation form
Beglaubigungsklausel *f* attestation clause
Beglaubigungsrecht *n* right of certification
Beglaubigungsschreiben *n* credentials
Beglaubigungsvermerk *m* note of certification
Beglaubigungszeuge *m* attesting witness
begleichen to pay, to settle, to discharge, to pay off *(bill, debt etc.)*
Begleichung *f* settlement, payment, discharge *(bill, debt etc.)*
~, vollständige full settlement; overall settlement
~ von Auslandsschulden settlement of foreign debts
Begleitadresse *f* despatch note; accompanying address
Begleitbrief *m s.* **Begleitschreiben**
Begleitpapiere *npl* accompanying documents
Begleitscheinverfahren *n* way-bill method; *(cust)* bond-note method
Begleitschreiben *n* letter of advice, covering [accompanying] letter
Begleitsortiment *n* accompanying range of goods; accompanying samples *(attached to an offer)*
Begleitware *f s.* **Begleitsortiment**
Begleitzettel *m* bill of delivery, waybill; *(cust)* customs clearance certificate
Begräbniskostenversicherung *f* burial [funeral] fund
begrenzen to limit, to restrict, to bound; to define *(concept etc.)*
begrenzt limited, restricted ◊ **nicht ~** unlimited, boundless
Begrenztheit *f* limitation; narrowness
Begrenzung *f* limitation, restriction, boundary; bounds, limit; definition *(concept etc.)*
Begrenzungsfrist *f* limitation period
Begriffsapparat *m* terms used
Begriffsfeld *n (d.pr.)* instruction array
Begriffs- und Qualitätsbestimmungen *fpl* definition of terms and quality standards

~, einheitliche uniform definition of terms and quality standards
begründen 1. to found, to set up, to establish, to start, to float *(business, company etc.)*; to lay the foundation of *(s.o.'s career, reputation etc.)*; 2. to substantiate, to give reasons for *(assertion, statement etc.)*; to create, to establish *(claim, right, charge etc.)* ◊ **eingehend ~** to give full reasons
Begründer *m* founder *(business etc.)*, promoter *(cause etc.)*
begründet well-founded, well-grounded, justified; substantiated *(assertion etc.)*; legitimate *(claim etc.)*, vested *(rights etc.)* ◊ **schlecht ~** ill--founded *(business venture etc.)*
Begründung *f* 1. founding, setting up, establishment *(business etc.)*, floating *(company etc.)*; laying (of) the foundation *(of s.o.'s career, reputation etc.)*; 2. substantiation, giving reasons for *(assertion, statement etc.)*; creation, establishment *(claim, right, charge etc.)* ◊ **mit der ~, daß** on the grounds that; **ohne jede ~** without giving any reasons; **zur ~** in support of
~ einer Auffassung statement of arguments
~ einer Klage *(jur)* statement of reasons
~ einer Verordnung preamble of a decree
~ eines Gesellschaftsverhältnisses establishment of a partnership
~ eines Gesetzes preamble of a law
~ eines Planes substantiation of a plan
~ eines Rechtes creation of a right
~ eines Vertreterverhältnisses creation of an agency
~ für angeforderte Etatmittel justification for budgetary means
~ von Schuldverhältnissen creation of obligations [debts]
begünstigen to favour, to show favour towards *(person)*, to be in favour of *(s.o.'s interests etc.)*; to encourage, to foster *(s.o.'s plan etc.)*, to facilitate, to promote *(progress etc.)*
begünstigt benefiting, beneficiary
Begünstigtenklausel *f* benefit clause
Begünstigter *m* beneficiary, accommodated party, recipient of a favour; accessory after the fact *(crime etc.)*
~ eines Versicherungsvertrages beneficiary of an insurance (policy)
~, wirklicher actual beneficiary
Begünstigung *f* favour, preferential treatment *(to s.o.)*; encouragement, fostering *(of s.o.'s plans etc.)*; facilitation, promotion *(progress etc.)*
Begünstigungsklausel *f s.* **Begünstigtenklausel**
Begünstigungszoll *m (cust)* preferential tariff [customs duties]
begutachten to give an opinion on *(s.th.)*; to have an expert's report made on *(s.th.)*, to

evaluate *(work done)*; *(ins)* to appraise, to evaluate *(damage)*
Begutachter *m* expert; valuer
Begutachtung *f* 1. giving an opinion on *(s.th.)*; having an expert's report made on *(s.th.)*, evaluation *(work done)*; *(ins)* appraisal, evaluation *(damage)*; 2. expert opinion, appraisal, expert's [examiner's] report
~, **sachverständige** expert opinion
begütert rich, wealthy, well-to-do; propertied
Behälter *m* container; holder *(gas, oil etc.)*; receptacle
Behälterfahrzeug *n* container vehicle [truck]
Behälterschiff *n* container ship
Behälterwagen *m* *(railw)* tank waggon [*(Am)* car]
behandeln to treat, to discuss, to deal with *(subject etc.)*; to handle, to manage *(situation etc.)* ⋄ **unterschiedlich ~** to discriminate
Behandlung *f* discussion, treatment, dealing with *(subject etc.)*; handling, management *(situation etc.)*
~, **menschliche** humane treatment
~ **von Arbeitsstreitigkeiten** handling of labour disputes
~, **zollamtliche** handling by the customs
Behandlungskosten *pl* handling charges
beheben to remove *(difficulty etc.)*, to put an end to *(abuse etc.)*, to redress *(wrong etc.)*, to remedy, to repair *(damage etc.)*, to rectify *(fault)*, to relieve *(traffic jam etc.)*
Behebung *f* removal *(difficulty etc.)*, putting an end to *(abuse etc.)*, redress *(wrong etc.)*, remedy, repair *(damage etc.)*, rectification *(fault)*, relief *(traffic jam etc.)*
Behelfslösung *f* makeshift [patch-up] solution
behelfsmäßig makeshift, improvised, temporary
beherbergen to house, to lodge, to accommodate
Beherbergung *f* housing, lodging, accommodation
Beherbergungsgewerbe *n* hotel trade
Beherbergungsstätte *f* inn; hostel; lodging
Beherbergungssteuer *f* lodging tax
beherrschen to rule *(country)*, to have sway over *(people)*, to dominate, to control *(market etc.)* ⋄ **allein ~** to monopolize; **sicher ~** to have a firm hold on
Beherrschung *f* rule *(country)*, sway over *(people)*, domination, control *(market etc.)*
~, **monopolistische** monopoly control
behindern to hinder, to impede, to hamper *(s.o., s.o.'s plans etc.)*; to block, to obstruct *(traffic opponent etc.)*
Behindertenbetreuung *f* looking after the handicapped, supervising [supervision of] the handicapped
Behindertenfürsorge *f* care of the handicapped

Behinderung *f* hindrance, impediment, hampering *(s.o., s.o.'s plans etc.)*; blocking, obstruction *(traffic, opponent etc.)*; physical disability
Behörde *f* (public) authority, board; agency ⋄ **etwas bei einer ~ anmelden** to notify an authority of s.th.
~, **örtliche** local authority
~, **zuständige** competent authority
Behördenapparat *m* governmental machinery
Behördenweg *m* official channels
behördlich governmental, official
Beihilfe *f* relief, aid, assistance, (financial) support; (social) allowance; subsidy; grant
~ **aus Mitteln der Sozialversicherung** relief paid by the social [national] insurance
~ **aus öffentlichen Mitteln** subsidy from public funds
~ **bei Umschulung** relief in the case of retraining
~ **bei zeitweiligem Verlust der Arbeitsfähigkeit** relief for temporary incapacity
~, **einmalige** non-recurring relief
~, **finanzielle** relief, subsidy, allowance, grant, grant-in-aid
~ **für Schwangere und Wöchnerinnen** maternity relief
~ **für Stillende** relief for nursing mothers
~, **gewerkschaftliche** relief paid by the trade union, (trade) union relief
~, **staatliche** government [state] allowance [grant]
Beilage *f* 1. supplement *(to newspaper etc.)*; appendix *(to report etc.)*; enclosure *(with letter)*; relevant papers, document *(forwarded with application etc.)*; 2. food served with main item, garnishing
beilegen 1. to annex, to join *(s.th. to report etc.)*, to enclose *(with letter)*; 2. to give, to attach *(importance to s.th. etc.)*; 3. to settle, to compose *(quarrel)*, to reconcile *(difference of opinion)*
Beilegung *f* settlement *(quarrel)*, reconciliation *(difference of opinion)*
~, **gütliche** amicable settlement [agreement]
beiliegend enclosed, under cover, herewith ⋄ ~ **erhalten Sie** enclosed please find
Beirat *m* advisory board [panel]
~, **juristischer** legal adviser
~, **wissenschaftlich-technischer** scientific-technological advisory board [panel]
Beiratsmitglied *n* member of the board [panel]
Beiratssitzung *f* board meeting
Beispielbetrieb *m* model plant [enterprise]
Beistand *m* help, assistance, aid
Beitrag *m* 1. contribution; 2. subscription *(to a party etc.)*, premium *(insurance)*, fee *(membership)*, dues *(trade union etc.)*; 3. paper *(presented*

Beitrag

at conferences etc.); speech *(delivered at conferences etc.)* ◊ **einen ~ leisten** to contribute; **einen schriftlichen ~ liefern** to present a paper *(conference etc.)*; **seinen ~ leisten** to pay one's contribution [share]
~, **anteilmäßiger** prorata contribution
~, **noch fälliger** contribution still due
~, **wesentlicher** substantial contribution
~, **wissenschaftlicher** paper
~ **zu wohltätigen Zwecken** contribution for charity
~ **zur Altersversorgung** contribution to a pension fund
Beiträge *mpl:*
◊ ~ **erheben** to collect dues; **durch freiwillige ~ unterhalten werden** to be supported by voluntary contributions
~, **freiwillige** voluntary contributions
beitragen 1. to contribute; 2. to subscribe to *(charity etc.)*; 3. to present *(paper at conferences etc.)*; to deliver (speech) *(at conferences etc.)*
beitragend contributory
Beitragsanteil *m* share, quota
Beitragsaufkommen *n* total amount of paid dues *(party members etc.)*, total amount of (membership) fees; *(ins)* total amount of paid premiums *(insured persons)*
Beitragsbefreiung *f* exemption from paying contribution [dues, membership fee]
Beitragsberechnung *f* calculation of contribution; *(ins)* calculation of premium
Beitragserhebung *f* collecting of subscriptions [premiums, fees, dues]
Beitragserhöhung *f* increase in contribution [dues, membership fee]; *(ins)* increase in premium
beitragsfrei non-contributory; without dues [membership fee]
Beitragsfreistellung *f s.* **Beitragsbefreiung**
Beitragsgruppe *f (ins)* premium category, category of premium
Beitragsklasse *f s.* **Beitragsgruppe**
Beitragsmarke *f* token
Beitragsmonat *m* month in [for] which contribution fees [dues] have to be paid
Beitragsperiode *f* period contribution is [has] to be paid for
Beitragspflicht *f* obligation to pay contribution, compulsory contribution
beitragspflichtig liable to contribution [subscription]
Beitragspflichtiger *m* contributor, person liable to pay dues [subscription]
Beitragsrückerstattung *f* reimbursement of contribution paid
Beitragssatz *m* rate of contribution; *(ins)* premium rate

Beitragsstaffelung *f (ins)* scale of premiums
Beitragsübertrag *m* contribution carried over [forward]; *(ins)* premium carried forward
Beitragszahlung *f* payment of dues; *(ins)* premium payment
beitreibbar recoverable ◊ **nicht ~** irrecoverable, unrecoverable *(debts)*; **nicht gerichtlich ~** unenforceable
beitreiben to recover *(debts)*, to enforce payment; to collect *(taxes)*
Beitreibung *f* recovery, enforcement of payment; collection *(taxes)*
Beitreibungskosten *pl* recovering expenses, cost(s) of enforcement; cost of tax collection
Beitreibungsordnung *f* rules for collection *(of money, taxes etc.)*
Beitreibungsverfahren *n (jur)* proceedings to recover debts
beitreten to join, to enter, to become a member *(party etc.)*; to accede to *(treaty etc.)*
Beitritt *m* joining *(party etc.)*; accession *(of a country to an international treaty)*; entry
Beitrittserklärung *f* application for membership; declaration of accession *(treaty etc.)*
Beitrittsgebühr *f* application fee
Beitrittsgeld *n s.* **Beitrittsgebühr**
Bekanntgabe *f* notification, announcement, making *s.th.* known, publication *(decree etc.)*; promulgation, proclamation *(law etc.)*
bekanntgeben to notify, to announce, to make *s.th.* known, to publish *(decree etc.)*; to promulgate, to proclaim *(law etc.)*
bekanntmachen to make *s.th.* known, to report, to disclose; to publish *(decrees etc.)*; to notify, to give notice of *s.th.*; to make public; to announce *(news, plans, etc.)*; to proclaim; to advertise ◊ **etwas amtlich ~** to announce *s.th.* officially, to make an official announcement
Bekanntmachung *f* publication, notification; announcement, proclamation; disclosure; advertisement ◊ **eine amtliche ~ verlesen** to read out [proclaim] an official announcement
Bekanntmachungstag *m* day of publication
Bekleidungsartikel *mpl* (articles of) clothing
Bekleidungsgeld *n* clothing allowance
Bekleidungsindustrie *f* garment [clothing] industry
beköstigen to board *(s.o.)*
Beköstigung *f* board(ing)
Beköstigungsgeld *n* allowance for board
bekräftigen to confirm, to affirm
Bekräftigung *f* confirmation, affirmation
Beladefrist *f* loading time
Beladekapazität *f* loading capacity
beladen to load, to charge (with) ◊ **wieder ~ to** reload

Beladepflicht *f* duty [obligation] to load *(within a specified time)*
Belader *m* loader, stevedore *(ships)*
Belade- und Entladegemeinschaft *f* cargo-handling [reloading] pool *(of enterprises by joint use of transport and handling facilities at railway stations)*
Beladevorschriften *fpl* loading instructions
Belang *m* importance, consequence; affair, concern, matter, issue ◊ **ohne ~** of no account [consequence]; irrelevant, immaterial; **von ~** of importance [consequence]; relevant, pertinent to; **von finanziellem ~** of financial interest
Belange *mpl* interests, concerns ◊ **jmds. ~ vertreten** to represent the interests of s.o.
~, soziale social issues [interests]
belastbar 1. loadable; 2. debitable, chargeable
Belastbarkeit *f* loading capacity
belasten 1. to load *s.th.*, to put a weight on *s.th.*; to be a burden to *s.o.*; to subject *s.th.* to stress; 2. *(acc)* to debit, to charge; 3. *(jur)* to incriminate *s.o.* ◊ **nachträglich ~** to charge [debit] later [subsequently]; **zu ~ mit** chargeable; **zu stark ~** to overcharge; **zu wenig ~** to undercharge
belastet 1. burdened; under stress [strain]; 2. debited, charged with; 3. incriminated
Belastung *f* 1. load, weight; burden; strain, stress; 2. *(acc)* debit, charge; encumbrance; 3. *(jur)* incrimination
~, ausstehende deferred charges
~ der Gewässer water pollution
~, feststehende fixed charges
~, finanzielle financial burden [strain]
~, geringste minimum load
~, gleichbleibende constant load
~, höchste maximum [peak] load *(power)*
~, steuerliche tax contribution *(of the individual)*; burden of taxation
~, übermäßige steuerliche overtaxation
~, unmittelbare direct charge
~, volle full load
~, zulässige maximum (permissible) load, safe load
Belastungen *fpl (com)* charges, debts ◊ **~ des Schuldendienstes tragen** to service debts; to meet debt service charges
Belastungsanzeige *f* 1. *(com)* debit advice [note]; 2. *(tech)* load indication
Belastungsdiagramm *n* load diagram
Belastungsfähigkeit *f s.* **Belastbarkeit**
Belastungsindex *m* load index
Belastungskennwert *m* loading indicator
Belastungsnote *f (com)* debit advice [note]
Belastungsplan *m* load schedule
Belastungsschaubild *n s.* **Belastungsdiagramm**

Belastungsspitze *f* peak hours [load]; maximum utilization *(equipment)*
Belastungsverhältnis *n s.* **Belastungsindex**
belaufen auf, sich to amount to, to come to, to run up to
beleben to revive, to stimulate *(market etc.)*
belebt *(st.ex.)* active, brisk
Belebung *f* revival, stimulation *(market etc.)*, *(st.ex.)* briskness
Beleg *m* voucher; receipt; documentary proof; *(jur)* supporting evidence ◊ **einen ~ abheften** to file a voucher
~, abgestempelter stamped voucher
~, anerkannter approved voucher
~, einmaliger single record [voucher]
~, fingierter fictitious record [voucher]
~, geprüfter audited voucher
~, interner internal record
~, ursprünglicher original voucher
belegbar provable
Belegdurchlauf *m (acc)* passage of voucher [document] *(from one department to another)*
Belegdurchlaufplan *m* schedule of the flow of records
~, geradliniger direct flow of records *(through bookkeeping departments)*
Belege *mpl*:
◊ **~ beibringen** to furnish evidence
~, innerbetriebliche *s.* **~, innere**
~, innere internal records
~, vereinheitlichte standardized vouchers
Belegerfassung *f* registration of records
Belegexemplar *n* specimen *(advertisement etc.)*; file copy; voucher copy; author's copy
Belegkarte *f* record card, voucher
Belegkontrolle *f* checking of records
belegmäßig by record
Belegregistratur *f* registry of vouchers, record office
Belegrevision *f s.* **Belegkontrolle**
Belegschaft *f* staff, personnel; workforce, labour force, employees, workers ◊ **zur ~ gehören** to be on the staff
~, gleichbleibende stable workforce
Belegschaftsaktie *f* employee's (single) share, *(Am)* employee stock
Belegschaftsaktiensystem *n* employee share scheme, employee's shares [*(Am)* stock purchase] plan
Belegschaftsfluktuation *f* personnel mobility
Belegschaftsstärke *f* strength of the labour force, number of employees
Belegschaftsversicherung *f* insurance of employees
Belegschein *m* voucher
Belegstandardisierung *f* standardization of vouchers

Belegsystem *n s.* **Belegwesen**
Belegungsfeinplan *m* detailed list of reservations *(hotel etc.)*
Belegungsplan *m* 1. reservation list *(hotel etc.)*; 2. *(tech)* loading schedule *(machine etc.)*
Belegungspotential *n* accommodation capacity
Belegwesen *n* system of vouchers
Belegzwang *m* obligation to record
beleihbar pledgeable *(security)*
beleihen to lend *(on securities etc.)*; to grant a loan *(on houses etc.)*; to raise a loan *(for an investment)*
Beleihung *f* lending; granting a loan *(on houses etc.)*; raising a loan *(for an investment)*
~ **einer Versicherung** granting a loan against life insurance policy
Beleihungsgrenze *f* limit to which money can be loaned *(on securities etc.)*
Beleihungswert *m* value placed on *s.th.* for a loan
beliefern to supply *(goods etc.)*, to provide, to furnish *(s.o. with s.th.)*
Belieferung *f* supply, delivery *(goods etc.)*
~, **ausreichende** adequate supply *(goods etc.)*
~ **des Marktes** supply of [to] the market
~, **dezentralisierte** decentralized supply *(goods etc.)*
~, **direkte** direct supply *(goods to retailer etc.)*
~, **diskontinuierliche** discontinuous supply *(goods etc.)*
~, **gegenseitige** mutual supply *(goods etc.)*
~, **konstante** constant supply
~, **kontinuierliche** continuous supply *(goods etc.)*
~, **kostenlose** supply without charge *(goods etc.)*
~, **planmäßige** supply according to schedule
~, **prompte** prompt supply *(goods etc.)*
~, **pünktliche** *s.* ~, **termingerechte**
~, **regelmäßige** regular supply *(goods etc.)*
~, **saisonmäßige** seasonal supply *(goods etc.)*
~, **schnelle** quick supply *(goods etc.)*
~, **ständige** permanent supply *(goods etc.)*
~, **störungsfreie** undisturbed supply *(goods etc.)*
~, **termingerechte** supply in due time; supply according to schedule
~, **unmittelbare** *s.* ~, **direkte**
~, **unregelmäßige** irregular supply
~, **unzureichende** insufficient supply *(goods etc.)*
~, **vertragsgemäße** contractual supply *(goods etc.)*, supply according to contract
~, **vorrangige** priority supply *(goods etc.)*
~, **zentrale** central supply *(goods etc.)*
~, **zentralisierte** centralized supply *(goods etc.)*
belohnen to reward *(s.o. for s.th.)*
Belohnung *f* reward
bemessen to measure *(s.th. by s.th.)*; to evaluate *(s.th. according to s.th.)*; to rate, to assess *(ability, property etc. for taxation etc.)*

Bemessung *f* measurement *(of s.th. by s.th.)*; evaluation *(of s.th. according to s.th.)*; rating, assessment *(of ability, property etc. for taxation etc.)*
~ **des Prämienfonds** calculation of the bonus fund
Bemessungseinheit *f* measuring unit
Bemessungsgrundlage *f* base data for assessment
Bemessungszeitraum *m* *(stats)* base period
benachrichtigen to inform, to notify *(s.o.)*; *(com)* to advise, to apprise
Benachrichtigung *f* information, notification; advice ◊ **mangels** ~ for want of advice; **ohne vorherige** ~ without (prior) notification; **ohne vorherige** ~ **zahlbar** payable without prior notification, payable on demand
~, **schriftliche** written communication
Benachrichtigungsschreiben *n* letter of notification; *(com)* letter of advice, advice note
benachteiligen to disadvantage, to deal unfairly with, to discriminate against *(s.o., goods of other countries etc.)*; to handicap *(s.o.)*
Benachteiligung *f* disadvantage, discrimination; handicap
~, **steuerliche** discriminatory taxation
benennen 1. to name *(person etc.)*, to designate *(s.th.)*; 2. to appoint, to set, to fix *(date etc.)*; to nominate *(person for an office etc.)*
benutzbar usable
Benutzbarkeit *f* usability
benutzen to use, to make use of; to utilize; to employ
Benutzer *m* user; reader *(library)*
~, **außerbetrieblicher** outside user
Benutzung *f* use; employment, utilization
~ **der Zwischenblock-Information** *(stats)* recovery of information
Benutzungsbefugnis *f* right to use
Benutzungsgebühr *f* charge, fee (for the use of *s.th.*)
Benutzungsgrad *m* degree [extent] of use
Benutzungsrecht *n* right of user, right to use *(s.th.)*
Benutzungsvorschrift *f* directions [instructions] for use
Benutzungszeit *f* utilization period
beobachten to observe, to keep to, to comply with, to adhere to *(rules, laws etc.)*
Beobachter *m* observer; watcher; spectator
Beobachterdelegation *f* (team of) observers
Beobachtung *f* observation; observance, keeping to, complying with, adherence to *(rules, laws etc.)*
~, **fiktive** *(stats)* dummy observation
~, **herausfallende** *(stats)* maverick
~, **notwendige** necessary observation

~, statistische statistical observation
Beobachtungsblatt *n* observation sheet
Beobachtungsbogen *m s.* **Beobachtungsblatt**
Beobachtungsfehler *m (stats)* ascertainment error, error of observation
Beobachtungsmaterial *n (stats)* data
~, nichtorthogonales *(stats)* non-orthogonal data
~, qualitatives *(stats)* qualitative data
~, quantitatives *(stats)* quantitative data
beraten 1. to advise *(s.o.)*, to give *s.o.* advice; 2. to discuss, to debate *(s.th.)*, to deliberate, to confer *(on s.th.)* ⋄ **schlecht ~ sein** to be ill-advised; **sich ~ lassen** to take the advice of *(s.o.)*
Berater *m* adviser, counsel(lor); consultant
~, technischer consultant, technical adviser
~, wirtschaftlicher economic adviser
Beratung *f* deliberation, discussion, consideration; advice *(technical etc.)*; *(jur)* consultation
~, technisch-ökonomische technical and economic advice, consultancy service
Beratungsdienst *m* advisory service, consultancy
Beratungsgremium *n* consultative [advisory] body [panel]
Beratungsstelle *f* information centre
~, berufliche vocational guidance office
Beratungs- und Vertragssystem *n* consultancy and contracting system
Beratungswesen *n:*
~, landwirtschaftliches advisory system in agriculture
berauben to rob; to deprive *(s.o. of s.th.)*
Beraubung *f* robbery; theft; deprivation
Beraubungsschaden *m* loss sustained by robbery
Beraubungsversicherung *f (ins)* insurance against theft
berechnen to calculate, to work out, to reckon *(price, cost etc.)*; to estimate, to assess, to compute, to appraise *(damage)*; to charge *(s.o. for s.th.)*
Berechnung *f* calculation, working out, reckoning *(price, cost etc.)*; estimation, assessment, computation, appraisal *(damage)*; charging *(s.o. for s.th.)*
~, angenäherte approximate calculation
~ der Einnahmen und Ausgaben calculation of income and expenditure
~ des Durchschnitts calculation of the average
~ des halben Preises invoicing half of the price
~ des vollen Preises invoicing the full price
~, direkte direct calculation; direct invoicing
~ eines günstigen Preises invoicing a favourable [special] price
~, fiktive fictitious invoicing
~, fortlaufende continuous calculation; cumulative calculation

~, iterative iterative calculation
~ mit fiktiven Größen calculation with fictitious figures
~, überschlägige rough calculation
Berechnungen *fpl:*
~, ökonomische economic calculations
~, technisch-ökonomische technical and economic calculations
~, volkswirtschaftliche national economic calculations
~, vorläufige provisional calculations
Berechnungsbasis *f* basis of calculation
Berechnungsdaten *pl* (calculating) data
Berechnungsgrundlage *f s.* **Berechnungsbasis**
Berechnungskennziffer *f* calculation index
Berechnungsmethode *f* method of calculation
Berechnungstabelle *f* calculating chart
Berechnungstafel *f (ins)* experience table
Bereich *m* sector *(economy)*; domain, field *(science, art etc.)*, province *(expert etc.)*, scope *(work, research, inquiry)*; sphere, orbit *(influence, control)*; range, extent *(knowledge, duty)*; purview *(authority etc.)*; region, area
~, analoger *(stats)* similar region
~, bester kritischer *(stats)* best critical region
~ der materiellen Produktion sector of material production
~, erfaßter *(stats)* coverage
~, führender leading sector
~, kritischer *(stats)* critical region
~, nichtmaterieller non-material sector
~, nichtproduktiver non-productive sector
~, nichtproduzierender non-producing sector
~, produktiver productive sector
~, produzierender producing sector
~, (stochastisch) ähnlicher *(stats)* similar region
~, überall wirksamer kritischer *(stats)* unbiased critical region
~, überdeckter *(stats)* coverage
~, volkswirtschaftlicher national economic sector
~, zulässiger range of tolerance
bereichern to enrich *(s.o., s.th.)*; **sich ~** to enrich o.s.
Bereicherung *f* enrichment
~, gesetzwidrige unlawful [illegal] enrichment
~, rechtswidrige *s. ~,* **gesetzwidrige**
~, ungerechtfertigte unjustified enrichment, fraudulent misuse *(funds etc.)*
~, ungesetzliche *s. ~,* **gesetzwidrige**
~, unrechtmäßige *s. ~,* **gesetzwidrige**
Bereicherungsabsicht *f* criminal intent to enrich *(o.s.)*
Bereicherungsmittel *n* means of enrichment
Bereicherungstrieb *m* urge to enrich *(o.s.)*
bereinigen *(acc)* to settle *(account, debts)*; *(stats)* to adjust

Bereinigung *f (acc)* settlement; *(stats)* adjustment
bereitgestellt provided, supplied; earmarked, allocated *(funds)*
Bereitschaftsdienst *m* stand-by duty; on call *(doctor etc.)*; operating a dispensing service out of hours; emergency service ◊ ~ **haben** to be on duty [call] *(doctor)*
Bereitschaftskosten *pl* stand-by charges [costs]
Bereitschaftszeit *f* stand-by time
bereitstellen to provide, to supply *(s.th.)*; to earmark, to allocate *(funds)*
Bereitstellung *f* provision, supply *(of s.th.)*; earmarking, allocation *(funds)*
~, jährliche annual provision
~ von Geldbeträgen appropriation of funds
~ von Kapital supply of capital
Bereitstellungsplan *m* plan of supply, supply plan *(goods)*; appropriation plan *(funds)*
Bergamt *n s.* **Bergbehörde**
Bergarbeiter *m* mine-worker, miner
Bergbau *m* mining (industry)
Bergbauberechtigung *f s.* **Bergbaukonzession**
Bergbaubesteuerung *f* taxation of mining
Bergbaubetrieb *m* mining enterprise
Bergbaudistrikt *m* mining district [area]
Bergbaufreiheit *f* rights of mining, mining rights
Bergbauingenieur *m* mining engineer
Bergbauinspektion *f* mining inspection; mining supervisory board
Bergbaukonzession *f* mining concession
Bergbauschutzgebiet *n* 1. protected mining area; 2. region where mining is prohibited
Bergbaustatistik *f* mining statistics
Bergbausteuer *f* mining tax
Bergbauunternehmen *n* mining company
Bergbauunternehmer *m* mining entrepreneur
Bergbauwirtschaft *f* mining industry
Bergbehörde *f* mining authority; mining supervisory board
Bergegeld *n s.* **Bergelohn**
Bergegut *n* salvage
Bergelohn *m* salvage money
Bergmann *m s.* **Bergarbeiter**
Bergmannsrente *f* miner's pension
Bergordnung *f s.* **Bergrecht**
Bergrecht *n* mining law(s)
Bergregal *n* royalty, mining rights
Bergrente *f* mining rent
Bergschaden *m* damage caused by mining operations *(agriculture, environment etc.)*
Bergsteuer *f s.* **Bergbausteuer**
Bergung *f* rescue *(persons)*; salvage *(ships and cargo)*
Bergungsentgelt *n s.* **Bergelohn**
Bergungsprämie *f s.* **Bergelohn**

Bergungsverluste *mpl* salvage losses
Bergwerk *n* mine; pit
Bergwerkskataster *m/n* mines register
Bergwerksrente *f s.* **Bergrente**
Bericht *m* report *(proceedings, speech, investigation etc.)*; account *(experience, historical event etc.)*; survey *(situation)*; paper *(scientific research etc.)*; commentary *(news, political situation etc.)*; statement, bulletin, communiqué; *(com)* advice; *(stats)* return ◊ **einen ~ abfassen** *s.* **einen ~ ausarbeiten**; **einen ~ ausarbeiten** to prepare [write, draft] a report; **einen ~ bestätigen** to confirm a report; **einen ~ einreichen** to submit a report; **einen ~ entgegennehmen** to hear a report; to accept a report; **einen ~ erstatten** *s.* **berichten**; **~ erstattet von** report delivered by; **einen ~ vorlegen** to submit a report
~, authentischer authentic report
~, eingehender detailed report [account]; detailed statement
~, gemeinsamer joint report; joint statement
~, genauer und sachlicher fair and accurate report
~, halbjährlicher half-yearly report
~, jährlicher annual report
~, kurzer summary
~, monatlicher monthly report
~, mündlich erstatteter verbatim report
~, täglicher daily report
~, tendenziöser tendentious report
~, vierteljährlicher quarterly report
~, wöchentlicher weekly report
berichten to report, to give [make] an account (of); to give [make] a report [statement]; to inform; to advise ◊ **über etwas ausführlich ~** to give full particulars on s.th., to report in detail on s.th.
Berichterstattung *f* reporting; report; commentary
~, gemeinsame joint report [account, statement]
~, operative current report [returns]
~, statistische statistical report, official returns
Berichterstattungspflicht *f* obligation to present a report
berichtigen to correct, to rectify *(mistake, statement etc.)*; to amend *(text etc.)*; to pay, to settle *(debt, account, bill etc.)*; to adjust *(frontier)*
Berichtigung *f* correction, rectification *(mistake, statement etc.)*; amendment *(text etc.)*; payment, settlement *(debt, account, bill etc.)*; adjustment *(frontier)*
~ von Buchungen correction of entries
~ von Steuerfestsetzungen correction of tax assessments
Berichtigungsanschlag *m* supplementary budget

Berichtigungsanzeige *f* notice of error
Berichtigungsbeiwert *m s.* **Berichtigungsfaktor**
Berichtigungsbuchung *f* correcting entry
Berichtigungsbudget *n* supplementary budget
Berichtigungsfaktor *m* corrective factor
Berichtigungskonto *n* suspensive account
Berichtigungsposten *m* correcting item
Berichtigungsveranlagung *f* reassessment of taxes
Berichtigungsvermerk *m* notice of correction
Berichtigungswert *m* correcting value
Berichtsabschnitt *m* paragraph of report
Berichtsanalyse *f* statistical (data) analysis; analysis of a report
Berichtsangaben *fpl* reported data
Berichtsbilanz *f (plan)* statistical balance (sheet) *(of the national economy or a particular industry)*
Berichtsbogen *m* report sheet
Berichtsdaten *pl s.* **Berichtsangaben**
Berichtsformular *n s.* **Berichtsbogen**
Berichtsheft *n* report book
Berichtsjahr *n* year under review [report]
Berichtskennziffer *f* indicator to be reported; indicator in the report
Berichtsmonat *m* month under review [report]
Berichtsunterlagen *fpl* documents of report
Berichtsverflechtungsbilanz *f* reporting input--output table
~, **betriebliche** post-plan input-output table
~ **für Bilanzbereiche** reporting input-output table of balancing organs [units]
~ **für Erzeugnisgruppen** reporting input-output table of groups of products
~ **für gleichartige Hauptrohstoffe und ihre Weiterverwendung** reporting input-output table of main raw materials and their further processing
~ **für Produktionskomplexe gleichartiger Finalprodukte** reporting input-output table for production complexes of final products of the same kind
Berichtswesen *n* system of statistical returns
Berichtszeitraum *m* reporting period, period under review
berieseln *(agric)* to irrigate with sewage; to water *(field etc., with spraying apparatus)*
Berieselung *f (agric)* irrigation with sewage; watering *(field etc., with spraying apparatus)*
Beruf *m* (regular) occupation, job, work, vocation, trade; profession *(usually with higher education)* ⋄ **einem ~ nachgehen** to pursue [follow] one's trade; to pursue [follow] one's profession; **einen ~ ausüben** *s.* **einem ~ nachgehen; einen ~ ergreifen** to take up a profession [career]; to enter [go into] a trade; **einen ~ erlernen** to learn a trade; to be trained in a profession; **im ~ stehen** *s.* **einem**

~ nachgehen; keinen ~ haben to have no trade; **keinen festen ~ haben** to have no regular job; **ohne ~** without a trade; without a profession; without an occupation; **seinen ~ verfehlt haben** to have taken up the wrong trade; **von ~** by trade; by profession; by occupation
~, **angelernter** semi-skilled trade
~, **ausgeübter** present occupation
~, **erlernter** the trade (one has learnt), the profession (in which one is trained)
~, **freier** free-lance occupation
~, **gesundheitsschädigender** occupation [profession] injurious to health
~, **handwerklicher** craft trade
~, **kaufmännischer** commercial occupation
~, **technischer** technical occupation
~, **zweiter** second [part-time] job; second occupation [profession]
berufen to call, to appoint *(lecturer etc.)*, to nominate *(s.o. to an office)*; **sich ~ auf** to appeal to *(s.th.)*, to refer to *(s.th.)*; ⋄ **~ sein** to be competent *(for s.th.)*, to be qualified *(for s.th.)*; **~ werden** to be called, to be authorized
beruflich vocational, occupational; professional
Berufsanalyse *f* vocation analysis *(of physical and mental requirements of a trade, its working conditions, training methods etc.)*
Berufsausbildung *f* vocational training
Berufsausbildungsbilanz *f* balance sheet of vocational training
Berufsausbildungspersonal *n* vocational training personnel *(teachers etc.)*
Berufsausbildungsverhältnis *n* apprenticeship
Berufsauslese *f* selection of vocation [trade]
Berufsaussichten *fpl* professional prospects
berufsbedingt occupational, vocational *(disease etc.)*; conditioned [influenced] by occupation *(expenses etc.)*
Berufsbekleidung *f* work(ing) clothes
Berufsberater *m* vocational counsellor
Berufsberatung *f* vocational guidance
Berufsberatungsstelle *f* vocational guidance office
Berufsbereinigung *f* measures to organize vocational training *(in enterprises under favourable conditions)*
Berufsbezeichnung *f* description of occupation; title
berufsbezogen in regard [related] to occupation
Berufsbild *n* description of vocation [trade]
Berufsbildung *f s.* **Berufsausbildung**
Berufsehre *f* professional honour
Berufseignung *f* vocational aptitude; qualification
Berufseignungsprüfung *f* qualification [aptitude] test for a trade [profession]

Berufsentwicklung *f* changes in job characteristics of a trade; changes in job characteristics of a profession
Berufserfahrung *f* professional [job] experience, experience in a trade [vocation]
Berufsethos *n* vocational [professional] ethics
Berufsfachschule *f s.* **Berufsschule**
Berufsfindung *f* choice of profession [vocation, trade]
berufsfremd not trained [untrained] for (the particular job)
Berufsgeheimnis *n* professional secret
Berufsgenossenschaft *f* professional association; trade association
Berufsgruppe *f* group of trades *(according to branches)*
Berufshaftpflichtversicherung *f* vocational liability insurance
Berufskrankenkasse *f* vocational health insurance (fund)
Berufskrankheit *f* occupational disease
Berufsleben *n* professional [active] life
Berufslenkung *f* occupational [vocational] guidance
berufslos *s.* **ohne Beruf**
berufsmäßig professional
Berufsnachwuchs *m* junior employees *(of some occupations etc.)*
Berufsordnung *f* sub-group of trades *(within a Berufsgruppe)*
Berufspädagogik *f* vocational pedagogics
Berufspraktikum *n* practical training (course) ⋄ **ein ~ absolvieren** to complete a course of practical training
Berufsschaden *m* occupational injury
Berufsschule *f* vocational training centre [school]
Berufsschüler *m* apprentice
Berufsschullehrer *m* vocational training teacher
Berufsschulpflicht *f* compulsory vocational training
Berufsstand *m* profession; trade
Berufsstatistik *f* occupational statistics
Berufsstolz *m* pride in one's job
Berufsstruktur *f* occupational structure *(of total labour force in an enterprise, industrial branch, etc.)*
Berufssystematik *f* catalogue of trades
berufstätig working, having employment [a job]
Berufstätige *pl* working [employed] population, working people
Berufstätigkeit *f* occupation, professional activity, job, employment
berufsunfähig disabled
Berufsunfähigkeit *f* disablement, disability
Berufsunfall *m* industrial accident, accident at work

Berufsverband *m* professional association
Berufsverbot *n* ban on pursuing one's trade [profession]
Berufsverkehr *m* 1. commuter service *(between enterprises and residential areas or quarters)*; 2. rush hours
Berufsverkehrsvertrag *m* commuter service [staff transport] contract *(between enterprise and transport company providing transport for employees to and from work)*
Berufswahl *f* choice of a profession [vocation, trade, career]
Berufswechsel *m* change of profession [job]
Berufswettbewerb *m* apprentice emulation contest [competition]
Berufszählung *f* employment census
Berufsziel *n* professional goal; intended career
Berufszweig *m* professional field [branch, line]
Berufung *f* call, appointment, nomination *(of s.o. to an office)*, reference (to), reliance (on); *(jur)* appeal ⋄ **~ einlegen** to file [lodge] an appeal; **eine ~ verwerfen** to refuse leave to appeal; **eine ~ zulassen** to give leave to appeal; **einer ~ stattgeben** to allow an appeal; **unter ~ auf** with reference to, referring to, on the authority of
Berufungsgericht *n* court of appeal
Berufungsklage *f* appeal
Berufungsrecht *n* right of appeal
Berufungsurteil *n* judgement on appeal
Berufungsverfahren *n* procedure on appeal; appeal proceedings
Berufungsvertrag *m* *(jur)* petition for leave to appeal
besamen to fertilize; to inseminate *(artificially)*; to pollinate *(plants)*
Besamung *f* fertilization; insemination *(artificially)*; pollination *(plants)*
Besamungsstation *f* *(agric)* insemination centre
Besatz *m* *(agric)* stock *(of s.th.)* per unit of farm land *(cattle, tractors, manpower etc.)*
Besatzung *f* 1. occupation *(country etc.)*; 2. crew *(ship etc.)*
Besatzungsbehörde *f* occupation authorities, military government [administration]
Besatzungskosten *pl* occupation costs
Besatzungszone *f* occupation zone, zone of occupation
beschädigen to damage, to injure, to do damage *(to s.o., to s.th.)*, to do an injury *(to s.o.)*; to soil *(textiles)*
beschädigt damaged, injured; soiled *(textiles)*; **beim Transport ~** damaged in transit; soiled in transit *(textiles)*; **leicht ~** slightly damaged [injured]; slightly soiled *(textiles)*; **schwer ~** seriously [extensively] damaged [injured]; badly soiled *(textiles)*

Beschädigtenbetreuung *f* welfare work for disabled people [the disabled]
Beschädigtenfürsorge *f* welfare service for disabled people [the disabled]
Beschädigung *f* damage, injury; soiling *(textiles)*
~, **absichtliche** wilful damage
~, **böswillige** malicious damage
beschaffen to procure; to provide; to supply; to make available; to raise *(money)*; to get, to find *(job, capital etc.)*
Beschaffenheit *f* state, condition; quality, property; nature; character, kind ⋄ **von guter** ~ in good condition; **von vorzüglicher** ~ of superior quality
~, **mangelhafte** defective condition; of poor quality
Beschaffung *f* procurement, procuring; provision, providing; supply; acquisition; raising *(money)*
~ **landwirtschaftlicher Erzeugnisse** procurement of agricultural produce [products]
Beschaffungskosten *pl* cost of acquisition
beschäftigen to keep *s.o.* busy, to occupy *s.o.*; to employ, to engage, to give work *(to s.o.)*; **sich** ~ **mit** to be busy [occupied] with, to be engaged in; to work at; to be concerned with, to deal with
beschäftigt busy (with), engaged (in); preoccupied; concerned (with) ⋄ ~ **sein bei** to be employed with, to be in the employ of, to work for
Beschäftigte *m/fpl* persons employed; economically active (population); employees
~, **nicht ständig** seasonal and casual workers, temporary workers
Beschäftigtenanteil *m* employment ratio
~ **der Bevölkerung** (population) employment ratio
~ **zur Sozialversicherung** employee's social insurance contribution, personal contribution to social insurance
Beschäftigtengrad *m* level of employment
Beschäftigtengruppe *f* occupational group *(classification of manpower in the various sectors of the economy for planning and statistics)*
Beschäftigtengruppenkatalog *m* job classification catalogue *(s.* **Beschäftigtengruppe***)*
Beschäftigtenkartei *f* card index of personnel [employees], personnel card index
Beschäftigtenkategorie *f* occupational category
Beschäftigtenkennziffer *f* employment index
Beschäftigtenrate *f* labour participation rate, employment rate
Beschäftigtenstand *m s.* **Beschäftigtenrate**
Beschäftigter *m* employee, employed person
~, **hauptamtlich** employee in main occupation
Beschäftigung *f* occupation, work, activity; employment, job ⋄ **eine** ~ **finden** to find a job [an employment]; **ohne** ~ unemployed
~, **einträgliche** gainful employment
~, **ganztägige** full-time job [employment]
~, **gelegentliche** casual job [employment]
~, **hauptamtliche** full-time job
~ **im Staatsdienst** in government employment, in the civil service
~ **in der Industrie** employment in industry
~ **in der Landwirtschaft** employment in agriculture
~ **in Kurzarbeit** short-time work
~, **leichte** light occupation
~, **nächtliche** night work
~, **regelmäßige** regular job [employment]
~, **sitzende** sedentary job [occupation]
~ **von Altersrentnern** employment of old age pensioners
~ **von Jugendlichen** juvenile employment
~ **von Kindern** child labour
~, **zeitweilige** temporary job [employment]
~, **zusätzliche** additional employment, extra job
Beschäftigungsgrad *m s.* **Beschäftigtengrad**
Beschäftigungslage *f* employment situation; labour situation
beschäftigungslos unemployed, out of work
Beschäftigungslosigkeit *f* unemployment
Beschäftigungsnachweis *m* certificate of employment
Beschäftigungspolitik *f* employment policy
Beschäftigungsschwankungen *fpl* fluctuation in employment
beschäftigungsunfähig unemployable
Beschäftigungsunfähigkeit *f* unemployability
Beschäftigungsverbot *n* prohibition of employment *(children etc.)*
Bescheid *m* answer; decision; information, instruction ⋄ **jmdm.** ~ **sagen** to give s.o. information, to inform [instruct] s.o.
~, **abschlägiger** refusal, negative reply; rebuff
~, **endgültiger** final decision
~, **schriftlicher** written reply, reply in writing
~, **vorläufiger** provisional decision
bescheinigen to certify, to attest; to confirm *s.th.* (in writing); to acknowledge *(receipt of letter etc.)*
Bescheinigung *f* certification; certificate; attestation; acknowledgement ⋄ **ohne amtliche** ~ uncertified
~, **amtliche** official certificate
~, **ärztliche** medical certificate
~, **behördliche** certificate from a public [government] authority
~, **gefälschte** forged certificate
~, **notarielle** certificate from a notary public
~, **zollamtliche** customs certificate

beschicken to supply *(market with goods)*; to exhibit, to send exhibits to *(fair etc.)*; to send *(deputies etc., to parliament)*
Beschickung *f* supply *(market with goods)*; exhibiting *(fair etc.)*; sending *(deputies etc., to parliament)* ⋄ **für turnusmäßige ~** for alternating participation
Beschickungsplan *m* participation plan
Beschickungsprogramm *n* participation programme (of the fair)
Beschlag *m s.* **Beschlagnahme**
Beschlagnahme *f* seizure, attachment *(real estate etc.)*; confiscation, impounding *(documents, goods etc.)*; embargo *(ship)*; *(jur)* sequestration *(property etc.)* ⋄ **der ~ unterliegend** seizable
beschlagnahmen to seize, to attach *(real estate etc.)*; to confiscate, to impound *(documents, goods etc.)*; to embargo *(ship)*; *(jur)* to sequester, to sequestrate *(property etc.)*
Beschlagnahmeverfügung *f (jur)* writ of sequestration
Beschlagnahmeversicherung *f* insurance against confiscation
beschleunigen to accelerate *(economic growth etc.)*, to speed up, to quicken the tempo *(work etc.)*, to hasten, to expedite *(undertaking etc.)*
Beschleunigung *f* acceleration *(economic growth etc.)*, speeding up, quickening the tempo *(work etc.)*, hastening, expediting *(undertaking etc.)*
beschließen 1. to end, to conclude, to close *(speech etc.)*; 2. to resolve, to determine upon, to decide *(s.th.)* ⋄ **einstimmig ~** to vote unanimously
Beschluß *m* decision, resolution; *(jur)* decree, order ⋄ **einen ~ ablehnen** to reject a resolution; **einen ~ aufheben** *(jur)* to rescind a decree; to revoke a decision; **einen ~ aussetzen** *(jur)* to stay [stop the execution of] a decree; to postpone the implementation of a decision; **einen ~ fassen** to arrive at a decision; to pass a resolution
~, bindender *(jur)* binding order; binding decision
~, gefaßter resolution adopted
~, gerichtlicher order of the court
~, widerspruchsvoller contradictory report [decision]
beschlußfähig competent to pass resolutions, having a quorum
Beschlußfassung *f* passing of a resolution
beschränken to limit, to restrict, to curtail *(expenditure, s.o.'s power etc.)*; **sich ~** to confine o.s. *(to subject etc.)*
beschränkend restrictive
beschränkt limited, restricted, confined
Beschränkung *f* limitation, restriction, curtailment *(of expenditure, of s.o.'s power etc.)*; confining *o.s.* to *(subject etc.)*

Beschränkungen *fpl*:
~, benachteiligende *s.* **~, diskriminierende**
~, diskriminierende discriminatory restrictions
~, finanzielle financial restrictions; fiscal restrictions
~, mengenmäßige quantitative restrictions
~, politische political restrictions
~, wirtschaftliche economic restrictions; business restrictions
Beschreibung *f* description; instructions *(directions for use of a product)*
~, technische technical description
Beschwerde *f* complaint; *(jur)* appeal; objection *(to court order, procedure etc.)* ⋄ **eine ~ einlegen** to make a complaint; **eine ~ einreichen** to lodge [file] a complaint; **eine ~ entgegennehmen** to receive a complaint; **eine ~ vorbringen** *s.* **eine ~ einreichen**; **eine ~ zulassen** to allow an appeal; **eine ~ zurückweisen** to dismiss an appeal; **einer ~ abhelfen** to deal with a grievance, to remove a cause of complaint; **Grund zur ~ haben** to complain with good reason; **keinen Grund zur ~ haben** to have no cause for complaint
~, berechtigte justifiable complaint
~, formelle formal complaint
Beschwerdeabteilung *f* complaints department
Beschwerdebuch *n* complaints book
Beschwerdebüro *n s.* **Beschwerdeabteilung**
Beschwerdefrist *f* time allowed for appeal
Beschwerdeführer *m* person who lodges a complaint, complainer; *(jur)* complainant
Beschwerdeführung *f* lodging of a complaint
Beschwerdegegenstand *m* subject of complaint
Beschwerdekommission *f* arbitration commission
Beschwerderecht *n* right of appeal, right to lodge a complaint
Beschwerdeschrift *f* written complaint; petition
Beschwerdeverfahren *n* appeal procedure; appeal proceedings
beschweren, sich to complain, to lodge a complaint *(about/against s.th.)*
beseitigen to remove, to eliminate *(source of trouble etc.)*, to correct, to put right *(mistakes etc.)*; to kill; to destroy, to get rid of *(pests in agriculture etc.)*; to do away with *(rule etc.)*
Beseitigung *f* removal, elimination *(source of trouble etc.)*, correcting [putting] right *(mistakes etc.)*; killing, destruction, getting rid of *(pests in agriculture etc.)*; doing away with *(rule etc.)*
~ der Zollschranken elimination [removal, lifting] of customs barriers [tariff barriers]
~ eines Mißstandes remedy of an abuse
~ übler Gerüche dispelling unpleasant odours
~ von Disproportionen elimination of disproportions

~ **von Elendsvierteln** slum clearance
~ **von Hindernissen** removal [brushing aside] of obstacles
~ **von Schäden** making good the damage
~ **von Schutt** removal of rubble
~ **von Schwierigkeiten** smoothing away [removal] of difficulties
~ **von Trümmern** removal of debris
besetzen 1. to occupy *(seat, table, position etc.)*; to fill (up) a post [vacancy]; 2. to occupy *(country etc.)*
besetzt 1. occupied *(seat, table etc.)*, filled *(post etc.)*, engaged *(telephone line etc.)*, taken *(seat etc.)*, full *(hotel etc.)*; 2. occupied *(country etc.)*
Besetzung *f* occupation *(country etc.)*
Besetzungsnorm *f* service norm *(a variant of the work norm stipulating number and qualification of operators of large equipment, plants, flow lines etc.)*
Besetzungsprobleme *npl (stats)* occupancy problems
Besetzungszahl *f (stats)* occupancy number
~ **eines Tabellenfeldes** *(stats)* cell frequency
besichtigen to visit, to look round, to go round *(fair etc.)*, to inspect *(factory etc.)*, to examine *(goods etc.)*
Besichtigung *f* visit, looking around, going round *(fair etc.)*; inspection *(factory etc.)* ⬥ **bei ~ gelieferter Waren** in examining the goods delivered; **bei näherer ~** on close [closer] inspection; **zur ~ freigegeben** be on view, be open to inspection *(articles on auction etc.)*
Besichtigungsbefugnis *f* power of inspection
Besichtigungsbericht *m* inspector's report
Besichtigungsfahrt *f s.* **Besichtigungstour**
Besichtigungsgebühren *fpl* entrance fee
Besichtigungsprotokoll *n* report of inspection
Besichtigungsrecht *n* right of inspection
Besichtigungsreise *f* sightseeing tour
Besichtigungsrunde *f* tour of inspection
Besichtigungstour *f* sightseeing excursion [tour]
Besichtigungsvermerk *m* notice of inspection
Besichtigungszeugnis *n* certificate of inspection
besiedeln to settle, to people, to populate *(region etc.)*; to colonize
besiedelt populated, peopled; **dicht ~** densely populated; **dünn ~** thinly populated
Besiedelung *f* settlement; colonization
~, **dichte** dense settlement of population, densely populated settlement
~, **dünne** sparse settlement (of population), sparsely populated settlement
Besiedelungsplan *m* settlement project
besiegeln to seal *(pact, alliance etc.)*, to set one's seal on *(contract etc.)*
Besiegelung *f* seal(ing)
Besitz *m* possession, occupancy *(land, house etc.)*; belongings *(personal things)*; holdings *(shares etc.)* ⬥ **etwas in ~ nehmen** *s.* **von etwas ~ ergreifen**; **im ~ einer Sache bleiben** to remain in [retain] possession of s.th.; **im ~ von Angaben (über)** in possession of data (regarding); **in ausländischem ~** in foreign possession; **under foreign ownership; in den ~ einer Sache kommen** to get possession of s.th., to come by s.th.; **in privatem ~ befindlich** privately owned (property); **in privaten ~ übergehen** to pass into private hands; **in staatlichem ~** under state ownership; state-owned; **in vollem ~ seiner geistigen Kräfte** in full possession of one's mental faculties; **jmdm. den ~ einer Sache streitig machen** to dispute s.o.'s ownership of s.th.; **jmdm. den ~ entziehen** to dispossess [expropriate] s.o. of s.th.; *(jur)* to eject [evict] s.o.; **ohne ~ without** possessions; **von etwas ~ ergreifen** to take possession of s.th.
~, **angenommener** constructive possession
~, **berechtigter** justified possession
~, **gemeinsamer** joint possession
~, **gewaltsam erworbener** possession gained by force
~, **in gutem Glauben erworbener** bona fide possession
~, **juristischer** juristical possession, possession in law
~, **nichtgerechtfertigter** unjustified possession
~, **öffentlicher** public property
~, **persönlicher** personal possessions [belongings, effects]
~, **privater** private property
~, **rechtmäßiger** legitimate [rightful] possession
~, **tatsächlicher** actual possession
~, **unbeweglicher** immovable possessions
~, **unerlaubter** illegal possession
~, **ungesetzlicher** *s.* ~, **unerlaubter**
~, **unmittelbarer** direct possession
~, **unrechtmäßiger** *s.* ~, **unerlaubter**
~, **unumstrittener** undisputed possession
~, **unveräußerlicher** inalienable possession
~ **von Aktien** holding of shares, shareholding, *(Am)* holding of stocks, stockholding
~, **zeitweiliger** temporary possession
Besitzabgabe *f s.* **Besitzsteuer**
Besitzabtretung *f* conveyance of possession
Besitzanspruch *m* claim for possession
besitzen to possess, to have, to be in possession of *(s.th.)*, to occupy *(land, houses etc.)*; to hold *(shares etc.)*
besitzend propertied
Besitzentziehung *f* dispossession; expropriation; *(jur)* disseizing
Besitzentziehungsklage *f (jur)* action of ejectment

Besitzer *m* possessor; occupier, occupant *(land, houses etc.)* ✧ **den ~ wechseln** to change hands
~, gutgläubiger bona fide possessor
~, nichtberechtigter *s.* **~, unrechtmäßiger**
~, rechtmäßiger legitimate [lawful] possessor
~, unrechtmäßiger illegitimate possessor
Besitzergreifung *f* taking possession; occupation; occupancy; seizure; *(jur)* entry by force
~, widerrechtliche unauthorized assumption of possession, usurpation
Besitzerrecht *n* possessor's right; owner's right
Besitz(er)wechsel *m* changing hands
~, mehrmaliger changing hands several times
Besitzerwerb *m* taking [coming into] possession
Besitzklage *f (jur)* action for possession, possessory action
besitzlos *s.* **ohne Besitz**
besitzmäßig possessory
Besitznachfolge *f* succession in possession
Besitznahme *f* taking [coming into] possession
Besitzpfandrecht *n* lien on property
Besitzrecht *n* right of possession
Besitzstand *m* possessory title; assets
Besitzsteuer *f* property tax
Besitzstörer *m (jur)* trespasser
Besitzstörung *f (jur)* trespass; disturbance; molestation; nuisance
Besitzstörungsklage *f (jur)* action to cease disturbance of possession; action for trespass
Besitztitel *m (jur)* title-deed
Besitztum *n* possession; property
~, immobiles *s.* **Besitz, unbeweglicher**
~, unbewegliches *s.* **Besitz, unbeweglicher**
~, unveräußerliches *s.* **Besitz, unveräußerlicher**
Besitzübernahme *f* taking (over) possession
Besitzübertragung *f* transfer (of possession)
Besitzveränderungsabgaben *fpl* transfer duty (on property)
Besitzveränderungssteuern *fpl s.* **Besitzveränderungsabgaben**
Besitzvererbung *f* leaving [bequeathing] of possession
Besitzverhältnisse *npl* ownership [property] relations
Besitzwechselsteuer *f s.* **Besitzveränderungsabgaben**
besolden to pay a salary *(civil servants etc.)*, to pay stipend *(magistrates, clergymen etc.)*, to pay *(soldiers etc.)*
Besoldung *f* salary, payment of salary *(civil servants etc.)*, stipend *(magistrates, clergymen etc.)*, payment *(soldiers etc.)*
Besoldungserhöhung *f* salary increase, increase in pay
Besoldungsgesetz *n* pay regulations

Besoldungsgruppe *f* salary class
Besoldungsordnung *f* scales of pay, pay regulations
Besoldungszulage *f* bonus; additional allowance *(added to pay)*
besorgen 1. to look after, to care for, to attend to *(s.o., animals etc.)*; to see to *(affairs, business etc.)*; to execute, to carry out *(order etc.)*; to do *(duty etc.)*; 2. to procure, to provide, to get; to buy
Besorgung *f* 1. looking after, caring for, attending to *(s.o., animals etc.)*; seeing to *(affairs, business etc.)*; execution, carrying out *(order etc.)*; doing *(duty etc.)*; 2. procurement, provision, getting; buying ✧ **eine ~ machen** to do an errand, to go [run] (on) an errand; to buy s.th.
Besorgungen *fpl* shopping ✧ **~ machen** to go shopping
besprechen to discuss, to talk *s.th.* over; to comment on, to review *(book etc.)*
Besprechung *f* talk, discussion, meeting; comment, review ✧ **eine ~ abhalten** to hold a meeting
~ auf höchster Ebene top-level meeting; summit meeting
~ auf höherer Ebene high-level talk
bessern, sich to improve *(situation, soil etc.)*, to better *(conditions etc.)*, to reform *(character etc.)*
Besserung *f* improvement *(situation, soil etc.)*, betterment *(conditions etc.)*, reform *(character etc.)* ✧ **~ zeigen** to show improvement
~, deutliche marked improvement *(market etc.)*
bestallen to install, to appoint *(s.o. to an office)*
Bestallung *f* installation, appointment *(of s.o. to an office)*
Bestallungsurkunde *f* certificate of appointment *(to an office)*
Bestand *m* 1. stock *(in hand)*, stock-in-trade; inventory *(stock-taking)*; cash balance, cash *(in hand)*; assets *(capital)*; holdings *(shares etc.)*; 2. *(agric)* livestock; crop; *(for)* stand *(timber etc.)*; 3. duration, permanence; stability, durability ✧ **den ~ aufnehmen** to take stock [an inventory]; **den ~ feststellen** *s.* **den ~ aufnehmen**; **über den ~ verkaufen** *(st.ex.)* to oversell
~ an Bargeld cash in hand
~ an Devisen foreign exchange reserve [stock]
~ an Diskonten discount holdings, bills discounted
~ an Waren stock of goods
~, buchmäßig ausgewiesener stock according to inventory
~, effektiver actual stock; actual amount
~, eiserner emergency ration
~, laufender current stock

~, **planwidriger** stocks exceeding the plan
~, **spekulativer** speculative stock
~, **transitorischer** suspense stock
~, **ungenutzter** unused stock
Bestände *mpl* stocks, supplies ◊ **alte ~ abstoßen** to get rid of old stocks; **alte ~ räumen** *s*. **alte ~ abstoßen**; **seine ~ auffüllen** to replenish one's stocks; **seine ~ erneuern** *s*. **seine ~ auffüllen**
~, **absatzfähige** saleable stocks
~, **alte** old stocks
~, **illiquide** non-cash assets
~, **liquide** liquid assets; fluid [available, ready] money [capital]
~, **plangebundene** planned stocks
~, **planwidrige** unplanned stocks
~, **unerschöpfliche** inexhaustible supplies
~, **unverkäufliche** dead stocks
Beständebilanz *f* balance sheet of stocks
Bestandsabbau *m s*. **Bestandsabgang**
Bestandsabgang *m* reduction of stocks
Bestandsänderung *f* change in stocks
Bestandsaufnahme *f* stock-taking, inventory ◊ **~ machen** to take stock [an inventory]
Bestandsausgleich *m* equalization of stocks
Bestandsbeleg *m* stock voucher
Bestandsbewegung *f* fluctuation of stocks
Bestandsbewertung *f* stock evaluation
Bestandsbilanz *f s*. **Beständebilanz**
Bestandsbildung *f* building up of stock(s)
Bestandsbuch *n* inventory, warehouse book
Bestandsbuchführung *f* stock accounting
Bestandsdichte *f (for)* crop density
Bestandsentwicklung *f* growth of stock(s) [inventory]
Bestandserfassung *f s*. **Bestandsaufnahme**
Bestandserhöhung *f* increase of [in] stocks
Bestandsermittlung *f s*. **Bestandsaufnahme**
Bestandsfehlbetrag *m* inventory shortage
Bestandsfinanzierung *f* financing of stock(s)
Bestandsgründung *f (for)* planting of a new stand of trees
Bestandshaltung *f* stockkeeping; stocking
~, **optimale** optimum stocking
Bestandshöhe *f* level of stock(s)
Bestandskarte *f (for, approx.)* coloured map showing distribution and age of trees in a plantation
Bestandskartei *f* card-index of stocks
Bestandskonto *n* stock account
Bestandskontrolle *f* stock [inventory] checking
Bestandskredit *m* credit for stock financing
Bestandsliste *f* stock-list, inventory
Bestandslockerung *f (for)* thinning out [clearing] of forest
Bestandsmasse *f* extent of stock; *(for)* total volume of timber in a stand
Bestandsnachweis *m s*. **Bestandsliste**

Bestandsnorm *f* standard (for the) amount of stock
Bestandsnormativ *n* stock standard [norm], (fixed) standard for the amount of stock
Bestandsnormierung *f* standardization of stock(s)
Bestandsnormung *f s*. **Bestandsnormierung**
Bestandsplan *m* plan of stocks
Bestandsplanung *f* planning of stocks
Bestandsposition *f* stock item, item of stock
Bestandsrichtsätze *mpl s*. **Bestandsnormativ**
Bestandsrichtwert *m* standard size [volume] of stock(s)
Bestandsschwankung *f* fluctuation of stock(s)
Bestandsstruktur *f* structure of stock
Bestandsüberwachung *f s*. **Bestandskontrolle**
Bestandsveränderung *f* change in stock [inventory]
Bestandsvermehrung *f s*. **Bestandserhöhung**
Bestandsverzeichnis *n s*. **Bestandsliste**
Bestandszahlen *fpl* inventory figures
Bestandszuwachs *m s*. **Bestandserhöhung**
Bestandteil *m* part, component; ingredient
~, **wesentlicher** essential part
Bestarbeiter *m* outstanding [exemplary] worker
bestätigen to confirm *(news, appointment, order etc.)*, to acknowledge *(receipt of s.th.)*; to approve, to sanction *(nomination, decision etc.)*; *(jur)* to corroborate *(evidence, statement etc.)*; to ratify, to validate *(deed, contract etc.)*, to uphold *(court sentence)*; **sich ~** to be confirmed, to prove (to be) true [correct], to hold good *(theory etc.)*
bestätigt confirmed; ratified
Bestätigung *f* confirmation *(news, appointment, order etc.)*; acknowledgement *(of receipt of s.th.)*; approval, sanction *(nomination, decision etc.)*; *(jur)* corroboration *(evidence, statement etc.)*; ratification, validation *(deed, contract etc.)*, upholding *(court sentence)*
Bestätigungskarte *f* card of acknowledgement
Bestätigungsrecht *n* right of certification
Bestätigungsschreiben *n* letter of confirmation [acknowledgement]
bestatten to bury, to inter
Bestattung *f* burial, interment, funeral
Bestattungsanstalt *f s*. **Bestattungsinstitut**
Bestattungsbeihilfe *f (ins)* funeral allowance
Bestattungsgebühren *fpl* funeral fees
Bestattungsinstitut *n* (firm of) undertakers
Bestattungskosten *pl* funeral expenses
Bestattungsversicherung *f* funeral insurance
Bestattungszuwendung *f s*. **Bestattungsbeihilfe**
Bestbietender *m* highest bidder
bestechen to bribe, to corrupt; *(jur)* to suborn *(witness etc.)*
Bestecher *m* briber; *(jur)* suborner

bestechlich bribable, corruptible
Bestechlichkeit *f* corrupt practices, corruptibility
Bestechung *f* bribery, corruption, *(Am)* graft; *(jur)* subornation *(witness etc.)* ◇ **der ~ zugänglich** open to bribery, corruptible **~, allgemeine** general corruption
Bestechungsfonds *m* slush fund
Bestechungsgeld *n* hush money, bribe
bestehen 1. to exist, to be; 2. to hold one's ground; 3. to pass *(test, examination etc.)* ◇ **~ auf** to insist on *(s.th.)*; **~ aus** to consist of *(s.th.)*, to be composed of *(s.th.)*; **~ in** to lie in *(difficulties etc.)*
Bestehen *n* 1. existence; 2. holding one's ground; 3. passing *(test, examination etc.)*; 4. insistence
bestellbar orderable
Bestellbuch *n* order-book
Bestelldienst *m* advance order shopping
bestellen 1. to deliver *(letter, message etc.)*; 2. to order *(goods, services)*; to ask *s.o.* to come *(for an interview etc.)*; to book, to reserve *(seat etc.)*; to subscribe to *(newspaper etc.)*; 3. *(agric)* to till, to cultivate; 4. *(jur)* to appoint *s.o. (as a guardian or trustee)*
Besteller *m* orderer; customer, buyer; subscriber *(newspaper etc.)*; messenger *(messages etc.)*
Bestellformular *n* order form
Bestellfrist *f* deadline for submitting order
Bestellkarte *f s.* **Bestellformular**
Bestellkatalogsystem *n* system of catalogue orders
Bestellschein *m s.* **Bestellformular**
Bestelltermin *m* date for placing orders
Bestellung *f* 1. delivery *(letter, message etc.)*; 2. order *(goods, services)*; asking *s.o.* to come *(interview etc.)*; booking, reservation *(seat etc.)*; subscription *(to newspaper etc.)*; 3. *(agric)* tillage, cultivation; 4. *(jur)* appointment *(of s.o. as a guardian/trustee)* ◇ **auf ~** on order; **auf ~ arbeiten** to work to order; **auf ~ anfertigen** to make to order, *(Am)* to custom; **auf ~ angefertigt** made to order, *(Am)* custom-made, custom-built; **bis auf weitere ~** until further notice; **eine ~ annehmen** to take an order; **eine ~ annullieren** to cancel an order; **eine ~ aufgeben** to place an order; **eine ~ ausführen** to deal with [execute] an order; **eine ~ buchen** to book an order; **eine ~ einholen** to call for an order; **eine ~ machen** *s.* **eine ~ aufgeben**; **eine ~ rückgängig machen** *s.* **eine ~ annullieren**; **gegen ~ erhältlich** obtainable on order; **laut ~** per order
~, dringende rush order
~ eines Treuhänders appointment of a custodian

~, laufende standing order
~, mündlich aufgegebene verbal order
~, nicht ausgeführte unfulfilled order
~, schriftliche written order
~, telefonisch aufgegebene telephone order
~ von Briefen delivery of letters
~ von Plätzen booking of seats
Bestellzettel *m s.* **Bestellformular**
bestens *(st.ex.)* best
besteuerbar taxable
besteuern to tax, to impose a tax on *s.th.*; to lay a rate on *(building etc.)*; to levy taxes
besteuert taxed ◇ **gering ~ sein** to be lightly taxed; **hoch ~ sein** to be heavily taxed
Besteuerung *f* taxation, imposition of taxes on *s.th.*; laying of rates on *(building etc.)*; levy ◇ **der ~ unterliegen** taxable, rateable
~, degressive degressive taxation
~, direkte direct taxation
~, einheitliche uniform taxation, flat rate
~, gestaffelte graduated taxation
~, indirekte indirect taxation
~, progressive progressive taxation
~, proportionale proportional taxation
~, regressive regressive taxation
~, unterschiedliche discriminatory taxation
~, zusätzliche additional [supplementary] taxation
Besteuerungsart *f* kind of taxation
Besteuerungsfreigrenze *f* tax exemption [immunity] limit, exemption
Besteuerungsgegenstand *m* object of taxation
Besteuerungsgrundlage *f* tax base, basis of taxation
Besteuerungsgrundsätze *mpl* principles of taxation
Besteuerungsmaßstab *m* tax scale, scale of taxation
Besteuerungsprinzipien *npl s.* **Besteuerungsgrundsätze**
Besteuerungsrecht *n* taxation law
Besteuerungsverfahren *n* method of taxation
bestimmen 1. to determine, to fix, to settle, to decide (up)on *(price, conditions etc.)*; to set *(time etc.)*, to appoint *(place etc.)*; 2. to designate, to nominate *(s.o. for post)*, to intend *(s.o. for office etc.)*; to appropriate, to set apart, to earmark, to allocate *(s.th. for certain use etc.)*; 3. to define *(concept etc.)* ◇ **etwas näher ~** to define s.th. more clearly; **über etwas ~** to give instructions [directions] in respect of s.th.
bestimmt 1. determined, fixed, settled, decided; 2. definite, distinct, well-defined; 3. firm, resolute
Bestimmtheit *f* 1. determination, firmness; 2. accuracy, precision; 3. certainty ◇ **mit ~** certainly, definitely

Bestimmtheitsgrundsatz *m (stats)* principle of determination
Bestimmtheitskoeffizient *m (stats)* coefficient of determination
Bestimmung *f* 1. determination, fixing, settlement, decision *(price, conditions etc.)*, setting *(time etc.)*, appointment *(place etc.)*; 2. designation, nomination *(of s.o. for post, office etc.)*, appropriation, setting apart, earmarking, allocation *(of s.th. for certain use)*; 3. stipulation, rule; 4. definition *(concept etc.)*
~ **des Einzelhandelspreises** setting the retail price
~, **eingefügte** inserted clause
~, **generelle** blanket clause
~, **unhaltbare** untenable stipulation, clause which cannot be upheld
Bestimmungen *fpl* regulations, stipulations; provisions
~, **allgemeine** general provisions
~, **gesetzliche** official regulations; legal provisions
~, **planmethodische** rules on the methodology of planning [plan drafting]
~, **polizeiliche** police regulations
Bestimmungsbahnhof *m* (railway) station of destination
Bestimmungsfaktor *m* defining factor
Bestimmungsflugplatz *m* airport of destination
Bestimmungsgröße *f* determinant, determinant magnitude [indicator]
~, **technisch-ökonomische** defining technical and economic magnitude
Bestimmungshafen *m* port of destination
Bestimmungsland *n* country of destination
Bestimmungslandprinzip *n* country of destination principle
Bestimmungsort *m* place [point] of destination
Bestleistung *f* record, outstanding [best] performance
bestmöglich *(st.ex.)* best possible
bestreiken to strike against *(firm etc.)*
bestreikt strike-bound
bestreitbar 1. contestable, disputable, challengeable *(right etc.)*; deniable *(facts, guilt etc.)*; controversial *(statement etc.)*; 2. payable, defrayable, bearable *(expenses, cost etc.)*
bestreiten 1. to contest, to dispute, to challenge *(right etc.)*; to deny *(facts, guilt etc.)*; 2. to pay, to defray, to bear, to meet *(expenses, cost etc.)*; to maintain *(livelihood, standard of living etc.)*
Bestreitung *f* 1. contestation, dispute, challenge *(right etc.)*; denial *(facts, guilt etc.)*; 2. payment, defrayal *(expenses, cost etc.)*; maintenance *(livelihood, standard of living etc.)*
Besttechnologie *f* advanced technology
Bestwert *m* advanced standard

~, **technologischer** advanced technological standard
Besuch *m* visit, visiting *(fair etc.)*, attendance *(meeting etc.)*; stay; sojourn; guest(s) ⋄ **einen ~ abstatten** to pay a visit, to call on *(s.o.)*; **einen ~ machen** s. **einen ~ abstatten**; **gültig für einen einmaligen ~** valid for a single admission
~ **eines Vertreters** visit from [by] a representative
~, **formeller** formal visit [call]
~, **offizieller** official visit
besuchen to visit, to call on *(s.o.)*, to attend *(meeting etc.)*
Besucher *m* visitor; caller; guest ⋄ ~ **anlocken** to attract visitors
~, **ausländischer** foreign visitor
~, **einheimischer** domestic visitor
~, **ständiger** regular [frequent] visitor
Besucherheft *n* visiting book
Besucherstrom *m* influx of visitors; flood of callers
Besuchszeit *f* visiting hours
Beta-Verteilung *f (stats)* beta distribution
beteiligen to give *s.o.* a share *in s.th.*, to make *s.o.* a party to *(undertaking, agreement etc.)*; **sich ~** to participate, to share *(in work to be done)*, to collaborate *(on book etc.)*, to contribute *(to collective work etc.)*; *(com)* to participate *(in business etc.)*
beteiligt interested, concerned
Beteiligter *m* interested [concerned] party
Beteiligung *f* participation *(in work to be done)*, collaboration *(on book etc.)*, contribution *(to collective work etc.)*; *(com)* share, participation *(in business etc.)*; partnership, holding *(in company etc.)* ⋄ ~ **erwerben** to secure an interest; to buy shares *(a share in the capital of an enterprise)*
~ **am Verlust** sharing the loss
~ **an der Geschäftsführung** management sharing
~ **an einem Konsortium** underwriting participation
~, **finanzielle** financial interest
~, **staatliche** state participation *(enterprise etc.)*; joint venture
~, **turnusmäßige** alternating participation
~, **verwaltete** holding under sequestration
Beteiligungsdauer *f* life of a partnership
Beteiligungserträge *mpl* earnings from capital participation
Beteiligungsgesellschaft *f* holding company
Beteiligungsinteresse *n* interest in participation
Beteiligungskosten *pl* cost of participation
Beteiligungsrekord *m* record attendance [participation]

Beteiligungssystem *n* quota [share] system
Betrag *m* amount, sum, total ⋄ **einen ~ abrunden** to round off a sum; **einen ~ absetzen** to set aside an amount [a sum]; **einen ~ abziehen** to deduct an amount; **einen ~ bei einer Bank einzahlen** to pay an amount into the bank; **einen ~ für Abnutzung absetzen** to write off an amount for wear and tear; **einen ~ bewilligen** to grant a sum of money, to allow *s.o.* a sum of money; to vote a sum; to pass a (special) item of expenditure; **einen ~ dem Reservefonds zuführen** to allocate an amount to the reserve fund; **einen ~ erhalten** to receive payment [a sum of money]; **einen ~ für etwas hinterlegen** to leave a deposit on s.th.; **einen ~ gleichmäßig aufteilen** to split a sum into equal shares; **einen ~ guthaben** to have a balance in one's favour; **einen ~ in Abzug bringen** *s.* **einen ~ abziehen**; **einen ~ kündigen** to call in a sum; **einen ~ vorschießen** to advance an amount [a sum]; **einen ~ zu Lasten eines Kontos vortragen** to charge a sum to the debit; **einen ~ zur Zahlung anweisen** to authorize the payment of a sum; **jmdm. einen ~ gutschreiben** to place an amount to s.o.'s credit, to pass an amount to the credit of s.o.; **jmdm. einen ~ kreditieren** to enter an amount to s.o.'s credit, to place an amount to the credit of s.o.; **jmdn. mit einem ~ belasten** to charge an amount to s.o.'s account, to pass an amount to the debit of s.o.; **um den erforderlichen ~ zu erreichen** to make up the required sum; **zum ~ von ... auflaufen** to amount to the sum of ...
~, **abgerundeter** amount rounded off
~, **abzuhebender** amount to be withdrawn
~, **als Sicherheit hinterlegter** surety; bail
~, **angezahlter** first instalment
~, **ausgemachter** sum agreed upon
~, **ausstehender** amount owing, outstanding amount
~, **beliebiger** any amount
~, **bestimmbarer** determinable amount
~, **bestimmter** definite sum
~, **einem Kreditbrief entnommener** amount withdrawn from a letter of credit
~, **doppelter** double the amount
~, **einbehaltener** amount withheld
~, **fälliger** amount [sum] due
~, **geschuldeter** sum owed [due, owing]
~, **gezeichneter** subscribed amount
~, **großer** large sum
~, **hinterlegter** deposited amount
~, **kleiner** small amount
~, **noch zur Verfügung stehender** unexpended balance, unspent amount

~, **offenstehender** *s.* ~, **ausstehender**
~, **pro forma angesetzter** nominal sum
~, **realisierter** realized amount
~, **restlicher** remaining sum [amount]
~, **steuerfreier** tax-free amount
~, **steuerpflichtiger** taxable amount [portion]
~, **strittiger** amount at issue [in dispute]
~, **überfälliger** amount overdue
~, **überzogener** overdraft, amount overdrawn
~, **ungedeckter** uncovered amount
~, **veranschlagter** estimate, estimated amount
~, **verfügbarer** amount available
~, **voller** full amount
~, **von der Bank abgehobener** sum withdrawn from the bank
~, **von der Versicherung gedeckter** amount covered by insurance
~, **vorausgezahlter** amount paid in advance
~, **zuviel berechneter** overcharge
Beträge *mpl*:
~, **im Haushaltsplan nicht inbegriffene** extra-budgetary funds
betragen 1. to amount to, to come to; 2. to behave, to conduct
betrauen:
⋄ **jmdn. mit etwas ~** to entrust s.o. with s.th.; to charge s.o. with s.th.; to commit [consign] s.th. to s.o.'s care
Betreff *m* reference ⋄ **einen ~ angeben** to quote a reference; **in betreff** with regard [respect] to, concerning, as to, in respect of *(s.th.)*
betreffen to affect, to concern *(s.o., s.th.)*; to be relevant to *(a matter)*; to hit *(town, country etc.)*
betreffend regarding, concerning
betreiben 1. to pursue, to follow, to carry on, to run, to manage *(trade, business etc.)*; 2. to run, to work *(machine, train etc., on oil, steam etc.)*
Betreiben *n*:
⋄ **auf jmds. ~ (hin)** at [by] the instigation of (s.o.), at the prompting of (s.o.)
betreuen to take care of *(s.o., s.th.)*, to attend (to) *(s.o.)*, to tend, to have (the) care of *(s.o.)*; to supervise *(work etc.)*
Betreuung *f* care; supervision
~, **medizinische** medical care
~, **soziale** social care [welfare service]
Betreuungseinrichtung *f* institution of welfare work, social welfare institution
Betreuungsgemeinkosten *pl* overhead costs of welfare work
Betreuungskosten *pl* costs of welfare work
Betrieb *m* 1. enterprise, firm, business, concern; factory, (manufacturing) plant, works; *(agric)* farm; 2. working, operation *(railway line etc.)* ⋄ **außer ~** out of order [action]; not working; **außer ~ setzen** to put out of operation, to stop, to close *(line etc.)*; **in einem ~ tätig sein**

to be in the employ of [employed in] an enterprise; **den ~ aufnehmen** to begin work(ing) *(business etc.)*; **den ~ einstellen** to cease work(ing), to close (down); **den ~ wieder aufnehmen** to resume work; **einen ~ führen** to run an enterprise; to manage an enterprise; **in ~ working**, in operation; **in ~ nehmen** to bring [put] into service [into operation] *(machinery, plant etc.)*, to put on the road *(bus etc.)*, to open *(railway line etc.)*; **in ~ sein** to be in service *(bus etc.)*, to work, to be in operation *(factory etc.)*; **in ~ setzen** to set [put] into operation, to set *(s.th.)* running, to start *(machine etc.)*; **in vollem ~** in full action

~, automatisierter automated factory [plant]
~, durcharbeitender day and night shift factory
~, durchgehender all-night service
~, einzelbäuerlicher individual farm, farm run individually *(as opposed to co-operative farm)*
~, forstwirtschaftlicher forestry
~, führender leading enterprise
~, gemeinsamer joint venture [enterprise]
~, genossenschaftlicher co-operative enterprise; co-operative farm
~, gewerblicher manufacturing establishment
~, großbäuerlicher large farm
~, großer large enterprise [factory]
~, gutgehender prosperous enterprise [business]
~, halbstaatlicher semi-state enterprise, enterprise with state participation
~, handwerklicher (private) small-scale manufacturing enterprise
~, kaufmännischer commercial [business, trading] firm [enterprise, concern]
~, kleiner small enterprise [factory]
~, landwirtschaftlicher farm; market-garden
~ mit staatlicher Beteiligung *s.* **halbstaatlicher**
~, mittelgroßer medium-sized enterprise [factory]
~, mittlerer *s.* **mittelgroßer**
~, öffentlicher public enterprise
~, organisationseigener enterprise belonging to a social organization *(trade union etc.)*
~, privater private enterprise
~, produzierender manufacturing enterprise
~, rentabler profitable enterprise [business]
~, staatlicher nationally-owned enterprise
~, verlustgeplanter enterprise with planned losses
Betriebe *mpl*:
~, lebenswichtige vital industries
betrieblich internal; operational
Betriebsabrechnung *f* manufacturing costs sheet, *(Am)* operating statement
Betriebsabrechnungsbogen *m* cost distribution sheet, cost accounting statement

Betriebsabschnitt *m* section of an enterprise [a factory]
Betriebsabteilung *f* department (of an enterprise)
Betriebsanalyse *f (fin)* operational [economic] analysis
Betriebsanforderungen *fpl* operating requirements
Betriebsangehöriger *m* employee (of an enterprise)
Betriebsanlage *f* (manufacturing) plant; *(railw)* working stock
Betriebsanlagen *fpl*:
~, nicht ausgenutzte idle equipment
Betriebsanlagewerte *mpl* plant assets
Betriebsanleitung *f* operating instructions
Betriebsanteil *m* share in a business [an enterprise]; capital share, share of stock
Betriebsassistent *m* personal assistant to the manager
Betriebsaufbau *m* enterprise structure
Betriebsaufstockung *f* enlargement [extension] of a farm
Betriebsaufwand *m* operating expenditure(s) *(money and material)*
Betriebsausgaben *fpl* operating expenses *(money)*
Betriebsausnutzung *f* plant utilization
Betriebsausschuß *m* shop committee
Betriebsausstattung *f* enterprise equipment and fittings, equipment and fittings of an enterprise, plant equipment
betriebsbedingt operational
Betriebsbedingungen *fpl* operating conditions *(machines etc.)*
Betriebsbegehung *f* works inspection *(to check measures of labour safety and health service)*
Betriebsbeirat *m* advisory board [panel] *(of an enterprise etc.)*
Betriebsberater *m* business [industrial management] consultant
Betriebsbericht *m* operating report
Betriebsberufsschule *f* vocational training centre (of an enterprice)
Betriebsbeschreibung *f (agric)* farm description *(containing indices of weather, fields, manpower etc.)*
Betriebsbesichtigung *f* factory visit
Betriebsbibliothek *f* enterprise [works] library
Betriebsbilanz *f* enterprise balance sheet [operating statement]
betriebsblind routine-inclined
Betriebsbuchführung *f s.* **Betriebsbuchhaltung**
Betriebsbuchhaltung *f* 1. bookkeeping (of enterprise); 2. accounts department
Betriebsbudget *n* enterprise operating budget
Betriebsdaten *pl* operating data

Betriebsdauer *f* 1. operating [working] time; 2. service life
Betriebsdelegierter *m* factory delegate
Betriebsdienst *m* technical service
Betriebsdirektor *m* factory [works, enterprise] manager; general manager
betriebseigen enterprise-owned
Betriebseigentümer *m* factory owner
Betriebseinheit *f* enterprise [factory] unit
Betriebseinnahmen *fpl* proceeds [earnings, receipts] of an enterprise
Betriebseinrichtungen *fpl* operating equipment
Betriebseinschränkung *f* cutting down a firm's activities
Betriebseinstellung *f* closing down, shut-down; discontinuation of operations
Betriebsergebnis *n* operating result
Betriebserlös *m* enterprise proceeds [receipts]
Betriebserweiterung *f* factory extension
Betriebsessen *n* canteen meals
Betriebsetat *m s.* **Betriebsbudget**
betriebsfähig in an operational state, in (good) working condition, serviceable
Betriebsfähigkeit *f* working capacity
Betriebsferien *pl* works holidays
betriebsfertig operational, fit [ready] for use
Betriebsfinanzierung *f* enterprise financing
Betriebsfläche *f* 1. (enterprise) floor space; 2. *(agric)* farm area *(s.* **Betriebsflächenverhältnis***)*
Betriebsflächenverhältnis *n (agric)* structure of farm area *(percentage of arable area, grassland, forest etc.)*
Betriebsform *f* 1. *(agric)* type of farm *(classification of farms according to type of ownership)*; 2. type of enterprise
Betriebsführung *f* (works) management
Betriebsgaststätte *f* canteen
Betriebsgeheimnis *n* trade [business] secret
Betriebsgemeinkosten *pl* enterprise overhead costs [overheads]; *(agric)* farm overheads
Betriebsgesundheitswesen *n* enterprise health service, health service in enterprise
Betriebsgewinn *m* operating profit; enterprise profit
~, einheitlicher overall (operating) enterprise profit
Betriebsgliederung *f (ind)* factory structure, structure of organization (of an enterprise); *(com)* structure of commercial enterprises *(according to technology, organization and management)*
Betriebsgröße *f* size of an enterprise, enterprise size; plant size; *(agric)* farm size
~, optimale optimum size of an enterprise
Betriebsgrößenstruktur *f* structure of enterprises according to size

Betriebshaftpflichtversicherung *f (ins)* third-party (liability) insurance of an enterprise, employer's (liability) insurance
Betriebshandwerker *m* craftsman (in an enterprise) *(electrician, plumber etc.)*
Betriebsheim *n* enterprise hostel
Betriebshygiene *f* industrial hygiene
Betriebsingenieur *m* production engineer
Betriebsinhaber *m s.* **Betriebseigentümer**
Betriebsinteresse *n* interest of an enterprise [a firm] ⋄ **im ~** in the interest of the enterprise; **im ~ liegen** to be in the interest of the enterprise, to be in the firm's interest
Betriebsjahr *n* business year
Betriebsjahresplan *m* annual enterprise plan
Betriebskapazität *f* capacity (of an enterprise)
Betriebskapital *n* working capital
~, kurzfristiges short-term working capital
Betriebskaufmann *m* commercial employee
Betriebsklasse *f* enterprise category *(classification of enterprises according to national economic importance)*
Betriebsklima *n* working atmosphere *(in an enterprise, institution etc.)*
Betriebskosten *pl* working expenses, operating [running] costs
~, laufende current operating [running] costs
Betriebslehre *f*:
~, landwirtschaftliche agricultural economics
Betriebsleistung *f* 1. performance of an enterprise; output; 2. operating efficiency
Betriebsleiter *m* enterprise manager; factory [works] manager
Betriebsleitung *f* enterprise management; factory [works] management
Betriebsleitungskosten *pl* (enterprise) management costs
Betriebsmaterial *n* working materials; *(railw)* rolling-stock
Betriebsmatrix *f* enterprise matrix
~, optimale optimal enterprise matrix
Betriebsmeß-, Steuerungs- und Regelungstechnik *f* precision measuring, testing and control equipment
Betriebsmethode *f* method of enterprise classification *(for national accounting by aggregating total production of all enterprises as opposed to finished products method)*
Betriebsmittel *npl* supplementary instruments of production
Betriebsmittelnormativ *n* standard [norm] of supplementary instruments of production
Betriebsmittelwirtschaft *f* 1. economy of supplementary instruments of production *(planning, designing, manufacturing and maintenance of devices, tools, gauges etc.)*; 2. department of supplementary instruments of production

Betriebsmodell *n (agric)* farm model
Betriebsobmann *m* head of works committee
Betriebsökonom *m* enterprise economist
Betriebsordnung *f* factory [plant] regulations
Betriebsorganisation *f* enterprise [industrial] organization
Betriebspaß *m* enterprise manual *(information on range of production, machinery used etc.)*
Betriebspension *f* company-financed pension
Betriebspensionsplan *m* company-financed pension scheme
Betriebspersonal *n* 1. employees, staff *(of an enterprise)*; 2. operators *(of a machine)*
Betriebsplan *m* enterprise plan, (economic) plan of an enterprise
Betriebsplanoptimierung *f* optimization of enterprise plans
Betriebsplanung *f* enterprise planning
~, **komplexe** comprehensive enterprise planning
~, **operative** current enterprise planning
Betriebspolitik *f* management policy; company labour policy
Betriebspraktikum *n* practical training (at an enterprise)
Betriebspreis *m* factory price
Betriebsprognose *f* enterprise long-term forecast
Betriebsprogramm *n* manufacturing programme
Betriebsprüfer *m* auditor
Betriebsprüfung *f* auditing
~, **steuerliche** auditing of enterprise by tax authorities
Betriebsprüfungsbericht *m* auditor's report on an enterprise
Betriebspsychologie *f* industrial psychology
Betriebsrat *m* works council [committee]
Betriebsrechenstation *f* enterprise computer centre
Betriebsreingewinn *m* net enterprise profit
Betriebsrevision *f s.* **Betriebsprüfung**
Betriebsrevisor *m s.* **Betriebsprüfer**
Betriebsschließung *f* shutdown, closing down (of an enterprise)
~, **saisonbedingte** seasonal shutdown
Betriebsschule *f* training centre (of an enterprise), factory [works] school *(for further education and training of adults)*
Betriebsschutz *m* enterprise [factory] guard(s)
betriebssicher safe (to operate), reliable (in operation), dependable in service
Betriebssicherheit *f* safety (in operation), reliability (in service/operation)
Betriebssoziologie *f* industrial sociology
Betriebssportgemeinschaft *f* sports [athletic] club of an enterprise
Betriebsstandort *m* location [site] (of an enterprise)
Betriebsstatistik *f* enterprise statistics

Betriebsstätte *f* premises *(business etc.)*; manufacturing unit *(industrial enterprise)*
Betriebsstillegung *f s.* **Betriebsschließung**
Betriebsstipendium *n* enterprise scholarship, scholarship granted by an enterprise
Betriebsstockung *f* interruption of work
Betriebsstörung *f* interruption of work *(factory etc.)*; dislocation *(train service etc.)*; breakdown *(machine, railway etc.)*
Betriebsstruktur *f* enterprise structure; *(agric)* farm layout
Betriebsstunden *fpl* operating hours *(machines etc.)*
Betriebssystem *n* 1. *(agric)* classification of farms; 2. *(d.pr.)* system of data processing
~, **landwirtschaftliches** classification of farms *(according to structure of production)*
Betriebssystematik *f* enterprise classification *(according to economic sectors, branches etc. for planning, accounting and statistical purposes)*
Betriebsteil *m* unit of an enterprise [a factory, works]
Betriebstransport *m* intra-works transport
Betriebstyp *m* type of enterprise
betriebstypisch typical of an enterprise
Betriebsumstellung *f* reorganization, changeover *(of an enterprise product line, production line etc.)*
Betriebsunfall *m* industrial accident, accident at work
Betriebsunfallversicherung *f* industrial accident insurance
Betriebsunkosten *pl* operating [working] expenses, running costs; maintenance costs
Betriebsuntersuchung *f* (economic) analysis of an enterprise
Betriebsvereinbarung *f* works [shop, company] agreement *(negotiated by the employer and the works council concerning working conditions)*
Betriebsverfassungsgesetz *n* industrial relations code
Betriebsverflechtungsbilanz *f* factory [works] input-output table
Betriebsverflechtungsmodell *n* input-output model of an enterprise
Betriebsvergleich *m* comparison of enterprises *(to use experiences and increase efficiency)*
Betriebsverhältnisse *npl* shopfloor [factory] working conditions; enterprise working conditions
Betriebsverkaufsstelle *f* retail shop (in an enterprise)
Betriebsverlagerung *f* change of location of an enterprise
Betriebsvermögen *n* enterprise property [assets]
Betriebsversammlung *f* workshop [works, workers and staff] meeting

Betriebswechsel *m* change of job [employment]
Betriebswirtschaft *f* business administration, industrial management
betriebswirtschaftlich operational; with regard to economic efficiency *(of an undertaking, industrial unit etc.)*; of business management, of practical economics; effecting operational efficiency *(factory etc.)*
Betriebswirtschaftslehre *f* science of industrial management; economic management theory
Betriebszeit *f* working hours *(enterprises, offices etc.)*; operating time *(machines)*
Betriebszustand *m* operating [working] conditions; state of machines [workshop]
Betriebszweig *m (ind)* branch of manufacturing [industry]; *(agric)* line [branch] of farm production
Betrug *m* fraud ⋄ **sich eines Betruges schuldig machen** to commit a fraudulent act
Beurkundung *f* attestation, authentication, certification *(statement, contract etc.)*
~, **notarielle** authentication by a solicitor [notary public]
beurlauben to give [grant] leave *(of absence)*; to suspend *(from office)*
Beurlaubung *f* suspension *(from office)*
Bevölkerung *f* population
~, **arbeitende** working [employed] population
~, **berufstätige** economically active [employed] population
~, **ländliche** rural population
~, **mittlere** average population
~, **nichtarbeitende** non-working [non-employed] population
~, **nichtbäuerliche** non-rural [*(Am)* non-farm] population
~, **nichtberufstätige** economically inactive population
~, **ortsansässige** residents
~, **stationäre** stationary population
Bevölkerungsabnahme *f* decrease in population
Bevölkerungsagglomeration *f* agglomeration of population
Bevölkerungsaufbau *m s.* **Bevölkerungsstruktur**
Bevölkerungsballung *f s.* **Bevölkerungsagglomeration**
Bevölkerungsbedarf *m* consumer demand *(for goods, services etc., of the general public)*
Bevölkerungsbewegung *f* population movement *(1. changes in the number and structure of the population; 2. migration)*
Bevölkerungsbilanz *f* population balance sheet *(of births, deaths, emigration, immigration according to sex and age)*
Bevölkerungsdichte *f* density of population
Bevölkerungsdruck *m* population pressure

Bevölkerungseinnahmen *fpl* total private income, income of the population
Bevölkerungsentwicklung *f* population development *(s.* **Bevölkerungsbewegung**)
~, **territorial differenzierte** population development according to regions
Bevölkerungsexplosion *f* population explosion
Bevölkerungsgesetz *n* population law
Bevölkerungsgruppe *f* population group [category]
Bevölkerungskonzentration *f* concentration of population
Bevölkerungskreise *mpl* groups [strata] of population
Bevölkerungspolitik *f* population policy
Bevölkerungsprobleme *npl* population problems
Bevölkerungsprognose *f* population forecast
Bevölkerungspyramide *f* population [age] pyramid
Bevölkerungsreproduktion *f* reproduction of population
~, **einfache** simple reproduction of population
~, **erweiterte** extended [expanded, enlarged] reproduction of population
~, **natürliche** natural [normal] reproduction of population
~, **regressive** regressive reproduction of population
Bevölkerungsschicht *f* social stratum
Bevölkerungsstand *m* population size *(at any given moment in a definite area)*
Bevölkerungsstatistik *f* population statistics
Bevölkerungsstruktur *f* population structure; structure of population
~, **demographische** (demographic) population structure *(according to age, sex etc.)*
Bevölkerungstheorie *f* population theory
Bevölkerungsüberschuß *m* population surplus, surplus of population
Bevölkerungsverbrauch *m* (general public) consumption *(of goods, services etc.)*
Bevölkerungsverteilung *f* distribution of population
~, **räumliche** regional distribution [location] of population
Bevölkerungsvorausberechnung *f* population forecast [projection]
Bevölkerungszunahme *f* increase in population
Bevölkerungszuwachs *m s.* **Bevölkerungszunahme**
bevollmächtigen to authorize, to empower
bevollmächtigt authorized, having power (of attorney)
Bevollmächtigter *m* authorized representative [agent]; attorney; plenipotentiary *(diplomat)*
bevorraten to stock up, to pile up reserves
Bevorratung *f* stockpiling

bevorrechtigen to grant a privilege *(to s.o.)*; *(com)* to give s.o. a prior claim
bevorrechtigt preferential, preferred; privileged
Bevorrechtigung *f* preference; privilege
bevorschussen to advance (money) *(to s.o. on s.th.)*
Bevorschussung *f* advance
Bevorzugungsbereich *m (stats)* zone of preference
bewässern to irrigate
Bewässerung *f* irrigation
~, **künstliche** artificial irrigation
~, **natürliche** natural irrigation
Bewässerungsanlage *f* irrigation works [plant]
Bewässerungslandwirtschaft *f* irrigation farming
Bewässerungssystem *n* irrigation system
Bewegung *f* movement; trend, tendency
~, **rückläufige** retrograde trend
Bewegungsgesetz *n* law of development
~, **inneres** law [principle] of endogenous development *(of a society)*
Beweis *m* 1. proof, evidence *(for s.th.)*; 2. token, sign, mark; 3. *(jur)* proof; (piece of) evidence; testimony, (testimonial) evidence; 4. (action of) proving, substantiation *(statement, claim etc.)*; 5. demonstration *(fact, theorem etc.)* ⋄ **als ~** as proof; **den ~ antreten** to offer proof; **den ~ erbringen** to prove; **den ~ führen** to prove one's argument; **durch ~ widerlegen** to rebut the argument; **einen ~ führen** to furnish (a) proof; *(jur)* to produce evidence; **etwas unter ~ stellen** to provide proof of s.th.; **mangels Beweises** for lack of evidence
~, **direkter** direct evidence
~, **dokumentarischer** proof by documentary evidence
~, **eindeutiger** conclusive proof
~, **einwandfreier** absolute proof, clear evidence
~, **formeller** formal proof
~, **indirekter** indirect evidence
~, **sachlicher** material evidence
~, **schriftlicher** written evidence, evidence in writing
~, **sicherer** positive proof
~, **urkundlicher** documentary evidence
~, **zulässiger** admissible evidence
Beweisantrag *m* motion to receive evidence
Beweisauflage *f (jur)* (judicial) injunction to produce proof [evidence]
Beweisaufnahme *f (jur)* taking [hearing] of evidence
beweisbar provable, demonstrable ⋄ **nicht ~** not provable
beweisen to prove, to substantiate *(statement, claim etc.)*; to demonstrate, to establish truth *(proposition etc.)*

Beweisführung *f* (line of) argument, argumentation; *(jur)* presentation [marshalling] of (the) evidence, presentation of one's case; *(maths)* proof
Beweislast *f (jur)* burden [onus] of proof
Beweismaterial *n (jur)* probative evidence
Beweismittel *n (jur)* (piece of) evidence, supporting evidence, proof
Beweisrecht *n (jur)* law of evidence
Beweisstück *n (jur)* (piece of) evidence, document in proof; exhibit
bewerben to apply for *(job etc.)*; to bid [tender] for *(contract)*; to canvass for *(orders, votes etc.)*; to stand [run] for *(candidacy)*
Bewerber *m* applicant; bidder, competitor *(tenders)*; candidate
Bewerbung *f* application *(job etc.)*; bidding, tender *(contract)*; canvassing *(order, votes etc.)*; standing [running] for *(candidacy)*
Bewerbungsschreiben *n* (letter of) application
bewerten to evaluate, to value, to assess, to estimate *(property etc.)*; to appraise *(achievement etc.)*; to rate *(taxes etc.)*
Bewertung *f* evaluation, valuation, assessment, estimate *(property etc.)*; appraisal *(achievement etc.)*; rating *(taxes etc.)*
~ **der Grundmittel** evaluation of fixed assets [capital]
~ **der Umlaufmittel** evaluation of working capital
~, **geldmäßige** evaluation in terms of money
~, **leistungsgerechte** evaluation according to performance
~, **objektiv bedingte** objectively determined evaluation
~, **optimale** optimum evaluation [rating]
Bewertungscharakteristika *npl* features [criteria] of evaluation
~, **funktionale** functional features [criteria] of evaluation
Bewertungskontinuität *f (acc)* continuity of balancing *(using the same structure of balance sheets and principles of evaluation over a long period)*
Bewertungsmethode *f* evaluation method, method of evaluation
Bewertungspreis *m* present money value *(expressed in current price)*
Bewertungsprinzip *n* evaluation principle
Bewertungsvorschriften *fpl* evaluation rules
bewilligen to grant *(s.o. s.th., s.th. to s.o.)*; to allocate, to allot *(financial and physical means)*; to permit; to consent to
Bewilligung *f* grant; allocation, allotment *(financial and physical resources)*; permission; concession
Bewilligungsverfahren *n* authorizing procedure

bewirtschaften 1. to ration *(food etc.)*; to control *(foreign exchange etc.)*; to register, to control *(rooms, flats to let etc.)*; 2. to farm *(land)*; to cultivate *(field)*; to manage *(farm)*; to run *(restaurant, hotel etc.)*
bewirtschaftet 1. rationed *(food etc.)*; controlled *(foreign exchange, distribution of goods etc.)*; 2. farmed *(land)*; cultivated *(field)*; managed *(farm)* ◊ **nicht ~** 1. non-rationed *(food)*; non--registered *(rooms or flats which can be let without permission of the housing authorities)*; 2. unfarmed *(land)*; uncultivated *(field)*
Bewirtschaftung *f* 1. rationing *(food etc.)*; control *(foreign exchange etc.)*; registration, control *(rooms, flats to let etc.)*; 2. farming *(land)*; cultivation *(field)*; management *(farm)*; running *(restaurant, hotel etc.)*
bezahlen to pay, to cash; to discharge, to repay *(debt)*, to honour *(bill, cheque etc.)* ◊ **bar ~** to pay cash down; to pay in cash; **im voraus ~** to pay in advance, to prepay; **in Raten ~** to pay by [in] instalments
Bezahlung *f* pay, payment; discharge, settlement, liquidation *(debt)*, honouring *(cheque, bill)* ◊ **gegen ~ von** on payment of
beziehbar ready for occupancy *(houses, flats etc.)*; *(com)* obtainable *(goods)*
beziehen to move into *(house)*, to occupy; *(com)* to obtain, to procure, to get, to buy *(goods)*; to draw *(salary etc.)*; **sich ~ auf** to refer to
Bezieher *m* purchaser *(goods, services etc.)*, subscriber *(newspaper etc.)*; *(fin)* buyer *(shares etc.)*
Beziehung *f* relation; reference ◊ **in ~ auf** with reference to; **in wirtschaftlicher ~** with reference to the economy, economically
Beziehungen *fpl*:
~, arbeitsteilige relations according to division of labour
~, diplomatische diplomatic relations
~, inoffizielle unofficial relations *(in diplomacy etc.)*
~, internationale international relations
~, internationale ökonomische international economic relations
~, offizielle official relations *(in diplomacy etc.)*
~, persönliche personal relations
~, zwischenmenschliche human relations
Bezirk *m* 1. district, region; administrative region; county; 2. field, scope, domain, sphere
~, ökonomischer economic region *(in regional planning an economic region as a rule does not coincide with an administrative region of the country)*
Bezirksdirektion *f* regional office
Bezirksdirektor *m* regional director
Bezirksgericht *n* county court, regional superior court

Bezirkshaushalt *m* county budget *(part of the state/central budget)*
Bezirksrat *m* 1. county councillor; 2. county council
Bezirksstraße *f* county road *(under the supervision of the respective county authority)*
Bezirkstag *m* county assembly
Bezirksverband *m* county association
Bezirksvorstand *m* county committee
Bezogener *m (com)* drawee
Bezug *m* 1. buying, purchase; supplies *(goods, services etc.)*; 2. income; 3. subscription *(newspaper etc.)*; 4. reference ◊ **auf etwas ~ nehmen** to refer to, to relate to, to have reference to; **in bezug auf** with regard [reference, respect] to
bezüglich relating, referring, relative, relevant; concerning, about, regarding, respecting, with respect [regard] to, as to
Bezugnahme *f* reference, referring ◊ **unter ~ auf** with reference to, referring to
Bezugsaktien *fpl* shares [*(Am)* stocks] of a new issue
Bezugsanweisung *f* order to deliver goods
Bezugsbasis *f* reference level; reference period; reference date
Bezugsbedingungen *fpl* terms of purchase [delivery, supply]
bezugsberechtigt entitled to draw *(a pension etc.)*; entitled to receive
Bezugsberechtigter *m* beneficiary
Bezugsdatum *n* reference date
Bezugsdauer *f* subscription period *(newspaper, journals etc.)*; duration of supply *(by enterprise etc.)*
Bezugsebene *f s.* **Bezugsbasis**
Bezugseinheit *f* reference unit
bezugsfertig ready to move into, ready for occupation *(houses, flats etc.)*
Bezugsgenossenschaft *f* co-operative purchasing association
~, landwirtschaftliche agricultural purchasing co-operative
Bezugsgröße *f* base
Bezugsgrundlage *f s.* **Bezugsbasis**
Bezugsjahr *n* base [basis] year
Bezugskosten *pl* delivery costs; procurement costs
Bezugsland *n* country of delivery
Bezugslinie *f (stats)* reference [datum] line
Bezugsmenge *f* quantity delivered
Bezugsperiode *f* duration of supply *(of goods etc. by enterprise etc.)*
Bezugsprämie *f (ins)* call premium
Bezugspreis *m* purchase price; subscription price *(periodicals etc.)*
Bezugspunkt *m (stats)* point of reference
Bezugsquelle *f* source of supply

Bezugsrecht *n* subscription right *(shares etc.)*, *(Am)* stock purchase warrant; *(fin)* application right; right of option
Bezugsschein *m* delivery order, materials requisition note [slip]; purchasing permit, coupon; subscription warrant *(shares etc.)*
Bezugs- und Absatzgenossenschaft *f* co-operative purchasing and sales association
Bezugs- und Liefergenossenschaft *f* **des Handwerks** co-operative purchasing and supply association of craft trades
Bezugs- und Lieferplan *m* purchasing and supply plan
Bezugsvereinigung *f* purchasing association
Bezugswert *m* relative [reference] value
Bezugswünsche *mpl* wants (of customers)
Bezugszahl *f* reference number
Bezugszeitraum *m* reference period
Bilanz *f* balance *(of accounts; between supply and demand etc.)*; balance sheet; statement of assets and liabilities [*(Am)* conditions] ⋄ **die ~ ausgleichen** to equalize the balance (sheet); to balance the account; **die ~ auswerten** to analyse the balance sheet; **die ~ frisieren** to cook the balance sheet; **die ~ verschleiern** *s.* **die ~ frisieren; die ~ ziehen** to strike the balance; **eine ~ anfertigen** *s.* **eine ~ aufstellen; eine ~ aufstellen** to prepare a balance sheet; **in der ~ ausweisen** to state [show] in the balance sheet
~, **abgeleitete** derived balance sheet
~, **aktive** credit balance
~ **der Anlagefonds** balance sheet of fixed assets
~ **der Arbeitskräfte** labour force [manpower] balance (sheet)
~ **der Aufwendungen und der Produktion** balance sheet of expenditure [costs] and production
~ **der Bodenschätze** balance sheet of mineral resources
~ **der Einnahmen und Ausgaben** income [revenue] and expenditure account [balance sheet]
~ **der Entstehung und Verwendung des gesellschaftlichen Gesamtprodukts** balance sheet of the formation and utilization of the gross social product
~ **der Entstehung und Verwendung des Realeinkommens** balance sheet of the formation and utilization of real income
~ **der Geldeinnahmen und -ausgaben der Bereiche und Zweige der Wirtschaft** balance (sheet) of money flows [income and expenditure] in economic sectors
~ **der Geldeinnahmen und -ausgaben der Bevölkerung** money income and expenditure balance sheet of the population
~ **der Grundfonds** *s.* **der Anlagefonds**
~ **der internationalen Verbindlichkeiten und Forderungen** balance sheet of international liabilities and outstanding debts
~ **der Konsumgüter** balance sheet of consumer goods
~ **der landwirtschaftlichen Produkte** balance sheet of agricultural products
~ **der natürlichen Ressourcen** balance sheet of natural resources
~ **der Produktion, Konsumtion und Akkumulation des gesellschaftlichen Gesamtprodukts** *s.* ~ **der Entstehung und Verwendung des gesellschaftlichen Gesamtprodukts**
~ **der Produktionskapazitäten** balance sheet of production capacities
~ **der Produktionsmittel** balance sheet of the means of production
~ **des Arbeitskräftepotentials** balance sheet of potential manpower resources, manpower balance sheet
~ **des Außenhandels** foreign trade balance (sheet)
~ **des gesellschaftlichen Gesamtprodukts** gross social product balance (sheet)
~ **des Marktaufkommens der Landwirtschaft** balance sheet of agricultural market production
~ **des Nationaleinkommens** balance (sheet) of the national income
~ **des Nationalreichtums** balance (sheet) of the national wealth
~ **des Staatshaushalts** state budget balance sheet
~ **des Volkseinkommens** *s.* ~ **des Nationaleinkommens**
~, **doppelte** duplicated balance sheet
~, **endgültige** final balance sheet
~, **genehmigte** approved balance (sheet)
~, **konsolidierte** consolidated balance sheet
~, **passive** debit balance
~, **provisorische** provisional balance sheet
~, **rohe** rough [draft] balance sheet
~, **schachbrettförmige** chess-board balance sheet
~, **unausgeglichene** unbalanced balance sheet
~, **vereinfachte** simplified balance sheet
~, **verschleierte** faked [cooked] balance sheet, tampered account
~, **vorläufige** preliminary balance sheet
~, **zusammengefaßte** aggregated balance sheet
Bilanzabschluß *m* closing of the balance sheet
Bilanzabschnitt *m* section of a balance sheet
Bilanzanalyse *f* analytical study of balance sheet
Bilanzänderung *f* making an alteration in the balance sheet

Bilanzarten *fpl* kinds of balance sheets
Bilanzaufbau *m* structure of the balance sheet
Bilanzaufbereitung *f s.* **Bilanzauswertung**
Bilanzaufstellung *f* preparation of the balance sheet
Bilanzauswertung *f* evaluation of balance sheets
Bilanzauszug *m* abstract of balance sheet
Bilanzberechnungen *fpl* accounting of balance sheets
Bilanzbereich *m* balancing organ [unit]
Bilanzberichtigung *f* correction in a balance sheet
Bilanzbestätigung *f* approval of a balance sheet
Bilanzbewertung *f s.* **Bilanzauswertung**
Bilanzbuch *n* ledger, *(Am)* statement book
Bilanzbuchhaltung *f* balance sheet department
Bilanzen *fpl*:
~, **buchhalterische** balance sheets of accounting
~ **der Berichtsperiode** balance sheets of the period under review
~ **der Geldbeziehungen und der Geldfonds** balance sheets of money flows and funds
~ **des Außenhandels** foreign trade balance sheets
~, **materielle** balance sheets in physical terms
~, **monatlich aufzustellende** monthly balance sheets
~, **statische** static balance sheets
~, **territoriale** regional balances [balance sheets]
~, **volkswirtschaftliche** national economic balance sheets
~, **wertmäßige** balance sheets in value terms
Bilanzentscheidungen *fpl* decisions on balance *(on the allocation of resources in making balance sheets)*
Bilanzergebnis *n* balance
Bilanzfaktor *m* item of a balance sheet
Bilanzfrisur *f s.* **Bilanzverschleierung**
Bilanzfunktion *f* function of balancing
Bilanzgenehmigung *f s.* **Bilanzbestätigung**
Bilanzgleichung *f* balance equation
Bilanzgliederung *f s.* **Bilanzaufbau**
Bilanzgruppe *f* group of balance sheets
bilanzieren to make out [draw up] a balance sheet; to balance *(supply and demand, sources and uses)*
Bilanzierung *f* balancing, making out [drawing up] a balance sheet
~ **der Erzeugnisse** balancing of products
~ **der Konsumgüter** balancing of consumer goods
~, **grobe** drawing up [making] a rough balance sheet
~, **materielle** physical balancing, making out [drawing up] balance sheets in physical terms
~, **territoriale** regional balancing

Bilanzierungsebene *f* level of balancing
Bilanzierungsfunktion *f* balancing function
Bilanzierungsgrundsätze *mpl s.* **Bilanzierungsprinzipien**
Bilanzierungsmethode *f* balancing method, method of making out balance sheets
Bilanzierungsperiode *f* balancing period
Bilanzierungsprinzipien *npl* principles of balancing, balancing principles
Bilanzierungsvorschriften *fpl* accounting rules *(for making balance sheets)*
Bilanzinformation *f* balancing information; balance sheet data
Bilanzjahr *n* financial year
Bilanzkomponente *f s.* **Bilanzposten**
Bilanzkontinuität *f* continuity of balance sheets
Bilanzkonto *n* balance sheet account
Bilanzkontrolle *f* follow-up [checking] of balances
Bilanzkurs *m s.* **Bilanzwert**
Bilanzmethode *f* method of using balance sheets
Bilanzmodell *n* model balance sheet
Bilanznomenklatur *f* classification of items subjects to balancing
Bilanzordnung *f* instructions [rules] for drawing up balances *(of raw materials, manufactured goods etc.)*
Bilanzorgan *n* balancing organ
Bilanzperiode *f s.* **Bilanzierungsperiode**
Bilanzposition *f s.* **Bilanzposten**
Bilanzposten *m* balance sheet item
Bilanzprüfer *m* auditor
Bilanzprüfung *f* auditing of balance sheets
Bilanzpyramide *f* (pyramid) system of balances [balance sheets]
Bilanzquadrant *m* quadrant of the input-output table
Bilanzreserve *f* unspecified item of a balance sheet *(part of the uses side of a balance sheet whose final use or allocation is decided during the plan period)*
Bilanzrevision *f s.* **Bilanzprüfung**
Bilanzsaldo *m* balance
Bilanzstichtag *m* fixed date for balance sheet items
Bilanzstruktur *f s.* **Bilanzaufbau**
Bilanzsumme *f* (total) sum of the balance
Bilanzsystem *n* system of balances [of balance sheets]
~, **territoriales** regional network of balances [balance sheets]
Bilanzverantwortung *f* responsibility in drawing up [making] balance sheets
Bilanzvereinheitlichung *f* standardization of balance sheets
Bilanzvergleich *m* comparison of balance sheets

Bilanzverordnung *f* rules [instructions] for making balance sheets
Bilanzverschleierung *f* dressing up [cooking of] the balance sheet; window dressing
Bilanzverzeichnis *n* list of balancing organs
Bilanzwert *m* balance sheet value
Bilanzzahl *f s.* Bilanzposten
Bilanzziffer *f s.* Bilanzposten
bilateral bilateral
bilden 1. to educate and train (systematically); 2. to form *(national income etc.)*; to create *(funds etc.)*; to found, to constitute *(association, committee etc.)*; **sich ~** to acquire knowledge and ability
Bildung *f* 1.(systematic) education and training; knowledge and ability; 2. formation *(national income etc.)*; creation *(funds etc.)*; foundation, constitution *(association, committee etc.)*
~, polytechnische polytechnical education and training
~, postgraduale postgraduate education
Bildungsanstalt *f s.* Bildungseinrichtung
Bildungsarbeit *f* educational work
Bildungsaufwand *m* expenditure for education and training
Bildungsausgaben *fpl* (monetary) expenditures on education and training
Bildungsbedürfnis *n* need for education and training
Bildungseffektivität *f* efficiency of education and training
Bildungseinrichtung *f* educational establishment [institution]
Bildungsfernsehen *n* educational television
Bildungsfonds *m* education budget
Bildungsforschung *f* research on education and training
Bildungsgang *m* (course of) education and training
Bildungsgrad *m s.* Bildungsniveau
Bildungsinvestition *f* educational investment, investment in education and training
Bildungskosten *pl* education and training costs, costs of training and education
Bildungsmonopol *n* monopoly of learning [education and training]
Bildungsniveau *n* level [standard] of education, educational level
Bildungsnotstand *m* worsening conditions in education and training
Bildungsökonomie *f* economics of education
Bildungsplanung *f* educational planning, planning of education and training
Bildungspolitik *f* education policy
Bildungsprivileg *n* educational privileges
Bildungsstand *m s.* Bildungsniveau
Bildungsstatistik *f* educational statistics
Bildungsstufe *f s.* Bildungsniveau
Bildungssystem *n* system of education and training, education service
~, einheitliches integrated system of education and training
Bildungswesen *n s.* Bildungssystem
billig cheap, inexpensive, low-priced
Billiglohnland *n* country with low [cheap] wages, low-wage country
Bimetallismus *m* bimetallism
binär *(d.pr.)* binary
Binär-Dezimal-Umsetzer *m* binary-to-decimal converter
Binär-Dezimal-Umwandlung *f (d.pr.)* binary-to-decimal conversion
Binär-Kode *m (d.pr)* binary code
~ für Dezimalziffern *(d.pr.)* binary-coded decimal code
Binäroperation *f (d.pr.)* binary operation
Binärspeicherstelle *f (d.pr.)* binary cell
Binärübertragung *f (d.pr.)* binary transfer
Binärzähler *m (d.pr.)* binary counter
Binärziffer *f (d.pr.)* binary digit, bit
binden to bind; to tie up *(money, capital etc.)*; to fix *(prices etc.)*; to compel, to oblige ◇ **sich an etwas ~** to bind o.s. [pledge one's word, commit o.s.] to s.th.
bindend binding *(agreement etc.)*
Bindung *f* binding; tying up *(money, capital etc.)*; fixing *(prices etc.)*; commitment, obligation
Bindungsklausel *f* price-maintenance clause
Binnenblock-Untergruppe *f (stats)* intrablock sub-group
Binnenfahrgastschiffahrt *f* passenger inland navigation
Binnenfischerei *f* freshwater fishing
Binnenfischereibetrieb *m* freshwater fishing enterprise
Binnenflotte *f* inland fleet
Binnenfrachtschiffahrt *f* waterway cargo transport
Binnengeld *n s.* Binnenwährung
Binnengewässer *n* inland water
Binnengroßhandel *m* domestic wholesale trade
Binnengroßhandelspreis *m* domestic wholesale price
Binnengruppenvarianz *f (stats)* within-group variance
Binnenhafen *m* inland harbour [port]
Binnenhafenordnung *f* inland harbour regulations
Binnenhandel *m* home [domestic] trade
Binnenhandelsmesse *f* domestic [home] trade fair
Binnenhandelsökonomik *f* economics of home [domestic] trade, home [domestic] trade economics

Binnenhandelspreisniveau *n* level of home trade prices
Binnenhandelsstatistik *f* statistics of home trade
Binnenklassenkorrelation *f (stats)* intra-class correlation
Binnenklassenvarianz *f (stats)* intra-class variance
Binnenkonnossement *n* inland [internal] bill of lading
Binnenkonsum *m* home [domestic, inland] consumption
Binnenland *n* inland; interior *(of a country)*
Binnenlotse *m* river pilot
Binnenmarkt *m* home [domestic] market
Binnenmarktforschung *f* domestic market research
Binnenmarktpreis *m* domestic price
Binnenpersonentransport *m* inland [domestic] passenger transport
Binnenschiff *n* river [canal] vessel; barge
Binnenschiffahrt *f* inland navigation
Binnenschiffsregister *n* river boat register
Binnenschiffstransport *m* river boat transport(ation); barge transport(ation)
Binnenschiffsverkehr *m* river boat traffic
Binnenschiffsversicherung *f* river [canal] vessel insurance, *(Am)* river boat insurance; barge insurance
Binnenschläge *mpl (agric)* fields nearest to the farmhouse
Binnentarif *m (transp)* domestic [inland] tariff; *(cust)* internal tariff
Binnentransportversicherung *f* inland transport insurance
Binnenverkehr *m* inland traffic [transport]
Binnenwährung *f* internal [unconvertible] currency
Binnenwanderung *f* domestic migration
Binnenwasserstraße *f* inland waterway
Binnenwasserstraßenverkehr *m* inland waterway traffic
Binnenwirtschaft *f* domestic economy *(system of material production, distribution, exchange and consumption of goods and services produced within a country)*
Binnenzoll *m* inland duty; internal tariff *(on goods traded in a customs union)*
Binomialstreuung *f s.* **Binomialverteilung**
Binomialverteilung *f (stats)* binomial distribution, point binomial
Bit *n (d.pr.)* bit *(binary digit)*
Black-box-Methode *f* black-box method
blanko blank, not filled in *(form etc.)*; *(com)* uncovered, unsecured
Blankoabgabe *f (st.ex.)* bearish operation
Blankoakzept *n* blank acceptance

Blank(o)formular *n* blank form, *(Am)* blank
Blankogiro *n s.* **Blankoindossament**
Blankoindossament *n* blank transfer, assignment [endorsement] in blank
Blankokauf *m* blank purchase
Blankokredit *m* blank [open] credit
Blankopapiere *npl* blank papers
Blankopolice *f* blank insurance policy
Blankoscheck *m* blank cheque
Blankounterschrift *f* blank signature
Blankoverkauf *m s.* **Blankoabgabe**
Blankovollmacht *f* unlimited power(s), full discretionary power, carte blanche
Blankowechsel *m* blank bill (of exchange)
Blindenanstalt *f* home for the blind
Blindenbetreuung *f* care of the blind
Blindenfürsorge *f s.* **Blindenbetreuung**
Blindenpflegegeld *n* nursing allowance (for the care of a blind person)
Block *m* 1. *(d.pr., plan, stats etc.)* block; 2. *(pol)* bloc, coalition; 3. block *(flats)*
~, **ausgewogener unvollständiger** *(stats)* balanced incomplete block
Blockade *f* blockade ◇ **eine ~ aufheben** to lift a blockade; **eine ~ durchbrechen** to run a blockade; **eine ~ verhängen** to impose a blockade
Blockadebrecher *m* blockade-runner
Blockdiagramm *n* block diagram
Blöcke *mpl* blocks
~, **gekoppelte** *(stats)* linked blocks
~, **im Dreieckssystem verkettete** *(stats)* triangular linked blocks
~ **mit zufälliger Zuteilung** *(stats)* randomised blocks
blockfrei non-aligned *(countries)*
blockieren to block *(accounts etc.)*
Blockierung *f* blocking *(accounts etc.)*
Block-Kartei *f* block index cards
Blockmatrix *f (maths)* block matrix
Blockmethode *f (d.pr.)* block method
Blockoptimierung *f* block optimization, optimization en bloc
Blockpolice *f (ins)* block premium
Blockprogrammierung *f (d.pr.)* block programming
Blockschema *n* block diagram
Blockversicherungsschein *m s.* **Blockpolice**
BMSR-Technik *f s.* **Betriebsmeß-, Steuerungs- und Regelungstechnik**
Boden *m* land, ground; *(agric)* soil, earth
Bodenabschätzung *f s.* **Bodenbewertung**
Bodenanalyse *f* soil analysis
Bodenanteil *m (agric)* 1. land brought (into) *(the co-operative farm when joining it)*; 2. income share according to land brought (into) *(the co-operative farm)*

Bodenart *f* type of soil
Bodenaufschwemmung *f* soil suspension
Bodenbearbeitung *f* tillage, tilling of the soil, cultivation of the land
Bodenbeschaffenheit *f* nature of the ground; *(agric)* condition [state] of the soil [ground]
Bodenbesitz *m* land ownership
Bodenbesitzer *m* landowner
Bodenbesitzung *f s.* **Bodenbesitz**
Bodenbestandteile *mpl* components of the soil
Bodenbewertung *f* evaluation of soil
Bodenbewirtschaftung *f* cultivation of the land, land cultivation
Bodenbonität *f* grade of fertility of soil
Bodenbuch *n* land registry *(of the agricultural co-operatives for registration of all areas cultivated by the co-operative according to property relations, kind of use, quantity and quality of the soil cultivated; basis for calculation of the* **Bodenanteil** *2.)*
Bodendecke *f* ground cover
~, **lebende** herbaceous soil covering
Bodeneigentümer *m s.* **Bodenbesitzer**
Bodeneinfluß *m* edaphic influence
Bodeneinkommen *n s.* **Bodenanteil** 2.
Bodenentseuchung *f* disinfection of the soil
Bodenentwässerung *f* land drainage, draining of the soil
Bodenerhitzung *f* heating of the soil
Bodenerosion *f* soil erosion
Bodenerschöpfung *f* exhaustion of soil
Bodenertrag *m* produce [yield] of a piece of land
~, **abnehmender** diminishing yield (of a piece of land)
Bodenertragsgesetz *n (agric)* law of diminishing returns
Bodenfauna *f* bottom fauna
Bodenfluß *m* soil movement
Bodenfonds *m* land resources
~ **einer landwirtschaftlichen Produktionsgenossenschaft** land resources of a co-operative farm
~, **staatlicher** state-owned land resources
Bodenfondsabgabe *f (agric)* levy on fertility of soil
Bodenfruchtbarkeit *f* fertility of soil
Bodengare *f* bacteriological ripeness of the soil
Bodengewinn *m* reclaimed land
Bodengewinnung *f* reclamation of land
Bodengrenze *f* edaphic limit
Bodengüte *f* quality of soil
Bodenimpfstoff *m* soil inoculant
Bodenimpfung *f* inoculation of the soil
Bodenkataster *m/n* land registry
Bodenklassifikation *f* classification of soil
Bodenklima *n* soil climate

Bodenkonzentration *f* land concentration, concentration of land
Bodenkraft *f* fertility
Bodenkredit *m* loan on landed property
Bodenkreditanstalt *f s.* **Bodenkreditbank**
Bodenkreditbank *f* land-mortgage bank
Bodenkreditinstitut *n s.* **Bodenkreditbank**
Bodenkreditpfandbrief *m* mortgage-deed; *(st.ex.)* mortgage debenture [*(Am)* bond]
Bodenkrume *f* surface soil
Bodenkunde *f* soil science
Bodenlockerung *f* loosening of the soil
Bodenluft *f* air in soil pores, entrapped air
Bodenmonopol *n* land monopoly
Bodenmüdigkeit *f s.* **Bodenerschöpfung**
Bodennährstoff *m* soil nutrient
Bodennutzung *f* land utilization
Bodennutzungsform *f* kind of land utilization
Bodennutzungsgebühr *f* rent for a piece of land
Bodennutzungsgemeinschaft *f* community using land jointly
Bodennutzungssystem *n* system of crop production
Bodenoberfläche *f* surface
Bodenpacht *f* 1. lease of land; 2. land rent *(payment for a leasehold)*
Bodenparzelle *f* plot (of land), parcel, allotment, *(Am)* lot
Bodenpflege *f* preservation of the soil
Bodenpolitik *f* land policy
Bodenpreis *m* land price, price of a piece of land
Bodenprofil *n* profile of the soil
Bodenrecht *n (agric)* land act; real property law
Bodenreform *f* agrarian [land] reform
~, **demokratische** democratic land reform
Bodenrente *f* ground-rent
Bodenschätze *mpl* mineral resources
Bodenschätzung *f s.* **Bodenbewertung**
Bodenschicht *f* bottom layer (of the soil)
Bodensenkung *f* subsidence of the ground
Bodenskelett *n* foundation of the soil
Bodenspekulation *f* land speculation, speculation on land
bodenständig indigenous *(culture etc.)*; autochthonous, settled, sedentary *(population)*; local *(custom)*
Bodensteuer *f* land tax
Bodentaxation *f s.* **Bodenbewertung**
Bodenübersichtskarte *f* soil-survey chart
Bodenuntersuchung *f s.* **Bodenanalyse**
Bodenverbesserung *f* soil improvement [amelioration]
Bodenverfestigung *f* soil stabilization
Bodenvergiftung *f* soil poisoning
Bodenverhältnisse *npl* soil conditions

106   Bodenverschiedenartigkeit

Bodenverschiedenartigkeit *f* soil heterogeneity
Bodenverschluß *m* compactness of the soil
Bodenverstaatlichung *f* nationalization of land
Bodenverwilderung *f* degeneration (into wild/ untilled state) of the soil
Bodenvorbereitung *f* preparation of fields *(for cultivation)*
Bodenwasser *n* ground water
Bodenwert *m s.* **Bodenbonität**
Bodenwertsteigerung *f s.* **Bodenwertzuwachs**
Boden(wert)zahl *f* index of soil quality
Bodenwertzuwachs *m* increase in the quality of soil
Bodenwiderstand *m* soil resistance
Bodenzersplitterung *f* land fragmentation
Bodenzins *m s.* **Bodenpacht**
Bodenzustand *m* condition of the soil
Bodmerei *f* bottomry
Bodmereianleihe *f* bottomry loan
Bodmereibrief *m* bottomry letter, letter of bottomry
Bodmereivertrag *m* bottomry agreement
Bon *m* voucher; credit slip, coupon; bonus, token
Bonifikation *f* allowance, rebate, reduction, reimbursement; compensation; *(fin)* commission; *(cust)* rebate on duty paid
bonifizieren to give *s.o.* an allowance, to allow *s.o.* a rebate, to compensate, to indemnify, to reimburse
Bonität *f* 1. solvency, reliability *(firm)*; 2. good quality *(article)*
Bonitätsauskunft *f* information on solvency [reliability] *(of a firm)*
Bonitierung *f* land [soil] assessment; grading *(breeding stock etc.)*
Bonsystem *n* voucher [coupon] system *(in self--service restaurants)*
Bonus *m* 1. bonus; 2. extra dividend
Boom *m* boom
Bootsbaubetrieb *m* boat-building enterprise
Bootsführer *m* boatswain, bos'n, bosun
Bootsladung *f* boatload
Bootswerft *f* boat-yard
Bord *m* board *(ship, aircraft)* ◊ **an ~ bringen** to take on board; **an ~ gehen** to go on board [aboard], to embark; **frei an ~** free on board (f.o.b.); **frei an ~ zu liefern** to deliver free on board; **über ~ gehen** to go by the board; **über ~ werfen** to throw overboard; to jettison *(lading)*
Bordbescheinigung *f* shipment certificate; board receipt
Bordkonnossement *n* (shipped) bill of lading, on board B/L
Bordpersonal *n* ship's crew; air-crew
Borg *m* borrowing; lending ◊ **auf ~** on credit

Borgkauf *m* credit buying [purchase], purchase of goods on credit
Börse *f* 1. purse; 2. stock exchange; stock market; money market; commodity market ◊ **an der ~** on the stock exchange; in the money market; **an der ~ handeln** to deal on the stock exchange; **an der ~ kaufen** to buy on the stock exchange; **an der ~ verkaufen** to sell on the stock exchange
~, amtliche official stock exchange
~, feste firm [strong, steady] market; constant rate on the stock market
Börsenabteilung *f* stock exchange department
Börsenaktion *f* stock exchange transaction
Börsenarbitrage *f* stock exchange arbitrage
Börsenauftrag *m* stock exchange order
Börsenausschuß *m* stock exchange committee
Börsenbehörde *f* stock exchange governing body
Börsenbeginn *m* start of trading, opening of market ◊ **bei ~** when trading starts, when the market opens
Börsenbericht *m* (money) market report, market comment, stock exchange news
Börsenbesuch *m* admission to [attendance at] the stock exchange
Börsenbesucher *m* visitor to the stock exchange; person authorized to enter the stock exchange
Börsenbetrieb *m* stock exchange; stock exchange business [transactions]
Börsenblatt *n* list of quotations; commercial newspaper
Börsenboom *m* boom on the stock market
Börsenbräuche *mpl* customs and practices of the stock exchange
Börsenbruch *m s.* **Börsenkrach**
Börsendiskont *m* discount on the stock market
Börseneffekten *pl s.* **Börsenpapiere**
Börsenehrengericht *n* court of honour of the stock exchange
Börseneinführung *f* introduction to the stock market
börsenfähig negotiable *(stock on the stock exchange)*; qualified *(to enter an exchange, to trade on an exchange)*
Börsenfähigkeit *f* negotiability *(stock on the stock exchange)*; qualification *(to enter an exchange, to trade on an exchange)*
Börsenferien *pl* stock exchange holidays
börsengängig quoted on the stock exchange
Börsengast *m* visitor to the stock exchange
Börsengeschäft *n* stock exchange transaction
~, indifferentes neutral stock exchange operation
Börsengesetz *n* law relating to stock exchanges and commodity markets, stock exchange act

Börsenhandel *m* stock exchange transaction(s)
Börsenhändler *m s.* **Börsenmakler**
Börsenhausse *f s.* **Börsenboom**
Börsenindex *m* stock price average, stock index
Börseninteressenten *mpl* prospective buyers on the stock market
Börsenjobber *m* stockjobber
Börsenkammer *f* chamber of stock exchange
Börsenkomitee *n s.* **Börsenausschuß**
Börsenkommissar *m* stock exchange commissioner
Börsenkommissionsgeschäft *n* commission business on the stock exchange [market]
Börsenkonsortium *n* syndicate of the stock market
Börsenkrach *m* stock exchange crash, collapse of the stock market
Börsenkreise *mpl* stock markets
Börsenkrise *f* crisis on the stock exchange
Börsenkurs *m* exchange rate, market price [rate] *(shares, obligations etc.)*
Börsenleitung *f* stock exchange management
Börsenmakler *m* stockbroker
~, **ungesetzlicher** illegal stockbroker
~, **unvereidigter** unsworn stockbroker
~, **vereidigter** sworn stockbroker
Börsenmanöver *n* market-rigging, market jobbery, stockjobbing; agiotage
Börsenmarkt *m* stock market
börsenmäßig in conformity with stock exchange rules
Börsennotierung *f* market [stock exchange] quotation
Börsenoperation *f s.* **Börsengeschäft**
Börsenordnung *f* stock exchange regulations
Börsenorganisation *f* organization of the stock market
Börsenpapiere *npl* listed securities [stocks, shares]
Börsenpreis *m* stock exchange price
Börsenpreisbildung *f* formation of stock exchange prices
Börsenprospekt *m* stock exchange prospectus
Börsenrat *m s.* **Börsenausschuß**
Börsenreform *f* stock exchange reform
Börsenregister *n* stock exchange register
Börsenschacher *m* stock market jobbery
Börsenschieber *m s.* **Börsenspekulant**
Börsenschiedsgericht *n* arbitration court of the stock exchange
Börsenschluß *m* close of the market
Börsenschwindel *m* fraudulent stock exchange transaction
Börsenspekulant *m* stockjobber, stock market speculator
Börsenspekulation *f* stock exchange speculation, speculation on the stock market

Branche 107

Börsenspiel *n* stockjobbing
Börsensteuer *f* stock exchange tax
Börsenstimmung *f* tone of the market
Börsensturz *m* crash on the stock market
Börsensyndikat *n s.* **Börsenkonsortium**
Börsensystem *n* stock exchange system
Börsentag *m* stock market day
Börsentendenz *f* trend of the (stock) market
Börsentermingeschäft *n* forward dealing [trading in futures] on an exchange; account dealing
Börsenterminhandel *m s.* **Börsentermingeschäft**
Börsentransaktion *f* stock exchange transaction
Börsentreiben *n* stock exchange business; bustle at the stock exchange
Börsenumsatz *m* (total) stock exchange dealings, total dealings on the stock exchange
Börsenumsatzsteuer *f* tax on stock exchange dealings; stamp duty
Börsenusancen *fpl s.* **Börsenbräuche**
Börsenverkehr *m* stock exchange business
Börsenvermittler *m s.* **Börsenmakler**
Börsenversammlung *f* stock exchange meeting [session]
Börsenvertreter *m* stock exchange agent
Börsenverwaltung *f s.* **Börsenleitung**
Börsenvorstand *m* governing committee of the stock exchange
Börsenwaren *fpl* stock exchange goods, marketable stocks
Börsenwert *m* market value
Börsenwesen *n s.* **Börsensystem**
Börsenzeit *f* business hours of the stock market, stock exchange hours
Börsenzeitung *f* financial paper
Börsenzettel *m* stock-list, price list of quotations
Börsenzulassung *f* listing at the stock exchange *(shares etc.)*
Botendienst *m* messenger service ⋄ ~ **leisten** to carry messages
Botenlohn *m* messenger's fee
Böttcherei *f* cooper's shop; cooperage
bourgeois bourgeois
Bourgeoisie *f* bourgeoisie
~, **nationale** national bourgeoisie
Boykott *m* boycott
boykottieren to boycott
Boykottierung *f* boycotting
brach *(agric)* fallow, uncultivated
Brache *f (agric)* fallow
Brachfeld *n s.* **Brachland**
Brachland *n* fallow land
brachlegen to lay fallow
brachliegen to lie fallow [idle]; to go to waste
Brachzeit *f* downtime, idle time *(machine)*
Branche *f* line of business; branch *(company etc.)*

Branchenausstellung *f* specialized exhibition
branchenbedingt due to conditions in the particular trade
Branchenbeteiligung *f* exhibition in trade groups
Branchenkenntnis *f* knowledge of the trade
branchenkundig experienced in the trade
branchenmäßig according to the line of business
Branchenmesse *f* specialized fair
Branchennomenklatur *f* branch nomenclature
Branchenrichtlinie *f* branch directives *(instructions for accounting issued by industrial organizations)*
Branchenspanne *f* special margin
Branchenspezialisierung *f* specialization in specific branches (of industry)
Branchenstatistik *f* (industrial) branch statistics
Branchenstruktur *f* (industrial) branch structure
branchenüblich usual in the industry concerned
Branchenverzeichnis *n* classified directory (of industrial branches)
Brand *m* 1. fire; conflagration; 2. refining *(gold, silver)*; distilling, distillation *(fruit etc.)*; 3. baking *(bricks)*; firing, kiln-drying, burning *(pottery)*; 4. brand, mark made by branding *(cattle, sheep etc.)* ◊ **in ~ setzen** to set on fire
Brandbekämpfung *f* fire fighting
Brandentschädigung *f (ins)* fire compensation, compensation for damage caused by fire
Brandgefahr *f* fire risk
Brandkasse *f* fire insurance
Brandschaden *m* fire damage, damage caused by fire
Brandschadenschätzung *f (ins)* appraisal of damage caused by fire
Brandschutz *m* fire protection
Brandschutzverordnung *f* fire protection regulations
Brandwirtschaft *f (agric)* burn-baiting, burn-beating
Branntweinabgabe *f s.* **Branntweinsteuer**
Branntweinaufschlag *m* excise on spirits; additional charge *(for off-licence sale)*
Branntweinbesteuerung *f* taxation of spirits
Branntweinbrenner *m* distiller
Branntweinbrennerei *f* distillery; distillation
Branntweinkonsum *m* consumption of spirits
Branntweinmonopol *n* state monopoly in spirits
Branntweinsteuer *f* tax on spirits
Branntweinverbrauch *m s.* **Branntweinkonsum**
Brauch *m* usage, custom
brauchbar useful; serviceable
Brauchbarkeit *f* usefulness; serviceability
Brauchbarkeitsgrad *m* degree of usefulness; degree of serviceability

Brauchbarkeitsprobe *f* test of usefulness
Brauchwasser *n* water for industrial use
Brauchwasserversorgung *f* supply of water for industrial use
brauen to brew
Brauerei *f* brewery
Braunkohle *f* lignite, brown [soft] coal
Braunkohlenbergbau *m* brown [soft] coal-mining, lignite mining
Braunkohlenkoks *m* lignite coke
Braunkohlentagebau *m* open-cast lignite mine
Bremspreis *m* curbing price *(to slow down consumption of certain goods)*
Brennstoff *m* fuel
Brennstoffbilanz *f* fuel balance sheet
Brennstoffkosten *pl* fuel costs
Brennstofflager *n* fuel store
Brennstoffressourcen *fpl* fuel resources
Brennstoff- und Energiebilanz *f* balance sheet of fuels and energy
Brennstoffverbrauch *m* fuel consumption
Brennstoffvorkommen *n* fuel deposits
Brennstoffwirtschaft *f* fuel economy
Brennwert *m* calorific value
Brief *m* 1. letter; 2. *(st.ex.)* offered (price), seller's (price)
~ und Geld *n (st.ex.)* asked and bid
Briefablage *f* (letter) file
Briefaufschrift *f* address
Briefgeheimnis *n* privacy of letters, secrecy of the mail
Briefgrundpfandrecht *n s.* **Briefhypothek**
Briefgrundschuld *f s.* **Briefhypothek**
Briefhypothek *f* unregistered [certified] mortgage *(secured by a letter)*
Briefkurs *m (st.ex.)* asked price, selling (price) rate
Brieftelegramm *n* letter telegram, *(Am)* lettergram
Briefträger *m* postman, *(Am)* mailman
Briefverkehr *m* correspondence
Brigade *f* work team, group of workers (in production)
Brigadeabrechnung *f* (work) team accounting *(of costs of material etc.)*
Brigadearbeit *f* team work
Brigadebereich *m* section of a work team [brigade]
Brigadeleistungslohn *m* intensive wage of a work team [brigade]
Brigadeleiter *m* (work) team leader, foreman
Brigadelohnsatz *m* wage rate of work teams
Brigademitglied *n* member of a work team
Brigadeordnung *f* rules pertaining to a work team
Brigadeorganisation *f* organization of work team

Brigadeplan *m* plan of a work team
Brigadestärke *f* strength of the work team
Brigadestücklohn *m* piece-rate wages of work team
Brigadewettbewerb *m* competition [emulation drive] of work teams
Brigadier *m s.* **Brigadeleiter**
Bringschuld *f* debt to be discharged at creditor's domicile
Bringsystem *n* system of discharging debts at the residence [domicile] of the creditor
Bruchteilversicherung *f* partial insurance
Brückengeld *n* bridge-toll
brutto gross ◊ ~ **für netto** gross for net
Bruttoakkumulation *f* gross accumulation
Bruttoaufschlag *m* gross extra charge
Bruttoausgaben *fpl* gross expenditure(s)
Bruttoausstoß *m* gross output
Bruttobeitrag *m (ins)* gross premium
Bruttobetrag *m* gross amount
Bruttobilanz *f* gross balance sheet
Bruttodevisenerlös *m* gross proceeds in foreign exchange
Bruttoeinkaufspreis *m* gross purchasing [gross cost] price
Bruttoeinkommen *n* gross income [earnings]
~, **landwirtschaftliches** gross farm income [earnings]
Bruttoeinnahmen *fpl* gross receipts [earnings, revenue, returns]
Bruttoenergieverbrauch *m* gross energy consumption
Bruttoerlöse *mpl* gross proceeds [receipts]
Bruttoerzeugung *f s.* **Bruttoproduktion**
Bruttofinanzierung *f* gross financing *(method of financing state administration and institutions where all expenditures are paid out by the respective budget and all revenues go to the state budget)*
Bruttofläche *f* total floor space (of building)
Bruttogehalt *n* gross salary
Bruttogehaltssumme *f* total gross salary
Bruttogeldeinnahmen *fpl* gross receipts [earnings, revenue] in money
Bruttogeldeinkommen *n* gross income in money
Bruttogeldeinkünfte *pl s.* **Bruttogeldeinkommen**
Bruttogewicht *n* gross weight
Bruttogewinn *m* gross profit
Bruttoinlandsprodukt *n* **(BIP)** gross domestic product (GDP)
Bruttoinvestition *f* gross investment
Bruttoinvestitionsfonds *m* gross investment fund
~, **einheitlicher** compound gross investment fund

Bruttokennziffer *f* gross index
Bruttoleistung *f* gross capacity [output]
Bruttolistenpreis *m* fixed gross price
Bruttolohn *m* gross wage
~, **nominaler** nominal gross wage
~, **realer** real gross wage
Bruttolohnermittlung *f s.* **Bruttolohnrechnung**
Bruttolohnrechnung *f* calculation of gross wages
Bruttolohnsumme *f* sum of gross wages
Bruttomasse *f s.* **Bruttogewicht**
Bruttonationaleinkommen *n* gross national income
Bruttoprämie *f s.* **Bruttobeitrag**
Bruttopreis *m* gross price
Bruttopreisliste *f* list of gross prices
Bruttoprinzip *n* gross principle of planning and accounting *(of receipts and expenditure without compensation — a typical method of financing non-self supporting institutions such as government administration etc.)*
Bruttoprodukt *n* gross product
~, **gesellschaftliches** gross social product
~, **reales nationales** real gross national product
Bruttoproduktion *f* gross production [output]
~, **industrielle** industrial gross production [output]
~, **landwirtschaftliche** gross agricultural production [output]
Bruttoproduktionsmethode *f* gross production method *(of calculating efficiency of production)*
Bruttoproduktionsvolumen *n* size of gross production [output]
Bruttoproduktionswert *m* value of gross production [output]
Bruttoproduktivität *f* gross productivity
Bruttoprofit *m s.* **Bruttogewinn**
Bruttoprofitrate *f* rate of gross profit
Bruttoregistertonne *f* **(BRT)** gross register(ed) ton (G.R.T.)
Bruttosatz *m* gross rate
Bruttosozialprodukt *n* **(BSP)** gross national product (GNP)
Bruttosumme *f* gross sum
Bruttotarif *m s.* **Bruttosatz**
Bruttotragfähigkeit *f* gross loading capacity
Bruttoumsatz *m* gross output *(of all productive departments of an enterprise regardless of whether it is marketed or consumed internally)*
Bruttoverdienst *m* gross income [earnings]
Bruttoverdienstspanne *f* margin of gross income [earnings]
Bruttoverkaufspreis *m* gross selling price
Bruttoversandgewicht *n* gross freight [shipping] weight
Bruttoverzollung *f* payment of duty on gross weight

Bruttowarenumsatz *m* gross commodity turnover
Bruttowert *m* gross value
Bruttozeit *f* gross working time *(incl. breaks)*
Bruttozins *m* gross interest
Buch *n (acc)* book, record; account; ledger ◊ **zu Buche schlagen** to show favourably in the books; **zu Buche stehen mit** to be valued at
Buchabschluß *m* closing [balancing] of the books
Buchbestand *m* stock according to ledger
buchen *(acc)* to book *(item, sum)*, to enter (transaction in the books); to book, to reserve *(room, flight etc.)* ◊ **als überfällig ~** to enter [put] as overdue; **kostenwirksam ~** to enter [put] as costs
Bücher *npl*:
◊ **die ~ abschließen** to close [balance] the accounts; **die ~ führen** to keep the books
Bücherabschluß *m s.* **Buchabschluß**
Bücherrevision *f* audit
Bücherrevisor *m s.* **Buchprüfer**
~, vereidigter chartered [*(Am)* certified public] accountant
Buchforderung *f* book claim, ledger-claim, *(Am)* accounts receivable
Buchführer *m s.* **Buchhalter**
Buchführung *f* bookkeeping, accountancy
~, doppelte double entry bookkeeping
~, einfache single entry bookkeeping
~, kameralistische *s.* **Buchhaltung, kameralistische**
~, kaufmännische commercial bookkeeping
~, nationale national (income and product) account
~, vollautomatische fully automated bookkeeping
Buchführungspflicht *f* statutory obligation to keep books
Buchführungsrichtlinien *fpl* principles of bookkeeping
Buchführungssystem *n* system of bookkeeping
Buchführungstechnik *f* method of bookkeeping; bookkeeping technique
Buchführungsunterlagen *fpl s.* **Buchungsunterlagen**
Buchführungsverordnung *f* regulation(s) of bookkeeping
Buchführungsvorschriften *fpl* rules of bookkeeping
Buchgeld *n* deposit [fiduciary] money
Buchgeldumlauf *m s.* **Buchgeldzirkulation**
Buchgeldvolumen *n* total amount of deposit money
Buchgeldzirkulation *f* circulation of deposit money
Buchgewerbe *n* book trade

Buchgewinn *m* book profit
Buchhalter *m* bookkeeper
Buchhaltung *f* bookkeeping, accountancy; accounts [accounting, bookkeeping] department
~, kameralistische budgetary bookkeeping, bookkeeping in the field of public finance
Buchhaltungsform *f* kind of bookkeeping
Buchhaltungsrichtlinien *fpl s.* **Buchführungsrichtlinien**
Buchhaltungssystem *n s.* **Buchführungssystem**
Buchhaltungsunterlagen *fpl s.* **Buchungsunterlagen**
Buchhandel *m* book trade
Buchhändler *m* bookseller
Buchhandlung *f* bookshop
Buchhypothek *f* registered mortgage
Buchkredit *m* credit on account, book credit
Buchladen *m s.* **Buchhandlung**
buchmäßig as shown by the books; bookkeeping, accountancy
Buchpreis *m* uniform price (of pressed coal)
Buchprüfer *m* auditor
~, vereidigter sworn auditor
Buchprüfung *f* audit
Buchrevision *f s.* **Buchprüfung**
Buchrevisor *m s.* **Buchprüfer**
Buchsaldo *m* book balance
Buchschuld *f* book debt
Büchsenwaren *fpl* tinned [canned] goods
Buchung *f (acc)* entry; booking, reservation *(room, flight etc.)* ◊ **laut unserer ~** according to our entry
Buchungsanweisung *f* booking order; order of making an entry
Buchungsanzeige *f* advice (of entry)
Buchungsautomat *m* automatic bookkeeping [accounting] machine
Buchungsbeleg *m* voucher, receipt
Buchungsfehler *m* error in the books
Buchungsformular *n* bookkeeping form
Buchungsjournal *n* ledger
Buchungskontrolle *f* auditing
Buchungsmaschine *f* bookkeeping machine
Buchungsnachweis *m s.* **Buchungsbeleg**
Buchungsnummer *f* number of entry
Buchungsorder *f s.* **Buchungsanweisung**
Buchungsposten *m* item, entry
Buchungsstation *f* accounting machine centre
Buchungsstelle *f* accountancy department
Buchungssystem *n* system of booking; bookkeeping system
Buchungstag *m* date [day] of entry
Buchungsunterlagen *fpl* (supporting) documents (in bookkeeping)
Buchungsverfahren *n* method of making entries
Buchungsverweis *m* reference (to an entry)

Buchungsvorfall *m s.* **Buchungsvorgang**
Buchungsvorgang *m* entry
Buchungszentrum *n s.* **Buchungsstation**
Buchungszwang *m* obligation to make an entry
Buchwert *m (acc)* book value
Bude *f* stall, booth (on the market)
Budget *n* budget *(s. a.* **Etat, Haushalt 1.**)
Budgetanweisungen *fpl* budgetary regulations
Budgetaufschlüsselung *f* budget [budgetary] allocation
Budgetausgleich *m* grants to local authorities (by the state/central budget)
Budgetausschuß *m* budget committee *(parliament, local council etc.)*
Budgetberatung *f* budget debate
Budgetdebatte *f s.* **Budgetberatung**
Budgetdefizit *n* budgetary deficit
Budgetgliederung *f* division of a budget
 ~ **nach Aufgabenbereichen** division of a budget according to spheres of responsibility
 ~ **nach Kapiteln** division of a budget according to chapters
Budgetjahr *n* fiscal [financial] year
Budgetkommission *f* budget commission [committee]
Budgetkontrolle *f* budget control *(s.* **Haushaltskontrolle**)
Budgetkürzung *f* budget cut
budgetmäßig according to the budget; budgetary, budget
Budgetmittel *npl* public funds, budgetary appropriation [means]
Budgetpolitik *f* budget(ary) policy
Budgetposten *m* budget item
Budgetrecht *n* budget regulations [law]
Budgetrestriktion *f* budget restriction
Budgetüberschuß *m* budget(ary) surplus
Bummelantentum *n* absenteeism
Bummelei *f* dawdling; loafing
Bummelstreik *m* go-slow; work-to-rule (campaign)
Bundesabgabe *f* federal levy
Bundesanwalt *m* Attorney of the Federal Supreme Court
Bundesarbeitsgericht *n* Federal Labour Court
Bundesbahn *f* Federal Railway
Bundesbank *f* Federal Bank
Bundesbankrat *m* Board of Governors of the Federal Reserve System [Federal Bank]
Bundesbehörde *f* Federal Authority
Bundesbürger *m* federal citizen
Bundesebene *f* federal level
bundeseigen federally-owned, federal
Bundesfinanzhof *m* Federal Finance Court
Bundesgebiet *n* federal territory
Bundesgericht *n* Federal Court
Bundesgerichtshof *m* Federal Supreme Court

Bundesgesetz *n* federal law
Bundesgesetzgebung *f* federal legislation
Bundeshaushalt *m* federal budget
Bundeskartellamt *n* Federal Cartel Office
Bundesland *n* federal country [state]
Bundesministerium *n* Federal Ministry
Bundesmittel *npl* federal financial resources
Bundespost *f* Federal Postal Service; Federal Postal Administration
Bundespräsident *m* Federal President
Bundespräsidialamt *n* Office of the Federal President
Bundesrat *m* Upper House (of Parliament)
Bundesrechnungshof *m* Federal Auditing Court
Bundesregierung *f* Federal Government
Bundesrepublik *f* Federal Republic
Bundesreservebank *f* Federal (Reserve) Bank (System)
Bundesrichter *m* Justice of the Federal Supreme Court
Bundesschatz *m* federal treasury
Bundesstaat *m* federal state; federation
bundesstaatlich federal
Bundessteuern *fpl* federal taxes
Bundesstraße *f* federal highway
Bundestag *m* Lower House (of Parliament)
Bundesverfassung *f* Federal Constitution
Bundesverfassungsgericht *n* Federal Constitutional Court
Bundesverwaltungsgericht *n* Federal Court of Justice for Administrative Affairs
Bundesvorstand *m* executive committee *(trade union etc.)*
Bündnis *n* alliance; pact
bündnisfrei non-aligned
Bündnispolitik *f* policy of alliance
Bunkerklausel *f* bunker clause
Bürge *m* 1. bail, bailsman, surety; 2. security, surety, guarantor ◊ **als ~ zugelassen werden** to be admitted as bail
bürgen to go bail for; to stand surety for, *(Am)* to bond
Bürger *m* citizen
Bürgerinitiative *f* citizens' action (committee)
bürgerlich civil; civic; middle class, bourgeois
Bürgermeister *m* mayor
Bürgerrechte *npl* civil rights
bürgerrechtlich civil-law
Bürgertum *n* (the) middle class
Bürgschaft *f (bank)* surety, guarantee; *(jur)* bail ◊ **eine ~ leisten** *(bank)* to stand surety [guarantee, security]; *(jur)* to stand bail; **eine ~ übernehmen** *s.* **~ leisten**
 ~, **gegenseitige** mutual surety
 ~, **persönliche** personal [private] surety
 ~, **selbstschuldnerische** surety on one's own account

Bürgschaftsbestellung *f* asking for surety
Bürgschaftserklärung *f* declaration of surety
Bürgschaftsforderung *f* claim resulting from given security
Bürgschaftskredit *m* guaranteed credit
Bürgschaftsleistung *f* suretyship; security; *(jur)* standing bail
Bürgschaftsprovision *f* commission on surety (given); commission on bank guarantee
Bürgschaftsschein *m s.* **Bürgschaftsschreiben**
Bürgschaftsschreiben *n* letter of surety, surety bond, guarantee; *(jur)* bail-bond
Bürgschaftsstellung *f* giving surety [security]; *(jur)* standing bail
Bürgschaftssumme *f* (amount of) security; *(jur)* bail
Bürgschaftsübernahme *f* provision of surety; guaranteeing a bill (of exchange)
Bürgschaftsurkunde *f* surety bond, guarantee, *(Am)* guaranty
Bürgschaftsverbindlichkeiten *fpl* liabilities resulting from (giving) surety
Bürgschaftsvergütung *f s.* **Bürgschaftsprovision**
Bürgschaftsvertrag *m* contract of surety
Bürgschaftswechsel *m* guaranteed bill of exchange
Büro *n* office; bureau
Büroangestellte *f* female clerk, female office worker
Büroangestellter *m* male clerk, male office worker
Büroarbeit *f* office-work
Büroausgaben *fpl* office expenditures
Büroausstattung *f* office equipment
Bürobedarf *m* (office) stationery
Bürochef *m s.* **Bürovorsteher**
Büroeinrichtung *f* office equipment [fittings]
Bürohaus *n* office building
Bürokraft *f* office-worker
Bürokratie *f* bureaucracy
Bürokratismus *m* red tape
Büromaschine(n) *f(pl)* office machine(s)
Büromöbel *pl* office furniture
Büropersonal *n* office personnel, clerical staff
Bürorechenmaschine *f* desk computer
Büroschluß *m* closing time (of office), office closing time ⋄ **nach ~** after office hours
Bürostunden *fpl* office hours
Bürotechnik *f* office equipment; office organization
Bürovorsteher *m* chief clerk
Bürozeit *f s.* **Bürostunden**
Buße *f* penitence, penance; sanction, penalty; forfeit *(money to be paid as penalty)*
Bußgeld *n* forfeit; fine, penalty

C

Callgeld *n (com)* call money
Campingschau *f* camping exhibition
Camping-, Wasser- und Wandersportbedarf *m* camping, water sports and hiking articles and equipment
Cauchy-Verteilung *f (stats)* Cauchy distribution
Charakter *m* character, nature; capacity
~ **der Arbeit** social nature of labour *(determined by the relations of production)*
~, **fundamentaler** fundamental nature
charakterisieren to characterize, to be characteristic of
Charakterisieren *n* characterizing
Charakterisierung *f* characterization; depiction (of character)
Charakteristik *f* characterization; portrait, delineation
Charakteristikum *n* distinguishing feature, characteristic (feature)
charakteristisch characteristic, typical
Charakterzug *m* distinguishing trait
Chargenproduktion *f* production in lots
Chartepartie *f* **(c/p)** charter-party *(cargo shipping)*
Charterauftrag *m* charter order
Charterer *m* charterer
Charterflug *m* charter flight
Charterfluggesellschaft *f s.* **Chartergesellschaft**
Charterfluglinie *f* charter air line
Chartergesellschaft *f* charter company
chartern to charter; to hire, to get hold of *(s.th.)*
Chartern *n* charter, chartering
~ **eines Flugzeugs** chartering an aircraft
Charterpartie *f s.* **Chartepartie**
Charterraten *fpl* charter transport rates [charges]
Charterverkehr *m* charter transport
Chartervertrag *m s.* **Chartepartie**
Chef *m* head, chief, boss
~ **der Verwaltung** head of the administration
Chefadministrator *m* chief administrator
Chefingenieur *m* chief engineer
Chefkonstrukteur *m* chief designer
Chefmontage *f* sub-contracted construction *(erection of a plant in which the contractor's employees act only to guide and supervise erection, as opposed to single-contractor construction or overall construction)*
Chemieausrüstungen *fpl* equipment for the chemical industry
Chemiefachmesse *f* chemical exhibition
Chemiefaserindustrie *f* artificial fibre industry
Chemiehandel *m* trade in chemicals

Chemieindustrie *f* chemical industry
Chemiemarkt *m* market for chemicals
Chemiewerte *mpl (st.ex.)* chemicals
Chemisierung *f* chemicalization, the pervasive influence [use] of chemistry *(in other sectors)*
Chemisierungsgrad *m* level of chemicalization
Chiffre *f* cipher
chiffrieren to encipher, to code
Chi-Maßzahl *f (stats)* Chi-statistic
Chip *m* chip
Chips *mpl* chips, dice *(e.g. per wafer)*
Chi-Quadrat-Maßzahl *f (stats)* Chi-squared statistic
Chi-Quadrat-Minimum-Methode *f (stats)* minimum Chi-squared method
Chi-Quadrat-Test *m (stats)* Chi-squared test
Chi-Quadrat-Verteilung *f (stats)* Chi-squared distribution
Christbaumschmuckindustrie *f* christmas tree decorations industry
cif-Agent *m* cif agent [agency]
cif-Geschäft *n* cif transaction
cif-Kalkulation *f* cif calculation
cif-Preis *m* cif price
Clearing *n (fin)* clearing
~, **bilaterales** bilateral clearing
~, **dreiseitiges** trilateral clearing
~ **mit konvertierbarem Saldo** clearing with convertible balance
~ **mit nichtkonvertierbarem Saldo** clearing with inconvertible balance
~, **multilaterales** multilateral clearing
Clearingabkommen *n* clearing agreement
Clearingbank *f* clearing bank
Clearingforderungen *fpl* clearing claims
Clearinghaus *n* clearing house
Clearingkonto *n* clearing account
Clearingkurs *m* rate of clearing
Clearingoperation *f* clearing transaction
Clearingorganisation *f* clearing organization [house]
Clearingsaldo *m* clearing balance
Clearingschuld *f* clearing debt
Clearingstelle *f s.* **Clearinghaus**
Clearingübereinkommen *n s.* **Clearingabkommen**
Clearing- und Zahlungsabkommen *n* clearing and payments agreement
Clearingverkehr *m* clearing (system)
Clearingverrechnung *f s.* **Clearing**
Clearingvorschuß *m* clearing advance
Clearingwährung *f* clearing [accounting, agreement] currency
Clearingzentrum *n s.* **Clearinghaus**
Closed-shop-Klausel *f* closed-shop clause
COBOL-Programm *n (d.pr.)* COBOL source program

COBOL-Programmiersprache *f (d.pr.)* common business oriented language (COBOL)
Code *m s.* **Kode**
Codex *m s.* **Kodex**
Compagnie *f* **(Co.)** company
Compagnon *m* partner, associate
Computer *m* computer
~ **mit festem Programm** fixed-program computer
~ **mit gespeichertem Programm** stored-program computer
~ **mit Pufferspeichern** buffer computer
~ **mit Sensoren** sensor-based computer
~ **mit verdrahtetem Programm** wired-program computer
~, **mittelgroßer** medium-scale computer
Computerentwurfsdaten *pl* computer design information
computergerecht computerized
computergesteuert computer-controlled [-operated, -driven, -automated], under computer control
computergestützt computer-assisted [-aided], computerized
Computerkommunikationssystem *n* computer communication system
Computersteuerungsprogramme *npl* computer control software
Computersystem *n* computer system
computerunterstützt *s.* **computergestützt**
COM-Verfahren *n* computer output microfilming (COM)
Consols *pl (fin)* consols
Container *m* container
Containerdienst *m* container service
Containerhafen *m* container port
Containerlager *n* container warehouse
Containerliegeplatz *m* container storage
Containerliniendienst *m* container shipping line
Containerschiff *n* container vessel
Containerservice *m s.* **Containerdienst**
Containertransport *m* container transport
Containertransportsystem *n* container transport system
Containerverkehr *m* container transport [traffic]
Conurbation *f* conurbation
Copyright *n* copyright
Cottagesystem *n* cottage industry system
Coupon *m s.* **Kupon**
Courtage *f (com)* brokerage, commission
courtagefrei free of brokerage
Courtagerechnung *f* brokerage account
Courtagesatz *m* commission rate, rate of commission
Courtagetarif *m* scale of commission
CPM-Methode *f s.* **Methode des kritischen Weges**

D

Dachdeckerarbeiten *fpl* roofing; tiling; slating; thatching
Dachgesellschaft *f* holding company
Dachgewerkschaft *f* parent union
Dachorganisation *f* holding organization; umbrella organization
Damenbekleidung *f* ladies wear
Damenkonfektion *f* ladies ready-made clothes
Damenschneiderei *f* ladies' tailoring; ladies' tailor shop
Damno *m/n* loss, discount *(on mortgages, securities etc.)*
Dampfer *m* steamer, steamship
Dampferlinie *f* steamship line
Dampfschiff *n s.* **Dampfer**
Dampfschiffahrt *f* steam navigaton
Dampfschiffahrtsgesellschaft *f* steamship company
Dämpfungsfaktor *m* *(stats)* damping factor
Darleh(e)n *n* loan ◇ **ein ~ aufnehmen** to raise a loan, to borrow money; **ein ~ geben** to grant a loan, to lend *s.o.* money; **ein ~ gewähren** *s.* **ein ~ geben**; **ein ~ kündigen** to call in a loan; **ein ~ tilgen** *s.* **ein ~ zurückzahlen**; **ein ~ zurückzahlen** to repay a loan
~, **abgeschriebenes** written-off loan
~ **an die Wirtschaft** commercial credit
~, **auf einmal in voller Höhe fälliges** straight loan
~, **bares** cash loan
~, **befristetes** loan for a fixed term
~ **einer Bank** bank loan
~, **eingefrorenes** dead loan
~, **fälliges** loan due
~, **gedecktes** secured loan
~ **gegen Lombardierung von Wertpapieren** loan on the collateral of securities
~ **gegen Pfand** loan against collateral
~ **gegen Sicherheiten** loan against security
~ **gegen Sichtwechsel** sight loan
~, **gesichertes** *s.* ~, **gedecktes**
~, **hypothekarisch gesichertes** mortgage loan
~, **jederzeit kündbares** call [demand] loan
~, **kündbares** loan at notice
~, **kurzfristiges** short-term loan
~, **langfristiges** long-term loan
~ **mit bestimmter Laufzeit** time loan
~, **mittelfristiges** medium-term loan
~, **nichtrückzahlbares** grant
~, **offenes** advance
~ **ohne Deckung** loan without security, unsecured loan
~, **rückzahlbares** loan
~, **sofort rückzahlbares** call loan

~, **täglich fälliges** day-to-day loan
~, **überfälliges** overdue loan
~, **unbefristetes** undated loan
~, **ungebundenes** untied loan
~, **ungedecktes** *s.* ~, **ungesichertes**
~, **ungesichertes** loan on trust, unsecured loan
~, **unkündbares** irredeemable loan
~, **unverzinsliches** *s.* ~, **zinsloses**
~, **verlorenes** *s.* ~, **abgeschriebenes**
~, **verzinsliches** loan on interest
~ **von mittlerer Laufzeit** *s.* ~, **mittelfristiges**
~, **zinsfreies** *s.* ~, **zinsloses**
~, **zinsloses** non-interest bearing loan
~ **zu Liquiditätszwecken** liquid loan
~ **zu Wucherzinsen** usurious loan
~, **zweckgebundenes** tied loan
Darleh(e)nsangebot *n* offer of a loan
Darleh(e)nsanspruch *m* claim to a loan
Darleh(e)nsansuchen *n s.* **Darleh(e)nsantrag**
Darleh(e)nsantrag *m* loan application
Darleh(e)nsbank *f* loan bank
Darleh(e)nsbegründung *f* grounds for a loan
Darleh(e)nsbewerber *m* loan applicant
Darleh(e)nsempfänger *m s.* **Darleh(e)nsnehmer**
Darleh(e)nsfinanzierung *f* financing of a loan
Darleh(e)nsfonds *m* loan fund
~, **sich erneuernder** revolving loan fund
Darleh(e)nsgeber *m* loaner, lender
Darleh(e)nsgenossenschaft *f* co-operative loan society
Darleh(e)nsgeschäft *n* loan transaction
Darleh(e)nsgesellschaft *f* loan society, *(Am)* credit corporation
Darleh(e)nsgewährung *f* granting of a loan
Darleh(e)nsgläubiger *m s.* **Darleh(e)nsgeber**
Darleh(e)nskasse *f* credit bank
Darleh(e)nskassenschein *m* loan certificate
Darleh(e)nskonto *n* loan account
Darleh(e)nsnehmer *m* loanee, borrower
Darleh(e)nsschein *m* loan certificate
Darleh(e)nsschuld *f* nominal amount of loan
Darleh(e)nsschuldner *m s.* **Darleh(e)nsnehmer**
Darleh(e)nssicherung *f* security for a loan
Darleh(e)nsverein *m* loan society
Darleh(e)nsversprechen *n* promise of a loan
Darleh(e)nsvertrag *m* bill of loan
Darleh(e)nsvorvertrag *m s.* **Darleh(e)nsversprechen**
darleh(e)nsweise as a loan
Darleh(e)nszins *m* interest on loan
Darleh(e)nszinssatz *m* rate of interest on loan
Darleiher *m s.* **Darleh(e)nsgeber**
Darstellung *f* representation; depiction, description; illustration; *(d.pr.)* delineation ◇ **eine ~ des Tatbestandes geben** to state the facts
~, **amtliche** official version

~, **äquivalente** *(maths)* equivalent representation
~, **axonometrische** *(stats)* axonometric chart
~, **bildliche** presentation in pictorial [graphic] form
~, **falsche** misrepresentation
~, **figürliche** *(stats)* pictogram
~, **gewöhnliche** *(maths)* ordinary representation
~, **graphische** graph; illustration (of an equation) by a graph
~ **im logarithmischen Netz** *(stats)* logarithmic chart
~, **irreduzible** *(maths)* irreducible representation
~, **modulare** *(maths)* modular representation
~, **reduzible** *(maths)* reducible representation
~, **statistische** illustration (of facts) by statistics; statistics
~, **symbolische** symbolic representation
~, **tabellarische** illustration (of figures) by a table; table
~, **zusammengefaßte** summary
Daten *pl (stats, d.pr.)* data; particulars *(curriculum vitae etc.)*; facts
~, **alphanumerische** *(d.pr.)* alpha-numerical data
~, **ankommende** *(d.pr.)* incoming data
~, **bearbeitete** *(d.pr.)* processed data
~, **erzeugnisbezogene** *(d.pr.)* product data
~, **gruppierte** grouped data
~, **primäre** primary data
~, **qualitative** qualitative data
~, **quantitative** quantitative data
~, **sekundäre** secondary data
~, **technische** technical data, specifications; performance specifications
~, **unverarbeitete** unprocessed [raw] data
~, **unvollständige** incomplete data
~, **verschlüsselte** *(stats)* coded data
~, **zusammengefaßte** *(stats)* integrated data
Datenadresse *f (d.pr.)* data address
Datenanforderung *f (d.pr.)* data request
Datenaufbereitung *f (d.pr.)* preparation of data, data preparation
Datenaufzeichnung *f (d.pr.)* data recording
Datenausgabe *f (d.pr.)* data output
Datenaustausch *m (d.pr.)* data communication
Datenauswahl *f (d.pr.)* selection of data, data selection
Datenauswertung *f (d.pr.)* data evaluation
Datenbank *f (d.pr.)* data bank
Datenbasis *f (d.pr.)* data base
~, **originäre** *(d.pr.)* source data base
~, **verwendete** *(d.pr.)* reference data base
Datenbearbeitung *f (d.pr.)* data handling
Datenbereitstellung *f* provision of data
Datendarstellung *f (d.pr.)* data representation
Datendurchlauf *m (d.pr.)* data throughput
Dateneingabe *f (d.pr.)* data input
~, **direkte** *(d.pr.)* direct data entry

~, **manuelle** *(d.pr.)* manual data input
Dateneinheit *f (d.pr.)* unit of data, data unit
~, **eingegebene** *(d.pr.)* data entry
~, **kleinste** *(d.pr.)* smallest unit of data
~, **logische** *(d.pr.)* logical unit of data
Datenempfänger *m (d.pr.)* data receiver
Datenerfassung *f* data collection
Datenerfassungsstelle *f (d.pr.)* data collection point
Datenerfassungssystem *n* system of data collection
Datenfernübertragung *f (d.pr.)* telecommunication
Datenfluß *m (d.pr.)* data flow, flow of information
~, **grenzüberschreitender** *(d.pr.)* transborder data flows
Datenflußplan *m (d.pr.)* data flowchart
Datengruppe *f (d.pr.)* group item
Datenkanal *m (d.pr.)* information channel
Datenregister *n (d.pr.)* data cartridge
Datenregistrierung *f (d.pr.)* data recording
Datensatz *m (d.pr.)* data record
Datenspeicher *m (d.pr.)* data storage
Datenstation *f (d.pr.)* data terminal station
Datenteil *m (d.pr.)* data division
Datenträger *m (d.pr.)* information carrier
Datenübermittlung *f s.* **Datenübertragung**
Datenübertragung *f (d.pr.)* data transfer [transmission]
Datenübertragungszeit *f (d.pr.)* data time
Datenumsetzer *m (d.pr.)* data translator
Datenumsetzung *f (d.pr.)* data conversion
Datenverarbeitung *f* data processing
~, **automatische** automatic data processing
~, **dezentrale** decentralized data processing
~, **elektronische (EDV)** electronic data processing
~, **grafische** *(d.pr.)* computer graphics
~, **indirekte** indirect data processing
~, **integrierte** integrated data processing
~, **maschinelle** mechanical data processing
~, **numerische** numerical data processing
~, **verteilte** distributed data processing
~, **zentralisierte** centralized data processing
Datenverarbeitungsanlage *f* data processing machine [equipment]
~, **elektronische (EDVA)** computer, electronic data processing machine
Datenverarbeitungseinheit *f (d.pr.)* processing unit
datenverarbeitungsgerecht meeting the requirements of data processing
Datenverarbeitungsstelle *f* processing station
Datenwähler *m (d.pr.)* data selector
Datenzwischenspeicher *m (d.pr.)* data synchronizer

dato after date, from today
Datoscheck *m* dated cheque
Datowechsel *m* day bill, bill after date
Datum *n* date ◊ **gestrigen Datums** of yesterday; **gleichen Datums** of the same date; **heutigen Datums** of today; **mit ~ versehen** to date; **morgigen Datums** of tomorrow; **neueren Datums** of recent date; **ohne ~** undated
~, äußerstes latest date
~ des Poststempels date of postmark
Datumsangabe *f* date
Dauer *f* length, duration *(stay etc.)*; period, term *(office etc.)*
Dauerabkommen *n* lasting settlement
Dauerakkreditiv *n* permanent (letter of) credit
Dauerarbeitslosigkeit *f* permanent [chronic] unemployment
Dauerauftrag *m (fin)* standing order *(to a bank etc.)*
Dauerausstellung *f* permanent exhibition
Dauerbelastung *f* permanent [*(Am)* constant] load
Dauerbeschäftigung *f* permanent employment, stable job
Dauerbesitz *m* permanent possession; *(st.ex.)* permanent portfolio
Dauerbetrieb *m* continuous working [operation]
Dauerertrag *m (com)* sustained return; *(agric)* sustained yield
Dauergarantie *f* continuing guarantee
Dauergüter *npl* durable goods, durables
dauerhaft durable, lasting; solid, fast
Dauerinvalidität *f* permanent disability
Dauerinvaliditätsversicherung *f* permanent disability insurance
Dauerkredit *m* permanent loan
Dauerleistung *f (tech)* continuous operation; continuous output, continuous (operational) performance
Dauermiete *f* permanent tenancy
Dauermieter *m* permanent tenant
Dauerprüfung *f* endurance test
Dauerrente *f* perpetual annuity
Dauerschaden *m (ins)* permanent injury
Dauerschuld *f* permanent debt
Dauerschuldverschreibung *f* perpetual debenture
Dauerstellung *f* permanent position [post]
Dauerwirkung *f* lasting [permanent] effect
Debent *m s.* **Debitor**
Debet *n* debit; *(acc)* debit [left-hand] side *(of balance sheet and ledger)* ◊ **im ~ stehen** to be on the debit side
Debetbeleg *m* debit voucher
Debetbuch *n* debit book
Debetbuchung *f* debit entry

Debetkonto *n* debit account
Debetmasse *f* bankrupt estate
Debetnote *f* debit note
Debetposten *m* entry on the debit side, item debited, debit entry
Debetsaldo *m* debit balance
Debetseite *f* debit [left-hand] side
Debetspalte *f* debit column
Debetzinsen *mpl* interest on debit balances
debitieren to debit
Debitor *m* debtor
Debitoren *mpl* 1. debtors *(bank customers)*; 2. receivables *(balance sheet)*
~, fällige receivables due
~, langfristige long-term receivables
~, sichere good debts
Debitorenabtretung *f* assignment of receivables
Debitorenaufstellung *f* statement on receivables
Debitorenkonto *n* debtor account, receivables
Debitorenprobe *f (tax)* checking of tax return
Debitverfahren *n* (legal) proceedings in bankruptcy
deblockieren to unfreeze, to deblock
Deblockierung *f* unfreezing, deblocking
Decharge *f* discharge *(cargo, debt)*
decken to cover *(needs etc.)*; to reimburse *(costs etc.)*; to guarantee *(for debt, loan etc.)*; to protect *(draft etc.)*
Deckfracht *f s.* **Deckladung**
Deckfrucht *f (agric)* cover crop
Deckkonto *n* fictitious account
Deckladung *f* on-deck-lading *(cargo shipping)*; deck cargo
Deckladungsversicherung *f* on-deck-lading insurance, deck cargo insurance
Deckung *f* cover, covering, coverage *(needs etc.)*; reimbursement *(costs etc.)*; surety, security *(for sum of money etc.)*; guarantee *(for debt, loan etc.)*; reserve fund *(for money in circulation)*; protection *(draft etc.)* ◊ **als ~ annehmen** to take as reimbursement; **mangels ~** for want of funds; **mit ~** cum funds; **ohne ~** without funds
~, automatische automatic coverage
~, bankmäßige note cover of bankable paper
~ des Bedarfs meeting the requirements [needs]
~, erforderliche requisite cover [guarantee, security, surety]
~, genügende ample security
~, ungenügende insufficient security [funds]
~, volle full cover(age)
~ von Banknoten backing of notes
~, vorgeschriebene *(ins)* legal reserve
~, zusätzliche additional cover
Deckungsbedürfnis *n* short interest; need to cover

Deckungsbeitragskostenrechnung *f* accounting of departmental participation in covering costs
Deckungsbestände *mpl (bank)* reserve fund, cover of notes in circulation
Deckungsbetrag *m* margin (of loss), cover
Deckungsbilanz *f* balance sheet showing cover of notes *(in circulation)*
Deckungseinzahlung *f* payment to cover
Deckungserfordernisse *npl* coverage requirements
Deckungsgeschäft *n* hedge, covering transaction
Deckungskapital *n* cover capital; *(ins)* reserve [cover] fund *(part of the premiums of insured persons)*
Deckungskauf *m* covering purchase
Deckungsklausel *f* cover clause *(on bill of exchange or draft)*
Deckungsmittel *npl (fin)* (covering) funds, cover
Deckungsorder *f (com)* covering order
Deckungspflicht *f* (business company's) pledge to cover its own debts
Deckungsquellen *fpl* (covering) resources
Deckungsrechnung *f* balancing of needs and resources
~, finanzielle balancing of financial needs and resources
Deckungsrücklage *f s.* Deckungskapital
Deckungsrückstellung *f s.* Deckungskapital
Deckungsstock *m (ins)* unearned premium reserve; *(bank)* guarantee stock
Deckungssumme *f (ins)* amount of unearned premium reserve
Deckungsverhältnis *n* reserve ratio
~, gesetzlich vorgeschriebenes legal reserve requirements
Deckungsverkauf *m (com)* covering sale
Deckungswechsel *m (fin)* security credit note
Deckungswerte *mpl* admitted assets
Deckungszusage *f (ins)* binding receipt
~, vorläufige *(ins)* cover(ing) note
De-facto-Anerkennung *f* de facto recognition
Defekt *m* 1. defect, flaw, fault, imperfection; deficiency; 2. *(fin)* deficit
Defektenprotokoll *n (fin)* (written) statement of deficit
Defensivzeichen *n* (defensive) trademark
Defizit *n* deficit ⋄ **ein ~ (ab)decken** to make good a deficiency; **ein ~ ausgleichen** to supply a deficiency; **ein ~ ausweisen** to show a deficit; **mit einem ~ abschließen** *s.* **ein ~ ausweisen**
Defizitfinanzierung *f* deficit spending *(in periods of economic crisis)*; deficit financing
Defizithaushalt *m* budget showing a deficit
Defizitressourcen *fpl* deficit [missing] resources
Defizitsaldo *m* deficit balance

Defizitware *f* goods in short supply
Defizitwirtschaft *f* deficit policy
Deflation *f* deflation ⋄ **eine ~ durchführen** to deflate a currency
deflationär deflationary
Deflationist *m* deflationist
deflationistisch *s.* **deflationär**
Deflationsbewegung *f* deflationary movement
Deflationskrise *f* deflationary crisis
Deflationslücke *f* deflationary gap
Deflationspolitik *f* deflationary policy
Deformation *f* deformation; distortion
deformieren to deform; to distort
Defraudant *m* defrauder, fraud
Defraudation *f* fraud
Deglomeration *f* deglomeration
Degression *f* degression
Degressionskurve *f* sloping curve
De-jure-Anerkennung *f* de jure recognition
Dekadenplan *m* decade plan
Dekapitalisierung *f* decapitalization
Dekartellisierung *f* decartelization
Deklaration *f* declaration
~ und Aktionsprogramm *n* **über die Errichtung einer neuen Internationalen Wirtschaftsordnung** Declaration and Programme of Action on the Establishment of a New International Economic Order
Deklarationsprinzip *n (cust)* principle of declaration
deklarieren *(cust)* to declare *(goods)*
Dekoder *m* decoder
dekodieren to decode
Dekolonisierung *f* decolonization
Dekonzentration *f* deconcentration
Dekonzentrationsprogramm *n* deconcentration programme
Dekorateur *m* window-dresser, decorateur
Dekoration *f* decoration; window display, window-dressing
Dekorationskosten *pl* decoration charges
Dekorationsware *f* goods on display
Delegation *f* delegation
Delegierung *f* delegating, delegation
~ von Verantwortung delegation of responsibility
Delegierungsvertrag *m* assignment contract, contract for the secondment of workers, contract of temporary employment in another enterprise
Delikatessengeschäft *n* delicatessen shop
Delikatessensortiment *n* (range of) high-quality foods
Delkredere *n* del credere, guarantee, security
⋄ **~ berechnen** to charge for del credere; **~ bieten** to stand security; **~ übernehmen** to give [stand] guarantee

Delkrederefonds *m* del credere [guarantee, security] fund
Delkrederekonto *n* del credere account
Delkredereprovision *f* del credere commission
Delkrederereserve *f* contingent fund
Delkredererückstellung *f s.* **Delkrederereserve**
Delkredereversicherung *f* del credere [credit] insurance
Delphimethode *f* Delphi-method
Demograph *m* demographer
Demographie *f* demography
demographisch demographic
Demokratie *f* democracy
~, **innergenossenschaftliche** inner democracy of co-operatives
~, **innergewerkschaftliche** inner trade-union democracy
~, **innerparteiliche** inner-party democracy
demokratisch democratic
demonetisieren to demonetize, to withdrawes from circulation
Demonetisierung *f* demonetization, withdrawal from circulation
Demontage *f* dismantling, dismantlement *(machine, factory etc.)*
Demontagearbeiten *fpl* dismantling (work)
Demontageliste *f* dismantling list
Demontageprogramm *n* dismantling programme
Demontageverfahren *n* process of dismantling, dismantling process
demontieren to take *s.th.* down; to disassemble, to dismantle
Demontieren *n* dismantlement
Denkmalspflege *f* recording and preservation of monuments
Denkmalspfleger *m* curator of monuments
Denomination *f* denomination
Deponent *m* 1. depositor *(of money in bank etc.)*; 2. *(jur)* bailor; deponent
~, **imaginärer** fictitious deponent
Deponie *f* refuse [garbage] dump, refuse disposal unit
~, **geordnete** refuse [garbage] dump according to ecological and regional requirements
~, **wilde** illegal dump
deponieren to (place on) deposit *(valuables etc.)*; to dump garbage [refuse]
Deponierung *f* deposit; deposition
Deport *m (st.ex.)* backwardation
Deportation *f* deportation
Deportgeschäft *n (st.ex.)* backwardation business
deportieren to deport
Deportierung *f s.* **Deportation**
Deportkurs *m (st.ex.)* backwardation rate
Depositalschein *m s.* **Depotschein**

Depositar *m s.* **Depotinhaber**
Depositen *pl* deposits
~, **nicht in Anspruch genommene** unclaimed deposits
~, **sofort fällige** demand deposits
Depositenabteilung *f (bank)* deposit department
Depositenbank *f* deposit bank
Depositenbuch *n* deposit book
Depositeneinlagen *fpl* deposits, trust-money
Depositenforderung *f* claim on deposits
Depositengelder *npl s.* **Depositeneinlagen**
Depositengeschäft *n* deposit transaction; deposit [commercial] banking
Depositenguthaben *n* balance on the deposit account
Depositenkapital *n* deposit funds
Depositenkasse *f* bank's branch office; deposit bank
Depositenkonto *n* deposit account
Depositenkunde *m* depositor
Depositenschein *m* deposit receipt
Depositenversicherung *f* bank guarantee for deposits
Depositenvertrag *m* deposit agreement
Depositenwechsel *m s.* **Depotwechsel**
Depositenzinsen *mpl* interest on deposits
Depot *n* storehouse; repository, depository, depot; *(bank)* deposit, safe-custody, *(Am)* custodianship (account); *(cust)* bonded warehouse
~, **festes** special deposit
~ **für unverzollte Waren** bonded warehouse
~, **gemeinschaftliches** joint deposit
~, **geschlossenes** trust deposit
~, **gesperrtes** blocked [frozen] deposit
~, **gewöhnliches** regular deposit
~, **irreguläres** irregular deposit
~, **offenes** open deposit
~, **totes** securities ledger
~, **verschlossenes** safe deposit
Depotabteilung *f* safe-custody [securities] department
Depotaufstellung *f s.* **Depotauszug**
Depotauszug *m* statement of a deposit position
Depotbescheinigung *f s.* **Depotschein**
Depotbuch *n s.* **Depot, totes**
Depoteffekten *pl s.* **Depotpapiere**
Depotempfangsbescheinigung *f s.* **Depotschein**
Depotgarantie *f* depository bond
Depotgebühr *f* safe deposit fee
Depotgeschäft *n* safe-custody business; safe--custody transaction
Depotinhaber *m* depositor
Depotkonto *n* safe-custody account *(for securities etc.)*
Depotmiete *f* safe-custody charges
Depotpapiere *npl* deposited securities

Depotquittung *f s.* **Depotschein**
Depotschein *m* deposit receipt
Depotsteuer *f* bank deposit tax
Depotstimmrecht *n* voting by proxy
Depotumbuchung *f* transfer of shares [*(Am)* stocks]
Depotversicherung *f* safe-custody box insurance
Depotvertrag *m* safe-custody agreement
Depotverwahrung *f* custody of securities
Depotverwaltungsgebühr *f s.* **Depotgebühr**
Depotverzeichnis *n* safe-custody slip
Depotwechsel *m* deposited bill
Depression *f* (economic) depression, slump; recession
~, **tiefe** deep depression
Depressionsperiode *f* (period of) depression
Deputat *n* allowance in kind *(free farm produce, coal etc.)*
Deputatlohn *m* payment in kind
Dequalifizierung *f* loss of skills
Deroute *f (st.ex.)* panic
Desaggregierung *f* disaggregation
Design *n* design
Designationsrecht *n* power of appointment
Designer *m* designer
designieren to designate
Desintegration *f* disintegration
Destabilisierung *f* destabilisation
Detailgeschäft *n* retail shop
Detailhandel *m* retail trade
Detailpreis *m* retail price
Detailverkauf *m* retail trade [trading]
Detailwaren *fpl* retail goods
Detailzwischenhändler *m* middleman for retail trade
Determinante *f (maths)* determinant
Devalorisierung *f* devalorization
Devalvation *f* devaluation
devalvieren to devalue, to devaluate
Devisen *pl* foreign currency [exchange] ◊ ~ **abführen** to surrender foreign currency; ~ **anmelden** to declare foreign currency; ~ **beantragen** to apply for foreign currency; **zahlbar in** ~ payable in hard currency
~, **blockierte** frozen [blocked] foreign exchange
~, **eingefrorene** *s.* ~, **blockierte**
~, **freie** hard [convertible] currency
Devisenabfluß *m* outflow of foreign exchange
Devisenabkommen *n* foreign exchange agreement
Devisenablieferung *f* surrender of currency
Devisenablieferungspflicht *f* obligation to surrender foreign currency
Devisenablieferungsprämie *f s.* **Devisenbonus**
Devisenabrechnungsstelle *f* foreign exchange clearing office

Devisenabteilung *f (bank)* foreign exchange department
Devisenanforderungen *fpl* currency demands, foreign exchange requirements
Devisenankauf *m* purchase of foreign currency [exchange]
Devisenanmeldung *f* declaration of foreign currency
Devisenarbitrage *f* foreign exchange arbitrage
Devisenarbitragegeschäft *n* currency arbitrage
Devisenarbitragetransaktion *f s.* **Devisenarbitragegeschäft**
Devisenaufkommen *n* foreign exchange resources
Devisenaufwand *m* foreign exchange expenditure
Devisenausfall *m* loss in foreign exchange
Devisenausfuhrverbot *n* ban on the export of foreign exchange
Devisenausgleichsfonds *m* foreign exchange equalization fund
Devisenausland *n* foreign country
Devisenausländer *m* non-resident (for currency purposes) *(person not liable to domestic currency regulations)*
Devisenbank *f* foreign exchange bank
Devisenbedarf *m* foreign currency needs
Devisenbehörde *f* foreign exchange (control) authority
Devisenberater *m* adviser on (matters affecting) foreign exchange
Devisenberechnung *f* calculation of foreign exchange
Devisenbeschaffung *f* earning foreign exchange; obtaining foreign currency
Devisenbescheinigung *f* foreign exchange [currency] permit
Devisenbeschränkungen *fpl* currency restrictions
Devisenbestand *m* foreign exchange reserve [holdings]
Devisenbestimmungen *fpl* foreign exchange (control) regulations
Devisenbewirtschaftung *f* foreign exchange control
Devisenbewirtschaftungsgesetz *n* foreign exchange law
Devisenbewirtschaftungsgesetzgebung *f s.* **Devisengesetzgebung**
Devisenbewirtschaftungsstelle *f s.* **Devisenbehörde**
Devisenbilanz *f* balance of foreign exchange payments
Devisenbonus *m* percentage allowance to earners of foreign currency [exchange]
Devisenbörse *f* foreign exchange market
devisenbringend foreign exchange earning

Devisenclearing n foreign exchange clearing
Devisendefizit n deficit in foreign exchange
Deviseneingang m receipt of foreign exchange, foreign exchange receipt
Deviseneinheitskurs m single exchange rate
Deviseneinnahmen fpl foreign exchange earnings [proceeds]
Deviseneinsparung f foreign exchange saving(s)
Devisenerklärung f foreign currency declaration
Devisenerlös m s. Deviseneinnahmen
Devisenerlöskennziffer f s. Devisenertragskennziffer
Devisenertrag m s. Deviseneinnahmen
Devisenertragskennziffer f index of proceeds in foreign exchange
Devisenerwerb m s. Devisenbeschaffung
Devisenerwirtschaftung f procurement of foreign exchange
Devisenfaktor m foreign exchange factor [impact]
Devisenfonds m foreign exchange fund
Devisenforderung f foreign exchange claim
Devisenfreibetrag m foreign currency allowance
Devisengegenwert m equivalent value in foreign exchange
Devisengenehmigung f authorization for foreign currency; foreign exchange permit
Devisengeschäft n foreign exchange business [transaction]
Devisengesetzgebung f foreign exchange (control) legislation
Devisengewinn m foreign exchange profit
Devisengrenze f s. Devisenplafond
devisengünstig easy to earn foreign exchange
Devisenguthaben n foreign exchange assets [holdings]
Devisenhandel m operations in foreign exchange, foreign currency [exchange] dealings
Devisenhandelsbeschränkungen fpl foreign exchange restrictions
Devisenhändler m foreign exchange dealer
Devisenhaushalt m s. Devisenlage
Devisenimportkredit m foreign exchange credit for imports
Devisenindex m foreign exchange index
Deviseninland n country of the currency
Deviseninländer m resident (for currency purposes) *(person liable to domestic currency regulations)*
Devisenkassakurse mpl spot (exchange) rates
Devisenkassengeschäfte npl exchange for spot delivery, spot exchange transactions
Devisenkauf m purchase of foreign exchange [currency]
Devisenknappheit f shortage of foreign exchange

Devisenkontingent n foreign exchange quota
Devisenkontingentierung f s. Devisenkontrolle
Devisenkonto n foreign exchange account
Devisenkontrollbestimmungen fpl s. Devisenbestimmungen
Devisenkontrolle f foreign exchange control
Devisenkontrollstelle f foreign exchange control office
Devisenkredit m foreign exchange credit
Devisenkurs m rate of exchange ⋄ **zum gegenwärtigen ~** at the current rate (of exchange)
~ **für kurzfristige Wechsel** short(-term) rate (of exchange)
~ **für langfristige Wechsel** long(-term) rate (of exchange)
~**, überbewerteter** over-valued rate of exchange
~**, unterbewerteter** under-valued rate of exchange
Devisenkursbericht m foreign exchange report
Devisenkursbildung f fixing of foreign exchange rates
Devisenkursnotierung f quotation of foreign exchange rates
Devisenkurszettel m foreign exchange list
Devisenlage f foreign exchange position
Devisenmakler m foreign exchange dealer
Devisenmangel m s. Devisenknappheit
Devisenmarkt m foreign exchange market
Devisenmittel npl foreign exchange [currency]
Devisenmonopol n state monopoly of foreign exchange
Devisennotierung f s. Devisenkursnotierung
Devisenoperation f foreign exchange transaction
Devisenordnung f exchange system, foreign currency legislation
Devisenplafond m foreign exchange limit
Devisenplan m foreign exchange plan
Devisenplanung f foreign exchange planning
Devisenpolitik f foreign exchange policy
Devisenpolster n foreign exchange reserve
Devisenprämie f s. Devisenbonus
Devisenpreis m foreign exchange price
Devisenpreiskalkulation f foreign exchange price calculation
Devisenprüfung f auditing of foreign exchange account
Devisenquoten fpl s. Devisenkontingent
Devisenrechnung f 1. calculation of foreign exchange; 2. foreign exchange invoice
Devisenrecht n foreign exchange regulations
devisenrechtlich relating to foreign exchange regulations; in accordance with foreign currency regulations
Devisenregelung f s. Devisenordnung
Devisenrentabilität f foreign exchange profitability

Dienst 121

Devisenreserve *f* foreign exchange reserve
Devisenrestriktionen *fpl s.* **Devisenbeschränkungen**
Devisenschieber *m* person who makes illegal transfer of foreign exchange, currency smuggler, illegal dealer in currency
Devisenschiebung *f* illegal transfer [smuggling] of foreign exchange [currency]
Devisenschmuggel *m* currency smuggling
Devisenschmuggler *m* currency smuggler
Devisenschwierigkeiten *fpl* difficulties in earning foreign exchange
Devisenschwindel *m* illegal dealings in foreign exchange
Devisenspekulation *f* speculation on the foreign exchange market
Devisensperre *f* exchange embargo, ban on foreign exchange transfer
Devisenstabilisierungsfonds *m* foreign exchange stabilization fund
Devisenstatus *m s.* **Devisenlage**
Devisenstelle *f* (foreign) exchange office
Devisenstock *m s.* **Devisenreserve**
Devisentermingeschäfte *npl* forward exchange deals [dealings, transactions]
Devisenterminhandel *m s.* **Devisentermingeschäfte**
Devisenterminmarkt *m* forward exchange market
Devisentransaktion *f s.* **Devisenoperation**
Devisentransfer *m* transfer of foreign exchange
~, **illegaler** illegal transfer of foreign exchange
~, **legaler** official transfer of foreign exchange
Devisenüberwachung *f s.* **Devisenkontrolle**
Devisenüberwachungsstelle *f* foreign exchange control office
Devisenumrechnungsfaktor *m* internal foreign exchange conversion factor
Devisenumrechnungskoeffizient *m* coefficient of foreign exchange conversion *(to modify the rate of exchange according to special circumstances)*
Devisenumrechnungssatz *m* foreign exchange conversion rate
Devisenumtauschbescheinigung *f* certificate of currency exchange
Devisen- und Sortenumrechnung *f* foreign exchange conversion
Devisenvergehen *n* currency offence, violation of foreign exchange regulations
Devisenverkauf *m* sale of foreign currency
Devisenverkehr *m* foreign currency operations [transactions]
~, **freier** free foreign currency exchange
Devisenverlust *m* foreign exchange loss
Devisenverpflichtungen *fpl* foreign exchange liabilities

Devisenverrechnungskonto *n* foreign exchange clearing account
Devisenverrechnungssystem *n* multiple currency system
Devisenverstoß *m s.* **Devisenvergehen**
Devisenvorschrift *f s.* **Devisenordnung**
Devisenwährung *f* currency exchange standard
Devisenwechsel *m* currency bill
~, **kurzfristiger** short exchange
~, **langfristiger** long exchange
Devisenwert *m* foreign exchange value
Devisenwirtschaft *f* foreign exchange sector
Devisenwirtschaftlichkeit *f s.* **Devisenrentabilität**
Devisenzufluß *m* inflow of foreign exchange
Devisenzuteilung *f* foreign currency [exchange] allocation [allowance]
Devisenzwangswirtschaft *f* (foreign) exchange control
dezentral decentral, decentralizing
Dezentralisation *f* decentralization
dezentralisieren to decentralize
Dezentralisierung *f s.* **Dezentralisation**
Dezentralismus *m* regionalism
Dezile *f (stats)* decile
Dezimalwährung *f* decimal coinage
Diagonalmatrix *f (maths)* diagonal matrix
Diagonal-Regression *f (stats)* diagonal regression
Diagonalreihe *f (maths)* diagonal sequence
Diagramm *n* diagram
~, **dreidimensionales** three-dimensional diagram
~, **logarithmisches** logarithmic diagram
~, **zweidimensionales** two-dimensional diagramm
Dialektik *f* dialectics
Diät *f* diet
Diäten *pl* daily allowance, remuneration *(especially for members of parliament)*
Diätengelder *npl s.* **Diäten**
Dichotomie *f* dichotomy
~, **doppelte** *(stats)* double dichotomy
dichtbesiedelt densely populated
dichtbewaldet heavily forested
Dichte *f* density *(population etc.)*; frequency *(traffic etc.)*
Dichtefunktion *f (stats)* density function
Diebstahl *m* larceny, theft
Diebstahlversicherung *f* burglary insurance
dienen to serve, to do service; to be useful
Dienst *m* service; duty, duties; employment; position, post ◊ **jmdn. aus dem ~ entlassen** to dismiss s.o. from his [her] post; **außer ~** off-duty; retired; **den ~ kündigen** to resign one's position; **den ~ verweigern** to refuse duty; **im ~** on duty; **in ~ stellen** to put into

service; **seinen ~ antreten** to take up one's duties; **seinen~ verrichten** to do one's work
~ am Kunden services offered to customers
~, gehobener s. **~, höherer**
~, höherer higher grade
~, mittlerer middle grade
~, öffentlicher civil [public] service *(working for the government)*
~, unterer lower grade
Dienstalter *n* seniority; length of service
Dienstangelegenheit *f* official matter; matter of business
Dienstanweisung *f* service instructions
Dienstaufsicht *f* supervision ◊ **~ führen** to be in charge of
Dienstaufsichtsverfahren *n* disciplinary proceedings
Dienstauftrag *m* official travel voucher
Dienstaufwand *m* ex officio expenditure
Dienstaufwandsentschädigung *f* expense allowance, repayment [reimbursement] of expenses
Dienstausweis *m* (workplace) identity card *(issued by enterprises, institutions etc.)*
Dienstbereich *m* competence, competency; sphere
dienstbereit ready to do one's duty; standing by, in readiness; open
Dienstbereitschaft *f* stand-by duty; after-hour service *(chemist's shop)* ◊ **~ haben** to be on duty [call] *(doctor)*
Dienstbesprechung *f* (business) discussion, consultation, departmental meeting
Dienstbezeichnung *f* designation (of a position/grade), rank
Dienstbezüge *mpl* earnings, emoluments, salary
Dienste *mpl*:
◊ **~ leisten** to render services
~, geleistete services rendered
~, technische technical services
Dienstfahrt *f* official tour [trip]
dienstfrei off-duty
Dienstgebrauch *m* official use ◊ **nur für den ~** for official use only, *(Am)* restricted
Dienstgeheimnis *n* business [professional, trade] secret
Dienstgespräch *n* official call
diensthabend on duty
Diensthabender *m* officer [person] on duty
Dienstjahre *npl* years of service
Dienstleistung *f* service
~, hauswirtschaftliche domestic service
~, kommerzielle commercial service
~, nichtkommerzielle non-commercial service
~, persönliche personal service
Dienstleistungen *fpl*:
~, bezahlte services with charges
~ gegen Entgelt s. **~, bezahlte**

~, industrielle industrial services
~, kommunale s. **~, stadtwirtschaftliche**
~, kostenlose free services, services without charge
~, materielle services offered involving material
~, produktive productive services
~, stadtwirtschaftliche municipal services
~, technische technical services
~, unentgeltliche s. **~, kostenlose**
Dienstleistungsabkommen *n* service agreement
Dienstleistungsabteilung *f* service department
Dienstleistungsanlagen *fpl* service equipment
Dienstleistungsbereich *m* service sector
Dienstleistungsbetrieb *m* service enterprise *(offering services in such fields as laundry, dry cleaning, repairing shoes, electric household appliances etc.)*
Dienstleistungsbilanz *f* balance (sheet) of services
Dienstleistungsgebühr *f* service charges
Dienstleistungsgesellschaft *f* economy based on trade and services
Dienstleistungsgewerbe *n* service industries
Dienstleistungskosten *pl* service costs
Dienstleistungspreis *m* price of services, service charge
Dienstleistungsrabatt *m* discount on services
Dienstleistungsrechenstation *f* commercial computer centre
Dienstleistungssektor *m* s. **Dienstleistungsbereich**
Dienstleistungssphäre *f* s. **Dienstleistungsbereich**
Dienstleistungstarif *m* service rates
Dienstleistungs- und Reparaturbetrieb *m* service and repair centre
Dienstleistungs- und Übertragungsbilanz *f* balance of services and transfers
Dienstleistungsunternehmen *n* s. **Dienstleistungsbetrieb**
Dienstleistungsvertrag *m* service contract
Dienstleistungszentrum *n* service centre
dienstlich official
Dienstlohn *m* wages, pay
Dienstordnung *f* official regulations
Dienstpersonal *n* personal [domestic] staff, servants
Dienstpflicht *f* official duty; liability for service; compulsory service
dienstpflichtig liable to service
Dienstplan *m* work schedule; duty roster
Dienstrang *m* grade, rank
Dienstrangsystem *n* system of grades
Dienstreise *f* business journey [trip]; official mission *(abroad)*
Dienstreisekosten *pl* travel(ling) expenses
Dienstsache *f* official matter

Dienstschluß *m* end of working hours ◊ **nach ~** after work
Dienstschreiben *n* official letter
Dienstsiegel *n* official seal [stamp]
Dienststelle *f* (government) office [department]
~, zuständige proper department, department concerned
Dienststellung *f* position
Dienststunden *fpl* office [working] hours
dienstunfähig *s.* **dienstuntauglich**
Dienstunfähigkeit *f s.* **Dienstuntauglichkeit**
dienstuntauglich unfit for work
Dienstuntauglichkeit *f* incapacity for work
Dienstvergehen *n* offence against rules and regulations
Dienstverhältnis *n* employment contract *(government officials etc.)*
dienstverpflichten to conscript
dienstverpflichtet conscripted
Dienstverpflichtung *f* conscription
Dienstvorschriften *fpl* official regulations
Dienstweg *m* official channels ◊ **auf dem ~** through official channels; **den ~ einhalten** to act through the proper channels
dienstwidrig contrary to rules and regulations
Dienstwidrigkeit *f* irregularity
Dienstwohnung *f* official quarters [residence]
Dienstzeit *f* period in office [of service]
Differentialaufwand *m* differential expenditure
Differentialaufwendungen *fpl s.* **Differentialaufwand**
Differentialeinkommen *n* differential income
Differentialfracht *f* discriminating freight
Differentialkosten *pl* differential costs
Differentialprozeß *m (stats)* differential process
Differentialrente *f* differential ground rent *(s.* **Differentialrente I, Differentialrente II)**
Differentialrente I *f* differential ground rent I *(based on soil fertility and situation)*
Differentialrente II *f* differential ground rent II *(based on varying capital investment)*
Differentialrenteneinkommen *n* income from differential ground rent
Differentialrentenmethode *f* method of fixing values according to differential ground rent
Differentialtarif *m (cust)* differential tariff; differential rates *(railway, road etc.)*
Differentialwert *m* differential value
Differentialzoll *m* differential tariff [duty]
Differenz *f* difference
~, absteigende *(stats)* forward difference
~, aufsteigende *(stats)* backward difference
~, echte *(stats)* proper difference
~, endliche *(stats)* finite difference
~, mittlere *(stats)* mean difference
~, mittlere quadratische sukzessive *(stats)* mean-square successive difference

~, signifikante significant difference
~, symmetrische *(stats)* symmetric difference
Differenzbetrag *m* balance
Differenzen *fpl*:
~, ausgewogene balanced differences
Differenzenmethode *f (stats)* method of difference; method of classification by non-apparent characteristics
Differenzenrechnung *f (stats)* calculus of differences
Differenzgeschäft *n (st.ex.)* speculation; buying on margin; time bargain; *(Am)* margin business [transaction]
Differenzgeschäfte *npl (st.ex.)* stag buying ◊ **~ machen** to stag
differenzierbar distinguishable; *(stats)* differentiable
Differenzierbarkeit *f* distinction; *(stats)* differentiability
~, stochastische *(stats)* stochastic differentiability
differenzieren to differentiate, to obtain the differential; to distinguish, to differentiate between
Differenziertheit *f* distinctiveness
Differenzierung *f* differentiation
~ der Zinssätze differentiation of interest rates
Differenzierungsprozeß *m* process of differentiation
~ zwischen Entwicklungsländern process of differentiation between developing countries *(in levels of development etc.)*
Differenzkonto *n* over-and-short account
Differenzmethode *f*:
~, Student-Anderson'sche *(stats)* variate-difference method
Differenztarif *m s.* **Differentialtarif**
Differenzzahlung *f (st.ex.)* marginal payment
Diffusionsprozeß *m (stats)* diffusion process
Diplom *n* diploma, certificate *(of university graduation)*
Diplomand *m* undergraduate
Diplomingenieur *m* (certified) engineer *(with a degree in engineering)*
Diplomingenieurökonom *m* (certified) industrial engineer *(with a degree in industrial engineering)*
Diplomökonom *m* economist *(with a degree in economics)*
Diplompraktikum *n* practical training *(in enterprise etc., to prepare for degree thesis)*
Diplomprüfung *f* (university) examination *(for a degree)*
Diplomwirtschaftler *m s.* **Diplomökonom**
Direktabnehmer *m* direct purchaser
Direktabsatz *m* direct marketing
Direktausfuhr *f s.* **Direktexport**

Direktberechnung *f* direct calculation *(costs, profits etc.)*
Direktbezieher *m s.* **Direktabnehmer**
Direktbeziehungen *fpl* direct relations *(of supply or delivery)*
Direktbezug *m* direct supply *(of goods from the producer to the retailer and/or consumer)*
Direktdiskont *m* discount (on a certain commodity)
Direkteinfuhr *f s.* **Direktimport**
Direkteinkauf *m s.* **Direktbezug**
Direkterzeuger *m s.* **Direktproduzent**
Direktexport *m* direct export
Direktfinanzierung *f* direct financing
Direktgeschäft *n* ex-factory transaction
Direkthandel *m* direct trade *(between producer and retailer)*
Direkthersteller *m s.* **Direktproduzent**
Direktimport *m* direct import
Direktinvestition *f* direct investment; original [initial] investment
Direktion *f* 1. manager's [director's] office; headmaster's office; 2. management, control *(business house etc.)*; running *(business etc.)*; administration *(hospital etc.)*; 3. board of directors [managers]
Direktionsbereich *m* management department
Direktionsbeschluß *m* management decision
Direktionsmitglied *n* member of the board (of directors)
Direktive *f* instruction, order, directive
~, **ministerielle** ministerial directive
Direktkauf *m* direct purchase
Direktor *m* director, manager *(company, bank etc.)*; head *(industrial concern etc.)*; principal, headmaster *(school etc.)*; governor *(prison)*
~, **geschäftsführender** acting [managing] director
~, **kaufmännischer** business manager
~, **ökonomischer** commercial manager, economic director
~, **stellvertretender** deputy director, assistant manager
~, **technischer** managing engineer
Direktorium *n* board of directors
Direktproduzent *m* direct producer
Direktschulden *fpl* direct debts
Direktverbindung *f* direct connection
Direktverkauf *m s.* **Direktabsatz**
Direktversand *m* direct shipment, through consignment
Direktversicherung *f* direct insurance
Direktwerbung *f* advertising in the media
dirigieren to direct, to give directions, to control; to dispatch *(goods to their destination)*
Dirigismus *m* state intervention in the economy
dirigistisch controlled, directed

Disagio *n* disagio, discount
Disagiogewinn *m* unamortized debt discount
Disagiokonto *n* discount account
Disagionotierung *f (st.ex.)* discount quotation
Diskont *m* discount; bank discount; discount rate, bank rate; discounting ◊ **abzüglich des Diskonts** minus the discount; **einen ~ absetzen** to deduct a discount; **einen ~ erhöhen** to raise a bank rate; **einen ~ gewähren** to allow a discount; **einen ~ herabsetzen** to mark down a bank rate; **einen ~ senken** *s.* **einen ~ herabsetzen**; **in ~ nehmen** to take on discount; **mit ~ kaufen** to buy at a discount; **mit ~ verkaufen** to sell at a discount; **zum ~ bringen** to present for discount
~, **handelsüblicher** commercial [customary, usual] discount
~, **nicht in Anspruch genommener** discount lost
Diskontabrechnung *f* statement of charges for discounted bills *(including discount)*
Diskontabzug *m* discount *(nominal value minus bank rate)*
Diskontbank *f* discount bank
Diskontbasis *f* discount basis
Diskontbedingungen *fpl* discount terms, terms
Diskontbestände *mpl* discount holdings
Diskontbestimmungen *fpl s.* **Diskontbedingungen**
Diskontbewegung *f* fluctuations in the bank rate
Diskonten *mpl* discounted bills (of exchange)
Diskonterhöhung *f* raising of the discount [bank] rate
diskontfähig discountable
Diskontgeschäft *n* discount(ing) business
Diskonthaus *n* discount house
diskontierbar *s.* **diskontfähig**
Diskontierbarkeit *f* discountability
diskontieren to discount
diskontiert discounted ◊ **~ werden** to be discounted
Diskontierung *f* discounting
~ von Wechseln discount marketing
Diskontierungsfaktor *m* rate of discount
Diskontierungszeitraum *m* discount period
diskontinuierlich discontinuous
Diskontinuität *f* discontinuity
Diskontkasse *f* discount office
Diskontkredit *m* discount credit *(on bills etc., minus bank rate)*
Diskontmakler *m* bill-broker
Diskontmarkt *m* discount market
Diskontmaterial *n* bills eligible for discount
Diskonto *m s.* **Diskont**
Diskontpolitik *f* discount [*(Am)* rediscount] policy

Diskontprovision *f* discount commission
Diskontrate *f s.* **Diskontsatz**
Diskontrechnung *f s.* **Diskontabrechnung**
Diskontsatz *m* discount [bank, *(Am)* rediscount] rate
Diskontsenkung *f* lowering of the discount [bank] rate
Diskontstelle *f s.* **Diskonthaus**
Diskonttag *m* date of discount
Diskonttage *mpl* discount days
Diskontumsatz *m* discount turnover
Diskontverbindlichkeiten *fpl* discounts
Diskontverkehr *m s.* **Diskontgeschäft**
Diskontwechsel *m* bill discounted
Diskontwert *m* discounted value
Diskordanz *f (stats)* discordance
Diskriminanzanalyse *f (stats)* discriminatory analysis
diskriminieren to discriminate
Diskriminierung *f* discrimination
Diskriminierungsmaßnahmen *fpl* discriminating measures
Diskriminierungspolitik *f* policy of discrimination, discriminating policy
Diskussion *f* discussion; debate ◊ **eine ~ führen** to make a discussion; **eine ~ schließen** to close [end] a discussion
Dispache *f (ins)* average adjustment [statement]; average bond
Dispacheur *m (ins)* average-stater, average--adjuster
dispachieren *(ins)* to adjust an average
Disparität *f* disparity, incongruity
Dispatcher *m* (production) supervisor *(s.* **Dispatcherdienst)**
Dispatcherbüro *n* supervisory service office
Dispatcherdienst *m* supervisory service *(following up implementation of plans, fulfilment of priority tasks and reporting breakdowns etc. to the responsible authorities)*
Dispatcherleitstelle *f s.* **Dispatcherzentrale**
Dispatchersystem *n* supervisory system *(s.* **Dispatcherdienst)**
Dispatcherzentrale *f* supervisory service centre
Dispens *m* dispensation, exemption; certificate of dispensation [exemption]
Dispensation *f s.* **Dispens**
dispensieren:
 ◊ **jmdn. von etwas ~** to dispense [excuse, exempt] s.o. from doing s.th.
Dispersion *f (stats)* dispersion
~, normale *(stats)* normal dispersion
~, übernormale *(stats)* hypernormal [supernormal] dispersion
~, unternormale *(stats)* sub-normal dispersion
Dispersionsmatrix *f (stats)* covariance [dispersion] matrix

Disponent *m* chief clerk
disponibel disposable, available
Disponibilität *f* disposability, availability
~ der Arbeiter mobility of workforce [manpower]
~ des Arbeiters mobility of a worker
disponieren to have *s.th./s.o.* at one's disposal, to dispose *(sum of money etc.)*; to make arrangements; to place orders
Disponieren *n* having *s.th./s.o.* at one's disposal; disposal *(sum of money etc.)*; making arrangements; placing orders
Disposition *f* 1. disposal *(sum of money etc.)*; making arrangements; placing of orders; 2. disposition, layout, plan
Dispositionsgruppe *f (com)* group of disposable commodities
Dispositionskartei *f* card index of stock
Dispositionsprozeß *m* process of preparing the supply of consumer goods *(in trading organizations)*
Dispositionsreserve *f (fin)* reserves of disposable financial means *(at lower budget levels)*
Dispositionsschein *m* banker's acknowledgement of a credit note
Dispositionsverfahren *n* method of preparing the supply of consumer goods *(in trading organizations)*
Disproportion *f* disproportion
Disproportionalität *f* disproportionality *(between sectors of the economy)*
disproportioniert disproportionate, out of proportion
Dissoziation *f* disassociation *(of a group of countries in the international division of labour according to a theory in development economics)*
Distanzfracht *f* rateable freight
Distanzgeschäft *n* forward delivery business
Distanzhandel *m* long-distance trade
Distanzkauf *m s.* **Distanzgeschäft**
Distanzscheck *m* cheque not drawn on the bank where the account is held
Distanztarif *m* distance rate
Distanztratte *f s.* **Distanzwechsel**
Distanzwechsel *m* bill of exchange payable elsewhere *(than at the place of issue)*
Distribution *f* distribution
Distributionsbeziehungen *fpl s.* **Distributionsverhältnisse**
Distributionsmethode *f* method of distribution
~, modifizierte modified method of distribution
Distributionsprozeß *m* process of distribution
Distributionssphäre *f* sector of distribution
Distributionstheorie *f* theory of distribution
Distributionsverhältnisse *npl* relations of distribution, distribution relationships
Distributionsweise *f* mode of distribution

Distrikt *m* district; region, area
Disziplin *f* 1. discipline; 2. branch, section
~, **technologische** technological [operating, working] system
Disziplinarbefugnis *f* disciplinary powers; authority to order disciplinary measures
Disziplinarbefugter *m* person vested with disciplinary powers; person with authority to order disciplinary measures
Disziplinarmaßnahme *f* disciplinary measure
Disziplinarordnung *f* disciplinary rules, rules of discipline
Disziplinarverfahren *n* disciplinary action [proceedings]
divergent divergent
Divergenz *f* divergence
Divergenzkoeffizient *m (stats)* coefficient of divergence
divergieren to diverge
divers diverse, different, varied; sundry
Diversa *pl s.* **Diverses**
Diverses *n* sundry goods; sundries
Diversifikation *f* diversification
Diversifizierungsprogramm *n* plan of diversification, diversification plan *(of production etc.)*
Dividende *f* dividend ◊ **eine ~ beschließen** to declare a dividend; **mit ~ cum** dividend; **ohne ~ ex** dividend, *(Am)* dividend off
~, **ausgeschüttete** distributed dividend
~, **außerordentliche** extraordinary [*(Am)* surplus] dividend
~, **fällige** dividend due
~, **festgestzte** declared dividend
~, **garantierte** guaranteed dividend
~, **gleichbleibende** stable dividend
~, **nicht ausgezahlte** unpaid dividend
~, **noch ausstehende** pending dividend
~, **noch nicht fällige** accrued dividend
~, **satzungsmäßige** statutory dividend
~, **steuerpflichtige** taxable dividend
~, **vorläufige** interim dividend
Dividendenabschlag *m* difference between the normal price and the ex-dividend price
Dividendenabschnitt *m s.* **Dividendenschein**
Dividendenaktie *f* participating share [*(Am)* stock]
Dividendenanspruch *m* right to a dividend
Dividendenausgleichskonto *n* dividends equalization account
Dividendenausgleichsreserve *f* dividends equalization fund
Dividendenausschüttung *f* distribution of dividends
Dividendenauszahlungsanweisung *f* dividend order
dividendenberechtigt entitled to receive dividends

Dividendenberechtigung *f* dividend rights
Dividendenbeschränkungen *fpl* limitation on dividends, dividend restriction
Dividendenbeteiligung *f* participation in dividends
Dividendenbogen *m* (dividend) coupon sheet
Dividendeneinkommen *n s.* **Dividendeneinnahmen**
Dividendeneinnahmen *fpl* dividend income
Dividendenerhöhung *f* increase of dividend
Dividendenerklärung *f* declaration of a dividend
Dividendenkonto *n* dividend account
Dividendenkürzung *f* reduction of dividend
Dividendenpapiere *npl s.* **Dividendenwerte**
Dividendenpolitik *f* dividend policy
Dividendenreserve *f* dividend reserve fund
Dividendenreservefonds *m s.* **Dividendenreserve**
Dividendenrücklage *f s.* **Dividendenreserve**
Dividendenrückstände *mpl* dividends in arrears
Dividendensatz *m* dividend rate
Dividendenschein *m* dividend warrant [coupon]
Dividendenstock *m s.* **Dividendenreserve**
Dividendenvorschlag *m* recommendation on dividends
Dividendenwerte *mpl* shares [*(Am)* stocks] carrying dividend
~, **börsengängige** dividend-paying securities
Dividendenzahlung *f* distribution of dividends
Divisionskalkulation *f* process cost accounting
Dock *n* dock, wharf, quay
Dockanlagen *fpl* docks; dock installations
Dockarbeiter *m* docker, dock worker, *(Am)* longshoreman
Dockgebühren *fpl* dockage, dock charges, wharf dues
Dockgeld *n* dock duty
Docklagermiete *f* dock rent
Dokument *n* document, record; *(jur)* (legal) instrument, deed ◊ **ein ~ mit einer Unterschrift versehen** to affix one's signature to a document
~, **amtliches** official document
~, **inoffizielles** unofficial document
~, **vertrauliches** confidential document
Dokumentation *f* documentation
~, **technische** technical documentation
~, **wissenschaftliche** documentation of results of scientific work
~, **wissenschaftsorganisatorische** documentation of R & D organization
Dokumentationszentrum *n* documentation centre
~, **technisches** technical documentation centre
Dokumente *npl* documents
~ **gegen Akzept** documents against acceptance

~ gegen Einlösung der Tratte *s.* ~ gegen Zahlung
~ gegen Zahlung documents against payment
Dokumentenakkreditiv *n* (documentary) letter of credit *(for goods trade)*
Dokumentendurchlauf *m* passage of a document
Dokumentendurchlaufzeit *f* time taken for the passage of a document
Dokumenteninkasso *n* documentary encashment *(through the bank of the seller)*
Dokumentenkredit *m* documentary credit
Dokumentenregulativ *n* instructions on documents to be submitted
Dokumententratte *f* documentary draft
dokumentieren to prove; to demonstrate
Dollar *m* dollar
Dollarabfluß *m* outflow of dollars
Dollaranleihe *f* dollar loan
Dollaraufkommen *n* dollar receipts
Dollarbilanz *f* dollar balance of payments
Dollarblock *m* dollar block
Dollardefizit *n* dollar deficit
Dollareinkommen *n* dollar income
Dollarguthaben *npl* dollar balance; assets held in dollars
Dollarklausel *f* dollar clause
Dollarknappheit *f* shortage of dollars
Dollarkrise *f* dollar crisis
Dollarlücke *f* dollar gap
Dollarpool *m* dollar pool
Dollarsphäre *f s.* **Dollarzone**
Dollarverknappung *f* shortage of dollars
~, **künstliche** artificial shortage of dollars
Dollarzahlungen *fpl* dollar payments
Dollarzone *f* dollar area
Domizil *n* domicile; *(com)* domicile, place of payment *(of a bill)*
Domizilakzept *n* domiciled acceptance
domizilieren to domiciliate *(a bill of exchange with a person or at a bank)*
Domizilwechsel *m* 1. change of residence; 2. *(st.ex.)* domiciled bill of exchange
Doppel *n* duplicate
Doppelanspruch *m* double claim
Doppelarbeit *f* duplicated work
Doppelauswahl *f (stats)* overlapping maps
~, **koordinierte** *(stats)* method of overlapping maps
Doppelbesteuerung *f* double taxation
~, **internationale** international double taxation
Doppelbesteuerungsabkommen *n* double taxation (avoidance) agreement *(to prevent double taxation)*
Doppelbuchung *f* double entry
Doppelcharakter *m* two-fold character
~ **der Arbeit** two-fold character of labour *(commodity-producing labour involving the unity of concrete and abstract labour)*
Doppelerfassung *f s.* **Doppelzählung**
Doppelfaktoren-Modell *n (stats)* bifactor model
Doppelschicht *f (ind)* double shift
Doppeltarif *m* dual rate
Doppelverdiener *m* person with two jobs; husband and wife who are both earning
Doppelverdienst double earnings
Doppelversicherung *f* double insurance
Doppelwährung *f* double standard
Doppelzählung *f* double counting
Doppik *f* double-entry book keeping
Dorfentwicklungsplan *m* village development plan
Dorfgemeinde *f* village [rural] community, country parish
Dorfgemeinschaft *f* village community
Dorfgenossenschaft *f* rural co-operative; village co-operative
Dorfverkaufsstelle *f* village shop [store]
dosieren to give *s.th.* in small amounts
Dosierung *f* dosage, dose
Dosis *f* dose
~, **äquivalente** *(stats)* equivalent dose
~, **effektive** *(stats)* median effective dose
~ **letalis** *(stats)* median lethal dose
Dosis-Metameter *n (stats)* dose metameter
Dosiswert *m s.* **Dosis**
~, **transformierter** *s.* **Dosis-Metameter**
Dotation *f* donation; endowment; financial allocation *(by the state to local authorities)*
dotieren to endow
Dotierung *f s.* **Dotation**
Dozent *m* reader, senior lecturer
Drahtadresse *f s.* **Drahtanschrift**
Drahtakzept *n* telegraphic acceptance
Drahtanschrift *f* telegraphic address
Drahtantwort *f* reply by telegram [wire]
Drahtanweisung *f* telegraphic money-order
Drahtaviso *n* cable advice
Drahtofferte *f* telegraphic offer
Drahtüberweisung *f* telegraphic transfer
Draufgabe *f* 1. earnest money; part payment in advance; 2. extra weight *(granted to customer)*
Draufgeld *n* earnest money; part payment in advance
Drechslerarbeit *f* turnery; turned work
Drechslerei *f s.* **Drechslerwerkstatt**
Drechslerwerkstatt *f* turner's shop
Dreckarbeit *f* dirty work
Dreckgeld *n* dirty money *(loading etc.)*
Dreiecksgeschäft *n (com)* triangular transaction
Dreiecksverteilung *f (stats)* triangular distribution
Dreifelderwirtschaft *f (agric)* three-course rotation [system]

Dreimächteabkommen *n* tripartite agreement
Dreimeilengrenze *f* three-mile limit
Dreimonatsakzept *n* three-month acceptance
Dreimonatsfrist *f* period of three months, three--month period
Dreimonatsgeld *n* ninety days' loan
Dreimonatspapier *n s.* **Dreimonatswechsel**
Dreimonatswechsel *m* three months' bill
Dreimonatsziel *n* three months after date
Drei-Punkte-Versuch *m (stats)* three-point essay
Drei-Reihen-Satz *m (stats)* three-series theorem
Dreischichtsystem *n* three-shift system
dreiseitig trilateral
Dreiviertelmehrheit *f* three quarters majority
Dreiviertelverlustklausel *f* three-fourth loss clause
Dreiviertelwertklausel *f* three-fourth value clause
dringlich urgent, pressing
Dringlichkeit *f* urgency
Dringlichkeitsantrag *m* application for priority [of urgency]
Dringlichkeitsbescheinigung *f* certificate of urgent need
Dringlichkeitsfrage *f* question of urgency
Dringlichkeitsliste *f* priority list
Dringlichkeitsstufe *f* priority
Dringlichkeitsvermerk *m* urgent note
Drittausfertigung *f* triplicate
Drittelbeteiligung *f* one-third interest
Dritter *m* third (person) ◊ **zugunsten eines Dritten** in favour of a third person [party]
Drittland *n* third country
Drittschuldner *m* garnishee
Druck *m* 1. pressure; 2. printing ◊ ~ **ausüben auf** to exert pressure on, to bring pressure to bear on; **in** ~ **geben** to send to the press; **in** ~ **gehen** to go to press; **sich im** ~ **befinden** gone to the press; **unter dem** ~ **der Armut** under the pressure of poverty; **unter** ~ **arbeiten** to work under pressure; **unter** ~ **handeln** to act under pressure; **unter** ~ **verhandeln** to negotiate under pressure
~, **finanzieller** financial pressure
~, **wirtschaftlicher** economic pressure
Druckarbeiten *fpl* printing work
Druckauftrag *m* printing order
Druckbewässerung *f (agric)* pump irrigation
drucken to print, to publish
drücken to press, to squeeze; to impress, to imprint, to stamp
Druckereigewerbe *n s.* **Druckgewerbe**
Druckerlaubnis *f* licence to print; permission to print
Druckgenehmigung *f s.* **Druckerlaubnis**
Druckgewerbe *n* printing trade [industry]
Druckkosten *pl* printing costs

Druckmittel *n* (means of) pressure
Drucksache *f* printed matter
Drusch *m (agric)* 1. threshing; 2. threshed corn
Druschgemeinschaft *f (agric)* threshing community
Dualaufgabe *f (d.pr.)* dual problem
Dualkarte *f (d.pr.)* binary dual card
Dualpreis *m* dual price
Dualstelle *f (stats)* bit
Dualsystem *n (d.pr.)* binary (number) system, binary code
Dualwert *m* dual value
Dualwirtschaft *f* dual economy
Dualzahl *f (d.pr.)* binary number
Dubiosen *pl* doubtful [bad] debts
Dubiosenkonto *n* bad debts account
Dumping *n* dumping ◊ ~ **betreiben** to dump
~, **verschleiertes** hidden dumping
Dumpingpreis *m* dumping price
Dumpingspanne *f* marginal dumping
Dumpingwaren *fpl* dumped goods
Düngemittel *n* fertilizer; manure
~, **chemisches** chemical fertilizer
~, **künstliches** artificial fertilizer
~, **organisches** manure
Düngemittelindustrie *f* fertilizer industry
Dünger *m* manure
Duplikat *n* duplicate, copy
durchdringen to penetrate, to pierce; to permeate, to pervade *(water, smell etc.)*
Durchdringung *f* penetration; permeation, pervasion *(water, smell etc.)*
~, **wirtschaftliche** economic penetration
Durchfahrt *f* passage; transit; thoroughfare *(street)* ◊ ~ **verboten** no transit; no thoroughfare *(street)*
Durchfahrtsrecht *n* right of passage
Durchfahrtzoll *m s.* **Durchfuhrzoll**
Durchflugrecht *n* air transit right
Durchfracht *f* through shipment, transit freight
Durchfrachtbrief *m* through bill of lading
Durchfrachtkonnossement *n s.* **Durchfrachtbrief**
Durchfuhr *f* transit; transit service
durchführbar practicable, workable, feasible, possible
Durchführbarkeit *f* practicability, workability, feasibility
Durchfuhrbeschränkungen *fpl* transit restrictions *(imposed on particular goods)*
durchführen 1. to lead [take] *s.o./s.th.* through; 2. to carry out [through]; to execute, to implement *(plan etc.)*, to enforce *(law etc.)*
Durchfuhrgüter *npl s.* **Durchgangsgüter**
Durchfuhrhandel *m* transit trade
Durchfuhrland *n* transit country
Durchfuhrrecht *n* right of passage

Durchfuhrtarif m transit transport rate [charges]
Durchführung f carrying out [through]; execution, implementation *(plan etc.)* enforcement *(law etc.)*
~ **des Haushalts, kassenmäßige** financial execution of the budget
~ **des Haushaltplanes** implementation of the budget
Durchführungsbestimmung f (implementing) regulation *(law etc.)*
Durchführungsverordnung f s. **Durchführungsbestimmung**
Durchführungsvorschrift f instructions for implementation [execution]
Durchfuhrverbot n transit embargo
Durchfuhrverkehr m traffic passing through, through-traffic
Durchfuhrwaren fpl s. **Durchgangsgüter**
Durchfuhrzoll m transit duty
Durchgang m passage *(bill through parliament etc.)*; transit *(goods)*
Durchgangsabgabe f s. **Durchfuhrzoll**
Durchgangsbahnhof m through [(Am) way] station
Durchgangsfracht f through shipment
Durchgangsfrachtbrief m through bill of lading, (Am) waybill
Durchgangsfrachtsatz m transit [through] rate
Durchgangsgebühr f transit charges
Durchgangsgüter npl transit goods ◊ **als ~ angeben** to enter goods as transit
Durchgangshandel m s. **Durchfuhrhandel**
Durchgangskonnossement n through-export bill of lading
Durchgangskonto n suspense account
Durchgangskosten pl transit costs
Durchgangslager n transit camp
Durchgangsland n country through which goods are conveyed in transit, transit country
Durchgangspassierschein m transit permit [pass]
Durchgangsposten m *(acc)* suspense item
Durchgangspostverkehr m transit mail service
Durchgangsreisender m through [transit] passenger
Durchgangssatz m transit [through] rate
Durchgangssendung f s. **Durchgangsfracht**
Durchgangsstadium n transition stage [period]
Durchgangsstation f through [(Am) way] station
Durchgangsstraße f through road
Durchgangsstrecke f transit [through] route
Durchgangstarif m s. **Durchgangssatz**
Durchgangsverkehr m s. **Durchfuhrverkehr**
Durchgangsvisum n transit visa
Durchgangswaren fpl s. **Durchgangsgüter**
Durchgangszertifikat n s. **Durchgangspassierschein**

Durchgangszoll m s. **Durchfuhrzoll**
Durchgangszug m through [express, non-stop] train
durchgeführt executed
durchgehen to go through *(application etc.)*; to go straight through *(persons)*; to be in transit *(goods)* ◊ **nicht ~** to fail to go through, to be defeated *(bill through parliament etc.)*; to fail *(examination, test)*
durchgehend:
◊ **~ geöffnet** open throughout
durchkommen to be passed *(application)*; to pass *(examination, test)*
Durchkonnossement n s. **Durchfrachtbrief**
durchlassen to allow s.o./s.th. to pass through
Durchlaßfähigkeit f capacity *(1. maximum quantity of products or services to be processed by a department within a certain period; 2. maximum number of transport units or quantity of goods which can pass through a transport route)*
Durchlaßschein m permit, pass
Durchlauf m *(d.pr.)* pass, run
Durchlaufdauer f passage time *(product)*
durchlaufen to run [go, pass] through [across] *(area etc.)*; to cover *(distance etc.)*; to filter through; *(d.pr.)* to traverse
Durchlaufkonto n interim account
Durchlaufplan m production schedule
Durchlaufplanung f production scheduling
Durchlaufproblem n optimal sequence problem *(work pieces etc.)*
Durchlaufzeit f passage time *(work piece, voucher etc.)*; *(d.pr.)* throughput time
Durchleitkredit m loan passed on, transmitted credit
Durchreise f passage, transit ◊ **auf der ~** on the way through
Durchreiseerlaubnis f transit certificate [pass]
durchreisen to pass through; to tour *(country)*
Durchreisesichtvermerk m s. **Durchreisevisum**
Durchreisevisum n transit visa
~, **einmaliges** transit visa for a single journey
~, **mehrmaliges** transit visa for repeated journeys
Durchsatz m input [consumption] of raw and other materials *(particularly in chemical industries)*
Durchschlupf m rate of low-quality goods (passing quality control unnoticed)
durchschmuggeln to smuggle
Durchschnitt m 1. average; mean; 2. section ◊ **im ~** on (an) average; **im ~ betragen** to average; **über dem ~** above average; **unter dem ~** below average
~, **annähernder** rough average
~, **fortschreitender** *(stats)* progressive averge
~, **gleitender** *(stats)* moving average

~, guter fair average
~, provisorischer *(stats)* working mean
~, ungefährer *s.* **~, annähernder**
durchschnittlich average; mean; ordinary, normal, middling, medium
Durchschnittsabgabepreis *m* average selling price
Durchschnittsabschreibungssatz *m* average rate of depreciation
Durchschnittsalter *n* average age
Durchschnittsarbeit *f* average work
Durchschnittsarbeitstag *m* average working day
Durchschnittsaufwand *m* average cost
Durchschnittsausgabe *f* average expenditure
Durchschnittsbelastung *f* average load
Durchschnittsbestand *m* average stock
Durchschnittsbetrag *m* average amount
Durchschnittseinkommen *n* average income
Durchschnittserlös *m* average proceeds
Durchschnittsertrag *m* *(com)* average return; *(agric)* average yield
Durchschnittserwerb *m s.* **Durchschnittseinkommen**
Durchschnittserzeugung *f* average production
Durchschnittsfamilie *f* average family
Durchschnittsgestehungspreis *m* average cost price
Durchschnittsgröße *f* average, average value [size]
~, gesellschaftliche social average *(cost, expenditure etc.)*
Durchschnittskapital *n* average capital
Durchschnittskonsum *m s.* **Durchschnittsverbrauch**
Durchschnittskosten *pl* average costs
Durchschnittskunde *m* average customer
Durchschnittskurs *m* average exchange rate
Durchschnittslebensdauer *f* average life expectancy, average span of life
Durchschnittsleistung *f* average performance; *(stats)* mean efficiency
Durchschnittslohn *m* average wage [salary]
Durchschnittslohngruppe *f* average wage-grade
Durchschnittslohnzuwachs *m* average wage [salary] growth
Durchschnittsmarktpreis *m* average market price
Durchschnittsmensch *m* average person
Durchschnittsnorm *f* average norm
Durchschnittsnotierung *f* average quotation
Durchschnittspassiva *pl* average liabilities [debts]
Durchschnittsprämie *f* 1. *(ins)* average premium; 2. average bonus
Durchschnittspreis *m* average price
Durchschnittsproduktion *f* average output [production]

Durchschnittsproduktivität *f* average productivity
Durchschnittsprozentsatz *m* average percentage
Durchschnittsqualität *f* average [standard] quality
~ der geprüften Liefermengen *(stats)* average outgoing quality level
Durchschnittsstundenlohn *m* average hourly earnings
Durchschnittsstundenverdienst *m s.* **Durchschnittsstundenlohn**
Durchschnittssumme *f* average sum
Durchschnittstransportkosten *pl* average transport cost; average haulage
Durchschnittsumsatz *m* average turnover
~, jährlicher average annual turnover, average turnover annually
Durchschnittsverbrauch *m* average consumption
Durchschnittsverbraucher *m* average consumer
Durchschnittsverdienst *m* average earnings
Durchschnittsverfallzeit *f* average (term of) maturity
Durchschnittsvorratsnorm *f* average norm of stocks *(either in physical or value terms)*
Durchschnittsware *f* standard quality goods
Durchschreibebuchführung *f* duplicate bookkeeping
Durchschreibebuchhaltung *f s.* **Durchschreibebuchführung**
durchsetzen to get *(plan etc.)* carried out, to put through *(plan etc.)*; to achieve *(one's end)*, to obtain *(what one wants)*; to force *(plan etc.)* through
Durchsetzung *f* getting *(plan etc.)* carried through, putting through *(plan etc.)*; achieving, achievement *(one's end)*, obtaining *(what one wants)*; forcing through *(plan etc.)*, enforcement *(claim)*; safeguarding *(rights)*
Dürre *f* drought; dryness
Dürreschadenversicherung *f* drought insurance
Dynamik *f* 1. dynamics; 2. vitality
~ der Bevölkerungsentwicklung dynamics of population development, demographic dynamics
Dynamisierung *f* dynamization *(economy etc.)*

E

Ebene *f* 1. plain, flat open country; 2. level; 3. *(maths)* plane ◊ **auf betrieblicher** ~ at enterprise level; **auf staatlicher** ~ at government [state] level; **auf volkswirtschaftlicher** ~ at national economic level
~, **fruchtbare** *(agric)* fertile plain
Echéance *f (fin)* term, falling due *(bill)*
echt genuine, real *(gold, stone, leather etc.)*; authentic *(document, text etc.)*
Echtheit *f* genuineness *(gold, stone, leather etc.)*; authenticity *(document, text etc.); (d.pr.)* validity
Echtheitsbeweis *m* proof of genuineness [authenticity]
Echtheitsprüfung *f* test of genuineness [authenticity]
Echtzeit *f (d.pr.)* real time
Echtzeitbetrieb *m (d.pr.)* real-time operation
Echtzeit-Rechner *m (d.pr.)* real time computer
Echtzeit-Simulator *m (d.pr.)* real-time simulator
Ecken-Test *m (stats)* corner test
Eckladen *m* corner-shop
Ecklohn *m* basic wage
Eckwert *m* threshold [base] rate
Edelmetall *n* precious metal
Edelvaluta *f* convertible currency
EDV-Anlage *f s.* **Datenverarbeitungsanlage, elektronische**
Effekt *m* effect, result; efficiency; benefit
~, **volkswirtschaftlicher** national economic result
Effekten *pl* 1. securities, stocks, bonds; 2. personal effects [belongings], movables, goods and chattels
Effektenabteilung *f* securities department *(bank)*
Effektenarbitrage *f* arbitrage in securities
Effektenbank *f* issuing house; investment bank
Effektenbesitzer *m* holder of securities
Effektenbestand *m* holdings (in securities)
Effektenbörse *f* stock exchange, security market
Effektengeschäft *n* stock-exchange business [transaction]
Effektenhandel *m* stock-exchange business [transactions], dealing in stocks
Effektenhändler *m (st.ex.)* stockbroker, jobber, stockjobber, stock dealer
Effektenkonto *n* stock account
Effektenkredit *m* loan on securities
Effektenkurs *m* market price of securities, quotation
Effektenlombard *m* advance on securities
Effektenlombardgeschäft *n s.* **Effektenlombardierung**
Effektenlombardierung *f* granting a loan on securities; raising a loan on securities
Effektenmakler *m (st.ex.)* stockbroker
Effektenmarkt *m* security market; stock exchange
Effektenpaket *n* block [parcel] of securities
Effektenrechnung *f s.* **Effektenkonto**
Effektenspekulation *f* speculation in securities
effektiv effective *(performance, industry etc.)*, efficacious *(action, remedy etc.)*; real, actual *(price, weight, value etc.)*
Effektivbestand *m* actual stock *(materials, goods etc.); (fin)* realizable assets
Effektivgeschäft *n* spot market transaction
Effektivhandel *m s.* **Effektivgeschäft**
Effektivität *f* effectiveness *(measures etc.)*; efficiency *(investments etc.)*
~, **ökonomische** economic efficiency
~, **volkswirtschaftliche** efficiency of the national economy, national economic efficiency
Effektivitätsausweis *m* statement of efficiency
Effektivitätsberechnung *f s.* **Effektivitätsrechnung**
Effektivitätsbewertung *f* evaluation of efficiency
Effektivitätseinschätzung *f* estimation of efficiency
Effektivitätsermittlung *f* ascertainment of efficiency
Effektivitätsfaktor *m* factor influencing efficiency
Effektivitätsgrad *m* rate of efficiency
Effektivitätskennziffer *f* indicator of efficiency, efficiency indicator
Effektivitätskoeffizient *m* coefficient of efficiency, efficiency coefficient
Effektivitätskriterien *npl* efficiency criteria
Effektivitätsmaß *n* measure of efficiency
Effektivitätsmessung *f* measurement [measuring] of efficiency
Effektivitätsnachweis *m* evidence of efficiency
Effektivitätsplanung *f* efficiency planning
Effektivitätsrechnung *f* efficiency calculation, calculation of efficiency
~, **komplexe** comprehensive calculation of efficiency
Effektivitätssteigerung *f* raising of efficiency
Effektivitätsverlust *m* loss in efficiency
Effektivitätswirkungen *fpl* efficiency effects
~ **von Strukturveränderungen** efficiency effects of structural changes *(in the economy)*
Effektivitätszuwachs *m* increase in efficiency
Effektivklausel *f* clause (on bill of exchange) *(that payment must be made in specified currency)*, actual currency clause
Effektivleistung *f* effective output *(industry etc.)*; effective performance *(machine etc.)*

Effektivlohn *m* actual wage
Effektivpreis *m* cash price *(basis for the average price)*
Effektivpreissystem *n* system of cash prices
Effektivstärke *f* effective strength
Effektivvermerk *m s.* **Effektivklausel**
Effektivverzinsung *f* actual (payment of) interest
Effektivwert *m* actual value
Effektivzahlung *f* (actual) payment (of a bill of exchange) *(in the specified currency)*
Effizienz *f* efficiency
~, **asymptotische** *(stats)* asymptotic efficiency
Effizienzfaktor *m (stats)* efficiency factor
Ehefrau *f* wife, married woman
~, **berufstätige** employed married woman, working wife
~, **mitarbeitende** *s.* **berufstätige**
~, **mitverdienende** *s.* **berufstätige**
~, **nicht berufstätige** non-working wife
~, **nicht mitarbeitende** *s.* **nicht berufstätige**
Ehegatte *m* marriage partner, spouse
Ehegattenermäßigung *f* spouse relief
Ehegattenversicherung *f (ins)* spouse insurance
Ehegattenzuschlag *f* spouse allowance *(additional payment of social insurance to social pension)*
Ehekontrakt *m* marriage contract
ehelich legitimate *(child etc.)*; matrimonial
Ehrenakzept *n* acceptance (of protested bill) for honour, acceptance supra protest
Ehrenakzeptor *m* acceptor (of protested bill) for honour
Ehrenamt *n* honorary post [function]
ehrenamtlich honorary, unpaid, unsalaried
Ehrenannahme *f s.* **Ehrenakzept**
Ehrenbürger *m* honorary citizen; freeman *(town, city)*
Ehrengast *m* guest of honour
Ehrenmitglied *n* honorary member
Ehrenpatenschaft *f* sponsorship (of honour)
Ehrenpension *f* pension of honour
Ehrenrente *f s.* **Ehrenpension**
Ehrenschuld *f* debt of honour
Ehrensold *m* honorarium
Ehrenzahler *m* payer for honour *(protested bill)*
Ehrenzahlung *f* payment (of protested bill) for honour
eichen to standardize, to verify *(weights etc.)*; to gauge *(measuring instruments)*
Eichfehlergrenze *f* gauging tolerance
Eichgebühr *f* gauging fee
Eichgeld *n s.* **Eichgebühr**
Eichgenauigkeit *f* calibration accuracy
Eichmaß *n* standard measure; gauge
Eichschein *m* certificate of gauging

Eichung *f* standardization, verification *(weights etc.)*; gauging *(measuring instruments)*
Eid *m* (solemn) oath ✧ **den ~ verweigern** to refuse to take the oath; **durch einen ~ gebunden** to be under oath; **einen ~ ablegen** *s.* **einen ~ leisten; einen ~ abnehmen** to administer an oath; **einen ~ leisten** to take an oath; **einen falschen ~ schwören** to swear a false oath; to commit perjury; **etwas unter ~ aussagen** to declare [state] s.th. under oath **jmdn. seines Eides entbinden** to release [relieve] s.o. from his oath; **seinen ~ brechen** to break one's oath; **unter ~** under [on, upon] oath; **unter ~ bezeugen** to testify under oath
~, **assertorischer** assertory oath
~, **falscher** false oath
~, **promissorischer** promissory oath
~, **vom Richter abgenommener** judicial oath
~, **wissentlich falscher** perjury
Eidbrecher *m* oath-breaker; perjurer
Eidbruch *m* violation [breaking] of an oath; perjury
eidbrüchig oath-breaking; forsworn, perjured ✧ **~ werden** to break one's oath
Eidesleistung *f* taking of an oath
eidesstattlich in lieu of oath
Eidesversicherung *f (jur)* statement on oath, sworn statement; affidavit *(in writing)*
Eigenaufkommen *n* domestic [local] resources
Eigenbau *m (ind)* in-house production [manufacture]; owner-built house
~ von Rationalisierungsmitteln in-house production [manufacture] of equipment for rationalisation purposes
Eigenbedarf *m* personal use; personal requirements; domestic [home] requirements *(country etc.)*
Eigenbedarfsdeckung *f* covering one's own requirements *(raw materials etc.)*
Eigenbesitz *m* proprietorship, (personal) ownership; proprietary possession, personal property
Eigenbesitzer *m* proprietary possessor; proprietor, owner
Eigenbewirtschaftung *f (agric)* individual [private] cultivation *(of a piece of land of a co-operative farm by a member's family)*
Eigenerwirtschaftung *f* self-generation *(resources etc.)*
~ der Mittel self-generation of financial resources
Eigenerzeugung *f* domestic [home] production *(of a country etc.)*; self-production, one's own production *(on farms etc.)*
Eigenexport *m* export business on one's own account *(a form of export transaction in which industrial enterprises establish direct contacts with foreign customers)*

Eigenfabrikat *n* self-produced article
Eigenfertigung *f* one's own production
Eigenfinanzierung *f* self-financing *(of enterprises and industrial organizations from their own proceeds)*
Eigengeschäft *n* 1. business [transaction] carried out on one's own account; 2. s. **Eigenexport**
eigengesetzlich having its own laws; acting in accordance with inherent laws
Eigengesetzlichkeit *f* determination by inherent laws
Eigengewicht *n* (own) weight *(container, object etc.)*; dead load [weight] *(bridge, building etc.)*; tare weight *(vehicle)*; light [unladen] weight *(ship)*; net weight
Eigenhandel *m* trade [business] carried out on one's own account
Eigenhändler *m* businessman trading on his own account; firm trading on its own account
Eigenheim *n* owner-occupied house; home of one's own
Eigenheimbau *m* building of owner-occupied houses
Eigenkapital *n* one's own capital; capital stock and reserves
Eigenkapitalbedarf *m* need for own capital
Eigenkonsum *m s.* **Eigenverbrauch**
Eigenkontrolle *f* internal economic control *(of and by enterprises etc.)*
Eigenkorrelation *f (stats)* autocorrelation
Eigenleistung *f* 1. enterprise net performance *(index reflecting the value added by an enterprise etc., in a given period)*; 2. personal contribution to housing *(manual labour and financial contribution by members of a* **Arbeiterwohnungsbaugenossenschaft**)
Eigenleistungsmethode *f* net performance method *(to derive labour productivity)*
Eigenmittel *npl* one's own resources [means, funds]
Eigenmittelabführung *f* payment (to the budget) out of one's own funds *(enterprise etc.)*
Eigenmittelanteil *m* proportion of one's own financial means [resources, funds]
Eigenmittelausstattung *f* allocation of funds *(to state-owned enterprises by the budget)*; one's own funds *(enterprise etc.)*
Eigenmittelbeteiligung *f* contribution (to investments) out of one's own funds *(enterprise etc.)*
Eigenmittelfinanzierung *f* self-financing *(of investments etc., from profits and amortization)*
Eigenmittelzuführung *f* increase in one's own funds *(by profit distribution)*
Eigenmontage *f* self-assembling
Eigennutz *m* self-interest
~, **strafbarer** unlawful action performed for personal profit, punishable act committed for personal gain
eigennützig self-interested; selfish
Eigenproduktion *f* national [domestic] production; *(agric)* farm output *(gross output less purchases in livestock, fodder and seeds)*
Eigenregression *f (stats)* autoregression
Eigenrevision *f* internal audit
Eigenschaft *f* quality *(of s.o.)*; property *(of s.th.)*; *(jur)* (legal) status
Eigenschaften *fpl*:
~, **zugesicherte** assured properties *(of goods according to contract)*, warrant of merchantability
Eigentum *n* property; ownership; proprietorship *(business, hotel etc.)*; belongings *(personal things)*; holdings *(shares etc.)*
~, **ausländisches** foreign [*(jur)* alien] property; foreign ownership
~, **bewegliches** movables
~, **geistiges** literary property; author's [composer's, artist's] work protected by copyright, intellectual [copyright] property
~, **gemeinschaftliches** joint [common] property; joint [common] ownership
~, **gemischtes** joint [mixed form of] property; joint [mixed form of] ownership; semi-socialized [state] property
~, **genossenschaftliches** co-operative property; co-operative ownership
~ **gesellschaftlicher Organisationen** property of social organizations
~, **gesellschaftliches** public property; social property; public ownership; social ownership
~, **individuelles** individual property; individual ownership
~, **kapitalistisches** capitalist property; capitalist ownership
~, **kollektives** collective property; collective ownership
~, **öffentliches** public property; public ownership
~, **persönliches** personal property; personal ownership
~, **privates** private property; private ownership
~, **privatkapitalistisches** *s.* ~, **kapitalistisches**
~, **sozialistisches** socialist property; socialist ownership
~, **staatliches** state property; state ownership
~, **staatlich-sozialistisches** socialist state property
~, **unbewegliches** immovables
~, **zwischenstaatliches** international property; international ownership
Eigentümer *m* owner; proprietor; holder
Eigentumsanspruch *m (jur)* claim of ownership; title to property

Eigentumsanteil *m* share of property
Eigentumsaufgabe *f* giving up [relinquishing] of ownership
Eigentumsbefugnis *f* right to use property *(land, car etc.)*
Eigentumsbeschränkung *f* restriction on property; restriction on ownership
Eigentumsdelikt *n* offence against property
Eigentumserwerb *m* acquisition of property; acquisition of ownership
Eigentumsform *f* form [type] of ownership
Eigentumsgrundschuld *f* owners land charges
Eigentumsklage *f* action claiming property for its owner
Eigentumsmeere *npl* territorial waters
Eigentumspfandrecht *n* lien on property
Eigentumsprivileg *n* privilege of ownership
Eigentumsrecht *n* right of ownership; proprietary right; title to ownership
Eigentumsschichtung *f* distribution of property *(in a society)*
Eigentumsschutz *m* protection of property
Eigentumssteuer *f* property tax
Eigentumsstörung *f (jur)* private nuisance; trespass
Eigentumsstreuung *f* dispersion of property
Eigentumstitel *m* title to property
Eigentumsübergang *m* passing of property; passing of ownership
Eigentumsübertragung *f* transfer of ownership
Eigentumsumschichtung *f* redistribution of property *(in a society)*
Eigentumsurkunde *f* title-deed
Eigentumsverbrechen *n s.* **Eigentumsdelikt**
Eigentumsverfügung *f* disposal of property
Eigentumsverfügungsrecht *n* right of disposal of property
Eigentumsvergehen *n s.* **Eigentumsdelikt**
Eigentumsverhältnisse *npl* ownership relations *(in the means of production)*
Eigentumsverletzung *f* damaging of s.o.'s property; trespass
Eigentumsverteilung *f* distribution of property
Eigentumsverzicht *m* giving up [relinquishing] of ownership; renunciation of property
Eigentumsvorbehalt *m* reservation of proprietary rights [title]
Eigentumswechsel *m* change(s) in ownership
Eigentumswohnung *f* freehold flat, owner-occupied apartment
eigenverantwortlich self-responsible
Eigenverantwortlichkeit *f s.* **Eigenverantwortung**
Eigenverantwortung *f* self-responsibility
Eigenverbrauch *m* domestic consumption *(of a country)*; intra-works consumption; on-farm consumption

Eigenvermögen *n* own assets [capital]
Eigenversorgung *f* self-supply, self-sufficiency; domestic supply
Eigenwechsel *m (com)* promissory note (P/N), note of hand
Eigenwert *m* actual value; intrinsic value; value of s.th. in itself; *(stats)* characteristic root
eignen, sich to be suited [suitable, qualified] *(for s.th.)*; to be fit *(for s.th.)*
Eigner *m* owner, proprietor
Eignung *f* suitability, qualification *(persons)*; suitability, appropriateness, applicability *(things)*
~, berufliche vocational qualification
Eignungsprüfung *f* qualification [aptitude] test
Eignungsuntersuchung *f* medical fitness test *(for job)*
Eilauftrag *m* express [rush] order
Eilavis *m/n* express advice
Eilbote *m* express messenger
Eilbrief *m* express letter, *(Am)* special delivery letter
Eilfracht *f* express goods, *(Am)* fast freight
Eilfrachtbrief *m* consignment note for express goods [*(Am)* fast freight]
Eilfrachter *m* express-delivery vehicle; express-cargo liner, *(Am)* express freighter
Eilfrachtgebühr *f* express [*(Am)* fast] freight charge
Eilgebühr *f* express charge, *(Am)* special delivery charge; expressage
Eilgut *n* railway express, fast freight; express goods; (by) express *(declaration)* ◊ **als ~ senden** to forward as express, to send by express
Eilgutabfertigung *f* 1. dispatch of express goods; 2. dispatch office *(for express goods)*
Eilgüterzug *m* express goods train
Eilgutfrachtsatz *m* express goods rate
Eilguttarif *m s.* **Eilgutfrachtsatz**
Eilgutverkehr *m* express goods transport(ation)
Eilpost *f* express [*(Am)* special] delivery
Eilsendung *f* express delivery; letter/parcel sent by express service
Eilzug *m* semi-fast train
Eilzugzuschlag *m* extra charge (for semi-fast train)
Eilzustellung *f* express [*(Am)* special] delivery
einarbeiten to work in advance *(e.g. working on Saturday to get another day off)*; to make up for *(lost time)* by extra work, *(Am)* to work in; **sich ~** to familiarize o.s. with *(work, subject etc.)*, to work o.s. in ◊ **etwas in eine Sache ~** to work s.th. into s.th.; **jmdn. ~** to make s.o. familiar with new work, to train s.o. (for a job); **sich in etwas ~** to familiarize o.s. with s.th.

Einarbeitung *f* familiarizing *s.o./o.s.* with new work, making *s.o.* familiar with new work, training *s.o.* (for a job); initiation (into a job); working new facts into *(a report etc.)*; incorporation *(of new facts in card index etc.)*
Einarbeitungszeit *f* time required for initiation into a job, period of vocational adjustment, initial period
Einbau *m* 1. installation, fitting, mounting; 2. built-in element; addition; incorporation; *(d.pr.)* addition, incorporation, drive-in
einbauen to install, to fit in, to mount; to build in; to incorporate
Einbauküche *f* built-in kitchen
Einbaumöbel *pl* built-in furniture
einbehalten to retain, to keep back, to withhold *(money, property etc.)*; to deduct *(taxes and social insurance contributions by employer)*
Einbehaltung *f* retention, keeping back, withholding *(money, property etc.)*; deduction *(of taxes and social insurance contributions by employer)*
~ **von Lohn** deduction from wage *(taxes and social insurance contributions by employer)*
einberufen to call, to convene *(meeting etc.)*, to convoke, to summon *(parliament etc.)*; to call up *(army)*
Einberufung *f* calling up *(meeting etc.)*; convocation, summoning *(parliament etc.)*; call-up, *(Am)* induction *(army)*
Einbranchen-Messe *f* highly specialized fair, fair devoted to a single trade
Einbruchdiebstahlversicherung *f* burglary insurance
Einbruchversicherung *f s.* **Einbruchdiebstahlversicherung**
einbürgern to naturalize *(alien)*; to establish *(commodities, methods etc., through use)*
Einbürgerung *f* naturalization *(alien)*; establishment *(of commodities, methods etc., through use)*
Einbuße *f* loss, forfeiture *(money etc.)*
einbüßen to lose, to forfeit *(money etc.)*
eindecken, sich to provide o.s. with, to get a supply of, to stock up(on); *(st. ex.)* to be long of
Einfach-Klassifikation *f* (nach einem Merkmal) *(stats)* one-way classification
Einfachverkehr *m* simple cashless transactions *(between banks directly connected by mutual accounts)*
Einfaktor-Theorie *f (stats)* single factor theory
Einfluß *m* influence *(on, upon, over s.o./s.th.)*; effect *(on, upon s.o./s.th.)*; *(pol)* pull, power ⋄ **seinen ~ geltend machen** to bring one's influence to bear upon
Einflußbereich *m s.* **Einflußsphäre**
Einflußgebiet *n s.* **Einflußsphäre**

Einflußnahme *f* influencing, exercise of influence
Einflußsphäre *f (com)* controlled market (area); *(pol)* sphere of influence
einforderbar claimable, demandable
einfordern to call in, to demand payment of *(debt etc., from s.o.)*, to claim debt *(from s.o.)*; to collect *(taxes etc.)*
Einforderung *f* calling-in *(of debt etc., from s.o.)*, call (for funds); collection *(taxes etc.)*
einfrieren 1. *(com)* to freeze, to block *(deposits, accounts etc.)*; 2. to become icebound *(ship, harbour etc.)*
Einfuhr *f* import(ation); import(s) *(s. a.* **Import**)
~, **begünstigte** favoured import(s)
~, **direkte** direct import(s)
~, **freie** uncontrolled [free] import(s)
~, **indirekte** indirect import(s)
~, **ungehinderte** unrestricted import(s)
~, **unmittelbare** *s.* ~, **direkte**
~, **zollfreie** duty-free import
Einfuhrabgaben *fpl* levies on imports
Einfuhrartikel *m* import article
Einfuhrauftrag *m* import order
einführbar importable
Einfuhrbedarf *m* import needs
Einfuhrbefugnis *f* right to import
Einfuhrbeschränkungen *fpl* import restrictions; restrictions on import(s)
Einfuhrbestimmung *f* import regulation
Einfuhrbewilligung *f* import licence [permit]
Einfuhrdeklaration *f* import declaration
einführen 1. to introduce; to establish *(new tax, law etc.)*, to initiate *(method, policy etc.)*, to inaugurate *(new system)*; 2. to import *(goods)*; 3. *(dr.pr.)* to insert, to enter, to lead in
Einfuhrerhöhung *f* increase in import(s)
Einfuhrerklärung *f s.* **Einfuhrdeklaration**
Einfuhrerlaubnis *f s.* **Einfuhrbewilligung**
Einfuhrerschwerung *f* rigorous import controls
Einfuhrerzeugnis *n* import product
Einfuhrfinanzierung *f* financing of imports, import financing
Einfuhrförderung *f* import promotion
Einfuhrfreiliste *f* list of free import goods
Einfuhrgenehmigung *f s.* **Einfuhrbewilligung**
Einfuhrgeschäft *n* import business [transaction]
Einfuhrgüter *npl* import goods
Einfuhrhafen *m* port of importation
Einfuhrhandel *m* import trade
Einfuhrhändler *m* importer, import dealer
Einfuhrkontingent *n* import quota
Einfuhrkontingentierung *f* fixing of import quotas
Einfuhrkontrolle *f* import control
Einfuhrkosten *pl* import costs; costs of importing

Einfuhrkredit *m* import credit
Einfuhrland *n* importing country
Einfuhrliste *f* import list, list of imports
Einfuhrlizenz *f s.* **Einfuhrbewilligung**
Einfuhrmeldung *f* statement of imports
Einfuhrmöglichkeiten *fpl* import capacity
Einfuhrmonopol *n* import monopoly
Einfuhrnebenabgaben *fpl* additional levies on imports
Einfuhrposition *f* import item
Einfuhrprämie *f* import bounty [bonus, premium]
Einfuhrpreis *m* import price
Einfuhrpreisindex *m* import price index, index of import prices
Einfuhrquote *f* share of imports *(in the overall domestic use of goods)*; import consumption ratio, import coefficient; import quota
Einfuhrregister *n* import schedule
Einfuhrrestriktionen *fpl s.* **Einfuhrbeschränkungen**
Einfuhrschein *m s.* **Einfuhrbewilligung**
Einfuhrsperre *f s.* **Einfuhrverbot**
Einfuhrstatistik *f* import statistics
Einfuhrsteuer *f* tax on imports
Einfuhrüberschuß *m* import surplus
Einfuhrumsatzsteuer *f* turnover tax on imports
Einfuhr- und Zahlungsbewilligung *f* import and payment approval
Einführung *f* introduction; establishment *(new tax, law etc.)*, initiation *(method, policy etc.)*; inauguration *(new system)*; 2. import(ation) *(goods)*
~ **in die Produktion** transfer into production, application in production *(innovations etc.)*
Einführungsaufgaben *fpl* establishing tasks *(to get newly produced goods into the market)*
Einführungspreis *m* establishing price *(to create markets for new commodities)*
Einführungsrabatt *m* establishing discount
Einführungswerbung *f* establishing [introductory] advertisement
Einführungszuschlag *m* establishing price support *(to equalize difference between cost and price of new product)*
Einfuhrverbot *n* ban on imports, import ban
Einfuhrverfahren *n* import regulations
Einfuhrvertrag *m* import contract [agreement]
Einfuhrvolumen *n* volume of imports, total import
Einfuhrware *f* import(ed) good [article]; import(ed) commodity
Einfuhrzoll *m* import duty, customs duty on importation
~, **protektionistischer** protective import duty
Einfuhrzollsatz *m* import tariff (rate)
Eingabe *f* 1. application, petition; 2. *(dr.pr.)* input, entry ◊ **eine ~ machen** to submit a petition
~ **eines Programms in einen Rechner** *(d.pr.)* loading of a program into a computer
~, **manuelle** *(d.pr.)* manual input; keyboard entry
~ **über Tastatur** *(d.pr.)* manual keyboard entry
Eingabe/Ausgabe *f (d.pr.)* input-output
Eingabe/Ausgabe-Anzeiger *m (d.pr.)* input--output indicator
Eingabe/Ausgabe-Befehl *m (d.pr.)* input-output statement
Eingabe/Ausgabe-Gerät *n (d.pr.)* input-output device
Eingabe/Ausgabe-Kanal *m (d.pr.)* input-output channel
Eingabe/Ausgabe-Puffer *m (d.pr.)* input-output synchronizer
Eingabe/Ausgabe-Pufferspeicher *m (d.pr.)* input-output buffer storage
Eingabe/Ausgabe-Register *n (d.pr.)* input--output register
Eingabe/Ausgabe-Routinen *fpl (d.pr.)* input--output support package
Eingabe/Ausgabe-Steuerung *f (d.pr.)* input--output control
Eingabe/Ausgabe-Steuerungssystem *n (d.pr.)* input-output control system
Eingabeband *n (d.pr.)* input tape
Eingabebereich *m (d.pr.)* input area
Eingabedatei *f (d.pr.)* input file
Eingabedaten *pl (d.pr.)* input data
Eingabedatenkanal *m (d.pr.)* digital input channel
Eingabeeinheit *f (d.pr.)* input unit
Eingabefrist *f* time limit for replying to petitions
Eingabegerät *n (d.pr.)* input device [equipment]
Eingabegeschwindigkeit *f (d.pr.)* input speed
Eingabeinformation *f (d.pr.)* input information
Eingabepuffer *m (d.pr.)* input buffer
Eingabetermin *m* last [closing] date for submitting an application [petition]
Eingabewerte *mpl s.* **Eingabedaten**
Eingang *m* 1. entrance, entry, door-way; 2. *(com)* arrival, entry *(goods)*, receipt *(letters, money etc.)*; 3. *(d.pr.)* input, entry ◊ ~ **vorbehalten** *(bank)* entry reserved, with proviso
Eingänge *mpl* incomings, receipts; in *(letter tray)*
~ **und Ausgänge** *fpl (acc)* incomings and outgoings, ins and outs
Eingangsabfertigung *f (cust)* customs examination
Eingangsabgaben *fpl* import dues
Eingangsanzeige *f* notice of arrival
Eingangsbestätigung *f* acknowledgement of receipt

Eingangsbilanz *f* initial statement of affairs
Eingangsbuch *n* book of entries [receipts]
Eingangsdaten *pl (d.pr.)* input data
Eingangsdatum *n* date of arrival [receipt] *(goods, money etc.)*, value date *(cheque)*
Eingangsfakturenbuch *n* invoice book
Eingangsgewicht *n* weight inwards [delivered]
Eingangsgröße *f (d.pr.)* input unit
Eingangshafen *m* port of entry
Eingangskontrolle *f* check-in
Eingangsmeldung *f* report on goods received; report of money received
Eingangsposition *f* receiving item; item delivered
Eingangsrechnung *f* invoice (of goods received)
Eingangsstempel *m* entry stamp
Eingangszoll *m* import duty, customs duty on importation
Eingangszollamt *n* customs office *(airport, railway station, port of arrival)*
eingeben to present, to hand in *(petition, application etc)*; *(d.pr.)* to enter, to read in, to feed; to type in, to key in; to load
eingebracht brought in *(capital etc.)*
eingedeckt:
 ⋄ ~ **sein** to be swamped with *(goods etc.)*
eingefroren frozen, blocked *(accounts etc.)*
eingehen 1. to go into *(details, matter etc.)*; 2. to accept, to agree to, to consent to *(arrangement, demand etc.)*, to fall in with *(request etc.)*, to submit to *(conditions of a treaty etc.)*, to accede to, to comply with *(terms etc.)*; 3. to enter into, to conclude *(contract etc.)*; to strike, to make, to clinch *(bargain)*; 4. to be received, to come in [to hand], to arrive *(money, goods, mail etc.)*
eingehend 1. incoming *(goods etc.)*; 2. thoroughly, in detail *(report etc.)*
eingeschrieben registered *(letter etc.)*; enrolled *(member)*
eingetragen registered *(trademark)*; incorporated, registered *(corporation, association)*; enrolled *(member)*
eingipflig *(stats)* unimodal
eingrenzen 1. to enclose, to close in *(piece of ground with wall etc.)*; to localize *(conflict etc.)*; 2. to define, to narrow down *(powers, field of research etc.)*; 3. *(d.pr.)* to track down; to localize, to isolate
Eingriff *m* encroachment, infringement *(of s.o.'s rights etc.)*; intervention, interference *(development etc.)*; disruption *(process etc.)*; *(d.pr.)* intervention; action
eingruppieren to group *(classifying people, objects)*
Eingruppierung *f* grouping *(classifying people, objects)*
Eingruppierungsunterlagen *fpl* employee classification documents, grading documents

einhalten to keep to, to adhere to *(timetable, fixed date etc.)*; to observe *(conditions etc.)*; to abide by *(contract etc.)*; to keep up *(payments)*; to maintain *(rules etc.)*; *(d.pr.)* to control
Einhaltung *f* keeping to, adherence to *(timetable, fixed date etc.)*; observance *(conditions etc.)*; abiding by *(contract etc.)*; keeping up *(payments)*; maintenance *(rules etc.)*
einheimisch home, domestic, inland *(trade, product etc.)*, home-produced *(goods etc.)*; local *(population, customs, industry)*; home-grown *(fruit etc.)*, home-bred *(farm-stock etc.)*, indigenous *(plant, animal etc.)*
Einheit *f* 1. *(pol)* unity; 2. unit *(measure, value etc.)*; entity; *(d.pr.)* module, component, device
~, **administrative** administrative unit
~ **der ersten Auswahlstufe** *(stats)* first-stage [primary] unit
~ **der Stichprobenauswahl** *(stats)* sampling unit
~ **der zweiten Auswahlstufe** *(stats)* secondary [second-stage] unit
~, **etatmäßige** budgetary unit
~, **komplexe** *(stats)* complex unit
~, **periphere** *(d.pr.)* peripheral unit
~, **statistische** statistical unit
~, **synchrone** *(d.pr.)* synchronous device
~, **technische** technical unit
~, **territoriale** regional unit; regional unity
~, **ursprüngliche** *(stats)* primary unit *(in sample surveys)*
~ **von Lehre und Forschung** unity of teaching and research
~ **von materieller und finanzieller Planung** unity of physical and financial planning *(principle taking into account the interdependence of physical and financial processes in the economy)*
~ **von Politik und Ökonomie** unity of politics and economy
~ **von Theorie und Praxis** unity of theory and practice
~, **widersprüchliche** contradictory unity
~, **wirtschaftliche** economic unit; economic unity *(territories)*
~, **zusammengesetzte** *s.* ~, **komplexe**
Einheiten *fpl*:
~, **abrechnungsfähige** accountable units *(of investments)*
einheitlich uniform *(standard, quality, tariff etc.)*; homogenous *(structure, design)*; standard *(price, rate of pay etc.)*; unitized; standardized
Einheitlichkeit *f* unity *(action, form)*; uniformity *(standard, quality, tariff etc.)*; homogeneity *(structure, design)*; consistency *(measures, plan)*
Einheitsbesteuerung *f* flat-rate taxation

Einheitsbestrebungen *fpl* tendencies towards unity [unification], unitary tendencies
Einheitsbewegung *f* movement towards unity, unitary movement
Einheitsbilanz *f* standard(ized) balance sheet
Einheitsbuchführung *f* standardized bookkeeping
Einheitsdurchschreibebuchführung *f* standardized duplicate bookkeeping
Einheitsformular *n* standard(ized) form
Einheitsfrachtsatz *m* standard freightage [freight rate]
Einheitsfront *f* united front *(parties etc.)*
Einheitsgebühr *f* general [standard] fee [charge]
Einheitsgewerkschaft *f* unified trade union
Einheitskontenrahmen *m* standardized system of accounts
Einheitskonto *n* standard account
Einheitskosten *pl* costs per unit *(of a product)*
Einheitskurs *m* *(st.ex.)* standard quotation; *(stats)* adjusted rate
Einheitslochkarte *f* standard(ized) punch(ing) card
Einheitsmaß *n* standard measure, standard *(weight etc.)*
Einheitsmatrix *f* *(math)* standard matrix
Einheitsmietvertrag *m* standard tenancy agreement
Einheitsmonat *m* *(stats)* month adjusted for calendar variation
Einheitspreis *m* uniform [standard] price
Einheitspreisgeschäft *n* one-price store
Einheitssatz *m* uniform [standard] rate
Einheitsscheck *m* standard(ized) cheque [*(Am)* check]
Einheitsschlüssel *m* standard code
Einheitssteuer *f* flat-rate tax
Einheitssystem *n* unitary system *(of products and highly productive technologies)*
Einheitstarif *m* standard rate [tariff]
Einheitsverpackung *f* standardized packing
Einheitsversicherung *f* all risks insurance
Einheitsvordruck *m s.* **Einheitsformular**
Einheitswährung *f* standard currency
Einheitsware *f* standard(ized) article
Einheitswert *m* standard value; unit of taxable value
Einheitszoll *m* uniform rate of duty, standard tariff
einigen to unite *(people etc.)*, to unify *(country etc.)*; **sich ~** to come to terms [an agreement, an understanding] *(with s.o. on/about s.th.)*, to agree on *(a certain price, conditions etc.)* ⋄ **sich gütlich ~** to come to a friendly [an amicable] agreement; to settle *s.th.* in a friendly way [manner], to settle *s.th.* amicably
Einigkeit *f* unity, union, concord, harmony

Einigung *f* 1. unity *(people etc.)*, unification *(country etc.)*; 2. agreement, settlement *(with s.o. about a matter, price etc.)*
Einigungsamt *n* conciliation board; arbitration board [tribunal]
Einigungsstelle *f s.* **Einigungsamt**
Einkammersystem *n* *(pol)* unicameral [single--chamber] system
einkassieren to collect *(contributions, money due etc.)*; to recover *(outstanding debt etc.)*; to take *(sum as daily total etc.)*
Einkassierung *f* collection, collecting *(bills of exchange, letters of credit, cheques etc.)*; *(ins)* collection of premiums
Einkauf *m* 1. purchase; purchasing, buying; 2. purchasing department *(of an enterprise)*
Einkäufe *mpl*:
 ⋄ **~ machen** to go shopping
einkaufen to buy, to purchase; to go shopping, to make one's purchases
Einkäufer *m* buyer *(for business house etc.)*; buying agent
Einkäuferbesuch *m* buyers' visit
Einkäuferinformation *f* information for buyers
Einkäuferinteresse *n* buyers' interest
Einkäuferwerbung *f* publicity for buyers
Einkaufsauftrag *m* buying order
Einkaufsbedingungen *fpl* terms of purchase, buying conditions
Einkaufsbeschränkung *f* purchase restriction
Einkaufsbruttopreis *m* gross purchasing price
Einkaufsbuch *n* *(acc)* invoice book; order book *(for purchases)*
Einkaufsbüro *n* buying office; purchasing agency
~, zentrales centralized purchasing agency
Einkaufserleichterungen *fpl* purchasing facilities
Einkaufsform *f* kind of buying
Einkaufsgemeinschaft *f* purchasing pool
Einkaufsgenossenschaft *f* co-operative purchasing society *(of private retailers in order to get favourable wholesale prices)*
Einkaufskartell *n* purchasing cartel
Einkaufskollektiv *n* advisory body for purchases *(in retail and wholesale trade)*
Einkaufskommission *f* purchasing committee
Einkaufskosten *pl* expenses in connection with a purchase *(commission to purchasing agent etc.)*
Einkaufsland *n* country of purchase
Einkaufsliste *f* shopping list
Einkaufsmöglichkeit *f* purchasing facility; shopping facility *(for individual consumers)*
Einkaufsmonopol *n* purchasing monopoly
Einkaufsplan *m* purchasing plan *(in retail trade to ensure quality and quantity of goods for sale)*
Einkaufsplanung *f* planning of purchases

Einkaufspreis *m* purchase [purchasing, cost] price
Einkaufsprovision *f* commission *(for buying s.th.)*
Einkaufsrabatt *m* purchase discount
Einkaufsrechnung *f* invoice
Einkaufsrechnungspreis *m s.* **Einkaufsbruttopreis**
Einkaufsselbstkosten *pl* purchase costs *(purchase price plus freight, insurance etc.)*
Einkaufsstunden *fpl* shopping hours
Einkaufstour *f* buying trip, shopping expedition
Einkaufs- und Absatzgenossenschaft *f s.* **Einkaufs- und Liefergenossenschaft**
Einkaufs- und Liefergenossenschaft *f* (ELG) co-operative purchasing and supply society *(of private tradesmen)*
Einkaufsverhältnisse *npl* buying conditions
Einkaufsvertreter *m* buying agent
Einkaufszentrum *n* shopping centre *(in cities)*; supermarket
einkellern to store [stock up] in the cellar, to lay in (the cellar)
Einkellerung *f* stocking-up in the cellar
einklagbar suable, actionable
einklagen to sue *(for outstanding debt etc.)*
einklarieren to clear in(wards)
Einklarierung *f* clearance inwards
Einkommen *n* income, earnings; revenue *(of the state)*; annuity *(fixed yearly income)*
~, **arbeitsloses** *s.* ~, **nicht erarbeitetes**
~ **aus Arbeit** earned income
~ **aus freiberuflicher Tätigkeit** earnings [income] from self-employment
~ **aus Handelstätigkeit** income from business activity
~ **aus Kapital** income from capital, unearned income, capital returns
~ **aus Unternehmertätigkeit** income from activities as entrepreneur
~ **aus verschiedenen Quellen** income from various sources
~ **aus wirtschaftlicher Tätigkeit** income from commercial activity
~, **beitragspflichtiges** income liable to contribution *(social insurance etc.)*
~, **direktes** primary income *(of individuals)*
~, **durch Arbeit erworbenes** *s.* ~ **aus Arbeit**
~, **durchschnittliches** average income
~, **dynamisches** dynamic income
~, **erarbeitetes** *s.* ~ **aus Arbeit**
~, **festes** fixed income
~, **fundiertes** well-founded income
~, **garantiertes** guaranteed income
~, **gebundenes** income bound (to)
~, **indirektes** indirect income
~, **konstantes** constant income

~, **lebenslängliches** income for life (time), lifelong income
~ **nach Abzug der Steuern** income after taxes, aftertax [net] income
~, **nicht erarbeitetes** unearned income
~, **produziertes** produced income
~, **ständiges** steady income
~, **statisches** *s.* ~, **konstantes**
~, **steuerpflichtiges** income liable to taxation
~, **unsicheres** malfounded income
~, **unsichtbares** invisible income
~, **ursprüngliches** primary income
~, **verfügbares** disposable income
~, **versteuerbares** taxable income
~ **vor Abzug der Steuern** pre-tax [gross] income
~, **wechselndes** changing income
Einkommen *npl*:
~, **höhere** higher incomes
~, **mittlere** middle incomes
~, **untere** lower incomes
einkommend incoming *(money, mail etc.)*; inward *(cargo, freight etc.)*
Einkommensangleichung *f* levelling of incomes
Einkommensausgleich *m* wage compensation, wage equalization payment
Einkommensbesteuerung *f* taxation of income
Einkommensbewegung *f* changes in income
Einkommensbezieher *m* income earner
einkommensbezogen earnings related *(pension etc.)*
Einkommensbilanz *f* income balance sheet
Einkommensbildung *f* income formation
Einkommenseinbuße *f* loss of income
Einkommenselastizität *f* income elasticity
~ **der Nachfrage** income elasticity of demand
Einkommensentwicklung *f* growth of incomes
Einkommensermittlung *f* assessment of income
~, **steuerliche** assessment of income for tax purposes
Einkommensfunktion *f* income function, function of income
Einkommensgliederung *f* structure of income
Einkommensgruppe *f* income group
~, **gehobene** higher income group
~, **höhere** *s.* ~, **gehobene**
~, **mittlere** medium income group
~, **untere** lower income group
Einkommenskonto *n* salary (bank) account
Einkommenskonzentration *f* concentration of income
Einkommenslage *f* social situation
Einkommensminderung *f* reduction of income
Einkommensnivellierung *f s.* **Einkommensangleichung**
einkommensorientiert income oriented
Einkommenspolitik *f* incomes policy

Einkommensposten *m* item of income *(in a national economic balance sheet)*
Einkommenspyramide *f* pyramid of income (distribution) *(structure of the population's income)*
Einkommensquelle *f* source of income
Einkommensrealisierung *f* materialization of income
Einkommensrelation *f* income proportion
Einkommensschichtung *f* income differentiation, differentiation of incomes
Einkommensschmälerung *f s.* **Einkommensminderung**
einkommensschwach with lower income
Einkommensschwankung *f s.* **Einkommensbewegung**
Einkommensskala *f* range of incomes
Einkommensstruktur *f* structure of income, income pattern
Einkommensteuer *f* income tax
~, **einheitliche** unifom income tax
~ **nach Tabelle** income tax according to tax table
~, **veranlagte** income tax according to (tax) assessment
Einkommensteuererklärung *f* income-tax return [*(Am)* statement]
Einkommensteuergesetz *n* law on income tax
Einkommensteuerrecht *n* law of taxation, tax laws
Einkommensteuersatz *m* rate of income tax
Einkommensteuertabelle *f* income-tax table
Einkommens- und Verbrauchsbilanz *f* balance (sheet) of income and consumption
Einkommensveränderung *f* changes in income
Einkommensverhältnisse *npl* income status *(of the population)*
Einkommensverteilung *f* distribution of income
Einkommensverwendung *f* utilization of income
Einkommenszuschlag *m* supplementary payment
~, **steuerfreier** tax-free supplementary payment
Einkommenszuwachs *m* increase in income
Einkontensystem *n* single account system
Einkünfte *pl* earnings *(persons, commercial undertakings etc.)*; income *(persons)*; revenue *(state)*; proceeds, receipts, takings *(enterprises)*
~ **aus freiberuflicher Tätigkeit** earnings [income] from self-employment
~ **aus gewerblicher Tätigkeit** industrial earnings [income]
~ **aus landwirtschaftlicher Tätigkeit** farm income
~, **außerordentliche** extra earnings [income]
~ **in Geld** money income, income in money, monetary income

~ **in Naturalien** earnings [income] in kind
~, **lohnsteuerpflichtige** income liable to income tax
~, **nebenberufliche** earnings [income] from secondary occupation
~, **nichtabgabepflichtige** non-taxable earnings [income]
~, **nichtwiederkehrende** non-regular income [earnings]
~, **persönliche** individual earnings [income]
~, **pfändbare** distrainable earnings [income]
~, **sonstige** miscellaneous earnings [income]
~, **steuerbegünstigte** earnings [income] with tax privileges
~, **steuerbegünstigte freiberufliche** free-lance income with tax privileges, income from self--employment with tax privileges
~, **steuerfreie** tax-free earnings [income]
~, **unpfändbare** unseizable earnings [income]
~, **wiederkehrende** regular earnings [income]
Einladebahnhof *m* loading station; station of origin
einladen 1. to load *(goods etc., onto a lorry, into a ship)*; to lade *(cargo etc.)*; 2. to invite *(s.o. to s.th.)*
Einladung *f* invitation
Einlage *f* 1. *(fin, com)* investment *(of capital)*; initial share *(in undertaking)*; money paid up *(on shares)*; *(bank)* deposit; 2. enclosure *(in letters etc.)* ◊ **seine ~ zurückziehen** to withdraw one's capital
~ **auf Depositenkonto** fixed deposit
~ **auf feste Kündigung** deposit for a fixed period
~, **befristete** time deposit
~ **bei einer Bank** deposit in a bank
~, **feste** fixed deposit
~, **gemeinschaftliche** joint deposit
~, **jederzeit kündbare** *s.* ~, **jederzeit rückzahlbare**
~, **jederzeit rückzahlbare** short deposit, deposit at short notice, day-to-day deposit
~, **kündbare** deposit at call
~, **kurzfristige** short-term deposit
~, **langfristige** long-term deposit
~, **mittelfristige** medium-term deposit
~, **unbefristete** *s.* ~, **jederzeit rückzahlbare**
Einlagebuch *n* pass-book, bank-book
Einlagegläubiger *m* depositor
Einlagekapital *n* capital invested; initial share; money paid up *(capital)*
Einlagekonto *n* deposit account
Einlagen *fpl* deposits
~ **auf das Grundkapital, ausstehende** uncalled capital
~ **auf Sicht** sight deposits
~, **fiktive** fictitious deposits

~, **öffentliche** public deposits
~, **verzinsliche** deposits bearing interest
Einlagenabfluß *m* outflow of deposits
Einlagenbestand *m* deposits
Einlagenbetrag *m* deposited amount
Einlagengeschäft *n* deposit business
Einlagenkonto *n* deposit account
Einlagenstand *m s.* **Einlagenbestand**
Einlagensumme *f* (total) amount of deposits
Einlagenzinsen *pl* (amount of) interest on deposits
Einlagenzinsfuß *m* interest rate on deposits
Einlagerer *m* depositor *(of goods in warehouse, repository etc.)*
einlagern to warehouse, to store (up), to put into stock; *(cust)* to bond
Einlagerung *f* warehousing, storage; *(cust)* bonding
Einlagerungsgewicht *n* storage weight
Einlagerungskapazität *f* storage capacity
Einlagerungskosten *pl* storage costs
Einlassung *f* *(jur)* (entering an) appearance, notice of one's intention to defend
Einlassungsfrist *f* *(jur)* period for entering appearance
einlaufen 1. to come in, to arrive *(train, ship)*, to enter (the port) *(ship)*; 2. to shrink *(textiles)*
Einlaufen *n* 1. arrival *(train, ship)*, entry *(ship)*; 2. shrinkage *(textiles)*
Einlauftest *m (d.pr.)* pre-test
einlegen 1. to deposit *(money with bank)*, to pay *(money into bank)*, to put *(money in bank)*; 2. to enclose *(s.th. in letters etc.)*; 3. to lodge, to make *(complaint etc.)*; 4. to preserve *(vegetables etc.)*
Einleger *m* depositor *(of money in bank etc.)*
einleiten to initiate, to open *(negotiations, relations etc.)*; to institute, to set up *(inquiry)*; to introduce *(system etc.)*
Einleitung *f* initiation, opening *(negotiations, relations etc.)*; introduction *(system etc.)*
einliefern to deliver *(s.th.)*; to post *(letters etc.)*; to deposit *(securities etc.)*; to take *s.o.* to *(hospital etc.)*
Einlieferung *f* delivery; posting *(letters etc.)*; depositing *(securities etc.)*; taking *s.o.* to *(hospital etc.)*
Einlieferungsschein *m* receipt of posting; certificate of receipt
einlösbar due, payable; redeemable; convertible *(bank notes)*
Einlösbarkeit *f* redemption; convertibility *(bank notes)*
einlösen to redeem *(mortgage, securities etc.)*; to convert *(foreign exchange)*; to discharge, to pay *(bill etc.)*; to meet, to take up, to honour *(bill of exchange etc.)*; to take out of pawn

Einlösung *f* redemption *(mortgage, securities etc.)*; conversion *(foreign exchange)*; discharge, payment *(bill etc.)*; taking up, honouring *(bill of exchange etc.)*; taking out of pawn
Einlösungsbetrag *m* amount of redemption
Einlösungsfonds *m* sinking [redemption] fund
Einlösungsfrist *f* term of redemption
Einlösungsgarantie *f* guarantee of redemption
Einlösungsklausel *f* redemption clause
Einlösungskurs *m* redemption rate
Einlösungspflicht *f (bank)* obligation to cash bank notes; obligation to honour a bill
Einlösungsprämie *f* redemption premium
Einmalbeitrag *m (ins)* non-recurring premium
Einmannarbeit *f* one-man work
Einmannbedienung *f* one-man attendance *(machines etc.)*
Einmanngesellschaft *f* one-man company
Einmannverkaufsstelle *f* one-man shop
einmieten *(agric)* to clamp, to silo; **sich ~** to take lodgings [room] *(with s.o.)*
Einnahmeausfall *m* loss of revenue
Einnahmebeleg *m* receipt
Einnahmebetrag *m* amount [sum] of receipts [takings, returns, proceeds, earnings]; amount [sum] of revenues
Einnahmen *fpl* receipts, takings, returns, proceeds *(firm, company etc.)*; earnings, income *(person)*; revenue *(state)*
~, **außerordentliche** extra-budgetary receipts, extra-budgetary revenues *(of the state budget)*
~, **außerplanmäßige** unplanned receipts
~ **des Staates** *(stats)* revenue
~, **geplante** planned receipts; planned revenues *(budget)*
~, **nebenberufliche** secondary [subsidiary] income
~, **öffentliche** public revenue
~, **ordentliche** planned revenue *(state budget)*
~, **regelmäßige** regular receipts
~, **staatliche** *s.* ~, **öffentliche**
~ **und Ausgaben** *fpl* **des Staates** revenue and expenditure of the state
Einnahmenbuch *n* book of receipts
Einnahmengliederung *f* classification [structure] of receipts
Einnahmenseite *f* credit side *(accounts etc.)*
Einnahmenstruktur *f* structure of receipts
Einnahmenteil *m s.* **Einnahmenseite**
Einnahmen- und Ausgabenbilanz *f* balance sheet of receipts and expenditure
Einnahmenvoranschlag *m* estimate of receipts
Einnahmeposition *f* receipts item
Einnahmequelle *f* source of income; source of revenue *(of the state)*
Einnahmeüberschuß *m* surplus of receipts; excess revenue *(budget)*

Einnahme- und Ausgabebuch *n* book of receipts and expenditure(s)
einnehmen to receive, to cash *(money)*; to collect *(taxes)*
Einnehmer *m* collector *(taxes etc.)*
einpacken to pack (up); to wrap up
Einparteiensystem *n* one-party system
Einpendler *m* commuter
Einpersonenhaushalt *m* single-person household
einplanen to include *(s.th. in a plan, programme etc.)*; to plan; to allow for *(exigencies etc.)*
einordnen to fit (detail) in *(report etc.)*; to arrange *s.th.* in proper order; to classify, to class *(s.th.)*; to file *(letter, document, index-cards etc., in proper order)*
Einordnung *f* fitting (detail) in *(report etc.)*; arrangement of *s.th.* in proper order; classification; filing *(letter, document, index-cards etc., in proper order)*
Einproduktbetrieb *m* one-product enterprise
Einproduktmodell *n* one-product model
einräumen to grant *(credit, loan etc.)*; to allow *(time, extension etc.)*; to concede *(right etc.)*; to admit *(mistake, fact etc.)*
Einräumung *f* grant *(credit, loan etc.)*; allowance *(time, extension etc.)*; concession *(right etc.)*; admission *(mistake, fact etc.)*
einrechnen to include *(s.th. in a plan, programme etc.)*; to take *s.th.* into account, to allow for *(s.th.)*
einreichen to present, to hand in, to submit *(petition etc.)*; to apply for *(s.th.)*
Einreichung *f* presentation, handing in, submission *(petition etc.)*; application for *(s.th.)*
~ **eines Antrages** filing of an application
Einreise *f* entry (into a country)
Einreisebewilligung *f s.* **Einreiseerlaubnis**
Einreiseerlaubnis *f* entry permit [visa]
Einreisegenehmigung *f s.* **Einreiseerlaubnis**
Einreisevisum *n* entry visa
einrichten 1. to arrange *(one's plan etc.)*; 2. to furnish *(house, room etc.)*; to fit out *(office, workshop etc.)*; 3. to set up *(irrigation system etc.)*; to establish *(agency, hospital, school etc.)*; 4. to adjust *(tool, instrument etc.)*
Einrichtezeit *f* tooling [set-up] time *(machine)*
Einrichtung *f* 1. arrangement *(of one's plan etc.)*; 2. furniture *(house, room etc.)*; 3. setting up [*(Am)* set-up] *(irrigation system etc.)*; establishment, institution *(agency, hospital, school etc.)*; 4. adjustment *(tool, instrument etc.)*; 5. appliance, device
~, **arbeitssparende** labour-saving appliance [device]
~ **des Einzelhandels** establishment of retail trade

~, **gastronomische** catering establishment
~, **gesellschaftliche** social institution [establishment]
~, **hochmechanisierte** highly mechanized device
~, **kommunale** municipal [local] institution [establishment]
~, **öffentliche** public institution
~, **staatliche** state(-owned) institution
~, **städtische** city [urban] institution
~, **wirtschaftliche** economic institution [establishment]
~, **zwischengenossenschaftliche** inter-co-operative establishment [institution]
Einrichtungshaus *n* departmental store for furniture and furnishings
Einrichtungskosten *pl* furnishing costs *(house, room etc.)*; setting-up [*(Am)* set-up] costs *(machine etc.)*
Einsatz *m* input, use, employment *(labour, resources, machines etc.)*; assignment, deployment *(manpower)*; application, use *(machines etc.)* ⋄ **im ~** in use, in operation; **zum ~ bereit** ready for use [operation] *(machine etc.)*; **zum ~ bringen** to use, to employ *(labour etc.)*, to bring into use, to put into operation *(machine etc.)*; **zum ~ kommen** to be used, to be employed, to be brought into use *(machine etc.)*
~, **komplexer** complex use [operation] *(building machine)*
~ **von Material, ökonomischer** economical use of material
Einsatz-Ausstoß-Analyse *f* input-output analysis
Einsatzbereitschaft *f* readiness for use [service] *(machine etc.)*; stand-by for duties *(person)*
einsatzfähig usable, serviceable *(machine etc.)*; employable *(person)*
Einsatzfolge *f* sequence of procedure [operations]
Einsatzgewicht *n* input weight
Einsatzgrad *m* degree of use [employment] *(machine etc.)*
Einsatzgruppe *f* (work)team; task force *(police etc.)*
Einsatzkoeffizient *m* input coefficient
Einsatzmaterial *n* input material
Einsatzmatrix *f* input matrix
Einsatzmenge *f* amount of input
Einsatznorm *f* input norm [standard]
Einsatzplan *m* operation plan
Einsatzverbot *n* ban on use [employment]
Einsatzvorbereitung *f* preparation prior to operating *(machine, plant etc.)*; preparation for assignment *(manpower)*
Einsatzzug *m* relief train

einschätzen to estimate *(value, budget revenue etc.)*, to assess *(taxes etc.)*, to appraise *(damages etc.)*; to form an estimate of *(s.o.)*
Einschätzung *f* estimation, estimate *(value, budget revenue etc.)*, assessment *(taxes etc.)*, appraisal *(damages etc.)*; estimation *(person's capabilities etc.)*
Einschichtarbeit *f* one-shift (work), day-shift (work)
Einschichtbetrieb *m* 1. one-shift [day-shift] enterprise; 2. one-shift operation
einschichtig single-shift, one-shift *(system of working)*
Einschichtsystem *n* single-shift [one-shift] system
einschiffen to ship; to embark; to take on board *(goods etc.)*; **sich ~** to embark *(for a place)*, to go on board *(passengers)*
Einschiffung *f* shipping, shipment *(goods etc.)*; embarkation *(passengers)*
Einschiffungshafen *m* port of shipment; port of embarkation
Einschiffungskosten *pl* shipping costs
Einschiffungstag *m* date of shipping; date of embarkation
einschränken to limit, to restrict, to reduce *(expenditure etc.)*; to curtail *(authority etc.)*; to curb, to restrain *(flow of foreign capital etc.)*; to modify, to qualify *(terms, rule, statement, condition etc.)*; **sich ~** to economize, to cut down expenses, to make retrenchments, to reduce one's standard of living
Einschränkung *f* limitation, restriction, reduction *(expenditure etc.)*; curtailment *(authority etc.)*; curbing, restraint *(flow of foreign capital etc.)*; modification, qualification *(terms, rule, statement, condition etc.)*
Einschreibebrief *m* registered letter
Einschreibegebühr *f* registration fee
Einschreibegeld *n s.* **Einschreibegebühr**
einschreiben to register *(letter etc.)*; to enrol *(as a member etc.)*; *(d.pr.)* to write in(to), to put in, to load, to clock in
Einschreiben *n* registered letter; *(d.pr.)* write-in
Einschreibporto *n s.* **Einschreibegebühr**
Einschreibsendung *f* registered mail [post]
Einschreibung *f* registration; enrolment *(university etc.)*
Einschuß *m* *(fin)* money [capital] invested; paid-in capital; *(st.ex.)* margin
Einsektorenmodell *n* one-sector model
einsenden to send in *(application, money etc.)*; to submit *(article etc.)*
Einsender *m* sender; submitter
Einsendung *f* sending in; submission
einsetzbar replaceable, interchangeable *(tool head etc.)*; usable *(workers etc.)*

einsetzen 1. to put in *(s.th.)*; to insert *(s.th.)*; 2. to use, to make use of *(st.th. or s.o.)*; 3. to appoint *(official, committee etc.)* 4. to stock a pond *(with fish)*
Einsetzung *f* 1. putting in; insertion; 2. using, making use of; 3. appointment
Einspaltenformular *n* one-column form
Einspaltentarif *m* one-column rate
einsparen to economize, to save *(material, labour etc.)*
Einsparung *f* economizing, saving *(material, labour etc.)*
Einsparungsbetrag *m* saved amount *(money)*
Einsparungseffekt *m* saving effect
Einsparungsprämie *f* economization bonus *(paid for economical use of money, material, fuel etc.)*
Einspruch *m* objection, protest, veto; *(jur)* demurrer ⋄ **einen ~ aufrechterhalten** to sustain an objection; **~ erheben gegen** to raise an objection to, to enter [make] a protest against, to put a veto on
Einstandspreis *m* cost price, prime cost
einstellen 1. to take on, to engage, to employ *(employee, worker)*; 2. to cease *(work)*, to stop *(work, payment etc.)*; 3. to set; to adjust
Einstellung *f* 1. engagement, employment *(employee, worker)*; 2. cessation, stoppage *(work, payment etc.)*; 3. attitude, outlook; 4. setting; adjustment
~, politische political attitude [opinion]
~ zur Arbeit attitude to work
Einstellungsbedingungen *fpl* conditions of employment
Einstellungsgespräch *n* employment interview, interview for a job
Einstellungsvermerk *m* entry in employment book; *(jur)* stamp of stay of proceedings
Einstellzeit *f* *(d.pr.)* setting [settling] time
Einströmen *n* inflow, influx *(capital etc.)*
~ von Kapital inflow [influx] of capital
einstufen to classify *(staff etc.)*; to grade *(goods according to quality)*; to rate, to assess *(taxation etc.)*
Einstufung *f* classification *(staff etc.)*; grading *(goods according to quality etc.)*; rating, assessment *(taxation etc.)*
~ nach der Leistungsfähigkeit performance rating; promotion according to performance [ability]
einstweilig temporary *(address etc.)*, provisional *(arrangement etc.)*, interim *(regulation etc.)*
einteilen to divide *(sum of money etc.)*; to classify *(population according to income etc.)*; to graduate *(scale etc.)*; to stratify *(groups in society etc.)* ⋄ **ordnungsgemäß ~** to arrange systematically

Einteilung *f* dividing *(sum of money etc.)*, division *(labour etc.)*; classification *(of population according to income etc.)*; graduation *(scale etc.)*; stratification *(of groups in society etc.)*
~ **nach einem Merkmal** *(stats)* one-way classification
~ **nach mehreren Merkmalen** *(stats)* manifold classification
~, **zweifache** *(stats)* two-way classification
Einteilungsgitter *n (stats)* grouping lattice
Eintrag *m* entry *(account-book, registry etc.)*; item
eintragen 1. to write [put] down, to enter *(name in/on list, order etc.)*; to register *(birth, deed, patent etc.)*; to enrol *(as a member)*; *(acc)* to enter (up), to post, to pass *(item in ledger etc.)*, to make an entry *(in account-book etc.)*; 2. to bring in, to bear, to yield *(profit etc.)*; 3. *(maths)* to plot *(point, curve etc.)*
einträglich lucrative, remunerative, profitable *(trade, occupation etc.)*; paying *(concern etc.)*
Einträglichkeit *f* lucrativeness, remunerativeness, profitableness *(trade, occupation etc.)*
Eintragung *f* writing [putting] down, entry *(of a name in/on a list, of an order etc.)*, recording *(facts etc.)*, registration *(birth, deed, patent etc.)*; enrolment *(as a member etc.)*; *(acc)* entry
eintreibbar recoverable
eintreiben to recover, to call in, to collect *(sum of money outstanding etc.)*
Eintreibung *f* recovery, collection *(sum of money outstanding etc.)*
~ **ausstehender Schulden** recovery of outstanding debts [amounts outstanding], debt collection
eintreten 1. to occur, to happen, to take place; to arise *(demand, difficulties etc.)*; 2. to join *(political party etc.)* ◊ **für jmdn.** ~ to take s.o.'s part [side]; to intercede for s.o.; to plead for s.o.
Eintritt *m* 1. occurence, happening; arising *(demand, difficulties)*; *(jur)* accrual; 2. entry, entrance, admission; 3. entrance [admission] fee [charge] ◊ ~ **erlangen** to get admission to, to gain admission into
Eintrittsgeld *n* entrance [admission] fee [charge]
Eintrittspreis *m s.* **Eintrittsgeld**
Ein- und Ausgangsbuch *n (acc)* book of incomings and outgoings
Ein- und Verkaufsbedingungen *fpl* conditions [terms] of purchase and sale
Ein- und Verkaufsländerprogramm *n (for.tr.)* programme of purchasing and selling countries
einverleiben to annex, to incorporate *(territory etc.)*
Einverleibung *f* annexation, incorporation *(territory etc.)*

Einvernehmen *n* (good) understanding, agreement, harmony ◊ **im** ~ **mit** in agreement [mutual understanding] with
einverstanden:
 ◊ ~ **sein** to agree [consent] to, to approve of *(s.th.)*; to agree, to be in agreement, to be one *(with s.o.)*
Einverständnis *n* consent; assent; approval
~, **geheimes** *s.* ~, **stillschweigendes**
~, **mündliches** verbal assent
~, **schriftliches** written consent
~, **stillschweigendes** tacit understanding [agreement]; connivance *(used negatively)*; collusion *(used negatively)*
Einwaage *f* 1. weight lost; 2. content *(by weight)*
Einwanderer *m* immigrant
einwandern to come into [enter] (a country), to immigrate
Einwanderung *f* immigration
Einwanderungsbehörde *f* immigration office
Einwanderungsbeschränkungen *fpl* restrictons on immigration
Einwanderungsbewilligung *f* immigration permit
Einwanderungsgesetz *n* immigration law
Einwandungserlaubnis *f s.* **Einwanderungsbewilligung**
Einwanderungskontingent *n* immigration quota
Einwanderungsland *n* country of immigration
Einwanderungspapiere *npl* immigration documents [papers]
Einwanderungspolitik *f* immigration policy
Einwanderungsverbot *n* immigration ban
einwandfrei faultless *(performance etc.)*; unimpeachable *(character etc.)*, impeccable, irreproachable *(conduct, quality etc.)*; incontestable, indubitable *(proof, evidence etc.)*
einwechseln to change *(foreign currency, bank note etc.)*; to exchange *(one thing for another)*; to cash *(cheque)*
Einwechslung *f* changing *(foreign currency, bank note etc.)*; exchange *(of one thing for another)*
Einwegverpackung *f* one-way [throw-away, non--returnable] package
einweisen to introduce *(s.o. to new job etc.)*; to instruct *(s.o. in duties etc.)*; to install *(s.o. in office)*
Einweisung *f* introduction *(to new job)*; instruction *(in duties etc.)*; installation *(in office)*
einwerfen to insert *(a coin in a slot-machine)*; to post, to mail *(a letter in a letter-box)*
einwilligen to consent, to agree
Einwilligung *f* consent, agreement
~, **elterliche** parental consent
einwirken to influence, to have an effect (up)on *(s.th.)*, to exercise [have] an influence on *(s.th.)*; to affect *(result, event)*

Einwirkung f influence, effect *(upon/on s.th.)*
Einwirkungsfaktor m influential factor
Einwohner m inhabitant
Einwohnermeldeamt n registration office
Einwohnerzahl f number of inhabitants
einzahlbar payable
einzahlen to pay in *(at post office, bank etc; taxes etc.)*; to deposit *(to an account)*
Einzahler m payer, depositor
Einzahlung f payment, paying-in *(at post office, bank etc.; taxes etc.)*; deposit *(to an account)*
Einzahlungsauftrag m order for payment
Einzahlungsbeleg m receipt; pay(ing)-in slip, *(Am)* deposit slip
Einzahlungsbescheinigung f s. **Einzahlungsbeleg**
Einzahlungsbogen m pay-in list
Einzahlungsbuch n (bank) pay(ing)-in book, *(Am)* bankbook
Einzahlungsfrist f period of payment
Einzahlungspflicht f pay-in obligation
Einzahlungsschalter m paying-in counter, *(Am)* collection window
Einzahlungsschein m s. **Einzahlungsbeleg**
Einzahlungstag m date of payment
Einzahlungstermin m s. **Einzahlungstag**
Einzahlungszettel m s. **Einzahlungsbeleg**
Einzelabkommen n separate compromise *(with creditors)*
Einzelabschreibung f single-item depreciation
Einzelakkord m individual rate (of piecework)
Einzelakkordsatz m s. **Einzelakkord**
Einzelanfertigung f job-work; production of single parts; specialized production
Einzelaufstellung f detailed enumeration, specification, *(Am)* itemized schedule
Einzelauftrag m individual order
Einzelbauer m individual farmer *(as distinct from collective or co-operative farmer)*
Einzelbauernwirtschaft f individual farm
Einzelbeitrag m *(ins)* individual premium
Einzelbeleg m single receipt [voucher]
Einzelbeteiligung f individual participation
Einzelberechnung f individual calculation
Einzelbericht m detailed report
Einzelbesitzer m individual owner
Einzelbetrieb m single plant [factory]
Einzelbewertung f individual [detailed] valuation
Einzelentscheidung f individual [one-man] decision
Einzelerscheinung f *(stats)* individual case
Einzelerzeugnis n single product
Einzelfall m isolated instance [case]; individual case; particular [special] case
Einzelfertigung f single-part production, single--piece work, *(Am)* individual construction

Einzelfirma f single firm; one-man firm
Einzelgehalt n special salary
Einzelgenehmigung f special permission; special permit; exclusive licence
Einzelgüter npl goods in units *(as opposed to bulk goods)*
Einzelhandel m retail trade ⋄ **über den ~ beziehen** to obtain from retail trade
~, genossenschaftlicher co-operative retail trade
~, privater private retail trade
Einzelhandelsbetrieb m retail trade enterprise *(departmental store, supermarket etc.)*
Einzelhandelseinrichtung f retail trade establishment
Einzelhandelsgeschäft n retail shop
Einzelhandelsnetz n network of retail shops
Einzelhandelsniederlassung f retail trade branch [agency]
Einzelhandelspackung f retail trade package
Einzelhandelspreis m retail price
Einzelhandelspreisbildung f retail pricing, formation of retail prices
Einzelhandelspreisindex m retail price index
Einzelhandelsrabatt m (retail trade) discount
Einzelhandelsspanne f retail (trade) margin
Einzelhandelsspezialisierung f specialization in retail trade *(on a small range of goods)*
Einzelhandelsstatistik f retail (trade) statistics
Einzelhandelstarif m retail (trade) wage rate
Einzelhandelsumsatz m retail (trade) turnover
Einzelhandelsumsatzplanung f planning of retail (trade) turnover
Einzelhandelsverkauf m retail trade [trading]
Einzelhandelsverkaufspreisbildung f. s. **Einzelhandelspreisbildung**
Einzelhandelsverkaufspreisniveau n level of retail prices
Einzelhandelsware f retail (trade) commodity
Einzelhändler m retailer, shopkeeper
~, privater private retailer
Einzelhandwerker m craftsman
Einzelhersteller m individual producer
Einzelherstellung f s. **Einzelfertigung**
Einzelkalkulation f cost calculation of a single product
Einzelkaufmann m salesman; sole trader
Einzelkonto n individual account
Einzelkosten pl direct unit [itemized] costs
Einzelleistung f performance of an individual, individual performance
Einzelleiter m individual manager
Einzelleitung f individual management
Einzellohnschein m wage slip
Einzelnorm f individual norm
Einzelplan m *(fin)* special plan *(for education, health service etc., forming part of the overall budget plan)*

Einzelpreis *m* price per unit
~, fester fixed price per unit
Einzelpreisbewilligung *f* approval of separate prices per unit
Einzelpreisbildung *f* non-standardized pricing
Einzelproduktion *f s.* **Einzelfertigung**
Einzelproduzent *m* individual producer
Einzelprüfung *f* detailed checking [*(acc)* audit]
Einzelqualitätskennziffer *f* indicator of a particular quality *(of a product)*
Einzelrechnung *f* single invoice
Einzelserienfertigung *f* single-lot production
Einzelteil *n* single [individual] part, component *(machinery etc.)*
Einzelteile *npl* component parts, components
Einzelteilfertigung *f* production of component parts [components]
~, zentrale centralized production of component parts [components]
Einzeltitel *m (fin)* single item
Einzel- und Sonderfertigung *f* piece and job lot production
Einzelunternehmen *n* single [one-man] enterprise
Einzelunternehmer *m* individual entrepreneur
Einzelverbraucher m (individual) consumer
Einzelverkauf *m* retail sale
Einzelverkäufer *m s.* **Einzelhändler**
Einzelverkaufsgeschäft *n s.* **Einzelhandelsgeschäft**
Einzelvermögen *n* individual wealth
Einzelverpackung *f* individual [unit] packing
Einzelvertrag *m* special [individual] contract *(for highly qualified scientists, technicians etc., with remuneration above general salary rates)*
Einzelvertrieb *m* privileged selling [sale]
Einzelverwahrung *f* special safe keeping *(documents etc.)*
Einzelvorratsnorm *f* single-item stock standard *(for a type of product)*
Einzelwerbung *f* advertisement for individual commodities; direct advertising
Einzelwert *m* individual [single] value
Einzelwettbewerb *m* individual competition *(as opposed to team competition)*
Einzelwirtschaft *f s.* **Einzelbauernwirtschaft**
einziehbar collectible *(debts, rents, taxes etc.)*, cashable *(money)*; seizable *(debts etc.)*
einziehen to collect, to get in *(debts, rents, taxes etc.)*; *(bank)* to call in *(money etc.)*, to withdraw *(money from circulation)*; to gather *(information)*; *(jur)* to confiscate *(property etc.)*
Einziehung *f* collection *(debts, rents, taxes etc.)*; *(bank)* withdrawal *(of money from circulation)*; *(jur)* confiscation *(property etc.)*
Einziehungsauftrag *m* transfer order *(in postal cheque service)*

Einzugsbereich *m* catchment area *(goods etc.)*; commuter belt *(persons)*
Einzugsgebiet *n s.* **Einzugsbereich**
Einzugsordnung *f* rules for collection *(money, taxes etc.)*
Einzweckmaschine *f* single-purpose machine
Eisenbahn *f* railway, *(Am)* railroad
Eisenbahnaktie *f* railway share
Eisenbahnanschluß *m* railway connection; railway junction
Eisenbahnarbeiter *m* railway employee, railwayman
Eisenbahnbau *m* railway construction
Eisenbahnbetrieb *m* railway service
Eisenbahner *m s.* **Eisenbahnarbeiter**
Eisenbahnergewerkschaft *f* railwaymen's trade union
Eisenbahnfährverkehr *m* railway ferry traffic
Eisenbahnfracht *f* rail(way) freight
Eisenbahnfrachtverkehr *m s.* **Eisenbahngüterverkehr**
Eisenbahnfrachtvertrag *m* contract on railway freight
Eisenbahngesellschaft *f* railway company
Eisenbahngütertarif *m* railway goods transport rate
Eisenbahngüterverkehr *m* railway goods [*(Am)* freight] traffic
Eisenbahnknotenpunkt *m* railway junction
Eisenbahnlinie *f* railway line [route]
Eisenbahnnetz *n* railway network [system]
Eisenbahnpersonenverkehr *m* railway passenger traffic
Eisenbahnstrecke *f* railway section [line]
Eisenbahntarif *m* railway transport rate
Eisenbahntransport *m* railway transport
Eisenbahnverbindung *f* rail connection
Eisenbahnverkehr *m* railway traffic [service]
Eisenbahnverkehrsordnung *f* railway traffic regulations
Eisenbahnwesen *n* railways, railway system
Eisenerzbergbau *m* iron-ore mining
Eisengießerei *f* iron-foundry
Eisenhandel *m* iron trade; ironmongery [hardware] business
Eisenhüttenwerk *n* ironworks, iron and steel works
Eisenindustrie *f* iron industry, heavy metallurgical industry
Eisenwaren *fpl* ironmongery, hardware
Eisenwarenhändler *m* ironmonger
Eisenwarenhandlung *f* ironmonger's [hardware] shop
Elastizität *f* elasticity
Elastizitätsfunktion *f* elasticity function
Elastizitätsgrenze *f* margin of elasticity
Elastizitätskoeffizient *m* elasticity coefficient

elektrifizieren to electrify
Elektrifizierung *f* electrification
Elektrifizierungsgrad *m* level [extent] of electrification
Elektrizitätserzeugung *f* production of electricity, generation of electric power
Elektrizitätsversorgung *f* electricity supply
Elektrizitätswerk *n* power station, electricity works
Elektrizitätswirtschaft *f s.* **Elektroenergiewirtschaft**
Elektrochemie *f* electro-chemistry
elektrochemisch electro-chemical
Elektroenergie *f* electric power, electrical energy *(s.a.* **Strom)**
Elektroenergieabnehmer *m* consumer of electricity
Elektroenergiebedarf *m* demand for electricity, power requirements
Elektroenergiebilanz *f* balance sheet of power supply and consumption
Elektroenergieentnahme *f* consumption of electricity; use of electricity
Elektroenergieerzeugung *f* generation of electric current [power, electricity]
Elektroenergiekontingent *n* quota of power supply
Elektroenergieprogramm *n* electric power programme
Elektroenergietarif *m* electricity rate(s)
Elektroenergieverbrauch *m* consumption of electricity, electricity consumption
Elektroenergieverbrauchsnorm *f* standard of electricity consumption
Elektroenergieversorgung *f* supply of current [electricity, power], power supply
Elektroenergieverteilungssystem *n* network of power distribution
Elektroenergiewirtschaft *f* electric power industry
Elektroindustrie *f* electrical industry
Elektromaschinenbau *f* electrical engineering industry
Elektromaschinenindustrie *f s.* **Elektromaschinenbau**
Elektrometallurgie *f* electrometallurgy
Elektronenbuchführung *f* computerization of [in] accounting
Elektronengehirn *n* electronic brain
Elektronenrechenmaschine *f s.* **Elektronenrechner**
Elektronenrechner *m* electronic computer
Elektronik *f* electronics
~, industrielle industrial electronics
Elektrotechnik *f* electrical engineering
Elektrotechniker *m* electrical technician; electrical engineer

Elektrowirtschaft *f s.* **Elektroenergiewirtschaft**
Element *n* element *(forces of nature, unit of labour etc.)*; component *(machine etc.)*
~ eines Potentials *(stats, maths)* compound of a potential
Elementargewalt *f* force of nature
Elementarschadenversicherung *f* insurance of elemental damages
Elend *n* extreme poverty, destitution, distress, misery ⋄ **im ~ leben** to live in misery
Elendsquartier *n* squalid dwelling; shanty
Elendsviertel *n* slum (quarter), slums; shanty-town
Eleve *m* student (of forestry); pupil; apprentice
Elfenbeinindustrie *f* ivory industry
Elfenbeinschnitzerei *f* ivory carving, ivory
Elite *f* elite, pick of society
Elitetheorie *f* theory of elites
Elternermäßigung *f* parents allowance
Elternvertretung *f* parent advisory council *(for school education)*
Emaillierarbeit *f* enamel work
emaillieren to enamel
Emaillierung *f* enamel(ling)
Emailware *f* enamel-ware
Emanzipation *f* emancipation; *(hist)* manumission *(slaves)*
emanzipieren to emancipate; *(hist)* to manumit *(slaves)*
Emballage *f* packing [wrapping] material
Embargo *n* embargo
Embargoliste *f* embargo list
Emigrant *m* emigrant
Emigrantentum *n* emigration; (the) emigrants
Emigration *f* emigration
~, innere passive resistance *(to a regime)*
emigrieren to emigrate
Emissär *m* emissary; issuer
Emission *f* 1. issue *(bank notes, shares etc.)*; 2. emission *(noxious particles, fumes)*
Emissionsabteilung *f* issue [issuing] department
Emissionsagio *n s.* **Emissionsprämie**
Emissionsbank *f* bank of issue, issuing house
Emissionsbilanz *f* balance sheet of issue
Emissionsfonds *m* fund of issue
Emissionsfunktion *f* issuing function *(of reserve banks)*
Emissionsgeschäft *n* issuing transaction(s); issuing; underwriting business
Emissionsgesetz *n* issue law
Emissionsgewinn *m* profit of issue
Emissionshaus *n* issuing house
Emissionskonsortium *n* issuing syndicate
Emissionskontrolle *f* control of capital issue
Emissionskosten *pl* share-issue [*(Am)* stock--issue] costs

10*

Emissionskredit *m* share-issue [*(Am)* stock-issue] credit
Emissionskurs *m* issue price
Emissionslenkung *f s.* **Emissionskontrolle**
Emissionsmarkt *m* capital market; market of (new) issues
Emissionsmodalitäten *fpl* terms of issue
Emissionsmonopol *n* right [privilege, prerogative] of issuing bank notes
Emissionsplan *m* plan of issue
Emissionspolitik *f* issuing policy
Emissionsprämie *f* premium on an issue
Emissionsprofit *m s.* **Emissionsgewinn**
Emissionsrecht *n* issuing right(s)
Emissionsregelung *f s.* **Emissionskontrolle**
Emissionsreserve *f* potential stock
Emissionssperre *f* restrictions on capital issue
Emissionsstatistik *f* issue statistics
Emissionsstelle *f s.* **Emissionshaus**
Emissionsstempel *m* stamp duty *(on the issue of securities)*
Emissionssteuer *f* issue tax
Emissionstätigkeit *f* capital issues
Emissionswert *m* issued value
Emissionszuwachs *m* increase of money in circulation
Emittent *m* issuer, emitter
emittierbar issuable
emittieren to issue *(bank notes, shares etc.)*
emittiert issued ◊ **nicht ~** unissued
Empfang *m* 1. receipt, acceptance [taking] of delivery *(goods etc.)*; reception *(guests, visitors etc.)*; 2. reception, reception desk *(hotels etc.)* ◊ **bei ~** on receipt of, on delivery of *(s.th.)*; **den ~ bescheinigen** to give a receipt for *(s.th.)*; to confirm receipt of *(goods etc.)*; **den ~ bestätigen** to acknowledge receipt of *(s.th.)*, to confirm receipt of *(s.th.)* (in writing); **in ~ nehmen** to receive; to accept [take] delivery of *(goods etc.)*; **nach ~** when received, after having received; **zahlbar bei ~** cash on delivery
empfangen to receive, to accept [take] delivery of *(goods etc.)*; to receive *(guests, visitors etc.)*
Empfänger *m* receiver, recipient; payee *(money, cheque etc.)*, consignee *(commodities)*, addressee *(letters)*, acceptor *(bill of exchange)*; benficiary *(legacy)* ◊ **~ bezahlt** cash on delivery; **frei ~** free consignee
Empfängeranweisung *f* consignee's order
Empfängerbetrieb *m* receiving enterprise, recipient
Empfängerland *n* receiving country, recipient
Empfängerverfügung *f (railw)* consignee's advice
Empfängervertrag *m (transp)* unloading contract

Empfängnis *f* conception *(of a child)*
empfängnisfähig capable of conceiving
Empfängnisoptimum *n* optimum fertility *(family planning)*; *(agric)* optimum fertilization
empfängnisverhütend contraceptive
Empfängnisverhütung *f* contraception; birth control
Empfängniszeit *f* period of possible conception
Empfangsabteilung *f* receiving department
Empfangsanzeige *f* advice of receipt
Empfangsbahnhof *m* destination
Empfangsberechtigter *m* authorized beneficiary [recipient]
Empfangsberechtigung *f* authorization of receipt
Empfangsbescheinigung *f* receipt
Empfangsbestätigung *f* acknowledgement of receipt
Empfangsbuch *n* book of receipts
Empfangsbüro *n* reception (desk), reception office
Empfangschef *m* receptionist, reception officer [*(Am)* clerk], *(Am)* room clerk
Empfangsdame *f* receptionist
Empfangsdaten *pl (d.pr.)* received data
Empfangsgebäude *n (approx.)* main building *(of a railway station)*
Empfangshalle *f* reception hall
Empfangskonnossement *n* (receiving) bill of lading
Empfangsprämie *f (st.ex.)* premium of receipt
Empfangsquittung *f* (accountable) receipt
Empfangsschein *m s.* **Empfangsbescheinigung**
Empfangsstation *f* point of destination, receiving station **frei ~** free (to) point of destination
Empfangstag *m* calling day, at-home day; *(com)* day of delivery
Empfangszimmer *n* reception room
empfehlen to recommend *(s.th. to s.o.)*; to recommend *(s.th./s.o. as; s.th./s.o. for)*; **sich ~** to take one's leave, to say goodbye
Empfehlung *f* recommendation; advice ◊ **auf ~ von** up(on) recommendation of *(s.o.)*
~, geschäftliche business reference
~, persönliche personal reference
Empfehlungsbrief *m s.* **Empfehlungsschreiben**
Empfehlungsschreiben *n* letter of recommendation
en bloc en bloc
Endabnehmer *m* final consumer; ultimate purchaser
Endabrechnung *f* final account
Endaufkommen *n* final yield *(taxes etc.)*
Endaufteilung *f* final partition
Endbahnhof *m* terminus, railhead, *(Am)* terminal (station)

Endbestand *m* final balance *(cash, deposits etc.)*, final stock *(goods etc.)*
Endbetrag *m* (final) amount
Endbezieher *m s.* **Endabnehmer**
Endbilanz *f* final balance sheet
Ende *n* end, close; termination ⋄ **am ~ des laufenden Monats** at the last instant; at the end of the (current) month; **zu ~ bringen** to bring to a close; **zu ~ gehen** to run out *(stocks etc.)*
Endeffekt *m* final effect
Endeinkommen *n* final income *(of classes, strata, individuals, enterprises etc., after distribution and redistribution of national income)*
Endentscheidung *f (stats)* terminal decision
Endergebnis *n* final [ultimate] result
Enderprobung *f* final test *(of a product)*
Enderzeugnis *n* final product
Enderzeugung *f* final production
en detail en detail
En-detail-Handel *m* retail trade
Endfertigung *f s.* **Enderzeugung**
Endfertigungsbetrieb *m s.* **Endhersteller**
Endfinanzierung *f* final financing
Endfläche *f* end [terminal] face; *(stats)* tail area
~ einer Verteilung *(stats)* tail area of a distribution
Endhafen *m* final port; home port
Endhersteller *m* final producer
Endherstellerbetrieb *m s.* **Endhersteller**
Endkalkulation *f* final [detailed] calculation
Endkäufer *m s.* **Endabnehmer**
Endkomplettierung *f* final completion
Endkontrolle *f* final checking
~, betriebliche final internal checking
Endkosten *pl* final cost(s)
Endkostenträger *m* final cost unit
Endlichkeit *f* finiteness, finitude *(space, time, capacity etc.)*
~ des Algorithmus finite algorithm
Endmontage *f* final assembly
Endprobe *f* final test
Endprodukt *n* 1. final product; 2. final production *(volume of commodities produced ready for investment, consumption and export)*
~, betriebliches final product of an enterprise
~ eines Zweiges final product of a branch
~, gesellschaftliches final social product [production]
~, volkswirtschaftliches national economic final product [production]
Endproduktion *f s.* **Enderzeugung**
Endproduzent *m* final producer
Endprüfung *f s.* **Endkontrolle**
Endpunkt *m* end; extremity; terminus, terminal point, (point of) destination *(of line etc.)*
Endsaldo *m* final balance
Endstation *f* terminus, *(Am)* terminal

Endsumme *f* (final) total, grand total
Endtermin *m* final [closing] date
Endunterzeichner *m* (the) undersigned
Endurteil *n* final decision; final judgement [verdict]
Endverbrauch *m* final [ultimate] consumption *(1. of material for producing a final product; 2. of consumer goods or means of production by the final user)*
Endverbraucher *m* final consumer
Endverbraucherpreis *m* retail price
Endverkauf *m* final sale
Endverteilung *f* final distribution *(national income)*
Endverwendung *f* final utilization *(national income)*
Endverwertung *f s.* **Endverwendung**
Endwert *m* final value
~ einer nachschüssigen Rente (total) amount of (an) ordinary annuity
~ einer Rente (total) amount of (an) annuity
~ einer vorschüssigen Rente (total) amount of (an) annuity due
Endzweck *m* final aim
Energetik *f* energetics
Energie *f* energy, power
Energieabgabe *f* release of energy; output of energy
Energieanwendung *f* use of energy
Energieaufwand *m* energy expenditure(s)
energieaufwendig energy-intensive
Energieausbeute *f* energy output, output of energy
Energiebeauftragter *m* person responsible for the control of use of energy
Energiebedarf *m* energy [power] requirements [needs]
Energiebereitstellung *f* provision of energy
Energiebetrieb *m* energy-producing enterprise *(electricity, gas, heating etc.)*
Energiebilanz *f* energy balance (sheet)
Energiebilanzierung *f* drawing up of an energy balance (sheet)
Energieeinsatz *m* input of energy
Energieeinsparung *f* economy [economizing] in energy consumption, saving [reduction] of energy consumption
Energieerzeugung *f* generation of energy
Energiegewinnung *f s.* **Energieerzeugung**
Energieindustrie *f* energy industry *(electricity, gas, heating etc.)*
Energieintensität *f* intensity of energy consumption, energy intensity, rate of use of energy
energieintensiv energy-intensive, of high energy consumption
Energiekontingent *n* energy quota

Energiekosten *pl* energy costs
Energielieferung *f* supply of energy
Energieplan *m* energy [power] plan
Energieplanung *f* energy [power] planning
Energiepolitik *f* energy policy
Energieprognose *f* energy forecast [prognosis]
Energieprogramm *n* energy [power] programme
Energiequelle *f* source of energy
Energiereserve *f* store of energy
Energieressourcen *fpl* energy resources
Energiespeicherung *f* storage [accumulation] of energy
Energiesystem *n* energy system
Energietarif *m* energy rates *(for electricity, gas, heating etc.)*
Energietechnik *f s.* **Energetik**
Energieträger *mpl* sources of energy *(coal, petroleum, nuclear power etc.)*
Energieübertragung *f* energy transmission
Energieübertragungsanlage *f* energy transmission installation [plant]
Energieumwandlung *f* power conversion, transformation of energy
Energieverbrauch *m* energy [power] consumption
Energieverbrauchsnorm *f* energy [power] consumption rate [norm]
Energieverbrauchsnormung *f* fixing the rate of energy consumption
Energieverlust *m* loss of energy
Energieversorgung *f* 1. energy [power] supply; 2. energy-supplying enterprises *(of a district)*
Energieversorgungsbetrieb *m* energy-supplying enterprise
Energieverteilung *f* energy distribution
Energieverwendung *f s.* **Energieanwendung**
Energiewirtschaft *f* (electric) power industry
Engagement *n* engagement; *(st.ex.)* commitment
Engpaß *m* bottleneck
Engpaßmaterial *n* material in short supply
Engpaßware *f* commodity in short supply
en gros wholesale
Engrosabnehmer *m* wholesale buyer [*(Am)* receiver]
Engrosabteilung *f* contract [wholesale] department
Engrosagent *m* wholesale commission agent
Engrosbezug *m* bulk buying, wholesale purchase
Engroseinkauf *m* wholesale purchase
Engrosgeschäft *n* wholesale business
Engroshandel *m* wholesale trade
Engroshändler *m* wholesale dealer, wholesaler
Engrosindex *m* wholesale price index
Engroskauf *m s.* **Engroseinkauf**
Engroskäufer *m* wholesale purchaser
Engroskaufmann *m s.* **Engroshändler**

Engroslager *n* wholesale store
Engrospreis *m* wholesale price
Engrosrabatt *m* trade discount
Engrosverkauf *m* (selling by) wholesale
Engrosvertreter *m s.* **Engrosagent**
Enklave *f* enclave *(sector, territory etc., separated from the national economy)*
Enquete *f* official investigation [inquiry]
Enquetemethode *f (stats)* survey method
Entballung *f* deglomeration *(of a region)*
entbinden to release *(s.o. from oath, responsibilities etc.)*
Entbindung *f* release *(from oath, responsibilities etc.)*
enteignen to expropriate, to dispossess
enteignet expropriated
Enteignung *f* expropriation, dispossession
~ **des Landes** appropriation of land *(by the state)*
~, **entschädigungslose** expropriation without compensation
~ **gegen Entschädigung** expropriation with compensation
Enteignungsanspruch *m (jur)* claim to expropriation
Enteignungsentschädigung *f* indemnity for expropriation
Enteignungsrecht *n* right to expropriate *(owner or property)*
Enteignungsverfahren *n* procedure of expropriation
enterben to disinherit *(s.o.)*; *(jur)* to exheredate *(s.o.)*
Enterbung *f* disinheritance; *(jur)* exheredation
entfalten 1. to unfold; 2. to display *(activities etc.)*
Entfaltung *f* display; development
~ **von Wert und Preis** development of value and price
entfernen to move *s.th.* to a distance; to remove *(s.th.)*, to take *s.th.* away; do dismiss *(s.o. from office etc.)*
Entfernung *f* removal *(of s.th.)*; distance *(between two points etc.)*; dismissal *(from office etc.)*
Entfernungstarif *m* transport rate according to distance
Entfernungszone *f* distance zone *(telephone etc.)*
Entfernungszuschlag *m* additional charge for distance
entflechten to disentangle, to decartelize, to deconcentrate, to decentralize
Entflechtung *f* disentanglement, decartelization, deconcentration, decentralization
entfremden:
  ⬦ **jmdm. etwas ~** to take s.th. away from s.o.;
  jmdm. jmdn. ~ to alienate [estrange] s.o. from s.o.
Entfremdung *f* alienation, estrangement

Entgegennahme *f* accepting, acceptance *(gift etc.)*; taking *(money etc.)*; receiving *(orders etc.)*
entgegennehmen to accept *(gift etc.)*; to take *(money etc.)*; to receive *(orders etc.)*
entgegenwirken to act [work] against *(s.th.)*; to counteract *(effect, influence etc.)*; to interfere (with), to counter
Entgelt *n* remuneration, payment, fee *(for services rendered)*; reward ⋄ **als** ~ as payment; **ohne** ~ without payment
~, **vereinbartes** payment agreed (upon)
~, **vereinnahmtes** payment received
Entgeltkatalog *m* list of incomes *(classification of all kinds of income for tax purposes)*
Entgeltnormen *fpl* norms of payment
Entgeltregelungen *fpl* payment regulations
entheben to relieve *(s.o. of obligations, doubts etc.)*; to release *(s.o. from responsibility etc.)*; to suspend *(s.o. from office temporarily)*; to dismiss *(s.o. from office)*
Enthebung *f* relief; release; suspension; dismissal
entkartellisieren to decartelize
Entkartellisierung *f* decartelization
Entkartellisierungsgesetz *n* decartelization law
Entladearbeiten *fpl* discharging *(cargo etc.)*; unloading (activities)
Entladebahnhof *m* unloading station; destination
Entladedauer *f* time [period] of unloading
Entladefrist *f* discharging [unloading] time
Entladegebühr *f* discharging fee; unloading fee
Entladehafen *m* unloading port; discharging port; port of destination
Entladekapazität *f* unloading capacitiy *(port)*; discharging capacity *(port)*
Entladekosten *pl* unloading expenses; discharging costs
entladen to unload; to discharge
Entladepflicht *f* duty to unload within free time
Entladestelle *f* unloading place
Entladezeit *f* time of unloading; duration of unloading
Entladung *f* unloading; discharge
Entlassung *f* dismissal, sacking, discharge *(worker, employee etc.)* ⋄ **seine** ~ **einreichen** to resign from one's position; **seine** ~ **erhalten** to be dismissed from *(office etc.)*
~, **begründete** dismissal for good reasons
~, **fristlose** dismissal without notice
~, **grundlose** dismissal without cause
~, **sofortige** instant dismissal
~, **vorübergehende** suspension from office
Entlassungsausgleich *m* compensation for dismissal
Entlassungsbescheid *m* notice of dismissal [removal]

Entlassungsentschädigung *f s.* **Entlassungsausgleich**
Entlassungsgeld *n* dismissal pay
Entlassungsgesuch *n* (letter of) resignation
Entlassungsgrund *m* reason(s) for dismissal [removal]
Entlassungspapiere *npl* testimonial and other employment documents
Entlassungsschein *m* certificate of discharge
Entlassungsschreiben *n* notice [letter] of dismissal
Entlassungszeugnis *n* testimonial; school-leaving certificate
entlasten to remove *(burden from s.o. or s.th.)*; to relieve *(s.o. from parts of his responsibility etc.)*; to ease, to lighten *(one's burden, conscience etc.)*; *(jur)* to exonerate, to exculpate
Entlastung *f* removal *(of burden from s.o. or s.th.)*; relief *(of s.o. from parts of his responsibility etc.)*; lightening *(one's burden, conscience etc.)*; *(jur)* exoneration, exculpation
~, **steuerliche** tax relief
~, **vollkommene** general release *(from duties etc.)*
Entlastungsantrag *m (jur)* petition of exoneration
Entlastungsbericht *m* record of release *(bankruptcy)*
Entlastungsbeweis *m (jur)* exonerating evidence
Entlastungsverkehr *m* relief transport
Entlastungszug *m* relief train
entleihen to borrow
Entleiher *m* borrower
entlohnen to pay *(workman etc.)*; to pay wages ⋄ **monatlich** ~ to pay by the month; **täglich** ~ to pay daily; **wochenweise** ~ to pay by the week
entlohnt paid
Entlohnung *f* payment; pay; remuneration ⋄ **gegen** ~ for remuneration
~, **differenzierte** differentiated remuneration
~, **erhöhte** increased remuneration
~, **gleiche** equal pay
~, **individuelle** individual remuneration
~, **kollektive** collective remuneration
~, **leistungsabhängige** remuneration according to performance
~ **mit Feiertagszuschlag** extra holiday pay
~ **nach der Leistung** *s.* ~, **leistungsabhängige**
~ **nach der (produzierten) Menge** *s.* ~ **nach der Stückzahl**
~ **nach der Stückzahl** payment according to pieces (produced) ; piece wage(s)
Entlohnungsform *f* kind of remuneration
Entlohnungsmethoden *fpl* methods of remuneration

Entlohnungssatz *m* wage rate
Entlohnungssystem *n* system of remuneration
Entlohnungstabelle *f* table of wage rates
entmündigen to disqualify; to incapacitate, to declare *s.o.* incapable of managing his/her affairs; to place *s.o.* under legal disability
entmündigt under (legal) disability, (legally) incapacitated
Entmündigter *m* (legally) incapacitated person
Entnahme *f* taking *(of s.th. from s.th.)*; drawing *(of s.th. from s.th.)*; using, use *(of electricity etc.)*; *(com)* withdrawal *(of money from account, cash etc.)*
Entnahmeschein *m* requisition (paper)
entnehmen 1. to take *(s.th. out of/from s.th.)*; to use *(electricity, gas etc.)*; *(com)* to take from, to withdraw *(money etc.)*; 2. to infer, to conclude, to understand, to learn *(from an article, news etc.)*
entpflichten to relieve *(official etc.)*; to give emeritus status *(professors)*
Entpflichtung *f* relief from duties; retirement
Entrepot *n* warehouse, store; *(cust)* bonded warehouse
Entrepreneur *m* entrepreneur; contractor
entrichten to pay *(contributions, taxes etc.)*
Entrichtung *f* payment *(contributions, taxes etc.)*
~ einer Schuld payment of a debt
entschädigen to compensate, to indemnify *(s.o. for s.th.)*; to pay *s.o.* damages *(for s.th.)*
Entschädigung *f* compensation, indemnification; indemnity; damages
~, einmalige non-recurring indemnification [damages]
~, nominelle nominal compensation
Entschädigungsanspruch *m* claim to compensation [damages]
Entschädigungsantrag *m* claim for compensation [damages]
entschädigungsberechtigt entitled to compensation [damages]
Entschädigungsberechtigter *m* person entitled to compensation [damages]
Entschädigungsbetrag *m* amount of damages
Entschädigungsgesetz *n* indemnity law
Entschädigungsgrundlage *f* basis of compensation [damages]
Entschädigungsklage *f* action for damages
Entschädigungskommission *f* *(ins)* compensation [damages] committee
Entschädigungsleistung *f* compensation, indemnification
entschädigungslos without compensation [indemnification, damages]
entschädigungspflichtig liable to pay compensation [damages]
Entschädigungssumme *f* compensation, indemnity, damages; dismissal pay *(to dismissed employees)*
Entschädigungszahlung *f* compensation, indemnification
entscheiden to decide, to settle *(question, dispute etc.)*, to determine on, to resolve upon *(s.th)*; **sich ~** to decide, to make up one's mind, to determine, to resolve, to come to a decision; to be decided [settled] *(matter etc.)*
Entscheidung *f* decision, settlement *(question, dispute etc.)*, determination ⋄ **eine ~ anfechten** to appeal against a decision; **eine ~ aufheben** to rescind a decision; **eine ~ bestätigen** to uphold a decision; **eine ~ fällen** to take [reach, come to] a decision; **eine ~ umstoßen** to overrule a decision; **sich die ~ vorbehalten** to reserve one's decision; **zu einer ~ kommen** to come to a decision [resolution]
~, abschließende *(stats)* terminal decision
~ am grünen Tisch armchair decision
~, endgültige final decision
~, gerichtliche judicial decision
~, gleichlautende congruent decision
~, kollektive collective decision
~, logische logical decision
~, mehrwertige *(stats)* multivalued decision
~, nichtprogrammierbare *(stats)* non-programmable decision
~, operative current decision
~, optimale optimum [optimal] decision
~, programmierbare *(stats)* programmable decision
~, schiedsrichterliche arbitrational decision
~, sofortige prompt [instant] decision
~, strategische strategic decision
~, taktische tactical decision
~, vorläufige preliminary decision
Entscheidungsalgorithmus *m* decision-making algorithm
Entscheidungsbefugnis *f* decision-making authority; *(jur)* competence, jurisdiction
Entscheidungsbereich *m* province [domain] of authority (to make decisions); *(stats)* zone of preference
Entscheidungsdurchsetzung *f* implementation [realization] of a decision
Entscheidungsebene *f* decision level
Entscheidungsereignis *n* event to be decided upon
Entscheidungsetappe *f* decision stage, stage of decision
Entscheidungsfaktor *m* decision-making factor
Entscheidungsfällender *m* decision-maker
~, risikofreudiger risk-prone decision-maker
~, risikomeidender risk-averse decision-maker
~, risikoneutraler risk-neutral decision-maker

Entscheidungsfeld *n* decision-making area
Entscheidungsfindung *f* decision-making
~, dezentralisierte decentralized decision-making
~, zentralisierte centralized decision-making
Entscheidungsforschung *f* decision research
~, mathematische mathematical decision research
~, nichtmathematische non-mathematical decision research
Entscheidungsfrage *f* categorical question *(demanding the answer 'yes' or 'no')*
Entscheidungsfreiheit *f* freedom in deciding, liberty of decision
Entscheidungsfunktion *f* *(stats)* decision function
~, als zulässig erklärte *(stats)* admissible decision function
~, gemischte *(stats)* randomized decision function
~, gleichmäßig bessere *(stats)* uniformly better decision function
~, ökonomische economic decision function
~, statistische statistical decision function
Entscheidungsgrund *m* reason for a decision; reason for a judicial decision
Entscheidungshierarchie *f* decision-making echelon [hierarchy, pyramid]
Entscheidungskompetenz *f* competence [scope] of decision-making
Entscheidungskriterium *n* decision criterion
Entscheidungsmatrix *f* decision matrix
~, horizontale horizontal decision matrix
~, vertikale vertical decision matrix
Entscheidungsmerkmal *n* criterion
Entscheidungsmethode *f* decision-making method, method of decision-making
Entscheidungsmittel *npl* aids to decision-making *(analysis, statistics etc.)*
Entscheidungsmodell *n* decision model
Entscheidungsmodellierung *f* modelling of decisions
Entscheidungsmöglichkeiten *fpl* variants of possible decisions
Entscheidungsnetzplan *m* net plan of decisions
Entscheidungsobjekt *n* object to be decided upon
Entscheidungsprozeß *m* decision-making process
~, einstufiger single-stage [single-phase] process of decision-making
~, mehrstufiger multi-stage [multi-phase] process of decision-making
Entscheidungsraum *m* decision scope; *(stats)* decision space
Entscheidungsrealisierung *f* implementation [realization] of decisions

Entscheidungsregel *f* decision principle
~, programmierte programmed decision principle
Entscheidungsspielraum *m* scope of [elbow-room for] decision-making
Entscheidungssubjekt *n* subject of decision
Entscheidungstabelle *f* decision diagram
Entscheidungstheorie *f* decision theory
~, statistische statistical decision theory
Entscheidungsträger *m s.* Entscheidungsfäller
Entscheidungsvariable *f* decision variable
Entscheidungsvariante *f* decision variant, alternative course of action
Entscheidungsvektor *m* decision vector
~, optimaler optimum [optimal] decision vector
Entscheidungsverlust *m* opportunity cost *(loss stemming from losing the opportunity to take advantage of an alternative by adopting a different course)*
Entscheidungsvorbereitung *f* decision preparation
Entscheidungsvorgang *m* process of decision-making
Entscheidungswahl *f* free choice (of decision)
Entscheidungszeitpunkt *m* date of decision
entschließen, sich to make up one's mind, to come to a decision, to decide, to determine, to resolve
Entschließung *f* resolution; decision ✧ eine ~ ablehnen to reject a resolution; eine ~ annehmen to pass [adopt] a resolution; eine ~ einbringen to move a resolution; eine ~ vorbereiten to draft a resolution
~, gemeinsame joint resolution
Entschließungsentwurf *m* draft of a resolution
Entschließungsfreiheit *f* liberty to move resolutions
Entschluß *m* resolution; decision; determination
entschlüsseln to decode
Entschlüsselung *f* decoding
entschulden to free s.o. of debts, to disencumber
Entschuldung *f* disencumbering, disencumberment, disencumbrance
entsenden to delegate, to depute *(s.o.)*
Entsendung *f* delegation, deputation
entsorgen to dispose of unclear [toxic, hazardous] waste; to decontaminate *(chemical substances etc.)*
Entsorgung *f* disposal of unclear [toxic, hazardous] waste; decontamination *(chemical substances etc.)*
entspannen, sich to ease (up) *(tension, political situation etc.)*; to relax, to find [take] relaxation
Entspannung *f* easing *(tension, political situation etc.)*; relaxation

~ **am Geldmarkt** ease on the money market
~ **der Konjunktur** easing of cyclical conditions
Entsprechungszahl *f (stats)* corresponding figure
entstehen to originate; to come into being, to come to birth, to be born *(ideas etc.)*; to arise, to spring up *(relations, friedship etc.)*, to emerge *(difficulties etc.)*
Entstehung *f* origin, origination; birth *(ideas etc.)*; rise, emergence *(difficulties etc.)*
Entstehungsprozeß *m* process of emergence
enttrümmern to clear away debris
Enttrümmerung *f* clearing away of debris
Enttrümmerungskosten *pl* cost of clearing away of debris
entvölkern to depopulate
Entvölkerung *f* depopulation
entwalden to deforest, to untimber *(land)*
Entwaldung *f* deforestation, untimbering *(land)*
entwässern to drain *(soil etc.)*
Entwässerung *f* drainage, draining *(soil etc.)*
Entwässerungsanlagen *fpl* drainage (installations)
Entwässerungsgebiet *n* drainage area
Entwässerungssystem *n* drainage system
entwerfen to sketch, to draw, to outline; to draw up *(document etc.)*, to draft *(plan etc.)*
Entwerfen *n* drawing up, drafting *(plan etc.)*
Entwerfer *m* planner, designer
entwerten to lower (the value); to depreciate; to devalu(at)e *(currency);* to cancel, to deface *(stamps etc.)*; to demonetize, to call in, to withdraw *(coins)*
entwertet depreciated; devaluated *(currency)*; cancelled, defaced *(stamps etc.)*; demonetized, called in, withdrawn *(coins)*
Entwertung *f* lowering (the value); depreciation; devaluation *(currency)*; cancellation *(stamps etc.)*; demonetization, calling in, withdrawal *(coins)*
~, **tatsächliche** physical depreciation
Entwertungsklausel *f* depreciation clause
Entwertungsrücklage *f* reserve for depreciation
entwickeln to develop, to enlarge on *(subject)*, to evolve *(plan etc.)*
entwickelt developed ◇ **voll** ~ full-fledged, fully developed
Entwicklung *f* development, growth; evolution; formation; trend
~, **computerunterstützte** computer-aided design (CAD)
~ **der Beschäftigtenlage** development on the labour market
~ **der Einkommen** growth in incomes
~ **der Einlagen** growth in deposits
~ **der Geburtenziffer** trend of births; growth of birthrate

~ **des Berufsbildes** changes in job characteristics to a higher level
~ **des geistig-kulturellen Lebens** development of intellectual and cultural life
~, **experimentelle** experimental development
~, **gesellschaftliche** social development
~, **gleichgewichtige** balanced development
~, **industrielle** industrial development
~, **konjunkturelle** cyclical development, economic [business] development [trend(s)]
~, **kurzfristige** short-term development
~, **langfristige** long-term development
~, **mittelfristige** medium-term development
~, **ökonomische** economic development
~, **planmäßige** development according to plan
~, **politische** political development
~, **rechnergestützte** *s.* ~, **computerunterstützte**
~, **rückläufige** negative development
~, **technologische** development in technologies, technological development
~, **volkswirtschaftliche** (national) economic development
~, **wirtschaftliche** economic development
~, **wissenschaftliche** scientific development
~, **zyklische** cyclical development
Entwicklungsablauf *m* (course of) development [evolution]
Entwicklungsabschnitt *m* development phase [period]
Entwicklungsalter *n* development age
Entwicklungsanalyse *f* development analysis
Entwicklungsanleihe *f* development loan
Entwicklungsanstoß *m* impetus [impulse] to development
Entwicklungsarbeit *f* development(al) work
Entwicklungsausgaben *fpl* development costs
Entwicklungsbank *f* development bank
Entwicklungsbericht *m (ind)* technical report
Entwicklungsbüro *n* design(ing) [project construction] office [bureau]
Entwicklungsdiagramm *n* process chart
Entwicklungserscheinung *f* sign [symptom] of development
Entwicklungsetappe *f* stage of development
entwicklungsfähig capable of development
Entwicklungsfähigkeit *f* capability of development
Entwicklungsfonds *m* development fund
Entwicklungsgang *m s.* **Entwicklungsablauf**
Entwicklungsgebiet *n* development area
Entwicklungsgeschichte *f* history of development, history of evolution
entwicklungsgeschichtlich associated with the history of development, seen from the point of view of the history of development; from the aspect of evolution
Entwicklungsgesetz *n* law of development

Entwicklungsgesetze *npl*:
~ in Natur und Gesellschaft laws of development of nature and society
Entwicklungshilfe *f* development aid
Entwickungsimpuls *m s.* Entwicklungsanstoß
Entwicklungsinvestitionen *fpl* development investments
Entwicklungskonzeption *f* development concept [idea]
Entwicklungskosten *pl* development costs, costs of development
Entwicklungskredit *m s.* Entwicklungsanleihe
Entwicklungsland *n* developing country
Entwicklungslinie *f (stats)* trend
entwicklungsmäßig developmental; evolutionary
Entwicklungsmodell *n* development model
Entwicklungsmöglichkeiten *fpl* development potentialities [possibilities]
Entwicklungsniveau *n* development level
Entwicklungsparameter *m* development parameter; *(d.pr.)* processing parameter
Entwicklungsperspektive *f* prospects [possibilities] of development
Entwicklungsphase *f* phase of development
Entwicklungsplan *m* development plan
Entwicklungspolitik *f* development policy [policies]
Entwicklungsproblem *n* problem of development
Entwicklungsprognose *f* long-term forecast of development
~, volkswirtschaftliche national economic development forecast, long-term forecast of national economic development
Entwicklungsprogramm *n* development programme
Entwicklungsprogrammierung *f* development programming
Entwicklungsprojekt *n* development project
Entwicklungsprozeß *m* development process; evolutionary process
Entwicklungsrate *f* rate of development
Entwicklungsreihe *f (stats)* series
Entwicklungsrichtung *f* direction of development
Entwicklungsstadium *n* stage of development; pilot stage
Entwicklungsstand *m* level of development
~, technischer level of technical development
Entwicklungsstörungen *fpl* developmental disturbances
Entwicklungsstrategie *f* development strategy, strategy of development *(country, sector etc.)*
Entwicklungsstufe *f* development stage
Entwicklungstempo *n* pace [rate] of development, development rate [tempo]

~, wirtschaftliches rate of economic development
Entwicklungstendenz *f* tendency [trend] of development
Entwicklungstheorie *f* development theory; theory of evolution
Entwicklungstrend *m s.* Entwicklungstendenz
Entwicklungs- und Anlaufkosten *pl* development and launching cost(s)
Entwicklungs- und Konstruktionsbüro *n* development and designing office
Entwicklungs- und Überleitungsvertrag *m* agreement on development and transfer of research results into production
Entwicklungsunterbrechung *f* interruption in development
Entwicklungsverfahren *n* developing process; developing method
Entwicklungsvorgang *m s.* Entwicklungsprozeß
Entwicklungsvorhaben *n* development scheme [project]
Entwicklungsvorhersage *f* development forecast
Entwicklungsweg *m* path [road] of development
~, volkswirtschaftlich günstiger optimum [favourable] path of development of the national economy
Entwicklungszeit *f* development time, period of development
Entwicklungszyklus *m* cycle of development
Entwurf *m* 1. draft, sketch, outline *(plan, design, pattern etc.)*; 2. design
~, endgültiger final draft
~, erster first draft
~, logischer *(d.pr.)* logic design
~, schriftlicher written draft
~, technischer technical draft [drawing]; engineering design
Entwurfsbüro *n* design(ing) [project construction] office [bureau]
Entwurfsstadium *n* drafting [blueprint] stage
entzerren to rectify, to correct *(statistical data etc.)*
Entzerrung *f* rectification, correction *(statistical data etc.)*
~ der Wechselkurse evening-out of exchange rates
entziehen:
◇ jmdm. etwas ~ to take s.th. away from s.o., to deprive s.o. of s.th., to withdraw s.th. from s.o., to withhold s.th. from s.o.
Entziehung *f* taking away, withdrawal; revoking *(licence etc.)*; deprivation *(drugs etc.)*; stopping *(allowance etc.)*
~ von Anlagekapital disinvestment
~ von Devisen drain on foreign exchange

erarbeiten to get *s.th.* by working, to work for *(s.th.)*; to work out, to elaborate
erarbeitet got by work
Erarbeitung *f* working out, elaboration
Erbanfall *m* inheritance; succession [reversion] of an estate
Erbanspruch *m* titel [claim] to an inheritance, hereditary title
Erbanteil *m s.* **Erbteil**
Erbantritt *m* assumption of succession
erbauen to construct, to erect, to build
Erbausschlagung *f s.* **Erbschaftsausschlagung**
Erbausschließung *f* exclusion from inheritance
Erbbaurecht *n* hereditary right to erect a building on s.o. else's property
Erbbauzins *m* rent paid for the right to erect a building on s.o. else's property
erbberechtigt entitled to inherit
Erbberechtigter *m* person entitled to inherit
Erbberechtigung *f* title to inheritance
Erbbescheinigung *f s.* **Erbschein**
Erbbesitz *m* inheritance, hereditament
Erbe *m* heir, successor
Erbe *n* inheritance, heritage
Erbeinigung *f* settlement of inheritance
Erbeinsetzung *f* appointment of an heir
erben to inherit
Erbengemeinschaft *f* (community of) joint heirs
Erbenhaftung *f* responsibility of the heir for the liabilities of the predecessor
erbenlos without an heir
erbfähig hereditable, inheritable
Erbfähigkeit *f* heritability, capability to inherit
Erbfall *m* (case of) succession
Erbfolge *f* succession *(by inheritance)*
~, **gesetzliche** legal succession
Erbfolgeordnung *f* order of succession
Erbgut *n* hereditament, heritage
Erbin *f* heiress
Erblasser *m* testator; predecessor; devisor *(of an estate)*
Erblasserin *f* testatrix; predecessor; devisor *(of an estate)*
Erbmasse *f s.* **Erbgut**
Erbpacht *f* heritable tenency
Erbrecht *n* law of inheritance [succession]; title of inheritance, right of succession
erbringen to produce, to adduce *(evidence for s.th.)*; to render service
Erbschaft *f* inheritance ⋄ **eine ~ antreten** to enter upon an inheritance; **eine ~ ausschlagen** to refuse an inheritance; **eine ~ machen** to come into an inheritance
Erbschaftsanfall *m* inheritance, succession
Erbschaftsanspruch *m* claim to inheritance
Erbschaftsausschlagung *f* renunciation of inheritance [a succession]

Erbschaftssteuer *f* death duty, inheritance tax
Erbschaftssteuerfreibetrag *m* exemption from death duty [inheritance tax]
Erbschein *m* certificate of heirship
Erbteil *n* share in the inheritance
Erbteilung *f* inheritance sharing, division of the inheritance
erbunfähig incapable of inheriting
Erbunfähigkeit *f* incapability of inheriting
erbunwürdig *s.* **erbunfähig**
Erbunwürdigkeit *f s.* **Erbunfähigkeit**
Erbvergleich *m* agreement between coheirs
Erbvertrag *m* contract of inheritance
Erbverzicht *m* renunciation of a succession [an inheritance]
Erdarbeiten *fpl* earthwork(s), excavation work
Erdöl *n* petroleum, mineral oil
~, **raffiniertes** refined oil
~, **rohes** crude oil
Erdölaktien *fpl* oil shares [*(Am)* stocks]
Erdölfeld *n* oil field
Erdölförderung *f* oil extraction; crude oil production *(amount)*
Erdölgebiet *n* oil-producing area
Erdölindustrie *f* oil industry
Erdölkartell *n* oil cartel
Erdölkonzession *f* oil rights
Erdölland *n* oil-producing country
Erdölleitung *f* pipeline
Erdölverarbeitung *f* oil [petroleum] refining
Erdölvorkommen *n* oil deposits
Erdölwerte *mpl (st.ex.)* oils
Erdölzone *f* oil belt
ereignen, sich to happen, to occur, to take place
Ereignis *n* event, occurrence, incident
~, **datiertes** *(stats)* dated event
~, **festgelegtes** *(stats)* fixed event
~, **kritisches** *(stats)* critical event
~, **nachfolgendes** *(stats)* succeeding event
~, **nichtkritisches** *(stats)* non-critical event
~, **unvorhersehbares** *(stats)* unforeseeable event
~, **vorhergehendes** *(stats)* preceding event
~, **wenig wahrscheinliches** *(stats)* event with little probability
~, **zufälliges** *(stats)* fortuitous event
Erfahrung *f* experience
~, **langjährige** long years of experience
Erfahrungen *fpl*:
 ⋄ **~ sammeln** to gather experience
Erfahrungsaustausch *m* exchange of experience
Erfahrungsnorm *f (stats)* empirical norm [standard]
~, **durchschnittliche** *(stats)* empirical average standard
Erfahrungsübermittlung *f s.* **Erfahrungsaustausch**
Erfahrungswert *m* empirical figure

erfassen 1. to seize, to grasp; to include, to take in; 2. to register, to list *(data etc.)*; *(d.pr.)* to acquire, to log; *(stats)* to cover, to collect, to compile; 3. *(agric)* to procure
Erfassen *n (d.pr.)* acquisition; detection; *(stats)* coverage
Erfassung *f* 1. inclusion *(of group for special purpose)*; 2. registering, registration, recording, listing *(data etc.)*; 3. *(stats)* coverage, collection, compilation; 4. *(agric)* procurement
~, **analytische** *(stats)* analytical compilation
~, **ausgewählte** *(stats)* selective compilation
~, **buchhalterische** registration in the books
~, **chronologische** chronological listing
~, **einmalige** *(stats)* non-recurring compilation
~, **erzeugnisbezogene** collection of data on products
~ **landwirtschaftlicher Erzeugnisse** procurement of agricultural goods
~, **laufende** *(stats)* current compilation
~, **listenmäßige** *(stats)* listing
~, **mengenmäßige** *(stats)* compilation in physical terms
~, **operative** *s.* ~, **laufende**
~, **periodische** *(stats)* periodical compilation
~, **primärstatistische** *(stats)* compilation of primary data
~, **regelmäßige** *(stats)* regular compilation
~, **statistische** statistical coverage [collection, compilation]
~, **steuerliche** taxation
~, **stichprobenweise** *(stats)* sample compilation
~, **wertmäßige** *(stats)* compilation in value terms
Erfassungseinheit *f (stats)* unit
Erfassungsfehler *m (stats)* compilation error
Erfassungsform *f (stats)* kind of compilation [coverage]
Erfassungsformular *n (stats)* compilation list
Erfassungsgruppe *f (stats)* cluster
~, **geschlossene** *s.* **Erfassungsgruppe**
Erfassungsorganisation *f* procurement organization
Erfassungsplan *m* plan of procurement
Erfassungspolitik *f* policy of procurement
Erfassungspreis *m (agric)* price of basic purchases
Erfassungssystem *n* 1. *(stats)* system of compilation [coverage, collection]; registration system *(persons etc.)*; 2. *(agric)* system of procurement (of agricultural produce)
Erfassungs- und Aufbereitungssystem *n* system of covering and preparing *(data etc.)*
Erfassungs- und Aufkaufbetrieb *m* enterprise for procurement and wholesale purchase (of agricultural produce)
Erfassungs- und Aufkaufplan *m* plan of procurement and wholesale purchase (of agricultural produce)
Erfassungsverfahren *n (stats)* method of coverage; compiling procedure
erfinden to invent, to devise
Erfinder *m* inventor
Erfinderbewegung *f* inventor's movement
Erfinderentgelt *n s.* **Erfindervergütung**
erfinderisch inventive *(talent, mind etc.)*; resourceful, imaginative, ingenious *(person)*
Erfinderleistung *f* inventor's performance
Erfinderpatent *n* patent for invention
Erfinderrecht *n* inventor's right
Erfindervergütung *f* monetary reward [payment] for invention
Erfindung *f* invention
~, **patentfähige** patentable invention
Erfindungsanmeldung *f* application [claim] for an invention
Erfindungsbeschreibung *f* description of an invention
Erfindungspatent *n s.* **Erfinderpatent**
Erfolg *m* success, achievement; result, effect *(work, efforts etc.)*
erfolglos unsuccessful, without success, vain, fruitless *(attempt etc.)*
Erfolglosigkeit *f* want of success; failure; miscarriage *(plan etc.)*
Erfolgsanteil *m* share in profit
Erfolgsanteilsystem *n* profit-sharing scheme; bonus system
Erfolgsbeteiligung *f s.* **Erfolgsanteil**
Erfolgsbilanz *f* profit and loss account, *(Am)* income account
Erfolgskonto *n s.* **Erfolgsbilanz**
Erfolgsrechnung *f s.* **Erfolgsbilanz**
erfolgversprechend promising
erforderlich necessary, required, requisite
erfordern to need, to require, to demand, to take *(time, money etc.)*; to call for *(care, tact etc.)*
Erfordernis *n* requirement, demand; exigence, exigency
Erfordernisse *npl* requirements, demands; exigencies; conditions ◊ **allen Erfordernissen entsprechen** to comply with [meet] all requirements; **allen Erfordernissen genügen** to satisfy all conditions
~, **technische** technical requirements
erforschen to try to find out, to discover *(facts behind a case etc.)*; to search for [into], to inquire into, to study *(causes etc.)*; to explore *(country etc.)*; to investigate *(cave etc.)*
Erforscher *m* explorer *(country etc.)*; investigator
Erforschung *f* inquiry, study, investigation, research *(causes etc.)*; exploration *(country etc.)*

erfüllen to fulfil, to carry out, to perform *(duty, promise etc.)*; to discharge *(obligation etc.)*; to comply with, to accede to *(request etc.)*; to implement *(plan, contract etc.)*; to meet *(requirements etc.)*
Erfüllung *f* fulfilment, implementation *(contract, plan)*; *(jur, com)* performance ⋄ **jmdn. zur ~ eines Vertrages auffordern** to summon s.o. to perform [fulfil] a contract
~, effektive *(jur)* specific performance
~, reale real fulfilment
~, vertragsgerechte performance according to contract
Erfüllungsanspruch *m* claim for performance *(of a contract etc.)*
Erfüllungsbericht *m* report of performance, performance report
Erfüllungseinschränkung *f* limitation of fulfilment
Erfüllungsgehilfe *m* debtor's agent
Erfüllungsgeschäft *n* delivery *(goods)*; settlement *(debts)*
Erfüllungsklage *f (jur)* action for performance
Erfüllungsort *m* place of fulfilment *(contract)*; place of payment [settlement] *(financial transaction)*; place of delivery *(purchase)*; place of performance *(delivery)*
Erfüllungstag *m s.* **Erfüllungstermin**
Erfüllungstermin *m* settlement day
~, vertraglicher settlement day fixed in the contract
Erfüllungszeit *f* time of performance; (final) date of contract fulfilment
ergänzen to complete *(collection etc.)*; to replenish *(stores, wardrobe etc.)*; to complement, to supplement
Ergänzung *f* completion *(collection etc.)*; replenishment *(stores, wardrobe etc.)*; complement, supplement
Ergänzungsabgabe *f (tax)* supplementary levy
Ergänzungsbedarf *m* supplementary needs; requirements for replacements
Ergänzungsbetrag *m* supplementary amount
Ergänzungsbilanz *f* supplementary balance (sheet)
Ergänzungsetat *m s.* **Ergänzungshaushalt**
Ergänzungshaushalt *m* suplementary budget
Ergänzungsinformation *f (stats)* supplementary information
Ergänzungskapital *n* supplementary capital; reserve of (working) capital
Ergänzungskredit *m* supplementary credit [loan]
Ergänzungslager *n* replenishing stock
Ergänzungsproduktion *f* completing production
Ergänzungssteuer *f* supplementary [additional] tax
Ergänzungsverfahren *n (stats)* missing-plot technique
~ fehlender Werte *s.* **Ergänzungsverfahren**
Ergänzungsversicherung *f* complementary insurance
Ergänzungszahlung *f* complementary payment
ergeben to establish, to show, to prove *(result, fact etc.)*; to result in; to yield, to produce *(profit etc.)*; to amount [come] to; **sich ~** to arise *(difficulties etc.)*; to follow, to ensue; to be the consequence [result] of s.th.
Ergebnis *n* result, outcome, effect; returns, receipts, yield; output *(production)*
~, abgerundetes result in round figures, round result
~, angenähertes approximate result
~, finanzielles financial result
~, greifbares tangible result
~, übriges miscellaneous returns [result]
~, vorläufiges preliminary result
~, zufallsbedingtes fortuitous result
Ergebnisanalyse *f* profit and loss analysis
Ergebnisbeeinflussung *f* interference with the result *(elections etc.)*
~ durch die Befrager *(stats)* interviewer bias
Ergebnisbilanz *f* profit and loss statement [account]
Ergebnisermittlung *f* profit and loss accounting
Ergebniskonto *n* profit and loss account
Ergebnisplanung *f* planning of economic results
Ergebnisrechnung *f* profit and loss accounting; profit and loss statement [account]
Ergebnistabelle *f s.* **Ergebnisbilanz**
ergebniswirksam affecting profit and loss
ergiebig productive *(soil, mine etc.)*; fertile *(soil)*; rich, abundant, plentiful *(source etc.)* ⋄ **wirtschaftlich ~** economically productive
Ergiebigkeit *f* productiveness *(soil, mine etc.)*; fertility *(soil)*; richness, abundance *(source etc.)*
Ergodizität *f (stats)* ergodicity
Ergonomie *f* ergonomics, *(Am)* human engineering
Erhalt *m* receipt *(letter, goods, order etc.)* ⋄ **den ~ einer Sendung bestätigen** to acknowledge receipt of a consignment
erhaltbar capable of being preserved
Erhaltbarkeit *f* preservability
erhalten to receive, to get *(letters etc.)*; to keep, to preserve, to maintain *(health, strength etc.)*; to take care of *(building, furniture etc.)* ⋄ **gut ~ sein** to be in good condition; to be in good repair *(building)*; to be well preserved *(archeological find etc.)*; **schlecht ~ sein** to be in poor condition; to be in a poor state of repair *(building)*; to be badly preserved *(archeological find etc.)*
erhältlich obtainable *(goods etc.)*

Erhaltung *f* maintenance *(fixed assets, soil fertility)*, conservation *(natural resources)*; support *(family)*; upkeep *(building)*
~ **der Anlagefonds** maintenance of fixed assets
Erhaltungsarbeiten *fpl* maintenance (work)
Erhaltungsaufwand *m* maintenance costs
Erhaltungskosten *pl s.* **Erhaltungsaufwand**
Erhaltungsmaßnahmen *fpl* maintenance measures *(repairs, general overhaul etc.)*, provision(s) for maintenance
Erhaltungszustand *m* state of preservation *(building etc.)*
erhebbar collectible
erheben to raise *(objection etc.)*; to make, to put forward *(claim etc.)*; *(fin)* to levy, to impose *(tax etc.)*; *(stats)* to collect *(data)*
Erhebung *f* imposition *(tax etc.)*; collection *(data)*; *(stats)* survey, inquiry, census
~, **einmalige** *(fin)* single [non-recurrent, non-recurring] collection
~, **periodische** *(stats)* periodical survey
~, **primärstatistische** *(stats)* survey of primary (statistical) data
~, **repräsentative** *(stats)* representative survey
~, **sekundärstatistische** *(stats)* survey of secondary (statistical) data
~, **statistische** survey of statistical data
~, **steuerliche** collection [levying] of taxes
~, **unvollständige** *(stats)* incomplete survey [census]
~ **von Abgaben** collection of levies [duties]
~ **von Zöllen** collection of customs duties
~, **wiederholte** *(stats)* repeated survey
Erhebungsart *f* *(fin)* kind of collection; *(stats)* kind of survey
Erhebungsbetrag *m* amount to be collected
Erhebungsblatt *n* *(stats)* survey
Erhebungsbogen *m* *(stats)* survey form
Erhebungsdatum *n* *(stats)* date of survey
Erhebungseinheit *f* *(stats)* survey unit
Erhebungsfehler *m* *(stats)* ascertainment error
Erhebungsform *f s.* **Erhebungsart**
Erhebungskosten *pl* costs [expenses] of (data) collection
Erhebungsplan *m* *(stats)* survey design
Erhebungsstichtag *m* *(stats)* fixed date of survey
Erhebungstermin *m* *(fin)* tax payment date
Erhebungsverfahren *n* *(fin)* taxation system
erhöhen to increase, to raise *(prices, taxes, wages, production etc.)*
Erhöhung *f* increase, rise *(prices, taxes, wages, production etc.)*
~ **der Ertragsfähigkeit** *(agric)* increase in productiveness [fertility]
~ **der Geburtenhäufigkeit** increase in the birth rate
~ **des Bankdiskonts** increase in the bank rate

~ **des Diskontsatzes** increase in the discount rate
erholen, sich to recover *(prices, market etc.)*; to be restored, to convalesce *(after illness, hard work etc.)*
Erholung *f* recovery, rest, relaxation, recreation
~ **des Marktes** recovery [improvement] (of the market)
~, **finanzielle** financial recovery
~, **schnelle** rapid recovery; *(st.ex.)* rally *(prices)*
~, **wirtschaftliche** economic recuperation *(after a depression)*
Erholungsaufenthalt *m* holiday, vacation
erholungsbedürftig in need of a rest, run down
Erholungseinrichtungen *fpl* recreational facilities
erholungsfähig buoyant *(market etc.)*
Erholungsfähigkeit *f* buoyancy *(market etc.)*
Erholungsgebiet *n* holiday resort; recreation area
Erholungsheim *n* holiday home; convalescent [rest] home
Erholungsmöglichkeiten *fpl* recreational facilities
Erholungspause *f* break, rest
~, **arbeitsbedingte** *(approx.)* break [rest] (to compensate stress load caused by working conditions)
Erholungsuchender *m* person seeking rest (and quiet)
Erholungsurlaub *m* holiday leave; convalescent leave
Erholungswesen *n* recreation system; system of convalescence
Erholungszentrum *n* recreation centre
erinnern to remind *(s.o. of s.th.)*
Erinnerung *f* remembrance, memory; recollection; *(jur)* appeal *(against payment of cost etc.)*
Erinnerungsposten *m* *(acc)* amount entered in a depreciation reserve account
Erinnerungsschreiben *n* (letter of) reminder
Erinnerungswert *m* reminder (value)
erkennen 1. to discern, to distinguish, to make out *(s.th.)*; to realize, to recognize, to perceive *(importance of s.th.)*; to appreciate *(value of s.th.)*; to identify *(s.o. etc.)*; to be alive to *(danger etc.)*; 2. *(jur)* to pass *(sentence)*; to give *(absolute discharge)*; to impose *(fine)*, to award *(damages)*
erkenntlich 1. grateful, obliged; 2. perceptible
◇ **sich jmdm. ~ zeigen** to show s.o. one's appreciation
Erkenntnis *f* 1. cognition, perception; recognition, knowledge; 2. *(jur)* judgement, sentence, finding
Erkenntnismodell *n* cognition [perception] model

erkenntnistheoretisch epistemological
Erkenntnistheorie *f* theory of cognition, epistemology
Erkenntnisvermögen *n* cognitive [perceptive] faculty, cognition, perception
erklären to explain; to interpret; to declare *(customs etc.)*; to state *(on oath etc.)*; **sich ~** to make a statement ◊ **für nichtig ~** to annul, to nullify; **für null und nichtig ~** to declare null and void; **jmdn. für tot ~** to allege s.o. to be dead; **für ungültig ~** to abrogate, to annul, to cancel *(contract etc.)*; **jmdn. für zahlungsunfähig ~** to declare s.o. insolvent; **sich für bankrott ~** to adjudge o.s. bankrupt
Erklärung *f* explanation; interpretation; declaration *(customs etc.)*; statement *(to the press etc.)* ◊ **eine ~ abgeben** to make a statement; to publish a statement; **eine ~ dementieren** to deny a statement; **jmdm. eine ~ schuldig sein** to owe s.o. an explanation; **von einer ~ Kenntnis nehmen** to take notice of a declaration
~, amtliche official statement
~, eidesstattliche statutory declaration, solemn affirmation
~, erläuternde explanatory declaration
~, formelle explicit declaration
~, öffentliche public statement
~, offizielle official statement
~, umfassende full statement
Erklärungstag *m (st.ex.)* contango day
erkunden to explore, to investigate *(ground, area, problems etc.)*; to find out *(name etc.)*
erkundigen, sich to inquire, to ask; to make inquiries *(about s.th.)*, to seek [gather] information *(on s.th.)*
Erkundigung *f* inquiry, information
Erkundigungen *fpl*:
  ◊ **~ einholen** to make inquiries *(about s.o. or s.th.)*; **~ einziehen** s. **~ einholen**
Erkundung *f* inquiry, search; exploration, investigation *(ground, area, problems etc.)*
  ~ und Förderung *f* **mineralischer Rohstoffe** prospecting for and production of mineral raw materials
Erkundungsaufwand *m* prospecting cost
Erkundungsforschung *f* exploratory research
Erkundungsprognose *f* preliminary forecast [prognosis]
Erlaß *m* 1. reduction, deduction *(prices)*; release, cancellation *(debts)*; exemption, remission *(taxes)*; 2. decree, edict, ordinance
erlassen to issue *(amnesty etc.)*; to set up, to lay down *(regulations etc.)*; to enact *(law etc.)* ◊ **jmdm. etwas ~** to let s.o. off [from], to release s.o. from, to relieve s.o. of *(obligation, debt etc.)*, to exempt s.o. from *(tax, fees etc.)*

Erlassung *f* remittal, remission, release *(penalty, debt etc.)*; exemption *(tax, examiniation etc.)*; acquittance *(debt)*; issuing *(amnesty etc.)*; setting up, laying down *(regulations)*; enaction, enactment *(law)*
erlauben to allow, to permit
Erlaubnis *f* 1. permission; leave *(to do s.th.)*; 2. permit, licence ◊ **eine ~ einholen** to obtain permission; **eine ~ geben** to give permission; **~ erhalten** to be authorized; **um ~ bitten** to request permission
~, allgemeine omnibus permit
~, besondere special permit [licence]
~, offizielle official permit
~, schriftliche written permit
Erlaubnisschein *m* (written) permission, permit, licence
Erlebensfall *m (ins)* case of survival
Erlebensfallversicherung *f* pure endowment assurance
Erlebenswahrscheinlichkeit *f (ins)* probability of survival
Erlebenszeit *f (ins)* endowment period
erledigen to settle *(matter etc.)*, to handle, to manage *(s.th.)*; to do, to finish off *(piece of work)*; to get through *(a great deal of work)*; to clear off *(arrears of work)*; to finish with *(business in hand etc.)* ◊ **ordnungsgemäß ~** to settle duly [properly]
erledigt settled, dealt with, done, finished
Erledigung *f* settlement *(matter etc.)*; arrangement, adjustment; disposal *(matter, piece of work etc.)*; dispatch *(matter etc.)* ◊ **zur ~** to be dealt with
~, umgehende immediate attention
Erleichterung *f* relief; facility
Erleichterungen *fpl* facilities
  ~ der Zahlungsbedingungen facilities for payment, payment facilities
  ~ für die Kreditaufnahme credit facilities
  ~ im Reiseverkehr travelling facilities
erlernbar (s.th. that) can be learned; learnable
erlernen to learn *(trade etc.)*; to acquire *(language etc.)*
Erliegen *n*:
  ◊ **zum ~ kommen** to close down *(business etc.)*; to be brought to a standstill *(traffic etc.)*; to fail *(strength etc.)*
Erlös *m* proceeds, receipts
~, absatzunabhängiger receipts not affected by sale
~ aus Export proceeds from export
~, finanzieller financial proceeds
Erlösausfall *m* deficiency of proceeds, deficit [loss] in proceeds
erlöschen to cease to exist *(firm etc.)*; to expire, to lapse *(contract, membership etc.)*

Erlöschen *n* extinction *(fire etc.)*; expiration, lapse, cancellation *(contract, membership etc.)*
~ **der Hinterlegung** forfeiture of deposit
~ **der Verjährung** expiration of limitation [prescription]
~ **der Verjährungsfrist** *s.* ~ **der Verjährung**
~ **einer Firma** extinction of a firm
~ **einer Schuld** cancellation of a debt
~ **eines Anspruchs** expiration of a claim
~ **eines Schuldverhältnisses** *s.* ~ **einer Schuld**
~, **vorzeitiges** premature expiration
Erlöse *mpl* proceeds, receipts
~ **aus Lizenzen** proceeds from licences
~ **künftiger Abrechnungszeiträume** transitory [suspense] proceeds
~, **leistungsunabhängige** proceeds not affected by production [performance]
~, **nichtplanbare** proceeds which cannot be planned, unplannable proceeds
~, **planbare** planned proceeds; plannable proceeds
~, **übrige** miscellaneous proceeds; sundries
Erlöserhöhung *f* increase in proceeds
Erlöskonto *n* proceeds account
Erlösschmälerung *f* reduction of proceeds
ermächtigen to empower, to authorize, to vest *s.o.* with authority [power]
Ermächtigung *f* 1. authorization; authority, power; 2. warrant, licence
~, **übertragene** delegated authority
ermäßigen to reduce, to lower, to cut, to mark down *(prices etc.)*
Ermäßigung *f* reduction, lowering, cut *(prices etc.)*; discount *(for cash)*, allowance *(for cash, taxes etc.)*
ermitteln to establish *(fact etc.)*; to ascertain, to find out, to discover *(s.o. or s.th.)*
Ermittlung *f* ascertainment; *(maths)* determination *(values etc.)*
Ermittlungen *fpl* investigations, inquiries ◊ ~ **anstellen** to instigate [start] investigations, to start [make] inquiries
~, **erfolglose** investigations without results
~, **polizeiliche** police investigations, investigations by the police
Ermittlungsausschuß *m* fact-finding commission
Ermittlungsdienst *m* investigation service
Ermittlungszeitraum *m* period under review
ermüden to exhaust, to wear down *(metal etc.)*; to get tired *(person)*
Ermüdung *f* fatigue *(metal etc.)*; tiredness *(person)*
ernähren to feed *(s.o., animals etc.)*; to nourish *(s.o., plant etc.)*; to support, to maintain *(family)*
Ernährer *m* provider; supporter, breadwinner

Ernährung *f* nutrition, nourishment, food, diet; support, maintenance *(family)*
~, **falsche** wrong diet
~, **künstliche** artificial feeding
~, **mangelhafte** malnutrition, undernourishment
~, **richtige** correct diet
~, **ungenügende** inadequate nutrition
Ernährungsniveau *n* nutritional level
Ernährungsökonomie *f* economics of food supply
Ernährungspolitik *f* food policy
Ernährungsproblem *n* food problem
Ernährungsstand *m s.* **Ernährungsniveau**
Ernährungsweise *f* feeding habits *(animals)*; form of nutrition; diet
Ernährungszustand *m* nutritional condition
ernennen to appoint, to nominate, to name *(s.o. to an office, post)*
Ernennung *f* appointment, nomination *(of s.o. to an office, post)*
Ernennungsurkunde *f* letter of appointment
erneuern to renew *(treaty, lease etc.)*, to replace *(part of machine etc.)*; to restore *(damaged building etc.)*, to renovate *(flats, rooms etc.)*; to repair *(road etc.)*; to repeat *(order etc.)*
Erneuerung *f* renewal *(treaty, lease etc.)*, replacement *(part of machine etc.)*, restoration *(damaged building etc.)*, renovation *(flats, rooms etc.)*; repair *(road etc.)*; repetition *(order etc.)*
~, **technische** technological replacements
Erneuerungsanspruch *m (ins)* right of reinstatement
Erneuerungsauftrag *m* reorder, renewal order
Erneuerungsbedarf *m* demand for replacements
erneuerungsfähig renewable
Erneuerungsfonds *m* reserve fund for replacements
Erneuerungsinvestition *f* replacing investment
Erneuerungskonto *n* reserve account for replacements
Erneuerungskosten *pl* renewal costs; cost of renovation
Erneuerungsprämie *f (ins)* renewal premium
Erneuerungsprozeß *m (stats)* birth and death process
Erneuerungsquote *f s.* **Erneuerungsrate**
Erneuerungsrate *f* renewal rate, rate of renewal *(products, equipment etc.)*
Erneuerungsrücklage *f* depreciation [investment, replacement] reserve
Erneuerungstheorie *f (stats)* renewal theory
Ernte *f* 1. harvesting, gathering, reaping *(corn etc.)*; picking *(fruit etc.)*; vintaging *(grapes etc.)*; 2. harvest time [season]; 3. harvest; crops
◊ **die ~ einbringen** to harvest, to get in the harvest
~ **auf dem Halm** standing crop

~, **erste** main crop
~, **frühe** forward crop
~, **gute** good crop [harvest]
~, **schlechte** bad [poor] crop [harvest]
Erntearbeit *f* harvesting, harvest work
Erntearbeiter *m* harvester, reaper, harvestman, harvest-hand
Ernteaussichten *fpl* crop prospects
Ernteertrag *m* produce, yield *(of field)*
Ernteertragsversicherung *f* crop yield insurance
Erntefläche *f* area under cultivation, sown area
Erntehelfer *m* volunteer harvester; seasonal labour *(for harvesting)*
Erntekampagne *f* harvest campaign
Erntekredit *m* crop loan
ernten to harvest, to reap *(corn etc.)*; to pick *(fruit etc.)*; to vintage, to pick *(grapes etc.)*
Ernteschätzung *f* crop estimate [forecast]
Erntestatistik *f* crop statistics
Ernteverlust *m* loss in harvesting
Ernteversicherung *f* crop insurance (scheme)
Erntevoranschlag *m s.* **Ernteschätzung**
Erntezeit *f* harvest time [period]
eröffnen to open *(account etc.)*; to unseal *(letter etc.)*; to institute *(bankruptcy proceedings etc.)*; to disclose *(secret etc.)*; to inform *(s.o. of s.th.)*; to inaugurate *(institutions, schools etc.)*
Eröffnung *f* opening *(account etc.)*; institution *(bankruptcy proceedings etc.)*; disclosure *(secret etc.)*; announcement *(information)*; inauguration *(institutions, schools etc.)*
Eröffnungsbestand *m* opening stock
Eröffnungsbilanz *f* opening balance sheet; initial statement of affairs *(at the beginning of financial year etc.)*
Eröffnungsbuchung *f* opening entry
Eröffnungskurs *m (st.ex.)* opening price
Eröffnungstag *m* opening day *(new shop etc.)*; inauguration day *(new institution etc.)*
Eröffnungstermin *m* opening date; date of institution; inauguration date
~ **für Angebote** first day for tenders [offers]
erpressen to blackmail
Erpresser *m* blackmailer
Erpressung *f* blackmail
erproben to test, to try, to prove; to try out *(new machines etc.)*
Erprobung *f* test, trial; try-out *(new machines etc.)*
~, **experimentelle** experimental test
Erprobungsbericht *m* test report *(machinery, equipment etc.)*
Erprobungsvertrag *m* test contract *(of machines, consumer goods etc., between producer and user to prove serviceability)*
errichten to erect, to set up *(scaffolding etc.)*; to construct, to build *(building etc.)*; to found, to establish *(institution etc.)*
Errichtung *f* erection *(scaffolding etc.)*; construction *(building etc.)*; establishment *(institution etc.)*
~ **eines Kontos** opening of an account
Errungenschaft *f* 1. achievement, acquisition *(property, goods)*; 2. *(tech)* device, convenience
Ersatz *m* substitute *(material)*; substitution, replacement; alternative; indemnification, indemnity; compensation; restitution ◊ ~ **leisten (für)** to supply a substitute; to make amends *(for damage caused)*; to compensate *(for s.th.)*, to make [give] compensation *(for s.th.)*, to make restitution *(of s.th.)*
~ **des aufgewandten Kapitals** replacement of capital spent
~ **des verausgabten Kapitals** *s.* ~ **des aufgewandten Kapitals**
~, **teilweiser** partial compensation
~, **wertmäßiger** compensation in value terms
Ersatzangebot *n* compensating offer
Ersatzanspruch *m* claim for damages
Ersatzausrüstung *f* replacement equipment
Ersatzausstattung *f s.* **Ersatzausrüstung**
Ersatzbedarf *m* replacement demand
Ersatzbeleg *m* substituting receipt
Ersatzbeschaffung *f* replacement supply
Ersatzerbe *m* substitute heir
Ersatzfonds *m* replacement fund *(for worn-out equipment etc.)*
~, **gesellschaftlicher** social replacement fund
Ersatzinvestitionen *fpl* replacement investments
Ersatzkasse *f* private sickness insurance company
Ersatzkosten *pl* compensation cost
Ersatzladung *f* substitute cargo
Ersatzleistung *f* compensation, indemnification, payment of damages
Ersatzlieferung *f* compensation delivery
Ersatzmittel *n* substitute, surrogate
Ersatzmodell *n* substitute model
Ersatzpflicht *f* liability for compensation; liability to pay damages
ersatzpflichtig liable for compensation
Ersatzpflichtiger *m* person liable for compensation
Ersatzstoff *m* substitute (material)
Ersatzstück *n s.* **Ersatzteil**
Ersatzteil *n* spare part, spare
Ersatzteilbelieferung *f* supply of spare parts
Ersatzteilfertigung *f* production of spare parts
Ersatzteilkatalog *m* catalogue [list] of spare parts
Ersatzteillager *n* store for spare parts
Ersatzteillieferung *f* delivery of spare parts
Ersatzteilliste *f* list of spare parts

Ersatzteilpreis *m* price of spare parts
Ersatzteilproduktion *f s.* **Ersatzteilfertigung**
Ersatzteiltypisierung *f* standardization of spare parts
Ersatzteilversorgung *f s.* **Ersatzteilbelieferung**
Ersatzteilvorrat *m* stock of spare parts
Ersatzteilwirtschaft *f* production and supply of spare parts
Ersatz- und Verschleißteiltypung *f s.* **Ersatzteiltypisierung**
Ersatzware *f* substitute (article)
ersatzweise by way of substitution
Ersatzwert *m* replacement value; *(ins)* full value
Ersatzzustellung *f (jur)* substituted service
erscheinen to appear, to occur; to be published *(report etc.)*; *(st.ex.)* to be issued
Erscheinung *f* appearance; publication *(report etc.)*; *(st.ex.)* issue; phenomenon
~, **gesellschaftliche** social phenomenon
Erscheinungsform *f* outward shape [form]; appearance, manifestation
~ **des Wertes** *(pol ec)* appearance of (the) value
~, **wirtschaftliche** manifestation of economic phenomenon
Erscheinungsweise *f* way of appearance
erschließen to open (up) *(new markets etc.)*, to make accessible; to develop *(building land)*
Erschließung *f* opening up, development *(market, country etc.)*
~, **industrielle** industrial development [opening up]
~ **neuer Absatzgebiete** opening up of new outlets
~ **von Reserven** mobilization of resources
Erschließungsaufwand *m* opening-up expenditure [costs], initial outlay
Erschöpfbarkeit *f* exhaustability
erschöpfen to exhaust, to use up, to consume (fully)
Erschöpfung *f* exhaustion
~ **natürlicher Ressourcen** exhaustion of natural resources
erschweren to make *s.th.* (more) difficult, to hinder *(work etc.)*; to impede *(progress etc.)*; to complicate *(matters etc.)*
Erschwernis *f* making *s.th.* (more) difficult, hindrance *(work etc.)*; impediment *(progress etc.)*; complication *(matters etc.)*
Erschwerniszulage *f* extra [additional] pay (for heavy work)
Erschwerung *f* added difficulty; impediment, hindrance
ersetzbar replaceable; reparable
ersetzen to take [fill] the place of *(s.th.)*, to serve as a substitute for *(s.o., s.th.)*; to replace *(s.th.)*; to make good *(s.th.)*, to compensate *(for damage etc.)*; to reimburse *(expenses)*

Ersetzung *f* taking [filling] the place of *(s.th.)*, serving as a substitute for *(s.o., s.th.)*; replacing *(s.th.)*; making good *(s.th.)*, compensation *(for damage etc.)*; reimbursing, reimbursement *(expenses)*
ersparen to save (up) *(money etc.)*, to save *(time etc.)*; to spare *(s.o., s.th.)*
Ersparnis *f* saving *(in time, in labour etc.)*
Ersparnisfunktion *f* savings function
Ersparnisprämie *f* bonus for economical use *(of materials etc.)*
erstatten to reimburse, to repay, to refund
Erstattung *f* reimbursement, refunding, repayment, restitution; delivery *(of a report)*
~, **teilweise** partial reimbursement *(costs etc.)*
~, **volle** full reimbursement *(costs etc.)*
Erstattungsanspruch *m* claim for restitution [refund]
Erstattungsantrag *m* application for restitution
Erstattungsverfahren *n* restitution suit
Erstausfertigung *f* original (copy)
Erstausführung *f* prototype, original model [pattern]
Erstausrüstung *f* initial equipment
Erstausstattung *f* original [initial] equipment
Erstausstattungspreis *m* price of the original equipment *(enterprise, workshop etc.)*
erstehen to purchase, to buy, to acquire
Erste-Hilfe-Leistung *f* first aid
Erstehung *f* purchase, acquisition
ersteigern to bargain, to purchase (at auction)
ersteigert bought by [at] auction
Ersteigerung *f* auction
Ersteinlage *f* original investment
erstellen to make *s.th.* available, to provide *(transport for tourists etc.)*; to construct, to erect *(building etc.)*; to draw up, to make out *(list etc.)*
Erstellung *f* making available *(s.th.)*, provision *(of transport for tourists etc.)*; construction, erection *(building etc.)*; drawing up, making out *(list etc.)*
Erstellungskosten *pl* cost of construction
Ersterfassung *f* first registration; *(acc)* first entry
Ersterfinder *m* original inventor
Ersterwerb *m* original acquisition
Ersterwerber *m* first purchaser; original subscriber
Erstfinanzierung *f* new [original] financing
erstgeboren first-born *(child)*
Erstgebot *n* first bid
Ersthypothek *f* senior mortgage
Erstkalkulation *f* original [first] calculation
erstklassig first-class, first-rate *(piece of work, hotel etc.)*; gilt-edged *(securities)*, prime *(bond)*
Erstlingsarbeit *f* first product [work] *(of an apprentice)*

Erstnutzung *f* first use
Erstpfändung *f* first attachment
Erstrisikoversicherung *f* first-risk insurance
Erstschrift *f* original
erteilen to give *(permission, information etc.)*, to grant *(permission)*
Erteilung *f* giving, granting
Ertrag *m* yield *(field, fruit-tree, mine)*; return, profit *(investment, enterprise etc.)*, proceeds *(from goods sold etc.)*
~, **fester** constant returns [profit, proceeds]
~ **je Flächeneinheit** yield per cultivated area
~, **periodenfremder** non-periodic returns [profit, proceeds]
ertragbringend productive, profitable
Erträge *mpl*:
~ **aus Beteiligungen** returns from holdings
~, **außerordentliche** extra proceeds
~, **betriebsfremde** outside proceeds
~, **sonstige** other proceeds [income]
~, **zukünftige** future earnings
ertragreich productive *(land, tree etc.)*; profitable, lucrative, paying *(business etc.)*
Ertragsanteil *m* royalty
Ertragsaufbesserung *f* improvement of proceeds, recovery of earnings
Ertragsaussichten *fpl* prospects of earnings
Ertragsberechnung *f s.* **Ertragsrechnung**
Ertragsbilanz *f* profit and loss account, *(Am)* income account
Ertragsergebnis *n s.* **Ertrag**
ertragsfähig capable of yielding (returns)
Ertragsfähigkeit *f* yield capacity *(forest, soil, mine etc.)*; return potential, earning capacity *(enterprise)*
Ertragsgrenze *f* margin of profit
Ertragshöhe *f* amount of proceeds
Ertragskraft *f* profit capacity
Ertragslage *f* situation of earnings and profits
Ertragsleistung *f (agric)* yield
Ertragsminderung *f* decline in earnings [proceeds]
Ertragsniveau *n* level of earnings [proceeds]
Ertragsprognose *f (agric)* (long-term) forecast of yields
Ertragsquelle *f* source of proceeds
Ertragsrechnung *f* calculation of proceeds
~, **laufende** current calculation of proceeds
Ertragsrückgang *m s.* **Ertragsminderung**
Ertragsspitze *f* peak yield
Ertragssteigerung *f* increase in returns [profit]; *(agric)* increase in yield
Ertragssteuer *f* tax on proceeds [profit]
Ertragsüberschüsse *mpl* unappropriated [unexpected] earnings [proceeds]
Ertrags-Umsatz-Verhältnis *n* earnings(-to)-sales ratio

Ertragsverbesserung *f* improvement of earnings [proceeds]
Ertragsvorschau *f* forecast of earnings [proceeds]
Ertragswert *m* capitalized value of potential returns [profit]
~, **voraussichtlicher** expected value *(of crops etc.)*
Ertragszuwachs *m (agric)* increase in yield
Erwachsenenbildung *f* adult education
Erwachsenenqualifizierung *f* adult training [education]
erwägen to consider, to weigh, to ponder, to think over *(matter, offer etc.)*; to deliberate on, to reflect on *(question etc.)*
erwägenswert worthy of consideration, worth considering [consideration] *(offer etc.)*
Erwägung *f* consideration; deliberation ⋄ **in ~ ziehen** to take into consideration
erwarten to expect; to wait for, to await
Erwartung *f* expectation
Erwartungskauf *m (st.ex.)* buy for a rise
erwartungstreu *(stats)* unbiased
Erwartungswert *m (stats)* expectation (value)
erweitern to widen *(road, channel etc.)*; to extend, to expand *(business, production, estate etc.)*; to improve *(range of knowledge etc.)*
Erweiterung *f* widening *(road, channel etc.)*; extension, expansion *(business, production, estate etc.)*; improvement *(range of knowledge etc.)*
Erweiterungsbau *m* building extension, addition to building
Erweiterungsbauten *mpl* extensions to buildings
Erweiterungsinvestition *f* capacity-expanding investment
Erweiterungskosten *pl* costs of expansion *(business, production etc.)*
Erweiterungsprogramm *n* expansion programme [plan]
Erweiterungsreserven *fpl* reserve for extension *(production etc.)*
Erweiterungsrücklagen *fpl s.* **Erweiterungsreserven**
Erwerb *m* earnings; acquisition; purchase; acquisition by inheritance
~, **gutgläubiger** innocent purchase; bona fide transaction
erwerben to acquire *(property etc.)*; to obtain *(rights etc.)*; to purchase *(goods, services etc.)*
erwerbsbehindert partially disabled
erwerbsfähig able to earn a livelihood, capable of gainful employment
Erwerbsfähigkeit *f* capability of gainful employment
Erwerbsgartenbau *m* commercial horticulture

erwerbslos unemployed, out of work
Erwerbslosenfürsorge *f* unemployment relief
Erwerbslosenquote *f* rate of unemployment, unemployment ratio
Erwerbslosenunterstützung *f* unemployment benefit
Erwerbslosenversicherung *f* unemployment insurance
Erwerbsloser *m* unemployed (person)
Erwerbslosigkeit *f* unemployment
Erwerbsminderung *f* reduction in earning capacity, reduction of working capacity
Erwerbsmöglichkeit *f* possibility of gainful employment
Erwerbsquelle *f* source of income
Erwerbssteuer *f* tax on profits [gains]
erwerbstätig working, gainfully employed
Erwerbstätiger *m* gainfully employed person
Erwerbstätigkeit *f* gainful employment
erwerbstüchtig capable of gainful employment, fit for work
erwerbsunfähig incapable of gainful employment, disabled, unfit for work
Erwerbsunfähigkeit *f* incapacity [inability] to earn one's living, disability, unfitness for work
~, **dauernde** permanent disability
~, **zeitweilige** temporary disability
Erwerbszweig *m* line of business
erwirtschaften to get [obtain] *s.th.* by careful management [by good economy], to make profits by careful management [by good economy]
Erzbergbau *m* ore mining
Erzbergwerk *n* ore mine
erzeugen to produce *(foodstuffs, meat etc.)*; to make, to manufacture *(industrial products, chemicals etc.)*; to generate *(electricity etc.)*
Erzeuger *m* producer
Erzeugerland *n* country of origin, producer country
Erzeugerpreis *m* producer price
~, **doppelter** *(agric)* two-level producer price
~, **einheitlicher** *(agric)* uniform price paid to farmers
Erzeugerrisiko *n* manufacturer's [producer's] risk
Erzeugnis *n* product, article, good; *(agric)* produce *(s. a. **Produkt**)*
~, **anmelde- und prüfpflichtiges** product requiring registration and testing
~, **arbeitsintensives** labour-intensive product
~, **artverwandtes** related product
~, **ausländisches** foreign product
~, **auswechselbares** replaceable product
~, **bearbeitetes** processed product
~, **branchenfremdes** product not typical of the industrial branch (concerned)

~, **branchentypisches** product typical of the industrial branch (concerned)
~ **des täglichen Bedarfs** article of daily consumption
~, **einfaches** simple product
~, **einheimisches** domestic [home, inland] product; *(agric)* home [inland] produce
~ **erster Qualität** first-class product
~, **fertiggestelltes** finished product
~, **forstwirtschaftliches** forest product
~ **für den Eigenverbrauch** *(agric)* produce [farm product] for self-consumption
~ **für einmalige Verwendung** one-way product
~ **für Mehrfachverwendung** multiple-use product
~, **gängiges** saleable article
~, **geistiges** intellectual product
~, **genormtes** standardized product
~, **geringwertiges** product of low value
~, **halbfertiges** semi-finished [intermediate, semi-manufactured, semi-processed, semi-fabricated, unfinished] product
~, **handelsübliches** product with the customary quality, product sold in accordance with normal trade
~, **hochwertiges** high-quality product
~, **industrielles** industrial product
~, **industriezweigfremdes** *s.* ~, **branchenfremdes**
~, **industriezweigtypisches** *s.* ~, **branchentypisches**
~, **inländisches** *s.* ~, **einheimisches**
~, **investitionsintensives** capital-intensive product
~, **kompliziertes** complicated product
~, **kunstgewerbliches** product of arts and crafts
~, **landwirtschaftliches** agricultural [farm] product, produce
~, **leicht verderbliches** easily perishable product [produce]
~, **materielles** physical product
~, **marktfähiges** (commercially) marketable product
~ **minderer Qualität** product of low quality, low-quality product
~ **mit hoher Zuverlässigkeit** high reliability product
~ **mit rascher modischer Weiterentwicklung** product changing with fashion
~ **mit rascher technischer Weiterentwicklung** product with rapid technical development
~ **mit Warenzeichen** trademark article
~ **mit Weltniveau** world-class product
~, **neues** new product
~, **nicht lagerfähiges** non-storable product
~, **nichtstandardisiertes** non-standardized product

Erzeugnis

~ **ohne Markenzeichen** unidentified product
~, **örtliches** local product
~, **patentrechtlich geschütztes** patented article
~, **pflanzliches** vegetable product; (farm) produce
~, **repräsentatives** representative product *(of a group of products of the same kind for calculating material, manpower and equipment needed)*
~, **saisonabhängiges** seasonal product
~, **saisonunabhängiges** all-season product
~, **schwer absetzbares** article [product] difficult to sell, drug on the market
~, **standardisiertes** standardized product
~, **strukturbestimmendes** product defining the profile (of an industrial branch)
~, **substituierbares** substitutable product
~, **technischen Anforderungen entsprechendes** product according to technical requirements
~, **teilstandardisiertes** semi-standard product
~, **tierisches** animal product
~, **typisiertes** *s.* ~, **standardisiertes**
~, **umsatzintensives** article [product] in great demand
~, **unfertiges** unprocessed product; unfinished product
~, **veraltetes** obsolete product
~, **veredeltes** refined product
~, **vereinheitlichtes** standardized product
~, **vergleichbares** comparable product
~, **volkswirtschaftlich strukturbestimmendes** product defining the profile of the national economy
~, **volkswirtschaftlich wichtiges** product of national economic importance
~ **von geringer Qualität** *s.* ~ **minderer Qualität**
~ **von hoher Qualität** *s.* ~, **hochwertiges**
~, **weiterverarbeitetes** upgraded product
Erzeugnisart *f* kind [type] of product
Erzeugnisauftrag *m* order for a product
Erzeugnisbilanz *f* product balance (sheet) *(showing supply and use of a product)*
Erzeugnisbilanzierung *f* product balancing
Erzeugniseinheit *f* unit of a product
Erzeugnisentwicklung *f* development of a product
erzeugnisgebunden related to a (particular) product
Erzeugnisgestaltung *f* product [industrial] design
Erzeugnisgliederung *f* classification [grouping] of products
Erzeugnisgruppe *f* group of products, product group
~, **repräsentative** representative group of products

Erzeugnisgruppenabrechnung *f* cost accounting of product groups *(special form of cost calculation)*
Erzeugnisgruppenarbeit *f* coordination of production and marketing *(between enterprises with similar product line)*
Erzeugnisgruppenbereich *m* group of enterprises with similar product line
Erzeugnisgruppenbilanz *f* balance (sheet) of groups of products
Erzeugnisgruppenkennziffer *f* indicator of groups of products, product groups indicator
Erzeugnisgruppenleitbetrieb *m* principal enterprise (of a group of enterprises with similar product line)
Erzeugnisgruppenprinzip *n* principle of product grouping (*s.* **Erzeugnisgruppenarbeit**)
Erzeugnisgruppenverflechtungsbilanz *f* input--output table of groups of products
Erzeugnishauptgruppe *f* main group of products
Erzeugniskalkulation *f* (cost) calculation of a product
Erzeugniskartei *f* card index on products
Erzeugnisklassifikation *f* classification of products
Erzeugnismenge *f* quantity of product(s)
Erzeugnisnomenklatur *f* catalogue [list] of products
Erzeugnisnorm *f* product standard
Erzeugnispaß *m* product characterization
Erzeugnisplanung *f* product planning
Erzeugnisprinzip *n* product principle *(organizing production flow according to the sequence of operations)*
Erzeugnisprognose *f* long-term forecast of the development of products
Erzeugnisprogramm *n* *s.* **Erzeugnissortiment**
Erzeugnisqualität *f* quality of a product
Erzeugnisse *npl*:
◇ ~ **absetzen** to market [sell, realize, dispose of] products
~ **der Industrie** industrial products [goods]
~ **der Landwirtschaft** agricultural [farm] produce
~ **des Handwerks** craftsmen's products
~, **devisenrentable** foreign-exchange-earning products
~, **gleichartige** equal products, products of the same kind
~, **haushaltstechnische** (technical) household articles, household appliances
~, **hochwertige** high-quality products [goods]
~, **neue und weiterentwickelte** new and advanced products
Erzeugnisselbstkosten *pl* prime costs per product

Erzeugnissortiment *n* range [assortment] of products, product line
erzeugnisspezialisiert specialized in the production of a certain product [certain products]
Erzeugnisstruktur *f* structure of production *(grouping of industrial production and/or enterprises according to technological characteristics of products)*
Erzeugnisstückzahl *f* number of products
Erzeugnissubstitution *f* substitution of product
Erzeugnissystematik *f s.* Erzeugnisnomenklatur
Erzeugnistyp *m* type of product
Erzeugnis- und Leistungsnomenklatur *f* classification [nomenclature] of products and services *(classification of all produced and imported goods and all material services according to similarity in technology and characteristics)*
Erzeugnisuntergruppe *f* sub-group of products
Erzeugnisverflechtungsbilanz *f* product input--output table
Erzeugnisvielfalt *f* broad range of products
Erzeugnisvorkalkulation *f* rough calculation per product
Erzeugung *f* production, manufacture, output; generation *(energy etc.) (s.a.* Produktion)
~, großtechnische large-scale production
~, industrielle industrial production
~, landwirtschaftliche agricultural [farm] production [output]
Erzeugungsdefizit *n* failing output
Erzeugungskapazität *f* production [manufacturing, productive] capacity
Erzeugungspreis *m* production price
Erz *n* ore
Erzförderung *f* output of ore
erziehen to educate; to train; to bring up
Erziehung *f* education; training; upbringing
Erziehungsbeihilfe *f* educational grant
Erziehungseinrichtung *f* educational institution [facility]
Erziehungswesen *n* system of education; educational matters
Etat *m* budget; finances *(country, local authority etc.) (s.a.* Budget, Haushalt 1.)
~, außerordentlicher extraordinary budget
Etatentwurf *m* draft budget, budget draft
Etatgesetz *n* budget law [appropriation act]
Etatjahr *n* fiscal [financial] year
Etatkostenvergleich *m* comparison of budget expenditure
etatmäßig budgetary
Etatposition *f* budget item
Etatposten *m s.* Etatposition
Etatrechnung *f* budget accounting *(s.* Haushaltsrechnung)
Etatrecht *n* budget regulations [law]

Etattitel *m s.* Etatposition
Etatüberschreitung *f* exceeding the budget
Etatüberschuß *m* budget(ary) surplus
Etikett *n* label; (price) tag
etikettieren to label; to tag *(article for sale)*
Etikettieren *n s.* Etikettierung
Etikettierung *f* labelling; tagging
~, übliche customary labelling
Etwapreis *m* rough price
Euro-Dollar *m* euro-dollar
Euro-Dollar-Markt *m* euro-dollar-market
Evalvation *f* evaluation
Eventualantrag *m* secondary motion
Eventualfall *m (jur)* contingency
Eventualforderung *f* contingent claim
Eventualkosten *pl* contingent cost [charge]
Eventualreserve *f* contingent reserve
Eventualschulden *fpl s.* Eventualverbindlichkeiten
Eventualverbindlichkeiten *fpl* contingent liabilities
Eventualverpflichtung *f* contingent liability
exakt exact, accurate *(result, calculation etc.)*; precise *(information etc.)*
Exaktheit *f* exactness, exactitude, accuracy *(result, calculation etc.)*; preciseness, precision *(information etc.)*
Exchangeorder *f (st.ex.)* order of exchange, exchange order
Exchequerbond *m* exchequer bond
Exekutivkomitee *n* executive committee
Existenz *f* existence; life; living
~, sichere secure living
~, unsichere precarious living
Existenzbedingungen *fpl* living conditions
Existenzform *f* kind of living
Existenzfrage *f* matter of life and death
Existenzgrundlage *f* livelihood, basis of existence
Existenzminimum *n* minimum subsistence level, living wage
~, steuerfreies tax-free living wage
Existenzmittel *npl* means of existence [subsistence]
Existenzsicherheit *f* security of life
Existenzunsicherheit *f* insecurity of life
Exklusivmodell *n* exclusive model
Exklusivrecht *n* exclusive right
Exklusivverkehr *m* exclusive traffic
Exklusivvertrag *m* exclusive agreement; tying contract
Exklusivvertreter *m* exclusive [sole] agent
exmittieren to evict, to eject *(tenant)*
Exmittierung *f* eviction *(tenant)*
Expansion *f* expansion
~, ökonomische *s.* ~, wirtschaftliche
~, wirtschaftliche economic expansion

Expansionspolitik *f* policy of expansion
Expansionsrate *f* rate of expansion
Expansionstempo *n* speed [tempo] of expansion
Expansionstheorie *f* theory of expansion
Expedient *m* dispatching clerk
Expedition *f* dispatching; dispatching department [service]
Expeditionsgebühr *f* dispatching charges [fees, duties]
Expeditor *m* dispatcher
Experiment *n* experiment ⋄ **ein ~ durchführen** to carry out an experiment
~, ökonomisches economic experiment
Experimentalmodell *n* experimental model
Experte *m* expert
Expertenauffassung *f* expert's opinion
Expertenbefragung *f* consultation of experts
Experteneinschätzung *f* expert's assessment [opinion]
Expertise *f* expertise
Exploitation *f* exploitation *(labour, mine etc.)*
Exploitationsgrad *m* rate of exploitation *(labour, mine etc.)*
~ der Arbeit rate of exploitation of labour
Exploitationsrate *f s.* **Exploitationsgrad**
Exponat *n* exhibit, article exhibited
Exponent *m* exponent, representative *(party, movement etc.)*
exponential *(maths, stats)* exponential
Exponentialfunktion *f (stats)* exponential function
Exponentialgleichung *f (maths, stats)* exponential equation
Exponentialgröße *f (maths, stats)* exponential (quantity)
Exponentialkurve *f (maths, stats)* exponential curve
~, modifizierte *(maths, stats)* modified exponential curve
Exponentialreihe *f (maths, stats)* exponential series
Exponentialverteilung *f (maths, stats)* exponential distribution
Export *m* export(ation); export(s) *(s. a.* **Ausfuhr)**
~, direkter direct export(s)
~, indirekter indirect export(s)
~, unmittelbarer *s.* **~, direkter**
~, unsichtbarer invisible export(s); invisibles
~ zu Schleuderpreisen dumping
exportabel *s.* **exportfähig**
Exportabgabe *f* levy on exports
Exportabrechnung *f* export accounting; export calculation
Exportabsatz *m* sales abroad, exports
Exportabschluß *m* export agreement
Exportabteilung *f* export department
Exportagent *m* export agent

Exportakkreditiv *n* export letter of credit
Exportangebot *n* export tender
Exportantrag *m* application for export
Exportartikel *m* export article
Exportauftrag *m* export order
Exportauftragsgeschäft *n* export order transaction [business]
Exportaufwand *m* cost of export goods, export costs; export equivalent
Exportaufwendungen *fpl s.* **Exportaufwand**
Exportaussichten *fpl* export prospects
Exportausstellung *f* export exhibition
Exportbedarf *m s.* **Exportnachfrage**
Exportbedingungen *fpl* terms [conditions] of export
Exportbegünstigungen *fpl* export facilities
Exportbeihilfe *f* support of export
Exportbeschränkung *f* export restriction
Exportbetrieb *m* exporter, exporting enterprise
Exportbonus *m* export bonus [premium]
Exportbürgschaft *f* export guarantee
Exportbüro *n* export office
Exportdokumente *npl* export documents
Exportdumping *n* export dumping
Exporteinnahmen *fpl* export earnings
Exporterlös *m* export proceeds [receipts]
Exporterzeugnis *n* export product
Exporteur *m* exporter; exporting company; exporting country
Exportexpansion *f* expansion of exports
exportfähig exportable
Exportfinanzierung *f* financing of exports, export financing
Exportfonds *m* export fund
Exportförderung *f* export promotion
Exportförderungsmaßnahmen *fpl* measures for export promotion
Exportförderungsstrategie *f* strategy of export promotion
Exportfunktion *f* export function
Exportgemeinschaft *f* export pool
Exportgenehmigung *f* export permission; export licence [permit]
Exportgeschäft *n* export business [transaction]
Exportgesellschaft *f* export company
Exportgewinn *m* export profit, profit from exports
Exportgrundpreis *m* fixed export price
Exportgüter *npl* export goods
Exporthandel *m* export trade
exportierbar *s.* **exportfähig**
exportieren to export
Export-Import-Firma *f* exporting and importing company
Export-Import-Rentabilität *f* export-import profitability
Exportindustrie *f* export industry

Exportintensität *f* export intensity
exportintensiv export intensive; highly dependent on exports
Exportkapazität *f* export capacity
Exportkartell *n* export cartel [ring]
Exportkaufmann *m* exporter, export sales manager
Exportkommissionsvertrag *m* contract on export commission transactions, export commission contract
Exportkontingent *n* export quota
Exportkontrolle *f* export control
Exportkosten *pl s.* **Exportaufwand**
Exportkredit *m* export credit
Exportkreditierung *f* crediting of exports
Exportkundendienst *m* export service
Exportlager *n* export warehouse [store]
Exportland *n* exporting country
Exportliste *f* list of exports
Exportlizenz *f* export licence [permit]
Exportmeldung *f* export declaration
Exportmesse *f* export fair
Exportmonopol *n* export monopoly
Exportmuster *n* export sample
Exportnachfrage *f* export demand
Exportorganisation *f* export organization
Exportplan *m* export plan
Exportplanrückstand *m* export plan arrears, backlog in export plan
Exportpolitik *f* export policy [policies]
Exportpotential *n* export capacity [potential]
Exportposition *f* export item
Exportprämie *f* export bounty [bonus]
Exportpreis *m* export price
~, durchschnittlicher average export price
Exportpreisänderung *f* change of export price
Exportpreisindex *m* export price index
Exportprodukt *n s.* **Exporterzeugnis**
Exportproduktion *f* production for export
Exportprogramm *n* export programme
Exportquote *f* export quota; export rate; share of export in overall domestic production
Exportregelung *f* export control
Exportrentabilität *f* export profitability, profitability of exports
Exportrentabilitätsberechnung *f* calculation of export profitability
Exportrentabilitätskennziffer *f* indicator of export profitability
Exportreserve *f* export reserve (stock)
Exportrestriktion *f s.* **Exportbeschränkung**
Exportsendung *f* export shipment
Exportstatistik *f* export statistics
Exportsteigerung *f* increase in export(s)
Exportstimulierung *f* export stimulation
Exportstreckengeschäft *n* triangular export transaction

Exportstruktur *f* export structure, structure of exports
Exportstützung *f* export subsidy
Exportsubvention *f s.* **Exportstützung**
Exportüberhang *m* excess export
Exportumsatz *m* export sales [volume]
Exportunternehmen *n s.* **Exportbetrieb**
Exportverbot *n* ban on exports, export ban
Exportvereinigung *f* exporting community
Exportverfahren *n* export regulations
Exportvergütung *f* export premium; *(cust)* drawback *(on certain goods)*; tax rebate *(to exporters)*
Exportverpackung *f* export packing
Exportvertrag *m* export contract [agreement]
Exportvertreter *m* export agent [agency]
Exportvolumen *n* volume of exports, total export
Exportware *f* export good [article]
Exportwarenfonds *m* goods earmarked for export
Exportwerbung *f* export(s) advertising
Exportzoll *m* export duty
Exportzuschuß *m s.* **Exportstützung**
Expreßgut *n* express parcel [good(s)], *(Am)* fast freight
Expreßgutverkehr *m* express delivery service
Expreßkarte *f* waybill for express parcels
Expropriation *f* expropriation
exproprieren to expropriate
extensiv extensive
Extensivinvestition *f* extensive investment *(for extensive reproduction)*
Extensivwirtschaft *f (agric)* extensive farming
Extraausgaben *fpl* extra expenditure
Extragewinn *m* extra profit
Extrakosten *pl* extra cost(s)
Extramehrwert *m* extra surplus value
Extrapolation *f (stats)* extrapolation
Extrapolationsmethode *f (stats)* method of extrapolation
Extrapreis *m* special price
Extremalquotient *m (stats)* extremal quotient
Extremwerte *mpl (stats)* extreme values
~ von Mittelwerten *(stats)* extreme mean

F

Fabrik *f* factory, works, plant; mill *(textiles, paper)* ◇ **ab ~** ex factory; **eine ~ betreiben** to run [operate] a factory; **eine ~ gründen** to found [establish] a factory; **eine ~ in Betrieb nehmen** to open a factory; **eine ~ leiten** to manage a factory; **eine ~ stillegen** to close

(down) a factory; **in der ~** in [at] the factory; **in einer ~ arbeiten** to work in [at] a factory
~, chemische chemical works
~, elektrotechnische electrical factory [works]
~, holzverarbeitende wood-processing factory
~, metallverarbeitende metal-processing factory
~, rentable profitable factory
~, unrentable unprofitable [non-profitable] factory
Fabrikabsatz *m* sales (of products) from the factory
~, direkter direct sales (of products) from the factory
Fabrikanlage *f* (manufacturing) plant, works
Fabrikant *m* factory-owner, manufacturer; mill-owner *(textiles, paper)*
Fabrikarbeit *f* 1. factory work; mill work; 2. factory-made [-produced] articles, manufactured goods
Fabrikat *n* make, product, brand, manufactured article
~, ausländisches foreign make [product, brand]
~, einheimisches domestic [home] make [product, brand]
~, erstklassiges first-class make [product, brand]
~, minderwertiges inferior make [product, brand]
Fabrikation *f* manufacturing; production; manufacture *(s. a.* **Herstellung, Produktion**)
Fabrikationsabteilung *f* manufacturing division
Fabrikationsanlage *f* production [manufacturing] plant [unit], production facilities
Fabrikationsanlagen *fpl* 1. productive assets; 2. production [manufacturing] plants [units], production facilities
Fabrikationsauftrag *m* factory [production, job] order
Fabrikationsbetrieb *m* manufacturing enterprise [plant]
Fabrikationseinrichtungen *fpl s.* **Fabrikationsanlagen** 2.
Fabrikationsfehler *m* maker's [factory] flaw, flaw [defect] in the making
Fabrikationsgeheimnis *n* production secret
Fabrikationsgemeinkosten *pl* factory overhead costs [overheads]
Fabrikationsjahr *n* year in which s.th. was built; date of building; year of construction *(ship etc.)*, year of manufacture *(machine, car etc.)*
Fabrikationskosten *pl* cost(s) of production, production costs
Fabrikationsleiter *m* production manager
Fabrikationslizenz *f* manufacturing licence
Fabrikationsmonopol *n* monopoly in production
Fabrikationsnummer *f* serial number *(machine etc.)*

Fabrikationsrechte *npl* production rights
fabrikationsreif ready for production
Fabrikationsreife *f* start-up for production
Fabrikbesitzer *m* factory [mill] owner
Fabrikbesuch *m* factory tour
Fabrikdirektor *m* factory [plant] manager
Fabrikgebäude *n* factory building [premises]
Fabrikgelände *n* factory property [site]
Fabrikgesetzgebung *f* factory legislation
Fabrikmarke *f* trade mark, brand
fabrikmäßig factory-made ✧ **~ hergestellt** factory-made, manufactured
fabrikneu brand-new *(car etc.)*, straight from the factory, new *(article)*
Fabrikordnung *f* factory rules and regulations
Fabrikpackung *f* original [ex-works] packing
Fabrikpreis *m* factory price
Fabrikschiff *n* factory-ship
Fabrikstrafen *fpl* factory penalties
Fabriksystem *n* system of factory production
Fabrikware *f* factory-produced article, factory product, manufactured article
fabrizieren to manufacture, to make, to produce *(machines etc.)*
Fach *n* province, branch, field *(activity)*; business, trade, line; speciality; subject *(study etc.)*
Fachabteilung *f* specialized department *(in enterprises, institutions etc.)*
Facharbeiter *m* skilled worker
Facharbeiterausbildung *f* vocational training
~, spezielle specialized vocational training
Facharbeiterbrief *m* skilled worker's certificate
Facharbeiterlohn *m* skilled worker's wage(s)
Facharbeiterprüfung *f* vocational (training) school [trade school] final examination
Facharbeiterweiterbildung *f* further [advanced, continued] education [training] of skilled workers
Facharbeiterzeugnis *n* vocational training [trade school] certificate
Fachausbildung *f* special(ized) [professional] training
Fachausdruck *m* technical term
Fachausschuß *m* committee of experts
Fachausstellung *f* specialized exhibition
Fachberater *m* technical adviser, consultant
Fachbereich *m* 1. section [part] of a department *(enterprise, institution etc.)*; 2. group of enterprises *(manufacturing similar products)*; 3. province, branch, field *(activity etc.)*
Fachbereichsleiter *m s.* **Fachgebietsleiter**
Fachbereichsstandard *m* special standard *(fixed for a special group of production enterprises)*
Fachbezeichnung *f s.* **Fachausdruck**
Fachbuch *n* specialized book; textbook
Fachbücherei *f* specialized [technical] library
Fachfiliale *f* specialized branch (shop)

Fachgebiet *n* province, branch, field *(activity)*; line; subject
Fachgebietsleiter *m* head of a section
Fachgeschäft *n* specialized dealer [shop], special(-line) shop
Fachgewerkschaft *f* craft union *(for each trade)*
Fachgruppe *f* trade group
Fachhandel *m* specialized trade
Fachhandelssortiment *n* range of goods in specialized trade
Fachhandelsspanne *f* trade margin of specialized dealers
Fachhändler *m* specialized dealer
Fachhochschule *f* college *(with university status in technical, economic or other subjects)*
Fachingenieur *m* engineer (specialized in a branch of engineering)
Fachkenntnis *f* technical [specialized, expert] knowledge
Fachkraft *f* skilled worker; specialist, expert
Fachkräfte *fpl*:
~, **wissenschaftlich-technische** trained technical personnel [staff]; science and technology experts
Fachkreis *m s.* **Fachkräfte**
fachkundig expert, competent
Fachlehrer *m* subject [specialist] teacher
Fachlehrgang *m* (short) technical [specialized] training course
fachlich technical; professional
Fachliteratur *f* specialized [technical] literature
Fachmann *m* expert, specialist
~, **erfahrener** expert with practical experience
fachmännisch expert; workmanlike; competent, professional
Fachmesse *f* specialized [specialist] fair
Fachnormenausschuß *m* engineering standards committee
Fachorgan *n* specialized executive body *(ministry, department of district council etc.)*; specialized committee *(parliament, district council etc.)*
Fachorganisation *f* specialized [professional] organization
~, **nationale** national specialized [professional] organization
Fachrichtung *f* special subject, field (of specialization)
Fachrichtungsnomenklatur *f* list of subjects
Fachschau *f* specialized display
Fachschulabschluß *m* (technical) school [college] graduation, graduation from a (technical) school [college]
Fachschulabschlußzeugnis *n* technical school [college] certificate
Fachschulabsolvent *m* graduate *(technical school, college)*
Fachschule *f* technical school [college]

Fachschulingenieur *m* engineer (with a technical institute training)
Fachschulreife *f* final examination (qualifying for admission to technical school)
Fachschulstudium *n* studies at a technical school [college]
Fachstudium *n* specialized studies
Fachunterricht *m* technical [specialized] instruction
Fachverband *m* professional [trade] association
Fachwissenschaft *f* branch [field] of science
Fachwörterbuch *n* technical [specialized] dictionary
Fachzeitschrift *f* periodical specializing in one subject; specialist periodical; technical journal; trade paper
fähig able, capable; fit for *(work, duty etc.)*; qualified; competent; talented, gifted
Fähigkeit *f* ability, capability; qualification, competence, efficiency; capacity; talent, faculty
~ **zu selbständiger Arbeit** ability to work independently
Fähigkeiten *fpl* abilities, capacities; talents
~, **berufliche** vocational ability, skill, skilfulness
~, **durchschnittliche berufliche** reasonable skill (in a trade)
~, **geistige** intellectual [mental] powers, intellectual capabilities, mental faculties
~, **handwerkliche** mechanical skill
~, **körperliche** physical capability
~, **körperliche und geistige** physical and intellectual [mental] abilities [capabilities]
~, **organisatorische** organizing ability
Fahne *f* 1. flag; 2. *(d.pr.)* flag *(an additional item of information added to a data item)*; lug
Fahrauftrag *m* transport order
Fahrausweis *m* ticket
Fährbahnhof *m* ferry-station
fahrbar movable; mobile
fahrbereit in running order *(vehicle)*; ready to drive *(car)*; ready to proceed *(ship)*
Fahrbereitschaft *f* 1. readiness for use *(car etc.)*; 2. transport supply service *(department of enterprises, institutions etc.)*
Fährbetrieb *m* ferry service; ferry business
Fahrbetriebsmittel *npl (railw)* rolling stock
Fährbootverkehr *m* ferry(-boat) service
Fahrdienst *m* 1. transport service; transport service department; 2. *(railw)* train service
Fährdienst *m s.* **Fährbootverkehr**
Fahrdienstleiter *m* transport officer; *(railw)* stationmaster
Fahrdienstvorschriften *fpl (railw)* train service regulations
Fähre *f* ferry(-boat)
Fahrer *m* driver *(car etc.)*; motor-cyclist; cyclist

Fahrerlaubnis *f* driving licence, *(Am)* driver's license
Fahrerlaubnisentzug *m* disqualification from driving
Fahrgast *m* passenger
Fahrgastschiff *n* liner, passenger-ship [-boat]
Fahrgastschiffahrt *f* passenger-ship [-boat] service
Fahrgastschiff- und Binnenhafenbetrieb *m* river-boat and port undertaking
Fahrgeld *n* fare; passage
Fährgeld *n* ferry dues, ferriage
Fahrgelderstattung *f* reimbursement [refunding] of fare [passage]
Fahrgeldstundung *f* respite of fare, charging at end of accounting period
Fährhafen *m* ferry-harbour
Fahrkarte *f* ticket ✧ **eine ~ lösen nach** to book [take] a ticket for
~, einfache single [*(Am)* one-way] ticket
~ hin und zurück return ticket
Fahrkartenausgabe *f* booking office *(railways, buses etc.)*
Fahrkartenautomat *m* automatic ticket machine
Fahrkilometer *mpl* mileage (covered)
Fahrkosten *pl s.* **Fahrtkosten**
fahrlässig negligent, careless
Fahrlässigkeit *f* negligence, neglect; carelessness
~, bewußte wilful negligence
~, grobe gross negligence
~, leichte ordinary negligence
~, unbewußte unwitting negligence
Fahrlässigkeitsklausel *f* negligence clause
Fahrlehrer *m* driving instructor
Fahrleistung *f* driving [road] performance
Fahrnisgemeinschaft *f* (jur) joint estate *(of husband and wife)*
Fahrpersonal *n* train crew; bus crew; tram crew
Fahrplan *m* timetable, *(Am)* schedule
fahrplanmäßig according to schedule, on time
Fahrpreis *m* fare
~, ermäßigter concessionary fare(s)
Fahrpreisermäßigung *f* reduction of fare, fare reduction
Fahrschein *m s.* **Fahrausweis**
Fährschiff *n* ferry, ferry-boat; train ferry
Fahrstrecke *f* route
Fahrtenbuch *n* driver's log-book
Fahrterlaubnisschein *m* certificate of seaworthiness
Fahrtkosten *pl* travelling expenses
Fährverkehr *m* ferry traffic
Fahrzeug *n* vehicle
Fahrzeugbau *m* vehicle construction (industry), automotive industry

Fahrzeugbrief *m* car registration document
Fahrzeughalter *m* car [vehicle] owner
Fahrzeugindustrie *f* motor industry, industry producing means of transport, *(Am)* automobile industry
Fahrzeugpapiere *npl* car registration papers
Fahrzeugpark *m* fleet of vehicles, vehicle fleet *(of an enterprise etc.)*
Fahrzeugverkehr *m* vehicular [wheeled] traffic
Fahrzeugzulassung *f* certificate of road worthiness, car licence
Faktor *m* 1. factor; 2. agent, middleman; manager; foreman
~, allgemeiner general factor
~, bestimmender determining [determinant] factor, determinant
~, bipolarer *(stats)* bipolar factor
~, gemeinsamer *(stats)* common factor
~, menschlicher human factor [element]
~, nichtorthogonaler *(stats)* oblique factor
~, persönlicher personal factor
~, preisbildender price-making factor
~, preiserhöhender price-raising factor
~, preissenkender price-reducing factor
~, primärer *(stats)* primary factor
~, sozialer social factor
~, spezifischer *(stats)* specific factor; unique factor
~, subjektiver subjective factor
~, unzuverlässiger unpredictable factor
Faktorbewertung *f* *(stats)* factor loading
Faktorei *f* factory; foreign trading station [depot]
Faktoren *mpl* factors
~, gebietsbedienende factors involved in serving a region *(services, retail trade, transport facilities etc.)*
~, gebietsbildende factors determining the character of a region *(such as centralizing effect of production, its degree of specialization, agricultural or industrial region etc.)*
~, gebührenbildende factors in calculating fees *(lawyers etc.)* [charges *(legal, postal etc.)*, dues *(harbour etc.)*, tolls *(bridge, pier, highway etc.)*]
~, markt- und warenspezifische specific market and commodity factors, specific factors of market and commodities
~, preisbildende price-making factors
~, städtebildende *s.* **~, gebietsbildende**
~, veränderliche variables
Faktorenanalyse *f* *(stats)* factor analysis
Faktorenlohn *m* factor wages [wage rates] *(fixed according to performance indicators especially in the chemical industry)*
Faktorenmatrix *f* factor matrix
Faktorenspeicher *m* *(d.pr.)* factor storage, read word

Faktorentabelle *f* table of factors
Faktorenumkehrprobe *f (stats)* factor reversal test
Faktorenwert *m (d.pr.)* factor value
Faktorgeschäft *n* transfer of claim(s) by purchase
Faktorgewicht *n (stats)* factor loading, test coefficient
Faktorindizes *mpl* factoral indices
Faktorkosten *pl* factor cost(s)
Faktorladung *f (stats)* factor loading
Faktur *f s.* **Faktura**
Faktura *f* invoice, bill (of sale)
Fakturenbuch *n* invoice book
fakturieren to invoice, to bill *(goods)*
Fakturiermaschine *f* invoicing machine
Fakultät *f* faculty
~, **ingenieurökonomische** faculty of industrial engineering
~, **juristische** faculty of law, law faculty
~, **ökonomische** *s.* ~, **wirtschaftswissenschaftliche**
~, **wirtschaftswissenschaftliche** faculty of economics, economics faculty
Fakultativklausel *f* optional clause
Fall *m* 1. *(com)* fall, drop, slump *(prices, rate of exchange etc.)*; 2. case, matter, affair ◊ **einen ~ bearbeiten** to handle [deal with, be in charge of] a case; **einen ~ schriftlich darlegen** to submit a written statement of a case
~ der Profitrate, tendenzieller tendency of the rate of profit to fall
fallen to fall, to drop, to go down; to tumble (down) *(prices, rates of exchange etc. going down quickly)* ◊ **unter etwas ~** to come within the scope of s.th. *(law etc.)*
fallieren to become insolvent, to go bankrupt, to fail to meet one's (financial) obligations
fällig due; payable *(invoice)*, collectible *(taxes)*, mature(d) *(bill of exchange)* ◊ **~ werden** to become due [payable]; **noch nicht ~** unmatured; **wenn ~** *s.* **bei Fälligkeit**
Fälligkeit *f* (date of) maturity; date of payment, settlement date ◊ **bei ~** at maturity, when due; **vor ~** prior to maturity
Fälligkeitsanspruch *m* claim within date of maturity
Fälligkeitsdatum *n* date of maturity
Fälligkeitsklausel *f* acceleration clause
Fälligkeitstag *m s.* **Fälligkeitsdatum**
Fälligkeitstermin *m s.* **Fälligkeitsdatum**
Fälligkeitswert *m* maturity value
Falliment *n* bankruptcy; insolvency
Fallissement *n s.* **Falliment**
fallit bankrupt; insolvent
Fallit *m* bankrupt
Fallmethode *f* case-study

Fallsammlung *f* table of cases
Fallstudie *f* case study
Falschbuchung *f* fraudulent entry
fälschen to falsify *(report etc.)*; to forge, to fake *(signature etc.)*; to counterfeit *(bank notes etc.)*; to tamper with *(invoice, account etc.)*; to adulterate *(food, wine etc.)*
Fälscher *m* falsifier *(report etc.)*; forger, faker *(signature etc.)*; counterfeiter *(bank notes etc.)*; adulterator *(food, wine etc.)*
Falschgeld *n* counterfeit [false, bogus] money
fälschlich wrong, mistaken, incorrect, erroneous
fälschlicherweise wrongly, mistakenly, incorrectly, erroneously
Falschmeldung *f* false information [report]
~, **strafbare** false information liable to punishment
Falschmünzer *m* counterfeiter
Falschmünzerei *f* counterfeiting
Fälschung *f* 1. falsification *(report etc.)*; counterfeiting *(bank notes etc.)*; 2. forgery, fake *(signature etc.)*; counterfeit money
Falsifikat *n s.* **Fälschung** 2.
Falsifikation *f s.* **Fälschung** 1.
falsifizieren *s.* **fälschen**
Faltung *f (stats)* convolution
Familie *f* family
~, **kinderreiche** family with many children
~, **vierköpfige** *(stats)* family of four
Familienangehöriger *m* member of a family, family member
~, **mithelfender** contributing family member *(working in a private economic establishment such as restaurants, shops etc., without fixed income, salary, wages etc.)*
Familienangelegenheit *f* family affair, domestic matter
Familienausgaben *fpl* family (budget) expenditure
Familienbeihilfe *f* family allowance [benefit]
Familienbesitz *m* family property [possession, estate]
Familienbetrieb *m* family enterprise; family shop; *(agric)* family farm
Familienbudget *n* family budget
Familieneinkommen *n* family income
Familienermäßigung *f* allowance [reduction] for families *(reduced fares, holiday rates etc.)*
Familienfahrkarte *f (railw)* family ticket
Familienforschung *f* genealogical research
Familienfürsorge *f* family welfare [care]
Familiengröße *f* family size, size of family
Familienhaushalt *m* family budget; family household
Familienhaushaltsplan *m s.* **Familienbudget**
Familienhaushaltsrechnung *f* family budgeting
Familienhilfe *f s.* **Familienbeihilfe**

Familienlohn *m s.* **Familieneinkommen**
Familienpackung *f* family-size package
Familienplanung *f* family planning
Familienpolitik *f* (state) policy towards family welfare
Familienstand *m* marital status
Familienstatistik *f* household statistics
Familienstruktur *f* family structure [pattern]
Familienunterhalt *m* upkeep of a family
Familienunternehmen *n s.* **Familienbetrieb**
Familienunterstützung *f* allowance payable in respect of dependants [a dependant]
Familienverhältnisse *npl* family background; home life; family relationships
Familienwochenhilfe *f* maternity benefit
Familienzulage *f s.* **Familienbeihilfe**
Familienzusammenführung *f* reunion of families
Familienzuschlag *m s.* **Familienbeihilfe**
Fangarbeit *f* 1. fishing; 2. *(min)* work of recovering drilling tools
Fangboot *n* fishing boat, trawler
Fanggebiet *n* fishing ground
Fangplatz *m* fishing spot
Fangzeit *f* fishing season; hunting season *(animals)*
Farm *f* farm
Farmer *m* farmer
Fassung *f* draft(ing) *(document, treaty etc.)*, wording *(clause, bill etc.)*, version *(book etc.)*
~, ursprüngliche original wording [version]
Fassungsvermögen *n* 1. (power of) comprehension, mental capacity, grasp; 2. *(tech)* capacity
faßweise by the cask [barrel]
Faustpfand *n* pledge, pawn
Faustregel *f* general rule; rough and ready formula; rule of thumb
~, Spearman'sche *(stats)* Spearman's footrule
Fehlanpassung *f* mismatch
Fehlanzeige *f* negative report
Fehlarbeit *f* faulty [imperfect] work
Fehlbestand *m* deficiency *(in stock etc.)*, shortage *(of goods etc.)*
Fehlbetrag *m* deficiency, deficit, missing amount
Fehldatierung *f* incorrect [wrong] dating, misdating
Fehldisposition *f* wrong disposition [planning]
Fehleinschätzung *f* false estimation
fehlen to miss; to be missing [short]; to be absent; to be lacking
Fehlen *n* absence; lack
~, begründetes absence on valid grounds
~, entschuldigtes absence with a valid excuse
~, unentschuldigtes absence without excuse
Fehlentscheidung *f* wrong decision
Fehlentwicklung *f* undesirable development

Fehler *m* mistake, error; *(tech)* fault; failing, defect
~, absoluter absolute error
~, asymptotischer mittlerer *(stats)* asymptotic standard error
~, ausgleichungsfähiger *s.* **~, kompensierender**
~, bereinigter corrected [adjusted] error
~, durchschnittlicher absoluter *(stats)* mean absolute error
~ eines Schätzwertes, mittlerer *(stats)* standard error of estimate
~, kompensierender *(stats)* compensating error
~, korrigierter *s.* **~, bereinigter**
~, kumulativer *(stats)* cumulative error
~, mittlerer standard error
~, mittlerer quadratischer *s.* **~, mittlerer**
~, stichprobenfremder *(stats)* non-sampling error
~, unverzerrter *(stats)* unbias(s)ed error
~, verzerrender systematischer *(stats)* bias
Fehlerberechnung *f* calculation of (the size of) an error
Fehlerbereich *m* *(stats)* error band
Fehlerbeseitigung *f* elimination [deletion] of an error [mistake]
Fehlereingrenzung *f (stats)* localization of a fault
Fehlerelement *n* element of error
Fehlererkennung *f* error detection [identification]; *(tech)* fault location
fehlerfrei correct, accurate, free from [of] mistakes [errors]; sound, faultless, flawless, free from defect(s) [fault(s)], without fault
Fehlerfreiheit *f* correctness, accuracy, freedom from mistakes [errors]; soundness, faultlessness, flawlessness, freedom from defect(s) [fault(s)]
Fehlerfunktion *f (maths)* Gaussian function
Fehlergesetz *n (maths)* law of error
Fehlergrenze *f* limit of error; *(tech)* tolerance
fehlerhaft faulty *(method etc.)*; incorrect, inaccurate, wrong, inexact *(calculation etc.)*; defective *(piece of work etc.)*
Fehlerhaftigkeit *f* inaccuracy, incorrectness; *(tech)* faultiness, defectiveness
Fehlerkarte *f (d.pr.)* error card
Fehlerkontrolle *f (d.pr.)* error control [checking]
Fehlerkorrektur *f* correction of error
Fehlermeldung *f (d.pr.)* error declaration [message]
Fehlerquadrat *n (maths)* square error
~, mittleres *(maths)* error mean square, mean square error
Fehlerquelle *f* source of error [mistake, defect]
Fehlerrechnung *f* calculation [calculus] of errors, method of calculating (accidental) errors

Fehlersuche *f* search [check] for a mistake [an error, a defect]; *(d.pr.)* error detection, debugging, trouble-shooting
Fehlertabelle *f* table of errors
Fehlertheorie *f* theory of errors
Fehlerverteilung *f (stats, maths)* Gaussian distribution
Fehlerverteilungsgesetz *n (stats, maths)* Gaussian distribution law
Fehlerwahrscheinlichkeit *f* probability of error
Fehlfabrikat *n* faulty [defective] article
Fehlfracht *f* dead freight
Fehlgeld *n* allowance for errors *(granted to cashiers)*
fehlgeleitet misdirected
Fehlgewicht *n* short weight
Fehlinterpretation *f* misinterpretation
Fehlinvestition *f* misdirected investment; unprofitable [uneconomic] investment
Fehljahr *n (agric)* bad year, year of bad harvest, *(Am)* fail year
Fehlkalkulation *f* miscalculation; miscomputation
Fehlkauf *m* bad buy
Fehlkonstruktion *f* faulty design; faulty construction
Fehlleistung *f* unsuccessful effort
fehlleiten to misdirect *(capital etc.)*
Fehlleitung *f* misdirection *(capital etc.)*
Fehlmenge *f* missing quantity, deficiency, shortage
Fehlmengenkosten *pl* cost of missing quantity
Fehlprodukt *n* faulty [defective] product
Fehlschaden *m (ins)* (case of) petty damages
Fehlschicht *f* missed shift; idle shift
Fehlschlag *m* failure *(plan, project etc.)* ⋄ **sich nach einem geschäftlichen ~ erholen** to recover from a business setback
Fehlschluß *m* incorrect [wrong] conclusion; wrong inference; fallacy, paralogism
Fehlspekulation *f* wrong [erroneous] speculation; erroneous assumption, misconception
Fehlstelle *f* unfulfilled vacancy
fehlsteuern *s.* **fehlleiten**
Fehlsteuerung *f s.* **Fehlleitung**
Fehlurteil *n* erroneous [error of] judgement, incorrect assessment; *(jur)* incorrect verdict; incorrect sentence
Fehlverbindung *f* wrong connection
Fehlversuch *m* unsuccessful [abortive] attempt
Fehlzeit *f* time lost through absenteeism *(workers etc.)*; time lost through technical defects *(machines etc.)*
Fehnkultur *f (agric)* cultivation of high-lying moor *(after removal of the peat)*
Fehnwirtschaft *f (agric)* system of cultivating high-lying moor and cutting the peat

Feierabend *m* finishing [closing] time (at work); leisure(-time), spare time [hours]
Feierabendarbeit *f* moonlighting, (additional) work during spare time
Feierabendheim *n* senior citizens' home
Feierschicht *f* cancelled [dropped] shift; unworked shift, shift lost through absenteeism
Feierschichten *fpl* unworked shifts; shifts lost through absenteeism; idle shifts ⋄ **~ einlegen** to drop shifts
Feiertag *m* public holiday
~, gesetzlicher legal [public] holiday
Feiertagsarbeit *f* work (done) on a public holiday
Feiertagslohn *m* payment for work (done) on a public holiday
Feiertagszuschlag *m* additional payment for work (done) on a public holiday
feilbieten to offer [put up] for sale
feilhalten *s.* **feilbieten**
feilschen to bargain, to haggle ⋄ **um etwas ~** to bargain for [over], to haggle about [over]
Feilschen *n* bargaining, haggling
Feilscher *m* bargainer, haggler, chafferer
Feinanalyse *f* accurate analysis
Feinbilanzierung *f* fine [detailed] balancing
Feingehalt *m* (degree of) fineness, (standard of) purity [titre] *(precious metals)*
Feingewicht *n* weight of fine metal, (degree of) fineness, (standard of) purity [title, titre]; precision weight
Feingold *n* pure [fine, refined] gold
Feingoldklausel *f* fine-gold clause
Feinkost *f* high-class groceries, delicatessen food
Feinkostgeschäft *n* high-class grocery shop [store], delicatessen shop [store], delicatessen
Feinkosthandlung *f s.* **Feinkostgeschäft**
Feinmechanik *f* precision engineering
Feinmechaniker *m* precision engineer; precision tool-maker
Feinplanung *f* detailed planning
Feinprojekt *n* final draft(ing) of a project
Feinsilber *n* pure [fine, refined] silver
Feinsortiment *n* specialized range of goods, specialized collection
Feinstbearbeitung *f* superfinishing, microfinish
Feld *n* field
~, bebautes cultivated [tilled] field
~, unbebautes uncultivated field
Feldarbeit *f* 1. agricultural work, farmwork; 2. field work *(sociology etc.)*
Feldbau *m* cultivation of fields, field farming, crop cultivation
Feldbausystem *n* field farming [cultivation] system
Feldbereinigung *f* re-allocation and re-grouping of land

Feldbestellung *f* tilling [tillage] of (the) fields
Feldeinteilung *f* division of arable land *(according to intended cultivation)*
Feld(er)gemeinschaft *f* collective ownership of farmland
Feldflur *f (agric)* open farmland, meadow land; open fields
Feldfrucht *f* field product
Feldfutteranbau *m* cultivation of forage crops, fodder cultivation
Feldfutterbau *m s.* **Feldfutteranbau**
Feldgemüse *n* field vegetable(s)
Feldgemüsebau *m* large-scale growing [cultivation] of vegetables
Feldgraswirtschaft *f* ley farming, grassland cultivation
Feldkapazität *f (agric)* field moisture [capacity]
Feldmark *f* (arable) land, fields *(of a community)*
Feldmaß *n* land-measure
Feldmesser *m* (land) surveyor
Feldrecht *n* laws relating to agricultural holdings; right to posses [cultivate] an agricultural holding
Feldversuch *m* field test *(of soil nutrient etc.)*
Feldvorräte *mpl* all growing plants *(in a farm)*
Feldwirtschaft *f* field farming
Fellauktion *f* fur auction
Fellhandel *m* trade in raw skins
Fellhändler *m* dealer in raw skins
fellverarbeitend skin processing *(industry etc.)*
Ferien *pl* holiday(s); vacation, leave; recess *(parliament etc.)*
Ferienadresse *f* holiday address
Ferienarbeit *f* holiday [vacation] work [job]
Ferienaufenthalt *m* holiday(s)
Ferienaustausch *m* holiday exchange
Feriendienst *m* holiday service
Feriendorf *n* holiday village
Feriengast *m* holiday visitor [guest]
Ferienheim *n* holiday home
Ferienkurs(us) *m* holiday [vacation] course
Ferienlager *n* holiday camp
Ferienort *m* holiday resort [spot]
Ferienplatz *m* holiday place [accommodation]
Ferienreise *f* holiday trip [tour]
Ferienreisender *m* holiday-maker
Feriensaison *f* holiday season, *(Am)* vacation time
Ferienscheck *m* holiday voucher
Feriensonderzug *m* special holiday train
Ferienwohnung *f* holiday flat
Ferienzeit *f* holiday [*(Am)* vacation] time
Fernamt *n* trunk [*(Am)* long-distance] exchange
fernbedienen to operate [handle] by remote control
Fernbedienung *f* remote control
fernbetätigen *s.* **fernbedienen**

fernbleiben to stay away from *(conference etc.)*
Fernbleiben *n* staying away from, absence, non-attendance *(conference etc.)*
Fernfahrer *m* long-distance lorry-driver, *(Am)* long-haul truck driver
Fernfahrt *f* long-distance run [trip]
Ferngas *n* grid gas
Ferngasleitung *f* grid-gas main
Ferngasversorgung *f* grid-gas [long-distance gas] supply
Ferngespräch *n* trunk [*(Am)* long-distance] call
 ⋄ **ein ~ anmelden** to book [*(Am)* place] a trunk [*(Am)* long-distance] call
Ferngiroverkehr *m* trunk [*(Am)* long-distance] giro transfer (business); transfer business between giro accounts in different localities
Ferngüterzug *m* long-distance freight train
Fernhandel *m* overseas trade *(especially used in England)*; trading over distances
Fernmeldeverkehr *m* telecommunication
Fernkurs *m* correspondence course
Fernlaster *m* long-distance lorry
Fernlastverkehr *m* long-distance road haulage
Fernlastwagen *m s.* **Fernlaster**
Fernlehrgang *m s.* **Fernkurs**
Fernleitung *f* long-distance power line *(grid supply system etc.)*; long-distance main *(gas)*; long-distance pipeline *(oil, natural gas etc.)*
Fernleitungsnetz *n* grid supply system *(for electricity, gas etc.)*; trunk main network *(of district heating system)*
Fernmeldeabkommen *n* telecommunication(s) agreement [convention]
Fernmeldeamt *n* district telecommunications centre
Fernmeldeanlage *f* telecommunication(s) installation [equipment]
Fernmeldedienst *m* telecommunication(s) service
Fernmeldegeheimnis *n* secrecy of telecommunication transmissions
Fernmeldeingenieur *m* telecommunications engineer
Fernmeldenetz *n* telecommunications network [system]
Fernmeldesatellit *m* (tele)communication(s) satellite
Fernmeldetarif *m* telegraphic telecommunication(s) rates
Fernmeldetechnik *f* telecommunications engineering, telecommunications
Fernmeldetechniker *m* telecommunications technician
Fernmeldeverein *m* telecommunication(s) union
Fernmeldevertrag *m* telecommunication agreement

Fernmeldewesen *n* telecommunications, telecommunications system
fernmündlich telephonic, by [over the] telephone
Fernpendler *m* long-distance commuter
Fernregelung *f s.* **Fernbedienung**
Fernregler *m* remote control device
Fernrohrleitung *f* long-distance main *(gas)*; long-distance pipeline *(oil)*; trunk main *(district heating)*
Fernschnellzug *m* (long-distance) express train
Fernschreibanschluß *m* teleprinter [*(Am)* teletype] connection, telex connection; telex *(on letter-head)*; tlx *(in telex message)*
Fernschreibdienst *m* teleprinter [*(Am)* teletype] service, telex service
Fernschreiben *n* telex, teleprint [*(Am)* teletype] message
Fernschreiber *m* teleprinter, *(Am)* teletypewriter, telex machine, ticker *(machine)*; teletyper *(person)*
Fernschreibgebühr *f* telex [*(Am)* teletype] charge(s)
Fernschreibgerät *n* teleprinter, *(Am)* teletypewriter, telex machine
Fernschreibleitung *f* teleprinter [*(Am)* teletype] line
Fernschreibnetz *n* teleprinter network
Fernschreibstelle *f* teleprinter [*(Am)* teletype] unit
Fernschreibteilnehmer *m* teleprinter [*(Am)* teletype] user [subscriber]
Fernschreibverkehr *m* teleprinter [*(Am)* teletype] communication(s)
Fernschreibvermittlung *f* telex exchange (office)
fernschriftlich by teleprinter [*(Am)* teletype], by telex
Fernsehen *n* television
~, **industrielles** industrial television
Fernsehgebühr *f* television licence fee
Fernsehindustrie *f* television industry
Fernsehingenieur *m* television engineer
Fernsehlotterie *f* television lottery
Fernsehmechaniker *m* television mechanic
Fernsehnetz *n* television network
Fernsehreklame *f* television advertising [advertisement]
Fernsehtechniker *m* television technician [engineer]
Fernsehwerbung *f s.* **Fernsehreklame**
Fernsendung *f* mail for delivery to other localities
Fernsprechamt *n* telephone exchange (office); trunk [*(Am)* long-distance] exchange
Fernsprechanlage *f* telephone equipment [installation]

Fernsprechanschluß *m* telephone connection, subscriber's line [station]
Fernsprechauftragsdienst *m* automatic telephone answering service
Fernsprechauskunftsdienst *m* telephone inquiry service
Fernsprechautomat *m* telephone kiosk [booth], coin-box telephone, *(Am)* coin [pay] telephone
Fernsprechbuch *n* telephone directory
Fernsprechdienst *m* telephone service
Fernsprechentstörungsdienst *m* telephone engineering fault complaint and repair service
Fernsprechentstörungsstelle *f s.* **Fernsprechentstörungsdienst**
Fernsprecher *m* telephone, phone
~, **öffentlicher** public telephone; public telephone box [booth]
Fernsprechgebühr *f* telephone charges
Fernsprechgrundgebühr *f* telephone subscription rate [fee]
Fernsprechkundendienst *m* telephone customer service *(information, talking clock etc.)*
Fernsprechleitung *f* telephone line [circuit]
Fernsprechnetz *n* telephone network
~, **öffentliches** public telephone network
Fernsprechteilnehmer *m* telephone subscriber
Fernsprechteilnehmerverzeichnis *n s.* **Fernsprechbuch**
Fernsprechverbindung *f* telephonic communication; telephone connection
Fernsprechverkehr *m* telephone service [communication]
Fernsprechverzeichnis *n s.* **Fernsprechbuch**
Fernsprechwesen *n* telephone service; telecommunications
Fernsprechzentrale *f* (public) telephone exchange, *(Am)* central (telephone) office; (private) (telephone) switch-board
Fernsteueranlage *f* remote control installation
Fernstudent *m* student taking correspondence courses
Fernstudium *n* correspondence course
Ferntransport *m* long-distance transport, *(Am)* long-haul traffic
Fernverbindung *f (transp)* long-distance rail service; *(transp)* long-distance bus service; trunk connection *(telephone)*
Fernverkehr *m* long-distance traffic, *(Am)* long-haul trucking
Fernverkehrsbereich *m (transp)* trunk zone; long-range call zone *(telecommunication)*
Fernverkehrslinie *f* 1. long-distance route; 2. long-distance (transport) service
Fernverkehrsomnibus *m* long-distance coach, cross-country bus
Fernverkehrsstraße *f* trunk road, *(Am)* highway
Fernversorgung *f* long-distance supply *(gas etc.)*

Fernwärme *f* central district heating
Fernwasserversorgung *f* long-distance water supply
Fernziel *n* long-term objective [aim], distant goal
Fernzug *m* long-distance train
fertig ready; finished *(piece of work etc.)*; accomplished *(qualification etc.)*
Fertigbau *m* prefabricated building
Fertigbauelement *n* prefabricated structural component
Fertigbauweise *f* prefabricated construction
Fertigbearbeitung *f* finishing, finish machining
Fertigbeton *m* ready-mixed concrete
Fertigerzeugnis *n s.* **Fertigprodukt**
Fertigfabrikat *n s.* **Fertigprodukt**
Fertiggericht *n* ready-to-serve [instant] meal
Fertiggewicht *n* finished weight *(product etc.)*
Fertighaus *n* prefabricated house
Fertigkeit *f* dexterity; skill; talent; proficiency
~, praktische practical skill
Fertigkleidung *f* ready-to-wear [ready-made] clothing
Fertigmontage *f* final assembly
Fertigprodukt *n* finished product [article]
fertigstellen to finish, to complete *(work, plan etc.)*
Fertigstellung *f* completion *(work, plan etc.)*
Fertigstellungsgrad *m s.* **Fertigungsstufe**
Fertigstellungsstufe *f s.* **Fertigungsstufe**
Fertigstellungstermin *m* completion date
Fertigstraße *f (tech)* finishing train
Fertigteil *n* prefabricated part [component]; manufactured building part, prefabricated constructional element
Fertigung *f* manufacture, production, making
~, computerunterstützte (CAM) computer-aided manufacturing
~, erzeugnisspezialisierte manufacture [production] according to products *(by using different types of machines for producing certain parts, sub-assembly groups or finished goods in one and the same production department)*
~, rechnergestützte *s.* **computergestützte**
~, verfahrensspezialisierte manufacture [production] according to particular production methods *(by concentrating similar types of machines in the same production department for producing goods from the first up to the last stage of production)*
~, zentrale centralized manufacture [production] *(concentration of production of components like gear-wheels etc., in special production units)*
~, zentralisierte *s.* **zentrale**
Fertigungsablauf *m* sequence of operations
Fertigungsabschnitt *m* section of production department [shop floor]
Fertigungsanlage *f* (manufacturing) plant

Fertigungsart *f* type of manufacture [production]
Fertigungsauftrag *m* production order
Fertigungsbereich *m* production department
Fertigungsbetrieb *m* factory, production plant
Fertigungsdauer *f s.* **Fertigungszeit**
Fertigungsdiagramm *n* process chart
Fertigungsdokumentation *f* technological documents [data, records]
Fertigungseinheit *f* production unit
Fertigungsfluß *m* production flow
Fertigungsgang *m* work(ing) cycle, (working) operation [process]; pass
Fertigungsgemeinkosten *pl* factory overhead costs
Fertigungsgemeinkostenkonto *n* factory overhead account
Fertigungsgrad *m* manufacturing [production, processing] stage
Fertigungsgruppe *f* manufacturing [production] group [unit]
Fertigungshilfsstelle *f* auxiliary [subsidiary] production department
Fertigungsindustrie *f* manufacturing industry
Fertigungsingenieur *m* production engineer
Fertigungsjahr *n* year of manufacture
Fertigungskapazität *f* manufacturing [production] capacity
Fertigungskette *f* production chain [line]
Fertigungskontrolle *f* production control
Fertigungskosten *pl* manufacturing [production] costs; processing costs
Fertigungsleiter *m* production manager
Fertigungslizenz *f* manufacturing licence
Fertigungslöhne *mpl* manufacturing wages; direct labour
Fertigungsmaterial *n* production [manufacturing] material
Fertigungsmethode *f* manufacturing [production, processing] technique, processing method
Fertigungsmittel *npl* supplementary instruments of production
Fertigungsmittelnormativ *n* standard [norm] of supplementary instruments of production
Fertigungsmittelwirtschaft *f* economy of supplementary instruments of production *(planning, designing, manufacturing and maintenance of devices, tools, gauges etc.)*; department of supplementary instruments of production
Fertigungsmuster *n* prototype
Fertigungsorganisation *f* organization of production, production organization
Fertigungsplan *m* production [manufacturing] schedule [plan]
Fertigungsplanung *f* production [manufacturing] planning
Fertigungsprinzip *n* type of manufacturing

Fertigungsprogramm *n* production [manufacturing] programme [plan]
fertigungsreif ready for production
Fertigungsreife *f* readiness for production
Fertigungsrhythmus *m* production rhythm
Fertigungsserie *f* production run
Fertigungssortiment *n* range of manufacturing
Fertigungsstand *m s.* **Fertigungsstufe**
Fertigungsstelle *f* production [manufacturing, processing] centre
Fertigungssteuerung *f* production control
Fertigungsstoffe *mpl* production [manufacturing] materials
Fertigungsstraße *f* production [assembly] line
Fertigungsstufe *f* manufacturing [production, processing] stage
Fertigungstechnik *f* production [manufacturing] engineering; production [manufacturing] technology
Fertigungstechnologie *f* production [manufacturing] technology, technology of production [manufacturing]
Fertigungsteil *n* production component
Fertigungsunterlagen *fpl s.* **Fertigungsdokumentation**
Fertigungsverfahren *n* manufacturing [production, processing] technique, processing method
Fertigungsvorbereitung *f* operations scheduling, preparation of production schedules
Fertigungsvorgang *m* manufacturing process
Fertigungszeit *f* production [manufacturing] time
Fertigungszuschlag *m s.* **Fertigungsgemeinkosten**
Fertigwaren *fpl* finished goods [manufactures]
Fertigwarenbestand *m* finished goods inventory
Fertigwarenlager *n* store [warehouse] for finished goods
Fertigwarenpreis *m* price of finished goods
Fertilität *f* fertility
fest solid *(fuel, food etc.)*; secure, firm *(lock, position, offer, order etc.)*; fixed *(prices etc.)*; binding *(contract etc.)*; *(st.ex.)* strong
Festangebot *n* firm [binding] offer
festangestellt established, in a permanent position
Festauftrag *m* firm order
festbesoldet (civil servant) with a fixed salary, salaried (civil servant)
Festbestellung *f s.* **Festauftrag**
Festbetrag *m* fixed amount
Festbezüge *mpl* fixed earnings [emoluments]
Festgeld *n* fixed [*(Am)* time] deposit
festgelegt tied [locked] up *(capital etc.)*; stipulated, stated *(agreement etc.)*
Festgeschäft *n* transaction for delivery at a fixed date; *(st.ex.)* future (deal), time bargain

festgesetzt fixed *(prices etc.)*, determined *(time, place etc.)*; decided upon, settled *(conditions etc.)*; assessed *(tax, fine etc.)* ◊ **vertraglich ~** stipulated in contract, laid down by contract, contractually fixed
festgestellt stated; liquidated *(debts etc.)* ◊ **amtlich ~** officially ascertained; officially stated
Festkauf *m* fixed [firm] purchase
Festkonto *n* blocked account; time deposit, deposit account
Festkurs *m* fixed rate *(bonds etc.)*; fixed rate of exchange *(currency)*
Festland *n* mainland; continent
Festlandsockel *m* continental shelf
festlegen to fix, to determine *(place, price, sum etc.)*, to decide (up)on, to settle *(conditions etc.)*, to set, to appoint *(time etc.)*; to lay down *(rules etc.)*; to define, to delimit; to demarcate *(frontier)*; to assess *(tax, fine etc.)*
Festlegung *f* fixing, determination *(place, price, sum etc.)*, decision, settlement *(conditions etc.)*; setting, appointment *(time etc.)*; laying down *(rules etc.)*; definition, delimitation; demarcation *(frontier)*; assessment *(tax, fine etc.)*
festliegend locked [tied] up *(capital etc.)*
Festmeter *n/m (for)* cubic metre (of solid timber)
Festorder *f s.* **Festauftrag**
Festpreis *m* fixed price
~, einheitlicher fixed standard price *(for commodities of a specific quality)*
Festpreisauftrag *m (st.ex.)* firm order, *(Am)* straight-fixed price contract *(to buy securities etc.)*
Festpreisbildung *f* formation of fixed prices
~, einheitliche formation of fixed standard prices
Festpreiskatalog *m* fixed price catalogue, list of fixed prices
Festpreissystem *n* fixed price system, system of fixed prices
festsetzen *s.* **festlegen**
Festsetzung *f s.* **Festlegung**
feststellen to establish, to ascertain, to find out, to discover *(fact etc.)*; to state, to perceive, to see; to set, to fix, to assess *(extent of damage)*
Feststellung *f* establishment. ascertainment, finding out, discovering *(fact etc.)*; statement, perception; setting, fixing, assessment *(extent of damage)*
Feststellungsbescheid *m (fin)* notice of tax assessment
Feststellungsgesetz *n (jur)* assessment law *(relating to payment of compensation for damages etc.)*
Feststellungsinteresse *n* interest in a declaratory judgement

Feststellungsklage *f (jur)* application for a declaratory judgement
Feststellungsurteil *n (jur)* declaratory judgement
Feststellungsverfahren *n (jur)* assessment proceedings
Festtag *m* (day of) festival; festive day
festtags on a public holiday
festverzinslich fixed-interest bearing
Festwährung *f* hard currency
Festwert *m* standard value
Fetischcharakter *m* fetishism
~ **der Ware** commodity fetishism
Fettgehalt *m* fat content *(milk, food etc.)*; grease content *(wool etc.)*
Fettmast *f (agric)* fattening, fatting
Fettweide *f (agric)* lush meadow
Fettwiese *f s.* **Fettweide**
feucht damp, moist, humid *(climate, soil etc.)*
Feuchtegrad *m s.* **Feuchtigkeitsgrad**
Feuchtigkeit *f* moisture (content), moistness *(soil, coal etc.)*; damp *(air, wall etc.)*; dampness, humidity *(atmosphere etc.)*; wetness *(concrete etc.)* ✧ **vor ~ schützen** keep dry
~, **absolute** absolute humidity
~, **relative** relative humidity
feuchtigkeitsbeständig damp-resisting [-resistant] *(paints, surface etc.)*; damp-proof *(wall etc.)*; moisture resistant *(substance)*
Feuchtigkeitsgehalt *m* moisture content *(coal etc.)*
Feuchtigkeitsgrad *m* degree of humidity *(atmosphere etc.)*
feuchtigkeitssicher damp-proof *(insulation etc.)*; moisture proof *(packing etc.)*
Feuchtigkeitswert *m (agric)* moisture equivalent
Feuchtigkeitszuschlag *m* moisture regain *(retail trade)*
feudal feudal
Feudalherr *m* feudal lord
Feudalherrschaft *f* feudalism, feudal regime [domination]
Feudalismus *m* feudalism
feudalistisch feudal
Feudallast *f* feudal burden
Feudalordnung *f* feudal order (of society), feudalism
Feudalrecht *n* feudal law; feudal right
Feudalrente *f* feudal (ground) rent
Feudalstaat *m* feudal state
Feudalsystem *n* feudal system
Feudalverfassung *f* feudal constitution [order]
Feudalwesen *n s.* **Feudalismus**
Feuer *n* fire
Feuerassekuranz *f s.***Feuerversicherung**
feuerbeständig fireproof
Feuerbeständigkeit *f* fireproof quality, fire-resistance; refractoriness *(construction)*

feuerfest *s.* **feuerbeständig**
Feuerfestigkeit *f s.* **Feuerbeständigkeit**
Feuerkasse *f s.* **Feuerversicherung**
Feuerpflichtversicherung *f* compulsory fire insurance
Feuerpolice *f (ins)* fire (insurance) police
Feuerrisiko *n (ins)* fire risk(s)
Feuerschaden *m* loss [damage] caused by fire ✧ **versichert gegen** ~ insured against fire
Feuerschutz *m* fire protection
feuersicher fireproof *(safe, strongroom etc.)*
Feuersicherheit *f* fireproof quality
Feuerversicherung *f* fire insurance
Feuerversicherungsgesellschaft *f* fire-insurance company
Feuerversicherungsprämie *f* fire-insurance premium
FE-Verfahren *n s.* **Forderungseinzugsverfahren**
Fideikommiß *n (jur)* fideicommissum; entail ✧ **ein ~ aufheben** to break an entail; **ein ~ errichten** to make [leave] an entail
Fiduzialgrenzen *fpl (stats)* fiducial limits
Fiduzialschluß *m (stats)* fiducial inference
Fiduzialverteilung *f (stats)* fiducial distribution
Fiduzialwahrscheinlichkeit *f (stats)* fiducial probability
Fiduziant *m (jur)* creator of a trust
Fiduziar *m* trustee
fiduziär fiduciary
Fiduziarerbe *m* fiduciary heir
fiduziarisch *s.* **fiduziär**
fiktiv fictitious *(assets, accounts etc.)*
Filialabschlüsse *mpl* branch transactions
Filialabteilung *f* branch office
Filialbank *f* branch bank
Filialbankbetrieb *m s.* **Filialbank**
Filialbanksystem *n s.* **Filialbankwesen**
Filialbankwesen *n* branch [chain] banking system
Filialbetrieb *m* branch establishment
Filialdirektor *m s.* **Filialleiter**
Filiale *f* branch (office)
~, **überseeische** overseas branch
Filialgeschäft *n* branch (office) *(shop);* multiple shop, chain [*(Am)* integrated] store; *(bank)* branch banking
Filialgruppe *f* branch group
Filialinventar *n* branch inventory
Filialkonto *n* branch account
Filialleiter *m* branch manager
Filialnetz *n* branch network *(banks, supermarkets etc.)*
Filialsystem *n* chain [branch] system
Filmindustrie *f* film industry, *(Am)* motion-picture industry
Filter *m (stats)* filter

Finalerzeugnis *n s.* **Finalprodukt**
Finalprodukt *n* finished good, final product
Finalproduktion *f* final production
Finalproduzent *m* final producer
Finanz *f* finance
Finanzabkommen *n* financial agreement, monetary convention
Finanzabteilung *f* finance department
Finanzakzept *n* accepted finance bill
Finanzamt *n* revenue [fiscal, *(Am)* tax] office
finanzamtlich by the fiscal authorities
Finanzamtsbescheid *m* tax assessment; tax demand, notice of tax assessment
Finanzanalyse *f* financial analysis
Finanzangelegenheiten *fpl* financial affairs; fiscal matters
Finanzapparat *m* budgetary system; financial system
Finanzaristokratie *f* finance [financial] aristocracy
Finanzausgleich *m* financial adjustment, equalization of financial burdens
~, **horizontaler** sharing [equalization] of financial burden between regions
~, **vertikaler** sharing [equalization] of burden within a region
Finanzausschuß *m* finance committee *(association etc.)*; Committee of Ways and Means *(Commonwealth countries)*, *(Am)* Revenue Board
Finanzausweis *m* financial statement
Finanzautonomie *f* financial independence
Finanzbearbeiter *m* accountant; bookkeeper
Finanzbedarf *m* financial requirements
Finanzbehörde *f* fiscal authority
Finanzbeirat *m* financial advisory board
Finanzberater *m* financial adviser
Finanzbericht *m* financial report [statement]
Finanzberichterstattung *f* delivery [submitting] of financial reports, financial reporting
Finanzbesprechungen *fpl* financial discussions
Finanzbeteiligung *f* financial participation [partnership]
Finanzbeziehung *f* financial relation
Finanzbilanz *f* financial balance sheet
Finanzbuchführung *f s.* **Finanzbuchhaltung**
Finanzbuchhalter *m* financial accountant; bookkeeper
Finanzbuchhaltung *f* financial accountancy; department of financial accountancy
Finanzdecke *f* financial cover [capacity]
Finanzdefizit *n* financial [budgetary] deficit
Finanzdelikt *n* financial [tax] offence
Finanzdisposition *f* financial set-up
Finanzdisziplin *f* discipline [correctness] in financial [tax] matters
Finanzeinnahmen *fpl* revenue, centralized (state) income

Finanzen *pl* finances ⋄ ~ **sanieren** to stabilize the finance *(company, economy etc.)*
~, **öffentliche** public finances
~, **staatliche** state finances
~, **zerrüttete** shattered finances
Finanzerträge *mpl* financial income
Finanzexperte *m* expert in finance, financial expert
Finanzfachmann *m s.* **Finanzexperte**
Finanzfonds *m* financial means [funds]
Finanzfrage *f* financial question [issue]
Finanzgebaren *n* management [conduct] of (public) finances
Finanzgebarung *f* fiscal policy
finanzgeplant financially planned
Finanzgericht *n* tax [fiscal, revenue] court
Finanzgeschäft *n* financing; investment banking
Finanzgesellschaft *f s.* **Finanzierungsgesellschaft**
Finanzgesetz *n* finance act; revenue act
Finanzgesetzgebung *f* financial legislation
Finanzgesetzvorlage *f* finance bill
Finanzgewalt *f s.* **Finanzhoheit**
Finanzgruppe *f* monopoly group of bankers, syndicate
Finanzhaushalt *m* state budget; financial budget *(of organizations etc.)*
Finanzherr *m s.* **Finanzier**
Finanzhilfe *f* financial aid [assistance]
~, **private** private financial aid
~, **staatliche** state financial aid
Finanzhof *m s.* **Finanzgericht**
Finanzhoheit *f* financial [fiscal] autonomy
finanziell financial; fiscal; pecuniary, monetary
⋄ ~ **gesund** financially sound, (financially) solvent; ~ **gut gestellt sein** to be well situated financially; ~ **interessiert sein** to be financially interested in *(s.th.)*; ~ **leistungsfähig** financially capable [able]; ~ **schlecht gestellt sein** to be badly situated financially; ~ **selbständig** financially independent; ~ **unabhängig** *s.* ~ **selbständig**
Finanzier *m* financier
finanzieren to finance
finanziert financed ⋄ **privat** ~ privately financed; **staatlich** ~ state-financed [-paid]
Finanzierung *f* financing
~, **auftragsgebundene** financing tied to orders (given)
~ **aus dem Haushalt** budgetary financing, financing from the budget
~, **ausreichende** sufficient financing [equipping with capital/funds]; sufficient capitalization
~ **durch Abtretung der Debitoren** debt [accounts receivable, receivables] financing
~ **durch die Bank** bank financing, financed by the bank

~, **fondsbezogene** financing related to production funds
~, **kurzfristige** short-term financing
~, **langfristige** long-term financing
~, **mittelfristige** medium-term financing
~ **mittels Forderungsabtretung** s. ~ **durch Abtretung der Debitoren**
~, **private** independent [private] financing
~, **ungenügende** insufficient financing [equipping with capital/funds]; insufficient capitalization
~, **zweckgebundene** tied financing
~, **zyklische** cyclical financing
Finanzierungsart f kind [type] of financing
Finanzierungsaufwand m financial expenditure(s)
Finanzierungsbank f issuing house
Finanzierungsbedarf m financial requirements
Finanzierungsbeihilfe f subsidy; relief *(social payment to families etc.)*
Finanzierungsbestimmungen fpl financing regulations [rules]
Finanzierungsbilanz f balance sheet of financing, statement on financing *(a project)*
Finanzierungsdienst m finance [financing] service
Finanzierungsfonds mpl financing funds; investment funds; financial funds
~, **operative** operational financial funds
Finanzierungsform f method of financing
Finanzierungsgemeinschaft f financing syndicate
Finanzierungsgeschäft n financial transaction; financing *(of companies etc.)*; investment banking
Finanzierungsgesellschaft f finance company; investment company
Finanzierungsgrundlage f basis of financing
Finanzierungsgrundsatz m principle of financing
Finanzierungshilfe f financial aid; assistance in financing
Finanzierungsinstitut n financing institution; financing bank; investment bank [company]
Finanzierungsinstrument n instrument of financing
Finanzierungslast f burden of financing
Finanzierungslimit n (upper) limit of financing
Finanzierungsmarkt m capital [investment] market
Finanzierungsmethode f method of financing
Finanzierungsmittel npl funds, financial means, credit instruments; capital
~, **zweckgebundene** tied means of financing, tied financial means
Finanzierungsmöglichkeit f possibility of financing; financial capability

Finanzierungsnachweis m statement on financing
Finanzierungsorgan n financing institution
Finanzierungsplan m finance plan, plan of financing
Finanzierungsplanung f planning of financing
Finanzierungsprogramm n programme of financing
Finanzierungsquellen fpl sources of financing; financial resources
~, **zweckgebundene** tied financial sources
Finanzierungsschema n financing scheme
Finanzierungsschwierigkeit f difficulties in financing, financial difficulties
Finanzierungssystem n system of financing
Finanzierungsträger m s. **Finanzierungsorgan**
Finanzierungsübersicht f financial survey, survey on financing
Finanzierungsverordnung f finance regulations *(for financing enterprises and institutions)*
Finanzierungszusage f commitment to finance *(project etc.)*
Finanzierungszuschuß m financial grant
Finanzinspektion f auditing; auditing authority
Finanzinstitution f finance institution
Finanzjahr n fiscal [financial] year
Finanzkapital n financial [finance, moneyed] capital
Finanzkasse f revenue office
Finanzkategorie f finance category
Finanzkennziffer f financial indicator [index]
Finanzkonsortium n financial consortium [syndicate]
Finanzkontrollbericht m auditor's (financial) report
Finanzkontrolle f financial auditing [control]
Finanzkontrollorgan n finance auditing [controlling] authority
Finanzkraft f financial power [capacity]
finanzkräftig financially strong
Finanzkreise mpl financial circles [quarters]
Finanzkrise f financial crisis
Finanzlage f financial position [situation, state]
~, **gute** financially strong position
~, **schlechte** weak financial position
Finanzlast f financial burden
Finanzmacht f financial power
Finanzmagnat m financial magnate
Finanzmakler m loan agent, money broker
Finanzmann m s. **Finanzmagnat**
Finanzmarkt m capital [long-term credit, stock] market, money market
Finanzmethode f s. **Finanzierungsmethode**
Finanzminister m Minister of Finance, Finance Minister; *(UK)* Chancellor of the Exchequer; *(USA)* Secretary of the Treasury
Finanzministerium n Ministry of Finance; *(UK)*

Treasury and Exchequer (and Audit) Department; *(USA)* Department of the Treasury
Finanzmittel *npl* financial resources [means]
Finanzmonopol *n* finance monopoly
Finanzökonomie *f* (public) finance; financial economics
Finanzökonomik *f* finance economics
Finanzoligarchie *f* finance oligarchy
Finanzoperation *f* financial operation [transaction]
Finanzorgan *n* finance organ, financial authority [body]
Finanzperiode *f* financial [fiscal] period; budgetary period
Finanzperspektivplan *m* long-term finance [financial] plan
Finanzplan *m* finance [financial] plan
~, **betrieblicher** finance [financial] plan of the enterprise
~, **detaillierter** detailed finance [financial] plan
~, **vorläufiger** tentative finance plan
Finanzplankalkulation *f* finance plan calculation
Finanzplanung *f* financial planning
Finanzplanvorschlag *m* draft of the finance plan
Finanzpolitik *f* financial [fiscal] policy
finanzpolitisch from the financial point of view
Finanzprognose *f* long-term financial forecast
Finanzprogramm *n* finance [financial] programme
Finanzprojekt *n* financial project
Finanzrechnung *f* financial accounting
Finanzrecht *n* law of public finance
Finanzreform *f* financial reform
Finanzreserve *f* financial reserves; undistributed budget resources
Finanzressourcen *pl s.* **Finanzierungsquellen**
Finanzrevision *f* finance [financial] auditing
~, **staatliche** governmental financial [state finance] auditing
Finanzrichtsatz *m* financial standard [norm]
Finanzsache *f* financial matter
Finanzsachverständiger *m s.* **Finanzexperte**
Finanzschuld *f* financial [monetary] debt
~, **gestundete** arrears given a respite for payment
Finanzschulddarleh(e)n *n* loan for financial [monetary] debts
finanzschwach financially weak
Finanzschwierigkeiten *fpl* financial difficulties [straits]
finanzstark financially strong
Finanzstatistik *f* finance statistics
Finanzstatus *m s.* **Finanzlage**
Finanzstrafe *f* fine
Finanzsystem *n* finance [financial] system

Finanztätigkeit *f* financing (activity)
finanztechnisch financial, fiscal
Finanzteil *m* financial part *(plans, newspapers etc.)*
Finanztheorie *f* theory of finance
Finanztransaktion *f* financial transaction
Finanzübersicht *f* financial statement [survey]
Finanz- und Kreditsystem *n* financial and crediting system
Finanzverfassung *f* financial system *(as stipulated in a country's laws)*
Finanzverhältnisse *npl s.* **Finanzlage**
~, **gesunde** sound financial position
Finanzverpflichtung *f* financial commitment
Finanzverwaltung *f* financial administration; fiscal authority
Finanzvoranschlag *m* budgetary estimate
Finanzvorlage *f* revenue bill *(to parliament etc.)*
Finanzwechsel *m* accommodation bill *(mainly between banks)*
Finanzwelt *f* financial world [circles]
Finanzwesen *n* financial system, public finance; finances; financial affairs
~, **öffentliches** public finance
Finanzwirtschaft *f* finances, public finance
finanzwirtschaftlich from the point of view of public finance
Finanzwirtschaftspolitik *f* fiscal policy
Finanzwissenschaft *f* finance economics, science of (public) finance
Finanzzentrum *n* financial centre
Finanzzoll *m* revenue-raising duty
Finanzzolltarif *m* customs tariff for raising revenue
Finanzzuweisung *f* allocation of (financial) funds
finden to find *(job etc.)*; to discover *(mistake etc.)*; to meet with *(approval, opposition etc.)*
Finder *m* finder; *(min)* discoverer *(mineral resources etc.)*
Finderlohn *m* reward to the finder (of lost property)
Finderrecht *n* law relating to objects found; right of the finder to the object found; *(min)* right of the discoverer to mineral resources
fingieren to feign; to simulate
fingiert feigned; fictitious *(bill etc.)*; simulated
Firma *f* firm, enterprise company ◊ **Ihre geschätzte** ~ your esteemed [valued] firm
~, **alteingesessene** old-established firm
~, **befreundete** firm [house] with which one has good relations
~, **bekannte** well-known firm
~, **bevollmächtigte** authorized firm
~, **eingetragene** registered firm
~, **erloschene** dissolved firm
~, **führende** leading firm

~, **gut renommierte** firm of good repute [reputation]
~, **marktbeherrschende** monopoly, monopoly firm; firm dictating the market
~, **solide** reliable firm
~, **teilnehmende** participating firm
~, **untersuchte** firm studied *(before granting a loan etc.)*; surveyed firm *(for statistics)*; investigated firm *(for fraud etc.)*
~, **unzuverlässige** unreliable [shaky] firm
~, **vertragsbrüchige** firm acting in breach of contract
~, **weltbekannte** firm of world renown [worldwide reputation], world-famous firm
~, **zahlungsfähige** solvent firm [house], sound business
~, **zahlungsunfähige** insolvent firm [house]
Firmenabsatz *m* sales of a firm
Firmenänderung *f* changing of the name of the [a] firm, name-change of a firm
Firmenangabe *f* name of the firm, business name
Firmenangehöriger *m* member of the firm, company worker [clerk]
Firmenanmeldung *f* firm's application
Firmenanteil *m* firm's share, share of the firm
Firmenausschließlichkeit *f (com, jur)* exclusive right to a firm's name
Firmenbezeichnung *f* name of firm, firm's name
Firmeneigentum *n* firm's property
Firmeneintragung *f* registration of a firm
Firmeneinzelstand *m* firm's individual stand
Firmengebrauch *m* use of a firm-name
~, **unbefugter** improper use of the [a] firm's name
Firmengemeinschaftsstand *m* collective stand of firms
Firmeninhaber *m* owner [principal] of a firm
Firmenmantel *m* legal title and registration of a firm
Firmenmarke *f s.* **Firmenzeichen**
Firmenmarkenverzeichnis *n* index of branded goods; register of trademarks
Firmenname *m* firm name, firm's [company, trading] name. title of business undertaking; trade name
Firmenöffentlichkeit *f (com, jur)* compulsory registration of a firm (commercial undertaking)
Firmenrechte *npl* trade rights
firmenrechtlich relating to the law on commercial undertakings
Firmenregister *n* register [list] of firms
Firmensanierung *f* reorganization of a firm
Firmenschutz *m* protection of registered names of firms

Firmensiegel *n s.* **Firmenstempel**
Firmenstempel *m* firm('s) [company] stamp
Firmenvermögen *n* firm's property [assets]
Firmenvertreter *m* firm's representative [agent]
Firmenverzeichnis *n* directory of names of firms (firm names)
Firmenwert *m* goodwill *(of a business)*
Firmenzeichen *n* trademark, brand
firmieren to use the name of a firm
Firmierung *f* firm name, trading name
Fischer *m* fisherman
Fischerei *f* 1. fishery *(industry);* 2. fishing
Fischereiausbildung *f* fishery training
Fischereibehörde *f* fishery authority
Fischereibetrieb *m* fishery, fishing enterprise
Fischereiflotte *f* fishing fleet
Fischereiforschung *f* research in fisheries
Fischereigebiet *n s.* **Fischfanggebiet**
Fischereigrenze *f* fishery limit
Fischereihafen *m* fishing port
Fischereipächter *m* holder of a fishing lease
Fischereiproduktionsgenossenschaft *f* **(FPG)** fishing co-operative
Fischereirecht *n* fishery laws
~, **internationales** international law of fisheries
Fischereistatistik *f* fishery statistics
Fischereiverband *m* association of fishermen
Fischereizone *f* fishing zone
Fischfang *m* fishing, (fish) catch, catch of fish
~ **und Fischverarbeitung** *f* fish catch and fish processing
Fischfanggebiet *n* fishing ground
Fischgründe *mpl* fishing grounds
Fischhandel *m* fishmongery (trade); fish trade; fish shop
Fischhändler *m* fishmonger; fish-merchant *(wholesale trade)*
Fischhandlung *f* fish [fishmonger's] shop
Fischindustrie *f* fish processing industry
Fischmarkt *m* fish-market
Fischsterben *n* death of fish(es) *(caused by industrial water-pollution)*
Fischwirtschaft *f* fishing, fishery
Fischzucht *f* pisciculture, fish-farming [-breeding, -hatching]
Fischzuchtanstalt *f* fish-farm, fish-breeding [*(Am)* fish raising] establishment
Fischzüchter *m* fish-farmer [-breeder]; pisciculturist
Fisher-Yates-Test *m (stats)* Fisher-Yates test
Fiskal *m* 1. fiscal, official of the Treasury; 2. public prosecutor
Fiskalat *n* 1. office of fiscal; 2. office of public prosecutor
Fiskaleinlagen *fpl* state deposits
fiskalisch fiscal
Fiskalität *f* fiscality

Fiskaljahr *n* fiscal [financial] year
Fiskalpolitik *f* budget(ary) policy
Fiskalschuld *f* fiscal [budgetary] debt
Fiskalzoll *m* revenue-raising duty
Fiskus *m* state treasury, financial authorities; the Crown *(in England)*; the Fisc *(in Scotland)*; the Treasury *(in the United States)*
Fixabkommen *n* firm agreement
Fixauftrag *m* firm order
fixen *(st.ex.)* to speculate for a fall, to sell short, to go bear
Fixer *m (st.ex.)* speculator for a fall, bear
Fixgeschäft *n* transaction for delivery at a fixed date; *(st.ex.)* future (deal), time bargain *(for a fixed date of delivery/acceptance)*
fixieren to fix *(time, place, appointment etc.)*; to determine *(price, quota etc.)*; to set *(limit etc.)*; to settle *(terms of contract etc.)*; to stipulate *(conditions etc.)*
Fixieren *n* fixing *(time, place, appointment etc.)*; determination *(price, quota etc.)*; setting *(limit etc.)*; settlement *(terms of contract etc.)*; stipulation *(conditions etc.)*
Fixierung *f s.* **Fixieren**
Fixkauf *m* firm purchase; purchase for delivery at a fixed date; *(st.ex.)* future (deal), time bargain
Fixklausel *f* fixed-date clause
Fixkosten *pl* fixed costs
Fixkostenkoeffizient *m* coefficient of fixed costs
Fixtermin *m* fixed date
Fixum *n* fixed [regular] salary
Fixverkauf *m* time sale
Fläche *f* surface; area; space *(trade fair etc.)*
~, **bebaute** built-up area
~, **gemietete** rented area
~, **nutzbare** usable space; *(agric)* usable area [field, land]
Flächenausdehnung *f* square [area] dimension *(town etc.)*
Flächenausnutzung *f* utilization per unit of area *(fair etc.)*; *(agric)* utilization per unit of arable land
Flächenbedarf *m* space [area] required
Flächenbuchung *f* booking of space *(fair etc.)*
Flächendiagramm *n (stats)* plane diagram
Flächeneinheit *f* unit of area; unit of surface measurement
Flächenerweiterung *f* extension of space [area]
Flächenleistung *f (agric)* output per unit of arable land; power per unit of area
Flächenmaß *n* square measure; measure of area
Flächennutzung *f* space utilization *(fair etc.)*; *(agric)* land development; land utilization
Flächennutzungsplan *m (agric)* plan of land utilization

Flächenproduktivität *f* output per hectare *(a misnomer for* **Flächenleistung***)*
Flächensteuer *f* land-tax *(on an area under cultivation)*
Flächenstichprobe *f (stats)* area sample
Flächenstichprobenverfahren *n (stats)* area sampling
Flächenzuteilung *f* allocation of space
Flagge *f* flag ⋄ **unter der ~ von ... fahren** to sail under the flag of ...
Flaggenattest *n* certificate of registry
Flaggenbuch *n* flag-book
Flaggenmißbrauch *m* improper display of a (national) flag
Flaggenrecht *n* law of the flag
Flaggenwechsel *m* re-registering *(of ship)* under a different (national) flag
Flaschenpfand *n* bottle deposit
flau *(com, fin, st.ex.)* dull, slack, lifeless, flat *(market etc.)*
Flauheit *f (com, fin, st.ex.)* dullness, lifelessness, slackness *(market etc.)*
Flaute *f (com)* slackness, slack period
~, **geschäftliche** slack times in business
~, **jahreszeitliche** seasonal slack
~, **wirtschaftliche** business depression
Fleischerhandwerk *n* butcher's trade
Fleischmarkt *m* meat market
flexibel flexible, pliable *(attitude, material etc.)*; adaptable *(persons etc.)*
Flexibilität *f* flexibility, pliability *(attitude, material etc.)*; adaptability *(persons etc.)*
Fließarbeit *f* production-line work, flow(-line) production, *(Am)* progressive manufacture
Fließband *n* conveyor belt; assembly [production] line
~, **grünes** *(agric)* green [fodder] conveyor belt *(covering all stages of green fodder production up to storage)*
Fließbandarbeit *f* assembly-line [production--line] work
Fließbandarbeiter *m* assembly-line [production--line] worker
Fließbanderzeugnis *n* assembly-line product
Fließbandfertigung *f* flow(-line) [beltline, conveyor-belt] production, *(Am)* progressive manufacture [assembly]
Fließbandmontage *f* flow-line [conveyor-line] assembly, *(Am)* progressive assembly
Fließbandverfahren *n* assembly-line method (of production)
Fließbild *n* flow diagram [chart, sheet]
Fließfertigung *f* flow(-line) production, *(Am)* progressive manufacture
~, **komplexe** comprehensive flow(-line) production, *(Am)* comprehensive progressive manufacture

Fließmontage *f* flow(-line) assembly
Fließprinzip *n* flow-line principle
Fließreihe *f s.* **Fließstraße**
Fließstraße *f* flow (production) line
~, automatische automated flow (production) line
Fließsystem *n* flow-line system
floaten to float *(currency)*
florieren to flourish, to prosper, to thrive *(business, trade etc.)*
Flotte *f* fleet
Flottenkapazität *f* fleet capacity [tonnage]
Flöz *n* layer, seam
Flucht *f* flight *(capital etc.)*; escape *(persons etc.)*
~ in Sachwerte flight to real values
Fluchtgeld *n s.* **Fluchtkapital**
Fluchtkapital *n* flight capital, hot [fugitive] money
Flüchtling *m* refugee; runaway; displaced person
Flüchtlingslager *n* refugee camp
Flug *m* flight; flying; air journey
Flugabkommen *n* air agreement
~, internationales international air agreement
Fluggast *m* air passenger
Fluggastversicherung *f* air passengers insurance
Flughafen *m* airport
Flughafengebühren *fpl* airport charges
Flughafensteuer *f* airport tax; airport service charge *(for passengers)*
Flugkarte *f* 1. air(-travel) [flight] ticket; 2. aviation [aeronautical] map [chart]
Flugkilometer *mpl* aircraft-kilometres; kilometres flown
Flugleistung *f* flight performance
Fluglinie *f* 1. airline (company); 2. air route
Flugliniennetz *n* network of air routes, airline network
Fluglinienverkehr *m* airline [airborne] traffic
Flugpassagier *m s.* **Fluggast**
Flugpersonal *n* flying [flight] personnel
Flugplan *m* 1. time-table [schedule] (of air service), *(Am)* flying schedule; 2. flight plan
Flugplatz *m* airport, airfield
Flugplatzversicherung *f* air service liability insurance
Flugpost *f* airmail
Flugpreis *m* air(-ticket) fare
Flugreise *f* air journey
Flugreisender *m s.* **Fluggast**
Flugroute *f* air route
Flugschein *m* 1. flight [air(-travel)] ticket; 2. pilot's licence
Flugstrecke *f* air route; covered distance, distance flown
Flugstreckennetz *n s.* **Flugliniennetz**
Flugverbindung *f* air connection; connecting flight

Flugverkehr *m* air traffic; air service
Flugverkehrsnetz *n s.* **Flugliniennetz**
Flugzeit *f* flight [flying] hours; flight season
Flugzeug *n* aircraft, aeroplane, plane, *(Am)* airplane ⋄ **per ~** by plane [air]
Flugzeugindustrie *f* aircraft industry
Flugzeugingenieur *m* aircraft engineer
Flugzeugkonstrukteur *m* aircraft designer
Flugzeugpark *m* aircraft fleet
Flugzeugschlosser *m* aircraft fitter
Flugziel *n* destination (of flight)
Fluktuation *f* fluctuation *(price, rate etc.)*; turnover *(labour force)*
~ der Arbeitskräfte manpower fluctuation, fluctuation [turnover] in the labour force
Fluktuationsarbeitslosigkeit *f* temporary unemployment *(caused by labour turnover)*
Fluktuationsklausel *f* fluctuation clause
Fluktuationskoeffizient *m* labour turnover rate
Fluktuationskosten *pl* costs caused by labour turnover
fluktuieren to fluctuate; to be mobile [on the move] *(population etc.)*
Flur *f (agric)* open farmland, meadow land; open fields
Flurbegehung *f (agric)* inspection and on-the--spot estimate *(of crops to be harvested)*
Flurbereinigung *f* re-allocation and re-grouping of land
Flurbereinigungsgesetz *n* law governing the re-allocation and re-grouping of land
Flurbuch *n (agric)* land register *(of agricultural holdings of a community)*
Flureinteilung *f (agric)* division of an agricultural holding
Flurform *f (agric)* layout of fields [farmland] *(in relation to a village)*
Flurgrenze *f* boundary [limit] of the holding of a village [community]
Flurholzanbau *m* growing [cultivation] of trees *(to benefit the land belonging to a village or community)*
Flurkarte *f* cadastral map *(of an agricultural holding)*
Flurneuordnung *f s.* **Flurbereinigung**
Flurregister *n* agricultural land register
Flurschaden *m (agric)* crop damage
Flurschlag *m (agric)* open tillage field
Flurumgang *m s.* **Flurbegehung**
Flurverfassung *f (agric)* system governing the use and ownership of a village holding
Flurzersplitterung *f (agric)* land fragmentation, parcellation of a holding
Flurzwang *m (agric)* obligation to conform to the rules governing an open-field system
Fluß *m* 1. river; stream; 2. flow, flowing *(traffic, goods etc.)*; 3. melting *(metal etc.)*

Flußbild *n* 1. general aspect of river; 2. *(ind)* flow chart [diagram, sheet]
~, **technologisches** technological flow chart
Flußdiagramm *n* flow diagram [chart, sheet]
Flußdichte *f (stats)* flux density
Flußfrachtgeschäft *n* river freight business
Flußfrachtsatz *m* river freight rate
Flußgüterversicherung *f* river transport insurance
Flußhafen *m* river port
flüssig liquid, fluid, available, ready, mobile *(money, capital etc.)*
Flüssigkeit *f* 1. liquid, fluid; *(ind)* liquor; liquidity *(solution etc.)*; fluidity *(liquid, substances etc.)*; 2. *(fin)* availability, mobility *(money etc.)*; liquidity *(assets etc.)*; liquidity, cash position *(bank etc.)*; ease *(capital market etc.)*
Flüssigkeitserfordernisse *npl* (commercial) standards of solvency
Flüssigkeitsgrad *m* degree of liquidity
Flüssigkeitsrate *f* reserve ratio *(central bank)*
Flüssigkeitsverhältnis *n (acc)* current position ratio *(to fixed capital)*
flüssigmachen to realize *(shares, obligations etc.)*, to disengage, to convert into cash *(money)*
Flußkargoversicherung *f s.* **Flußgüterversicherung**
Flußkaskoversicherung *f* additional river boat insurance, insurance on hull *(of river boats)*
Flußladeschein *m* river bill of lading
Flußregulierung *f* regulation of a river
Flußrisiko *n* danger on [from] the river, river risks
Flußrisikoversicherung *f* river risk insurance
Flußschiffahrt *f* river traffic [navigation, shipping]
Flußtransport *m* river transport(ation)
Flußtransportversicherung *f* river transport insurance
Flußverkehr *m* river traffic
Flußverunreinigung *f* river pollution
Flutkraft *f* tidal power
Flutkraftwerk *n* tidal power station
fob f.o.b. (free on board)
fob-Kalkulation *f* f.o.b. calculation
fob-Klausel *f* f.o.b. clause
fob-Lieferung *f* f.o.b. delivery; delivery f.o.b.
fob-Preis *m* f.o.b. price
föderalisieren to federalize; **sich ~** to federate, to form a federation; to become federalized; to form a confederacy *(temporary union of parties, persons etc.)*
Föderalismus *m* federalism
föderalistisch federalist
Föderation *f* federation; confederation *(states etc.)*; confederacy *(parties, persons etc.)*

föderativ federal, federative
Föderativstaat *m* federal state; federation
föderieren to federate, to federalize *(number of states)*; **sich ~** *s.* **sich föderalisieren**
föderiert federated, federate
Folge *f* result, upshot, outcome, effect; succession, sequence; order; series; continuation, instalment; consequence ⋄ **~ leisten** to comply with *(request etc.);* to accept *(invitation etc.);* to answer *(summons etc.);* to follow, to obey *(instructions etc.);* **in der ~** subsequently; **in dichter ~** in close succession; **in rascher ~** in quick [rapid] succession; **in ungezwungener ~** in no particular order
~, **abnehmende** *s.* ~, **fallende**
~, **chronologische** chronological order
~, **fallende** descending order
~, **steigende** ascending order
~, **technologische** technological sequence [order]
~, **übergreifende** spillover
~, **unmittelbare** direct result
~, **unvermeidliche** inevitable consequence [result]
~, **zunehmende** *s.* ~, **steigende**
Folgebedarf *m* resulting demand
Folgebeitrag *m (ins)* renewal premium
Folgedichte *f (agric)* rate of recurrence of crops
Folgeereignis *n* result, resulting effect [event], consequence
Folgeinvestition *f* (con)sequential investment
~, **mittelbare** indirect sequential investment
~, **standortbedingte** (con)sequential infrastructure investment
~, **unmittelbare** direct [consequential] investment
Folgen *fpl*:
⋄ **die ~ tragen** to bear the consequences
~, **katastrophale** disastrous consequences
~, **schwerwiegende** serious consequences
~, **unangenehme** unpleasant consequences
~, **verheerende** devastating effects
~, **weittragende** far-reaching consequences
Folgeprämie *f s.* **Folgebeitrag**
Folgeprozeß *m* sequential process
Folgeprüfung *f (stats)* sequential test
Folgerecht *n (jur)* right of stoppage in transit
Folgeschaden *m (ins)* consequential damage
~, **mittelbarer** *(ins)* indirect consequential damage
~, **unmittelbarer** *(ins)* direct consequential damage
Folgeschätzung *f (stats)* sequential estimation
Folgetest *m (stats)* sequential test
folio *(acc)* folio
Folio *n (acc)* folio

Fonds *m* fund *(expressed primarily in money terms),* (financial) fund [resources]; (disposable) capital; stock *(physical)*
~ **der Erhaltung der Grundmittel** fund for maintaining fixed assets, maintenance capital
~ **der Erweiterung der Grundmittel** fund for expanding fixed assets
~ **der Erweiterung der Produktion** fund for expanding production
~ **der Erweiterung des nichtproduktiven Bereichs** fund for expanding the non-productive sector
~ **der individuellen Konsumtion** resources for individual consumption *(disposable income of the population and total stock of consumer goods and services)*
~ **für die gesellschaftliche Konsumtion** resources for social consumption
~ **für die staatliche Verwaltung** (central) government administrative resources
~ **für die Vergütung nach der Arbeitsleistung** piece-rate wage fund
~ **für das Handelsrisiko** business risk fund *(of trading enterprises to cover reduction in prices, costs of re-processing and non-planned expenditures by suppliers)*
~ **für Investitionen** *s.* ~ **der Erweiterung der Grundmittel**
~ **für Wissenschaft und Technik** science and technology fund
~, **unteilbarer** non-disbursable fund *(of co-operatives etc., to members but may be used for investment)*
Fonds *mpl* funds, resources *(stock of equipment, material or financial resources available over a definite period of time),* (disposable) capital; stocks
~, **aktive betrieblich genutzte** directly employed enterprise funds [capital]
~, **ausländische** foreign funds
~, **betriebliche** enterprise funds [capital]
~ **der nichtproduktiven Konsumtion** resources for non-productive consumption
~ **der nichtproduktiven Sphäre** funds of the non-productive sector *(of the national economy)*
~ **des Betriebes, eigene** enterprise's own funds [capital]
~, **finanzielle** funds, financial resources; capital
~, **fremde** outside [external] funds [capital]
~, **geliehene** borrowed funds [capital]
~, **genossenschaftliche** co-operative funds [capital], funds [capital] of the co-operative (society)
~, **geplante** planned funds
~, **gesellschaftlich notwendige produktive** socially necessary productive funds [capital]
~, **gesellschaftliche** social funds

~, **konsolidierte** consolidated funds [capital]
~, **materielle** physical resources; capital assets
~, **nichtproduktive** non-productive funds [capital]
~, **öffentliche** public funds
~, **produktive** productive funds [capital]
~, **schwarze** black money
~, **unproduktive** *s.* ~, **nichtproduktive**
~, **zweckgebundene** earmarked [tied] funds *(only to be used for planned purposes)*
Fondsabführung *f* transfer of funds [capital]
Fondsabgabe *f* 1. tax on funds [capital]; 2. *s.* **Fondsabführung**
Fondsausnutzung *f* utilization of funds [capital]
Fondsausstattung *f* provision with funds [capital]
Fondsausstattungsgrad *m* level of provision with funds [capital]
Fondsbesitzer *m* fund owner, owner of funds
Fondsbestand *m* stock of funds [capital]
fondsbezogen relating to funds [capital]
Fondsbildung *f* formation of funds [capital]
Fondsbörse *f* stock exchange
Fondseffektivität *f* efficiency of funds [capital]
Fondseinsatz *m* utilization of funds [capital], fund [capital] utilization
Fondsentwicklung *f* growth of funds [capital]
Fondsergiebigkeit *f s.* **Fondseffektivität**
Fondsertrag *m* investment return, capital yield
~, **differentialer** differential investment return [capital yield]
Fondsinhaber *m s.* **Fondsbesitzer**
Fondsintensität *f* capital-output ratio, funds intensity
fondsintensiv funds [capital] intensive
Fondspreis *m* price related to an effective prime cost
Fondsquote *f* output-capital ratio
Fondsrate *f (approx.)* ratio of net income to wages, prime costs etc.
Fondsrentabilität *f* return on funds [capital] employed
Fondsrentabilitätsrate *f* rate of return on funds [capital] employed
Fondsstruktur *f* structure of funds [capital]
Fondsumschlag *m* fund [capital] circulation, circulation of funds [capital]
Fondsverbrauch *m* consumption of (material) funds
Fondsverminderung *f* reduction of funds [capital]
Fondsverwendung *f* expenditure of money funds
Fondsverzehr *m s.* **Fondsverbrauch**
Fondsverzinsung *f* interest on funds [capital]
Fondsvorschuß *m* advanced funds [capital]
Fondswirksamkeit *f s.* **Fondseffektivität**

Fondszuführung *f* supply of funds [capital]
Fondszuwachs *m* increase in funds [capital]; increase in (the) resources *(for individual consumption etc.)*
Förderanlage *f* conveying [mechanical handling] plant; conveying [mechanical handling] equipment; *(min)* winding [hauling] plant; *(min)* winding [hauling] equipment
Förderband *n* conveyor belt; *(manuf)* assembly line
Förderer *m* 1. furtherer, promoter; supporter, patron; 2. *(min)* haulier, onsetter
Fördergebiet *n* mining [drilling] area
Fördergut *n* *(min)* material to be hoisted [brought up]; material brought up
Förderkosten *pl* *(min)* costs of winding
Förderkurs *m* extension [sandwich] course
Förderleistung *f* capacity *(conveyor etc.)*; delivery, discharge *(pump etc.)*; *(min)* production, output; rate of winding; tonnage wound
Fördermenge *f* quantity conveyed *(conveyor etc.)*; delivery, discharge *(pump etc.)*; *(min)* quantity produced, output; tonnage
Fördermittel *n* *(min)* conveyor
fordern to claim *(damages, compensation etc.)*; to demand *(s.th.)*, to call for *(s.th.)*; to require *(s.th.)*
fördern 1. to advance *(science, s.o.'s interests etc.)*; to promote *(project, growth etc.)*, to further *(cause, movement etc.)*; to encourage *(development etc.)*; 2. to convey, to handle *(raw materials etc.)*; *(min)* to haul *(coal etc.)*
Fördertechnik *f* conveying engineering
Forderung *f* claim; debt; demand, requirement
◇ **eine ~ abbuchen** to wipe off a debt [claim, debit balance]; **eine ~ ablehnen** to turn down a claim; **eine ~ abtreten** to cede a debt [claim]; **eine ~ an jmdn. abtreten** to assign [transfer] a claim to s.o.; **eine ~ an jmdn. haben** to have a claim on s.o.; **eine ~ anerkennen** to admit a claim; to acknowledge a debt; **eine ~ anmelden** to bring forward [submit] a claim; to lodge a proof of debt [a claim]; **eine ~ auf etwas erheben** to lay claim to s.th.; **eine ~ auf jmdn. übertragen** to assign [transfer] a claim to s.o.; to transfer a debt; **eine ~ aufgeben** to abandon [renounce] a claim; **eine ~ beanstanden** to demur to; **eine ~ befriedigen** to pay [settle] a claim; **eine ~ belegen** to prove a claim; **eine ~ bestreiten** to dispute a claim, to put a claim in question; **eine ~ durchsetzen** to push through a claim; **eine ~ einklagen** to take legal proceedings for the recovery of a debt, to litigate a claim; **eine ~ einreichen** to make a claim, to lay claim to; **eine ~ eintreiben** to recover [enforce] a debt; **eine ~ einziehen** to collect a debt; **eine ~ erfüllen** to answer [meet] a claim; **eine ~ erheben** to lodge a claim; **eine ~ erlassen** to release a claim; **eine ~ gegen jmdn. geltend machen** to claim s.th. from s.o.; **eine ~ nicht anerkennen** to disallow a claim; **eine ~ übertragen** to assign [transfer] a claim; **eine ~ vorbringen** to raise [make] a claim; **eine ~ zulassen** to admit [allow] a claim; **eine ~ zurückweisen** to turn down [reject] a claim; **seine ~ geltend machen** to assert [enforce] one's claim

~, **abgetretene** assigned claim
~, **ältere** old claim
~, **anmeldefähige** provable claim
~, **anmeldepflichtige** notifiable debt [claim]
~, **ausstehende** outstanding debt
~, **begründete** just [equitable] claim
~, **berechtigte** *s.* ~, **begründete**
~, **betagte** *s.* ~, **ältere**
~ **bevorrechtigte** preferential debt
~, **bevorzugt zu befriedigende** *s.* ~, **bevorrechtigte**
~, **blockierte** blocked debt
~, **buchmäßige** book claim
~, **dubiose** doubtful debt
~, **eingefrorene** frozen [blocked] debt
~, **einklagbare** legal [recoverable] debt
~, **fällige** debt due
~, **fingierte** simulated [bogus] claim
~, **gesicherte** secured debt [claim]
~, **gesperrte** *s.* ~, **blockierte**
~, **getilgte** claim [debt] paid
~, **gültige** existent debt [claim]
~, **hypothekarische** mortgage claim
~, **jederzeit realisierbare** solvent debt
~, **kurzfristige** short-term debt [claim]
~, **langfristige** long-term debt [claim]
~, **laufende** current account
~, **mittelfristige** medium-term debt [claim]
~ **nach Lohnerhöhung** demand for wage increase
~, **nachgewiesene** proved debt [claim]
~, **nachweisbare** provable claim
~, **nicht beitreibbare** *s.* ~, **uneinbringliche**
~, **nicht bevorrechtigte** non-preferential debt
~, **nicht durchgesetzte** dormant claim
~, **offenstehende** *s.* ~, **ausstehende**
~, **private** private [civil] claim
~, **privilegierte** *s.* ~, **bevorrechtigte**
~, **rechtmäßige** legal claim
~, **rückständige** debt overdue [in arrears]
~, **sofort fällige** liquid debt
~, **strittige** disputed claim
~, **übertriebene** excessive [unreasonable] demand
~, **unbegründete** unfounded debt [claim]

~, **unberechtigte** non-provable debt [claim]
~, **uneinbringliche** bad [irrecoverable] debt
~, **unsichere** doubtful claim
~, **unverzinsliche** debt without interest
~, **verfallene** forfeited [lapsed] claim
~, **verjährte** expired claim; stale debt
~, **vertraglich begründete** claim [debt] founded on contract
~, **verzinsliche** debt bearing interest
~, **vollstreckbare** enforceable claim
~, **wucherische** exorbitant [excessive] charge
~, **zweifelhafte** doubtful debt
Förderung f 1. advancement; promotion, furtherance; encouragement; 2. (min) haulage (coal etc.); delivery, discharge (fluid, gas etc.); output, production
~, **betriebliche** in-service [on-the-job] training
~, **wirtschaftliche** business promotion
Forderungen fpl claims; demands; debts; (acc) accounts receivable ◊ **den ~ entsprechen** to meet the requirements (quality of goods etc.); ~ **einklagen** to sue for debts; **gegenseitige ~ ausgleichen** to set off claims; **seine ~ belegen** to prove (one's) debts; **von seinen ~ abgehen** to withdraw one's claim
~ **an Kunden** (acc) trade account receivables
~ **aus laufender Rechnung** (acc) debts founded on open account
~, **ausstehende** outstanding debts
~ **aus Warenlieferungen und Leistungen** claims arising from commodity deliveries and services
~, **diverse** (acc) sundry debt(or)s
~, **gegenseitige** mutual debts; mutual claims
~, **sonstige** (acc) other accounts
~ **und Verbindlichkeiten** fpl (acc) debtors and creditors, receivables and payables
~, **verschiedene** s. ~, diverse
Forderungsabtretung f assignment [assignation, transfer] of a claim [debt]
Forderungsberechtigter m rightful claimant; beneficiary (under an insurance policy etc.)
Forderungsbestand m amount of debts
Forderungsbetrag m amount of claims
Forderungseinziehung f collection of debts
Forderungseinzugsverfahren n method of collecting customers' debts by the bank (by cashless transfer from the account of the recipient to the account of the supplier)
Förderungsgebiet n development area
Forderungskonto n debt account
Forderungskredit m bank loan for financing commodity turnover
Förderungsmaßnahmen fpl promotion measures, measures of encouragement
Forderungspapier n (fin) instrument entitling s.o. to a claim upon payment of money/delivery of goods (check, bill of exchange, bill of lading etc.)
Forderungspfändung f (jur) garnishment
Forderungspfändungsbeschluß m garnishee order
Forderungspfändungsverfahren n garnishee proceeding(s)
Forderungsrecht n right to claim; claim
Förderungssystem n promotion system
Forderungsteilbetrag m portion of claim [debt]
Forderungstitel m claim
Forderungsübertragung f s. **Forderungsabtretung**
Forderungsvermächtnis n (jur) testamentary disposition of claims
Forderungsverzeichnis n schedule of (a bankrupt's) estate
Forderungsverzicht m remission of a claim
Forderungswert m (monetary) value of a claim
Förderzeit f (materials) handling time
Förderziffer f (min) output [production] figure
Form f 1. form; shape; design; outline (car etc.); style (layout etc.); 2. mode (living etc.); type (government etc.); pattern (civilization etc.); 3. form, condition (persons etc.); 4. mould, frame (foundry etc.) ◊ **in mündlicher ~** orally; **in notarieller ~** before a notary; **in rechtsgültiger ~** in due form; **in schriftlicher ~** in writing; **schriftliche ~ erfordern** to require written evidence
~, **binäre** (d.pr.) binary quantic
~, **geschlossene** closed form (economy etc.)
~, **kubische** (maths) cubic quantic
~, **offene** open form (economy etc.)
~, **quadratische** (maths) quadric quantic
~, **schriftliche** written evidence
~, **vorgeschriebene** prescribed form, formality
formal formal (cause, reason etc.)
formalrechtlich in accordance with the letter of the law
Formalvertrag m formal contract
Format n size
Formation f formation; unit; system, order; period
~, **gesellschaftliche** social formation
Formblatt n form, (Am) blank ◊ **ein ~ ausfüllen** to fill up [in] a form, (Am) to fill out a blank
~, **amtliches** official [legal] form [(Am) blank]
Formel f formula
~, **Spearman-Brown'sche** (stats) Spearman-Brown formula
formell formal
Formen fpl 1. forms; shapes; designs (car etc.); 2. modes (living etc.); types (government etc.); patterns (civilization etc.); 3. moulds, frames (foundry etc.)

~ der **Bedürfnisbefriedigung** ways of meeting requirements [needs]
~ des **gesellschaftlichen Lebens** forms of social life
~, **gesellschaftliche** social conventions
Formfehler *m* flaw, irregularity *(document, procedure)*, technical defect *(contract etc.)*
formfrei *s.* formlos
Formgeber *m* industrial designer
formgebunden s.th. that must comply with legal formalities
Formgebung *f* forming, shaping, designing
~, **industrielle** industrial designing
formgemäß *s.* formgerecht
formgerecht in proper [due] form
Formgestalter *m* industrial designer
Formgestaltung *f* (industrial) designing
förmlich formal
formlos formless, informal *(contract, procedure, receipt etc.)*
Formlosigkeit *f* formlessness, informality, lack of form *(contract, document etc.)*
Formmangel *m* lack of form, want of legal form, informality *(document, procedure etc.)*
formnichtig invalid *(document etc. because of want of legal form)*
Formnichtigkeit *f* invalidity *(document etc. because of want of legal form)*
Formular *n s.* Formblatt
formulieren to formulate *(regulation, theorem, law of nature etc.)*, to word, to phrase *(contract etc.)*
Formulierung *f* formulation *(regulation, theorem, law of nature etc.)*, wording, phrasing *(contract etc.)*
Formung *f* forming, shaping *(metal etc.)*; modelling *(wax etc.)*; moulding *(material, character etc.)*
~, **spanabhebende** cutting shaping, shaping by cutting
~, **spanende** *s.* ~, spanabhebende
~, **spangebende** *s.* ~, spanabhebende
~, **spanlose** non-cutting shaping, shaping without cutting
Formvorschrift *f (jur)* formality, formal requirement
formwidrig incorrectly drawn up *(document etc.)*, not in accordance with [not in compliance with] formal requirements
Formzwang *m* obligation to comply with the statutory form
forschen to search (for), to investigate; to do research work
Forscher *m* researcher, research worker
Forscherdrang *m* urge to do research [to scholarly inquiry]
Forschergeist *m* spirit of research, inquiring (scholarly) mind

Forschergruppe *f* research unit, research team
Forschertrieb *m s.* Forscherdrang
Forschung *f* research (work)
~, **angewandte** applied research
~, **auftragsgebundene** commissioned research
~, **außerbetriebliche** external research
~, **betriebswirtschaftliche** business research
~, **ergonomische** research on human engineering [ergonomics]
~, **experimentelle** experimental research, experiment
~, **gemeinsame** joint research
~, **interdisziplinäre** interdisciplinary research
~, **kurzfristige** short-term research
~, **langfristige** long-term research
~, **naturwissenschaftliche** research in (the field of) natural science
~, **ökologische** ecological research
~, **ökonomische** economic research
~, ‚**reine**' pure research
~, **technische** engineering [industrial] research
~ und **Entwicklung** *f* research and development (R & D)
~ und **Lehre** *f* research and teaching
~, **wissenschaftliche** scientific research
~, **wissenschaftstheoretische** science-theory research, research in science of science
Forschungsablauf *m* flow [process] of research
Forschungsabteilung *f* research department [division]
Forschungsanstalt *f* research establishment [institute, centre, station]
Forschungsarbeit *f* research (work)
~, **selbständige wissenschaftliche** independent scientific research work
~, **wissenschaftliche** scientific research activities
Forschungsart *f* kind of research
Forschungsaufgabe *f* research work [task]
Forschungsaufgaben *fpl*:
~, **ausgewählte langfristige** selected long-term [long-range] research tasks [work]
Forschungsauftrag *m* research commission; research assignment
Forschungsaufwand *m* research expenditure(s) *(in terms of money, material, time etc.)*
~, **einmaliger** non-recurring [one-time] expenditure on research
~, **laufender** current expenditure on research; current expenditure on research and development
~, **nichtproduktiver** unproductive expenditure on research; unproductive expenditure on research and development
~, **produktiver** productive expenditure on research; productive expenditure on research and development

Forschungsausgaben *fpl* research expenditure(s) *(in terms of money only)*
Forschungsausrüstungen *fpl* research equipment
Forschungsbedarf *m* demand for research
Forschungsbeirat *m* advisory board for research
Forschungsbudget *n* research budget
Forschungsdauer *f* period of research
Forschungseffektivität *f* research efficiency; research and development efficiency
Forschungseinrichtung *f* research institution [centre, establishment]
Forschungsergebnisse *npl* research (results), results of research work [scientific investigation]
Forschungsfinanzierung *f* financing of research
~, **aufgabenbezogene** goal-oriented financing of research
Forschungsfonds *m* research fund
~, **betrieblicher** enterprise research fund
Forschungsfondsintensität *f* intensity of research funds
Forschungsgebiet *n* field of research
Forschungsgemeinschaft *f* research team; joint venture in research
Forschungsgegenstand *m* subject [field] of research
Forschungsgerät *n* research apparatus
Forschungsgrundfonds *m* fixed assets for research work, research capital
Forschungsgrundfondseffektivität *f* capital--output ratio in research
Forschungshaushalt *m* research budget
Forschungsingenieur *m* research engineer
Forschungsinstitut *n* research institute
Forschungsintensität *f* research intensity, intensity of research
Forschungsinvestitionen *fpl* (capital) investment(s) in science, science investment(s)
Forschungskapazität *f* research capacity
Forschungskooperation *f* co-operation in research
~, **internationale** international co-operation in research
Forschungskoordinierung *f* co-ordination of research
Forschungskosten *pl* research costs
Forschungskostenindex *m* cost-of-research index
Forschungslabor *n* research laboratory
Forschungsmethode *f* method of research
~, **allgemeine** general research method
~, **experimentelle** experimental research method
Forschungsmethodik *f* research methods [system]
Forschungsmilieu *n* research environment
Forschungsmittel *npl* resources for research

Forschungsobjekt *n* object [subject] of research
Forschungsökonomie *f* research economics *(planning, financing, organization etc., of research and development)*
Forschungsorganisation *f* organization of research
Forschungsorientierung *f* orientation of research
Forschungspersonal *n* research personnel [staff]
Forschungsplanung *f* planning of research
Forschungspolitik *f* research policy
Forschungspotential *n* research potential
Forschungsprognose *f* research forecast, prognosis of research
Forschungsprogramm *n* research programme
Forschungsprojekt *n* research project
~, **gemeinsames** joint research project
Forschungsrat *m* advisory board for research; research council
Forschungsreise *f* study tour
Forschungsrichtung *f* trend of research; school of research
Forschungsrisiko *n* research risk(s)
Forschungsschiff *n* research vessel [ship]
Forschungsstatistik *f* research statistics
Forschungsstätte *f* research institution [centre, station]
Forschungsstelle *f s.* **Forschungsstätte**
Forschungsstudium *n* research studies
Forschungstätigkeit *f* research (work) activities
Forschungsteam *n* research team
Forschungstechnologie *f* research technology
Forschungsthema *n* subject of research
Forschungsvertrag *m* research contract
Forschungsvorhaben *n* research project
Forschungszeit *f* period of research
Forschungszentrum *n* research centre
Forst *m* forest
Forstakademie *f* school of forestry
Forstamt *n* (local) forest superintendent's office
Forstarbeit *f* forestry work
Forstarbeiter *m* forestry worker
Forstbeamter *m* forest(ry) official [officer]
Forstbehörde *f* forest authority
Forstbenutzung *f s.* **Forstnutzung**
Forstberechtigung *f* forest right(s); right of utilizing [exploiting] forest products [resources]
Forstberuf *m* forestry occupation
Forstbetrieb *m* forestry enterprise [undertaking]
Forstbezirk *m* forest range
Forstdienst *m* forest service
Forsteleve *m* student [trainee] of forestry
Förster *m* forester; forest guard, *(Am)* (forest) ranger
Forstfach *n* forestry
Forstfrevel *m (jur)* (trespass involving) damage to a forest

Forstgarten *m* nursery (of young trees), arboretum
Forsthaus *n* forester's lodge [house]
Forsthoheit *f* exclusive right to the use of a forest
Forstkarte *f* forestry map
Forstmann *m* forester; forest worker
Forstmeister *m* head forester
Forstnebennutzung *f* utilization of secondary forest products
Forstnutzung *f* forest utilization
Forstökonomie *f s.* **Forstwirtschaft**
Forstordnung *f* forestry regulations
Forstrecht *n* forest law; forest rights
Forstrevier *n* forest district [range]; beat (of a forest)
Forstschädling *m* forest pest
Forstschule *f* forest training school, school of forestry
Forstschutz *m* forest protection
Forstverwaltung *f* forest administration
Forstwart *m* assistant forester
Forstwesen *n* forestry
Forstwirt *m* forestry expert, sylviculturist
Forstwirtschaft *f* forestry
forstwirtschaftlich forestry *(school, training, statistics etc.)*, sylvicultural *(methods, problems etc.)*, relating to forestry
Forstwirtschaftsjahr *n* forest year
Forstwirtschaftslehre *f* forest economics
Forstwissenschaft *f* science of forestry
Fortbestand *m* continued existence; continuation, continuance
fortbestehen to continue, to endure, to subsist; to remain in existence
fortbilden, sich to improve one's knowledge, to continue one's education [training]
Fortbildung *f* further [advanced, continued] education [training]
~, berufliche further vocational training
~, betriebliche on-the-job [in-service] training
Fortbildungskosten *pl* cost(s) of further education
Fortbildungskurs(us) *m* further education course; refresher course *(teacher etc.)*
Fortbildungslehrgang *m s.* **Fortbildungskurs**
Fortbildungsprogramm *n* programme of further education [training]
Fortbildungsschule *f* college of further education
fortentwickeln to develop further *(idea, design, character etc.)*; to develop, to expand *(industry etc.)*; **sich ~** to develop further
fortführen to carry on *(business etc.)*
Fortführung *f* continuation *(business etc.)*
Fortführungsinvestition *f* carry-over investment
fortgeschritten advanced

Fortkommen *n* progress *(in one's profession, business etc.)*; advancement *(in one's career)*
fortschreiben to project to a subsequent date *(plans etc.)*; to extrapolate *(statistical data)*; to adjust *(value of property etc.)*
Fortschreibung *f* adjustment *(value of property etc.)*; *(stats)* extrapolation; projection *(value of property, size of population etc.)*; continuation (of planning)
Fortschritt *m* progress, advance
~, gesellschaftlicher social progress
~, kultureller cultural progress
~, technischer technological progress
~, wirtschaftlicher economic progress
~, wissenschaftlich-technischer scientific and technological progress
fortschrittlich progressive *(ideas)*, advanced *(opinions, educational methods etc.)*
Fortschrittlichkeit *f* progressiveness *(institutions, parties etc.)*; advanced state *(thinking, ideas, educational methods etc.)*
fortschrittsfeindlich anti-progressive
Fortschrittsgedanke *m* conception of progress
Fortschrittskontrolle *f* following-up of technological progress
Fortschrittsrate *f* rate of development
fortzahlen to pay further
Fortzahlung *f* further payment
Fracht *f* 1. load, freight, goods; cargo *(ship)*; 2. carriage, freight(age), cartage ⋄ **~ aufnehmen** to take on freight; **~ berechnen** to charge freight; **~ bezahlt** carriage [freight] paid; **~ führen** to carry goods [freight]; **~ vorausbezahlt** carriage [freight] prepaid; **in ~ geben** to freight; **in ~ nehmen** to charter; **ohne ~** without freight, empty *(lorry etc.)*
~, durchgehende through-freight
~ gegen Nachnahme freight against cash on delivery (c.o.d.), freight forward
~, gestundete freight payment with respite
~, nicht lohnende unremunerative freight
~, tote dead freight
~, unterwegs befindliche freight in transit; floating cargo
~, verlorene lost freight
~, volle full cargo
~, zuviel erhobene freight overcharge
Frachtabnahme *f* acceptance of freight [*(Am)* shipment]
Frachtangebot *n* freight offered
Frachtaufschlag *m* extra carriage
Frachtausgleich *m* adjustment of freight rates
Frachtbasis *f s.* **Frachtparität**
Frachtbeförderung *f* transport of freight [goods]
Frachtbegünstigung *f s.* **Frachtermäßigung**
Frachtbenachrichtigung *f* arrival [landing] notice (of freight)

Frachtberechnung *f* calculation of freight (rates)
Frachtbörse *f* freight exchange
Frachtbrief *m* consignment note, way-bill, *(Am)* bill of lading
~, durchgehender through way-bill
~, erloschener spent bill of lading
~, internationaler international consignment note
Frachtbriefduplikat *n* duplicate consignment note [way-bill], *(Am)* duplicate bill of lading
Frachtbuch *n* freight book; book of cargo [lading, loading]
Frachtdampfer *m s.* **Frachter** 1.
Frachtdienst *m* freight service; shipping service
Frachteingangsbenachrichtigung *f s.* **Frachtbenachrichtigung**
Frachteinkommen *n* freight revenue [earnings]
Frachteinkünfte *pl s.* **Frachteinkommen**
Frachtempfänger *m* consignee
Frachtenausgleich *m* equalization of freight costs [rates]
Frachtenindex *m* freight rate index
Frachteninkasso *n* collection of freight charges
Fracht(en)makler *m* freight broker
Frachtenmarkt *m* freight market
Frachtenumschlag *m* freight turnover
Frachter *m* 1. freighter, cargo boat [vessel]; 2. freight [cargo] aircraft, air freighter
Frachtermäßigung *f* freight reduction
Fracht-Fahrgast-Schiff *n* passenger-cargo boat
Frachtflugzeug *n s.* **Frachter** 2.
Frachtforderung *f* freight claim
frachtfrei *s.* **Fracht vorausbezahlt**
Frachtführer *m* carrier
~, öffentlicher common carrier
Frachtführerpfandrecht *n* carrier's lien
Frachtfuhrunternehmen *n* carrying [carrier's] business [undertaking]
Frachtgebühr *f* carriage, freight(age)
Frachtgeld *n s.* **Frachtgebühr**
Frachtgeschäft *n* carrying trade; freight business; chartering business *(sea transport)*
Frachtgewicht *n* freight weight
Frachtgut *n* freight, (freight) goods; cargo, shipload
~, leicht verderbliches perishable freight
Frachtgutsendung *f* consignment
Frachtkalkulation *f* calculation of freight costs; calculation of carriage [freightage]
Frachtkilometer *m* freight kilometre
Frachtkonto *n* freight account
Frachtkontrakt *m s.* **Frachtvertrag**
Frachtkosten *pl* freight charges [costs], carriage, cartage, freightage ⋄ **~ bezahlen** to pay freight charges; **~ übernehmen** to take over freight charges, to take charge of freight costs

Frachtliste *f* freight list
Frachtlohn *m s.* **Frachtgebühr**
Frachtmeile *f* freight mile *(measurement according to freight kilometre)*
Frachtnachlaß *m s.* **Frachtermäßigung**
Frachtnote *f* freight note
Frachtpapiere *npl* freight documents; shipping documents
Frachtparität *f* freight parity (charge)
Frachtrabatt *m* freight discount [rebate(ment)]
Frachtrate *f* freight tariff [rate]
Frachtratenindex *m s.* **Frachtenindex**
Frachtraum *m* cargo compartment, hold *(of a ship)*; freight capacity
Frachtrechnung *f* freight bill [account, invoice]
Frachtsatz *m* freight tariff [rate], rate of freight, freightage
~, erhöhter increased (freight) rate
Frachtschiff *n s.* **Frachter** 1.
Frachtsendung *f* consignment
Frachtspediteur *m* freight forwarder, carrier
Frachtspesen *pl s.* **Frachtkosten**
Frachtstellung *f* terms of freight *(free on rail, free on board, free alongside ship etc.)*
Frachtstrecke *f* (freight) line [route]
Frachtstück *n* package, parcel; bale *(cotton)*
Frachtstundung *f* delay of carriage
Frachttarif *m* freight rates
~, amtlich genehmigter official (freight) rate
~, behördlich genehmigter *s.* **~, amtlich genehmigter**
~ mit ausgeschlossenem Risiko conditional (freight) rate
Frachttransport *m* transport of goods, goods traffic
Frachtunkosten *pl s.* **Frachtkosten**
Frachtvergütung *f* reimbursement of freight
Frachtverkehr *m* goods [*(Am)* freight] traffic
Frachtversender *m* consignor
Frachtversicherung *f* freight [cargo] insurance
Frachtvertrag *m* freight contract; charter-party *(ship)*
Frachtvorschuß *m* advance(d) freight [payment of freight(age)]
Frachtzahlung *f* freight payment
Frachtzettel *m* way-bill, freight note
Frachtzoll *m* customs duty on freight [cargo]
Frachtzuschlag *m* additional [extra] freight(age)
Frachtzustellung *f* delivery (of freight)
Frage *f* question; issue; problem; doubt ⋄ **außer ~ stehen** to be beyond question [doubt], there is no question [doubt] about *(s.th.)*; **eine ~ auf die Tagesordnung setzen** to place [put] a question on the agenda; **eine ~ aufwerfen** to raise a question; **eine ~ entscheiden** to solve a problem; to resolve a question; **es ist eine ~ der Zeit** it is a matter of time; **in ~ kommen**

to be possible; **in ~ stellen** to doubt; to call in(to) question; **nicht in ~ kommen** to be out of (the) question; **ohne (jede) ~** without (any) doubt; undoubtedly
~, brennende burning issue [question]
~, entscheidende crucial [decisive] question
~, freibeantwortbare s. **~ ohne vorgegebene Antwortmöglichkeiten**
~, geschlossene s. **~ mit vorgegebenen Antwortmöglichkeiten**
~ mit vorgegebenen Antwortmöglichkeiten *(stats)* closed-ended question
~, nationale national question [issue]
~, offene open(-ended) question
~ ohne vorgegebene Antwortmöglichkeiten *(stats)* open-ended question
~, politische political issue [question, problem]
~, schwebende unsettled [pending] question [problem]
~, soziale social question [issue]
~, strittige controversial question [issue]
~, ungelöste unsolved [unresolved] question [problem]
~, wirtschaftliche economic issue [question, problem]
Fragebogen *m* questionnaire, inquiry form
⋄ **einen ~ ausfüllen** to fill in a questionnaire
Fragen *fpl* questions; problems
~, allgemein interessierende questions of common interest [public concern]
~, gemeinsam interessierende questions of mutual interest
Fragenkomplex *m* complex of questions
Fragenkreis *m* range of questions
Fragenmethode *f* inquiry by questionnaire
Fragesteller *m* questioner
Fragestellung *f* formulation [statement, framing] of the question
Fragestunde *f* question time *(parliament etc.)*
Fraktion *f (pol)* parliamentary group [party]
Fraktionsführer *m* leader [chairman, chairperson] of the parliamentary group [party]
Fraktionsmitglied *n* member of the parliamentary group [party]
Fraktionssitzung *f* meeting of the parliamentary group [party]
Fraktionszwang *m* obligation to vote according to group policy, group discipline; *(UK)* control by Party Whips
Franchise *f (ins)* franchise
Frankatur *f (post)* 1. prepayment, franking; 2. postage
Frankaturzwang *m* obligation to prepay, compulsory prepayment of freight
frankieren to prepay; to stamp, to put stamps on, to frank *(letter etc.)*
frankiert prepaid, post-paid, stamped

Frankierung *f* prepayment (of postage); stamping
franko post-paid, prepaid; carriage paid *(parcels etc.)*; free of charges
Frankobrief *m* prepaid letter
Frankopreis *m* free of cost
Frankoumschlag *m* stamped envelope
Frankovermerk *m* notice of prepayment
Frau *f* woman, female; wife; Mrs., Ms. *(address)*
~, berufstätige working woman
~, geschiedene divorcee, divorced woman
~, ledige unmarried woman, single (woman)
~, unverheiratete s. **~, ledige**
~, verheiratete married woman
Frauenarbeit *f* female work
Frauenarbeitsschutz *m* women's labour protection
Frauenausschuß *m* women's committee
Frauenberuf *m* women's occupation
Frauenbeschäftigtengrad *m* female employment ratio
Frauenbeschäftigung *f* female employment
Frauenbewegung *f* women's movement; feminist movement
Frauenemanzipation *f* women's emancipation, emancipation of women
Frauenorganisation *f* women's organization
~, internationale international women's organization
Frauenqualifizierung *f* further [advanced, continued] training of women *(system of sponsoring women's activities in professional and public affairs)*
Frauenrechte *npl* women's rights
Frauenstimmrecht *n* s. **Frauenwahlrecht**
Frauenwahlrecht *n* women's [female] suffrage
Fautfracht *f* dead freight
frei free; prepaid *(postage)*; clear *(road etc.)*; gratis, gratuitous, free of charge *(not to be paid for)*; independent *(country, peoples etc.)*; blank *(paper etc.)*; vacant *(position, post etc.)*; unrationed, non-rationed *(goods etc.)*
Freiaktie *f* bonus share [*(Am)* stock]
freiberuflich freelance ⋄ **~ arbeiten** s. **~ tätig sein**; **~ tätig sein** to work as a freelance, to freelance
Freibetrag *m* tax-free amount; allowance *(of currency exported without restriction etc.)*
freibleibend subject to being sold; subject to alteration without notice ⋄ **~ anbieten** to make a conditional offer
Freifahrt *f* free travel *(granted to railway personnel etc.)*
Freifahr(t)schein *m* free (travel) ticket
Freifläche *f* open space *(town and city planning)*
Freiflächenausstellung *f* outdoor display [exhibition]

Freiflächenstand *m* open-air stand
Freigabe *f* derequisition *(attached goods etc.)*, decontrol *(rationed goods)*, deblocking *(funds, accounts etc.)*, floating *(exchange rates)*
freigeben to derequisition *(attached goods etc.)*, to decontrol *(rationed goods)*, to deblock *(accounts)*, to float *(exchange rates)*
Freigeländeausstellung *f s.* **Freiflächenausstellung**
Freigeländefläche *f* open-air space
Freigepäck *n* free luggage
Freigrenze *f* free quota, tax-free limit, limit of tax-free income
Freigut *n* duty-free goods
Freihafen *m* free port
Freihafengebiet *n* free (trade) zone
Freihandel *m* free trade
Freihandelspolitik *f* free trade policy
Freihandelstheorie *f* free trade theory
Freihandelszone *f* free trade area
Frei-Haus-Lieferung *f* carriage paid delivery
Freiheit *f* freedom, liberty
~, **persönliche** personal liberty
~, **politische** political freedom [liberty]
Freiheiten *fpl* liberties
~, **bürgerliche** civil liberties
Freiheitskampf *m* freedom struggle, struggle for freedom
Freikarte *f* free ticket
Freilager *n* bonded warehouse
Freiland *n* open land; outdoors
Freilandgemüse *n* outdoor vegetables
Freiliste *f (cust)* free list
freimachen to prepay; to stamp, to put stamps on, to frank (letter etc.)
Freimachung *f* prepayment (of postage); stamping
Freischicht *f* cancelled shift
Freisetzung *f* release
~ **von Arbeitskräften** release of manpower
Freisetzungseffekt *m* release effect *(manpower)*
freisprechen *(jur)* to acquit *(s.o. of/on s.th.)*
Freisprechung *f s.* **Freispruch**
Freispruch *m* acquittal
freistellen to release *(workers etc.)*; to give *s.o.* leave *(for training etc.)*; to leave the choice [decision] open *(to s.o.)*
Freistellung *f* release *(workers etc.)*; leave *(for training etc.)*
~, **bezahlte** paid leave *(for training etc.)*
Freiverkehr *m* unofficial trading
Freiverkehrsbörse *f* kerb market
Freivermerk *m* postage paid, note of prepayment (of freight)
freiwillig voluntary *(service, work, saving, contribution, participation, decision, insurance etc.)*, non-compulsory *(insurance etc.)*

Freizeichnung *f* stipulation of exemption from liability
Freizeichnungsklausel *f* saving clause; *(ins)* memorandum clause
Freizeit *f* leisure, spare time
Freizeitgestaltung *f* recreational [leisure] activities, planned recreation
~, **sinnvolle** meaningful recreational [leisure] activities
Freizeitindustrie *f* recreation [leisure] industry
Freizeitverlust *m* loss of leisure
Freizone *f* free (trade) zone
freizügig *(bank)* unrestricted
Freizügigkeit *f* liberty to move; free movement *(labour etc.)*; freedom *(movement of capital etc.)*
Freizügigkeitsverkehr *m* all-banks savings account system *(entitling holder to deposit or withdraw money at any bank or post office)*
fremd foreign *(country etc.)*; alien *(person, custom etc.)*; strange *(idea etc.)*; *(fin)* outside, borrowed *(money, capital etc.)*
Fremdarbeiter *m* foreign worker
Fremdaufwendungen *fpl* extraneous expenses
Fremdbesitz *m* property held in custody
Fremdbezug *m* supplies of goods from outside
fremdenfeindlich hostile to strangers [foreigners]
Fremdenfeindlichkeit *f* hostility to strangers [foreigners]
Fremdenführer *m* tourist guide
Fremdengesetz *n* alien's act
Fremdenheim *n* boarding [guest] house
Fremdenindustrie *f* tourist industry
Fremdenverkehr *m* tourism; tourist trade; tourist traffic
Fremdenverkehrsabgabe *f* tax levied in a tourist centre
Fremdenverkehrsgewerbe *n* tourist trade [industry]
Fremdenverkehrsstatistik *f* tourist statistics
Fremdenverkehrsverband *m* regional tourist association
Fremdenverkehrsverein *m* local tourist association
Fremdenverkehrswerbung *f* tourist advertising
Fremdenverkehrswirtschaft *f* tourist business sector; tourist trade
Fremdfinanzierung *f* financing through credits [with outside capital], outside financing
Fremdgeld *n* trust money [funds]; liabilities
Fremdgeschäft *n* transaction for third account
Fremdherrschaft *f* foreign rule [domination]
Fremdkapital *n* borrowed [outside] capital
Fremdkapitalanteil *m* share of borrowed [outside] capital
Fremdversicherung *f* insurance by proxy, third--party insurance *(insurance policy taken by s.o. other than the person to be insured)*

Fremdwährung *f* foreign currency
Fremdwährungsschuldverschreibung *f* foreign exchange bond
Fremdwährungsversicherung *f* foreign currency insurance
Fremdwährungswechsel *m* foreign exchange bill
Fremdwerte *mpl (bank)* deposits
Frequenzmethode *f (stats)* frequency method
Freundschaftswechsel *m* accommodation bill
Frieden *m* peace ⋄ ~ **schließen** to make peace
Friedensbewegung *f* peace movement
Friedenspolitik *f* peace policy
Friedensproduktion *f* peace-time production
Friedensprogramm *n* peace programme
Friedensrat *m* peace council
Friedenssicherung *f* safeguarding of peace
Friedensverhandlungen *fpl* peace negotiations
Friedensvertrag *m* peace treaty
Friedenswirtschaft *f* peace-time economy
Frischgewicht *n* green weight *(vegetables, skins etc.)*
Frischhaltepackung *f* air-tight [keep-fresh] packet
Frischwarenmarkt *m* perishable [fresh] goods market
Frist *f* deadline, closing date; fixed [limited] period [space] of time, time allowed *(for completion of work, payment of a debt etc.)*, term *(payment, notice etc.)*, time-limit, date, time *(payment, completion of task etc.)* ⋄ **eine ~ einhalten** to meet the deadline; **eine ~ einräumen** to grant a respite; **eine ~ setzen** to fix [set] a time-limit; **eine ~ verlängern** to extend the time-limit; **eine ~ versäumen** to fail to comply with a term; **eine ~ zugestehen** to grant [accord] a respite; **in der vorgeschriebenen ~** within the required time [prescribed period]; **in kürzester ~** within a very short time; **innerhalb einer gewissen ~** within a certain (period of) time; **nach Ablauf der ~** after expiration of this period; **unter Einhaltung einer ~** keeping within a period of time; **vor Ablauf der ~** before expiration of this period
~, **abgelaufene** expired time
~, **angemessene** reasonable length of time
~, **äußerste** final [ultimate] date
~, **kurze** short term [period (of time)]
~, **lange** long term [period (of time)]
~, **letzte** final respite
~, **obligatorische** obligatory [traditional] period (of time)
~, **vertragliche** contractual period (of time); contractually fixed date
Fristablauf *m* expiration [expiry] of term; end [expiration] of a (fixed) period

Fristberechnung *f* calculation of payment deadline
Fristbewilligung *f* grant(ing) of time [a respite]
Fristen- und Terminplan *m* time and date schedule
Frist(en)- und Terminplanung *f* time and date scheduling [planning]
fristgemäß in due time, within a prescribed period [term]
fristgerecht *s.* **fristgemäß**
Fristgesuch *n (jur)* request for time; request for a respite
fristlos without notice [warning]
Fristsetzung *f* setting of a time limit
Fristüberschreitung *f* exceeding the time limit, failure to observe a time limit [to meet the deadline]
Fristverlängerung *f* extension of time, prolongation of a term; extension of term of payment
Fristversäumnis *n* failure to observe a time limit
Fristwechsel *m* time-bill
frostbeständig *(agric)* frost-resistant *(plants etc.)*
Frostbeständigkeit *f (agric)* frost resistance *(plants etc.)*
frostempfindlich frost-tender
frosten to freeze *(goods etc.)*
frostgeschädigt damaged [injured] by frost
Frostschaden *m* frost damage
Frostschadenversicherung *f* frost damage insurance
Frostzone *f (agric)* freezing zone *(soil etc.)*
Frucht *f* fruit; crop, produce; corn, cereals ⋄ **die ~ auf dem Halm verkaufen** to sell the crop standing; **die ~ steht gut** the corn looks good [well]
Fruchtart *f* type [kind] of fruit
fruchtbar fertile *(soil etc.)*; prolific *(species, breed etc.)*; fruitful *(discussion etc.)*
Fruchtbarkeit *f* fertility *(soil etc.)*; prolificacy, fecundity *(species, breed etc.)*, fruitfulness *(discussion, idea etc.)*
Fruchtbarkeitsziffer *f* fertility index
Früchte *fpl* fruit, fruits; rewards, results *(work, research, industry etc.)*
~ **der Arbeit** rewards [results] of work [labour]
~, **getrocknete** dried fruit
~, **reife** ripe fruit
~, **unreife** unripe fruit
Früchteverarbeitung *f* fruit processing
Früchteverarbeitungsindustrie *f* fruit processing industry
Fruchtfolge *f* crop rotation
Fruchtwechsel *m s.* **Fruchtfolge**
Fruchtwechselwirtschaft *f* crop rotation farming; system of crop rotation

Frühaussaat *f s.* **Frühjahrsaussaat**
Frühbezugspreis *m* subscription price
Frühbezugsrabatt *m* subscription discount
Frühbörse *f (st.ex.)* morning [early] market
Frühdienst *m* (early) morning duty
Frühgeburt *f* premature birth
Frühgemüse *n* early vegetable(s)
Frühinvalidität *f* disablement before retirement
Frühjahrsaussaat *f* spring-time [early] sowing
Frühjahrsbestellung *f* spring-time cultivation, seed-bed preparation and sowing
Frühjahrsmesse *f* spring (trade) fair
Frühkapitalismus *m* early capitalism
Frühpost *f* morning [first] mail
Frühschicht *f* (early) morning shift
frühtragend *(agric)* early-fruiting *(variety etc.)*
Frühverkaufsstelle *f* early opening shop
Frühzustellung *f s.* **Frühpost**
F-Test *m (stats)* variance-ratio test
Fuhre *f* carriage-load; cart-load; waggon-load
Führerschein *m* driving licence, *(Am)* driver's license
~, **internationaler** international driving licence
Führerscheinentzug *m* disqualification from driving; suspension of s.o.'s driving licence *(for a certain period of time)*
Fuhrgeld *n s.* **Fuhrlohn**
Fuhrgeschäft *n s.* **Fuhrunternehmen**
Fuhrkosten *pl s.* **Fuhrlohn**
Fuhrlohn *m* cartage, carriage
Fuhrpark *m* fleet of vehicles
Führung *f* 1. management *(enterprise etc.)*; leadership *(team of workers, party etc.)*; guidance, guiding *(people etc.)*; 2. conduct *(negotiations etc.)*; 3. conduct, behaviour; 4. use *(title etc.)*; 5. *(tech)* guide(way); 6. *(fin)* keeping, conducting, carrying *(account etc.)* ◇ **mit der ~ der Geschäfte beauftragt** charged with running the business; charged with conducting the affairs *(diplomatic service)*
~ **der Bücher** bookkeeping
~ **der Geschäfte** running (of) the business; conducting [conduct of] the affairs *(diplomatic service)*
~ **der Kassengeschäfte** managing [keeping] the cash transactions
~, **kollektive** collective leadership
~ **von Konten** keeping of accounts
Führungsaufgabe *f* executive function
Führungsbereich *m* managerial [management] department
Führungsebene *f* managerial [management] level
~, **höhere** higher management
~, **mittlere** middle management
~, **oberste** top management
~, **untere** lower management

Führungseigenschaften *fpl* managerial [executive] qualities; leadership qualities *(government, party)*
Führungsentscheidung *f* management [managerial] decision
Führungsfunktion *f (com)* management [managerial] function; *(pol)* leadership function
Führungsgremium *n s.* **Führungsgruppe**
Führungsgröße *f (d.pr.)* control quantity; *(tech)* reference input (signal)
Führungsgruppe *f* managerial group *(in enterprises etc.)*; leading [executive] body *(parties etc.)*
Führungshierarchie *f* management hierarchy, echelon
Führungsinstrumente *npl* 1. management methods [techniques]; 2. machines and devices used in management and administration *(computers, data bank etc.)*
Führungskraft *f* manager, executive *(enterprise etc.)*; leader *(party etc.)*; leading force (leadership) *(in a country, movement etc.)*; office-bearer *(association etc.)*
~, **kaufmännische** business executive
~, **technische** technical executive
Führungskräfte *fpl* management [managerial] personnel [staff] *(enterprise etc.)*; leaders *(party, country etc.)*
Führungskrise *f* leadership crisis, crisis of leadership
Führungslehre *f* theory of management
Führungsmannschaft *f* management team
Führungsnachwuchs *m* junior managerial staff, junior executives; potential leaders *(party etc.)*
Führungsorgan *n* management [managerial] body; controlling body
Führungsposition *f* management [managerial] position *(in enterprises etc.)*; position of leadership, leading position *(party, country etc.)*
Führungsrolle *f* leading role [part]
Führungsschicht *f* managerial section; management; leading stratum; group [stratum] of leaders
Führungsspitze *f* top management *(enterprises etc.)*; top leadership [leaders]; top echelon *(party, country etc.)*
Führungsstab *m* operational staff
Führungsstil *m* style of leadership [management]
Führungstätigkeit *f* managerial activity
Führungswissenschaft *f* science of management
Führungszeugnis *n* certificate of conduct
Fuhrunternehmen *n* carrier, trucking company, haulage contracting firm, firm of hauliers
Füllgewicht *n* net weight *(contents of tin, bottle etc.)*; capacity (in weight) *(washing machine etc.)*; weight of filling *(quilt etc.)*

Füllgut *n* contents *(container etc.)*; charge *(furnace etc.)*
Füllmenge *f* capacity *(tank etc.)*
Füllprogramm *n* (co-ordinated) production programme
~, optimales optimum [optimal] production programme
Fund *m* find *(of s.th.)*; discovery *(oil, gold etc.)*
Fundbüro *n* lost-property office
fundieren to fund, to consolidate *(loan, debt etc.)*
fundiert funded *(debt, bill of exchange etc.)*; well-established *(business etc.)*
Fündigkeit *f (min)* presence of workable ore [oil]
Fundlohn *m* reward to the finder (of lost property)
Fundmeldung *f* notification of a find
Fundort *m* place where an object is [was] found
Fundrecht *n* law relating to objects found; right of the finder to the object found; *(min)* right of the discoverer to mineral resources
Fundsache *f* object found, (piece of) lost property
Fundstätte *f s.* **Fundort**
Fundstelle *f s.* **Fundort**
Fundstück *n s.* **Fundsache**
Fundunterschlagung *f* stealing [larceny] by finding
Fundus *m* 1. piece [plot] of land; property; ground(s), land; 2. fund *(knowledge etc.)*; resources *(money etc.)*; 3. equipment *(including costumes, props etc.; in theatres)*
Fünfjahrplan *m* five-year plan
Fünfjahrplanabschnitt *m* five-year plan section, section of the five-year plan
Fünfkanal-Lochstreifen *m (d.pr.)* five-channel perforated tape
Fünftage(arbeits)woche *f* five-day (working) week
Fungibilität *f* interchangeability, fungibility *(goods etc.)*
fungieren to function *(as head of an office etc.)*; to act, to officiate *(as an official etc.)*; to serve, to do *(in place of s.th.)*
Funkanlage *f* radio installation [equipment, facilities], wireless installation
Funkausstellung *f* radio exhibition
Funkdienst *m* radio (communication) service
Funkeinrichtung *f s.* **Funkanlage**
Funkempfangsanlage *f s.* **Funkanlage**
Funker *m* radio [wireless] operator
Funkfernschreiber *m* radio teletyper
Funkfernsprecher *m* radio telephone
Funklotterie *f* radio lottery
Funkmechaniker *m* radio mechanic
Funksendeanlage *f s.* **Funkanlage**
Funksprechverkehr *m* radio [wireless] telecommunications

Funkstation *f s.* **Funkstelle**
Funkstelle *f* radio [broadcasting] station
Funktaxi *n* radio taxi
Funktechnik *f* radio [wireless] engineering; radio technology
Funktechniker *m* radio engineer
Funktelefonie *f* radiotelephony, wireless telephony
Funktelegrafie *f* radio [wireless] telegraphy
Funktelegramm *n* radio telegram, radiogram
Funktion *f* 1. function; office, duties *(person etc.)*; 2. *(maths)* function; 3. corollary, result, product *(thought etc.)* ⋄ **eine ~ auf jmdn. übertragen** to devolve authority to s.o.; **in der ~ als** in the function as *(head of department etc.)*; **in ~ treten** to assume duties
~, ausübende executive function
~, Boolesche *(stats)* Boolean function
~, charakteristische *(stats)* characteristic function
~, einstweilige provisional function [duty]
~, erzeugende *(stats)* generating function
~, Gaußsche *(stats)* Gaussian function
~, gesellschaftliche function in a political [social] organization
~, hyperbolische *(maths)* hyperbolic function
~, inverse *(maths)* inverse function
~, kubische *(maths)* cube function
~, logarithmische *(maths)* logarithmic function
~, logische *(stats)* logical variable
~, mathematische mathematical function
~, momenterzeugende *(stats)* moment generating function
~, quadratische *(maths)* square function
~, staatliche governmental function
~, tetrachorische *(stats)* tetrachoric function
~, vollziehende *s.* **~, ausübende**
funktional functional
Funktionalabteilung *f* operational department *(production department, service department etc.)*
Funktionalanalyse *f (stats, maths)* functional analysis
Funktionalgleichung *f (stats, maths)* functional equation
Funktionalismus *m* functionalism
Funktionalmatrix *f (maths)* functional matrix
Funktionalorgan *n s.* **Funktionalabteilung**
Funktionalsystem *n* staff management system
Funktionalzusammenhang *m* interdependence, functional coherence
Funktionär *m* functionary, office-holder, office-bearer *(in a political organization)*
Funktionen *fpl*:
~ des Geldes functions of money
~, orthogonale *(stats)* orthogonal functions
funktionieren to function, to work *(machine etc.)*
Funktionieren *n* functioning *(economy etc.)*

Funktionsbild *n* job profile
Funktionsdauer *f* total [overall] operating time
Funktionsdiagramm *n* (*stats*) functional diagram
funktionsfähig functionable, workable; capable of operating [working]; in order
Funktionsfähigkeit *f* workability; capability of operating [working]
Funktionsfeld *n* radius of action
Funktionsgleichung *f s.* **Funktionalgleichung**
Funktionsmodell *n* function model
Funktionsmuster *n* pattern of function; function model
Funktionsplan *m* job description (*contains all tasks and powers of an employee within a certain sphere of responsibility*)
Funktionsprobe *f* operational test
~, **technische** technical service test
Funktionsprüfung *f* operational checking; (*d.pr.*) functional check [test]
funktionssicher fail-safe
Funktionssicherheit *f* fail-safety
Funktionsspiegel *m s.* **Funktionsplan**
Funktionsstörung *f* malfunction (*system, machine etc.*), defect, trouble
Funktionstafel *f* list of functions
funktionstüchtig in operating condition
Funktionstüchtigkeit *f s.* **Funktionssicherheit**
Funktionswechsel *m* change(s) in function (*redistribution of tasks of office-holders, officials etc.*)
Funktionswert *m* 1. (*stats, maths*) value of a function; 2. (*ind*) operation [operating] value (*machine etc.*)
Funktionszeichen *n* (*maths*) functional symbol
Funktionszeit *f* operating time; (*d.pr.*) action period (*store*)
Funktionszulage *f* allowance (*for managerial personnel in institutions, government bodies, etc. for extra responsibilities*)
Funktionszyklus *m* operational cycle
Funkverkehr *m* radio communication(s)
~, **kommerzieller** commercial radio communication(s)
Funkwerbung *f* radio advertising
Funkzeugnis *n* radio telecommunication licence
Furchenbewässerung *f* (*agric*) furrow irrigation
Fürsorge *f* care, solicitude; welfare, welfare work [service(s)]
~, **ärztliche** medical care; under the care of a doctor
~, **behördliche** public welfare service(s)
~, **freie** voluntary welfare service(s)
~ **für Körperbehinderte** welfare service(s) for (the) physically handicapped (persons)
~ **für Strafentlassene** after-care for discharged prisoners

~, **geschlossene** institutional care
~, **offene** (financial) assistance (*in the form of pensions, reliefs, benefits etc.*)
~, **öffentliche** public welfare work; public relief (*as money*)
~, **private** voluntary welfare work
Fürsorgeamt *n* welfare centre
Fürsorgeanstalt *f* reformatory
Fürsorgearbeit *f* social work
Fürsorgeausgaben *fpl* welfare expenditure(s)
Fürsorgeausschuß *m* (public) welfare committee
Fürsorgebehörde *f* (state) welfare authority
fürsorgeberechtigt eligible for public relief
Fürsorgeeinrichtung *f* welfare institution [establishment]
Fürsorgeempfänger *m* recipient of public relief
Fürsorgeerziehung *f* treatment of young offenders
Fürsorgelasten *fpl* funds used for welfare services; (public) welfare expenditure(s)
Fürsorgepflicht *f* obligation to provide welfare services
Fürsorgeprogramm *n* welfare programme
Fürsorger *m* social [welfare] worker
Fürsorgerecht *n* legislation relating to welfare services; welfare service law(s)
Fürsorgerin *f* woman social [welfare] worker, woman welfare officer
fürsorgerisch welfare
Fürsorgestaat *m* welfare state
Fürsorgestelle *f* welfare centre
Fürsorgeunterstützung *f* public relief
Fürsorgeverband *m* welfare association
Fürsorgeverein *m* (voluntary) welfare organization
Fürsorgewesen *n* social welfare (system)
fürsorglich solicitous; thoughtful; considerate
Fürsorglichkeit *f* solicitude; thoughtfulness; considerateness
Fusion *f* fusion, merger, consolidation
fusionieren to merge, to combine, to fuse, to consolidate
Fusionist *m* fusionist
fusionistisch fusionist (*tendency etc.*)
Fusionsanhänger *m s.* **Fusionist**
Fusionsbedingungen *fpl* terms of merger
Fusionsbilanz *f* balance sheet for merger; consolidated balance sheet
Fusionsgewinn *m* consolidation profit(s)
Fusionskosten *pl* costs of merger, consolidation costs
Fusionsüberschuß *m s.* **Fusionsgewinn**
Fusionsvertrag *m* deed of amalgamation
Fußbodenleger *m* floor-layer
Fußgänger *m* pedestrian
Fußgängerbrücke *f* foot-bridge

Fußgängerüberweg *m* pedestrian crossing; zebra crossing
Fußgängerunterführung *f* pedestrian subway, *(Am)* underpass
Fußgängerverkehr *m* pedestrian traffic
Fußgängerzone *f* pedestrian area [zone, precinct], traffic-free zone [area] *(usually in city shopping centres)*
Fußpfleger *m* chiropodist
Fustage *f* 1. empty barrels *(crates, sacks etc.)*; 2. charge for containers
Fusti *pl* 1. impurities *(contained in goods delivered)*; 2. allowance [reduction, rebate] for impurities *(contained in goods delivered)*
Futter *n* 1. *(agric)* food, feed, fodder, forage; 2. *(ind)* lining *(coat, furnace, window etc.)*; chuck *(lathe etc.)* ⋄ **gut im ~ sein** *(agric)* to be well fattened
~, **frisches** fresh forage [fodder]
~, **grünes** green (fodder)
Futteranbau *m* cultivation [growing] of fodder
Futteraufnahmevermögen *n* feeding capacity *(animals)*
Futteraufriß *m (agric)* fodder diagram *(comparing fodder consumption and milk yield)*
Futterausnutzung *f* utilization of forage [fodder]
Futterautomat *m (agric)* automatic feeder
Futterbau *m s.* **Futteranbau**
Futterbedarf *m* fodder [feed, forage] requirement(s)
Futterbereitung *f* preparation of (animal) feed [food]
Futtereinheit *f* fodder unit
Futterfläche *f* forage crop area
Futtergerste *f* fodder barley
Futtergetreide *n* fodder cereals, feed grain
Futterkalender *m (agric)* feeding manual
Futterkartoffeln *fpl* fodder potatoes
Futterkuchen *m* feed(ing) cake
Futtermangel *m* lack of fodder [forage]; shortage [scarcity] of fodder [forage]
Futtermittel *n* feed(stuff), fodder
Futtermittelanbau *m* cultivation of feed [feedstuff(s), feeding stuff(s)]
Futtermittelbewertung *f* feed(stuffs) [feeding stuffs] evaluation, evaluation of feed [feedstuff(s), feeding stuff(s)]
~ **in Naturalform** evaluation of feed [feedstuff(s), feeding stuff(s)] in physical terms
~, **wertmäßige** evaluation of feed [feedstuff(s), feeding stuff(s)] in value terms *(for the purpose of cost accounting)*
Futtermittelbilanz *f* balance sheet of fodder sources and uses
Futtermittelbuch *n* feeding-stuff book *(registration of fodder delivered by an agricultural co--operative to its members)*

Futtermitteleinheit *f* feedstuff unit, unit of feedstuff(s)
Futtermittelfonds *m* stock of fodder [feed, feedstuff(s), feeding stuff(s)]
Futtermittelindustrie *f* feedstuffs industry
Futtermittelmarkt *m* feedstuffs market
Futtermittelproduktion *f* feed(stuffs) production
Futtermittelverordnung *f* feedstuffs regulation *(regulating feedstuff production etc.)*
füttern 1. to feed; 2. to line *(coat etc.)*
Futternorm *f* daily maintenance energy requirement
Futterpflanzen *fpl* fodder [forage] crops
Futterplan *m* feeding plan
Futterplatz *m* feeding place [area]
Futterreserve *f* reserve fodder
Futtersilo *m/n* silo (for fodder)
Fütterung *f* feeding
Fütterungsnorm *f s.* **Futternorm**
Futterverarbeitung *f s.* **Futterverwertung**
Futterverwerter *m (agric)* fodder utilizer
Futterverwertung *f* utilization of fodder [forage, feed]
Futterwert *m* feeding [nutritive] value
Futterwerttabelle *f* table [list] of feeding values
Futterwirtschaft *f* fooder farming *(organization of production, distribution and storage of fodder and feeding of livestock)*
Futterzeit *f s.* **Fütterzeit**
Fütterzeit *f* feeding time
Futterzubereitung *f* preparation of feeding stuffs [food, feed, foodstuffs]
Futurismus *m* futurism
Futurist *m* futurist
futuristisch futuristic
F-Verteilung *f (stats)* F-distribution, variance--ratio distribution
~, **nicht zentrale** *(stats)* non-central F-distribution

G

Gabe *f* 1. gift; present; donation; 2. gift, natural ability, talent
gabeln to fork up, to pick up with a fork *(hay etc.)*; **sich ~** to bifurcate, to divide *(road, river etc.)*
Gabelung *f* forking, bifurcation *(road, river etc.)*
Gage *f* salary, pay
Galanterieartikel *mpl s.* **Galanteriewaren**
Galanteriewaren *fpl* fancy goods; (costume) jewellery; novelties

Galanteriewarenhändler *m* fancy goods dealer; (cheap) jeweller; dealer in novelties
Gallone *f* gallon *(measure for liquids)*
Gallup-Befragung *f* Gallup poll
Gallup-Institut *n* Gallup Institute *(of public opinion poll)*
Galvaniseur *m* worker in electroplating
Gamma-Funktion *f (stats)* gamma function
~, **unvollständige** *(stats)* incomplete gamma function
Gamma-Koeffizient *m (stats)* gamma coefficient
Gamma-Verteilung *f (stats)* gamma distribution
Gang *m* 1. walk, gait *(persons etc.)*; 2. course *(events, meal etc.)*; 3. turn *(screw etc.)*; gear *(engine etc.)*; 4. corridor; gangway *(aircraft etc.)*; passage; 5. *(min)* vein, seam, lode; lead *(metal)*; reef *(gold)*; ✧ **etwas in ~ bringen** s. **etwas in ~ setzen**; **etwas in ~ halten** to keep s.th. running [in operation] *(machine etc.)*; to keep s.th. going [alive] *(debate etc.)*; **etwas in ~ setzen** to set s.th. in action, to actuate, to set to work, to start *(machine etc.)*; to bring [call] s.th. into action, to set s.th. on foot [in train] *(process etc.)*; to get s.th. going *(debate etc.)*; **in vollem ~ sein** to be in full swing; to be in full operation *(factory, scheme etc.)*; to be in progress, to be in train *(negotiations etc.)*
~ **der Ereignisse** course of events
~, **säkularer** *(stats)* secular trend
~, **überdeckter** covered passage [way]
~, **unterirdischer** underground [subterranean] passage
gangbar 1. feasible, practicable *(plan. etc.)*; 2. current *(money etc.)*; saleable, marketable *(goods)*
Gangbarkeit *f* 1. feasibility, practicability *(plan etc.)*; 2. currency *(money etc.)*; saleability *(goods etc.)*
gängig s. **gangbar** 2.
Gängigkeit *f* s. **Gangbarkeit** 2.
ganz all; whole, entire, complete, undivided; altogether ✧ **im ganzen** in all [full], altogether, all told; in the aggregate; in the lump; in bulk; **im ganzen bezahlen** to pay in full; **im ganzen gesehen** on balance, taking one thing with another, taking it by and large, all things considered; **im ganzen kaufen** to buy in bulk
Ganzfabrikat *n* finished product [article]
Ganzholzbauweise *f* (method of) all-wood construction
ganzjährig lasting a full [whole] year; operating all the year (round)
Ganzmetallkonstruktion *f* all-metal construction
Ganzpacht *f (approx.)* farm from which the tenant enjoys the entire profits, full profit-keeping tenancy

ganzseitig full-page *(advertisement etc.)*, covering a whole page
Ganzstahlkonstruktion *f* all-steel construction
ganztägig all-day, full-time ✧ ~ **arbeiten** to work full-time
Ganztagsarbeit *f* s. **Ganztagsbeschäftigung**
Ganztagsbeschäftigung *f* full-time job [employment]
Ganztagsschule *f* whole-day school; (system of) whole-day schooling
Ganztagsversorgung *f* round-the-clock [day--and-night] catering
ganzzahlig *(maths)* integral *(number, value etc.)*
Ganzzahligkeit *f (maths)* integrity *(number, value etc.)*
Garage *f* garage
Garagenbesitzer *m* garage owner
Garagenbesitzerhaftpflichtversicherung *f* garage owner's liability insurance
Garagenhaftpflichtversicherung *f* garage liability insurance
Garagenmiete *f* garage rent
Garant *m* guarantor; surety
Garantie *f* guarantee, warranty, security guaranty; pledge *(execution of contracts)* ✧ **ein Jahr ~ haben** to be guaranteed for one year; **für jmds. Verhalten ~ übernehmen** to vouch for s.o.'s good conduct; ~ **für etwas übernehmen** to guarantee s.th., to warrant s.th.; to stand surety for *(debt)*; ~ **gewähren** to guarantee; ~ **leisten** to guarantee, to warrant; ~ **stellen** to give guarantee; ~ **verlangen** to ask for a guarantee; **keine ~ übernehmen** to give no guarantee; **mit ~** with guarantee; **ohne ~** without guarantee
~, **ausdrückliche** express warranty
~, **sichere** reliable guarantee
~, **stillschweigend gewährte** implied warranty
Garantieabkommen *n* covenant to warranty
Garantieaktie *f (st.ex.)* deposited stock
Garantieangebot *n* guarantee offer
Garantieanleihe *f* security loan
Garantiearbeit *f* guarantee work *(executed under a guarantee)*
Garantiebetrag *m* amount guaranteed
Garantiebrief *m* s. **Garantieerklärung**
Garantiedauer *f* guarantee period
Garantiedepot *n* collateral security
Garantiedienst *m* guarantee service
Garantiedurchschrift *f* copy of guarantee
Garantiedurchsicht *f* guarantee inspection; guarantee overhaul
Garantieerklärung *f* guarantee, warranty
Garantiefall *m* case of warranty
Garantiefonds *m* guarantee fund
Garantieforderung *f* claim resulting from guarantee (given), guarantee claim

Garantiefrist *f* period of validity of guarantee, term of guarantee
Garantiegeber *m* guarantor, warrantor
Garantiegesellschaft *f* guarantee company; underwriters
Garantiehinterlegung *f* giving of security
Garantiekapital *n* security capital
Garantieklausel *f* warranty clause
Garantiekonsortium *n* underwriters
Garantiekosten *pl* guarantee costs
Garantiekredit *m* security credit [loan]
Garantieleistung *f* giving of guarantee [*(jur)* surety]; guarantee work *(executed under a guarantee)*
Garantieleistungsvertrag *m s.* **Garantievertrag**
Garantielohn *m* guaranteed wage
Garantien *fpl* safeguards ⋄ ~ **erhalten** to obtain safeguards *(in treaty etc.)*
Garantiepflicht *f* obligation to give guarantee
garantieren to guarantee, to warrant; to vouch for *(s.th.)* ⋄ **(für) etwas ~** to guarantee s.th.; **für jmdn. ~** to stand surety for s.o., to act as guarantor for s.o.; to vouch for s.o.
Garantieschein *m* guarantee [warranty] certificate [coupon]; surety bond
Garantieschreiben *n s.* **Garantieerklärung**
Garantiesumme *f* amount guaranteed
Garantiesyndikat *n* underwriters, underwriting syndicate
Garantiesystem *n* system of guarantee [warranty]
Garantieübernahme *f* standing of surety *(for s.o. or s.th.)*
Garantieumfang *m* extent of warranty
Garantie- und Nacharbeit *f* guarantee and refinishing work
Garantievereinbarung *f* del credere agreement
Garantievermerk *m* guarantee mark
Garantieverpflichtung *f* warranty of quality
Garantievertrag *m* guarantee contract, contract of guarantee
Garantievorrat *m* protective [reserve, standard, inventory] stock
Garantiewechsel *m* security bill
Garantiewert *m* value guaranteed; security value
Garantiezeit *f* guarantee period, period of guarantee
Garbe *f (agric)* sheaf *(corn etc.)*
Garderobe *f* wardrobe, (personal) stock of clothes; cloakroom, *(Am)* checkroom
Garderobenfrau *f* cloakroom attendant, *(Am)* checkroom woman
Garderobenmarke *f* cloakroom ticket, *(Am)* check
Gare *f* 1. *(ind)* finished state *(processed material)*; refined state *(steel)*; 2. *(agric)* readiness (of the soil) for cultivation; mellowness of the soil; favourable soil conditions; 3. dressing of skins; bundle *(measurement of skins)*
gären to ferment
Gären *n* fermenting; fermentation
Gärerzeugnis *n* fermentation product, product of fermentation
Gärfutter *n (agric)* silage
Garten *m* garden
Gartenarbeit *f* gardening
Gartenarchitekt *m* landscape gardener
Gartenbau *m* horticulture; gardening
Gartenbauausstellung *f* horticultural show [exhibition]
Gartenbaubetrieb *m* horticultural enterprise
Gartenbaugesellschaft *f* horticultural society
Gartenfrüchte *fpl* garden produce, horticultural products
Gartenland *n* horticultural [garden] land
Gartenschau *f* horticultural show
Gartenwirtschaft *f* 1. horticulture; 2. garden restaurant
Gärtner *m* gardener
Gärtnerei *f* 1. gardening; horticulture; 2. market garden, *(Am)* truck garden; nursery *(trees)*
Gärung *f* fermentation
Gas *n* gas
Gasanstalt *f s.* **Gaswerk**
Gaserzeugung *f (ind)* gas-making, gas production; gas generation
Gasfernversorgung *f* long-distance gas supply
Gasgebühr *f* gas rate
Gasindustrie *f* gas industry
Gast *m* guest; visitor; customer *(restaurant etc.)*
Gastarbeiter *m* foreign worker
Gastdozent *m* guest [visiting] lecturer
Gästebuch *n* guest book *(restaurant etc.)*; visitors' book *(museum etc.)*
Gästehaus *n* guesthouse
Gastgeber *m* host
Gasthaus *n* inn; (small) hotel
Gastland *n* host country
Gastprofessor *m* guest [visiting] professor
Gastrecht *n* right of [to] hospitality
Gastronom *m* innkeeper; hotel-keeper; restaurant manager; catering specialist
Gastronomie *f* catering trade
Gaststätte *f* restaurant *(in the broadest sense of the word including café, public-house, teashop, inn etc.)*
Gaststättenaufschlag *m* restaurant margin *(between retail price and restaurant price)*
Gaststättenbetrieb *m* restaurant; restaurant business
Gaststätteneinrichtung *f* 1. restaurant *(s.* **Gaststätte***)*; 2. restaurant furniture and fittings
Gaststättenerlös *m* restaurant proceeds [profit]

Gaststättengewerbe *n* restaurant industry; catering trade
Gaststättenkosten *pl* restaurant costs
Gaststättenkultur *f* quality of restaurant service
Gaststättennetz *n* restaurant network
Gaststättenpreis *m* restaurant (sales) price *(for meals, beverages etc.)*
Gaststättenpreisniveau *n* level of restaurant (sales) prices *(s.* **Gaststättenpreis**)
Gaststättenspanne *f s.* **Gaststättenaufschlag**
Gaststättenumsatz *m* restaurant (sales) turnover
Gaststättenverkaufspreis *m s.* **Gaststättenpreis**
Gaststättenwesen *n* catering trade, restaurant industry
Gastwirt *m* innkeeper; hotel-keeper
Gastwirtschaft *f s.* **Gasthaus**
Gasverbrauch *m* gas consumption
Gasverbrauchsnorm *f* standard rate of gas consumption
Gaswerk *n* gasworks
GATT-Liberalisierung *f* GATT liberalization
GATT-Raum *m* GATT area
Gattung *f* family; species; race; kind, sort, type; genus
Gattungskauf *m* purchase of an article [goods] by simple designation *(without indication of quality)*
Gattungsschuld *f* obligation to supply unascertained goods
Gattungswaren *fpl* unascertained goods
Gebäude *n* building, structure; edifice ◇ **ein ~ sanieren** to restore [reconstruct] a building
~, **abgerissenes** demolished building
~, **baufälliges** derelict [dilapidated] building
~, **gut erhaltenes** well-maintained building
~, **hoch besteuertes** heavily rated building
~, **leerstehendes** unoccupied [vacant, empty] building
~, **öffentliches** public building
~, **städtisches** municipal building
Gebäudeabnahme *f* final architect's certificate
Gebäudeabschreibungen *fpl* depreciation of buildings
Gebäudeausrüstung *f* equipment of buildings *(power, water etc.)*
Gebäudebesteuerung *f* taxation of buildings
Gebäudeentschuldungssteuer *f* tax (levied) on house rent *(especially in respect of houses built with subsidies)*
Gebäudeertragssteuer *f s.* **Gebäudesteuer**
Gebäudeinstandsetzung *f* repair [restoration] of a building
Gebäudekomplex *m* complex of buildings
Gebäudekonto *n* building account
Gebäudereiniger *m* building cleaner
Gebäudeschaden *m* damage to a building [buildings]

Gebäudesteuer *f* tax on buildings; house-property tax
Gebäudeteil *m* part of a building
Gebäudeunterhaltung *f* building maintenance
Gebäudeversicherung *f* building [house] insurance
Gebäudeverwalter *m* house-property agent [manager]
Gebäudeverwaltung *f* house-property management
Gebäudewert *m* value of a building
Gebäudewerterhöhungen *fpl* improvements of [to] buildings
Gebäudezählung *f* survey of buildings
geben to give, to present, to bestow; to afford, to provide *(opportunity etc.)*; to deliver, to hand over
Geber *m* giver, donor; dispenser, distributor *(charity etc.)*
~ *mpl* **und Nehmer** *mpl (st.ex.)* sellers and buyers
gebessert improved *(rate of exchange etc.)*
Gebiet *n* territory; area; district; region; field, domain, province, sphere *(science, research, knowledge etc.)* ◇ **auf landwirtschaftlichem ~** in the field of agriculture; **auf wirtschaftlichem ~** in the economic field; **sich auf ein ~ spezialisieren** to specialize in a subject [an area of study]
~, **abgetretenes** ceded territory
~, **bebautes** built-up area
~, **besetztes** occupied territory
~, **besiedeltes** populated area
~, **dicht besiedeltes** congested [densely populated] area
~, **dünn besiedeltes** thinly populated area
~, **erzreiches** area rich in ore
~, **fruchtbares** fertile district
~, **geräumtes** evacuated area
~, **kohlenreiches** area rich in coal
~, **kornreiches** rich corn-district [corn-land], *(Am)* rich grain-district [grain-land]
~, **kritisches** *(stats)* critical region
~, **ländliches** rural area
~, **landwirtschaftliches** agricultural area
~, **neutrales** neutral territory
~, **politisches** sphere of politics, political sphere
~, **unbewohntes** uninhabited area
~, **unerschlossenes** undeveloped area
~, **unterentwickeltes** underdeveloped area
~, **vom Krieg betroffenes** war-stricken area
~, **wasserreiches** area rich in water
~, **wirtschaftliches** economic field
~, **wissenschaftliches** scientific field
~, **zurückgebliebenes** backward area
Gebietsabgrenzung *f* zoning
Gebietsabtretung *f* cession of territory

Gebietsanspruch *m* territorial claim
Gebietsbeauftragter *m* regional commissioner
Gebietseinteilung *f* regional division
~, administrative division into administrative regions; regional administrative division
~, ökonomische division into economic regions; regional economic division
~, wirtschaftliche *s.* ~, ökonomische
Gebietsentwicklung *f* regional development
Gebietsentwicklungsplan *m* development plan of a region, regional development plan
Gebietsentwicklungsprogramm *n* regional development programme
Gebietserweiterung *f* territorial expansion
Gebietsforderung *f s.* Gebietsanspruch
Gebietsgrundsatz *m* territorial [regional] principle
Gebietshoheit *f* territorial sovereignty
Gebietskartell *n* localized cartel
Gebietskörperschaft *f* area authority
Gebietsökonomie *f* regional economy [economics] *(s.* Territorialökonomie)
Gebietsorganisation *f* regional organization
Gebietsplan *m s.* Gebietsentwicklungsplan
Gebietsplanung *f* regional planning
Gebietsprognose *f* regional forecast [prognosis]
Gebietsressourcen *pl* regional resources
Gebietsspezialisierung *f* regional specialization
Gebietsstruktur *f* regional structure
Gebietstyp *m* type of region
Gebietsveränderung *f* border changes
Gebietsverflechtungsbilanz *f* regional input--output table
Gebietsverflechtungsmodell *n* regional input--output model
Gebietswirtschaft *f* regional economy
gebietswirtschaftlich from the point of view of regional economy
gebildet 1. educated; cultured; cultivated; *(person)* of education; *(person)* of culture; 2. formed *(fund etc.)*; organized, established *(organization etc.)*
Gebildete *mpl/fpl* educated [lettered] (people)
Gebildeter *m* educated person
Gebirgsbewohner *m* mountain-dweller, highlander
Gebirgsland *n* mountainous country
geboren born
Geborenenüberschuß *m* excess of births *(over deaths)*, excess of the birth rate
Geborenenziffer *f* birth rate
~, nicht aufgegliederte crude birth rate
geborgen salvaged *(ship)*
Gebot *n* bid ⋄ ein ~ machen to make a bid
~, erstes first [opening, starting] bid
~, festes firm bid
~, geringstes lowest bid

~, höheres higher [further] bid
~, letztes last [final] bid
~, niedrigstes *s.* ~, geringstes
Gebrauch *m* use, employment; usage; custom; practice ⋄ allgemein in ~ in common use; außer ~ not in use, out of use; außer ~ kommen to fall into disuse, to go out of use, to become obsolete; etwas in ~ nehmen to put s.th. into use; für den einheimischen ~ for home consumption; für den privaten ~ for personal use; in ~ kommen to come into use; sparsam im ~ economical in use; von etwas ~ machen to make use of s.th., to avail o.s. of s.th., to use s.th.; vor ~ schütteln shake before using; zum äußeren ~ for external application; zum eigenen ~ for private use; zum inneren ~ for internal use; zum persönlichen ~ for personal use
~, dauernder constant use
~ eines Firmennamens use of a firm name
~, gewöhnlicher ordinary use
~, täglicher daily use
gebrauchen to use, to make use of *(s.th.)*; to employ *(s.th.)*; to utilize *(s.th.)*
gebräuchlich ordinary, usual, customary *(procedure etc.)*; general, common, current *(expression etc.)*
Gebrauchsanleitung *f s.* Gebrauchsanweisung
Gebrauchsanmaßung *f (jur)* illegal (temporary) use of s.o. else's property; illegal use of property held in pawn
Gebrauchsanweisung *f* directions [instructions] for use
Gebrauchsartikel *m* article for daily use, utility article
Gebrauchsausführung *f* utility type
Gebrauchsbedingungen *fpl* conditions of use
Gebrauchsdauer *f* service life
Gebrauchsdiebstahl *m s.* Gebrauchsanmaßung
Gebrauchseigenschaften *fpl* characteristics of goods [products]
Gebrauchseignung *f s.* Gebrauchsfähigkeit
gebrauchsfähig usable, serviceable
Gebrauchsfähigkeit *f* usability, serviceableness; utilizability
Gebrauchsfahrzeug *n* utility vehicle
gebrauchsfertig ready for use, instant *(foods etc.)*
Gebrauchsgegenstand *m* article for daily use; personal article
Gebrauchsgraphik *f* commercial art
Gebrauchsgraphiker *m* commercial artist
Gebrauchsgut *n s.* Gebrauchsgegenstand
Gebrauchsgüter *npl* articles of daily use
~, langlebige (consumer) durables
Gebrauchsmuster *n* (commercial) sample; sample for experimental use [test]; registered design, utility model

Gebrauchsmusterschutz *m* legal protection of (registered) design
Gebrauchsrecht *n* right to use *(product)*
gebrauchsunfähig unusable, unserviceable; not utilizable
Gebrauchsvorschrift *f s.* **Gebrauchsanweisung**
Gebrauchsware *f s.* **Gebrauchsgegenstand**
Gebrauchswasser *n* water for domestic use; water for industrial use; tap-water
Gebrauchswerber *m* commercial advertiser
Gebrauchswerbung *f* commercial advertising
Gebrauchswert *m* use-value; utility value
Gebrauchswerteigenschaften *fpl s.* **Gebrauchseigenschaften**
Gebrauchswert-Kostenanalyse *f* **(GKA)** use--value cost analysis *(optimization of costs and quality of goods produced)*
Gebrauchswertminderung *f* decrease of use--value *(due to defects)*
Gebrauchszweck *m* purpose, intended use
gebraucht used, second-hand *(furniture etc.)*
Gebrauchtwagen *m* second-hand [used] car
Gebrauchtwagenhandel *m* trade in second--hand [used] cars
Gebrauchtwaren *fpl* second-hand goods
Gebrauchtwarenhandel *m* second-hand trade
Gebrauchtwarenpreis *m* price of second-hand goods
Gebühr *f* charge, fee; due; toll *(roads etc.)*; commission *(trade)*; rate, tariff *(customs)*; royalty *(for utilization of s.th., for licences etc.)* ⋄ **eine ~ berechnen** to charge a fee; **eine ~ zurückvergüten** to refund a fee [charge]; **für eine ~ von** at a charge of; **~ zahlt Empfänger** charges paid by the receiver; **gegen eine geringe ~** for a small fee; **zu einer herabgesetzten ~** at a reduced rate
~ der öffentlichen Versorgungsbetriebe public utility charges [rates]
~, doppelte double rate
~, ermäßigte reduced rate
~, feste fixed duty
~, zuviel berechnete excessive charge
Gebühren *fpl* charges, fees; dues; tolls *(roads etc.)*; commission *(trade)*; rates, tariffs *(customs)* royalties *(for utilization of s.th., for licences etc.)* ⋄ **~ einziehen** to collect charges [fees]; **~ entrichten** to pay charges [fees]; **~ vorausbezahlt** charges prepaid; **gegen ~ aushändigen** to hand over on payment of charges [fees]
~, amtliche official charges [fees]
~, fällige fees due
~, überhöhte excessive charges
~ und Abgaben *fpl* rates and taxes
Gebührenabkommen *n* agreement on charges and fees

Gebührenaufstellung *f* table [list] of charges
Gebührenaufteilung *f* allocation of charges [fees]
Gebührenbefreiung *f s.* **Gebührenerlaß**
Gebührenberechnung *f* charging a fee
Gebühreneinheit *f* unit (of charge) *(telephone)*
Gebührenerhebung *f* collection of charge(s)
Gebührenerhöhung *f* increase in charges [fees]
Gebührenerlaß *m* remission of charges [fees]
Gebührenermäßigung *f* reduction of charges [fees]
Gebührenerstattung *f* return of charges [fees]
gebührenfrei free of charge, without fee; *(cust)* duty-free; *(post)* postage-free; non-chargeable, *(Am)* toll-free *(telephone)*
Gebührenfreiheit *f* exemption from charges [fees]
Gebührenmarke *f* revenue stamp, fee-stamp
Gebührenordnung *f* list [schedule, scale] of charges [fees]
Gebührenpauschale *f* flat rate
gebührenpflichtig chargeable, liable [subject] to a charge [fee]
Gebührensatz *m* rate of charges [fees]
Gebührentabelle *f* table of rates
Gebührentafel *f (cust)* tariff scale
Gebührenverzeichnis *n s.* **Gebührentabelle**
Gebührenzone *f* (rate) area *(for telephone calls, parcels etc.)*
Gebührenzuschlag *m* additional charge
gebunden 1. tied *(credits etc.)*; controlled *(capital etc.)*; earmarked *(funds etc.)*; bound by *(contract etc.)*; 2. bound *(volume etc.)*
Geburry-Prozeß *m (stats)* birth process
Geburt *f* birth ⋄ **eine ~ anmelden** to register a birth
Geburten *fpl* births
~ und Todesfälle *mpl (stats)* births and deaths
Geburtenabnahme *f s.* **Geburtenrückgang**
Geburtenanstieg *m* increase in the birth rate
Geburtenanzeige *f* announcement of a birth
Geburtenausfall *m s.* **Geburtenrückgang**
Geburtenbeihilfe *f* maternity benefits
Geburtenbeschränkung *f s.* **Geburtenkontrolle**
Geburtenbuch *n s.* **Geburtenregister**
Geburtenentwicklung *f* growth in birth rate
Geburtenhäufigkeit *f* frequency of births
Geburtenkontrolle *f* birth control
Geburtenliste *f s.* **Geburtenregister**
Geburtenrate *f* birth rate, natality
Geburtenregelung *f s.* **Geburtenkontrolle**
Geburtenregister *n* register of births
Geburtenrückgang *m* fall [decline, drop] in the birth rate ⋄ **einen ~ erzielen** to bring down the birth rate
geburtenschwach with a low birth rate *(year, area etc.)*

geburtenstark with a high birth rate *(year, area etc.)*
Geburtenstatistik *f* birth rate [natality] statistics
Geburtentafel *f* table of births
Geburtenüberschuß *m* excess of births *(over deaths)*, excess of the birth rate
Geburtenverhältnis *n s.* **Geburtenrate**
Geburtenzahl *f* number of births
Geburtenziffer *f s.* **Geburtenrate**
Geburtsbeihilfe *f s.* **Geburtenbeihilfe**
Geburtsdatum *n* date of birth
Geburtsjahr *n* year of birth
Geburtsjahrgang *m* age class [cohort]
Geburtsland *n* country of birth
Geburtsort *m* place of birth, birthplace
Geburtsrate *f s.* **Geburtenrate**
Geburtsrecht *n* birthright
Geburtsschein *m s.* **Geburtsurkunde**
Geburtstag *m* birthday
Geburtsurkunde *f* birth certificate
gechartert chartered
Gedanke *m* thought; idea; notion; conception; intention
~, **schöpferischer** creative idea
Gedankenaustausch *m* exchange of ideas; brainstorming
Gedankenfülle *f* wealth of ideas; fertility of thought
Gedankengut *n* (stock of) ideas
gedeckt covered *(needs, cheques etc.)*; secured *(bill etc.)*; guaranteed *(loan etc.)*; protected
gedeihen to prosper, to be prosperous *(persons etc.)*; to thrive, to do well, to grow well *(plants etc.)*; to flourish, to succeed *(business etc.)*; to make good progress *(negotiations etc.)*
Gedeihen *n* prosperity *(persons etc.)*; rapid growth *(plants etc.)*; success *(business etc.)*; good progress *(negotiations etc.)*
Gedinge *n (min)* piecework; contract [agreement]; *(hist)* tribute; contract
Gedingearbeit *f (min)* piecework
Gedingearbeiter *m (min)* pieceworker
Gedingelohn *m (min)* piecewage, pay [wage] for piecework
Gedingenehmer *m s.* **Gedingearbeiter**
Gedingestufe *f (min)* piecework rate
gedruckt printed
gedungen hired
geehrt honoured *(person)*
geeignet appropriate, fitting, suitable *(occasion etc.)*; qualified, eligible *(for post etc.)*; convenient *(time etc.)*
Gefahr *f* danger; peril; jeopardy; risk; hazard; threat; menace ⋄ **auf eigene ~** at one's own risk; **auf ~ des Absenders** at sender's risk; **auf jede ~ hin** at all hazards; **die ~ übernehmen** to take the risk; **etwas auf eigene ~**

tun to do st.h. at one's own risk; **in ~ bringen** to imperil, to jeopardize; **in ~ sein** to be in danger; to be in peril *(of losing rights, liberties etc.)*; to be in jeopardy *(of losing one's life etc.)*; **ohne ~** free from danger [risk]; safe
~, **augenscheinliche** apparent danger
~ **beim Eigentümer** owner's risk
~, **einem Beruf eigentümliche** risk incident to employment
~, **gemeinsame** common danger [peril]
~, **mögliche** potential risk
~, **übernommene** subscribed risk
~, **übersehbare** perceptible risk
~, **unmittelbare** imminent danger
gefährden to expose *s.o./s.th.* to danger, to risk; to endanger, to imperil *(s.o./s.th.)*, to jeopardize *(s.o.'s freedom/future)*
Gefährdetenfürsorge *f (approx.)* care and protection of young persons *(who are in moral danger)*
gefahrdrohend dangerous; perilous, threatening, menacing *(situation etc.)*
Gefährdung *f* exposure to danger [risk] *(goods in transit etc.)*
Gefährdungshaftung *f* liability arising from unforeseeable causes
Gefahren *fpl* dangers; perils; risks; hazards; threats ⋄ **versichert gegen alle ~** insured against all risks
~, **inflationistische** risks of inflation; inflationary risks
Gefahrenänderung *f* alteration [changes] in risk
Gefahrenbereich *m* danger area
Gefahreneinteilung *f* classification of risks
Gefahrenerhöhung *f (ins)* increase in risk(s)
Gefahrengeld *n* danger money
Gefahrengemeinschaft *f (ins)* common safety arrangement for vessel and cargo; *(ins)* society covering common risks
Gefahrenherd *m* (constant) source of danger
Gefahrenhöhe *f* degree of risk
Gefahrenklasse *f (ins)* class of risks
Gefahrenklassifizierung *f* classification of risks
Gefahrenklausel *f* risk clause
Gefahrenpunkt *m* danger point [spot]; critical point
Gefahrenquelle *f* source of danger
Gefahrenrückversicherung *f* reinsurance of risk
Gefahrenschutz *m* (measures for the) prevention of (industrial) accidents
Gefahrenstelle *f* danger spot
Gefahrentarif *m (ins)* danger rate
Gefahrenübergang *m s.* **Gefahrübergang**
Gefahrenzone *f* danger zone, zone of danger
Gefahrenzulage *f* danger [hazard] money, hazard [danger zone] bonus

Gefahrenzuschlag *m* danger money
gefährlich dangerous; perilous; risky, hazardous *(mission etc.)*; threatening, menacing *(situation etc.)*
Gefährlichkeit *f* dangerousness, dangerous nature; perilousness; gravity
gefahrlos free from danger [risk], without risk; safe
Gefahrlosigkeit *f* freedom from danger [risk]; safeness, safety
Gefahrmeldeanlage *f* danger warning [alarm] system
Gefahrtragung *f* risk of loss
Gefahrübergang *m* passing of risk
Gefahrübernahme *f* assumption of risk
gefahrvoll full of danger
Gefälle *n* 1. differential *(wage)*, gap *(price)*, margin *(between interest rates)*; 2. *(min)* amount of material produced, yield
Gefälligkeitsadresse *f* accommodation address
Gefälligkeitsakzept *n s.* **Gefälligkeitswechsel**
Gefälligkeitsbrief *m* introductory letter
Gefälligkeitsflagge *f* flag of convenience
Gefälligkeitsgirant *m* accommodation endorser
Gefälligkeitsgiro *n s.* **Gefälligkeitsindossament**
Gefälligkeitsindossament *n* accommodation indorsement
Gefälligkeitspapier *n* accommodation paper
Gefälligkeitspartei *f* accommodation party
Gefälligkeitswechsel *m* accomodation bill
gefälscht falsified *(report etc.)*, forged *(document etc.)*, counterfeited *(bank note etc.)*, faked *(result etc.)*, tampered *(account etc.)*; adulterated *(food etc.)*
Gefangenenarbeit *f* prison labour
Gefangenenfürsorge *f* prison welfare
Geflügel *n* poultry
Geflügelausstellung *f* poultry show
Geflügelfarm *f* poultry farm
Geflügelhaltung *f* poultry keeping; poultry husbandry [farming]
Geflügelhändler *m* poulterer
Geflügelhandlung *f* poulterer's shop
Geflügelzucht *f* 1. poultry breeding; poultry farming; 2. poultry farm
Geflügelzüchter *m* poultry breeder
Gefolgschaft *f* 1. allegiance; 2. adherents, followers *(leader etc.)*, partisans *(government etc.)*
gefragt asked for, sought after, in demand *(goods etc.)* ◊ **sehr ~** in great demand *(goods etc.)*; **wenig ~** in less demand *(goods etc.)*
Gefrieranlage *f* refrigeration [refrigerating] plant; (deep-)freezing plant
Gefriergut *n* frozen goods
Gefrierkette *f* chain of cold storage and transportation

Gefrierlagerung *f* cold [freezing] storage
Gefrierpackung *f* package of frozen food
Gefrierraum *m* refrigerating [refrigerator] room; freezing [refrigerating] chamber; cold room [store]
Gefrierschiff *n* refrigerating ship
Gefrierwaren *fpl s.* **Gefriergut**
gefroren (deep-)frozen, chilled *(food etc.)*
Gefüge *n* structure, set-up *(society etc.)*
~, soziales social structure, (the whole) fabric of society
Gefühlswert *m (ins)* sentimental value *(piece of jewellery etc.)*
geführt stocked *(articles etc.)*
gegebenenfalls should the case occur, if need be, if possible; if applicable *(on printed forms etc.)*
gegen towards; about, approximately; compared with; for, against, on *(payment etc.)*
Gegenangebot *n* counteroffer
Gegenanspruch *m* counterclaim
Gegenantrag *m* counterproposal, counterproposition; countermotion *(parliament etc.)*
Gegenauftrag *m* counterorder
Gegenauslese *f (ins)* anti-selection
Gegenbedingung *f* counterstipulation
Gegenbeweis *m* proof [evidence] to the contrary; argument to the contrary, counterargument; *(jur)* counterevidence
Gegenbuchung *f* cross entry; set-off
Gegenbürge *m (jur)* countersurety
Gegenbürgschaft *f* countersurety, countersecurity
Gegend *f* region; district; area; locality; vicinity, neighbourhood
~, dicht bevölkerte densely populated region
~, fruchtbare fertile region [area]
~, gebirgige mountainous region [area, district]
~, (rein) landwirtschaftliche (purely) agricultural region [area]
Gegendarstellung *f* counterstatement
Gegendeckung *f* countersecurity; hedging
Gegenentwurf *m* counterdraft
Gegenerklärung *f* counterstatement, counterdeclaration; disclaimer
Gegenforderung *f* counterclaim ◊ **als ~** per contra
Gegengebot *n* counterbid; counteroffer
Gegengeschäft *n (com)* contra transaction; *(ins)* return business
Gegengeschenk *n* return present
Gegengewicht *n* counterbalance, counterweight
Gegenhypothese *f (stats)* alternative [non-null] hypothesis
Gegenkandidat *m* rival [opposition] candidate
Gegenklage *f (jur)* cross-action; countercharge, counterclaim

Gegenkläger *m (jur)* bringer of a cross-action
Gegenkonto *n* counteraccount
Gegenkontrolle *f* cross-checking
Gegenkraft *f* counterforce
Gegenleistung *f* return service; quid pro quo; *(jur)* valuable consideration
~, **angemessene** good [valuable] consideration
~, **fällige** consideration due
~, **formale** formal consideration
Gegenmaßnahme *f* countermeasure
Gegenmittel *n* counterremedy
Gegenmuster *n* countersample
Gegenofferte *f* counteroffer; counterorder
Gegenpartei *f* adverse party, the other side, opposite party
Gegenposten *m (acc)* contra entry, set-off
Gegenprobe *f* reverse check
Gegenquittung *f* counterreceipt
gegenrechnen to account for checking purposes
Gegenrechnung *f* check-account, *(Am)* controlling account ◇ **durch ~ ausgleichen** to counterbalance; **eine ~ aufmachen** to make out a contra account
Gegenrevolution *f* counterrevolution
Gegensaldo *m* counterbalance
Gegensatz *m* contrast; opposition, antagonism
~ **zwischen körperlicher und geistiger Arbeit** contrast between physical and mental [intellectual] labour
~ **zwischen Stadt und Land** contrast between town and country(side)
gegensätzlich opposite, contrary; antagonistic
Gegensätzlichkeit *f* opposite [contrary] nature
Gegenschuld *f* reciprocal debt; debt owed by a creditor
Gegenseite *f* opposite [other] side [party]; reverse *(coin)*
gegenseitig mutual, reciprocal *(aid etc.)*
Gegenseitigkeit *f* mutuality; reciprocity ◇ **auf ~** on mutual terms
Gegenseitigkeitsabkommen *n* reciprocal trade agreement
Gegenseitigkeitsgeschäft *n* barter transaction
Gegenseitigkeitsgesellschaft *f* mutual benefit society, benevolent society
Gegenseitigkeitsklausel *f* reciprocity clause
Gegenseitigkeitskonto *n* mutual account
Gegenseitigkeitspakt *m* mutual assistance pact
Gegenseitigkeitsprinzip *n* principle of reciprocity
Gegenseitigkeitsverein *m* mutual benefit society; benevolent society
Gegenseitigkeitsvereinbarung *f* bilateral [reciprocal] agreement
Gegenseitigkeitsvertrag *m* bilateral treaty
Gegensicherheit *f* counterbond ◇ **~ leisten** to put up a counterbond

Gegensiegel *n (jur)* counterseal
Gegenspionage *f* counterespionage
Gegenstand *m* 1. object *(material)*, (material) thing; article, item; 2. subject; (subject) matter *(report etc.)*; item, theme *(discussion etc.)*; issue, matter *(under discussion)*
~, **besprochener** subject under discussion
~ **der Kritik** object of criticism
~ **des täglichen Bedarfs** article for daily use [of prime necessity]
~, **gepfändeter** thing seized in distraining, distress
~, **versicherter** insured object [matter], subject matter insured
~ **von Verhandlungen** subject of negotiations
Gegenstände *mpl*:
~, **bewegliche** movable things, movables
~, **gebrauchte** articles that have been used [worn], second-hand articles
~, **nicht übertragbare** non-negotiable objects
~, **persönliche** personal effects
~, **technische** technical equipment
~, **übertragbare** negotiable objects
~, **unbewegliche** immovable things, immovables
~, **vererbliche** corporeal hereditament
~, **verlorene** lost property
~, **verpfändete** pledged chattels
~, **vom Versicherungsschutz ausgeschlossene** memorandum articles
gegenständlich objective *(thinking etc.)*; concrete *(term etc.)*
Gegenständlichkeit *f* objectivity *(thinking etc.)*; concreteness *(term etc.)*
gegenstandslos baseless, groundless, unfounded, without substance *(argument, criticism etc.)*; irrelevant, no longer pertinent *(when issue etc. is no longer valid)*
Gegenstimme *f* adverse vote, vote to the contrary, vote against ◇ **mit einer ~** with one vote against; **ohne ~** unanimously
Gegenstück *n* counterpart
Gegenteil *n* (the) contrary [reverse, opposite]
gegenteilig contrary, opposite *(statement etc.)*; opposing *(party etc.)*
Gegentransaktion *f (st.ex.)* countertransaction, *(Am)* straddle
Gegenüberstellung *f* comparison; confrontation
Gegenunterschrift *f* countersignature
Gegenuntersuchung *f (jur)* counter inquiry
Gegenverpflichtung *f* counterobligation
Gegenverschreibung *f (jur)* counterbond
Gegenversicherung *f* counterinsurance, reciprocal insurance, reinsurance
Gegenvormund *m* co-guardian, *(Am)* (joint) guardian
Gegenvormundschaft *f* co-guardianship, *(Am)* (joint) guardianship

Gegenvorschlag *m* counterproposal, counter-proposition
Gegenvorstellung *f* counter-representation
Gegenwartswert *m* present-day value *(property etc.)*
Gegenwechsel *m* counter-exchange; redraft, re-exchange
Gegenwert *m* equivalent (value), *(Am)* avails
Gegenwertfonds *m* counterpart fund
Gegenwertmittel *npl* counterpart funds
gegenzeichnen to countersign
Gegenzeichnung *f* countersigning, countersignature
Gegenzeuge *m (jur)* witness to the contrary [for the other side]
Gegner *m* adversary, opponent; opposing party
gegnerisch adverse; opposing
Gehalt *m* 1. content; capacity, volume; standard *(of a coin etc.)*; 2. substance, content *(intellectual, inner etc.)*
~ **an Gold/Silber, gesetzlicher** legal standard of fineness *(gold/silver coinage)*
Gehalt *n* salary, pay, remuneration *(s.a.* **Lohn)** ◊ **das ~ aufbessern** to raise the salary; **ein ~ beziehen** to receive [draw, be paid] a salary; **ein ~ festsetzen** to fix a salary; **~ zahlen** to salary, to pay salary
~, **festes** regular salary
Gehälter *npl*:
~ **für Büroangestellte** office salaries
~ **kaufmännischer Angestellter** clerical salaries
~ **leitender Angestellter** executive salaries
Gehaltsabbau *m* reduction of salary, salary reduction
Gehaltsabrechnung *f* salary accounting; statement of salaries
Gehaltsabteilung *f* pay [wages] office
Gehaltsabzug *m* deduction from salary
Gehaltsangabe *f* salary statement
Gehaltsangebot *n* offer of salary, salary offer(ed)
Gehaltsangleichung *f* adjustment of salaries
Gehaltsanspruch *m* salary claim
Gehaltsansprüche *mpl*:
◊ ~ **stellen** to state the salary expected
Gehaltsanstieg *m s.* **Gehaltserhöhung**
Gehaltsaufbesserung *f s.* **Gehaltserhöhung**
Gehaltsauszahlung *f s.* **Gehaltszahlung**
Gehaltsbestimmung *f* 1. fixing of (a) salary; 2. determination of content [fineness] *(gold etc.)*
~ **mit parallelen Wirkungsgeraden** *(stats)* parallel line essay
Gehaltsbezüge *mpl* total salary drawn
Gehaltseingruppierung *f s.* **Gehaltseinstufung**
Gehaltseinstufung *f* salary classification

Gehaltsempfänger *m* person in receipt of a salary, salaried worker
Gehaltsempfänger *mpl* salaried workers, the salariat
Gehaltsentwicklung *f* growth of salary
Gehaltserhöhung *f* salary increase, rise [*(Am)* raise] in salary
~, **altersbedingte** increase of salary based on length of service
~, **automatische** automatic salary increase
Gehaltsfestlegung *f* fixing of (a) salary
Gehaltsfestsetzung *f s.* **Gehaltsfestlegung**
Gehaltsfonds *m* salary fund
Gehaltsforderung *f s.* **Gehaltsanspruch**
Gehaltsgruppe *f* salary scale [bracket]
Gehaltsgruppenkatalog *m* list of salary scales according to job
Gehaltshöhe *f* salary level; amount of salary
~, **leistungsbedingte** salary depending on efficiency
Gehaltsklasse *f* salary grade [bracket]
Gehaltskonto *n* salary (bank) account
Gehaltskürzung *f* reduction in salary, salary cut
Gehaltsliste *f* payroll
Gehaltsnachzahlung *f* (salary) back pay; additional payment of salary
Gehaltsperiode *f* pay [payroll] period
Gehaltspfändung *f* seizure [attachment, distress] of salary
Gehaltspolitik *f* salary [pay] policy
Gehaltsrückstände *mpl* accrued salaries
Gehaltssatz *m* salary rate [scale]
Gehaltssenkung *f* reduction in salary, drop in salary
Gehaltssteigerung *f s.* **Gehaltserhöhung**
Gehaltsstelle *f* payroll office
Gehaltsstreifen *m* salary slip
Gehaltsstufe *f* salary level
Gehaltstabelle *f* table of salary scales
Gehaltstag *m* payday
Gehaltsverbesserung *f s.* **Gehaltserhöhung**
Gehaltsvorschuß *m* advance (on salary)
Gehaltsvorstellungen *fpl* salary required; salary expected
Gehaltswünsche *mpl s.* **Gehaltsvorstellungen**
Gehaltszahlung *f* payment of salary
Gehaltszulage *f* addition to salary, increase [rise] in salary; supplementary allowance ◊
~ **bekommen** to get a rise in salary
Gehaltszuschlag *m* additional [extra] salary [pay] *(for overtime etc.)*
gehandelt *(st.ex.)* traded [*(Am)* listed] on the stock exchange (market)
geheim secret *(information etc.)*; covert *(agreement etc.)*; occult *(science etc.)*; esoteric *(doctrine etc.)*; clandestine, surreptitious *(dealings etc.)* ◊
streng ~ top secret

Geheimabkommen *n* secret agreement, secret treaty *(between countries)*
Geheimbericht *m* secret [confidential] report
Geheimbote *m* (secret) emissary
Geheimbündnis *n* secret alliance *(between firms)*
Geheimdienst *m* secret [intelligence] service
Geheimdiplomatie *f* secret diplomacy
geheimhalten to keep *s.th.* secret, to keep quiet *(about s.th.)*; to conceal *(s.th.)*
Geheimhaltung *f* keeping *s.th.* secret; concealing, concealment; (observance of) secrecy
Geheimhaltungsklausel *f* secrecy clause
Geheimhaltungspflicht *f* obligation to maintain secrecy
Geheimhaltungsstufe *f* degree of security; security grading
Geheimhaltungssystem *n* system of secrecy, secrecy [security] system
Geheimkartell *n* secret cartel
Geheimkonto *n* secret [private] account
Geheimnis *n* secret; mystery ◊ **ein ~ bewahren** to keep a secret; **ein ~ verraten** to betray [reveal, disclose] a secret
Geheimnisverletzung *f* violation of secrecy
Geheimpatent *n* secret patent
Geheimsache *f* secret matter, matter of secrecy
Geheimvertrag *m* secret agreement [contract]; secret treaty *(between countries)*
Geheimvorbehalt *m* mental reservation *(in a contract etc.)*
Gehilfe *m* helper, assistant *(in shop etc.)*
Geistesarbeit *f* intellectual work, brainwork
Geistesarbeiter *m* brainworker
Geisteswissenschaften *fpl* the arts, the humanities
Geisteswissenschaftler *m* scholar in the field of the humanities
geisteswissenschaftlich concerned with the humanities
Gelände *n* ground, terrain; tract *(land)*; area *(factory etc.)*, site *(building etc.)*
~, **bebautes** built-up area
~, **unbebautes** undeveloped area
Geländeerschließung *f* land development
Gelbgießer *m* brass-founder
Geld *n* money; cash; currency; coins ◊ **gegen bares** ~ **for cash**; ~ **abheben** to withdraw money; ~ **akkumulieren** to accumulate money; ~ **anlegen** to invest money; ~ **auf Zinsen ausleihen** to lend money at interest, to put money out (at interest); ~ **aufnehmen** to borrow [take up] money; ~ **ausleihen** to lend money; ~ **erwerben** to earn money; ~ **gegen Zinsen verleihen** to lend money on interest; ~ **unterschlagen** to misappropriate money, to convert money to one's own use; ~ **verschaffen** to procure money; ~ **ver-**

schieben to transfer money illegally; ~ **wechseln** to change money *(into small coins)*; to exchange money *(currency)*; ~ **zurückerstatten** to refund money
~, **abgenutztes** worn currency
~, **angelegtes** invested money
~, **anvertrautes** money in trust
~, **bares** cash, ready money, money in hand
~, **bereitliegendes** cash in hand
~, **billiges** easy money
~, **disponibles** available funds
~, **echtes** good [genuine] money
~, **effektives** real money *(as opposed to substitutes like bill of exchange etc.)*
~, **eigenes** own money
~, **eingezahltes** deposit
~, **erspartes** savings
~, **festes** time money
~, **flüssiges** ready money, funds on hand
~, **fremdes** foreign money
~, **gangbares** current [good] money
~, **gefälschtes** counterfeit [false, bogus] money
~, **geliehenes** borrowed money
~, **gemünztes** coin
~, **gutes** sound currency
~, **hartes** hard currency
~, **Geld heckendes** *(pol ec)* money-breeding money
~, **heißes** hot money
~, **hinausgeworfenes** wasted money
~, **kleines** change
~, **knappes** dear money
~, **konvertierbares** convertible money [currency]
~, **kursierendes** current money
~, **kurzfristiges** money at short notice, short-term loan
~, **langfristiges** time deposit, time money
~, **minderwertiges** debased currency
~, **mit Kündigungsfrist angelegtes** time deposit
~, **sicher angelegtes** money safely invested, safely invested money
~, **tägliches** daily [call] money
~, **teures** dear money
~, **überschüssiges** surplus money
~, **umlaufendes** current money, money in circulation
~ **und Brief** *m* asked and bid
~, **ungültiges** money that is no longer current
~, **verfügbares** disposable funds
~, **wertbeständiges** money of stable value
~, **zinstragendes** interest-bearing money
~, **zirkulierendes** money in circulation
Geldabfindung *f* monetary compensation, cash settlement
Geldabfluß *m* drain [efflux, outflow] of money, withdrawal of money *(from account)*

Geldabhebung f withdrawal of money
Geldabhebungsvollmacht f *(bank)* authority to draw *(on an account)*
Geldabschöpfung f absorption of purchasing power
Geldabwertung f devaluation [devalorization] (of currency)
Geldakkumulation f monetary accumulation
Geldanforderung f demand [claim, request] for money; currency demand
Geldangebot n supply of money, money supply
Geldangelegenheit f money [financial] matter
Geldanhäufung f accumulation of money; accumulation of currency
Geldanlage f investment, employment of money
Geldanleihe f loan (of money), money loan
Geldansprüche mpl demand for money; monetary claims; outstanding debts
Geldanweisung f remittance (of money), money order
~, telegrafische telegraphic money order
Geldaristokratie f plutocracy
Geldarmut f (financial) poverty; dearth of money
Geldart f type [variety] of money [currency]
Geldaufbringung f raising of money
Geldaufnahme f raising of money; borrowing (of money)
~, kurzfristige short-term borrowings
~, langfristige long-term borrowings
Geldaufwand m monetary expenditure(s), expenditure of money, expense
Geldaufwertung f revaluation (of money)
Geldausdruck m monetary expression
~ des Wertes monetary expression of value
Geldausfuhr f export of money
Geldausfuhrverbot n money export embargo, embargo on the export of money
Geldausgabe f 1. disbursement, expenditure, expense; 2. emission (of money)
Geldauslage f (financial) outlay
Geldausleihe f money lending
Geldausleiher m money lender
Geldausweitung f creation of new currency; monetary expansion
Geldauszahler m *(bank)* paying-out cashier, paying teller
Geldauszahlung f payment (of money)
Geldbedarf m currency demands, demand for currency *(on the market)*; financial needs [requirements]
Geldbeitrag m financial contribution
Geldbelohnung f remuneration *(in cash)*; reward *(in cash for finder etc.)*
Geldbeschaffung f provision of money
Geldbestand m monetary holdings [stock] *(of a country)*; cash balance *(cashbox, till etc.)*

Geldbetrag m amount [sum] (of money)
Geldbewegung f circulation of money, money circulation; movement of money
Geldbewilligung f grant (of money)
Geldbeziehung f monetary relation
Geldbilanz f monetary balance sheet
Geldbörse f 1. money market; 2. purse
Geldbuße f s. **Geldstrafe**
Gelddarleh(e)n n loan (in cash)
Gelddepositen pl deposits
Geldeingänge mpl takings, receipts
Geldeinheit f monetary unit
Geldeinkommen n money income, income in money, monetary income
Geldeinkünfte pl s. **Geldeinkommen**
Geldeinlage f deposit
Geldeinnahme f receipt (of money)
Geldeinnahmen fpl (cash) receipts, takings; revenue
Geldeinnehmer m cashier; *(bank)* receiving teller; treasurer
Geldeinziehung f collecting [collection] of money
Geldeinzug m s. **Geldeinziehung**
Geldemission f emission of money
Geldempfänger m remittee
Geldentschädigung f pecuniary [monetary] compensation, indemnity *(for loss etc.)*
Geldentwertung f depreciation of money, inflation
Gelder npl money; debts; deposits; funds; capital
~, aufgenommene borrowed money, borrowings
~, ausstehende outstanding money [debts]
~, durchlaufende transitory money
~, fremde foreign money; borrowings; *(bank)* deposits by customers
~, öffentliche public funds
Gelderlös m money proceeds
Geldersatz m substitute for money
Geldersatzmittel npl substitutes for money, means of payment other than cash *(cheque, bill of exchange etc.)*
Geldersparnisse fpl money savings
Geldertrag m (monetary) yield(s) *(from investment etc.)*; return(s), profit *(from enterprise etc.)*; proceeds *(from goods sold etc.)*; revenue *(from estate, annuity etc.)*
Gelderwerb m acquisition of money; (way of) making [getting] money
Geldfälscher m counterfeiter
Geldfälschung f 1. counterfeit, false [bogus] money; 2. counterfeiting (of money)
Geldfetisch m money fetishism
Geldfetischismus m s. **Geldfetisch**
Geldflüssigkeit f liquidity; ready flow of money *(on the money market)*

Geldfonds *mpl* monetary funds
~, fremde outside monetary funds, borrowings
~, gesellschaftliche social [public] monetary funds
Geldfondsentwicklung *f* growth of monetary funds
Geldforderung *f* money due, outstanding debt; demand for money; claim for money, monetary claim
Geldforderungen *fpl*:
~, gegenseitige reciprocal debts
~, sich gegenseitig ausgleichende reciprocally compensating debts
~, wechselseitige *s.* ~, gegenseitige
Geldform *f* monetary form
~ des Wertes monetary form of value
Geldfrage *f* financial matter [question]; question of money
Geldfülle *f* abundance of money
Geldfunktion *f* function of money
Geldgeber *m* lender of money, financial backer, investor
Geldgeschäft *n* money transaction, financial operation
Geldgeschenk *n* present of money; donation in cash
Geldhandel *m* traffic in money; financial (banking) business
Geldhändler *m* money-broker, banker
Geldhandlungskapital *n* banking capital, bank stock [funds, assets]
Geldhandlungsprofit *m* banker's profit, profit of the bank
Geldherrschaft *f s.* Geldaristokratie
Geldhilfe *f* financial aid
Geldhort *m* (monetary) treasure
Geldhortung *f* currency hoarding
Geldinstitut *n* financial institution; bank; savings bank
Geldkapital *n* money capital
Geldkasse *f* cash-box; cash-register
Geldkassette *f* strong-box, cash-box
Geldkaufkraft *f* purchasing power of money
Geldknappheit *f* shortage of money; scarcity of money, financial stringency
Geldkredit *m s.* Gelddarleh(e)n
Geldkreislauf *m* circulation of money;, money-cycle
Geldkrise *f* monetary crisis; financial crisis
Geldkurs *m* rate of exchange; *(st.ex.)* bid price, buying rate
Geldeinsatz *m* rate for loans, bank rate
Geldleistung *f* money payment; *(ins)* cash benefit
geldlich pecuniary, financial, monetary
Geldlohn *m* money [monetary] wage, wage
Geldlohnrate *f* money wage rate

Geldmacht *f* financial power
Geldmakler *m* money broker; bill broker
Geldmangel *m* scarcity [lack, dearth] of money, financial stringency
Geldmarkt *m* money market
geldmarktempfindlich sensitive to the state of the money market
Geldmarktentwicklung *f* tendency of the money market
Geldmarktgeschäft *n* money market business; transaction on the money market
Geldmarktpapier *n* money market security
Geldmarktschwankungen *fpl* fluctuations in the money market
Geldmarkttitel *m s.* Geldmarktpapier
Geldmasse *f s.* Geldmenge
Geldmenge *f* quantity of money; stock of money supply *(usually by the central bank)*; volume of money *(in circulation)*
Geldmengentheorie *f* quantity (of money)
Geldmittel *npl* financial resources [means, funds]
~, öffentliche public funds
~, verfügbare available funds
~, zeitweilig freie temporarily free financial resources
Geldmünze *f* coin
Geldnachfrage *f* demand for money [currency]
Geldnebenkosten *pl* additional monetary costs *(interest, bank charges etc.)*
Geldnehmer *m* borrower; mortgagor
Geldneuordnung *f s.* Geldreform
Geldnot *f* money difficulties, financial straits
Geldopfer *n* monetary sacrifice
Geldordnung *f s.* Geldsystem
Geldpapier *n* financial document
Geldpolitik *f* monetary policy
geldpolitisch from the point of view of monetary policy
Geldposten *m* sum of money; *(acc)* item
Geldprämie *f* money [cash] bonus
Geldpreis *m* 1. interest on loans; rate of exchange; 2. money [cash] price
Geldquantum *n s.* Geldmenge
Geldquelle *f* source of money [capital]
Geldreform *f* monetary reform
Geldregulierung *f* money market control
Geldreserve *f* money reserve
Geldrolle *f* roll of coins, rouleau
Geldsache *f* money matter, matter of money
Geldsammlung *f* raising of funds; collection of money
Geldsatz *m* money rate
Geldschein *m* bank [currency] note
Geldschöpfung *f* creation of currency [money]
Geldschöpfungspolitik *f* policy of money creation

Geldschöpfungstheorie *f* theory of money creation
Geldschrank *m* safe
Geldschuld *f* (money) debt
Geldschuldner *m* debtor
Geldschwemme *f* glut of money
Geldschwierigkeiten *fpl* pecuniary difficulties; financial difficulties [straits] ◊ **in ~ sein** to be in financial [pecuniary] difficulties
Geldsendung *f* cash remittance
Geldsorgen *fpl* money troubles, pecuniary embarrassment(s)
Geldsorte *f* denomination *(of notes and coins)*
Geldsorten *fpl* notes and coins
~, ausländische foreign notes and coins, foreign currency
Geldsortenschuld *f* debt to be paid in a specified currency
Geldspende *f* donation, (money) contribution, subscription *(to a charity etc.)*
Geldstabilität *f s.* **Geldwertstabilität**
Geldstrafe *f* fine
Geldstrom *m* money flow, flow of money
Geldstromanalyse *f* analysis of money flow
Geldstück *n* coin
Geldstückelung *f* denomination of money [currency]
Geldsumme *f* sum (of money)
Geldsurrogat *n s.* **Geldersatz**
Geldsystem *n* monetary system
Geldtausch *m s.* **Geldumtausch**
Geldtelegramm *n s.* **Geldanweisung, telegrafische**
Geldtheorie *f* money theory
Geldüberfluß *m* excess of money
Geldüberhang *m* surplus money, excessive supply of money
Geldüberweisung *f* money order, remittance
Geldumlauf *m* money circulation
Geldumlaufformel *f* money circulation formula
Geldumlaufgeschwindigkeit *f* velocity of money circulation
Geldumlaufgesetz *n* law of money (in) circulation
Geldumlaufplanung *f* planning of money (in) circulation *(to maintain equilibrium between money in circulation and goods and services offered)*
Geldumsatz *m* turnover of money *(in circulation)*
Geldumstellung *f* currency conversion
Geldumtausch *m* exchange of money *(especially foreign currency)*; currency conversion
Geldumtauschstelle *f s.* **Geldwechselstelle**
Geld- und Kreditsystem *n* system of money and credit
Geld- und Sachleistungen *fpl* payments in cash and kind

Geldunterstützung *f* financial support [subvention], pecuniary aid
Geldverbilligung *f* cheapening of money
Geldverdiener *m* earner (of money)
Geldverfassung *f* monetary system *(as stipulated by the laws of a country)*
Geldverflechtungsbilanz *f* monetary input-output table
Geldverkehr *m* money [monetary] transactions
Geldverknappung *f* (growing) scarcity [tightness] of money
Geldverleih *m* money-lending
Geldverleiher *m* money-lender
Geldverlust *m* loss of money; financial [pecuniary] loss
Geldvermehrung *f* increase of money [currency], increase in the supply of money
Geldvermittler *m* money broker
Geldvermögen *n* monetary assets
Geldvermögenswert *m* financial asset
Geldverschwendung *f* waste of money
Geldvolumen *n* volume of money; (total) supply of money
Geldvorrat *m* (monetary) funds, available funds; cash reserve; *(bank)* cash in vault; supply of money *(on the money market)*
Geldvorschuß *m* cash advance
Geldwanderung *f* migration of money *(to holiday areas, regional shopping centres etc.)*
Geldware *f* money commodity
Geldwechsel *m* exchange of money; change for loose money
Geldwechselgeschäft *n* exchange transaction; exchange business
Geldwechselstelle *f* (currency) exchange (office)
Geldwechsler *m* money changer
Geldwert *m* monetary [cash] value; value of money [(the) currency]
~, äußerer international value of (the) currency
~, innerer national value of (the) currency
Geldwertentwicklung *f* development [tendency] of the value of currency
Geldwertschuld *f* claim payable in original value
Geldwertschwankungen *fpl* fluctuations in the value of money
Geldwertstabilität *f* stability of (the) value of money
Geldwertverbesserung *f* increase in the value of money
Geldwertverschlechterung *f* decline in the value of money
Geldwesen *n* monetary [financial] system
Geldwirtschaft *f* money economy; trade on a monetary basis *(as distinct from barter)*
geldwirtschaftlich from the point of view of monetary conditions

Geldwucher *m* usury
Geldwucherer *m* usurer
Geldzahlung *f* payment (in cash)
Geldzeichen *n* monetary token *(coin, bank note, cheque etc.)*
Geldzins *m* money interest
Geldzirkulation *f* circulation of money, money circulation
Geldzufluß *m* influx of money [currency]
Geldzulage *f* supplementary payment; additional [extra] pay
Geldzuwachs *m s.* **Geldvermehrung**
Geldzuweisung *f* allocation of funds
Gelegenheit *f* opportunity, occasion; chance
Gelegenheitsarbeit *f* casual [occasional, odd] job
Gelegenheitsarbeiter *m* casual labourer [worker], odd-job man
Gelegenheitsauftrag *m* casual commission; odd job
Gelegenheitsgeschäft *n* chance business; good bargain
Gelegenheitskauf *m* chance purchase, (good) bargain
Gelegenheitskäufer *m* chance purchaser
Gelegenheitsprobe *f s.* **Gelegenheits-Stichprobenverfahren**
Gelegenheits-Stichprobenverfahren *n (stats)* chunk sampling
gelenkt controlled, administered *(economy, prices etc.)*
geliehen borrowed *(capital, money etc.)*
gelöscht 1. landed *(goods from ship)*; unloaded, unshipped; 2. extinguished *(fire, light etc.)*; 3. cancelled *(claim, debt etc.)*; cleared *(mortgage)*; closed *(account)*
gelten to hold good [true]; to be applicable, to apply *(quality etc.)*; to be valid *(stamp, ticket etc.)*; to be in force, to be operative [effective] *(law, regulation etc.)*; to be current *(coins etc.)*
geltend valid *(contract, law etc.)*; prevailing, accepted, recognized *(custom, opinion etc.)*; operative, effective *(law, regulation etc.)* ⋄ ~ **machen** to assert, to enforce *(claim, right etc.)*; to exert, to exercise *(influence etc.)*; to urge *(reason, excuse etc.)*
Geltendmachen *n s.* **Geltendmachung**
Geltendmachung *f* exercise *(influence etc.)*; assertion, enforcement *(claim, right etc.)*; insistence, vindication *(prerogative, privilege etc.)*
Geltung *f* validity *(stamp, ticket etc.)*; currency *(money)*; accepted [recognized] value *(opinion, theory etc.)*; credit, repute, esteem, importance *(persons, qualities etc.)*
Geltungsbereich *m* scope *(law etc.)*, purview *(theory etc.)*, field of application *(principles etc.)*
Geltungsdauer *f* period of validity *(passport etc.)*

Geltungsgebiet *n* area in which a law [regulation] is in force
Gemarkung *f* administrative area *(of a community)*; boundaries *(of a community)*
Gemeinbesitz *m* common property; communal property; public property; joint property
Gemeinde *f* municipality *(local government of town/city)*; community *(of people in a specific locality etc.)*; parish *(subdivision of a district in rural areas etc.)*
Gemeindeabgaben *fpl* local (authority) taxes, local rates
Gemeindeamt *n* municipal office; municipal authority; rural administrative authority
Gemeindeangelegenheiten *fpl* municipal affairs; rural affairs
Gemeindeangestellter *m* municipal employee [worker]
Gemeindeanleihe *f* municipal loan
Gemeindearbeiter *m* municipal worker
Gemeindeausgaben *fpl* local authority budget expenditures
Gemeindeausschuß *m* local [municipal] committee
Gemeindebehörde *f* local government authority, rural [municipal] authority
Gemeindebetrieb *m* municipal undertaking [enterprise]
gemeindeeigen municipal *(property, enterprise etc.)*; communally-owned
Gemeindeeigentum *n* municipal [local authority] property
Gemeindeeinnahmen *fpl* local (government) revenue
Gemeindeeinrichtung *f* municipal [rural] institution
Gemeindefinanzen *pl* local finance(s)
Gemeindehaus *n* village hall; community centre
Gemeindehaushalt *m* municipal [local government] budget
Gemeindekasse *f* municipal funds; municipal finance office
Gemeindeland *n* common land
Gemeindeobligationen *fpl* municipal bonds
Gemeindeordnung *f* municipal code
Gemeinderat *m* municipal council; parish council
Gemeindeselbstverwaltung *f* municipal [local] self-government
Gemeindesteuer *f* local rate [tax]
Gemeindesteuersystem *n* rating system
Gemeindetyp *m* type of municipality
Gemeindeunterstützung *f* public assistance
Gemeindeverband *m* association of municipalities
Gemeindevermögen *n* municipal property
Gemeindevertreter *m* rural councillor

Gemeindevertretung *f* parish [local] assembly
Gemeindeverwaltung *f* local [municipal, rural] administration [government]; local [municipal, rural] authority
Gemeindewahl *f* local [municipal] election
Gemeindewald *m* communal forest
Gemeindewiese *f* communal pasture; village green
Gemeindewirtschaft *f* municipal economy; administration of a municipality's business affairs
Gemeindeeigentum *n* communal property *(especially communal land)*; public ownership *(land, natural resources etc.)*
Gemeingebrauch *m (jur)* common use
Gemeingläubiger *m* non-preferential creditor *(in case of bankruptcy)*
Gemeingut *n* common [communal, public] property
Gemeinkapital *n* joint stock *(of a company etc.)*
Gemeinkosten *pl* overhead costs [expenses], overheads
~, **technologische** indirect production costs *(depreciation, energy costs etc.)*
Gemeinkostenabweichung *f* overhead variance
Gemeinkostenanalyse *f* overhead cost analysis
Gemeinkostenanteil *m* rate of overheads, proportion of overhead costs *(in total costs)*
Gemeinkostenart *f* type of overhead costs
Gemeinkostenbereich *m* centre of overhead costs
Gemeinkostendeckung *f* covering of overhead costs
Gemeinkostennormativ *n* standard rate of overhead costs
Gemeinkostenplanung *f* planning of overhead costs
Gemeinkostenrechnung *f* accounting of overhead costs
Gemeinkostensatz *m* rate of overhead costs
Gemeinkostensenkung *f* decrease in overhead costs
Gemeinkostenumlage *f* distribution of overhead costs, apportioning [apportionment] of indirect cost(s)
Gemeinkostenzuschlag *m* rate of overhead costs
Gemeinlast *f (ins)* common burden *(shared by various funds)*
Gemeinnutz *m* public interest [benefit]
gemeinnützig in the public interest, for the public benefit, to the advantage of all, in the interest(s) of the community; non-profit-making *(organization etc.)*
Gemeinnützigkeit *f* usefulness in the public interest, advantageousness for the public; non--profitmaking character *(organization etc.)*

Gemeinsamkeitsgrad *m (stats)* communality
Gemeinschaft *f* team; community; union, association
gemeinschaftlich common *(property etc.)*, mutual *(interests etc.)*, joint *(undertaking etc.)*, collective *(action, efforts etc.)*, united *(activities etc.)*
Gemeinschaftlichkeit *f* community of possessions [interests]; participation in common activities; sharing of common ideas; solidarity *(national groups etc.)*
Gemeinschaftsanlage *f* joint investment
~, **landwirtschaftliche** joint agricultural establishment *(coldstorage plants, fruit-processing plants etc.)*
Gemeinschaftsanschluß *m* party line *(telephone)*
Gemeinschaftsantenne *f* joint antenna [aerial]
Gemeinschaftsarbeit *f* teamwork; piece of co--operative work
Gemeinschaftsbeteiligung *f* collective [joint] participation
Gemeinschaftsbilanz *f* consolidated balance sheet
Gemeinschaftsdepot *n* joint deposit *(of securities etc.)*
Gemeinschaftseinkauf *m* co-operative purchasing
Gemeinschaftseinrichtung *f* joint establishment
~, **hauswirtschaftliche** (public) service centre *(e.g. laundry, household repairs etc.)*
Gemeinschaftsemission *f* joint issue
Gemeinschaftsessen *n* cafeteria [canteen] meals
Gemeinschaftsfinanzierung *f* group financing
Gemeinschaftsforschung *f* joint research
Gemeinschaftsgeist *m* team spirit, solidarity
Gemeinschaftsgründung *f* joint founding [foundation]
Gemeinschaftshaftung *f* joint responsibility [liability]
Gemeinschaftskonto *n* joint account
Gemeinschaftsküche *f* canteen, central kitchen
Gemeinschaftsproduktion *f* co-production
Gemeinschaftsraum *m* recreation [common] room
Gemeinschaftsschau *f* collective display
Gemeinschaftsverpflegung *f* common [public] catering
Gemeinschaftswerbung *f* co-operative advertising; joint advertising *(of different types of products)*
Gemeinschuldner *m* declared bankrupt, common debtor
Gemeinwert *m* (normal) market value
Gemeinwesen *n* (the) community; (the) commonwealth
~, **dörfliches** village [rural] community
~, **politisches** the state; the body politic
~, **städtisches** town [urban] community

Gemeinwirtschaft *f* economy directed towards public advantage *(rather than private profit)*
Gemeinwohl *n* general [common, public] weal
Gemischtbauweise *f* composite construction
Gemischtwaren *fpl* groceries (and general goods), *(Am)* general merchandise
Gemischtwarenhandel *m* grocery (and general goods) trade; trade in groceries and general goods; *(Am)* general merchandise trade
Gemischtwarenhandlung *f* grocer's shop, grocery, general shop [store], *(Am)* general merchandise store
Gemüseanbau *m* cultivation [growing] of vegetables, vegetable gardening; market gardening, *(Am)* truck farming
Gemüsebau *m s.* **Gemüseanbau**
Gemüsehandel *m* trade in vegetables; vegetable trade
Gemüsehändler *m* greengrocer *(retail trade);* vegetable dealer *(wholesale trade)*
Gemüsehandlung *f* greengrocer's (shop)
Gemüsemarkt *m* vegetable market
Gemüse- und Obstgürtel *m* vegetable and fruit zone *(cultivation of vegetables and fruits near centres of consumption)*
Genauigkeit *f* accuracy; precision
Genauigkeitsgrad *m* degree of accuracy
genehmigen to grant *(application)*, to approve; to assent; to accept; to permit
Genehmigung *f* granting, approval *(of s.th.);* assent *(to s.th.);* acceptance *(of s.th.);* licence, permission *(for s.th.);* authorization
Genehmigungsbehörde *f* authorizing agency [body]; authority that issues [grants, permits] the right to do st.h.
Genehmigungsbescheid *m* notice of approval
Genehmigungspflicht *f* duty to obtain authorization [permission, approval]
genehmigungspflichtig requiring official approval [permission, sanction]
Genehmigungsverfahren *n* authorizing procedure
Genehmigungsvermerk *m* 'approved' endorsement [stamp] *(on application etc.)*
Generalagent *m* general agent [representative]
Generalauftragnehmer *m* chief contractor, chief [main] acceptor of order
Generalauftragnehmervergütung *f* remuneration of the chief contractor [chief acceptor of order]
Generalbebauungsplan *m* master plan *(town and city planning)*
Generalbevollmächtigter *m (jur)* universal [general] agent *(with unlimited power of attorney)*
Generaldirektion *f* head office, central administrative office; central management; board of directors *(central banks etc.);* central board

Generaldirektor *m* general manager; director--general
Generalindex *m (stats)* composite index-number
Generalinstandsetzung *f s.* **Generalreparatur**
Generalinvestor *m* general investor
Generalklausel *f (jur)* general [blanket] clause
Generalkonsul *m* consul-general
Generalkonsulat *n* consulate-general
Generallinie *f* central policy, general line
Generalplan *m* general development plan *(town)*
Generalpolice *f* comprehensive insurance; floating [open] policy *(marine insurance)*
Generalreparatur *f* general [major] overhaul [repair] *(machines etc.)*
Generalsekretär *m* Secretary-General *(United Nations);* general secretary *(political parties etc.)*
Generalstaatsanwalt *m* chief public prosecutor
generalüberholen to give *s.th.* a major [thorough, complete] overhaul, to recondition
Generalüberholung *f* major [thorough, complete] overhaul
Generalverkehrsplan *m* long-term traffic development plan
Generalverkehrsplanung *f* long-term traffic development planning
Generalversammlung *f* General Assembly *(UN);* general meeting *(companies etc.)*
Generalvertreter *m (com)* general agent *(as opposed to sole agent)*
Generalvollmacht *f (jur)* full [unlimited] power (of attorney)
Generation *f* generation *(population etc.)*
Generationsabstand *m* generation gap, space between generations
Generationsproblem *n* generation problem, problem of the difference(s) between generations
genormt standardized, unitized
Genossenschaft *f* co-operative, (co-operative) society
~, **eingetragene** incorporated society
~, **gewerbliche** industrial co-operative society
~, **landwirtschaftliche** agricultural co-operative (society)
Genossenschaftler *m* member of a co-operative society
genossenschaftlich co-operative
Genossenschaftsanteil *m* share in a co-operative society
Genossenschaftsbank *f* co-operative bank [banking association]
Genossenschaftsbauer *m* co-operative farmer, member of a co-operative farm
Genossenschaftsbewegung *f* co-operative movement
Genossenschaftsbildung *f* formation of co--operative societies

Genossenschaftsfirma f co-operative enterprise
Genossenschaftsgesetz n co-operative association law
Genossenschaftsmitglied n s. **Genossenschaftler**
Genossenschaftsplan m co-operative plan
Genossenschaftsrecht n law of associations; co-operative act
Genossenschaftsregister n register of co-operative societies
Genossenschaftssektor m co-operative sector
Genossenschaftssteuern fpl taxes on co-operatives [co-operative societies]
Genossenschaftsverband m co-operative union
Genossenschaftsvertrag m articles of association of a society
Genossenschaftswesen n (system of) co-operative societies
Genußmittel npl luxuries, luxury articles, non--essential food and drink (wines, spirits, tobacco and the like)
Geographie f geography
~, **ökonomische** economic geography
~, **politische** political geography
Gepäck n luggage, (Am) baggage
Gepäckabfertigung f registering of luggage, checking of baggage; (cust) clearing
Gepäckaufbewahrung f left luggage office
Gepäckschein m luggage [cloakroom] ticket
Gepäcktarif m luggage [(Am) baggage] rates
Gepäckversicherung f luggage [(Am) baggage] insurance
Gepflogenheiten fpl habits
~, **gesellschaftliche** social habits [conventions]
~, **kommerzielle** commercial usage [practice]
Gerätebau m equipment [instrument] making
Gerätemonteur m fitter for (electrical) household appliances
Gerätesystem n system of equipment [instruments]
gerecht just, fair (person etc.), equitable (decision, settlement etc.), legitimate (right, claim, doubt etc.), deserved (punishment etc.), merited (praise etc.)
Gerechtigkeit f justness, fairness (person etc.), justice, equity (decision, settlement etc.), legitimacy (right, claim, doubt etc.), just deserts (punishment etc.), merit (praise etc.)
~, **soziale** social justice
Gericht n 1. judgement; court (of law/justice); 2. dish
gerichtlich court, of the court
Gerichtsakte f documents [papers] relating to an action at law
Gerichtsbarkeit f jurisdiction; judicial power [authority]
Gerichtsbeschluß m court decision

Gerichtsgebühren fpl court fees
Gerichtshof m high court of law
Gerichtskosten pl legal costs
Gerichtsort m s. **Gerichtsstand**
Gerichtsstand m legal domicile (person, firm etc.); legal venue [jurisdiction]
Gerichtsstandvereinbarung f jurisdiction clause
~, **internationale** international jurisdiction clause
Gerichtsurteil n verdict; judgement (of the court)
Gerichtsverfahren n action (at law); legal proceedings
Gerichtsverhandlung f legal proceedings; hearing; trial
Gerichtsvollzieher m bailiff
Gerichtsweg m legal proceedings ⋄ **auf dem ~** by (means of) legal proceedings; **den ~ gehen** to take legal proceedings
geringwertig low-value (goods, food etc.); low--grade (mineral, fuel etc.)
Gerüstbauer m scaffolder
gesamt whole, entire, all (inhabitants, property etc.); complete; total, overall, aggregate (costs etc.)
Gesamtabsatz m total sales
Gesamtabschreibungen fpl accrued depreciation
Gesamtabtretung f general assignment
Gesamtaktie f share certificate
Gesamtaktiva pl total [overall] assets
Gesamtanalyse f overall analysis
Gesamtangebot n total supply
Gesamtanordnung f general arrangement (display etc.)
Gesamtarbeitsvertrag m collective agreement
Gesamtaufkommen n total yield (tax etc.)
Gesamtaufstellung f general statement
Gesamtauftrag m bulk order; block booking (tickets etc.)
Gesamtaufwand m total expenditure(s) [outlay]
Gesamtaufwandskennziffer f index [indicator] of total expenditure(s)
Gesamtausbeute f total output
Gesamtausfuhr f total exports
Gesamtausgaben fpl total expenditure(s)
Gesamtauslagen fpl total expenses
Gesamtausstoß m total (production) output
Gesamtauswahlsatz m (stats) overall sampling fraction
Gesamtbearbeitungszeit f (total) operating time
Gesamtbedarf m total demand [requirement]
Gesamtbedingungen fpl overall conditions
Gesamtbeschäftigte pl total number of employees [workers]
Gesamtbeschäftigtenzahl f s. **Gesamtbeschäftigte**

Gesamtbesitz *m* total property; entirety of estate
Gesamtbestand *m* total stock
Gesamtbetrag *m* total (amount), grand [sum] total, aggregate amount
Gesamtbevölkerung *f* total population
Gesamtbilanz *f* overall balance
~, **volkswirtschaftliche** national economic account
Gesamtbürgschaft *f* joint surety
Gesamtdurchschnitt *m* total average
Gesamteigentum *n* joint property
Gesamteigentümer *mpl* joint owners
Gesamteinfuhr *f* total imports
Gesamteinfuhrkontingent *n* overall import quota
Gesamteingänge *mpl* total receipts
Gesamteinkommen *n* total income; total revenue
Gesamteinkünfte *pl* total income
Gesamteinnahmen *fpl* total receipts
Gesamteinzahlungen *fpl* total deposits
Gesamtentwicklung *f* general trend [tendency]
Gesamtergebnis *n* total result *(production etc.)*
Gesamterlös *m* total proceeds [returns]; *(agric)* total produce [harvest]
Gesamterzeugung *f (ind)* total output
Gesamtfinanzierungsmodell *n* overall model of financing
Gesamtgefüge *n* overall set-up
~, **territoriales** overall regional set-up
Gesamtgewicht *n* total weight
Gesamtgewinn *m* total profits
Gesamtgläubiger *m* general [joint] creditor
Gesamtgut *n (jur)* joint property
Gesamthaftung *f* joint liability
Gesamthand *f s.* **Gesamthandseigentum**
Gesamthandseigentum *n* co-ownership
Gesamthandsgemeinschaft *f* (community of) joint owners
Gesamtheit *f* (the) whole, entirety, totality; *(stats)* population
~ **mit endlichem Umfang** *(stats)* finite population
~, **sich erneuernde** *(stats)* self-renewing aggregate
Gesamthypothek *f* blanket mortgage
Gesamtindex *m* overall index
Gesamtkapital *n* joint capital
Gesamtkosten *pl* total costs
Gesamtkostenrechnung *f* accounting of total costs
Gesamtmontage *f* single-contractor construction; overall construction
Gesamtnutzeffekt *m* overall efficiency
Gesamtnutzen *m* overall [total] efficiency
~, **ökonomischer** overall economic efficiency
Gesamtnutzung *f* use of common land

Gesamtoptimierungsmodell *n* overall [comprehensive] optimization model
Gesamtplanung *f* overall planning
Gesamtpreis *m* lump-sum price; total price
Gesamtprodukt *n* gross (national) product (GNP)
Gesamtproduktion *f* total (production) output
Gesamtprokura *f* joint [general] power of attorney
Gesamtrechnung *f* overall account(ing)
~, **betriebliche** overall business accounting *(system of accounting and statistics)*
~, **perspektivische** long-term national accounting
~, **prognostische** national account projection
~, **territoriale** regional aggregate accounting
~, **volkswirtschaftliche** national (income and product) account
Gesamtregelung *f* overall settlement
Gesamtschaden *m* total damage, *(ins)* total loss
Gesamtschätzung *f* overall estimate
Gesamtschau *f* general display
Gesamtschuld *f* joint liability [debt]
Gesamtschuldner *m* general [joint] debtor
gesamtschuldnerisch joint
Gesamtselbstkosten *pl* total costs [expenditures]
Gesamtstruktur *f* overall structure; total range *(supply etc.)*
~ **der Wirtschaft** structure of the national economy
Gesamtsumme *f* sum total, total (amount)
Gesamtsystem *n* overall system
Gesamttonnage *f* total tonnage
Gesamtüberschuß *m* total surplus
Gesamtumsatz *m* total turnover
~ **des Außenhandels** total exports and imports, total turnover of foreign trade
Gesamtverband *m* general association
Gesamtverbrauch *m* total consumption
Gesamtverdienst *m* total earnings
Gesamtvereinbarung *f s.* **Gesamtarbeitsvertrag**
Gesamtverflechtungsbilanz *f* input-output table of the national economy
Gesamtvermögen *n* aggregate property
Gesamtversicherung *f* comprehensive [all-in] insurance
gesamtvolkswirtschaftlich from a general economic point of view
Gesamtvollmacht *f s.* **Gesamtprokura**
Gesamtwert *m* total value
Gesamtwirkung *f* general effect
Gesamtwirtschaft *f* overall [whole] national economy
Gesamtzeit *f* total time; *(d.pr.)* overhead time
Gesamtzeitaufwand *m* total expenditure of time

Gesandter *m* envoy, representative on a special mission; diplomatic agent; minister
~, außerodentlicher envoy extraordinary
~, ständiger envoy, minister
Gesandtschaft *f* legation, mission
Gesandtschaftsrat *m* counsellor of legation
Gesandtschaftssekretär *m* secretary of a legation
Geschädigter *m (ins)* injured person
Geschäft *n* 1. business; transaction, operation, deal; 2. firm, enterprise, concern, company; shop ⋄ **ein ~ abschließen** to make a deal; **ein ~ betreiben** to carry on a business; **ein ~ eröffnen** to open a shop [firm]; **ein ~ führen** to run a shop [firm]; **ein ~ leiten** to manage a shop [firm]; **ein ~ schließen** to close a shop *(for the day)*; to close down a shop [firm] *(permanently)*
Geschäfte *npl* dealings, transactions, operations
Geschäftemacher *m* profiteer
Geschäftemacherei *f* profiteering
geschäftlich business, commercial
Geschäftsabschluß *m* 1. (business) transaction, deal; 2. (annual) closing of accounts
Geschäftsanteil *m* share [interest] in limited company
Geschäftsanteilschein *m* share certificate
Geschäftsaufgabe *f* retirement from business
Geschäftsaussichten *fpl* business prospects [outlook]
Geschäftsausstattung *f* office [shop] inventory
Geschäftsbank *f* commercial bank
Geschäftsbankgeld *n* commercial bank deposit money
Geschäftsbedingungen *fpl* (business) conditions; terms of trade
~, Allgemeine (AGB) General Terms [Conditions] of Trade
Geschäftsbericht *m* company report, annual report of board of management
Geschäftsbeziehungen *fpl* trade [business] relations
Geschäftsbrief *m* business letter
Geschäftsbücher *npl* account books, accounts
Geschäftseröffnung *f* opening of a shop [business]
geschäftsfähig legally able [competent] to make contracts
Geschäftsfähigkeit *f* (legal) capacity to contract, (legal) contractual capacity; (legal) capacity to act in law
Geschäftsfrau *f* businesswoman
Geschäftsfreund *m* business friend; colleague
Geschäftsführer *m* manager *(shop etc.)*, managing director *(limited company)*; company secretary; secretary *(institution)*
Geschäftsführung *f* (business) management

Geschäftsgebaren *n* business [commercial] practices
Geschäftsgeheimnis *n* business [trade] secret
Geschäftsinhaber *m* owner of a firm, principal; shop-keeper
Geschäftsinteresse *n* interest in commercial [business] matters
Geschäftsjahr *n* business year
Geschäftskapital *n* capital
Geschäftskonto *n* business account
Geschäftskosten *pl* business expense(s)
Geschäftslage *f* business situation
Geschäftsleben *n* business life
Geschäftsleiter *m* manager
Geschäftsleitung *f* 1. management, management committee, board of management; 2. management, conduct of business
Geschäftsmann *m* businessman
geschäftsmäßig businesslike *(manner etc.)*
Geschäftsmiete *f* shop rent; rent of business premises
Geschäftsoperation *f* trade transaction
Geschäftsordnung *f* standing orders *(parliament etc.)*; rules of procedure *(association etc.)*
Geschäftspapiere *npl* business [commercial] papers
Geschäftspartner *m* business partner; party to a transaction
Geschäftspersonal *n* staff, employees
Geschäftsprüfung *f* auditing
Geschäftsstelle *f* office; *(bank)* branch
Geschäftsstellenleiter *m s.* **Geschäftsleiter**
Geschäftsstrategie *f* business strategy
Geschäftsstunden *fpl s.* **Geschäftszeit**
Geschäftstätigkeit *f* business [commercial] activities
Geschäftsträger *m* chargé d'affaires
geschäftstüchtig capable, efficient
Geschäftstüchtigkeit *f* business efficiency
Geschäftsübernahme *f* take-over (of a shop), taking over a shop [business]
geschäftsunfähig incapable of acting in law; unable [incompetent] to make contracts
Geschäftsunfähigkeit *f* (legal) incapacity, incapacity to act in law; (legal) incapacity to contract
Geschäftsunkosten *pl s.* **Geschäftskosten**
Geschäftsverbindung *f* business contact [connection]
Geschäftsverbindungen *fpl*:
⋄ **~ pflegen** to have [entertain] business relations (with other firms)
Geschäftsverkehr *m* business dealings [transactions]
Geschäftsverlauf *m* trend of business
Geschäftszeit *f* business hours
Geschäftszweig *m* branch [line] of business

Geschenk *n* gift, present; donation
Geschenkartikel *mpl* gifts, fancy goods, souvenirs
Geschenkartikelgeschäft *n* gift [souvenir] shop
Geschenkpackung *f* gift pack [wrapping]
Geschenksendung *f* gift parcel
Geschichte *f* 1. history; 2. story, tale
~ der politischen Ökonomie history of political economy
Geschlechterverhältnis *n (stats)* sex ratio
Geschworene *mpl/fpl (jur)* the jury
Geschworenenbank *f (jur)* the jury box
Geschworener *m (jur)* member of a jury, jury member
Geselle *m* journeyman
Gesellschaft *f* 1. (human) society; 2. company, *(Am)* corporation; partnership
~, bürgerliche bourgeois [capitalist] society
~, klassenlose classless society
~, matriarchalische matriarchal society
~, menschliche human society
~ mit beschränkter Haftung (GmbH) limited (liability) company
~ mit unbeschränkter Haftung (GmuH) company with unlimited liability
~ mit unbeschränkter Haftung, eingetragene (eGmuH) incorporated [registered] company with unlimited liability
~, patriarchalische patriarchal society
~, postindustrielle post-industrial society
~, private proprietary company, *(Am)* private corporation
~, sozialistische socialist society
Gesellschafter *m* partner, associate *(limited company etc.)*; shareholder, *(Am)* stockholder
~, beschränkt haftender partner with limited liability [liable with limitation]
~, persönlich haftender general partner, personally liable partner
~, stiller sleeping [silent] partner
~, unbeschränkt haftender partner with unlimited liability [liable without limitation]
~, vollhaftender *s.* ~, unbeschränkt haftender
Gesellschafteranteil *m* share (in a limited company)
Gesellschafterbeschluß *m* decision of the shareholders meeting
Gesellschafterdarleh(e)n *n* loan granted to a company by one of the shareholders
Gesellschafterliste *f* register of shareholders
Gesellschafterversammlung *f* (general) meeting of shareholders [partners], shareholders' meeting
gesellschaftlich social *(structure, life etc.)*
Gesellschaftsanteil *m* share (in a company's capital)
Gesellschaftsform *f* form of society

Gesellschaftsformation *f* social formation
~, ökonomische socio-economic formation
Gesellschaftsgläubiger *m* creditor of a company
Gesellschaftskapital *n* capital stock (of a company)
Gesellschaftsordnung *f* social system [order]
Gesellschaftspolitik *f* social policy
gesellschaftspolitisch social-policy *(measures, ideas etc.)*
Gesellschaftsrecht *n (jur)* company law; *(com)* right of a member to a certain proportion of the profits and assets of a company
Gesellschaftsreise *f* conducted [party] tour, group outing
Gesellschaftsschicht *f* social stratum
Gesellschaftsstruktur *f* social structure, structure of society
Gesellschaftssystem *n* social system
~, kapitalistisches capitalist social system
~, sozialistisches socialist social system
Gesellschaftsvermögen *n* company assets, assets of a company
Gesellschaftsvertrag *m* memorandum and articles of association
Gesellschaftswissenschaften *fpl* social sciences
Gesetz *n* law; act; statute ◊ ein ~ durchbringen to pass a law
~ der großen Zahlen *(stats)* law of large numbers
~ der großen Zahlen, starkes *(stats)* strong law of large numbers
~ der kapitalistischen Akkumulation, allgemeines *(pol ec)* general (economic) law of capitalist accumulation
~ der kleinen Zahlen *(stats)* law of small numbers
~ der Konzentration und Zentralisation des Kapitals *(pol ec)* (economic) law of concentration and centralization of capital
~ der Ökonomie der Zeit *(pol ec)* law of the economy of time
~ der planmäßigen proportionalen Entwicklung der Volkswirtschaft (economic) law of planned and proportionate [balanced] development of the national economy *(economic theory)*
~ der seltenen Ereignisse *(stats)* Poisson distribution
~ der stetigen Steigerung der Arbeitsproduktivität (economic) law of permanent increase of labour productivity *(economic theory)*
~ der Übereinstimmung der Produktionsverhältnisse mit dem Charakter der Produktivkräfte law of conformity between production relations and the character of productive forces *(economic theory)*

Gesetz

- **der ungleichmäßigen ökonomischen und politischen Entwicklung des Kapitalismus** law of uneven economic and political development of capitalism *(economic theory)*
- **der Verteilung nach der Arbeitsleistung** law of distribution of income according to (labour) performance *(economic theory)*
- **des tendenziellen Falls der Profitrate** *(pol ec)* (economic) law of the tendency of the profit rate to fall
- **des vorrangigen Wachstums der Produktion von Produktionsmitteln gegenüber der Produktion von Konsumtionsmitteln** (economic) law of priority [accelerated] development [growth] of means of production in comparison with consumer goods *(economic theory)*
- **~, objektives** objective law
- **~, ökonomisches** economic law
- **~, Parkinsonsches** Parkinson's Law
- **vom abnehmenden Bodenertrag** *(agric)* law of diminishing returns
- **von Angebot und Nachfrage** (economic) law of supply and demand
- **von der Konkurrenz und Anarchie der kapitalistischen Produktion** (economic) law of competition and anarchy of capitalist production *(economic theory)*

Gesetzblatt *n* law gazette
Gesetzbuch *n* (legal) code
~, bürgerliches code of civil law, civil code
Gesetzentwurf *m* draft bill ⋄ **einen ~ ablehnen** to reject a (draft) bill; **einen ~ annehmen** to pass a bill, to carry [adopt] a bill; **einen ~ einbringen** to introduce [bring in, present] a (draft) bill
Gesetzeskraft *f* force of (a) law, force of laws
Gesetzeslücke *f* loophole [defect] in the law
Gesetzesvorlage *f* bill
gesetzgebend legislative *(body etc.)*
Gesetzgeber *m* legislator
gesetzgeberisch legislatorial *(measures etc.)*
Gesetzgebung *f* legislation
Gesetzgebungsverfahren *n* legislative procedure, procedure of legislation
gesetzlich legal *(measures etc.)*; statutory *(holidays etc.)*
Gesetzlichkeit *f* legality
gesetzmäßig regular, following a set pattern, based on a principle [law]; legal, legitimate *(power, title, claim etc.)*; lawful *(procedure etc.)*
Gesetzmäßigkeit *f* objective trend [development]; law (of development), regularity; lawfulness, legality, legitimacy
gesetzwidrig illegal, unlawful
Gesetzwidrigkeit *f* illegality, unlawfulness
Gespräch *n* talk; conversation; discourse; (telephone) conversation; (telephone) call ⋄ **ein ~ anmelden** to book [*(Am)* place] a call *(telephone)*
~, dienstliches business call
~, dringendes urgent call *(telephone)*
Gespräche *npl (pol)* talks
- **auf höchster Ebene** *(pol)* talks at the highest level; *(pol)* summit talks
Gesprächspartner *m* person with whom one is talking [conversing]; interlocutor; party to a (telephone) call
Gestalt *f* shape, form; appearance; figure; build; frame
gestalten to fashion, to form *(s.th.)*; to model *(clay figure etc.)*; to shape *(workpiece etc.)*; to mould *(character etc.)*; to arrange *(programme, exhibition etc.)*, to organize *(activities, conference etc.)*; to create, to produce *(work of art etc.)*; to frame *(ideas etc.)*; to design *(window display, manufactured article etc.)*, to dress *(window)*
Gestaltung *f* fashioning, formation *(of s.th.)*; modelling *(clay figure etc.)*; shaping *(workpiece etc.)*; moulding *(character etc.)*; arrangement *(programme, exhibition etc.)*; creation, production *(work of art etc.)*; framing *(ideas etc.)*; design *(window display, manufactured article etc.)*; configuration *(coast, mountain range etc.)*; structure *(organism etc.)*; development
- **der Arbeits- und Lebensbedingungen** development of working and living conditions
Gestehungskosten *pl* cost(s) of production, production costs
Gestehungspreis *m* production price
Gesuch *n* (formal) request; *(jur)* application; *(jur)* petition ⋄ **ein ~ abschlagen** to refuse [turn down] a request; **ein ~ bewilligen** to grant an application; **einem ~ entsprechen** to comply with a request
Gesundheit *f* health, healthiness *(person, body, organ etc.)*; fitness *(person)*; soundness *(body, animal, plant etc.)*
~, geistige mental health; soundness of mind, sanity
~, körperliche physical [bodily] health; physical fitness
~, öffentliche public health; public hygiene
gesundheitlich concerning [relating to] health; hygienic *(measures etc.)*; sanitary *(conditions etc.)*
Gesundheitsamt *n* public health department [office], *(Am)* health department
Gesundheitsattest *n* health certificate
Gesundheitserziehung *f* health education
Gesundheitsfürsorge *f* medical welfare work [service]; public health service
Gesundheitsschädigung *f* injury to health
~, arbeitsbedingte injury to health caused by working conditions

Gesundheitsstatistik *f* health statistics
Gesundheits- und Arbeitsschutz *m* health and labour protection
Gesundheitswesen *n* public health, health service
Gesundung *f* recovery *(health, economy etc.)*; recuperation; convalescence
Getränkeindustrie *f* drinks [beverage] industry
Getränkekontor *n* wholesale (trade) company for beverages
Getränkesteuer *f* tax on alcoholic beverages
Getreide *n* grain, corn; cereals
Getreideablieferung *f* (compulsory) delivery of grain *(to the state)*
Getreideablieferungssoll *n* grain-delivery quota
Getreideanbau *m* cultivation [growing] of grain [cereals], corn-growing
Getreideanbaufläche *f* corn-growing area
Getreideart *f* type of grain
Getreideaufkauf *m* purchase of grain
Getreideausfuhr *f* export of grain, grain export
Getreidebau *m s.* Getreideanbau
Getreidebeschaffung *f s.* Getreideerfassung
Getreidebörse *f* corn [grain] exchange
Getreideeinfuhr *f* import of grain, grain import
Getreideerfassung *f* procurement of grain
Getreideernte *f* harvesting (of the grain); grain harvest [crop], corn harvest [crop]
Getreideerzeugung *f* grain production
Getreideexport *m s.* Getreideausfuhr
Getreidehandel *m* grain trade, trade in grain; grain merchant's business [firm]
Getreidehändler *m* grain merchant [dealer]
Getreidehandlung *f* grain merchant's shop
Getreideimport *m s.* Getreideeinfuhr
Getreidekrise *f* corn crisis
Getreideland *n* corn-growing area, corn-growing [corn-producing] country
Getreidemakler *m* grain broker, corn broker
Getreidemarkt *m* grain market
Getreidemühle *f* flour-mill; corn-mill
Getreidepreis *m* grain-price, price of grain
Getreideproduktion *f s.* Getreideerzeugung
Getreidesoll *n s.* Getreideablieferungssoll
Getreidesorte *f s.* Getreideart
Getreidespeicher *m* granary, storehouse for grain
Getreidespeicherung *f* grain storage
Getreidetrocknung *f* grain drying
Getreidewirtschaft *f* 1. grain [cereal] producing; 2. grain production and marketing administration
Getreidezoll *m* customs duty on grain, cereals [grain] duty
Gewächshaus *n* greenhouse, glasshouse, hothouse
Gewähr *f* guarantee; security; *(jur)* warranty, guaranty ◇ **ohne ~** without (any) [with no] guarantee
gewähren to grant *(request, right, postponement etc.)*, to allow *(discount, rebate etc.)*
gewährleisten to guarantee, to ensure *(peace, rights of citizens etc.)*; *(jur)* to guarantee, to warrant *(liability of the seller to repair or make good a defective article sold)*
Gewährleistung *f* guarantee, ensuring *(peace, right of citizens etc.)*; *(jur)* guarantee, warranty *(liability of the seller to repair or make good a defective article sold)*
~ **der Durchschnittsqualität** average quality protection
~ **der Qualität eines Herstellungspostens** lot quality protection
~, **nicht eingehaltene** breach of warranty
Gewährleistungsanspruch *m* claim to guarantee; claim resulting from guarantee
Gewährleistungsfrist *f* period of guarantee [warranty]
Gewährleistungsklausel *f* guarantee clause
Gewährleistungskosten *pl* guarantee costs
Gewährleistungspflicht *f* guarantee, warranty
Gewahrsam *m* safekeeping; custody
Gewahrsamsinhaber *m* bailee
Gewährsmangel *m* (serious) fault [defect] constituting a breach of the seller's guarantee
Gewährspflicht *f* warranty ◇ **eine ~ übernehmen** to give a warranty
Gewährsträger *m* guarantor
Gewährung *f* granting *(request, right, postponement etc.)*; allowing *(discount, rebate etc.)*
Gewährvertrag *m* contract of guarantee
Gewalt *f* power; authority; control; force, violence ◇ **auf ~ verzichten** to renounce the use of force; **~ anwenden** to use force; **~ haben über etwas** to have s.th. under control; **mit ~** by force
~, **ausführende** executive power [authority]
~, **außerökonomische** extra-economic power
~, **exekutive** *s.* ~, **ausführende**
~, **gesellschaftliche** social power
~, **gesetzgebende** legislative power [authority]
~, **höhere** force majeure, influence beyond one's control, Act of God
~, **konsularische** consular power
~, **ökonomische** economic power
~, **richterliche** judicial power
~, **sachliche** actual control
~, **soziale** *s.* ~, **gesellschaftliche**
~, **unumschränkte** sovereign [absolute] power
~, **vollziehende** *s.* ~, **ausführende**
Gewaltakt *m* act of violence, violent [extreme] measure
Gewaltandrohung *f* threat of violence
Gewaltanwendung *f* use of force

Gewaltenteilung *f* separation of powers
Gewaltentrennung *f s.* **Gewaltenteilung**
Gewaltherrschaft *f* despotism, tyranny; despotic [tyrannical] rule
Gewässer *n* stretch of water; pool; pond; small lake
Gewässer *npl* waters; bodies of water; lakes, rivers and canals
~, **fließende** (bodies of) flowing [running] water
~, **inländische** inland waters
~, **künstliche** (small) artificial lakes
~, **oberirdische** surface waters
~, **schiffbare** navigable waters
~, **stehende** stagnant waters
~, **territoriale** territorial waters
~, **unterirdische** underground [subterranean, subsurface] waters
~, **verschmutzte** polluted waters
Gewässerinstandhaltung *f* maintenance [upkeep] of waters
Gewässerschutz *m* prevention of water pollution
Gewässerverzeichnis *n* list of waters
Gewehrschäfter *m* gun-stock maker
Gewerbe *n* business, trade; occupation ⋄ **ein ~ anmelden** to register a business [trade]; **ein ~ ausüben** to pursue [carry on] a trade; **ein ~ betreiben** to carry on a business; to follow [ply] a trade
~, **ambulantes** itinerant trade
~, **konzessioniertes** licensed trade
~, **stehendes** business [trade] carried on in a permanent establishment
Gewerbeanmeldung *f* registration of a business [trade]
Gewerbeaufsicht *f* industrial inspection; administration of labour legislation and industrial law
Gewerbeaufsichtsamt *n* industrial inspection board
Gewerbeausstellung *f* industrial exhibition
Gewerbebank *f* trade bank
Gewerbeberechtigung *f* right to carry on a business [trade]; trading licence
Gewerbebetrieb *m* trade [business] establishment
Gewerbeerlaubnis *f s.* **Gewerbeberechtigung**
Gewerbeertrag *m* trading [business] profit
Gewerbeertragssteuer *f* (trade) profit tax
Gewerbefreiheit *f* freedom of trade
Gewerbekapital *n* trade [business] capital
Gewerbelehrer *m* vocational teacher
Gewerbeordnung *f* industrial code, trade regulations
Gewerberaumbilanz *f* balance sheet of industrially used buildings
Gewerberolle *f* trade [business] register

Gewerbeschein *m* trade licence
Gewerbesteuer *f* trade tax *(tax paid for carrying on a trade)*
Gewerbetätigkeit *f* industrial activity
gewerbetreibend carrying on a business [trade]
Gewerbetreibender *m* person carrying on a business [trade]; tradesman; craftsman; manufacturer
Gewerbezweig *m* branch of trade [industry]
gewerblich industrial, commercial
gewerbsmäßig professional; carried on for gain [profit]
gewerbstätig *s.* **gewerbetreibend**
Gewerbszweig *m s.* **Gewerbezweig**
Gewerk *n* 1. trade; craft; 2. trade [craft] guild
Gewerkschaft *f* trade union
Gewerkschafter *m s.* **Gewerkschaftler**
Gewerkschaftler *m* trade unionist
gewerkschaftlich trade union ⋄ **~ organisiert** unionized
Gewerkschaftsbank *f* trade union bank, *(Am)* labor bank
Gewerkschaftsbeitrag *m* (trade) union dues [subscription]
Gewerkschaftsbewegung *f* trade union movement, trade unionism
~, **internationale** international trade union movement
Gewerkschaftsbund *m* federation of trade unions, *(Am)* federation of labor unions
gewerkschaftsfeindlich anti-union(ist)
Gewerkschaftsfunktionär *m* (trade) union official
Gewerkschaftsgruppe *f* trade union group
Gewerkschaftskasse *f* trade union fund
Gewerkschaftskongreß *m* trades union congress
Gewerkschaftsmitglied *n* member of trade [*(Am)* labor] union, trade unionist
Gewerkschaftsmittel *npl* trade union resources [funds]
Gewerkschaftspolitik *f* trade union policy
Gewerkschaftspresse *f* trade union press
Gewerkschaftsschule *f* trade union school
Gewerkschaftsverband *m* federation of trade unions
Gewerkschaftsvermögen *n* trade union funds
Gewerkschaftswahl *f* trade union election
Gewerkschaftswesen *n* system of trade unions; trade unionism
Gewerkschaftszeitung *f* trade union paper [journal]
Gewicht *n* importance, significance; weight ⋄ **ins ~ fallen** to be of importance; to bear [carry] weight; **nach ~** by weight; **nach ~ verkaufen** to sell by weight; **unter ~ verkaufen** to sell below weight

~, **fehlendes** short weight
~, **frachtpflichtiges** chargeable weight
~, **lebendes** live weight
~, **spezifisches** specific weight
~, **statistisches** statistical weight
~, **totes** dead weight
Gewichte *npl*:
~, **gleitende** *(stats)* moving weights
gewichten *(stats)* to weight
Gewichtseinheit *f* unit of weight
Gewichtseinheitstarif *m (cust)* uniform weight tariff
Gewichtsfaktor *m s.* **Gewichtskoeffizient**
Gewichtsfunktion *f (stats)* weight function
Gewichtskoeffizient *m (stats)* weighting coefficient
Gewichtssystem *n (stats)* weighting system
Gewichtstoleranz *f* tolerance of weight
Gewichtsverhältnis *n* weight ratio, ratio of weight
Gewichtsverlust *m* loss of weight *(vegetables etc.)*
Gewichtszoll *m* weight [specific] duty
Gewichtung *f (stats)* weighting
Gewichtungsfehler *m (stats)* weight bias
Gewinn *m* profit; earnings; returns *(investment etc.)*; proceeds *(sales etc.)*; yield; gain; benefit, advantage ◊ **am ~ beteiligt sein** to have a share in profits; **einen ~ ausweisen** to show a profit; **~ erwirtschaften** *s.* **~ erzielen;** **~ erzielen** to make [realize] profit; **mit ~ arbeiten** to operate at a profit; **mit ~ verkaufen** to sell at a profit
~, **akkumulierter** accumulated profit
~, **anfallender** accruing profit
~ **aus Warenlieferungen** profit resulting from sale (of goods)
~, **ausgeschütteter** distributed [divided] profit
~, **bereinigter** *s.* **~, reiner**
~, **bilanzmäßiger** *s.* **~, buchmäßiger**
~, **buchmäßiger** book profit
~, **durch technische Neuerungen erzielter** profit from innovation, innovational profit
~, **durchschnittlicher** average profit
~, **effektiver** real profit
~, **entgangener** lost profit
~, **erhoffter** anticipated profit
~, **erwarteter** expected profit
~, **erwirtschafteter** *s.* **~, erzielter**
~, **erzielter** (actual) profit made [realized]
~, **geplanter** planned profit
~, **industrieller** industrial profit
~, **jährlicher** annual profit
~, **kalkulatorischer** calculated profit
~, **kommerzieller** commercial [trading] profit
~, **nicht ausgeschütteter** undistributed [undivided] profit
~, **periodenfremder** profit from previous years

~, **realisierter** *s.* **~, erzielter**
~, **reiner** net profit
~, **spekulativer** speculative profit
~, **steuerpflichtiger** taxable profit, profit liable to taxation
~, **überplanmäßiger** excess profit, profit exceeding the plan (target)
~, **unerwarteter** unexpected profit
~, **ungerechtfertigter** unjustified [unwarranted] profit
~, **unversteuerter** pre-tax profit
~, **vorjähriger** *s.* **~, periodenfremder**
~, **zu versteuernder** taxable profit
Gewinnabführung *f* profit transfer [payment]
Gewinnabschlag *m* profit reduction *(for goods of low quality etc.)*
Gewinnabschöpfung *f* skimming [syphoning off] (of) excess profits
Gewinnabsicht *f* intention of making profit, gainful intent; profit motive
Gewinnanalyse *f* profit analysis
Gewinnanspruch *m* dividend [profit] right
Gewinnanteil *m* share in (the) profits, dividend per [on] share; *(ins)* profit commission
Gewinnanteilschein *m* dividend coupon [warrant]
Gewinnaufschlag *m* mark-up
Gewinnaufstellung *f* statement on profits
Gewinnaufstockung *f* increase of capital resources out of profits
Gewinnausgleich *m* compensation for lost profit
Gewinnausschließungsvereinbarung *f* non--profit [profit exclusion] agreement
Gewinnausschluß *m* exclusion of profits
Gewinnausschüttung *f* distribution of profits
Gewinnaussicht *f* chance of making a profit; chance of winning *(lottery etc.)*
Gewinnbemessungsgrundlage *f* basis for accounting profit
gewinnberechtigt entitled to share in profits
Gewinnberechtigung *f* profit-sharing right, right to a share in profits
Gewinnbeteiligung *f* profit-sharing, sharing of profits; *(ins)* profit commission
~ **der Arbeiter** worker profit-sharing
gewinnbringend profitable, paying, lucrative
Gewinnentnahme *f* withdrawal of profits; profits taken out
Gewinnentwicklung *f* growth of profit
Gewinnerhöhung *f* increase in profit
Gewinnermittlung *f* determination of profits
Gewinnerzielung *f* making of profits
Gewinngeld *n* money won, winnings *(lottery etc.)*
Gewinngemeinschaft *f* group sharing pooled profits
Gewinnhöhe *f* (amount of) profit
Gewinnkonto *n* profit account

Gewinnlage *f* situation of earnings and profits
Gewinnmarge *f s.* **Gewinnspanne**
Gewinnmasse *f s.* **Gewinnhöhe**
Gewinnmaximierung *f* maximization of profit
gewinnmindernd profit-reducing *(factors etc.)*
Gewinnminderung *f* decrease [decline] in profit
Gewinnnormativ *n* standard rate of profit
Gewinnplan *m* plan of profit, profit plan
Gewinnplanung *f* profit planning
Gewinnposten *m (acc)* profit item
Gewinnquote *f* profit margin; prize *(lottery)*; dividend *(football pool etc.)*
Gewinnrate *f* rate of profit
~, normative standard rate of profit
Gewinnrealisation *f s.* **Gewinnrealisierung**
Gewinnrealisierung *f* realization of profit(s)
Gewinnrechnung *f s.* **Gewinnkonto**
Gewinnsaldo *m* profit balance
Gewinnsatz *m s.* **Gewinnspanne**
Gewinnspanne *f* margin of profit, profit margin
Gewinnsteuer *f* profit tax
Gewinnstreben *n* profit drive, pursuit of profit
Gewinnsucht *f* greed for profit [gain]
gewinnsüchtig profit-seeking
Gewinnteilung *f* profit-sharing *(companies etc.)*; sharing of winnings *(lottery etc.)*
Gewinntransfer *m* profit transfer
Gewinnumverteilung *f* redistribution of profit
Gewinn- und Verlustbeteiligung *f* sharing of profits and losses
Gewinn- und Verlustkonto *n s.* **Gewinn- und Verlustrechnung**
Gewinn- und Verlustrechnung *f* profit and loss account, *(Am)* income account
Gewinnung *f* production, extraction *(mineral resources)*; reclamation *(land)*
Gewinnungskosten *pl* cost(s) of extraction [production] *(coal, oil etc.)*
Gewinnverteilung *f* distribution of profit
~, umsatzabhängige distribution of profits according to sales [turnover]
Gewinnverteilungsquote *f* rate of profit distribution
Gewinnverwendung *f* utilization of profit
Gewinnverwendungsfonds *m* fund of profit utilization
Gewinnvortrag *m (acc)* profit carried forward
Gewinnzuschlag *m* mark-up; additional rate of profit
Gewinnzuwachs *m* increase in profit
Gewohnheitsrecht *n* common law
Gießerei *f* foundry
Gießereibetrieb *m s.* **Gießerei**
Gießereiindustrie *f* foundry [founding] industry
Giftmüll *m* toxic waste
Gilde *f (hist)* (trade) guild
Gipfelkonferenz *f* summit (conference)

Gipfeltreffen *n* summit (meeting)
Gipfelwert *m (stats)* top [maximum] value
giral *(bank)* by way of transfer on the giro system
Giralgeld *n* deposit money
Girant *m* endorser, indorser
~, nachfolgender succeeding [following] endorser [indorser]
~, vorhergehender preceding endorser [indorser]
Girat *m* endorsee, indorsee
girierbar endorsable, indorsable
girieren to endorse, to indorse
Girierung *f* endorsement, indorsement
Giriervermerk *m s.* **Girierung**
Giro *n* giro system; endorsement, indorsement *(on bill, cheque etc.)*; bank transfer ◊ **~ fehlt** endorsement [indorsement] required; **~ ungenau** endorsement [indorsement] irregular
~, beschränktes restrictive endorsement [indorsement]
~, offenes endorsement [indorsement] in blank
Giroabteilung *f* giro department
Giroauftrag *m* giro transfer instruction [order]
Giroausgleichstelle *f s.* **Girozentrale**
Girobank *f* clearing bank
Giroeinlagen *fpl* deposits (on a giro transfer account)
Girogeld *n s.* **Giralgeld**
Girogeschäft *n* clearing business
Giroguthaben *n* balance of a giro transfer account, giro account balance
Girokarte *f* giro transfer card
Girokasse *f* clearing house [office]
Girokonto *n* giro (transfer) account
Gironetz *n* giro (transfer) network
Girooblige *n* contingent liability incurred by the endorser [indorser] *(of a bill)*
Girosammeldepot *n* central depository of securities
Giroscheck *m* giro cheque
Girosystem *n* giro system
Giroüberweisung *f* giro transfer
Giroverbindlichkeit *f s.* **Girooblige**
Giroverkehr *m* giro transfer business; clearing system
Girovertrag *m* giro clearing agreement
Girowechsel *m* giro bill (of exchange)
Girozahlung *f* payment by means of a giro bank transfer
Girozentrale *f* central clearing house, giro institution
Gitter *n (stats)* lattice
~, ausgewogenes quadratisches *(stats)* balanced lattice square
~, dreidimensionales *(stats)* three-dimensional lattice
~, dreifaches *(stats)* triple lattice

~, **kubisches** *(stats)* cubic lattice
~, **quadratisches** *(stats)* square lattice
~, **rechteckiges** *(stats)* rectangular lattice
~, **teilweise ausgewogenes quadratisches** *(stats)* partially balanced lattice square
Gitterplan *m (stats)* lattice design
Gitter-Stichprobenverfahren *n (stats)* grid sampling
Glasbläser *m* glass-blower
Glaser *m* glazier
Glasgraveur *m* glass engraver
Glasindustrie *f* glass industry
Glasmacher *m* glassmaker
Glasmaler *m* glass painter
Glasschmuckmacher *m* trinket-maker
Glasveredler *m* cut-glass maker
Glasversicherung *f* plate-glass insurance
Glätten *n (stats)* smoothing
Glättungsfähigkeit *f (stats)* smoothing power
Glaube *m* faith, belief ⋄ **im guten Glauben** bona fide
Gläubiger *m* creditor ⋄ **einem ~ Sicherheit bieten** to secure a creditor; **einen ~ bevorrechtigen** to prefer one creditor over others
~, **bevorrechtigter** preferential [preferred] creditor
~, **gerichtlich anerkannter** judgement creditor
~, **hypothekarischer** mortgage creditor
~, **sichergestellter** secured creditor
Gläubigeranspruch *m* creditor's claim
Gläubigerantrag *m* creditor's bankruptcy petition
Gläubigeraufgebot *n* calling of a meeting of creditors
Gläubigerausgleich *m* composition with creditors *(in the case of bankruptcy)*
Gläubigerausschuß *m* committee of inspection, *(Am)* creditors' committee *(in the case of bankruptcy)*
Gläubigerbank *f* creditor bank
Gläubigerbegünstigung *f* fraudulent preference (of a creditor) *(in the case of bankruptcy)*
Gläubigerforderung *f* creditor's claim
Gläubigergefährdung *f* jeopardizing a creditor's interest
Gläubigergemeinschaft *f* body of creditors *(in the case of bankruptcy)*
Gläubigergenehmigung *f* creditor's assent *(to the transfer of a debt from the original debtor to a third party)*
Gläubigerland *n* creditor country
Gläubigerpapiere *npl* creditor's documents
Gläubigerposten *m* credit entry
Gläubigerschaft *f* body of creditors
Gläubigerschutz *m* protection of creditors
Gläubigerstaat *m s.* **Gläubigerland**
Gläubigervergleich *m s.* **Gläubigerausgleich**

Gläubigerversammlung *f* meeting of creditors
Gläubigervertrag *m* contract between a creditor and a third party
Gläubigerverzeichnis *n* list of creditors
Gläubigerverzug *m* creditor's delay
Gläubigerwechsel *m* subrogation (of a creditor)
Glaubwürdigkeitsgrad *m (stats)* degree of belief
gleichaltrig of the same age
gleichartig similar *(character, feeling etc.)*; analogous *(case etc.)*; homogeneous *(structure etc.)*
Gleichartigkeit *f* similarity *(character, feeling etc.)*; homogeneity *(structure etc.)*
Gleichaufteilungsgerade *f (stats, maths)* line of equidistribution
gleichberechtigt having equal rights; equally entitled; *(jur)* concurrent *(claims)*
Gleichberechtigung *f* equality (of rights), equal rights
~ **der Frau** equal rights for women
~ **von Mann und Frau** equal rights of men and women
Gleichgewicht *n* balance, equilibrium
~ **der Kräfte** balance of power
~, **dynamisches** dynamic balance
~, **labiles** unstable equilibrium
~, **monetäres** monetary equilibrium
~, **ökonomisches** economic equilibrium [balance]
~, **partielles** partial equilibrium
~, **politisches** political equilibrium [balance]
~, **relatives** relative [unstable] equilibrium
~, **stabiles** stable equilibrium
~, **statisches** static equilibrium
~, **wirtschaftliches** *s.* ~, **ökonomisches**
Gleichgewichtsbedingungen *fpl* conditions of equilibrium
~, **volkswirtschaftliche** conditions of economic equilibrium
Gleichgewichtskonstante *f (stats)* equilibrium constant
Gleichgewichtsmechanismus *m* balancing mechanism
Gleichgewichtspreis *m* balancing price *(demand and supply)*
Gleichgewichtssituation *f* (situation of) equilibrium
Gleichgewichtsstörung *f* disturbance of equilibrium, disturbed balance [equilibrium]
Gleichgewichtszustand *m* state of equilibrium *(between supply and demand etc.)*
Gleichheit *f* equality *(of interest, before the law etc.)*
Gleichmacherei *f* egalitarianism
gleichmäßig regular *(intervals etc.)*; even, equal *(distribution etc.)*; constant *(pressure etc.)*
Gleichmäßigkeit *f* regularity
~ **der Besteuerung** proportionate taxation

Gleichungssystem

Gleichungssystem *n* system of equations
~, lineares linear system of equations
~, ökonometrisches econmectric system of equations
~, vollständiges complete system of equations
Gleichverteilung *f (stats)* uniform distribution
gleichwertig of the same value; of the same quality
Gleichwertigkeit *f* equivalence, equality *(methods, systems etc.)*; equal standard [quality] *(performances etc.)*
Gleisbauarbeiter *m* worker in tracklaying
Gleitmittelverfahren *n (stats)* method of moving average
Gleitpreis *m* sliding price
Gleitpreisklausel *f* price escalator clause
Gleitzoll *m* sliding-scale tariff
gliedern to order, to arrange; to divide
Gliederung *f* arrangement, construction; division; organization, structure
~ der volkswirtschaftlichen Proportionen structure of (the) national economic proportions
~ des Arbeitsganges organization of the operation (process)
~ des Produktionsprozesses, horizontale horizontal organization of the production process
~ des Produktionsprozesses, vertikale vertical organization of the production process
~ des Volkswirtschaftsplanes structure of the national economic plan
~ eines Systems, innere inner structure of a system
~ nach Kostenelementen structure of cost elements; arrangement according to cost elements
Gliederungszahl *f (stats)* number *(men, workers, cars produced etc., expressed as a percentage)*
Gliedstaat *m* member state *(of a treaty system etc.)*
Globalabkommen *n* general agreement [contract]
Globalabschreibung *f* global depreciation
Globalaktie *f* share certificate
Globalbetrag *m* lump sum
Globalgenehmigung *f* general permission
Globalgröße *f* global magnitude [figure]
Globalkontingent *n* global quota
Globalkredit *m* block credit, lump-sum loan *(to be distributed to a number of borrowers)*
Globalvertrag *m s.* Globalabkommen
Globalwarenbegleitschein *m* general waybill [*(Am)* shipping note]
Glockengießer *m* bell founder [caster]
Gold *n* gold
~, gemünztes minted gold
~, pures pure gold

Goldabfluß *m* outflow [efflux, exodus] of gold, gold outflow [efflux]
Goldabwanderung *f s.* Goldabfluß
Goldagio *n* premium on gold
Goldankauf *m* purchase [purchasing] of gold
Goldankaufpreis *m* purchase price of gold
Goldanleihe *f* gold loan
Goldarbitrage *f* arbitrage in gold
Goldaufkaufpreis *m s.* Goldankaufpreis
Goldaufkommen *n s.* Goldproduktion
Goldausfuhr *f* gold export(s)
Goldautomatismus *m* gold automatism, controlling effect of a gold standard
Goldbarren *m* gold bar [ingot], gold bullion
Goldbasis *f* gold basis
Goldbestand *m* gold stock [reserve]
Goldblockländer *npl* gold bloc countries
Goldbörse *f* bullion market
Golddeckung *f* gold cover(age)
Golddevisen *pl* gold exchanges
Golddevisenwährung *f* gold-exchange standard
Goldeinfuhr *f* gold import(s)
Goldeinheit *f* unit of gold
Goldgehalt *m* gold content, proportion of gold *(coins)*
Goldgeld *n* gold money
Goldhandel *m* gold trade, trade in gold
Goldkernwährung *f* gold bullion standard
Goldklausel *f* gold clause
Goldkurs *m* gold rate
Goldmarkt *m* gold market
Goldmechanismus *m* gold-standard mechanism
Goldmünze *f* gold coin
Goldmünzfuß *m* standard of gold coinage
Goldmünzstandard *m s.* Goldmünzfuß
Goldparität *f* gold parity
Goldpreis *m* price of gold, gold price
Goldproduktion *f* gold production, production of gold
Goldreserven *fpl* gold reserves
Goldschatz *m* gold treasure, hoard of gold
Goldschläger *m* gold-beater
Goldsendung *f* gold shipment, shipment of gold
Goldstandard *m* gold standard
Goldstück *n* gold coin [piece]
Goldumlauf *m* gold circulation, circulation of gold
Goldumlaufwährung *f* gold (specie) standard
Goldverknappung *f* scarcity of gold
Goldversendung *f* shipping [shipment] of gold
Goldversorgung *f* supply of gold, gold supply
Goldvorrat *m* stock of gold, gold holdings
Goldwährung *f s.* Goldstandard
Goldwert *m* value of gold; value in gold *(equivalent)*
Goldwertklausel *f s.* Goldklausel
Goldzahlung *f* gold payment

Goldzertifikat *n* gold certificate
Goldzirkulation *f* gold circulation
Goldzufluß *m* inflow [influx] of gold, gold inflow [influx]
Grad *m* degree *(intensity, university etc.)*; grade *(rank etc.)*; level *(mechanization etc.)*
~ **der gesellschaftlichen Arbeitsteilung** level of social division of labour
gratis gratis, for nothing, free of charge
~ **und franko** free of charge and postage paid
Gratisaktie *f* bonus share
Gratisangebot *n* free offer, offer free of charge
Gratismuster *n s.* **Gratisprobe**
Gratisprobe *f* free sample
Graveur *m* engraver
Grenzabfertigung *f* customs clearance *(at the frontier)*
Grenzaustrittsbahnhof *m* border station (of departure)
Grenzbedingung *f* marginal condition
Grenzbelastung *f* marginal [critical] load
Grenze *f* boundary *(territory, estate etc.)*; border *(country, district etc.)*, frontier *(state)*; *(maths)* limit ◊ **frei ~ Lieferland** free to frontier of supplier's country
Grenzeintrittsbahnhof *m* border station (of arrival)
Grenzen *fpl*:
~, **nationale** national frontiers
~, **stochastisch definierte** *(stats)* probability limits
Grenzerlös *m* marginal revenue [receipts]
Grenzertrag *m* marginal return *(investment etc.)*
Grenzfall *m* borderline case; marginal case; limiting case; critical case
Grenzfluß *m* frontier river, river forming the boundary [frontier, border] *(between two countries)*
Grenzforderung *f* territorial claim
Grenzgänger *m* border crosser; frontier commuter *(for work)*
Grenzgebiet *n* 1. frontier [border] area, borderland; 2. allied [related] field *(of study)*
Grenzgenauigkeit *f* accuracy
~, **innewohnende** *(stats)* intrinsic accuracy
Grenzgewässer *n* frontier watercourse [lake]
Grenzkommission *f* frontier [border] commission
Grenzkonflikt *m* frontier [border] dispute
Grenzkontrolle *f* frontier [border] control, *(Am)* border inspection check
Grenzkontrollstelle *f* frontier [border] control point, checkpoint
Grenzkosten *pl* marginal cost
Grenzkostentheorie *f* marginal cost theory
Grenzlinie *f* boundary [frontier] line, borderline, line of demarcation; dividing line

Grenzmal *n s.* **Grenzzeichen**
Grenzmark *f s.* **Grenzzeichen**
Grenznutzen *m* marginal utility
Grenznutzentheorie *f* theory of marginal utility
Grenzparameter *m* limiting parameter
Grenzpreis *m* marginal price
Grenzprodukt *n* marginal product
Grenzproduktion *f* marginal production
Grenzproduktivität *f* marginal productivity
Grenzproduktivitätstheorie *f* theory of marginal productivity
Grenzpunkt *m (stats, maths)* limit(ing) point
Grenzrate *f* marginal rate
Grenzrecht *n* law of boundaries
Grenzscheide *f* boundary (line)
Grenzscheidung *f* demarcation [delimitation] of boundaries
Grenzschein *m* frontier pass
Grenzschließung *f s.* **Grenzsperre**
Grenzschutz *m* 1. frontier [border] protection; 2. frontier [border] guard
Grenzsperre *f* closing of the frontier(s); ban on border traffic
Grenzstaat *m* frontier [border] state; neighbouring state
Grenzstadt *f* frontier [border] town
Grenzstation *f* frontier [border] station
Grenzstein *m* boundary stone
Grenzstreifen *m* frontier [border] zone
Grenzstreit *m* boundary dispute; frontier [border] dispute
Grenzstreitigkeit *f s.* **Grenzstreit**
Grenzstrom *m s.* **Grenzfluß**
Grenzüberbau *m* encroachment *(by building on a neighbour's land)*
Grenzübergang *m* 1. crossing of the frontier [border], frontier [border] crossing; 2. frontier [border] crossing point
Grenzübergangsbahnhof *m* rail frontier point
Grenzübergangsstelle *f* frontier [border] crossing point
grenzüberschreitend frontier-crossing *(goods, vehicles etc.)*
Grenzüberschreitung *f* 1. crossing of the frontier [border]; 2. encroachment *(on a neighbour's land)*; trespass *(on land)*
Grenzverkehr *m* traffic across the frontier(s), frontier traffic
~, **kleiner** local frontier traffic
Grenzverletzung *f* violation of the frontier [border, boundary]
Grenzverteilung *f (stats)* asymptotic distribution
Grenzvertrag *m* boundary treaty
Grenzwert *m* marginal value; *(maths)* limit, limiting value; threshold value
~, **oberer** *(maths)* upper limit
~, **unterer** *(maths)* lower limit

Grenzwertproduktivität *f* marginal-value productivity
Grenzwertsatz *m* limit theorem
~, **erster** *(stats)* first limit theorem
~, **zentraler** *(stats)* central limit theorem
Grenzzeichen *n* boundary mark, landmark
Grenzziehung *f* determination [fixing, delimitation, demarcation] of the boundary (line) [frontier]
Grenzzoll *m* customs duty *(levied on goods crossing a frontier)*
Grenzzollamt *n* (frontier) customs office
Grenzzollbehörde *f* (frontier) customs authorities
Grenzzone *f* frontier [border] zone
Grenzzwischenfall *m* frontier [border] incident
Grobablaufplan *m* rough timing [working] schedule
Grobanalyse *f* rough analysis
Grobberechnung *f* rough calculation
Grobbilanzierung *f* rough balancing
grobfahrlässig grossly negligent
Grobplanung *f* rough [outline] planning
Grobprojekt *n* rough outline of a project
Grobsortiment *n* general range [assortment] of goods
Großabnehmer *m* bulk purchaser
Großagrarier *m* big landlord [landowner]
Großaktionär *m* major [big] shareholder
Großankauf *m s.* **Großeinkauf**
Großauftrag *m* large order
Großbank *f* large [major] bank
Großbauer *m* big farmer
großbäuerlich large-scale agricultural *(enterprise etc.)*
Großbaustelle *f* large building site
Großbehälter *m* (large) container
Großbeteiligung *f* large-scale participation, participation on a large scale
Großbetrieb *m* large enterprise
~, **genossenschaftlicher** large co-operative enterprise
~, **landwirtschaftlicher** large farm
Großbezieher *m s.* **Großabnehmer**
Großblockbauweise *f* large(-sized) block construction
Großbourgeoisie *f* big bourgeoisie
großbürgerlich upper middle-class
Großbürgertum *n* upper middle class
Großcomputer *m* large computer; mainframe computer
Größe *f* size; quantity; value; magnitude; amount ◊ **eine unbekannte ~ bestimmen** to determine an unknown quantity; **nach ~ sortieren** to sort out according to size
~, **abgeleitete statistische** *(stats)* derived statistic

~, **bekannte** known quantity
~, **dynamische** dynamic magnitude
~, **endliche** finite quantity [number]
~, **gesuchte** *s.* ~, **unbekannte**
~, **gleichbleibende** *s.* ~, **konstante**
~, **heterograde** *(stats)* extensive magnitude
~, **homograde** *(stats)* intensive magnitude
~, **inkommensurable** incommensurable quantity
~, **komplexe** complex quantity
~, **konstante** constant quantity
~, **numerische** numeric quantity
~, **optimale** optimum quantity; optimum size
~, **physikalische** physical quantity
~, **regellose** *(stats)* random variable
~, **relative** relative magnitude
~, **skalare** scalar quantity
~, **statische** static quantity
~, **unbekannte** unknown quantity
~, **unendliche** infinite quantity [number]
~, **unvergleichbare** *s.* ~, **inkommensurable**
~, **variable** variable (quantity)
~, **volkswirtschaftliche** economic quantity *(optimization etc.)*; (national) economic magnitude *(national income etc.)*
~, **vorgegebene** given quantity [number]
Großeinkauf *m* bulk buying [purchasing]; bulk purchase
Großeinkaufspreis *m s.* **Großhandelspreis**
Größen *fpl*:
~, **qualitative** *(stats)* qualitative data
~, **quantitative** *(stats)* extensive magnitudes
Größenangabe *f* dimensional information
Größenanordnungswert *m (stats)* grade
Größenbereich *m* range of magnitudes
Größenfehler *m* dimensional error
Größenklasse *f* size; magnitude
Größenordnung *f* order (of magnitude)
Größentoleranz *f* size [dimensional] tolerance
Größenverteilung *f* size distribution
Großerzeuger *m* large-scale [mass] producer
Großfabrikation *f* mass production, large-scale manufacture
Großfamilie *f* extended family
Großfertigung *f s.* **Großfabrikation**
Großfinanz *f* high finance
großflächig large-area
Großflughafen *m* major airport
Großforschung *f* major [large-scale] research
Großforschungszentrum *n* centre of large-scale research
Großgrundbesitz *m* big land ownership; large landed property
Großgrundbesitzer *m* big landowner
Großhandel *m* wholesale trade
~, **staatlicher** state(-owned) wholesale trade
Großhandelsabgabepreis *m* **(GAP)** wholesale (delivery) price

Großhandelsabschlag *m* discount on wholesale trade (delivery) prices
Großhandelsaufschlag *m* wholesale trade margin *(calculated as a surcharge on the industry delivery price)*
Großhandelsbetrieb *m* wholesale trading enterprise
~, kommunaler municipal wholesale trading enterprise
Großhandelseinkaufspreis *m* wholesale prime cost
Großhandelsgeschäft *n* wholesale business [company, firm] ⋄ **ein ~ betreiben** to do [run] a wholesale business
Großhandelsgesellschaft *f* **(GHG)** wholesale trading company
Großhandelsindex *m* wholesale price index
Großhandelslager *n* wholesale warehouse, (wholesale) storage house
Großhandelsnetz *n* wholesale network *(including offices, warehouses, cargo handling points etc.)*
Großhandelsplanung *f* wholesale trade planning
Großhandelspreis *m* wholesale price
Großhandelspreisindex *m s.* **Großhandelsindex**
Großhandelspreisliste *f* list of wholesale prices, wholesale price list
Großhandelspreisreform *f* reform of wholesale prices, wholesale price reform
Großhandelsrabatt *m* wholesale (trade) discount
Großhandelssortiment *n* range of wholesale trade goods
Großhandelsspanne *f* wholesale trade margin
Großhandelsspezialisierung *f* specialization in wholesale trade
Großhandelsstatistik *f* wholesale trade statistics
Großhandelsumsatz *m* wholesale turnover
Großhandelsverkaufspreis *m s.* **Großhandelspreis**
Großhandelsvertreter *m* wholesale trade agent
Großhändler *m* wholesale dealer, wholesaler
Großhandlung *f* wholesale business
Großindustrie *f* large-scale industry
großindustriell large-scale (industrial) *(production etc.)*
Großindustrieller *m* big industrialist, industrial magnate
Grossist *m* wholesale dealer, wholesaler
Großkapital *n* big business; high finance
Großkapitalist *m* big capitalist
Großkaufzentrum *n* hypermarket
Großkonzern *m* big concern
Großkraftwerk *n* large power station
Großküche *f* large catering establishment; canteen

Großmacht *f* great power
Großmarkt *m* central market, supermarket
Großplattenbau *m* large-panel construction method [system]
Großproduktion *f* large-scale production
Großraumbüro *n* open-plan office
Großraumverkaufsstelle *f* open-plan shop
Großraumwagen *m* large-capacity [high--capacity] waggon
Großraumwirtschaft *f* large-area economy
Großrechner *m s.* **Großcomputer**
Großreparatur *f* major [big] repair
Großschaden *m (ins)* heavy loss; major damage
Großschiffahrtsweg *m* major waterway
Großserie *f* large series *(of a product)*
Großserienfertigung *f* large-scale manufacture [production]
Großserienherstellung *f s.* **Großserienfertigung**
Großserienproduktion *f s.* **Großserienfertigung**
Großstadt *f* large town, city
Großstadtgebiet *n* metropolitan area
großstädtisch of a large town [city]
Großstadtverkehr *m* city traffic
Großunternehmen *n* large-scale [big] enterprise
Großunternehmer *m* big industrialist [manufacturer], large-scale entrepreneur
Großverbraucher *m* large [bulk] consumer *(enterprises or institutions buying large quantities of goods)*
Großverdiener *m* high-income earner
Großversand *m* mail-order business
Großversandgeschäft *n* mail-order house
Großverteiler *m* wholesaler, large-scale distributor
Großvertrieb *m* large-scale distribution
Großvieh *n* cattle and horses
Großvieheinheit *f* unit of cattle
Großviehhaltung *f* cattle and horse farming [rearing]
Großviehproduktion *f* cattle and horse raising
Großzählung *f* census
Grube *f* mine, pit; colliery *(coal)*
Grubenanteil *m* mining share
Grubenarbeiter *m* miner
Grubenbetrieb *m* 1. mining, underground working; 2. mine, mining concern
Grubenförderung *f* underground haulage; output of a mine
Grubengelände *n* site of a mine
Grubenrettungswesen *n* mine rescue organization
Grummet *n (agric)* second crop of hay
Grummeternte *f (agric)* second hay harvest
Grünanlagen *fpl* parks and lawns, open spaces *(in large town)*

Grund *m* 1. bottom *(river, ocean etc.)*; 2. ground, soil; land; 3. foundation(s) *(house, theory etc.)*; 4. reason
Grundabgabe *f* land tax
Grundarbeitszeit *f* basic working time
Grundausbildung *f* basic instruction [training]
~, **berufliche** basic vocational training
Grundbedarf *m* basic needs
Grundberuf *m* vocation, trade
Grundbesitz *m* landed property; land ownership
~, **für Wohnzwecke genutzter** residential property
Grundbesitzer *m* landed proprietor, landowner, estate owner
Grundbestand *m* normal stock
Grundbetrag *m* basic [original] amount
Grundbuch *n* land register
Grundbuchamt *n* land registry, land registration office
Grundbuchauszug *m* abstract of title, land certificate
Grundbuchberichtigung *f* rectification of land register
Grundbucheintragung *f* entry in the land register
Grundbuchordnung *f* land registration act
Grundbuchrecht *n* law of land registration
Grunddaten *pl* basic data
Grundeigentum *n s.* **Grundbesitz**
~, **belastetes** encumbered [burdened] estate; imperfect ownership
~, **unbelastetes** unencumbered [unburdened] estate; perfect ownership
Grundeigentümer *m s.* **Grundbesitzer**
Grundeigentumsmonopol *n* monopoly of private ownership of land
Grundeigentumstitel *m* title to landed property [ownership]
Grundeinheit *f* basic unit
Grundeinkommen *n* basic income
gründen to found *(economic community etc.)*, to promote, to float *(company etc.)*, to establish, to set up *(business etc.)*
Gründer *m* founder, promoter; originator
Gründeraktien *fpl* founders' [promoters'] shares
Gründeranteile *mpl s.* **Gründeraktien**
Gründerbericht *m* founders' report
Gründergesellschaft *f* association of founders
Gründergewinn *m* founders' profit
Gründerlohn *m* founder's fee *(for services during the formation of a company)*
Gründerrechte *npl* founders' preference rights
Grundertragssteuer *f* farmers' tax
Gründerversammlung *f* founders' meeting
Grunderwerb *m* purchase [acquisition] of land
Grunderwerbskosten *pl* purchase cost of real estate

Grunderwerbssteuer *f* tax on the acquisition [transfer] of real property
Grunderzeugnis *n* primary product
Grundfischerei *f* ground [bottom] fishing
Grundfonds *m* fund of fixed assets [capital] *(monetary expression of fixed assets)*
Grundfonds *mpl*:
~, **ausgesonderte** discarded fixed assets [capital]
~, **stillgelegte** (temporarily) idle fixed assets [capital]
~, **verschlissene** worn-out fixed assets
~, **zur Nutzung überlassene** hired-out fixed assets [capital]
Grundfondsabgabe *f* levy on fixed assets [capital]
Grundfondsausnutzung *f* utilization of fixed assets [capital]
Grundfondsausstattung *f* endowment with fixed assets [capital]
Grundfondsbewegung *f* changes in fixed assets [capital]
Grundfondsbilanz *f* balance (sheet) of fixed assets [capital]
Grundfondseffektivität *f* efficiency of fixed assets [capital]
Grundfondseinheit *f* unit of fixed assets [capital]
Grundfondseinsatzkoeffizient *m* coefficient of the utilization of fixed assets [capital]
Grundfondsintensität *f* capital-output ratio
grundfondsintensiv with a high proportion of fixed assets [capital]
Grundfondsökonomie *f* 1. economics of fixed assets; 2. effective utilization of fixed assets [capital]
Grundfondsplanung *f* planning of fixed assets [capital]
Grundfondsquote *f* output-capital ratio
Grundfondsrentabilität *f* profitability of fixed assets [capital] *(ratio of profit to fixed assets)*
Grundfondsreproduktion *f* reproduction of fixed assets [capital] *(discard, supply and maintenance of fixed assets, investments etc.)*
Grundfondsstatistik *f* statistics of fixed assets [capital]
Grundfondsverschleiß *m* wear and tear of fixed assets [capital]
Grundfondswirtschaft *f* supply and maintenance of fixed assets [capital]
Grundfondszuwachs *m* increase [growth, increment] of fixed assets [capital]
Grundfutter *n (agric)* staple [basic] fodder
Grundgebühr *f* basic rate [fee], flat rate; *(post)* rental, charge, basic rate
Grundgehalt *n* basic salary
Grundgesamtheit *f (stats)* (parent) population, universe

~, **endliche** *(stats)* finite population
~, **hypothetische** *(stats)* hypothetical population
~, **kontinuierliche** *(stats)* continuous population
~, **nicht normal verteilte** *(stats)* non-normal population
~, **unendliche** *(stats)* infinite population
Grundgeschäft *n* underlying transaction
Grundgesetz *n* constitution; constitutional law; basic [fundamental] law; statute
~, **ökonomisches** basic economic law *(economic theory: objective economic law characterizing the essence and the fundamental trends of development in a society)*
Grundgewicht *n* basic weight
Grundgröße *f (d.pr.)* base item
Grundindustrie *f* basic industry
Grundinteresse *n* basic interest
Grundinvestition *f* basic investment
Grundkapital *n* original capital [stock]
Grundkosten *pl* real [basic] costs *(incurred in the immediate manufacturing process)*
~, **direkte** direct real [basic] costs *(s.* **Grundkosten***)*
~, **indirekte** indirect real [basic] costs *(s.* **Grundkosten***)*
Grundkredit *m* real estate loan
Grundkreditanstalt *f* land-mortgage bank
Grundkreditbank *f s.* **Grundkreditanstalt**
Grundkreditinstitut *n s.* **Grundkreditanstalt**
Grundkreditpfandbriefe *mpl* real estate bonds
Grundlage *f* base, foundation, ground; basis *(theory, existence, calculation etc.)* ◊ **auf der ~ der Gleichberechtigung** on the basis of equality, on an equal footing; **auf genossenschaftlicher ~** on a co-operative basis; **auf gesetzlicher ~** on a statutory basis [footing]
~, **wirtschaftliche** economic basis
Grundlagenforschung *f* basic research
Grundlagenvertrag *m* basic treaty
Grundlasten *fpl* taxes and rates on real estate
Grundlinie *f (stats)* base line
Grundlohn *m* basic wage(s); basic wage rate
~, **leistungsorientierter** efficiency-oriented basic wage; wage linked to (work) performance
Grundlohnfonds *m* base wage fund
Grundlohnformen *fpl* types [kinds] of base wages
Grundlohnsatz *m* base wage rate
Grundlohntarif *m s.* **Grundlohnsatz**
Grundmaß *n (stats)* basic dimensions
Grundmaterial *n* direct [productive] material; basic materials directly used in production
Grundmittel *npl* fixed assets [capital], capital assets
~, **in Nutzung befindliche** fixed assets [capital] employed
~, **stillgelegte** *s.* **Grundfonds, stillgelegte**

~, **vermietete und verpachtete** fixed assets leased out
Grundmittelarten *fpl* types of fixed assets [capital]
Grundmittelaufwand *m* expenditure(s) of fixed assets [capital]
Grundmittelausnutzung *f* utilization of fixed assets [capital]
Grundmittelaussonderung *f* discard of fixed assets [capital]
Grundmittelbestand *m* stock of fixed assets [capital]
Grundmittelbewertung *f* valuation of fixed assets [capital] *(ascertainment of monetary value of available stock of fixed assets in accountancy)*
Grundmittelbilanz *f s.* **Grundfondsbilanz**
Grundmitteleinsatz *m* utilization of fixed assets [capital]
Grundmittelfonds *m* fund of fixed assets [capital] *(monetary expression of net value of fixed assets in ledger)*
Grundmittelgruppen *fpl* groups of fixed assets [capital] *(classification according to productive and non-productive sectors)*
Grundmittelintensität *f s.* **Grundfondsintensität**
Grundmittelkartei *f* card index of fixed assets [capital]
Grundmittelkonto *n* fixed assets [capital] account
Grundmittelkredit *m* investment credit
Grundmittelnachweis *m s.* **Grundmittelrechnung**
Grundmittelquote *f s.* **Grundfondsquote**
Grundmittelrechnung *f* accounting of fixed assets [capital] *(of stocks, wastage of and increase in fixed assets as well as their utilization in production including depreciation)*
Grundmittelrentabilität *f* profitability of fixed assets [capital] *(s.* **Grundfondsrentabilität***)*
Grundmittelreproduktion *f s.* **Grundfondsreproduktion**
Grundmittelstatistik *f* statistics of fixed assets [capital]
Grundmittelstruktur *f* structure of fixed assets [capital] *(share of various types of fixed assets in the sum total of fixed assets)*
Grundmittelumbewertung *f* revaluation of fixed assets [capital]
Grundmittelumsetzung *f* relocation of fixed assets [capital] *(moving fixed assets from one enterprise to another in connection with specialization and concentration of production)*
Grundmittelverkauf *m* sale of fixed assets [capital]
Grundmittelvermietung *f* leasing [farming out] of fixed assets [capital]

Grundmittelverzeichnis *n* inventory [list] of fixed assets [capital]
Grundmittelwirtschaft *f s.* **Grundfondswirtschaft**
Grundmodell *n* basic model
~ **der Verflechtungsbilanz** basic model of input-output table
Grundnahrungsmittel *n* basic food (stuff)
Grundnorm *f* basic [fundamental] standard *(conduct etc.)*; basic industrial standard; basic norm
Grundnormativ *n* basic (industrial) standard
Grundordnung *f* fundamental constitutional order
Grundpfand *n* mortgage on real estate; real estate security
Grundpfandrecht *n* mortgage lien, hypothecary right
Grundprämie *f (ins)* basic premium [rate]
Grundpreis *m* basic price
Grundproportionen *fpl* basic proportions
~, **volkswirtschaftliche** basic national economic proportions *(such as between population, manpower and fixed assets etc.)*
Grundprozesse *mpl* basic processes
~, **volkswirtschaftliche** basic national economic processes
Grundrechte *npl* basic [constitutional] rights
~, **bürgerliche** civil [civic] liberties
Grundreihe *f (manuf)* basic [standard] series *(of sizes in mass production)*
Grundrente *f* 1. basic pension; 2. *(agric)* ground rent
~, **absolute** *(agric)* absolute ground rent
Grundrichtung *f* general tendency *(economic development etc.)*
Grundriß *m* 1. outline, sketch *(scientific subject etc.)*; 2. floor plan *(building)*, ground plan *(building, mine working etc.)*
Grundsatz *m* (fundamental) principle
Grundsatzentscheidung *f* decision on principle
Grundsatzerklärung *f* declaration of principle
Grundsatzfrage *f* fundamental [cardinal] issue
Grundsatzprogramm *n* basic programme; policy statement *(parties, trade unions etc.)*
Grundschulbildung *f* primary (school) education
Grundschuld *f* land charge; real estate liability
Grundschuldbrief *m* land charge deed
Grundschule *f* primary school
Grundschullehrer *m* primary school teacher
Grundsortiment *n* basic range of goods *(as opposed to specialized range)*, basic assortment
Grundsteuer *f* land tax, property [real estate] tax
Grundsteuerveranlagung *f* assessment on landed property

Grundstimmung *f* prevailing tone *(capital market etc.)*
Grundstock *m* basis, foundation; basic stock, original fund
Grundstoff *m* primary material, (basic) raw material
Grundstoffindustrie *f* basic industry
Grundstoffpreise *mpl* raw material prices
Grundstück *n* piece [plot] of land; (building) site
~, **baureifes** building estate [site]
~, **bebautes** built-up property
~, **belastetes** mortgaged estate [property]
~, **belastungsfähiges** property [land] that can be mortgaged
~, **enteignetes** expropriated property
~, **freies** vacant property
~, **gemeinschaftliches** joint property [real estate]
~, **genutztes** used land
~, **gepachtetes** rented property
~, **gewerblich genutztes** industrial property
~, **grundsteuerpflichtiges** rateable estate [property]
~, **landwirtschaftlich genutztes** agricultural [arable] land
~, **städtisches** town lot; municipal property
~, **unbebautes** undeveloped property
~, **unbelastetes** clear estate, estate free from encumbrances
~, **ungenutztes** unused land
~, **verpachtetes** leased (out) property
Grundstücksabschätzung *f* valuation of an estate, real estate assessment
Grundstücksabschreibung *f* depreciation on land
Grundstücksanteil *m* portion of an estate
Grundstücksauflassung *f* conveyance of real estate, transfer of title to land
Grundstücksbelastung *f* mortgage of land
Grundstücksbeteiligungen *fpl* real estate holdings
Grundstücksbewertung *f s.* **Grundstücksabschätzung**
Grundstückseigentümer *m* real estate owner, owner of (building) site
Grundstücksentwicklungskosten *pl s.* **Grundstückserschließungskosten**
Grundstückserschließung *f* land [property] development
Grundstückserschließungskosten *pl* property development cost(s)
Grundstücksgeschäft *n* real estate transaction, *(Am)* land deal
Grundstückshandel *m* trade in real estate, real estate trade
Grundstückshypothek *f* real estate [land] mortgage

Grundstückskauf *m* purchase of land [property]
Grundstückskonto *n* property account
Grundstücksmakler *m* estate agent
Grundstücksmarkt *m* property market
Grundstücksparzelle *f* plot of land, allotment
Grundstückspreis *m* real estate price, price of a piece of land
Grundstücksrecht *n* land law, law concerning real property
Grundstücksspekulant *m* land jobber
Grundstücksspekulation *f* land jobbing, speculation in real estate
Grundstückssteuer *f s.* **Grundsteuer**
Grundstücksübereignung *f s.* **Grundstücksauflassung**
Grundstücksübertragung *f s.* **Grundstücksauflassung**
Grundstücksumschreibung *f* alienation of an estate
Grundstücksunterhaltungskosten *pl* maintenance cost(s) of an estate
Grundstücksverkauf *m* sale of a piece of land; real estate dealing [selling, marketing]
Grundstücksverwalter *m* property manager
Grundstücksverwaltung *f* property management
Grundstückswert *m* value of land
Grundstufe *f* elementary grade *(school)*
Grundstufenlehrer *m* elementary grade teacher
Grundsystematik *f* basic classification *(used in planning)*
Grundumsatz *m* basic turnover
Grund- und Leistungspreis *m* basic and direct service charges *(telephone, gas, electricity etc.)*
Gründung *f* founding, foundation *(economic community etc.)*, promotion, floating *(company etc.)*, establishment, setting up *(business etc.)*
Gründungsakt *m* foundation, establishment
Gründungsaktien *fpl* founders' shares
Gründungsbilanz *f* formation statement [balance sheet]
Gründungseinlage *f* original investment
Gründungsjahr *n* year of foundation
Gründungskapital *n* capital on formation, original capital
Gründungskonsortium *n* syndicate [association] of founders
Gründungskosten *pl* promotion expense(s)
Gründungsmitglied *n* founder [foundation, charter] member
Gründungsurkunde *f* foundation deed *(institution etc.)*; memorandum of association *(company)*
Gründungsversammlung *f* founders' meeting
Gründungsvertrag *m* memorandum [articles] of association
Grundurlaub *m* minimum leave [vacation]

Grundverfahren *n* unit operation *(in manufacturing processes)*
Grundvergütung *f* basic pay; basic remuneration
Grundvermögen *n* 1. basic assets; 2. (landed) property, real estate
Grundvertrag *m* basic treaty [agreement]
Grundwasser *n* ground-water
Grundwassernutzung *f* utilization of ground--water
Grundwerkstoff *m* basic material
Grundwert *m* 1. land value; 2. basic [fundamental] value; 3. *(maths)* original number *(of which another number is a percentage)*; *(stats)* base (value)
Grundwiderspruch *m* basic contradiction
Grundzahl *f* basic number [figure]; *(maths)* base (number)
Grundzeit *f* basic time
~ **Hand** *(manuf)* basic time of manual operations
~ **Maschine** *(manuf)* basic time of mechanical operations
~ **Maschine/Hand** *(manuf)* basic time of mechanical and manual operations
Grundzins *m* ground rent
grundzinspflichtig tributary; liable to (pay) ground rent; subject to ground rent
Grundzinssatz *m* basic rate of interest
Grundzollsatz *m* basic customs tariff
Grundzüge *mpl* main [principal] features; distinctive marks [features]; principles
Grünfläche *f* grass- and tree-covered open space *(town and city planning)*
Grünfutter *n* *(agric)* green fodder [forage]
Grünfütterung *f* *(agric)* feeding (of animals) with greenstuff
Grüngürtel *m* green belt *(town and city planning)*
Grünland *n* *(agric)* grassland, meadowland
Grünlandanteil *m* *(agric)* ratio of grassland *(to the total land of a farm or an agricultural co--operative)*
Gründlandwirtschaft *f* *(agric)* ley [grass, grassland] farming
Gruppe *f* group *(sociological group and/or category)*; class *(people etc.)*
~, **endliche** *(stats)* finite group
~, **politische** political group
~, **unendliche** infinite group
Gruppen *fpl*: ⋄ ~ **bilden** to form groups, to group; **in** ~ **einteilen** to divide [sort] s.th. into groups [classes], to group, to classify *(s.th)*; **nach** ~ **einteilen** *s.* **in** ~ **einteilen**
~, **berufsgleiche** job families
~, **konkurrierende** competing groups
~, **nichtkonkurrierende** non-competing groups
Gruppenabschreibung *f* group depreciation
Gruppenakkord *m* collective piecerate

Gruppenakkordlohn *m* group piece wage(s)
Gruppenarbeit *f* teamwork, group work; gang work *(civil engineering etc.)*
Gruppenausbildung *f* group training
Gruppenbildung *f* group formation, formation of [into] groups
Gruppenbindung *f* group cohesion
Gruppenbreite *f (stats)* interval
Gruppendynamik *f* group dynamics
Gruppeneigentum *n* group property
Gruppenfaktor *m (stats)* group factor
Gruppeninteresse *n* interest of a group [team], sectional interest
Gruppenlebensversicherung *f* group-term life insurance
Gruppenleistung *f* group performance
Gruppenleistungslohn *m* group performance rate
Gruppenleistungslohnsystem *n* group piecework system
Gruppenlohn *m* group wage (rate)
Gruppenmerkmal *n (stats)* group characteristic
Gruppenmitte *f (stats)* group average
Gruppenmittelwert *m s.* **Gruppenmitte**
Gruppenpreis *m* cost of group tour
Gruppenproduktion *f* group production
Gruppenprüfung *f* group test
Gruppenschau *f* collective display
Gruppensoziologie *f* group sociology
Gruppenstücklohn *m* group piece wage
Gruppentarif *m* party [group] rate [tariff]
Gruppentechnologie *f* group technology
Gruppenvergleich *m (stats)* group comparison
Gruppenversicherung *f* group [collective] insurance
Gruppenwechselplan *m (stats)* cross-over [switchback] design, change-over trial
gruppieren to group, to arrange in a group [in groups]
Gruppieren *n s.* **Gruppierung**
Gruppierung *f* grouping, arrangement in a group [in groups]; grouping, group *(within a party etc.)*
~ **der Erzeugnisse nach der Nutzungsdauer** grouping of products according to service life
~**, mehrstufige** multi-stage grouping
~ **nach der ökonomischen Verwendung der Produktion** grouping according to (the) economic utilization of production
~ **nach einem Merkmal** grouping according to one criterion
~ **nach qualitativen Merkmalen** grouping according to qualitative criteria
~ **nach quantitativen Merkmalen** grouping according to quantitative criteria
Gruppierungsfaktor *m (stats)* factor of grouping; *(d.pr.)* blocking factor

Gruppierungsgitter *n (stats)* grouping lattice
Gruppierungsgrundsätze *mpl s.* **Gruppierungsprinzipien**
Gruppierungskorrektur *f (stats)* correction for grouping
Gruppierungsmerkmal *n* characteristic [criterion] of grouping
Gruppierungsparameter *m* sorting parameter
Gruppierungsprinzipien *npl (stats)* (fundamental) principles of grouping
Gruppierungstabelle *f (stats)* grouping table
gültig valid *(contract, cheque, passport etc.)*; effective, operative, in force *(law, decree, treaty etc.)*; current *(money)*
Gültigkeit *f* validity *(contract, cheque, passport etc.)*; legal force *(law, decree, treaty etc.)*; currency *(money)* ◊ **die ~ aufheben** to invalidate; **die ~ bestreiten** to contest [dispute] the validity *(of s.th.)*; to contest, to dispute *(s.th.) (will etc.)*; **die ~ eines Testamentes bestätigen** to prove a will; **die ~ eines Testamentes bestreiten** to dispute a will; **die ~ verlängern** to extend the validity; **die ~ verlieren** to become invalid; to expire; **~ erlangen** to attain validity, to become valid; to become operative [effective]; **~ haben** to be valid; to be current *(money)*, to be legal tender *(money)*; to be operative [effective, in force] *(law etc.)*; **keine ~ mehr haben** to be no longer valid, to have expired
~**, allgemeine** universal validity *(rule, theory etc.)*
~ **einer Offerte** *s.* ~ **eines Angebots**
~ **eines Angebots** validity of an offer
~ **eines Vertrages** force of a contract [an agreement]; validity [force] of a treaty *(between countries or groups of countries)*
~**, empirische** *(stats)* empirical validity
~**, logische** *(stats)* logical validity
~**, teilweise** particular [partial] validity
Gültigkeitsbereich *m* range of validity, scope *(theory, law etc.)*
Gültigkeitsdauer *f* period of validity ◊ **die ~ verlängern** *s.* **die Gültigkeit verlängern**
Gültigkeitserklärung *f* validation, legalization
Gültigkeitskontrolle *f (d.pr.)* validity check
Gültigkeitsvermerk *m* certification *(on a bill, cheque etc.)*
Gunst *f* favour, goodwill ◊ **sich zu jmds. Gunsten verrechnen** to make a mistake in s.o.'s favour; **zu Gunsten buchen** to enter on the credit side; **zu Gunsten von** in favour of; **zu jmds. Gunsten** in s.o.'s favour, to s.o.'s advantage
Gut *n* property, possession; farm; estate; assets ◊ **Hab und ~** property, possessions; goods; belongings
~**, anvertrautes** trust

~, **bewegliches** s. **Güter, bewegliche**
~, **eingebrachtes** brought-in property *(in marriage)*
~, **fremdes** other people's property
~, **gerettetes** salvage
~, **herrenloses** abandoned property, goods unclaimed
~, **schwimmendes** venture
~, **unbewegliches** s. **Güter, unbewegliche**
~, **veränderliches** *(ins)* shifting property
~, **volkseigenes (VEG)** nationally-owned farm *(producing seeds, seedlings, pedigree cattle and propagating modern methods of farming in the former GDR)*
Gutachten *n* (expert) opinion, opinion [evidence] of an expert; examiner's report
Gutachter *m* expert; *(ins)* appraiser
Gutbereich *m (stats)* acceptance region
gutbringen *(acc)* to credit
Güte *f* quality ⋄ **(von) erster** ~ (of) top quality; **(von) verschiedener** ~ (of) varying quality
~ **der Anpassung** *(stats)* goodness of fit
~, **durchschnittliche** standard quality
~ **einer Schätzung** *(stats)* closeness in estimation
Güteanforderung *f* standard of quality
Güteeigenschaften *fpl* properties of product *(for classification)*
Güteeinteilung *f* classification *(of products etc.)* according to quality, grading
Gütefaktor *m* quality factor
Gütegrad *m* quality, grade
Güteklasse *f* class, grade; standard of quality
Gütekontrolle *f* 1. quality inspection; 2. (quality) inspection department
Gütemerkmal *n* quality feature [characteristic] *(for product classification)*
Güteprüfung *f* quality test [inspection], test for quality
Güter *npl* goods, products, commodities, merchandise
~, **austauschbare** substitutable goods; exchangeable goods
~, **bahnlagernde** goods at the railway depot
~, **bewegliche** movables
~, **bewirtschaftete** rationed goods
~, **eingelagerte** stored goods
~, **haltbare** durable goods, durables
~, **hochwertige** high-grade [high-quality] goods
~, **im Inland hergestellte** home-produced [inland] goods
~, **konsumtionsfähige** consumable goods
~, **kurzlebige** non-durables
~, **lagerfähige** storable goods
~, **langlebige** s. ~, **haltbare**
~, **lebenswichtige** essential goods
~, **leicht verderbliche** easily perishable goods

~, **sperrige** bulky goods
~, **strategische** strategic goods [commodities]
~, **unbewegliche** immovables
~ **unter Zollverschluß** bonded (warehouse) goods
~, **unterwegs befindliche** goods in transit
~, **verderbliche** perishable goods, perishables
~, **vertretbare** fungible goods [things], fungibles
~, **zollpflichtige** dutiable goods
Güterabfertigung *f* 1. dispatch of goods; 2. goods department, goods [freight, forwarding] office
Güterabsatz *m* sale of goods [commodities]
Güterannahme(stelle) *f* goods [*(Am)* freight] (receiving) office
Güterausgabe(stelle) *f* goods [*(Am)* freight] (delivery) office
Güteraustausch *m* exchange of goods; barter
Güterbahnhof *m* goods station [yard], *(Am)* rail freight yard
Güterbeförderung *f* transport of goods, goods traffic
Güterbegleitschein *m* waybill; shipping note
Güterbewegung *f* movement of goods
Gütereinteilung *f* classification of goods
Gütererzeugung *f* production [manufacturing] of goods
Güterfernverkehr *m* long-distance goods traffic, *(Am)* long haul trucking
Gütergemeinschaft *f* joint ownership of property
Güterkraftverkehr *m* road haulage, *(Am)* trucking
Güterkraftverkehrstarif *m* goods traffic rate
Gütermenge *f* quantity [volume] of goods
Güternahverkehr *m* short-distance goods [freight] traffic
Güterproduktion *f* s. **Gütererzeugung**
Güterrecht *n* law of property
Güterstrom *m* flow of goods
~, **einläufiger** one-way flow of goods
~, **gegenläufiger** two-way flow of goods
Güterstromoptimierung *f* optimization of flow of goods
Gütertarif *m* goods (transport) rate, goods [*(Am)* freight] tariff
Gütertarifbahnhof *m (railw)* goods loading station
Gütertaxi *n* hired van [lorry]
Gütertransport *m* transport of goods, goods traffic
Gütertransportleistung *f* goods transport performance
Gütertransportplan *m* transport plan of goods
Gütertransportpreis *m* goods transport charges
Gütertransportversicherung *f* goods transport [*(Am)* freight] insurance

Gütertrennung f separation of property
Güterumschlag m cargo [freight] handling
Güterverkehr m goods [(Am) freight] traffic
~, **zentralisierter** centralized transport of goods
~, **zwischenstaatlicher** inter-state goods transport
Güterverkehrstarif m goods traffic [transport] rate
Güterversand m dispatching of goods
Güterverteilung f distribution of (consumer) goods; distribution of property [wealth]
Güterwagen m goods [railway] waggon, (Am) freight car
Güterwagenpark m goods waggon [(Am) freight car] pool
~, **gemeinsamer** common [joint] goods waggon [(Am) freight car] pool
Güterwirtschaft f merchandising
Güterzug m goods [(Am) freight] train
Güteschutz m quality protection
Gütesicherung f s. **Güteschutz**
Güteüberwachung f quality control
~, **statistische** quality control (for statistical purposes)
Güte- und Lieferbedingungen fpl quality and delivery terms (of commodities)
Güteverfahren n (jur) conciliatory proceedings
Gütevorschlag m (jur) conciliatory proposal
Gütevorschrift f quality specification, specification as to quality
Gütevorschriften fpl **und Lieferbedingungen** fpl, **Technische** (TGL) Technical Standards, Standards of Quality and Terms of Delivery
Gütewert m s. **Gütefaktor**
Gütezeichen n quality mark [seal]
gutgehend flourishing, thriving (business etc.); (s.th.) that sells well (goods etc.)
Gutgewicht n extra weight (granted to customers)
gutgläubig (jur) acting in good faith (person); done in good faith (action etc.); bona fide (person, action etc.)
guthaben to have (sum of money) to one's credit; to have credit for (s.th.)
Guthaben n credit (balance), (bank) balance; account; assets
~, **eingefrorenes** frozen account
~, **gesperrtes** blocked credit balance
~ **im Ausland** deposits held abroad; reserves held abroad
~, **jederzeit verfügbares** s. ~, **täglich abhebbares**
~, **täglich abhebbares** call money
~, **verfügbares** s. ~, **zur Verfügung stehendes**
~, **zinsloses** balance without interest; non-interest-bearing deposit
~, **zur Verfügung stehendes** amount standing to the credit

Guthaben npl assets; accounts; deposits
~, **antizipative** deferred credits
~, **ausländische** foreign deposits
~, **dubiose** doubtful accounts
~, **öffentliche** public deposits
Guthabenkonto n credit [deposit] account
Guthabenüberschuß m credit balance
gütlich amicable, friendly (agreement, settlement etc.)
Gutsbesitzer m owner of an estate, estate owner
Gutschein m credit note; coupon; gift token
gutschreiben s. **gutbringen**
Gutschrift f (bank) credit(ing); credit item [entry]; credit voucher [slip]
Gutschriftanzeige f (bank) credit note, advice of amount credited
Gutschriftposten m (bank) credit item
Gutsinspektor m s. **Gutsverwalter**
Gutspächter m tenant of an estate, tenant farmer
Gutsverwalter m manager of an estate; landlord's manager
Gutsverwaltung f management of an estate; estate management

H

Habe f property; possessions, belongings
~, **liegende** s. ~, **unbewegliche**
~, **persönliche** personal belongings [possessions]
~, **unbewegliche** immovables, real estate [property]
Haben n (acc) credit (side) ⋄ **im** ~ **buchen** to enter on the credit side
Habenbestände mpl (acc) assets
Habenbuchung f (acc) credit entry
Habenposition f s. **Habenposten**
Habenposten m credit item [entry]
Habensaldo m (acc) credit balance (of an account)
Habenseite f (acc) credit side ⋄ **auf die** ~ **buchen** s. **im Haben buchen**
Habenzins(en) m(pl) credit interest
Habilitation f habilitation (post-doctoral thesis at German universities)
habilitieren to habilitate (to acquire a professorship)
Habseligkeiten fpl belongings, effects, things
Hackbau m (agric) hoe culture; hoe-farming
hacken (agric) to hoe
Hackfrüchte fpl root crops and tubers
Hackfrüchteanbau m cultivation of root crops and tubers

Hackkultur *f s.* **Hackfrüchte**
Hafen *m* harbour; port ◊ **aus dem ~ auslaufen** to clear the port; **in den ~ einlaufen** to drop into port, to enter the harbour, to enter port
~, geschlossener dock-port
~, innerer dock area
~ mit Zollfreilager bonded port
~, natürlicher natural harbour
Hafenabgaben *fpl* harbour-dues, port charges, port-dues
Hafenamt *n* port authority
Hafenanlagen *fpl* port [harbour] installations, docks
Hafenarbeiter *m* port worker, docker, *(Am)* longshoreman
Hafenaufsichtsamt *n s.* **Hafenamt**
Hafenbehörde *f s.* **Hafenamt**
Hafenbereich *m* port area
Hafengebühren *fpl s.* **Hafenabgaben**
Hafengeld *n* groundage, keelage
Hafenkonnossement *n* ocean bill of lading
Hafenkosten *pl s.* **Hafengeld**
Hafenliegegeld *n* moorage, mooring dues; groundage, keelage
Hafenliegezeit *f* lay-days
Hafenordnung *f* port and harbour regulations
Hafenrisiko *n (ins)* port risk
Hafensperre *f* embargo; blockade
Hafenstadt *f* seaport; river-port; port(town)
Hafenumschlag *m* port transshipment
Hafenusancen *fpl* customs and usages of (the) port
Hafenverwaltung *f* port administration
Hafenviertel *n* dock-area, water-front
Hafenzeit *f s.* **Hafenliegezeit**
Hafenzoll *m* customs duties at the port of entry [departure]
Haft *f (jur)* detention; custody; imprisonment
Haftanstalt *f* jail, prison; detention centre; remand home
haftbar (legally) responsible; *(jur)* (legally) liable
Haftbarkeit *f s.* **Haftung**
haften to be (legally) responsible [liable, answerable] for; to guarantee ◊ **beschränkt ~ to** accept limited liability; **für etwas ~ to** guarantee s.th.; **für jmdn. ~** to answer for s.o.; to be responsible for s.o.; **persönlich ~ to** accept personal liability; **unbeschränkt ~ to** accept unlimited liability
Haftpflicht *f (jur)* liability ◊ **es besteht keine ~** there is no liability
~ des Arbeitgebers employer's liability
Haftpflichtanteil *m* proportion of liability
Haftpflichtausschluß *m* non-liability
Haftpflichthöchstgrenze *f* maximum liability
haftpflichtig *(jur)* liable
Haftpflichtmindestgrenze *f* minimum liability

Haftpflichtpolice *f* third party (liability) insurance policy
~, allgemeine general liability (insurance) policy
Haftpflichtumfang *m* liability coverage
Haftpflicht-, Unfall- und Kraftfahrversicherung *f* **(HUK)** liability, accident and motor vehicle insurance
Haftpflichtversicherung *f* third party (liability) insurance
Haftpflichtversicherungspolice *f s.* **Haftpflichtpolice**
Haftung *f* (legal) responsibility; *(jur)* liability ◊ **ohne ~** without liability
~, anteilmäßige prorata liability
~, beschränkte limited liability
~, beschränkte persönliche limited personal liability
~, direkte primary liability
~, doppelte double liability
~, erhöhte additional responsibility
~, finanzielle financial responsibility
~, gegenseitige cross liability *(shipping)*
~, gemeinsame joint liability
~, gesamtschuldnerische joint and several liability
~, gesetzliche legal liability
~, obligatorische *s.* **~, vertragliche**
~, persönliche personal liability
~, solidarische *s.* **~, gemeinsame**
~, unbeschränkte unlimited liability
~, unbeschränkte persönliche unlimited personal liability
~, unmittelbare *s.* **~, direkte**
~, verschuldensunabhängige strict liability in tort
~, vertragliche contractual obligation
Haftungsausschluß *m* non-liability
Haftungsausschlußklausel *f* non-liability clause
Haftungsbeschränkung *f* limitation of liability
Haftungsübernahme *f* assumption of liability
Haftungsumfang *m* extent of liability, liability coverage
Hagelschaden *m* damage caused by hail
Hagelschadenversicherung *f* hail (storm) insurance
halbamtlich semi-official, quasi-official
halbautomatisch semi-automatic
Halbfabrikat *n s.* **Halbfertigerzeugnis**
halbfertig semi-finished, semi-fabricated, semi-manufactured, semi-processed, unfinished
Halbfertigerzeugnis *n* semi-finished [intermediate, semi-manufactured, semi-processed, semi-fabricated, unfinished] product
Halbfertigware *f* intermediate [semi-finished, semi-fabricated, semi-manufactured, semi-processed, unfinished] good

Halbierungslinie

Halbierungslinie *f (stats)* median line
Halbierungsmethode *f (stats)* split-half [split-test] method
Halbinvariante *f (stats)* cumulant, half-invariant, semi-invariant
Halbjahresabschluß *m* half-yearly [mid-year, semi-annual] settlement
Halbjahresausweis *m* half-yearly [semi-annual, mid-year] statement
Halbjahresbilanz *f* half-yearly balance sheet
Halbjahr(es)plan *m* half-yearly [six-month, six-months'] plan
Halbjahresrate *f* half-yearly [semi-annual] instalment
Halbjahresrechnung *f s.* **Habjahresabschluß**
Halbjahreszahlung *f* half-yearly [semi-annual] payment
halbjährlich half-yearly, semi-annual *(payments etc.)*
halbmonatlich twice-monthly, semi-monthly, fortnightly, half-monthly *(report etc.)*
Halbpacht *f* half-share farming; *(Am)* share-crop system, 'metayage' system *(by which farmer pays half the yield as rent in some countries)*
Halbpächter *m* share-cropper, 'metayer', farmer who pays rent in kind
Halb-Quartilspanne *f (stats)* semi-interquartile range
halbstaatlich semi-state
halbtags part-time, half-day
Halbtagsarbeit *f* half-day [part-time] employment [job]
Halbtagsbeschäftigung *f s.* **Halbtagsarbeit**
Halbtagskraft *f* person working part-time
Halbtagsstelle *f* half-day [part-time] job
Halbwert *m (stats)* median
Halbzeug *n* half-finished [semi-finished, semi-processed, semi-manufactured] product
Halde *f (min)* dump, dump-heap ◇ **auf ~ produzieren** *(min)* to stockpile *(coal, ore etc.)*
Haldenbestände *mpl (min)* dump stocks, stocks on the dumps
Haldenbevorratung *f (min)* stockpiling *(coal, ore etc.)*
Hallenkapazität *f* hall capacity
Halm *m:*
  ◇ **auf dem ~ verkaufen** *(agric)* to sell the crop standing
haltbar durable, hard-wearing, lasting *(material etc.);* fast *(colour);* imperishable *(food)*
Haltbarkeit *f* durability, lasting qualities *(material etc.);* fastness *(colour);* good keeping qualities *(food)*
halten to keep *(s.th.);* to hold *(position etc.);* to maintain *(prices, standard etc.);* to abide by *(promise etc.);* to observe *(law etc.);* to stick to [by] *(principle etc.)*

Halter *m* holder, keeper
haltlos untenable *(assertion etc.);* baseless, without foundation *(theory etc.)*
Haltung *f* 1. keeping *(s.th.);* attitude *(towards s.th./s.o.);* posture; 2. *(st.ex.)* tone *(of the market)*
Hand *f:*
  ◇ **aus erster ~** first-hand; **aus zweiter ~** second-hand; **etwas aus erster ~ kaufen** to buy s.th. direct [first-hand] *(from producer);* **etwas aus zweiter ~ kaufen** to buy s.th. through an intermediary [through a middleman]; to buy s.th. second-hand; **in privater ~** in private hands; **unter der ~ verkaufen** to sell unofficially [under the counter]; **von ~ verarbeiten** to process manually
~, öffentliche public authorities, the state
Handakten *fpl (jur)* reference files
Handarbeit *f* 1. manual work [labour], work done by hand; handicraft; handwork; handiwork; 2. (piece of) needlework, knitting
Handarbeiter *m* manual labourer [worker]; handworker; handicraftsman; artisan
Handbetrieb *m* manual operation; hand control; hand working, working by hand
Handbuch *n* manual, handbook; textbook; guide
Hände *fpl:*
  ◇ **zu Händen von** for the attention of *(in correspondence)*
Handel *m* commerce, trade; business; transaction, deal, bargain
~, ambulanter itinerant trade
~, beweglicher *s.* **~, ambulanter**
~, bilateraler bilateral trade
~, direkter direct supply *(of goods from the producer to the retailer and/or consumer)*
~, freier free trade
~, genossenschaftlicher co-operative trade *(mainly consumer co-operatives and farmers' trading co-operatives)*
~, innerer home [domestic] trade
~, internationaler international trade
~ mit Drittländern trade with third countries
~ mit Gebrauchtwaren trade in second-hand goods
~, multilateraler multilateral trade
~, örtlicher local trade
~, privater private trade
~, rechtswidriger illegal trade [traffic]
~, reger brisk [lively] trade
~, schwarzer black-market business
~, spekulativer speculation
~, spezialisierter specialized trade
~, staatlicher state trading system [sector]
~, überseeischer overseas trade
~, unsichtbarer trade in invisibles, invisibles

~, **vermittelnder** agency business
~, **volkseigener** nationally-owned (wholesale and retail) trade *(in the former GDR)*
~, **zweiseitiger** *s.* ~, **bilateraler**
~, **zwischenstaatlicher** *s.* ~, **internationaler**
handeln 1. *(com)* to trade, to deal [do business] with *(s.o.)*; 2. to act, to take action; to proceed; to behave ⋄ **um etwas** ~ to bargain [haggle] for s.th.
Handelsabgaben *fpl* taxes and levies on trade
Handelsabkommen *n* trade agreement
~, **zweiseitiges** bilateral trade agreement
Handelsabordnung *f* trade delegation
Handelsabschlag *m* discount, rebate; deduction
Handelsadreßbuch *n* commercial directory
Handelsagent *m* commercial agent; commercial traveller; representative
Handelsakzept *n* trade acceptance
Handelsarten *fpl* kinds of trade
Handelsartikel *m* article of commerce, commercial article; commodity; merchandise
Handelsattaché *m* commercial attaché
Handelsaufschlag *m* trade surcharge
Handelsaufwand *m s.* **Handelskosten**
Handelsausgaben *fpl s.* **Handelskosten**
Handelsauskünfte *fpl* trade [commercial] information
Handelsauskunftsbüro *n* trade inquiry bureau [desk], commercial information stand
Handelsausrüstungen *fpl* equipment of trading institutions
Handelsaustausch *m* foreign trade, export and import; international barter (trade)
Handelsausweitung *f* trade expansion
Handelsbank *f* commercial bank
Handelsbedingungen *fpl* conditions [terms] of trade
Handelsberechtigung *f s.* **Handelserlaubnis**
Handelsbereich *m* trade group *(of shops with different ranges of goods according to regional aspects)*
Handelsbeschränkung *f* trade restriction
Handelsbeschränkungen *fpl:*
⋄ ~ **aufheben** to lift [remove] trade restrictions; ~ **verhängen** to impose trade restrictions
Handelsbesprechungen *fpl* trade talks [negotiations]
Handelsbestimmungen *fpl* trade regulations
Handelsbetrieb *m* 1. commercial enterprise, business, firm; concern; 2. trade, commerce
~, **genossenschaftlicher** co-operative (store)
~, **privater** private shop
~, **staatlicher** state trading organization [enterprise]; state-owned shop
Handelsbetriebswirtschaft *f* commercial administration

Handelsbetriebswirtschaftslehre *f* theory of commercial administration
Handelsbevollmächtigter *m (com)* attorney, agent (holding power of attorney)
Handelsbezeichnung *f* trade name, brand
Handelsbeziehungen *fpl* trade relations
Handelsbilanz *f* balance of trade, trade balance
~, **aktive** favourable trade balance
~, **ausgeglichene** even trade balance
~, **passive** unfavourable [adverse] trade balance
Handelsbilanztheorie *f* balance of trade theory
Handelsblockade *f* trade blockade
Handelsbourgeoisie *f* trade [trading, commercial] bourgeoisie
Handelsboykott *m* trade boycott
Handelsbrauch *m* business [trade] code; trade custom [usage]
Handelsbrief *m* business letter
Handelsbuchführung *f* commercial bookkeeping
Handelsbündnis *n* trade alliance
Handelsdefizit *n* trade deficit
Handelsdelegation *f* trade mission [delegation]
Handelsdiskriminierung *f* trade discrimination
Handelsdisponent *m* chief clerk *(in commerce)*
Handelseinbuße *f* loss of trade
Handelseinheit *f* unit of trade, trade unit
Handelseinkommen *n* trade income
Handelseinschränkung *f* trade restraint [restriction], restraint [restriction] on trade
Handelsembargo *n* embargo
Handelserlaubnis *f* trading [trade] licence
Handelserlös *m* trade proceeds
Handelsertrag *m s.* **Handelserlös**
Handelsexpansion *f s.* **Handelsausweitung**
Handelsfach *n* commercial subject
handelsfähig negotiable *(bond, security etc.)*
Handelsfaktur(a) *f* commercial invoice
Handelsfirma *f* firm, business, business house
Handelsfixkauf *m* firm purchase; purchase for delivery at a fixed date; *(st.ex.)* future (deal), time bargain
Handelsflagge *f* merchant flag
Handelsflaute *f (com)* slackness, slack period
Handelsflotte *f* merchant fleet [navy]
Handelsfondsabgabe *f* trading fund levy *(on profits of trading organizations)*
Handelsförderung *f* trade promotion
Handelsförderungsmaßnahme *f* trade promotion measure
Handelsforum *n* trade forum
Handelsfreiheit *f* freedom of trade; free trading
Handelsfunktion *f* trading function
handelsgängig marketable *(article etc.)*, commercial *(article, product etc.)*
Handelsgarten *m* market garden, *(Am)* truck garden [farm]

Handelsgärtner *m* market gardener
Handelsgärtnerei *f* market [*(Am)* truck] gardening; market [*(Am)* truck] garden
Handelsgegenstand *m s.* **Handelsartikel**
Handelsgemeinkosten *pl* overhead costs in trade
Handelsgenossenschaft *f* trading co-operative
Handelsgepflogenheit *f s.* **Handelsbrauch**
Handelsgericht *n* commercial court
Handelsgerichtsbarkeit *f* commercial jurisdiction
Handelsgeschäft *n* 1. commercial transaction; 2. (business) firm [house]; shop
Handelsgesellschaft *f* commercial company [firm]
~, offene general partnership company *(with full liability of all members)*
Handelsgesetz *n* commercial [trade] law
Handelsgesetzbuch *n* **(HGB)** trade code
Handelsgesetzgebung *f* commercial [trade] legislation
Handelsgewerbe *n* business, trade
Handelsgewicht *n* commercial weight; commercial standard of weights; avoirdupois weight
Handelsgewinn *m* trading profit
Handelsgewohnheit *f s.* **Handelsbrauch**
Handelsgut *n s.* **Handelsartikel**
Handelshafen *m* commercial [trading] port
Handelshaus *n s.* **Handelsfirma**
Handelshindernisse *npl* obstacles to trade, trade obstacles
Handelskapital *n* trading [commercial] capital; stock in trade
Handelskette *f* chain of stores [shops]
Handelsklasse *f* group of goods traded *(according to a classification)*
Handelsklausel *f* trade clause [stipulation]
Handelsklauseln *fpl* commercial terms
~, Internationale International Commercial Terms (Incoterms)
Handelskonferenz *f* trade conference
Handelskontakte *mpl* business contacts
Handelskonvention *f* (international) trade convention
Handelskooperation *f* co-operation in trade; trading co-operation
Handelskorrespondenz *f* commercial correspondence
Handelskosten *pl* trade costs
Handelskostenanalyse *f* trade costs analysis
Handelskredit *m* commercial credit
Handelskreise *mpl* commercial [trade] circles
Handelskrieg *m* trade war
Handelskrise *f* commercial crisis; trade crisis
Handelskultur *f* standard of retail service
Handelskunde *f* business *(as a subject)*
Handelslehre *f s.* **Handelskunde**

Handelsmacht *f* mercantile nation
Handelsmakler *m* commercial [mercantile] broker
Handelsmarine *f* merchant fleet [navy]
Handelsmarke *f* trademark, brand
Handelsmesse *f* trade fair
Handelsmetropole *f* commercial metropolis [centre]
Handelsminister *m* Minister of Commerce, President of the Board of Trade, *(Am)* Secretary of Commerce
Handelsministerium *n* Ministry of Commerce, Board of Trade, *(Am)* Departement of Commerce
Handelsmißbräuche *mpl* trade abuses
Handelsmission *f* trade mission
Handelsmonopol *n* trade monopoly
Handelsname *m s.* **Handelsbezeichnung**
Handelsnetz *n* trade network
Handelsniederlassung *f* business establishment; registered seat *(of a firm)*; branch, trading post *(abroad)*
Handelsoperation *f* commercial transaction [activity]
Handelsorgan *n* business establishment
Handelsorganisation *f* trading organization
Handelspapiere *npl (st.ex.)* negotiable papers
Handelspartner *m* trade [trading] partner
Handelsperspektive *f* trade prospects
Handelsplanung *f* trade planning
Handelsplatz *m* trading [commercial] centre, trading-post
Handelspolitik *f* commercial [trade] policy
handelspolitisch pertaining to commercial [trade] policy
Handelspraktiken *fpl* trade practices
Handelspreis *m* trade price
Handelspreisbildung *f* trade price-fixing
Handelspreisbindung *f* price maintenance
Handelspreiskatalog *m* trade price list
Handelsprivileg *n* trade privilege
Handelsprodukt *n* commercial product; commodity; merchandise
Handelsprofit *m* trade profit
Handelsprogramm *n* trade programme
Handelsprovision *f* commission; brokerage
Handelsrabatt *m* discount; rebate; deduction
Handelsrat *m* commercial [trade] counsellor
Handelsrecht *n* commercial [mercantile] law
handelsrechtlich in accordance with [pertaining to] commercial law
Handelsregister *n* commercial [trade] register
Handelsreisender *m* travelling salesman, commercial traveller
Handelsrestriktionen *fpl s.* **Handelsbeschränkungen**
Handelsrisiko *n* business [commercial] risk

Handelssache *f (jur)* commercial [trade] dispute [case]
Handelsschiff *n* merchant vessel [ship], merchantman
Handelsschiffahrt *f* merchant shipping
Handelsschranke *f* trade barrier, barrier to trade
Handelssortiment *n* range of goods for sale
Handelsspanne *f* trade margin
Handelsspannennormativ *n* (standard) norm of trade margin, trade margin normative
Handelsspannenteilung *f* trade margin sharing
Handelssperre *f* embargo *(on export and import)*
Handelsstadt *f* commercial [trading] town, trade centre
Handelsstand *m* merchant [trading] class; merchants, traders
Handelsstatistik *f* trade statistics
Handelsstraße *f* trade-route
Handelsstützpunkt *m* trading base
Handelssystem *n* trading system
Handelstätigkeit *f* commercial activities, commerce
Handelstechnik *f* 1. shop equipment and fittings; 2. documents and ways of conducting foreign trade
Handelstreffpunkt *m* trade [business] centre; trade fair
handelsüblich customary [usual] in (the) trade, commercial *(quality, practice, discount etc.)*
Handelsumsatz *m* trade turnover
Handels- und Kreditgenossenschaft *f* trade and loan co-operative
Handels- und Schiffahrtsvertrag *m* trade and shipping agreement
Handels- und Zahlungsabkommen *n* trade and payments agreement
Handelsunternehmen *n s.* **Handelsbetrieb**
Handelsusancen *fpl* trade customs [usage, practices]
Handelsverband *m* trade association
Handelsverbindungen *fpl* trade connections
Handelsverbot *n* prohibition of trade
Handelsverein *m s.* **Handelsvereinigung**
Handelsvereinbarung *f s.* **Handelsabkommen**
Handelsvereinigung *f* trade association
Handelsverkehr *m* commerce, trading, commercial intercourse
Handelsverluste *mpl* losses in trade
Handelsvertrag *m* commercial treaty [contract], trade agreement
Handelsvertreter *m* trade representative; mercantile agent; travelling salesman, commercial traveller
Handelsvertretung *f* trade [commercial] mission [representation]
Handelsvollmacht *f (com)* limited authority to act and sign

Handelsvolumen *n* trade volume, volume of trade; total exports and imports
Handelsvorräte *mpl* stock-in-trade
Handelsvorschriften *fpl* trade regulations
Handelswaren *fpl* goods, commodities, merchandise
Handelswechsel *m* trade [commercial] bill
Handelswege *mpl* trade [commercial] channels; trade-routes
Handelswerbung *f* commercial advertising
Handelswert *m* trade [commercial] value
Handelswissenschaft *f* commercial science
Handelszeichen *n* trademark
Handelszentrum *n* trading centre
Handelszweig *m* line of business, branch of trade
handeltreibend trading, mercantile
Handfertigkeit *f* manual skill, dexterity
Handfließfertigung *f* manual flow production
handgearbeitet hand-made
handgefertigt *s.* **handgearbeitet**
Handgeld *n* earnest-money
handgemacht *s.* **handgearbeitet**
handgerecht handy
Handgriff *m* 1. grip, handle; 2. grip, movement (of the hand), manipulation, motion
Handklöppler *m* lace-bobbin maker
Handlanger *m* helper, unskilled workman; handy-man
Händler *m* trader, dealer, merchant; tradesman; shopkeeper
Handlung *f* 1. action, activity, deed; 2. shop, store
~, **fahrlässige** negligent act
~, **feindselige** hostile act
~, **gesetzwidrige** unlawful act
~, **strafbare** punishable offence
Handlungsablauf *m* (course of) action
Handlungsbeauftragter *m* agent
Handlungsbevollmächtigter *m* attorney, agent *(holding power of attorney)*
handlungsfähig capable of acting
Handlungsfähigkeit *f* capacity to act
Handlungsfreiheit *f* free scope [rein], freedom [liberty] of action
~, **völlige** full liberty to act
Handlungsgehilfe *m* employee; (commercial) clerk; shop-assistant
Handlungsreisender *m s.* **Handelsreisender**
Handlungsspielraum *m* scope (of action)
handlungsunfähig incompetent to act
Handlungsunfähigkeit *f* incapacity to act
Handlungsvollmacht *f* power to act [of procuration]
Handwerk *n* trade, craft
~, **genossenschaftliches** co-operative craft [trade]

244 Handwerk

~, **privates** private craft [trade]
~, **produzierendes** productive crafts *(as opposed to craft services)*
Handwerker *m* craftsman, artisan; skilled worker
Handwerkergenossenschaft *f* co-operative society of craftsmen [tradesmen]
Handwerkerinnung *f* craftsmen's [tradesmen's] guild
Handwerkerpreis *m* craftsman's delivery price *(goods, services etc.)*
Handwerkerproduktionsgenossenschaft *f* production co-operative (society) of craftsmen
Handwerkerrolle *f s.* **Handwerksrolle**
Handwerkerschaft *f* craftsmen, tradesmen
Handwerkervereinigung *f* association of craftsmen [tradesmen]
Handwerkerzunft *f s.* **Handwerkerinnung**
handwerklich of crafts, of the craftsman
Handwerksberuf *m* skilled craft [trade]
Handwerksbetrieb *m* craftsman's business [establishment]
Handwerksgeselle *m* journeyman
Handwerkskammer *f* Chamber of Crafts [Trades]
Handwerksleistungen *fpl* output and services of crafts [trades]
handwerksmäßig workmanlike
Handwerksmeister *m* master craftsman
Handwerkspreis *m s.* **Handwerkerpreis**
Handwerkspreisanordnung(en) *f(pl)* regulation(s) of craftsman's delivery prices
Handwerksproduktion *f* output of crafts [trades]
Handwerksrolle *f* trade register, register of trades
Handwerkssteuer *f* income tax levied on crafts
Handwerks- und Gewerbebetrieb *m* craftsman's business [establishment]
Handzeit *f* manual working time
Hansa *f s.* **Hanse**
Hanse *f* 1. *(hist)* Hanseatic League, Hansa, Hanse *(league of towns of northern Germany and adjacent countries for the promotion and protection of trade during the later part of the Middle Ages)*; 2. guild of merchants; 3. Hansa [Hanse, Hanseatic] towns
Hanseat *m* citizen of a Hansa [Hanse, Hanseatic] town; Hanseatic merchant
Hansebund *m* 1. Hanseatic League; 2. the Hanseatic Confederation *(of German commerce and industry, 1909)*
Hansestadt *f* Hanseatic town [city]
Hardware-Handel *m* trade in hardware, hardware trade
Hartgeld *n* metal money, coins
Hartwährung *f* hard currency

Hättekalkulation *f* cost calculation (under conditions presumed)
Häufigkeit *f* frequency
~, **absolute** *(stats)* absolute frequency
~, **bei Unabhängigkeit erwartete** *(stats)* independence frequency
~ **der Teilnahme** frequency of participation *(fairs etc.)*
~, **proportionale** *(stats)* proportional frequency
~, **relative** *(stats)* relative frequency
Häufigkeiten *fpl:*
~, **theoretische** *(stats)* theoretical frequencies
Häufigkeitsdichte *f (stats)* frequency density
Häufigkeitsfläche *f (stats)* frequency surface
Häufigkeitsfunktion *f (stats)* frequency function
~, **kumulative** *(stats)* cumulative frequency function
Häufigkeitskurve *f (stats)* frequency curve
~, **anormale** *(stats)* abnormal frequency curve
~, **kumulative** *(stats)* cumulative frequency curve
Häufigkeitsmoment *n (stats)* frequency moment
Häufigkeitspolygon *n (stats)* frequency polygon
Häufigkeitsstufen *fpl (stats)* quantiles
Häufigkeitstabelle *f (stats)* frequency table
Häufigkeitstheorie *f* frequency theory
~ **der Wahrscheinlichkeit** *(stats)* frequency theory of probability
Häufigkeitsverteilung *f (stats)* frequency distribution
~, **kumulative** *(stats)* cumulative frequency distribution
~, **überlagerte** *(stats)* compound frequency distribution
Häufigkeitszahl *f* frequency number
Hauptabnehmer *m* main contract buyer
Hauptabrechnung *f* drawing up and settlement of periodical accounts
Hauptabschluß *m (acc)* annual statement of accounts
Hauptabteilung *f* main [chief] department
Hauptabteilungsleiter *m* head of main department
Hauptaktionär *m* principal shareholder [*(Am)* stockholder]
hauptamtlich full-time *(functionary, occupation etc.)*, on a full-time basis
Hauptanteil *m* principal [decisive] share
Hauptarbeit *f* main (part of the) work
Hauptaufgabe *f* main task; prime function
~, **ökonomische** central economic policy
Hauptauftraggeber *m* main investor
Hauptauftragnehmer *m* main executor *(investment etc.)*, person who accepts a commission, main [prime] contractor
Hauptausfuhr *f* main [chief, bulk of] export(s)
Hauptausfuhrgüter *npl* chief [main] exports

Hauptausfuhrland *n* main exporting country
Hauptbausaison *f* peak construction season
Hauptbebauungsplan *m* general building plan
Hauptbelastung *f* peak load *(carried by power station, road, railway etc.)*; main [heavy] burden *(financial etc.)*
Hauptbelastungszeit *f* peak load period
Hauptberuf *m* full-time [regular] occupation
hauptberuflich full-time, regular *(functionary, occupation etc.)*
Hauptbeschäftigung *f* main [regular] occupation
Hauptbestandteil *m* main constituent [part]; chief ingredient
Hauptbetrieb *m* main [leading] enterprise
Hauptbeweggrund *m* prime [chief, leading] motive
Hauptbilanz *f* general balance sheet
Hauptbuch *n* (general) ledger
Hauptbuchhalter *m* chief bookkeeper; accountant
Hauptbuchhaltung *f* main accounting [accounts] department
Hauptdirektion *f* head office
Hauptdiskussionsredner *m* main speaker, principal in a debate
Haupteffekt *m (stats)* main effect
Haupteigentümer *m* general owner, senior partner *(business etc.)*
Haupteinfuhr *f* main [chief, bulk of] import(s)
Haupteinfuhrwaren *fpl* main [principal] imports
Haupteinkommen *n* principal income
Haupteinnahmequelle *f* major part of revenue
Haupterzeugnis *n* principal [main] product, staple product
Hauptexportartikel *m* main export (article), major export item
Hauptexportland *n s.* **Hauptausfuhrland**
Hauptexportposten *m s.* **Hauptexportartikel**
Hauptfach *n* main subject
Hauptfaktoren *mpl* primary factors
Hauptfrage *f* main issue, cardinal question
Hauptfristenplan *m* general [main] time schedule
Hauptgeschäft *n* main business [dealings, transaction]; main [leading] shop
Hauptgeschäftssitz *m* commercial domicile, principal place of business; headquarters, seat of the firm [concern]
Hauptgeschäftsstelle *f* head [central] office *(insurance etc.)*
Hauptgeschäftsviertel *n* main commercial district [quarter]
Hauptgeschäftszeit *f* rush-hour(s), main business hours
Hauptgeschäftszentrum *n* main [central, key] shopping area

Hauptgewinn *m (com)* main profit; first prize *(lottery)*
Hauptgläubiger *m* principal [main] creditor
Hauptinteresse *n* main [chief, first] interest
Hauptinvestition *f* main investment
Hauptinvestitionsträger *m s.* **Hauptauftraggeber**
Hauptkartei *f* master file
Hauptkasse *f* central pay office *(state)*; box-office *(theatre etc.)*
Hauptkassierer *m* chief [head] cashier
Hauptkäufer *m s.* **Hauptabnehmer**
Hauptkennziffer *f* main indicator
Hauptkomponenten *fpl (stats)* principal components
Hauptkonsument *m* main [principal] consumer
Hauptkredit *m* primary loan
Hauptleistung *f* main performance; main output [production]
Hauptlieferant *m* main supplier
Hauptmarkt *m* main [chief] market
Hauptmechanik *f* (general) department of repairs and power supply *(ancillary department reponsible for supervising and repairing machines and electrical equipment etc.)*
Hauptmechaniker *m* head of (general) department of repairs and power supply
Hauptmerkmal *n* salient [main] feature [characteristic]
Hauptmieter *m* principal tenant
Hauptmontage *f* main assembly
Hauptniederlassung *f* head [central] office
Hauptnutzer *m* main user *(patent etc.)*
Hauptpostamt *n* general [*(Am)* main] post office
Hauptposten *m* principal item
Hauptpostscheckamt *n* principal [main] postal cheque office
Hauptprodukt *n* main [chief, staple] product
Hauptproduktion *f* main production [output]
Hauptproduktionsbereich *m (agric)* main line of production
Hauptproduktionsprozeß *m* main production process
Hauptproduktionsrichtung *f s.* **Hauptproduktionsbereich**
Hauptproduktivkraft *f* main productive force *(labour, human power)*
Hauptprojektant *m* chief contractor for designing project
Hauptrechner *m* host computer
Hauptreferat *n* keynote address
Hauptreparatur *f* main [major] repair, refitting, refit *(ship)*
Hauptrichtungen *fpl* main directions [trends]
Hauptsaison *f* peak season
Hauptschuld *f* 1. principal debt; 2. principal blame; principal guilt

Hauptschuldner *m* principal debtor
Hauptsitz *m* registered office, principal place of business
Hauptstadt *f* capital (city)
Hauptstrecke *f* main route; *(railw)* main line
Haupttätigkeit *f* main [chief] occupation
Haupttechnologe *m* chief technologist
Hauptteilhaber *m* principal shareholder
Hauptterminplan *m* schedule of dates for the main production process
Haupttrend *m* main trend *(fashion, market etc.)*
Haupttriebkraft *f* main motive [driving] force
Hauptunterschied *m* main [chief, principal, essential, cardinal] difference
Hauptverbraucher *m s.* **Hauptkonsument**
Hauptverdiener *m* principal earner *(of a family)*
Hauptverkehr *m* major part of the traffic; rush--hour [peak-hour] traffic
Hauptverkehrsstraße *f* main road; main highway, *(Am)* highway, trunk road
Hauptverkehrsstunde *f s.* **Hauptverkehrszeit**
Hauptverkehrszeit *f* rush hour(s); peak hour(s)
Hauptversammlung *f* general meeting *(shareholders etc.)*
~, **außerordentliche** extraordinary meeting *(shareholders etc.)*
~, **ordentliche** *s.* **Hauptversammlung**
Hauptvertrag *m* main contract
Hauptvertreter *m* general agent *(insurance, travel office etc.)*; main protagonist *(theory etc.)*
Hauptvertretung *f* general agency
Hauptverwaltung *f* head office, central headquarters
Hauptvorstand *m* governing board
Hauptwarengruppe *f* main group of commodities, major trade group
Hauptwarenmarkt *m* main commodity market
Hauptwarenmarktpreis *m* price on the main commodity market
Hauptwerk *n* main plant [factory]
Hauptwirkung *f* main effect
Hauptziel *n* main [principal] aim [objective, target]
Hauptzollamt *n* Customs and Excise Office
Haus *n* house; domicile ⋄ **ein ~ auf Leibrente kaufen** to buy a house on an instalment system contracting to give the seller a life annuity; **ein ~ auf Leibrente verkaufen** to sell a house on an instalment system contracting to give the seller a life annuity; **frei ~** delivered free, carriage paid; franco domicile; **frei ~ liefern** to deliver free house; **ins ~ liefern** to deliver to (the) buyer's residence
Hausabfälle *mpl* household refuse [rubbish]
Hausangestellte(r) *f(m)* domestic (servant), household help(er), house worker
Hausarbeit *f* housework, household-work

Hausarbeitstag *m* day off *(allowed to most working housewives once a month in the former GDR)*
Hausarbeitszeit *f* time for housework [household-work]
Hausbank *f* firm's bank
Hausbau *m* house-building
~, **billiger** low-cost home construction
Hausbedarf *m* domestic use
Hausbelieferung *f* door-to-door delivery
Hausbesitz *m* ownership [possession] of a house; house-property
Hausbewohner *m* occupant [occupier] of a house
Häuserblock *m* block of houses; block of flats, *(Am)* apartments
Hausgehilfe *m s.* **Hausangestellte(r)**
Hausgehilfin *f s.* **Hausangestellte(r)**
Hausgemeinschaft *f* community of flat dwellers (in a house); people living in the different flats of a house
Hausgrundstück *n* house plot
Haushalt *m* 1. budget; finances *(of a country, local authority etc.) (s.a.* **Budget, Etat**); 2. household ⋄ **den ~ führen** to manage [run] the household; **einen gemeinschaftlichen ~ führen** to keep house together
~, **ausgeglichener** balanced budget
~, **außerordentlicher** extraordinary budget
~, **gemeinsamer** common household
~, **individueller** private household
~, **kommunaler** local budget
~, **nicht ausgeglichener** unbalanced budget
~, **öffentlicher** public budget
~, **ordentlicher** (ordinary) budget
~, **örtlicher** *s.* ~, **kommunaler**
~, **privater** private household
~, **städtischer** *s.* ~, **kommunaler**
~, **zentraler** central [state] budget
Haushaltsabfälle *mpl* household refuse [rubbish]
Haushaltsabführung *f* payment to the budget, budget levy; profit transfer to the budget *(all kinds of payments of nationally-owned enterprises in the former GDR to the budget)*
Haushaltsabrechnung *f* budget accounting
Haushaltsabstriche *mpl* budget cuts
Haushaltsabteilung *f* finance department
Haushaltsakkumulation *f* budget accumulation, public savings
Haushaltsanalyse *f* analysis of (the) budget
Haushaltsansatz *m* budget estimates
Haushaltsartikel *m* household [domestic] article
Haushaltsaufbau *m* structure of the budget
Haushaltsaufschlag *m* excise (duty)
Haushaltsaufstellung *f* drafting [drawing up] of the budget (plan)
Haushaltsausgaben *fpl* budget expenditure(s)

Haushaltsausgleich *m* grants to local authorities *(by the state/central budget)*
Haushaltsausschuß *m* budget committee *(parliament, local council etc.)*
Haushaltsausstattung *f* furnishing of homes; household equipment standard *(proportion of households with refrigerators, TV sets etc.)*
Haushaltsbearbeiter *m* clerk responsible for the budget *(of an institution)*
Haushaltsbedarf *m* household requirements; domestic needs
Haushaltsberatung *f* budget debate
Haushaltsbericht *m* budget report
Haushaltsbeschränkungen *fpl* budgetary restrictions [restraints]
Haushaltsbesteuerung *f* taxation of family income
Haushaltsbewilligung *f* budget approval
Haushaltsbeziehungen *fpl* budgetary relations *(between enterprises and institutions and the budget)*
Haushaltsbilanz *f* budget revenue and expenditure balance sheet
Haushaltsbilanzierung *f* drawing up of budget revenue and expenditure balance sheets; budget balancing
Haushaltsbuch *n* housekeeping (account) book
Haushaltsbuchführung *f* budgetary book keeping
Haushaltsdebatte *f (pol)* budget debate
Haushaltsdefizit *n* budget(ary) deficit
Haushaltsdisziplin *f* keeping to the budget (plan)
Haushaltsdurchführung *f* implementation of the budget (plan)
Haushaltseinkommen *n* family income
Haushaltseinnahmen *fpl* budget revenue
Haushaltsentwurf *m* draft budget, budget draft
Haushaltsergebnis *n* (financial) result of the budget year
Haushaltsfehlbetrag *m s.* **Haushaltsdefizit**
haushaltsfinanziert financed by the budget
Haushaltsfinanzierung *f* financing by the budget; budget financing
Haushaltsführung *f* 1. housekeeping, maintenance of a household; 2. budgeting
Haushaltsgeld *n* housekeeping money
Haushaltsgesetz *n* budget law [appropriation act]
Haushaltsgröße *f* size of the budget
Haushaltsgrundsätze *mpl* principles of budgeting
Haushaltsjahr *n* fiscal [financial] year
Haushaltskennziffer *f* budget index [figure], indicator of (the) budget
Haushaltskonto *n* budget account *(bank account of institutions used to settle business)*

Haushaltskontrolle *f* budget control *(by higher financial authorities to ensure drafting and implementation of the budget);* budget auditing *(checking inflows and outflows of budgetary resources)*
Haushaltskreditierung *f* credit financing of the budget
haushaltsmäßig budgetary
Haushaltsmethode *f* method of financing institutions by the budget
Haushaltsmittel *npl* public funds, budgetary appropriations [means]
~, **eingesparte** saved public funds
~, **geplante** planned budgetary means [resources]
~, **nicht ausgenutzte** unused budgetary means [resources]
~, **veranschlagte** *s.* ~, **geplante**
Haushaltsnachtrag *m* supplementary budget
Haushaltsnorm *f* budget norm
Haushaltsordnung *f* budgetary rules and regulations
Haushaltsorgane *npl* budget authorities
Haushaltspackung *f* family-size package
Haushaltsperiode *f* budget period
Haushaltsplan *m* budget
~, **außerordentlicher** extraordinary budget
~, **ordentlicher** ordinary budget
Haushaltsplanansatz *m* draft budget, budget draft
Haushaltsplanentwurf *m* (budget) estimates
Haushaltsplanung *f* budget planning, budgeting
~, **kurzfristige** short-term budget planning
~, **langfristige** long-term budget planning
~, **mittelfristige** medium-term budget planning
Haushaltspolitik *f* budget(ary) policy
Haushaltsposten *m* budget item
Haushaltsprinzipien *npl* budgeting principles
Haushaltsprognose *f* long-term budget(ary) forecast
Haushaltsrechnung *f* budget accounting *(statistical summary classifying revenue and expenditures of state authorities according to composition, sources, purposes etc.)*
Haushaltsrechnungsführung *f* budgetary accounting
Haushaltsrecht *n* budget regulations [law]
Haushaltsreform *f* budget reform
Haushaltsreserve *f* undistributed budget funds, budgetary reserve
Haushaltsschema *n* budgetary scheme *(showing budgetary partial plans and their subdivision according to items)*
Haushaltssystem *n* budget system
Haushaltssystematik *f* classification of (the) budget *(breakdown of the state budget according to economic, political and administrative aspects)*
Haushaltstitel *m* budget item

Haushaltsüberschreitung *f* exceeding the budget
Haushaltsüberschuß *m* budget(ary) surplus
Haushalts- und Familieneinkommen *n* household and family income
Haushalts- und Finanzreform *f* budget and finance reform
Haushaltsverbrauch *m* household consumption
Haushaltsvergleich *m* comparative budget analysis
Haushaltsversicherung *f* household insurance
Haushaltsvolumen *n* total budget [budgetary means]
Haushaltsvoranschlag *m* budgetary estimate
Haushaltswaren *fpl* household articles
Haushaltszuschuß *m* budget subsidy
Haushaltszuweisung *f* budgetary appropriation(s)
Haushaltung *f* 1. household; 2. housekeeping
Haushaltungsbuch *n* housekeeping book
Haushaltungskosten *pl* household expenses
Haus-Haus-Gepäckverkehr *m (railw)* door-to-door (luggage) service
Haus-Haus-Verkehr *m* door-to-door service
Hausindustrie *f* cottage industry
Hauslieferung *f s.* **Hausbelieferung**
Hausmarke *f* (firm's) own brand [make], special brand
Hausordnung *f* house rules
Hausse *f* rise ◊ **auf ~ spekulieren** to buy for a rise
Haussteuer *f* house tax
Haus- und Grundsteuer *f* house and land tax
Hausverwalter *m* house administrator
Hauswirtschaft *f* 1. domestic science, home economics; 2. housekeeping; 3. *(agric)* private holding
~, geschlossene closed household economy, subsistence economy
~, persönliche household plot, farmer's private holding *(of co-operative farmer for family supply of garden produce)*
Havarie *f (ins)* average; collision; accident; damage by sea ◊ **eine ~ andienen** *(ins)* to notify average; **eine ~ aufmachen** *(ins)* to adjust [settle] the average
~, besondere *(ins)* particular average
~, große *(ins)* general average
~, kleine *(ins)* petty average
Havarieberechnung *f (ins)* average adjustment
Havariegelder *npl (ins)* average charges
Havarie-große-Einschuß *m (ins)* general average deposit
Havarie-(große)-Klausel *f (ins)* (general) average clause
Havariegutachten *n (ins)* damage [average] survey

Havarieinspektion *f (ins)* claims agency
Havarieklausel *f (ins)* average clause
Havariekommissar *m (ins)* average adjuster; claims agent; settling agent
Havarieschadenaufstellung *f (ins)* statement of average
Havarieverfahren *n (ins)* average procedure
Havarievertrag *m (ins)* average agreement
Havariezertifikat *n (ins)* (average) survey report
Haverei *f (ins)* average and costs
Havereigelderversicherung *f* average and costs insurance
Hebegebühr *f (ins)* collection charge
Hebel *m* lever; incentive
~, ökonomischer economic incentive [stimulus, stimulant, inducement, lever]
Hebelfunktion *f* incentive [stimulation] function *(price, tariffs etc.)*
Hebelwirkung *f* incentive [stimulating] effect
Heimarbeit *f* homework, outwork
Heimarbeiter *m* homeworker, outworker
Heimarbeiterzuschlag *m* extra pay for homework [outwork] *(to compensate expenses for heating, lighting etc.)*
Heimatanschrift *f* home address
Heimatbahnhof *m* home station
Heimathafen *m* home port, port of registry *(merchant ship)*
Heimelektrik *f* domestic lighting and electrical appliances
Heimelektronik *f* consumer electronics
Heimfracht *f* homeward-bound cargo
Heimfürsorge *f* home-care *(of old or sick people)*
Heimindustrie *f* cottage industry
Heimschule *f* boarding school
Heiratsversicherung *f* marriage insurance
Heizungsinstallateur *m* fitter for heating installations
Hektarertrag *m* yield per hectare
Helfer *m* helper, help; assistant; aid; *(com)* adviser
~ in Steuersachen tax adviser [consultant]
hemmen to impede, to hinder, to slow down *(economic growth etc.)*; to stop, to arrest *(movement, activity, development etc.)*; to check, to stem *(flow etc.)*
Hemmnis *n* obstacle, hindrance, impediment
Hemmung *f* impeding, impediment, hindering, hindrance, slowing down *(economic growth etc.)*; stopping, arresting *(movement, activity, development etc.)*; checking, stemming *(flow etc.)*
herabdrücken to force down, to depress *(prices etc.)*; *(st.ex)* to bear *(market etc.)*
herabmindern to lower, to diminish *(value, quality etc.)*; to belittle, to disparage *(s.o.'s achievement etc.)*

herabsetzen to reduce, to lower, to cut *(price, tariff etc.)*, to diminish *(value, quality etc.)*
Herabsetzung *f* reduction, lowering, cutting *(price, tariff etc.)*, diminution *(value, quality etc.)*
Herangehen *n* approach
~, **induktives** inductive approach
~, **interdisziplinäres** inter-disciplinary approach
~, **klassenmäßiges** class approach
~, **komplexes** complex [comprehensive] approach
~, **morphologisches** morphological approach
~, **praktisches** practical approach
~, **problemorientiertes** problem-oriented approach
~, **strukturlogisches** structural-logical approach
~, **system-kybernetisches** system-cybernetic approach
~, **theoretisch-informationelles** theoretical--information method of approach
heraufsetzen to raise, to increase, to put up *(prices etc.)*
Heraufsetzung *f* increase *(prices etc.)*
Herbstbestellung *f* autumn sowing
Herbstmesse *f* autumn (trade) fair
Herkunft *f* 1. origin; 2. *(agric)* strain *(clover, potato etc.)*; 3. background *(social)*
Herkunftsbezeichnung *f* mark of origin; designation of place of origin
Herkunftsland *n* country of origin
herrenlos ownerless *(goods etc.)*
Herrenmaßschneider *m* (gentle)men's tailor
Herrschaftsbereich *m* purview, domain *(economic law etc.)*
Herrschaftsform *f* type of rule
herstellen to make, to manufacture, to produce *(goods etc.)*; to establish, to create *(order, peace, relationship etc.)*
Hersteller *m* manufacturer, maker *(goods etc.)*
Herstellerabgabepreis *m* manufacturer's selling price
Herstellerbetrieb *m* manufacturing enterprise [firm]
Herstellerfirma *f s.* Herstellerbetrieb
Herstellerland *n* country of origin [manufacture]
Herstellerrisiko *n* manufacturer's risk
Herstellkosten *pl* cost(s) of production, production costs
Herstellung *f* manufacture, production *(goods etc.)*; establishment *(connection, relationship etc.)*, fabrication *(mark etc.)* ⋄ **die ~ einschränken** to curtail production
~, **fabrikmäßige** *s.* ~, **serienmäßige**
~, **großtechnische** large-scale manufacture
~, **serienmäßige** serial [mass] production
Herstellungsabteilung *f* production department
Herstellungsanlage *f* manufacturing [production, fabrication] facility [plant]

Herstellungsart *f* method of manufacture [production]
Herstellungsaufwand *m* manufacturing cost [expenditure]
Herstellungsberechnung *f* cost accounting, costing
Herstellungsbeschränkungen *fpl* production [manufacturing] restrictions
Herstellungsbetrieb *m s.* Herstellerbetrieb
Herstellungsdauer *f* production time
Herstellungsfehler *m* manufacturing defect
Herstellungsgang *m* manufacturing process
Herstellungsgenehmigung *f* manufacturing licence
Herstellungsjahr *n* year of manufacture
Herstellungskosten *pl* cost(s) of production, production costs
Herstellungsland *n s.* Herstellerland
Herstellungslizenz *f* manufacturing licence
Herstellungslos *n* lot
Herstellungsmethode *f* method of production, production method
Herstellungsmöglichkeiten *fpl* production possibilities [prospects]
Herstellungsmonopol *n* monopoly in production
Herstellungsmuster *n* pilot [pre-production] model
Herstellungsort *m* place of production
Herstellungsposten *m s.* Herstellungslos
Herstellungspreis *m* production price
Herstellungsprogramm *n* production programme
Herstellungsprojekt *n* manufacturing project
Herstellungsrechte *npl* manufacturing rights
Herstellungsstadium *n* stage of production
Herstellungstechnik *f* manufacturing technology
Herstellungsunternehmen *n* manufacturing [producing] enterprise, factory
Herstellungsverfahren *n* manufacturing [production, processing] technique [method], method of processing
Herstellungswerk *n s.* Herstellerbetrieb
Herstellungswert *m* purchase price
Herstellungszeichen *n* trademark
Herstellungszeit *f* production [manufacturing] time; *(d.pr.)* process time
herunterwirtschaften to ruin, to bring down
heterogen heterogeneous
Heterogenität *f* heterogeneity *(property relations etc.)*
Heterograd *m (stats)* heterograde
Heuer *f* seamen's pay
Heuristik *f* heuristics
~, **negative** negative heuristics
~, **positive** positive heuristics

heuristisch heuristical
Hierarchie *f* hierarchy
Hierarchiesystem *n* hierarchical system
Hilfe *f* help, assistance, aid; support
~, **finanzielle** financial aid [assistance]
~ **für Autofahrer, technische** mobile breakdown service
~, **gegenseitige** mutual aid [assistance]
~, **materielle** material support
~, **technische** technical aid [assistance]
Hilfeleistung *f* help, assistance, aid; support; subsidies
Hilfsabteilung *f* ancillary [auxiliary] department
Hilfsaktion *f* relief scheme; campaign to aid [help] *(disabled etc.)*
Hilfsarbeit *f* unskilled work [labour]
Hilfsarbeiter *m* unskilled worker, labourer
Hilfsausrüstung *f* auxiliary equipment
hilfsbedürftig in need of help; needy
Hilfsbedürftigkeit *f* need (of help)
hilfsbereit ready to help, helpful
Hilfsbereitschaft *f* readiness to help; helpfulness
Hilfsbetrieb *m (agric)* farm workshop
Hilfsdienst *m* auxiliary service; *(manuf)* ancillary service *(repair shop, transport etc.)*
Hilfsfonds *m* relief fund
Hilfsfunktion *f* auxiliary function
Hilfsgelder *npl* subsidies
Hilfsgerät *n* labour-saving appliance [implement, device]
Hilfskasse *f* relief fund
Hilfskonto *n* adjunct account; relief account
Hilfskraft *f* additional [temporary] worker; help(er), assistant
Hilfsleistung *f* ancillary [auxiliary] productions *(s.* **Hilfsproduktion***)*
Hilfsleistungskosten *pl* ancillary production costs
Hilfslohn *m* indirect labour cost
Hilfsmaßnahme *f* relief measure
Hilfsmaterial *n (manuf)* auxiliary material; *(acc)* indirect material
Hilfsmaterialverbrauch *m* consumption of auxiliary material
Hilfsmaterialverbrauchsnorm *f* consumption standard of auxiliary material
Hilfsmittel *n* device, aid; auxiliary material
Hilfsorganisation *f* relief organization
Hilfspersonal *n* ancillary [auxiliary] personnel *(employed in ancillary jobs)*
Hilfsprodukte *npl* ancillary products
Hilfsproduktion *f* ancillary production *(production at an ancillary plant in an industrial enterprise for the supply and support of the principal production process)*
Hilfsprogramm *n* aid programme

Hilfsprozeß *m* auxiliary process
Hilfsquelle *f* resource; source of help
Hilfsquellen *fpl*:
~, **natürliche** natural resources
Hilfsschule *f* school for educationally subnormal [mentally retarded] children
Hilfsspeicher *m (d.pr.)* auxiliary [secondary] storage
Hilfsstoffe *mpl s.* **Hilfsmaterial**
Hilfswerk *n* welfare [relief] organization
Hilfswissenschaft *f* auxiliary science, complementary science [subject]
Hilfszeit *f* auxiliary time
~, **manuelle** auxiliary manual time *(setting a workpiece in a holding device by hand etc.)*
~, **maschinelle** auxiliary machine time *(setting a workpiece in a holding device by machine etc.)*
Hinterbliebenenrente *f* pension for surviving dependants
Hintergrundauftrag *m (d.pr.)* background job
Hintergrundprogramm *n (d.pr.)* background program
Hintergrundprogrammierung *f (d.pr.)* background programming
Hintergrundverarbeitung *f (d.pr.)* background processing
hinterlegen to deposit
Hinterleger *m* depositor; *(jur)* bailor
Hinterlegung *f* deposit; *(jur)* bail
Histogramm *n* block diagram, histogram
Hitzearbeit *f* work in conditions of high temperature
Hitzezuschlag *m* bonus for work in conditions of high temperature
Hobler *m* planer; shaper
Hochbau *m* surface [structural, constructional] engineering; construction of multistorey buildings
Hochbetrieb *m* great [big] rush *(shops, railway station etc.)*
hochbezahlt highly paid *(job etc.)*
hochentwickelt highly developed
Hochfinanz *f* high finance
Hochflut *f* high tide [water]
Hochhaus *n* skyscraper, high-rise [multistorey] building
Hochkonjunktur *f* boom
Hochkonjunkturphase *f* phase of the boom, boom (phase)
Hochleistung *f* great [high] achievement *(science etc.)*; *(ind)* high output; high power [performance] *(engine etc.)*
hochmechanisiert highly mechanized
hochqualifiziert highly skilled *(worker)*; highly qualified *(professional)*
Hochsaison *f* peak season, height of the season
Hochschulabsolvent *m* graduate

Hochschulausbildung f university education
Hochschulbildung f university education
Hochschule f university; institution of university status *(providing for specialized study or research)*; academy, college *(music)*
~, **pädagogische** college of education
~, **technische** college for advanced technology, *(Am)* institute of technology
Hochschulforschung f university research
Hochschulkader m (university) graduate
Hochschullehrer m university [college] teacher, professor, reader, lecturer
Hochschulreform f university [higher education] reform
Hochschulreife f entrance level for higher education, matriculation standard
Hochschulstatistik f statistics of higher education
Hochseefischerei f deep-sea fishing [fishery], off-shore fishery
Hochseeschiffahrt f ocean shipping
Höchstauslastung f maximum utilization *(capacity etc.)*
Höchstbeanspruchung f peak load; high degree of stress
Höchstbedarf m maximum demand
Höchstbelastung f 1. *(tech)* peak [maximum] load; 2. high degree of stress *(people)*
Höchstbestand m maximum stock
Höchstbetrag m maximum amount [sum]
Höchstgebot n highest bid [offer]
Höchstgewicht n maximum weight
Höchstgrenze f (maximum) limit *(prices etc.)*
Höchstkurs m maximum price [rate]
Höchstleistung f maximum [top] performance; *(ind)* maximum output
Höchstlohn m maximum wage(s)
Höchstpreis m ceiling [maximum] price
Höchstpreisliste f list of maximum prices
Höchstrente f maximum pension
Höchstsatz m maximum rate, ceiling
Höchststand m highest level
~, **wissenschaftlich-technischer** top [highest] level of technology; top [highest] engineering level; top quality
Höchstwert m maximum value
Höchstwertprinzip n *(ins)* maximum value principle
Höchstzinssatz m maximum rate (of interest)
Höchstzoll m *(cust)* maximum duty
Hoch- und Fachschulkader mpl university and college graduates
Hoch- und Fachschulwesen n higher education
Hoch- und Tiefbau m *(approx.)* structural and civil engineering
hochverzinslich high-interest-bearing
Hochwasser n flood, high water

Hochwassergebiet n flood(ed) area
Hochwasserschutz m flood protection
Hochwasser- und Überschwemmungsversicherung f s. **Hochwasserversicherung**
Hochwasserversicherung f flood insurance
hochwertig high-quality, top-grade
Höflichkeitsbesuch m courtesy call
Hoheitsgewässer npl territorial waters
Hoheitsrechte npl sovereign rights
Hoheitszeichen n national emblem
Holding(gesellschaft) f holding company
Holschuld f debt to be discharged at the domicile of the debtor
Holzabfuhr f wood [timber] haulage
Holzabhieb m felling [cutting down, chopping down] of trees [timber], *(Am)* logging
Holzablage f 1. depositing of wood [timber]; 2. wood [timber] yard, *(Am)* lumber yard; timber [forest] depot *(in the forest)*
Holzabsatz m sale [disposal] of wood [timber]
Holzanbau m cultivation of trees [timber]; silviculture
Holzarbeit f 1. woodwork(ing); felling of trees, timber cutting, *(Am)* lumbering, logging; 2. timber-work, structural woodwork *(in construction)*; 3. article made of wood, wooden article; wood-carving, carving in wood
Holzarbeiter m woodworker, worker in wood [timber]; woodcutter, woodman *(Am)* lumberjack; lumberer, logger
holzarm scarcely timbered *(country etc.)*
Holzart f kind [species] of wood [timber]
Holzartenwechsel m rotation of timber crops
Holzaufbereiter m wood preparer; wood [timber] converter
Holzaufbereitung f preparation [preparatory treatment] of wood *(pulp manufacture etc.)*; conversion [cutting up] of wood [timber] *(for sale etc.)*
Holzaufnahme f registration [recording] of (felled) wood [timber], registration [recording] of the fell [cut]
Holzausbau m finishing [completion] of the interior woodwork *(building etc.)*; *(min)* timbering, planking, casing, lining *(shaft etc.)*; timber framework
Holzausformung f conversion [cutting up] of wood [timber] *(for sale)*
Holzaushaltung f s. **Holzausformung**
holzbearbeitend woodworking *(industry)*; timber converting [semi-processing], *(Am)* lumber manufacture
Holzbearbeitungsindustrie f woodworking industry, *(Am)* lumber(ing) industry
Holzberechtigter m holder of (right of) common of estovers
Holzberechtigung f right of common of estovers

Holzbestand *m (for)* standing crop [standing growth] of timber; stock [supply] of timber [wood]
Holzbildhauer *m* wood-carver
Holzblasinstrumentenmacher *m* wood-wind instrument maker
Holzeinschlag *m* felling of trees [timber], wood--cutting, timber-cutting; *(Am)* logging (amount of) wood [timber] felled; felling rate, fell
Holzentnahmegerechtigkeit *f* (right of) common of estovers
Holzerzeugung *f* wood [timber] production
Holzfällen *n* felling [cutting down] of trees, wood-cutting, timber-cutting, *(Am)* logging, lumbering
Holzfäller *m* woodcutter, woodman, *(Am)* lumberjack, lumberer, logger
Holzfällerlager *n* logging [lumber] camp
Holzfloß *n* log [timber] raft [float], *(Am)* lumber raft; wooden raft *(for transporting goods etc.)*
Holzflößer *m* log [river] driver
Holzflößerei *f* rafting of timber, logrunning, log-driving
Holzgefälle *n* yield of wood [timber]
Holzgerechtigkeit *f* common of estovers
Holzgewinnung *f* wood [timber, *(Am)* lumber] production
Holzhandel *m* timber trade
Holzindustrie *f* wood [*(Am)* lumber] industry
Holzkontor *n* timber ward
Holzlager *n* wood [timber, *(Am)* lumber] yard, wood [timber] store, timber warehouse; timber dock *(in sawmill); (for)* timber [forest] depot, stock of timber, timber stock
Holzmasse *f* volume of wood [timber]
Holzmassenaufnahme *f* recording of the volume of (standing) timber
Holzmassenermittlung *f* determination of the volume of (standing) timber
Holznutzung *f* exploitation [utilization] of the wood and timber resources
Holznutzungsrecht *n* right of exploiting [utilizing] the wood and timber resources
Holzrecht *n* right of cutting wood *(in a forest)*; right of common of estovers
holzreich well-timbered *(country etc.)*
Holztechnik *f* woodworking [wood] technology [technique]
Holztransport *m* wood [timber] transport
holzverarbeitend woodworking *(industry, craft etc.)*; wood-processing *(industry etc.)*
Holzverarbeitung *f* woodworking; wood processing
Holzverarbeitungsindustrie *f* woodworking industry
Holzveredlung *f* refining [refinement] of wood; wood processing

Holzvorräte *mpl* timber stocks
Holzwirtschaft *f* timber industry
Holzzuwachs *m* forest growth
~, **jährlicher** annual growth [increase] of wood
Homograd *m (stats)* homograde
Honorar *n* fee, remuneration *(physician etc.)*, royalties *(author)*, honorarium
Honorarsteuer *f* tax on fees [royalties]
Honorarvertrag *m* honorarium contract, agreement on royalties
honorieren to pay (a fee) for, to remunerate; to honour, to meet *(bill of exchange)*
Honorierung *f* remuneration, payment; acceptance *(bill of exchange)*
Hopfenanbaugebiet *n* hop-growing district
Hort *m* before-and-after-school centre for school-children
Hortung *f* hoarding
Hortungskauf *m* hoarding purchase
Hotel *n* hotel
Hotelerlöse *mpl* hotel proceeds
Hotelier *m* hotel-keeper, hotelier
Hotelnetz *n* network of hotels
Hotel- und Gaststättengewerbe *n* hotel and catering trades
Hotelwesen *n* hotel business [affairs], hotels
Hotelzimmer *n* hotel room
Huckepackverkehr *m* road-rail service; road and ferry service
Hühnerhaltung *f* chicken farming
Hühnerzucht *f* chicken farming [breeding]
Humanismus *m* humanism
Humanität *f* humanity; humaneness
Hungerlohn *m* starvation wage
Hungersnot *f* famine, starvation
Hüttenwerker *m* blast furnace worker
Hut- und Mützenmacher *m* hat and cap maker
Hybridrechner *m* hybrid computer
Hydromelioration *f* hydro-amelioration
Hygiene *f* hygiene
Hygieneinspektion *f* sanitary inspection
Hygienekleidung *f* sanitary [protective] clothing
Hygienenorm *f* hygienic standard
Hygieneüberwachung *f* hygienic control
Hypothek *f* mortgage ⋄ **eine ~ aufnehmen** to raise a mortgage; **mit einer ~ belasten** to mortgage, to encumber with a mortgage
~ **auf Grund und Boden** mortgage on real estate
~, **erste** first mortgage
hypothekarisch by [on] mortgage, hypothecary ⋄ ~ **belastet** mortgaged; ~ **gesichert** on mortgage security
Hypothekenanstalt *f s.* **Hypothekenbank**
Hypothekenbank *f* mortgage bank
Hypothekenbrief *m* mortgage (deed)
Hypothekendarleh(e)n *n* mortgage loan

Hypothekenforderung *f* mortgage claim
hypothekenfrei unencumbered, unmortgaged
Hypothekengeschäft *n* mortgage business
Hypothekengläubiger *m* mortgagee
Hypothekenpfandbrief *m* mortgage bond
Hypothekenschuld *f* mortgage debt
Hypothekenschuldner *m* mortgagor
Hypothese *f* hypothesis
~, **einfache** simple hypothesis
~, **lineare** linear hypothesis
~, **statistische** statistical hypothesis
~, **Student'sche** *(stats)* "Student's" hypothesis
~, **zulässige** admissible hypothesis
~, **zusammengesetzte** composite hypothesis

I

Idealismus *m* idealism
Idee *f* idea; concept; thought, notion
ideenarm poor [lacking] in ideas; lacking in imagination
Ideenarmut *f* poverty [lack] of ideas; lack of imagination
Ideenfülle *f* wealth of ideas
Ideengut *n* ideas; intellectual goods
Ideenkonferenz *f* brain-storming
ideenlos *s.* **ideenarm**
Ideenlosigkeit *f s.* **Ideenarmut**
Ideenprojekt *n* outline of a project
ideenreich full of ideas
Ideenreichtum *m* wealth of ideas; fertility of thought; fertility of imagination
Ideenskizze *f* outline [sketch] of ideas
Identifizierbarkeit *f (d.pr.)* detectability
identifizieren to identify
Identifizierung *f* identification
Identifizierungskennzeichen *n (d.pr.)* tag
Identität *f* identity
Identitätsausweis *m s.* **Identitätskarte**
Identitätskarte *f* identity card
Identitätskennzeichen *n* identity mark; *(d.pr.)* label
Identitätsnachweis *m* proof of identity; *(cust)* certificate of origin
Identitätsvergleich *m (d.pr.)* logical comparison, matching operation
Ideologie *f* ideology
~, **bürgerliche** bourgeois ideology
~, **kleinbürgerliche** petit-bourgeois [petty-bourgeois] ideology
~, **marxistische** Marxist ideology
~, **sozialistische** socialist ideology
ideologisch ideological

ignorieren to ignore, to disregard
illegal illegal, unlawful
Illegalität *f* illegality, unlawfulness
illiquid insolvent; illiquid, non-liquid
Illiquidität *f* insolvency; illiquidity; unavailability of funds [assets]; shortage of liquid assets
Imbißgaststätte *f* snack bar, *(Am)* snackbar, quick-lunch bar
Imbißraum *m* refreshment room
Imbißstand *m* refreshment stall
Imbißstube *f s.* **Imbißraum**
Imbißzustelldienst *m* catering, refreshment delivery service
Imitation *f* imitation, copy(ing) *(design etc.)*
imitieren to imitate, to copy *(design etc.)*
Imker *m* bee-keeper, apiarist
Immaterialgüter *npl* intangible goods [assets]; immaterial things
immateriell immaterial, intangible *(asset etc.)*
Immatrikulation *f* enrol(l)ment (at a university)
immatrikulieren to enrol(l) (at a university)
Immigrant *m* immigrant
Immigration *f* immigration
immigrieren to immigrate; to migrate into (an area) *(from rural area to urban centre etc.)*
Immission *f* 1. appointment *(to an office)*; 2. *(jur)* intromission *(of water etc. into neighbouring property)*
immobil immobile, immovable; stationary *(vehicles)*
Immobiliarbesitz *m* immovables
Immobiliarkredit *m* loan on real estate [landed property]
Immobiliarpfändung *f* seizure of real estate [landed property]
Immobiliarvermögen *n* real estate [property], realty
Immobiliarversicherung *f* insurance of buildings; real property [estate] insurance
Immobilien *pl* immovables, real estate, landed property
Immobiliengesellschaft *f* real estate company
Immobilienhandel *m* real estate business
Immobilienhändler *m s.* **Immobilienmakler**
Immobilienmakler *m* estate agent [broker]
Immobilienmarkt *m* real estate market
Immobiliensteuer *f* tax on real estate
Immobilienverkauf *m* sale of property
Immobilisation *f (jur)* conversion into realty
immobilisieren *(jur)* to convert into realty
Immobilität *f* immobility
Immunität *f* immunity
Imperialismus *m* imperialism
Imperialist *m* imperialist
imperialistisch imperialist
Imperium *n* empire

Import *m* import(ation); import(s) (*s.a.* **Einfuhr**)
~, **direkter** direct import(s)
~, **indirekter** indirect import(s)
~, **mittelbarer** *s.* ~, **indirekter**
~, **ungehinderter** unrestricted import(s)
~, **unmittelbarer** *s.* ~, **direkter**
~, **unsichtbarer** invisible import(s); invisibles
Importabgaben *fpl* levies on imports
Importabgabepreis *m* import delivery price *(at which imported goods are sold to local consumers)*
Importabteilung *f* import department
Importanteil *m* share of import *(in capital goods, consumer goods etc.)*
Importartikel *m* import article
Importauftrag *m* import order
Importaufwand *m* costs of import goods, import costs; import equivalent
Importaufwendungen *fpl s.* **Importaufwand**
Importbedarf *m* import needs
Importbedürfnisse *npl s.* **Importbedarf**
Importbefugnis *f* right to import
Importbeschränkungen *fpl* import restrictions, restrictions on import(s) ◇ ~ **auferlegen** to impose import restrictions [restrictions on import(s)]
Importbestimmungen *fpl* import regulations
Importbewilligung *f* import licence [permit]
Importdeklaration *f* import declaration
Importdokumente *npl* import documents [papers]
Importe *mpl* imports, goods imported, imported goods
Importerhöhung *f* increase in import(s)
Importerlaubnis *f s.* **Importbewilligung**
Importerschwerung *f* rigorous import controls
Importerzeugnis *n* import product
Importeur *m* importer; importing company; importing country
Import-Export-Koordinierung *f* import-export co-ordination *(method of management to balance export and import)*
importfähig *s.* **importierbar**
Importfinanzierung *f* financing of imports, import financing
Importfirma *f* importer, importing firm
Importförderung *f* import promotion
Importfunktion *f* import function
Importgenehmigung *f s.* **Importbewilligung**
Importgeschäft *n* import business [transaction]
Importgüter *npl* import goods
Importhafen *m* port of importation
Importhandel *m* import trade
Importhaus *n s.* **Importfirma**
importierbar importable
importieren to import
Importindustrie *f* import industry

Importintensität *f* import intensity *(level of dependence of domestic consumption on imports)*; share of imports in total domestic consumption of a product
Importkapazität *f* import capacity
Importkaufmann *m* importer; import clerk
Importkoeffizient *m* import coefficient *(share of imports in total domestic consumption of a product)*
Importkonnossement *n* inward bill of lading
Importkontingent *n* import quota
Importkonto *n* import account
Importkontrolle *f* import control
Importkosten *pl* import costs; costs of importing
Importkredit *m* import credit
Importkreditbrief *m* import letter of credit
Importlager *n* import warehouse
Importland *n* importing country
Importliste *f* import list, list of imports
Importlizenz *f s.* **Importbewilligung**
Importmaterial *n* imported material *(raw material, semi-finished goods)*
Importmaterialaufwand *m* input of imported material *(raw material, semi-finished goods)*
Importmeldung *f* statement of imports
Importmöglichkeiten *fpl s.* **Importkapazität**
Importmonopol *n* import monopoly
Importplan *m* import plan
Importposition *f* import item
Importposten *m s.* **Importposition**
Importpotential *n* import potential; import capacity
Importprämie *f* import bounty [bonus, premium]
Importpreis *m* import price
Importpreisindex *m* import price index, index of import prices
Importprodukt *n s.* **Importerzeugnis**
Importquote *f* import quota; share of imports *(in the overall domestic use of goods)*; import consumption ratio, import coefficient
Importrestriktionen *fpl s.* **Importbeschränkungen**
Importrückgang *m* decline [drop] in imports
Importsperre *f s.* **Importverbot**
Importstatistik *f* import statistics
Importsteuer *f* tax on imports
Importstruktur *f* import structure, structure of imports
Importsubvention *f* import subsidy
Importtarif *m* 1. import tariff; 2. *(railw)* import transport rates *(for certain imports)*
Importüberschuß *m* import surplus
Importumsatz *m* import turnover
Importunternehmen *n s.* **Importfirma**
Importverbot *n* ban on imports, import ban
Importverfahren *n* import regulations

indizieren 255

Importvertrag *m* import contract [agreement]
Importvertreter *m* import agent
Importvolumen *n* volume of imports, total import
Importware *f* import(ed) good [article]; import(ed) commodity
Importwünsche *mpl s.* **Importbedarf**
Importzoll *m* import duty, customs duty on importation
Impulskauf *m* impulsive purchase [buying], buying on impulse
Inanspruchnahme *f* 1. making demands *(on s.th.)*; laying claim *(to s.th.)*; use, utilization, employment *(material, funds etc.)*; reliance *(on aid etc.)*; 2. compulsory purchase of land *(by the state for mining, road construction etc.)*
~ **ausländischer Hilfe** use of foreign aid
~ **fremder Leistungen** use of outside services [sub-contracted work]
inäquivalent non-equivalent
Inäquivalenz *f* inequivalence, non-equivalence
Inbesitznahme *f* taking possession *(of s.th.)*; taking over, take-over
Inbetriebnahme *f* bringing [putting] into service *(new machinery, plant etc.)*; putting on the road *(bus etc.)*; opening *(railway line etc.)*; starting [beginning] of work *(new pit etc.)*; *(d.pr.)* start-up procedure
Inbetriebsetzung *f* setting in operation [action]; starting up, start-up *(machine etc.)*
Incoterms *pl* International Commercial Terms, Incoterms
Indemnität *f* indemnity; indemnification, compensation *(for loss suffered etc.)*
Indentgeschäft *n* indent business *(with overseas buyer)*
Indentvertrag *m* indent contract *(with overseas buyer)*
Index *m* 1. index (number); indicator; code; *(maths)* index; 2. list of banned books
~, **arithmetischer** *(stats)* arithmetic index
~ **der Anormalität** *(stats)* index of abnormality
~ **der durchschnittlichen Veränderung** *(stats)* index of average changes
~ **der Industrieproduktion** index of industrial production
~ **der Leistungsfähigkeit einer Voraussage** *(stats)* index of forecasting efficiency
~, **einfacher** *(stats)* simple index
~, **gekreuzter** *s.* ~ **mit gekreuzten Gewichten**
~, **geometrischer** *(stats)* geometric index
~, **gewichteter** *(stats)* weighted index (number)
~, **gewogener** *s.* ~, **gewichteter**
~, **harmonischer** *(stats)* harmonic index
~, **hochgestellter** *s.* ~, **oberer**
~, **kontravarianter** *(maths)* contravariant index
~, **kovarianter** *(maths)* covariant index

~ **mit fester Basis** *(stats)* fixed base index
~ **mit gekreuzten Gewichten** *(stats)* crossed--weight index (number)
~ **mit veränderlicher Basis** *(stats)* index with variable basis
~, **oberer** *(maths)* superscript, power exponent
~, **tiefgestellter** *s.* ~, **unterer**
~, **unbewerteter** *s.* ~, **ungewogener**
~, **ungewogener** *(stats)* unweighted index (number)
~, **unterer** subscript
~, **verketteter** *(stats)* chain index
~, **zusammengesetzter** *(stats)* composite index (number)
Indexbildung *f* indexing
Indexfamilie *f* *(stats)* index family
Indexgewichte *npl* *(stats)* index weights
Indexkarte *f* index card
Indexkriterien *npl* index criteria
Indexlohn *m* wage tied to cost of living index
Indexmethode *f* index method
Indexregister *n* *(d.pr.)* index register
Indexsystem *n* *(stats)* index system
Indextheorie *f* index theory
Indexverkettung *f* *(stats)* chaining of indices
Indexverknüpfung *f* *(stats)* combination of indices
Indexversicherung *f* index insurance *(premium tied to certain indices, especially cost of living)*
Indexwährung *f* index-linked currency; isometric standard; managed currency
Indexzahl *f* *(stats)* index number [figure]
~ **mit fester Basis** *(stats)* fixed base index number [figure]
~ **mit veränderlicher Basis** *(stats)* index number [figure] with variable basis
Indexziffer *f s.* **Indexzahl**
Indienststellung *f* 1. putting into service *(bus etc.)*; putting into commission *(ship etc.)*; 2. installing *(person in office)*
Indifferenzbereich *m* *(stats)* region of indifference
Indifferenzintervall *n* *(stats)* interval of indifference
Indifferenzzone *f s.* **Indifferenzbereich**
Indikator *m* indicator; index
indirekt indirect; *(d.pr.)* off line
indisponibel not available, not at one's disposal; inalienable *(property)*
Individualbesitz *m* personal property; personal ownership
Individualverkehr *m* individual motorized transport
Individualversicherung *f* individual insurance *(separate from national/social insurance)*
Indizienbeweis *m* *(jur)* circumstantial evidence
indizieren to index

Indizierung *f s.* **Indexbildung**
indossabel *s.* **indossierbar**
Indossament *n* endorsement, indorsement
~, **beschränktes** conditional [qualified] endorsement
~, **fiduziarisches** fiduciary endorsement
~, **gefälschtes** forged endorsement
~, **in der Form abweichendes** irregular endorsement
~, **unvollständiges** incomplete endorsement
~, **vollständiges** complete endorsement
Indossant *m* endorser, indorser
~, **nachfolgender** subsequent endorser
~, **vorhergehender** previous endorser
Indossat *m* endorsee, indorsee
Indossement *n s.* **Indossament**
Indossent *m s.* **Indossant**
indossierbar endorsable, indorsable ◊ **nicht ~** not do be endorsed
Indossierbarkeit *f* negotiability
indossieren to endorse, to indorse
Induktion *f* induction
~, **statistische** statistic induction
industrialisieren to industrialize
Industrialisierung *f* industrialization
~, **selbsttragende** self-sustaining industrialization
Industrialisierungsgrad *m* level of industrialization
Industrialisierungspolitik *f* industrialization policy
Industrie *f* industry
~, **arbeitsintensive** labour-intensive industry
~, **bezirksgeleitete** regionally-managed industry
~, **einheimische** domestic [home] industry
~, **energieerzeugende** energy (producing) industry *(electricity, gas, heating etc.)*
~, **exportintensive** export-intensive industry
~, **exportorientierte** export-oriented industry
~, **extraktive** extractive industry
~, **genossenschaftliche** co-operative industry
~, **inländische** *s.* ~, **einheimische**
~, **kapitalintensive** capital-intensive industry
~, **lebenswichtige** vital industry
~, **leistungsfähige** efficient industry
~, **lohnintensive** wage-intensive industry
~, **materialintensive** material-intensive industry
~, **örtliche** local industry; industry managed [run] by local authorities
~, **ortsansässige** *s.* ~, **örtliche**
~, **private** private industry
~, **produktionswichtige** essential industry
~, **saisonbedingte** seasonal industry
~, **schutzzollbedürftige** infant industry, industry in need of protection
~, **staatlich subventionierte** state subsidized industry
~, **traditionelle** traditional industry
~, **verarbeitende** manufacturing [processing] industry
~, **verstaatlichte** nationalized industry
~, **volkseigene** nationally-owned industry
~, **weiterverarbeitende** *s.* ~, **verarbeitende**
~, **zentralgeleitete** centrally-managed [centrally--run] industry
~, **zollpolitisch geschützte** sheltered [protected] industry
Industrieabfälle *mpl* industrial wastes
Industrieabgabepreis *m* **(IAP)** industry delivery price *(of goods sold by industrial enterprises to other industries and sectors on the basis of the average prime cost plus profit)*
Industrieabgabepreisindex *m* index of industry delivery price
Industrieabkommen *n* industrial agreement
Industrieabnehmer *m* industrial customer
Industrieabsatz *m* industry sales
Industrieabwasser *n* industrial waste water
Industrie-Agrar-Komplex *m* industrial-agricultural complex
Industrie-Agrarland *n* industrial-agricultural [industrial-agrarian] country
Industrieaktie *f* industrial share [*(Am)* stock]
Industrieaktiengesellschaft *f* industrial company [*(Am)* corporation]
Industrieaktienindex *m* index of industrial shares
Industrieanlage *f* industrial plant
Industrieanlagenexport *m* export of industrial plants
Industrieansiedlung *f* industrial settlement
Industriearbeit *f* industrial work
Industriearbeiter *m* industrial worker
Industrieartikel *m* industrial article [good]
Industrieausdehnung *f* industrial expansion
Industrieausfuhr *f* industrial export(s), export of manufactured goods
Industrieausrüstungen *fpl* industrial equipment
Industrieausstellung *f* industrial exhibition
Industrieausstoß *m* industrial output
Industrieausweitung *f s.* **Industrieausdehnung**
Industriebahn *f* works [factory, industrial] railway
Industrieballung *f* industrial agglomeration [centre]
Industriebank *f* industrial bank
Industriebankfiliale *f* industrial bank branch office
Industriebau *m* 1. industrial construction; 2. industrial building
Industriebaubilanz *f* balance sheet of industrial building construction
Industriebedarf *m* needs of industry; demand for industrial goods

Industrieberater *m* industrial consultant
Industriebereich *m* industrial sector
Industriebericht *m* industrial report
Industrieberichterstattung *f* industrial statistical reporting
Industriebeschäftigter *m* person employed in industry, industrial employee
Industriebetrieb *m* industrial enterprise [undertaking, establishment]
Industriebevölkerung *f* industrial population
Industriebezirk *m* industrial region
Industriebörse *f (st.ex.)* commodity market; produce exchange
Industriedemontage *f* industrial dismantling, dismantling of industries
Industrieentwicklung *f* industrial development
Industrieerzeugnis *n* industrial product, manufactured article, manufacture
Industrieerzeugung *f* industrial production
Industriefinanzierung *f* financing of industry
Industriefinanzierungsgesellschaft *f* industrial finance company
Industriefirma *f* industrial firm
Industriefläche *f* industrial estate; area for industrial development
Industrieförderung *f* promotion of industry
Industrieformgestaltung *f* industrial design, design of industrial goods
Industrieforschung *f* industrial research
Industriegebiet *n* industrial area [region, district]
Industriegelände *n* industrial estate
Industriegemeinde *f* industrial community
Industriegesellschaft *f* 1. industrial company; 2. industrial society
Industriegruppe *f* industrial group, group of industries
Industriegüter *npl* industrial goods
Industrieinvestitionen *fpl* investments in industry
Industriekapazität *f* industrial capacity
Industriekapital *n* industrial capital
Industriekapitalismus *m* industrial capitalism
Industriekapitän *m* captain of industry
Industriekartell *n* industrial cartel
Industriekaufmann *m* clerk in industry
Industriekombinat *n* industrial combine [trust]
Industriekomplex *m* industrial centre; industrial complex
Industriekonzentration *f* concentration of industries
Industriekonzern *m* industrial concern
Industriekooperation *f* industrial co-operation
Industriekraftwerk *n* industrial power station
Industriekredit *m* industrial loan, loan to industry
Industriekreditbank *f* industrial credit bank

Industriekreise *mpl* industrial circles
Industriekrise *f* crisis in industry
Industrieladen *m* factory-to-consumer shop
Industrieland *n* industrial country
industriell industrial
Industrieller *m* industrialist, (industrial) capitalist
Industriemacht *f* industrial power
Industriemagnat *m* industrial magnate [tycoon]
Industriemanager *m* industrial manager
Industriemarkt *m* market in industrial stocks and shares
industriemäßig on an industrial scale, industrialized
Industriemeister *m* factory foreman
Industriemesse *f* industrial fair
Industrieministerium *n* industrial ministry
Industriemonopol *n* industry monopoly
Industrienorm *f* industrial standard
Industrieobligationen *fpl* industrial debentures; industrial bonds
Industrieökonomie *f* industrial economics
Industriepapiere *npl (st.ex.)* industrial papers [securities], industrials
Industrieplanung *f* planning of industry, industrial planning
Industriepolitik *f* industrial policy
Industriepotential *n* industrial potential [capacity]
Industriepreis *m* industry [industrial] price
~, fondsbezogener industry price based on funds used
Industriepreisänderung *f* changes in industry prices
~, planmäßige planned changes in industry prices
Industriepreisbildung *f* industry price formation
Industriepreisindex *m* industry price index
Industriepreiskalkulation *f* calculation of prices in industry
Industriepreiskontrolle *f* control of industry prices
Industriepreisniveau *n* level of industry prices
Industriepreisplanung *f* industry price planning
Industriepreispolitik *f* industry price policy
Industriepreisreform *f* industry price reform
Industriepreisregelsystem *n* system of regulating industry prices
Industrieprodukt *n* industrial product
Industrieproduktion *f* industrial production [output]
Industrieproduktionsstruktur *f* structure of industrial production [output]
Industrieproletariat *n* industrial proletariat
Industrieschäden *mpl* environmental damage caused by industries

Industrieschmied *m* industry [industrial] smith
Industriesoziologie *f* industrial sociology
Industriespezialisierung *f* industrial specialization
Industriespionage *f* industrial espionage
Industriestaat *m s.* **Industrieland**
Industriestadt *f* industrial town
Industriestandort *m* location of industry
Industriestatistik *f* industrial statistics
Industriestruktur *f* industrial structure
Industrieunternehmen *n* industrial enterprise
Industrieunternehmer *m s.* **Industrieller**
Industrieverband *m* 1. industrial trade union; 2. industrial employer's association
Industrievereinigung *f* industrial association
Industrieverlagerung *f* transfer [deployment] of industries
Industrievertrieb *m* (industrial) marketing organization
Industrievertriebsnetz *n* network of industrial marketing organizations
Industriewaren *fpl* industrial consumer goods
Industriewarenabteilung *f* department of industrial consumer goods
Industriewarenverbrauch *m* consumption of industrial consumer goods
Industriewasser *n* water for industrial consumption [use]
Industriewasserversorgung *f* supply of water for industries
Industriewerbung *f* industrial advertising
Industriewerk *n s.* **Industriebetrieb**
Industriewerte *mpl s.* **Industriepapiere**
Industriezählung *f* census of industrial enterprises
Industriezentrum *n* industrial centre
Industriezölle *mpl* (customs) duties on industrial goods
Industriezone *f s.* **Industriegelände**
Industriezweig *m* industrial branch [sector]
~, **strukturbestimmender** economic structure-determinant industrial branch, industrial branch determining the structure
~, **zollpolitisch geschützter** sheltered industry [industrial branch]
Industriezweigforschung *f* industrial branch research
industriezweigfremd untypical line of production of an industrial branch
Industriezweiggliederung *f* classification of industrial branches
Industriezweiginstitut *n* institute of an industrial branch [sector]
Industriezweigleitung *f* management of an industrial branch
Industriezweigplanung *f* planning of an industrial branch

Industriezweigstruktur *f* industrial branch structure
industriezweigtypisch typical line of production of an industrial branch
induzieren to induce, to bring *s.th.* about, to give rise to *(s.th.)*
Inflation *f* inflation ◊ **der ~ Einhalt gebieten** to check inflation; **die ~ eindämmen** to curb inflation
~, **galoppierende** galloping inflation
~, **importierte** imported inflation
~, **latente** *s.* ~, **schleichende**
~, **schleichende** creeping [latent] inflation
~, **versteckte** hidden inflation
inflationär inflationary
inflationistisch *s.* **inflationär**
Inflationsdruck *m* inflationary pressure
Inflationserscheinung *f* inflationary symptom
Inflationsfaktor *m* inflationary factor
inflationsfeindlich anti-inflationary
Inflationsgefahr *f* danger of inflation
inflationsgeschützt inflation-hedged
Inflationsgewinn *m* profit resulting from inflation
Inflationspolitik *f* inflationary policy
Inflationsspirale *f* inflationary spiral
Inflationstendenzen *fpl* inflationary tendencies
Inflationszeit *f* period of inflation
inflatorisch *s.* **inflationär**
Informant *m* informant; informer
Informatik *f* information science, informatics
Informatiker *m* information [data] processor; (computer) software programmer
Information *f* information; news; data ◊ **zu Ihrer ~** for your information
~, **assoziative** associative information
~, **auf ihren Zuverlässigkeitsgrad bewertete** confidence-rated information
~, **beschreibende** descriptive information
~, **bewertete** rated information
~, **bibliographische** bibliographic information
~, **diskrete** discreet information
~, **elementare** elementary information
~, **empirische** empirical information
~, **heuristische** heuristic(al) information
~, **industrielle** industrial information
~, **irrelevante** irrelevant information
~, **komplexe** complex information
~, **laufende** current information
~, **mündlich übermittelte** oral information
~, **nichtfixierte** non-fixed information
~, **offene** evident information
~, **ökonomische** economic information
~, **periodische** periodic information
~, **politische** political information
~, **relevante** relevant information
~, **retrospektive** retrospective information

~, **selektive** selective information
~, **soziale** social information
~, **statistische** statistical information
~, **strategische** strategic information
~, **technische** technical information
~ **und Dokumentation** *f* information and documentation
~, **unvollständige** incomplete information
~, **verdichtete** condensed information
~, **versteckte** latent [hidden] information
~, **vollständige** complete [full] information
~, **wahre** true [reliable] information
~, **wissenschaftliche** scientific information
~, **wissenschaftlich-technische** scientific-technical information
~, **zusammenfassende** summary information
~, **zusätzliche** supplementary information
~, **zweigspezifische** specialized branch information
Informationen *fpl* information ⋄ **nach den neuesten** ~ according to the latest information [news]; ~ **einholen [einziehen]** to gather information, to make inquiries
Informationsabteilung *f* information department
Informationsanalyse *f* information [data] analysis, analysis of information [data]
Informationsausgabe *f (d.pr.)* information output
Informationsaustausch *m* exchange of information, communication, information interchange
~, **internationaler** international exchange of information
Informationsauswertung *f* utilization of information
Informationsballast *m* superfluous information
Informationsbank *f (d.pr.)* data bank
Informationsbarriere *f* information barrier
Informationsbasis *f* basis [source] of information [data]
Informationsbearbeitung *f* processing of information [data]
Informationsbedarf *m* need for information
~, **objektiver** objective need for information
~, **subjektiver** subjective need for information
Informationsbericht *m* report
Informationsbesuch *m* visit to gain information
Informationsbewertung *f* assessment [evaluation] of information
Informationsbeziehungen *fpl* communication(s)
Informationsbroschüre *f* brochure, prospectus
Informationsbulletin *n* bulletin
Informationsbüro *n* information bureau, inquiry office
Informationsdefizit *n* lack of information
Informationsdichte *f* information density; *(d.pr.)* packing density

Informationsdienst *m* information service
~, **technischer** technical information service
Informationsebene *f* information level
Informationseffekt *m* information effect
Informationseingabe *f (d.pr.)* information input
Informationseinheit *f* unit of information
Informationseinrichtung *f* information department [bureau, office]
Informationsempfänger *m* receiver of information
Informationsentropie *f* information entropy
Informationserschließung *f* collection and documentation of information
Informationsfluß *m* flow of information
Informationsfonds *m* information file; data array
Informationsgehalt *m* content of information, information (content)
Informationsgewinnung *f* accumulation [collection] of information
Informationsgrundlage *f s.* **Informationsbasis**
Informationskanal *m* channel of information
Informationskosten *pl* cost(s) of information
Informationsmangel *m* lack [shortage] of information
Informationsmarkt *m* information market
Informationsmaterial *n* information material; (information) data
Informationsmatrix *f (stats)* information matrix
Informationsmenge *f* amount [volume] of information
Informationsmethode *f* method of giving information; method of collecting information
Informationsmittel *npl* means of information [communication]
Informationsmodell *n* information model
Informationsnetz *n* information network
Informationsniveau *n* information standard
Informationsnutzer *m* user of information
Informationsnutzung *f* utilization of information
Informationsprozeß *m* information process
Informationsquelle *f* source of information
Informationsrecherche *f (d.pr.)* information retrieval
~, **automatisierte** *(d.pr.)* automatic information retrieval
Informationsrecherchesprache *f (d.pr.)* information retrieval [indexing] language
Informationsreise *f* information trip
Informationsreserve *f* information resources
Informationssammlung *f* accumulation [collection] of information
Informationsschau *f* information display
Informationsspeicher *m (d.pr.)* (information) memory
Informationsspeicherung *f* information storage

Informationsstand *m* information desk [stall, stand, counter]
Informationsstelle *f* information bureau [office]
Informationsstrom *m s.* **Informationsfluß**
Informationssystem *n* information system, system of information
~, **internationales** international system of information
Informationstechnik *f* information technique
Informationstechnologie *f* information technology
Informationstheorie *f* information theory
Informationsübertragung *f* transmission [conveyance] of information
Informationsübertragungsgenauigkeit *f* reliability in transmission of information
Informationsübertragungskanal *m* information transmission channel
Informationsumfang *m* amount of information
Informationsumwandlung *f* conversion of information
Informations- und Dokumentationswissenschaft *f* informatics
Informations- und Nachweissystem *n* information and reference system
Informations- und Organisationstechnik *f* information and organization techniques
Informationsverarbeitung *f* information [data] processing
Informationsverarbeitungssystem *n* system of information [data] processing
Informationsverarbeitungstechnik *f* information [data] processing techniques; computer hardware
Informationsverbreitung *f* dissemination of information
~, **selektive** selective dissemination of information
Informationsverdichtung *f* condensation of information
Informationsverlust *m* loss of information
Informationsvermittlung *f* information conveyance, conveyance of information
Informationsversorgung *f* information service
Informationsverwendung *f* use of information
Informationsvorrat *m* stock of information
Informationswissenschaft *f* information science
Informationszentrum *n* information centre
Informationszuwachs *m* growth in information
Informationszyklus *m* information cycle
Infrastruktur *f* infrastructure
~ **der Wissenschaft** infrastructure of science
~, **soziale** social infrastructure
~, **technische** technical infrastructure
Infrastrukturinvestitionen *fpl* infrastructural investments

Ingenieur *m* engineer
Ingenieurbau *m* 1. constructional [civil] engineering; 2. engineering construction
Ingenieurbüro *n* engineering office
Ingenieurhochschule *f* engineering college
Ingenieurökonomie *f* engineering economics
Ingenieurpsychologie *f* industrial psychology
Ingenieurschule *f* engineering school, technical institute *(without university status)*
Inhaber *m* owner, proprietor *(business, shop etc.);* holder *(licence, passport etc.);* bearer *(cheque etc.);* tenant, occupier, occupant *(building, flat etc.);* possessor ◇ **zahlbar an (den)** ~ payable to (the) bearer *(cheque)*
Inhaberaktie *f* bearer share
Inhabergrundschuld *f (jur)* land charge *(for which the deed is made out to bearer)*
Inhaberhypothek *f* mortgage made out to bearer
Inhaberindossament *n* endorsement [indorsement] (made out) to bearer
Inhaberklausel *f* bearer clause
Inhaberkreditbrief *m* open letter of credit
Inhaberobligation *f* bearer bond
Inhaberpapiere *npl* bearer credit instruments
Inhaberpolice *f* bearer insurance policy, insurance policy made out to bearer
Inhaberscheck *m* bearer cheque
Inhaberschuldverschreibung *f s.* **Inhaberobligation**
Inhabersparguthaben *n* savings balance of bearer's account
Inhabersparkonto *n* bearer's savings account
Inhaberwechsel *m* bearer bill (of exchange)
Inhalt *m* content(s); subject matter, substance *(report etc.);* point, meaning *(life etc.);* capacity *(of filled vessel etc.); (maths)* area, volume
~ **der Arbeit** content(s) of work
Inhaltserklärung *f (post, cust)* declaration [list] of contents
Inhaltsverzeichnis *n* list of contents *(parcel etc.);* table of contents *(book etc.)*
Initiative *f* initiative
Inkasso *n* collection, collecting *(bills of exchange, letters of credit, cheques etc.); (ins)* collection of premiums ◇ **das** ~ **haben** *(ins)* to have the authority to collect premiums; **zum** ~ for collection
Inkassoakzept *n (bank)* acceptance for collection
Inkassobüro *n (ins)* collection agency
Inkassogebühren *fpl (bank)* collection charges
Inkassogeschäft *n (bank, ins)* collection business
Inkassokonto *n* collection account
Inkassoprovision *f (ins)* commission for collecting premiums

Inkassospesen *pl (ins)* expenses of collection
Inkassovollmacht *f (ins)* power to collect premiums; *(bank)* authorization to collect debts
Inkassowechsel *m* bill for collection
inklusive inclusive (of), including *(transport costs etc.)*
Inklusivpreise *mpl* inclusive terms
inkonvertibel inconvertible, non-convertible
Inkrafttreten *n* coming into effect [force] *(regulation, law etc.)*
Inkurssetzung *f* putting into circulation *(shares, money etc.)*
Inland *n* home country; interior of the country
⋄ **für das ~ bestimmt** for home consumption; for home use; **im ~ hergestellt** produced domestically [nationally]
Inlandguthaben *n* domestic assets
Inländer *m* national, inhabitant of the home country
Inländerkonvertibilität *f* convertibility for residents
inländisch home, domestic, inland, internal *(trade etc.)*; indigenous *(industries, products etc.)*
Inlandluftverkehr *m* inland [domestic] air traffic
Inlandsabsatz *m* home sales, sales in the home market
Inlandsanleihe *f* domestic [internal] loan
Inlandsaufkommen *n* domestic output
Inlandsauftrag *m* inland order, order for the home market
Inlandsaufwand *m* inland [domestic] cost(s)
Inlandsaussteller *m* local [home, domestic] exhibitor
Inlandsbedarf *m* domestic needs, home requirements
Inlandsdienst *m* inland [*(Am)* domestic] service
Inlandserlös *m* domestic proceeds *(from sale of imported goods)*
Inlandserzeugnis *n* domestic [home, inland, indigenous] product; domestic produce
Inlandsgebühr *f* inland [*(Am)* domestic] charge
Inlandsgeschäft *n* inland [internal, domestic] business [trade]; domestic [internal] transaction
Inlandshandel *m* home [domestic, inland, internal] trade
Inlandskredite *mpl* domestic credits
Inlandsmarkt *m* home market
Inlandsmarktanalyse *f* home market analysis
Inlandsmarktforschung *f* home market research
Inlandsnachfrage *f* home [domestic] demand
Inlandspost *f* inland [*(Am)* domestic] mail
Inlandspreis *m* domestic price, price in the home market
Inlandspreisbildung *f* formation of domestic prices

Inlandspreisindex *m* domestic price index
Inlandspreisniveau *n* level of domestic prices
Inlandspreisvergleich *m* comparison of domestic prices
Inlandsprodukt *n* home [domestic] product
Inlandsproduktion *f* home [domestic, inland, internal] production
Inlandsschuld *f* internal debt; national debt
Inlandsumsatz *m* inland [domestic] turnover
Inlandsverbrauch *m* home [domestic, inland] consumption
Inlandsverkauf *m s.* **Inlandsabsatz**
Inlandsverkehr *m* inland [domestic] traffic
Inlandsverschuldung *f* national debts
Inlandswährung *f* internal [inland] currency
Inlandsware *f* home [domestic] product
Inlandswechsel *m* inland [domestic] bill (of exchange)
Inlandszoll *m* inland [domestic] duty
Inlandszollsatz *m* domestic customs rate [tariff]
in natura in kind
Innenabsatz *m* internal sales
Innenarchitekt *m* interior designer
Innenausgestaltung *f* interior decoration
Innenausstattung *f* interior fittings [equipment]; interior decoration and furnishing
Innendekorateur *m* interior decorator
Inneneinrichtung *f* interior furnishings
Innenmechanisierung *f (agric)* livestock farming mechanization
Innenpolitik *f* home [domestic] policy
Innenrevision *f* internal control [auditing]
Innenstadt *f* town centre; city centre; central area of town [city]
Innenumsatz *m* internal turnover [re-input] *(of goods produced in the same enterprise, farm etc.)*; turnover from inter-company sales
Innenwirtschaft *f* internal farm activities
innerbetrieblich internal, intra-enterprise, intra-plant, intracompany; in-plant, in-house *(training etc.)*
innerdienstlich internal
innergenossenschaftlich inner co-operative
innerregional inner regional
innerstaatlich domestic, internal *(matter, affair etc.)*
innerstädtisch inner-urban, within the town
innerzweiglich intra-branch *(co-operation etc.)*; within the branch, inner-branch
Innovation *f* innovation
innovativ innovative
Innung *f* trade [craft] guild
Innungsmitglied *n* member of a trade [craft] guild
Innungsverband *m* union of trade [craft] guilds
Innungswesen *n* guild system
Input *m* input

Input-Output-Analyse *f* input-output analysis
Input-Output-Koeffizient *m* input-output coefficient
Input-Output-Modell *n* input-output model
Input-Output-Rechnung *f* input-output calculation
Input-Output-Schema *n* input-output diagram [model]
Input-Output-Tabelle *f* input-output table
Insassenversicherung *f* passenger insurance
Insektenbekämpfungsmittel *n* insecticide
Inselbewohner *m* island inhabitant, islander
Inserat *n* advertisement; announcement, notice *(of change of address etc.)*
Inseratenannahme *f* advertising office
Inseratenbüro *n* advertising agency; advertising office
Inserent *m* advertiser
inserieren to advertise, to put [insert, place] an advertisement *(in a paper etc.)*
insolvent insolvent
Insolvenz *f* insolvency
Inspekteur *m* inspector, inspecting officer
Inspektion *f* inspection *(factory etc);* examination; survey, surveying *(mines, buildings etc.)*
inspizieren to inspect *(factory etc.);* to survey *(mines, buildings etc.)*
instabil unstable
Instabilität *f* lack of stability, instability
Installateur *m* fitter; plumber; electrician
Installation *f* installing, installation
Installationskosten *pl* installation costs
Installationsplan *m* installation scheme [plan]
Installationsplanung *f* installation planning
installieren to instal(l), to fix, to set up
instand halten to maintain *(roads etc.);* to service *(car etc.);* to keep up *(house etc.)*
Instandhaltung *f* maintenance *(roads etc.);* servicing *(car etc.);* upkeep *(house etc.);* care *(books etc.)*
~, laufende normal maintenance; normal servicing; normal repairs
~, vorbeugende maintenance (repairs)
Instandhaltungsabteilung *f* maintenance department
Instandhaltungsbetrieb *m* maintenance works
Instandhaltungsfonds *m* fund for repairs
Instandhaltungskosten *pl* maintenance costs
Instandhaltungsmaßnahme *f* maintenance measure, steps taken to maintain s.th.
Instandhaltungsmechaniker *m* maintenance mechanic
Instandhaltungsplan *m* maintenance plan
Instandhaltungsprozeß *m* maintenance
Instandhaltungsrichtwerte *mpl* maintenance standard norms *(used in planning maintenance work)*

Instandhaltungszyklus *m* maintenance cycle
instand setzen to repair *(machine etc.);* to renovate *(building etc.)*
Instandsetzung *f* repair *(machine etc.);* renovation *(building etc.)*
Instandsetzungsabteilung *f* repair department
Instandsetzungsarbeiten *fpl* repairs, repair work
Instandsetzungsdienst *m* maintenance and repair service
Instandsetzungskosten *pl* costs of repair
Instandsetzungswerkstatt *f* repair shop; service station, garage *(for cars)*
Instanz *f* authority; *(jur)* instance, stage of proceedings
~, höchste highest authority; *(jur)* highest court
~, letzte *(jur)* last stage of appeal; final court of appeal
Instanzenweg *m* normal [prescribed] channels
Institut *n* institute
Institution *f* institution
Instrument *n* instrument, device, tool
Instrumentarium *n* instruments, tools *(policy etc.)*
~, finanzpolitisches instruments [tools] of fiscal policy
~, kreditpolitisches instruments [tools] of credit policy
Instrumentenschleifer *m* instrument grinder
Intarsienschneider *m* intarsia cutter
Integration *f* integration
~, horizontale horizontal integration
~, ökonomische economic integration
~, soziale social integration
~, vertikale vertical integration
~, wissenschaftlich-technische scientific-technological integration
Integrationsform *f* type of integration
Integrationsgrad *m* scale [level] of integration
~, extrem hoher *(d.pr.)* giant-scale integration (GSI)
~, geringer *(d.pr.)* small-scale integration (SSI)
~, hoher *(d.pr.)* large-scale integration (LSI)
~, mittlerer *(d.pr.)* medium-scale integration (MSI)
Integrationsmaßnahmen *fpl* integration projects [measures]
~, mehrseitige multilateral integration projects [measures]
Integrationsniveau *n s.* Integrationsgrad
Integrationspolitik *f* integration policy
Integrationsprozeß *m* process of integration, integration process
Integrierbarkeit *f* integrability
~, stochastische *(stats)* stochastic integrability
integrieren to integrate *(into/within s.th.)*
Intelligenz *f* 1. intelligentsia; 2. intelligence
~, technische graduate engineers

Intensität *f* intensity *(labour etc.)*
Intensitätsgrenze *f* intensity limit
intensiv intensive *(labour etc.)*
Intensivgewässer *npl* fish-rearing waters
Intensivhaltung *f* *(agric)* battery [intensive] breeding, intensive rearing
intensivieren to intensify *(production etc.)*
Intensivierung *f* intensification *(production etc.)*
Intensivierungsfaktoren *mpl* factors to intensify production *(application of results of advanced technology, better utilization of fixed assets etc.)*
Intensivierungskonzeption *f* draft outline of intensification plan *(of production)*
Intensivinvestitionen *fpl* investments for intensification [rationalization] *(of production)*
Intensivkurs *m* intensive [crash] course
Intensivwirtschaft *f* *(agric)* intensive farming
Interdependenz-Matrix *f* *(stats)* interdependence matrix
~, **technologische** *(stats)* technological interdependence matrix
Interesse *n* interest
~, **betriebliches** interest of the enterprise
~, **gesellschaftliches** social interest
~, **individuelles** individual interest
~, **kollektives** collective interest
~, **materielles** material interest
~, **ökonomisches** economic interest
~, **persönliches** personal interest
~, **staatliches** state interest
~, **versicherbares** insurable [assurable] interest
~, **volkswirtschaftliches** interest of the national economy, national economic interest
Interessengemeinschaft *f* community of interests
Interessengruppe *f* interest group *(firms etc.)*; pressure group *(of people for a cause etc.)*; group of lobbyists
Interessenkollision *f* clash of interests
Interessenkonflikt *m* conflict of interests
Interessent *m* party interested, prospective customer
Interessenübereinstimmung *f* coincidence [consistency] of interests
Interessenvertretung *f* representation of interests
Interessiertheit *f* interest, interestedness
~, **materielle** interest in material incentives
~, **moralisch-ideelle** interest in non-material incentives
Interimsabkommen *n* interim [provisional, temporary] agreement
Interimsaktie *f* provisional share, *(Am)* interim stock
Interimsdividende *f* interim dividend
Interimshaushalt *m* interim budget
Interimskonto *n* suspense account

Interimsregierung *f* interim [provisional] government
Interimsschein *m* interim certificate, scrip
Interimsvertrag *m* provisional contract
Interimswechsel *m* provisional [interim] bill (of exchange)
Interkalationskriterium *n* *(stats)* circular test
Interline-Abkommen *n* interline agreement
international international; inter-governmental
internationalisieren to internationalize
Internationalisierung *f* internationalization; transnationalization
~ **der Produktion** internationalization of production
~ **des Wirtschaftslebens** internationalization of economic life
Internationalismus *m* internationalism
Interpolation *f* *(stats)* interpolation
interregional interregional
Intervallplanung *f* interval planning
Intervallprognose *f* interval forecast [prognosis]
Intervallschätzung *f* *(stats)* interval estimation
Intervenient *m* *(com)* acceptor (of bill) for honour
intervenieren to intervene *(in market etc.)*
Intervention *f* 1. intervention, intervening *(in market etc.)*; 2. acceptance (of protested bill) for honour
Interventionspreis *m* intervention price
Interventionspunkt *m* intervention point *(at which the central bank intervenes in the exchange market)*
Interview *n* interview
interviewen to interview
Interviewer *m* interviewer
Interviewmethode *f* interviewing method
Interviewter *m* person interviewed
Interzonenhandel *m* interzonal trade
Interzonenverkehr *m* interzonal traffic
invalid(e) invalid, infirm; disabled
Invalide *m* invalid, disabled person
Invalidenrente *f* disability pension
Invalidenversicherung *f* disablement [disability] insurance
invalidisieren to retire *s.o.* due to ill health
Invalidität *f* disablement, disability, incapacity for work (due to ill health)
Invaliditätsentschädigung *f* disablement compensation *(in private accident insurance schemes)*
Invaliditätsfall *m* case of disablement [disability]
Invaliditätsgruppe *f* class of disablement, disability class
Invaliditätszusatzversicherung *f* additional disablement insurance
invariant *(stats)* invariant
Invarianz *f* *(stats)* invariance

Inventar *n* inventory *(list);* stock *(goods, fixtures and livestock etc.)* ❖ **das ~ aufnehmen** to take [draw up, compile] an inventory, to draw up a list of all assets and liabilities
~, **aktives** capitalized stock
~, **buchmäßiges** book stock [property, assets]
~, **festes** fixtures
~, **landwirtschaftliches** farm stock
~, **laufend geführtes** current inventory
~, **lebendes** livestock
~, **tatsächlich aufgenommenes** registered stock
~, **totes** dead stock
~, **unbewegliches** immobile stock, installed property
Inventaraufnahme *f* stock-taking, inventory-taking
Inventaraufstellung *f* 1. list of current assets, list of stores and equipment, stock book; 2. stock-taking, making [taking] of an inventory
Inventarbeitrag *m* contribution to the stock *(paid in cash or kind to a co-operative farm by a prospective member)*
~, **zusätzlicher** additional contribution to the stock *(s.* **Inventarbeitrag***)*
Inventarbewertung *f* valuation of stock
Inventarbuch *n* stock book [ledger]; inventory book *(library etc.);* register *(museum etc.)*
inventarisieren to take [draw up, compile] an inventory; to enter in the inventory
Inventarliste *f s.* **Inventarverzeichnis**
Inventarnummer *f* inventory number; accession number *(library, museum etc.)*
Inventarobjekt *n s.* **Inventarstück**
Inventarstück *n* item of the furnishings and fixtures *(house, office etc.);* item of farm equipment [stock]; item of implements and machinery *(factory etc.)*
Inventarverzeichnis *n* inventory
Inventur *f* stock-taking, making [taking] of an inventory
Inventurausverkauf *m* stock-taking [clearance] sale
Inventurauswertung *f* assessment of stock-taking [inventory]
Inventurbestand *m* stock of goods after inventory [stock-taking]
Inventurbilanz *f* stock balance sheet
Inventurbuch *n* stock book [ledger]
Inventurdifferenz *f* discrepancy in inventory
~, **negative** minus difference in stock
~, **positive** excess stock
Inventurliste *f* stock list
Inventurpark *m* rolling stock *(of a transport enterprise at the time of inventory)*
Inventurprotokoll *n* inventory record
Inventurprüfung *f* stock-checking

Inventurverkauf *m s.* **Inventurausverkauf**
Inventurvorschriften *fpl* stock-taking rules
Investant *m* investor
Investbeitrag *m* 1. investment loan *(granted by agricultural co-operative members to the co-operative out of their private savings);* 2. investment contribution *(to be paid by members of agricultural co-operatives of type I when transforming it into or joining type III in the former GDR)*
Investentscheidung *f* investment decision
investieren to invest
Investition *f* investment
~, **landwirtschaftliche** agricultural investment
~, **unsichere** insecure investment
~ **zur Schaffung eines Reservebestandes** investment for reserve stock
~, **zusätzliche** additional investment
Investitionen *fpl:*
~, **ausländische** foreign investments
~, **dezentrale** decentralized investments
~, **direkte** direct investments
~, **effektive** effective investments
~, **gemeinsame** joint investments
~, **gewinnbringende** profitable investments
~ **in Warenbeständen** inventory investments
~, **indirekte** indirect investments
~, **industrielle** industrial investments
~, **kurzfristige** short-term investments
~, **langfristige** long-range [long-term] investments
~, **laufende** running [current] investments
~, **materielle** material investments
~ **mit kurzer Amortisationsdauer** short-life investments
~ **mit langer Amortisationsdauer** long-life investments
~, **mittelfristige** medium-term investments
~, **nicht fertiggestellte** *s.* ~, **unvollendete**
~, **nichtmaterielle** non-material investments
~, **nichtplanmäßige** unplanned investments
~, **planfreie** investments exempt from planning
~, **planmäßige** investments according to (the) plan
~, **private** private investments
~, **produktive** productive investments
~, **spezifische** investments per unit *(of output etc.)*
~, **staatliche** public [state] investments
~, **tatsächliche** effective [actual] investments
~, **übermäßige** excessive investments
~, **unproduktive** non-productive investments
~, **unvollendete** unfinished investments
~, **wirksame** effective investments
Investitionsabnahme *f* quality inspection of an investment project
Investitionsabrechnung *f* investment accounting

Investitionsabteilung *f* investment department
Investitionsanleihe *f* investment loan
Investitionsarbeiten *fpl* investment activities
Investitionsaufgabe *f* investment project
Investitionsauftraggeber *m* investor, person [institution] who gives an order for an investment
Investitionsauftragnehmer *m* investment enterprise [firm], executor of investment(s); *(build)* contractor
Investitionsaufwand *m* investment expenditure(s), expenditure(s) on investments
Investitionsaufwandskoeffizient *m* input coefficient of investments
Investitionsausmaß *n* extent of investments
Investitionsbank *f* investment bank
Investitionsbaubilanz *f* construction balance sheet of investments
~, **örtliche** local construction balance sheet of investments
Investitionsbedarf *m* investment needs
Investitionsbereitschaft *f s.* **Investitionsneigung**
Investitionsbeteiligung *f* participation in investments, investment participation
Investitionsbilanz *f* investment balance sheet
Investitionsboom *m* investment boom
Investitionsdurchführung *f* implementation [carrying out] of an investment
Investitionseffekt *m* investment effect *(e.g. ratio of incremental output to investment)*
Investitionseinsparung *f* saving in investments
Investitionsentscheidung *f* decision on investment, investment decision
Investitionsfinanzierung *f* investment financing
Investitionsfonds *m* investment fund
Investitionsgeschehen *n* investments, investment business
Investitionsgesellschaft *f* investment company
Investitionsgüter *npl* capital [investment] goods
Investitionsgüterangebot *n* supply of capital [investment] goods; capital goods in show, display of capital equipment *(fair etc.)*
Investitionsgütererzeugung *f* production of capital [investment] goods
Investitionsgüterindustrie *f* capital [investment] goods industry
Investitionsgüternachfrage *f* demand for capital [investment] goods
Investitionshaushalt *m* investment budget
Investitionshilfe *f* investment assistance [aid]
Investitionshöhe *f s.* **Investitionsausmaß**
Investitionsintensität *f* investment intensity
investitionsintensiv investment-intensive
Investitionskoeffizient *m* investment coefficient
Investitionskomplex *m* complex of investments *(of different sectors in one area)*

Investitionskonjunktur *f s.* **Investitionsboom**
Investitionskontrolle *f* investment control [follow-up]
Investitionskonzept *n s.* **Investitionskonzeption**
Investitionskonzeption *f* investment project outline [programme]
Investitionskoordinierung *f* investment co-ordination, co-ordination of investments
~, **territoriale** regional co-ordination of investments
Investitionskosten *pl* investment costs
Investitionskostensenkung *f* reduction in investment costs
Investitionskraft *f* investment capacity
Investitionskredit *m* investment credit
Investitionsleistungen *fpl* work done in implementing an investment project *(mainly construction and assembly work)*
Investitionsleistungsvertrag *m* investment contract *(between investor and executor of investment project detailing certain conditions)*
Investitionslenkung *f* steering of investments
Investitionsmaßnahme *f* investment (measure)
Investitionsmittel *npl* investment resources [capital]
Investitionsmittelrechnung *f* calculation of investment resources [capital]
Investitionsmodell *n* investment model
Investitionsmultiplikator *m* investment multiplier *(as an effect on following investments)*
Investitionsneigung *f* propensity to invest
Investitionsniveau *n* level of investments
Investitionsnorm *f* standard rate of investment cost(s) for one unit of capacity
Investitionsnutzeffekt *m* investment efficiency
Investitionsordnung *f* investment regulations
Investitionsplan *m* investment plan
Investitionsplanung *f* planning of investments, investment planning
~, **perspektivische** long-term investment planning
Investitionspolitik *f* investment policy
Investitionsprognose *f* investment forecast [prognosis]
Investitionsprogramm *n* investment programme
Investitionsprojekt *n* investment project
Investitionsquote *f* (incremental) output investment ratio
Investitionsrate *f* investment rate *(ratio between investment and national income plus amortization)*
Investitionsrechnung *f* investment calculation(s)
Investitionsreserve *f* investment reserve fund
Investitionsruine *f* misinvestment, aborted investment project

Investitionsstatistik *f* investment statistics
Investitionssteuer *f* investment tax
Investitionsstruktur *f* investment structure
Investitionstätigkeit *f* investment activities
Investitionstermin *m* date for implementation of investment(s)
Investitionsträger *m* investor
Investitionsumfang *m s.* **Investitionsausmaß**
Investitionsvariante *f* investment variant
Investitionsverordnung *f* investment regulations *(related to planning, financing, carrying out etc., of investment projects)*
Investitionsvervielfacher *m s.* **Investitionsmultiplikator**
Investitionsvolumen *n s.* **Investitionsausmaß**
Investitionsvorbereitung *f* preparation of investment (project)
Investitionsvorhaben *n* investment project
Investitionszuwachsrate *f* growth rate of investments
Investment *n* investment
Investmentbank *f* investment bank
Investmentfonds *m* investment fund
Investmentgesellschaft *f* investment company
Investmentschein *m* investment bond
Investmentsparen *n* saving through investment trusts
Investmittel *npl s.* **Investitionsmittel**
Investor *m* investor
Invisibles *pl* invisibles
Inzahlungnahme *f* trade-in
Irrtum *m* error, mistake; fallacy
~, rechtlicher mistake of law
~, tatsächlicher mistake of fact
Irrtümer *mpl*:
 ◊ **~ und Auslassungen vorbehalten (I. u. A. v.)** errors and omissions excepted (E. & O. E., e. & o. e.)
Irrtumswahrscheinlichkeit *f (stats)* level of significance
Isoliermonteur *m* fitter for insulation
Ist *n* actual incomings and outgoings
Istabrechnung *f* accounting of actual costs
Istaufkommen *n* actual yield [quota delivered]
Istaufwand *m* actual expenses
Istausgaben *fpl* actual expenditures
Istbestand *m* actual balance [stock]
Istbilanz *f* actual balance sheet
Isteinnahmen *fpl* actual receipts [takings]
Isterlös *m* actual proceeds [receipts]
Istgehalt *m* real [actual] contents
Istgehalt *n* actual salary
Istgewinn *m* actual profit
Istgröße *f* actual figure *(production etc.)*, actual number *(flats constructed etc.)*; actual size *(suits etc.)*
Istkalkulation *f* calculation of actual costs

Istkapazität *f* actual capacity
Istkosten *pl* actual costs
Istkostenrechnung *f* accounting of actual costs
Istlohn *m* actual wages
Ist-Prinzip-Abrechnung *f (home tr)* accounting of the actual commodity turnover
Istproduktion *f* actual output [production]
Istselbstkosten *pl* actual prime costs
Istspanne *f* actual margin
Iststärke *f* effective strength
Iststunden *fpl* actual hours *(worked etc.)*
Istverbrauch *m* actual consumption
Istverdienst *m* actual earnings
Istwert *m* actual value
Istzahlen *fpl* actual figures
Istzeit *f* actual [real] time
Iteration *f (maths)* iteration; *(stats)* run
Iterationsindex *m* cycle index
Iterationsmethode *f* iteration method
Iterationsprozeß *m* iteration process
Iterationstest *m (stats)* iteration test
~, Wald-Wolfowitz'scher *(stats)* Wald-Wolfowitz test
Iterationsverfahren *n* iteration procedure; successive approximation
IWF-Beauflagung *f* IMF conditionality *(imposed on countries getting IMF loans)*

J

Jagd *f* hunting
Jagdaufseher *m* gamekeeper, *(Am)* game-warden
jagdberechtigt authorized to hunt
Jagdberechtigung *f* authorization to hunt
Jagdfrevel *m* poaching, game trespass
Jagdfrevler *m* poacher
Jagdgebiet *n* hunting ground [district]
Jagdgerechtigkeit *f* hunting rights
Jagdgesetz *n* game law
Jagdhoheit *f* right to hunt
Jagdhüter *m s.* **Jagdaufseher**
Jagdpacht *f* tenancy [rent] of a shoot
Jagdpächter *m* game tenant
Jagdrecht *n* game laws
Jagdrevier *n s.* **Jagdgebiet**
Jagdschaden *m* damage caused by hunters
Jagdschein *m* hunting permit, shooting licence
Jagdsteuer *f* tax on hunting
Jagdwaffenmechaniker *m* hunting-gun maker
Jagdzeit *f* hunting season
jagen to hunt *(game)*; to shoot *(duck etc.)*
Jahr *n* year

Jahrbuch *n* yearbook, annual
~, **statistisches** statistical yearbook
Jahre *npl:*
~, **geburtenarme** years of low birthrate
~, **geburtenstarke** years of high birthrate
Jahresabkommen *n* annual agreement
Jahresabonnement *n* annual [yearly] subscription
Jahresabrechnung *f* annual balance sheet, annual settlement *(of accounts);* annual statement
Jahresabschluß *m* annual settlement of an account; annual statement of accounts, annual balance sheet
Jahresabschlußbericht *m* annual report
Jahresabschlußbilanz *f* annual balance (sheet)
Jahresabschlußprüfung *f* annual auditing
Jahresanalyse *f* annual (economic) analysis
Jahresanfangsbestand *m* stock at the beginning of the year
Jahresarbeitsverdienst *m* annual wages
Jahresarbeitsvertrag *m* annual working contract *(between industrial enterprises for co-operation in production);* annual co-operative contract *(between co-operative farm and co-operation council)*
Jahresaufkommen *n* annual output
Jahresausgaben *fpl* annual expenditure(s)
Jahresausstoß *m s.* **Jahresaufkommen**
Jahresbedarf *m* annual requirements
Jahresbeitrag *m* annual fee [contribution]
Jahresbericht *m* annual report
Jahresberichterstattung *f* annual reporting
Jahresbilanz *f* annual balance (sheet)
Jahresbudget *n* annual budget
Jahresdurchschnitt *m* annual average
Jahresdurchschnittsbestand *m* annual average stock
Jahresdurchschnittseinkommen *n* annual average income
Jahresdurchschnittsleistung *f* annual average output; *(tech)* annual average performance
Jahreseinkommen *n* yearly income
Jahresendabrechnung *f* annual settlement (of accounts)
Jahresendprämie *f* end-of-the-year bonus
Jahreserhebung *f (fin)* annual tax collection; annual tax assessment; *(stats)* annual survey
Jahresfrist *f* period [time] of a year ⋄ **binnen** ~ within a year; **nach** ~ after one year, in a year's time
Jahresgehalt *n* salary per annum, annual salary
Jahresgeschäftsbericht *m* annual business report
Jahresgewinn *m* annual profit
Jahreshauptversammlung *f* annual (general) meeting

Jahreshaushalt *m s.* **Jahresbudget**
Jahreshaushaltsbericht *m* annual statement of the budget
Jahreshaushaltsplan *m* annual budget plan
Jahreshaushaltsrechnung *f* annual budget accounting
Jahreskapazität *f* annual capacity
Jahreskongreß *m* annual congress
Jahreskontrollbericht *m s.* **Jahresbericht**
Jahreskreditvertrag *m* annual credit agreement
Jahreslohn *m* annual wages
Jahreslohnfonds *m* annual wage fund
Jahresmaschinenzeitfonds *m* annual machine capacity *(expressed in terms of hours)*
Jahresmietvertrag *m* annual rental agreement
Jahresmitgliederversammlung *f* annual membership meeting
Jahresmitgliedskarte *f* annual membership card
Jahresmittel *n* annual mean *(rain etc.)*
Jahresnorm *f* yearly norm
Jahrespacht *f* yearly lease; annual letting
Jahrespauschale *f* yearly lumpsum
Jahresplan *m* annual plan
Jahresplanbestand *m* planned stock per annum
Jahresplanentwurf *m* annual plan draft
Jahresplanerfüllung *f* annual plan fulfilment
Jahresplanmodell *n* annual plan model
Jahresplanung *f* annual planning
Jahresprämie *f* annual bonus; *(ins)* annual premium
Jahresprodukt *n* annual product
Jahresproduktion *f* annual output [production]
Jahresproduktionsplan *m* annual production plan
Jahresrate *f* yearly quota [share] *(imports etc.);* annual instalment, yearly payment
Jahresrechnung *f* annual account
Jahresrente *f* annuity
Jahresselbstkosten *pl* annual prime cost
Jahressoll *n* yearly planned task *(production, sale etc.)*
Jahrestag *m* anniversary
Jahresumsatz *m* annual turnover
Jahresumschlag *m s.* **Jahresumsatz**
Jahresverbrauch *m* annual consumption
Jahresverlust *m* annual loss
Jahresversammlung *f* annual meeting
Jahresvertrag *m* annual agreement [contract]
Jahresvolkswirtschaftsplan *m* annual national economic plan
Jahresvorratsnorm *f* annual rate of stocks
Jahreswirtschaftsbericht *m* yearly economic report
Jahreswirtschaftsplan *m s.* **Jahresvolkswirtschaftsplan**
Jahreszinsen *mpl* annual interest
Jahreszuwachs *m* annual increase

Jahreszuwachsrate *f* annual rate of growth
Jahrfünft *n* period of five years
Jahrgang *m* age-class, age-group; year *(persons born in any particular year)*
Jahrhundert *n* century
jährlich annually
Jahrzehnt *n* decade
Journal *n* journal, magazine, periodical; *(com)* daybook; logbook *(ships)*
Journalist *m* journalist
Jubiläum *n* jubilee
Jubiläumsausgabe *f* jubilee edition
Jubiläumsausstellung *f* jubilee exhibition
Jubiläumsmesse *f* jubilee fair
Jugendaktiv *n* team of young activists
Jugendamt *n* youth welfare office
Jugendarbeit *f* youth work
Jugendarbeitslosigkeit *f* youth unemployment
Jugendarbeitsschutz *m* youth labour safety
Jugendausschuß *m* youth committee
Jugendbewegung *f* youth movement
Jugendfürsorge *f* young people's welfare; youth welfare department
Jugendfürsorger *m* youth welfare officer
Jugendgericht *n* juvenile court
Jugendherberge *f* youth hostel
Jugendkommission *f* committee for youth
Jugendlicher *m* young person
Jugendobjekt *n* youth project
Jugendorganisation *f* youth organization
~, **internationale** international youth organization
Jugendrecht *n* juvenile [youth] code
Jugendschutz *m* protection of the young
Jugendschutzgesetz *n* Children and Young Persons Act
Jugendweihe *f* youth initiation ceremony
Jungarbeiter *m* young worker
Jungvieh *n* young stock [cattle]
Junker *m* *(hist)* junker *(s.* **Junkertum***)*
Junkertum *n* *(hist)* the junkers, junkerdom *(system of military landlords in former Prussia)*
Junktim *n* package deal
Jurisdiktion *f* jurisdiction
Jurist *m* lawyer; jurist; legal expert
Jury *f* selection committee, panel of judges [adjudicators]
justieren to adjust; *(d.pr.)* to align
Justierung *f* adjustment; *(d.pr.)* alignment, registration
Justitiar *m* legal adviser [consultant]
Justiz *f* justice; administration of justice
Justizbeamter *m* court official
Justizbehörde *f* judicial [legal] authority
Justizgewalt *f* judicial power; judicature
Justizhoheit *f* supreme judicial sovereignty
Justizwesen *n* legal [judicial] system

K

Kabel *n* cable; cable(gram)
Kabeladresse *f* cable address
Kabelanweisung *f* cable money order
Kabelbahn *f* cable-railway
Kabelweg *m:*
  ◊ **auf dem ~** by cable
Kabinett *n* 1. special-purpose teaching room; 2. *(pol)* cabinet
~, **technisches** class-room equipped with technical aids and literature
Kabinettssitzung *f* cabinet meeting
Kabinettsumbildung *f* changes in the cabinet
Kabotage *f* cabotage
Kader *m* staff member; cadre *(political party etc.)*
Kader *mpl* personnel, staff *(s. a.* **Personal***)*
Kahlfraß *m* *(for)* complete defoliation *(by insects);* *(agric)* complete destruction of the leaf area *(by intense grazing)*
Kahlschlag *m* *(for)* cut-over land; complete deforestation, clear-felling
Kahlschlagwirtschaft *f* methodical deforestation *(followed by replanting)*
Kahnführer *m* boatswain, bosun; bargee
Kahnladung *f* boatload
Kai *m/n* quay, wharf ◊ **ab ~** ex quay [wharf]; **frei ~** free quay
Kaiarbeiter *m* wharfman, docker
Kaigebühr *f* quayage, quay dues, wharfage
Kaigeld *n s.* **Kaigebühr**
Kailager *n* quay store
Kailagergeld *n* quay rent
Kälberaufzucht *f* calf-breeding
Kälberaufzuchtbetrieb *m* calf-breeding farm
Kalenderjahr *n* calendar year
Kaliindustrie *f* potash industry
Kalkül *n/m* 1. (rough) calculation, estimate; 2. *(maths)* calculus
Kalkulation *f* calculation, computation; estimate ◊ **eine ~ aufstellen** to make a calculation, to calculate, to work out the figures
~, **knappe** close calculation
~, **vorsichtige** conservative estimate
Kalkulationsansatz *m* basis of (cost/price) calculation
Kalkulationsart *f* kind of (cost/price) calculation
Kalkulationsaufschlag *m s.* **Kalkulationszuschlag**
Kalkulationsaufschlagsatz *m* rate of mark-up
Kalkulationsbestandteil *m* element of (cost/price) calculation
Kalkulationsdifferenz *f* discrepancy in calculations *(difference between primary and final calculation)*

Kalkulationseinheit *f* unit of calculation (cost/price)
Kalkulationselement *n* element of (cost/price) calculation
Kalkulationsfaktor *m s.* **Kalkulationselement**
Kalkulationsfehler *m* calculating error
Kalkulationslocher *m (d.pr.)* calculation punch
Kalkulationsmethode *f* method of calculation
Kalkulationspreis *m* calculated price
Kalkulationsprüfung *f* checking of estimates
Kalkulationsquote *f s.* **Kalkulationsaufschlagssatz**
Kalkulationsrichtlinien *fpl* guide-lines for calculation
Kalkulationsschema *n* calculation scheme
Kalkulationsverfahren *n* method of calculation
Kalkulationszuschlag *m* mark-up
Kalkulator *m* calculator; accountant; bookkeeper
kalkulatorisch calculatory
kalkulieren to calculate, to reckon, to estimate
kalorienarm poor in [containing few] calories
Kaloriengehalt *m* calorie content
kalorienreich rich in calories
Kalorienwert *m* calorific value
kältebeständig cold-resistant, frost-resistant
Kältebeständigkeit *f* resistance to cold [frost]
Kälteindustrie *f* refrigeration industry
kältekonserviert preserved by refrigeration; frozen *(goods etc.)*
Kältekonservierung *f* preservation by refrigeration
Kältetechnik *f* refrigeration engineering
Kälte- und Klimaanlagenmonteur *m* fitter for refrigeration and air-conditioning plants
Kälteverfahren *n* refrigeration method [process]
Kammer *f* chamber *(court etc.)*; board *(organizations etc.)*
Kämmerei *f* finance department *(of local authorities)*
Kämmerer *m* finance official *(of local authorities)*
Kampf *m* fight, struggle
~, **ideologischer** ideological struggle
~, **politischer** political struggle
~ **um den Absatz** fight for the market
~ **um die Macht** fight [struggle] for power, power struggle
~ **um Märkte** *s.* ~ **um den Absatz**
Kampfabstimmung *f* crucial vote *(in important debate)*; vote *(by workers on whether to strike or not)*
Kämpfer *m* fighter *(for ideas etc.)*; champion *(for rights etc.)*
Kampfmaßnahmen *fpl* combative measures
~ **der Gewerkschaft** trade union combative measures
Kampfpreis *m* cut-throat price

Kampfrate *f* fighting rate *(competitive shipment charges)*
Kampfzoll *m* retaliatory duty [tariff]
Kanal *m* canal; channel; drain
~, **formeller** official [formal] channel
~, **geschlossener** canal with locks
~, **halboffizieller** semi-official [semi-formal] channel
~, **künstlicher** canal, artificial waterway
~, **offener** canal without locks
~, **offizieller** official channel
Kanalabgaben *fpl s.* **Kanalgebühr**
Kanäle *mpl:*
~, **diplomatische** diplomatic channels
Kanalgebühr *f* canal toll [dues]
Kanalisation *f* canalization *(river)*; sewerage; sewage system *(town)*; drainage ◊ **an die ~ angeschlossen sein** to be on main drainage, to be connected to the municipal sewerage system
Kanalisationsanschluß *m* sewerage connection
Kanalisationsnetz *n* network [system] of sewers, sewerage
kanalisieren to canalize *(river)*; to construct sewers *(town)*
Kanalisierung *f* canalization; installation of sewers
Kanalschiffahrt *f* canal navigation [shipping]
Kanalsystem *n* canal [sewage] system
Kanalverkehr *m* canal traffic
Kandidat *m* candidate *(for an examination, in an election etc.)*; applicant *(for a position, an office, a political party etc.)* ◊ **jmdn. als ~ ablehnen** to turn down [reject] s.o. as candidate; **jmdn. als ~ aufstellen** to put s.o. up as candidate; **jmdn. als ~ unterstützen** to back (up) [support] s.o. as candidate; **jmdn. als ~ vorschlagen** to propose s.o as a candidate; **als ~ zurücktreten** to withdraw one's candidature, to withdraw as a candidate; **den Kandidaten prüfen** to examine s.o. as candidate; **sich als ~ vorstellen** to come forward as a candidate
~, **aufgestellter** nominee; nominated candidate
~, **einziger** sole candidate
~, **geeigneter** eligible candidate
Kandidatenliste *f* list of candidates; list of applicants ◊ **eine ~ aufstellen** to put forward a list of candidates
Kandidatur *f* candidature, *(Am)* candidacy
kandidieren to stand as a candidate, *(Am)* to run for office
Kann-Bestimmung *f* discretionary clause
Kann-Vorschrift *f s.* **Kann-Bestimmung**
Kantine *f* canteen, mess, cafeteria
Kantorowitschmethode *f* Kantorovich method *(of linear optimization of transport problems)*
Kanzler *m* chancellor

Kapazität *f* capacity
- ~ **eines Betriebes** plant capacity
- ~, **freie** spare [idle] capacity
- ~, **projektierte** projected [rated] capacity
- ~, **technische** machine capacity
- ~, **ungenutzte** idle capacity
- ~, **voll ausgenutzte** fully utilized capacity

Kapazitätsauslastung *f* capacity utilization
- ~, **volle** working to full capacity

Kapazitätsausnutzung *f s.* **Kapazitätsauslastung**

Kapazitätsausnutzungsgrad *m* rate [extent] of capacity utilization

Kapazitätsausnutzungsnorm *f* standard rate of capacity utilization

Kapazitätsausweitung *f* capacity expansion

Kapazitätsbilanz *f* capacity balance sheet

Kapazitätseffekt *m* impact on capacity
- ~ **der Investitionen** impact of investments on capacity expansion

Kapazitätsermittlung *f s.* **Kapazitätsmessung**

Kapazitätserweiterung *f* expansion of capacity

Kapazitätskosten *pl* standby-charges [costs]

Kapazitätsmessung *f* measuring of capacity

Kapazitätsplanung *f* capacity planning

Kapazitätsreserve *f* reserve [spare] capacities

Kapazitätsverlust *m* loss of capacity

Kapazitätszuwachs *m* increase [growth] in capacity

Kapital *n* capital ⋄ **in ~ umwandeln** to convert into capital, to capitalize; ~ **abschreiben** to write off capital; ~ **abziehen** to withdraw capital; ~ **anlegen** to invest capital; ~ **anlocken** to attract capital; ~ **aufbringen** to raise capital; ~ **aus dem Ausland zurückführen** *s.* ~ **repatriieren**; ~ **aus etwas schlagen** to make money out of s.th.; to make propaganda out of s.th., to exploit s.th.; ~ **ausführen** *s.* ~ **exportieren**; ~ **bereitstellen** to furnish (with) capital; ~ **einbringen** to bring in capital; ~ **einziehen** to call in [up] capital; ~ **erhöhen** to increase capital; ~ **exportieren** to export capital; ~ **fest anlegen** to lock up [immobilize] capital; ~ **freisetzen** to set capital free; ~ **flüssigmachen** to mobilize capital; ~ **hineinstecken** *s.* ~ **anlegen**; ~ **investieren** *s.* ~ **anlegen**; ~ **kündigen** to recall capital; ~ **repatriieren** to repatriate capital; ~ **übernehmen** to take over capital; ~ **umsetzen** to turn over capital; to realize capital; to transfer capital *(from one branch to another etc.)*; **mit ~ ausstatten** to furnish (with) [provide] capital; **neues ~ aufnehmen** to raise fresh [additional] capital; **vom ~ leben** to live on capital
- ~, **amortisiertes** sunk capital
- ~, **angegebenes** declared capital
- ~, **angelegtes** invested capital
- ~, **arbeitendes** productive [employed] capital
- ~, **aufgenommenes** borrowed money
- ~, **ausgegebenes** issued capital
- ~, **ausländisches** foreign capital
- ~, **autorisiertes** authorized capital
- ~, **begebenes** issued capital [*(Am)* stock]
- ~, **betriebsnotwendiges** necessary operating capital
- ~, **bewilligtes** authorized capital [*(Am)* stock]
- ~, **brachliegendes** dead [idle] capital, unemployed funds
- ~, **deklariertes** declared capital
- ~, **dividendenberechtigtes** capital entitled to a dividend
- ~, **eingebrachtes** brought-in capital
- ~, **eingetragenes** registered capital
- ~, **eingezahltes** paid-up [paid-in] capital
- ~, **eisernes** (absolute) minimum capital
- ~, **fälliges** matured capital
- ~, **festgelegtes** locked-up capital
- ~, **festliegendes** frozen capital
- ~, **fiktives** fictitious capital
- ~, **fixes** fixed capital
- ~, **flüssiges** liquid capital
- ~, **freies** unemployed capital
- ~, **fungierendes** industrial and trading capital *(as opposed to finance capital)*
- ~, **geistiges** intellectual capital, fund of knowledge
- ~, **genehmigtes** authorized [approved] capital [*(Am)* stock]
- ~, **gezeichnetes** subscribed capital
- ~, **herabgesetztes** reduced capital
- ~, **in Wertpapieren angelegtes** capital invested in securities
- ~, **industrielles** industrial capital
- ~, **konstantes** constant capital
- ~, **kurzfristig angelegtes** short-term invested capital
- ~, **langfristig angelegtes** long-term invested capital
- ~, **latentes** latent capital *(as stocks of commodities, material and money)*
- ~, **nicht realisierbares** locked-up capital
- ~, **nicht voll eingezahltes** partly paid-in capital
- ~, **noch nicht eingezahltes** unpaid capital
- ~, **potentielles** potential capital *(kind of dead capital)*
- ~, **produktives** productive capital
- ~, **registriertes** registered capital
- ~, **schrumpfendes** shrinking capital
- ~, **stehendes** *s.* ~, **konstantes**
- ~, **tatsächlich eingezahltes** real paid-in capital
- ~, **totes** dead [unemployed, idle] capital
- ~, **umlaufendes** circulating capital
- ~, **unaufgerufenes** uncalled capital
- ~, **unbeschäftigtes** unemployed capital

~ **und Arbeit** *f* capital and labour
~ **und Zinsen** *mpl* capital and interest; principal and interest
~, **unkündbares** irredeemable capital
~, **unproduktives** dead capital
~, **ursprüngliches** original capital
~, **variables** variable capital
~, **verfügbares** available capital [funds]
~, **vermindertes** *s.* ~, **herabgesetztes**
~, **verwässertes** hidden capital *(to conceal taxation)*
~, **verzinsliches** *s.* ~, **zinstragendes**
~, **voll eingezahltes** fully paid-in capital
~, **vorgeschossenes** advanced capital
~, **wechselndes** changing capital
~, **zinsfreies** non-interest-bearing capital
~, **zinstragendes** interest-bearing capital
~, **zurückgezahltes** redeemed [paid-back] capital
Kapitalabfindung *f* lump sum settlement of capital
Kapitalabfluß *m* capital outflow
Kapitalabgabe *f* capital levy
Kapitalabnutzung *f* depreciation of capital
Kapitalabschöpfung *f* absorption of capital
Kapitalabschreibung *f* capital item disallowed for income tax purposes
Kapitalabwanderung *f* exodus [efflux] of capital
Kapitalabzug *m* withdrawal of capital
Kapitalakkumulation *f* accumulation of capital
Kapitaländerung *f s.* **Kapitalveränderungen**
Kapitalanhäufung *f s.* **Kapitalakkumulation**
Kapitalanlage *f* investment of capital, capital investment
~, **außerbetriebliche** outside investment
~, **kurzfristige** short-term capital investment
~, **langfristige** long-term capital investment
~, **leicht realisierbare** liquid investment
~, **lohnende** paying [profitable] investment
~, **mündelsichere** gilt-edged investment
~, **unproduktive** unproductive investment; dead assets
Kapitalanlagegesellschaft *f* investment trust
Kapitalanlagegüter *npl* capital assets, investment goods
Kapitalanlagekonto *n* capital assets account
Kapitalanlagenbewertung *f* appreciation of assets
Kapitalanleger *m* investor
Kapitalansammlung *f* capital accumulation
Kapitalanteil *m* shareholding, stockholding *(in company etc.)*; portion of capital *(per unit of production)*
Kapitalanteilschein *m* stock certificate
kapitalarm short of capital [funds]
Kapitalaufbringung *f* raising of capital
Kapitalaufnahme *f s.* **Kapitalaufstockung**

Kapitalaufstockung *f* increase of capital [*(Am)* capital stock]
Kapitalaufwand *m* capital expenditure [outlay]
Kapitalaufwendungen *fpl* capital disbursements
Kapitalausfuhr *f* export of capital
Kapitalausnutzung *f s.* **Kapitalverwertung**
Kapitalausstattung *f* capital [fund] resources; capital endowment [equipment]
Kapitalausweitung *f* capital expansion
Kapitalauszahlung *f* capital payment
Kapitalbasis *f* financial basis
Kapitalbedarf *m* capital requirement
~, **langfristiger** demand for long-term investment (capital)
Kapitalbedürfnisse *npl* capital requirements
Kapitalbeitrag *m* contribution to capital
Kapitalbereitstellung *f* provision of capital
Kapitalberichtigung *f* adjustment of capital
Kapitalberichtigungskonto *n* capital adjustment account
Kapitalbeschaffung *f* raising [procurement] of capital
Kapitalbesitzer *m* owner of shares [*(Am)* stocks]
Kapitalbeteiligung *f* participation (in a business firm), financial interest; stock subscription
Kapitalbetrag *m* amount of capital
~ **einer Anleihe** principal of a loan
Kapitalbewegung *f* capital movement
~, **internationale** international movement of capital
Kapitalbewegungen *fpl*:
~, **kurzfristige** short-term capital movements
~, **langfristige** long-term capital movements
~, **nationale** inter-branch capital movements (within the country)
Kapitalbewertung *f* capital valuation
Kapitalbilanz *f* balance sheet of capital transactions
Kapitalbildung *f* capital formation
Kapitaldecke *f* capital cover
Kapitaldeckung *f* covering of capital
Kapitaldienst *m* capital service
Kapitaldisposition *f* provision of capital
Kapitaldividende *f* dividend on capital
Kapitaleinbringung *f* bringing in of capital
Kapitaleinfuhr *f* import of capital
Kapitaleinkommen *n* income from capital investment, investment [unearned] income
Kapitaleinkünfte *pl s.* **Kapitaleinkommen**
Kapitaleinlage *f* invested capital, paid-in share
Kapitaleinsatz *m* employment of capital
Kapitaleinschuß *m s.* **Kapitalspritze**
Kapitaleinzahlung *f* paying in of capital
Kapitaleinziehung *f* recall [calling in] of capital
Kapitalemission *f* capital issue
Kapitalentblößung *f* depletion of capital
Kapitalentnahme *f* withdrawal of capital

Kapitalentschädigung *f s.* **Kapitalabfindung**
Kapitalentwertung *f* depreciation of capital
Kapitalerhöhung *f* increase of capital ◇ **eine ~ vornehmen** to make a new issue of capital
Kapitalertrag *m* capital return [yield], income from capital investment
Kapitalertragssteuer *f* capital yield tax *(on dividends etc.)* ◇ **~ erheben** to raise [collect] capital yield tax
Kapitalertragswert *m* capitalized value
Kapitalexport *m* export of capital, capital export
Kapitalfehlbetrag *m* amount of shortage of capital, capital deficit
Kapitalfetischismus *m* capital fetishism
Kapitalflucht *f* flight [exodus, outflow] of capital
Kapitalfluß *m* flow of capital [funds]
Kapitalforderung *f* claim on capital
Kapitalfreisetzung *f* release [setting free] of capital
Kapitalgeber *m* financer, investor
Kapitalgesellschaft *f* limited (liability) company, *(Am)* joint stock company
Kapitalgewinn *m* investment profit, capital gain
Kapitalgewinnabgabe *f* capital gains levy
Kapitalgewinnkonto *n* capital gains [*(Am)* surplus] account
Kapitalgüter *npl* capital goods
Kapitalgüterindustrie *f* capital goods industry
Kapitalherabsetzung *f* reduction of capital
Kapitalhöhe *f* amount of capital
Kapitalien *npl* capital funds, (financial) resources
Kapitalimport *m* import of capital
Kapitalintensität *f* capital intensity, employment of large capital assets, high proportion of fixed capital costs in production costs
kapitalintensiv capital-intensive
Kapitalinvestition *f* capital investment
kapitalisierbar capitalizable
kapitalisieren to capitalize
kapitalisiert capitalized ◇ **nicht genügend ~** under-capitalized
Kapitalisierung *f* capitalization
Kapitalisierungsanleihe *f* funding loan
Kapitalisierungsmethode *f* method of capitalization
Kapitalismus *m* capitalism
~, monopolistischer monopoly capitalism
~, staatsmonopolistischer state monopoly capitalism
~, vormonopolistischer pre-monopoly capitalism
Kapitalist *m* capitalist
kapitalistisch capitalist
Kapitalknappheit *f* capital shortage, lack of capital

Kapitalkoeffizient *m* capital coefficient, capital to output ratio
Kapitalkonto *n* capital account
~, vermindertes reduced capital account
Kapitalkonzentration *f* concentration of capital, capital concentration
Kapitalkosten *pl* (real) capital costs, cost of capital, price of capital funds
Kapitalkraft *f* financial power [strength, capacity]
kapitalkräftig well provided with capital, wealthy, sound *(business)*
Kapitalkrise *f* capital crisis
Kapitallenkung *f* steering of capital *(to certain sectors)*
Kapitalmangel *m* lack [shortage] of capital
Kapitalmarkt *m* capital [long-term credit, stock] market
~, freier open market
Kapitalmarktpolitik *f* capital market policy
Kapitalmarktzins *m* capital market rate, price of money
kapitalmäßig according to capital
Kapitalmehrheit *f* controlling financial interest *(in company etc.)*, majority stockholding, majority in shares, *(Am)* majority stocks ◇ **~ eines Unternehmens erwerben** to acquire a controlling interest in a concern
Kapitalmenge *f* amount of capital
Kapitalnachfrage *f* demand for capital
Kapitalnettoertrag *m* net capital gain
Kapitalnettoverlust *m* net capital loss
Kapitalprämie *f (ins)* capitalized premium (in life insurance)
Kapitalquellen *fpl* sources of capital
Kapitalrealisierung *f s.* **Kapitalverwertung**
Kapitalrente *f* unearned income; annuity; revenue from capital investments
Kapitalreserven *fpl* accumulated surplus, capital reserve(s)
Kapitalrückfluß *m* reflux of capital
Kapitalrückführung *f* repatriation of capital
Kapitalrückzahlung *f* repayment of capital
Kapitalschöpfung *f* creation of capital
Kapitalschöpfungskoeffizient *m* coefficient of capital creation
Kapitalschutzabkommen *n* agreement on (capital) investment protection
kapitalschwach financially weak
Kapitalschwund *m* dwindling assets
Kapitalsicherheit *f* capital security
Kapitalspritze *f* injection of capital
kapitalstark financially strong *(company etc.)*; well-capitalized *(firm etc.)*
Kapitalstärke *f* financial strength *(company etc.)*
Kapitalsteuer *f* capital levy, tax on capital, property tax

Kapitalstock *m* capital stock [fund]
Kapitalstrom *m* flow of capital [funds]
Kapitalstruktur *f* structure [composition] of capital *(company etc.)*
Kapitalsumme *f* sum of capital; total amount of capital *(in balance sheet etc.)*; insurance principal
Kapitaltransaktion *f* capital transaction
Kapitaltransfer *m* transfer of capital, capital transfer
Kapitalüberschuß *m* surplus capital
Kapitalübertragung *f s.* **Kapitaltransfer**
Kapitalumdisposition *f* reinvestment of capital
Kapitalumlauf *m* circulation of capital
Kapitalumlenkung *f* re-direction of capital *(usually from one geographical area to another)*; re-allocation of capital *(usually from one sector to another)*
Kapitalumsatz *m (st.ex.)* turnover of shares [stocks] *(in a definite length of time)*
Kapitalumsatzrate *f (st.ex.)* ratio of turnover of shares [stocks] *(s.* **Kapitalumsatz***)*
Kapitalumschichtung *f s.* **Kapitalumlenkung**
Kapitalumschlag *m* turnover of capital, capital turnover; capital transactions
Kapitalumstellung *f* reorganization of capital
Kapitalveränderungen *fpl* changes in capital
Kapitalverbrauch *m* capital consumption
Kapitalverflechtung *f* interlocking of capital
Kapitalverflüssigung *f* making capital liquid
Kapitalverhältnis *n* 1. relation(ship) of capital *(with labour)*; 2. ratio of capital, capital ratio *(to output etc.)*
Kapitalverkauf *m (st.ex.)* sales of shares [stocks]
Kapitalverkehr *m* capital transactions
Kapitalverkehrssteuer *f* tax on capital transactions
Kapitalverlust *m* capital loss
Kapitalvermehrung *f* increase of capital; increase of shares [stocks]
Kapitalverminderung *f* reduction of capital; reduction of shares [stocks]
Kapitalvermittlung *f* intermediary service in the provision of capital
Kapitalvermögen *n* capital, capital assets
Kapitalverpflichtung *f* capital liability
Kapitalversicherung *f* insurance for a lump sum *(as opposed to national/social pension scheme)*
Kapitalverwässerung *f* watering down of shares [stocks]
Kapitalverwendung *f s.* **Kapitalverwertung**
Kapitalverwertung *f* utilization [employment, realization] of capital
Kapitalverzehr *m s.* **Kapitalverbrauch**
Kapitalverzinsung *f* interest on capital, investment return

Kapitalvorschuß *m* advanced capital
Kapitalwanderung *f* migration of capital
Kapitalwert *m* capitalized value *(firm)*; capital value *(shares)*
Kapitalzahlung *f (ins)* commutation
Kapitalzeichnung *f* subscription to shares [stocks]
Kapitalzins *m* rate of interest (on capital)
Kapitalzinsen *mpl* interest on capital
Kapitalzufluß *m* influx of capital
Kapitalzufuhr *f* inflow of capital; import of capital
Kapitalzurückzahlung *f* repayment of principal
Kapitalzusammenballung *f s.* **Kapitalkonzentration**
Kapitalzusammenlegung *f* fusion [merger] of capital
Kapitalzusammensetzung *f* structure [composition] of capital
Kapitalzuschuß *m* addition to capital
Kapitalzuwachs *m* growth in capital
Kapitän *m* captain
~ **der Handelsmarine** captain [master] of a merchant ship
Kapitänspatent *n* master's certificate
Kapitel *n (fin)* budget code
Karenzzeit *f (ins)* waiting period
Kargo *m* cargo, freight
Kargoversicherung *f* cargo [sea freight] insurance, *(Am)* ocean freight insurance
Karte *f* card *(index etc.)*; ticket *(railway, bus etc.)*; map
Kartei *f* card-index; card filling system
Karteikarte *f* index-card, filing-card, file-card
Karteikasten *m* filing box [drawer], card-index box [drawer]
Kartell *n* cartel, ring, *(Am)* trust ◊ **ein ~ auflösen** to dissolve a cartel; **ein ~ bilden** to form a cartel, *(Am)* to cartelize; **ein ~ entflechten** to decartelize; **sich einem ~ anschließen** to join a cartel
~, **horizontales** horizontal cartel
~, **internationales** international cartel
~, **vertikales** vertical cartel
Kartellabkommen *n* cartel agreement
Kartellabsprache *f* cartel arrangement
Kartellaufsicht *f* control [supervision] of cartels; office for the control [supervision] of cartels
Kartellaußenseiter *m* outsider (of a cartel)
Kartellbestimmungen *fpl* cartel rules
Kartellbeteiligung *f* cartel participation
Kartellbildung *f* formation of cartel
Kartellentflechtung *f* decartelization
Kartellgesetz *n* cartel act [law], act [law] to control cartels
Kartellgesetzgebung *f* legislation on cartels, *(Am)* anti-trust laws [legislation]

kartellieren to form *(industries, firms etc.)* into a cartel, to bring *(market, production of raw material, manufacture of goods etc.)* under the control of a cartel; to cartelize
Kartellierung *f* cartelization
Kartellkonvention *f* international agreement on cartels
Kartellmanipulation *f* cartel manipulation
Kartellmitglied *n* member of a cartel
Kartellpolitik *f* (government's) policy on cartels
Kartellpreis *m* price fixed by a cartel
~, gebundener fixed cartel price
Kartellquote *f* (production) quota of a member of a cartel
Kartellrecht *n* cartel law
Kartellverbot *n* ban on cartels
Kartellvereinbarung *f* cartel agreement [arrangement], contract in restraint of trade
Kartellverordnung *f* decree to control cartels, cartel decree
Kartellvertrag *m* cartel contract
Kartellvorschriften *fpl* cartel regulations
Kartellwesen *n* cartel system, cartels
Kartenausgabe *f* booking office, *(Am)* ticket window
Kasko *m* hull (of ship)
Kaskopolice *f* hull insurance policy, comprehensive insurance policy
Kasko-Teilversicherung *f* limited comprehensive insurance
Kasko- und Gepäckversicherung *f* comprehensive and luggage insurance
Kaskoversicherung *f* comprehensive (vehicle) insurance; insurance on hull *(ship)*
~ mit Selbstbeteiligung comprehensive insurance with part-contribution
~ ohne Selbstbeteiligung comprehensive insurance without part-contribution
Kasko-Vollversicherung *f* complete comprehensive insurance
Kassa *f* 1. cash; 2. cashier's counter [desk]
⋄ **gegen ~** for (ready) cash; **per ~ bezahlen** to pay in cash
Kassaabzug *m* cash discount
Kassaanweisung *f* cash order
Kassabuch *n* cash book
~, kleines petty cash book
Kassadiskont *m* cash discount
Kassafrist *f* time within which cash payment must be made
Kassafuß *m* cash value *(of currencies with fluctuating exchange rates)*
Kassageschäft *n* cash transaction [operation, sale], cash [ready money] business
Kassakauf *m* cash purchase, buying for cash
Kassakäufer *m* cash buyer [purchaser]
Kassakonto *n* petty cash account

Kassakurs *m* spot quotation [price] *(stocks, securities)*; spot rate *(currencies)*
Kassalieferung *f* spot delivery
Kassamarkt *m* spot market
Kassaobligationen *fpl* medium-term bonds, medium-term debenture bonds, cash bonds
Kassaorder *f* cash order
Kassaposten *m* cash item [entry]
Kassapreis *m* cash price
Kassaverkauf *m* cash sale
Kassawerte *mpl* securities dealt on the spot market
Kassazahlung *f* cash payment
Kasse *f* cash-box, petty cash-box *(in office)*, till *(in shop)*, cash [pay] desk *(in shop, restaurant etc.)*; *(bank)* cashier's desk, *(railw)* booking office, box office *(theatre)* ⋄ **an der ~** at the cash-desk *(supermarket etc.)*; at the counter [window] *(bank etc.)*; at the box office *(cinema, theatre etc.)*; **die ~ abschließen** 1. to count the receipts; 2. to lock the cash-box; **die ~ führen** to be in charge of the cash, to act as cashier, to keep the cash; **die ~ schließen** to close the counter; **gegen ~** *s.* **gegen Kassa**; **gegen ~ kaufen** to buy for cash, to buy cash down; **gegen ~ verkaufen** to sell for cash, to sell cash down; **gegen sofortige ~** prompt [spot] cash; **~ machen** to balance the cash
~, auszahlende paying office
~ bei Lieferung cash on delivery (c.o.d.)
~ gegen Dokumente cash against documents
Kassekonto *n* cash account
Kassenabschluß *m* closing [balancing] of cash accounts
Kassenabwicklung *f* winding up [*(Am)* wind-up] of cash accounts
Kassenanweisung *f* cash order; *(fin)* treasury bill
Kassenarzt *m* panel doctor
Kassenausgänge *mpl* cash disbursements
Kassenauszahlung *f* cash disbursement, outward payment
Kassenbarbestand *m* ready cash balance
Kassenbeleg *m* cash voucher
Kassenbericht *m* cash report
Kassenbestand *m* 1. cash in hand, cash balance; 2. planned surplus in a budget
Kassenbilanz *f* cash balance sheet
Kassenbon *m* sales slip, *(Am)* sales check
Kassenbote *m* bank-messenger
Kassenbuch *n* cashbook
Kassenbucheintragung *f* cashbook entry
Kassenbuchung *f s.* **Kasseneintragung**
Kassendefizit *n* cash deficit; adverse cash balance *(bookkeeping)*
Kassendifferenz *f* cash balance *(surplus or deficit)*

Kasseneingänge *mpl s.* **Kasseneinnahme**
Kasseneinnahme *f* cash receipts, takings
Kasseneintragung *f* cash entry
Kasseneinzahlung *f* inward payment in cash
Kassenendbestand *m* final cash balance
Kassenfehlbetrag *m* cash deficit
Kassenführer *m* cashier
Kassenführung *f* cash management, cash keeping; treasurership *(party etc.)*
Kassengeschäft *n* cash transaction [operation, sale], cash [ready money] business
Kassenkauf *m* cash buying [purchase]
Kassenkonto *n s.* **Kassekonto**
Kassenkontrolle *f* cash audit
Kassenkredit *m* cash credit [advance]
Kassenleistung *f* benefit paid by the social insurance
Kassenlimit *n* cash limit
Kassenmanko *n s.* **Kassenfehlbetrag**
Kassenobligation *f* medium-term bond, medium-term debenture bond, cash bond *(Swiss Bank)*
Kassenordnung *f* finance regulations
Kassenpatient *m* social insurance patient
Kassenplan *m* cash plan; *(ins)* plan of budgetary relations *(between budget and insurance institutions quarterly)*
Kassenplanbestand *m* planned cash money
Kassenplanung *f* cash planning
Kassenpreis *m* cash price
Kassenprotokoll *n* cash register *(of daily takings and broken down according to various denominations)*
Kassenprüfer *m* auditor
Kassenprüfung *f* auditing
Kassenquittung *f* sales slip [*(Am)* check]
Kassenrabatt *m s.* **Kassadiskont**
Kassenraum *m* cashier's counter [hall]; counter room *(bank etc.)*
Kassenreserve *f* cash reserve, reserve in cash
Kassenrevision *f* cash audit
Kassenrevisor *m* cash auditor
Kassensaldo *m* cash balance
Kassenschalter *m (railw)* booking office; box office *(theatre)*; *(post)* counter; *(bank)* cashier's desk [counter]
Kassenscheck *m* open [uncrossed] cheque
Kassenschein *m (com)* receipt; *(fin)* treasury bill
Kassenschrank *m* safe
Kassenstunden *fpl* business hours, opening hours of booking [box, paying] office
Kassensturz *m* cash checking, counting one's cash ⋄ **~ machen** to carry out an audit of the cash accounts; spot check of cash (in hand)
Kassenüberschuß *m* cash surplus, surplus [excess] cash; cash over
Kassenübersicht *f* cash balance sheet

Kassenumsatz *m* cash turnover
Kassenverkehr *m* over the counter business [transactions]
Kassenverwalter *m* cashier, cash clerk; treasurer *(party, organization etc.)*
Kassenvorschuß *m* cash advance
Kassenwart *m* treasurer *(association etc.)*
Kassenzettel *m* sales slip, *(Am)* cash check
kassieren 1. to cash, to take (in) *(money from customer etc.)*; to collect *(contributions, money due etc.)*; 2. to confiscate, to take away; 3. *(jur)* to annul, to cancel, to make void *(judgement, decision etc.)*; to rescind *(document)*
Kassierer *m (bank)* cashier; dues collector, treasurer *(organization, club etc.)*; *(railw)* booking clerk; box office clerk *(theatre etc.)*
Kassierung *f* collection *(money, contribution, member fees etc.)*
Katalog *m* catalogue
~, **alphabetischer** alphabetic(al) catalogue
~, **systematischer** subject catalogue
Kataloggeschäft *n* catalogue [mail-order] sale, mail-order business ⋄ **durch ~** by mail order
katalogisieren to catalogue *(books, commodities etc.)*
Katalognummer *f* catalogue number
Katalogpreis *m* catalogue price
Kataster *m/n* land register, cadastre
Katasteramt *n* land registry office
Katasterauszug *m* extract from the land register
Katasterfläche *f* (registered) land area
Katasterkarte *f* cadastral map
katastermäßig cadastral
Katastersteuer *f* cadastral tax [levy]
katastrieren to register *(land property etc.)*, to enter on the land register
Katastrophe *f* disaster, catastrophe
Katastrophenbekämpfung *f* disaster relief activities
Katastropheneinsatz *m* disaster operation
Katastrophengebiet *n* disaster area ⋄ **zum ~ erklären** to declare (region) as a disaster area
Katastrophengefahr *f* disaster risk
Katastrophenrisiko *n (ins)* disaster risk
Katastrophenrückstellung *f (ins)* disaster reserve fund
Katastrophenschaden *m* disaster loss
Katastrophenschutz *m* protection against disasters
Katastrophenwagnis *n (ins)* disaster [catastrophe] risk
Kategorie *f* category; class; concept
~, **historische** historical category
~, **ökonomische** economic category
~, **soziale** social category
kategorisieren to categorize, to classify
Kategorisierung *f* categorization, classification

Kauf *m* purchase, purchasing, buying; bargain ◊ **durch ~** by purchase; **einen ~ abschließen** to complete a purchase; to close a bargain; **einen ~ tätigen** to effect [negotiate, make] a purchase; to strike a bargain; **etwas mit in ~ nehmen** to put up with s.th., to take s.th. into the bargain; **von einem ~ zurücktreten** to withdraw an offer to buy; **zum ~ anbieten** to offer for sale
~ **auf Abruf** purchase on call
~ **auf Abzahlung** hire purchase; purchase by instalments, instalment purchase, deferred payment system
~ **auf Baisse** *(st.ex.)* purchase for a fall
~ **auf Besicht** purchase on inspection
~ **auf Hausse** *(st.ex.)* purchase for a rise
~ **auf Kredit** purchase on account
~ **auf Lieferung** purchase for future delivery; forward purchase
~ **auf Probe** purchase as per sample [on approval]
~ **auf Rechnung** purchase on account
~ **auf Voranmeldung** purchase after registration [on waiting list]
~ **auf Wechsel** purchase on bill of exchange
~ **auf Zeit** forward purchase, purchase on credit, time bargain *(securities etc.)*; forward exchange *(currency)*
~ **auf Ziel** *(st.ex.)* fixed term purchase
~ **aus erster Hand** first-hand purchase
~ **aus zweiter Hand** second-hand purchase
~, **fingierter** sham purchase
~ **gegen bar** cash purchase
~, **günstiger** (good) bargain
~, **guter** (good) bargain, good buy
~ **mit Rückgaberecht** purchase with right of return
~ **nach Muster** purchase according to sample
~ **nach Probe** purchase after a trial run
~, **schlechter** a bad buy; a bad bargain
~, **teurer** expensive purchase
~ **und Verkauf** *m* buying and selling
~ **unter Eigentumsvorbehalt** conditional sale
Kaufabneigung *f* resistance to buy(ing), consumer resistance
Kaufabschluß *m* conclusion of a purchase contract ◊ **beim ~** at the time of purchase, when making the purchasing contract; **einen ~ tätigen** to conclude a purchasing contract
Kaufandrang *m* buying pressure
Kaufangebot *n* offer to buy; bid
Kaufanlaß *m s.* **Kaufmotiv**
Kaufanweisung *f s.* **Kaufauftrag**
Kaufauftrag *m* buying order
kaufbar purchasable
Kaufbedingungen *fpl* terms [conditions] of purchase

Kaufbereitschaft *f* consumer acceptance
Kaufbestimmungen *fpl s.* **Kaufbedingungen**
Kaufbrief *m (jur, com)* deed of purchase; title deed *(for real estate)*; bill of sale *(for ships)*
kaufen to buy, to purchase ◊ **billig ~** to buy cheap, to make a bargain; **etwas alt ~** *s.* **etwas gebraucht ~**; **etwas gebraucht ~** to buy s.th. second-hand; **etwas neu ~** to buy s.th. new; **fertig ~** to buy ready-made; **fest ~** *(st.ex.)* to buy firm; **teuer ~** to pay a high price
Käufer *m* buyer, purchaser; customer; taker *(at auction etc.)*; *(jur)* vendee
~ **aus zweiter Hand** second-hand buyer
~ **beim Räumungsverkauf** buyer at clearance sale
~, **bösgläubiger** mala fide buyer
~, **gutgläubiger** buyer [purchaser] in good faith
~, **möglicher** potential buyer [purchaser, customer]
~, **ortsansässiger** resident buyer
~, **umsichtiger** discriminating buyer
~, **ungenannter** undisclosed buyer [purchaser, customer]
Käufergruppe *f* customer group
Käuferland *n* buying country; buyer's country
Käufermarkt *m* buyer's market
Käuferrecht *n* purchaser's right(s)
Käuferschicht *f* class of buyers
Käuferstreik *m* buyer's strike
Kauffahrer *m* 1. *s.* **Kauffahrteischiff**; 2. master [owner] of a trading vessel
Kauffahrtei *f* maritime trade [trading]
Kauffahrteiflotte *f* trading [merchant] fleet
Kauffahrteischiff *n* merchantman, merchant ship [vessel]
Kauffahrteischiffahrt *f s.* **Kauffahrtei**
Kauffonds *m* disposable income
~ **der Bevölkerung** disposable income of the population
Kaufgegenstand *m* article to be bought [purchased]
Kaufgeld *n* purchase money
Kaufgelegenheit *f* opportunity to buy
Kaufgenehmigung *f* permission to buy [to purchase]
Kaufgesuch *n* offer to buy
Kaufgewohnheiten *fpl* buying habits
Kaufhalle *f* supermarket
Kaufhallenverband *m* association of supermarkets
Kaufhandlung *f* purchasing, buying
Kaufhaus *n* department(al) store
Kaufhemmung *f* buyer's resistance
Kaufinteresse *n* inclination to buy
Kaufinteressent *m* prospective purchaser, potential buyer

Kaufkontingent *n* buying [purchase] quota
Kaufkontrakt *m s.* **Kaufvertrag**
Kaufkraft *f* purchasing power *(money)*; spending power *(consumer)* ◊ **überschüssige ~ abschöpfen** to absorb surplus spending power
~ der Bevölkerung spending power of the population
~ des Geldes purchasing power of money
~, nominelle nominal purchasing power
~, überschüssige surplus spending power
kaufkräftig able to buy, well-funded; with purchasing power *(money)*; with spending power *(consumer)*
Kaufkraftindex *m* index of purchasing power
Kaufkraftlenkung *f* steering of spending power
Kaufkraftparität *f* purchasing power parity
Kaufkraftschwund *m* dwindling of purchasing power
Kaufkraftüberhang *m* excessive spending power
Kaufkraftvergleich *m* comparison of purchasing [spending] power
Kaufkraftverschlechterung *f* deterioration of the purchasing value of money
Kaufkraftwert *m s.* **Kaufkraft**
Kaufkurs *m* buying rate
Kaufladen *m* shop, store
käuflich purchasable, available for sale; open to bribery, venal, corruptible ◊ **~ erwerben** to buy, to acquire by purchase; **~ überlassen** to sell
Kauflust *f* inclination to buy; *(st.ex.)* buoyancy ◊ **die ~ hat nachgelassen** buying has fallen off
~, fallende falling buying
~, geringe little activity among buyers, little buying
~, steigende wave of selling
Kaufmann *m* businessman; merchant, wholesaler; retailer, grocer, shopkeeper, storekeeper; commercial clerk
kaufmännisch commercial, business
Kaufmannsgehilfe *m* commercial clerk; shop-assistant
Kaufmannskapital *n* commercial capital
Kaufmannslehre *f* commercial apprenticeship
Kaufmannslehrling *m* commercial apprentice
Kaufmittel *n* purchasing medium
Kaufmotiv *n* motive for buying
Kaufmuster *n* sample
Kaufneigung *f* propensity to buy
Kaufnota *f (st.ex.)* bought note; *(com)* sales note
Kaufnote *f s.* **Kaufnota**
Kaufobjekt *n s.* **Kaufgegenstand**
Kaufoption *f* option to buy
Kauforder *f (st.ex.)* buying [purchasing] order
Kaufort *m* place of purchase
Kaufpotential *n s.* **Kaufkraft**

Kaufpreis *m* purchase price ◊ **den ~ zurückerstatten** to refund the purchase price
Kaufpreisminderung *f* purchase price reduction
Kaufrecht *n* right of purchase
Kaufsumme *f* purchase price; purchase money
Kaufunlust *f* disinclination to buy, consumers' resistance
Kaufurkunde *f* deed of purchase; title deed *(real estate)*; bill of sale *(ships)*
Kaufvereinbarung *f* sales agreement
Kaufvertrag *m* contract of purchase, sales [purchase] contract; deed of purchase; title deed *(real estate)*; bill of sale *(ships)* ◊ **~ mit Eigentumsvorbehalt** conditional sales agreement; **vom ~ zurücktreten** to rescind a sales contract
Kaufwert *m* purchase value
kaufwillig prepared [willing] to buy
Kaufwunsch *m* inclination to buy
Kaufzentrum *n* shopping centre
Kaufzwang *m* obligation to buy ◊ **kein ~** free inspection invited
Kaution *f* money [securities] deposited as a guarantee; *(jur)* surety, security, guarantee; bail *(for release of prisoner)* ◊ **gegen ~** against security; on bail; **gegen ~ freigelassen** to be let out on bail; **gegen ~ freilassen** to release on bail; **~ hinterlegen** to provide security [surety]; to furnish [put up] a guarantee; **~ leisten** to pay a guarantee; **~ stellen** to give security; **~ verlangen** to ask for security [surety]; **~ zulassen** to grant bail
~, hinterlegte caution money
~, hohe ample bail
Kautionseffekten *pl* securities deposited as a guarantee
kautionsfähig able to provide security [surety]; *(jur)* competent to stand bail
Kautionshypothek *f* mortgage given as security
Kautionskredit *m* collateral loan
kautionspflichtig liable to provide security [surety]; *(jur)* liable to stand bail
Kautionsstellung *f (com)* depositing of security; depositing of money [securities] as a guarantee; *(jur)* provision of security [surety]
Kautionssumme *f* (amount of) security [surety]; sum deposited as a guarantee; *(jur)* (amount of) bail
Kautionsversicherung *f* fidelity insurance *(against default of employee)*
Kautionswechsel *m* security bill, bill of exchange given as security
Kehrwert *m* reciprocal value
Keim *m* seeds *(discord etc.)*; germ *(life etc.)*
Keller *m (bank)* vault; cellar
Kellermeister *m* head cellarman *(brewery)*; cellar manager *(hotel)*

Kellerwechsel *m* fictitious [accommodation] bill, kite
Kellner *m* waiter; steward *(ship)*
Kenndaten *pl* characteristic data, specific details
Kenner *m* authority; expert *(in field of knowledge)*; connoisseur *(in matters of taste)*
Kenngröße *f* characteristic measurement; *(maths)* characteristic quantity
Kennkarte *f* identity card
kenntlich:

⋄ ~ **machen** to label, to mark; to identify, to distinguish
Kenntlichmachung *f* labelling, marking; identification
Kenntnis *f* knowledge *(of facts etc.)*; information *(on s.th.)*; perception, awareness *(of situation etc.)*; notice, awareness *(of statement etc.)*
⋄ **etwas zur ~ nehmen** to note s.th., to take note [notice] of s.th.; **jmdn. in ~ setzen** to inform [advise, notify] s.o.; **jmdn. von etwas in ~ setzen** to inform s.o. of s.th.; **keine ~ (von etwas) haben** to know nothing (of s.th.); **sich ~ verschaffen über etwas** to obtain information on s.th.; **~ von etwas haben** to have information on s.th., to be informed on s.th.; **zu Ihrer gefälligen ~** for your kind attention; **zur ~** for information, for the attention of *(s.o.)*; **zur ~ und weiteren Veranlassung** for information and further action
Kenntnisnahme *f* taking notice, noting of s.th.
Kenntnisniveau *n* level of knowledge
Kenntnisse *fpl* knowledge; information; attainments, accomplishments, skills; know-how
⋄ **besondere ~ nicht erforderlich** special knowledge not required; **~ aneignen** to acquire knowledge; **~ anhäufen** to accumulate knowledge; **~ erweitern** to widen knowledge; **~ erwerben** to acquire knowledge
~, geringe small stock of knowledge
~, gründliche thorough [profound] knowledge
~, oberflächliche superficial knowledge
~, technische technical knowledge
~, umfassende all-round [comprehensive] knowledge
Kennummer *f* reference [identification] number
Kennwort *n* reference *(in letter)*
Kennzahl *f* index figure; indicator; *(com)* code number; *(maths)* characteristic; index *(of logarithm)*; exchange number *(teleprinter)*
Kennzahlen *fpl*:
~ der Arbeitsleistung indicators of performance
Kennzeichen *n* (distinguishing/identifying) mark [feature]; characteristic; hall-mark *(indicating genuineness, especially of gold and silver articles etc.)*; keynote *(speech etc.)*; *(agric)* brand *(on cattle etc.)*, earmark *(on pigs etc.)*; identification *(birds etc.)*; registration (number) *(vehicle)*
~, polizeiliches registration [*(Am)* license] number
Kennzeichen *npl*:
~, besondere particular characteristics
kennzeichnen to mark (out), to characterize, to distinguish; to typify; to label *(goods etc.)*; *(agric)* to brand *(cattle etc.)*, to earmark *(pigs etc.)*; to identify *(birds etc.)*
Kennzeichnung *f* marking; *(d.pr.)* qualification
Kennzeichnungspflicht *f* compulsory identification
Kennziffer *f* index, indicator; index number [figure]; *(d.pr.)* key number
~, erzeugnisbezogene product index
~, fondsbezogene index [indicator] related to a fund
~, industriezweigtypische typical branch indicator [index]
~, ökonomische economic indicator [index]
~, quantitative quantitative indicator [index] *(related to the quantity of goods or commodities and expressed in kilos, metres etc.)*
~, statistische statistical indicator
~, synthetische aggregate indicator
~, technisch-wirtschaftliche technological and economic index *(quantified and precisely defined technological and economic indicator, e.g. volume of commodity production in currency units, steel production in metric tons etc.)*
Kennziffern *fpl*:
~, absolute indices [indicators] in absolute value *(output per year etc.)*
~, analytische analytical indices [indicators]
~, betriebliche enterprise [firm] indices [indicators]
~ der Arbeitskräfte und des Lohnes indices [indexes, indicators] of labour force and wages
~ der Entwicklung des Lebensniveaus index numbers of standard of living
~ der Finanzen indices [indicators] of finance
~ der materiellen Stimulierung indices [indicators] of material incentives
~, finanzielle financial indices [indicators]
~, materielle material indices [indicators]
~, personelle personal indices [indicators]
~, qualitative qualitative indices [indicators]
~, relative index numbers [figures]; relative indices [indicators] *(of the relative level compared with 100)*
~, technisch-ökonomische technological-economic indices [indicators]
~, territoriale regional indices [indicators]
~, verantwortungsbereichsbezogene indices [indicators] related to the field of responsibility *(ministry, district etc.)*

~, **volkswirtschaftliche** national economic indices [indicators]
~, **vorhaben- bzw. aufgabenbezogene** project indices [indicators], indices [indicators] related to a project
~, **wertmäßige** value indices [indicators]
~, **zweigliche** s. ~, zweigspezifische
~, **zweigspezifische** sectoral [branch] indices [indicators]
Kennziffernkomplex *m* set of indices
Kennziffernnomenklatur *f* classification of indices [indicators] *(for planning, accounting etc.)*
Kennziffernprogramm *n* list of indicators
Kennziffernpyramide *f* pyramid of indicators [indices]
Kennziffernsystem *n* system of indicators [indices]
Kennziffernsystematik *f* classification of indicators [indices]
Keramikindustrie *f* ceramics industry
Kerammaler und -dekorierer *m* ceramics painter
Kern *m* nucleus *(party etc.)*, core *(team etc.)*; heart *(city etc.)*; essence *(argument etc.)*
Kernenergie *f* nuclear [atomic] energy
Kernforschung *f* nuclear research
Kernkraft *f* nuclear force; nuclear power
Kernkraftwerk *n* nuclear power plant [station]
Kette *f* chain; bond, fetter; string, train *(followers)*; sequence, succession *(ideas, events)*
~, **Markoff'sche** *(stats)* Markoff chain
Kettengeschäft *n* chain store
Kettenhandel *m* middleman trade, chain transaction
Kettenindex *m* chain index
Kettenladen s. **Kettengeschäft**
Kettenwirkung *f* chain reaction
Kinderabteilung *f* children's department *(store etc.)*
Kinderarbeit *f* child labour
Kinderbedarf *m* articles for children
Kinderbeihilfe *f* maternity allowance *(a lump sum paid by the state at the birth of every child)*
Kinderbekleidung *f* children's wear
Kindereinrichtung *f* facility for children *(crèche, kindergarten, children's home etc.)*
Kinderermäßigung *f* allowance for children *(in income tax assessment)*; reduction for children *(fare etc.)*
Kinderernährung *f* infant feeding
Kindererziehung *f* education [upbringing] of children
Kinderferiengestaltung *f* organization of vacation for children *(in holiday camps etc.)*
Kinderferienheim *n* holiday home for children
Kinderferienlager *n* children's holiday camp

Kinderfreibetrag *m* non-taxable allowance for children
Kinderfürsorge *f* child welfare (centre)
Kindergarten *m* kindergarten, nursery (school)
Kindergeld *n* children's allowance *(paid monthly by the state for every child up to the age of 18 at different rates according to the number of children)*
Kinderheim *n* children's home, orphanage
Kinderkrippe *f* crèche
kinderreich having many children
Kindersterblichkeit *f* infant mortality
Kindertagesstätte *f* day nursery
Kinderzuschlag *m* children's allowance
klagbar actionable *(matter, statement etc.)*; suable *(claim, debt etc.)*
Klagbarkeit *f* actionability *(matter, statement etc.)*; admissibility for legal action *(claim, debt etc.)*
Klage *f* complaint; *(jur)* legal action; suit ◊ **eine ~ anstrengen** to bring [enter] an action *(against s.o.)*, to take [institute] legal proceedings *(against s.o.)*; to sue *(s.o.)*; **eine ~ begründen** to make out a case; to substantiate a claim; **eine ~ einreichen** to lodge [make] a formal complaint; to file a petition [suit]; **eine ~ führen über** to complain about; **eine ~ zurücknehmen** to withdraw an action; **einer ~ stattgeben** to substain an action
~ **auf Erfüllung des Vertrages** action for specific performance of contract
~ **auf Schadenersatz** action [suit] for damages
~ **auf Unterhalt** maintenance suit
~ **auf Zahlung** action for payment
~ **wegen Vertragsverletzung** action for breach of contract
Klageabweisung *f* dismissal of an action [suit]
Klageandrohung *f* threat of legal action
Klageanspruch *m* plaintiff's claim
Klageantrag *m* plaintiff's application for relief
Klagebeantwortung *f* answer to a charge
Klagebefugnis *f* right of action
Klagebegründung *f* making out a case, substantiation of a claim
Klageerhebungsfrist *f* time limit for plaintiff's action
Klagefrist *f* plaintiff's actionable time
Klagegegenstand *m* subject of an action [suit]
Klagegrund *m* grounds [cause] for complaint
klagen to complain; *(jur)* to sue in court, to institute legal proceedings
Kläger *m* accuser; *(jur)* plaintiff, complainant; petitioner *(divorce)*; private prosecutor
Klagerecht *n* right of action
Klagerücknahme *f* discontinuance of an action
Klagesache *f* lawsuit, action
Klageschrift *f* statement of claim

Klageweg *m*:
⋄ **auf dem ~** by bringing [entering] an action
Klagezustellung *f* service of the statement of claim (to defendant)
klarieren to clear a ship at the customs-house
Klarierer *m* ship-broker who arranges clearance of ship
Klarierung *f* clearance of a ship at the customs--house
Klarierungsbrief *m s.* **Klarierungsschein**
Klarierungsschein *m* certificate of clearance (of ship), clearance certificate (of ship)
Klasse *f* class; category; grade; group ⋄ **zu einer ~ gehören** to belong to a class
~, arbeitende working class
~, besitzende property-owning class *(primarily the means of production)*
~, einseitig offene *(stats)* open-ended class
~, halboffene *s.* **~, einseitig offene**
~, herrschende ruling class
~, nicht arbeitende non-working class
~, privilegierte privileged class
~, vollständige *(stats)* complete class
Klassen *fpl*:
⋄ **nach ~ sortieren** to classify *(goods according to features etc.)*
Klassenantagonismus *m* class antagonism
Klassenauseinandersetzung *f* class struggle
klassenbewußt class conscious
Klassenbewußtsein *n* class consciousness
Klassenbeziehungen *fpl* class relations
Klasseneinteilung *f* division into classes
Klassengegensatz *m s.* **Klassenantagonismus**
Klassengesellschaft *f* class society
Klassenhäufigkeit *f (stats)* cell frequency
Klassenherrschaft *f* class rule
Klasseninteresse *n* class interest
Klassenkampf *m* class struggle
Klassenmitte *f (stats)* class mark
Klassenstandpunkt *m* class standpoint
Klassenstruktur *f* class structure
~ der Gesellschaft class structure of society
Klassenunterschied *m* class distinction; class difference, difference between classes
Klassenzugehörigkeit *f* belonging to a class
Klassifikation *f* classification
~, allgemeine general classification
Klausel *f* clause; condition, stipulation, proviso
⋄ **eine ~ in einen Vertrag aufnehmen** to insert a clause in a contract; **eine ~ in einen Vertrag einfügen** to embody a clause in a treaty; to add a clause to a contract [an agreement]
~, eingefügte inserted clause
~, einschränkende restrictive clause
~, handelsübliche customary clause
~, übliche common clause

Klausurtagung *f* closed meeting [conference], private session
Klaviermacher *m* piano-maker
Kleidergeld *n* clothing allowance
Kleinaktie *f* low par-value share, baby share
Kleinaktionär *m* small shareholder [*(Am)* stockholder]
Kleinanzeige *f* small [classified] advertisement, 'small ad'
Kleinarbeit *f* painstaking work
Kleinautomatisierung *f* small-scale automation
Kleinbahn *f* light [minor, narrow gauge] railway
Kleinbauer *m* smallholder, small farmer
kleinbäuerlich smallholding
Kleinbauernhof *m* smallholding, small farm
Kleinbetrieb *m* small enterprise [firm]; *(agric)* small farm, smallholding
Kleinbürger *m* lower middle-class person, petty bourgeois
kleinbürgerlich lower middle-class, petty bourgeois
Kleinbürgertum *n* lower middle-class, petty bourgeoisie
Kleineisenwaren *fpl* ironmongery
Kleinfamilie *f* nuclear [small] family
Kleingarten *m* allotment garden
Kleingärtner *m* allotment-holder
Kleingeld *n* small change; coins
kleingestückelt of low denomination
Kleingewässer *n* small stretch [bodies] of water, small waters; small pool [pond, lake]
Kleingewerbe *n* small-scale trade [business] ⋄ **ein ~ betreiben** to carry on a small trade [business]
Kleingewerbetreibender *m* person carrying on a small trade [business]
Kleingutverkehr *m* parcel post
Kleinhandel *m* retail trade
Kleinhandelsbetrieb *m* retail shop [*(Am)* store]
Kleinhandelspreis *m* retail price
Kleinhandelsrabatt *m* retail discount
Kleinhandelsverkauf *m* retail sale
Kleinhändler *m* retailer
Kleinindustrie *f* cottage [small] industry
Kleininvestitionen *fpl* small-scale investments
Kleinkredit *m* small loan
Kleinmaterial *n* low-value material(s)
Kleinmechanisierung *f* small-scale mechanization
Kleinproduktion *f* small-scale production
~, industrielle small-scale production in industry, small-scale industrial production
~, landwirtschaftliche small-scale production in agriculture, small-scale agricultural production
Kleinrechner *m* mini-computer, small computer
Kleinserienfertigung *f* small batch production
Kleinsparer *m* small saver

Kleinstadt *f* small town
Kleinstbetrag *m* very small amount
Kleintier *n* small domestic animal
Kleintierzucht *f* breeding of small domestic animals
Kleinunternehmen *n* small business
Kleinverbraucher *m* small-scale consumer
Kleinverkauf *m* retail trade
Kleinvieh *n* small farm animals, small livestock
Kleinware *f* hardware
Kleinzeitverfahren *n* methods time measurement
Klempner und Installateur *m* plumber and gasfitter
klimabeständig unaffected by climatic conditions *(material etc.)*
Klimabeständigkeit *f* ability to withstand different climatic conditions *(material etc.)*
Klimafaktor *m* climatic factor *(food production etc.)*
Klimaprüfung *f* test to withstand different climatic conditions *(materials etc.)*
Klimaschutzzeichen *n* climate quality mark *(for ability of products to withstand different climatic conditions)*
Klumpen *m (stats)* cluster
~ **in letzter Ordnung** *(stats)* ultimate cluster
~ **in numerierten Einheiten** *(stats)* serial cluster
~ **in weiterer Nachbarschaft liegender Einheiten** *(stats)* quasi-compact cluster
~ **in zusammenhängenden Einheiten** *(stats)* compact cluster
~ **in zusammenhängenden Einheiten mit eingeschränktem Wertebereich** *(stats)* patch, contour level
Klumpenauswahl *f (stats)* cluster sample
Klumpenauswahlverfahren *n (stats)* cluster sample
Klumpenstichprobe *f (stats)* cluster, sampling
Knappheit *f* shortage, scarcity *(provisions etc.)*; narrowness *(in lead in R & D etc.)*; conciseness *(account, speech etc.)*
Knappschaft *f* 1. miners' fraternity [society, guild]; 2. miners' and employees' insurance fund
Knappschaftskasse *f* miner's insurance fund
Knappschaftsrente *f* miners' pension
Knappschaftsversicherung *f* miners' insurance
Knechtschaft *f* servitude; slavery; bondage
koalieren to form a coalition *(parties etc.)*; to unite, to combine
Koalition *f* coalition *(parties etc.)*; association, combination *(workers, employees etc.)*
Koalitionsbildung *f* formation of a coalition *(parties etc.)*
Koalitionsgespräche *npl* coalition talks

Koalitionspartei *f* coalition party
Koalitionsrecht *n* right of combination *(workers, employees etc.)*
Koalitionsregierung *f* coalition government
Koalitionsverhandlung *f* negotiation on forming a coalition (government)
Koch *m* cook
kochfertig ready-to-cook *(food)*
Kode *m* code
Kodegruppe *f (d.pr.)* code group
Kodeprüfung *f (d.pr.)* code check
Kodestruktur *f (d.pr.)* code structure
Kodeübersetzer *m (d.pr.)* code translator
Kodeumsetzer *m (d.pr.)* code converter
Kodeumsetzung *f (d.pr.)* code conversion
Kodeumwandlung *f (d.pr.)* code translation
Kodewort *n* code word
Kodex *m* code *(of conduct for multinationals etc.)*
kodieren to code, to encode
Kodieren *n* coding
Kodierer *m* coder
Kodierung *f s.* **Kodieren**
Kodifikation *f (jur)* codification
kodifizieren *(jur)* to codify (a law)
Koeffizient *m* coefficient
~ **der totalen Bestimmtheit** *(stats)* coefficient of total determination
~ **des direkten Aufwandes** coefficient of direct inputs
~ **des vollen Aufwandes** coefficient of total inputs *(direct and indirect)*
Koeffizientenmatrix *f* coefficient matrix
Koeffizientenmethode *f* coefficient method
Koexistenz *f* co-existence
~, **friedliche** peaceful co-existence
Kohlenbergbau *m* coal mining
Kohlenbergwerk *n* coal mine
Kohlenversorgung *f* supply of coal
Kohlevorkommen *n* coal deposit
Kohorte *f (stats)* cohort
Kokillengießer *m* die caster
Kollege *m* colleague
Kollegin *f s.* **Kollege**
Kollegium *n* council, committee, board
~ **der Rechtsanwälte** lawyers' group *(co-operative institution of practising lawyers, i.a., organizes social and technical work of members of the group)*
Kollektion *f* collection, range; selection, assortment
Kollektiv *n* collective, co-operative unit; work team
~, **irreguläres** *(stats)* irregular collective
Kollektivabschreibung *f* depreciation of groups of machines
Kollektivaussteller *m* collective exhibitor
Kollektivausstellung *f* collective display

Kollektivbewußtsein *n* collective consciousness
Kollektiveigentum *n* collective property; collective ownership
Kollektiventscheidung *f* collective decision
Kollektiverziehung *f* education of the individual by the collective
Kollektivgeist *m* collective spirit [mind]
kollektivieren to collectivize
Kollektivierung *f* collectivization
~ **der Landwirtschaft** collectivization of agriculture
Kollektivinteresse *n* collective interest
Kollektivität *f* collectivity, collectiveness
Kollektivprokura *f* joint power of attorney
Kollektivstand *m* group stand
Kollektivverpflichtung *f* collective undertaking
Kollektivversicherung *f* group insurance
Kollektivvertrag *m* collective agreement
Kollektivvollmacht *f* joint power of attorney
Kollektivwerbung *f* collective advertising
Kollektivwettbewerb *m* collective emulation [competition]
Kollektivwirtschaft *f* collective farming; collective farm
Kollision *f* collision; clash *(opinions, interests etc.)*; conflict *(laws, rules etc.)*
Kolonialbesitz *m* colonial possessions
Kolonialgebiet *n* colonial territory
Kolonialhandel *m* colonial trade
Kolonialherrschaft *f* colonial rule
Kolonialismus *m* colonialism
Kolonialmacht *f* colonial power
Kolonialpolitik *f* colonial policy
Kolonialregierung *f* colonial government
Kolonialsystem *n* colonial system
Kolonie *f* colony
Kolonisierung *f* colonization
~, **kulturelle** cultural colonization
Kombinat *n* trust, combine ⋄ **ein** ~ **leiten** to run [be in charge of] a trust [combine]
Kombination *f* 1. combination; 2. deduction; conjecture, speculation
~ **der landwirtschaftlichen Produktion** combination of live-stock and crop farming
~ **der Produktion** combination of production *(merger of successive production stages or main production with by-production in one enterprise)*
Kombinatsbildung *f* merger of enterprises *(into a trust)*
Kombinatsdirektor *m* director [manager] of a trust
Komitee *n* committee
Kommanditaktionär *m* limited-liability shareholder *(in partnership limited by shares)*
Kommanditanteil *m s.* **Kommanditeinlage**
Kommanditär *m* managing partner (of a limited partnership company)

Kommanditeinlage *f* limited partner's capital contribution
Kommanditgesellschaft *f* limited partnership company *(where one partner has unlimited liability while the others have limited liability)*
~ **auf Aktien** limited company by shares *(where one partner has unlimited liability)*
Kommanditist *m* limited [sleeping] partner
Kommanditscheck *m* cheque [*(Am)* check] drawn by one branch of a firm on another
Kommanditsumme *f* limited partner's contribution *(amount for which the limited partner is liable)*
Kommanditvertrag *m* partnership agreement *(limited partnership)*
Kommerz *m* commerce; trade
kommerzialisieren to commercialize; to convert (public debt) into a negotiable loan *(debt)*
Kommerzialisierung *f* commercialization; conversion of (public debt) into a negotiable loan
kommerziell commercial
kommissarisch temporary, provisional
Kommission *f* commission; committee; board ⋄ **in** ~ on commission, in consignment; **in** ~ **geben** to give on commission; **in** ~ **nehmen** to take on commission
~, **gemischte** joint commission [committee]
~, **paritätische** committee on a parity basis
Kommissionär *m* commission agent; wholesale bookseller *(book trade)*
Kommissionsagent *m s.* **Kommissionär**
Kommissionsbasis *f*:
⋄ **auf** ~ on a commission basis, on commission
Kommissionsbericht *m* committee('s) report
Kommissionsbuch *n* commission agent's order book
Kommissionsfirma *f* commission house
Kommissionsgebühr *f* commission, factorage
Kommissionsgeschäft *n* commission business; business on commission
Kommissionsgut *n* goods consigned to a commission agent; book on sale or return
Kommissionshandel *m* commission trade, buying and selling of goods on commission
Kommissionshandelsvertrag *m* commission trade contract [agreement]
Kommissionshändler *m* commission agent
Kommissionskonto *n* commission account
Kommissionslager *n* consignment stock
Kommissionsmakler *m* commission broker
Kommissionsmitglied *n* committee member
Kommissionsnummer *f* commission agent's order number
Kommissionspreis *m* commission price
Kommissionsprovision *f* commission on sales effected

Kommissionsreisender *m* commercial traveller
Kommissionssatz *m* rate of commission
Kommissionsverkauf *m* sale on commission
Kommissionsvertrag *m* commission agency agreement
Kommissionsvertreter *m s.* **Kommissionär**
Kommissionsware *f s.* **Kommissionsgut**
kommissionsweise on commission
Kommittent *m* principal (of commission agency)
kommittieren to commission, to authorize (a commission agency)
kommunal municipal, local
Kommunalabgaben *fpl* local rates [*(Am)* taxes]
Kommunalangelegenheiten *fpl* local government affairs
Kommunalanleihe *f* municipal loan
Kommunalausgaben *fpl* municipal [local authority] expenditures
Kommunalbank *f* municipal bank
Kommunalbehörde *f* local authorities
Kommunalfinanzen *pl* local government finances
Kommunalgebühr *f* fee paid to local authority *(for stamps on documents etc.)*
Kommunalkredit *m* credit [loan] to a local authority
Kommunalobligation *f* municipal bond
Kommunalpolitik *f* local politics; local government policy
Kommunalpolitiker *m* politician concerned with local government affairs
Kommunalsteuern *fpl* municipal [local] taxes
Kommunalverband *m* association of municipalities
Kommunalverwaltung *f* municipal [local] authority
Kommunalwahl *f* local election
Kommunalwirtschaft *f* municipal utilities [services]
Kommune *f* community; commune
Kommunikation *f* communication
Kommunikationsmittel *npl* mass media; means of communication
Kommunismus *m* communism
Kompaktbau *m* compact building
Kompaniegeschäft *n* joint business, partnership, joint venture
komparativ comparative
Kompensation *f* compensation; set-off *(claims)*
Kompensationsabkommen *n* barter agreement [arrangement]
Kompensationsgeschäft *n* compensation business [transaction]; barter trade
Kompensationsverkehr *m* compensation [barter] trade
kompensieren to compensate for, to offset, to balance, to counterbalance

Kompetenz *f* authority, powers *(persons etc.)*, responsibility *(authority etc.)*, competence, jurisdiction *(court etc.)*
Kompetenzbereich *m* (sphere of) authority [responsibility; jurisdiction]
Kompetenzstreit *m* conflict of responsibility [authority]; conflict of jurisdiction *(between courts)*
Kompetenzstreitigkeit *f s.* **Kompetenzstreit**
Komplementär *m* managing partner [director] *(in limited partnership)*; general partner (with unlimited liability)
Komplex *m* complex *(questions, traits, buildings, industry etc.)*; set *(laws, characteristics etc.)*; group *(countries etc.)*
Komplexautomatisierung *f* complex automation
Komplexbefehl *m (d.pr.)* complex instruction
Komplexbrigade *f* inter-trade work team *(of various trades in construction, mining etc.)*
Komplexeinsatz *m* complex use [operation] *(building machine, combine harvester etc.)*
Komplexität *f* complexity *(structure, society etc.)*
~ **der Planung** complexity of planning
Komplexitätsgrad *m* degree of complexity
Komplexkosten *pl* complex costs *(of technology, departmental management, sales etc.)*
Komplexmechanisierung *f* complex mechanization
Komplexnorm *f* comprehensive work standard *(comprising work standards of successive activities)*
Komplexpreis *m* complex price *(of a complex of performances in building industry)*
Komplexstudie *f* comprehensive job analysis
Kompliziertheit *f* complexity
~ **der Arbeit** complexity of labour
Kompliziertheitsgrad *m* level of complexity
Komponentenanalyse *f (stats)* component analysis
Komponentenzerlegung *f s.* **Komponentenanalyse**
Kompromiß *m* compromise ◊ **einen ~ eingehen** to make a compromise, to compromise
kompromißlos without a compromise, uncompromising
Kompromißlösung *f* compromise (solution)
Kompromißvorschlag *m* compromise proposal, proposed compromise ◊ **der ~ wurde angenommen** the proposed compromise was accepted
konditionell conditional
Konditionen *fpl* terms, conditions
Konditionsgeschäft *n* business [transaction] conducted on a sale or return basis
Konfektion *f* 1. ready-made clothes; 2. manufacture of ready-made clothes

konfektionieren to manufacture clothing
konfektioniert ready-made
Konfektionsgeschäft *n* ready-made [ready-to-wear] clothes shop, ladies' [gentlemen's] outfitters
Konfektionsgröße *f* size [number] of ready-made clothes
Konfektionsindustrie *f* ready-made clothes industry
Konfektionswaren *fpl* ready-made [ready-to-wear] articles of clothing [garments]
Konferenz *f* conference, meeting ✧ **an einer ~ teilnehmen** to take part in a conference [meeting]; **eine ~ abhalten** to hold a conference; **eine ~ einberufen** to call a conference [meeting]; **eine ~ leiten** to preside over a conference [meeting]
Konferenzbeitrag *m* conference paper [contribution]
Konferenzbericht *m* conference report
Konferenzmaterial *n* conference material
Konferenzteilnehmer *m* member of [participant in] a conference, *(Am)* conferee
konferieren to confer, to hold [have] a conference
Konfidenzbereich *m (stats)* confidence region
Konfidenzgrenzen *fpl (stats)* confidence limits
Konfidenzgürtel *m (stats)* confidence belt
Konfidenzintervall *n (stats)* confidence interval
Konfidenzintervalle *npl*:
~, kürzeste *(stats)* shortest confidence intervals
Konfiskation *f* confiscation, seizure, sequestration *(goods, property etc.)*
konfiszieren to confiscate, to seize, to sequestrate *(goods, property etc.)*
konfisziert confiscated, seized, sequestrated *(goods, property etc.)*
Konfiszierung *f s.* **Konfiskation**
Konflikt *m* conflict, clash *(between political parties, nations etc.)*, dispute *(between individuals etc.)*
Konfliktsituation *f* conflict situation
Konglomerat *n* conglomerate *(concern with diverse products and services)*
Kongreß *m* congress, *(Am)* convention *(parties, representatives etc.)*; conference
Konjunktur *f* trade [business] cycle; economic [business] situation [outlook] ✧ **die ~ dämpfen** to curb [place a check on] (the) boom
~, aufsteigende increasing economic [business] activity
~, günstige favourable economic situation [trend]
~, inflationistische inflationary boom
~, rückläufige declining economic activity, business slump

~, scheinbare specious boom
~, sinkende slump, recession
~, steigende upward economic [business] trend, economic [business] revival
~, ungünstige unfavourable economic situation [trend]
Konjunkturablauf *m* (course of the) trade cycle; trend of economic [business] activity
Konjunkturabschwächung *f* downward movement [downswing] of the trade cycle; decline in economic [business] activity; business slowdown
Konjunkturanalyse *f* business cycle analysis, (economic) trend analysis
Konjunkturanregung *f* stimulation of economic [business] activity
Konjunkturanstieg *m* increase in economic [business] activity, economic upturn [revival, upward trend]
Konjunkturaufschwung *m* upswing of the trade cycle; economic upturn [revival, upward trend]; business expansion
Konjunkturauftrieb *m s.* **Konjunkturanregung**
Konjunkturausgleich *m* smoothing out of cyclical fluctuations; seasonal cyclical [business cycle] adjustment
Konjunkturaussichten *fpl* economic [business] prospects [outlook]
Konjunkturbarometer *n* business barometer
konjunkturbedingt cyclical, due to the economic situation
Konjunkturbedingungen *fpl* boom conditions
Konjunkturbelebung *f s.* **Konjunkturaufschwung**
Konjunkturbericht *m* report on business conditions, economic report [survey]
Konjunkturbewegung *f* trade [business] cycle; cyclical movement
konjunkturdämpfend countercyclical *(policy, measures etc.)*, designed to check excessive economic [business] activity
Konjunkturdiagnose *f s.* **Konjunkturanalyse**
Konjunktureinflüsse *mpl* cyclical influences
konjunkturell cyclical *(movements, variations etc.)*; economic, business *(developments, situation etc.)*
konjunkturempfindlich cyclical *(industry, trade etc.)*; easily affected by [sensitive to] economic fluctuations
Konjunkturempfindlichkeit *f* sensitivity to economic fluctuations
Konjunkturentwicklung *f* economic [business] development [trend]
Konjunkturfaktoren *mpl* cyclical factors
Konjunkturforschung *f* trade cycle studies; economic [business] research
konjunkturgerecht cyclically correct

Konjunkturgewinn *m* boom profits, profits due to the favourable economic [business] situation
Konjunkturindikator *m* economic [business] indicator
Konjunkturjahr *n* boom year
Konjunkturklima *n* economic [business] climate
Konjunkturkrise *f* economic crisis; economic [trade] depression
Konjunkturkurve *f* cyclical trend
Konjunkturlage *f* economic [business] situation
Konjunkturphase *f* phase of the trade cycle
Konjunkturpolitik *f* trade cycle policy, policy for controlling the level of economic activity
konjunkturpolitisch of a policy for controlling the level of economic activity
Konjunkturprognose *f* economic [business] forecast
Konjunkturrückgang *m* slump (in trade); (economic) recession, business slump
Konjunkturschwankung *f* cyclical fluctuation, economic [business] fluctuation
Konjunkturspritze *f* shot in the arm to stimulate economic [business] activity
Konjunkturstabilisierung *f* economic [business] stabilization
Konjunktursturz *m s.* **Konjunkturrückgang**
Konjunkturstützung *f* maintaining the level of economic [business] activity
Konjunkturtheorie *f* theory of the trade cycle, business cycle theory
Konjunkturüberhitzung *f* excessive level of economic [business] activity, overheating of the economy
Konjunkturverkauf *m* seasonal sale
Konjunkturverlauf *m s.* **Konjunkturablauf**
Konjunkturzyklus *m* trade cycle; business cycle
Konkomitanz *f (stats)* concomitance
Konkordanz *f (stats)* concordance
Konkordanzkoeffizient *m (stats)* coefficient of concordance
Konkurrent *m* competitor, rival
Konkurrenz *f* competition, rivalry ⋄ **die ~ unterbieten** to undercut competitors; **sich gegenseitig ~ machen** to compete with one another
~, freie free [open] competition
~, heftige fierce [severe] competition
~, monopolistische monopolistic [monopoly] competition
~, preisdrückende price-cut competition
~, ruinöse ruinous [destructive] competition
~, scharfe stiff [keen] competition
~, schwache weak competition
~, starke strong [vigorous] competition
~, unlautere unfair competition
~, unvollkommene imperfect competition

~, vollkommene perfect competition
Konkurrenzangebot *n* competitive bid
Konkurrenzausschaltung *f* elimination of competition
Konkurrenzausschreibung *f* invitation to tender
Konkurrenzbedingungen *fpl* competitive conditions
Konkurrenzbeschränkung *f* restriction [restraint] of competition
Konkurrenzbetrieb *m* rival [competing] enterprise
Konkurrenzerzeugnis *n* rival product
konkurrenzfähig competitive
Konkurrenzfähigkeit *f* competitiveness
Konkurrenzfirma *f* rival [competing] firm [enterprise]
Konkurrenzgeschäft *n* competing business
Konkurrenzkampf *m* (fierce) competition, rivalry
Konkurrenzklausel *f* agreement [contract] clause in restraint of trade *(subsequent to the termination of service)*
konkurrenzlos unrivalled, unbeatable, without competition
Konkurrenzpreis *m* competitive price
Konkurrenzunternehmen *n s.* **Konkurrenzfirma**
Konkurrenzwirtschaft *f* competitive economy
konkurrieren to compete
konkurrierend competitive, competing
Konkurs *m* bankruptcy; insolvency ⋄ **einen ~ abwenden** to avoid bankruptcy; **in ~ gehen** to go into bankruptcy, to be under receivership, to go into liquidation *(company)*; **~ anmelden** to file a petition in bankruptcy, to declare o.s. bankrupt; **~ eröffnen** to institute bankruptcy proceedings, to adjudicate s.o. bankrupt, to be adjudged [adjudicated] bankrupt; **~ machen** to go bankrupt
~, freiwilliger voluntary bankruptcy
Konkursanmeldung *f* filing of a bankruptcy petition, filing of a petition for winding up *(company)*
Konkursantrag *m* petition in bankruptcy
Konkursaufhebung *f* close of a bankruptcy; annulment of adjudication (in bankruptcy)
Konkursbeauftragter *m* trustee in bankruptcy, liquidator *(company)*
Konkurserklärung *f* declaration of bankruptcy
Konkurseröffnung *f* adjudication in bankruptcy
Konkursforderung *f*:
  ⋄ **eine ~ zulassen** to admit [allow] a claim
Konkursgericht *n* bankruptcy court
Konkursgläubiger *m* creditor of a bankrupt [company in liquidation]
Konkursmasse *f* estate [assets] of a bankrupt

Konkursordnung *f* bankruptcy act
Konkursrecht *n* law of bankruptcy
Konkursschuldner *m* (declared) bankrupt, debtor
Konkursverfahren *n* (legal) proceedings in bankruptcy ◇ **ein ~ eröffnen** to institute bankruptcy proceedings; **ein ~ aufheben** to annul adjudication in bankruptcy
Konkursverwalter *m* accountant [trustee] in bankruptcy; (official) liquidator [receiver]
Können *n* knowledge; ability
~, handwerkliches manual skill
~, technisches know-how
Konnossement *n* bill of lading (B/L)
Konsens *m* consent *(of contracting parties)*; assent *(by contracting parties to an agreement)*
Konsensprinzip *n* principle of the unanimous vote
Konsensus *m* consensus *(of opinion etc.)*
Konservator *m* curator, keeper *(museum etc.)*
Konservenindustrie *f* canning industry
konservieren to preserve *(fruit, meat, vegetables etc.)*; to cure *(skins etc.)*
Konsignant *m* consigner, consignor
Konsignatär *m* consignee
Konsignation *f* 1. consignment; 2. address *(of bill of lading etc.)*
Konsignationsfaktura *f* pro-forma invoice
Konsignationsgeschäft *n* buying and selling of goods on consignment; transaction carried out by a commission agent *(for a principal)*
Konsignationsgut *n* goods consigned *(in overseas trade)*
Konsignationshandel *m* buying and selling of goods on consignment
Konsignationskonto *n* consignment account
Konsignationslager *n* consignment stock(s)
Konsignationssendung *f* consignment of goods on commission
Konsignationsverkauf *m* selling on consignment; consignment sale
Konsignationsware *f* goods consigned (to a commission agent) *(in overseas trade)*
Konsignator *m s.* **Konsignatär**
konsignieren to consign; to address a ship *(to s.o.)*
Konsistenzkoeffizient *m (stats)* coefficient of consistence
konsolidieren to fund *(debt etc.)*; to consolidate *(stocks etc.)*; to merge, to amalgamate *(mines etc.)*
konsolidiert consolidated *(funds etc.)*
Konsolidierung *f* funding *(debt etc.)*; consolidation *(stocks etc.)*; merger, amalgamation *(mines etc.)*
Konsols *pl* consols, *(Am)* consolidated government bonds

Konsorten *mpl* members of an underwriting syndicate
Konsortialanteil *m* underwriting share
Konsortialbank *f* syndicate bank, member bank of a syndicate
Konsortialbeteiligung *f* syndicate participation
Konsortialführer *m* leading bank of a syndicate
Konsortialgeschäft *n* syndicate operation, transaction by a syndicate
Konsortialgewinn *m* underwriting profit
Konsortialkonto *n* joint account *(carried by the leading member bank of a syndicate)*
Konsortialkredit *m* loan [credit] granted by a syndicate of banks
Konsortialkurs *m* syndicate price
Konsortialmitglied *n* member of a syndicate
Konsortialprovision *f* underwriters' commission
Konsortialquote *f* share of the joint profit *(received by a member bank of a syndicate)*
Konsortialvertrag *m* banking syndicate agreement
Konsortium *n* syndicate, consortium
konstituieren to constitute, to appoint, to institute *(committee etc.)*, to set up *(constituent assembly etc.)*
konstruieren to design *(car, aircraft etc.)*; to build *(machine, bridge, ship etc.)*; to fabricate, to invent *(alibi etc.)*; *(maths)* to construct *(triangle etc.)*
Konstruieren *n*:
~, rechnergestütztes computer-aided design (CAD)
Konstrukteur *m* designer, designing engineer
Konstruktion *f* 1. designing *(car, aircraft etc.)*; building *(machine, bridge, ship etc.)*; 2. construction, structure, building
Konstruktionsabteilung *f* projection and drawing department, designing department
Konstruktionsänderung *f* design change
Konstruktionsarbeit *f* designing (work)
Konstruktionsauftrag *m* construction contract; building contract
Konstruktionsbüro *n* designing [drawing] office, *(Am)* drafting office
Konstruktionsfehler *m* defect [flaw] in construction; faulty design
Konstruktionskosten *pl* construction costs; building costs
Konstruktionsmerkmal *n* constructional feature *(machine etc.)*; structural feature *(bridge etc.)*; design feature *(car etc.)*
konstruktionstechnisch constructional
Konstruktionsteil *n* component [element] of a construction [design]
Konstruktionsunterlagen *fpl* construction papers *(production drawings, calculation charts etc.)*

Konstruktionsvertrag *m* contract related to construction design
Konstruktionszeichnung *f* production [workshop] drawing
konstruktiv *(tech)* constructional; constructive *(methods, policy etc.)*
Konsularabkommen *n* consular convention
Konsularabteilung *f* consular department [section]
Konsularbezirk *m* consular district
Konsulargebühren *fpl* consular fees
konsularisch consular
Konsularvertretung *f* consular representation
Konsulat *n* consulate
Konsultation *f* consultation
Konsultationspunkt *m (agric)* demonstration farm
Konsultationstätigkeit *f* consultancy, consulting
Konsum *m* 1. consumption *(consumer goods etc.)*; 2. consumers' co-operative
Konsumartikel *mpl* consumer goods
Konsumausgaben *fpl* consumption expenditure [expenses]
Konsumbereitschaft *f s.* **Konsumneigung**
Konsumdarleh(e)n *n s.* **Konsumentenkredit**
Konsument *m* consumer *(goods etc.)*; user *(services etc.)*
~, **gesellschaftlicher** social [*(Am)* communal] consumer *(institutions etc.)*
~, **individueller** individual consumer
~, **nichtproduktiver** non-productive consumer
~, **produktiver** productive consumer *(consuming means of production and other goods for productive purposes)*
Konsumentenbedarf *m* consumer demand
Konsumentenbefragung *f* consumer research; consumer research survey
Konsumentengruppe *f* consumer group, group of consumers
Konsumentenideologie *f* consumerism
Konsumentenkaufkraft *f* consumer purchasing power
Konsumentenkredit *m* consumer credit
Konsumentenkreditbeschränkungen *fpl* restrictions on consumer credit
Konsumentennachfrage *f* consumer demand
Konsumfreudigkeit *f s.* **Konsumneigung**
Konsumfunktion *f* consumption function
Konsumgenossenschaft *f* consumer co-operative (society)
Konsumgenossenschaftsverband *m* association of consumer co-operatives
Konsumgesellschaft *f* consumer society
Konsumgewohnheiten *fpl* consumer habits
Konsumgüter *npl* consumer goods
~, **kurzlebige** non-durables
~, **langlebige** consumer durables

Konsumgüterausstellung *f* exhibition of consumer goods, consumer goods exhibition
Konsumgüteraustausch *m* trade in consumer goods
Konsumgüterbilanz *f* balance sheet of consumer goods
Konsumgüterbinnenhandel *m* local [domestic] trade in consumer goods
Konsumgüterbinnenmarkt *m* local [domestic] market for consumer goods
Konsumgütergroßhandel *m* wholesale trade in consumer goods
Konsumgütergruppe *f* group of consumer goods
Konsumgüterindustrie *f* consumer goods industry
Konsumgütermarkt *m* consumer goods market
Konsumgütermesse *f* consumer goods fair
Konsumgüternachfrage *f* demand for consumer goods
Konsumgüterpreis *m* consumer goods price; retail price
Konsumgüterproduktion *f* production of consumer goods
Konsumgüterprogramm *n* programme of consumer goods
Konsumgütersektor *m* consumer goods sector
Konsumgütersphäre *f s.* **Konsumgütersektor**
Konsumgüterverbrauch *m* consumption of consumer goods
Konsumgüterwerbung *f* advertising of consumer goods
Konsumgüterzweig *m* branch of consumer goods
konsumierbar consumable
konsumieren to consume
Konsumladen *m* co-operative shop [store]
Konsumneigung *f* propensity to consume
Konsumquote *f* consumption ratio *(between consumption expenditure and income)*
Konsumsteigerung *f* increase [rise] in consumption
Konsumsteuer *f* consumption tax, excise tax (on consumer goods)
Konsumtion *f* consumption
~, **gesellschaftliche** social consumption
~, **individuelle** individual consumption
~, **lebensstandardwirksame** consumption raising the standard of living
~, **nichtproduktive** non-productive consumption
~, **produktive** productive consumption
Konsumtionsabgabe *f* levy on the consumption of consumer goods and services
Konsumtionsbilanz *f* (national) consumption plan *(set of detailed indicators etc. of the national economic plan for planning volume and structure of individual and social consumption)*

Konsumtionsfonds m (national) consumption fund *(part of the national income which is earmarked and/or used for individual and social consumption)*
Konsumtionsforschung f consumer research
Konsumtionsgewohnheiten fpl s. **Konsumgewohnheiten**
Konsumtionsmittel npl s. **Konsumgüter**
Konsumtionsmittelpreis m consumer goods price
Konsumtionsniveau n level of consumption
Konsumtionsplanung f planning of consumption
Konsumtionsprognose f (national) consumption forecast [prognosis]
Konsumtionsrate f rate of consumption *(share of consumption in the national income)*
Konsumtionssphäre f consumption sector *(non-productive sector)*
Kontakt m contact; connection
Kontaktaufnahme f establishing contacts
Kontaktbesuch m contact-establishing visit
Kontaktgespräch n introductory talk
Kontaktpflege f maintaining contacts
kontant *(st.ex.)* for cash [money]
Kontanten pl foreign notes and coins; cash, ready money
Kontantgeschäft n *(st.ex.)* cash business [transaction]
Kontantkauf m cash purchase *(securities)*; *(st.ex)* purchase for cash
Konten npl:
⋄ ~ **manipulieren** to manipulate accounts
Kontenabrechnung f settlement of accounts
Kontenabschluß m balancing of accounts
Kontenabstimmung f reconciliation of accounts
Kontenanalyse f auditing of accounts; (internal) checking of accounts
Kontenbewegung f changes in an account
Kontenblatt n account(s)-sheet
kontenführend accounting
Kontenführung f accounting
Kontenführungspflicht f obligation to keep a bank account
Kontengliederung f classification of accounts
Kontengruppe f group of accounts
Kontenklasse f class of accounts
Kontenplan m list of accounts
Kontenrahmen m (general) system of accounts
Kontensaldo m balance in bank account
Kontensperre f blocking of (bank) accounts
Kontenübertragung f transfer (from one account to another)
Kontenüberziehung f overdrawn account; overdraft
Kontenverfügung f drawing money out of an account

Kontenverfügungsgewalt f right to draw money out of an account
Konterbande f contraband (goods)
Kontingent n quota *(export etc.)*; share; allocation *(material etc.)*
kontingentieren 1. to allocate *(material etc.)*; to fix a quota; to impose (a system of) quotas *(exports etc.)*; 2. to ration *(foreign currency etc.)*; to restrict by means of quotas *(output of goods in cartels etc.)*; *(bank)* to limit the fiduciary issue; to limit the total issue of notes
Kontingentierung f 1. allocation *(material etc.)*; fixing of quotas; imposition of (a system of) quotas *(exports etc.)*; 2. rationing *(foreign currency etc.)*; restriction by means of quotas *(output of goods in cartels etc.)*; *(bank)* limitation of the fiduciary issue; limitation of the total issue of notes
Kontingentierungsgrundlage f quota basis
Kontingentierungssatz m quota
Kontingentierungssystem n s. **Kontingentsystem**
Kontingentsantrag m application for a quota
Kontingentsfestsetzung f s. **Kontingentierung**
Kontingentssystem n quota system [scheme]
Kontingentträger m enterprise [institution, person] given a quota *(materials etc.)*
Kontingentzuweisung f allocation of a quota
Kontingenz f *(stats)* contingency
~, **mittlere quadratische** *(stats)* mean-square contingency
~, **partielle** *(stats)* partial contingency
~, **quadratische** *(stats)* square contingency
Kontingenzkoeffizient m *(stats)* coefficient of contingency
Kontingenztafel f *(stats)* contingency table
Kontinuität f continuity
~ **der Planung** continuity of planning
Konto n account ⋄ **ein ~ auflösen** to close an account; **ein ~ ausgleichen** to settle [balance] an account; **ein ~ bei einer Bank haben** to keep an account with a bank; **ein ~ belasten** to charge [debit] an account; **ein ~ einrichten** to open an account; **ein ~ eröffnen (bei)** to open an account (with); **ein ~ eröffnen (zugunsten von)** to open an account (in favour of); **ein ~ führen** to keep an account; **ein ~ sanieren** to improve solvency; **ein ~ schließen** to close an account; **ein ~ sperren** to block an account; **ein ~ überziehen** to overdraw an account; **über ein ~ verfügen** to draw money out of an account
~, **abgeschlossenes** closed account
~, **abgetretenes** assigned account
~, **antizipatives** suspense account
~, **ausgeglichenes** blanched account
~, **debitorisches** debit account

Kontrollsystem 289

~, **doppeltes** duplicate account
~, **dubioses** insolvent account
~, **eingefrorenes** frozen account
~, **fingiertes** proforma account
~, **gebundenes** deposit account, *(Am)* time deposit
~, **gedecktes** secured account
~, **gemeinsames** joint account
~, **gemeinschaftliches** *s.* ~, **gemeinsames**
~, **gesperrtes** blocked account
~, **im Inland geführtes** inland account
~, **kreditorisches** credit account
~ **laufender Ausgaben** current expense account
~, **laufendes** current [*(Am)* drawing] account
~, **offenes** open account
~, **persönliches** private account
~ **pro Diverse** sundry creditors' account; sundry debtors' account
~, **revolvierendes** revolving account
~, **tägliches** *s.* ~, **laufendes**
~, **transitorisches** *s.* ~, **antizipatives**
~, **überzogenes** overdrawn account
~, **ungedecktes** unsecured account
Kontoauszug *m (bank)* statement of account, bank slip, abstract of account
Kontobuch *n* account book; pass [*(Am)* deposit] book
kontoführend *s.* **kontenführend**
Kontoführer *m* bookkeeper
Kontogegenbuch *n* passbook *(of client)*
Kontoguthaben *n* credit balance (in bank account)
Kontoinhaber *m* bank depositor
Kontokorrent *n* current account, *(Am)* account current
Kontokorrentauszug *m* statement of current account
Kontokorrentgeschäft *n* current account business; current account transaction
Kontokorrentkartei *f* index card of current accounts
Kontokorrentkonto *n* current [running] account, *(Am)* demand deposit
Kontokorrentkredit *m* advance on current account, credit on current account
Kontokorrentverbindlichkeiten *fpl* deposit liabilities
Kontokorrentverkehr *m* current account business
Kontokorrentvertrag *m* agreement [contract] following the opening of a current account
Kontonummer *f* bank account number
Kontor *n* office; department
Kontordirektor *m* head of department; company manager of a state trading company
Kontorist *m* (office) clerk
Kontosperre *f s.* **Kontensperre**

Kontospesen *pl* account charges
Kontostand *m* state of an account
Kontoveränderung *f* change in account
Kontozahlung *f* payment on account
Kontrahent *m* 1. contractor, contracting party; 2. opponent
kontrahieren to contract *(loan etc.)*
Kontrakt *m* contract, formal agreement ◊ **einen ~ abschließen** to enter into an agreement [contract]; **laut ~** as per contract, according to contract
Kontraktbruch *m* breach of contract
kontraktbrüchig breaking a contract
kontraktlich contractual *(obligation etc.)*; stipulated by contract *(settlement etc.)*
Kontrollabschnitt *m* counterfoil, *(Am)* stub
Kontrollapparat *m* control machinery
Kontrollausschuß *m* supervisory committee
Kontrollbefehl *m (d.pr.)* supervisory instruction
Kontrollbehörde *f* control authority
Kontrollberatung *f* discussion after auditing
Kontrollbericht *m* auditor's report
Kontrollbescheid *m* auditor's decision
Kontrolldaten *pl (d.pr.)* inspection data
Kontrolle *f* control *(crowd etc.)*; verification, auditing *(account etc.)*; checking *(admittance etc.)*; supervision *(work etc.)*; examination *(customs etc.)*; inspection *(building site etc.)* ◊ **sich einer ~ entziehen** to get out of control; **unter ~ bekommen** to get *s.th.* under control
~, **gesellschaftliche** public inspection
~, **mitlaufende** continuous checking
~, **staatliche** state control
~, **vorbeugende** (preventive) inspection *(buildings etc.)*
Kontrollergebnis *n (d.pr.)* inspection result
Kontrolleur *m* controller; conducter *(tram etc.)*
Kontrollfehler *m (d.pr.)* inspection error
Kontrollgesellschaft *f* holding company
Kontrollgrenze *f (stats)* control limit
~, **obere** *(stats)* upper control limit
~, **untere** *(stats)* lower control limit
Kontrollgrenzen *fpl*:
~, **eingeengte** *(stats)* compressed limits
kontrollieren to controll *(crowd etc.)*; to verify, to audit *(account etc.)*; to check *(admittance etc.)*; to supervise *(work etc.)*; to examine *(customs etc.)*; to inspect *(building site etc.)*
Kontrollkarte *f (stats)* control chart
Kontrollkommission *f* control commission
Kontrollorgan *n* control authority; auditing board
Kontrollpunkt *m* check-point; *(stats)* point of control
Kontrollrat *m* control council
Kontrollsystem *n* control [auditing, checking, supervising] system

Kontrolltätigkeit *f* controlling [verifying, auditing, checking, supervising, examining, inspecting] activities
Kontroll- und Revisionsapparat *m* board of auditors
Kontrollverfahren *n* control [verification, auditing, checking, supervising, examining, inspecting] method
Kontrollziffern *fpl* orientation data [indicators]
Konvention *f* convention; international agreement
Konventionalstrafe *f* penalty for breach of contract; liquidated damages
Konventionaltarif *m* (*cust*) conventional tariff
Konvergenz *f* convergence
~ **nach Maß** (*stats*) convergence in measure
~ **nach Wahrscheinlichkeit** (*stats*) convergence in probability
~, **stochastische** (*stats*) convergence in probability, stochastic convergence
Konvergenztheorie *f* convergence theory
Konversion *f* conversion (*debt, loan etc.*)
Konvertibilität *f* convertibility (*currency etc.*)
konvertierbar convertible ◊ **begrenzt** ~ partially convertible; **frei** ~ freely convertible; **nicht** ~ inconvertible; **voll** ~ fully convertible
Konvertierbarkeit *f* convertibility
konvertieren to convert
Konvertierung *f* conversion (*debt, loan etc.*)
Konzentration *f* concentration (*population, industry etc.*); integration (*firms etc.*)
~ **der Produktion** concentration of production
~ **der Wirtschaftskraft, übermäßige** excessive concentration of economic power
~ **des Kapitals** concentration of capital
~, **horizontale** horizontal integration
~, **landwirtschaftliche** concentration in agriculture
~, **vertikale** vertical integration
~ **wirtschaftlicher Macht** concentration of economic power
Konzentrationsbewegung *f* concentration movement (*capital etc.*); integration movement (*firms etc.*)
Konzentrationsindex *m* (*stats*) index of concentration
Konzentrationskoeffizient *m* (*stats*) coefficient of concentration
Konzentrationskurve *f* (*stats*) curve of concentration
Konzentrationsmaß *n* extent of concentration
Konzentrationsprozeß *m* process of concentration; process of integration
Konzentrationstendenz *f* trend of concentration (*capital etc.*); trend of integration (*firms etc.*)
Konzentrationstheorie *f* theory of concentration; theory of integration

konzentrieren to concentrate (*population, industry etc.*); to integrate (*firms etc.*)
Konzept *n* concept; rough copy, first draft (*speech, document etc.*)
Konzeption *f* (draft) policy outline; plan, programme; idea, concept, conception
~, **strukturpolitische** long-term programme for developing production structure
~, **volkswirtschaftliche** long-term comprehensive development programme of the national economy
~, **wissenschaftlich-technische** scientific and technological programme
Konzern *m* concern, firm; trust
~, **horizontaler** horizontally integrated concern [trust]
~, **vertikaler** vertically integrated concern [trust]
Konzernbetrieb *m* affiliated company, subsidiary
Konzernbilanz *f* consolidated balance sheet of a concern
Konzernbildung *f* formation of concerns
Konzernentflechtung *f* decartelization, deconcentration of a concern
Konzerngebilde *n* concern, trust
Konzerngruppe *f* group of concerns [trusts]
Konzernverflechtung *f* interlocking of concerns
Konzession *f* 1. concession; 2. licence
konzessionieren to grant a licence, to license
konzessioniert licensed, authorized
Konzessionsentziehung *f* revocation of a licence
Konzessionserteilung *f* granting of a licence, licensing
Konzessionsgebühren *fpl* licensing fees
Konzessionsinhaber *m* concessionaire; licensee
Konzessionsnehmer *m s.* **Konzessionsinhaber**
Kooperation *f* co-operation
~, **horizontale** horizontal co-operation
~, **internationale** international co-operation
~, **mehrseitige** multilateral co-operation
~, **soziale** social co-operation
~, **vertikale** vertical co-operation
~, **zwischenbetriebliche** inter-enterprise co-operation
Kooperationsbeziehungen *fpl* co-operation, relations of co-operation
Kooperationsgemeinschaft *f* (*ind*) inter-enterprise co-operation; (*agric*) inter-farm co-operation; farm-enterprise co-operation (*between processing enterprises and co-operative farms*)
Kooperationsgrad *m* degree of co-operation
Kooperationskette *f* chain of inter-enterprise co-operation; chain of farm-enterprise co-operation
Kooperationskoeffizient *m* co-operation co-efficient

Kooperationsleitstelle *f* head office of co-operation *(co-ordinating idle capacities)*
Kooperationsorganisation *f* organization of co-operation
Kooperationspartner *m* partner in co-operation
Kooperationsplan *m* plan of co-operation
Kooperationsplanung *f* planning of co-operation
Kooperationsrat *m* *(agric)* co-operation council
Kooperationsverband *m* chain of co-operation *(between co-operative and state farms, processing enterprises and trade in the former GDR)*
Kooperationsvereinbarung *f* co-operation agreement
Kooperationsvertrag *m* agreement on co-operation, co-operation agreement
~, **internationaler** international agreement on co-operation
Koordinierung *f* co-ordination
~ **der Forschung** co-ordination of research
~, **internationale** international co-ordination
~, **territoriale** regional co-ordination
~, **zweigliche** inter-branch co-ordination
Koordinierungsplan *m* co-ordination plan
Koordinierungsvereinbarung *f* co-ordination agreement, agreement on co-ordination
Kopf *m*:
◊ **pro** ~ per head [capita]
Kopfarbeit *f* brain [intellectual] work
Kopfarbeiter *m* brain worker, worker by brain
Kopie *f* copy, duplicate *(document etc.)*
Koppelprodukte *npl* *(agric)* farm products produced as a unit *(e.g. beef and milk, wool and mutton)*
Koppelwirtschaft *f* *(agric)* (system of) alternate husbandry
Kopplungsgeschäft *n* tie-in arrangement, tying agreement
Kopplungsmatrix *f* *(maths)* double matrix
Kopplungsverkauf *m* tie-in sale
Kopplungsvertrag *m* tie-in contract
Koproduktion *f* co-production
Korbmacher *m* basket-maker, basket-weaver
körperbehindert (physically) disabled
Körperbehinderung *f* (physical) disability
Körperschaft *f* body *(persons)*; body corporate, corporate body, corporation *(artifical persons)*; legal entity
~, **beratende** advisory body
~ **des öffentlichen Rechts** body incorporated under public law
~, **gemeinnützige** non-profit-making body
~, **gesetzgebende** legislative body
~, **öffentliche** public corporation
~, **parlamentarische** parliamentary body
~, **wissenschaftliche** scientific body
körperschaftlich corporate, incorporated

Körperschaftseinkommen *n* corporate income
Körperschaftsgewinn *m* corporate profits [earnings]
Körperschaftssteuer *f* corporation (income) tax
Körperschaftssteuererklärung *f* corporation (income) tax return
Körperschutzmittel *n* body protective gear
Korrektur *f* correction; reading of proof
~ **zur Klassenbildung** *(stats)* correction for grouping
Korrekturen *fpl*:
~ **der Extremwerte** *(stats)* end corrections
~, **im Mittel treffende** *(stats)* average corrections
~, **Sheppard'sche** *(stats)* Sheppard's corrections
Korrekturfaktor *m* *(stats)* comparability factor
~ **für endliche Gesamtheiten** *(stats)* finite sampling correction
~, **regionaler** *(stats)* area comparability factor
~, **zeitlicher** *(stats)* time comparability factor
Korrelation *f* *(stats)* correlation
~ **der Größenanordnungswerte** *(stats)* great correlation
~, **lineare** *(stats)* linear correlation
~, **multiple nichtlineare** *(stats)* multiple curvilinear correlation
~, **negative** *(stats)* inverse correlation
~, **nichtlineare** *(stats)* curvilinear [non-linear] correlation
~, **partielle** *(stats)* partial correlation
~, **positive** *(stats)* direct correlation
~, **schiefe** *(stats)* skew correlation
~, **sinnlose** *(stats)* nonsense correlation
~, **vorgetäuschte** *(stats)* spurious correlation
~ **zwischen den Klassen** *(stats)* inter-class correlation
Korrelationsanalyse *f* *(stats)* correlation analysis
Korrelationsbild *n* *(stats)* scatter diagram
Korrelationsfläche *f* *(stats)* correlation surface
Korrelationsfunktion *f* *(stats)* correlation function
Korrelationsindex *m* *(stats)* correlation index
Korrelationskoeffizient *m* *(stats)* correlation coefficient
Korrelationsmatrix *f* *(stats)* correlation matrix
Korrelationsrechnung *f* *(stats)* correlation calculus [calculation]
Korrelationstabelle *f* *(stats)* table of correlation
Korrelationstafel *f s.* **Korrelationstabelle**
Korrelationsverhältnis *n* *(stats)* ratio of correlation
Korrelogramm *n* *(stats)* correlogram
Korrespondenzbank *f* corresponding bank
korrespondieren to correspond
korrumpieren to corrupt, to bribe
korrupt corrupt, bribable
Korruption *f* corruption, bribery

Kosmetikerin *f* cosmetician; beautician
Kost *f* food; board; diet
~, **freie** free meals [board]
~ **und Logis** *n* board and lodging
~ **und Lohn** *m* wages with free meals included
kosten to cost
Kosten *pl* cost(s), expense(s), expenditure, charge(s) ◊ **abzüglich der** ~ **für** minus costs of; **als** ~ **buchen** to enter [put] as costs; **auf eigene** ~ at one's own expense [cost]; **auf gemeinsame** ~ at joint expense, dividing the expenses [cost]; **auf** ~ **der Allgemeinheit** at the public expense; **auf** ~ **der Qualität** at the cost of quality; **auf** ~ **von** at the cost [expense] of; **auf meine** ~ at my expense; **ausschließlich der** ~ exclusive of costs; **die** ~ **bewegen sich zwischen** (the) costs range between; **die** ~ **tragen** to bear [pay, meet] the costs; **einen Teil der** ~ **übernehmen** to contribute to the cost; **jmdn.** ~ **aufbürden** to award the cost against s.o.; **keine** ~ **sparen** to spare no expense; ~ **absetzen** to deduct costs; ~ **auf die Abteilungen verrechnen** to charge costs to the departments; ~ **auferlegen** to impose costs; ~ **aufgliedern** to classify costs, *(Am)* to itemize costs; ~ **aufschlüsseln** to break down costs; ~ **aufteilen** to allocate [apportion] costs; ~ **berechnen** to calculate costs; ~ **berücksichtigen** to take the cost into account, to consider the cost; ~ **bestreiten** to meet the costs [expenses]; ~ **decken** to cover costs [expenses]; ~ **einsparen** to save costs [expenses]; ~ **tragen** to defray costs [expenses]; ~ **übernehmen** to pay the costs [expenses]; ~ **umlegen** to reallocate costs; ~ **veranschlagen** to precalculate costs; ~ **verursachen** to incur costs [expenses]; ~ **zurückerstatten** to pay back costs [expenses], to refund expenses; **mit geringen** ~ at a slight cost; **ohne** ~ free of charge
~, **abnehmende** declining [decreasing] cost(s)
~, **abschreibungsfähige** debitable costs, costs that can be written off
~, **abzugsfähige** deductible costs
~, **aufgelaufene** accumulated costs
~, **auftragsfixe** costs fixed in the order
~ **aus schlechter Führungstätigkeit** costs incurred by bad management
~, **außerordentliche** special costs
~, **außerplanmäßige** unscheduled costs
~, **beeinflußbare** controllable cost(s)
~, **betrieblich notwendige** operationally necessary costs
~, **betriebliche** operational costs
~, **betriebsfixe** operationally fixed costs
~, **degressive** degressive costs
~, **direkte** direct cost(s)

~, **direkte technologische** direct technological cost(s)
~, **durch Wartezeiten bedingte** cost of idleness *(machines)*
~, **effektive** real costs
~, **entstandene** cost incurred, accrued cost
~, **erstattungsfähige** chargeable cost
~, **feste** *s.* ~, **fixe**
~, **fiktive** shadow [fictitious] costs
~, **fixe** fixed costs
~, **flexible** flexible costs
~ **für Ausschuß** cost of scrap products
~ **für den Aufwand an lebendiger Arbeit** costs of using living labour *(wages and salaries)*
~ **für den Aufwand an vergegenständlichter Arbeit** costs of using materialized labour *(depreciation, material)*
~ **für den Verbrauch produktiver Leistungen** costs of value-adding services; jobbing costs
~ **für Energie** cost of energy
~ **für Forschung und Entwicklung** research and development costs
~ **für Garantieleistungen** costs of after-sales service
~ **für geringwertige und schnellverschleißende Arbeitsmittel** costs of low-value und short-service-life tools
~ **für Hilfsmaterial** cost of ancillaries [auxiliaries]
~ **für Hilfs- und Nebenleistungen** ancillary performance costs
~ **für Nacharbeiten** cost of extra [additional] work, reworking costs, cost(s) of refinishing
~ **für technologisch bedingten Ausschuß, Nacharbeit und Garantieverpflichtungen (ANG-Kosten)** costs of scrap products, refinishing and after-sales service
~ **für Vorleistungen** cost of advance performances
~, **gesellschaftlich notwendige** socially necessary costs
~, **indirekte** indirect cost(s)
~, **indirekte technologische** indirect technological (cost(s)
~, **indirekte variable** indirect variable cost(s)
~, **innerbetriebliche** internal costs
~ **je Einheit des Erzeugnisses (je Erzeugniseinheit)** cost per unit (of product)
~, **kalkulationsfähige** calculable cost(s)
~, **kalkulatorische** imputed costs
~, **komparative** comparative cost(s)
~, **konstante** constant costs
~, **kumulative** cumulative costs
~, **kurzfristige** short-term costs
~, **langfristige** long-term costs
~, **laufende** running costs [expenses]
~, **nicht erstattungsfähige** non-chargeable cost

~, **nicht kalkulationsfähige** incalculable cost(s)
~, **nicht planbare** costs which cannot be planned
~ **per Einheit** unit costs, costs per unit
~, **planbare** costs to be planned
~ **pro Kopf** per capita costs
~, **progressive** progressive costs
~, **proportionale** proportionate costs
~, **regressive** regressive costs
~, **sonstige** miscellaneous [other] costs
~, **sonstige produktionsbedingte** other costs conditioned by production
~, **spezifische** special cost
~, **spezifizierte** specified (direct) cost
~, **ständige** standing [recurring] costs
~, **steigende** rising costs
~, **steuerabzugsfähige** tax deductible costs
~, **technologische** technological costs
~, **unvorhergesehene** incidental costs [expenses]
~, **variable** variable costs
~, **vermeidbare** avoidable costs
~, **Versicherung** *f* **und Fracht** *f* cost, insurance and freight (c.i.f.)
~, **voraussichtliche** probable costs
~, **vorkalkulierte** predetermined cost
~, **wirkliche** actual cost
~, **zunehmende** increasing costs
~, **zusätzliche** additional costs [expenses]
Kostenabbau *m* reduction of costs [expenses]
Kostenabgrenzung *f* cost definition
Kostenabrechnung *f* cost accounting
Kostenabrechnungssystem *n* system of cost accounting
Kostenabrechnungsverfahren *n* method of cost accounting
Kostenabweichung *f* cost deviation
Kostenanalyse *f* cost analysis
Kostenansatz *m* amount of costs charged
Kostenanschlag *m* estimate of cost, cost estimate ◇ **einen ~ machen** to estimate costs
Kostenanstieg *m* rise [increase] in [of] costs
Kostenanteil *m* cost fraction, proportion of cost
Kostenart *f* type [kind] of cost
Kostenartenabgrenzung *f* definition of types of cost
Kostenartengliederung *f* classification according to types of cost
Kostenartengruppe *f* group of types of cost
Kostenartenrechnung *f* calculation of cost according to types
Kostenaufgliederung *f* breakdown of costs; classification of costs
Kostenaufschlüsselung *f* classification of costs
Kostenaufstellung *f* statement of cost, costing record, cost account
Kostenaufwand *m* expediture, expense, cost; outlay

Kostenausgleichung *f* balance of expense
Kostenbeitrag *m* contribution to expenses
Kostenbeleg *m* cost record
Kostenberechnung *f* cost account, costing
Kostenbereich *m* cost area *(area where costs arise)*
Kostenbestandteil *m* part of costs, cost element
Kostenbeteiligung *f* cost sharing
Kostenbetrag *m* amount of costs [expenses]
Kostenblatt *n* cost sheet
kostendeckend cost-covering
Kostendeckung *f* covering of costs [expenses]
Kostendeckungskoeffizient *m* coefficient of cost covering
Kostendegression *f* regressive cost trend
Kostendiagramm *n* break-even chart
Kostendynamik *f* dynamics of costs
Kosteneinheit *f* cost unit
Kosteneinsparung *f* cost saving
Kostenelastizität *f* elasticity of cost
Kostenelement *n* cost element
Kostenelemente *npl*:
~, **normierte** standardized elements of cost
Kostenentwicklung *f* growth in [of] cost(s)
Kostenerfassung *f* recording of cost(s)
Kostenermittlung *f* cost ascertainment
Kostenersatz *m* compensation for outlay (incurred), reimbursement [refund] of cost(s)
Kostenersparnis *f* saving of cost(s)
Kostenerstattung *f* reimbursement of expenses
Kostenfaktor *m* cost factor
Kostenfestsetzung *f* cost fixing, costing
Kostenfeststellung *f* cost finding, costing
Kostenfolge *f* sequence of costs
Kostenfrage *f* question of costs
kostenfrei free of charge, free, gratis
Kostenfunktion *f* cost function
Kostengliederung *f* classification of costs
kostengünstig at favourable costs
Kostenindex *m* cost index
Kosteninflation *f* cost inflation
Kosteninformation *f* information on costs
Kostenkalkulation *f* calculation of cost, costing
Kostenkoeffizient *m* cost coefficient
Kostenkontrolle *f* auditing, cost control
Kostenlimit *n* cost limit
kostenlos free, free of charge
kostenmäßig in terms of costs, as far as costs are concerned
Kostenmiete *f* minimum economic rent
Kostenminimierung *f* minimization of costs
Kostennachweis *m* indication of cost
Kostenniveau *n* level of cost
Kostennorm *f* cost norm [standard]
Kostennormativ *n* normative cost *(for a certain unit of goods and/or performances)*
Kosten-Nutzen-Analyse *f* cost-benefit analysis

Kosten-Nutzen-Rechnung *f* cost-benefit calculation
Kostenoptimierung *f* optimization of costs
Kostenoptimum *n* optimum of cost
Kostenordnung *f* scale of fees and charges
kostenpflichtig with costs
Kostenplan *m* plan of costs
Kostenplaner *m* cost planner
Kostenplanung *f* planning of costs
Kostenpreis *m* cost-price; prime cost
Kostenpreisbildung *f* formation of cost-prices
Kosten-Preis-Schere *f* cost-and-price scissors
Kostenprognose *f* long-term forecast of costs
Kostenpunkt *m* matter of expense
Kostenrechner *m* cost accountant
Kostenrechnung *f* calculation of cost, cost accounting
Kostensatz *m* cost unit rate; turnover [costs] ratio
Kostensatzmethode *f* unit cost method
Kostensenkung *f* reduction of cost
Kostensenkungsauflage *f* imposition of cost reduction
kostensparend cost-saving
Kostenstatistik *f* statistics of costs, cost statistics
Kostensteigerung *f* increase in [of] cost(s)
Kostenstelle *f* cost centre
Kostenstellenabrechnungsbogen *m* form for cost centre accounting
Kostenstellenbereich *m* cost centre area *(of several cost centres)*
Kostenstellenplan *m* plan of cost centres
Kostenstellenplanung *f* planning of cost centres
Kostenstellenrechnung *f* allocation of expenses to cost centres
Kostensteuern *fpl* cost taxes *(land-tax, sales tax and turnover tax)*
Kostenstruktur *f* structure of cost(s)
Kostensummenmethode *f* total cost method *(overall or partial for calculating the costs during a certain period)*
Kostentheorie *f* cost theory
Kostenträger *m* 1. *(acc)* cost unit, unit of costs; 2. financing authority for costs incurred *(in implementation of social tasks)*; 3. bearer of costs
Kostenträgerabrechnungsbogen *m* form for accounting cost units
Kostenträgergruppe *f* group of cost units
Kostenträgermethode *f* cost unit method
Kostenträgerplan *m* plan of cost units
Kostenträgerrechnung *f* cost unit accounting *(apportioning all costs to products and performances)*
Kostenträgerstückrechnung *f* cost unit accounting per piece

Kostenträgerzeitrechnung *f* cost unit accounting in a period
Kostentrend *m* cost trend, trend of costs
Kostenübernahme *f* cost absorption
Kostenüberschlag *m* estimate (of cost)
Kostenüberschreitung *f* excess of cost
Kostenübersicht *f* cost survey
Kosten- und Industriepreiskalkulation *f* calculation of cost(s) and industry prices
Kosten- und Preisarbeit *f* costing and pricing
Kosten- und Preisvorgabe *f* cost and price instruction
Kostenunterlagen *fpl* cost data
Kostenunterschreitung *f* saving of cost(s)
Kostenvergleich *m* comparison of costs, cost comparison
~, **normativer** comparison of standard costs
Kostenverrechnung *f* cost allocation [apportionment]
Kosten *pl*, **Versicherung** *f* **und Fracht** *f* cost, insurance and freight (c.i.f., c.i.&f.) *(delivery clause)*
Kosten *pl*, **Versicherung** *f*, **Fracht** *f* **und Provision** *f* cost, insurance, freight and commission (c.i.f.&c., c.i.f.c.) *(delivery clause)*
Kosten *pl*, **Versicherung** *f*, **Fracht** *f*, **Zinsen** *mpl*, **Provision** *f* cost, insurance, freight, interest and commission (c.i.f.i.c.) *(delivery clause)*
Kostenverteilung *f* cost allocation
Kostenverteilungsplan *m* plan of cost allocation
Kostenverteilungsverfahren *n* method of cost allocation
Kostenvoranschlag *m* estimated cost, estimate (of cost)
Kostenvorausrechnung *f* precalculation of cost, cost prediction
Kostenvorgabe *f* given cost
Kostenvorschuß *m* advance on cost payment
Kostenvorteil *m* cost advantage
~, **absoluter** absolute cost advantage
~, **komparativer** comparative cost advantage
~, **relativer** relative cost advantage
Kostenwahrheit *f* reality of cost
Kostenwert *m* cost value
Kostenzahl *f* cost figure
Kostenzuschlag *m* additional cost
Kostenzuwachskoeffizient *m* cost growth coefficient
Kostgeld *n* board (allowance); *(st.ex.)* contango
Kostgeschäft *n* contango, continuation [carrying over] business
Kostpreis *m* cost-price
kostspielig expensive, costly
Kraft *f* 1. strength; power; energy; force; 2. worker ⋄ **außer ~** repealed; **außer ~**

setzen to repeal, to invalidate, to cancel; to annul *(contract etc.)*; to abrogate *(treaty etc.)*; to suspend *(rights etc.)*; **außer ~ treten** to cease to be effective, to expire; **in ~** in force; **in ~ treten** to come into force
~, hauptamtliche permanent staff member
Kraftanlagen *fpl* power plant
Kraftaufwand *m* expenditure of energy [effort]
Kräfte *fpl* 1. forces, powers; 2. forces *(political, military)*; personnel, staff members, workers ⋄ **nach besten Kräften** to the best of one's ability
~, geistige mental [intellectual] powers
~, hauptamtliche permanent personnel [staff members]
~, körperliche physical strength
~, lebendige kinetic energy
~, politische political forces
~, schöpferische creative power
~, technische technical personnel [workers]
~, ungenutzte latent power
~, wirtschaftliche economic forces
Kräftebedarf *m* manpower [labour] requirements
Kräfteverhältnis *n* balance of power [forces] *(country etc.)*, comparative [relative] strength *(political parties etc.)*
~, internationales international balance of power
Kraftfahrdienst *m* motor transport service, vehicle pool
Kraftfahrer *m* driver; chauffeur
Kraftfahrhaftpflichtversicherung *f* third party motor vehicle insurance
Kraftfahrzeugbau *m* automobile [*(Am)* automotive] engineering
Kraftfahrzeugdichte *f* density of motor vehicles
Kraftfahrzeug-Elektriker *m* car electrician
Kraftfahrzeugführer *m* driver of a vehicle
Kraftfahrzeughaftung *f* driver's third party liability
Kraftfahrzeughalter *m* motor vehicle owner; person in charge of a motor vehicle
Kraftfahrzeughandwerker *m* motor vehicle mechanic, motor [car] mechanic, *(Am)* automobile mechanic
Kraftfahrzeugindustrie *f* motor (vehicle) industry, *(Am)* automobile industry
Kraftfahrzeuginstandhaltungsbetrieb *m* motor vehicle repair shop
Kraftfahrzeugpark *m* fleet of motor vehicles
Kraftfahrzeugsachverständiger *m (ins)* expert on motor vehicles and motor vehicles regulations
Kraftfahrzeugsammelversicherung *f* vehicle fleet insurance
Kraftfahrzeugschlosser *m* vehicle mechanic; car mechanic

Kraftfahrzeugsteuer *f* motor vehicle tax
Kraftfahrzeugversicherung *f* motor vehicle insurance
Kraftfahrzeugzulassung *f* motor vehicle licence
kräftig strong, powerful *(constitution etc.)*; nutritious, rich *(food etc.)*; sharp, vigorous *(rise in prices etc.)*; big *(drop in turnover etc.)*
Kraftomnibusverkehr *m* bus traffic [service]
Kraftprobe *f* trial of strength; endurance test
Kraftstoff *m* fuel; petrol
Kraftstoffkosten *pl* cost of fuel [petrol]
Kraftstoffverbrauch *m* fuel consumption
Kraftstoffverbrauchsnorm *f* standard rate of fuel consumption
Kraftstoffverbrauchssatz *m* rate of fuel consumption
Kraftverkehr *m* motor traffic
Kraftverkehrsbetrieb *m* motor transport enterprise
Kraftverkehrsordnung *f* motor traffic regulations
Kraftverkehrstarif *m* (vehicle) transport rate
Kraftwagenpark *m s.* **Kraftfahrzeugpark**
Kraftwerk *n* power station
Kranbau *m* crane construction (industry)
Kranführer *m* crane driver [operator]
Krangeld *n* cranage
krank sick *(persons, economy etc.)*; ill *(persons etc.)*; diseased *(organ etc.)*; unhealthy, sickly *(plant etc.)*; ailing *(firm etc.)*
Krankenanstalt *f s.* **Krankenhaus**
Krankenbehandlung *f* treatment of a patient
Krankenbesuch *m* visit to a patient
Krankenfürsorge *f* care of the sick
Krankengeld *n* sick [sickness] benefit [pay, allowance]
Krankengeldgewährung *f* payment of sick benefit
Krankengeldzuschlag *m* supplementary sick benefit
Krankenhaus *n* hospital
Krankenhausarzt *m* physician at a hospital
Krankenhausaufenthalt *m* stay in hospital, *(Am)* hospitalization
Krankenhausbehandlung *f* hospital treatment
Krankenhauskosten *pl* hospital costs
Krankenhauszuschuß *m* hospital benefits
Krankenkasse *f* national sickness insurance scheme; sickness insurance fund
Krankenschein *m* medical certificate
Krankenstand *m* sickness figure *(for country etc.)*, number of persons sick *(away from work in a firm etc.)*
Krankenversicherung *f* health insurance
~, private private health insurance
~, soziale national [social] health insurance
Kranker *m* sick person; patient

Krankheit f illness; disease; complaint
~, **meldepflichtige** notifiable disease
Krankheitsfall m case (of illness)
krankheitshalber owing to illness
Krankheitsverhütung f prevention of an illness
Kreativität f creativity, creativeness
Kreativitätsforschung f creativity research
Kredit m credit; loan ✧ **auf ~ on** credit; **auf ~ geben** to give on credit; **auf ~ kaufen** to buy on credit; **auf ~ verkaufen** to sell on credit; **einen ~ aufnehmen** to raise a loan, to borrow money; to accept a credit; **einen ~ beantragen** to request [ask for] a loan; **einen ~ einräumen** to grant a credit; **einen ~ einrichten** to extend a credit; **einen ~ eröffnen** to open [lodge] a credit; **einen ~ gegen Sicherheit gewähren** to grant a credit [loan] against security; **einen ~ gewähren** to grant a loan; **einen ~ kündigen** to withdraw a credit; **einen ~ prolongieren** to renew [extend] a credit; **einen ~ schöpfen** to create credit; **einen ~ überziehen** to overdraw one's account; **einen ~ zinslos gewähren** to grant an interest-free loan [credit]; **einen ~ zurückzahlen** to repay a loan; **etwas auf ~ liefern** to deliver [supply] s.th. on account; **gegen ~** on credit; **ohne ~** without credit
~, **begrenzter** limited credit [loan]
~, **bestätigter** confirmed credit
~, **eingefrorener** frozen [blocked] credit [loan]
~, **fälliger** credit due
~, **gedeckter** covered loan
~, **genehmigter** authorized loan
~, **gesicherter** secured [covered] credit
~, **hypothekarischer** mortgage
~, **in Anspruch genommener** credit used
~, **kommerzieller** commercial credit
~, **kurzfristiger** short-term credit [loan]
~, **landwirtschaftlicher** farm loan
~, **langfristiger** long-term credit [loan]
~, **laufender** open credit
~, **mittelfristiger** medium-term credit
~, **offener** bank [open] credit
~, **prolongierter** extended credit
~, **revolvierender** revolving credit
~, **staatlicher** state credit [loan]
~, **unbegrenzter** unlimited credit
~, **unbestätigter** unconfirmed credit
~, **ungedeckter** s. ~, **ungesicherter**
~, **ungesicherter** unsecured [uncovered] credit
~, **unwiderruflicher** credit not subject to call, non-callable credit, irrevocable (letter of) credit
~, **widerruflicher** revocable (letter of) credit
~, **zinsloser** interest-free loan
~ **zu günstigen Bedingungen** credit [loan] on favourable terms

Kreditabkommen n credit [loan] agreement
Kreditabteilung f credit department
Kreditanalyse f checking the use of a loan
Kreditangebot n credit [loan] offer
Kreditanspruch m credit claim, claim for credit
Kreditanstalt f credit institution [bank], bank
Kreditantrag m loan [credit] application
✧ **einen ~ stellen** to apply for a loan
Kreditarten fpl kinds of credit
Kreditaufnahme f raising [acceptance] of credit, borrowing ✧ **die ~ bei der Bank erhöhen** to increase the borrowings at the bank
Kreditauftrag m credit order
Kreditausdehnung f extension of a loan [credit]
~, **inflationistische** credit inflation
Kreditausreichung f granting (of) credits [loans]; disbursement of loan
Kreditausreichungsform f method of granting credits
Kreditausweitung f credit expansion
Kreditbank f credit bank
~, **landwirtschaftliche** agricultural [rural] bank, (Am) agricultural credit corporation
Kreditbeanspruchung f (actual) disbursement of loan
Kreditbedarf m credit needs [requirements]
Kreditbedingungen fpl credit conditions, terms of a loan [credit]
Kreditbereitstellung f provision of credit
Kreditbeschränkung f credit restriction
Kreditbestand m credit stock
Kreditbestandsbilanz f balance sheet of credit stock
Kreditbetrag m amount of credit
Kreditbetrug m fraudulent obtaining of credit, obtaining credit by false pretences
Kreditbewegung f credit circulation
Kreditbewegungsbilanz f balance sheet of credit circulation
Kreditbewegungsplan m plan of credit circulation
Kreditbewilligung f granting of a credit [loan]
Kreditbeziehungen fpl credit relations
Kreditbilanz f credit balance, balance sheet of credits
~ **nach außen** foreign credit balance
Kreditbrief m letter of credit
Kreditbürgschaft f credit guarantee
Kreditdrosselung f credit restrictions [squeeze]
Kreditentscheidung f decision on credit
Krediteröffnung f opening of a credit
kreditfähig solvent, financially sound, credit-worthy
Kreditfähigkeit f solvency, financial soundness, credit-worthiness
Kreditfinanzierung f financing by credit
Kreditfonds m credit fund

Kreditfrist *f* duration [period] of a credit
Kreditfunktion *f* credit function
Kreditgarantie *f* credit surety
Kreditgeber *m* lender, creditor, credit grantor
Kreditgebung *f* granting of credit(s)
Kreditgeld *n* credit [bank] money; loan
Kreditgeldzeichen *n* bank note
Kreditgenossenschaft *f* (co-operative) credit society
~, **landwirtschaftliche** co-operative farm credit society
Kreditgeschäft *n* credit transaction [operation]
Kreditgewährung *f* granting [giving] of credits
Kreditgrenze *f* credit ceiling [limit]
Kreditgrundsätze *mpl* credit principles, principles of granting credit
Kredithilfe *f* financial aid
Kredithöhe *f* amount [volume] of credit
kreditieren to enter [place] an amount (to s.o.'s credit), to credit s.o.'s account; to give [extend, allow] credit
Kreditierung *f* entering [placing] an amount (to s.o.'s credit), to credit s.o.'s account; giving [extending, allowing] credit
~, **fondsbezogene** crediting related to production funds
~ **nach dem Gesamtbedarf** crediting according to total (financial) needs
~, **objektbezogene** projected [earmarked] crediting
Kreditinanspruchnahme *f* recourse [resorting] to credits; use of loan
Kreditinflation *f* credit inflation
Kreditinstitut *n s.* **Kreditanstalt**
Kreditinstrument *n* credit instrument
Kreditkarte *f* credit card
Kreditkauf *m* credit buying [purchase], purchase of goods on credit
Kreditkaufbrief *m* letter of credit
Kreditkennziffer *f* (*stats*) credit index number; (*plan*) credit indicator
Kreditknappheit *n* credit stringency [tightness]
Kreditkontingent *n* credit quota
Kreditkontingentierung *f* credit rationing
Kreditkonto *n* credit account
Kreditkontrolle *f* credit control; regulation of credit (*by government, bank etc.*); supervision of credit transactions (*within firm etc.*)
Kreditlaufzeit *f* duration [period], life] of a credit
Kreditlimit *n* credit limit [ceiling]
Kreditlockerung *f* credit relaxation
kreditlos creditless
Kreditmarkt *m* credit market
Kreditmechanismus *m* credit mechanism
Kreditmethode *f* credit method, crediting method

Kreditmittel *npl* credit funds [means]
Kreditnachfrage *f* demand for credits, credit demand
Kreditnahme *f* raising of credit, borrowing
Kreditnehmer *m* borrower
Kreditobjekt *n* object of credit, credited object
Kreditoperationen *fpl* lending operations
Kreditor *m* creditor, credit grantor
Kreditorenkonto *n* creditor account
Kreditpapier *n* credit instrument [bond]
Kreditplafond *m* credit [loan] ceiling
Kreditplan *m* credit plan
Kreditplankennziffer *f* credit plan indicator
Kreditplanung *f* credit planning
Kreditpolitik *f* credit policy (*government, firm etc.*), lending [loan] policy (*central and international banks etc.*)
kreditpolitisch relating to credit [lending, loan] policy
Kreditposten *m* credit item
Kreditprinzip *n* credit principle
Kreditprüfung *f* examination of credit standing
Kreditquelle *f* credit source
Kreditreserve *f* credit reserve
Kreditrestriktionen *fpl* credit restrictions
Kreditrisiko *n* credit risk
Kreditrückfluß *m* backflow [reflux, backward flow] of credits
Kreditrückzahlung *f* credit repayment [reimbursement]
Kreditsaldo *m* credit balance
Kreditschöpfung *f* credit creation
Kreditschraube *f* credit squeeze
Kreditschutz *m* safeguarding [protection] of credit, credit protection
Kreditseite *f* credit side
Kreditsicherheit *f* credit security
Kreditsperre *f* credit ban, ban on credit(s)
Kreditspritze *f* credit injection
Kreditsystem *n* credit system
Kredittilgung *f* redemption [repayment] of a credit, credit redemption
Kreditvergabe *f* granting of credit(s)
Kreditverhältnis *n* creditor-debtor relationship
Kreditverkauf *m* selling [sale] on credit
Kreditverkehr *m* credit transactions
Kreditverknappung *f* credit stringency, tightness of credit
Kreditverlängerung *f* prolongation of credit, credit extension
Kreditvertrag *m* credit agreement [contract]
Kreditverweigerung *f* refusal of credit
Kreditverwendung *f* use of credits, credit utilization, application [employment] of credit
Kreditvolumen *n* volume [amount] of credits, credit volume
Kreditvoraussage *f* credit forecast

Kreditwesen *n* credit system
Kreditwirtschaft *f s.* **Kreditwesen**
kreditwürdig credit-worthy, trustworthy, financially sound
Kreditwürdigkeit *f* credit-worthiness, creditability, *(Am)* credit rating
Kreditzinsen *mpl* credit interest, interest on credit
Kreditzinssatz *m* interest rate on credit
Kreditzusage *f* credit commitment
Kreditzweck *m* purpose of credit
Kreis *m* 1. circle *(associates etc.)*; 2. district
Kreisbauamt *n* district building office
Kreisdiagramm *n* (*stats*) circular chart
Kreishaushalt *m* district budget
Kreislauf *m* cycle, cyclical movement
~ **der Fonds** cirulation of funds
~ **des Kapitals** capital circulation, circulation of capital
Kreissparkasse *f* district savings bank
Kreistag *m* district assembly
Kreistagsabgeordneter *m* member of district assembly
Kriegswirtschaft *f* war economy
Krippenplatz *m* place in a crèche
Krise *f* crisis
~ **des Kapitalismus, allgemeine** general crisis of capitalism *(economic theory)*
~, **partielle** partial crisis
~, **zyklische** cyclical crisis
Krisenherd *m* centre of crisis; political storm-centre, trouble spot
Krisentheorie *f* theory of crisis
Krisenzyklus *m* crisis cycle
Kriterium *n* criterion
~, **Carleman'sches** (*stats*) Carleman's criterion
~, **ökonomisches** economic criterion
Kritik *f* criticism; critique; review *(book etc.)*
Küchenabfälle *mpl* kitchen waste [refuse, rubbish]
Küchenpersonal *n* kitchen personnel
Küchenproduktion *f* food produced in a restaurant
Kühlanlage *f* refrigeration [cold storage] plant
Kühlgutversicherung *f* cold-storage insurance
Kühlhaus *n* cold store, cold-storage depot
Kühllagerung *f* cold storage
Kühlleistung *f* cooling capacity [power]
Kühlraum *m* cold room [store], refrigerator room
Kühlschiff *n* refrigerator [cold storage] ship [vessel]
Kühl- und Lagerwirtschaft *f* refrigeration and storage (facilities)
Kühlwagen *m* (*railw*) refrigerator wagon [(*Am*) car]; (*road transp*) refrigerator van [lorry, (*Am*) truck]

Kükenaufzucht *f* chicken-rearing
kulant obliging, accommodating *(person)*; generous *(offer)*
kultivieren to cultivate *(garden etc.)*; to till *(field etc.)*; to farm *(land)*; to breed *(plants etc.)*; to refine *(taste, style etc.)*; to improve *(mind etc.)*
Kultivierung *f* cultivation *(garden etc.)*; tillage *(field etc.)*; farming *(land)*; breeding *(plants etc.)*; refinement *(taste, style etc.)*; improvement *(mind etc.)*
Kultur *f* culture; civilization
Kulturabgabe *f* entertainment tax
Kulturabkommen *n* cultural agreement
Kulturarbeit *f* cultural work [activity, activities]
Kulturaustausch *m* cultural exchange
Kultureinrichtung *f* leisure facility
Kulturerbe *n* cultural heritage
Kulturfläche *f* (*agric*) cultivated area
Kulturfonds *m* (monetary) fund for financing cultural activities
Kulturgut *n* cultural asset [value]
Kulturhaus *n* clubhouse *(in towns and villages for cultural activities)*
Kulturpflanze *f* cultivated plant
Kulturpolitik *f* cultural policy
kulturpolitisch relating to cultural policy
Kulturreferent *m* person [official] in charge of cultural affairs
Kulturwaren *fpl* toys, sports articles and jewellery
Kulturzentrum *n* cultural centre
Kumulante *f* (*stats*) cumulant
~, **faktoriale** (*stats*) factorial cumulant
kumulativ cumulative
kündbar terminable *(agreement, contract)*, subject to notice
Kunde *m* customer; client
~, **bar zahlender** cash customer
Kundenakzept *n* trade acceptance
Kundenberater *m* customer consultant [adviser]
Kundenberatung *f* advisory service *(for customers)*
Kundenbuch *n* customer's book
Kundendienst *m* service to the customer; after-sales service; delivery service *(as part of service)*
~ **im Export** customer service in export
Kundendienstbedingungen *fpl* terms of customer service
Kundendienstbüro *n* customer service office
Kundendienststützpunkt *m* branch office of customer service
Kundendienstvertrag *m* service contract, contract on service to the customer
Kundenfläche *f* shoppers' floor space
Kundenkartei *f* customers' card index
Kundenkreis *m* clientele, customers

Kundenproduktion *f* made-to-order production
Kundenstamm *m* regular clientele [customers]
Kundenstruktur *f* structure of clientele
Kundenwechsel *m* 1. trade (commercial) bill; 2. change of customers
Kundenwerbung *f* advertising publicity
kündigen to give *s.o.* notice, to give *s.o.* notice of termination *(employment, service, lease agreement)*; to terminate, to cancel *(contract)*; to give notice of withdrawal, to call in *(loan etc.)*; to give notice (to the tenant) to quit; to give notice (to the lessor) of giving up the flat; to call for redemption *(bond, mortgage etc.)*
Kündigung *f* notice, notice of termination *(employment, service, lease, agreement)*; termination, cancellation *(contract)*; giving notice of withdrawal *(loan etc.)*; denunciation *(treaty etc.)*; giving notice (to the tenant) to quit; giving notice (to the lessor) of giving up the flat; call for redemption *(bond, mortgage etc.)*
~ **des Kredits** calling in of a credit, notice of withdrawal of a credit
~, **fristgemäße** due notice; due notice of termination
~, **schriftliche** written notice
Kündigungsfrist *f* period of notice
~, **gesetzliche** statutory period of notice
~, **halbjährliche** six months' notice
~, **jährliche** twelve months' notice
~, **vierteljährliche** three months' [quarterly] notice
~, **vierzehntägige** two weeks' notice
Kündigungsgrund *m* reason for giving notice
Kündigungsrecht *n* right to give notice *(to terminate agreement, contract etc.)*
Kündigungsschutz *m* protection against dismissal
Kündigungstermin *m* last day for giving notice *(to terminate employment, contract etc.)*, last day for calling in *(bond, loan etc.)*, cancellation date
Kundschaft *f* customers; clientele
Kunstblumenmacher *m* artificial flowermaker
Kunstfasern *fpl* artificial [synthetic] fibres
Kunstgewerbe *n* arts and crafts
Kunsthandel *m* art trade, trade in works of art and objects d'art
Kunsthandlung *f* art dealer's shop
Kunsthandwerk *n* arts and crafts
Kunstschaffen *n* artistic creation, creation of works of art; works of art
Kunstschlosser *m* art metal worker
Kunstschmied *m* art smith
Kunststoff *m* plastics, plastic [synthetic, man--made] material
Kunststofferzeugnis *n* plastic product
Kunststoffschrott *m* waste of plastic materials

Kupferschmied *m* coppersmith, brazier
Kupieren *n* *(stats)* truncation
Kupon *m* voucher; counterfoil; coupon
Kuppelprodukt *n* joint product
Kuppelproduktion *f* production of joint products *(gas and coke etc.)*
Kur *f* cure *(at a spa etc.)*; course of treatment
Kuraufenthalt *m* stay at a spa [health-resort]
Kurheim *n* sanatorium, spa home; convalescent home
Kurhotel *n* spa hotel, hotel at a health-resort
Kurort *m* health-resort; spa
Kurs *m* 1. rate of exchange, exchange rate *(currency)*; *(st.ex.)* quotation, price; 2. policy *(government etc.)*, line *(official etc.)*; 3. course *(ship etc.)* ⋄ **außer ~** out of circulation; **außer ~ setzen** to withdraw from circulation; **hoch im ~ stehen** to be at a premium, to be in great demand; **in ~ setzen** to set in circulation; **zum gegenwärtigen ~** at the present [current] rate of exchange; **zum ~ von** at the rate of; **zum mittleren ~** *(fin)* at the parity rate, at par
~, **multipler** multiple rate of exchange
~, **nichtkommerzieller** non-commercial rate of exchange *(special exchange rate based on governmental agreements for tourists and non-commercial transactions)*
~, **variabler** variable rate of exchange
Kursabschlag *m* *(st.ex.)* backwardation
Kursabschwächung *f* *(st.ex.)* weakness of prices
Kursberechnung *f* 1. calculation of the rate of exchange *(currency)*; *(st.ex.)* calculation of rates [prices]; 2. calculation [computation] of the course *(ship etc.)*
Kursbericht *m* market quotations, market-report
Kursbestimmung *f* 1. fixing of rates of exchange *(currency)*; *(st. ex.)* rate [price] fixing; 2. fixing [calculation, computation] of course *(ship etc.)*
Kursbuch *n* (railway) timetable
Kürschner *m* furrier
Kursdifferenz *f* difference in the rate of exchange *(currency)*; *(st.ex.)* difference in rates [prices]
Kurse *mpl*:
⋄ **die ~ manipulieren** *(st.ex.)* to manipulate the prices; **die ~ sind gefallen** *(st.ex.)* prices have dropped; **die ~ sind gestiegen** *(st.ex.)* prices have risen
Kurseinbuße *f* *(st.ex.)* price decline
Kursentwicklung *f* trend of the rate of exchange *(currency)*; *(st.ex.)* trend of rates [prices]
Kursfestsetzung *f* fixing of the rate of exchange *(currency)*; *(st.ex.)* rate [price] fixing
Kursgefüge *n* structure of exchange rates *(currency)*; *(st.ex.)* structure of rates

Kursgewinn *m (st.ex.)* price gain
kursieren to circulate *(money, bills etc.)*
Kursniveau *n* level of rates of exchange *(currency)*; *(st.ex.)* price level
Kursnotierung *f* market quotation
Kursparität *f* exchange parity, parity of exchange rates
Kursrückgang *m (st.ex.)* decline in prices
Kursschwankungen *fpl* exchange fluctuations *(currency)*; *(st.ex.)* price [rate] fluctuations
Kursstabilität *f* stability of the rate of exchange *(currency)*; *(st.ex.)* rate [price] stability
Kurssteigerung *f (st.ex.)* price increase
Kurssturz *m (st.ex.)* sharp fall in prices
Kursstützung *f* exchange pegging *(currency)*; *(st.ex.)* price support [pegging]
Kursus *m* study-course, course of instruction
Kursverlust *m (st.ex.)* loss on the exchange
Kurswechsel *m* reorientation; *(pol)* change of policy; change of course *(ship etc.)*
Kurswert *m (st.ex.)* market value [price]
Kurszettel *m* stock-exchange list
Kurtaxe *f* tax on visitors to spas
Kur- und Bäderwesen *n* sanatoria and spas
Kurve *f* curve
~, **autokatalytische** *(stats)* auto-catalytic curve
~ **der mittleren Dichte** *(stats)* curve of mean density
~ **der mittleren Dichtefunktion** *s.* ~ **der mittleren Dichte**
~ **der Verteilungsfunktion** *(stats)* distribution curve
~ **des mittleren Stichprobenumfanges** *(stats)* average sample number curve
~ **gleicher Schärfe** *s.* ~ **gleicher Teststärke**
~ **gleicher Teststärke** *(stats)* curve of equidetectability
~ **höherer Ordnung** *(stats, maths)* curve of higher order
~, **logistische** *(stats)* auto-catalytic [logistic] curve
~, **skedastische** *(stats)* scedastic curve
~ **zweiter Ordnung** *(stats)* curve of the second order
Kurvenanpassung *f (stats)* curve fitting
~ **an ausgewählte Punkte** *(stats)* method of selected points
~ **an den Trend** *(stats)* trend fitting
~ **für den Trend** *s.* ~ **an den Trend**
Kurvenbild *n (maths)* curve diagram [graph]
Kurvenbüschel *n (maths)* pencil of curves
Kurvendarstellung *f s.* **Kurvenbild**
Kurvenform *f (maths)* curve form
kurvenförmig curviform
Kurvenintegral *n (maths)* curvilinear integral
Kurvenkrümmung *f (maths)* curvature of a curve

Kurvenordinate *f (maths)* ordinate of a curve
Kurvenparameter *m (maths)* parameter of a family of curves
Kurvenpunkt *m (maths)* point of a curve
Kurvenradius *m (maths)* radius of a curvature
Kurvenschar *f (maths)* family of curves
Kurvenverlauf *m (maths)* course [path] of a curve
Kurzarbeit *f* short-time work
kurzarbeiten to work short-time
Kurzarbeiter *m* short-time worker
kurzfristig short-term *(credit, borrowing etc.)*; at short notice ◊ ~ **lieferbar** available for prompt delivery; can be delivered within a short time
kurzlebig short-lived; perishable *(goods)*
Kurzlebigkeit *f* perishability *(goods)*
Kurzlehrgang *m* short study-course
Kurzleistung *f* short peak output [performance] *(machine)*
Kurzwaren *fpl* haberdashery
Küstenbefestigung *f* protection [reinforcement] of the coast; coastal protective works
Küstenfischerei *f* inshore [coastal] fishery [fishing]
Küstengebiet *n* coastal area [region, zone]
Küstengewässer *n* coastal [inshore] waters
Küstenhandel *m* coastal trade
Küstenlinie *f* coastline, shoreline
Küstenprovinz *f* maritime [coastal] province
Küstenschiffahrt *f* coastal shipping, coasting [coastwise] trade
Küstenschutz *m* coast [shore] protection
Küstenstreifen *m* coastal strip
Küstenverlauf *m* coastline, shoreline
Kybernetik *f* cybernetics
~, **ökonomische** economic cybernetics

L

labil unstable *(economy, situation etc.)*; labile *(character etc.)*; delicate, poor *(health etc.)*; weak *(person etc.)*
Labilität *f* instability *(economy, situation etc.)*; lability *(character etc.)*; delicateness, poorness *(health etc.)*; weakness *(person etc.)*
Laborant *m* laboratory assistant
Lackarbeit *f* 1. *(techn)* varnishing; enamelling *(work)*; spraying, painting *(car etc.)*; 2. lacquer ware, lacquer; piece of lacquer work [lacquer ware]; inlaid lacquer work [lacquer ware]
Lackierer *m* lacquerer

Ladeanlagen *fpl* loading facilities
ladebereit ready to be loaded, ready to take cargo *(ship)*
Ladebereitschaft *f* readiness to be loaded, readiness to take cargo *(ship)* ◇ **vorbehaltlich der ~** subject to load readiness
Ladebrief *m* bill of lading
Ladebuch *n* cargo book
Ladeeinheit *f* loading unit
Ladeerlaubnis *f* loading permission; loading permit
Ladefähigkeit *f s.* **Ladekapazität**
Ladefläche *f* loading space [area]
Ladefrist *f* time allowed for loading, loading time
Ladegebühr *f s.* **Ladegeld**
Ladegeld *n* loading charges
Ladegemeinschaft *f* loading pool
Ladegeschäft *n* loading and unloading
Ladegewicht *n* payload; maximum load; *(railw)* loading weight; tonnage *(ship, aircraft)*; weight loaded *(actual weight of cargo)*
Ladegut *n* freight; load
Ladekapazität *f* loading [carrying] capacity; tonnage *(ship)*
Ladelinie *f* load line *(ship)*
Ladeliste *f* loading [cargo] list
Lademaß *n* loading gauge; maximum dimensions of a load
Lademenge *f* load, freight
laden 1. to load, to freight; to ship; *(d.pr.)* to feed; 2. *(jur)* to cite before a court, to summon
Laden *n* loading
Laden *m* shop, *(Am)* store ◇ **den ~ öffnen** to open the shop; **den ~ schließen** to close the shop; **einen ~ aufmachen** to set up a shop
Ladenauslage *f* store display [layout]
Ladenausstattung *f s.* **Ladeneinrichtung**
Ladenausstellung *f* store display *(merchandise)*
Ladenbau *m* shop fitting
Ladenbesitzer *m* owner [proprietor] of a shop; shopkeeper, *(Am)* storekeeper
Ladendieb *m* shoplifter
Ladendiebstahl *m* shoplifting
Ladeneinbruch *m* shopbreaking
Ladeneinrichtung *f* shop fittings [equipment]
Ladenhüter *m* non-seller; dead stock
Ladeninhaber *m s.* **Ladenbesitzer**
Ladenkasse *f* till; cash desk
Ladenkette *f* chain of stores
Ladenmiete *f* shop rent
Ladenpreis *m* retail [selling] price
Ladenschild *n* shop sign
Ladenschluß *m* shop closing, (shop) closing time ◇ **kurz vor ~** shortly before closing time; **nach ~** after closing time, after hours

Ladenschlußgesetz *n* shop-closing law; law governing trading hours
Ladenschlußzeit *f s.* **Ladenschluß**
Ladenstraße *f* shopping street
~, verkehrsfreie shopping precinct
Ladenstunden *fpl* shop [business] hours
Ladentisch *m* (shop) counter ◇ **etwas unter dem ~ verkaufen** to sell s.th. under the (shop) counter
Ladentischverkauf *m* over-the-counter sale
Ladepapier *n* shipping document
Ladeplatz *m* loading bay [area]
Lader *m* loader
Laderampe *f* loading platform [ramp]
Laderaum *m* loading space *(truck etc.)*; (ship's) hold; tonnage *(measurement of ships)*; stowage compartment *(plane)*
Ladeschein *m* bill of lading [loading]
Ladestelle *f* loading point [place]
Ladestraße *f* loading strip *(lorries)*
Lade- und Transportgemeinschaft *f* loading and transport pool
Ladevermögen *n* loading capacity
Ladeverzeichnis *n* freight list; *(cust)* shipper's manifest
Ladevorrichtung *f* loading equipment
Ladezeit *f* loading time
~, gebührenfreie free loading time
Ladung *f* 1. load, freight; cargo *(ship)*; shipment; carload; 2. *(jur)* summons, citation ◇ **jmdm. eine ~ zustellen** *(jur)* to serve s.o. with a summons; **einer ~ Folge leisten** *(jur)* to answer a summons; **~ aufnehmen** to load; to take in cargo *(ship, plane)*; **~ löschen** to discharge a cargo; **ohne ~** freightless; in ballast *(ship)*
~, abgehende outward freight; outward cargo
~, erneute *(jur)* resummons
~, förmliche *(jur)* formal summons
~, geborgene cargo saved
~, gemischte mixed cargo
~, gestapelte stacked cargo
~, schwimmende cargo on the way
~, sperrige bulk load; bulky cargo *(ship)*
~, unterwegs befindliche load on the way; floating cargo *(timber)*
~, verderbliche perishable freight; perishable cargo *(ship)*
~, volle full load; full cargo *(ship)*
~, wertvolle valuable load; valuable cargo *(ship)*
Ladungskosten *pl* lading [shipping] charges
Ladungsverzeichnis *n* freight list, carrier's manifest; [*(Am)* ocean] manifest
Lag *n* *(stats)* lag
Lage *f* 1. situation *(financial etc.)*; position *(economic etc.)*; site *(building etc.)*; location; 2. layer ◇ **die ~ hat sich geändert** the situation has changed; **die ~ hat sich gebessert**

the situation has improved; **die ~ hat sich verschlechtert** the situation has worsened; **in günstiger ~** well-situated, well-positioned; **in schwieriger ~** in a difficult situation [position]; **in zentraler ~** in a central position, centrally situated
~, allgemeine general situation
~, angespannte tense situation
~, bedrängte embarrassment
~, finanzielle financial situation
~, geschäftliche business situation
~, günstige favourable situation
~, politische political situation
~, rechtliche legal status; legal situation
~, verkehrsgünstige favourable situation [convenient position] concerning transport facilities
~, wirtschaftliche economic situation
Lager *n* 1. warehouse, store(house), depot; dump; 2. stock (of goods), stocks, stores; 3. bed, layer, deposit *(coal, ore etc.)*; 4. camp ◊ **ab ~** ex warehouse [store]; **am ~** in stock; **auf ~ arbeiten** to work on stock; **auf ~ bleiben** to remain in stock; **auf ~ bringen** to stock; **auf ~ haben** to have in stock; **auf ~ halten** to hold in store, to keep in stock; **auf ~ legen** to lay in stock; **auf ~ nehmen** to stock, to warehouse; **das ~ räumen** to clear off old stock, to sell out; **ein ~ abbauen** to reduce stock [inventory]; **ein ~ anlegen** to lay in stock, to stock; **ein ~ auffüllen** to restock, to replenish the stock; **ein ~ aufnehmen** to take an inventory; **ein ~ aufstocken** to increase stock; **ein reichhaltiges ~ haben** to be heavily stocked; **nicht auf ~** not in stock; **nicht auf ~ haben** to be out of stock, not to have in stock; **nur gängige Sorten auf ~ haben** to have only a conventional range of articles in stock; **sein ~ räumen** to clear one's stock
~, offenes open warehouse [storehouse]
~, reich sortiertes well-assorted stock
Lageranfertigung *f* production for stock
Lagerangleichung *f* inventory adjustment
Lagerarbeiten *fpl* storing (work)
Lagerarbeiter *m* warehouseman
Lagerauffüllung *f* replenishment of stock
Lageraufnahme *f* stocktaking, inventory
Lageraufnahmefähigkeit *f* storage capacity
Lagerauftrag *m* stock order
Lagerbestand *m* stock (in hand), inventory ◊ **ohne ~** unstocked
~, durchschnittlicher average stock
lagerbeständig suitable for [unaffected by] storage
Lagerbestandsbericht *m* inventory [stock] report
Lagerbestandsverzeichnis *n* inventory ◊ **ein ~ aufnehmen** to make up an inventory

Lagerbestellung *f* stock order
Lagerbetrieb *m* warehousing business
Lagerbewegung *f* stock fluctuation
Lagerbewegungsliste *f* list of stock fluctuations
Lagerbewertung *f* valuation of inventory
Lagerbuch *n* stock ledger [book]
Lagerbuchhalter *m* store-ledger clerk
Lagerbuchhaltung *f* store accounting
Lagerdisposition *f* inventory control
lagerfähig storable, suitable for storage
Lagerfähigkeit *f* 1. storage capacity *(area)*; 2. suitability for storage; shelf life
Lagerfertigung *f* production on stock
Lagerfläche *f* floor space
Lagerfrist *f* time [period] for storage (of goods); time [period] for stock of goods
Lagergebühren *fpl* storage charges
Lagergeld *n* warehouse charges, storage
Lagergeschäft *n* storage [warehouse] business, warehousing; sales ex store
Lagerglied *n* storage point *(between producer and retail enterprise)*
Lagergut *n* stock, goods in storage, stored goods
Lagerhalle *f* warehouse, large storeroom
Lagerhalter *m* stockkeeper, warehouseman, stock clerk, *(Am)* storeman
Lagerhaltung *f* stockkeeping, storing, warehousing
~, optimale optimum stockkeeping
Lagerhaltungskosten *pl* stockkeeping costs
Lagerhaltungszeit *f* storage time
Lagerhaus *n* warehouse; storehouse
~, öffentliches public warehouse
Lagerist *m* stockkeeper, warehouseman, stock--clerk, *(Am)* storeman
Lagerkapazität *f* storage capacity
Lagerkartei *f* stock card index
Lagerkontrolle *f* stock checking; storehouse checking
Lagerkosten *pl* storage costs
Lagerleiter *m* 1. warehouse manager; 2. holiday--camp supervisor
Lagermiete *f* storage (charges)
Lagermöglichkeiten *fpl* storing facilities
lagern 1. to store, to stock; to stack *(in the open)*; 2. to camp
Lagerordnung *f* camp rules *(holiday camps etc.)*
Lagerpersonal *n* 1. warehouse staff [personnel]; 2. personnel of holiday camp
Lagerpfandschein *m* warehouse receipt
Lagerplatz *m* 1. storage area, yard, depot; dump; 2. camp site *(holiday camps etc.)*
Lagerprozeß *m* storage process
Lagerraum *m* storage, storeroom, stock room, depot
Lagerschein *m* warehouse receipt
Lagerschuppen *m* storage shed

Lagerstätte *f* deposit *(coal, ore etc.)*
~, **mineralische** mineral deposit
Lagerstättenbilanz *f* deposit balance (sheet)
Lagersystem *n* storage system
Lagertechnik *f* 1. storage equipment; 2. storage method
Lagertechnologie *f* storage technology
Lagerüberwachung *f* stock control
Lagerumsatz *m s.* **Lagerumschlag**
Lagerumschlag *m* turnover in stock, stock turnover
Lagerung *f* 1. storage, storing, warehousing; seasoning *(maturation)*; 2. stratification *(coal etc.)*
~, **technisch bedingte** storage involving further processing [seasoning]
~, **unsachgemäße** careless storage
Lagerungsprozeß *m* storing, process of storage
Lagerungsschaden *m* damage sustained during storage
Lagerungsverlust *m* storage loss
Lagervertrag *m* storage contract [agreement]
Lagerverwalter *m* stockkeeper, storekeeper
Lagerverwaltung *f* storage [warehouse] management
Lagerverzeichnis *n* inventory record
Lagervorrat *m* stock, inventory
~ **in der Verkaufsabteilung** forward stock
Lagervorrichtungen *fpl* storage [warehousing] facilities
Lagervorschriften *fpl* storage regulations [rules]
Lagerware *f* storage goods [merchandise]
Lagerwert *m* inventory value
Lagerwirtschaft *f* storage, warehousing
Lagerzeit *f* time [period] of storage
Lagerzugänge *mpl* stock receipts
Land *n* 1. land; soil, ground, arable land; 2. country, state ✧ **an ~ bringen** to land; **auf dem Lande** in the country(side); **auf dem Lande leben** to live in the country(side); **außer Landes** abroad; **außer Landes gehen** to leave the country, to go abroad; **jmdn. des Landes verweisen** to expel s.o. from the country, to banish s.o.; ~ **gewinnen** to recover [reclaim] land; ~ **parzellieren** to divide land into smallholdings, to parcel out land; ~ **sanieren** to reclaim land; to improve land; ~ **urbar machen** to clear land; ~ **veräußern** to sell [dispose] land; **zu Lande** by land
~, **angeschwemmtes** alluvian, alluvial land
~, **armes** poor country
~, **assoziiertes** associated country
~, **bebautes** cultivated land; built-up area
~, **besetztes** occupied country
~, **festes** dry land, terra firma
~, **fruchtbares** fertile land [soil]
~, **gutes** good land [soil]
~, **melioriertes** improved land

~, **ökonomisch schwachentwickeltes** economically less developed country
~, **reiches** rich country
~, **rückständiges** backward country
~, **saures** acid soil
~, **teilnehmendes** participating country [nation] *(fair etc.)*
~, **trockenes** dry land; dry soil
~, **übernehmendes** recipient country
~, **überseeisches** overseas country
~, **unbebautes** virgin [*(Am)* new] land; uncultivated land [field]
~, **unfruchtbares** infertile land [soil]
~, **urbares** arable land
Landambulatorium *n* rural outpatient department, rural medical centre
Landarbeit *f* farm work, agricultural work
Landarbeiter *m* farmhand, farm worker [labourer]
Landarzt *m* country doctor
Landaufenthalt *m* stay in the country(side)
Landbau *m* agriculture; farming, husbandry
Landbaukombinat *n* rural construction combine
Landbesitz *m* 1. land ownership, ownership of land; 2. landed property, real estate
Landbesitzer *m* landowner, landed proprietor
Landbevölkerung *f* rural population
Landbewohner *m* countryman, country-dweller
Landbezirk *m* country [rural] district
Landbuch *n* land register
Landeerlaubnis *f* permission to land; landing permit
Landegebühren *fpl* landing charges
Landeigentum *n s.* **Landbesitz**
Landeigentümer *m s.* **Landbesitzer**
landen to land
Länder *npl* countries; Länder *(Federal Republic of Germany)*, States *(constituent members of a federal state)*
Länderanalyse *f* country analysis *(in foreign trade planning)*
Länderbericht *m* country report; information on countries
Länderbeteiligung *f* participation of countries; national participation *(fair etc.)*
länderbezogen related to countries
Ländereien *pl* landed property, land(s), estate(s)
Ländergruppe *f* group of countries, country group
Länderkollektivstand *m* national collective display *(fair, exhibition etc.)*
Länderpavillon *m* national pavilion *(fair, exhibition etc.)*
Länderregierung *f* state government
Länderschau *f* national display [exhibition]
Landerschließung *f* developing of a new area; opening up of a country *(for trade etc.)*

Länderstruktur *f* country structure, country-wise classification *(in foreign trade)*
Ländertypen *mpl* types of countries
Länderverfassung *f* state constitution
Landesanleihe *f* domestic loan
Landesausschuß *m* national committee
Landesbank *f* national bank; regional bank
Landesbedarf *m* needs of the country ⋄ **den ~ decken** to supply [cover] the needs of the country
Landesbehörde *f* state authority
landeseigen state-owned
Landeserzeugnis *n (ind)* domestic [home] product; *(agric)* domestic [home] produce
Landesgebiet *n* national territory
Landesgrenze *f* frontier, national border
Landeshauptstadt *f* capital *(of a country)*
Landeshoheit *f* sovereignty
Landesinneres *n* interior of a country
Landeskultur *f* strategy of environmental ecology *(planning and implementation of measures to maintain and improve natural conditions of life and production)*
Landeskunde *f* 1. knowledge of the manners and customs of a country; 2. study of the geography and civilisation of a country; regional studies
Landesprodukt *n s.* **Landeserzeugnis**
Landesproduktion *f* national production
Landesregierung *f* central [state] government
Landesschuld *f* national debt
Landessprache *f* national language
landesüblich customary, usual (in a country/region)
Landesvaluta *f* national currency
Landesverfassung *f* national constitution
Landesversicherungsanstalt *f* regional social insurance authority
Landesverteidigung *f* national defence
Landesverwaltung *f* national administration; state administration
Landeswährung *f* national currency, legal tender
Landeszentralbank *f* national reserve bank, central bank *(of a country)*
Landflucht *f* migration from the country *(to the towns)*, rural exodus
Landfunk *m* rural radio broadcast, radio service for rural population
Landgemeinde *f* rural community
Landgewinn *m* reclaimed land *(for agricultural purposes etc.)*
Landgewinnung *f* reclamation of land
Landgut *n* estate
Landhunger *m* urgent [pressing] demand for land *(for cultivation by landless peasants)*
Landkreis *m* rural district

landläufig generally accepted [held] *(opinion etc.)*; popular *(view, idea etc.)*; customary, common, usual *(practice etc.)*; widely-used *(expression etc.)*
Landleben *n* country life
ländlich rural, country *(life etc.)*; pastoral *(existence etc.)*
landlos landless
Landmann *m* countryman, farmer
Landmaschine *f* farming equipment, agricultural machine
Landmaschinenausstellung *f* exhibition of agricultural machines
Landmaschinenbau *m* agricultural machinery construction; agricultural engineering industry
Landmaschinenindustrie *f* agricultural engineering industry
Landmaschinenmesse *f* agricultural machinery fair
Landmaschinenschlosser *m* farm-machine mechanic
Landnot *f* shortage of land
Landnutzung *f* land utilization
Landpacht *f* tenancy of agricultural land, holding of agricultural land on lease; lease of agricultural land
Landreform *f* land reform
Landschaft *f* 1. region; tract of country; 2. countryside; environs, environment *(of a town)*; rural district *(surrounding a town)*; 3. landscape
landschaftlich regional
Landschaftsgärtner *m* landscape gardener
Landschaftspflege *f* care of the landscape
Landschaftsschutz *m* conservation (of land), protection of landscape features
Landschaftsschutzgebiet *n* nature reserve
Landstadt *f* country town
Landtechnik *f* 1. agricultural technology; 2. farm [agricultural] machinery
Landtransport *m* overland transport
Land- und Forstwirtschaft *f* agriculture and forestry
Land- und Nahrungsgütertechnik *f* agricultural and food machinery
Land- und Nahrungsgüterwirtschaft *f* agricultural and food industry
Landung *f* landing
Landvermessung *f* land surveying, ordnance survey
Landvermesser *m* (land) surveyor
Landverteilung *f* distribution of land, land distribution
Landwarenhaus *n* rural department(al) store
Landweg *m* country road; country path; (over)land route ⋄ **auf dem ~** by [over] land
Landwirt *m* farmer; agronomist; farm economist

Landwirtschaft *f* 1. agriculture; farming; 2. farm *(estate)*
~, **extensive** extensive (land) cultivation; extensive farming
~, **intensive** intensive (land) cultivation; intensive farming
landwirtschaftlich agricultural *(country, machines etc.)*; farming *(methods, activities etc.)*; farm *(buildings, implements etc.)*; agronomic *(research, adviser etc.)*
landwirtschaftlich-technisch of agricultural technology
Landwirtschaftsausstellung *f* agricultural exhibition
Landwirtschaftsbank *f* agricultural bank; rural bank; *(Am)* land bank
Landwirtschaftsbetrieb *m* farm, farm (enterprise)
~, **örtlicher** local farm (enterprise)
Landwirtschaftserzeugnisse *npl* agricultural [farm] products [produce]
Landwirtschaftskredit *m* agricultural credit, farm loan
Landwirtschaftsmesse *f* agricultural fair
Landwirtschaftsplanung *f* planning of agriculture
Landwirtschaftspolitik *f* agricultural policy; farm policy
Landwirtschaftspreis *m* agricultural price
Landwirtschaftswissenschaften *fpl* agricultural sciences
Landzuteilung *f* allotment of land, *(Am)* land grant
langfristig long-term; in the long run
langjährig long-term *(contract etc.)*; long-standing, of long duration *(friendship etc.)*; long-established *(tradition etc.)*; many years' *(experience etc.)*
langlebig long-living *(person, animal etc.)*; long-lasting *(fashion etc.)*; long-standing, long-established *(custom etc.)*; durable *(product etc.)*
Langlebigkeit *f* longevity *(person, animal etc.)*; durability *(product etc.)*
langwierig protracted *(negotiations etc.)*; lengthy *(preparations etc.)*
Laplace-Verteilung *f (stats)* Laplace distribution
Lärm *m* noise; din; row
Lärmbekämpfung *f* noise abatement
Lärmbelästigung *f* noise nuisance, annoying [disturbing] noise
lärmgeschädigt injured by exposure to noise
Lärmgeschädigter *m* person injured by exposure to noise
Lärmintensität *f* noise intensity [level]
Lärmpegel *m* noise level
~, **erträglicher** tolerable noise level
~, **unerträglicher** intolerable noise level
~, **unzumutbarer** unacceptable noise level
~, **zumutbarer** acceptable noise level
Lärmschaden *m* injury by exposure to noise
Lärmschutz *m* protection against noise; noise barrier
Lärmschwerhörigkeit *f* partial deafness caused by noise
Lärmtabelle *f* table of noise intensity
Last *f* 1. burden; weight; load; cargo, freight; 2. *(fin)* encumbrance, burden; charge; 3. trouble; nuisance
~, **bewegliche** live load
~, **finanzielle** financial burden
~, **ruhende** dead load
~, **tote** *s.* ~, **ruhende**
Lasten *fpl* encumbrances, burdens; charges; taxes and rates ⋄ **zu ~ buchen** to enter on the debit side; **zu unseren ~** to our debit
~, **öffentliche** public charges
~, **soziale** social burdens
~, **steuerliche** tax burdens
Lastenausgleich *m* equalization of burdens
Lastenausgleichsabgabe *f* equalization-of--burdens levy
Lastenausgleichsfonds *m* equalization-of--burdens fund
Lastenbeförderung *f* carriage [conveyance, transport] of goods
Lastenbeihilfe *f* financial assistance
lastenfrei free of charge; unencumbered, free from encumbrances
Lastkahn *m* barge, lighter
Lastkilometer *m* load kilometre
Lastkraftwagen *m* **(LKW)** lorry, *(Am)* (motor) truck
Lastkraftwagenversicherung *f* motor transport insurance
Lastschrift *f* debit item [entry]; debit note [advice]
Lastschriftanzeige *f* debit note
Lastschriftauftrag *m* debit order
Lastschriftbeleg *m* debit voucher
Lastschriftposten *m* debit item
Lastschriftverfahren *n* method of debit transaction
Lastwagen *m s.* **Lastkraftwagen**
Lastwagenladung *f* truck load
Lastwagentransport *m* lorry transport
Lastzug *m* (motor) lorry [*(Am)* truck] and trailer(s), tractor-trailer unit
Latifundienbesitz *m s.* **Latifundium**
Latifundium *n* latifundium
Lauf *m* course *(time, river etc.)*; running *(engine etc.)* ⋄ **im Laufe der Zeit** in the course of time; **im Laufe von** in the course of
~ **der Ereignisse** course of events

Laufbahn *f* career
~, berufliche business career
laufend current *(prices, expenditure etc.)*; continuous *(stocktaking etc.)*; regular *(payments etc.)*; consecutive, serial *(number etc.)* ◇ **auf dem laufenden sein** to be fully informed; **jmdn. auf dem laufenden halten** to keep s.o. currently informed
Laufkunde *m* casual [chance] customer
Laufkundschaft *f* casual customers, passing trade
Laufzeit *f* duration *(lease etc.)*, term *(bill of exchange etc.)*, validity, period *(licence etc.)*; *(tech)* hours of operation; *(tech)* life ◇ **die ~ verlängern** to extend the term *(patent etc.)*
Laufzettel *m* circular; inter-departmental circular for termination of employment *(to confirm the person has returned property belonging to firm etc.)*
Laurent-Prozeß *m (stats)* Laurent process
laut as per, in accordance with, according to
lauten to read, to run ◇ **~ auf** to be made out to
leben to live, to be alive, to exist; to stay *(somewhere)*; to reside, to dwell ◇ **bescheiden ~** to live modestly; **üppig ~** to live in affluence
Leben *n* life, existence, being ◇ **im öffentlichen ~ stehen** to be in the public eye, to be a public figure
~, geistiges intellectual [spiritual] life
~, geistig-kulturelles intellectual and cultural life
~, kulturelles cultural life [activities]
~, öffentliches public life
Lebendgeburt *f* live [viable] birth
Lebendgeburtenziffer *f* natality
Lebendgewicht *n* live weight
lebendig brisk *(business etc.)*
Lebendmasse *f* live weight *(livestock)*
Lebendvermarktung *f* selling alive
Lebensalter *n* age
Lebensanschauung *f* outlook (up)on life
Lebensaussichten *fpl* expectancy [prospects] of life
Lebensbaum *m* tree of life
Lebensbedingungen *fpl* living conditions *(people)*, conditions essential to life *(animals, plants)*
~, gesellschaftliche social conditions of life
~, materielle material conditions of life
~, natürliche natural conditions of life
~, soziale social conditions of life
Lebensbedürfnisse *npl* essentials of life
Lebensdauer *f* lifetime, life span, duration of life *(humankind)*; service life *(machines etc.)*; durability *(cutting tools etc.)*
~, begrenzte limited service life
~ der Grundmittel service life of fixed assets

~, durchschnittliche average lifetime; standard service life *(machines)*
~, lange longevity *(person)*; long life-span *(persons, animals etc.)*; long service [working] life *(machines etc.)*; long (shelf) life, durability *(goods)*
~, mittlere average lifetime; average service time
~, mutmaßliche probable expectation [anticipation] of life; probable service life
~, normale average lifetime; average service life *(machines)*
~, unterdurchschnittliche sub-standard service life
~, wirtschaftliche economic service life
Lebenserwartung *f* life expectancy
lebensfähig viable *(industry, firm, organization etc.)*; able to survive, capable of survival *(community etc.)*
Lebensfähigkeit *f* viability *(industry etc.)*; ability to survive *(community etc.)*
lebensfeindlich hostile to life
Lebensfrage *f* vital question [issue, matter]
Lebensfrist *f* term [span] of life
Lebensführung *f* manner of life, style of living
Lebensgefahr *f* mortal danger, danger to life
lebensgefährlich (highly) dangerous to life
Lebensgemeinschaft *f* partnership for life, life partnership
Lebensgewohnheit *f* way [habit] of living
Lebensgewohnheiten *fpl* traditional life; habits
Lebenshaltung *f* standard of living
Lebenshaltungsindex *m* cost-of-living index
Lebenshaltungskosten *pl* cost of living
~, gestiegene increased cost of living
Lebenshaltungskostenindex *m* cost-of-living index; consumer price index
Lebenskurve *f (stats)* life curve
~, aggregierte *(stats)* aggregate life curve
Lebenslauf *m* career; curriculum vitae; history *(engine etc.)*
Lebensmittel *pl* foodstuffs, food, nourishment; victuals, provisions ◇ **~ rationieren** to ration food
~, leicht verderbliche very perishable goods
Lebensmittelausstellung *f* food exhibition
Lebensmittelbedarf *m* food requirements
Lebensmittelbevorratung *f* stockpiling of foodstuffs
Lebensmittelchemielaborant *m* food laboratory assistant
Lebensmitteleinfuhr *f* food import
Lebensmittelgeschäft *n* grocer's shop, grocery; food shop [*(Am)* store]
Lebensmittelgroßhandel *m* wholesale provision business
Lebensmittelgroßhändler *m* wholesale grocer, provision merchant

Lebensmittelgroßhandlung *f* wholesale provision enterprise
Lebensmittelhandel *m* grocery [provision] trade; grocery [provision] business
Lebensmittelhandlung *f s.* **Lebensmittelgeschäft**
Lebensmittelherstellung *f* food manufacture [processing]
Lebensmittelindustrie *f* foodstuffs [food manufacturing, food processing] industry
Lebensmittelkarte *f* (food) ration card
Lebensmittelknappheit *f* food shortage, shortage of food
Lebensmittelkontrolle *f* food control; control (of the purity and hygiene) of food
Lebensmittelmangel *m* shortage of food
Lebensmittelpaket *n* food parcel
Lebensmittelproduktion *f* food production
Lebensmittelration *f* food ration
Lebensmittelrationierung *f* food rationing
Lebensmittelsendung *f* consignment of food
Lebensmittelüberwachung *f s.* **Lebensmittelkontrolle**
Lebensmittel- und Feinkostausstellung *f* exhibition of food and high-class provisions, food and drink exhibition
Lebensmittelverarbeitung *f* food processing
Lebensmittelvergiftung *f* food poisoning
Lebensmittelverkauf *m* sale of foodstuffs [provisions]
Lebensmittelversorgung *f* supplying with food, food supply
Lebensmittelvorrat *m* stock of food [provisions]
Lebensniveau *n* standard of living
Lebensphase *f* phase of life
Lebensqualität *f* quality of life
Lebensraum *m* living space
Lebensrente *f* life annuity
Lebensspanne *f* span of life
Lebensstandard *m* standard of living
~, **hoher** high standard of living
~, **niedriger** low standard of living
~, **notwendiger** necessary standard of living
~, **tatsächlicher** actual standard of living
Lebensstandardforschung *f* research in standard of living
Lebensstandardplanung *f* planning of the standard of living
Lebensstandardprognose *f* long-term forecast of the living standard
Lebensstandardvergleich *m* comparison of living standards
Lebensunterhalt *m* living, livelihood, subsistence ◊ **seinen ~ verdienen** to earn one's living
~, **notwendiger** minimum subsistence
Lebensunterhaltskosten *pl* living expenses

Lebensunterhaltskostenzuschuß *m* cost of living allowance
Lebensverhältnisse *npl* conditions of life; living conditions
~, **gesellschaftliche** social conditions of life; social conditions of living
Lebensversicherung *f* life insurance
~, **abgekürzte** ordinary endowment policy *(deferred annuity)*
~ **auf den Erlebensfall** endowment policy
~ **auf den Erlebens- und Todesfall, gemischte** combined endowment and whole life insurance
~ **auf den Todesfall** whole life insurance
~, **aufgeschobene** deferred life insurance
~, **erneuerungsfähige** renewable term insurance
~ **mit gleichbleibenden Prämien** ordinary life policy
~, **unkündbare** non-cancellable insurance
~, **voll eingezahlte** paid-up insurance
Lebensversicherungsanstalt *f* life insurance office
Lebensversicherungsgesellschaft *f* life insurance company
~ **auf Gegenseitigkeit** mutual life insurance company
Lebensversicherungspolice *f* life insurance policy
~ **auf den Todesfall** whole life policy
~, **erneuerungsfähige** renewable term policy
~, **jährlich kündbare** permanent life policy
~, **umwandelbare** convertible term policy
~, **zeitlich befristete** term policy
Lebensversicherungsprämie *f* life insurance premium
Lebensversicherungsvertrag *m* life insurance contract
Lebenswahrscheinlichkeit *f* life expectation
Lebensweise *f* way of life [living], mode of life
~, **gesunde** healthy living, healthy way of life
~, **kulturvolle** cultured way of life
~, **nomadische** nomadic mode of life
~, **vernünftige** sensible way of living, sensible living, sensible habits
lebenswichtig vital, essential
Lebenszeit *f* lifetime; service life *(machines)* ◊ **auf ~** for life
~ **eines Erzeugnisses** service life of a product
Lebenszyklus *m* life cycle
Ledererzeugung *f* manufacture of leather
Ledergeschäft *n* leather business; leather shop
Lederhandel *m* leather trade
Lederhandlung *f* leather shop
Lederindustrie *f* leather industry
Ledermesse *f* leather fair
Lederwaren *fpl* leather goods
Lederwarenindustrie *f* leather goods industry

Lederwarenmesse *f* leather goods fair
leer empty *(containers etc.)*, blank *(form, paper etc.)*, vacant *(house etc.)* ◊ **~ stehen** to be vacant, to stand empty; **~ zurück** to be returned empty *(bottles, cases etc.)*
leeren to empty *(sack, refuse bin etc.)*; to clear *(postbox etc.)*, to collect *(mail etc.)*
Leerfahrt *f* empty run
Leerfracht *f* dead freight
Leergewicht *n* tare *(container, cases etc.)*, empty weight *(vehicles etc.)*, deadweight
Leergut *n* empties
Leergutlagerung *f* storing of empty cases
Leerguttransport *m* transport of empties
Leerkilometer *m* *(transp)* distance covered without load
Leerkosten *pl* cost apportioned to idle capacity
Leerlauf *m* *(tech)* idling, idle running [motion]; no-load operation
Leerlaufverlust *m* loss of earnings caused by idle time [capacity] *(of an enterprise)*
Leerlaufzeit *f* idle running [motion] time
Leerpackung *f* dummy, empty package
leerstehend empty, vacant, unoccupied
Leerstellen *fpl* *(d.pr.)* blank spaces
Leertonnage *f* deadweight tonnage
Leerung *f* emptying *(sack, refuse bin etc.)*; clearance *(postbox etc.)*, collection *(mail etc.)*
~, nächste *(post)* next collection
Leerungszeit *f* *(post)* collection time
Leerverkauf *m* short sale
Leerwagen *m* empty waggon
Leerwohnung *f* unfurnished flat
Leerzimmer *n* unfurnished room
Leerzug *m* empty goods [freight] train
legal legal, legitimate *(government etc.)*
legalisieren to legalize *(relationship etc.)*; to authenticate *(document etc.)*
Legalisierung *f* legalization *(relationship etc.)*; authentication *(document etc.)*
Legalisierungsklausel *f* attestation clause
Legat *n* legacy; devise *(real property)* ◊ **ein ~ aussetzen** to leave a legacy; **ein ~ einbehalten** to hold back a legacy
legislativ legislative
Legislative *f* legislature, legislative body [assembly]; legislative power
Legislaturperiode *f* legislative period, lifetime of a parliament
legitim legitimate, lawful *(claim etc.)*; justified *(objection, criticism)*
Legitimation *f* authentication *(documents etc.)*; legalization *(action etc.)*; legitimation *(child etc.)*; authorization; identification
Legitimationskarte *f* licence *(permitting the buying or offering of goods)*; (official) congress [conference] card

Legitimationsnachweis *m* proof of identity
Legitimationspapiere *npl* identification papers; *(jur)* bearer instruments
Legitimationsprüfung *f* proving of identity
Legitimationsübertragung *f* transfer of rights
legitimieren to authenticate *(documents etc.)*; to legalize *(action etc.)*; to legitimate *(child etc.)*; to authorize *(s.o.)*; **sich ~** to prove one's identity, to show one's papers
legitimiert authorized
Legitimierung *f s.* **Legitimation**
Legitimität *f* legitimacy
Lehen *n* *(hist)* fief, feoff, feudal tenure; benefice
Lehnswesen *n* *(hist)* feudal system
Lehrabschluß *m* completion of an apprenticeship
Lehrabschlußzeugnis *n* certificate of completion of apprenticeship
Lehramt *n* teaching profession
Lehranstalt *f* educational establishment
Lehrauftrag *m* teaching assignment; lectureship *(university)*
Lehrausbilder *m* teacher at a vocational training centre
Lehrausbildung *f* training of apprentices
Lehrausbildungsprogramm *n* apprenticeship programme
Lehrbefähigung *f* competence to teach
Lehrberechtigung *f* authority to teach
Lehrberuf *m* 1. vocation, trade, occupation, craft *(requiring vocational training)*; 2. teaching profession
Lehrbetrieb *m* 1. training enterprise; enterprise where apprentices are trained; training shop, apprentice workshop; 2. teaching; lectures *(university)*
Lehre *f* 1. teaching, doctrine; theory; 2. rule, precept; hint, lesson, warning; conclusion; 3. apprenticeship ◊ **die ~ aufnehmen** to start working as an apprentice, to start apprenticeship; **die ~ beenden** to finish apprenticeship; **in der ~ sein** to serve an apprenticeship
~, kaufmännische commercial apprenticeship [training]
Lehrerbildungsanstalt *f* teachers' training college [institution]
Lehrfach *n* (teaching) subject
Lehrfacharbeiter *m* (highly qualified) skilled worker with responsibility for training apprentices on the shop floor *(under guidance of a foreman)*
Lehrgang *m* course (of instruction), course (of study); (training) course
Lehrjahr *n* year of apprenticeship
Lehrkabinett *n* teaching laboratory *(for vocational training)*
Lehrkraft *f* teacher

Lehrling *m* apprentice
Lehrlingsausbilder *m s.* **Lehrausbilder**
Lehrlingsausbildung *f s.* **Lehrausbildung**
Lehrlingseinstellung *f* engagement of apprentices
Lehrlingsentgelt *n* (monthly) pay for apprentices
Lehrlingsheim *n* hostel for apprentices
Lehrlingsnorm *f* work standard of apprentices *(according to the stage of training)*
Lehrlingsvergütung *f s.* **Lehrlingsentgelt**
Lehrlingswohnheim *n s.* **Lehrlingsheim**
Lehrmeinung *f* (academic) thinking; academically accepted opinions [views]
~, **ökonomische** opinions [views] held on an economic issue; academic opinions [views] held on an economic issue
Lehrmeister *m* teacher for vocational training
Lehrobermeister *m* head teacher for vocational training
Lehrpersonal *n* teaching staff
Lehrplan *m* (teaching) syllabus, curriculum
Lehrproduktion *f* production by apprentices in vocational training centres *(as part of the training programme)*
Lehrsatz *m* doctrine; *(maths)* theorem
Lehrstätte *f* training centre, vocational training school
Lehrstelle *f* apprenticeship (place)
~, **offene** vacancy for an apprentice
Lehrstellenverzeichnis *n* register of apprenticeship *(in a district, town etc.)*
Lehr- und Ausbildungsjahr *n* year of apprenticeship
Lehr- und Versuchsgut *n* teaching and experimental farm
Lehrverhältnis *n* apprenticeship
Lehrvertrag *m* apprenticeship contract, contract of apprenticeship
Lehrwerkstatt *f* training (work)shop, apprentice workshop
Lehrzeit *f* (term of) apprenticeship
Lehrzeugnis *n s.* **Lehrabschlußzeugnis**
Leibeigener *m (hist)* bondman, serf
Leibeigenschaft *f (hist)* bondage, serfdom
Leibeigentum *n (hist)* (human) property *(of feudal lord etc.)*
Leibrente *f* (life) annuity ⋄ **jmdm. eine ~ aussetzen** to settle a life annuity on s.o.
~, **abgekürzte** temporary life annuity
~, **aufgeschobene** deferred annuity
~, **lebenslängliche** life annuity
~, **zeitweilige** terminable annuity
Leibrentenempfänger *m* annuitant
Leibrentenrecht *n* law appertaining to annuities; right to an annuity
Leichtbauweise *f* light-weight construction

leichtbeschädigt slightly damaged *(machines, goods etc.)*; slightly injured *(person)*
Leichter *m* lighter, barge
Leichtergebühr *f* lighterage
Leichtindustrie *f* light industry
Leichtmatrose *m* ordinary seaman
Leichtmetallbau *m* light (metal) construction, light alloy construction
leichtverderblich easily perishable *(produce etc.)*
leichtverdient easily earned
leichtverkäuflich easy to sell, saleable
Leihanstalt *f* loan-office; pawnshop
Leihe *f* loan; *(jur)* gratuitous loan for use; pawnshop
Leihemballage *f* containers to be returned [on loan]
leihen to lend, to loan *(s.o. s.th., s.th. to s.o.)* ⋄ **jmdm. etwas ~** to rent [hire] s.th. (out) to s.o.; **sich etwas bei [von] jmdm. ~** to borrow s.th. from s.o.; to hire [rent] s.th. from s.o.
Leihfrist *f* lending period
Leihgabe *f* loan *(work of art etc.)*
Leihgebühr *f* lending fee, hire charge
Leihgeld *n* loan(s)
Leihgeschäft *n* money-lending business, loan business
Leihhaus *n s.* **Leihanstalt**
Leihkapital *n* loan capital
Leihpacht *f* lend-lease
Leihpachtsystem *n* lend-lease system
Leihsache *f* chattel lend for use
Leihschein *m* pawn-ticket
Leih- und Pachtgesetz *n (hist)* Lend-Lease Act
Leihvertrag *m* loan contract
leihweise by way of a loan, as a loan
Leihzins *m* interest on a loan
Leinenindustrie *f* linen industry
leisten to perform *(duty etc.)*; to carry out, to execute *(project etc.)*; to fulfil *(target etc.)*; to achieve, to accomplish, to do, to render *(services etc.)*; to make, to effect *(payments)*
Leistung *f* performance; achievement, accomplishment, attainment; work (done); result(s); output *(enterprise, machine, worker)*; *(agric)* yield *(milk etc.)*; production capacity; workmanship; efficiency; power, capacity *(machine etc.)*; contribution *(fees etc.)*, service(s); payment; benefit *(insurance etc.)* ⋄ **eine gute ~ vollbringen** to do one's best, to do a good job
~, **abrechenbare** accountable performance
~, **finanzielle** financial performance
~ **für die Wiedergutmachung** indemnification payment and services
~, **gute gestalterische** good design
~, **höchste** best performance
~, **höchstmögliche** maximum [best] performance

~, **industrielle** industrial performance; industrial output; industrial capacity
~, **installierte** installed capacity
~, **kleine** small achievement
~, **mangelhafte** poor performance
~, **materielle** physical performance
~, **mengenmäßige** output *(worker etc.)*
~, **nicht industrielle** non-industrial performance; non-industrial output; non-industrial results; non-industrial capacity *(transport, communication, trade etc.)*
~, **nicht qualitätsgerechte** performance not according to quality standards
~, **normale** standard performance; normal rate [level] of performance
~, **qualitätsmäßige** (good) workmanship
~, **produktive** productive performance
~, **technische** technical performance; engineering feat
~, **unentgeltliche** unpaid service(s)
~, **unvollendete** unfinished work [performance]
~, **volkswirtschaftliche** total output of the economy
~, **von einem Vertragspartner zu erbringende** obligation incumbent on a contracting partner
Leistungen *fpl*:
~ **der Sozialversicherung** payments [service(s)] of the national [social] insurance
~, **innerbetriebliche** intra-enterprise performance(s)
~, **wissenschaftlich-technische** scientific and technological achievements
Leistungsabfall *m* decline [falling off] of work [performance]; decline [falling off] in output
~ **in der Produktion** decline [decrease, drop] in production
Leistungsabweichung *f* differences in performance
Leistungsangabe *f* performance data; output data *(machine etc.)*
Leistungsanreiz *m* incentive
~, **finanzieller** monetary [financial] incentive
~, **materieller** material incentive
~, **moralisch-ideeller** non-material [moral] incentive
~, **nichtfinanzieller** non-monetary [non-financial] incentive
Leistungsart *f* type of production activity *(classification of productive or service activities)*
Leistungsaufnahme *f (tech)* power input
Leistungsbedarf *m (tech)* power requirement
Leistungsbehinderungen *fpl* circumstances interfering with performance
Leistungsbereich *m (tech)* range of capacity [performance]
Leistungsbereitschaft *f* readiness for work [performance]

Leistungsbewertung *f* evaluation [rating] of performance, evaluation of work (done); evaluation of result(s); rating of production capacity; evaluation of efficiency
~, **betriebliche** evaluation of performance [results, efficiency] of an enterprise
~, **individuelle** evaluation of individual performance
Leistungsbilanz *f* balance of current account *(balance sheet of exports and imports of goods, services and transfers)*
Leistungsdenken *n* performance orientation
Leistungsdruck *m* stress; pressure to produce results
leistungsfähig efficient; productive; capable of performance [high output] *(machine etc.)*; financially strong; physically fit, vigorous *(worker)*
Leistungsfähigkeit *f* efficiency; productive power *(machine etc.)*; capacity; capability of performance; financial strength; fitness, vigour *(worker)*
~, **asymptotische** *(stats)* asymptotic efficiency
~, **menschliche** human performance capacity, fitness, vigour
~, **relative** relative efficiency
Leistungsfähigkeitsfaktor *m (stats)* efficiency factor
Leistungsfaktor *m* efficiency [performance, rating] factor, power factor
Leistungsfonds *m* fund (of enterprises) to improve working and living conditions
Leistungsgesellschaft *f* performance-oriented society
Leistungsgrad *m* level of performance *(employee etc.)*, operator's performance, output *(per shift, machine etc.)*
Leistungsgrenze *f* limit of performance [capacity, output]
Leistungsinanspruchnahme *f* use [utilization] of capacity; use of services; use of benefits *(insurance etc.)*
Leistungskennziffer *f* performance index [indicator]
Leistungsklage *f (jur)* action for satisfaction
Leistungsklasse *f* class [category] based on standard of performance
Leistungsknick *m* sudden drop in efficiency; sudden drop in one's mental and physical powers
Leistungskontrolle *f* efficiency test; check on efficiency, efficiency check
~, **laufende** constant check on efficiency
Leistungskraft *f* efficiency *(machines etc.)*
Leistungskriterien *npl* performance criteria; output criteria; capacity criteria; service criteria

Leistungskurve *f* performance curve [chart, graph]
Leistungslohn *m* incentive wage(s)
Leistungslohnsystem *n* incentive payment system
Leistungslohn-Zeitlohn-Verhältnis *n* ratio between piece-rate wages and time-rate wages
Leistungsminderung *f* decline [drop] in efficiency
Leistungsniveau *n* performance level; level of efficiency
Leistungsnorm *f* standard of performance
Leistungsparameter *m* performance parameter; output [capacity] parameter
Leistungspflicht *f* obligation to perform a contract; obligation to render a service
leistungspflichtig under an obligation to perform a contract; under obligation to render a service
Leistungsprämie *f* efficiency bonus [pay, payment]; merit bonus
Leistungspreis *m* cost of workmanship; price of energy consumed
Leistungsprinzip *n* performance principle
Leistungsprüfung *f* efficiency test; proficiency test; check on the standard of performance; achievement test *(school etc.)*
Leistungsrechnung *f* output and services accounting *(of demand, output and utilization of goods and services)*
Leistungsreserven *fpl* reserves of capacity
Leistungsrückgang *m* decrease in performance
Leistungsschau *f* (industrial) fair [exhibition]
Leistungsschub *m*:
~, **qualitativer** boost in efficiency [performance]
~, **quantitativer** boost in productivity
Leistungssoll *n* (production) target; *(tech)* target rating
Leistungsstand *m* (current) performance level
leistungsstark powerful *(engine, machine etc.)*, high-performance; with a high output; with a high productivity
leistungssteigernd efficiency-boosting; increasing efficiency [performance, output]; incentive; *(agric)* high-yielding *(milch cow etc.)*
Leistungssteigerung *f* increase in performance; increase in output; increase in efficiency; increase in capacity
Leistungsstimulierung *f* utilization of incentives *(to increase performance, output etc.)*
Leistungstarif *m* consumption rate (of energy)
Leistungs- und Haushaltsplan *m* budget, general service and financial disbursement plan
Leistungsverbesserung *f* improvement in performance, performance improvement
Leistungsvergleich *m* comparison of performance [efficiency]

Leistungsvergütung *f* payment according to performance
Leistungsverhältnis *n* efficiency ratio
Leistungsverlust *m* loss of efficiency
Leistungsvermögen *n* s. **Leistungsfähigkeit**
Leistungsverpflichtung *f* obligation to fulfil task; obligation to fulfil output (norm)
Leistungsversprechen *n* promise to fulfil task; promise to fulfil output (norm)
Leistungsvertrag *m* general service contract *(services, construction work, scientific-technological research etc.)*
Leistungsverweigerung *f* rejection of performance; rejection of payment
Leistungsverzeichnis *n* bill of quantities *(construction)*; articles and conditions *(production etc.)*
Leistungsverzug *m* delay in fulfilling a contract; delay in discharging a duty; delay in payment
Leistungsvolumen *n* capacity
Leistungswettbewerb *m* efficiency contest
Leistungszulage *f* merit salary increase, efficiency bonus
Leistungszuwachs *m* increase in efficiency [productivity]
Leitbetrieb *m* principal enterprise *(charged with organizing joint activities in the field of research and development, production, sales etc., within a group of enterprises engaged in similar production)*
leiten to lead, to guide; to manage, to run, to be in charge of *(enterprise etc.)*; to head *(group)*; to supervise; to govern, to rule *(country)*; to route over *(transport)*; to channel *(information etc.)*; to preside over, to chair *(meeting)*; to steer, to pilot; *(tech)* to convey, to pass, to lead
leitend leading; managerial, executive *(position)*
Leiter *m* head, chief (executive); manager, director *(enterprise)*, works manager; leader *(delegation, team etc.)*; chairperson, chairman, president *(meeting)* ◊ **einen ~ abberufen** to remove a manager; **einen ~ einsetzen** to appoint a manager
~ **der Absatzabteilung** marketing [sales] manager
~ **der Forschungsabteilung** head of research department
~ **der Gütekontrolle** head of quality control
~ **der Personalabteilung** head of personnel department
~ **des Fuhrparks** (chief) transport officer
~ **eines Kollektivs** head of a team
~ **eines landwirtschaftlichen Betriebes** farm manager
~, **geschäftsführender** acting manager

~, **kaufmännischer** business manager
~, **staatlicher** state-appointed manager *(enterprise etc.)*, state-appointed director *(institution etc.)*
~, **stellvertretender** deputy [assistant] manager
~, **technischer** technical manager; manager of engineering works; head of technical department
Leitereigenschaften *fpl* characteristics of a manager [director, leader, executive]
Leitfiliale *f* main branch office *(bank)*
Leitgedanke *m* main idea
Leitmotiv *n* keynote
~, **politisches** keynote of a policy
Leitpostamt *n* head post office *(in a region)*
Leitstelle *f* head office
Leitstudie *f* pilot study *(marketing etc.)*
Leitung *f* 1. management *(enterprise etc.)*; administration *(institution etc.)*; leadership *(party)*; steering committee *(meeting etc.)*; 2. line *(telephone etc.)*; piping, pipes, pipeline *(oil etc.)*; mains *(water, electricity etc.)* ⋄ **die ~ übernehmen** to take over management; **unter neuer ~** under new management
~, **allgemeine** general management
~ **der Produktion** production management
~ **der Wirtschaft, planmäßige** planned management of the economy
~ **durch Motivierung** management by motivation
~ **durch Zielvorgaben** management by objectives
~, **gemeinschaftliche** joint management
~, **gesellschaftliche** social management
~, **kollektive** collective method of management
~ **nach dem Ausnahmeprinzip** management by exception
~ **nach dem Delegierungsprinzip** management by delegation
~ **nach Ergebnissen** management by results
~, **oberste** top management
~, **operative** operational management
~, **staatliche** management [administration] representing the government
~, **systemorientierte** management according to a system
~, **territoriale** regional management; regional administration
~ **und Belegschaft** *f* management and labour
~ **und Planung** *f* management and planning
~ **und Planung, dezentrale** decentralized management and planning
~ **und Planung, zentrale** central management and planning *(economy etc.)*
Leitungsapparat *m* management machinery
Leitungsaufbau *m* management [administrative] structure
Leitungsaufgabe *f* managerial [administrative] task [job]; managerial [administrative] business [responsibility]
Leitungsbereich *m* scope of competence
Leitungsebene *f* management [managerial] level
~, **höchste** top management
~, **höhere** higher level of management
~, **mittlere** medium level of management
~, **untere** lower level of management
~, **unterste** lowest level of management
Leitungsentscheidung *f* management [managerial] decision
Leitungsfunktion *f* management [managerial] function
Leitungshierarchie *f* management [managerial] hierarchy
Leitungsinstrument *n* management [managerial] instrument [tool]
Leitungskonzeption *f* management [managerial] programme
Leitungskosten *pl* management cost(s)
Leitungskräfte *fpl* management [managerial] personnel [staff]
Leitungsmechanismus *m* management mechanism
Leitungsmethode *f* management method; management technique
~, **moderne** modern method of management; modern technique of management
Leitungsmethodik *f* management methodology
Leitungsorganisation *f* organization of management [administration]
Leitungsprinzip *n* management [managerial] principle
Leitungsprinzipien *npl* management principles; code of conduct for management
Leitungspyramide *f* management [managerial] pyramid
Leitungsstab *m* management [managerial] staff
Leitungsstil *m* management style, style of management
Leitungsstruktur *f* management [managerial] structure [set-up]
Leitungsstufe *f s.* **Leitungsebene**
Leitungssystem *n* system of management
~, **zweistufiges** two-tier system of management
Leitungstätigkeit *f* management [managerial] work
Leitungstheorie *f* theory of management, management theory
Leitungs- und Kontrollmechanismus *m* management and control mechanism
Leitungswissenschaft *f* science of management
Leumund *m* reputation, repute
Leumundsnachweis *m* character evidence
Leumundszeuge *m* character witness
liberalisieren to liberalize, to decontrol *(prices, imports etc.)*

Liberalisierung *f* liberalization, decontrol *(prices, imports etc.)*
Liberalisierungsabkommen *n* liberalization agreement
Liberalismus *m* liberalism
Liebhaberpreis *m* collector's price
Liebhaberwert *m* souvenir value
Lieferabkommen *n* supply [delivery] contract
Lieferangebot *n* supply offer, offer of delivery [supply], offer to deliver [supply]; tender, bid ◊ **ein ~ machen** to tender
Lieferannahme *f* acceptance of delivery
Lieferant *m* supplier; contractor; caterer, purveyor *(of food)*
Lieferantenbuch *n* (subsidiary) ledger of accounts of suppliers
Lieferantenfinanzierung *f* financing of suppliers
Lieferantenkartei *f* card index of suppliers
Lieferantenkonten *npl* suppliers' accounts
Lieferantenkredit *m* supplier's credit
Lieferantenliste *f* list of suppliers
Lieferantenrechnung *f* supplier's invoice
Lieferantenschuld *f* debt due to a supplier
Lieferantenskonto *n* discount allowed by suppliers
Lieferanweisung *f* delivery order
Lieferaufschub *m* deferred delivery
Lieferauftrag *m* order for delivery
lieferbar deliverable, available ◊ **kurzfristig ~** for short delivery; **nicht ~** undeliverable, non-available, not to be had; **nicht mehr ~** no longer on sale
Lieferbarkeit *f* deliverability, availability
Lieferbarkeitsbescheinigung *f* certificate of negotiability *(securities etc.)*
Lieferbasis *f* basis of delivery
Lieferbedingungen *fpl* terms of delivery
lieferbereit ready for delivery
Lieferbereitschaft *f* readiness for delivery
Lieferbetrieb *m* (firm of) suppliers, contractors
Lieferbeziehungen *fpl* delivery relations
Lieferbezirk *m* area of supply
Lieferbuch *n* delivery book
Lieferdatum *n* date of delivery
Lieferdienst *m* delivery service
Lieferer *m s.* **Lieferant**
Liefererkonto *n* supplier's account
lieferfähig deliverable, available; able to deliver
Lieferfähigkeit *f* deliverability, availability
Lieferfirma *f s.* **Lieferbetrieb**
Lieferfrist *f* term [time] of delivery ◊ **die ~ einhalten** to keep [adhere to] the time of delivery; **die ~ verkürzen** to reduce the time of delivery; **die ~ verlängern** to extend the time of delivery; **eine ~ setzen** to fix a time for delivery

Lieferfristüberschreitung *f* delayed delivery
Liefergarantie *f* guarantee of delivery
Liefergebiet *n* delivery area; service area
Liefergenossenschaft *f* wholesale co-operative society
Liefergeschäft *n* transaction for the supply of goods; *(st.ex.)* time-bargain, *(Am)* futures; option deal
Liefergewicht *n* net weight
Liefergrafik *f* delivery graph
Liefergrenze *f* bounds of deliveries, boundary of delivery
Lieferhafen *m* port of delivery
Lieferklausel *f* clause of delivery, delivery clause
Lieferkonsortium *n* suppliers' syndicate
Lieferkosten *pl* cost of delivery
Lieferkredit *m* supplier's credit
Lieferland *n* supplying country, country of delivery
Liefermenge *f* quantity of delivery, lot; quantity delivered; quantity ordered
Liefermöglichkeit *f* capacity to deliver; prospects of delivery
liefern to deliver; to supply; to provide, to purvey *(food)*; to yield *(raw material etc.)*; to give, to provide, to furnish *(evidence)* ◊ **gegen bar ~** payment on delivery; **sofort ~** to deliver immediately; **termingemäß ~** to deliver within the time stipulated [fixed]
Liefernormen *fpl* standards of delivery
Lieferort *m* place of delivery
Lieferparität *f s.* **Lieferbasis**
Lieferpflicht *f* obligation to supply
Lieferplan *m* delivery plan
Lieferposten *m* delivery item
Lieferpreis *m* delivery price
Lieferprogramm *n* supply programme
Lieferrhythmus *m* frequency [rhythm] of deliveries
Lieferschein *m* delivery note, bill of delivery
Lieferschwierigkeiten *fpl* difficulties in delivery
Liefersoll *n (agric)* (fixed) quota of delivery
Liefersperre *f* suspension of supplies; embargo
Lieferstopp *m* stoppage of supplies
Liefertag *m* delivery day
Liefertermin *m* date of delivery ◊ **den ~ verschieben** to postpone the date of delivery; **~, festgesetzter** fixed date of delivery
Liefer- und Leistungsbedingungen *fpl* terms of supply and service
Liefer- und Leistungsgarantie *f* delivery and service warranty [guarantee]
Liefer- und Montagevertrag *m* delivery and assembly contract *(of equipment, plant etc.)*
Liefer- und Zahlungsbedingungen *fpl* terms of delivery and payment

Lieferung *f* delivery; supply; provision, purveyance *(food)*; consignment, *(Am)* shipment ◊ **auf ~ kaufen** to buy on future delivery; **auf sofortige ~ verkaufen** to sell with immediate delivery; **auf spätere ~ kaufen** to buy with deferred delivery; **auf zukünftige ~ verkaufen** to sell with deferred delivery; **bei ~** on delivery; **die ~ abnehmen** to take [accept] delivery *(of s.th.)*; **die ~ anmelden** to advise delivery; **die ~ durchführen [vornehmen]** to effect delivery, to deliver; **gegen sofortige ~ kaufen** to buy with immediate delivery; **~ ab Kai** delivery from the quay; **~ frei Bahnhof** delivery free station; **~ frei Grenze** delivery free border, free delivery to frontier; **~ frei Haus** delivery free house; **~ frei Seehafen** delivery free port; **~ gegen bar** payment on delivery; **~ gegen Nachnahme** cash on delivery; **~ in Raten** delivery in instalments; **~ nur an Wiederverkäufer** supply to the trade only; **nach erfolgter ~** when delivered; **zahlbar bei ~** payable on delivery [at time of delivery]; *(post)* cash on delivery (COD)
~, aufgeschobene deferred delivery
~, beschleunigte expedited delivery
~, innerbetriebliche internal delivery
~, komplette complete delivery
~, kostenlose delivery free of charge
~, künftige future delivery
~, kurzfristige short-term delivery
~, mangelhafte bad delivery
~, monatliche monthly delivery
~, nicht erfolgte lack of delivery
~, prompte spot delivery
~, quartalsweise quarterly delivery
~, rechtzeitige delivery in time
~, rückständige delivery in arrears, back order
~, sofortige immediate delivery
~, spätere deferred delivery
~, tägliche daily delivery
~, unverzügliche delivery without delay
~, unvollständige incomplete delivery
~, verzögerte delayed delivery
~, wöchentliche weekly delivery
Lieferungs- *s.* **Liefer-**
Lieferungskauf *m (st.ex.)* purchase for future delivery
Lieferungspreis *m (st.ex.)* quotation for futures
Lieferungsverkauf *m (st.ex.)* sale for future delivery
lieferungsweise according to delivery
Liefervertrag *m* delivery [supply] contract
~, befristeter term delivery contract
~, unbefristeter open-end delivery contract
Lieferverzögerung *f* deferred delivery
Lieferverzug *m* delay in delivery
Lieferwerk *n s.* **Lieferbetrieb**

Lieferwert *m* declared value; value of goods delivered
Lieferwertangabe *f* declaration of the value of goods
Lieferzeit *f* delivery time ◊ **die ~ einhalten** to deliver within the specified time [period]
Lieferzettel *m* delivery note
Lieferzwang *m* compulsory delivery
Lieferzyklus *m* delivery interval
Liegegebühren *fpl s.* **Liegegeld**
Liegegeld *n* demurrage
Liegegeldsatz *m* rate of demurrage
liegen to lie; to be situated, to be located
liegengeblieben uncleared *(stocks, correspondence etc.)*
Liegenschaften *fpl* immovables, *(Am)* realty
Liegenschaftskonto *n* real estate account
Liegenschaftsrecht *n* law of real property
Liegenschaftsübertragung *f* conveyance of real estate
Liegeplatz *m* berth
Liegetage *mpl s.* **Liegezeit**
Liegezeit *f* lay days ◊ **die ~ überschreiten** to be on demurrage; **frei ~** free lay days
Likelihood-Verhältnistest *m (stats)* likelihood-ratio test
Limit *n* limit ◊ **das ~ einhalten** to stick to the limit; **das ~ einschränken** to reduce the limit; **das ~ erhöhen** to raise the limit; **das ~ festsetzen** to fix the limit; **das ~ überschreiten** to exceed the limit
~, ausführbares feasible limit
~, ausgedehntes large limit
~, erreichbares attainable limit
~, knappes narrow limit
~, oberstes maximum limit, ceiling *(land holdings etc.)*
~, unteres lower limit
~, unterstes minimum limit, floor *(land holdings etc.)*
limitieren to limit
limitiert limited ◊ **nicht ~** unlimited
Limitierung *f* limitation
Limitkalkulation *f* calculation to fix the limit *(pricing etc.)*
Limitpreis *m* price limit
Limitschätzkalkulation *f* estimate of the limit
Linie *f* line; course; *(transp)* route, regular service ◊ **auf breiter ~** over a wide field; **eine ~ befliegen** *(transp)* to fly on a route; **eine ~ eröffnen** *(transp)* to start a service (line); **~ stillegen** to close a line *(railway)*, to stop a service *(bus etc.)*; **eine mittlere ~ einhalten** to pursue a middle course
~, absteigende line of descent, descending line
~, gerade direct line
~, offene unused portion *(credit)*

~, politische political line [course], policy *(party etc.)*
Linienbus *m* regular bus, public service bus
Liniendienst *m* liner service
Linienorganisation *f* line organization *(business, factory etc.)*
Linienschiffahrt *f* liner shipping
Linienstichprobenverfahren *n* *(stats)* line sampling
Liniensystem *n* line system *(method of forecasting)*
Linke, die *(pol)* the Left; left wing *(of a party)*
Linkskurs *m* left-wing policy *(party etc.)*; policy tending towards the left *(government etc.)*
liquid fluid, available, ready *(capital etc.)* mobile, liquid, in hand *(money)* ◊ **nicht ~** illiquid, not liquid, insolvent
Liquidation *f* 1. liquidation, winding up *(firm)*; settlement, liquidation *(debt)*; 2. fee, bill *(doctors, lawyers etc.)* ◊ **in ~** in liquidation; **in ~ befindlich** in liquidation [winding up]; **in ~ gehen** to go into liquidation
~, freiwillige voluntary winding up
~, gerichtliche liquidation subject to the supervision of the court
~, gütliche winding up by arrangement
~, stille de facto liquidation [dissolution]
Liquidationsanordnung *f* liquidation order
Liquidationsanteil *m* liquidating dividend
Liquidationsanteilschein *m* share certificate confirming participation in liquidation
Liquidationsantrag *m* petition for liquidation
Liquidationsaufwand *m* liquidation costs
Liquidationsbedingungen *fpl (st.ex.)* settlement terms
Liquidationsbeschluß *m* winding-up resolution [order]
Liquidationsbilanz *f* statement of realization and liquidation
Liquidationsbüro *n* clearing house
Liquidationsgewinn *m* profit made during liquidation proceedings
Liquidationsguthaben *n* clearing balance
Liquidationsquote *f* liquidating dividend
Liquidationsrate *f s.* **Liquidationsquote**
Liquidationstag *m (st.ex.)* ticket day
Liquidationsverfahren *n* liquidation proceedings, winding up, *(Am)* wind up
Liquidationsvergleich *m* composition in winding up proceedings *(when creditors accept partial settlement)*
Liquidationsverkauf *m* sale of bankrupt assets
Liquidationsverlust *m* loss made in the realization of assets *(during liquidation proceedings)*
Liquidationswert *m* total value of assets in liquidation proceedings; *(st.ex.)* realization value

Liquidator *m* liquidator
~, gerichtlich bestellter official liquidator [*(Am)* receiver]
liquidierbar payable, due
Liquidierbarkeit *f* liquidity, convertibility *(assets, resources, estates etc.)*
liquidieren 1. to liquidate, to dissolve, to wind up; to sell off, to realize; to settle; 2. to charge
Liquidierung *f s.* **Liquidation**
liquidisieren to increase the liquidity
Liquidisierung *f* increase in liquidity
Liquidität *f* liquidity *(assets, resources etc.)*, fluidity, availability, mobility *(money, capital, financial resources etc.)*; ease *(money market, capital market)*; solvency *(company etc.)*
~ einer Bank liquidity of a bank
Liquiditätsanspannung *f* decrease in liquidity
Liquiditätsausstattung *f* allocation of financial funds
Liquiditätsbedürfnis *n* need for liquidity
Liquiditätsbilanz *f* balance sheet of liquidity, statement of current assets and liabilities
Liquiditätserhaltung *f* maintenance of liquidity
Liquiditätsgrad *m* degree of liquidity
Liquiditätsguthaben *n* liquid assets *(credit institutions)*
Liquiditätskontrolle *f* control of liquidity
Liquiditätskredit *m* liquid loan
Liquiditätslage *f* liquid position
Liquiditätsmaßnahmen *fpl* easy money policy
Liquiditätsneigung *f* liquidity preference
Liquiditätspolitik *f* liquidity policy
Liquiditätsreserve *f* reserve of liquid assets
Liquiditätsstatus *m* liquid [current] position
Liquiditätsstreben *n s.* **Liquiditätsneigung**
Liquiditätsüberhang *m* monetary reserves, surplus liquidity
Liquiditätsverkauf *m* sale in order to raise liquidity
Liquiditätsvorschriften *fpl* liquidity rules
Liste *f* list ◊ **eine ~ aufstellen** to draw up [make out] a list; **eine ~ eröffnen** to head a list; **eine ~ schließen** to close a list; **etwas auf eine ~ setzen** to put s.th. on a list; **etwas auf eine schwarze ~ setzen** to blacklist s.th.; **etwas auf einer ~ abhaken** to tick of [*(Am)* check off] s.th. in [on] a list; **etwas aus einer ~ streichen** to take s.th. off a list; **in eine ~ eintragen** to list, to enter on a list, to register
~, amtliche register
~ offener Posten statement of open items
listenmäßig according to a list, as listed
Listenpreis *m* list [catalogue] price, price listed
Lizenz *f* licence ◊ **die ~ für ein Buch erwerben** to acquire the rights to produce and publish a book; **eine ~ einziehen** to

revoke a licence; **eine ~ erteilen** to give [grant] a licence; **eine ~ erwerben** to take out a licence; **eine ~ vergeben** to grant a licence; **in ~ hergestellt** manufactured under licence; **ohne ~** without licence, non-licensed; **sich um eine ~ bewerben** to apply for a licence
~, ausschließliche sole [exclusive] licence
Lizenzabführung *f* royalty
Lizenzabkommen *n* licence agreement; agreement for sale of rights *(copyright)*
Lizenzausgabe *f* licensed edition *(book)*
Lizenzaustausch *m* exchange of licences
Lizenzbau *m* licensed construction, manufacture under lincence
Lizenzbedingungen *fpl* terms of a licence
Lizenzentzug *m* revocation of a licence
Lizenzerteilung *f* granting of a licence, licensing
Lizenzexport *m* licence export
Lizenzfertigung *f* manufacture under licence
Lizenzforschung *f* research under licence
lizenzfrei royalty-free *(production)*
Lizenzgeber *m* licensor
Lizenzgebühr *f* royalty
~, einmalige lump sum payment of royalty
Lizenzgeschäft *n* licence deal; licence trade
Lizenzhandel *m* licence trade
lizenzieren to licence, to grant a licence
Lizenzimport *m* licence import
Lizenzinhaber *m* holder of a licence, licensee
Lizenzmonopol *n* licence monopoly
Lizenznahme *f* taking out a licence, acquisition of a licence
Lizenznehmer *m* licensee
Lizenzpaß *m* licence (certificate)
Lizenzpolitik *f* licence policy
Lizenzproduktion *f* production under licence
Lizenzrecht *n* licence law
Lizenzträger *m s.* **Lizenzinhaber**
Lizenzvergabe *f* licensing, granting of a licence
Lizenzvertrag *m* licence contract; contract for sale of rights *(copyright)*
Lizenzwesen *n* licensing system, licensing
Lochkarte *f* punch(ed) card
Lochkartenanlage *f* punch card equipment; punched card system
Lochkartenbuchführung *f* punch card accounting
Lochkartenmaschine *f* punch card machine
Lochkartenschlüssel *m* punch card code
Lochkartenverfahren *n* punch card method
Lochstreifen *m* punch(ed) tape
loco on [in] stock; loco, spot ◊ **Kaffee ~ Hamburg** coffee for delivery at Hamburg
Locogeschäft *n* spot deal [transaction]; spot [cash] business

Locomarkt *m* spot market
Locopreis *m* spot price
Locoverkehr *m* spot [cash] business
Locowaren *fpl* spots, spot goods
logarithmieren to take [calculate] the logarithm of *(a number etc.)*
logarithmisch logarithmic *(function etc.)*
Logarithmus *m* logarithm
Logbuch *n* log-book
Lohn *m* wage(s); pay(ment), remuneration *(s.a.* **Gehalt)** ◊ **~ festsetzen** to set wage rates [wages]; **~ pfänden** to attach wage(s); **vom ~ abziehen** to deduct from wage(s)
~, festgesetzter fixed wage(s)
~, geltender current [prevailing] wage(s)
~, gleicher equal pay
~, höchster maximum [top] wage(s)
~, inflationärer inflationary wage(s)
~, konstanter fixed [set] wage(s)
~, niedrigster minimum wage(s)
~, ortsüblicher local wage rate
~, rückständiger outstanding wages
~, vertragsmäßiger contractual wages(s)
Lohnabbau *m* wage cuts, reduction of wage(s)
lohnabhängig wage-dependent, wage-earning
Lohnabhängiger *m* wage-earner
Lohnabkommen *n* wage agreement
Lohnabrechnung *f* payroll accounting; wage(s) statement; pay slip
Lohnabrechnungsperiode *f* accounting period of wages
Lohnabschlagzahlung *f* (wage) payment on account
Lohnabtretung *f* assignment of wage(s)
Lohnabzug *m* deduction from wages, wage deduction
Lohnanalyse *f* wage analysis
Lohnangleichung *f* equalization of wage(s); cost-of-living and wage adjustment
Lohnanstieg *m* rise in wages, wage increase
Lohnarbeit *f* wage [hired] labour
Lohnarbeiter *m* wage earner, wageworker
Lohnauftrag *m* job(bing) order
Lohnaufträge *mpl*:
◊ **~ vergeben** to farm out work to subcontractors
Lohnaufwand *m* expenditure on wages
Lohnaufwandskennziffer *f* index [indicator] of expenditure on wages
Lohnausfall *m* lost pay
Lohnausgaben *fpl s.* **Lohnaufwand**
Lohnausgleich *m* wage compensation, wage equalization payment
Lohnauszahlung *f* payment of wages
Lohnbedingungen *fpl* wage conditions
Lohnbeleg *m* wage statement
Lohnberechnung *f* calculation of wages

Lohnbestandteile *mpl* wage elements *(for the various types of wages like direct and indirect labour costs etc.)*
Lohnbewegung *f* wage trend
Lohnbuch *n* wages book
Lohnbuchhalter *m* wages [payroll] clerk
Lohnbuchhaltung *f* 1. pay [wages] office; 2. wage(s) [payroll] accounting
Lohnbüro *n* pay [wages] office
Löhne *mpl*:
⋄ ~ **abbauen** to cut wages; ~ **angleichen** to equalize [level up] wages; ~ **anpassen** to adjust wages; ~ **einbehalten** to hold back wages; ~ **einfrieren** to freeze wages; ~ **kürzen** to cut wages
Lohneinbehaltung *f* partial withholding of wage(s)
Lohneinkünfte *fpl* wage earnings
Lohneinnahmen *fpl s.* Lohneinkünfte
Lohnempfänger *m* wage earner, wageworker
Lohnentwicklung *f* growth of wages
Lohnerhöhung *f* wage increase [rise]
Lohnfestlegungen *fpl* fixing of wages
~, **rechtswidrige** unlawful fixing of wages; wage decisions contrary to law
Lohnfonds *m* wage fund
Lohnfondsinanspruchnahme *f* actual wage fund used
Lohnfondskontrolle *f* auditing of the wage fund
Lohnfondsplanung *f* planning of wage fund
Lohnfondszuwachs *m* growth [increase] of wage fund
Lohnforderung *f* wage claim
Lohnform *f* wage form, type of wage(s) *(piece rate wage, time wage etc.)*
~, **direkte** direct wage form
~, **indirekte** indirect wage form
~, **individuelle** individual wage form
~, **kollektive** collective wage form, group wage(s)
~, **kombinierte** combined wage form *(individual and collective forms of wages)*
Lohnformel *f* wage formula
Lohnfortzahlung *f* continued payment of wage(s) *(in case of sickness etc.)*
Lohngefälle *n* wage differential
Lohngefüge *n* structure [composition] of wage(s), wage structure
Lohngemeinkosten *pl* overhead wage [labour] costs
Lohngestaltung *f* fixing of wage forms *(according to conditions of production)*
Lohngruppe *f* wage scale
Lohngruppenkatalog *m* list of wage scales according to trade [job]
Lohnhöchstgrenze *f* wage ceiling
Lohnhöhe *f* wage level
Lohnindex *m* wage index

Lohnintensität *f* wage intensity
lohnintensiv wage-intensive
Lohnkampf *m* strike for higher wages, wage dispute
Lohnklasse *f* wage scale
Lohnkosten *pl* wage [labour] costs
Lohnkostenanteil *m* wage factor in cost, wage cost factor
Lohnkostennorm *f s.* Lohnkostennormativ
Lohnkostennormativ *n* wage [labour] cost standard
Lohnkurve *f* wage curve
Lohnkürzung *f* reduction in wages, pay-out
Lohnleitlinien *fpl* wage guidelines
Lohnlimit *n s.* Lohnhöchstgrenze
Lohnliste *f* payroll; wages sheet
Lohnniveau *n* wage level
Lohnpause *f* pay pause
Lohnpfändung *f* seizure [attachment, distress] of wage(s)
Lohnplanung *f* wage planning
Lohnpolitik *f* wage [pay] policy
~, **leistungsorientierte** performance-oriented wage policy
Lohnprämie *f* incentive bonus
Lohn-Preis-Spirale *f* wage-price spiral
Lohnrechnung *f* wage calculation, accounting of labour costs
Lohnregelung *f* wage regulations
Lohnregulierung *f* regulation of wages, wage regulation
Lohnrückforderung *f* repayment [recovery] of wage(s)
Lohnsatz *m* rate of pay, wage rate
Lohnsenkung *f* reduction in wages
Lohnskala *f* wage scale
~, **gleitende** sliding wage scale
Lohnspitze *f s.* Lohnhöchstgrenze
Lohnstatistik *f* statistics on wages, wage statistics
Lohnsteuer *f* income tax *(levied on wages and salaries)*
Lohnsteuerberechnung *f* calculation of income tax
lohnsteuerfrei not subject to income tax, tax-free
Lohnsteuerkarte *f* card showing pay and tax deducted
Lohnsteuerpflicht *f* liability of an employee to pay income tax
lohnsteuerpflichtig subject to income tax
Lohnsteuertabelle *f* income tax table *(for earned income)*
Lohnsteuerverordnung *f* regulations of income tax
Lohnstopp *m* wage freeze
Lohnstreifen *m* pay slip

Lohnstreit *m* wage dispute
Lohnstruktur *f* wage structure
Lohnstufe *f* wage level
Lohnsumme *f* wage fund *(of an enterprise)*; total sum of wages and salaries *(paid by an enterprise)*
Lohnsystem *n* wage system; system of wage payment
Lohntabelle *f* table of wage scales
Lohntag *m* payday
Lohntarif *m* wage rate
Lohntüte *f* wage [pay] packet
Lohn- und Gehaltsempfänger *mpl* salaried and wage-earning employees
Lohnunterschied *m* wage differential
Lohnveredlung *f* 1. product upgrading, upgrading of product *(by further processing etc.)*; 2. job-processing by farmed-out labour, sub-contracting; cross-border sub-contracting *(where a product is processed usually in a foreign country or an industrial free trade zone)*
~, aktive executing jobbing order from outside (the borders of) the country; importing bonded processing *(often in a free trade zone)*
~, passive giving jobbing order [farming] out labour] (to a firm) outside the country
Lohnvereinbarung *f* wage [pay] agreement
Lohnverlauf *m* relation of incentive bonus to performance
Lohnverhandlungen *fpl* wage negotiations
Lohnvorschuß *m* wage advance
Lohnzahltag *m* payday
Lohnzahlung *f* payment of wages
~, vertraglich vereinbarte wage payment according to contract
Lohnzahlungsperiode *f* payroll period
Lohnzahlungszeitraum *m* *s.* **Lohnzahlungsperiode**
Lohnzettel *m* *s.* **Lohnstreifen**
Lohnzuschlag *m* additional [extra] wage [pay] *(for overtime etc.)*
Lohnzuwachs *m* wage increase [increment]
loko *s.* **loco**
Lombard *m/n* loan against security; lending on securities
Lombardanleihe *f* loan on collateral [personal] securities
Lombardbank *f* loan bank
Lombardbestände *mpl* collateral holding [deposits]
Lombarddarleh(e)n *n* loan on collateral security
Lombarddeckung *f* security, *(Am)* collateral
Lombarddepot *n* collateral deposit
lombardfähig suitable for loans, *(Am)* eligible to serve as collateral ⋄ **nicht ~** unsuitable for loans, *(Am)* not eligible to serve as collateral

Lombardforderung *f* collateral claim
Lombardgeschäft *n* loan business on securities; collateral loan transaction
lombardieren to grant a loan on collateral [personal] securities; to pledge collateral [personal] securities for a loan
Lombardierungsgrenze *f* ceiling on loan upon collateral security
Lombardierungswert *m* collateral value
Lombardkredit *m* loan on collateral [personal] securities ⋄ **einen ~ aufnehmen** to borrow on collateral; **einen ~ gewähren** to lend on collateral
Lombardliste *f* list of stocks and shares acceptable as securities for loans
Lombardsatz *m* interest rate on a loan on collateral [personal] securities
Lombardschein *m* qualifying agreement, *(Am)* hypothecation certificate
Lombardschuld *f* collateral debt
Lombardvertrag *m* collateral trust indenture
Lombardverzeichnis *n* *s.* **Lombardliste**
Lombardvorschuß *m* advance upon collateral securities, *(Am)* collateral advances
Lombardwechsel *m* advance [*(Am)* collateral] bill (of exchange)
Lombardwert *m* loan [*(Am)* collateral] value
Lombardzettel *m* pawn ticket
Lombardzinsfuß *m* *s.* **Lombardsatz**
Lombardzinssatz *m* *s.* **Lombardsatz**
Los *n* 1. lot, batch *(in production)*; 2. lottery ticket
Löschanlage *f* 1. unloading installation *(for ships etc.)*; 2. fire extinguishing system
Löscharbeit(en) *fpl* unloading *(ship etc.)*
löschen 1. to unload, to discharge *(cargo etc.)*; 2. to close *(account)*; to delete, to cancel *(items from account)*; to remove *(s.o. from the register)*; (jur) to abandon, to extinguish *(right to property etc.)*; to erase, to wipe out *(recording, tape, information etc.)*; 3. to put out, to extinguish *(fire etc.)*
Löscherlaubnis *f* discharging permission; discharging permit
Löschgeld *n* discharging dues, landing charges
Löschgebühren *fpl* *s.* **Löschgeld**
Löschhafen *m* port of discharge
Löschplatz *m* *s.* **Löschhafen**
Löschung *f* 1. unloading, discharging, discharge *(cargo etc.)*; 2. closure *(account)*; deletion, cancellation *(of items from account)*; removing *(s.o. from the register)*; (jur) abandonment, extinguishment *(of right to property etc.)*; erasure, wiping out *(recording, tape, information etc.)*; 3. extinction *(fire etc.)*
Löschungsgebühren *fpl* *s.* **Löschgeld**
Löschzeit *f* discharging time *(ship)*

lose loose, unpacked *(goods)*
Loseblattsystem *n* loose-leaf system
Lösegeld *n* ransom ◇ **gegen ein ~** on payment of a ransom
lösen 1. to solve *(problems etc.)*, to resolve *(difficulties, conflicts etc.)*; 2. to buy, to get *(ticket etc.)*; to book, to reserve seat *(in train etc.)*; 3. to withdraw *(from a treaty, one's commitment etc.)*; 4. to ease, to relax *(tension etc.)*
Losgröße *f* lot [batch] size *(in production etc.)*
~, optimale optimum lot [batch]
~, wirtschaftliche economic lot [batch]
Lösung *f* solution *(problems etc.)*, resolution, settlement *(difficulties, conflicts etc.)*
~, endgültige final solution
~, numerische numerical solution
Lotse *m* pilot
lotsen to pilot *(ship into harbour)*
Lotsenamt *n* pilot office
Lotsenboot *n* pilot boat
Lotsengebühr *f* pilotage
Lotsenzwang *m* compulsory pilotage
Lotterie *f* lottery
Lotteriegewinn *m* lottery winnings, prize
Lotterieprämie *f* lottery premium
Lotteriesteuer *f* lottery tax
LPG-Fonds *mpl* funds of an agricultural co-operative, co-operative farm funds
LPG-Gebiet *n* area of a co-operative farm; co-operative farm land
LPG-Gesetz *n* co-operative farm code *(regulates/regulated the social and legal status of the farm and, i.a., the aims, rights and duties of co-operative labour)*
LPG-Mitglied *n* co-operative farm member, member of a co-operative farm
LPG-Mitgliederversammlung *f* general assembly of co-operative farmers *(the highest authority of an agricultural co-operative farm which takes decisions on all major issues such as the statute of the co-operative, election of the chairman, plan of the co-operative etc.)*
LPG-Organe *npl* co-operative farm governing bodies
LPG-Typ *m* type of co-operative farm
LPG-Versicherung *f* insurance of co-operative farms
LPG-Vorsitzender *m* co-operative farm chairman *(elected by the general assembly of the members of the co-operative farm)*
LPG-Vorstand *m* administrative committee of a co-operative farm, co-operative farm administrative committee
Luftbeförderung *f* air transport, transportation by air
Luftfahrt *f* aviation
~, zivile civil aviation

Luftfahrtregister *n* civil airways register *(national register of civil aeroplanes, flight personnel and airports)*
Luftflotte *f* air fleet
Luftfracht *f* air carriage [*(Am)* freight] ◇ **per ~** by air freight [air cargo]; by air carriage; **per ~ senden** to send by air freight [air cargo]
Luftfrachtbrief *m* air consignment note, air waybill
Luftfrachtdienst *m* air freight service
Luftfrachttarif *m* air freight tariff
Luftfrachtverkehr *m* air freight transport, transportation of freight by air
Luftfrachtversicherung *f* air freight insurance
Luftpost *f* airmail ◇ **per ~** by airmail; **per ~ senden** to send by airmail
Luftpostdienst *m* airmail service
Luftposttarif *m* airmail rates
Luftpostzuschlag *m* additional airmail charge
Luftrecht *n* air (traffic) regulations
Lufttransport *m* air transport [carriage]
Luftverkehr *m* air traffic
~, internationaler international air traffic
Luftverkehrsbetrieb *m* airline (company)
Luftverkehrspassagiertarif *m* passenger rates in air transport
Luftverkehrstarif *m* air rates
Luftverkehrsunternehmen *n s.* **Luftverkehrsbetrieb**
Luftverschmutzung *f* air pollution
Luftweg *m* air(line) route, air lane; airway
Lustbarkeitssteuer *f* entertainment tax
Luxusartikel *m* luxury article, luxury
Luxusausführung *f* de luxe model, luxury model; de luxe finish
Luxusbesteuerung *f* luxury taxation
Luxusgüter *npl* luxury articles, luxuries
Luxusindustrie *f* luxury goods industry
Luxuskonsumtion *f* luxury consumption
Luxussteuer *f* tax on luxury goods
Luxuswaren *fpl s* **Luxusgüter**
Luxuszoll *m* duty on luxury goods

M

Macherlohn *m* charge for [cost of] making *(garments etc.)*; labour charge
Macht *f* power; authority; strength, might ◇ **sich der ~ der Tatsachen beugen** to acknowledge the evidence of the facts
Machtanspruch *m* claim to power

Machtapparat *m* machinery of power
Machtausübung *f* exercise of power
Machtbefugnis *f* authority, competence
Machtbereich *m* sphere of influence
Machtblock *m* power bloc
Machtentfaltung *f* growth of power
Machtergreifung *f* seizure of power
Machtfrage *f* question of power
Machthaber *mpl* the rulers, the powers-that-be
mächtig powerful; mighty; massive; terriffic, tremendous
Mächtigkeit *f* 1. powerfulness; mightiness; 2. *(min)* thickness *(of coal seam/stratum)*; 3. *(stats)* power; 4. *(maths)* cardinality of set
Machtinstrument *n* instrument of power
Machtkampf *m* power struggle, struggle for power
machtlos powerless
Machtlosigkeit *f* impotence
Machtmittel *npl* means of exercising power
Machtpolitik *f* power politics
machtpolitisch power political
Machtposition *f* position of power
Machtprobe *f* trial of strength
Machtstreben *n* drive [striving] for power
Machtübernahme *f* assumption of power
Machtverschiebung *f* shift to power
Machtverhältnisse *npl* balance of power
machtvoll powerful
Machtzentrum *n* centre of power, power centre
Machtzuwachs *m* increase in power
Magazin *n* warehouse, storehouse, depot
Magazinarbeiter *m* warehouseman
Magazinverwalter *m* storekeeper
Magistrat *m* city council, municipal authority, municipality
Mahnbrief *m* demand-note, dunning letter, reminder
mahnen to remind *(s.o.)*; to admonish *(s.o. on account of s.th.)*
Mahnfrist *f* time allowed for payment
Mahngebühr *f* charges for reminder, reminder charge
Mahnschreiben *n s.* **Mahnbrief**
Mahnung *f* dunning, request for payment, reminder; warning; admonition; exhortation
Mahnwesen *n* arrears billing
Mahnzettel *m* reminder
Majorität *f* majority
Majoritätsbeschluß *m* majority decision
Majoritätsbeteiligung *f* majority holding
MAK-Bilanzen *fpl* physical balances *(of materials, equipments and consumer goods)*
makellos spotless *(cleanliness etc.)*; unimpeachable *(character etc.)*; flawless, perfect *(figure, product etc.)*; immaculate *(dress etc.)*
Makellosigkeit *f* spotlessness *(cleanliness etc.)*; unimpeachability *(character etc.)*; flawlessness *(figure, product etc.)*; immaculateness *(dress etc.)*
Makler *m* broker, agent
~, amtlicher official broker
~, freier outside broker
Maklerausschuß *m (st.ex.)* brokerage board
Maklerbank *f (st.ex.)* brokerage house, broking firm
Maklerbezirk *m (st.ex.)* broker's territory
Maklerbuch *n (st.ex.)* broker's dealings [jobbing] book
Maklerbüro *n* broker's office
Maklerdarleh(e)n *n (st.ex.)* stockbroker's loan
Maklerfirma *f (st.ex.)* stockbroking house
Maklergebühr *f (st.ex.)* brokerage, broker's commission
Maklergeschäft *n (st.ex.)* brokerage operation; broking [jobbing] business
~, freies *(st.ex.)* outside brokerage
Maklergruppe *f (st.ex.)* group of brokers
Maklergutachten *n (st.ex.)* broker's report
Maklerlohn *m s.* **Maklerprovision**
Maklerprovision *f* broker's commission; *(st.ex.)* brokerage, stockbroker's commission
Maklersyndikat *n (st.ex.)* board of brokers; multiple listing *(dealers in immobiles)*
Maklervertrag *m* broker's contract
Makroanalyse *f* macro-analysis
Makrobefehl *m (d.pr.)* macro-instruction
Makromodell *n* macro-model
Makrorayon *m* macro-region
Makrostandort *m* macro-location
Maler *m* painter
Mandat *n (pol)* mandate; *(jur)* order; (parliamentary) seat; *(jur)* brief
Mangel *m* shortage, scarcity *(goods, jobs etc.)*, lack *(experience, opportunity, confidence etc.)*; shortcoming *(book, persons etc.)*, deficiency *(design etc.)*, fault; defect, flaw, imperfection *(articles etc.)* ⬥ **einen ~ beseitigen** to rectify a defect; **für einen ~ haften** to warrant for a defect
~ an Arbeitskräften manpower shortage, shortage [lack] of manpower
~, an Mitteln lack of funds
~, offensichtlicher apparent [obvious] defect
~, unsichtbarer invisible defect
~, versteckter latent defect
Mängel *mpl*:
~, offene apparent defects
Mängelanzeige *f* notification of defects
Mangelberuf *m* scarce job
Mängelbeseitigung *f* rectification of defects
Mängeleinrede *f* rejection on account of defects
Mängeleinspruch *m s* **Mängeleinrede**
Mangelerscheinung *f* deficiency symptom

mangelfrei free from defects [flaws, faults]
Mangelgewähr *f* warranty for defects
mangelhaft defective, faulty, *(articles etc.)*, incomplete, imperfect; insufficient, inadequate *(training, experience, packing etc.)*
Mängelhaftung *f* warranty for defects *(goods etc.)*
Mangelkrankheit *f* deficiency disease
mangeln to lack, to be short of
mangelnd missing, wanting
Mängelrüge *f s.* **Mängelanzeige**
Mangelware *f* scarce commodity [goods], goods in short supply
Manifest *n* (ship's) manifest; manifesto
Manipulation *f* manipulation, handling, managing *(s.th. in an artful way)*, preparation of goods *(by sorting, bottling, packaging to create artificial demand)*
~, **geschickte** skilful manipulation
~, **zweifelhafte** dubious manipulation
Manipulationsbestand *m* general adjustment fund
Manipulationsfonds *m s.* **Manipulationsbestand**
Manipulationsgebühr *f* handling charge
manipulieren to manipulate, to handle, to manage *(s.th. in an artful way)*, to prepare goods *(by sorting, bottling, packaging to create artificial demand)*
Manipulierung *f:*
~ **der Preise** manipulation of prices
Manko *n* deficit; deficiency ⋄ **ein ~ aufweisen** to show a deficit
Mankogeld *n* (cashier's) allowance for shortages
männlich male
Mantel *m* *(st.ex.)* share certificate; legal title and registration of a firm
Manteltarifvertrag *m* skeleton contract, *(Am)* master agreement *(wage rates)*
Manufaktur *f* manufacture; (manu)factory
Manufakturbetrieb *m* (manu)factory
Manufakturwaren *fpl* piece-goods, *(Am)* yard goods
Marge *f* margin
Marginalien *fpl* marginal notes
Marginalprinzip *n* principle of marginal utility
Mark *f* mark
Marke *f* 1. token *(dues, cloak-room etc.)*; stamp *(letters, co-op etc.)*; 2. mark, trademark, make, brand; 3. coupon *(rationed articles etc.)*; (identification) disc [tag]
~, **eingetragene** registered trademark
~, **gut eingeführte** popular make
Marken *fpl:*
⋄ **auf ~** (obtainable) with coupons [stamps] *(food etc.)*
Markenartikel *m* branded article; proprietary article

Markenartikelpreisbindung *f* price maintenance of branded article
Markenbezeichnung *f* trade [brand] name
Markenerzeugnis *n s.* **Markenartikel**
Markenfabrikate *npl* trademarked goods
Markenfirma *f* manufacturer of branded goods
markenfrei unrationed
markenpflichtig rationed
Markenprodukt *n s.* **Markenartikel**
Markenschutz *m* protection of trademarks
Markenschutzabkommen *n* agreement on protection of trademarks
Markenware *f s.* **Markenartikel**
Markenzeichen *n* trademark
Marketing *n* marketing
Marketingaktivitäten *fpl s.* **Marktarbeit**
Marketingfachmann *m s.* **Marktbearbeiter**
Marketingspezialist *m s.* **Marktbearbeiter**
Markoff-Prozeß *m (stats)* Markoff process
~, **mehrfacher** *(stats)* multiple Markoff process
Markscheide *f (min)* boundary
Markscheider *m (min)* mining surveyor
Markt *m* market; marketplace, market square ⋄ **am offenen ~ kaufen** to buy in [on] the open market; **auf dem ~ erscheinen** to come into [enter] the market; **auf dem ~ intervenieren** to interfere with the market; **auf dem schwarzen ~ verkaufen** to sell on the black market; **auf den ~ bringen** to bring [put] on the market; **den ~ beeinflussen** to influence the market; **den ~ beherrschen** to dominate the market; **den ~ beschicken** to send goods to the market; **den ~ beurteilen** to gauge the market; **den ~ drücken** to depress the market; **den ~ durch Aufkäufe beherrschen** to corner the market; **den ~ erobern** to conquer the market; **den ~ erschließen** to tap the market; **den ~ kennen** to be acquainted with the market; **den ~ manipulieren** to manipulate the market; **den ~ mit Waren überschwemmen** to flood [congest] the market; **den ~ überschwemmen** to glut the market *(goods, money etc.)*; **einen ~ abhalten** to hold a market; **einen ~ schaffen** to create a market; **vom ~ verschwinden** to disappear from the market
~, **abgeschwächter** sagging market
~, **aufnahmefähiger** ready market
~, **ausländischer** foreign market
~, **bedingt aufnahmefähiger** limited market
~, **beständiger** steady market
~, **effektiver** effective market
~, **einheimischer** *s.* ~, **innerer**
~, **fester** firm [steady] market
~, **flauer** dull market
~, **freier** free market
~ **für Anlagewerte** investment market

Markt

~ **für landwirtschaftliche Erzeugnisse** market for agricultural [farm] goods
~ **für mitlaufende Basisdaten, internationaler** *(d.pr.)* international on-line data-base market
~ **für Staatspapiere** *(st.ex.)* consols market
~ **für tägliches Geld** call-money market
~ **für Termingeschäfte** *(st.ex.)* market for futures
~, **gedrückter** depressed market
~, **gemeinsamer** common market
~, **gesättigter** saturated market
~, **grauer** grey market
~, **gut beschickter** market well-stocked with goods
~, **heimischer** *s.* ~, **innerer**
~, **im Freien abgehaltener** open-air market
~, **innerer** internal [home] market
~, **jungfräulicher** virgin market
~, **kontrollierter** controlled market
~, **lebhafter** active market
~, **lustloser** inactive market
~, **nationaler** national market
~, **nicht kontrollierter** uncontrolled market
~, **nicht mehr aufnahmefähiger** *s.* ~, **gesättigter**
~, **offener** open market
~, **organisierter** organized market
~, **potentieller** potential market
~, **schlecht bestückter** poor market
~, **schrumpfender** contracting market
~, **schwacher** weak market
~, **schwarzer** black market
~, **sich ausdehnender** expanding market
~, **stagnierender** stagnant market
~, **steigender** growing market
~, **übersättigter** over-stocked market
~, **überseeischer** overseas market
~, **umfangreicher** extensive [broad] market
~, **unkontrollierter** *s.* ~, **nicht kontrollierter**
~, **unveränderlicher** constant market; *(st.ex.)* pegged market
~, **unvollkommener** imperfect market
~, **vollkommener** perfect market
~, **vom Käufer beherrschter** buyer's market
~, **vom Verkäufer beherrschter** seller's market
~, **widerstandsfähiger** resistant market
Marktabgaben *fpl* market dues; market-stall charges
Marktabsprache *f* cartel agreement; marketing arrangement
Marktanalyse *f* market analysis
Marktangebot *n* market supply
Marktanteil *m* market share
Marktanweisung *f* market order
Marktarbeit *f* marketing (activities)
Marktaufnahmefähigkeit *f* absorptive capacity of the market

Marktaufteilung *f* division of the market; market-sharing
Marktbearbeiter *m* marketing specialist
Marktbedingungen *fpl* market conditions
Marktbeeinflussung *f* influencing a market
Marktbeherrschung *f* control of the market
Marktbelebung *f* buoyancy of the market
Marktbelieferung *f* supplying the market
Marktbeobachtung *f* monitoring the market, study of the market
Marktbericht *m* market report
Marktberichte *mpl*:
~, **tägliche** daily market reports
Marktbesucher *m* (market) stall-keeper *(seller)*; customer
Marktbewegung *f* market fluctuation
Marktbewertung *f* market evaluation
Marktbeziehungen *fpl* market relations
Marktbude *f* market stall [stand, booth]
Markteinführung *f* marketing a new product
Markteinstandspreis *m* market cost price
Marktentfernung *f* market accessibility [distance]
Marktentfremdung *f* alienation from the market
Marktentwicklung *f* growth [development] of the market
Markterholung *f* market recovery; rallying of the market, market rally
Markterkundung *f* study of the market
Markterschließung *f* tapping of a market, opening-up of (new) markets
marktfähig marketable, saleable *(product)* ✧ ~ **machen** to market, to commercialize; **nicht** ~ unmarketable, unsaleable
Marktfähigkeit *f* marketability
Marktfaktor *m* market factor
marktfertig ready for marketing *(product)*
Marktflecken *m* small market town
Marktforschung *f* market research
~, **operative** current market research
~, **perspektivische** research [analysis] on long-term market trends
~, **subjektbezogene** research on consumer demand
~, **territoriale** regional market research
Marktforschungsinstitut *n* market research institute
marktgängig *s.* **marktfähig**
Marktgängigkeit *f s.* **Marktfähigkeit**
Marktgebühren *fpl s.* **Marktabgaben**
Marktgefüge *n* market structure
Marktgeltung *f* market position; reputation
marktgerecht in line with market conditions
Markthalle *f* bazaar, covered market
Marktinformation *f* market information
marktkonform compatible with the free market

Marktkonstellation *f* state of the market
marktkonträr incompatible with the (free) market
Marktkontrolle *f* control of the market
Marktkonzeption *f* marketing programme
Marktkurs *m* *(st.ex.)* market price
Marktlage *f* market situation, state of the market
Marktlücke *f* untapped market
Marktmechanismus *m* market mechanism
Marktordnung *f* market regulations; regulation of the market
Marktorientierung *f* orientation to the market
Marktpflege *f* measures to maintain position in the market
Marktplatz *m* marketplace, market square
Marktposition *f* position in the market
Marktpreis *m* (current) market price
~, **freier** open market price
~, **gängiger** normal market price
Marktproduktion *f* market production
~, **landwirtschaftliche** agricultural market production, agricultural sales
Marktproduktionspreis *m* market production price
Marktprognose *f* market forecast [prognosis]
Marktregulierung *f* regulation of the market
Marktsättigung *f* saturation of the market
Marktschwäche *f* weakness of the market
Marktschwankungen *fpl* fluctuations in the market
Marktsituation *f s.* **Marktlage**
Marktstand *m* market stand
Marktstellung *f s.* **Marktposition**
Marktstruktur *f* market structure
Marktstudie *f* market (trend) analysis
Marktstützung *f* measures to support the market
Markttag *m* market-day
Markttendenz *f* market trend
Marktuntersuchung *f s.* **Marktstudie**
Marktveränderungen *fpl* changes in the market
Marktvergrößerung *f* expansion of the market
Marktverkehr *m* market trading
Marktvoraussagen *fpl* market forecasts
Marktvorbereitung *f* preparatory marketing activities
Marktwert *m* market value
~, **gegenwärtiger** current market value
~, **internationaler** international market value
Marktwerte *mpl*:
~, **führende** *(st.ex.)* leaders
~, **veränderliche** fluctuating market values
Marktwirtschaft *f* market economy
~, **freie** free market economy
~, **soziale** social market economy
marktwirtschaftlich free market

Marxismus *m* Marxism
Marxismus-Leninismus *m* Marxism-Leninism
marxistisch Marxist
marxistisch-leninistisch Marxist-Leninist
Maschine *f* machine, engine; typewriter ⋄ **(mit der)** ~ **schreiben** to type
~, **arbeitssparende** labour-saving machine
~, **automatische** automatic machine
~, **halbautomatische** semi-automatic machine
~, **landwirtschaftliche** agricultural [farm] machine
~, **numerisch gesteuerte** numerically controlled machine
Maschinen *fpl* machines, engines, machinery
~, **nicht ausgelastete** under-utilized machines [machinery]; idle machines [machinery]
maschinell mechanical ⋄ ~ **hergestellt** machine-made
Maschinenanlage *f* plant, machinery; machine unit
Maschinenantrieb *m* machine drive ⋄ **mit** ~ machine-driven
Maschinenarbeit *f* machine work; mechanized work
Maschinenausfall *m* stoppage; breakdown; standstill *(of machines)*
Maschinenauslastung *f* use of machine to capacity, utilization of machine
Maschinenausnutzungsnorm *f* standard rate of machine utilization
Maschinenbau *m* machine building; construction of machines; (mechanical) engineering
Maschinenbauer *m* mechanical engineering fitter; mechanic assembling machinery
Maschinenbauingenieur *m* mechanical engineer
Maschinenbauzeichner *m* mechanical engineering draughtsman
Maschinenbelegung *f*:
~, **optimale** optimal allocation [distribution] of work (orders) to machines *(in machine shop)*
Maschinenbelegungsplan *m* allocation [distribution] plan of work (orders) to machines
Maschinenbesatz *m s.* **Maschinenbestand**
Maschinenbestand *m* stock of machines
Maschinenfabrik *f* machine factory
Maschinenhaus *n* power house
Maschinenlaufstunden *fpl s.* **Maschinenlaufzeit**
Maschinenlaufzeit *f* machine running time
Maschinenpark *m* machinery, stock of machines, mechanical equipment
Maschinenpaß *m* technical manual *(for machine)*
Maschinenpflege *f* maintenance [service] of machines [engines]
Maschinenraum *m* machine shop; engine-room; press-room

21*

Maschinensaal *m* s. **Maschinenraum**
Maschinensatz *m* 1. machine unit generator set; set of connected machines; 2. machine composition; matter set by machine
Maschinenschaden *m* mechanical breakdown, mechanical [engine] trouble, engine breakdown
Maschinenschlosser *m* engine [machine] fitter; mechanic
Maschinenschreiber *m* typist
Maschinenstunde *f* machine hour
Maschinenstundenkostennormativ *n* standard rate of machining cost per hour
Maschinenstundenkostenrechnung *f* calculation of machining cost per hour
Maschinenstundensatz *m* rate of machining cost per hour
Maschinensystem *n* machinery; system of machines
Maschinen- und Anlagenmonteur *m* machine and plant fitter
Maschinen- und Anlagenzeitfonds *m* rated capacity of fixed assets *(in hours)*
Maschinenwärter *m* operator, machine attendant
Maschinenzeitfonds *m* rated capacity of machines *(in hours)*
Maschinerie *f* machinery
Maschinist *m* machinist, machine operator; *(railw)* engine driver
Maß *n* scale; measurement, measure; size; proportion
~ **der Arbeit** measure of work
~ **der Werte** measure of value
~, **Pearson'sches schiefes** *(stats)* Pearson measure of skewness
Maßabteilung *f* made-to-measure department
Maßarbeit *f* s.th. made to measure
Maße *npl*:
~ **und Gewichte** *npl* weights and measures
Masse *f* mass *(of people, errors etc)*; crowd; bulk of the population
Maßeinheit *f* unit of measure(ment)
Maßeinteilung *f* scale
Masse-Leistung-Verhältnis *n* **(der Erzeugnisse)** weight-efficiency ratio (of products)
Massen *fpl* masses; large quantities [numbers] *(of products on the market etc.)*; (jur) assets; estate
Massenabfertigung *f* mass treatment *(shops, hospital etc.)*
Massenabsatz *m* mass sales
Massenandrang *m* massive rush; huge crowd
Massenangebot *n* large-scale supply
Massenanspruch *m* (jur) preferential claim *(against the assets of a bankrupt)*
Massenansturm *m* s. **Massenandrang**

Massenarbeitslosigkeit *f* mass unemployment
Massenartikel *m* bulk [mass-produced] article
Massenbedarf *m* 1. mass demand; 2. s. **Massenbedarfsartikel**
Massenbedarfsartikel *m* article in mass demand; mass consumer article
Massenbedarfsartikel *mpl* basic consumer goods
Massenbedarfsdeckung *f* meeting the needs in basic consumer goods
Massenbedarfsgüter *npl* basic consumer goods
Massenbedarfsgüterproduktion *f* production of basic consumer goods
Massenbeförderungsmittel *n* means of mass transport(ation)
Massenelend *n* mass poverty
Massenentlassung *f* mass dismissals
Massenerhebung *f* mass survey
Massenerzeugnis *n* mass-produced article
Massenfabrikation *f* mass production
Massenfertigung *f* s. **Massenfabrikation**
Massenfilialbetrieb *m* multiple shop [chain store] business
Massenfilialsystem *n* multiple shop [chain store] system
Massenfließfertigung *f* mass flow [serial] production
Massengüter *npl* bulk goods [load]
Massengüterindustrie *f* mass-production industry
Massengutfrachtschiff *n* bulk carrier
massenhaft in bulk, in large numbers
Massenhersteller *m* mass producer
Massenherstellung *f* s. **Massenfabrikation**
Masseninitiative *f* rank and file initiative
Massenkarambolage *f* multiple car crash, pile-up
Massenkaufkraft *f* mass purchasing power
Massenkommunikationsmittel *n* means of mass communication
Massenkonsum *m* mass consumption
Massenmedien *npl* mass media
Massenorganisation *f* mass organization
Massenstreik *m* general strike
Massentransport *m* transport in bulk
Massenverbrauch *m* mass consumption
Massenverbraucher *m* large-scale consumer
Massenverkauf *m* bulk sale
Massenverkehr *m* bulk transport *(coal, ore, grain etc.)*
Massenversammlung *f* mass meeting
Massenverteilung *f* mass distribution
massenweise in bulk, in large numbers
Massenwerbung *f* 1. *(com)* mass advertising; 2. large-scale labour recruitment
Massenwettbewerb *m* mass emulation [competition]

Massenwirkung f mass effect; mass appeal
Masseschuldner m debtor of a bankrupt's estate
Masseur m masseur
Masseverlust m shrinkage
Masseverwalter m trustee in bankruptcy
Masseverzeichnis n statement of affairs *(in bankruptcy)*
Maßgabe f:
 ⋄ **nach ~** in accordance with
maßgebend authoritative
maßgeblich determinative, decisive *(influence, role etc.)*, important *(contribution etc.)*
Maßgröße f unit of measurement
maßhalten to be moderate
Maßhalten n moderation
Maßhaltepolitik f policy of moderation
mäßig moderate, reasonable *(prices etc.)*
Mäßigkeit f moderation, reasonableness *(prices etc.)*
massiv massive *(aid etc.)*, large-scale *(increase in price etc.)*, severe *(criticism etc.)*, grave *(accusation etc.)*, heavy *(attack etc.)*, enormous *(scale etc.)*
Maßnahme f measure, step
~, **außerordentliche** emergency measure
~, **organisatorische** organizational measure [step]
~, **vorbeugende** preventive measure [step]
~, **vorläufige** preliminary measure [step]
~, **vorübergehende** temporary measure
Maßnahmen fpl:
 ⋄ **~ beschließen** to pass measures; **~ ergreifen** to take measures [steps]; **~ treffen** s. **~ ergreifen**
~, **bevölkerungspolitische** demographic measures
~, **disziplinäre** disciplinary measures
~, **einschneidende** incisive measures
~, **finanzielle** financial measures; fiscal measures
~, **gerichtliche** legal measures
~, **gesetzliche** legislative measures
~, **handelspolitische** trade measures
~, **ökonomische** economic measures
~, **politische** policy measures; political measures
~, **preisstabilisierende** price stabilization measures
~, **prophylaktische und vorsorgende veterinärmedizinische** prophylactic and curative veterinary measures
~, **protektionistische** protectionist measures
~, **sozialpolitische** social policy measures
~, **staatliche** governmental measures
~, **steuerliche** taxation measures
~, **vorbeugende** preventive steps [measures]
~, **wirtschaftliche** economic measures [regulations]

~, **wirtschaftspolitische** measures (in the field) of economic policy
Maßnahmeplan m plan of action
Maßstab m measure, standard, yardstick, gauge; scale; criterion
~ der Preise scale of prices
~, **vergrößerter** enlarged scale
~, **verkleinerter** reduced scale
maßstabgerecht true to scale
Maßsystem n system of units
Maß- und Gewichtsgesetz n Weights and Measures Act
Maßverhältnis n ratio of measurement
Maßzahl f *(stats)* statistic; numerical value
~, **abgeleitete statistische** *(stats)* derived statistic
~, **aus Stichproben gewonnene** *(stats)* sample statistic
~, **bedingte statistische** *(stats)* conditional statistic
~, **beste statistische** *(stats)* optimum statistic
~, **der mittleren Lage** *(stats)* measure of location
~, **dimensionslose** *(stats)* absolute measure
~, **lineare systematische** *(stats)* linear systematic statistic
~, **statistische** *(stats)* statistic
~, **unwirksame** *(stats)* inefficient statistic
mästen to fatten
mastfähig of good fattening potential, growth potential
Mastfähigkeit f fattening capacity [quality]
Mastferkel n fattening pig
Mastfutter n fattening food [fodder]
Mastgans f table goose
Masthähnchen n broiler chicken
Mastjahr n mast year *(of fattening livestock)*
Mastkalb n veal calf
Mastochse m feeding bullock
Mastrasse f beef breed
Mastrind n beef cattle
Mastschwein n feeding [fattened] pig
Maststall m fattening pen
Maststier m fattening bull
Mästung f fattening
Mastvieh n fat stock
Mastwirtschaft f beef breeding
Mastzeit f mast season [time]
Material n material ⋄ **~ beschaffen** to get materials
~, **angearbeitetes** material in process
~, **angefordertes** requisitioned material
~, **ausgewähltes** selected material
~, **bereitgestelltes** reserved material
~, **bestelltes** material on order
~, **bezogenes** material delivered
~, **eingelagertes** material on hand [in stock]

Material

~, **geeignetes** suitable material
~, **hergestelltes** fabricated material
~, **knappes** scarce material
~, **lieferbares** deliverable material
~, **metrisches** *(in Einheiten des Dezimalsystems)* metric material
~, **rollendes** *(railw)* rolling stock
~, **statistisches** statistical data
~, **strategisches** strategic material
~, **veraltetes** obsolete material
~, **vorhandenes** available material
~, **vorrätiges** s. ~, **vorhandenes**
~, **zugeteiltes** apportioned material
Materialabrechnung f accounting of materials
Materialangebot n offer of material
Materialart f sort [type] of material
Materialaufkommen n material available *(in a particular period)*
Materialaufwand m material expenditure, expenditure of material
~, **direkter** direct costs of materials
Materialaufwandskoeffizient m coefficient of material expenditure
Materialausgabe f issue of material
Materialausnutzung f utilization of material
Materialausnutzungskoeffizient m coefficient of utilization of material
Materialausnutzungsnorm f standard rate of utilization of material
Materialaustausch m substitution of material
Materialbedarf f requirements of material, material requirements; demand for material
Materialbedarfsdeckung f meeting of material requirements; meeting of demand for material
Materialbedarfsermittlung f calculation of material requirements; calculation of demand for materials
Materialbedarfsplanung f planning of material requirements; planning of demand for material
Materialbeleg m voucher for material
Materialbereitstellung f provision [supply] of material(s)
Materialbeschaffenheit f quality of material
Materialbeschaffung f s. **Materialversorgung**
Materialbestand m stock of materials
Materialbestandskonto n materials stores account
Materialbestandskontrolle f stock-taking of materials
Materialbestandsnorm f standard rate of stocks of materials, standard stock level
Materialbestandsplan m plan of inventory in stocks of material
Materialbestandsplanung f planning of inventory in stocks of material

Materialbewegung f movement of material(s)
Materialbewirtschaftung f rationing of materials
Materialbilanz f balance sheet of material
Materialbörse f exchange market for material and machinery
Materialbruttoverbrauch m gross consumption of material
Materialbuchführung f materials accounting, stock [inventory] accounting *(of materials)*, book keeping of material stocks
Materialbuchhaltung f book keeping of material
Materialdisposition f allocation of material
Materialeinkauf m purchasing of material
Materialeinkaufskonto n purchase account of material(s)
Materialeinsatz m consumption [input, use] of material(s)
~, **rationeller** rational input of material(s)
Materialeinsatzkoeffizient m coefficient of consumption [input] of material(s)
Materialeinsatzschlüssel m s. **Materialeinsatzkoeffizient**
Materialeinsparung f saving [economy in the use] of material
Materialentnahme f materials requisition
Materialentnahmeschein m s. **Materialbeleg**
Materialermüdung f metal fatigue
Materialertragssteuer f tax based on the estimated output of goods from the quantity of materials used
Materialfehler m fault [flaw] in the material
Materialfluß m flow of materials
Materialflußbild n flow chart of material
Materialfonds m material available
Materialgemeinkosten pl overhead costs of materials
Materialintensität f material intensity
materialintensiv material-intensive, material--consuming
Materialismus m materialism
~, **dialektischer** dialectical materialism
~, **historischer** historical materialism
materialistisch materialistic
Materialknappheit f shortage of materials
Materialkontingent n quota of material(s)
Materialkonto n s. **Materialbestandskonto**
Materialkontrolle f checking of economical use [utilization] of material
Materialkosten pl cost(s) of material(s)
~, **direkt zurechenbare** direct cost(s) of materials
~, **indirekt zurechenbare** indirect cost(s) of materials
Materialkostenanteil m share [portion] of material cost in total cost

Materialkostennorm *f* standard of material costs
Materialkostenreduzierung *f* reduction in the cost of material(s)
Materiallager *n* storehouse [store room] for materials, material stores
Materialökonomie *f* economical use of material
Materialplan *m* material procurement plan *(comprising demand and sources of supply of material)*
Materialplanung *f* material planning, planning of material
Materialpreis *m* price of material
Materialpreisdifferenz *f* difference in the price of material(s)
Materialprobleme *npl* difficulties in procuring materials
Materialprüfung *f* testing of material
Materialrechnung *f* calculation of material
Materialreserve *f* reserve of material
Materialressourcen *fpl* material resources
Materialschaden *m* damage to material
Materialstatistik *f* statistics on resources and uses of material
Materialstruktur *f* structure of material inputs
Materialsubstitution *f* substitution of material
Materialuntersuchung *f s.* **Materialprüfung**
Materialverbrauch *m* consumption of material, material consumption
Materialverbrauchsnorm *f* standard rate of material consumption
Materialverbrauchsplan *m* plan of material consumption
Materialverbrauchsplanung *f* planning of material consumption
Materialverbrauchsrechnung *f s.* **Materialrechnung**
Materialverbrauchsstudie *f* analysis of material consumption
Materialverflechtungsbilanz *f* input-output table of materials
Materialverflechtungsmodell *n* input-output table of material in terms of prices
Materialverlust *m* loss [waste] of material
~, **technologisch-bedingter** loss of material due to technical reasons
Materialverlustnorm *f* standard rate of loss of material
Materialverrechnungspreis *m* accounting price of material(s)
Materialverrechnungspreisdifferenz *f* difference in the accounting price of material(s)
Materialversorgung *f* supply of materials; material procurement
Materialversorgungsbilanz *f* material supply balance sheet
Materialverteilung *f* distribution of material

Materialverwendung *f* use of material; utilization of material
Materialvorrat *m s.* **Materialbestand**
Materialvorratsnorm *f s.* **Materialbestandsnorm**
Materialwirtschaft *f* 1. material economics *(part of economics dealing with planning and accounting of material etc.)*; 2. procurement and utilization of materials
Materialzufuhr *f* supply of material
Materialzuschnitt *m* cut of material
matriarchalisch matriarchal
Matriarchat *n* matriarchy
Matrix *f* matrix
~ **der Momente** *(stats)* moment matrix
~, **quadratische** *(stats)* square matrix
~, **rechteckige** *(stats)* rectangular matrix
~, **reguläre** *(stats)* non-singular matrix
~, **stochastische** *(stats)* stochastic matrix
Matrixelement *n* *(stats)* matrix element
Matrizenrechnung *f* matrix algebra
Matrizenumkehrung *f* matrix inversion
Matrose *m* sailor, seaman
Matrose *m* **der Binnenschiffahrt** inland waterways boatman
Matrose *m* **der Handelsschiffahrt** merchant seaman
Maurer *m* bricklayer
maximal maximum
Maximalbelastung *f* maximum load
Maximalbestand *m* maximum stock
Maximalbetrag *m* limit, maximum amount
Maximalforderung *f* maximum demand
Maximalgewicht *n* maximum weight
Maximalhöhe *f* maximum height
Maximalleistung *f* maximum output
Maximallohn *m* maximum wage
Maximalpreis *m* maximum [ceiling, top] price
Maximalprofit *m* maximum profit
~, **langfristiger** maximum long-term profit
Maximaltarif *m* maximum tariff
Maximalvorrat *m* maximum (reserve) stock
Maximalwert *m* maximum value
Maximierung *f* maximization
Maximum *n* maximum
Maximumstelle *f (stats)* mode
Mechaniker *m* mechanic
~ **für Bergbautechnik** mining mechanic
~ **für Datenverarbeitungs- und Büromaschinen** mechanic for computers and office equipment
mechanisiert mechanized
Mechanisierung *f* mechanization
Mechanisierungsgrad *m* degree of mechanization
Mechanisierungskoeffizient *m* coefficient of mechanization

Mechanisierungsniveau *n* level [degree] of mechanization
Mechanisierungsstufe *f* stage of mechanization
Medialtest *m (stats)* medial test
Median(wert) *m (stats)* median
medio middle of the month
Medioabrechnung *f* fortnightly settlement
Mediofälligkeiten *fpl* fortnightly liabilities [commitments]
Mediogeld *n* fortnightly loans
Mediogeschäft *n* futures transaction to be completed on the 15th of the month
Medioliquidation *f s.* **Medioabrechnung**
Medioprolongation *f* fortnightly continuation
Mediowechsel *m* bill of exchange maturing for payment on the 15th of the month
Medium *n* medium
Mehr *n* surplus, excess, increase
Mehrangebot *n* additional offer [supply]
Mehrarbeit *f* 1. extra [additional] work; 2. surplus labour
Mehraufwand *m* additional expenditure
Mehrausgaben *fpl* additional expenditure, excess costs
Mehrbedarf *m* additional [extra] demand
Mehrbelastung *f* extra charge; overloading
Mehrbestand *m* additional [extra] stock
Mehrbetrag *m* additional [extra, excess] amount, excess sum *(money)*
Mehrbietender *m* higher bidder
Mehrbranchenmesse *f* multi-trade fair
mehrdimensional multi-dimensional
Mehreinnahmen *fpl* additional receipts [revenue]
mehren to increase, to multiply, to augment
Mehrergebnis *n* surplus proceeds
Mehrerlös *m* excess [surplus] proceeds
Mehrerlösabführung *f* levy on excess proceeds
mehrfach multiple, multi-, manifold, repeated
Mehrfacharbitrage *f* compound arbitrage
Mehrfachbeobachtung *f (stats)* multiple observation
Mehrfachebenenzielbaum *m (stats)* multi-level relevance tree scheme
~, **integrierter** *(stats)* integrated multi-level tree scheme
Mehrfacheinteilung *f (stats)* manifold classification
Mehrfachklassifizierung *f (stats)* multiple classification
Mehrfachkorrelation *f (stats)* multiple correlation
Mehrfachkorrelationskoeffizient *m (stats)* coefficient of multiple correlation
Mehrfachqualifikation *f* multiple job skills; several qualifications
Mehrfachregression *f (stats)* multiple regression

Mehrfachspezialisierung *f* multiple specialization
Mehrfachversicherung *f* multiple(-line) system of insurance
Mehrfachziele *npl* multiple objectives
~, **sich widersprechende** competitive multiple objectives
Mehrfachzoll *m* multiple tariff
Mehrfaktorenanalyse *f (stats)* multiple factor analysis
Mehrfaktorenversuch *m (stats)* factorial experiment
Mehrfracht *f* excess cargo [freight]
Mehrgebot *n* higher bid, overbid
Mehrgepäck *n* excess luggage
mehrgeschossig multi-storey
Mehrgewicht *n* excess weight
Mehrgewinn *m* additional [excess] profit(s)
Mehrgewinnsteuer *f* capital gains tax
Mehrheit *f* majority
~, **absolute** absolute majority
~, **anteilmäßige** proportional majority
~, **arbeitsfähige** working majority
~, **einfache** simple majority
~, **geringe** small majority
~, **große** large majority
~, **knappe** narrow [bare] majority
~, **relative** relative majority
~, **überwältigende** overwhelming majority
~, **zahlenmäßige** majority in numbers
Mehrheitsabstimmung *f* majority vote
Mehrheitsaktionär *m* majority shareholder [*(Am)* stockholder]
Mehrheitsbeschluß *m* majority decision
Mehrheitsbeteiligung *f* majority holding
Mehrheitsentscheidung *f* majority decision
Mehrkosten *pl* additional [excess] costs
Mehrleistung *f* increased [higher] performance
Mehrleistungsfonds *m* supplementary incentive fund
Mehrleistungslohn *m* productivity [incentive] bonus
Mehrleistungsprämie *f* productivity [efficiency, incentive] bonus
Mehrlohn *m* extra [additional] pay
Mehrlohnprämie *f* efficiency [incentive] bonus
Mehrlohnverlauf *m* relation of incentive bonus to performance
Mehrmaschinenbedienung *f* multiple machine operation
Mehrparteiensystem *n* multiple-party system
Mehrphasenstichprobenverfahren *n (stats)* multiphase sampling
Mehrpreis *m* higher price
Mehrprodukt *n* surplus product
Mehrproduktion *f* 1. increased output; 2. surplus production

Mehrschichtarbeit *f* multi-shift work
Mehrschichtenbetrieb *m* multiple-shift operation; multiple-shift enterprise
mehrschichtig multi-shift
Mehrschichtsystem *n* multi-shift system
Mehrstimmenwahlrecht *n* multiple vote
Mehrstimmrechtsaktie *f* multiple voting share
Mehrumsatz *m* increased [additional] turnover
Mehrvariantenplanung *f* planning with several variants
Mehrverbrauch *m* increase in consumption, additional consumption
Mehrverdienst *m* additional earnings
Mehrversicherung *f s.* **Mehrfachversicherung**
Mehrwegverpackung *f* multi-way packing
Mehrwert *m* 1. surplus value; 2. increase in value; additional value; value added
~, **absoluter** absolute surplus value
~, **relativer** relative surplus value
Mehrwertgesetz *n* law of surplus value
Mehrwertmasse *f* volume of surplus value
Mehrwertrate *f* rate of surplus value
Mehrwertsteuer *f* value-added tax
Mehrwerttheorie *f* theory of surplus value
Meineid *m* false oath, perjury
meineidig perjured ⋄ ~ **werden** to commit perjury
Meinung *f* opinion
~, **abweichende** dissenting opinion
~, **allgemeine** common opinion
~, **eigene** personal opinion
~, **herrschende** prevailing opinion
~, **öffentliche** public opinion
~, **vorgefaßte** biased [prejudiced] opinion
Meinungsänderung *f* change of opinion
Meinungsäußerung *f* expression of one's opinion
Meinungsaustausch *m* exchange of views
Meinungsbefragung *f (stats)* opinion survey; consensus of opinion
Meinungsforscher *m* opinion pollster
Meinungsforschung *f* opinion research
Meinungskauf *m (st.ex.)* speculative buying
Meinungsstreit *m* conflict of opinions
Meinungsumfrage *f* (public) opinion poll [survey]
Meinungsumschwung *m* swing of opinion
Meinungsverschiedenheit *f* difference of opinion
Meinungsverkäufe *mpl (st.ex.)* speculative sellings
Meinungswechsel *m s.* **Meinungsänderung**
meistbegünstigt most-favoured
Meistbegünstigung *f* most-favoured-nation treatment
Meistbegünstigungsklausel *f* most-favoured--nation clause

meistbietend bidding most ⋄ ~ **verkaufen** to sell to the highest bidder
Meistbietender *m* highest bidder
Meister *m* foreman, master ⋄ **seinen** ~ **machen** to become a master *(baker, tailor etc.)*; *(ind)* to become a foreman
~ **seines Faches** to be a master of his craft
Meisterbereich *m* foreman's sphere [section]; foreman's purview [authority]
Meisterbrief *m* guild diploma, master craftsman's certificate
Meisterleistung *f* masterly performance
Meisterprüfung *f* master craftsman's examination *(to certify proficiency in one's trade)*
Meisterschulung *f* advanced training [retraining] of foremen
Meisterstück *n* masterpiece
Meistertitel *m* title of a master, master's title
Meisterwürde *f* rank of master craftsman
Meistgebot *n* highest bid
Meldeamt *n s.* **Meldestelle**
Meldebehörde *f s.* **Meldestelle**
Meldekartei *f* registration cards [card index] *(containing registration of people in a locality)*
Meldemenge *f (stats)* quantity to be reported, reported quantity
melden to report *(s.o./s.th.)*; to notify *(authority of birth etc.)*; to announce *(s.o.)*; **sich** ~ to register *(with s.o.)*; to report *(to s.o.)*, to contact *(s.o.)*, to get in touch *(with s.o.)*
Meldepflicht *f* obligation to register
meldepflichtig obliged to register
Melderegister *n* register *(residents, goods etc.)*
Meldeschein *m* registration form
Meldeschluß *m* closing date *(applications etc.)*
Meldestelle *f* resident's registration centre; registration office
Meldung *f* registration *(of s.th./with s.o.)*; notification *(birth etc.)*; announcement *(arrival etc.)*; news; report; announcement; message
Meldewesen *n* system of registration
Meldezettel *m s.* **Meldeschein**
Melioration *f* melioration, land improvement, soil conditioning
Meliorationsgenossenschaft *f* land improvement co-operative
meliorieren to improve *(land)*
Memorandum *n* memorandum
Memorial *n (acc)* diary, journal
Memorialbuchführung *f* memorial bookkeeping
Menge *f* 1. quantity; amount; set; a lot *(of money etc.)*; 2. crowd ⋄ **der** ~ **nach** quantitative, in terms of quantity; **eine** ~ **für etwas bezahlen** to pay quite a lot for s.th.
~, **abzählbar unendliche** *(stats)* countably infinite set

~, **abzählbare** *(stats)* countable set
~ **der Transformationen eines lateinischen Quadrats** *(stats)* transformation set of Latin squares
~, **disjunkte** *(stats)* disjoint set
~, **endliche** *(stats)* finite set
~, **erhebliche** considerable quantities [amounts]
~, **geordnete** *(stats)* ordered set
~, **gleichmächtige** *(stats)* equipotent quantity
~, **große** lump; large quantity
~, **leere** *(stats)* null [empty] set
~, **mögliche** *(stats)* feasible set
~, **nicht abzählbare** *(stats)* odd set
~, **unendliche** *(stats)* infinite set
~, **ungeordnete** *(stats)* uncleared set
~, **unrichtige** wrong quantity
~, **vertraglich vereinbarte** contracted quantity
~, **wohlgeordnete** *s.* ~, **geordnete**
Mengen *fpl*:
 ⋄ **in großen** ~ in large quantities; **in kleinen** ~ in small quantities [amounts]
Mengenabsatz *m* sale in terms of quantity; large-scale sale
Mengenabschlag *m s.* **Mengenrabatt**
Mengenabschreibung *f* depreciation (based on quantitative output)
Mengenangabe *f* indication of quantity
Mengenbegriff *m* term of quantity; *(stats)* concept of sets
Mengenbestimmung *f* quantitative determination [analysis]
Mengenbezeichnung *f* term of quantity
Mengendiskont *m s.* **Mengenrabatt**
Mengeneinheit *f* unit of quantity
Mengeneinkauf *m* bulk buying
Mengenerlös *m* quantity proceeds
Mengenertrag *m s.* **Mengenerlös**
Mengenindex *m (stats)* quantum index
Mengenkennziffer *f* volume index
Mengenkontrolle *f* quantitative control
Mengenkosten *pl* charges varying in proportion to the quantity of goods handled
Mengenkurs *m (st.ex.)* indirect rate of exchange
Mengenlehre *f (maths)* theory of sets
Mengenleistung *f* quantitative output *(machines, plants etc.)*
mengenmäßig quantitative, in terms of quantity
Mengenmessung *f* quantitative measurement
Mengenmeßziffer *f (stats)* quantum relative
Mengennachlaß *m s.* **Mengenrabatt**
Mengennorm *f* quantity standard [quota, norm]
Mengennotierung *f (st.ex.)* quotation of the indirect rate of exchange
Mengenpreis *m* bulk price
Mengenprodukt *n (stats)* product of sets
Mengenrabatt *m* quantity rebate [discount]
Mengenrabattpreis *m* quantity rebate price

Mengensystem *n (stats)* family of sets
Mengentarif *m* quantity rate
Mengentheorie *f s.* **Mengenlehre**
Mengentoleranz *f s.* **Mengenabweichung**
Mengenverhältnis *n* ratio, proportion
Mengenvorgabe *f* quantity standard
Mengenzoll *m* specific duty
Menschenführung *f* human management, guidance [leadership, management] of people
Menschengruppe *f* group of people
Menschenhandel *m* trade in human beings
Menschenhändler *m* trader in human beings
Menschenkraft *f* manpower
Menschenleben *n* human life; lifetime
Menschenpotential *n* manpower reserves
Menschenrechte *npl* human rights
Menschenwürde *f* human dignity
menschenwürdig worthy of human beings ⋄ ~ **leben** to live in conditions fit for human beings
Menschheit *f* humankind; humanity
menschlich human
Menschlichkeit *f* humanity
Mensch-Maschine-Dialog *m* man-machine dialogue
Mensch-Maschine-Modell *n* man-machine model
merkantil mercantile
Merkantilismus *m* mercantilism
Merkantilist *m* mercantilist
merkantilistisch mercantilist
Merkantilsystem *n* mercantile system
Merkblatt *n* sheet [leaflet] of instructions, reminder
Merkmal *n* mark; sign; feature, attribute, character
~, **charakteristisches** characteristic feature
~, **dominantes** dominant feature
~, **hervorstechendes** outstanding feature
~, **heterogrades** *(stats)* variable
~, **homogrades** *(stats)* attribute
~, **qualitatives** *s.* ~, **homogrades**
~, **quantitatives** *(stats)* variable
~, **rezessives** *(stats)* characteristic, attribute
~, **unterscheidendes** criterion, distinguishing feature; *(stats)* criterion
Merkmale *npl*:
~, **besondere** distinguishing features
~, **diskrete** *(stats)* discrete variables
~, **stetige** *(stats)* continuous variables
Merkmalsanalyse *f* character analysis
Merkmalsgruppe *f* group of features
Merkmalsiterationen *fpl (stats)* runs
Merkmalsklasse *f (stats)* category
Merkmalspaar *n (stats)* pair of features
Merkmalsunterschiedlichkeit *f (stats)* variability

Merkposten *m (acc)* monitory item
meßbar measurable, mensurable *(quantity, function, distance etc.)*
Meßbarkeit *f* measurability, mensurability *(quantity, function, distance etc.)*
Meßbereich *m* measuring range
Messe *f* fair, exhibition ◊ **die ~ besuchen** to attend a fair; **eine ~ abhalten** to hold [stage] a fair; **eine ~ beschicken** to participate in a fair
~ des Kunsthandwerks handicrafts fair
~, internationale international (trade) fair
~, landwirtschaftliche agricultural fair
~, technische technical fair
Messeablauf *m* course of the fair
Messeabschlüsse *mpl* fair transactions concluded
Messeabzeichen *n* fair badge
Messeamt *n* (trade) fair office
Messeangebot *n* goods offered at a fair
Messeareal *n s.* **Messegelände**
Messeaufträge *mpl* fair orders
Messeaufwand *m* fair expenses; fair costs
Messeauskunft *f* information on a fair, fair information
Messeausweis *m* fair card
~ für Aussteller fair card for exhibitors
Messebauten *pl* fair buildings
Messebestimmungen *fpl* fair regulations
Messebesuch *m* visit to the fair; fair attendance
Messebesucher *m* visitor to a fair
Messebeteiligung *f* participation in a fair
Messedienst *m* fair service; international trade centre
Messedirektverkehr *m* direct fair transport
Messedispositionen *fpl* fair arrangements
Messeeinrichtungen *fpl* trade fair installations
Messeerfolg *m* success of a fair; success at a fair
Messeerleichterungen *fpl* fair facilities
Messeexponat *n* fair exhibit
Messefläche *f* fair space [area]
Messegelände *n* fairgrounds, exhibition grounds
Messegeschäft *n* fair business; fair transaction
Messegruppen *fpl* display groups at a fair
Messegut *n* exhibits
Messeguttransport *m* dispatch of exhibits
Messegutversicherung *f* insurance of exhibits
Messegutzollschein *m* fair customs document
Messehalle *f* exhibition hall
Messehaus *n* fair building
Messekalender *m* fair calendar
Messekatalog *m* fair catalogue
Messekaufvertrag *m* sales contract concluded at a fair
Messekontingent *n* quota of goods to be exhibited

Messekontingentschein *m* certificate of quota of goods to be exhibited
Messekosten *pl* exhibition costs
Messekundschaft *f* fair customers
Messeleitung *f* fair management
Messemiete *f* rent for fair space
Messemuster *n* fair sample
messen to measure, to gauge *(pressure, volume, area etc.)*, to take the measurements; to survey *(land etc.)*
Messen *n* measurement, measuring *(temperature)*
Messeneuheiten *fpl* novelties (at a fair)
Messeordnung *f* rules and regulations of a fair
Messepavillon *m* fair pavilion
Messepersonal *n* staff of a fair
Messeplakat *n* fair poster
Messeplakette *f* fair tag [logo]
Messeplan *m* 1. fair programme; 2. fair map
Messeplatz *m* fair place [town, city]
Messeprivileg *n* fair privilege
Messeprogramm *n* fair programme
Messepublikum *n s.* **Messebesucher**
Messequartier *n* lodging for a fair visitor
Messerundgang *m* tour of a fair hall [ground]
Messespediteur *m* fair forwarding agent
Messespesen *pl* fair expenses
Messestadt *f* fair town [city]
Messestand *m* booth, stall (at a fair)
Messetarif *m* (concessionary) fair rates
Messeteilnehmer *m* participant at [in] a fair
Messeunterlagen *fpl* fair documents
Messeversicherung *f* fair insurance
Messevertretung *f* fair agency
Messeverwaltung *f* fair administration
Messevisum *n* fair visa
Messewechselstelle *f* fair exchange bureau
Messewerbung *f* fair advertising
Messewesen *n* matters concerning a fair
Messezeitung *f* fair news bulletin
Messezollpapiere *npl* fair customs documents
Meßfehler *m* error in measurement
Meßgerät *n* measuring instrument, gauge; meter
Meßgröße *f* quantity to be measured; measurable quantity; measured quantity
Meßinstrument *n s.* **Meßgerät**
Meßmethode *f* method of measurement
Meß-, Steuer- und Regelungstechnik *f* measurement and process control, control engineering
Meßtechnik *f* 1. measuring technique; 2. (science of) measuring
Meß- und Steuertechnik *f*:
~, computerunterstützte computer-aided measurement and control
Messung *f* measurement *(activity, results)*
~ der Arbeitsproduktivität measuring labour productivity

~ **der gesellschaftlichen Wertgröße** measuring the magnitude of social value
~, **direkte** direct measurement
~, **indirekte** indirect measurement
Meßwert *m* measured value
Meßzahl *f s.* **Meßziffer**
Meßziffer *f (stats)* index, index-number, relative
Metageschäft *n* joint transaction
Metakonto *n* joint account
Metall *n* metal
Metallabfall *m* scrap-metal, waste metal
Metallarbeit *f* metalwork
Metallarbeiter *m* metalworker
Metallbau *m* metal construction
Metallbauweise *f* method of metal construction
Metallbearbeitung *f* metalworking
Metallbearbeitungsverfahren *n* metalworking technique; metalworking process
Metallberufe *mpl* occupations in the metal industry
Metallbestand *m (bank)* bullion reserve
Metallblasinstrumentenmacher *m* metal wind instruments maker
Metallbörse *f* metal exchange
Metalldeckung *f* metallic cover
Metalle *npl*:
~, **edle** precious [noble] metals
~, **unedle** base metals
Metallerzbergbau *m* metalliferous mining
Metallerzeuger *m* metal manufacturer, producer of metals
Metallgeld *n* coins, metal [metallic] money
Metallgeldsystem *n* system of coin circulation
Metallgeldumlauf *m* coin circulation
Metallgewebemacher *m* wire gauze maker
Metallgewerbe *n* metal trades
Metallgewinnung *f* extraction of metal
Metallgießer *m* metal founder
Metallgießerei *f* metal foundry
Metallhandel *m* metal trade, trade in metals
Metallindustrie *f* metal industry
Metallkonstruktion *f* metal construction
Metallmarkt *m* metal market
Metallmünze *f* metal coin
Metallnotierungen *fpl (st.ex.)* metals quotations
Metallproduktion *f* metal production
Metallschleifer und -polierer *m* metal grinder and polisher
Metallumlaufwährung *f* metal money, metallic currency
Metallurg *m* metallurgist
Metallurgie *f* metallurgy
metallurgisch metallurgical
metallverarbeitend metalworking
Metallverarbeitung *f* metalworking
Metallvorrat *m s.* **Metallbestand**
Metallwährung *f* metallic standard [currency]

Metallwaren *fpl* metal articles [goods], metalware, hardware
Metallwarenfabrik *f* metalware factory
Metallwarenhandel *m* trade in metal goods, hardware trade
Metallwarenindustrie *f* metal goods industry
Metallwert *m* (intrinsic) metallic value
~ **der Ware** metamorphosis of commodities *(changes of commodities into money and money again into commodities)*
Meterkilogramm *n* kilogram-metre, metre-kilogram
Meter-Kilogramm-Sekunde-System *n* metre--kilogram-second system, MKS-system
Meterkilopond *n s.* **Meterkilogramm**
Metermaß *n* metric measure(ment)
Meterware *f* goods sold by the metre
meterweise by the metre
Methode *f* method
~, **algorithmische** algorithmic method
~, **analytische** analytical method
~ **der analytisch-experimentellen Arbeitsnormung** analytical method of fixing work standards
~ **der analytisch-rechnerischen Arbeitsnormung** synthesizing method of fixing work standards
~, **axiomatische** axiomatic method
~, **biographische** biographic method
~, **Brownsche** *(stats)* Brown's method
~, **deduktiv-axiomatische** deductive-axiomatic method
~ **der Arbeitsnormung** method of work rating
~ **der aufsteigenden Indizes** *(stats)* method of rising indices
~ **der durchschnittlichen Rangzahlen** *(stats)* mid-rank method
~ **der eingeschränkten Informationsverwendung** *(stats)* limited information method
~ **der Erzeugnisreihen** method of series of products
~ **der Fehlerschranken** *(stats)* method of limiting [limited] errors
~ **der gleitenden Durchschnitte** *s.* ~ **der gleitenden Mittel**
~ **der gleitenden Mittel** *(stats)* moving average method
~ **der Halbreihenmittelwerte** *(stats)* method of semi-averages
~ **der harmonischen Gewichte** *(stats)* method of harmonic weights
~ **der kleinsten Quadrate** *(stats)* least-squares method
~ **der kollektiven Expertenbegutachtung** method of joint consultation of experts
~ **der koordinierten Doppelauswahl** *(stats)* method of overlapping maps

- der maximalen Mutmaßlichkeit *(stats)* maximum likelihood method
- der Momente *(stats)* method of moments
- der Pfadkoeffizienten *(stats)* method of path coefficients
- der reduzierten Form *(stats)* reduced form method
- der Routendifferenzen *(stats)* method of route differences
- der Trendkorrektur *(stats)* method of trends correction
- der ungewogenen Durchschnitte *(stats)* unweighted means method *(in variance analysis)*
- des kritischen Weges critical path method (CPM)
- ~, erfahrungsstatistische *(stats)* discretionary statistical method *(method of obtaining the rate of material consumption)*
- ~, finite finite method
- geteilter Parzellen *(stats)* split-plot method
- ~, heuristische heuristic method
- ~, interdisziplinäre inter-disciplinary approach
- ~, mathematisch-ökonomische mathematical--economic method
- ~, normative normative method
- ~, parametrische *(stats)* parametric method
- ~, qualitative qualitative method
- ~, quantitative quantitative method
- ~, Spearman-Kärber'sche *(stats)* Spearman--Kärber method
- der Preisbildung, normative standard method of price formation

Methodenlehre *f s.* **Methodologie**
Methodik *f* methodology, methods
Methodologie *f* methodology
Metra-Potential-Methode *f* Metra-potential method
metrisch metric(al)
Mietanzahlung *f* key money, advance rent
Mietaufhebung *f* order to end a tenancy
Mietaufhebungsklage *f* action to end a tenancy
Mietaufkündigung *f* notice to quit a tenancy
Mietaufschlag *m* rent supplement
Mietaufwand *m* rent expenses
Mietausfall *m* loss of rent
Mietausfallversicherung *f* rent and rental value insurance
Mietauto *n s.* **Mietwagen**
mietbar rentable *(flat etc.)*, for hire *(boat, car etc.)*
Mietbasis *f*:
⋄ **auf ~** on a hire basis
Mietbedingungen *fpl* conditions [terms] of hire
Mietbehälter *m (post)* box on hire; cask on hire *(brewery)*
Mietbeihilfe *f* rent allowance [grant]; rent subsidy

Mietbeschränkungen *fpl* rent restrictions
Mietbetrag *m* amount of rent; rental fee
Mietdauer *f* period of tenancy
Miete *f* 1. rent *(flat etc.)*, hire charge *(boat, car etc.)*; renting, hiring; 2. *(agric)* clamp ⋄ **zur ~** on lease
~, **angemessene** fair rent
~, **fällige** rent due
~, **rückständige** back rent
Mieteinkommen *n* income from rents
Mieteinnahme *f* amount received as rent
mieten to rent, to hire; to take on lease; to engage *(taxi etc.)*; to charter *(ship etc.)*
Mietentschädigung *f* rent subsidy *(tenants)*; compensation for loss of rent *(landlord)*
Mieter *m* tenant; lodger; lessee; hirer ⋄ **einem ~ kündigen** to give s.o. notice to quit; **einen ~ exmittieren** to evict [turn out] a tenant
~, **alleiniger** sole tenant
~, **ausziehender** outgoing tenant
~, **exmittierter** evicted tenant
~, **neu einziehender** incoming tenant
mieterhöhend rent-raising
Mieterhöhung *f* increase in rent, rent rise
Mieterlös *m* income from rent
Mietermäßigung *f* rent reduction, reduction of rent
Mieterpflicht *f* tenant's obligation
Mieterschutz *m* tenant's protection; rent control
Mieterschutzbestimmungen *fpl* terms covering the protection of tenants
Mieterschutzgesetz *n* law protecting tenants
Mieterselbstverwaltung *f* tenant's self-management
Mietertrag *m* rental
Mietertragswert *m* rental value
Mietfahrzeug *m* vehicle for hire
Mietfläche *f* rented space; space to let
mietfrei rent-free
Mietgebühr *f* rent *(housing)*; charge *(hiring)*
Mietgeld *n* (amount of) rent
Mietgesetz *n* rent act
Miethöchstpreis *m* rent ceiling, ceiling on rent
Mietinkasso *n* collection of rents
Mietkauf *m* hire-purchase
Mietkaufvertrag *m* hire-purchase contract
Mietkonto *n* rent account
Mietkontrakt *m s.* **Mietvertrag**
Mietkosten *pl s.* **Mietaufwand**
Mietkündigung *f* notice to quit
Mietnachlaß *m s.* **Mietermäßigung**
Mietpartei *f* tenant
Mietpfändung *f* distress for non-payment of rent
mietpflichtig for rent
Mietpreis *m* rent; hire charge; rental
Mietpreisbindung *f* rent restriction [control]

Mietpreislenkung *f* rent control
Mietpreisminderung *f s.* **Mietsenkung**
Mietpreispolitik *f* (policy of) rent control
Mietpreisrecht *n* law concerning control of rents
Mietrecht *n* law of landlord and tenant
Mietrückstand *m* rent arrears
Mietsache *f* property let; object hired
Mietschuld *f* 1. rent due; 2. *s.* **Mietrückstand**
Mietschuldner *m* defaulting tenant
Mietsenkung *f* rent reduction, reduction of rent *(general)*
Mietshaus *n* rented house; block of flats
Mietskaserne *f* tenement house
Mietspeicher *m* warehouse (for hire)
Mietsteigerung *f* rent increase
Mietstreitigkeit *f* rent dispute
Mietsumme *f* (amount of) rent
Mietvereinbarung *f* rent agreement
Mietverhältnis *n* tenancy ⋄ **ein ~ abschließen** to enter into a lease; **ein ~ aufheben** to terminate a lease
Mietverlust *m* loss of rent
Mietvertrag *m* lease (contract); contract of tenancy *(flats etc.)*; charter contract *(cars etc.)* ⋄ **einen ~ abschließen** to sign a lease; **einen ~ aufkündigen** to terminate a lease; **einen ~ verlängern** to extend a lease
~ für gewerblich genutzte Räume commercial lease
~, jährlich kündbarer annual tenancy, annual lease
~, kurzfristiger short lease
~, langfristiger long lease
~, monatlich kündbarer monthly tenancy (lease)
~, verlängerter renewed lease
Mietvertragsbestimmungen *fpl* provisions in the lease
Mietvertragsdauer *f* life of a lease
Mietvorauszahlung *f* advance payment of rent
Mietwagen *m* hired [*(Am)* rented] car
Mietwagenverleih *m* car-hire service, *(Am)* rent--a-car service
Mietwäsche *f* rented linen
mietweise for rent [hire]
Mietwert *m* rental value
Mietwohnung *f* rented flat; flat to let
Mietwucher *m* charging of exorbitant rents
Mietzahlung *f* payment of rent
Mietzahlungstag *m* rent day
Mietzeit *f* lease, term of tenancy
Mietzins *m* rent, rental
mietzinspflichtig subject to rent
Mietzuschuß *m* rent subsidy
Migration *f* migration
Mikroanalyse *f* micro-analysis

Mikrocomputer *m* mini-computer, small computer
Mikrodokumentation *f* microphotographic documentation
Mikroelektronik *f* microelectronics
mikroelektronisch microelectronic
Mikrofilmlesegerät *n* microfilm reader
Mikroklima *n* microclimate
Mikromethode *f* micro-method
Mikroökonomie *f* micro-economics
Mikrostandort *m* micro-location
Mikrostruktur *f* microstructure
Mikrozensus *m* sample census
Milchertrag *m s.* **Milchleistung**
Milcherzeugung *f* milk production
Milchgeschäft *n* dairy
Milchgewinnung *f s.* **Milcherzeugung**
Milchhandel *m* milk trade; dairy business
Milchhändler *m* milkman; milk retailer, dairy--man
Milchkontrolle *f* milk control
Milchkuh *f* dairy [milking, milch] cow
Milchleistung *f* milk yield
Milchleitung *f* milk pipe [pipeline]
Milchproduktion *f s.* **Milcherzeugung**
Milchprüfung *f* milk testing
Milchsammelstelle *f* milk collecting centre
Milchverarbeitung *f* milk processing
Milchversorgung *f* milk supply
Milchverwertung *f* utilization of milk
Milchvieh *n* dairy cattle
Milchwirtschaft *f* dairy farming
Milchwirtschaftsbetrieb *m* dairy farm
Milieu *n* environment, social surroundings, atmosphere
~ der Großstadt city life
~, soziales social environment
milieubedingt environmental
Milieuforschung *f* environmental research
milieugeschädigt deprived
Milieugeschädigter *m* victim of bad environment
Milieutheorie *f* environmental theory
Mille *n:*
⋄ **pro ~** per thousand
Milliarde *f* a thousand million, *(Am)* billion
Millionär *m* millionaire
Minderaufkommen *n* deficit
Minderausgaben *fpl* reduced expenditure(s); reduction in expenditures
Minderbedarf *m* reduced demand
minderbegütert *s.* **minderbemittelt**
minderbemittelt of limited means, with a low income
Minderbetrag *m* deficit
Minderbewertung *f* undervaluation; depreciation

Mindereinnahme *f* shortfall in earnings [takings, receipts]
Minderergebnis *n* reduction in proceeds [yields]
Minderertrag *m* shortfall; *(ind)* drop in output, *(agric)* decrease in yield
Mindergebot *n* underbid
Mindergewicht *n* short weight, underweight
Mindergewinn *m* reduction in profits
Minderheit *f* minority
Minderheitenfrage *f* minority issue [question]
Minderheitenproblem *n* minority problem
Minderheitenschutz *m* protection of minorities
Minderheitsaktionär *m* minority shareholder [*(Am)* stockholder]
Minderheitsbeteiligung *f* minority interest
Minderheitspaket *n* minority holding
Minderheitsrecht *n* right of a minority
minderjährig under age
Minderjähriger *m* minor
Minderjährigkeit *f* minority
Minderleistung *f* reduced output
Minderlieferung *f* short delivery; short shipment
Mindermengenzuschlag *m* surcharge on commodities bought in smaller quantities
mindern to lessen *(pain etc.)*, to ease *(poverty etc.)*, to diminish *(strength etc.)*, to reduce *(price etc.)*
Minderqualität *f* low [poor] quality
Minderumsatz *m* decrease in turnover, falling-off in sales
Minderung *f* reduction, reducing *(price etc.)*, diminishing *(strength etc.)*, lessening *(pain etc.)*, easing *(poverty etc.)*
~ der Erwerbsfähigkeit reduction of working capacity
~ der Verdienstfähigkeit reduction of earning capacity
Minderwert *m* reduced value
minderwertig inferior, of inferior value [quality], low-grade, substandard
Minderwertigkeit *f* inferiority
Mindestabsatz *m* minimum sales
Mindestabsatzvorrat *m* minimum sales stock
Mindestakkordsatz *m* minimum job rate
Mindestalter *n* minimum age
Mindestanforderungen *fpl* minimum requirements
Mindestangebot *n* lowest tender
Mindestanzahl *f* minimum number
Mindestarbeitszeit *f* minimum working time
Mindestbedarf *m* minimum demand; minimum needs
Mindestbestand *m* lowest [minimum] stock
Mindestbesteuerung *f* minimum taxation
Mindestbetrag *m* minimum (amount)
Mindestbezahlung *f* minimum [guaranteed] pay

mindestbietend making the lowest bid
Mindestbietender *m* lowest bidder
Mindesteinkommen *n* minimum income
Mindesteinlage *f* *(bank)* minimum deposit; *(ind)* minimum investment
Mindesterleichterungen *fpl* minimum facilities
Mindestertrag *m* lowest yield
Mindestfläche *f* minimum area
Mindestforderung *f* minimum claim
Mindestfracht *f* minimum freight
Mindestfrachtsatz *m* minimum freight rate
Mindestfreibetrag *m* exemption minimum *(taxation)*
Mindestgebot *n* reserved price *(auction)*; upset price *(usually half the estimated value)*
Mindestgebühr *f* minimum charge [fee]
Mindestgehalt *n* 1. minimum salary; 2. minimum content *(metal, fluid etc.)*
Mindestgesprächsgebühr *f* minimum charge *(for telephone call)*
Mindestgewicht *n* minimum weight
Mindestgrenze *f* minimum limit; *(ins)* franchise
Mindestguthaben *n* minimum balance
Mindestkapital *n* minimum capital
Mindestkassenreserve *f* minimum reserve in cash
Mindestkosten *pl* minimum cost
Mindestkurs *m* minimum rate
Mindestleistung *f* (minimum) task *(worker)*, minimum performance *(machine etc.)*
Mindestlohn *m* minimum wage
Mindestlohnsatz *m* minimum wage rate
~, **betrieblicher** minimum plant wage rate (in an enterprise)
~, **garantierter** guaranteed basic wage rate
~, **gesetzlicher** legal minimum wage rate
Mindestmaß *n* minimum
Mindestmenge *f* minimum quantity
Mindestpflichtversicherung *f* obligatory minimum insurance
Mindestprämie *f* *(ins)* natural premium
Mindestpreis *m* minimum [lowest] price; reserved price *(auction)*
Mindestprovision *f* minimum commission
Mindestprovisionssatz *m* minimum commission rate
Mindestrente *f* minimum pension
Mindestreserve(n) *f(pl)* minimum reserve(s)
~, **vorgeschriebene** fractional reserves
Mindestreservenerhöhung *f* increase in minimum reserves
Mindestreservepolitik *f* minimum reserve policy
Mindestreservesatz *m* minimum reserve rate
Mindestsatz *m* minimum rate
Mindestschaden *m* minimum damage
Mindestskalenwert *m* minimum scale value

Mindeststandfläche *f* minimum stand space *(exhibition, fairs etc.)*
Mindeststandgröße *f* minimum size of a stand
Mindeststückgutgewicht *n* minimum carload weight
Mindeststücklohntarif *m* minimum piece (wage) rate
Mindeststundenlohn *m* minimum hourly rate of pay
Mindesttarif *m* minimum rate
Mindestumtausch *m* minimum exchange
Mindestverdienst *m* minimum pay
Mindestverkaufspreis *m* reserved price *(auction)*
Mindestverpflichtungen *fpl* minimum liabilities
Mindestversicherungsleistung *f* minimum term and period of insurance
Mindestversorgung *f* minimum supply
Mindestvertragsstrafe *f* minimum penalty *(for breach of contract)*
Mindestvorrat *m* minimum stock [store; supply]
Mindestwert *m* minimum value
Mindestzeichnungsbetrag *m* *(st.ex.)* minimum (amount of) subscription
Mindestzeitlohn *m* minimum time wage
Mindestzeitlohntarif *m* minimum time (wage) rate
Mindestzinssatz *m* minimum rate of interest
Mindestzoll *m* minimum customs duty
Mindestzollsatz *m* minimum tariff
Mineral *n* mineral
Mineralablagerung *f* deposit of minerals
Mineralboden *m* mineral soil
Mineraldünger *m* mineral fertilizer
mineralisch mineral
Mineralöl *n* mineral oil
Mineralölaufbereitung *f* refining of mineral oil
Mineralölgewinnung *f* extraction of mineral oils
Mineralölsteuer *f* mineral oil tax
minimal minimum, minimal
Minimalbelastung *f* minimum load
Minimalbestand *m* minimum stock
Minimalbetrag *m* minimum (amount)
Minimalfracht *f* minimum freight
Minimalgewicht *n* minimum weight
Minimalkosten *pl* minimum costs
Minimalsatz *m* lowest [minimum] rate
Minimaltarif *m* minimum rate
Minimalvorrat *m* minimum reserve [stock]
Minimalwert *m* minimum value
Minimaxentscheidungsfunktion *f* minimax decision function
Minimaxlösung *f* minimax solution
Minimaxprinzip *n* minimax principle
Minimaxschätzung *f* minimax estimation
Minimaxstrategie *f* minimax strategy
Minimaxtheorem *n* minimax theorem

Minimierung *f* minimization
Minimum *n* minimum
~, **relatives** *(stats)* through
~, **steuerfreies** tax-free minimum
Minimumstelle *f* *(stats)* antimode
Minister *m* minister
ministerial ministerial
Ministerialprinzip *n* departmental principle *(division of budgetary receipts and expenditure according to sphere of responsibility)*
ministeriell *s.* **ministerial**
Ministerium *n* ministry
Ministerpräsident *m* Prime Minister, Chairman of the Council of Ministers
Ministerratsbeschluß *m* decision of the Council of Ministers
Minorität *f* minority
Minoritätsaktionär *m* minority shareholder [*(Am)* stockholder]
Minoritätsbeteiligung *f* minority interest
minus minus
Minusbetrag *m* deficit
Minuteneinkauf *m* purchase on advanced order
Mischdünger *m* compound fertilizer
Mischfutter *n* mixed fodder
Mischfutterindustrie *f* mixed fodder industry
Mischkonten *npl* mixed accounts
Mischkultur *f* mixed cultivation
Mischladung *f* mixed cargo
Mise *f* *(ins)* single premium
Mißerfolg *m* failure
~, **finanzieller** financial failure
~, **wirtschaftlicher** flop
Mißernte *f* bad harvest
Mission *f* mission ⋄ **in geheimer** ~ on a secret mission
~, **diplomatische** (diplomatic) mission
Mißkredit *m* discredit, bad reputation
Mißwirtschaft *f* mismanagement, bad management
Mitarbeit *f* collaboration, help, assistance ⋄ **unter** ~ **von** in collaboration with
~, **freiwillige** voluntary work
~, **kostenlose** unpaid work
mitarbeiten to assist, to collaborate *(in s.th.)*; to contribute *(to s.th.)*
Mitarbeiter *m* collaborator, assistant, co-worker; colleague
~ **der Geschäftsleitung** managerial assistant
~, **freier** freelance worker
~, **kaufmännischer** clerk
~, **technischer** technical assistant; technician
~, **wissenschaftlicher** scientific assistant, research worker [fellow]
Mitarbeiterstab *m* staff (of competent people) *(for a particular purpose)*; task force *(for a project etc.)*, team *(of research workers etc.)*

Mitbegründer *m* co-founder
mitbenutzen to share in the use of
Mitbenutzung *f* joint utilization [use]
Mitbenutzungsrecht *n* right to joint use
Mitbesitz *m* joint occupancy, co-ownership, joint property
Mitbesitzer *m* co-occupier; co-owner, joint owner
mitbestimmen to have a voice *(in s.th.)*, to co-determine, to have a determining influence *(on s.th.)*
Mitbestimmung *f* co-determination
~, **betriebliche** participation [co-determination] in management
~, **personelle** co-determination in matters concerning personnel
~, **soziale** co-determination of conditions of employment
~, **wirtschaftliche** co-determination of business policy
Mitbestimmungsrecht *n* right to co-determine
mitbeteiligen to give *s.o.* a share *(in s.th.)*; to give *s.o.* a say *(in s.th.)*; **sich ~** to go in *(with s.th.)*, to participate, to join, to take part *(in s.th.)*
mitbeteiligt participating, taking part *(in s.th.)*
Mitbeteiligter *m* participant
Mitbeteiligung *f* participation, partnership
mitbewerben, sich to compete
Mitbewerber *m* competitor, rival (tenderer)
mitbewohnen to occupy [live in] as well
Mitbewohner *m* other occupant *(house, room etc.)*, other resident *(housing estate etc.)*
mitbezahlen to share the cost of *(s.th.)*; to pay at the same time
mitbieten to bid as well
Miteigentum *n* joint ownership [property]
Miteigentümer *m* joint owner, co-proprietor, co-owner
Miteigentumswert *m* equity
mitentscheiden to decide *(s.th.)* with *(s.o.)*; to decide at the same time; to have a say in deciding *(s.th.)*
Miterbe *m* co-heir, joint heir
mitfinanzieren to help (to) finance *(s.th.)*, to co-finance
Mitfinanzierung *f* co-financing
Mitgebrauch *m* joint use
Mitgift *f* dowry
Mitglied *n* member
~, **ausscheidendes** retiring [outgoing] member
~, **außerordentliches** associate member
~, **eingetragenes** enrolled member
~, **förderndes** paying member
~, **korrespondierendes** associate [corresponding] member
~, **nichtständiges** part-time member

~, **ordentliches** full [regular] member
~, **ständiges** permanent member
~, **stimmberechtigtes** *s.* ~, **wahlberechtigtes**
~, **vollberechtigtes** fully qualified member
~, **wahlberechtigtes** voting member
~, **zahlendes** paying [subscribing] member
Mitgliederbanken *fpl* member banks
Mitgliederhaftung *f* liability of members
Mitgliederversammlung *f* general meeting, meeting of members
Mitgliedsbeitrag *m* member's subscription, membership fee
Mitgliedschaft *f* membership
Mitgliedschaftsantrag *m* application for membership
Mitgliedsfirma *f* member-firm
Mitgliedskarte *f* membership-card
Mitgliedsnummer *f* membership number
Mitgliedsstaat *m* member state
Mithaftung *f* joint liability
Mitinhaber *m* co-partner, co-owner
Mitmieter *m s.* **Mitpächter**
Mitpächter *m* co-tenant
Mitschuldner *m* joint debtor
Mitschuldverhältnis *n* joint obligation
Mitteilung *f* notification, information, announcement, notice; message
~, **mündliche** message
~, **schriftliche** written notification [information, announcement], notice
~, **telefonische** telephone message
~, **vertrauliche** confidential information
Mitteilungspflicht *f* duty to inform *(s.o.)*
Mittel *n* 1. medium; mean, average *(rainfall etc.)*; *(maths)* mean value, mean; 2. means *(of negotiations to achieve s.th.)*; 3. product, agent *(for cleansing etc.)*; preparation *(cosmetics etc.)*
~, **arithmetisches** arithmetic mean
~ **der Grundgesamtheit** *(stats)* true mean
~, **fortschreitendes** *(stats)* progressive average
~, **geometrisches** *(stats)* geometric mean
~, **gewogenes** *(stats)* weighted average
~, **gewogenes arithmetisches** weighted arithmetic mean
~, **gleitendes** *(stats)* moving average
~, **harmonisches** *(stats)* harmonic mean
~, **jährliches** annual average
~, **korrigiertes** *(stats)* adjusted mean
~, **provisorisches** *(stats)* assumed mean
~, **quadratisches** *(stats)* quadratic mean
~, **ungewogenes** *(stats)* unweighted mean
~, **wahres** *(stats)* true mean
~, **wirksames** effective means
Mittel *npl* (financial) resources [means]; funds, ◇ **aus Mangel an Mitteln** because of shortage of (financial) resources [means], for lack of (financial) resources [funds]; **~ aufbringen**

to mobilize resources [funds]; **~ und Wege finden** to find ways and means; **notwendige ~ bereitstellen** to provide the necessary funds; **öffentliche ~ beanspruchen dürfen** to have recourse to public money; **ohne ~ sein** to be without means; **über ausreichende ~ verfügen** to have substantial resources [means] at one's disposal
~, ausländische external [foreign] resources; foreign capital
~, beschränkte limited (financial) resources
~, empfängnisverhütende contraceptives
~, erforderliche necessary [required] resources *(financial)*
~, finanzielle financial resources [means]; funds
~, flüssige liquid assets; fluid [available, ready] money [capital]
~, fremde borrowed funds [capital], capital from external sources
~, geringfügige *s.* **~, beschränkte**
~, greifbare *s.* **~, verfügbare**
~, knappe *s.* **~, beschränkte**
~, kurzfristige money at short notice, short-term loan
~, langfristige time deposit, time money
~, laufende current assets
~, liquide *s.* **~, verfügbare**
~, nicht ausreichende inadequate resources [funds, means]
~, nicht verteilte unallocated funds
~, nicht verwendete unemployed [unused] funds
~, öffentliche public funds [money]
~, sofort verfügbare spot cash
~, überschüssige surplus funds
~, unbedeutende insignificant resources
~, unzureichende slender means
~, verfügbare available resources [funds, means]
~, zweckbestimmte funds earmarked *(for s.th.)*, earmarked funds
Mittelaufbringung *f* mobilization of resources
Mittelaufkommen *n* accumulation of resources
mittelbar indirect
Mittelbauer *m* medium farmer
Mittelbetrieb *m* medium-sized enterprise
Mittelbewirtschaftung *f* regulation [control, rationing] of resources [means]
Mitteleinsatz *m* employment of resources [funds]
Mittelentscheidung *f* decision on disposal of resources [funds]
mittelfristig medium-term *(loan, credit, contract etc.)*; medium-dated *(bill of exchange etc.)*; medium-range *(planning, forecast etc.)*
Mittelgröße *f* medium size
Mittelkurs *m* mean rate, middle market price; middle course

mittellos without means, poor
Mittellosigkeit *f* lack of means
Mittelmaß *n* medium [average] size
mittelmäßig average, moderate, fair, mediocre
Mittelmäßigkeit *f* mediocrity
Mittelpreisklasse *f* medium price range
Mittelpunkt *m* focus, central point, centre
Mittelrückführung *f* repayment of funds [money]
Mittelschichten *fpl s.* **Mittelstand**
Mittelsmann *m* middleman, intermediary, go--between; broker
Mittelsorte *f* medium quality
Mittelsperson *f* mediator, intermediary, middleman, go-between
Mittelstadt *f* medium-sized town
Mittelstand *m* middle classes
~, gehobener upper middle classes
Mittelweg *m* middle way; middle course
Mittelwert *m* average, mean (value)
~, bereinigter *s.* **Mittel, korrigiertes**
~, errechneter (calculated) mean
~, extremer *(stats)* extreme mean
~, gewogener *(stats)* weighted mean [average]
~, größter oder kleinster *(stats)* largest or smallest mean
~, korrigierter *s.* **Mittel, korrigiertes**
Mittelzuweisung *f* allocation of resources [funds]
Mittler *m s.* **Mittelsmann**
Mitschuldner *m* co-debtor
Mitunternehmer *m* partner
Mitunternehmerschaft *f* partnership; co-partnership
Mitunterzeichner *m* co-signatory
mitverantworten to be jointly responsible
mitverantwortlich co-responsible, jointly responsible
Mitverantwortung *f* joint responsibility
mitverdienen to earn (money) with s.o. *(husband, wife etc.)*
Mitverdienerin *f* working wife
Mitverschluß *m (bank)* dual-control lock
Mitverschulden *n* contributory negligence
Mitversicherer *m* co-insurer
mitversichern to insure s.o. along with s.o. else, to insure s.o./s.th. as well
mitversichert insured along with s.o. else, co--insured
Mitversicherter *m* co-insured person
Mitversicherung *f* co-insurance
mitwirken to help *(to do s.th.)*, to take part in *(s.th.)*, to participate, to play a part in *(s.th.)*, to co-operate
Mitwirkung *f* help, participation, co-operation
Mitwirkungspflicht *f* duty to co-operate *(of insured persons)*

Mitwirkungsrecht *n* right of participation
Möbel *n* furniture
Möbelbau *m* furniture making [production]
Möbelgeschäft *n* furniture shop
Möbelhändler *m* furniture dealer, dealer in furniture
Möbelhandlung *f s.* Möbelgeschäft
Möbelindustrie *f* furniture industry
Möbellager *n* furniture warehouse [store]
Möbelmesse *f* furniture fair
Möbeltransport *m* furniture removal
Möbeltransportgeschäft *n* firm of furniture removers
Möbelversand *m* furniture transport; selling of furniture by mail order
Mobiliar *n* furniture; movable goods, movables
Mobiliarkredit *m* loan on movables
Mobiliarvermögen *n* movable property
Mobiliarversicherung *f* insurance of movable goods
Mobilisation *f s.* Mobilisierung
mobilisieren to mobilize
Mobilisierung *f* mobilization
Mobilisierungsfunktion *f* mobilizing function
~ der Staatsfinanzen mobilizing function of state finance
Mobilität *f* mobility
~ der Arbeitskräfte mobility of labour force [manpower]
~, soziale social mobility
möblieren to furnish *(room, flat etc.)*
möbliert furnished
Modalitäten *fpl* terms *(agreement, loan etc.)*; procedure, ways and means *(for implementing regulation etc.)*
Modalwert *m (stats)* mode, modal value
Mode *f* fashion ◊ aus der ~ kommen to go out of fashion; der ~ unterworfen sein to depend on the fashion; in ~ sein to be in fashion; mit der ~ gehen to follow the fashion; ~ machen to lead [determine] the fashion
~, herrschende prevailing fashion
~, neue new fashion [style]
Modeartikel *m* fashionable article
Modeausstellung *f* fashion show
modebewußt fashion-conscious
Modeentwicklung *f* fashion trend
Modegeschäft *n* fashion store [shop]
Modehandel *m* fashion trade
Modehaus *n* fashion house
Modell *n* 1. model; pattern; shape, design; prototype; type; scheme; 2. mannequin
~, abgeschlossenes sequentielles *(stats)* closed sequential scheme
~, analytisches *(stats)* analytical model
~, begrenztes sequentielles *(stats)* closed sequential scheme [model]

~, determiniertes *(stats)* determined model
~, deterministisches deterministic model
~, durch mehrere Gleichungen bestimmtes *(stats)* multi-equational model
~, dynamisches *(stats)* dynamic model
~, formales formal model
~, gegenständliches material model
~, gemischtes *(stats)* mixed model
~, graphisches graph, graphic model
~, ideelles ideal model
~, inneres internal model
~, internes *s.* ~, inneres
~, komplexes ökonomisches complex [composite] economic model
~, lineares *(stats)* linear model
~, maßstabgerechtes full-scale model
~, mathematisches mathematical model
~ mit simultanen Gleichungen simultaneous equations model
~, offenes sequentielles *(stats)* open sequential scheme
~, ökonomisches economic model
~, ökonomisch-mathematisches economic-mathematical model
~, sequentielles *(stats)* sequential scheme
~, statisches *(stats)* static model
~, statistisches *(stats)* statistic model
~, stochastisches *(stats)* stochastic model
~, strategisches strategic model
~, verkleinertes reduced-scale model
~, visuelles visual model
~, zusammengesetztes *(stats)* aggregative model
Modellanalyse *f* model analysis
Modellaufbau *m* structure of a model
Modellbauer *m* model-maker; pattern-maker *(metalworking)*
Modelldimension *f* dimension of a model
Modellexperiment *n* model experiment
Modell-Identifikation *f* model identification
modellieren to model, to draw up a model; form, shape, mould
Modellierung *f* model(l)ing
~, kybernetische cybernetic model(l)ing
~, mathematische mathematical model(l)ing
~, prognostische forecast model(l)ing
Modellkopplung *f* linking of models
Modellmethode *f* model method
Modellmodenschau *f* mannequin parade
Modellplanung *f* model planning
Modellprojektierung *f* designing of a model
Modellprüfung *f* test of a model, model testing
Modellschau *f* display [exhibition] of samples, sample show
Modellsystem *n* model system
Modelltest *m* model test
Modelltheorie *f* model theory
Modelltyp *m* type of model(s)

Modell- und Bilanzsystem *n* system of models and balance sheets
~ **der zentralen Planung** system of models and balance sheets of (the) central planning
~, **territoriales** system of regional models and balance sheets
Modellverknüpfung *f* linkage of models
Modemesse *f* fashion fair
Modenschau *f* fashion show
modern modern *(style etc.)*, up-to-date *(method etc.)*
Moderne *f* modern times [age], modern spirit; modern trend, modernity *(art)*
modernisieren to modernize
Modernisierung *f* modernization
Modernisierungskredit *m* modernization loan
Modeschöpfer *m* couturier, fashion designer
Modeschöpfung *f* new creation
Modestil *m* style in fashion
Modewaren *fpl* fashion goods
Modifikation *f* modification
modifizierbar modifiable
modifizieren to modify
Modifizierung *f s.* **Modifikation**
modisch fashionable, stylish
Modistin *f* dealer in fashion articles
Modul *m (maths)* modulus; module *(construction)*
modular modular *(design, system etc.)*
Modulfunktion *f* modular function
Modus *m* mode, method
möglich possible, practicable, feasible; potential
Möglichkeit *f* possibility *(of event happening etc.);* feasibility, practicability *(of method etc.);* chance *(to study etc.);* opportunity, prospect *(of travelling etc.)*
~, **finanzielle** financial capacity [capability]
~, **potentielle** potentiality
~, **technische** technical possibility
~, **technologische** technological possibility
Möglichkeiten *fpl*:
  ⋄ **alle ~ einkalkulieren** to allow for all contingencies [possibilities]; **seinen ~ entsprechend** according to his means
~, **geschäftliche** business opportunities
~, **schwache** off chance
Möglichkeitsbereich *m* range of possibilities
~, **objektiver** objective range of possibilities
Molkerei *f* dairy
Molkereierzeugnisse *npl* dairy produce
Molkereigenossenschaft *f* dairy co-operative, co-operative dairy society; co-operative dairy factory
Molkereiprodukt *n* dairy product
Molkereiprodukte *npl s.* **Molkereierzeugnisse**
Moment *n* moment
~, **aus einer Stichprobe bestimmtes** *(stats)* sample moment

~ **einer Stichprobenverteilung** *(stats)* sampling moment
Momentanwert *m* present value
Momentengleichung *f (stats)* moment equation
Momentenkurve *f (stats)* bending moment diagram
Momentenlinie *f s.* **Momentenkurve**
Momentenmethode *f (stats)* moment method
Monatsabonnement *n* monthly subscription
Monatsabrechnung *f* monthly account
Monatsabschluß *m* monthly settlement; monthly balance sheet
Monatsabstimmung *f (acc)* monthly reconciliation
Monatsaufstellung *f* monthly statement
Monatsausweis *m (bank)* monthly statement [return]
Monatsbedarf *m* a month's supply
Monatsbericht *m* monthly report
Monatsbilanz *f* monthly balance sheet
Monatsdurchschnitt *m* monthly average
Monatsdurchschnittsverfahren *n* monthly average method
Monatsfahrkarte *f* monthly season-ticket
Monatsfrist *f* period of a month ⋄ **nach ~** after one month, in a month's time
Monatsgehalt *n* monthly salary
Monatsgeld *n* monthly allowance; monthly loan, loan repayable in a month's time
Monatskarte *f s.* **Monatsfahrkarte**
Monatslohn *m* monthly wages
Monatsprämie *f (ins)* monthly premium
Monatsproduktion *f* monthly production
Monatsrate *f* monthly instalment [payment]
Monatssteuertarif *m* monthly tax rate
Monatsübersicht *f s.* **Monatsaufstellung**
Monatsumsatz *m* monthly turnover
Monatsverdienst *m* monthly earnings
Monatswechsel *m* one month's bill; monthly allowance
monieren to criticize *(s.th.);* to complain about *(s.th.);* to make a complaint about *(goods etc.);* to query, to question *(invoice etc.)*
Monitum *n* complaint; reminder
Monokultur *f* monoculture
Monometallismus *m* monometallism
monometallistisch monometallic
Monopol *n* monopoly; oligopoly ⋄ **ein ~ ausüben** to enforce a monopoly; to exercise a monopoly
~, **ausländisches** foreign monopoly
~, **gesetzliches** legal monopoly
~, **inländisches** national [local] monopoly
~, **staatliches** state monopoly
~, **unvollständiges** partial monopoly, oligopoly
Monopolabgabe *f* monopoly tax
Monopolabkommen *n* monopoly agreement

monopolähnlich semi-monopoly
Monopolbetrieb *m* monopoly, company having a monopoly
Monopolbourgeoisie *f* monopoly bourgeoisie
monopolfeindlich anti-monopoly
Monopolgewinn *m s.* **Monopolprofit**
Monopolindustrie *f* monopolized industry
Monopolinhaber *m* monopolist
monopolisieren to monopolize
Monopolisierung *f* monopolization
Monopolisierungstendenzen *fpl* tendencies towards monopoly; oligopoly tendencies
Monopolist *m* monopolist
monopolistisch monopoly *(price, profit etc.)*, monopolistic *(company, competition etc.)*; oligopoly, oligopolistic
Monopolkapital *n* monopoly capital
Monopolkapitalismus *m* monopoly capitalism
Monopolkapitalist *m* monopoly capitalist
monopolkapitalistisch monopoly capitalist
Monopolmißbrauch *m* abuse of monopoly
Monopolpreis *m* monopoly price
Monopolprofit *m* monopoly profit
Monopolrecht *n* monopoly right
Monopolrente *f* monopoly rent
Monopolstellung *f* monopoly (position)
Monopolunternehmen *n* monopoly (enterprise), oligopolistic enterprise
Monopolverwaltung *f* state authority for producing and marketing of a product
Monotoniewirkung *f* effect of monotony
Montage *f* assembly, assemblage, setting up *(machine etc.)*; fitting, mounting *(crane, apparatus etc.)*; erection *(prefabricated building etc.)*; installation *(boiler etc.)*
Montageabteilung *f* assembly department [section]
Montagebau *m* industrialized building method, building method using prefabricated units
Montagebauweise *f s.* **Montagebau**
Montagebedingungen *fpl* terms of assembling; assembling conditions
Montagebetrieb *m* assembly enterprise [plant]
Montageeinheit *f* assembly unit
Montagefließfertigung *f* assembly mass production
Montagehalle *f* assembly room [shop]
Montagekapazität *f* assembly capacity
Montagekosten *pl* assembly costs; cost of installation [erection]
Montageleistung *f* assembly work
Montageorganisation *f* organization of assembly
Montageplan *m* assembly plan
Montageplanung *f* assembly planning
Montageschlosser *m* assembly fitter
Montagestraße *f* assembly line

Montagewerk *n s.* **Montagebetrieb**
Montagewerkstatt *f* assembling [assembly] shop
Montanaktie *f* mining share [*(Am)* stock]
Montanindustrie *f* coal, iron and steel industries
Montanmarkt *m* mining market
Montanpapiere *npl* mining shares
Montanunternehmen *n* mining concern [trust]
Montanvertrag *m* Treaty on European Coal and Steel Community
Montanwerte *mpl* mining securities
Monteur *m* fitter
montieren to assemble, to set up *(machine parts etc.)*; to fit, to mount *(crane, apparatus etc.)*; to erect *(prefabricated building etc.)*; to install *(boiler etc.)*
Moorkultur *f* marshland cultivation
Moorland *n* moorland, marshland
Moratorium *n* moratorium
Morbiditätsstatistik *f* morbidity statistics
Mortalitätsstatistik *f* mortality statistics
Mosaiksetzer *m* mosaic setter
Motiv *n* motive
Motivation *f* motivation
~, **äußere** external motivation
~, **innere** internal motivation
~, **sekundäre** *s.* ~, **äußere**
Motivforschung *f* motivation research
Motivierung *f s.* **Motivation**
motorisieren to motorize
motorisiert motorized
Motorisierung *f* motorization
Mühle *f* mill *(flour etc.)*, grinding mill *(ore etc.)*, grinder
Mühlenbauer *m* millwright
Mühlenbetrieb *m* flour-mill
Mühlenindustrie *f* flour-milling industry
Müll *m* refuse, rubbish, garbage
Müllabfuhr *f* 1. dust-cart, refuse collection, *(Am)* garbage collection; 2. refuse collection department
Müllaufbereitung *f* treatment of garbage
Müllbeseitigung *f* removal of refuse [garbage]
Mülldeponie *f* refuse [rubbish] heap; refuse [rubbish] site [dump]
Müller *m* miller
Müllhalde *f s.* **Mülldeponie**
Müllkippe *f* rubbish tip
Müllkompostierung *f* refuse composting, compost-making from refuse
Müllplatz *m* rubbish dump
Müllrecycling *n* waste [refuse] recycling
Müllverbrennung *f* refuse incineration
Müllverbrennungsanlage *f* refuse incinerator
Müllverwertung *f* utilization of garbage, refuse [garbage] disposal
Multikollinearität *f (stats)* multicollinearity

multilateral multilateral
Multimomentverfahren n multi-moment method
multinational multinational
Multiplikator m multiplier
~ **für endliche Grundgesamtheiten** *(stats)* finite multiplier
Multi-Ziel-Optimierung f multi-objective optimization
Mündel n ward
Mündelgeld n trust money *(for ward)*
mündelsicher *(jur)* eligible for investment of trust money *(in securities, papers etc.)*
Mündelsicherheit f *(jur)* suitability for investment of trust money *(in securities, papers etc.)*
Mündelvermögen n trust fund [money, property]
mündig of age; mature, responsible
Mündigkeit f full age; majority
Münzamt n mint
Münzanstalt f s. **Münzamt**
Münzautomat m slot machine
Münze f 1. coin; 2. mint
~, **falsche** false coin
~, **nachgemachte** counterfeit coin
~, **unechte** spurious coin
Münzen fpl:
◊ ~ **prägen** to strike coins; ~ **schlagen** s. ~ **prägen**; **nachgemachte** ~ **in den Verkehr bringen** to put counterfeit coins into circulation
Münzeinheit f unit of currency, monetary unit; coin denomination
münzen to coin
Münzfälscher m counterfeiter
Münzfälschung f forging [counterfeiting] of coin
Münzfernsprecher m coin-box telephone
Münzfreiheit f right to strike coins
Münzfuß m standard of coinage *(ratio of the standard weight of gold etc. to the number of coins to be struck)*
Münzgeld n metallic money [coins]
Münzgewicht n standard weight *(of coins)*
Münzgewinn m seigniorage, seigneurage
Münzgold n monetary gold
Münzhandel m dealings in gold and silver coins *(not in currency)*
Münzhoheit f coin prerogative
Münzkonvention f monetary agreement
Münzmetall n coinage metal
Münzparität f *(bank)* mint par of exchange
Münzprägung f striking of coins, mintage
Münzpreis m mint price
Münzrolle f *(bank)* rouleau (of coins)
Münzsammlung f coin collection
Münzsorte f *(bank)* foreign coins
Münzstandard m monetary standard

Münzstätte f s. **Münzamt**
Münzstückelung f *(bank)* coin denomination
Münzsystem n coinage
Münzumlauf m coin circulation
Münzunion f monetary union
Münzwechsler m coin changer, change-giving machine
Münzwert m assay value
Münzwesen n coinage; minting
Münzzähler m coin meter
Münzzeichen n mint mark
Mußvorschrift f mandatory clause
Muster n sample; pattern, model, protosample *(merchandise etc.)*; pattern *(cultural, dressmaking etc.)*; model *(layout, tailoring etc.)*; industrial design *(patent etc.)*; prototype *(device etc.)*; specimen *(signature, product etc.)* ◊ **dem ~ entsprechend** up to sample, according to the sample; according to pattern; **laut ~** true to specimen; **Waren nach ~ bestellen** to order goods from the sample; **etwas nach ~ kaufen** to buy s.th. from sample
~, **eingetragenes** registered design
~ **ohne Wert** sample of no value
~, **übliches** conventional design
Musteranlage f pilot plant
Musterartikel mpl line of samples
Musterausstellung f sample fair [show, exhibition]
Musterbestellung f sample order
Musterbetrieb m model plant [enterprise]; model farm
Musterbilanz f standard balance sheet
Mustereinfuhr f import of samples, prototype import
Musterfarm f demonstration [model] farm
Musterfertigung f prototype [sample] production
mustergemäß up [according] to sample
Musterkollektion f range of samples; collection of patterns *(knitting machines etc.)*
Musterlager n sample show room; sample stock
Mustermesse f sample fair
Musterpaß m *(cust)* permit exempting samples from customs duty
Musterrabatt m discount on samples
Mustersatzung f standard statute
Musterschau f display [exhibition] of samples, sample show
Musterschutz m design copyright
Mustersendung f consignment of samples
Musterstatut n s. **Mustersatzung**
Musterstichprobe f *(stats)* master sample
Mustertarif m standard rate
Musterverkauf m sale of samples
Mustervertrag m standard contract
Musterwirtschaft f s. **Musterfarm**

Mutmaßlichkeit f *(stats)* likelihood
Mutmaßlichkeitsfunktion f *(stats)* likelihood function
Mutmaßlichkeitsverhältnis n *(stats)* likelihood ratio
Mutter f mother
Mütterberatung f mother-and-child advisory service, maternity care
Mütterberatungsdienst m maternity welfare service
Mütterberatungsstelle f infants welfare [maternity] centre, child welfare centre
Mütterfürsorge f maternity welfare
Müttergenesungsheim n convalescent home for mothers, maternity convalescent home
Muttergesellschaft f parent company
Mütterheim n maternity home
Mutterschaftsgeld n maternity benefits [allowance]
Mutterschaftshilfe f s. **Mutterschaftsgeld**
Mutterschaftsurlaub m maternity leave
Mutterschutz m protection of motherhood
Muttersterblichkeit f maternal mortality
Mutter- und Kinderschutz m protection of children and motherhood
Mutungsbereich m *(stats)* confidence belt; confidence interval; confidence region
Mutungsgrenzen fpl *(stats)* confidence limits; fiducial limits

N

Nacharbeit f retouching, refinishing; repair, maintenance
nacharbeiten to retouch, to refinish; to repair, to maintain; to work from [copy] a model
Nacharbeitskosten pl costs of refinishing
Nachauftragnehmer m subcontractor
Nachbargebiet n neighbouring [adjoining] district [region]; allied [neighbouring] field *(study etc.)*
Nachbargrundstück n neighbouring [adjoining] piece of land
Nachbarindustrie f surrounding industry
Nachbarland n neighbouring country; neighbouring piece of land
Nachbarort m neighbouring town [village]
Nachbarstand m neighbouring [adjoining, adjacent] stand [stall]
Nachbau m reproduction *(engines etc.)*, imitation *(type of house etc.)*
nachbauen to reconstruct *(engine etc.)*, to imitate *(type of house etc.)*

nachbearbeiten to process further, to rework, to redress; to finish *(s.th.)*, to touch up
Nachbearbeitung f further processing, rework, redressing; finishing *(of s.th.)*, touching-up
nachbehandeln to apply a subsequent [further] treatment *(to s.th.)*
Nachbehandlung f after-treatment, subsequent [further] treatment
Nachbeitrag m *(ins)* additional premium *(paid after the accounting period to meet coverage not envisaged earlier)*
nachbelasten to make an additional charge
Nachbelastung f additional charge
nachberechnen s. **nachbelasten**
Nachberechnung f s. **Nachbelastung**
nachbessern to touch up
Nachbesserung f refinishing
nachbestellen to reorder, to repeat an order
Nachbestellung f reorder, additional [repeat] order
nachbewilligen to grant additionally
Nachbewilligung f additional allowance
nachbezahlen to pay afterwards [subsequently]
Nachbezahlung f subsequent payment
nachbeziehen to obtain an additional [a further] supply
Nachbezug m obtaining an additional [a further] supply
Nachbezugsrecht n entitlement (of a shareholder) to receive arrears of dividend (on cumulative preference shares)
nachbilden to copy, to imitate; to make a replica *(of s.th.)*
Nachbildung f copy, limitation, reproduction
Nachbörse f *(st.ex.)* business conducted after official hours, kerb [street] market
nachbuchen to enter an additional item
Nachbuchung f additional entry
Nachbürge m surety for a surety; *(st.ex.)* subsequent endorser
Nachbürgschaft f surety for a surety
nachdatieren to postdate, to backdate
Nacherbe m reversionary [next] heir
Nacherbfall m succession of a reversionary heir
Nacherbfolge f s. **Nacherbfall**
Nacherbschaft f inheritance in reversion
nacherheben to assess for an additional payment
Nacherhebung f additional assessment
Nachernte f second crop, aftercrop; gleanings
Nachfolge f succession; following
Nachfolgebedarf m sequential demand
nachfolgeberechtigt entitled to succeed
Nachfolgegesellschaft f successor company
Nachfolgeinstitut n successor institution
nachfolgen to follow
Nachfolgeorganisation f successor organization

Nachfolger *m* successor ⋄ **einen ~ ernennen** to appoint [designate] a successor
Nachfolgestaat *m* succession state
nachfordern to make a further [an additional] claim
Nachforderung *f* subsequent claim, extra charge
nachforschen to inquire; to investigate
Nachforschung *f* inquiry; investigation
Nachfrage *f* inquiry; *(com)* demand ⋄ **die ~ befriedigen** to meet [cover] the demand *(for s.th.)*; **es herrscht ~ (nach)** there is a demand (for); **sich der ~ erfreuen** to be in demand
~, abnehmende decreasing demand
~, anhaltende steady demand
~, aperiodische non-periodic demand
~, elastische elastic demand
~, fiktive fictitious demand
~, geringe limited demand
~, gleichbleibende constant demand
~, häufige frequent demand
~, laufende current demand
~, periodische periodic demand
~, saisonbedingte seasonal demand
~, schwankende fluctuating demand
~, spärliche slack demand
~, starke great [brisk] demand
~, unelastische inelastic demand
~, ungeheure huge demand
~, wachsende increasing demand
Nachfragebelebung *f* growth of demand
Nachfragedynamik *f* dynamics of demand
Nachfrageelastizität *f* elasticity of demand
Nachfrageentwicklung *f* development of demand
Nachfrageerhöhung *f* increase in demand
Nachfragefunktion *f* demand function
Nachfrageintensität *f* intensity of demand
Nachfrageintensitätskoeffizient *m* demand intensity coefficient
Nachfragekurve *f* demand curve
Nachfragemenge *f* quantity demanded
Nachfragemonopol *n* monopsony
nachfragen to inqure, to make inquiries; to demand
Nachfrageoligopol *n* oligopsony
Nachfrageperiodizität *f* periodicity of demand
Nachfrageprognose *f* long-term forecast of demand
Nachfrager *m* (potential) buyer
Nachfragerückgang *m* decline in [decreasing] demand
Nachfragestruktur *f* structure of demand
Nachfrageüberhang *m* excess demand
Nachfrist *f* extension of the original term, additional term
Nachfrucht *f* succeeding crop, aftercrop
Nachgebot *n* later bid

Nachgebühr *f s.* **Nachporto**
nachgemacht copied, imitated
Nachgeschäft *n (st.ex.)* 'call of more' dealing; 'put of more' dealing
Nachgirant *m* endorser
Nachgiro *n* subsequent endorsement
Nachholebedarf *m* backlog demand
Nachkalkulation *f* secondary [final] calculation
Nachkomme *m* descendant
Nachkommen *mpl*:
⋄ **ohne ~** issueless
~, erbberechtigte issue entitled to inherit
Nachkommenschaft *f* descendance
Nachkriegsbedürfnisse *npl* postwar needs
Nachkriegsentwicklung *f* postwar development
Nachkriegskonjunktur *f* postwar boom
Nachkriegskrise *f* postwar crisis [recession]
Nachkriegsrezession *f s.* **Nachkriegskrise**
Nachlaß *m* heritage, legacy, deceased's estate; remission, reduction, rebate, discount
Nachlaßangelegenheit *f* matter of estate
Nachlaßanspruch *m* claim against the estate
Nachlaßauseinandersetzung *f* distribution of the estate
Nachlaßberechtigter *m* distributee
Nachlaßforderung *f* claim on the estate
Nachlaßgegenstand *m* item forming part of the estate
Nachlaßgericht *n* probate court
Nachlaßgläubiger *m* creditor of the estate
Nachlaßhaftung *f* responsibility of the heir (for the liabilities of the predecessor)
Nachlaßinventar *n* inventory of the estate
nachlässig careless, negligent
Nachlässigkeit *f* carelessness, negligence
Nachlaßkonkurs *m* bankruptcy of the estate
Nachlaßkonkursverwalter *m* trustee of a bankrupt's estate
Nachlaßkosten *pl* charges on an estate
Nachlaßpfleger *m* administrator of the estate
Nachlaßpflegschaft *f* administration of the estate
Nachlaßregelung *f* settlement of an estate
Nachlaßsache *f (jur)* testamentary cause
Nachlaßschuld *f* debt to be paid out of the estate
Nachlaßsteuer *f* death duty, inheritance tax
Nachlaßstiftung *f* testamentary trust
Nachlaßverbindlichkeit *f* liability arising from an inheritance
Nachlaßverfahren *n* probate proceedings
Nachlaßvergleich *m* voluntary partition of an estate
Nachlaßversteigerung *f* disposal of an estate by auction
Nachlaßverteilung *f s.* **Nachlaßauseinandersetzung**

Nachlaßvertreter *m* personal representative of an estate
Nachlaßverwalter *m* administrator of an estate
Nachlaßverwaltung *f* administration of an estate
Nachlaßverwaltungskosten *pl* administration costs of an estate
Nachlaßwert *m* value of an estate
Nachleistungen *fpl (acc)* subsequent costs *(obligation to be discharged in a later accounting period than the one to which payment for it has been allocated)*
nachliefern to deliver subsequently
Nachlieferung *f* subsequent delivery
Nachlösegebühr *f* sum charged when paying one's fare on the train; penalty for travelling without a ticket
Nachlösekarte *f* ticket bought on the train; excess fare ticket
nachlösen to pay one's fare on the train; to pay the excess fare
nachmachen to copy, to imitate; to make a replica *(of s.th.)*
Nachmittagsschicht *f* afternoon [second] shift
Nachmodell *n* secondary model
Nachnahme *f* cash on delivery (c.o.d.); trade charge ⋄ **gegen ~ liefern** cash on delivery; **per ~** cash on delivery
Nachnahmebetrag *m* amount to be collected on delivery; (amount of the) trade charge
Nachnahmebrief *m* cash on delivery letter
Nachnahmedienst *m* cash on delivery service
Nachnahmegebühr *f* cash on delivery fee
Nachnahmepaket *n* cash on delivery parcel
Nachnahmesendung *f* cash on delivery consignment
Nachnutzung *f* utilization of non-patented scientific and technical achievements *(by other enterprises)*
Nachnutzungsentgelt *n s.* **Nachnutzungsgebühr**
Nachnutzungsgebühr *f* charges for utilization of non-patented scientific and technical achievements
Nachnutzungsvertrag *m* agreement on the utilization of non-patented scientific and technical achievements
nachpfänden to make a second distress
Nachpfänden *n* second distress
Nachpfändung *f s.* **Nachpfänden**
Nachporto *n* surcharge, additional charge *(for an unfranked or insufficiently franked letter)*
nachprägen to remint; to imitate, to copy *(coin)*
nachprüfen to check *(account etc.)*, to verify *(statement, data etc.)*, to scrutinize *(votes etc.)*, to examine, to re-examine; to inspect *(machine etc.)*; (jur) to review *(decision, case etc.)*

Nachprüfen *n* check, checking *(account etc.)*, verification *(statement, data etc.)*, scrutiny *(votes etc.)*, examination, re-examination; inspection *(machine etc.)*; (jur) review *(decision, case etc.)*
Nachprüfer *m* controller, supervisor
Nachprüfung *f s.* **Nachprüfen**
nachrechnen to check *(calculation etc.)*, to re-calculate
Nachricht *f* news, information, report, notice, communication
Nachrichten *fpl:* ⋄ **jmdn. mit ~ versorgen** to furnish s.o. with information
Nachrichtenagentur *f* news agency
Nachrichtenbeförderung *f* postal transport *(excluding packets, parcels etc.)*
Nachrichtenbüro *n* news agency
Nachrichtendienst *m* news service
Nachrichtenfluß *m* flow of information
Nachrichteningenieur *m* telecommunications engineer
Nachrichtenkanal *m* information channel
Nachrichtentechniker *m* telecommunications technician
Nachrichtensatellit *m* communications satellite
Nachrichtenstrom *m* stream of information
Nachrichtentechnik *f* telecommunication(s)
Nachrichtentheorie *f* communication theory
Nachrichtenübermittlung *f s.* **Nachrichtenübertragung**
Nachrichtenübertragung *f* transmission of news [intelligence]
~ mit Satelliten communication via satellite
Nachrichtenverarbeitung *f* data processing; information processing
Nachrichtenverkehr *m* communications
Nachrichtenverkehrsleistung *f* communications service
Nachrichtenwesen *n* telecommunication(s)
Nachsaison *f* off-season, after-season
nachschicken *s.* **nachsenden**
Nachschrift *f* post scriptum, postscript; marginal note, annotation
nachsenden to reforward, to redirect, to send on
Nachsendung *f* forwarding; additional consignment [*(Am)* shipment]
Nächstgebot *n* nearest bid
Nachtarbeit *f* night-work
Nachtarbeiter *m* night-worker
Nachtarbeitszuschlag *m* night-work supplementary pay
Nachtdienst *m* night duty
Nachteil *m* disadvantage, drawback
nachteilig disadvantageous
Nachtflug *m* night flight
Nachtrag *m* supplement, addendum, postscript
Nachtragsbuchung *f* supplementary entry
Nachtragsbudget *n s.* **Nachtragsetat**

Nachtragsetat *m* supplementary budget
Nachtragshaushalt *m s.* **Nachtragsetat**
Nachtragshaushaltsvorlage *f* bill of supplementary budget
Nachtragspolice *f (ins)* additional policy
Nachtragszahlung *f* additional payment
Nachtsafe *m* night safe
Nachtschicht *f* night shift
Nachtschichtprämie *f* night-shift bonus
Nachtschichtvergütung *f* night-shift pay [wages]
Nachtschichtwechsel *m* night-shift change-over
Nachttarif *m* night-rate, night-tariff
Nachttresor *m s.* **Nachtsafe**
Nachunternehmer *m* subcontractor
Nachurlaub *m* additional leave
Nachveranlagung *f* supplementary assessment
Nachvergütung *f* 1. payment of a dividend based on a member's contribution to the society; 2. later payment
Nachvermächtnis *n* reversionary legacy
nachversichern to take out an additional insurance *(on s.th.)*
Nachversicherung *f* additional insurance
nachversteuern to tax at a later date
Nachversteuerung *f* taxation at a later date
Nachweis *m* proof, demonstration, statement
~ **der Arbeitszeit** statement on working time
~ **der Investitionen** statement on investments
~ **der Versicherungsfähigkeit** evidence of insurability satisfactory to company
~ **der Warenbestände** statement on stocks
~ **des Arbeitslohnes** statement on wages
~ **des Materialbedarfs** statement on the demand for material
~ **des Materialverbrauchs** statement on material consumption
~ **des Nutzens der Aufwendungen für wissenschaftlich-technischen Fortschritt** statement on the benefit of outlays for scientific-technological progress
nachweisbar provable
nachweisen to state, to prove
Nachweiskosten *pl* accountable costs
Nachweismakler *m (st.ex.)* intermediate broker
Nachweispflicht *f* accountability, obligation to account
nachwiegen to check the weight
Nachwirkung *f* after-effect, aftermath; *(stats)* lag
~, **verteilte** *(stats)* distributed lag
~ **von Behandlungen** *(stats)* residual treatment effect
Nachwuchs *m* junior staff
Nachwuchskraft *f* junior worker [employee]; trainee
~ **für Führungsfunktionen** management trainee
Nachwuchslenkung *f* guidance of trainees

Nachwuchsregelung *f* birth control
nachzählen to count *s.th.* again, to recount
Nachzahlung *f* additional [supplementary] payment
nachzeichnen to subscribe
Nachzeichnung *f* further subscription
Näherei *f* 1. sewing, needlework; piece of sewing [needlework]; 2. machining section *(clothing factory)*; dress factory
Naherholung *f* recreation at local resorts
Naherholungsgebiet *n* local recreation area
Naherholungsverkehr *m* local recreation traffic
Naherholungszentrum *n* local recreation centre
Näherung *f* approximation
Näherungsfehler *m* approximation error
Näherungslösung *f* approximate solution
Näherungsrechnung *f* approximation calculus [calculation]
Näherungsverfahren *n* approximation method
Näherungswert *m* approximate value
Nahgüterverkehr *m* short-distance goods traffic
Nähmaschinenindustrie *f* sewing machine industry
Nährboden *m* fertile soil
Nährkraft *f* nutritive power
Nährmittel *npl* cereal products
Nährmittelindustrie *f* cereal products industry
Nährstoff *m* nutrient
Nährstoffaufwand *m* nutrient expenditures
Nährstoffbedarf *m* nutrient requirements
Nährstoffertrag *m* nutrient yield
Nährstoffgehalt *m* nutrient content
nährstoffreich rich in nutrients, nutritious
Nährstoffverhältnis *n* nutrient ratio
Nahrung *f* nourishment, nutriment, food, nutrition
Nahrungsbedarf *m* food requirements
Nahrungsgüterressourcen *pl* food resources
Nahrungsgüterwirtschaft *f* food economy
Nahrungsmangel *m* shortage of food, food shortage
Nahrungsmittel *npl* food(s), foodstuff(s)
~, **hochwertige** food(s) of high nutritive value
~, **pflanzliche** vegetable food products
~, **tierische** animal food products
~, **unentbehrliche** indispensable food(s)
Nahrungsmittelchemie *f* food chemistry
Nahrungsmittelchemiker *m* food chemist
Nahrungsmitteleinfuhr *f* food import
Nahrungsmittelfälschung *f* food adulteration
Nahrungsmittelgesetz *n* food act
Nahrungsmittelindustrie *f* food industry
Nahrungsmittelmangel *m s.* **Nahrungsmangel**
Nahrungsmittelsendung *f* consignment of food, *(Am)* food shipment
Nahrungsmittelverbrauch *m* food consumption
Nahrungsmittelvergiftung *f* food poisoning

Nahrungsquelle *f* source of food
Nahrungsreserve *f* food resources
Nahrungs- und Genußmittel *npl* foods, beverages and tobacco
Nahrungs- und Genußmittelausstellung *f* exhibition of foods, beverages and tobacco
Nahrungs- und Genußmittelindustrie *f* foods, beverages and tobacco industry
Nahrungs- und Genußmittelmesse *f* fair of foods, beverages and tobacco
Nährwert *m* nutritive value
Nahschnellverkehr *m* fast local passenger traffic
Nahverkehr *m* local traffic
~, **städtischer** urban traffic
Nahverkehrsmittel *npl* means of local transport
~, **städtische** means of urban transport
Nahverkehrszone *f* local traffic zone
Namensaktie *f* registered share [*(Am)* stock]
Namensliste *f* list of names
Namenspapier *n* registered security
Namenspfandbriefe *mpl* registered debentures [*(Am)* bonds]
Namensschuldverschreibung *f s.* **Namenspfandbriefe**
Namensverzeichnis *n s.* **Namensliste**
Nämlichkeitsmittel *n (cust)* means of identification *(seal, stamp, number etc.)*
Nämlichkeitsnachweis *m (cust)* proof of identification
Natalität *f* natality
Nation *f* nation
Nationalbank *f* national bank
Nationaleinkommen *n* national income
~, **produziertes** produced national income
Nationaleinkommensbilanz *f* balance sheet of national income
Nationaleinkommensbilanzierung *f* balancing the national income
Nationaleinkommensprognose *f* forecast of national income
Nationaleinkommensvergleich *m* comparison of national incomes
~, **internationaler** international comparison of national incomes
Nationaleinkommenszuwachs *m* growth in national income
Nationalisierung *f* nationalization
Nationalismus *m* nationalism
Nationalreichtum *m* national wealth
~, **potentieller** potential national wealth
Nationalschuld *f* national debt
Nationalstaat *m* national state
~, **junger** newly independent country
Nationalvermögen *n* national property
Nationalversammlung *f* national assembly
Nationalwährung *f* national currency
Naturalabgabe *f* tax [levy] in kind

Naturalakkumulation *f (agric)* physical accumulation, accumulation in kind
Naturalausgleich *m* settlement in kind
Naturalsaustausch *m* natural exchange, exchange in kind
Naturalbezüge *mpl* earnings received in kind
Naturaleinheit *f* physical unit
Naturaleinkommen *n* income in kind
Naturaleinkünfte *pl s.* **Naturaleinkommen**
Naturalentschädigung *f* restitution [replacement] in kind
Naturalertrag *m* natural yield
Naturalform *f* physical form [shape]
Naturalgeld *n* money in kind
Naturalkennzahl *f* indicator in kind
Naturallasten *fpl* charges to be paid in kind
Naturallohn *m* remuneration in kind
Naturalleistungen *fpl* payment in kind; *(ins)* benefit in the form of services
Naturalmasse *f* natural mass [weight]
Naturalmethode *f* method of evaluating in physical terms
Naturalobligation *f (jur)* imperfect obligation
Naturalpacht *f* rent paid in kind
Naturalrente *f s.* **Naturalpacht**
Naturalsteuer *f* tax paid in kind
Naturalverflechtungsbilanz *f* input-output table in physical terms
Naturalvergütung *f* payment in kind
Naturalverteilung *f* distribution in kind *(of produce, products)*
Natural-Wert-Verflechtungsbilanz *f* input--output table in physical and value terms
Naturalwirtschaft *f* subsistence economy
Naturalzins *m* rent payable in kind
Naturbedingungen *fpl* natural conditions
Naturenergie *f* natural energy
Naturkraft *f* natural force [energy]
~ **der Arbeit** physical attributes of labour
Naturmilieu *n* natural environment
Naturreichtum *m* natural wealth
Naturressourcen *pl* natural resources
Naturressourcenabgabe *f* tax on use of natural resources
Naturschätze *mpl* natural wealth [resources]; mineral resources
Naturschutz *m* nature conservancy [conservation]
Naturschutzgebiet *n* nature conservation area
Naturschutzpark *m* national park
Naturstoffe *mpl* natural materials
Naturwissenschaften *fpl* (natural) sciences
Nebenabgaben *fpl* additional [supplementary] taxes
Nebenabteilung *f* secondary [auxiliary] department
Nebenadresse *f* alternative address

Nebenamt *n* sub-office
nebenamtlich in addition to one's official duties
Nebenanlage *f* subsidiary plant
Nebenanspruch *m* second right
Nebenarbeit *f* extra work
Nebenbedingung *f* secondary condition
Nebenberuf *m* secondary occupation, second job
nebenberuflich done as a secondary occupation
Nebenbeschäftigung *f* spare-time [part-time] occupation, side-line job
Nebenbestandteil *m* secondary ingredient
Nebenbestimmung *f* additional clause
Nebenbetrieb *m* subsidiary enterprise
Nebenbeweis *m* additional proof, corroborative evidence
Nebenbezüge *pl* additional income
Nebenbuch *n* *(acc)* auxiliary book(s)
Nebenbürge *m* co-surety; co-guarantor
Nebeneinkommen *n s.* **Nebenbezüge**
Nebeneinkünfte *pl s.* **Nebenbezüge**
Nebeneinnahmen *fpl* additional income [earnings]
Nebenergebnis *n* by-product (of research work), spin-off
Nebenerwerb *m* side-job, secondary occupation
Nebenerwerbsbetrieb *m* *(agric)* smallholding
Nebenforderung *f* accessory claim
Nebengebühren *fpl* additional charges [fees]
Nebengeschäft *n* side business; branch office; branch shop
Nebengewinn *m* extra [additional] profit
Nebeninformation *f* secondary information
Nebenkasse *f* petty cash; branch pay-office
Nebenkonto *n* second account
Nebenkosten *pl* additional cost(s) [expenditure, expenses, charges]
Nebenkostenstelle *f* additional cost centre
Nebenleistung *f* 1. *(ind)* manufacture [processing] of by-products; 2. supplementary payment; fringe benefits *(for personnel etc.)*
Nebenparameter *m* secondary parameter
Nebenplatz *m* *(bank)* branch
Nebenpostamt *n* sub-post office
Nebenprodukt *n* by-product
Nebenprozeß *m* ancillary process *(production)*; *(jur)* subsidiary process
Nebenschuldner *m* co-debtor
Nebensicherheit *f* collateral security
Nebenstelle *f* branch office
Nebenursache *f* incidental cause, secondary reason
Nebenverbraucher *m* secondary consumer
Nebenverdienst *m* additional earnings
Nebenvereinbarung *f* supplementary agreement
Nebenvergütung *f* supplementary payment
Nebenverpflichtung *f* *(jur)* obligation to perform an additional service

Nebenversicherung *f* collateral insurance
Nebenvertrag *m* subcontract
Nebenvormund *m* joint guardian, co-guardian
Nebenvormundschaft *f* joint guardianship, co--guardianship
Nebenwerte *mpl (st.ex.)* sundry securities
Nebenwiderspruch *m* secondary contradiction
Nebenwirkung *f* secondary effect
Nebenzweck *m* secondary aim
Nebenzweig *m* ancillary branch
Negation *f* negation
Negotiation *f* negotiation *(bill of exchange)*, purchase, sale *(foreign draft, securities)*
negoziabel negotiable; marketable
negoziieren to negotiate *(bill of exchange)*, to purchase *(foreign draft)*; to sell *(securities)*; to be in commerce [trade]
neigen to incline, to have a tendency to *(s.th.)*
Neigung *f* inclination, propensity, trend, tendency
NE-Metallurgie *f* non-ferrous metallurgy
Nennbelastung *f* nominal load
Nennbetrag *m* nominal amount
Nennleistung *f* nominal output
Nennwert *m* nominal [face] value ⋄ **über dem ~** above par; **unter dem ~** below par; **zum ~** at par
Nennwertaktie *f* par value share [*(Am)* stock]
Nennwertparität *f* nominal parity
Neokolonialismus *m* neo-colonialism
Nestfertigung *f* production in batches
Nestmontage *f* group assembly
netto net
Nettoabsatz *m* net sales
Nettoakkumulation *f* net accumulation
Nettobeitrag *m (ins)* net insurance policy refund *(total amount due to policy holder minus incidental charges)*
Nettobetrag *m* net amount
Nettobilanz *f (acc)* balance of balances
Nettodeviseneinerlös *m* net proceeds in foreign exchange
Nettodurchschnittsverdienst *m* average net earnings
Nettoeinkaufspreis *m* net purchase price
Nettoeinkommen *n* net income
Nettoeinnahme *f* net receipt
Nettoerlös *m* net proceeds
Nettoertrag *m* net proceeds [yield]
Nettofinanzierung *f* net financing
Nettofläche *f* net floor space
Nettogehalt *n* net salary
Nettogeldeinkommen *n* net money income
Nettogeldeinkünfte *pl s.* **Nettogeldeinkommen**
Nettogeldeinnahmen *fpl s.* **Nettogeldeinkommen**
Nettogewicht *n* net weight

Nettogewinn *m* net profit
Nettogewinnabführung *f* net profit transfer [payment]
Nettogewinnabführungsnormativ *n* standard rate of net profit transfer
Nettogewinnmaximierung *f* maximization of net profits
Nettogewinnverteilung *f* distribution of net profits
Nettogewinnverwendung *f* distribution of net profits
Nettogewinnzuwachs *m* net profit increase
Nettoinvestition *f* net investment
Nettokennziffer *f* net indicator
Nettolohn *m* net wage
Nettomasse *f* net weight [volume]
Nettomiete *f* net rent
Nettoprämie *f (ins)* net premium
Nettopreis *m* net price
Nettoprinzip *n* net accounting principle *(transfers to and from budget as net amounts)*
Nettoprodukt *n* net product
~, gesellschaftliches net national product, national income
Nettoproduktionsmethode *f* net production method *(statistical method for measuring the efficiency of social labour)*
Nettoproduktionswert *m* net production value
Nettoprovision *f* net commission
Nettorate *f* net rate *(shipping)*
Nettoregistertonne *f* net registered ton
Nettorohstoffeinsatznorm *f* net standard rate of material consumption
Nettosozialprodukt *n* net national product
Nettotonnage *f* net tonnage
Nettotonne *f* net ton
Nettotonnenkilometer *mpl* net-ton kilometres
Nettoumsatz *m* net turnover
Nettovalutaerlös *m* net proceeds [earnings] in convertible [foreign] currency
Nettoverdienst *m* net earnings
Nettoverkauf *m* net sale
Nettoverkaufserlös *m* net profit on sales
Nettoverkaufspreis *m* net sales price
Nettoverlust *m* net loss
Nettovermögen *n* net assets
Nettoverteilung *f* net distribution
Nettoverzinsung *f* net [pure] interest
Nettowert *m* net value
Nettozins *m s.* **Nettoverzinsung**
Nettozinsfuß *m* net rate of interest
Nettozinsrate *f s.* **Nettozinsfuß**
Nettozinssatz *m s.* **Nettozinsfuß**
Netz *n* net, network *(posts, telegraphs etc.)*; grid *(electricity etc.)*
~ der Versorgungseinrichtungen network of service centres [establishments]

~ von Rechenstationen network of computer [computation] centres
Netzdichte *f* density *(of roads, railways etc. in a certain area)*
Netzplankalkulation *f* network calculation
Neztplantechnik *f* network planning *(CPM, PERT)*
Netzwerk *n* network
Netzwerkanalyse *f* network analysis
Netzwerkdiagramm *n* network diagram
Netzwerktechnik *f* network technique
Neuabschlüsse *mpl* new orders [transactions]
Neuanlage *f* new plant; reinvestment
Neuanmeldung *f* new application
Neuanschaffung *f* new purchase [acquisition]
Neuanschaffungskosten *pl (ins)* replacement costs
Neuanschaffungswert *m (ins)* replacement value
Neuansiedlung *f* resettlement
Neuaufbau *m* rebuilding, reconstruction; reorganization, restructuring, reshaping *(organizations etc.)*
neuaufgelegt re-edited; reprinted
Neuauflage *f* new edition
~, unveränderte reprint
~, veränderte (new) revised edition
~, verbesserte new revised edition
Neuaufschluß *m* exposure *(area)* ; *(min)* open lode
Neuausgabe *f s.* **Neuauflage**
neuausrüsten to re-equip
Neuausrüstung *f* re-equipment
Neuaussaat *f* resowing; new seeds [seedlings]
Neuausstattung *f* 1. re-equipping *(factory etc.)*; refitting *(shop etc.)*; refurnishing; 2. new equipment *(factory etc.)*; new fittings *(shop etc.)*; new furnishings *(flats etc.)*
Neuaussteller *m* new exhibitor
Neubau *m* rebuilding, reconstruction *(street, bridge etc.)*; new building
Neubauer *m* new farm settler
Neubauernprogramm *n* new farm settler's programme
Neubauplan *m* new building plan
Neubauten *mpl* new buildings
Neubauwohnung *f* flat in a newly built house [block]
neubearbeitet revised *(book etc.)*; newly arranged *(programme etc.)*
Neubearbeitung *f* revision; new arrangement
Neubegebung *f* new issue *(securities etc.)*
Neubelebung *f* revival *(market etc.)*
Neuberechnung *f* recalculation
Neubesetzung *f* filling of a post [an office] (with a new person), appointment (of a new person) to a post [an office]
Neubestellung *f* new order, reorder

neubewerten to re-evaluate; to revalorize
Neubewertung f re-evaluation, revaluation; revalorization
~ **des Anlagevermögens** revaluation of assets
~ **von Wertpapieren** *(st.ex.)* markdown [markup] of securities
Neubildung f reshaping, reorganization; new formation
~ **einer Gesellschaft** new formation of a company [society]; reorganization of a company [society]
Neueinstellung f engagement of new person(s)
Neueinstufung f regrading *(salaries etc.)*; *(stats)* reclassification
Neueinteilung f reclassification *(categories etc.)*; regrouping *(parties, forces etc.)*; redivision *(land etc.)*
Neueintragung f new registration; *(acc)* new entry
Neuemission f new issue, reissue
Neuentdeckung f recent discovery, rediscovery
Neuentwicklung f new development [design, product]
Neuerer m innovator
Neuereraktiv n innovators' team
Neuereraktivitäten fpl innovative activities
Neuereraufgabe f innovators' task
Neuererbewegung f innovators' movement
Neuererbrigade f innovators' team [group]
Neuererbüro n bureau of innovations
Neuererinstrukteur m instructor for innovations *(in technology and able to direct their introduction in other enterprises)*
Neuererkonferenz f innovators' conference
Neuererleistung f innovator's performance
Neuerermethode f innovation, new technology
Neuererpaß m innovator's record-book
Neuererplan m plan of innovations
Neuererrat m advisory body on innovations
Neuererrecht n rules and regulations on innovations
Neuererstammkarte f innovator's index card
Neuerertätigkeit f innovator's activities
Neuerertum n s. **Neuererbewegung**
Neuerervereinbarung f innovators' agreement [contract]
Neuerervergütung f innovator's reward
Neuerervorschlag m proposal of an innovation
Neuererzentrum n innovators' centre
Neuertragssorte f high yielding variety (HYV) *(rice, wheat etc.)*
Neuerung f innovation
~, **technische** technical innovation
~, **technologische** technological innovation, innovation in technology
Neuerungsvorschlag m s. **Neuerervorschlag**
Neuerwerbung f new acquisition

Neufassung f redrafting *(documents etc.)*, revison *(text etc.)*; revised version
Neufestsetzung f fresh settlement *(prices etc.)*, setting, resetting *(rate of exchange etc.)*
~ **von Quoten** adjustment of quotas
Neufinanzierung f refinancing, recapitalization
Neufundierung f refunding
~ **einer Anleihe** refunding of a loan
Neugestaltung f reorganization
Neugründung f foundation of a new company [organization]; new foundation
Neugruppierung f regrouping, reshuffling
Neuheit f newness *(houses, articles etc.)*; novelty, innovation, new development
~, **letzte** latest novelty
~, **technische** s. **Neuerung, technische**
Neuheitenangebot n offer of new products
Neuheitenausstellung f novelty fair
Neuheitenliste f list of new developments
Neuheitenschau f s. **Neuheitenausstellung**
Neuheitenzentrum n novelty centre
Neuheitswert m novelty value
Neuigkeit f 1. newness *(houses, articles etc.)*; novelty *(idea etc.)*; 2. (piece of) news
Neuigkeitsgrad m degree of newness
Neuigkeitswert m value of newness
Neuinvestition f new investment; reinvestment
Neukalkulation f revised calculation, recalculation
Neukapitalisierung f recapitalization
Neukonstruktion f new design; reconstruction
Neuland n reclaimed land; virgin soil; new territory
Neulandgewinnung f reclamation of land, land reclamation
Neulieferung f new delivery
Neuordnung f reorganization, reshaping
~ **der Planung** reorganization of planning
Neuorganisation f reorganization
Neuorientierung f reorientation *(political party etc.)*, rethinking *(policy, theory etc.)*; *(com)* readjustment
Neupreis m new price
Neuproduktion f new production
Neuprofilierung f reshaping, remoulding, reshuffling, rearrangement, refashioning
Neuregelung f revision *(regulation etc.)*, reform *(law etc.)*; new regulation [provision]
Neuschaffung f new creation
neutral neutral
Neutralität f neutrality
~, **aktive** active neutrality
Neutralitätserklärung f declaration of neutrality
Neutralitätsverletzung f violation of neutrality
Neuveranlagung f reassessment, re-evaluation
Neuvermessung f fresh survey *(land)*

Neuverteilung f redistribution, reallocation
Neuwert m 1. *(pol ec)* newly created value *(part of the value of a commodity or of the social gross product created by living labour)*; 2. *(ins)* original value
Neuwertversicherung f insurance at original value
~, gleitende *(ins)* floating policy
Neuwertentschädigung f *(ins)* damages equal to original value
Neuzüchtung f new strain [variety] *(grain etc.)*; new breed *(animals)*
Neuzugang m new admission; new member
Neuzuteilung f reallocation
Nichtabnahme f nonacceptance, rejection
nichtabzugsfähig nondeductible
Nichtachtung f disregard, lack of regard *(rules etc.)*, nonobservance
nichtamtlich unofficial
Nichtanerkennung f nonrecognition
~ einer Schuld, einseitige unilateral repudiation of a debt
Nichtangriffspakt m nonaggression treaty [pact]
Nichtannahme f nonacceptance
Nichtäquivalentenaustausch m nonequivalent exchange
Nichtäquivalenz f nonequivalence
Nichtauslastung f underutilization, underemployment *(of production capacity)*
Nichtauslieferung f nondelivery; *(jur)* nonextradition
Nichtausnutzung f nonutilization *(licence etc.)*
Nichtballungsgebiet n nonagglomeration area
Nichtbeachtung f nonobservance *(of validity etc.)*
~ von Bestimmungen disregard of stipulations
Nichtbeantwortung f nonresponse
Nichtbefolgung f nonobservance, noncompliance; disregard
~ der Vorschriften breach [nonobservance] of regulations
Nichtbelegung f nonoccupation
Nichtberechtigter m unauthorized person, person having no title, person not entitled *(to s.th.)*
nichtbeschränkt unrestricted, unlimited
Nichtbeteiligung f nonparticipation
Nichtbezahlung f nonpayment
nichteingeschränkt unrestricted, unlimited
Nichteinhaltung f noncompliance
Nichteinmischung f noninterference, nonintervention
Nichteisenmetall n nonferrous metal
Nichteisenmetallurgie f nonferrous metallurgy
Nichterfüllung f nonfulfilment *(plan etc.)*, nonperformance, default *(contract etc.)*
~ einer Verpflichtung nonfulfilment of an obligation; *(jur)* nonfeasance

nichtig invalid, void
Nichtigkeit f nullity, voidness
Nichtigkeitsbeschwerde f plea of nullity
Nichtigkeitserklärung f nullification, annulment
Nichtigkeitsklage f nullity action [suit]
nichtkommerziell noncommercial
Nichtlediger m nonsingle (person)
Nichtlieferung f nondelivery
nichtmateriell nonmaterial; immaterial
Nichtmitglied n nonmember
nichtpaktgebunden nonaligned
nichtparametrisch nonparametric
Nichtzahlung f s. **Nichtbezahlung**
Nichtzustellung f nondelivery *(of mail)*
niederlassen, sich to establish o.s., to settle down, to take up one's residence [domicile]; to set up, to open *(branch, agency etc.)*
Niederlassung f establishment, settlement; branch, agency *(bank, firm etc.)*
Niederlassungsfreiheit f freedom of residence; freedom of establishment *(branch, agency etc.)*
Niederlassungsrecht n right to freedom of residence; right of establishment *(branch, agency etc.)*
niederlegen to resign from *(office etc.)*, to renounce, to give up *(leadership etc.)* ◊ **die Arbeit ~** to stop work(ing), to down tools, to strike
Niederlegung f resignation *(from office etc.)*, renunciation, giving up *(leadership etc.)*; strike *(action)*
niederschlagen to waive *(claim etc.)*, to cancel *(taxes etc.)*; *(jur)* to stay, to quash *(criminal proceedings)*
Niederschlagung f waiver *(claim etc.)*, cancellation *(taxes etc.)*; *(jur)* quashing *(criminal proceedings)*
Niederstwert m lowest value
Niederstwertprinzip n principle that stock-in--trade should be assessed at cost, cost or market price whichever is the lower
Niederung f flats; marsh
Nießbrauch m usufruct
~ an einem Grundstück, lebenslänglicher tenancy for life
~, lebenslänglicher life estate
~, uneingeschränkter perfect usufruct
Nießbraucher m usufructuary, beneficiary
Nießbrauchrecht n usufructuary right
Niveau n level, standard
~, technisches technological level
Niveauanalyse f analysis of level [standard] *(of productivity, efficiency, national income etc.)*
Niveauangleichung f levelling up *(in terms of national income, labour productivity etc.)*

Niveaukennziffer *f* level index [indicator] *(used in planning as orientation data)*
Niveauunterschied *m* difference in levels
Niveauvergleich *m* comparison of levels
nivellieren to level, to even up
Nivellierung *f* levelling
Nochgeschäft *n (st.ex.)* 'call of more' dealing; 'put of more' dealing
Nomade *m* nomad
Nomadenleben *n* nomadic life
Nomadenvolk *n* nomadic people
nomadisch nomad(ic)
nomadisieren to lead a nomadic existence
Nomenklatur *f* nomenclature
~ **der Planung** classification of planning items, planning classification
Nomenklaturposition *f* item of nomenclature
nominal nominal
Nominalbetrag *m* nominal sum
Nominaleinkommen *n* nominal [money] income
Nominalismus *m* nominalism
Nominalkapital *n* nominal [authorized] capital
Nominalkurs *m (st.ex.)* nominal price
Nominallohn *m* nominal wages
Nominalnennwert *m* nominal value
Nominalparikurs *m (st.ex.)* nominal par of exchange
Nominalpreis *m* nominal price
Nominalpreisindex *m* nominal price index
Nominalsatz *m* nominal rate
Nominalverzinsung *f* nominal interest
Nominalwert *m* s. **Nominalnennwert**
Nominalzins *m* nominal rate of interest
nominieren to nominate, to name
Nominierung *f* nomination, naming, appointment
Norm *f* norm, standard; quota ⋄ **als ~ gelten** to serve as a norm [standard]; **der ~ entsprechen** to conform to the standard; **die ~ erfüllen** to fulfil a quota; **eine ~ aufstellen** to set up a standard
normal normal *(behaviour, development etc.)*, standard *(size, weight, state etc.)*
Normalabweichung *f (stats)* normal deviate
Normalarbeitstag *m* normal working day
Normalarbeitswoche *f* normal working week
Normalarbeitszeit *f* normal working hours
Normalausführung *f* standard design
Normalausstattung *f* standard equipment *(factories etc.)*; standard furnishing *(hotel rooms etc.)*
Normalbelastung *f* normal load
Normalbestand *m* normal stock
Normalfahrpreis *m* standard fare
Normalfertigungsmittel *npl* general tools
Normalfrachtsatz *m* standard freight rate
Normalgebühr *f* normal charges [fees]
Normalgewicht *n* standard weight

Normalgrad *m* standard rate
~ **der Arbeitsintensität** standard rate of labour intensity
Normalgröße *f* standard size
normalisieren to normalize, to standardize
Normalisieren *n* s. **Normalisierung**
Normalisierung *f* normalization, standardization
~ **einer Häufigkeitsfunktion** *(stats)* normalization of frequency function
~ **von Punktziffern** *(stats)* normalization of scores
Normalkalkulation *f* costing based on normal standards
Normalkonnossement *n* uniform bill of lading
Normalkontenplan *m* standard scheme of accounts
Normalkosten *pl* standard costs
Normalkostenrechnung *f* calculation of standard cost(s)
Normalkredit *m* commercial credit [loan]
Normalkurve *f (stats)* normal curve
Normalleistung *f* standard performance
Normallohn *m* standard [regular] wage
Normalmaß *n* standard measure
Normalpolice *f (ins)* ordinary policy
Normalpreis *m* standard [normal, regular] price
Normalverbrauch *m* normal [average] consumption
Normalverbraucher *m* average consumer
Normalverdienst *m* average earnings
Normalverteilung *f (stats)* standard distribution
Normalverzinsung *f* ordinary interest
Normalwert *m* standard value, standard
Normativ *n* standard, (standard) norm
~, **arbeitshygienisches** standard of factory hygiene
~, **betriebliches** (standard) norm of an enterprise
~ **der Fondsausnutzung** (standard) norm of utilization of funds
~ **der Gewinnbildung** (standard) norm of profit formation
~ **der Materialvorratshaltung** (standard) norm of storage of materials
~ **der Nettogewinnabführung** (standard) norm of net profit transfer [payment]
~ **des Materialverbrauchs, technisch-ökonomisch begründetes** technical-economic (standard) norm of material consumption
~ **Exportgewinnanteil** standard share in export receipts
~, **kalkulatorisches** (standard) norm to be calculated
~, **ökonomisches** economic (standard) norm *(planned or given indicator quantifying economic conditions, connections or results)*

~, **technisch-ökonomisches** technical-economic (standard) norm
~, **volkswirtschaftliches** national economic (standard) norm
Normativakt *m* guiding principle [stipulation]
Normativausgabenfinanzierung *f* (standard) norm cost financing
Normativbesteuerung *f* taxation at a fixed rate *(based on average income or profit)*
Normativbestimmungen *fpl* provisions, rules *(agreement etc.)*; rules and regulations *(company etc.)*
Normativkoeffizient *m* normative coefficient
Normativkosten *pl* normative costs *(planned costs of products, construction groups etc. on the basis of technological documents)*
Normativkostenblatt *n* normative costs sheet *(form used in cost calculation)*
Normativkostenrechnung *f* normative costs calculation
Normativnutzungsdauer *f* standard utilization time [period]
Normativ-Prämienfonds *m* standard bonus fund
Normativsteuer *f* tax at a fixed rate
Normenarbeit *f* fixing of labour [work] standards [norms]
Normenkatalog *m* catalogue of standards norms
Normenkommission *f* committee for standards [norms]
Normenstatistik *f* statistics of standards [norms]
Normerfüllung *f* fulfilment of standards [norms]
normgerecht according to standard
normieren to standardize, to fix norms
Normierung *f* standardization, fixing of standards [norms]
Normsatz *m* standard rate
Normteile *npl* standard [standardized] parts
Normtype *f* standard
Normübererfüllung *f* overfulfilment of norms
Normung *f s.* **Normierung**
Normuntererfüllung *f* nonfulfilment of norms
Normzeit *f* standard [mean] time *(for doing a job)*
~, **technisch begründete** technologically based standard time
Normzeitermittlung *f* measurement [establishment] of standard working times
Nostroeffekten *pl* own securities *(held by a bank at another bank)*
Nostrogeschäft *n* business done for one's own account
Nostroguthaben *n* credit balance on a nostro account
Nostrokonto *n* nostro [*(Am)* our] account
Nostrotransaktion *f* operation for one's own account

Nostroverpflichtung *f* debit balance on a nostro account
Not *f* 1. need, want, poverty, hardship; 2. trouble, difficulty, distress; 3. necessity ◊ **im Fall der** ~ in case of need; **in** ~ in need, in needy circumstances; **in** ~ **geraten** to be reduced to poverty, to encounter hard times; to get into serious difficulties; **jmds.** ~ **lindern** to alleviate s.o.'s poverty [hardship]; ~ **leiden** to suffer want [hardship]
~, **drückende** dire need
Nota *f* bill, note, invoice ◊ **laut** ~ as per note
Notabgabe *f* emergency tax
Notabilität *f* notability, high repute
Notadressat *m* referee in case of need
Notadresse *f* emergency address; *(com)* nomination of a referee in case of need
Notakzept *n* collateral acceptance, acceptance in case of need
Notanzeige *f* notice of dishonour *(bill of exchange)*
Notar *m* notary (public); commissioner of oaths
~, **beurkundender** solicitor, conveyancing lawyer
Notariat *n* notary's office; notariat
Notariatsbescheinigung *f* notarial instrument
Notariatsgebühren *fpl* lawyer's fees; notarial fees
notariell notarial ◊ ~ **beglaubigt** attested by a solicitor
notarisch *s.* **notariell**
Notation *f* notation
Notdienst *m* emergency service
Note *f* 1. bank note [*(Am)* bill]; 2. (diplomatic) note; 3. mark *(school etc.)*
Notenausgabe *f* note issue
Notenaustausch *m* exchange of notes
Notenbank *f* bank of issue, central bank
Notenbankausweis *m* statement of the bank of issue, bank return
Notenbankpolitik *f* central bank policy
Notendeckung *f* cover of note circulation *(gold, silver etc.)*, backing of notes
Notendruck *m* printing of bank notes
Noteneinlösung *f* conversion of bank notes
Notenemission *f* issue of bank notes
Notenkontingent *n* fixed fiduciary issue; fixed issue of notes
Notenprivileg *n* note-issuing privilege
Notenreserve *f* statutory reserve of bank notes *(margin between the number of notes in circulation and the authorized note issue)*
Notenstückelung *f* denomination of bank notes
Notenumlauf *m* note circulation
~, **tatsächlicher** active note circulation
Notenwechsel *m* exchange of (diplomatic) notes
Noterbe *m* lawful heir

Notfall *m* case of need [emergency]
Notgeld *n* emergency [necessity] money *(issued during the period of severe inflation)*
Notgesetz *n* s. **Notstandsgesetz**
Notgesetzgebung *f* s. **Notstandsgesetzgebung**
Nothafen *m* port of refuge [distress]
Nothelfer *m* helper in time of need
Nothilfe *f* help in time of need; first-aid; emergency relief
~, technische rescue team (with technical aids)
notierbar *(st.ex.)* quotable, *(Am)* listable
notieren 1. to note *(s.th. down)*, to make a note *(of s.th.)*; 2. *(st.ex.)* to quote; to stand at *(share etc.)*
Notieren *n* notation
notiert quoted, *(Am)* listed ⋄ **amtlich ~** officially quoted [*(Am)* listed]; **fortlaufend variabel ~** consecutively noted [*(Am)* bunched]; **nicht ~** not quoted [*(Am)* listed], *(Am)* unlisted
Notierung *f* notation; *(st.ex.)* quotation ⋄ **zur ~ kommen** to be quoted officially, *(Am)* to be listed on the stock exchange
~, amtliche official quotation
~, einheitliche regular quotation
~, erste first call, opening quotation
~, fortlaufende variable quotation of currently adjusted rates
~, letzte previous quotation; closing price
~, uneinheitliche split quotation
Notifikation *f* notification; *(com)* notice of dishonour
notifizieren to notify
Notiz *f* 1. note, notice; 2. *(st.ex.)* quotation
Notklausel *f* escalator clause
Notlage *f* plight, difficult [precarious] position
~, finanzielle financial difficulties
~, wirtschaftliche economic plight
notleidend needy, poor *(persons etc.)*, suffering *(industry etc.)*
Notlösung *f* temporary solution
Notmaßnahme *f* emergency measure
Notopfer *n* emergency levy [contribution]
Notreparatur *f* emergency repair [maintenance]
Notstand *m* state of emergency, emergency situation
Notstandsarbeiten *fpl* relief works
Notstandsarbeiter *m* relief worker
Notstandsbestimmungen *fpl* emergency provisions
Notstandsfonds *m* emergency fund
Notstandsgebiet *n* disaster area; depressed [deprived] area
Notstandsgesetz *n* emergency bill [law]
Notstandsgesetzgebung *f* emergency legislation
Notstandskredit *m* relief loan
Notstandsmaßnahmen *fpl* emergency measures

Notstandsprogramm *n* relief programme
Notunterkunft *f* emergency [temporary] accommodation [dwelling]
Notverkauf *m* forced [compulsory] sale
Notverordnung *f* emergency decree
Notwährung *f* emergency currency
Notwohnung *f* s. **Notunterkunft**
Notzeit *f* time of need
Notzeiten *fpl* times of need
Novation *f* novation *(substitution of a new obligation for an old one)*
Novelle *f* *(jur)* amendment, supplementary addition (to an existing law), new bill *(modifying an existing law)*
null nil, zero, nought
~ und nichtig null and void ⋄ **als ~ und nichtig betrachten** to consider null and void; **für ~ und nichtig erklären** to declare null and void
Nullabweichung *f* zero error
Nullage *f* zero position *(indicators)*
Nullast *f* no load
Nullastpunkt *m* *(stats)* arbitrary origin
Nullfunktion *f* nil function
Nullinie *f* zero line
Nullmatrix *f* zero matrix
Nullmethode *f* zero method
Nullniveau *n* zero level
Nullpunkt *m* zero point [position]; zero level *(resources etc.)*
Nullsaldo *m* zero balance
Nullserie *f* pilot lot
Nulltarif *m* free fares; free public transport, free admission *(to hall etc.)*
Nullverfahren *n* s. **Nullmethode**
Nullwachstum *n* zero growth
Nullwert *m* zero, nought
nullwertig nonvalent, avalent
Nullwertigkeit *f* zero valency
numerieren to number ⋄ **fortlaufend ~** to number consecutively
Numerieren *n* numeration
Numerierung *f* numbering; numeration
numerisch numerical
Numero *n* number
Nummer *f* number; size *(hat, shoes etc.)*
~, laufende consecutive number
Nummernkonto *n* numbered account
Nutzanteil *m* profit share
Nutzanwendung *f* *(practical)* application
Nutzarbeit *f* effective [useful] work
nutzbar useful, productive; profitable; *(agric)* arable, cultivable
Nutzbarkeit *f* use; exploitability; profitableness
Nutzbarmachung *f* utilization; *(agric)* cultivation
nutzbringend profitable, advantageous

Nutzeffekt *m* efficiency; effectiveness
~ **der Arbeit** efficiency of labour
~ **der Arbeitsteilung** efficiency of division of labour
~ **der Automatisierung** efficiency of automation
~ **der Investitionen** efficiency of investment(s)
~ **der lebendigen Arbeit** efficiency of (living) labour
~ **der Produktion** efficiency of production
~ **des Außenhandels** efficiency of foreign [external] trade
~ **des wissenschaftlich-technischen Fortschritts** efficiency of scientific-technical progress
~, **gebietswirtschaftlicher** regional economic efficiency
~, **gesellschaftlicher** national [social] efficiency
~, **ökonomischer** economic efficiency
Nutzeffektsanalyse *f* efficiency analysis
Nutzeffektsberechnung *f s.* **Nutzeffektsermittlung**
Nutzeffektsermittlung *f* efficiency calculation, calculation of efficiency
Nutzeffektskennziffer *f* efficiency index [indicator]
Nutzeffektskoeffizient *m* efficiency coefficient
~, **normativer** coefficient of standard rate of efficiency
Nutzeffektskriterium *n* efficiency criterion
Nutzeffektsnachweis *m* report on efficiency, certificate of efficiency
Nutzeffektsnorm *f* standard rate of efficiency
Nutzeffektsnormativ *n* efficiency (standard) norm
Nutzeffektsuntersuchung *f* analysis of efficiency
Nutzeffektsvergleich *m* comparison of efficiency, efficiency analysis
nutzen to use, to make use of, to utilize
nützen to be of use, to be useful
Nutzen *m* use; benefit, advantage, gain, profit, yield ⋄ **mit einem ~ von** leaving a margin of; **ohne ~** profitless; **zum ~ von** for the benefit of
~, **wirtschaftlicher** economic gain
Nutzensabrechnung *f* efficiency accounting
Nutzensanteil *m* share of benefits; share of profits
Nutzensberechnung *f* efficiency calculation
Nutzensbeteiligung *f* benefit [profit] sharing
Nutzensermittlung *f* benefit calculation
Nutzensmaximierung *f* maximization of efficiency
Nutzensmaximum *n* maximum utility
Nutzensnachweis *m* report [statement] on efficiency

Nutzensrechnung *f* benefit calculation
Nutzensteilung *f* benefit sharing
Nutzer *m* user
Nutzertrag *m* benefit, profit, yield
Nutzfahrt *f* loaded run [trip]
Nutzfahrzeug *n* commercial [utility] vehicle
Nutzfläche *f* useful [effective] area
~, **landwirtschaftliche** land [area] under cultivation, arable land
Nutzflächenverhältnis *n* (agric) ratio of farm crops to arable land
Nutzholz *n* timber
Nutzkilometer *mpl* kilometres covered with load
Nutzkosten *pl* fixed costs apportioned to productive capacity
Nutzladefaktor *m* loading capacity factor
Nutzlast *f* payload, service [working] load
Nutzleistung *f* effective capacity [output]
Nützlichkeitspreis *m* utility price
Nützlichkeitswert *m* utilitarian value
nutzlos useless, futile, ineffectual
Nutzlosigkeit *f* uselessness, futility
nutznießen to make use of; to hold in usufruct
Nutznießer *m* user, beneficiary; (jur) usufructuary
Nutznießung *f* use; (jur) usufruct ⋄ **die ~ haben** to enjoy the usufruct (of)
Nutzpflanze *f* (agric) useful plant
Nutzrate *f* (agric) net income-input ratio (ratio between the co-operative's net income and fixed assets and working capital)
Nutzung *f* use, utilization; (jur) enjoyment
Nutzungsart *f* type [kind] of use
Nutzungsbefugnis *f* right of use
Nutzungsberechtigter *m* beneficiary, usufructuary
Nutzungsbilanz *f* residuary benefit
Nutzungsdauer *f* service life
Nutzungseigentum *n* joint ownership in which only one co-owner enjoys the fruits and advantages (of property)
Nutzungsentgelt *n* rental, hire
Nutzungsgebühr *f* fee [charges] for use
Nutzungsgemeinschaft *f* community holding land in common
Nutzungsgrad *m* degree of utilization (of fixed assets)
Nutzungsgrenze *f* (agric) natural limit of (economically) cultivable land
Nutzungshauptzeit *f* machine running time
Nutzungsjahre *npl* service life [time]
Nutzungskoeffizient *m* utilization coefficient (of plant and equipment)
Nutzungsnebenzeit *f* machine ancillary time
Nutzungsperiode *f* utilization period
Nutzungspfand *n* antichretic pledge
Nutzungspflicht *f* duty [obligation] to use

Nutzungsplanung *f (agric)* cultivation planning *(of the most suitable or effective cultivation of land)*; *(for)* long-term planning of tree-felling
Nutzungsprozent *n* utilization percentage
Nutzungsrecht *n* usufructuary rights, right of use
Nutzungsschaden *m* damage [wrong] occasioned by deprivation of the use of s.th.
Nutzungstausch *m* exchange of usufructuary rights
Nutzungsvertrag *m* usufructuary contract
Nutzungswert *m* rental value
Nutzungszeit *f* machine running plus ancillary time
Nutzvieh *n* livestock
Nutzwald *m* commercial forest
Nutzwert *m* economic value
Nutzwertklasse *f* category of economic value
Nutzwirkung *f* useful effect

O

Oase *f* oasis
Oasenanbau *m* cultivation of oases, oasis cultivation
Oasenbauer *m* oasis farmer [cultivator]
Oasenkultur *f* oasis crop
Obdach *n* shelter ◊ ~ **finden** to find shelter *(with s.o.)*; **jmdm. ~ gewähren** to grant s.o. shelter; ~ **suchen** to seek shelter
obdachlos homeless
Obdachlosenasyl *n* hostel for the homeless
Obdachlosenfürsorge *f* care of the homeless
Obdachlosenheim *n s.* **Obdachlosenasyl**
Obdachloser *m* homeless person
Obdachlosigkeit *f* homelessness
Oberaufseher *m* general supervisor
Oberaufsicht *f* general supervision
Oberbau *m* superstructure
Oberbuchhalter *m* chief accountant
Oberbürgermeister *m* mayor of large city, Lord Mayor
Oberfläche *f* surface
Oberflächenbeschaffenheit *f*:
~ **des Bodens** *(agric)* nature of the soil
Oberflächenkultur *f (agric)* surface cultivation
Oberklasse *f* upper class *(society)*; higher [senior] form [class] *(school)*; *(maths)* upper bounds *(of Dedekind's cut)*
Oberschicht *f* 1. upper stratum, upper classes [strata] *(society)*; 2. *(agric)* surface soil, top layer of soil, topsoil

Oberschulbildung *f* secondary (school) education
Oberschule *f* secondary school
Oberstaatsanwalt *m* attorney-general
Objekt *n* object; project *(investment etc.)*; transaction *(business etc.)*; property
Objektanalyse *f* product analysis
Objektbeauflagung *f* plan target [indicator] related to a special project
Objektbesteuerung *f* impersonal taxation, taxation on items of value
Objekte *npl*:
~, **beliehene** mortgage properties
Objektgliederung *f* product organisation *(in which the operational activities are divided on a product basis)*
Objektkollektiv *n* project construction team
Objektlohn *m* group piece-rate wage scheme *(type of collective piece-rate wages in project construction)*
Objektplanung *f* project planning
Objektprinzip *n* principle of product organization *(dividing operational activities on a product basis)*
Objektprogramm *n (d.pr.)* object program
Objektstandort *m* project location, site
Objektsteuer *f* tax levied on (individual) items of value
Objekt-Subjekt-Dialektik *f* interrelation(ship) between objective and subjective factors *(history, economy etc.)*
Objekttaktstraße *f* project assembly line
Objektterminplan *m* project schedule
Objektvergleich *m* project analysis [comparison]
Obligation *f (fin)* bond, *(Am)* debenture (bond); *(jur)* obligation, liability
Obligationen *fpl*:
~, **auf den Inhaber lautende** bearer [*(Am)* coupon] bonds
~, **auf den Namen lautende** registered bonds
~, **ausstehende** outstanding bonds
~, **eigene** own bonds
~, **einlösbare** optional bonds
~, **endgültige** definitive bonds
~, **festverzinsliche** active bonds
~, **frei verfügbare** free bonds
~, **garantierte** guaranteed bonds
~, **gekündigte** called bonds
~, **getilgte** cancelled bonds
~, **gezogene** drawn bonds
~, **hypothekarisch gesicherte** mortgage bonds
~, **kündbare** callable [*(Am)* redeemable] bonds
~, **kurzfristige** short-term bonds
~, **langfristige** long-term bonds
~, **mittelfristige** medium-term bonds
~ **mit Zinsschein** coupon bonds
~, **mündelsichere** trustee [*(Am)* legal] bonds

~, nicht eingelöste unpaid bonds
~, nicht übertragbare s. ~, auf den Namen lautende
~, öffentlich-rechtliche public bonds
~, steuerfreie tax exempt bonds
~, tilgbare s. ~, kündbare
~, übertragbare s. ~, auf den Inhaber lautende
~, ungültige disabled bonds
~, unverzinsliche non-interest-bearing bonds
~, vorläufige temporary bonds
~, zinstragende interest-bearing bonds
Obligationsanleihe f debenture loan
Obligationsausgabe f bond issue
Obligationsbuch n bond register
Obligationsfinanzierung f financing through bonds
Obligationsgläubiger m bond [debenture] holder, (Am) obligee
Obligationshandel m trade in bonds, bond trading
Obligationsinhaber m bond [debenture] holder
Obligationskonto n debenture account
Obligationsschein m bond
Obligationsschuld f fixed debt
Obligationsschulden fpl bonds payable (in balance sheet)
Obligationsschuldner m bond debtor, (Am) obligor
Obligationstilgung f bond redemption
Obligationsverpflichtung f bond obligation
Obligationszinsen mpl bond interest, interest on bonds, (Am) debenture interest
Obligationszinsschein m bond coupon
Obligo n liability (e.g. of a bank towards the Federal Bank); guarantee (on bill of exchange)
◊ ohne ~ without liability [recourse]
Obligobuch n discount ledger
Obligokartei f liability card index (used in investment accounting for registering allocation of duties in investment projects)
Obligoliste f list of commitments
Obstanbau m s. Obstbau
Obstanbaugebiet n area under fruit cultivation
Obstbau m fruit growing, fruit farming
Obstbaubetrieb m fruit-growing farm
Obstbauer m fruit farmer [grower]
Obsternte f fruit crop [harvest]
Obsterzeugnis n fruit product
Obsterzeugung f fruit production
Obsthandel m fruit trade
Obsthändler m fruiterer
Obsthandlung f fruiterer's shop
Ödland n waste [uncultivated, barren] land
Ödlandkultivierung f cultivation of waste [barren] land
Ofenbauer m kiln-maker; stove-maker; stove fitter

Offenbarungseid m poverty affidavit; insolvent debtor's oath, oath of manifestation [disclosure]
Offenbarungspflicht f contractual obligation to state conditions of work
Offenbarungsschuldner m bankrupt [trustee] debtor (who has made a sworn declaration as to the true state of his financial affairs)
Offenlegungspflicht f (approx.) bank's legal duty to ascertain the solvency and standing of a borrower
Offenmarktoperationen fpl open-market operations
Offenmarktpapier n open-market paper
Offenmarktpolitik f open-market policy
Öffentlichkeitsarbeit f public relations (work/activities)
Öffentlichkeitsgrundsatz m (approx.) obligation to apply for registration of a commercial business
Öffentlichkeitsprinzip n (jur) principle of open trial
öffentlich-rechtlich under public law
offerieren to offer, to make an offer; to tender; to bid
Offerte f offer; tender; bid (s. a. Angebot)
◊ eine ~ abgeben to make an offer
~, freibleibende open offer
~, gültige valid offer
~, unverbindliche offer without commitment
~, verbindliche binding [firm] offer
Öffnungstag m opening day
Öffnungszeiten fpl business [office] hours; hours of opening, opening time
off-line (d.pr.) off-line
Off-line-System n (d.pr.) off-line system
Off-shore-Auftrag m offshore purchase order
Off-shore-Bohrung f offshore drilling; offshore borehole [bore]
Off-shore-Kauf m offshore purchase
Ökologie f ecology
ökologisch ecological
Ökonom m economist
Ökonometrie f econometrics
ökonometrisch econometrical
Ökonomie f 1. economy (1. general term, covering the sphere of material production and the economy in general; 2. efficient utilization of social labour, material etc.) 3. economics (as a science)
~, bürgerliche politische bourgeois political economy
~ der Entwicklungsländer, politische political economy of developing countries
~ der Zeit economy of time
~ des Kapitalismus, politische political economy of capitalism

~ des Sozialismus, politische political economy of socialism
~, klassische bürgerliche politische classical bourgeois political economy
~, marxistische politische Marxist political economy
~, neoklassische bürgerliche politische neoclassical bourgeois political economy
~, politische political economy
Ökonomik f (national) economy; economics
ökonomisch economic; economical
ökonomisch-mathematisch economic-mathematical
ökonomisieren to economize, to make s.th. more economical
Ökonomisierung f economizing
Ökonomismus m economism
Ökosphäre f ecosphere
Ökosystem n ecosystem
Oktalsystem n (maths) octal notation
Öl n (mineral) oil; petroleum; shale-oil; (edible) oil (palm etc.)
Ölaktie f oil share [(Am) stock]
Ölbedarf m need for oil; demand for oil; oil consumption
ölbeheizt oil-fired
Ölbeheizung f oil heating (system)
Ölbohrung f oil drilling
Ölembargo n oil embargo
Ölersatz m oil substitute
Ölfabrik f oil mill (for edible oil)
Ölfeld n oil field
Ölfeuerung f oil firing; oil-firing system
Ölförderland n oil producing country
Ölfrucht f oleaginous fruit
Ölgas n oil gas
Ölgasteer m oil-gas tar
Ölgesellschaft f oil company [concern]
Ölgewinnung f oil production; oil extraction
Ölhafen m oil tanker terminal
ölhaltig containing oil; oleiferous, oleaginous (plant)
Ölhandel m oil trade, trade in oil
Ölheizung f oil heating
Oligopol n oligopoly
Oligopreis m oligopoly price
Ölindustrie f oil industry
Ölkonzession f oil concession
Ölland n oil exporting country
Ölleitung f oil pipeline; oil pipe
Ölmenge f amount of oil
Ölpest f s. Ölverschmutzung
Ölpflanze f oil plant, oil-yielding plant, oil-producing plant
Ölpreis m oil price
Ölproduzent m oil producer
ölproduzierend oil producing

Ölraffinerie f oil refinery
Ölsaaten fpl oil-bearing seeds
Ölsand m oil sand, oil-bearing sand
Ölsuche f oil prospecting
Öltanker m oil tanker
Ölverarbeitung f 1. oil processing; oil [petroleum] refining; 2. oil milling (edible oil); (edible) oil processing
Ölverbrauch m oil consumption
Ölverseuchung f s. Ölverschmutzung
Ölverschmutzung f oil pollution
Ölvorkommen n oil resources [deposits]
Ölwirtschaft f oil economy; oil industry
Omnibus m (omni)bus
Omnibusbahnhof m bus depot; bus terminus [terminal]
Omnibuslinie f bus-route
Omnibuslinienverkehr m bus-route service
Omnibuspark m bus fleet
Omnibusverkehr m bus traffic
Omniumpolice f (ins) all-risk policy
Omniumversicherung f all-risk insurance
on-line (d.pr.) on-line
On-line-Entwurf m (d.pr.) on-line design
On-line-System n (d.pr.) on-line system
Operand m (d.pr.) operand
Operateur m operator
Operation f operation; (st.ex.) transaction
~, arithmetische arithmetic operation
Operationsforschung f operations research
~, angewandte applied operations research
Operationsmodell n operation model
Operationsteil m (d.pr.) operation [instruction] part
Operationszeit f operating time
Operativberatung f short meeting
Operativinformation f information given at meeting called at short notice
Operativplan m working plan [programme]; emergency plan [programme]
Operator m operator
~, abgeschlossener (maths) closed operator
~, abschließbarer (maths) closable operator
~, additiver (maths) additive operator
~, adjungierter (maths) adjoined operator
~, beschränkter (maths) bounded operator
~, einfacher (maths) simple operator
~, fast beschränkter (maths) quasi-bounded operator
~, invertierbarer (maths) invertible operator
~, logischer (maths) logic operator
~, unbeschränkter (maths) unbounded operator
optimal optimum, optimal
Optimalgröße f optimum size
Optimalität f optimality
Optimalitätsaufgabe f optimality task
Optimalitätskriterium n optimality criterion

Optimalitätsprinzip *n* optimum principle
~, **volkswirtschaftliches** national economic optimum principle
Optimalleistung *f* optimum performance
Optimallösung *f* optimum solution
Optimalplanung *f* optimum planning
Optimalpreis *m* optimum [optimal] price
Optimalpreiskonzeption *f* optimum [optimal] price concept
Optimalpreissystem *n* optimum [optimal] price system
Optimalstrategie *f* optimum strategy
Optimalwert *m* optimum value
Optimierung *f* optimization; programming
~, **diskrete** discrete programming
~, **dynamische** dynamic optimization
~, **einparametrische** one-parameter optimization
~, **ganzzahlige** integer programming
~, **heuristische** heuristical optimization
~, **hyperbolische** hyperbolic optimization
~, **konvexe** convex optimization
~, **lineare** linear programming
~, **mathematische** mathematical optimization
~, **mehrparametrische** optimization on the basis of various parameters
~, **nichtlineare** non-linear optimization
~, **parametrische** parametric optimization
~, **quadratische** quadratic optimization
~, **skalierte** single-objective optimization
~, **stochastische** stochastic optimization
Optimierungsaufgabe *f* optimization
Optimierungskriterium *n* optimization [optimality] criterion
Optimierungsmodell *n* optimization model
~, **mathematisches** mathematical optimization model
~, **volkswirtschaftliches** national economic optimization model *(reflection of the most essential components and relations of the national economy by means of a mathematical model)*
Optimierungsrechnung *f* optimization (calculation)
Optimierungszeitraum *m* optimization period
Optimum *n* optimum
~, **volkswirtschaftliches** national economic optimum
Option *f* option ◊ **eine ~ aufgeben** to renounce an option; **eine ~ ausüben** to exercise an option
~, **gemeinsam ausgeübte** joint option
Optionsanleihe *f* optional bond
Optionsausübung *f* exercise of options
Optionsberechtigter *m* optionee, holder [owner] of an option
Optionsdauer *f* option period
Optionsempfänger *m (approx.)* person who has the option of either accepting or refusing the offer of a specific quantity of goods at a specific price
Optionsfixierer *m (approx.)* person offering a specific quantity of goods at a specific price
Optionsgeber *m* giver of an option, optioner
Optionsgeschäft *n (st.ex.)* option dealing
Optionsklausel *f* optional clause
Optionsnehmer *m* taker of an option
Optionsrecht *n* right of option
Optionsvertrag *m* option
Order *f* order; commission ◊ **an (die) ~ von** to the order of; **an eigene ~** to one's own order; **an fremde ~** to order of a third party; **an ~ lautend** payable to order; to be made out to order; **auf ~ und Rechnung von** by order and account of; **bis auf weitere ~** until further orders; **eine ~ annullieren** to cancel [withdraw] an order; **eine ~ ausführen** to execute an order; **eine ~ erteilen** to place an order; **laut ~** according to order; **nicht an ~** not to order, not transferable; **zahlbar an ~** payable to order
~, **begrenzte** limited order
~, **freibleibende** open order
~, **laufende** standing order
~, **limitierte** *s.* ~, **begrenzte**
~, **mündliche** oral order
~, **schriftliche** written order
~, **unlimitierte** unlimited order
Orderbuch *n* order book; book of commission
Orderklausel *f* pay-to-order clause
Orderkonnossement *n* bill of lading drawn to order
Orderpapier *n* order document, instrument (made out) to order (and transferable by endorsement)
Orderscheck *m* order cheque
Orderschuldverschreibung *f (fin)* registered bond (made out) to order
Ordertratte *f* promissory note made out to order
Orderzettel *m* order slip
ordnen to put [set] *(s.th.)* in order; to arrange *(s.th.)*
Ordnen *n* putting [setting] *(s.th.)* in order; arrangement
Ordnung *f* order *(public, state of affairs etc.)*; arrangement *(papers, books etc.)*; rank, order *(classification etc.)*; code *(road etc.)*; rules (in--house etc.); regulations *(implementing principles etc.)*; law; structure; pattern; system; *(maths)* order; ordered set; ordering
~, **exponentielle** *(maths)* exponential order
~, **gesellschaftliche** social order
~, **logische** logical order
~, **räumliche** layout *(forest nursery etc.)*
~, **systematische** systematical arrangement

~, **wirtschaftliche** economic structure [system, order]
Ordnungsdienst *m* 1. steward's work [job]; 2. stewards
ordnungsgemäß in compliance [accordance] with regulations; official, proper *(vote etc.)*; correct, proper *(documents etc.)*; regular, systematic *(accounting etc.)* ◇ ~ **ausgefüllt** duly completed; ~ **ausgestellt** duly drawn; ~ **bestellt** duly appointed *(representative etc.)*; ~ **unterschrieben** duly signed
ordnungsmäßig in a certain order *(arrangement etc.)*; ordered, systematic *(classification, division etc.)*
Ordnungsmerkmal *n (stats)* aid to classification
Ordnungsnummer *f* reference number
Ordnungsprinzip *n* order [organizing] principle
Ordnungsrelation *f (maths)* ordering relation
Ordnungsstrafe *f* penalty for infringement of regulations *(police etc.)*, fine
Ordnungsstrafverfahren *n* proceedings for infringement of regulations *(police etc.)*
Ordnungssystem *n* system of classification, classification system
ordnungswidrig contrary to regulations; incorrect *(behaviour)*
Ordnungswidrigkeit *f* infringement of regulations
Ordnungszahl *f (maths)* ordinal (number)
Organ *n* 1. authority, agency, institution; 2. organ, publication, medium
~, **ausführendes** executive authority
~, **bilanzierendes** (planning) authority responsible for balancing *(resources in physical terms)*
~ **der Staatsmacht, örtliches** local (government) authority
~, **öffentliches** public authority
~, **offizielles** bulletin
~, **vollziehendes** *s.* ~, **ausführendes**
~, **wirtschaftsleitendes** economic management authority
Organisation *f* organization; setup; structure
~ **der Arbeit** organization of labour [work], work organization
~ **der Produktion** organization of production, production organization
~ **des Industriebetriebes** organization of an industrial enterprise
~, **fehlerhafte** faulty set-up
~, **gemeinnützige** non-profit-making organization
~, **gesellschaftliche** social organization; non-governmental organization (NGO)
~, **innerbetriebliche** intra-enterprise organization
~, **innergebietliche** intra-regional organization *(related to problems inside regions)*

~, **mit Profit arbeitende** profit-making organization
~, **ohne Profit arbeitende** *s.* ~, **gemeinnützige**
~, **profitorientierte** profit-oriented organization
~, **supranationale** supra-national organization
~, **unzureichende** inadequate arrangement
Organisationsablauf *m* organizational procedure
Organisationsanweisung *f* instruction [directive] for organizing [managing] *(s.th.)*
Organisationsarbeit *f* organizational work
Organisationsaufbau *m* structure [set-up] (of an organization)
Organisationsaufgabe *f* organizational task
Organisationsbüro *n* secretariat
Organisationsebene *f* organizational level
Organisationseffekt *f* efficiency of organization
Organisationseinheit *f* unit of organization
Organisationsfehler *m* fault in the organization
Organisationsform *f* organizational form [structure]
Organisationsfragen *fpl* organizational matters
Organisationsgemeinschaft *f (ins)* association of insurance companies
Organisationsgrad *m* level of organization
Organisationsgrundlage *f* organizational basis
Organisationsgrundsatz *m* organizational principle, principle of organization
Organisationsinstrument *n* instrument of organization, organizational tool
Organisationskybernetik *f* organization cybernetics
Organisationslehre *f* study of industrial organization methods
Organisationsleitung *f* management of an organization
Organisationsmethode *f* method of organization
Organisationsmittel *npl* technical aids for the organization of office work
Organisationsniveau *n* level of organization
Organisationsplan *m* organizational plan [chart]
Organisationsprinzip *n s.* **Organisationsgrundsatz**
Organisationsprogramm *n* organization programme
Organisationsprojekt *n (approx.)* draft for the organization of the production line; draft of the study of management structure
Organisationsrichtlinie *f* organizational guidelines
Organisationsschaubild *n* organization chart
Organisationsschema *n* organization scheme
Organisationsschwierigkeiten *fpl* difficulties of organization
Organisationsstab *m* management committee *(for organizational matters)*

Organisationsstruktur *f* organizational structure [chart]
Organisationsstufe *f* stage of organization
Organisationssystem *n* system of organization
Organisationstätigkeit *f* organizational activity
Organisationstechnik *f* organizational technique
Organisationsträger *m* sponsor, parent organization
Organisationstyp *m* type of organization
Organisationsumstellung *f* reorganization
Organisations- und Rechenzentrum *n* (ORZ) organizational and computer centre
Organisationsverfahren *n* method of organization
Organisationsvertrag *m* contract [agreement] of foundation *(organization etc.)*
Organisationswissenschaft *f* science of organizing the process of social development
Organisationszentrum *n* business efficiency department
Organisator *m* organizer
organisatorisch organizational *(problem etc.)*; organizing *(ability)*
organisieren to organize
organisiert organized; affiliated to an organization ⋄ **genossenschaftlich ~** organized in a co-operative; **gesellschaftlich ~** organized socially *(party, trade union etc.)*; **gewerkschaftlich ~** organized in a trade union; **nicht ~** nonorganized, nonunionized; **politisch ~** organized politically
Organkonto *n* inter-company account
Organkredit *m* loan to members of the board *(of a credit organization etc.)*
Orgelbauer *m* organ-builder
orientieren to orientate, to inform; to instruct, to brief *(s.o.)*; **sich ~** to gather information; to get o.s. informed
Orientierung *f* orientation; information, instruction; guidelines
~, preispolitische guidelines for price policy; price policy
Orientierungsdaten *pl* background information, data providing guidelines, guidance data, guidelines
Orientierungskennzahlen *fpl s.* **Orientierungskennziffern**
Orientierungskennziffern *fpl* orientation data [indicators]
Orientierungspunkt *m* landmark, checkpoint, reference point
Orientierungstafel *f* information panel [board]
Orientierungszentrum *n* information centre
original original
Original *n* original ⋄ **mit dem ~ übereinstimmend** corresponding to the original

Originalausgabe *f* first edition
Originalbuchung *f* original entry
Originaldaten *pl* source data; *(d.pr.)* raw data
Originalfaktura *f* original invoice
Originalgröße *f* original size
Originalpackung *f* original package
Originalpreis *m* original price
Originalprogramm *n (d.pr.)* source program
Originalquittung *f* original receipt
Originalscheck *m* original cheque [*(Am)* check]
Originalsendung *f* original consignment
Originaltara *f* tare determined by the sender
Originalunterlagen *fpl* original data
Originalverpackung *f* original wrapping [pack(ag)ing] ⋄ **in ~** factory-packed
Originalwechsel *m* original bill
originär native, inborn; original
Ort *m* place, site; village; *(min)* coal [mining, winning] face ⋄ **vor ~** on the spot; *(min)* at the (pit) face
~ der Lieferung place of delivery
Orthonormierung *f* orthonormalization
Orthopädiemechaniker *m* worker making orthopaedic aids; artificial limb maker
Orthopädieschuhmacher *m* orthopaedic shoemaker
örtlich local; regional ⋄ **~ begrenzen** to localize
Örtlichkeit *f* locality, place
ortsansässig local, resident
Ortsanschluß *m* local telephone connection
Ortsbauplan *m* plan of a town [village] *(giving projected building developments)*
Ortsbehörde *f* local authority
Ortschaft *f* (inhabited) place, village
Ortsgespräch *n* local telephone call
Ortsgewerkschaftsleitung *f* local trade union committee
Ortsklasse *f* regional wage differential
Ortsklassenzuschuß *m* cost-of-living allowance of a locality
Ortskrankenkasse *f* sickness benefit fund of a locality
Ortssendung *f* mail for local delivery *(letter, parcel)*
Ortsstatut *n* bye-law
Ortstarif *m* regional wage rate
Ortsteil *m* suburb, part of village
Ortsteilnehmer *m* local subscriber *(telephone)*
Ortsveränderung *f* change of place, migration
Ortsverband *m* local association; association of villages [communities]
Ortsverkehr *m* 1. local telephone calls; 2. local traffic
Ortszeit *f* local time
Ortszulage *f* residential allowance *(supplementary allowance paid in certain professions for those people working in a specific area)*

Ortszuschlag *m s.* **Ortsklassenzuschuß**
Ortszustellbereich *m* (postal) delivery area
Ortszustellung *f (post)* local delivery
Ost-West-Handel *m* East-West trade

P

Pacht *f* 1. lease, leasehold; tenancy; 2. rent ✧ auf ~ *s.* in ~; die ~ läuft ab the lease expires; eine ~ abschließen to enter into a lease; eine ~ aufheben to terminate a lease; eine ~ verlängern to extend a lease; in ~ on [under, by] lease; in ~ geben to let (out) on lease; to put out to lease; in ~ haben to have on lease, to hold under [on, by] (a) lease; in ~ nehmen to take on lease, to take a lease of
~ **auf Lebenszeit** lifetime lease
~ **auf unbegrenzte Zeit** (perpetual) lease
~ **auf Zeit** time lease
~, **gemeinsame** joint lease
~, **individuelle** single lease
~, **rückständige** rent in arrears
~ **und Leihe** *f* Lend-Lease *(an arrangement authorized by U.S. Congress in March 1941 by which the U.S. government gave material aid and other services to the Allies during World War II)*
Pachtablauf *m* expiration of lease
pachtbar tenantable
Pachtbedingungen *fpl* leasehold terms [conditions], terms of a lease
Pachtbesitz *m* leasehold (property); tenancy, tenure on [by] lease
Pachtbetrieb *m* farm (held) on lease, leasehold estate [farm], tenant farm
Pachtbrief *m s.* **Pachtvertrag**
Pachtdauer *f* duration [term, life] of (a) lease; tenancy
pachten to take *(s.th.)* on lease, to lease *(s.th.)*; to rent
Pächter *m* lessee, leaseholder, *(esp. Am)* renter; *(agric.)* tenant (farmer)
Pachtertrag *m* rental(s)
Pachtfläche *f* leased area
pachtfrei rent-free
Pachtgebühr *f* rent, rental
Pachtgeld *n s.* **Pachtgebühr**
Pachtgrundstück *n* leasehold [leased] property, real property held by tenure
Pachtgut *n* tenant farm; leasehold property [estate]
Pachthof *m s.* **Pachtgut**
Pachtkontrakt *m s.* **Pachtvertrag**

Pachtkosten *pl* rent [rental] (paid)
Pachtland *n s.* **Pachtgrundstück**
Pachtpreis *m s.* **Pachtgebühr**
Pachtschutz *m* (legal) protection of leaseholders
Pachtsumme *f* (amount of) rent, rental
Pacht- und Leihgesetz *n* Lend-Lease Act *(s.* **Pacht und Leihe**)
Pacht- und Leihleistungen *fpl* lend-lease
Pacht- und Leihvertrag *m* Lend-Lease Agreement *(s.* **Pacht und Leihe**)
Pachtung *f* taking on lease; leasehold
Pachtverhältnis *n* tenancy, lease ✧ **von einem** ~ **zurücktreten** to give up a lease
Pachtverlängerung *f* extension [renewal] of lease
Pachtvertrag *m* (contract of) lease ✧ **einen** ~ **abschließen** to enter into a lease; to sign a lease; **einen** ~ **aufsetzen** to draw up a lease; **einen** ~ **verlängern** *s.* **eine Pacht verlängern**
~, **landwirtschaftlicher** farming lease
~, **langfristiger** long(-term) lease
pachtweise on [by] lease
Pachtwert *m* rental value
Pachtzahlung *f* payment of rent
Pachtzeit *f s.* **Pachtdauer**
Pachtzins *m s.* **Pachtgebühr**
Päckchen *n* small parcel, *(Am)* packet
packen to pack *(s.th.),* to put *s.th.* into *(box etc.)*; to wrap *s.th.* (up) *(in paper)*
Packen *m* large packet [parcel, bundle]; pile; stack
Packer *m* packer, wrapper
Packerei *f* packing room; packing department
Packerlohn *m* packer's wages
Packkiste *f* packing case [box]
Packkosten *pl* packing costs
Packliste *f* packing list
Packmaterial *n* packing material(s), wrappings, wrappage
Packraum *m s.* **Packerei**
Packung *f* package, packet
Packwagen *m* luggage van, *(Am)* baggage car
Packzettel *m* packing label [slip]; list of contents
Pädagogik *f* (science of) education; pedagogics
Paket *n* parcel, package; *(pol)* package (deal); *(st.ex.)* parcel [block] of shares
Paketannahme *f* 1. parcels receiving office, parcel (post) counter; 2. acceptance of parcels
Paketannahmestelle *f* parcels receiving office, parcel (post) counter
Paketausgabe *f* parcels issuing counter [office]
Paketausgabeschalter *m* parcels issuing counter
Paketauslieferung *f* delivery of parcels
Paketbeförderung *f* parcel(s) delivery
Paketgebühr *f* parcel(s) rate [postage]
paketieren to make packets *(of cigarettes etc.)*; to pack *(goods)*

Paketkarte *f* parcel bill, parcel dispatch note [slip]
Paketpolice *f (ins)* package policy
Paketpost *f* parcel post [*(Am)* mail]
Paketpostamt *n* parcel post office
Paketschalter *m* parcel counter
Paketsendung *f* 1. parcel, package; 2. parcel delivery
Paketumschlagstelle *f* parcels sorting office
Pakt *m* pact; treaty
paktfrei non-aligned
Palette *f* 1. range *(goods)*; 2. *(tech)* pallet
~, **breite** wide range *(goods)*
Palettentransport *m* transport by pallets
Palettenumschlag *m* turnover of pallets
Panne *f* breakdown; engine trouble [failure]
Pannendienst *m* breakdown service
pannensicher foolproof, failsafe
Panzergewölbe *n (bank)* strong room
Panzerschrank *m* safe
Papier *n* paper
Papierabfälle *mpl* waste paper
Papiere *npl* documents, papers; securities, stock(s) ⋄ ~ **auf dem Kapitalmarkt unterbringen** to market securities
~, **ausländische** *(st.ex.)* foreign papers
~, **börsenfähige** *(st.ex.)* marketable papers
~, **diskontfähige** *(st.ex.)* eligible papers
~, **festverzinsliche** *(st.ex.)* fixed-interest securities; investment bonds
~, **fundierte** *(st.ex.)* consolidated stock
~, **konsolidierte** *s.* ~, **fundierte**
~, **kurzfristige** *(st.ex.)* short-dated papers
~, **langfristige** *(st.ex.)* long-dated papers
~, **mündelsichere** gilt-edged securities [stocks], gilts, absolutely safe securities [papers, stocks]
~, **nicht diskontfähige** *(st.ex.)* ineligible papers
~, **nicht zinstragende** *(st.ex.)* non-interest bearing stock(s), non-dividend paying stock(s)
~, **öffentliche** state bonds
~, **schlecht gehende** *(st.ex.)* dull performers
~, **sichere** *(st.ex.)* first-rate stock, blue-chip stock; gilt-edged securities, gilts
~, **übertragbare** *(st.ex.)* negotiable instruments
~, **zinstragende** *(st.ex.)* interest-bearing papers; dividend-paying papers
Papierfabrik *f* paper mill
Papierfabrikation *f* papermaking, paper manufacture
Papiergeld *n* paper money, bank notes, *(Am)* bills
~, **konvertierbares** convertible paper money
~, **nicht konvertierbares** inconvertible paper money
Papiergeldausgabe *f s.* **Papiergeldemission**
Papiergeldemission *f* issue of bank notes [paper money]

Papiergeldkurs *m* exchange rate (of paper money)
Papiergeldumlauf *m* bank note circulation
Papiergeldzeichen *n* bank note, *(Am)* (bank) bill
Papiergeldzirkulation *f s.* **Papiergeldumlauf**
Papierherstellung *f s.* **Papierfabrikation**
Papierindustrie *f* paper industry
papierverarbeitend paper processing
Papierwährung *f* paper currency
Papierwaren *fpl* stationery
Papierwarenhändler *m* stationer
Papierwarenhandlung *f* stationer's (shop), stationery (shop)
Parallelbetrieb *m* 1. parallel production; 2. *(d.pr.)* parallel operation
Parallelbuchung *f* parallel entry [posting]
Parallel-Eingabe-Ausgabe-Funktion *f (d.pr.)* parallel input-output function
Parallelfertigung *f* parallel production
Parallelität *f* parallelism
~ **von Arbeitsoperationen** simultaneity of operations
Parallellauf *m (d.pr.)* parallel operation
Parallelmarkt *m* 1. parallel market; 2. free foreign exchange market *(as opposed to the official or authorized institutions)*
Parallelprinzip *n (d.pr.)* parallel principle
Parallelprogrammierung *f (d.pr.)* parallel programming
Parallelregister *n* parallel register ⋄ **ein ~ führen** to keep a parallel register
Parallel-Seriendarstellung *f (d.pr.)* parallel-serial notation
Parallel-Stichprobe *f (stats)* duplicate sample
Parallelübertragung *f (d.pr.)* parallel transfer
parallelverarbeitend *(d.pr.)* parallel-processing
Parallelverarbeitung *f* 1. simultaneous processing; 2. *(d.pr.)* parallel processing
Parallelverlauf *m* parallel course
Parallelversuch *m (stats)* replication
Parallelwährung *f* parallel standard *(gold and silver etc.)*
Parameter *m* parameter
~, **absoluter** *(stats)* absolute parameter
~ **der Lage** *(stats)* parameter of location
~ **der Leistung** performance data *(machines etc.)*
~ **der Nachfrage** *(stats)* demand parameter
~ **der Verteilung** *(stats)* parameter of distribution
~, **geschätzter** *(stats)* estimated parameter
~, **konstanter** *(stats)* constant parameter
~, **kritischer** *(stats)* critical parameter
~, **lästiger** *(stats)* nuisance parameter
~, **numerischer** *(stats)* numerical parameter
~, **optimaler** *(stats)* optimum [optimal] parameter

~, **qualitativer** *(stats)* qualitative parameter
~, **quantitativer** *(stats)* quantitative parameter
~, **relativer** *(stats)* relative parameter
~, **schätzbarer** *(stats)* estimable parameter
~, **statistischer** *(stats)* statistical parameter
~, **stochastischer** *(stats)* random parameter
~, **technologischer** technological parameter
~, **veränderlicher** *(stats)* variable parameter
~, **zeitabhängiger** *(stats)* time-dependent parameter; time-varying parameter
parameterfrei *(stats)* non-parametric
parametergesteuert *(d.pr.)* parameter-controlled
Parameterpreis *m* price based on indicators
Parameterpreisbildung *f* pricing [formation of prices] on the basis of indicators
Parameterpunkt *m* *(stats)* parameter point
Parameterschätzung *f* *(stats)* parameter estimation [estimate]
Parasitismus *m* parasitism
pari par ⟡ **auf** ~ at par; **über** ~ above par, at a premium; **unter** ~ below par, at a discount
Pari-Emission *f* par issue
Parikurs *m* par value price; par rate (of exchange)
Parität *f* parity
Paritätenkurs *m s.* **Parikurs**
paritätisch proportional, on a par, parity, with equal representation *(committee etc.)*
Paritätskurs *m s.* **Parikurs**
Paritätsprüfung *f (d.pr.)* parity check(ing)
Paritätstabelle *f* parity table
Pariwert *m* par value
Parkettleger *m* parquet layer
Parkgebühr *f* parking fee [charge]
Parkplatz *m* parking place, car park, parking lot; parking (space)
Parkplatzversicherung *f* car-park insurance
Parlament *n* parliament
Parlamentarier *m* parliamentarian
parlamentarisch parliamentary
Parlamentarismus *m* parliamentar(ian)ism
Parlamentsabgeordneter *m* member of parliament (MP)
Parlamentsausschuß *m* parliamentary committee
Parlamentsbeschluß *m* 1. act of parliament; 2. parliamentary decision [resolution]
Parlamentssitzung *f* parliamentary session
Part *m* 1. part, share; 2. share in the ownership of a vessel
Partei *f* party ⟡ **in eine ~ eintreten** to join a party
~, **gegnerische** opponent(s)
~, **vertragschließende** contracting party
Parteiapparat *m* party machine
Parteiarbeit *f* party work
Parteiaufbau *m* party set-up [structure]

Parteiensystem *n* system of parties, party system
Parteigruppe *f* party group
Parteikonferenz *f* party conference
Parteileitung *f* party committee
parteilich according to party principles
Parteilichkeit *f* accordance with party principles; taking sides, partisanship
parteilos non-party, belonging to no party; independent; neutral
Parteiloser *m* non-party member
Parteimitglied *n* party member
Parteinorm *f* party norm
Parteiorgan *n* 1. party committee [authority], party body; 2. party newspaper
Parteiorganisation *f* party organization
Parteipolitik *f* party politics
Parteiprogramm *n* party programme, (party) platform
Parteisekretär *m* party secretary
Parteistruktur *f* party structure [set-up]
Parteitag *m* party congress
Parteiversammlung *f* party meeting
Parteninhaber *m* part owner (of a ship)
Partialkalkulation *f* partial calculation
Partie *f* lot *(of goods)*, parcel; consignment; batch
Partiegröße *f* lot size
Partien *fpl*:
⟡ **in ~ von** in lots of
Partiepreis *m* special price for the lot
Partieware *f* sub-standard goods, job goods; remainders
Partikularismus *m* particularism
Partizipationsgeschäft *n* business on joint account, joint transaction
Partner *m* partner; party *(to an agreement etc.)*
Partnerbetrieb *m* co-operating enterprise
Partnergemeinde *f* twin municipality
Partnerministerium *n* counterpart ministry; co-operating ministry
Partnerschaftsbeziehungen *fpl*:
~, **ökonomische** relations of economic co-operation
Partnerstadt *f* twin town
Parzelle *f* parcel (of land), plot, allotment, *(Am)* lot
~ **mit Klumpenerfassungs-Merkmal** *(stats)* entry plot
Parzellenpacht *f* allotment [plot] rent
parzellieren to parcel (out); to divide into lots
Passage *f* passage
Passagier *m* passenger
Passagierflugzeug *n* passenger plane, airliner
Passagiergut *n* luggage, *(Am)* baggage
Passagierliste *f* list of passengers
Passagierschiff *n* passenger ship

Passagierschiffahrt *f* passenger shipping
Passagierstrom *m* passenger stream
Passagierverkehr *m* passenger transport
Passagierversicherung *f* insurance of passengers
Passiergewicht *n* (legally required) minimum weight (of coin)
Passierschein *m* pass, permit
Passierstelle *f* crossing point
Passiva *pl* liabilities
~, ständige permanent liabilities
Passivgeschäft *n* transaction creating a liability, borrowing transaction
Passivhandel *m* excess of imports over exports
passivieren to enter (item) on the debit [liability] side, to carry as liability
Passivposten *m* debit item [entry]
Passivsaldo *m* debit balance; deficit [adverse] balance, deficit
Passivseite *f* debit side (of balance sheet), liabilities side
Passivzinsen *mpl* interest (on debts) payable (to creditors)
Paßkontrolle *f* passport check [examination, inspection]
Paßstelle *f* passport office
Paßzwang *m* obligation to carry a passport
Patenbetrieb *m* sponsoring enterprise
Patenbrigade *f* sponsoring work team
Patenschaft *f* sponsorship
Patenschaftsvertrag *m* sponsorship agreement
Patent *n* patent *(for s.th.)* ◊ **auf ein ~ verzichten** to abandon a patent; **durch ~ geschützt** patented, protected (by patent); **ein ~ abtreten** to assign a patent *(to another firm etc.)*; **ein ~ anfechten** to contest [oppose, challenge] a patent; **ein ~ anmelden** to apply for a patent; to file an application for a patent; **ein ~ annullieren** to annul a patent; **ein ~ anwenden** to exercise a patent; **ein ~ aufgeben** to surrender a patent; **ein ~ aufrechterhalten** to keep a patent alive [in force]; to maintain a patent; **ein ~ bekanntmachen** to publish a patent; **ein ~ besitzen** to hold a patent; **ein ~ erhalten** to receive a patent; **ein ~ erneuern** to renew a patent; **ein ~ erteilen** to issue [grant] a patent; **ein ~ erweitern** to extend a patent; **ein ~ löschen** to cancel a patent; **ein ~ mit allen Rechten verkaufen** to sell a patent outright; **ein ~ nutzen** to employ a patent; **ein ~ ungenutzt lassen** to shelve a patent; **ein ~ verletzen** to infringe a patent; **ein ~ verweigern** to refuse [reject, withhold] a patent; **ein ~ verwerten** to exploit a patent; **ein ~ widerrufen** to revoke a patent; **ein ~ zurückziehen** to withdraw a patent

~, abgelaufenes expired patent
~, angemeldetes patent applied for [pending]
~, endgültiges complete patent
~, für ungültig erklärtes invalidated patent
~, gültiges patent in force, valid patent
~, laufendes unexpired patent
~, strittiges litigious patent
~, ungültiges void patent
~, verfallenes lapsed patent
Patentabkommen *n* patent agreement
Patentamt *n* patent office
Patentanmelder *m* applicant for a patent, patent applicant
Patentanmeldung *f* patent application; filing (of) a patent application ◊ **eine ~ einreichen** to file an application for a patent [a patent application]
Patentanspruch *m* patent claim
Patentanwalt *m* patent lawyer, patent agent, *(Am)* patent attorney
Patentaustausch *m* cross-licensing of patents; exchange of patents
Patentbeschreibung *f* patent specification
Patentbrief *m s.* **Patenturkunde**
Patentdauer *f* life [term] of a patent
Patentdiebstahl *m* patent piracy
Patentdokumentation *f* patent papers
Patenterteilung *f* grant(ing) [issue] of a patent, patent granting [issue]
patentfähig patentable
Patentgebühr *f* patent fee
Patentgegenstand *m* object (matter) of a patent
Patentgemeinschaft *f* joint patentees [patent holders], patent pool
Patentgericht *n* patent court, court adjudicating patent matters
Patentgesetz *n* patent act [law]
Patenthandel *m* patent trade
patentierbar patentable
patentieren to patent, to grant [issue] a patent on [for] s.th. ◊ **etwas ~ lassen** to take out [obtain] a patent for [on] s.th.
patentiert patented
Patentinformation *f* information on patents
Patentingenieur *m* patent engineer
Patentinhaber *m* patent holder, patentee, owner of a patent
Patentkosten *pl* patent costs [charges]; royalties
Patentliste *f s.* **Patentrolle**
Patentlizenz *f* patent licence
Patentpool *m* patent pool [holding]
Patentprüfer *m* patent examiner
Patentprüfung *f* patent examination
Patentrecht *n* 1. patent law; 2. patent rights
patentrechtlich under patent law ◊ **~ geschützt** patented, protected (by patent)
Patentrolle *f* register of patents, patent register

Patentschrift *f* patent specification
Patentschutz *m* protection by patent, patent coverage
Patentschutzgesetz *n s.* **Patentgesetz**
Patentstreit *m* patent litigation
Patentträger *m s.* **Patentinhaber**
Patenturkunde *f* (letters) patent
Patentverfahren *n* patenting, patent procedure
Patentvergütung *f* remuneration [payment] for a patent
Patentverletzung *f* patent infringement, piracy
Patentvertrag *m* patent agreement, agreement on patents
Patentverwertung *f* exploitation of a patent
Patentwesen *n* patent system; patent matters
Patient *m* patient
~, **ambulant behandelter** out-patient
~, **stationär behandelter** in-patient
Patt *n* stalemate; deadlock
Pauperismus *m* pauperism
Pauschalabschreibung *f* depreciation based on average figures, group depreciation
Pauschalbetrag *m* lump sum, global amount, flat charge [rate]; all-inclusive price, all-in price
~, **steuerfreier** tax-free lump sum
Pauschaldeckung *f* (ins) blanket coverage
Pauschale *f s.* **Pauschalbetrag**
Pauschalgebühr *f* flat rate [charge], blanket rate, all-in rate
Pauschalierung *f* consolidation of amounts into a lump sum; taxation based on average figures; lump sum taxation
~, **steuerliche** taxation based on average figures; lump sum taxation
Pauschalkauf *m* purchase in bulk, basket purchase
Pauschalpolice *f* open [blanket] policy
Pauschalpreis *m* lump sum (price)
Pauschalreise *f* package [all-in] tour
Pauschalsatz *m s.* **Pauschalgebühr**
Pauschalsteuer *f* tax based on average figures; lump sum tax; comprehensive tax
Pauschalsumme *f s.* **Pauschalbetrag**
Pauschalversicherung *f* blanket [package] insurance
Pauschalzahlung *f* lump sum payment; composition payment
Pausengestaltung *f* (work-)break arrangement
Pausenplan *m* work-break timetable
pekuniär pecuniary, financial *(difficulties etc.)*
Pelzhandel *m* fur trade
Pelzhändler *m* furrier
Pelznäher *m* **und Staffierer** *m (approx.)* stitcher and fur-liner
Pelztierzucht *f* fur farming
Pelzwaren *fpl* furs

Pendelmethode *f (stats)* up-and-down method
pendeln *(transp)* to commute
Pendelverkehr *m* 1. *(transp)* shuttle service; 2. commuter traffic
Pendelwanderung *f (transp)* commuting *(of workers etc. between residence and place of work)*
Pendelzug *m* 1. *(transp)* shuttle train; commuter train
Pendler *m (transp)* commuter
Pension *f* 1. (old-age) pension; 2. boarding house, small private hotel ✧ **in ~ gehen** to retire; **in ~ sein** to be retired, to live in retirement
Pensionär *m* 1. (old-age) pensioner, retiree; 2. boarder
pensionieren to pension (off), to retire, to superannuate
pensioniert retired, in retirement
Pensionierung *f* pensioning (off); retirement
Pensionierungsgrenze *f s.* **Pensionsalter**
Pensionsalter *n* retiring [retirement, pension(able)] age
Pensionsbeitrag *m* pension fund [scheme] contribution, contribution to the pension scheme
pensionsberechtigt pensionable, eligible for [entitled to] a pension
Pensionsberechtigung *f* right [entitlement] to a pension
Pensionsfonds *m* pension [retirement, superannuation] fund
Pensionsgeschäft *n* deposit of bills of exchange [stocks] *(as a security for a loan, often with a foreign bank)*, repurchase operation
Pensionskasse *f s.* **Pensionsfonds**
Pensionsliste *f* retired list
Pensionspreis *m* charge for [price of] board and lodging
Periode *f* period; cycle; *(maths)* repetend, recurring figure(s), period
~ **der Wiederkehr** *(stats)* return period
~, **verborgene** *(stats)* hidden periodicity
Periodendauer *f* cycle duration
Periodenkosten *pl* period cost(s)
periodisch periodic(al)
Periodisierung *f* periodization
Periodizität *f* periodicity
~ **der Krisen** periodicity of crises
Periodogramm *n (stats)* periodogram
~, **Schuster'sches** *(stats)* Schuster periodogram
peripher peripheral
Peripheriespeicher *m (d.pr.)* peripheral memory
Peripheriesteuer-Software *f (d.pr.)* peripheral-driving software
permanent permanent *(position, peace, crisis etc.)*, constant, continual, perpetual *(danger, anxiety, inventory etc.)*
Permanenz *f* permanence, permanency

Permutation *f* permutation
Persistenz *f* persistency
Person *f* person
~, **fingierte** fictitious person
~, **juristische** juristic [artificial, juridical] person, legal entity, corporation, body corporate
~, **natürliche** natural person
Personal *n* personnel; staff; workers, employees, labour force, workforce *(factory etc.)*; personnel *(train, airport etc.)*, staff *(shop, hotel etc.)*; crew *(train, bus etc.)*; domestic staff, servants ⋄ **gut mit ~ ausgestattet sein** to be well staffed; **mit ~ versehen** to staff *(institution etc.)*; **~ abbauen** to reduce (the) personnel, to cut staff, to slim [trim] (the) workforce, to make staff [workers, jobs] redundant, *(coll)* to axe [shed] jobs; **~ einstellen** to employ [take on, engage, hire] personnel [workers, staff]; **~ entlassen** to dismiss personnel [staff, workers], to make staff [workers, jobs] redundant; *(coll)* to axe [shed] jobs; **zum ~ gehören von** to be on staff of
~, **dienstältestes** longest-serving staff (member)
~, **fliegendes** (air) crew(s)
~, **freiwilliges** voluntary personnel
~, **geschultes** skilled [trained] personnel
~, **ingenieurtechnisches** engineers and technicians
~, **ortsansässiges** local personnel
~, **ständiges** permanent [regular] personnel
~, **zeitweiliges** temporary personnel
Personalabbau *m* reduction of personnel [staff], cut(s) in employment [staff], slimming [trimming] of (the) workforce [manning levels], manpower [staff] reduction, *(coll)* (job) axe
Personalabfluß *m* exodus of personnel [staff]
Personalabteilung *f* personnel department, *(Am)* personnel division, human resources [industrial relations] department
Personalakte *f* personal [personnel] file [records]; (personal) dossier
Personalanalyse *f* assessment and classification of personnel [staff]
Personalangaben *fpl* personal data, particulars
Personalarbeit *f* 1. staff recruitment policy; 2. training and promotion of personnel [staff]
Personalausbildung *f* staff training
Personalausgaben *fpl* expenditure on personnel
Personalauswahl *f* selection of personnel [staff]
Personalbedarf *m* staff requirements
Personalbedarfsplan *m* staff requirement plan
Personalbestand *m* (number of) personnel [employees], workforce, labour force, staff (size), manning
Personalbüro *n s.* **Personalabteilung**
Personalchef *m* personnel [staff] manager, head of (the) personnel department

Personal-Computer *m* **(PC)** personal computer (PC)
Personaleinsatz *m* placement of personnel [staff]
Personalentwicklung *f s.* **Personalausbildung**
Personalentwicklungs- und -einsatzplan *m* training and placement plan of personnel [staff]
Personalfluktuation *f* fluctuation of personnel [staff]
Personalgewinnung *f* recruitment of personnel [staff]
Personalien *pl s.* **Personalangaben**
Personalkartei *f* personnel index
Personalkosten *pl* personnel [labour, staff, employment] cost(s), personnel expenditure [expenses], payroll costs
Personalkredit *m* personal loan [credit]
Personalleitung *f* personnel managment
Personalmangel *m* shortage of personnel [manpower], staff shortage, undermanning, manpower deficit ⋄ **an ~ leiden** to be short of personnel; to be understaffed [undermanned]
Personalplanung *f* personnel [manpower, human resources] planning
Personalpolitik *f* personnel [employment] policy
Personalprogramm *n* staff recruitment, training and promotion programme
Personalraum *m* rest room
Personalreserve *f* staff envisaged for higher appointments
Personalstärke *f* strength of staff employed
Personalsteuer *f* personal [individual] tax
Personalstruktur *f* grading of staff
Personalunion *f* holding two positions; *(pol)* personal union
Personalunterlagen *fpl* personnel files
Personalverwaltung *f* 1. personnel [manpower] management [administration]; 2. personnel department
Personalwerbung *f* advertising for recruitment of personnel [staff]
Personenbahnhof *m* (passenger) station
Personenbeförderung *f* passenger transport(ation), conveyance of passengers
Personenbeförderungsgesetz *n* law relating to passenger transport
Personenbeförderungsleistung *f* passenger transport performance
Personenbeförderungstarif *m s.* **Personentarif**
Personenbeförderungsvertrag *m* passenger transport contract
Personenbeförderungszahl *f* number of passengers transported
Personen(garantie)versicherung *f* fidelity (guarantee) insurance, *(Am)* suretyship insurance

Personenkilometer *m* (**Pkm**) passenger-
-kilometer *(unit of transport = approx. 0,62 passenger-miles)*
Personenkonto *n* personal account
Personenkraftverkehr *m* passenger motor traffic; passenger motor transport(ation)
Personenkraftverkehrstarif *m* (**PKT**) table of fares for passenger transport *(by car, bus etc.)*
Personennahverkehr *m* short-distance [local] passenger transport *(railway)*; short-haul passenger transport *(car)*; commuter traffic
~ **mit Kraftfahrzeugen** short-haul passenger motor transport
Personenschaden *m* personal [physical] injury [damage]
Personenschadenhaftung *f* liability for personal injury
Personenstand *m* civil state, legal status, (person's) status
Personenstandsregister *n* register of births, deaths and marriages
Personensteuer *f* personal tax *(income tax etc.)*
Personentarif *m* table of fares for passenger transport
~, **einheitlicher internationaler** uniform international table of fares for passenger transport
Personentaxiverkehr *m* passenger taxi transport
Personenverkehr *m* passenger transport(ation), passenger traffic
~, **kommunaler** municipal passenger transport [service]
Personenverkehrstarif *m s.* **Personentarif**
Personenversicherung *f* insurance of individuals, personal insurance
Personenverzeichnis *n* list of persons; directory *(personnel)*
Personenwagen *m* *(railw)* (passenger) coach [carriage], *(Am)* (passenger) car
Personenwagenpark *m* number of railway coaches [carriages]; car pool
Personenzug *m* 1. passenger train; 2. slow train
Persönlichkeit *f* personality, well-known [leading] figure
~, **führende** (leading) personality [figure]
Persönlichkeitsrecht *n* personal [individual] right
Perspektiventscheidung *f* long-term decision
Perspektivplan *m* long-term plan
Perspektivplanansatz *m* long-term draft plan
Perspektivplanbilanz *f* balance sheet of long-
-term plan
Perspektivplanbilanzierung *f* balancing a long-
-term plan
Perspektivplankonzeption *f* draft outline of a long-term plan
Perspektivplanmodell *n* model of a long-term plan

Perspektivplanung *f* long-term planning
~, **betriebliche** long-term planning in enterprises, enterprise long-term planning
~, **finanzielle** financial long-term planning
~, **territoriale** regional long-term planning
~, **volkswirtschaftliche** national economic perspective [long-term] planning
Perspektivplanzeitraum *m* period of a long-
-term plan
Perspektivvertrag *m* long-term contract
Perzentile *n* *(stats)* percentile
Pfadkoeffizient *m* *(stats)* path coefficient
Pfand *n* pledge, security; pawn; lien; hypothec; deposit *(for bottles etc.)*
pfändbar distrainable *(goods, property etc.)*, attachable *(debts etc.)*
Pfändbarkeit *f* distrainability *(goods, property etc.)*, attachability *(debts etc.)*
Pfandbenachrichtigung *f* notice of lien
Pfandbesitzer *m* pledgee, pawnee, holder of a pledge
Pfandbestellung *f* pledging, pawning, creation of lien
Pfandbrief *m* mortgage debenture [*(Am)* bond]; security, mortgage deed ⋄ **einen ~ aus dem Verkehr ziehen** to retire a bond; **einen ~ unterbringen** to offer a bond for sale, to place a bond on the market; **einen ~ zeichnen** to subscribe a bond
Pfandbriefanstalt *f* (public) mortgage bank
Pfandbriefausgabe *f* (mortgage) bond issue, issue of bonds
Pfandbriefbesitz *m* bond holdings
Pfandbriefbesitzer *m* bondholder
Pfandbriefdarleh(e)n *n* loan on mortgage, loan in the form of a mortgage bond
Pfandbriefdisagio *n* bond discount
Pfandbriefemission *f s.* **Pfandbriefausgabe**
Pfandbriefgesetz *n* laws relating to mortgage bonds [debentures]
Pfandbriefgläubiger *m* bond creditor, debenture holder
Pfandbriefinstitut *n s.* **Pfandbriefanstalt**
Pfandbriefkauf *m* purchase of bonds
Pfandbriefmarkt *m* *(st.ex.)* mortgage bond [debenture] market
Pfandbriefschuldner *m* bond debtor
Pfandbriefumlauf *m* circulation of bonds
Pfandbriefverkehr *m* dealings in mortgage bonds
Pfandbruch *m* fraudulent removal, concealment of [damage to] goods taken in execution
Pfandbuch *n* pawnbroker's book [register]
Pfanddepot *n* safe custody of securities *(on which a banker has a lien)*; pledged-securities deposit
Pfandeffekten *pl* pledged (negotiable) securities

pfänden to distrain upon *(goods etc.)*, to attach *(wages, debts etc.)* ⋄ **jmdn. ~ lassen** to garnish s.o., to distrain upon s.o., to levy a distraint [distress] upon s.o.
Pfandentstrickung *f s.* **Pfandbruch**
Pfandforderung *f* hypothecary claim
pfandfrei pledge-free; free of deposit *(bottles etc.)*
Pfandfreigabe *f* restoration of goods taken in distraint [distress], replevin
Pfandgeber *m* pawner, pledger, hypothecary debtor
Pfandgebühr *f* pledge money
Pfandgegenstand *m* pledge, article put up as security, pledged item, *(Am)* hypothec; distraint article, article taken in execution
Pfandgeld *n* compensation *(received by impounder from trespasser)*; deposit *(for bottles etc.)*
Pfandgeschäft *n* pawnbroking, pawnbrokery
Pfandgläubiger *m* holder of a pledge [lien], pledgee, secured creditor, *(Am)* hypothecary creditor; pawnee *(pawnshop)*; mortgagee
Pfandhalter *m* holder of a pledge [security]
Pfandhaus *n* pawnshop
Pfandhinterlegung *f* deposit of a pledge
Pfandindossament *n (bank)* restrictive [pledging] endorsement *(by which an instrument payable to order becomes a pledge)*
Pfandinhaber *m s.* **Pfandgläubiger**
Pfandklage *f* action of replevin
Pfandklausel *f* clause giving the bank a lien
Pfandkredit *m* loan on a pledge
Pfandleihanstalt *f s.* **Pfandhaus**
Pfandleihe *f s.* **Pfandhaus**
Pfandleiher *m* pawnbroker
Pfandleihgewerbe *n* pawnbroking
Pfandmißbrauch *m* abuse of distraint [distress]
Pfandnahme *f* pawn-taking
Pfandnehmer *m s.* **Pfandgläubiger**
Pfandobjekt *n* pledged article, lien
Pfandrecht *n* 1. lien; 2. law of liens and pledges, *(Am)* hypothecary law ⋄ **ein ~ aufheben** to vacate a lien; **ein ~ begründen** to constitute a lien; **ein ~ bestellen** to create a lien; **ein ~ erweitern** to spread a lien; **ein ~ geltend machen** to enforce a lien on s.o.'s property; **ein ~ verlieren** to lose a lien; **sein ~ ausüben** to exercise one's right of lien
~ an beweglichen Sachen lien on movable chattels
~ an Forderungen right of a judgement creditor to satisfy himself with money in the garnishee's possession
~, eingetragenes registered lien
~, erstes first lien
~, nachrangiges second lien
pfandrechtlich hypothecary
Pfandsache *f s.* **Pfand**

Pfandschein *m* pawn ticket; certificate of pledge
Pfandschuld *f* mortgage debt, debt on a mortgage
Pfandschuldner *m s.* **Pfandgeber**
Pfandsicherheit *f* collateral security
Pfandsiegel *n* bailiff's stamp
Pfandstück *n s.* **Pfandgegenstand**
Pfändung *f* distraining, distraint *(of s.o./s.th.)*; attaching, attachment *(of wages etc.)*; execution, seizure *(of s.th.)*, distress *(of s.th.)*
~ von beweglichen Sachen seizure of movable property (under execution), distress of movable property
~ von Forderungen garnishment
~ von Löhnen attachment of wages
Pfändungsankündigung *f* notice of a garnishee [attachment] order
Pfändungsantrag *m* application for a writ of execution; application for a garnishee order
Pfändungsbefehl *m* distress warrant, warrant of distress
Pfändungsbeschluß *m (jur)* distress decision; order of attachment, garnishee order
Pfändungsbeschränkungen *fpl* restrictions on distress
Pfändungsgesuch *n s.* **Pfändungsantrag**
Pfändungsschutz *m* protection from distress, exemption from attachment
Pfändungsverfügung *f* garnishee [attachment] order, distress warrant [order]
Pfandverkauf *m* sale of a pledge
Pfandvertrag *m* contract of lien; mortgage deed
Pfandverwahrung *f* keeping [custody] of a pledge [security, an article taken in execution, an attached article]
Pfandverwertung *f* realization [disposition] of a pledge [security, an article taken in execution, an attached article]
pfandweise on mortgage [pawn], *(Am)* as collateral
Pfandwert *m* value of pawned article
Pfandzettel *m s.* **Pfandschein**
Pfandzinsen *mpl* chattel interest
Pferdezucht *f* 1. horse-breeding; 2. stud farm
Pferdezüchter *m* horse breeder
Pflanzenbau *m* crop [plant] cultivation [farming]
Pflanzeneiweiß *n* vegetable protein
Pflanzenproduktion *f* crop production [cultivation]
Pflanzenschädling *m* plant pest
Pflanzenschutz *m* plant protection, control of plant pests and diseases
Pflanzenschutzmittel *n* plant protective (agent), pesticide, insecticide
Pflanzenzucht *f* crop [plant] cultivation [breeding]
Pflanzenzüchter *m* plant breeder

Pflanzenzüchtung *f s.* **Pflanzenzucht**
Pflanzer *m* planter
Pflanzgut *n* seedlings, vegetative propagation stock
pflanzlich vegetable
Pflanzung *f* 1. planting; 2. plantation
Pflege *f (agric)* cultivation, tending; *(tech)* maintenance, tending; care, looking after *(persons)* ◇ **ein Kind in ~ geben** to place a child in care; to put a child to nurse [board]; **ein Kind in ~ nehmen** to take charge of a child, to take a child into care
~ und Wartung service [servicing] and maintenance
Pflegeamt *n* 1. public health department; 2. hospital management committee
Pflegeanstalt *f* nursing home, hospice; mental home
Pflegearbeiten *fpl (agric)* cultivation (work)
pflegearm *(agric)* easy to tend [cultivate] *(crops)*; easy to clean, wash-and-wear, crease-resistant and drip-dry, easy-care *(textiles)*
pflegebedürftig needing care, in need of care *(person etc.)*; in need of nursing *(old and sick persons)*
Pflegeeltern *pl* foster parents
Pflegeerlaubnis *f* permission to act as foster parents
Pflegefall *m* case requiring nursing [care]
Pflegegeld *n* nursing allowance
Pflegeheim *n s.* **Pflegeanstalt**
Pflegeklasse *f* category of nursing care
Pflegekosten *pl* maintenance expenses (of foster child/old people in nursing homes); nursing expenses [fees]
pflegeleicht *s.* **pflegearm**
pflegen to tend, to take care of, to look after; *(agric)* to cultivate; *(tech)* to maintain, to service *(machine)*
Pflegeperson *f* attendant, nurse, *(Am)* caretaker; keeper *(zoo)*; *(jur)* curator, guardian
Pflegepersonal *n* service personnel; nursing personnel [staff]
Pfleger *m s.* **Pflegeperson**
Pflegesatz *m* hospital allowance
Pflegestation *f* 1. medical care unit *(in some senior citizens' homes)*; 2. *(agric)* maintenance workshop
Pflegevertrag *m (tech)* maintenance agreement; *(agric)* cultivation agreement; nursing agreement *(persons)*
Pflegschaft *f* curatorship, custodial care, guardianship, tutelage; receivership *(administration)*
Pflicht *f* duty, obligation
~, gesellschaftliche social obligation [commitment]
~, häusliche domestic duty [task]
~, rechtliche legal obligation
~, staatsbürgerliche civic duty, duty of the citizen
~, vertragliche contractual obligation
~, vorvertragliche pre-contractual obligation
Pflichtablieferung *f* obligatory deliveries
Pflichtaktie *f* qualifying share
Pflichtanteil *m* contingent quota
Pflichtarbeit *f* compulsory work
Pflichtbeitrag *m* compulsory contribution *(to social insurance etc.)*
~ zur Sozialversicherung compulsory [obligatory] contribution to social insurance; *(Brit)* national insurance contribution (NIC)
pflichtbewußt dutiful, responsible
Pflichtbewußtsein *n* sense of duty
Pflichteinlage *f* limited partner's share [contribution]
Pflichteinstellung *f* compulsory employment (of registered disabled persons)
Pflichtenheft *n (d.pr.)* specification(s) of product requirements
Pflichtenkreis *m* (scope of) responsibilities, duties, functions
Pflichterfüllung *f* performance [fulfilment] of a duty
Pflichtgrenze *f (ins)* income limit for compulsory national insurance
Pflichtkrankenkasse *f* compulsory health insurance scheme
Pflichtleistung *f* standard insurance benefit
Pflichtmitglied *n* compulsory member
Pflichtmigliedschaft *f* compulsory membership
Pflichtprüfung *f* compulsory audit(ing)
Pflichtreserve(n) *f(pl) (bank)* statutory [minimum] reserves
Pflichtsortiment *n* compulsory range of goods
Pflichtteil *m* statutory [legal, legitimate, minimum] portion (of an inheritance); lawful share
Pflichtteilanspruch *m* claim (of a disinherited heir) to (his) legal [statutory] portion
Pflichtteilberechtigter *m* person entitled to a legal [statutory, minimum] portion
Pflichtteilentziehung *f* deprivation of legal [statutory, legitimate, minimum] portion [lawful share]
Pflichtteilfestsetzung *f* fixing the legal [statutory, legitimate, minimum] portion [lawful share]
Pflichtverletzung *f* failure to carry out [comply with] one's duty, neglect of one's duty; abuse of a position of authority
pflichtversichert compulsorily insured
Pflichtversicherung *f* compulsory insurance
Pflichtverteidiger *m* assigned [court-appointed] counsel, counsel for the defence

pflichtwidrig contrary to [in defiance of] one's duty; disloyal
Pflichtwidrigkeit *f s.* **Pflichtverletzung**
Pflug *m* plough, *(Am)* plow
pflügen to plough, *(Am)* to plow
Pflüger *m* ploughman, *(Am)* plowman
Pflugland *n* arable [ploughable, *(Am)* plowable] land, ploughland
Pförtner *m* gateman *(factory etc.)*; doorman *(hotel etc.)*; caretaker *(block of flats etc.)*; porter *(school etc.)*; gatekeeper *(park etc.)*
Pfründe *f* benefice, living; sinecure
Pfund *n* pound
Pfundabwertung *f* devaluation of the pound [of sterling]
Pfundanleihe *f* sterling loan
Pfundguthaben *n* sterling account
Pfundkonto *n* sterling account
Pfundnote *f* pound note
Pfundschwäche *f* weakness of the pound
Pfundzone *f* sterling area
Pfusch *m (coll)* botched job, shoddy work, mess
pfuschen *(coll)* to botch (up), to bungle, to mess up, to make a mess of *(job etc.)*
Phänomen *n* phenomenon, *(pl)* phenomena
Phantasiebeziehung *f* fancy [fanciful] tradename
Phantasiepreis *m* fancy [*(Am)* sky-rocketing] price
Phase *f* phase, stage
~, **analytische** analytical stage
~, **direktive** directive stage *(planning etc.)*
~, **konzeptionelle** conceptual stage
Phasendiagramm *n (stats)* phase diagram
Phasenebene *f (stats)* phase plane
Phasengliederung *f* division into phases [stages] *(production)*
Phasenintegral *n (stats)* phase integral
Phasenkurve *f (stats)* phase curve, path traced by the motion of a point *(in a phase space)*
Phasenpauschalierung *f (fin)* single-stage taxation
Phasenprodukt *n* semi-finished product; intermediate product
Phasenpunkt *m (stats)* phase point
Phasenraum *m (stats)* phase space
Phasenverschiebung *f (stats)* phase displacement
Phasenwechsel *m* change from one phase to another
Philosophie *f* philosophy
~, **bürgerliche** bourgeois philosophy
~, **idealistische** idealistic philosophy
~, **marxistisch-leninistische** Marxist-Leninist philosophy
~, **materialistische** materialist(ic) philosophy
Physiklaborant *m* physics laboratory assistant

Piktogramm *n* 1. ideogram; 2. *(stats)* pictogram
Pilotanlage *f* pilot plant
Pilotstudie *f* pilot study
Pionier *m* pioneer
Pionierarbeit *f* pioneer work
Pionierentwicklung *f* pioneering development
Pionierinvestitionen *fpl* pioneer investment(s)
Pionierleistung *f* pioneering performance [deed, exploit]
PKW-Einheit *f* motor car unit *(statistical figure comparing the road area required by different types of vehicles)*
plädieren to plead; to make the final speech ✧ **für etwas ~** to plead for s.th., to advocate s.th., to hold a brief for s.th.
Plädoyer *n* plea, pleading; counsel's (concluding) speech
Plafond *m (bank)* (upper) limit, ceiling
Plafondbesteuerung *f* maximum [ceiling] taxation
Plagiat *n* plagiarism ✧ **ein ~ begehen** *s.* **plagiieren**
Plagiator *m* plagiarist
plagiatorisch plagiaristic
plagiieren to plagiarize, to commit plagiarism
Plakat *n* poster, placard, bill ✧ **ein ~ ankleben** to put up [stick up] a poster [placard, bill]
Plakatanschlag *m* poster advertising; bill posting
Plakate *npl*:
✧ **~ ankleben verboten** stick no bills
Plakatentwurf *m* poster [placard] design
Plakatfläche *f* hoarding, *(Am)* bill-board
plakatieren to advertise *(s.th.)* with posters; to put up posters
Plakatsäule *f* advertising [advertisement, poster] pillar
Plakatwand *f s.* **Plakatfläche**
Plakatwerbung *f* advertising with posters, poster publicity
Plan *m* 1. plan; scheme; project; blueprint; schedule; 2. diagram; graph; 3. map; chart ✧ **alles geht nach ~** everything is going according to schedule; *(plan)* everything is going according to plan; **einen (bestimmten) ~ verfolgen** to pursue a (definite) plan; **einen ~ abändern** to modify a plan; **einen ~ aufgeben** to renounce a plan; **einen ~ ausarbeiten** to draw up [draft, prepare] a plan; **einen ~ ausführen** to carry out [implement, execute] a plan; **einen ~ einreichen** to submit a plan; **einen ~ entwerfen** *s.* **einen ~ ausarbeiten**; **einen ~ erfüllen** to fulfil(l) [implement] a plan; to reach (plan) targets; **einen ~ unterstützen** to promote a scheme; **einen ~ vereiteln** to thwart a plan [design]; **einen ~ verwirklichen** to realize a scheme; *(plan)* to

carry out [implement, realize] a plan; **einen ~ vorlegen** to present [submit] a plan; **einen ~ zeichnen** to draw up a plan; to draw a map; **nach ~ abfahren** to start [leave, depart] according to timetable; **nach ~ arbeiten** to work according to a schedule; *(plan)* to work according to a plan
~, **abänderungsfähiger** plan liable to modification
~, **angespannter** tight plan
~, **anspruchsvoller** exacting plan
~, **bestätigter** confirmed [approved] plan
~, **bilanzierter** balanced plan
~ **der Forschungs- und Entwicklungsarbeiten** plan of research and development (R & D)
~ **der Marktarbeit** marketing plan *(of methods and kinds of marketing such as market research, market formation etc.)*
~ **der materiell-technischen Versorgung** plan of material supply
~ **der Positionen** plan of items *(compilation of budget accounts according to national economic aspects)*
~ **der Volkswirtschaft, langfristiger** long-term plan of the national economy
~, **detaillierter** detailed plan
~, **gekürzter** shortened plan
~, **graphischer** graph
~, **konsistenter** fully balanced plan
~, **kurzfristiger** short-term plan
~, **langfristiger** long-term plan
~, **laufender** current plan
~, **mittelfristiger** medium-term plan
~, **optimaler** optimum plan
~, **undurchführbarer** impossible plan
~, **verlängerter** extended plan
~ **Wissenschaft und Technik** plan of science and technology
~, **wohldurchdachter** well-thought-out plan
~, **zusammengefaßter** aggregated plan
Planablauf *m* plan sequence *(1. process of working out a plan in various stages; 2. process of plan implementation, control and analysis of plan fulfilment)*
Planabrechnung *f* statement [report] on plan implementation
Planabschnitt *m* section of plan; plan period; *(fin)* budget period
Planabstimmung *f* plan co-ordination
~, **betriebliche** plan co-ordination in an enterprise
~, **internationale** *s.* **Plankoordinierung, internationale**
~, **interministerielle** inter-ministerial co-ordination of plans
~, **intersektorale** inter-sectoral plan co-ordination

~, **territoriale** regional plan co-ordination
Planabweichung *f* deviation from the plan, plan deviation; *(fin)* budget variance
Planadressat *m* plan addressee *(enterprise or institution receiving plan tasks from higher echelons)*
Plananalyse *f* plan analysis
Planänderung *f* plan modification
Planangebot *n* draft plan *(of enterprises etc.)*
Plananlauf *m* plan take-off *(initial stage of plan implementation)*
Planansatz *m*:
~, **volkswirtschaftlicher** (national economic) draft plan, suggested planning data *(result of the first and formative stage in preparing the plan)*
Planarbeit *f* planning
Planaufbau *m* structure of a plan, plan structure
Planaufgabe *f* plan task [target]
Planauflage *f* plan(ned) target [quota]
~, **staatliche** state plan target [task] *(assigned to partial systems of the national economy)*
~, **verbindliche** binding plan target [task]
Planaufschlüsselung *f* allocation of plan targets and tasks *(according to temporal and spatial aspects)*
Planaufstellung *f* plan drafting [preparation]
Planausarbeitung *f* plan elaboration [preparation]
planbar plannable
Planbarkeit *f* possibility of planning
Planbegründung *f* substantiation of a plan *(or draft submitted to higher planning authority)*
Planberatungen *fpl* plan discussions
Planberechnung *f* plan calculation
Planbericht *m* report on the plan, plan report
Planberichtigung *f* correction to the plan, plan correction
Planbestand *m* planned stocks
Planbestätigung *f* plan confirmation
Planbeziehungen *fpl* planned relationships
~, **horizontale** planned horizontal relationships
~, **vertikale** planned vertical relationships
Planbilanz *f* plan balance sheet
Planbilanzberechnung(en) *f(pl)* calculation of plan balance sheet(s)
Planbilanzierung *f* plan balancing, balancing of a plan
Plandirektive *f* plan directive
Plandiskussion *f* plan discussion *(discussion of the draft plan at all levels)*
Plandisziplin *f* adherence to the plan
Plandurchführung *f* plan implementation
Pläne *mpl*:
~ **komplexer Aufgaben, langfristige** long-term plans of complex tasks
planen to plan; to drawn up [make] a schedule

Planentscheidung *f* plan decision
Planentwurf *m* draft plan, plan draft
Planer *m* planner
Planerfüllung *f* plan fulfilment [implementation], fulfilment of targets [quotas]
~, **mengenmäßige** quantitative fulfilment of the plan
~, **sortimentsgerechte** plan fulfilment according to the range of goods envisaged
~, **vorfristige** plan fulfilment ahead of schedule
Planfehler *m* planning error
Planfertigungskosten *pl* standard production costs
Planfortschreibung *f* plan extension; rolling planning
plangemäß *s.* **planmäßig**
plangerecht *s.* **planmäßig**
Plangewinn *m* planned profit
Planinformationen *fpl* plan information *(set of indices worked out at lower levels and passed on to the higher echelons)*
Planinformationssystem *n* system of plan information
Plan-Ist-Abrechnung *f* cost accounting according to planned and actual costs
Plan-Ist-Kostenrechnung *f s.* **Plan-Ist-Abrechnung**
Plan-Ist-Vergleich *m* comparison of planned and realized targets
Planjahr *n* plan year
Plankalkulation *f* plan calculation
Plankapitalismus *m* planned capitalism
Plankennziffer *f* plan indicator [index number]
~, **staatliche** state plan indicator
~, **verbindliche** binding plan indicator
Plankommission *f* planning commission
Plankonkretisierung *f* fixing the details of the plan
Plankontinuität *f* continuity of plans
Plankontrolle *f* follow-up of plan
Plankonzeption *f* outline of a draft plan
Plankoordinierung *f s.* **Planabstimmung**
~, **internationale** international co-ordination of plans
~, **volkswirtschaftliche** national economic plan co-ordination
Plankorrektur *f* plan modification
Plankosten *pl* planned costs
Plankostenbeleg *m* standard costs record
Plankostenentwicklung *f* development of planned costs
Plankostenrechnung *f* accounting of planned costs; standard costing
Plankostensatz *m* rate of planned costs
Plankostenvorgabe *f* estimate, estimated costs *(applied in standard costing)*
Plankredit *m* general plan credit

Planlohnfonds *m* planned wage fund
planlos without (a) plan; without (a) method, unsystematic; aimless; haphazard
Planlosigkeit *f* lack of plan(ning); aimlessness; haphazard approach
planmäßig according to plan; on schedule; systematic, methodical; budgetary
Planmäßigkeit *f* consistency in planning; method; system(atic approach)
Planmethodik *f* plan methodology
planmethodisch according to planning method
Planmittel *npl* planned resources
Plannorm *f* plan norm
Planoptimierung *f* plan optimization
Planoptimierungsmodell *n* plan optimization model
Planperiode *f* planning period; *(fin)* budgeted period
Planposition *f* plan item *(1. plan task in the plan document expressed in physical terms; 2. item of product classification)*
Planpreis *m* planned price
~, **konstanter (KPP)** constant planned price
~, **unveränderlicher (UPP)** *s.* ~, **konstanter**
Planproduktion *f* planned production
Planprojekt *n* plan project
Planrealisierung *f s.* **Planerfüllung**
Planrechnung *f* plan calculation
Planreserven *fpl* untapped planned resources
Planrückstand *m* plan arrears [non-fulfilment]
Planschulden *fpl* arrears in plan fulfilment
Planselbstkosten *pl* planned prime cost
Plansoll *n s.* **Planauflage**
Planspiel *n* business [planning] game
Planstelle *f* established [permanent, regular] post, post authorized (in the budget)
~, **freie** vacancy
Planstellenanforderungen *fpl* demand for additional personnel [staff]; requirements expected in filling vacancies
Plantage *f* plantation; large orchard
Plantagenwirtschaft *f* plantation agriculture; plantation system
Planteil *m* plan component
Planübererfüllung *f* overfulfilment of the plan, plan overfulfilment
Planung *f* planning; budgeting
~, **auftraggebundene** planning according to order
~, **eigenverantwortliche** self-responsible planning
~, **erzeugnisbezogene** *s.* ~, **erzeugnisgebundene**
~, **erzeugnisgebundene** product-related planning
~, **finanzielle** finance [financial] planning
~, **gemeinsame** joint planning

~, **gleitende** sliding planning
~, **innerbetriebliche** intra-enterprise [in-house] planning
~, **komplexe** comprehensive planning
~, **komplex-territoriale** comprehensive regional planning
~, **kurzfristige** short-term planning
~, **langfristige** long-term planning
~, **mittelfristige** medium-term planning
~, **operative** current (short-term) planning
~, **optimale** optimum [optimal] planning
~, **perspektivische** long-term planning
~, **prognostische** long-term forecasting [prognosis]
~, **regionale** regional planning
~, **rollende** rolling [continuous] planning
~, **soziale** social planning
~ **sozialer Prozesse** planning of social processes
~, **staatliche** state [government] planning
~ **und Leitung** f **der Volkswirtschaft** planning and management of the (national) economy
~, **volkswirtschaftliche** national economic planning
~, **zentrale** central planning
~, **zentrale staatliche** central state planning
~, **zentralisierte** centralized planning
Planungsablauf m planning procedure; sequence of planning activities
Planungsabteilung f planning department
Planungsbehörde f planning authority [board]
Planungsdokumente npl plan documents
Planungsebene f planning level, level of planning
Planungseinheit f planning unit
Planungsetappe f stage of planning
Planungsfehler m planning error
Planungsfunktionen fpl planning functions
Planungsgegenstand m object of planning
Planungsgerät n planning table (for balancing production programmes)
Planungsinstrument n planning instrument [tool]
Planungsinstrumentarium n (set of) planning tools [instruments]
Planungskennziffer f planning indicator
Planungskomitee n planning committee
Planungslimit n plan limit (quantity which must not be exceeded in the process of plan preparation and implementation)
Planungsmappe f planning file
Planungsmaßnahme f measure adopted in planning, planning measure
Planungsmethode f planning method, method of planning
Planungsmethodik f planning methodology
Planungsmethodologie f s. **Planungsmethodik**

Planungsmodell n planning model
Planungsnormativ n planning standard [target]
Planungsobjekt n s. **Planungsgegenstand**
Planungsordnung f regulations for planning
Planungsorgan n planning body [authority, organ]
Planungsorganisation f planning organization; organziation of planning
Planungsphase f phase [stage] of planning
Planungsprinzip n planning principle
Planungsprozeß m planning process
Planungsrechnung f plan calculation [computation]
~, **lineare** linear plan calculation [computation]
Planungsrichtlinie f planning instructions
Planungsstab m planning board
Planungssystem n planning system, system of planning
~, **automatisiertes** automated system of planning
~, **rechnergestütztes** computer-aided system of planning
Planungstätigkeit f planning activities
Planungstheorie f planning theory, theory of planning
Planungsunterlagen fpl planning documents
Planungszeitraum m planning period [horizon]
Planungszyklus m planning cycle
Planuntererfüllung f non-achievement of the (plan) target(s)
Planunterlage f plan document
Planvariante f plan variant
Planverbrauch m planned consumption, consumption according to plan (materials etc.)
Planverflechtungsbilanz f plan input-output table
Planverflechtungsbilanzierung f drawing up plan input-output tables
Planvergleich m comparison of plans
Planverletzung f non-adherence to the plan
Planverlust m planned loss
Planverstoß m s. **Planverletzung**
Planverteidigung f plan vindication [defence]
Planvolumen n planned volume [amount] (goods and services etc.)
Planvorgabe f initial planning targets
Planvorlauf m 1. lead in plan fulfilment; advance fulfilment of (plan) targets; 2. preliminary plan drafting
Planvorschlag m plan proposal
Planvorsprung m ⋄ **einen ~ erarbeiten** to fulfil (plan) target(s) in advance
Planwert m planned value
planwidrig contrary to plan
Planwirtschaft f planned economy
Planzahlen fpl plan(ned) figures, targets
Planzeitraum m plan(ned) [planning] period

Planziel *n* (plan) target [quota]
Planziffern *fpl s.* **Planzahlen**
Planzins *m* interest according to plan; interest on planned credits
Planzinssatz *m* interest (rate) on planned credits [according to plan]
Plaste-Industrie *f s.* **Plastindustrie**
Plastindustrie *f* plastics industry
Platz *m* 1. place, spot; site *(building, storage)*; centre *(trade etc.)*; 2. space, room; 3. seat ◊ **am Platze** in the market; **einen ~ reservieren lassen** to reserve [book] a seat
~, abgelegener remote place
~, bestellter reserved seat
Platzabschluß *m* spot contract
Platzagent *m s.* **Platzvertreter**
Platzakzept *n (st.ex.)* local acceptance
Platzanforderung *f* demand for space *(exhibition hall etc.)*
Platzangebot *n* spot offer
Platzaufschlag *m* extra charge for (good) position *(exhibition hall etc.)*
Platzbedarf *m* need for space, space required
Platzbeschränkung *f* limitation of space
Platzbestellung *f* reservation, booking (of seats)
platzen to bounce, to be dishonoured *(bill of exchange)*
Platzgeschäft *n* local (business) transaction; *(st.ex.)* spot deal [contract]
Platzkarte *f* seat reservation ticket
platzkartenpflichtig seat reservation required
Platzkäufer *m (st.ex.)* local [spot] purchaser
Platzkilometer *mpl* seat kilometres *(covered kilometres multiplied by the number of seats available in a vehicle)*
Platzkostenrechnung *f* job [workplace, workbench] cost accounting [costing]
Platzkredit *m* local credit
Platzkurs *m* spot market price [rate]
Platzmiete *f* renting *(football ground etc.)*, hiring *(tennis court etc.)*; charge *(parking etc.)*; stall rent, stallage
Platzmietvertrag *m* stand rent contract
Platzreservierung *f* reservation [booking] of seats, seat reservation
Platz- und Empfangsgroßhandel *m* local wholesale trade *(in fruits, vegetables and other perishables directly at the place of production)*
Platzverkauf *m* sale on the spot, spot sale
Platzverkehr *m* local bank operations
Platzvertreter *m* local agent
Platzwechsel *m (st.ex.)* bill (of exchange) payable at place of issue, local bill
plazieren to place, to position *(s.o.)*; to invest *(capital)*; to (find a) market (for), to sell *(goods)*; to negotiate *(bill of exchange)*
Plazierung *f* placing; showing *(s.o.)* to a table *(restaurant)*; deployment *(personnel etc.)*; placement, investment *(capital etc.)*
~, bevorzugte preferred position
~ einer Anleihe placement [negotiation] of a loan
Pleite *f* bankruptcy, insolvency, (business) failure; flop, washout *(model of a product etc.)* ◊ **~ machen** to go bankrupt; *(coll)* to go broke, to go bust, to go to the wall
pleite bankrupt, *(coll)* broke, bust ◊ **~ sein** to be broke
Plenarsitzung *f* plenary session [meeting]
Plenarversammlung *f* plenary [general] assembly
Plenum *n* full [plenary] session, plenum
plombieren to seal, to affix a seal
plombiert sealed
Plombierung *f (cust)* sealing *(container, goods wagon etc.)*
Poissonprozeß *m (stats)* Poisson process
Poissonverteilung *f (stats)* Poisson distribution
~, doppelte *(stats)* double Poisson distribution
~, überlagerte *(stats)* compound Poisson distribution
Polarisation *f* polarization
polarisieren to polarize
Polemik *f* controversy, polemics
Police *f (ins)* policy
~, abgelaufene expired policy
~ auf eine bestimmte Summe value policy
~, befristete time policy
~, beitragsfreie free policy
~, benannte named policy
~, durchschnittliche standard policy
~, eingetragene registered policy
~, gemischte mixed policy
~, geschlossene closed policy
~, gewinnberechtigte participating policy
~, laufende floating policy
~ mit Wertangabe valued policy
~, nicht gewinnberechtigte non-participating policy
~, offene open policy
~ ohne Wertangabe open [unvalued] policy
~, perspektivische future policy
~, prämienfreie *s.* **~, beitragsfreie**
~, verfallene lapsed policy
Policenausfertigung *f* issue of policy
Policenbeleihung *f* policy loan
Policenbesitzer *m* policy holder
Policenbuch *n* policy book
Policendatum *n* date of policy
Policenformular *n* policy form, blank policy
Policenkündigung *f* cancellation of policy
Poliklinik *f* outpatient department *(often of hospital)*; polyclinic
Politbüro *n* political bureau, politburo, politbureau

Politik *f* policy; politics
- der **Bündnisfreiheit** policy of non-alliance
- der **friedlichen Koexistenz** policy of peaceful coexistence
- der **Nichtpaktgebundenheit** policy of non-alignment
- der **Vollbeschäftigung** policy of full employment
- des **Abwartens** wait-and-see policy
- des **billigen Geldes** policy of cheap money, cheap money policy
- ~, **langfristige** long-term policy
- ~, **ökonomische** economic policy

Politiker *m* politician; statesman
Politikerin *f* stateswoman
Politikum *n* political issue, matter of politics
Politikwissenschaft *f* political science
politisch political; policy *(statement etc.)*
politisieren 1. to politicize; to give *(s.th.)* a political character; 2. to talk (about) politics
Politisieren *n* talking politics
Politisierung *f* politicization
Politökonomie *f* political economy
Politologe *m* political scientist
Politologie *f* political science
politologisch in (the field of) political science, from the point of view of political science
Polsterer *m* upholster
Pólya-Prozeß *m (stats)* Pólya process
Pólya-Verteilung *f (stats)* Pólya distribution
Polygon-Melkstand *m (agric)* polygonal milking parlour
Polynome *npl*:
~, **Charlier'sche** *(stats)* Charlier polynomials
Polytechnikum *n* polytechnic
Pool *m* pool
Population *f* population
Populationsanalyse *f* population analysis
Populationsdichte *f* population density
Populationsdynamik *f* population dynamics
Populationsgenetik *f* population genetics
Populationslehre *f* demography
Populationsmaß *n (stats)* population parameter
Populationstheorie *f* population theory
Populationsumkehr *f (stats)* population inversion
Portefeuille *n* portfolio
Portefeuille-Effekten *pl* portfolio securities
~ **industrieller Werte** portfolio of industrial shares
Portier *m* gateman *(factory etc.)*; doorman *(hotel etc.)*; caretaker *(block of flats etc.)*
Portion *f* portion, share
portionsweise in portions
Porto *n* postage (rate); (parcels) carriage ◇ **einschließlich** ~ postage included
~, **gewöhnliches** ordinary postage

Portoablösung *f* settling of postal charges by block payment
Portoauslagen *fpl* postage (expenses)
Portobuch *n* postage book
Portoermäßigung *f* reduction in the postal rate
portofrei post(age)-free; prepaid, postpaid; carriage paid *(parcels)*
Portofreiheit *f* exemption from postage
Portogebühren *fpl s.* **Porto**
Portokasse *f* petty cash; petty-cash box
Portokosten *pl* postage expenses
portopflichtig liable to postage [postal charges]
Portorechnung *f* postage account
Portorückvergütung *f* refunding of postage
Portospesen *pl s.* **Portokosten**
Portozuschlag *m* additional [extra] postage; surcharge
Porzellangestalter *m* porcelain designer
Porzellanmaler *m* china-painter
Posamentierer *m* passementarie maker
Position *f* 1. position; 2. *(acc)* item, entry; 3. *(social)* standing, status
~, **führende** *s.* ~, **leitende**
~, **gehobene** advanced position
~, **gesellschaftliche** social position
~, **leitende** leading [policy-making] position
~, **verantwortliche** position of responsibility, responsible position
positionieren *(d.pr.)* to position, to place, to locate
Positionspapier *n* position paper
Post *f* 1. postal service; post office; 2. post, mail; 3. correspondence, letters ◇ **eingegangene ~ erledigen** to attend to the correspondence; **etwas zur ~ bringen** to take s.th. to the post office; **mit der heutigen ~** by today's post [*(Am)* mail]; **mit der ~ schicken** to post, *(Am)* mail, to send by post [*(Am)* mail]; **mit gewöhnlicher ~** by surface mail; **mit gleicher [getrennter] ~** under separate cover; **mit umgehender ~** by return (of post/mail), *(Am)* by return mail; **per ~** by post [mail]
Postabholer *m* (post) caller, caller for mail
Postabkommen *n* postal convention
Postablage *f* filing of letters; letter rack
Postablieferungsschein *m* notification of postal collection
Postabonnement *n* postal subscription
Postabschnitt *m s.* **Posteinlieferungsschein**
Postabteilung *f* postal department; mailing department
Postadresse *f* postal address, *(Am)* mailing address
Postagentur *f* sub-post office
postalisch postal; by post [mail]
Postamt *n* post office
~, **fahrbares** mobile post office

postamtlich postal
Postangelegenheit *f* postal matter
Postangestellter *m* postal clerk [employee]
Postanschluß *m* telephone connection
Postanschrift *f s.* **Postadresse**
Postanstalt *f s.* **Postamt**
Postanweisung *f* postal [money] order, postal remittance
~, gebührenfreie service money order (without charges)
~, telegrafische telegraphic (postal) order
Postanweisungsformular *n* money order form
Postauftrag *m* postal collection order, order for collection of a debt by the post office
Postausgang *m* 1. outgoing [leaving] mail; 2. out-tray
Postausgangsbuch *n* register of outgoing mail
Postauslieferung *f* postal delivery
Postbarscheck *m* postal cheque [*(Am)* check], (national) giro payment order
Postbeamter *m* post-office clerk, *(Am)* postal clerk; counter clerk
Postbeförderung *f* postal [mail] delivery [transport]; conveyance of mail
Postbegleitschein *m* post office dispatch note
Postbetrieb *m* 1. postal services; 2. postal institution
Postdienst *m* postal service
Posteingang *m* 1. incoming mail; 2. in-tray
Posteingangsbuch *n* register of incoming mail
Posteingangsstempel *m* (rubber) stamp for incoming mail
Posteinlieferungsschein *m* postal [post-office] receipt
Posten *m* 1. post, place; position, job, situation; 2. *(acc)* entry, item; 3. *(com)* lot, parcel; 4. amount, sum; 5. *(strike)* picket ✧ **einen ~ aufgeben** to resign from a position, to retire; **einen ~ austragen** *(acc)* to cancel an entry; **einen ~ belasten** to debit an item; **einen ~ eintragen** to make an entry; **einen ~ gutschreiben** to credit an item; **einen ~ löschen** *s.* **einen ~ austragen; einen ~ manipulieren** to handle an item; **einen ~ nachtragen** to book an omitted item; **einen ~ neu besetzen** to fill a vacancy; **einen ~ stornieren** *s.* **einen ~ austragen; einen ~ streichen** *s.* **einen ~ austragen; einen ~ übertragen** to carry over an entry; **einen ~ umbuchen** to transfer an amount [an entry] to another account; to transfer an amount to s.o. else's name; **jmdn. für einen ~ bestimmen** to appoint s.o. to a post
~, absetzbarer deductible item
~, antizipativer accrued item
~, ausstehender receivable item, item still uncovered
~, bestreitbarer debatable item
~, debitorischer *s.* **~, ausstehender**
~ der Rechnungsabgrenzung deferred item(s) [asset(s)]; deferred charges
~, durchlaufender in-transit item, item in transit
~, eingetragener booked item
~, einmaliger non-recurring item
~, großer 1. *(acc)* major item; 2. large lot *(articles etc.)*
~, innerbetrieblicher intra-enterprise [intra-company, in-house] item
~, kleiner *(acc)* minor item; small lot *(articles etc.)*
~, offener unpaid [uncovered] item
~, transitorischer suspense [deferred] item
~, unbeglichener item not squared [paid for], item (still) uncovered
~, unbesetzter vacancy, vacant position
postenweise by items, in [by] lots
Postfach *n* post-office box (P.O.B.), P.O. box
postfertig ready for posting [mailing]
Postgebühren *fpl* postal charges [rates] *(s. a.* **Porto***)*
Postgeheimnis *n* secrecy of (the) post [mail], postal secrecy
Postgesetz *n* postal law
Postgiroverkehr *m* postal [post-office] giro transactions; postal [post-office] giro service
Postgut *n* mail, postal matters, goods conveyed by post [mail]
Postkarte *f* postcard
~ mit Rückantwort reply-paid postcard
Postkraftverkehr *m* postal transport service
postlagernd poste restante, (mail) to be called for
Postleitgebiet *n* postal region [zone], *(Am)* zip area
Postleitzahl *f* postal [*(Am)* zip] code, post-code
Postliste *f* mailing list
Postmietbehälter *m* post hire box *(for parcels)*
Postnachnahme *f* cash [*(Am)* collect] on delivery (system) (c.o.d.)
Postnachnahmesendung *f* cash [*(Am)* collect] on delivery (c.o.d.) mail [consignment; parcel]
Postnebenstelle *f s.* **Postagentur**
Postordnung *f* postal regulations
Postrecht *n* legal provisions concerning postal services
Postscheck *m* giro cheque, postal cheque [*(Am)* check]; giro, *(Brit)* National Giro *(system)*
Postscheckamt *n* post giro office, postal cheque [*(Am)* check] office, *(Brit)* Giro Centre
Postscheckdienst *m* postal cheque [*(Am)* check] service; *(Brit)* (National) Giro
Postscheckguthaben *n* (postal) giro (account) balance

Postscheckkonto *n* (postal) giro account, postal cheque [*(Am)* check] account
Postscheckkunde *m* (postal) giro account holder, *(Brit)* National Giro account holder
Postscheckübeweisung *f* (postal) giro transfer
Postscheckverkehr *m* (postal) giro [*(Am)* check] system
Postschließfach *n* post-office box (P.O.B.), P.O. box
Postschnellgut *n* express parcel
Postsendung *f* post, mail
~, **unzustellbare** undeliverable mail
Postsortieranlage *f* mail sorting equipment
Postsparbuch *n* post-office savings book
Postsparer *m* post-office [*(Am)* postal] saver
Postsparkasse *f* post-office savings bank, *(Am)* postal savings office
Postsparkonto *n* post-office [*(Am)* postal] savings account
Postsperre *f* suspension of mail services
Poststelle *f* mailing room *(enterprises, institutions etc.)*; sub-post office
Posttarif *m* postal rates
Postüberweisung *f* postal giro [*(Am)* check] transfer
Post- und Fernmeldegebühr *f* postal and telegraphic charges
Post- und Fernmeldewesen *n* post(al) and (tele)communications (system), posts and (tele)communications
Postverkehr *m* postal [mail] service [traffic]
Postvermerk *m* official endorsement *(on envelope etc.)*
Postversand *m* dispatch of mail
Postverspätung *f* postal delays
Postverwaltung *f* post-office [postal] administration [authorities]
Postvollmacht *f* (written) authorization to receive mail on behalf of another person; postal procuration
postwendend by return (of post/mail), *(Am)* by return mail
Postwerbung *f* postal advertising; junk mail
Postwertversicherung *f* registered mail insurance
Postwertzeichen *n* (postage) stamp
Postwesen *n* postal system; postal services
Postwurfsendung *f* mail advertising; mail circular; sample packet; *(coll)* junk mail
Postzahlungsverkehr *m* postal money order [remittance] service
Postzeitungsvertrieb *m* postal newspaper (and periodical delivery) service
Postzentrale *f* mailing department *(in enterprises etc.)*
Postzustellung *f* postal [mail] delivery
Postzustellungsdienst *m* postal service

Postzwang *m* postal principle (obligation to use the post for the conveyance of letters)
Potential *n* 1. potential; capacity *(of factory etc.)*; 2. manpower
~ **an Arbeitskräften** potential labour force [humanpower, manpower]
~, **industrielles** industrial potential [capacity]
~, **ökonomisches** economic potential
~, **technisches** technology potential
~, **technologisches** s. ~, **technisches**
~, **wissenschaftliches** scientific potential
~, **wissenschaftlich-technisches** science and technology potential
Potentialfaktor *m* fixed factor *(production etc.)*
Potentialfunktion *f* *(stats)* potential function
Potentialgleichung *f* *(stats)* differential equation describing the potential *(especially Laplace equation, Poisson equation)*
Potentialtheorie *f* *(stats)* potential theory
Potentialvektor *m* *(maths)* potential vector
potentiell potential
Potenz *f* potency, strength; *(maths)* power
~, **ökonomische** economic strength
~, **relative** *(stats)* relative potency
Potenzexponent *m* exponent, power index
Potenzfunktion *f* *(maths, stats)* power function
potenzieren to strengthen, to intensify, to increase the strength [potential]; *(maths)* to raise *(s.th.)* to a power
Potenzieren *n* *(maths)* raising *(s.th.)* to a power
Potenzmenge *f* *(stats)* power sum
Potenzmittel *n* *(stats)* power mean
~, **kombinatorisches** *(stats)* combinatorial power mean
Potenzmoment *n* *(stats)* power moment
Potenzreihe *f* *(stats)* power series
Potenzsumme *f* power sum
Potenzwert *m* *(stats)* value of a power
Potestativbedingung *f* *(jur)* potestative condition
P_1-**Produktion** *f* production at one's own expense
P_2-**Produktion** *f* jobbing production *(based on materials supplied by another enterprise)*
Präambel *f* preamble
Präferenz *f* preference, preferential treatment
Präferenzabmachung *f* preferential agreement
Präferenzanspruch *m* preferential claim, claim to preferential treatment
Präferenzen *fpl*:
◇ **einem Partner ~ einräumen** to give preference to a partner
~, **steuerliche** (preferential) tax concessions, preferential tax rate
Präferenzpreis *m* preferential price
Präferenzspanne *f* difference between preferential and general tariff, margin of preference

Präferenzsystem *n* preferential [preference] system
Präferenzzoll *m* preferential tariff [duty]
Prägeanstalt *f* mint
Prägegebühr *f* mintage, brassage
prägen to shape, to mould *(experience, character etc.)*; to have one's mark *(on s.th.)*; to mint, to strike, to coin *(metals)*
Prägen *n* minting, striking, coining; mintage, coinage
Prägeort *m* mint
Prägerecht n seignorage, royalty
Prägung *f* mintage, coinmaking
Praktikant *m* trainee
Praktiken *fpl* practices
~, **unfaire** sharp practices
Praktiker *m* practician; practitioner *(largely confined to professions)*; practical(ly-minded) person
Praktikum *n* practical training (course); practical work [studies]; *(coll)* practical ⋄ **ein ~ machen** to undergo one's practical training, *(coll)* to do one's practical
Prämie *f* 1. bonus, extra [*(Am)* premium] pay; bounty 2. *(ins)* premium; contribution; 3. *(st.ex.)* option money, premium
~, **angegebene** *(ins)* specified premium
~, **anteilige** *(ins)* pro-rata rate
~, **ausstehende** *(ins)* outstanding premium
~, **bedungene** *(ins)* stipulated premium
~, **einheitliche** *(ins)* flat premium rate
~, **fällige** *(ins)* premium due
~, **feste** *(ins)* fixed [stable] premium
~ **für langjährige Betriebszugehörigkeit** long-service bonus
~, **gleichbleibende** *(ins)* level premium
~, **gleitende** *(ins)* sliding-scale premium
~, **hohe** *(ins)* high premium
~, **jährliche** *(ins)* annual premium
~, **nicht produktionsgebundene** non-production bonus
~, **niedrige** *(ins)* low premium
~, **noch nicht fällige** *(ins)* deferred premium
~, **produktionsgebundene** production bonus
~, **rückständige** *(ins)* premium arrears
~, **zusätzliche** *(ins)* additional premium
Prämienakkordsystem *n* system of incentive piece-wage rates
Prämienangleichungsklausel *f (ins)* variable premium rates clause
Prämienanleihe *f* lottery [premium] bond
Prämienanteil *m* pro-rata premium
Prämienaufkommen *n (ins)* premium income, earned premium
Prämienaufwendungen *fpl (ins)* premium costs
Prämienbedingungen *fpl* conditions for awarding a bonus

prämienbegünstigt under a bonus scheme, bonus-linked, premium-aided
Prämienberechnung *f (ins)* calculation [rating] of premiums
Prämienbeteiligung *f (ins)* special settlement dividend
Prämienbetrag *m (ins)* (amount of) premium
Prämienbildung *f (ins)* calculation of premium, rate setting [making], rating
Prämienbrief *m (st.ex.)* option contract
Prämiendepot *n (ins)* unearned premium reserve *(interest-bearing deposit from which premiums are deducted when payment is due)*
Prämieneinnahmen *fpl (ins)* earned premium
Prämieneinzahlung *f (ins)* payment of premium; premium deposit
Prämieneinziehung *f (ins)* collection of premiums
Prämienempfänger *m* person awarded a bonus
Prämienerklärung *f (st.ex.)* declaration of option(s)
Prämienerklärungstag *m (st.ex.)* option declaration date, *(Am)* option day
Prämienfälligkeitstag *m (st.ex.)* premium-due date
Prämienfestsetzung *f s.* **Prämienbildung**
Prämienfonds *m* bonus fund
Prämienform *f* kind of bonus payment
prämienfrei *(ins)* free (of premium)
Prämiengeld *n* bonus; *(st.ex.)* option money
Prämiengeschäft *n (st.ex.)* option dealing
~, **doppeltes** *(st.ex.)* compound option
~, **einfaches** *(st.ex.)* single option
Prämiengewährpolice *f (ins)* return premium policy
Prämiengleichheit *f (st.ex.)* rate equity
Prämiengrundbetrag *m (ins)* rate basis (of premium)
Prämienhandel *m (st.ex.)* trading in puts and calls [*(Am)* in privileges]
Prämienhändler *m (ins)* option dealer
Prämienherabsetzung *f (ins)* reduction of premiums
Prämienhöhe *f s.* **Prämienbetrag**
Prämienkauf *m (st.ex.)* purchase of an option
Prämienkäufer *m (st.ex.)* option buyer
Prämienkennzahl *f* performance indicator
Prämienkonto *n* bonus account
Prämienkurs *m (st.ex.)* option rate [price]
Prämienleistung *f (ins)* payment of premiums
Prämienlohn *m* incentive wage, time rate plus bonus wage
Prämienlohnsatz *m* incentive wage rate
Prämienlohnsystem *n* incentive wage system, bonus system [scheme]
Prämienmakler *m (st.ex.)* option [*(Am)* privilege] broker

Prämienmarkt *m (st.ex.)* option market
Prämienmittel *pl s.* **Prämienfonds**
Prämienobligationen *fpl (ins)* premium bonds [*(Am)* debentures]
Prämienordnung *f* rules for bonus payment
Prämienpfandbriefe *mpl* lottery mortgage bonds [*(Am)* debentures]
Prämienplan *m* bonus plan; *(ins)* premium (savings) plan
Prämienrabatt *m (ins)* premium rebate
Prämienrechnung *f (ins)* premium note, renewal notice
Prämienregulierung *f (ins)* rate adjustment of premiums
Prämienreserve *f (ins)* premium reserve (fund), policy reserve
Prämienrückerstattung *f (ins)* (no-claim) premium refund
Prämienrückgewähr *f (ins)* guarantee of return of premiums
Prämienrückstände *mpl (ins)* arrears in premiums
Prämiensatz *m (ins)* premium [life] rate *(life insurance)*; *(st.ex.)* option rate [price]
Prämienschein *m (ins)* premium bond [token]
Prämiensparen *n* saving under a bonus system, premium-aided saving
Prämienstaffelung *f* fixing of different rates of bonus payments; *(ins)* scale of premiums
Prämiensteuer *f (fin)* premium tax
Prämienstücklohn *m* piece-rate wage with bonus
Prämienstundung *f (ins)* deferment of payment of premiums
Prämiensystem *n* bonus system
~, kollektives group bonus system
Prämientarif *m (ins)* premium rate [scale]
Prämienüberschüsse *mpl (ins)* net premium income
Prämienvereinbarung *f* agreement on bonus payment
Prämienvergütung *f (ins)* bonus payment
Prämienverkauf *m (st.ex.)* option sale
Prämienverkäufer *m (st.ex.)* taker of an option
Prämienversicherung *f (ins)* proprietary insurance
~, reine *(ins)* non-participating insurance
Prämienverteilung *f* distribution of bonuses, bonus distribution
Prämienverzeichnis *n (ins)* premium catalogue
Prämienverzicht *m (ins)* abandonment of premiums
Prämienvorauszahlung *f (ins)* advance (payment of) premium(s)
Prämienware *f (st.ex.)* securities dealt on the option market, option stock
Prämienwerte *mpl s.* **Prämienware**

Prämienzahlung *f* bonus payment; *(ins)* payment of premium
~, einmalige *(ins)* single payment (of premium)
~, laufende *(ins)* regular payment of premiums
Prämienzeitlohn *m* time-rate wage with bonus
Prämienzettel *m s.* **Prämienschein**
Prämienzuschlag *m (ins)* extra premium
prämiieren to award a bonus for *(better performances etc.)*
Prämiieren *n* awarding a bonus *(for better performance etc.)*
Prämiierung *f* award
pränumerando in advance, before a given date, beforehand
Pränumerandozahlung *f* payment in advance [before a given date]
Präsentant *m* presenter
Präsentation *f* presentation; presentment *(bill of exchange etc.)*
Präsentationsfrist *f* (fixed) period [time] for [of] presentment *(bill of exchange etc.)*
Präsentationsklausel *f* presentment for acceptance clause *(on bill of exchange etc.)*
Präsentationspflicht *f* obligation to present within a specified time *(bill of exchange etc.)*
Präsentationsrecht *n (jur)* right of presentation; advowson
Präsentdatum *n* date of presentment *(of document etc.)*
präsentieren to present *(bill of exchange etc.)*
Präsentierung *f* presentation; presentment *(bill of exchange etc.)*
Präsenzgelder *npl* attendance fees
Präsident *m* president; chairman, chairperson *(sessions etc.)*; *(bank)* governor; *(jur)* presiding judge
~, amtierender acting president; acting chairman
~, stellvertretender vice-president
Präsidentschaft *f* presidency; chairmanship
Präsidentschaftskandidat *m* candidate for the presidency, presidential candidate
Präsidentschaftswahl *f* presidential election
präsidial presidential
Präsidialregierung *f* presidential (form of) government
Präsidialsystem *n* presidential system [(form of) government]
präsidieren to preside over [at] *(meeting, committee etc.)*, to hold [be in] the chair, to act as chairman
Präsidium *n* 1. presiding [managing] committee; presidium *(party etc.)*; executive body [council]; presidency; 2. (police) headquarters
Prävention *f (ins)* prevention *(ill health etc.)*; *(jur)* right of a court to claim jurisdiction over others

Praxis *f* practice *(also of lawyers, doctors etc.)*; field *(sociology etc.)*
~, gesellschaftliche social practice
Praxisanwendung *f* application in practice, practical application
praxisbezogen practical, in step with (actual) practice, practice-oriented
Praxisbezogenheit *f* practicality, keeping in step with (actual) practice
Praxiserfahrung *f* (practical) experience
praxisfern out of step with (actual) practice, academic
praxisorientiert oriented towards practical application
Präzision *f* precision, accuracy
~, innewohnende maximale *(stats)* intrinsic accuracy
Präzisionsarbeit *f* precision work; piece of precision work
Präzisionsindustrie *f* precision engineering (industry)
Präzisionsmaß *n* *(stats)* modulus of precision
Präziswechsel *m* fixed bill (of exchange)
Preis *m* 1. price *(goods etc.)*; charge, fee, cost, rate *(services etc.)*; 2. prize *(award etc.)*; reward ⋄ **als ~ fordern** to name a price; **auf den ~ aufschlagen** to add to the price; **bis zum ~ von** *(to buy/sell s.th.)* as high as; **den ersten ~ erhalten** to get the first prize; to obtain the first place; **den höchsten ~ erzielen** to fetch the maximum [highest] price; **den ~ angeben** to quote [state] the price; **den ~ anheben** to raise [increase, jack up] the price; **den ~ berechnen** to calculate the price; to charge *(s.o.)* a price; **den ~ bestimmen** to fix the price; **den ~ drücken** to send the price down, to depress the price, to force down the price; **den ~ erfragen** to inquire (about) the price; **den ~ erhöhen** to increase [advance, raise] the price; to mark up; **den ~ ermitteln** to derive the price; **den ~ festlegen** to fix [set] the price; **den ~ herabdrücken** *s.* **den ~ drücken**; **den ~ hinaufschrauben** to send the price up; **den ~ in die Höhe treiben** to force up the price; **den ~ kalkulieren** *s.* **den ~ berechnen**; **den ~ notieren** *(st.ex.)* to quote the rate; **einen ~ aushandeln** to negotiate a price, to bargain; **einen ~ ausmachen** to agree (up)on a price; **einen ~ aussetzen** to put a prize; **einen ~ bieten** to offer a price; **einen ~ erzielen** to obtain [fetch] a price; **einen ~ gewinnen** to obtain a prize; **einen ~ vereinbaren** to agree on a price; **jmdm. einen ~ verleihen** to award s.o. a prize, to present a prize to s.o.; **im ~ fallen** to fall in price; **im ~ herabsetzen** to cut the price; **im ~ sinken** *s.* **im ~ fallen**; **im ~ steigen** to advance [rise] in price; **mit dem ~ einverstanden sein** to agree with a price, to accept a price, to be willing to pay a price *(buyer)*; **nach dem ~ fragen** *s.* **den ~ erfragen**; **~ freibleibend** open price; **seinen ~ behalten** to hold its price; **seinen ~ haben** to have its price; **sich auf einen ~ einigen** *s.* **einen ~ ausmachen**; **über ~ verkaufen** to sell above (the) price; **um den ~ feilschen** to haggle over the price; **um jeden ~** at any price [cost], at all costs; **um keinen ~** not at any price; not for anything; **unter ~ kaufen** to buy below the price; **unter ~ verkaufen** to sell below the price; **vom ~ nachlassen** to make a reduction in price; **zu einem festen ~** at a firm price; **zu einem guten ~** at a good price; **zu jedem ~** *s.* **um jeden ~**; **zum amtlich festgesetzten ~** at the officially fixed price; **zum gleichen ~** at the same price; **zum halben ~** at half price, for half the price; **zum ~ von** at a price of; **zum vollen ~** at full price
~ ab Hersteller (ex) factory price, ex works price
~ ab Kai price ex quay
~ ab Kai Bestimmungshafen price ex quay port of destination
~ ab Schacht pithead price
~ ab Speicher ex warehouse price
~ ab Versandbahnhof at station price
~ ab Werk *s.* **~ ab Hersteller**
~ ab Zeche *s.* **~ ab Schacht**
~, abgemachter *s.* **~, vereinbarter**
~, allerniedrigster *(coll)* rock-bottom price
~, allgemeingültiger all-round price
~, amtlich festgesetzter controlled price
~, amtlicher legal [official] price
~, angebotener price offered
~, angemessener reasonable [fair] price
~, angesetzter *(st.ex.)* quoted price
~, aufgeblähter inflated price
~, ausbedungener price agreed upon
~ ausschließlich Verpackung price excluding packing
~ außerhalb der Saison off-season price
~, äußerster lowest/highest (possible) price; keenest price
~ bei Barzahlung cash price
~ bei Ratenzahlung hire-purchase price
~ bei sofortiger Lieferung spot price [quotation]
~, bestätigter confirmed price
~, betriebsindividueller enterprise [factory] price
~, beweglicher elastic price
~, bisheriger price hitherto
~ des Basiszeitraums price at base period
~ des Planzeitraums price at planning period

~, **durchschnittlich gewogener** weighted average price
~, **durchschnittlicher** average price
~, **echter** real price
~, **effektiver** real [effective] price
~, **einheitlicher** uniform price
~, **einmaliger** unique price
~ **einschließlich Gemeinkosten** price including overhead (costs)
~, **empfohlener** recommended price
~, **endgültiger** final price
~, **erhöhter** increased [advanced] price
~, **ermäßigter** reduced price
~, **ermittelter** derived price
~, **erzielter** price obtained
~, **faktischer** actual price
~, **fester** fixed price
~, **festgesetzter** stated [fixed] price
~, **fingierter** fictitious price
~, **fixer** s. ~, **fester**
~, **fondsbezogener** price relating to production funds
~ **frei an Bord** price free on board
~ **frei Bestimmungshafen** price free port of destination
~ **frei ein und aus** price free in and out
~ **frei Empfangsstation** price free station of destination
~ **frei Frachtführer** price free carrier
~ **frei Grenze Ausfuhrland** price free frontier [border] of exporting country
~ **frei Grenze Einfuhrland** price free frontier [border] of importing country
~ **frei Haus** mailing [door-to-door] price, price free to the door
~ **frei Kai (Versandhafen)** price free on quay (shipping port)
~ **frei Lager des Käufers** price free buyer's warehouse
~ **frei Lager des Lieferers** price free supplier's warehouse
~ **frei Längsseite (des) Schiff(es)** price free alongside ship
~ **frei Lastkahn (Versandhafen)** price free into barge (shipping port)
~ **frei LKW** price free on truck
~ **frei Schiff Bestimmungshafen** price free on ship [steamer] port of destination
~ **frei Verladerampe des Versenders** price free loading platform of consignor
~ **frei Waggon Empfangsstation** price free on rail (waggon) receiving station
~ **frei Waggon Versandstation** price free on rail (waggon) forwarding station
~ **für künftige Lieferung** forward price
~, **gebotener** bid price, price offered
~, **gebundener** controlled price; cartel price

~, **geforderter** asking price, price asked
~, **gegenwärtiger** current [prevailing] price
~, **geltender** s. ~, **gegenwärtiger**
~, **genehmigter** approved price
~, **genormter** standardized price
~, **gerechter** fair [moderate] price
~, **gesenkter** reduced price
~, **gesetzlicher** legal price
~, **gestaffelter** scheduled price
~, **gesteuerter** controlled price; manipulated price
~, **gestützter** subsidized [supported] price
~, **gewöhnlicher** usual price
~, **gleitender** sliding price
~, **gültiger** s. ~, **geltender**
~, **halber** half price
~, **handelsüblicher** prevailing market price
~, **herabgesetzter** s. ~, **ermäßigter**
~, **heraufgesetzter** marked-up price
~, **inländischer** domestic price
~, **konkurrenzloser** unrivalled price
~, **labiler** unstable price
~, **laufender** s. ~, **gegenwärtiger**
~, **letzter** lowest price; (st.ex.) latest price [rate]
~, **marktgerechter** fair market price
~, **mittlerer** s. ~, **durchschnittlicher**
~, **nicht amtlicher** unofficial price
~, **niedrigster** lowest [minimum, floor] price
~, **notierter** (st.ex.) quoted rate
~, **optimaler** optimum price
~, **örtlicher** local price
~, **reduzierter** s. ~, **gesenkter**
~, **reeller** s. ~, **gerechter**
~, **regulärer** regular price
~, **regulierter** regulated price
~, **rückläufiger** regressive price
~, **scharf kalkulierter** cut-rate price
~, **sinkender** s. ~, **rückläufiger**
~, **staatlich festgesetzter** price fixed by the state
~, **subventionierter** s. ~, **gestützter**
~, **üblicher** usual [customary] price
~, **unverbindlicher** price subject to alteration, price not binding
~, **vereinbarter** agreed price
~, **verlustbringender** losing price, price entailing a loss
~, **vertraglich vereinbarter** contractual price, price agreed upon by contract
~, **voraussichtlicher** probable price
~, **vorläufiger** preliminary price
~, **wahrscheinlicher** s. ~, **voraussichtlicher**
~, **zeitweiliger** temporary price
~, **zonaler** zonal price
Preisabbau *m* cut [reduction] in prices
Preisabfall *m* decline in prices
Preisabkommen *n* price(-fixing) agreement

Preisabmachung f s. **Preisabkommen**
Preisabrede f s. **Preisabsprache**
Preis-Absatz-Funktion f price-demand function
Preis-Absatz-Kurve f price-demand curve
Preisabschlag m discount, price deduction
Preisabschwächung f decrease in prices
Preisabschwächungstendenz f decreasing [downward] tendency in prices
Preisabsprache f price agreement
Preisabstand m disparity in prices
Preisabstufung f graduation of prices
Preisabweichung f variation in prices, price variance
Preisamt n pricing authority [office]; price(-control) board [authority]
Preisanalyse f analysis of prices
Preisänderung f price change, change [alteration] in price(s) ⋄ **~ vorbehalten** (prices are) subject to change (without notice)
Preisänderungsbilanz f balance sheet of price changes
Preisänderungsklauseln fpl price-alteration clause(s)
Preisänderungskoeffizient m coefficient of price changes
Preisänderungsrücklage f monetary [money] reserve for price changes
Preisanfrage f inquiry about prices, price inquiry
Preisangabe f (price) quotation
Preisangebot n price offered; (price) quotation, quote(d price) ⋄ **ein ~ machen** to offer a price, to quote
~, freibleibendes open price offer
~, offenes s. **~, freibleibendes**
~, unverbindliches prices without commitment
~, verbindliches binding price offer
Preisangleichung f levelling out of prices
Preisanhebung f raising of prices, price rise [increase]
Preisankündigung f announcement of prices
Preisanordnung f instructions for fixing prices, pricing instructions
Preisanpassung f s. **Preisangleichung**
Preisanreiz m price incentive
Preisansatz m basis of fixing prices
Preisanstieg m rise in prices, price increase
Preisantrag m application to fix prices
Preisantragsverfahren n method [procedure] of making price proposals
Preisargumentation f substantiation for fixing prices
Preisart f kind of price
Preisaufbau m price structure, structure of price
Preisaufschlag m extra [additional] charge, extra price, surcharge; (price) mark-up ⋄ **mit ~** with an extra charge; **ohne ~** without extra charge

Preisaufsicht f price control
Preisauftrieb m upward trend of prices, tendency of prices to rise
Preisausgleich m price compensation
Preisausgleichsabführung f payment of price compensation *(to the budget)*
Preisausgleichsfonds m price compensatory fund
Preisausgleichskasse f s. **Preisausgleichsfonds**
Preisausgleichsprinzip n principle of compensatory prices
Preisausgleichsstelle f price adjustment board
Preisausgleichszuführung f payment of price compensation *(to enterprises)*
Preisauskunft f price information, information on prices
Preisauskunftspflicht f obligation to give information on prices
Preisausschreiben n competition; prize contest
Preisaussichten fpl price outlook [anticipations]
Preisauszeichnung f marking with a price, price marking [labelling]
Preisauszeichnungspflicht f obligation to mark (articles) with prices
Preisband n price range, spread of prices
Preisbarometer n price barometer
Preisbasis f price basis, basis of prices [quotation]
Preisbeanstandung f price reclamation [complaint]
preisbedingt relating to prices
Preisbedingungen fpl terms of prices
Preisbegünstigung f favourable terms of prices
preisbeherrschend price determining
Preisbehörde f s. **Preisamt**
Preisbeirat m price advisory board [panel]
Preisbeobachtung f monitoring of prices
Preisberechnung f calculation of prices, pricing, costing
Preisberechnungsgrundlage f basis of pricing
Preisbereinigung f adjustment of prices
~ der Zirkulationskosten adjustment of prices of circulation costs
~ des Warenumsatzes adjustment of prices of commodity turnover
Preisberichtigung f adjustment of prices
Preisbeschränkung f price restraint
Preisbesserung f improvement in prices
Preisbestandteil m (constituent) part of the price, price component
Preisbestätigung f price confirmation
~, zentrale staatliche price confirmation by the central authorities
preisbestimmend price determining
Preisbestimmung f s. **Preisberechnung**
Preisbestimmungen fpl rules for pricing, pricing regulations

Preisbestimmungsgrundlage *f s.* **Preisberechnungsgrundlage**
Preisbestimmungstabelle *f* pricing table
Preisbewegung *f* price movement [fluctuation]
Preisbewilligung *f* approval of prices
Preisbewilligungsorgan *n* price approving authority
Preisbewilligungsverfahren *n* price approving procedure
preisbewußt price-conscious
Preisbeziehung *f* price relation
Preisbezugsbasis *f* price reference base, reference base of prices
Preisbilanz *f s.* **Preisverflechtungsbilanz**
preisbildend price-forming
Preisbildung *f* price fixing [formation], pricing
~, **dynamische** dynamic price formation
~, **freie** free formation of prices
~ **nach technischen und ökonomischen Parametern** price formation according to technical and economic parameters
Preisbildungsamt *n s.* **Preisamt**
Preisbildungsart *f* kind of price formation
Preisbildungsbefugnis *f* right of fixing prices
Preisbildungsfaktor *m* price determinant [determining factor]
Preisbildungsfunktion *f* price formation [pricing] function
Preisbildungsgesetz *n* law of price formation
Preisbildungsgrundsatz *m s.* **Preisbildungsprinzipien**
Preisbildungsklausel *f* price formation clause
Preisbildungskonzeption *f* policy outline for price formation [pricing]
Preisbildungsmechanismus *m* mechanism of price formation
Preisbildungsmethode *f* method of price fixing [formation]
Preisbildungsnormativ *n* standard norm for pricing
Preisbildungsorgan *n* pricing authority [office]
Preisbildungsprinzip *n* principle of price formation
Preisbildungsprozeß *m* process of price formation
Preisbildungsunterlagen *fpl* pricing documents [papers]
Preisbildungssystem *n* system of price formation
Preisbildungsvorschriften *fpl* rules of price formation
Preisbindung *f* price maintenance
~, **horizontale** collective resale price maintenance
~ **im Einzelhandel** retail price maintenance
~ **(in) zweiter Hand** resale price maintenance
~, **unberechtigte** unreasonable price restraint

Preisbindungsabkommen *n* fair-trade agreement
Preisbindungsabsprache *f* agreement on maintenance of prices
Preisbindungsklausel *f* price-maintenance clause
Preisbindungsrevers *m* additional contract on price maintenance
Preisbindungsvereinbarungen *fpl s.* **Preisbindungsabkommen**
Preisbindungsverordnung *f* rule on price maintenance
Preisbindungsvertrag *m* price-fixing contract
Preisblatt *n s.* **Preisliste**
Preisbrecher *m* price cutter *(person, firm, article undercutting competitors)*
Preisdeflation *f* price deflation
Preisdegression *f* degression of prices
Preisdifferenz *f* difference in prices, price difference
Preisdifferenzierung *f* price differential [discrimination] *(according to quality etc.)*; price discrimination *(against countries etc.)*
~, **räumliche** area price differential [discrimination] *(according to quality etc.)*
~, **zeitliche** temporary price differential [discrimination] *(according to season)*
Preisdifferenzierungsmerkmal *n* characteristic of price differential [discrimination]
Preisdifferenzkonto *n (acc)* price variance account
Preisdifferenzrücklage *f* money [monetary] reserve for price differences
Preisdiktat *n* price dictation; price dictate
~, **monopolistisches** monopoly price dictation; monopoly price dictate
Preisdiskriminierung *f* price discrimination *(against countries etc.)*; discriminatory pricing
Preisdisparität *f* disparity [inequality] of [in] prices
Preisdisziplin *f* adherence to pricing rules
Preisdokument *n* price document
Preisdokumentation *f* price documentation
Preisdruck *m* pressure on prices
Preisdrücker *m* price dumper
Preisdumping *n* (price) dumping
Preisdynamik *f* dynamics of price movement
Preise *mpl*:
◇ **bei sinkenden Preisen** with declining prices; ~ **abbauen** to cut [reduce] prices; ~ **ermäßigen** *s.* ~ **senken**; ~ **hinauftreiben** [**hochtreiben**] to boost [force up, bid up, push up] prices; ~ **senken** to reduce prices; ~ **unterbieten** to undercut prices; **zu ermäßigten Preisen** at reduced prices; **zu ermäßigten Preisen verkaufen** to sell at reduced prices; **zu festen Preisen verkaufen** to sell at

fixed prices; **zu herabgesetzten Preisen** s. **zu ermäßigten Preisen**
Preisebene f s. **Preisniveau**
Preiseinbruch m depression of prices, slump (in prices), (sharp/sudden) fall [dip] in/of prices
Preiseinflüsse mpl price influences
Preiseinhaltungsklausel f price maintenance clause
Preiseinstufung f graduation of prices
Preiselastizität f price elasticity
Preiselement n price component *(e.g. cost, profit, trade margin etc.)*
Preisempfehlung f price recommendation; recommended price
~, unverbindliche optional price recommendation
preisempfindlich susceptible to changes in prices
preisentscheidend price-deciding
Preisentscheidung f price decision
Preisentwicklung f price development [movement, trend]
~, inflationistische inflationary price development, inflationary trend of [in] prices [price trend]
Preisentwicklungslinie f price trend
Preisentwicklungsplan m price development plan
Preiserhöhung f price increase, increase [rise] in price(s), upward price movement; price hike
Preiserhöhungstendenz f rising tendency in prices
Preiserholung f recovery of prices
Preisermäßigung f discount, price cut [abatement], price reduction, reduction in price(s)
Preisermittlung f pricing; price calculation
~ **auf der Grundlage der Selbstkosten** pricing on the basis of prime costs
Preisermittlungspflicht f obligation to calculate prices
Preiserrechnungsvorschriften fpl rules for price calculation
Preisersatzkennziffer f substitutive price indicator
Preiserstarrung f price freeze
Preisertragsverhältnis n price-returns ratio
Preiserwartungen fpl s. **Preisaussichten**
Preisexplosion f price explosion [jump]
Preisfaktoren mpl price [cost] factors
Preisfestlegung f s. **Preisfestsetzung**
Preisfestsetzung f fixing [setting] of prices, pricing
~ **nach Zonen** zone pricing, fixing of prices according to zones
Preisfestsetzungsrichtlinien fpl s. **Preiserrechnungsvorschriften**

Preisfeststellung f s. **Preisermittlung**
Preisfixierung f s. **Preisfestsetzung**
Preisflexibilität f flexibility [responsiveness] of prices
Preisforderung f price demanded; *(st.ex.)* asked price
Preisform f kind [form] of price(s)
Preisformel f price formula
Preisforschung f research on prices
Preisfrage f price issue [matter]
Preisfreigabe f unfreezing of prices
Preisfreigabeanordnung f rules for unfreezing prices
Preisführerschaft f price leadership
Preisfunktion f price function
Preisgabe f revelation, giving away [up], disclosure *(of secrets etc.)*; abandonment
~ **der Sicherheit** abandonment of security
~ **eines Rechtes** abandonment [surrender, relinquishment] of a right
Preisgaberecht n right of abandonment [to abandon]
Preisgarantie f price guarantee
preisgeben to reveal, to give away [up] *(a secret etc.)*; to abandon, to surrender *(territory etc.)*; to relinquish *(right etc.)*
Preisgebiet n price area [zone]
preisgebunden subject to resale price maintenance, price-maintained, price-controlled
Preisgefälle n price gap [differential], disparity in prices
Preisgefüge n price structure, pattern of prices
~, inneres system [pattern] of home prices
Preisgegenüberstellung f s. **Preisvergleich**
preisgemindert reduced in price
Preisgenehmigung f price approval
preisgerecht according to prices
Preisgesetzgebung f price legislation, legislation on prices
Preisgestaltung f price formation [making], price fixing, pricing
preisgestoppt price-frozen
Preisgleichgewicht n price equilibrium
Preisgleitklausel f price variation [*(Am)* escalator] clause
Preisgrenze f price limit ⋄ **die ~ überschreiten** to exceed the price limit
~, feste firm price limit
~, obere maximum [ceiling] price, (price) ceiling
~, untere minimum [floor] price, price floor, bottom price
Preisgrundlage f s. **Preisbasis**
Preisgruppe f price group; price class [category]
Preisgruppenplanung f planning of groups of prices
Preisgruppenstruktur f structure [pattern] of price groups

25 Ök. Wörterb. Deutsch–Englisch

preisgünstig cheap, reasonably-priced, good value for money
Preisherabsetzung *f s.* **Preissenkung**
Preishindernis *n* price obstacle
Preishöhe *f* price level
Preisindex *m* price index
~ **der Lebenshaltung** cost-of-living price index
~, **gewogener** weighted price index
Preisindexzahl *f* price index number
Preisinflation *f* inflation of prices, (price) inflation
Preisinspektor *m s.* **Preisprüfer**
Preiskalkulation *f* price calculation
Preiskampf *m* price war
Preiskarteiblatt *n* price sheet
Preiskartell *n* price cartel, price-fixing agreement (between cartel members)
Preiskatalog *m* price catalogue
Preiskategorie *f s.* **Preisgruppe**
Preiskennziffer *f* price indicator
Preisklasse *f* price range
Preisklausel *f* price clause
Preiskoeffizient *m* price coefficient
Preiskomitee *n* pricing committee
Preiskonjunktur *f* period of rising prices, price(-led) boom
Preiskonkurrenz *f* price competition, competition in prices
Preis-Konsum-Funktion *f* price-consumption function
Preiskontrolle *f* price control
~, **betriebliche** enterprise price control
~, **staatliche** government price control
Preiskontrollmethode *f* method of price control
Preiskontrollorgan *n* price control authority [office]
Preiskonvention *f s.* **Preisabsprache**
Preiskonzeption *f* price policy outline, price conception
~, **länderbezogene** price policy outline [price conception] relating to countries
~, **warenbezogene** price-policy outline relating to commodities
Preiskonzession *f* price concession
Preiskoordinierung *f* co-ordination of prices, price co-ordination
Preiskoordinierungsorgan *n* price co-ordinating authority
Preiskorrektur *f* price modification, adjustment of price(s)
Preiskotierung *f s.* **Preisnotierung**
Preiskrieg *m s.* **Preiskampf**
Preiskurant *m s.* **Preisliste**
Preiskurve *f* price curve
Preislage *f* price range ⋄ **in derselben** ~ in the same price range; **in jeder** ~ in every price range, at all prices

Preislawine *f* avalanche of price increases, price explosion
Preis-Leistung-Verhältnis *n* price-efficiency ratio *(in price formation)*
Preislenkung *f s.* **Preiskontrolle**
preislich in price; related to prices, price *(fluctuations etc.)*
Preislimit *n s.* **Preisgrenze**
Preislimitierung *f* price limitation
Preisliste *f* price list
Preismanipulation *f* manipulation of prices
Preismaßnahmen *fpl* price measures [policies]
Preismaßstab *m* price scale
Preismechanismus *m* price [pricing] mechanism
Preismeßziffer *f* price relative
Preismethode *f (stats)* price method
~, **repräsentative** *(stats)* representative price method
Preisminderung *f* price reduction
Preismodell *n* price [pricing] model
Preisnachlaß *m* deduction from the stated price, price reduction, discount ⋄ ~ **gewähren** to give [allow] a discount
Preisnachweis *m* statement on prices
Preisnachweispflicht *f* obligation to draw up a statement on prices
Preisneuordnung *f s.* **Preisreform**
Preisniveau *n* price level ⋄ **das** ~ **aufrechterhalten** to keep up prices
~, **allgemeines** general price level
~, **regional einheitliches** uniform regional price level
Preisniveaukennziffer *f* price level indicator
Preisniveauunterschied *m* differences in the price level(s)
Preisnivellierung *f* levelling of prices
Preisnormativ *n* price standard
Preisnotierung *f (st.ex.)* quotation of prices *(commodities)*, quotation of rate of exchange
Preisobergrenze *f* (price) ceiling, maximum price
Preisorgan *n* pricing office [authority]
Preisperiode *f* base price period
Preisplanung *f* price planning, planning of prices
~, **perspektivische** long-term price planning
~, **prognostische** long-term forecast of prices
Preisplanungssystem *n* price planning system
Preispolitik *f* price [pricing] policy
preispolitisch pertaining [related] to price policy, price policy *(principles, measures etc.)*
Preisprinzipien *npl* pricing principles
Preis-Profit-Rate *f* price-profit ratio
Preisprognose *f* price forecast
Preisprüfer *m* price controller
Preisprüfung *f* price control
Preisrecht *n* pricing rules and regulations

preisrechtlich concerning pricing rules and regulations
Preisreduzierung *f s.* **Preissenkung**
Preisreform *f* price reform
Preisregelung *f* price regulation
Preisregulierung *f* regulation of prices
Preisrelation *f* price proportion
Preisrevision *f* price modification [change], recalculation of prices
Preisrevisionsklausel *f* price recalculation [change] clause
Preisrichtlinien *fpl* guidelines for pricing
Preisrisiko *n* price risk; risks involved in pricing *(product etc.)*
Preisrückerstattung *f* price repayment
Preisrückgang *m* fall [decline, drop] in prices, price recession
Preisrückvergütung *f* discount; refunding (of price)
Preisschere *f* price scissors, price gap
Preisschild *n* price tag [label, ticket]
Preisschleuderei *f* slashing of prices
Preisschraube *f s.* **Preisspirale**
Preisschwankung *f* price fluctuation
Preisschwankungsklausel *f* price fluctuation clause
preissenkend price-lowering, price-reducing
Preissenkung *f* price reduction, lowering of prices, price cut, markdown
Preissenkungsauflage *f* price reduction normative
Preissenkungsnormativ *n* standard norm of price reduction
Preissicherung *f* ensuring correct prices
Preisskala *f* scale of prices
~, **gleitende** sliding scale of prices
Preisspanne *f* price margin [spread, range]
Preisspekulation *f* speculation in prices
Preisspiegel *m* reflection of the level of prices
Preisspirale *f* price [inflationary] spiral
preisstabil stable in price
preisstabilisierend price-stabilizing
Preisstabilisierung *f* stabilization of prices
Preisstabilität *f* stability of prices, price stability, stable prices
Preisstaffel *f* range of prices
Preisstaffelung *f* differentiation of prices, price differentiation
Preisstatistik *f* price statistics
preissteigernd price-raising
Preissteigerung *f* price increase [rise], rise in prices, rising prices, price hike
~, **allgemeine** all-round increase in prices
~, **plötzliche** sudden increase in prices
Preissteigerungsrücklage *f* (money) reserve for price increases
Preisstellung *f* specification of prices, pricing

Preisstellungsklausel *f* pricing clause
Preisstopp *m* price freeze
Preisstopp-Stichtag *m* date set for freezing (of) prices
Preisstrategie *f* pricing strategy
Preisstruktur *f* price structure
Preisstufe *f* price rating *(hotels, restaurants etc.)*
Preissturz *m* slump [sudden fall] in prices
Preisstützung *f* price support; subsidy
~, **produktgebundene** price support for a product; product-related subsidy
~, **staatliche** government price support; government subsidy
Preisstützungsgesetz *n* price-support law
Preisstützungsmaßnahmen *fpl* price-support measures
Preisstützungsprogramm *n* programme of price support, price-supporting programme
Preissumme *f* sum of prices
Preissummenmethode *f* method of adding prices
Preissystem *n* price system
~, **doppeltes** dual price system
Preistabelle *f* table of prices [charges]
Preistafel *f* price list
Preistaxe *f* fixed price [fee, charge]
Preisteilverflechtungsmodell *n* partial input--output model in terms of prices
Preistendenz *f* price tendency [trend]; *(st.ex.)* market trend
Preistheorie *f* price theory
preistreibend forcing prices up, price-raising, price-boosting
Preistreiber *m* price booster; *(st.ex.)* bull
Preistreiberei *f* forcing up [boosting] (of) prices
Preistrend *m* price trend
Preistyp *m* type of prices
Preisübereinstimmung *f* uniformity of prices
Preisüberhöhung *f (st.ex.)* excessive quotation
Preisüberprüfung *f* checking of prices
Preisüberschreitung *f* exceeding the price limit
Preisüberwachung *f s.* **Preiskontrolle**
Preisüberwachungsstelle *f* price controlling office
Preisumgehung *f* evasion of prices
Preisumschwung *m* reversal of prices
Preisunterbieter *m* price cutter
Preisunterbietung *f* price cutting, underselling, undercutting, dumping
Preisuntergrenze *f* minimum price (limit), bottom [floor] price
Preisunterlagen *fpl* price data; pricing documents [papers]
Preisunterschreitung *f* undercutting of prices
Preisveränderung *f* price change(s)
Preisverantwortung *f* responsibility for fixing (stable) prices

Preisverband *m* (price) cartel
Preisvereinbarung *f* price (fixing) agreement
Preisverfall *m* downward trend [collapse, plummeting] of prices
Preisverflechtung *f* interlocking of prices
Preisverflechtungsbilanz *f* input-output table in terms of prices
Preisverflechtungsbilanzierung *f* drawing up input-output tables in terms of prices
Preisverflechtungskoeffizient *m* price coefficient in input-output table
Preisverflechtungsmodell *n* input-output model in terms of prices
Preisvergleich *m* comparison of prices
Preisverhältnisse *npl* price situation [relations]
Preisverhältniszahl *f s.* **Preismeßziffer**
Preisverhandlung *f* negotiation on prices
Preisverlauf *m s.* **Preistrend**
Preisverordnung *f* price decree
Preisverständigung *f s.* **Preisabsprache**
Preisverstoß *m* infringement of price regulations
Preisverzeichnis *n s.* **Preisliste**
Preisvolumen *n s.* **Preissumme**
Preisvoraussage *f* price forecast
Preisvorbehalt *m* rights reserved in changing prices
Preisvorbehaltsklausel *f* price reserve clause
Preisvorschlag *m* price offer, proposed price
Preisvorschrift *f* pricing rules
Preisvorteil *m* price advantage
Preiswechsel *m s.* **Preisveränderung**
preiswert worth the money, cheap, moderately priced, low-priced, inexpensive
Preiswettbewerb *m* competition in prices
Preiswirkung *f* effect of prices
Preiswucher *m* charging (of) exorbitant prices
Preiszettel *m s.* **Preisschild**
Preiszone *f* price zone *(regional differentiation of prices)*
Preiszugeständnis *n* price concession
Preiszusammenbruch *m* collapse of prices
Preiszuschlag *m* additional charge, price mark-up
~, produktgebundener additional charge for a product
Preiszuschuß *m* subsidy
Presse *f* the press, newspapers
Presseabteilung *f* press department [office]
Presseagentur *f* news [press] agency
Presseamt *n* press office
Pressearbeit *f* public relations (PR)
Presseattaché *m* press attaché
Presseausweis *m* press card
Pressebericht *m* press report, report in the press; (official) bulletin
Pressedienst *m* press service; news agency

Presseerklärung *f* statement to the press; *(written)* handout ⋄ **eine ~ abgeben** to make a statement to the press
Presseinformation *f* press information [release]
Pressekampagne *f* press campaign
Pressekarte *f s.* **Presseausweis**
Pressekommuniqué *n* press communiqué
Pressekonferenz *f* press [news] conference ⋄ **eine ~ abhalten** to hold a press conference
Pressemeldung *f* news item
Pressenotiz *f* press release
Presseorgan *n* press
Pressesprecher *m* press officer, spokesman
Pressevertreter *m* reporter, newsman
Pressewesen *n* the press; journalism
Pressezentrum *n* press centre
Prestigeschau *f* prestige display
prima first-class *(goods, quality etc.)*; first-rate *(report etc.)*; great, marvellous *(wine etc.)*
Primabankakzept *n* prime bank(ers') acceptance
Primadiskonten *pl* first-class bills of exchange, *(Am)* prime bills
Primage *f* primage
Primanota *f (bank)* daybook
Primapapiere *npl (fin)* first-class [blue-chip] papers
Primaqualität *f* prime quality
primär primary *(task, problem etc.)*
Primäraufkommen *n* primary resources
Primärbeleg *m (d.pr.)* primary voucher [record]
Primärberechnung *f* primary calculation
Primärdaten *pl* primary data
Primärdatenerfassung *f (d.pr.)* collection of primary [source] data
Primärdatengewinnung *f* obtaining primary data
Primärdokumentation *f* primary documentation
Primäreinheit *f (stats)* first-stage unit
Primäreinkommen *n* primary income
Primärenergieträger *m* primary source(s) of energy
Primärenergieverbrauch *m* consumption of primary energy
Primärerfassung *f* collection of primary data
Primärerhebung *f* primary survey
Primärgruppe *f* primary group
Primärinformation *f* primary information [data]
Primärkosten *pl* primary costs
Primärliquidität *f* liquidity of assets *(cash, foreign exchange, bills, short-term credits etc. with the central bank)*
Primärprogramm *n (d.pr.)* source program
Primärquellen *fpl* primary sources
Primärverteilung *f* primary distribution
Primasorte *f* first quality
Primat *n* primacy, priority

Primaware *f* first-class product
Prima-Warenakzept *n* prime goods acceptance
Primawechsel *m (com)* first of exchange
Primgeld *n s.* **Primage**
Prinzip *n* principle
~ **der Branchenkonzentration** principle of concentration in trade groups
~ **der eigenverantwortlichen Leitung** principle of self-responsible management
~ **der Einzelleitung** principle of one-man management
~ **der Gewaltenteilung** principle of separation of powers
~ **der Leistung und Gegenleistung** principle of quid pro quo
~ **der materiellen Interessiertheit** principle of material incentive(s) [interest]
~ **der Meistbegünstigung** most-favoured-nation principle
~ **der Praxisbezogenheit** principle of keeping in step with actual practice
~ **der Praxisorientierung** principle of orientation towards practical application
~**, föderalistisches** federal principle
~**, zentralistisches** centralist principle
Prinzipal *m* principal, head, chief
Prinzipalgläubiger *m* principal creditor
Prinzipdarstellung *f* principal scheme
Prinzipformel *f* principal formula
Prinziplösung *f* principle solution, solution in principle
Prinzipmodell *n* principal model
Prinzipschema *n s.* **Prinzipdarstellung**
Priorität *f* priority, preference, precedence ⋄ ~ **beanspruchen** to claim priority; ~ **genießen** to enjoy preference
Prioritäten *fpl* preference debentures [*(Am)* bonds]
~ **zweiten Ranges** second debentures [bonds]
Prioritätenskala *f* order of priorities
Prioritätsaktie *f* preference share [*(Am)* bond, stock]
Prioritätsanleihe *f* preference loan [bond]
Prioritätsanspruch *m* prior(ity) claim
Prioritätsentscheidung *f* award of priority *(patents etc.)*
Prioritätsfrist *f* period of priority
Prioritätsgesetz *n* law of priority
Prioritätsgläubiger *m* priority [preferential, preferred] creditor
Prioritätsgrundsatz *m s.* **Prioritätsprinzip**
Prioritätsintervall *n s.* **Prioritätsfrist**
Prioritätsliste *f* priority list; list of priorities
Prioritätsobligation *f* preference [priority] bond
Prioritätsordnung *f s.* **Prioritätenskala**
Prioritätspapiere *npl s.* **Prioritäten**
Prioritätsprinzip *n* principle of priority

Prioritätsrecht *n* right of priority *(patents etc.)*
Prioritätstag *m* priority date
Prise *f* prize
Prisenanteil *m s.* **Prisengeld**
Prisengeld *n* prize money
Prisengericht *n* prize court
Prisengut *n* prize goods
Prisenkommando *n* prize crew
Prisenrecht *n* prize law
Prisenverteilung *f* distribution of prizes
privat private; personal; individual; confidential
Privatabkommen *n* private agreement
Privatabmachung *f s.* **Privatabkommen**
Privatadresse *f* private [home] address
Privatangelegenheit *f* personal [private] matter [affair, concern]
Privatanleihe *f* personal [private] loan
Privatanschrift *f s.* **Privatadresse**
Privatausgaben *fpl* private expenses
Privatbahn *f* private railway [railroad] (company)
Privatbank *f* private bank
Privatbankier *m* (private) banker
Privatbedarf *m* private [personal] needs
Privatbesitz *m* private ownership; private property ⋄ **in** ~ **(befindlich)** privately owned; **in** ~ **übergehen** to pass into private hands, to be privatized [denationalized]
Privatbesitzer *m* private owner
Privatbetrieb *m* private enterprise [firm, company]
Privatdarleh(e)n *n s.* **Privatanleihe**
Privatdiskont *m* discount rate for first-class bills (of exchange), prime acceptance rate
Privatdiskonten *pl* first-class bills (of exchange), prime acceptances
Privatdiskontsatz *m* market rate of discount; prime acceptance rate
Privateigentum *n* private property [ownership]
~ **an Grund und Boden** private ownership in land
~ **an Produktionsmitteln** private ownership in (the) means of production
Privateigentümer *m s.* **Privatbesitzer**
Privateigentumsrecht *n* law of real property
Privateinkommen *n* private [personal] income
Privateinkünfte *pl s.* **Privateinkommen**
Privateinlage *f* private paid-in capital
Privateinzelhandel *m* private retail trade
Privatentnahme *f* money withdrawn (from business capital) for private use
Privaterbfolge *f* succession by will
Privatfirma *f* private firm [company]
Privatforderung *f* personal claim
Privatgebrauch *m* personal [private] use
Privatgeschäft *n* private [privately-owned] shop
Privatgewässer *npl* private waters

Privatgläubiger m creditor for private debt
Privathand f:
◊ **in ~** in private hands; privately owned
Privathandel m private (retail) trade
Privathändler m private retailer [trader]
Privathaushalt m 1. private household; 2. private budget
Privathersteller m (private) manufacturer [maker]
Privatier m rentier, person who lives on (his) private income [means]
Privatindustrie f private(ly-owned) industry
Privatinformation f confidential report
Privatinitiative f private initiative; private enterprise
Privatinteresse n personal [private] interest
Privatinvestition f private (sector) investment
privatisieren to privatize, to transfer to private ownership [(in)to private hands], to denationalize
Privatisierung f privatization, transfer (in)to private ownership [private hands], denationalization
Privatkapital n private capital; private industry
Privatkapitalismus m (private) capitalism
Privatkapitalist m capitalist
privatkapitalistisch capitalist
Privatklage f private action [prosecution]
Privatkläger m plaintiff in a private action, private complainant [prosecutor]
Privatklinik f private hospital [clinic]
Privatkonsum m s. **Privatverbrauch**
Privatkonto n private [personal] account
Privatkredit m trade credit; private credit
Privatladen m s. **Privatgeschäft**
Privatpatient m private patient
Privatperson f private individual [person]
Privatpfändung f impounding
Privatpraxis f private practice *(doctors etc.)*
Privatproduzent m s. **Privathersteller**
Privatquartier n private accommodation
Privatrecht n civil [private] law
~, internationales private international law
privatrechtlich civil-law, private-law
Privatsache f s. **Privatangelegenheit**
Privatsatz m s. **Privatdiskont**
Privatschulden fpl private [personal, individual] debts
Privatschuldverschreibung f private bond
Privatsektor m private sector
Privatsphäre f private life, privacy
Privatunternehmen n s. **Privatbetrieb**
Privatunternehmer m entrepreneur; private contractor
Privatunternehmerschaft f entrepreneurship, owners of private enterprises
Privatunternehmertum n private sector

Privatverbrauch m private [personal] consumption
Privatverkauf m private sale
Privatverkehr m private transport; *(st.ex.)* unofficial dealings, kerb market
Privatvermögen n private [personal] property [assets, means]
Privatversicherung f private insurance
Privatwald m privately-owned wood, private woodlands
Privatwechsel m private bill of exchange
Privatwirtschaft f s. **Privatsektor**
privatwirtschaftlich private(-sector)
Privatwohnung f private residence
Privatzins m preferential rate of interest
Privileg n privilege
Probe f 1. test, trial; 2. specimen; sample, pattern *(article)* ◊ **der ~ entsprechen** to be up to the sample; **eine ~ bestehen** to stand [pass] a test; **eine ~ entnehmen** to take a sample; **eine ~ nehmen** s. **eine ~ entnehmen**; **gemäß ~** according to sample; **jmdn. auf ~ einstellen** to employ s.o. on trial; **laut beiliegender ~** as per sample enclosed; **nach ~ s. gemäß ~**; **streng nach der ~** strictly up to sample; **zur ~** on trial
~, entnommene picked sample
~, entscheidende crucial test
~, kostenlose free trial; free sample
~, vorgelegte sample displayed
~, vorgezeigte sample shown
Probeabschluß m s. **Probebilanz**
Probeanfertigung f sample; producing a sample
Probeanstellung f probationary employment
Probearbeit f sample [specimen] (of s.o.'s work); test piece [paper]
Probearbeitsverhältnis n employment on a probationary basis
Probeauftrag m trial [sample] order
Probeauswahl f s. **Probeentnahme**
Probebelastung f test load; trial of strength
Probebeschäftigung f s. **Probeanstellung**
Probebestellung f s. **Probeauftrag**
Probebetrieb m 1. pilot plant *(scale production)*; 2. trial run [operation]
Probebilanz f *(acc)* trial balance (sheet)
~, bereinigte *(acc)* closing trial balance
~, geordnete *(acc)* classified trial balance
Probeentnahme f sampling, taking of samples
Probeerfassung f *(stats)* pilot survey
Probeerhebung f *(stats)* pilot [exploratory] survey
Probeexemplar n specimen (copy)
Probefahrt f test drive, trial run
Probefall m test case
Probejahr n probationary year
Probekauf m purchase on trial

Probelauf *m* test [trial, dry] run
Probelieferung *f* trial delivery [shipment]
Probemaschine *f* test machine
Probemuster *n* give-away sample
Probenahme *f s.* **Probeentnahme**
Probenteilung *f (stats)* sample division
Probepackung *f* trial [sample] package
Probesendung *f* sample sent on approval, *(Am)* trial shipment
Probestück *n* specimen, sample [item]; test piece
probeweise on trial; on probation *(person)*; on approval *(goods)*
Probezeit *f* time of probation; trial [try-out] period
probieren to try, to test
Probiergewicht *n* (degree of) fineness *(of coins)*
Probierverfahren *n* trial method
Probit *m (stats)* probit
Probit-Analyse *f (stats)* probit analysis
Probit-Differenz *f (stats)* probit difference
Probit-Wert *m (stats)* probit (value)
Problem *n* problem ◊ **ein ~ anpacken** to tackle a problem; **sich mit einem ~ auseinandersetzen** to deal with a problem
~ **der Betriebsführung** managerial problem
~ **der mehrfachen Entscheidung** *(stats)* multi--decision problem
~ **von k-Stichproben** *(stats)* k-samples problem
~**, wirtschaftspolitisches** economic policy problem
Problemanalyse *f* problem analysis
Problemanalytiker *m* problem analyst
Problematik *f* problems, problematical nature
problematisch problematic(al), difficult
Problembeschreibung *f (d.pr.)* problem definition [description]
problembewußt aware of a problem
Problembewußtheit *f s.* **Problembewußtsein**
Problembewußtsein *n* awareness of a problem
Problemfall *m* problem(atic) case
Problemforschung *f* research on a problem [a set of problems]
Problemkatalog *m* catalogue [list] of problems
Problemlösung *f* solution to [of] a problem
Problemlösungsverhalten *n* problem-solving attitude
Problemorganisation *f* problem organization *(managerial method of solving problems)*
problemorientiert *(d.pr.)* problem-oriented
Problemprognose *f* forecast of a problem
Problemrat *m* advisory panel for solving a problem
Problemsituation *f* situation of a problem
Problemstellung *f* 1. problem(s), task; 2. formulation of a problem
Problemstruktur *f* structure of a problem

Problemtheorie *f* theory of problems
Produkt *n* 1. product, article, good; *(agric)* produce; 2. outcome, result
~**, abgesetztes** sold product
~ **des Ackerbaus** (agricultural) produce
~**, fertiges** finished product
~ **für die Gesellschaft** product for the needs of (the) society
~ **für sich** product for individual needs
~**, gefälschtes** adulterated product *(food)*; forge(d product), counterfeit (product)
~**, gesellschaftliches** social product
~**, handwerkliches** handicraft product
~**, heimisches** domestic [home, inland] product; *(agric)* home [inland] produce
~**, hochwertiges** high-quality product
~**, indifferentes** imaginary product
~**, individuell angeeignetes** individually appropriated product
~**, inländisches** *s.* ~**, einheimisches**
~**, leichtverderbliches** easily perishable product [produce]
~**, modisches** fashion article
~**, notwendiges** necessary product
~**, standardisiertes** standardized product
Produktanalyse *f* product analysis
Produkte *npl*:
~**, pflanzliche** vegetable products, (farm) produce
~**, tierische** animal products
Produktenaustausch *m* exchange in kind
Produktenbörse *f* commodity [goods, produce] exchange
Produkteneinheit *f* unit of a product
Produktenfluß *m* flow of products
Produktengroßhandelsbörse *f* wholesale produce market
Produktenhandel *m* trade in agricultural [farm] produce, produce trade
Produktenhandlung *f* scrap shop [yard]
Produktenhändler *m* dealer in farm produce; dealer in rags, ragman, scrap merchant
Produktenmakler *m* produce broker
Produktenmarkt *m* produce market
Produktenmasse *f s.* **Produktenmenge**
Produktenmenge *f* amount of products
Produktenrente *f* ground-rent paid in kind
Produktenwert *m* (total) value of a product
Produktform *f* form of a product
Produktgestaltung *f* product design
Produktion *f* production; manufacturing; output ◊ **aus der ~ ziehen** to withdraw from production; **die ~ abbremsen** to curtail production; **die ~ abwürgen** to throttle production; **die ~ aufnehmen** to start [begin] operation, to open, to go on stream; **die ~ drosseln** to cut back [throttle] production; **die ~ einstellen** to

Produktion

stop production; to shut (down); **die ~ steigern** to increase [step up] production; **die ~ stillegen** to stop production; to shut (down) *(enterprise)*; **die ~ umstellen** to switch production *(to s.th.)*
~, **abgesetzte** sold production
~, **arbeitsintensive** labour-intensive production
~, **arbeitsteilige** production with a division of labour
~, **außerplanmäßige** unplanned production
~, **automatische** automated production
~, **billige** low-cost production
~ **des Mehrwertes** production of surplus value
~, **einheimische** home [domestic] production
~ **für eigene Rechnung** production at one's own expense
~ **für fremde Rechnung** jobbing production *(based on materials supplied by another enterprise)*
~, **geistige** brain [mental] production
~, **genormte** standardized production
~, **genossenschaftliche** co-operative production
~, **geplante** planned production
~, **gesellschaftliche** social production
~, **gewerbliche** factory production
~, **gleichartige** production of the same kind
~, **großtechnische** large-scale production
~, **handwerkliche** (handi)craft production
~, **industrielle** s. ~, **industriemäßige**
~, **industriemäßige** industrial-scale production, production on an industrial scale
~, **industriezweigfremde** production untypical of a(n industrial) branch
~, **industriezweigtypische** typical production of a branch (of industry)
~, **inländische** s. ~, **einheimische**
~ **in Naturaleinheiten** production in units
~, **intelligenzintensive** knowledge-intensive production
~, **jährliche** annual [yearly] production
~, **landwirtschaftliche** agricultural [farm] production [output]
~, **laufende** current production [output]
~, **marktgerechte** marketable production
~, **materielle** physical [material] production
~ **materieller Güter** production of physical goods
~, **mittelbare** indirect production
~, **nationale** s. ~, **einheimische**
~, **nichtnormgerechte** non-standard production
~, **patentamtlich geschützte** patented production
~, **pflanzliche** crop production
~, **serienmäßige** serial production
~, **standardisierte** s. ~, **genormte**
~, **stetige** continuous production
~, **teure** high-cost production

~, **tierische** livestock [animal] production
~, **überplanmäßige** production exceeding [overfulfilling] plan [planned] targets
~, **unfertige** s. ~, **unvollendete**
~, **unvollendete** unfinished production
~, **verbundene** joint production, production of joint products *(gas and coke etc.)*
~, **wirkliche** real [actual] production
~, **zersplitterte** dispersed production; split production
~, **zweigfremde** s. ~, **industriezweigfremde**
~, **zweigtypische** s. ~, **industriezweigtypische**
Produktionsabfall *m* scrap, waste
Produktionsabgabe *f* production levy
Produktionsabgabesatz *m* rate of production levy
Produktionsabkommen *n* production agreement; agreement between producers
Produktionsablauf *m* production flow [sequence]
Produktionsablaufplan *m* manufacturing time schedule
Produktionsablaufplanung *f* planning of flow of production, production sequencing
Produktionsabnahme *f* production decline
Produktionsabsatz *m* sale of production
Produktionsabschnitt *m* manufacturing section
Produktionsabschwächung *f* dwindling production
Produktionsabstimmung *f* co-ordination of production; adjustment of production
Produktionsabteilung *f* production department [floor]
Produktionsagenzien *npl* s. **Produktionsfaktoren**
Produktionsangleichung *f* levelling up of production
Produktionsanlage *f* production [manufacturing] plant [unit], production facilities
~, **direktschreibende** *(d.pr.)* direct-write production system
Produktionsanlagefonds *m* fixed (productive) assets
Produktionsanlagen *fpl* 1. production assets; 2. production [manufacturing] plants [units], production facilities
Produktionsanlauf *m* launching of production
Produktionsanstieg *m* rise [increase] in production [output]
Produktionsanstrengungen *fpl* efforts to increase production, productive efforts
Produktionsarbeiter *m* production [blue-collar] worker
Produktionsästhetik *f* aesthetics in production
Produktionsaufgabe *f* production task
~, **staatliche** production target [assignment] (set by the state)

Produktionsfinanzierung 393

Produktionsaufgebot *n* movement to increase production
Produktionsaufkommen *n* output
Produktionsauflage *f* production target
Produktionsaufnahme *f* starting [commencement] of production
Produktionsaufsicht *f* supervision of production
Produktionsauftrag *m* production order
Produktionsaufwand *m* production cost(s)
~, **materieller** material input
Produktionsaufwendungen *fpl s.* **Produktionsaufwand**
Produktionsausbildung *f* on-the-job training, shop-floor training, training in production
Produktionsausfall *m* loss of production [in output]
Produktionsausgaben *fpl* production expenses
Produktionsausmaß *n* extent [amount] of production
Produktionsausrüstungen *fpl* productive machinery and equipment
Produktionsausstattung *f* productive equipment
Produktionsausstoß *m* (production) output
Produktionsbasis *f* basis of production
~, **materielle** physical [material] basis of production
Produktionsbedarf *m* production needs
produktionsbedingt owing to production
Produktionsbedingungen *fpl* production conditions
~, **gesellschaftliche** social conditions of production
~, **materielle** physical [material] conditions of production
~, **sachliche** *s.* ~, **materielle**
Produktionsbeginn *m* start(ing) of production
Produktionsbegrenzung *f* restriction [limitation] of output [production]
Produktionsbelebung *f* revival of production
Produktionsbeleg *m* (production) requisition (form)
Produktionsberatung *f* production meeting
Produktionsbereich *m* production department [line, sector]
Produktionsbericht *m* production report
Produktionsbeschränkung *f s.* **Produktionseinschränkung**
Produktionsbeschränkungen *fpl* restrictions [limitations] on production
Produktionsbetrieb *m* manufacturing [producing] enterprise, factory
Produktionsbeziehungen *fpl s.* **Produktionsverhältnisse**
produktionsbezogen relating to production, production-related, production-oriented

Produktionsbilanz *f* statement on production
Produktionsbreite *f* range of production
Produktionsbrigade *f* work team
Produktionschef *m* production manager
Produktionsdauer *f* duration of production
Produktionsdefizit *n* failing output
Produktionsdirektor *m* production manager
Produktions-Dispatcherabteilung *f* production monitoring department
Produktionsdisposition *f* production plan
Produktionsdiversifizierung *f* diversification of production
Produktionsdrosselung *f* cutting back of production, production cutback
Produktionsdurchlauf *m s.* **Produktionsablauf**
Produktionsdurchlaufplan *m s.* **Produktionsablaufplan**
Produktionsdurchlaufzeit *f* manufacturing time (of a product)
Produktionsdynamik *f* dynamics of production
Produktionseffektivität *f* efficiency in production
Produktionseinheit *f* production unit; unit of output, work unit
Produktionseinrichtung *f* factory
Produktionseinrichtungen *fpl* production equipment [facilities]
Produktionseinschränkung *f* cut(back) in production, production cut(back), restriction [limitation] of production [output], reduction in output
Produktionseinstellung *f* standstill [stoppage, abandonment] of production
Produktionsentwicklung *f* growth in production
Produktionserfahrung *f* industrial [manufacturing] experience [know-how]
Produktionsergebnis *n* total output [production], (production) output
Produktionserhöhung *f* increase in production
Produktionserlaubnis *f* production licence; permission to produce s.th.
Produktionserlös *m* proceeds of production
produktionserschwerend making production more difficult
Produktionserweiterung *f* expansion of production
produktionsfähig ready for production
Produktionsfaktor *m* factor of production, production factor
Produktionsfaktorentheorie *f* theory of production factors
Produktionsfehler *m* manufacturing defect
Produktionsfeld *n* field of production
Produktionsfertigkeit *f* production skill(s)
Produktionsfinanzierung *f* financing of production

Produktionsfläche *f* production floor [area]
Produktionsfluß *m* flow of production
Produktionsfonds *mpl* production assets
Produktionsfondsabgabe *f* levy on production assets
Produktionsfondsausnutzung *f* employment [exploitation] of production assets
Produktionsfondsintensität *f* intensity in the use of production assets; production assets per unit of output [production], capital-output ratio
Produktionsfondsquote *f* rate of use [production per unit] of production assets, output-capital ratio
Produktionsfondsrentabilität *f* profit per unit of productive assets, profit-capital ratio
produktionsfördernd production-raising
Produktionsfunktion *f* production function
Produktionsgebäude *n* production building
Produktionsgebiet *n s.* **Produktionsfeld**
Produktionsgeheimnis *n* production secret
Produktionsgenossenschaft *f* production co-operative, producer(s') co-operative
 ~ **des Handwerks (PGH)** craftsmen's production co-operative *(crafts, retail, bakery and service sector co-operatives)*
 ~, **gärtnerische (GPG)** horticultural (production) co-operative
 ~, **landwirtschaftliche (LPG)** agricultural production co-operative, co-operative farm
 ~ **werktätiger Fischer (PwF)** fishermen's production co-operative
Produktionsgesamtmenge *f* total output
Produktionsgliederung *f s.* **Produktionsstruktur**
Produktionsgröße *f* 1. level of production; 2. size *(garment etc.)*
Produktionsgrundarbeiter *m* production worker
Produktionsgrundfonds *mpl* fixed [capital] assets
Produktionsgrundlagen *fpl s.* **Produktionsbasis**
Produktionsgut *n s.* **Produktionsgüter**
Produktionsgüte *f* quality of production
Produktionsgüter *npl* producer [capital] goods
Produktionsgüterbetrieb *m* producer [capital] goods enterprise
Produktionsgüterindustrie *f* producer [capital] goods industry
Produktionshilfsarbeiter *m* auxiliary production worker
Produktionshöchstleistung *f* maximum capacity in production
Produktionshöchststand *m* record [maximum] level of production
Produktionshöhe *f* level of production [output]
Produktionsindex *m* production index

Produktionsinstrumente *npl* instruments of production
Produktionskapazität *f* production [manufacturing, productive] capacity
Produktionskartell *n* production cartel
Produktionskennziffern *fpl* production indicators
Produktionskette *f* production chain
Produktionskoeffizient *m* production coefficient, coefficient of production
Produktionskollektiv *n* production team
Produktionskomplex *m* production complex
Produktionskonto *n* product(ion) account
Produktionskontrolle *f* production supervision [control]
Produktionskontroll- und Produktionslenkungsanlage *f* system of production control [supervision and steering]
Produktionskonzentration *f* concentration [pooling] of production
Produktionskooperation *f* co-operation in production
 ~, **internationale** international co-operation in production
Produktionskosten *pl* cost(s) of production, production costs
 ~, **einmalige** non-recurring production costs
 ~, **gesellschaftliche** cost(s) of social production
Produktionskostenaufstellung *f* production cost sheet; statement of production costs
Produktionskostensenkung *f* reduction of production costs
Produktionskostentheorie *f* cost-of-production theory
Produktionskraft *f* (production) capacity; productive force
Produktionskredit *m* production credit *(used for financing working capital)*
 ~, **laufender** current production credit
Produktionskreislauf *m s.* **Produktionszyklus**
Produktionskultur *f* working conditions in production
Produktionskurve *f* production curve
Produktionsland *n* producing country, country of origin
Produktionsleistung *f* 1. output; *(agric)* output per worker; 2. production capacity
 ~ **je Arbeitsstunde** output per man-hour
 ~, **volkswirtschaftliche** national product
Produktionsleiter *m* production manager
Produktionsleitung *f* production management
Produktionslenkung *f* production control [steering]
Produktionslinie *f* production line, line of production
Produktionslizenz *f* production [manufacturing] licence

Produktionsmaßstab *m* production scale
Produktionsmenge *f* quantity of production, output; *(agric)* yield
Produktionsmethode *f* method of production, production method
Produktionsmethoden *fpl*:
~ **in der Landwirtschaft, industriemäßige** methods of industrial production in agriculture
Produktionsminderung *f s.* **Produktionsdrosselung**
Produktionsmittel *npl* means of production, production [capital] goods
Produktionsmittelbezüge *mpl* purchase of producer [capital] goods
Produktionsmittelhandel *m* trade in producer [capital] goods
Produktionsmittelindustrie *f* producer [capital] goods industry
Produktionsmittelmarkt *m* market for producer [capital] goods
Produktionsmittelpreis *m* price of producer [capital] goods
Produktionsmittelproduktion *f* production of producer [capital] goods
Produktionsmittelvorrat *m* stock of producer [capital] goods
Produktionsmittelzirkulation *f* circulation of producer [capital] goods
Produktionsmöglichkeiten *fpl* production possibilities [prospects]
Produktionsmonopol *n* monopoly in production
Produktionsniveau *n* production level
Produktionsnomenklatur *f* nomenclature of production
Produktionsnorm *f* production norm
Produktionsnutzeffekt *m* production efficiency
Produktionsoptimierung *f* optimization of production
Produktionsoptimierungsmodell *n* production optimization model
Produktionsoptimum *n* optimum output
Produktionsorganisation *f* organization of production, production organization
Produktionsperiode *f* production period
Produktionsperspektive *f* production prospects
Produktionsphase *f* production stage, stage of production
Produktionsplan *m* production plan
~, **operativer** current production plan
~, **optimaler** optimum production plan
Produktionsplanung *f* production planning
~, **operative** current planning of production
Produktionspotential *n* production potential, production [productive] capacity
Produktionspotenz *f* production capacity [potential]

Produktionspraxis *f* experience in production; production
Produktionspreis *m* production price
~, **gesellschaftlicher** social cost of production
Produktionsprinzip *n* production principle *(principle of management based on the structure of production)*
Produktionsprofil *n* profile of production *(range of goods produced in an enterprise)*
Produktionsprognose *f* long-term forecast [prognosis] of production
Produktionsprogramm *n* production programme
Produktionspropaganda *f* propagation of new techniques and methods of production
Produktionsprozeß *m* production process
~ **des Kapitals** production process of capital
~, **wissenschaftlich-disponierter** science-oriented process of production
Produktionsqualität *f* production quality, quality of production
Produktionsquellen *fpl* productive resources
Produktionsquote *f* production [output] quota
Produktionsrahmen *m* range of production
Produktionsrationalisierung *f* rationalization of production, production rationalization
Produktionsrechte *npl* production rights
Produktionsregulierung *f* regulation of production
produktionsreif ready for production
Produktionsreife *f* start-up for production
Produktionsreserve *f* idle capacity, capacity reserve(s)
Produktionsreserven *fpl* idle resources, capacity reserves
Produktionsressourcen *fpl* (material and financial) resources for production
Produktionsrhythmus *m* production rhythm
Produktionsrisiko *n* producer's [production] risk
Produktionsrückgang *m* decline [drop] in production [output]
~, **saisonbedingter** seasonal decline in production
~, **scharfer** slump in production
Produktionsschwankung *f* fluctuation in production
Produktionsschwerpunkt *m* product emphasis
Produktionsschwierigkeiten *fpl* difficulties in production
Produktionssektor *m* production sector
Produktionsselbstkosten *pl* prime cost of production
Produktionssoll *n s.* **Produktionsauflage**
Produktionssortiment *n* range [assortment] of production
Produktionsspezialisierung *f* specialization of production

Produktionssphäre f sector of production, production sector
Produktionsspitze f (all-time) production record
Produktionsstand m production level, level of production
Produktionsstandard m standard of production
Produktionsstandort m location of production
Produktionsstatistik f production statistics, census of production
Produktionsstätte f place of production, manufacturing [production] plant
Produktionssteigerung f s. **Produktionserhöhung**
Produktionsstelle f s. **Produktionsstätte**
Produktionssteuer f production [manufacturing] tax
Produktionssteuerung f production control [steering]
Produktionssteuerungsplan m production control scheme
Produktionsstockung f production breakdown, interruption in production
Produktionsstörung f production disruption; production breakdown
Produktionsstraße f s. **Produktionslinie**
Produktionsstruktur f production structure [pattern]
Produktionsstückzahl f number of product(ion) units
Produktionsstufe f stage of production
~, **nachgelagerte** downstream production stage, forward linkage
~, **vorgelagerte** upstream production stage, backward linkage
Produktionssystem n system of production
Produktionstätigkeit f manufacturing (activity)
~, **saisonbedingte** seasonal production
Produktionstechnik f production engineering
produktionstechnisch technological
Produktionstechnologie f manufacturing technology
Produktionstempo n pace [tempo] of production; growth rate
Produktionstheorie f production theory
Produktionstransport m transport in production
Produktionsüberleitung f transfer of production (from one location to another)
Produktionsüberleitungsvertrag m agreement on production transfer
Produktionsüberschuß m production surplus
Produktionsübersicht f production return
Produktionsüberwachung f production control
Produktionsumfang m volume of production
~, **mengenmäßiger** physical volume of production
~, **wertmäßiger** volume of production in terms of value

Produktionsumlauffonds m working [circulating] capital
Produktionsumstellung f production changeover
produktionsunabhängig non-production
Produktions- und Betriebskosten pl production and operational costs
Produktions- und Erzeugnisstruktur f structure of production and products
Produktions- und Leistungskennziffern fpl output indicators
Produktions- und Realisierungsbedingungen fpl terms of production and sale
Produktionsunterbrechung f s. **Produktionsstockung**
Produktionsunterlagen fpl production documents
Produktionsvektor m production vector
Produktionsveränderung f change in production
Produktionsverbesserung f improvement in production
Produktionsverbindungen fpl links in production; relations involved in production; production linkages
Produktionsverbot n ban on production
Produktionsverbrauch m input, productive consumption
Produktionsverbrauchsintensität f input intensity
Produktionsvereinigung f association of producers
Produktionsverfahren n manufacturing [production, processing] technique [method], method of processing
Produktionsverflechtung f interlocking of production, production input-output linkage
Produktionsverflechtungsbilanz f production input-output table
Produktionsverflechtungsbilanzierung f working out [drawing up] of production input-output tables
Produktionsverflechtungsmodell n production input-output model
Produktionsverflechtungsmodellierung f working out of production input-output models
Produktionsverflechtungsstruktur f interlocking structure of production
Produktionsvergleich m comparison of output
Produktionsverhältnisse npl relations of production, production relations
Produktionsverlagerung f transfer of production
Produktionsverlauf m production schedule
Produktionsverlust m loss in production, production loss

Produktionsverpflichtung *f* commitment [undertaking] (given) to raise production
Produktionsverteilung *f* allocation of production
Produktionsvolumen *n* output, volume of production
Produktionsvorausplanung *f* advance [forward] production planning, pre-planning of production
Produktionsvoraussetzung *f* pre-condition of production
Produktionsvorbereitung *f* preparation of production
~, **organisatorische** organizational preparation of production
~, **technische** technical preparation of production
Produktionsvorbereitungskosten *pl* preparation costs of production
Produktionsvorbereitungszeit *f* preparing [preparation] time for production
Produktionsvorgabe *f s.* **Produktionsauflage**
Produktionsvorgang *m s.* **Produktionsprozeß**
Produktionsvorhaben *n* (production) project
Produktionsvorlauf *m* lead [head start] in production ◊ **einen ~ schaffen** to create a lead [head start] in production
Produktionsvorrat *m* production stocks
Produktionsvorschau *f* production outlook
Produktionsvorschriften *fpl* directions of production
Produktionswachstum *n* growth in production
Produktionsweise *f* mode of production
Produktionswerkzeuge *npl* tools of production
Produktionswert *m* value of goods produced [of production]; *(acc)* production cost value *(of goods produced in a given period)*
Produktionswettbewerb *m* emulation in production
Produktionswiederaufnahme *f* resumption of production *(after a stoppage etc.)*
produktionswirksam affecting production
Produktionswirksamkeit *f* production efficiency *(of investments)*
Produktionszahlen *fpl* production figures
Produktionszeit *f* production time
Produktionszeitmaß *n* production time measurement
Produktionszeitplan *m* production timetable [schedule]
Produktionszeitplanung *f* production time planning
Produktionszentrum *n* centre of production
Produktionszersplitterung *f* dispersal of production
Produktionsziel *n* (production) target
Produktionsziffer *f* output [production] figure

Produktionszone *f* production area
Produktionszunahme *f s.* **Produktionszuwachs**
Produktionszunahmerate *f* rate of increase in production
Produktionszusammenarbeit *f* co-operation in production
Produktionszusammenschluß *m (agric)* pooling of production
Produktionszuschuß *m* grant given for production purposes
Produktionszuwachs *m* increase in production, production growth
Produktionszuwachsprämie *f* bonus for increase in (agricultural) production
Produktionszweck *m* purpose of production
Produktionszweig *m* industry, line [branch] of production
Produktionszweigstruktur *f* production branch structure
Produktionszyklus *m* production cycle
produktiv productive ◊ **~arbeiten** to work productively; **~ tätig sein** to be productive; **~ zusammenarbeiten** to co-operate productively
Produktivgenossenschaft *f s.* **Produktionsgenossenschaft**
Produktivität *f* productivity, (production) efficiency
~ **der wissenschaftlichen Arbeit** productivity in scientific work
~, **geistige** creative [mental, intellectual] productivity
~, **geplante** planned productivity
~, **gesellschaftliche** social productivity
~, **individuelle** individual productivity
~, **potentielle** potential productivity
~, **wachsende** growing productivity
Produktivitätsabnahme *f* decline in productivity
Produktivitätsanalyse *f* productivity analysis
Produktivitätseffekt *m* productivity effect
Produktivitätsentwicklung *f* growth in productivity
Produktivitätserhöhung *f s.* **Produktivitätssteigerung**
Produktivitätsfaktor *m* productivity factor
Produktivitätsfortschritt *m* growth of [gain, improvement, progress in] productivity
Produktivitätsgefälle *n* productivity differential [gap]
Produktivitätsgesetz *n* law of productivity
Produktivitätsgrenze *f* productivity limit [ceiling]
Produktivitätshöhe *f s.* **Produktivitätsniveau**
Produktivitätsindex *m* productivity index
Produktivitätskurve *f* productivity curve
Produktivitätsmessung *f* measurement of productivity

Produktivitätsniveau *n* level of productivity
Produktivitätsplanung *f* productivity planning, planning of productivity
Produktivitätsrate *f* rate of productivity
Produktivitätsreserve *f* reserves in productivity, productivity reserve
Produktivitätsstand *m s.* **Produktivitätsniveau**
Produktivitätssteigerung *f* increase [rise] in productivity
Produktivitätsstudie *f* productivity study, study on productivity
Produktivitätstheorie *f* productivity theory
Produktivitätstrend *m* trend in productivity
Produktivitätsunterschied *m* difference(s) in productivity
Produktivitätsveränderung *f* change(s) in productivity
Produktivitätsverbesserung *f s.* **Produktivitätssteigerung**
Produktivitätsvergleich *m* comparison of productivity
Produktivitätswert *m* productivity value
produktivitätswirksam productivity-raising
Produktivitätszunahme *f s.* **Produktivitätszuwachs**
Produktivitätszuwachs *m* rise [gain, increase] in productivity
Produktivkapital *n* productive capital
Produktivkraft *f* productive force
~ **Mensch** people [humankind] as (a) productive force
~ **Wissenschaft** science as (a) productive force
Produktivkredit *m* production loan [credit]; performing loan *(used in investments to increase productivity)*
Produktmanager *m* product manager
Produktmoment *n (stats)* joint [multivariate] moment, product moment
Produktmomentkorrelation *f (stats)* product-moment correlation
Produktplanung *f* product planning
Produzent *m* producer, manufacturer, maker; grower
~, **selbständiger** independent [private] producer
~, **unmittelbarer** direct producer
Produzenten *mpl*:
~, **assoziierte** associated producers
Produzentenkartell *n* producer(s') cartel
Produzentenkollektiv *n* team of producers
Produzentenkredit *m* producer loan [credit]
Produzentenrente *f (agric)* producer's rent
Produzentenrisiko *n* producer's risk
Produzentenverband *m* producers' association
produzierbar producible
produzieren to produce, to make, to manufacture
produzierend producing

Profil *n* profile
profilbestimmend profile-determinant
profilbildend forming the profile
profilieren to profile *(moulding etc.)*; to mould *(character etc.)*; to shape *(trend etc.)*; **sich ~** to show one's worth, to distinguish o.s.; to develop along specialist lines *(person, enterprise etc.)*
Profilieren *n s.* **Profilierung**
profiliert profiled, distinguished, well-formed
Profilierung *f* showing (one's) worth; distinguishing *(o.s.)*; developing [development] along specialist lines *(person, enterprise etc.)*; moulding *(character etc.)*
Profit *m* profit, gain *(s. a.* **Gewinn)** ◇ **mit ~ arbeiten** *s.* **machen**; **ohne ~ arbeiten** to work without making profit; **~ abwerfen** to bring profit; **~ erwirtschaften** to earn profit; to derive profit *(from s.th.)*; **~ machen** to make profit
~, **allgemeiner** general rate of profit
~, **angefallener** accrued profit
~, **entgangener** lost profit
~, **erwirtschafteter** earned profit
~, **industrieller** industrial profit
~, **kommerzieller** commercial profit
~, **konjunkturbedingter** boom profit, profit made during the boom
~, **nicht erwirtschafteter** unearned profit
~, **verborgener** concealed [disguised] profit
profitabel profitable
Profitaneignung *f* appropriation of profit
Profitaufteilung *f* profit sharing
Profitberechnung *f* calculation of profit(s)
Profitbesteuerung *f* taxation on profit(s)
profitbringend profitable; lucrative
Profitentwicklung *f* growth of profit(s)
Profitwirtschaftung *f* making of profit
Profitexplosion *f* profit explosion
Profitfunktion *f* profit function, function of profit
Profitgesetz *n* law of profit
Profitgier *f* greed for profit
profitgierig profit-seeking
Profithöhe *f s.* **Profitmasse**
profitieren to make a profit, to profit [benefit, gain] (from)
Profitinteresse *n* interest in profit
Profitjäger *m* profiteer
Profitkalkulation *f s.* **Profitberechnung**
Profitmacher *m s.* **Profitjäger**
Profitmasse *f* amount of profit
Profitquelle *f* source of profit
Profitrate *f* rate of profit
Profitrategesetz *n* law of the rate of profit
Profitsteigerungstendenz *f* tendency of the rate of profit to rise

Profitsteuer *f* tax on profit
Profitstreben *n* seeking [drive] for profit
Profitsucht *f s.* Profitgier
Profittransfer *m* transfer of profit, profit transfer
Profitverschleierung *f* concealing profit(s)
Proformarechnung *f* pro forma invoice
Prognose *f* (long-term) forecast, prognosis
~, bedingte uncertain forecast
~ der Entwicklung der Technik forecast of technological development
~ der Entwicklung von Wissenschaft und Technik forecast of scientific and technological development
~ der volkswirtschaftlich strukturbestimmenden Aufgaben (long-term) forecast of tasks determining the national economic structure
~, detaillierte detailed forecast
~, finanzökonomische (long-term) financial forecast
~, gesamtvolkswirtschaftliche national economic forecast
~, komplexe comprehensive [complex] forecast
~ mit hohem Wahrscheinlichkeitsgrad high--confidence forecast
~, operative current forecast
~, simultane simultaneous forecast
~, technische technological forecast
~, territoriale (long-term) regional forecast
~, unternehmerische business forecast
~, volkswirtschaftliche *s.* ~, gesamtvolkswirtschaftliche
~, wissenschaftliche scientific forecast
~, wissenschaftlich-technische forecast in science and technology
Prognoseabteilung *f* forecasting department
Prognosearbeit *f* forecasting
Prognoseart *f* kind of (long-term) forecast
Prognoseauftrag *m* order to work out a forecast
Prognoseausarbeitung *f* working out [elaboration of] (long-term) forecasts
Prognosebasiswert *m* base value of a forecast
Prognosebudget *n* budget estimates
Prognoseelemente *npl* parts of a forecast
Prognoseentscheidung *f* forecasting decision
Prognoseetappe *f* stage of forecasting
Prognoseexperiment *n* experiment in forecasting
Prognosefaktoren *mpl* forecasting factors
Prognosefehler *m* forecast(ing) error
Prognosefehlerquelle *f* source of forecast(ing) error
Prognoseforschung *f* research on forecasting
Prognosefunktion *f* function of (long-term) forecast
~, mathematische mathematical prognosis [forecasting] function

Prognosegegenstand *m s.* Prognoseobjekt
Prognosegenauigkeit *f* accuracy of a forecast
Prognosegraph *m* graph of a forecast
Prognosegruppe *f* team of (long-term) forecasters
Prognosehorizont *m* horizon of (long-term) forecast
Prognoseinformation *f* information on (long--term) forecast
Prognosekomponenten *fpl s.* Prognoseelemente
Prognosekorrektur *f* correction [modification] of a forecast
Prognosekosten *pl* 1. costs based on expected trends, estimated costs; 2. forecasting costs
Prognoselehre *f* theory of forecasting
Prognosemethode *f* method of forecasting
~, heuristische heuristic method of forecasting
~, ökonometrische econometric method of forecasting
Prognosemethodik *f s.* Prognosemethodologie
Prognosemethodologie *f* methodology of forecasting
Prognosemodell *n* model of a (long-term) forecast
~, einsektorales one-sector model of a (long--term) forecast
~, mehrsektorales multi-sectoral model of a (long-term) forecast
Prognoseobjekt *n* subject of (long-term) forecasting
Prognoseperiode *f s.* Prognosezeitraum
Prognoserechnung *f* calculation of costs based on expected trends; budget estimation
Prognosesicherheit *f* certainty of a forecast
Prognosestellung *f* task of (long-term) forecasting
Prognosesystem *n* system of forecasts
Prognosetätigkeit *f* forecasting, predicting; prognosticating
~, systembezogene forecasting within [related to] a system
~, technische technological forecasting
~, wissenschaftlich-technische forecasting in science and technology
Prognosetechnik *f s.* Prognosemethode
Prognosetendenz *f* trend of a forecast, forecast trend
Prognosetheorie *f s.* Prognoselehre
Prognosevariable *f* variable of a forecast
Prognosevariante *f* variant of a forecast
Prognoseverfahren *n* process of forecasting
~, statistisches statistical method of forecasting
Prognosevorgaben *fpl* tasks given in long-term forecasting
Prognosewahrscheinlichkeit *f* probability of forecasts

Prognosezeitraum *m* period of a forecast
Prognosezuverlässigkeit *f* reliability of forecasts
Prognostik *f* prognosis
prognostisch prognostic(al), predictive
Prognostiziertechnik *f s.* **Prognosemethode**
prognostizieren to forecast, to predict; to prognosticate
Prognostizieren *n s.* **Prognosetätigkeit**
Prognostizierung *f s.* **Prognosetätigkeit**
Prognostizierungsmethode *f s.* **Prognosemethode**
Prognostizierungssystem *n s.* **Prognosesystem**
Programm *n* programme, (*Am*) program; range (*goods etc.*); *(d.pr.)* program ⋄ **ein ~ einstellen** *(d.pr.)* to set a program; **ein ~ herstellen** *s.* **programmieren**; **ein ~ testen** *(d.pr.)* to debug a program
~, alleinoperierendes *(d.pr.)* stand-alone program
~, allgemeines general program; *(d.pr.)* general routine
~, angehaltenes *(d.pr.)* suspended program
~, arithmetisches *(d.pr.)* arithmetic routine
~, erweiterbares *(d.pr.)* open-end program
~, gemeinsames common programme
~, geschlossenes *(d.pr.)* closed routine
~, interpretierendes *(d.pr.)* interpretive program, interpreter
~, iteratives *(d.pr.)* iterative routine
~, kodiertes *(d.pr.)* coded program
~, offenes *(d.pr.)* open routine; direct [insert] routine
~, politisches political programme, platform
~, umfassendes comprehensive programme
Programmabarbeitung *f (d.pr.)* program execution
programmabhängig *(d.pr.)* program dependent [sensitive]
Programmablauf *m (d.pr.)* computer operation, control sequence, program flow [run]
Programmablaufplan *m (d.pr.)* program flow chart
Programmabruf *m (d.pr.)* program fetch
Programmabschnitt *m (d.pr.)* control section
Programmänderung *f* change of programme; *(d.pr.)* program modification
Programmanfang *m (d.pr.)* program start
Programmaufbau *m (d.pr.)* program structure
Programmausarbeitung *f* drafting [elaboration] of a programme; *(d.pr.)* working out a program
Programm-Auswahlkarte *f (d.pr.)* run-card
Programmband *n (d.pr.)* program [sequence control] tape
Programmbandkanal *m (d.pr.)* program tape channel
Programmbefehl *m (d.pr.)* program instruction

Programmbeschreibung *f (d.pr.)* program description
Programmbewertung *f (d.pr.)* program evaluation
Programmbewertungs- und Prüfverfahren *n* Program Evaluation and Review Technique (PERT)
Programmbezeichnung *f (d.pr.)* program identification
Programmbibliothek *f (d.pr.)* program library
Programmdokumentation *f (d.pr.)* program documentation
Programmeinheit *f (d.pr.)* program unit
Programmeinstellung *f (d.pr.)* program setting
Programmentwurf *m* draft programme
Programmfehler *m (d.pr.)* program(ming) error, bug
Programmfehlerbeseitigung *f (d.pr.)* program debugging
Programmfolge *f (d.pr.)* program sequence
Programmformulierung *f (d.pr.)* programming, coding
Programmforschung *f (d.pr.)* program research
Programmfortschaltung *f (d.pr.)* program advance
Programmgang *m (d.pr.)* program cycle
programmgemäß according to programme
Programmgenerator *m (d.pr.)* program generator
programmgesteuert computer-controlled
Programm-Gruppenabschaltung *f (d.pr.)* group suppression
Programmiereinheit *f (d.pr.)* programmer unit
programmieren to program
Programmieren *n* programming
Programmierer *m (d.pr.)* programmer; coder
Programmierprinzip *n (d.pr.)* programming principle
Programmiersprache *f (d.pr.)* program(ming) language
~, problemorientierte *(d.pr.)* problem-oriented language
Programmiersystem *n (d.pr.)* programming system
Programmierung *f (d.pr.)* programming
~, dynamische *(d.pr.)* dynamic programming
~, heuristische heuristic programming
~, lineare linear programming
~ mit kürzester Wartezeit *(d.pr.)* minimum latency programming
~ mit kürzester Zugriffszeit *(d.pr.)* minimum access programming
~, nichtlineare non-linear programming
~, parametrische *(d.pr.)* parametric programming
~, schnelle *(d.pr.)* minimum access programming
~, stochastische *(d.pr.)* stochastic programming

Programmiertechnik *f (d.pr.)* programming technique
Programmierungsaufgabe *f (d.pr.)* programming problem
Programmierungsaufwand *m (d.pr.)* programming costs
Programmierungsfehler *m (d.pr.)* programming error
Programmierungsfeld *n (d.pr.)* patch bag
Programmierungsmethode *f (d.pr.)* programming method
Programmierungssprache *f s.* **Programmiersprache**
Programmierungsunterlagen *fpl (d.pr.)* programming documents
Programmierverfahren *n (d.pr.)* programming method
Programminformation *f (d.pr.)* program information
Programminstruktion *f (d.pr.)* program instruction
Programmkarte *f (d.pr.)* program card
Programm-Kennzahl *f (d.pr.)* call number
Programmkompatibilität *f (d.pr.)* program compatibility
Programmkontrolle *f (d.pr.)* program control
Programmlauf *m (d.pr.)* program run
Programmname *m (d.pr.)* program name
Programmnumerierung *f (d.pr.)* program numbering
Programmoptimierung *f (d.pr.)* program optimization
Programmothek *f s.* **Programmbibliothek**
Programmplanung *f (d.pr.)* programming
Programmprüfung *f (d.pr.)* program review [testing]
Programmregister *n (d.pr.)* program register
Programmsatz *m (d.pr.)* sentence
Programmschleife *f (d.pr.)* program loop
Programmschritt *m (d.pr.)* program step
Programmschrittüberlappung *f (d.pr.)* program exit overlap
Programmschrittzähler *m (d.pr.)* sequence counter
Programmselektor *m (d.pr.)* calculate selector
Programmspeicher *m (d.pr.)* program memory (storage)
Programmspur *f (d.pr.)* program track
Programmsteuerung *f (d.pr.)* program control
~ des Rechners *(d.pr.)* computer program control
~, elektronische *(d.pr.)* electronic program control
~ mit Lochkarte *(d.pr.)* punch card programming
Programmstreifenlocher *m (d.pr.)* program tape punch

Programmstufe *f (d.pr.)* level of program, program level
Programmtafel *f (d.pr.)* plug board, program panel
Programmtrommel *f (d.pr.)* program drum
Programmüberblender *m (d.pr.)* date in-and-out control
Programmüberprüfung *f (d.pr.)* proof reading
Programmübersicht *f (d.pr.)* sequence chart
Programmumsetzer *m (d.pr.)* assembler
Programmunterbrechung *f* interruption of programme; *(d.pr.)* program interrupt
Programmverteiler *m (d.pr.)* program distributor
Programmvorbereitung *f (d.pr.)* program preparation
Programmvorwahl *f (d.pr.)* program preselection
Programmwähler *m (d.pr.)* program selector
Programmwiederholung *f (d.pr.)* program repeat
Programmzähler *m (d.pr.)* program counter
Programmzeit *f (d.pr.)* programming time; processing speed
Programmzeitschalter *m (d.pr.)* timer switch
Programmzeitverkürzer *m (d.pr.)* data processing accelerator
Programmzeitverkürzung *f (d.pr.)* increase of processing speed
Programmzentrale *f (d.pr.)* program centre
Programmzuführung *f (d.pr.)* program supply
Progression *f* progression; *(tax also)* progressive scale
Progressionssatz *m* rate of progression *(taxation etc.)*
progressiv progressive
Progressivbesteuerung *f* progressive [graduated] taxation
Progressivität *f* progressiveness *(taxation etc.)*
Progressivsteuer *f* progressive [graduated] tax
prohibitieren to prohibit
prohibitiv prohibitive
Prohibitivpreis *m* prohibitive price
Prohibitivsätze *mpl* discriminatory (tariff) rates
Prohibitivsteuer *f* prohibitive tax
Prohibitivsystem *n* prohibitive system
Prohibitivtarif *m s.* **Prohibitivsätze**
Prohibitivzoll *m* prohibitive (customs) duty [tariff]
Projekt *n* project ◊ **ein ~ ausarbeiten** to plan a project; **ein ~ durchführen** to realize [implement] a project; **ein ~ fallenlassen** to drop [abandon] a project
~, gemeinsames joint project
Projektablauf *m* project sequence
Projektanalyse *f* project analysis
Projektanalyse- und Projektkontrollverfahren *n* project analysis and control technique (PACT)

Projektant *m* 1. (investment) project planning enterprise *(including preparation etc.)*; 2. (project) planner
Projektaufgabe *f s.* **Projektierungsauftrag**
Projektdaten *pl* (investment) project data
Projektfinanzierung *f* financing [funding] of a project, project financing [funding]
projektieren to project, to plan
Projektierung *f* investment project preparation, project planning
Projektierungsarbeit *f* project planning
Projektierungsauftrag *m* project order [assignment]
Projektierungsaufwand *m* (investment) project preparation cost, cost of preparing an investment project
Projektierungsbetrieb *m s.* **Projektant**
Projektierungsbüro *n* project drawing office
Projektierungseinrichtung *f s.* **Projektierungsbüro**
Projektierungsfinanzierung *f* financing [funding] of an investment project preparation
Projektierungsinstitut *n* project drawing institute
Projektierungskollektiv *n* (investment) project preparation team
Projektierungskosten *pl s.* **Projektierungsaufwand**
Projektierungsleistung *f* (investment) project preparation (performance) *(feasibility studies etc.)*
Projektierungsmethode *f* method of (investment) project preparation
Projektierungsplan *m* (investment) project preparation plan
Projektierungs- und Entwicklungsarbeiten *fpl* project research and development
Projektierungs- und Konstruktionsarbeiten *fpl* (investment) project drafting and designing
Projektierungsunterlagen *fpl* (investment) project documents
Projektierungsvertrag *m* (investment) project contract
Projektierungszeit *f s.* **Projektierungszeitraum**
Projektierungszeitraum *m* (investment) project period
Projektinformation *f* project information
Projektingenieur *m* project engineer
Projektkosten *pl* project cost(s)
Projektleiter *m* project manager
Projektleitung *f* (investment) project management
Projektleitungsmethode *f* method of (investment) project management
Projektlösung *f* variant of a project completion
Projektorganisation *f* (investment) project organization

Projektplanung *f* (investment) project planning
Projektplanungsmethode *f* method of (investment) project planning
Projektpreis *m* project price, price of a project
Projektträger *m* project administrator [sponsor]
Projektvorbereitung *f* (investment) project preparation
Pro-Kopf-Leistung *f* per capita performance
Pro-Kopf-Produktion *f* per capita production
Pro-Kopf-Quote *f* per capita quota
Pro-Kopf-Umsatz *m* per capita turnover
Pro-Kopf-Verbrauch *m* per capita consumption
Prokura *f* general [full] power of attorney; procuration ⋄ **die ~ entziehen** to cancel (the) (full) power of attorney [procuration]; **jmdm. die ~ erteilen** to give s.o. (full) power of attorney [procuration]; **per ~ unterzeichnen** to sign by procuration; **~ haben** to hold (full) power of attorney [procuration]
Prokurist *m* chief clerk *(usually)*; *(Am)* executive secretary
Proletariat *n* proletariat(e)
Proletarier *m* proletarian
proletarisch proletarian
proletarisieren to proletarianize
Proletarisierung *f* proletarianization
Prolongation *f* prolongation, renewal *(bill etc.)*; extension *(credit etc.)*; *(st.ex.)* carry-over, continuation, contango, backwardation
Prolongationsabkommen *n* extension agreement
Prolongationsakzept *n s.* **Prolongationswechsel**
prolongationsfähig renewable
Prolongationsgebühr *f (st.ex.)* contango (rate) *(paid by operator for a rise)*; backwardation *(paid by operator for a fall)*; renewal charge *(bill etc.)*
Prolongationsgeschäft *n (st.ex.)* continuation business, contango (business), backwardation, carry-over business
Prolongationsklausel *f* continuation clause
Prolongationskosten *pl* renewal cost
Prolongationspreis *m* making-up price
Prolongationsprovision *f* renewal rate
Prolongationsrecht *n* right of renewal
Prolongationssatz *m (st.ex.)* continuation [carry-over] rate
Prolongationswechsel *m* renewed bill (of exchange), renewal bill
prolongierbar *s.* **prolongationsfähig**
prolongieren to extend; to renew *(a bill etc.)*; *(st.ex.)* to carry over
prolongiert extended; renewed *(bill etc.)*
Promesse *f* promissory note
Promessengeschäft *n* selling of a share in a lottery ticket

Promptgeschäft *n* delivery without delay, *(st.ex.)* sale for quick [prompt] delivery
Promptware *f* commodity to be delivered without delay
Propergeschäft *n* business [transaction] carried out on one's own account
Properhandel *m s.* **Propergeschäft**
Proportion *f* proportion, ratio
~, **innerzweigliche** intra-branch proportion
~, **volkswirtschaftliche** national economic proportion
proportional proportional, proportionate, pro rata
Proportionalbesteuerung *f* proportional taxation
Proportionalität *f* proportionality
Proportionalitätsbedingung *f* proportionality condition
Proportionalitätsfaktor *m* proportionality factor [constant]
Proportionalitätsgesetz *n* law of proportionality
Proportionalitätsgrenze *f* proportional limit
Proportionalitätstheorie *f* theory of proportionality
Proportionalsteuer *f* proportional tax
Proportionalsystem *n* proportional [proportionate] system
Proportionen *fpl*:
~, **optimale** optimum proportions
~, **territoriale** regional proportions
proportionieren to proportion
Proportionierungskonzeption *f* proportioning concept [outline]
Proportionierungsvariante *f* proportioning variant
pro rata *(lat)* pro rata
Prospekt *m* prospectus, leaflet, folder
prospektieren to prospect for *(minerals etc.)*
Prospektieren *n* prospecting
Prospektierung *f* prospecting for *(minerals etc.)*
prospektiv prospective
Prospektwerbung *f* advertising by prospectus(ses) [leaflets]
prosperieren to prosper, to flourish
Prosperität *f* prosperity
Pro-Stunden-Quote *f* per hour quota
Protektionismus *m* protectionism
Protektionist *m* protectionist
protektionistisch protectionist
Protektionswirtschaft *f* favouritism; nepotism
Protektorat *n* protectorate
Protest *m* (act of) protest ◊ **mangel Protestes** in the absence of protest; **ohne ~ protest waived**; **zu ~ gehen** to go to protest
~, **rechtzeitiger** due protest
~, **verspäteter** retarded [delayed] protest
Protestanzeige *f* notice of protest [dishono(u)r]

Protestbenachrichtigung *f s.* **Protestanzeige**
Protestgebühr *f* protest fee [charges]
Protestgläubiger *m* protester
protestieren to protest
Protestkosten *pl s.* **Protestgebühr**
Protestnote *f s.* **Protestanzeige**
Protestschreiben *n* letter of protest
Protestspesen *pl* protest fees [charges]
Proteststreik *m* protest strike
Protesturkunde *f* certificate of protest [dishono(u)r]
Protestverzicht(erklärung *f)* *m* waiver of protest
Protestzahlung *f* payment under protest
Protokoll *n* 1. minutes, report *(of meetings etc.)*; record *(of proceedings etc.)*; 2. protocol *(diplomacy)*; 3. *(d.pr.)* audit, listing, log ◊ **das ~ führen** to take (down) the minutes; **das ~ verlesen** to read (out) the minutes; **ein ~ aufnehmen (über)** to make [keep] a record (of), to record *(s.th.)*; **im ~ vermerken** to enter in the record; **zu ~ geben** to put [place] on record; to make a statement; **zu ~ nehmen** to record, to take down minutes
~, **amtliches** official report
~, **gedrucktes** printed report
~, **gerichtliches** public record
Protokollabteilung *f* protocol department
Protokollant *m* minutes secretary, person who takes (down) the minutes
Protokollbuch *n* minute book; *(jur)* records
Protokollchef *m* Chief of Protocol
Protokollführer *m s.* **Protokollant**
Protokollprogramm *n* 1. *(pol)* protocol (programme); 2. *(d.pr.)* trace program
protokollieren to take (down) [keep] the minutes, to make [keep] a record *(of s.th.)*, to record *(s.th.)*; to enter *(s.th.)* in the minutes [record]; *(jur)* to take down (on record)
Provenienz *f* provenance, origin
Proviant *m* provisions, victuals, food; rations
Provinzialabgaben *fpl* provincial [regional] taxes
Provinzialbank *f* provincial [regional] bank
Provinzialbörse *f* provincial [regional] (market of) exchange
Provision *f* commission; brokerage ◊ **auf ~** on (a) commission; **mit ~** with commission; **ohne ~** without commission; **~ berechnen** to charge a commission; **~ gewähren** to accord [give] a commission
~, **geteilte** split commission
~, **halbe** half commission
~, **ungeteilte** full commission
Provisionsanspruch *m* claim for commission
Provisionsbasis *f s.* **Provisionssatz**
Provisionsberechnung *f* statement of commission

Provisionseinnahmen *fpl* commission earnings, commission(s) received [earned]
Provisionsforderung *f* accrued commission, commission(s) receivable
provisionsfrei free of commission
Provisionsgebühr *f* commission (fee)
Provisionsgeschäft *n* commission business, business on a commission basis
Provisionslohn *m* commission
Provisionssatz *m* commission rate, rate of commission
Provisionsvergütung *f s.* Provision
Provisionsvertreter *m* commission agent
Provisionszahlung *f* payment of commission
Proximitätssatz *m (stats)* proximity theorem
Prozedur *f* procedure
Prozeduranweisung *f (d.pr.)* procedural [procedure] statement
Prozedurbezeichnung *f* (d.pr.) procedure identifier
Prozedurprogrammsatz *m (d.pr.)* procedural sentence
Prozent *n* per cent, *(Am)* percent
Prozentdiagramm *n* percentage diagram
Prozente *npl*:
 ⋄ **gegen ~** on a percentage basis; **in Prozenten** in per cent; **~ abwerfen** to yield a percentage
Prozentkurs *m (st.ex.)* percentage quotation, price expressed as a percentage of the nominal value
Prozentnotierung *f s.* Prozentkurs
Prozentpunkt *m* percentage point
Prozentrechnung *f* percentage calculation [arithmetic]
Prozentsatz *m* percentage
Prozentspanne *f* percentage margin
Prozenttara *f* percentage tare
prozentual percentage, proportional
Prozentverteilung *f (stats)* percentage distribution
Prozeß *m* 1. process; 2. *(jur)* lawsuit; (legal) proceedings, action, litigation; trial *(hearing)*
 ⋄ **einen ~ anstrengen** *(jur)* to institute [initiate] legal proceedings, to bring a lawsuit [an action] *(against s.o.)*, to sue *(s.o.)*; **einen ~ aufnehmen** *(jur)* to take a case; **einen ~ aussetzen** *(jur)* to postpone a case; **einen ~ betreiben** *(jur)* to take legal proceedings [action] *(against s.o.)*, to conduct litigation; **einen ~ durchführen** *(jur)* to sustain an action; **einen ~ einstellen** *(jur)* to stop an action [a case]; **einen ~ fortsetzen** *(jur)* to maintain a suit
~, anditiver *(stats)* additive [random walk] process
~, anhängiger *(jur)* pending suit

~, arbeitsaufwendiger labour-intensive process
~, arbeitssparender labour-saving process
~, arbeitsteiliger process involving a division of labour
~, autoregressiver autoregressive process
~, betriebssicherer safe(ly) running) process
~ der gleitenden Mittel *(stats)* moving-average process
~ der Zufallsimpulse *(stats)* random impulse process
~, determinierter defined process
~, diskreter stochastischer *(stats)* discrete process
~, konservativer *(stats)* conservative process
~, kostenaufwendiger cost-intensive process
~, kostspieliger *(jur)* expensive lawsuit
~, latent-deterministischer *(stats)* crypto-deterministic process
~, laufender *(jur)* pending case
~, linearer linear process
~, lohnaufwendiger process involving high wage costs
~, Martingaler *(stats)* Martingale
~, materialaufwendiger material-intensive process
~, materialsparender material-saving process
~, mehrphasiger *(stats)* multiple phase process
~ mit unabhängigen Zuwachsen *(stats)* differential process
~ mit unbestimmten Anfangsbedingungen, deterministischer *s.* **~, latent-deterministischer**
~, multiplikativer *(stats)* multiplicative process
~, nichtstationärer *(stats)* evolutionary process
~ ohne Zu- und Abgang *s.* **~, konservativer**
~, orthogonaler *(stats)* orthogonal process
~, periodischer stationary process
~, stationärer *(stats)* stationary process
~, stofflicher physical process
~, stoffumwandelnder process of treating materials, material treatment process
~, stoffverformender process of shaping material, material-shaping process
~, streitiger *(jur)* contentions [litigious, adversary] suit
~, streng stationärer *(stats)* strictly stationary process
~, zeitlich homogener *(stats)* temporally homogeneous process
~, zeitlich kontinuierlicher *(stats)* temporally continuous process
Prozeßakte(n) *f(pl) (jur)* case file(s) [record(s)], documents relating to case
Prozeßautomatisierung *f* process automation
Prozeßbeginn *m (jur)* institution of proceedings [a (law)suit, a case]
Prozeßbeteiligter *m (jur)* party to a lawsuit, liti-

gant, contending [opposing, litigant, contesting] party
Prozeßbevollmächtigter *m* lawyer, solicitor, authorized proxy [representative], *(Am)* attorney at law, attorney-in-fact
prozeßfähig actionable *(matter etc.)*; capable to sue and be sued
Prozeßfähigkeit *f (jur)* capacity to act in legal proceedings [to sue and be sued]
Prozeßforschung *f* process research
prozeßführend *(jur)* litigant
Prozeßführung *f (jur)* conduct of a case; litigation
Prozeßgebühr *f* legal costs
Prozeßgegenstand *m (jur)* subject of an action
Prozeßgegner *m (jur)* opposing party
prozessieren *(jur)* to bring an action [take action] *(against s.o.)*
Prozeßkosten *pl* cost(s) of litigation [a lawsuit, an action]
Prozeßkostenrechnung *f (jur)* bills of costs of an action
Prozeßmaterial *n (jur)* grounds for litigation
Prozessor *m (d.pr.)* (data) processor
prozessorabhängig *(d.pr.)* processor-dependent *(interrupt)*
prozessorgesteuert *(d.pr.)* processor-controlled
Prozeßorganisation *f* organization of a process
Prozeßpartei *f s.* **Prozeßbeteiligter**
Prozeßrechner *m* process control computer
Prozeßsteuersystem *n* system of process control [steering]
Prozeßsteuerung *f* process control [steering]
Prozeßstruktur *f* process structure
Prozeßunfähigkeit *f (jur)* incapacity to act in legal proceedings [to sue and be sued]
Prozeßunterlagen *fpl (jur)* papers [documents] in the case
Prüfanzeiger *m (d.pr.)* check indicator
Prüfaufgabe *f (d.pr.)* check problem
Prüfbedingungen *fpl (d.pr.)* sense conditions
Prüfbefehl *m (d.pr.)* examine statement
Prüfbefund *m* report on technical examination
Prüfbeleg *m s.* **Prüfungsbescheinigung**
Prüfbericht *m s.* **Prüfungsbericht**
Prüf-Bit *n (d.pr.)* check [redundancy, parity bit
Prüfeinrichtung *f (d.pr.)* checking feature
prüfen to examine, to check, to test, to inspect *(goods etc.)*, to taste *(wine etc.)*; to verify *(data etc.)*, to investigate *(complaints etc.)*; *(acc)* to audit; *(jur)* to review
Prüfer *m (ind)* tester, checker, inspector *(quality control etc.)*, taster *(wine etc.)*; *(acc)* auditor; examiner *(patents; schools etc.)*; *(d.pr.)* verifier
~, **betriebseigener** enterprise accountant
~, **leitender** accountant in charge
~, **staatlicher** government auditor

Prüfergebnis *n s.* **Prüfungsergebnis**
Prüfgröße *f (stats)* test statistic
Prüfgruppe *f* test group
Prüfkontrolle *f (d.pr.)* test control
Prüfliste *f* checklist
Prüflos *n (stats)* (inspection) lot
Prüfmaß *n s.* **Prüfgröße**
Prüfpflicht *f* obligation to check
Prüfposten *m s.* **Prüflos**
Prüfprogramm *n* test program(me); *(d.pr.)* test routine; *(acc)* audit programme
Prüfumfang *m (stats)* amount of inspection
~, **mittlerer** *(stats)* average amount of inspection
Prüfung *f* examination, test, testing, inspection *(goods etc.)*, tasting *(wine etc.)*; verification *(data etc.)*, investigation *(complaints etc.)*, *(acc)* audit; *(jur)* review ⋄ **eine ~ ablegen** to take [*(Brit)* sit for] an examination; **eine ~ bestehen** to pass an examination; **eine ~ nicht bestehen** to fail (in) an examination; **zur ~ zugelassen** admitted to take part in examination
~, **abgebrochene** curtailed inspection
~, **betriebseigene** *(acc)* internal audit
~, **betriebsfremde** *(acc)* external audit
~, **eingehende** *(acc)* detailed audit
~, **innerbetriebliche** *s.* ~, **betriebseigene**
~, **laufend durchgeführte** *(acc)* continuous audit
~, **losweise** *(stats)* lot-by-lot inspection
~, **mündliche** oral examination
~, **planmäßige** routine testing
~, **rechnerische** checking the figures *(bill etc.)*
~, **reduzierte** reduced inspection
~, **sachliche** checking the items *(bill etc.)*
~, **schriftliche** written examination
~, **stichprobenartige** *(acc)* audit test
~, **zerstörende** destructive test
~, **zollamtliche** customs examination [check(ing)]
Prüfungsablauf *m (acc)* audit procedure
Prüfungsabschnitt *m (acc)* period under audit
Prüfungsabteilung *f (acc)* inspection department; *(acc)* auditing department
Prüfungsanweisung *f (acc)* audit instructions
Prüfungsauftrag *m (acc)* audit(ing) assignment
Prüfungsausschuß *m* board of examiners
Prüfungsbedingungen *fpl* test conditions; conditions for the admission of a candidate (to an examination)
Prüfungsbericht *m* test report, report on a test; *(acc)* audit(or's) report, accountant's report
Prüfungsbescheinigung *f* inspection [test] certificate; *(acc)* accountant's certificate
Prüfungsbestimmungen *fpl* examination regulations [rules]
Prüfungsbogen *m (acc)* auditing form [paper]

Prüfungsdiagramm *n* inspection diagram
Prüfungsergebnis *n* result of a test [an inspection, an investigation, an audit]; examination result
Prüfungsgebühr *f* examination fee
Prüfungsgesellschaft *f (acc)* firm of auditors, auditing company [firm]
Prüfungsgrenze *f (stats)* control limit
Prüfungsgrundsätze *mpl (acc)* standards [principles] of auditing
Prüfungskommission *f s.* **Prüfungsausschuß**
Prüfungskosten *pl* testing cost(s); *(acc)* audit(or's) fees, audit(ing) cost(s)
Prüfungsordnung *f* examination rules [regulations]
Prüfungspflicht *f* obligatory inspection
prüfungspflichtig subject to inspection
Prüfungsplan *m* examination plan [schedule]
Prüfungsprogramm *n* examination programme; *(acc)* audit programme
Prüfungsprotokoll *n* certificate of inspection; *(acc)* accountant's certificate
Prüfungsrichtlinie(n) *f(pl)* instructions for conducting an examination; *(acc)* auditing standards
Prüfungstabelle *f (stats)* control chart
Prüfungstermin *m* meeting of creditors *(bankruptcy etc.)*; *(acc)* date of auditing
Prüfungsverband *m* auditing board
Prüfungsverfahren *n* method of testing *(machines etc.)*; examination procedure *(patents etc.)*
Prüfungsvermerk *m (acc)* certificate of audit
Prüfungsvorschriften *fpl (acc)* rules of auditing
Prüfungswesen *n (acc)* (system of) auditing
Prüfungszeitraum *m s.* **Prüfungsabschnitt**
Prüfverfahren *n s.* **Prüfungsverfahren**
Prüfzeichen *n* test [certification] mark; *(d.pr.)* check character
Prüfziffer *f (d.pr.)* check digit
Pseudoadresse *f (d.pr.)* symbolic address
Pseudobefehl *m (d.pr.)* pseudo instruction
Pseudomarxismus *m* pseudo-Marxism
Pseudoprogramm *n (d.pr.)* symbolic program
Puffer *m (d.pr.)* buffer, synchronizer
Pufferbestände *mpl* buffer stock
Punkt *m* point, item
Punktbewertungssystem *n* points rating method
pünktlich punctual, prompt, in [on] time
Pünktlichkeit *f* punctuality, promptness
Punktschätzung *f (stats)* point estimate
Punktstichprobe *f (stats)* point sample
Punktstichprobenverfahren *n (stats)* point sampling
Punktwert *m (stats)* score
Punktzahl *f s.* **Punktwert**

Q

Quader-Gitter-Plan *m (stats)* cuboidal lattice design
Quadrat *n* square
~ **des Variationskoeffizienten** *(stats)* relative variance
~, **halblateinisches** *(stats)* semi-Latin square
~, **Knut-Wik'sches** *(stats)* Knut-Wik square
~, **lateinisches** *(stats)* Latin square
~ **mit systematischer Anordung** *(stats)* systematic square
~, **quasi-lateinisches** *(stats)* quasi-Latin square
~, **selbstkonjugiertes lateinisches** *(stats)* self-conjugate Latin square
~, **systematisches** *s.* ~ **mit systematischer Anordnung**
~, **unvollständiges lateinisches** *(stats)* incomplete Latin square
Quadrate *npl*:
~, **innere kleinste** *(stats)* internal least squares
~, **konjugierte** *(stats)* conjugate squares
~, **konjugierte lateinische** *(stats)* conjugate Latin squares
~, **orthogonale** *(stats)* orthogonal squares
Qualifikation *f* qualification *(educational achievements, skills etc.)*; characterization, description *(of s.o., of s.th., as s.th.)*; qualification *(statement etc.)*
Qualifikationsanalyse *f* analysis of qualification *(personnel etc.)*
Qualifikationsanforderungen *fpl* qualification requirements; qualification required
Qualifikationsart *f* kind of qualification
qualifikationsbedingt due to one's qualification
Qualifikationsgrad *m* level [standard] of qualification
Qualifikationsgruppe *f* qualification group
Qualifikationsmerkmale *npl* qualifications *(of a person for classification purposes)*
Qualifikationsnachweis *m* proof of qualification; certificate (of qualification)
Qualifikationsniveau *n s.* **Qualifikationsgrad**
Qualifikationsnorm *f* qualifying standard
Qualifikationsprogramm *n* training programme
Qualifikationsstand *m s.* **Qualifikationsgrad**
Qualifikationsstufe *f* stage of qualification
Qualifikationsstruktur *f* qualification pattern
Qualifikationsunterschiede *mpl* differences in the level of qualification
qualifizieren to train, to educate; to upgrade; to improve *(plan etc.)*; to characterize, to describe *(s.o., s.th., as s.th.)*; to qualify *(statement etc.)*; **sich** ~ to qualify o.s. *(for s.th.)*
qualifiziert qualified; highly trained, skilled

Qualifizierung *f* training, education; upgrading; improvement *(plan etc.)*; qualification *(for post etc.)*; characterization, description *(of s.o., of s.th., as s.th.)*; qualification *(statement etc.)*
~ **am Arbeitsplatz** on-the-job training
~, **berufliche** professional skill; trade skill
~ **des Systems der Volkswirtschaftsplanung** improvement in [of] the system of national economic planning
~, **fachliche** *s.* ~, **berufliche**
~ **leitender Mitarbeiter** training of managerial staff
~ **während der Arbeitszeit** *s.* ~ **am Arbeitsplatz**
~, **wissenschaftliche** professional qualification
Qualifizierungseinrichtungen *fpl* training institutions [centres]
Qualifizierungsgespräch *n* management--employee discussion on further training
Qualifizierungsgrad *m s.* **Qualifikationsgrad**
Qualifizierungskosten *pl* training costs
Qualifizierungslehrgang *m* refresher [extension, upgrading] course
Qualifizierungsmaßnahmen *fpl* training programme
Qualifizierungsplan *m* training [upgrading] programme [plan]
Qualifizierungsprogramm *n* training programme; refresher course
Qualifizierungsvertrag *m* management--employee agreement on training (measures)
Qualität *f* quality, grade; kind, sort ⋄ **nach ~ sortieren** to grade (according to quality)
~, **abfallende** inferior quality
~, **ausbedungene** stipulated quality
~, **auserlesene** prime quality
~, **ausgesuchte** choice quality
~, **beste** first-class [first-rate, superior] quality, grade A, top quality
~, **durchschnittliche** (fair) average quality, standard quality, medium grade
~, **gute** good quality
~, **handelsübliche** normal quality
~, **hohe** high quality [grade]
~, **leichtere** milder quality *(spirits, tobacco etc.)*
~, **mangelnde** low [cheap, inferior] quality
~, **mindere** inferior [lower] quality
~, **mittlere** medium [middling] quality [grade]
~, **schlechte** poor quality [workmanship]
~, **verbesserte** improved quality
qualitativ qualitative
Qualitätsabfall *m s.* **Qualitätsminderung**
Qualitätsabnahme *f s.* **Qualitätsminderung**
Qualitätsabschlag *m* discount for substandard article [quality]
Qualitätsabweichung *f* variation in quality, quality tolerance

Qualitätsanalyse *f* quality analysis
Qualitätsänderung *f s.* **Qualitätsveränderung**
Qualitätsanforderungen *fpl* standards of quality, quality requirements
Qualitätsanspruch *m* right [fair claim] to quality
Qualitätsarbeit *f* (high-)quality work, (superior) workmanship
Qualitätsbeanstandung *f* complaint about quality
Qualitätsbescheinigung *f* quality certificate, certificate of quality
Qualitätsbestimmung *f* defining [definition] of quality
Qualitätsbeurteilung *f* judging the quality, judgement of quality
Qualitätsbewegung *f* movement for improving the quality of products
Qualitätsbewertung *f* grading *(product etc.)*
qualitätsbewußt quality-conscious
Qualitätsbezeichnung *f* quality mark; quality description
Qualitätsdifferenzierung *f* quality differentiation
Qualitätseinstufung *f s.* **Qualitätsbewertung**
Qualitätselastizität *f* elasticity [tolerance] of quality
Qualitätsentwicklung *f* development of quality
Qualitätserhöhung *f* improvement [increase, rise] in quality
Qualitätserzeugnis *n* high-quality [high-class] article [product]
Qualitätsexpertise *f s.* **Qualitätsbescheinigung**
Qualitätsfunktion *f (stats)* quality function
Qualitätsgarantie *f* guarantee of quality
qualitätsgemäß *s.* **qualitätsgerecht**
qualitätsgerecht according to (standard) quality
Qualitätsgrad *m* (quality) grade
Qualitätsgutachten *n s.* **Qualitätsbescheinigung**
Qualitätsindex *m* quality index
Qualitätskennziffer *f* quality indicator [standard]
Qualitätsklasse *f* (quality) grade [class]
Qualitätsklausel *f* quality clause
Qualitätskontrolle *f* quality control
~ **bei mehreren Variablen** *(stats)* multivariate quality control
~, **betriebliche** intra-enterprise quality control
~ **durch Probieren** testing and quality control
~ **durch Stichproben** random control of quality
~, **statistische** statistical quality control, quality control for statistical purposes
Qualitätskontrollorgan *n* quality control institution [office]
Qualitätsmangel *m* flaw, low [defective] quality, quality failure

Qualitätsmarke *f* (quality) brand
qualitätsmäßig in terms of quality
Qualitätsmaßstab *m* standard of quality
Qualitätsmerkmal *n* quality characteristic [mark]
Qualitätsmessung *f* measuring of quality, quality grading
Qualitätsminderung *f* deterioration in [lowering of] quality
Qualitätsmuster *n* representative sample; quality sample
Qualitätsniveau *n* quality level
~, toleriertes *(stats)* acceptable quality level
~, zulässiges *s.* **~, toleriertes**
Qualitätsparameter *mpl* quality criteria
Qualitätsplanung *f* quality planning
Qualitätsprobe *f* 1. quality test; 2. sample
Qualitätsproduktion *f* quality production
Qualitätsprüfung *f* quality test [inspection]
Qualitätsrente *f* differential ground rent
Qualitätsrisiko *n* quality risk
Qualitätsschutz *m* quality protection
Qualitätssicherung *f* ensuring (good) quality, quality assurance
Qualitätsstandard *m* standard of quality, quality standard
Qualitätssteigerung *f* improving [raising] the quality, quality improvement
Qualitätsstufe *f* grade, class *(of product)*
Qualitätstest *m* quality test
Qualitätsüberwachung *f s.* **Qualitätskontrolle**
Qualitätsunterschied *m* difference in quality
Qualitätsuntersuchung *f s.* **Qualitätskontrolle**
Qualitätsveränderung *f* change in quality
Qualitätsverbesserung *f* quality improvement
Qualitätsvereinbarung *f* agreement on quality
Qualitätsverlust *m s.* **Qualitätsminderung**
Qualitätsverschlechterung *f* deterioration in quality
Qualitätsvorschriften *fpl* quality rules [specifications]
Qualitätsware *f s.* **Qualitätserzeugnis**
Qualitätswaren *fpl* high-quality [high-class] goods
Qualitätszeichen *n* quality mark
Qualitätszertifikat *n s.* **Qualitätsbescheinigung**
Qualitätszeugnis *n s.* **Qualitätsbescheinigung**
Qualitätszuschlag *m* additional charge for quality
Qualitätszuwachs *m s.* **Qualitätsverbesserung**
quanteln to quantize *(quantity, energy etc.)*
Quantelung *f* quantization *(quantity, energy etc.)*
Quantifikation *f s.* **Quantifizierung**
quantifizierbar quantifiable
quantifizieren to quantify
Quantifizierung *f* quantification
Quantil *n (stats)* fractile, quantile

quantisieren *s.* **quanteln**
Quantisierung *f s.* **Quantelung**
Quantität *f* quantity
quantitativ quantitative
Quantitätsbestimmung *f* fixing [defining] the quantity
Quantitätsfunktion *f (stats)* quantity function
Quantitätsgleichung *f (stats)* quantity equation
Quantitätskontrolle *f* quantity check, checking the quantity
Quantitätstheorie *f* quantity theory *(of money)*
Quantitätszuwachs *m* increase in quantity
Quantum *n* quantity, amount, quantum; portion, share
Quarantäne *f* quarantine
Quarantänegelder *npl* quarantine charges
Quartal *n* quarter (of a year); term *(school)*
Quartalsabrechnung *f* quarterly account(ing); quarterly balance (sheet); quarterly statement (of accounts)
Quartalsabschluß *m* quarterly balance (sheet); quarterly statement (of accounts)
Quartalsanalyse *f* quarterly analysis
Quartalsbericht *m* quarterly statement
Quartalsdividende *f* quarterly dividend
Quartalskassenplan *m* quarterly cash plan
Quartalskreditplan *m* quarterly credit plan
quartalsmäßig quarterly
Quartalsplan *m* quarterly plan
~, operativer current quarterly plan
Quartalsprämie *f* quarterly bonus
Quartalsumsatz *m* quarterly turnover [sales]
Quartalsverrechnung *f* quarterly clearing [settlement]
Quartalsversorgungsplan *m* quarterly plan of provision *(goods and services)*
quartalsweise quarterly
Quartalszahlung *f* quarterly payment
Quartiergeld *n* lodging money
Quartil *n (stats)* quartile
~, oberes *(stats)* upper quartile
~, unteres *(stats)* lower quartile
Quartilabstand *m (stats)* quartile deviation, interquartile range
~, halber *(stats)* semi-interquartile range
Quasimonopol *n* quasi monopoly
Quelle *f* source *(data, river etc.)*; origin *(report etc.)*; spring; well
Quellenprogramm *n (d.pr.)* source program
Querkontrolle *f* cross-checking
Querkorrelation *f* **(zwischen geordneten Reihen)** *(stats)* cross-correlation
Querprüfung *f (d.pr.)* vertical redundancy check
Querrechnung *f (d.pr.)* cross footing
Querschnitt *m* cross section *(people, goods in display etc.)*; representative sample *(population etc.)*; profile *(moulding etc.)*

Querschnittsabteilung *f* general management [administrative] department *(e.g. finance, planning, general administration, as opposed to production departments etc.)*
Querschnittsanalyse *f* cross-section analysis [study]
Querschnittsprognose *f* general long-term forecast
Querschnittsprogramm *n* general programme
Querschnittsstichprobe *f (stats)* general random sample method
Querschnittsuntersuchung *f s.* **Querschnittsanalyse**
querschreiben to cross *(cheque)*; to accept *(bill of exchange)*
QUEST-Methode *f* QUEST method *(QUEST = quantitative utility estimate for science and technology)*
quittieren 1. to receipt *(bill)*; to sign for *(sum of money etc.)*; 2. to resign [retire] from, to leave *(business, work etc.)*
Quittung *f* receipt; voucher ⋄ **eine ~ ausstellen** to make [write] out a receipt; **gegen ~** on receipt; **laut ~** as per receipt
~, gültige good [valid] receipt
~, ordnungsgemäße receipt in due form
Quittungsbuch *n* receipt book
Quittungsduplikat *n* duplicate receipt
Quittungsformular *n* receipt form
Quittungskarte *f* receipt card
Quittungsvordruck *m s.* **Quittungsformular**
Quote *f* quota; share, (pro)portion
~ des Inlandsabsatzes domestic tariff area sales ratio (DTASR)
Quotenaktie *f* no-par-value share [stock], share of no par value
Quotenerhöhung *f* increase in the quota
Quotenheraufsetzung *f s.* **Quotenerhöhung**
Quotenkampf *m* competition for more favourable quotas
Quotenkartell *n* quota cartel, cartel in which output quotas are allocated to the member firms, *(Am)* commodity restriction scheme
Quotenrückversicherung *f (ins)* quota-share reinsurance
Quotenstichprobe *f (stats)* quota sample
Quoten-Stichprobenverfahren *n (stats)* quota sample method
Quotensystem *n* quota system
Quotenverfahren *n (stats)* quota sampling
Quotient *m* quotient
quotieren to quote *(price etc.)*
Quotierung *f* quotation
Quotitätssteuer *f* tax levied according to a fixed rate, percentage tax

R

Rabatt *m* discount; rebate; deduction ⋄ **einem ~ unterliegen** to be subject to a discount; **einen ~ gewähren** to allow [grant, give] a discount *(on s.th.)*; **mit ~ verkaufen** to sell at a discount; **mit 10% ~** at a discount [reduction] of 10 per cent, at a 10 per cent discount
~ bei Großbestellung large-order discount, quantity [volume] discount
~ für Barzahlung discount for cash, cash discount
~ für vorfristige Zahlung anticipative discount
~, nachträglich gegebener discount given subsequently
~, verschleierter hidden discount
~, zusätzlicher additional discount
Rabattberechnung *f* discount calculation
Rabattbuch *n* discount book
Rabattgabe *f s.* **Rabattgewährung**
Rabattgewährung *f* granting of discount
Rabattgruppe *f* discount group *(commodities etc.)*
rabattieren to give [grant, allow] a discount [reduction] *(on s.th.)*
Rabattkartell *n* discount(ing) cartel
Rabattklausel *f* discount clause
Rabattmarke *f* trading stamp, discount token [stamp]
Rabattsatz *m* discount rate
Rabattsparmarke *f s.* **Rabattmarke**
radikal radical, drastic *(measure, change etc.)*; extreme *(action etc.)*; ruthless *(pursuit of aims etc.)*; complete *(abolition, change etc.)*; absolute *(rejection etc.)*
radikalisieren to radicalize
Radikalismus *m* radicalism, extremism
Raffinerie *f* refinery
raffinieren to refine
Raffprobe *f (stats)* chunk sampling
Rahmen *m* frame(work); scope; *(stats)* framed structure
Rahmenabkommen *n* general [framework, overall, basic, skeleton] agreement
Rahmenfunktionsplan *m* general [skeleton] job description *(s.* **Funktionsplan***)*
Rahmengebühr *f* general rate
Rahmengesetz *n* law providing the framework for specific legislation, framework law
Rahmenkatalog *m* skeleton catalogue
Rahmenkennziffernprogramm *n* general [skeleton] programme of indices [indicators]
Rahmenkollektivvertrag *m* general collective agreement
Rahmenkreditvertrag *m* global [general] credit agreement

Rahmenlieferungsabkommen *n* general agreement on deliveries
Rahmenmerkmal *n* general characteristic
Rahmenmethodik *f* general [skeleton] methods
~, vorläufige provisional general [skeleton] methods
Rahmennetzplan *m* general network
Rahmenordnung *f s.* **Rahmenvorschriften**
Rahmenstellenplan *m* general [skeleton] job plan
Rahmenstrukturplan *m* general structure *(of organization etc.)*
Rahmentarif *m* framework [skeleton] wage scale
Rahmentechnologie *f* general technology
Rahmenvertrag *m s.* **Rahmenabkommen**
Rahmenvorschriften *fpl* general regulations
Ramsch *m* junk (goods), job goods ◊ **im ~ kaufen** to buy in (job) lots; **im ~ verkaufen** sell as a job lot
Ramschgeschäft *n* 1. junk business; 2. junk shop
Ramschhandel *m* junk trade
Ramschhändler *m* junk dealer
Ramschhandlung *f s.* **Ramschladen**
Ramschkauf *m* buying in job lots
Ramschladen *m* junk shop
Ramschware *f s.* **Ramsch**
Ramschverkauf *m* sale in job lots
Rand *m* outskirts, periphery, *(town etc.)*; margin *(page etc.)*; *(stats)* barrier
~, absorbierender *(stats)* absorbing barrier
~, quadratischer *(stats)* quadrat
Randbedingungen *fpl* marginal terms [conditions]; *(maths)* boundary conditions
Randbereinigung *f (stats)* end corrections
Randbevölkerung *f* fringe population
Randeinteilung *f (stats)* marginal classification
Randgebiet *n* fringe *(area, subject)*; outskirts (town); border area, borderland *(country)*
Randgruppe *f* fringe (group)
Randklasse *f (stats)* marginal category
Randlochkarte *f* edge-punched card
Randomisierung *f (stats)* randomization
Randsiedlung *f* suburban housing estate, *(Am)* suburban settlement
Randzone *f* marginal [peripheral] zone
Rang *m* grade, rate *(remuneration)*; order, priority, rank *(precedence)*; rank, standing, status *(position)*; quality, class, grade *(product)*; class *(lottery, dividend)*
Rangänderung *f* change(s) in the order of precedence; alteration [change] in the order of priorities, change of priority *(mortgages etc.)*
Rangfolge *f* (order of) precedence, order (of rank); priority
Rangierbahnhof *m* shunting [marshalling] yard, *(Am)* switchyard

rangieren 1. to rank *(before or behind s.o./s.th.)*; 2. *(railw)* to shunt, *(Am)* to switch
Rangiergebühr *f* shunting [*(Am)* switching] charge
Rangklasse *f* rank grouping
Rangkorrelation *f (stats)* rank correlation
~, partielle *(stats)* partial rank correlation
Rangkorrelationskoeffizient *m (stats)* Kendall's tau, coefficient of rank correlation
~, Spearman'scher *(stats)* Spearman's coefficient of rank correlation
Rangliste *f* ranking list, rankings
Rangordnung *f* hierarchy, order of priorities [precedence], ranking (order)
~, konjugierte *(stats)* conjugate ranking
Rangordnungsgrad *m (stats)* grade
Rangordnungsmaßzahlen *fpl (stats)* rank order statistics
Rangordnungsmerkmal *n (stats)* characteristic of ranking
Rangordnungsnummer *f (stats)* rank
Rangordnungsproblem *n*:
~, Galton'sches *(stats)* Galton's individual difference problem
Rangstufe *f* (degree of) rank; priority
Rangsummentest *m*:
~, Mann-Whitney'scher *(stats)* Mann-Whitney test
~, Wilcoxon's *(stats)* Wilcoxon's test
Rangzahl *f s.* **Rangordnungsnummer**
Rankit *n (stats)* rankit
Rapport *m* (regular) report *(to head of office etc.)*
Rapprochement *n* rapprochement, reconciliation
Rarität *f* rarity; rare specimen [article], curio(sity)
Raritätenhandel *m* trade in rare articles [curios]
Rasse *f* race; breed *(animals etc.)*; subspecies *(plants etc.)*
Rassendiskriminierung *f* racial [race] discrimination
Rassenfrage *f* racial issue
Rassenkreuzung *f (agric)* crossbreeding
Rassenpolitik *f* racial policy
Rassenproblem *n* racial [race] problem *(of discrimination)*
Rassentrennung *f* racial segregation
Rassevieh *n* pedigree [registered] cattle
Raststätte *f* motorway restaurant, roadhouse
Rat *m* 1. (piece of) advice, counsel; suggestion; recommendation; 2. council, board; 3. councillor
~ der Gemeinde village [parish] council; municipal council
~ der Stadt town [city] council, municipal council
~ des Bezirks county council

~ des Kreises district council
~ des Stadtbezirks urban district [borough] council, district [borough] council *(of a town/ city)*
~, örtlicher local [municipal] council
~, pädagogischer teachers' council; teachers' staff meeting
~, wissenschaftlicher academic council
Rate *f* instalment; rate *(of growth etc.)*; freight rate, freight, freightage
~ der Verwertung rate of exploitation
~ des Mehrprodukts rate of surplus product
~ des Mehrwerts rate of surplus value
~ des Zinsfußes rate of interest
~, jährliche yearly [annual] instalment
~, monatliche monthly instalment
~, offene unpaid instalment
~, vierteljährliche quarterly instalment
Raten *fpl*:
  ◇ auf ~ kaufen to buy by instalments [on the instalment system, on hire-purchase]; **in festen ~** by fixed instalments; **in festgesetzten ~** by stated [in specified] instalments; **in ~ zahlen** to pay by instalments; **rückzahlbar in ~** repayable by [in] instalments
Ratenanleihe *f* instalment loan, loan to be repaid in (annual) instalments
Ratenanstieg *m* increase in the number of instalments
Ratenbrief *m* instalment purchase agreement [contract]
Ratenerhöhung *f* increase in freight rates
Ratengeschäft *n* instalment trading; hire purchase
Ratenhandel *m s.* **Ratengeschäft**
Ratenhypothek *f* mortgage with equal annual capital repayments, instalment mortgage
Ratenkauf *m* hire purchase; purchase by instalments, instalment purchase, deferred payment system
Ratenkredit *m* credit for financing hire purchase; consumer [instalment] credit
Ratenschulden *fpl* instalment debts
Ratensparvertrag *m* contract for saving in fixed instalments
Ratentermin *m* date for paying instalment
Ratentilgung *f* repayment of instalments
Ratenverkauf *m* instalment sale
Ratenwechsel *m* bill of exchange payable by instalments, multi-maturity bill of exchange
ratenweise in [by] instalments
Ratenzahlung *f* payment by instalments ◇ **auf ~** on the hire purchase [instalment] system [*(Am)* plan]
Ratenzahlungsgeschäft *n* hire purchase business; hire purchase transaction
Ratenzahlungskredit *m s.* **Ratenkredit**

Räterepublik *f* republic governed by workers' councils
Rätesystem *n* system of government by workers' councils
Rathaus *n* town [*(Am)* city] hall
Ratifikation *f* ratification
Ratifikationsurkunde *f* (document of) ratification ◇ **die ~ hinterlegen** to deposit the (document of) ratification
ratifizieren to ratify
Ratifizierung *f s.* **Ratifikation**
Ration *f* ration
rational rational
Rationalisatorenbewegung *f* drive for rationalization (in production)
rationalisieren to rationalize, to streamline
Rationalisierung *f* rationalization
~, komplexe comprehensive rationalization
~, territoriale regional rationalization
Rationalisierungsaufwand *m* rationalization expenditure
Rationalisierungsbüro *n* rationalization office
Rationalisierungseffekt *m* rationalization effect
Rationalisierungsfachmann *m* efficiency [rationalization] expert; time-and-motion--study man; industrial engineer
Rationalisierungsfinanzierung *f* financing of rationalization
Rationalisierungsfonds *m* rationalization fund
Rationalisierungsgrad *m* degree [level] of rationalization
Rationalisierungsinvestition *f* investment for rationalization, rationalization investment; modernization investment
Rationalisierungskonzeption *f* programme of rationalization
Rationalisierungskosten *pl* rationalization costs
Rationalisierungskredit *m* rationalization credit
Rationalisierungsmaßnahme *f* rationalization measure
Rationalisierungsmethode *f* method of rationalization
Rationalisierungsmittel *npl* rationalization resources *(financial and material)*
Rationalisierungsnutzen *m* benefit of rationalization (measures), returns on rationalization
Rationalisierungsprogramm *n* rationalization programme
Rationalisierungsvorhaben *n* rationalization project
Rationalisierungsvorschlag *m* proposal of a rationalization measure [an innovation]
Rationalisierungswesen *n* system of rationalization
rationell efficient, economical *(method, planning, organization etc.)*
rationieren to ration; to allot *(stocks, securities)*

Rationierung f rationing
~ **von Devisen** foreign exchange rationing
~ **von Lebensmitteln** food rationing
~ **von Waren** rationing of goods
Ratssitzung f s. **Ratstagung**
Ratstagung f council meeting
Ratsversammlung f 1. council, assembly; 2. council meeting
Raub m 1. robbery; 2. booty, plunder, spoils, loot
Raubbau m over-exploitation, exhaustion *(of natural resources etc.)* ⋄ ~ **treiben** to over--exploit, to exploit ruthlessly
rauben to rob
räuberisch rapacious, predatory
Räucherwaren *fpl* smoked meat; smoked fish
Rauchversicherung f smoke insurance
Rauchwaren *fpl* 1. tobacco products; 2. furs, pelts
Rauchwarenauktion f auction of furs and pelts
Rauchwarenbörse f s. **Rauchwarenauktion**
Rauhgewicht n (gross) weight *(piece of jewellery etc., made of an alloy of a precious metal)*
Raum m room, space; area, district, zone; locality; hall
~, **besetzter** space occupied [taken up]
~, **erforderlicher** space required
~, **gewerblich genutzter** space used for commercial purposes
~, **in Anspruch genommener** s. ~, **besetzter**
~, **umbauter** enclosed area
Raumanordnung f layout of rooms, floor plan
Raumausnutzung f space utilization
Raumausstattung f 1. equipping of a room; 2. equipment in a room
Raumbedarf m (amount of) space required; storage factor *(ship)*
Raumeinheit f spatial unit
räumen to clear *(snow, rubble etc.)*; to remove *(obstacles etc.)*; to vacate *(flat etc.)*; to evacuate *(building, town etc.)*; to dredge *(port, river etc.)*
Raumersparnis f saving (in) space
Raumgestalter m interior decorator [designer]
Raumgestaltung f interior decoration [design]
Raumgewicht n volumetric weight
Rauminhalt m volume, capacity, cubic content
raumintensiv requiring a lot of space
räumlich spatial, of [relating to] space; three--dimensional
Räumlichkeit f premises, room(s); spatiality
Raummangel m lack of room [space]; restricted space
Raumordnung f regional [area] (development) planning; regional [area] development
Raumplanung f 1. regional [area] (development) planning; spatial planning; 2. (planned) allocation [distribution] of rooms

raumsparend space-saving
Räumung f clearance *(room etc.)*; removal *(obstacles etc.)*; *(jur)* eviction, *(Am)* ejectment; evacuation *(building, town etc.)*; dredging *(port, river etc.)*
Räumungsarbeiten *fpl* clearing operations
Räumungsausverkauf m clearance sale
Räumungsbefehl m eviction notice, *(Am)* writ of ejectment
Räumungsfrist f period within which a tenant has to quit premises, time (set) for moving out [for vacating rented property]
Räumungsklage f action for eviction [*(Am)* ejectment]
Räumungspreis m clearance price
Räumungsurteil n eviction order
Räumungsverkauf m clearance sale, (enforced) sale of stock *(due to damage to goods etc.)*; liquidation [closing-down] sale *(when liquidating a business)*
Raumverschwendung f waste of space
Raumverteilung f 1. planned use of space; allocation [distribution] of rooms; 2. space [spatial] distribution; layout *(of room(s) etc.)*
Rauschgift n narcotic (drug), drug
Rauschgifthandel m drug traffic
Rauschgifthändler m drug trafficker; drug dealer
Rayon m district, area
Reaktion f reaction, response *(to s.th.)*; *(pol)* reaction
~ **der Konsumenten, günstige** favourable reaction from consumers
~ **der Konsumenten, ungünstige** adverse reaction from consumers
~, **quadratische** *(stats)* quadratic response
~, **quantitative** *(stats)* quantitative response
Reaktionär m *(pol)* reactionary
Reaktionszeit f *(stats)* response time
Reaktionszeiten-Verteilung f *(stats)* response--time distribution
Realakkumulation f real accumulation
Realbesitz m landed property
Realeinkommen n real income [earnings]
~, **verbrauchswirksames** real income spent on wage goods
~, **verfügbares** real income available
~, **verwendetes** real income used (up)
Realeinkommensbilanz f balance sheet of the formation and utilization of real income
Realeinkommensindex m real income index
realisierbar realizable; practicable
Realisierbarkeit f realizability
realisieren to implement, to carry out *(plan etc.)*, to realize; to convert (into money); to effect *(sale)*, to sell; to materialize
Realisierung f implementation *(plan etc.)*, realization; sale; materialization

Realisierungsbedingungen *fpl* conditions of realization [implementation]
Realisierungsfrist *f* (appointed period of) time for implementation [realization]; gestation period *(project)*
Realisierungsmethode *f* method of realization [implementation]
Realisierungsphase *f* stage of realization [implementation]
Realisierungsrisiko *n* implementation risk, risk involved in realization
Realisierungsschwierigkeiten *fpl* difficulties in realization [implementation]
Realisierungstermin *m s.* **Realisierungsfrist**
Realisierungsvereinbarung *f* innovation realization agreement
Realisierungswert *m* realized value
Realität *f* reality
~, **objektive** objective reality
Realkapital *n* 1. real capital; 2. real estate
Realkosten *pl* real costs
Realkostenindex *m* index of real costs
Realkredit *m* credit on real estate, real estate loan
Realkreditinstitut *n* mortgage bank
Reallast(en) *f(pl)* recurrent charges on real estate
Reallohn *m* real wages
Reallohnentwicklung *f* development of real wages
Reallohnerhöhung *f* increase in [growth of] real wages
Reallohnindex *m* index of real wages
Reallohnsenkung *f* decrease in real wages
Realobligationen *fpl* real estate bonds
Realpfandrecht *n* mortgage lien, hypothecary right
Realpreis *m* real price
Realpreisindex *m* index of real prices
Realprodukt *n* real product
Realrecht *n (agric)* land act; real property law
Realsteuer *f* non-personal tax, tax on real estate; trade tax
Realvermögen *n* real estate
Realwert *m* real value
Realzins *m* real (rate of) interest, interest (rate) in real terms
Rechenanlage *f* computer
~, **programmgesteuerte** program-controlled computer
Rechenaufwand *m* 1. computing expenses [costs]; 2. computing time
Rechenautomat *m s.* **Rechenanlage**
Rechenbefehl *m (d.pr.)* arithmetic instruction
Rechenbetrieb *m s.* **Rechenzentrum**
Recheneinheit *f (d.pr.)* arithmetic unit
Rechengeschwindigkeit *f (d.pr.)* calculating [computing] speed

Rechenlocher *m (d.pr.)* calculating punch(er)
Rechenmaschine *f* calculating machine, calculator; computer
Rechenpreis *m* price indicator
Rechen-Probit *m (stats)* working probit
Rechenprogramm *n s.* **Rechnerprogramm**
Rechenschaft *f* account ◊ ~ **ablegen** to give [render] (an) account *(of s.th.)*; to account, to answer *(for s.th.)*
Rechenschaftsbericht *m* account, statement (of accounts); report (of activities); accounts rendered
Rechenschaftslegung *f* reporting, rendering an account
Rechenschaftspflicht *f* accountability
rechenschaftspflichtig accountable *(to s.o.)*, answerable *(to s.o.)*
Rechenstation *f s.* **Rechenzentrum**
Rechenverfahren *n* method of calculation
Rechenwerk *n (d.pr.)* arithmetic section [element, unit]
Rechenzeit *f* computing time
Rechenzentrum *n* computer centre
Recherche *f* inquiry, investigation; (official) search *(for prior patent specifications)*
Recherchemethode *f* method of investigation
Recherchemittel *n* means [instrument] of investigation [inquiry]
rechnen to reckon, to calculate, to compute; to count
Rechnen *n* calculation, reckoning; arithmetic
~, **maschinelles** computer-based calculation
Rechner *m s.* **Rechenanlage**
rechnergesteuert computer-controlled
rechnergestützt computer-aided; computer--assisted, computerized
rechnerisch mathematical, arithmetical, computational, by way of calculation
Rechnerkapazität *f* computer power
Rechnerprogramm *n* computer program
Rechnersprache *f* computer [machine] language
Rechnersteuerung *f* computer forward control
Rechnersystem *n* computer system
rechnerunterstützt *s.* **rechnergestützt**
Rechnerverbund *m* computer network
Rechnerverbundbetrieb *m* multiprocessing
Rechnerverbundnetz *n* distributed processing system
Rechnerverbundsystem *n* multiprocessing system
Rechnerzeit *f* computing time
Rechnung *f* 1. calculation, reckoning, computation; 2. account, bill, invoice ◊ **auf eigene ~** on [for] s.o.'s own account; **auf feste ~ kaufen** *(st.ex.)* to buy firm; **auf fremde ~** on [for] the account of another *(person etc.)*; **auf gemeinschaftliche ~** on [for] joint account;

auf Ihre ~ on [for] your account; **auf Ihre ~ und Gefahr** on your account and risk; **auf neue ~** on new account; **auf ~** on account; **auf ~ eines Dritten** on account of a third person [party]; **auf ~ kaufen** to buy on account [credit]; **eine ~ ausstellen** to make out a bill; to draw [make out] an account **eine ~ beanstanden** to query [question] an invoice; **eine ~ begleichen** to settle [balance] an account, to pay [settle] a bill; **für feste ~ kaufen** s. **auf feste ~ kaufen**; **jmdm. etwas in ~ stellen** to charge s.o. with s.th., to charge [debit, place, put] s.th. to s.o.'s account; **laut ~** as per invoice; **~ (ab)legen** to render (an) account *(of s.th.)*

~, fällige invoice due, payable invoice
~, fingierte fictitious invoice
~, laufende current account
~, offene outstanding account [bill, invoice]
~, provisorische s. **~, vorläufige**
~, spezifizierte specified invoice
~, vorläufige temporary [provisional] bill
Rechnungsabgrenzung *f* separation of items applicable to a future accounting period, apportionment of [between] accounting periods, accruals and deferrals
Rechnungsabgrenzungsposten *m* deferred item, item applicable to a future period, accounting apportionment item
Rechnungsabschluß *m* 1. closing of accounts; final settlement (of accounts); account settled; 2. statement of account
Rechnungsausschuß *m* audit committee
Rechnungsauszug *m* statement of account; extract of account
Rechnungsbeleg *m* voucher
Rechnungsbetrag *m* amount invoiced [of invoice]
Rechnungsbuch *n* account book, book of accounts, invoice book
Rechnungsdatum *n* date of invoice
Rechnungsdefizit *n* accounting deficit
Rechnungsdoppel *n* duplicate invoice
Rechnungseinheit *f* accounting unit; unit of account
Rechnungserteilung *f* invoicing
Rechnungsführer *m* accountant
Rechnungsführung *f* accountancy, accounting
~, wirtschaftliche economic accountancy [accounting]
Rechnungshof *m* audit office
Rechnungsjahr *n* financial [fiscal] year
Rechnungslegung *f* rendering of accounts
Rechnungsposten *m* item of account [(a) bill], invoice item
Rechnungspreis *m* invoice price
Rechnungsprüfer *m* auditor

Rechnungsprüfung *f* audit(ing) (of accounts); checking (of accounts)
Rechnungsstellung *f* s. **Rechnungserteilung**
Rechnungsüberschuß *m* accounting surplus
Rechnungswert *m* invoice value, value as per invoice
Rechnungswesen *n* accounting, accountancy
Recht *n* law *(of statute etc.)*; right, privilege; claim, interest; power, authority *(of jurisdiction etc.)*; title ◊ **auf ein ~ verzichten** to abandon [disclaim, waive] a right; **auf seinem ~ bestehen** to assert [insist on, stand on] one's right(s); **das ~ auf seiner Seite haben** to be within one's rights, to be in the right; **ein ~ ausüben** to exercise a right [power]; **ein ~ geltend machen** to assert [uphold] a right; to vindicate a right; **ein ~ haben (auf etwas)** to have right [claim] (to s.th.); to be entitled *(to/to do s.th.)*; to be eligible *(for/to do s.th.)*; **jmdm. sein ~ geben** to give s.o. his right(s); **nach geltendem ~** under law in force; **zu ~ bestehen** to be valid [justified, legally founded]; **zu seinem ~ kommen** to come into one's own right(s)

~, abtretbares transferable right
~ an einer Erfindung right to an invention
~, angeborenes inherent right
~, alleiniges sole right
~ auf Arbeit right to work
~ auf Auskunftserteilung right to demand information; right to obtain information
~ auf Bildung right of education and training
~ auf Erholung und Freizeit right of recreation and leisure time
~ auf medizinische Versorgung right to medical care
~ auf Mitbestimmung right of co-determination; right of participation in decision-making
~ des Besitzes right of possession, possessory right
~, feststehendes vested right *(not related to special conditions)*
~, geltendes existing [prevailing] law, law in force
~, internationales international law
~, unangreifbares indefeasible right
~, vertraglich begründetes contractual right
Rechte, die *(pol)* Right, right wing *(party etc.)*
Rechte *npl*:
  ◊ **alle ~ vorbehalten** all rights reserved; **die ~ berühren** to affect the rights; **gleiche ~ gewähren** to give equal rights; **in jmds. ~ eintreten** to succeed to s.o.'s rights
~ Dritter third-party rights
~, materielle substantive rights
~ und Pflichten *fpl* rights and obligations [liabilities] (under a contract)

Rechteck *n* rectangle
~, lateinisches *(stats)* Latin rectangle
Rechtecksverteilung *f (stats)* uniform [rectangular] distribution
rechtlich legal; lawful, legitimate; valid ◊ **~ erheblich** relevant (in law) [(to the issue)]; **~ unerheblich** irrelevant (in law) [(to the issue)]; **~ verpflichtet** bound by (the) law
rechtlos without rights, rightless
Rechtlosigkeit *f* rightlessness, (total) absence of rights; lawlessness
rechtmäßig legal, legitimate; lawful; rightful; just, fair, fair and proper ◊ **für ~ erklären** to legitimate, to legalize
Rechtmäßigkeit *f* legality, legitimacy; lawfulness; rightfulness; validity
Rechtsabteilung *f* legal department
Rechtsangelegenheit *f* legal matter
Rechtsanspruch *m* legal claim *(on/to s.th.)*, title *(to s.th.)*
Rechtsanwalt *m* lawyer; solicitor; (legal) counsel, barrister, *(Am)* attorney(-at-law)
Rechtsauffassung *f* conception of the law; interpretation of (the) law
Rechtsausdruck *m* legal term
Rechtsauslegung *f* legal interpretation, interpretation of the law
Rechtsausschuß *m* judicial committee; committee on legal affairs
Rechtsbefugnis *f* competence
Rechtsbeistand *m s.* **Rechtsberater**
Rechtsberater *m* legal adviser [consultant] (legal) counsel
Rechtsberatungsstelle *f* legal advisory board
Rechtsbeschwerde *f* appeal
Rechtsbestimmungen *fpl* provisions of the law, legal provisions
Rechtsbeugung *f* perversion of justice; (intentional) misconstruction of the law
Rechtsbruch *m* breach [infringement] of (the) law
Rechtseinwand *m* demurrer, objection
rechtsfähig having legal capacity [status]; capable of rights and duties
Rechtsfähigkeit *f* legal capacity [status]
Rechtsfall *m* court case
~, analoger *(jur)* precedent
Rechtsform *f* legal form
Rechtsfrage *f* point [issue, question] of law, legal issue [question]
Rechtsgeschäft *n* legal transaction [act]
Rechtsgrund *m* legal argument; title *(claim)*
Rechtsgrundlage *f* legal basis [grounds]
Rechtsgrundsatz *m* legal maxim
rechtsgültig valid, good [valid] in law, legally effective, having legal force, *(Am)* entitled to full faith and credit

Rechtsgültigkeit *f* validity; legality
Rechtsgutachten *n* (legal) opinion, counsel's opinion
Rechtshilfe *f* legal assistance [aid]
Rechtsirrtum *m* error [mistake] in law
Rechtskraft *f* legal force [effect(iveness)], (legal) validity ◊ **~ erlangen** to become effective [final], to enter into effect; **~ haben** to be conclusive
rechtskräftig legal, legally binding [effective], valid; final, non-appealable *(judgement)*
rechtskundig legally trained
Rechtslage *f* legal position [status]
Rechtsmangel *m* defect [deficiency] in a title *(goods etc.)*
Rechtsmittel *n* legal remedy [relief]; right of appeal ◊ **~ einlegen** to lodge [take] an appeal
Rechtsmittelbelehrung *f (jur)* information on the means and period of appeal *(given when court's decision is announced)*
Rechtsmittelgericht *n* appellate court
Rechtsmittelverfahren *n* appeal procedure
Rechtsmittelverzicht *m* waiver of legal remedy
Rechtsnachfolge *f* (legal) succession, succession in title
Rechtsnachfolger *m* (legal) successor, successor in interest [title], assign(ee)
Rechtsnorm *f* legal norm [standard], established law
Rechtsordnung *f* legal system, established law
Rechtspflege *f* administration of justice, judicature
Rechtsprechung *f* jurisdication, administration of justice; court decisions
Rechtsprinzipien *npl* legal principles
Rechtsquelle *f* source of law, legal source
~, formelle formal legal source
~, materielle material legal source
rechtsradikal extreme right-wing
Rechtsradikaler *m* right-wing extremist
Rechtssache *f* (legal) case [matter]
Rechtsschutz *m* legal protection
~, gewerblicher protection of inventions
Rechtssicherheit *f* unequivocal administration of the law, predictability of legal decisions; legal certainty, undisputed legal position
Rechtsspruch *m* legal decision; judgement *(civil law)*; sentence *(criminal law)*; verdict *(jury)*
Rechtsstaat *m* constitutional state
rechtsstaatlich constitutional, in conformity with the rule of law
Rechtsstaatlichkeit *f* constitutionality, rule of law
Rechtsstellung *f* legal status [position]
Rechtsstreit *m* (legal) action, (law) suit, litigation
Rechtssystem *n* legal system

Rechtstheorie *f* legal theory
Rechtsträger *m* legal entity
rechtsunfähig having no legal status
Rechtsunfähigkeit *f* legal incapacity
rechtsungültig invalid; illegal
rechtsunwirksam (legally) ineffective, without legal force, invalid
Rechtsunwirksamkeit *f* legal ineffectiveness
rechtsverbindlich legally binding *(on s.o.)*
Rechtsverfahren *n* legal procedure; legal action [proceedings]
Rechtsverhältnis *n* legal relationship
Rechtsverhältnisse *npl* legal relations
Rechtsverkehr *m* 1. *(jur)* legal procedure; 2. right-hand traffic
Rechtsverletzung *f* infringement [violation] of a right; infringement [violation] of a law
Rechtsverordnung *f* statutory instrument
Rechtsvertreter *m* legal representative
Rechtsvorschriften *fpl* legal provisions
Rechtsweg *m* legal action, recourse to the law [the courts] ◊ **auf dem ~** by legal action; **den ~ beschreiten** to take legal action [steps, measures]
rechtswidrig illegal, unlawful, contrary to (the) law
Rechtswidrigkeit *f* illegality, unlawfulness; unlawful [wrongful] act
rechtswirksam s. **rechtskräftig**
Rediskont *m* rediscount
rediskontfähig eligible for rediscount, rediscountable
rediskontieren to rediscount
Rediskontsatz *m* rediscount rate
Reduktion *f* reduction *(prices etc.)*
Redundanzprüfung *f (d.pr.)* redundancy check
reduzierbar reducible *(price, tariff etc.)*
reduzieren to cut, to reduce, to lower *(price, tariff etc.)*; to lower, to diminish *(value, quality etc.)*; to cut down, to reduce *(expenditure etc.)*
Reduzierung *f* reduction *(price, tariff etc.)*
Reede *f* roadstead, roads
Reeder *m* shipowner
Reederei *f* shipping company
Reexport *m* re-export(ation)
Reexportgeschäft *n* re-exports; re-export business
Reexportklausel *f* re-export clause
REFA-Mann *m* time-and-methods study man
Referendum *n* referendum
Referent *m* person presenting a paper [report]; official in charge *(of a subject or department)*
refinanzieren to refinance; to rediscount
Refinanzierung *f* refinancing
Refinanzierungskredit *m* credit for refinancing
Reform *f* reform
~, einschneidende stringent reform

~, radikale radical reform
~, steuerliche reform of tax laws
~, tiefgreifende far-reaching reform
reformbedürftig in need of reform(s)
Reformbestrebungen *fpl* efforts towards reforms
Reformbewegung *f* reform movement
Reformgesetz *n* reform bill; reform law
Reformhaus *n* health-food shop
reformieren to reform *(institution, law etc.)*
Reformkurs *m* policy [line] of reform
Reformpolitik *f* policy of reform
Reformwaren *fpl* health foods; health products
Regel *f* rule; (guiding) rule [principle]
Regelabweichung *f* deviation from the rule
Regelbelastung *f* normal load
Regeleinrichtung *f* control device
Regelfall *m* normal case
Regelgröße *f (d.pr.)* controlled variable
Regelkreis *m (d.pr.)* regulating circuit; feedback control system, feedback [control] loop
Regelleistung *f* standard work performed; *(ins)* normal [minimum] benefit
Regelleistungspreise *mpl* cost of standard work performed
Regelmechanismus *m* 1. (economic) regulating mechanism; 2. *(tech)* control device [mechanism]
regeln to settle *(matter, debt etc.)*; to fix *(date, price etc.)*; to put in order *(affairs, finances etc.)*; *(jur)* to regulate *(procedure, succession etc. by law)*; *(tech)* to regulate *(speed etc.)*, to control *(volume etc.)*
Regelparameter *m* control parameter
Regelsystem *n* control system
Regeltarif *m* normal rate *(charges etc.)*
Regeltechnik *f* control engineering
Regelung *f* settlement *(matter, debt etc.)*; fixing *(date, price etc.)*; putting in order *(affairs, finances etc.)*; *(jur)* regulation *(of procedure, succession etc. by law)*; *(tech)* regulation *(speed etc.)*, control *(volume etc.)*
Regelungstechnik *f s.* **Regeltechnik**
Regelungstheorie *f* theory of (automatic) control
Regelvorrichtung *f* control device
Regeneration *f* regeneration *(fibres, oil etc.)*; reclaiming *(rubber etc.)*; recycling *(waste material etc.)*
regenerieren to regenerate *(fibres, oil etc.)*; to reclaim *(rubber etc.)*; to recycle *(waste material etc.)*
Regenversicherung *f* rain insurance
Regie *f* control; management, administration; production, direction *(esp. film, theatre)* ◊ **in eigener ~** on one's own account
Regiekosten *pl* overhead costs [expenses], overhead administrative cost(s)

regieren to rule, to govern *(country, people etc.)*
Regierung *f* government, administration ⋄ **an der ~** in power; **an die ~ gelangen** to come (in)to power; **eine ~ bilden** to form a government; **unter der ~ von** under the government of
Regierungsabkommen *n* government(al) [intergovernmental] agreement, agreement between governments
Regierungsanleihe *f* government [state] loan
Regierungsauftrag *m* government(al) order [contract]
Regierungsbeamter *m* government official, civil servant
Regierungsbezirk *m* administrative district
regierungseigen government-owned
Regierungsform *f* form of government
Regierungsgarantie *f* state guarantee
Regierungskäufe *mpl* government(al) purchases
Regierungskommission *f* government(al) commission
~, paritätische parity government(al) commission
Regierungsstelle *f* government agency [office]
Regierungssystem *n* system of government
Region *f* region
regional regional
Regionalanalyse *f* regional analysis *(production, population etc.)*
Regionalbank *f* regional bank
Regionalplanung *f* regional (economic) planning
Regionalreihen *fpl* *(stats)* regional series
Regionalstatistik *f* regional statistics
Regionalstruktur *f* regional structure
~ der Volkswirtschaft regional structure of the national economy
Regionalwirtschaft *f* regional economy
Register *n* register; record; list
~ der volkseigenen Wirtschaft register of nationally-owned enterprises
Registertonne *f* register ton
Registrator *m* registrar
Registratur *f* 1. registration; 2. filing department, registry, record office, registrar's office
registrieren to register, to record, *(d.pr. also)* to log
Registrierkasse *f* cash register
Registriernummer *f* registration number *(application etc.)*; licence number *(cars etc.)*
Registrierung *f* registration
Reglement *n* regulations
reglementieren to regiment *(people)*; to regularize *(work etc.)*
Reglementierung *f* regimentation *(people)*; regularization *(work etc.)*
Regredient *m s.* **Regreßberechtigter**

Regreß *m* recourse; recovery ⋄ **ohne ~** without recourse; **~ gegen(über)** recourse against [to] *(s.o.)*
Regreßanspruch *m* right of recourse
Regressant *m s.* **Regreßberechtigter**
Regressat *m s.* **Regreßschuldner**
Regreßberechtigter *m* person entitled to recourse
Regression *f* regression
~, analytische *(stats)* analytical regression
~, bedingte *(stats)* conditional regression
~ der Kosten cost regression
~, diagonale *(stats)* diagonal regression
~, einfache *(stats)* simple regression
~, exponentielle *(stats)* exponential regression
~, fehlerfreie *(stats)* true regression
~, gewogene *(stats)* weighted regression
~, innere *(stats)* internal regression
~, lineare *(stats)* linear regression
~, mehrfache *(stats)* multiple regression
~, nichtlineare *(stats)* non-linear regression
~, orthogonale *(stats)* orthogonal regression
~, partielle *(stats)* partial regression
Regressionsanalyse *f* regression analysis
Regressionsfläche *f* *(stats)* regression surface
Regressionsfunktion *f* *(stats)* regression function
Regressionsgerade *f* *(stats)* (straight) line of regression
Regressionsgleichung *f* *(stats)* regression equation
Regressionskoeffizient *m* *(stats)* regression coefficient
Regressionskurve *f* *(stats)* regression curve
Regressionslinie *f* *(stats)* regression line
Regressionsmethode *f* *(stats)* method of regression
Regressionsprognose *f* *(stats)* (long-term) regression forecast
Regressionsrechnung *f* *(stats)* regression calculus
Regressionsschätzwert *m* *(stats)* regression estimate
regressiv regressive
Regressor *m* *(stats)* predicted variable, regressor
regreßpflichtig liable to recourse
Regreßrecht *n* right of recourse
Regreßschuldner *m* person liable to recourse, recourse debtor
Regreßverzicht *m* renunciation of recourse
Regreßverzichtabkommen *n* agreement on renunciation of recourse
regulativ regulative, regulating, regulatory *(effect, mechanism etc.)*
Regulativ *n* directive; regulating mechanism, regulator
regulierbar controllable; adjustable

regulieren to settle *(bill, claim etc.)*, to discharge, to pay *(debt etc.)*; *(tech)* to regulate *(volume, speed etc.)*
Regulierung *f* settlement *(bill, claim etc.)*, discharge, payment *(debt etc.)*; *(tech)* regulation *(volume, speed etc.)*
~, **nach kritischen Parametern** *(stats)* control according to critical parameters
~, **ökonomische** economic regulation
Regulierungsfunktion *f* regulating [regulation] function
~ **der Staatsfinanzen** regulating [regulation] function of state finances
Regulierungskonto *n* regulating account
Regulierungsmechanismus *m* regulating mechanism
~, **direkter** direct regulating mechanism
~, **indirekter** indirect regulating mechanism
Regulierungssystem *n* regulating system
Regulierungszölle *mpl* regulating duties
Rehabilitation *f* rehabilitation
rehabilitieren to rehabilitate
Rehabilitierung *f s.* **Rehabilitation**
reichbegütert very wealthy, affluent
reichhaltig well-stocked, abundant *(range of goods etc.)*
Reichtum *m* riches, wealth; affluence; fortune; richness, abundance
~, **gesellschaftlicher** national wealth
~, **materieller** material wealth
Reife *f* ripeness *(situation, fruit, corn etc.)*; maturity *(judgement, person, wine etc.)*
~, **technologische** technological maturity
Reifegrad *m* degree of ripeness [maturity]
reifen to ripen *(situation, fruit, corn ect.)*; to mature *(judgement, person, wine etc.)*
Reifeprüfung *f* school leaving examination *(s.* **Reifezeugnis**)
Reifezeit *f (agric)* time of ripening [maturing]
Reifezeugnis *n* school leaving certificate *(approx, equivalent to A-Level or O-Level of General Certificate of Secondary Education – GCSE)*; *(Am)* graduation diploma *(of Senior High School)*
Reifung *f* ripening; maturation
Reihe *f* row *(seats, trees etc.)*; line *(people etc.)*; number *(years etc.)*; series
~, **arithmetische** arithmetic series
~, **autoregressive** *(stats)* autoregressive series
~, **dynamische** *(stats)* dynamic series
~, **empirische** *(stats)* empirical series
~, **endliche** finite series
~, **harmonische** *(stats)* harmonic series
~, **statische** static series
~, **statistische** statistical series
~, **steigende** ascending series
~, **unendliche** infinite series

Reihenanordnung *f* tandem arrangement *(machines etc.)*
Reihenbau *m* row of terrace(d) houses
Reihendüngung *f (agric)* side dressing
Reihenfabrikation *f s.* **Reihenfertigung**
Reihenfertigung *f* series production, flow (shop) production
Reihenfolge *f* order; succession, sequence ✧ **in der richtigen** ~ in the right order; **in umgekehrter** ~ in inverse order
~, **optimale** optimum sequence
~, **technologische** technological order *(machines)*
~, **zeitliche** chronological order
Reihenhaus *n* terrace(d) house; *(Am)* row [attached] house
Reihenkorrelation *f (stats)* serial correlation
Reihenkorrelationskoeffizient *m (stats)* serial correlation coefficient
~, **zirkulärer** *(stats)* circular serial correlation coefficient
Reihenkultur *f (agric)* row crop cultivation
reihenmäßig *s.* **reihenweise**
Reihenpflanzung *f (agric)* row crop planting
Reihenprobit *m (stats)* corrected probit
Reihenregreß *m* recourse to a bill *(against the other parties in consecutive order)*, recourse sequence *(following chain of endorsers)*
Reihensaat *f (agric)* drill sowing
Reihenschiffahrt *f* shipping along a shared route *(operated in turn by the companies involved)*
Reihenuntersuchung *f* mass screening; mass examination
Reihenverteilung *f*:
~, **logarithmische** *(stats)* logarithmic series distribution
reihenweise in rows [lines]; in series; in large numbers
Reimport *m* re-import(ation)
Reinausgaben *fpl* net expenditure
Reineinkommen *n* net income [earnings]
~ **der Gesellschaft** national net income
~ **des Betriebes** net income of the enterprise
~, **zentralisiertes** centralized net income
Reineinkommensverteilung *f* distribution of net income
Reineinkommensverwendung *f* utilization of net income
Reineinnahme *f* net receipts [income]
Reineinsparung *f* net economies *(in materials etc.)*
Reinerlös *m* net proceeds
Reinertrag *m* net proceeds [returns] *(from investment etc.)*; *(agric)* net yield; net output
Reingewicht *n* net weight
Reingewinn *m* net profit [earnings], net margin
Reingewinnsatz *m* rate of net profit

Reingewinnverteilung *f* distribution of net profit
Reinhaltung *f* keeping clean *(room etc.)*; prevention of pollution *(air, river etc.)*
Reinheit *f* purity *(air, water etc.)*
Reinheitsgrad *m* level of purity *(air, water etc.)*
reinigen to clean *(room, street, grain etc.)*; to cleanse *(utensil etc.)*; to purify, to clear *(air, water etc.)*; to clarify *(liquid)*; to refine *(metal etc.)*
Reinigung *f* 1. cleaning *(room, street, grain etc.)*; cleansing *(utensil etc.)*; purification, clearing *(air, water etc.)*; clarification *(liquid)*; refinement *(metal etc.)*; 2. cleaners *(enterprise)*
~, chemische 1. dry cleaning; 2. dry cleaners
~ und Färberei *f* cleaners and dyers
Reinigungsanstalt *f* (dry) cleaners
Reininvestition *f* net investment
Reinmasse *f* net weight
Reinsaat *f* *(agric)* pure crop; crop seeded without a nurse crop
Reinschrift *f* fair copy
Reinumsatz *m* net turnover
Reinverlust *m* net loss
Reinvermögen *n* net capital; net assets; net property
reinvestieren to reinvest, to plough [*(Am)* plow] back *(profits into business)*
Reinvestition *f* reinvestment, ploughback [*(Am)* plowback]; replacement investment
Reinzucht *f* pure-line breeding
Reise *f* journey, trip; tour; voyage
Reiseabkommen *n* travel agreement
Reiseagentur *f s.* **Reisebüro**
Reisebedarf *m* travel requisites
Reisebescheinigung *f* travel document
Reisebeschränkungen *fpl* travelling restrictions
Reisebüro *n* travel agency [agent(s)], tourist office
Reisedevisen *pl* foreign currency for travelling (purposes)
Reiseerleichterungen *fpl* travel facilities
Reisefreibetrag *m* travel allowance (free of charge); duty-free imports *(by travellers)*
Reisefreigrenze *f* (limit of) travel allowance; limit of goods imported or exported duty-free *(by travellers)*
Reisegeld *n* travel money
Reisegepäck *n* luggage, *(Am)* baggage
Reisegepäckbeförderung *f* transport of luggage, *(Am)* transportation of baggage
Reisegepäckversicherung *f* luggage [*(Am)* baggage] insurance
Reisegesellschaft *f s.* **Reisegruppe**
Reisegruppe *f* tourist group, party of tourists
Reisehandel *m* tourist trade; travelling salesman's trade

Reisekosten *pl* travel(ling) expenses
Reisekostenabrechnung *f* travel(ling) costs accounting
Reisekostenberechnung *f* calculation of travel(ling) costs
Reisekostenvorschuß *m* advance for travel(ling) costs
Reisekreditbrief *m* traveller's letter of credit
Reiseland *n* tourist country
Reiseleiter *m* tourists' guide
reisen to travel ⋄ **geschäftlich ~** to travel on business
Reisen *n* travel(ling)
Reisender *m* traveller; voyager *(sea)*; tourist; passenger *(train, coach etc.)*; travelling salesman
Reisepapiere *npl* travel documents
Reisepaß *m* passport
Reiseplan *m* itinerary for a journey [trip]
Reiseprospekt *m* travel brochure [leaflet, folder]
Reiseroute *f* travel route; itinerary
Reisescheck *m* traveller's cheque [*(Am)* check]
Reisespesen *pl* travel expenses
Reisestrom *m* flow of tourists
Reiseunfallversicherung *f* traveller's accident insurance
Reiseverkehr *m* passenger traffic; tourist traffic [travel]; holiday traffic
Reiseversicherung *f* travel insurance; tourist policy
Reisevertreter *m* commercial traveller; sales representative; travelling salesman
Reisezahlungsmittel *pl s.* **Reisedevisen**
Reisezeit *f* tourist [travel] season
Reiseziel *n* destination
Reisezug *m* passenger train
Reisezugkilometer *m/n* passenger train kilometre
Reitwechsel *m (com)* kite ⋄ **einen ~ ausstellen** to fly a kite
Reklamant *m* complainant
Reklamation *f* complaint, claim ⋄ **eine ~ annehmen** to admit a claim; **eine ~ einlegen** to make [lodge] a complaint *(about s.th.)*; **eine ~ entgegennehmen** to receive a complaint; **eine ~ vorbringen** *s.* **eine ~ einlegen**
~, berechtigte legitimate [justified] complaint
~, spätere subsequent claim
Reklamationsanspruch *m* right to complain *(about s.th.)*
Reklamationsfrist *f* deadline for complaints
Reklamationsprotokoll *n* record of complaints
Reklamationssumme *f s.* **Reklamationswert**
Reklamationsverfahren *n* complaints procedure
Reklamationswert *m* value of the goods complained about
Reklame *f* 1. advertising; publicity; (sales) promotion; 2. advertisement, *(coll)* ad; com-

Reklame

mercial, spot *(on radio and television)* ◊ **für etwas ~ machen** to advertise s.th., to make publicity for s.th., to publicize [promote] s.th.
Reklameartikel *m* advertising gift [novelty]
Reklameaufwendungen *fpl s.* **Reklamekosten**
Reklamechef *m* advertising [publicity] manager
Reklamefachmann *m* advertising [publicity, promotion] expert [man], *(coll)* adman
Reklamefeldzug *m* advertising [publicity] campaign, publicity drive
Reklamekosten *pl* advertising [publicity] expenses [cost]
Reklamepreis *m* bargain price
Reklamesteuern *fpl* advertising tax
reklamieren to complain *(about s.th.)*, to lodge [make] a complaint *(about s.th.)*; to object *(to s.th.)*, to protest *(against s.th.)*
rekommerzialisieren to recommercialize
Rekommerzialisierung *f* recommercialization
Rekompensation *f* compensation; recompense
Rekompensationsgeschäfte *npl* compensation transactions
rekompensieren to compensate *(s.o.)*; to indemnify *(s.o.)*; to recompense *(s.o.)*
rekonstruieren to reconstruct
Rekonstruktion *f* reconstruction
Rekonstruktionsperiode *f* reconstruction period, period of reconstruction
Rekonstruktionsplan *m* reconstruction plan
Rekonstruktionsvorhaben *n* project of reconstruction, reconstruction project
Rekordbeteiligung *f* record attendance [participation]
Rekordernte *f* record [bumper] crop
Rekordpreis *m* record price
Rektagiro *n s.* **Rektaindossament**
Rektaindossament *n* restrictive endorsement *(prohibiting further negotiation)*
Rektaklausel *f* restrictive [non-negotiable] clause
Rektakonnossement *n* straight [restrictive] bill of lading *(ships)*
Rektaladeschein *m s.* **Rektakonnossement**
Rektapapiere *npl* non-negotiable instruments; registered securities
Rektascheck *m* non-negotiable cheque [*(Am)* check]; cheque [*(Am)* check] payable to named payee
Rektawechsel *m* non-negotiable bill of exchange
Rektifikation *f* rectification
rektifizieren to rectify
rekultivieren to recultivate
Rekultivierung *f* recultivation
Relation *f* relation(ship); ratio; proportion
Relationen *fpl:*
~, strukturelle structural proportions
~ zwischen Lohngruppen proportions between wage groups
Relationspreis *m* relative price
relativ relative
relativieren to relativize; to qualify *(statement etc.)*
Relativität *f* relativity
Relativmaximum *n (stats)* relative maximum
Relativwert *m s.* **Relativzahl**
Relativzahl *f* relative number
Reliberalisierung *f* liberalization
Rembours *m* reimbursement; *(bank)* payment by documentary acceptance credit [documentary bill]
Remboursbank *f* commercial [accepting] bank
Remboursement *n s.* **Rembours**
Remboursgeschäft *n* financing by documentary acceptance credit
Rembourskredit *m* documentary acceptance credit
Remboursregreß *m* recourse of an endorser against prior endorsers; reimbursement recourse
Remboursewechsel *m* documentary bill [draft]
Remittent *m* payee *(of a bill of exchange)*
remittieren to return, to send back *(goods etc.)*
remonetisieren to remonetize
Remonetisierung *f* remonetization
Rendement *n* yield (from raw material) *(expressed as a percentage);* purity *(of raw material) (expressed as a precentage)*
Rendite *f* (net) yield, return *(on investment etc.)*
renovieren to renovate; to redecorate *(rooms)*
Renovierung *f* renovation; redecoration *(of rooms)*
Renovierungsarbeiten *fpl* renovation; redecoration *(rooms)*
rentabel profitable *(business, investment etc.)*; paying *(scheme, business etc.)*; economically paying *(investment etc.)*
Rentabilität *f* profitability *(business, investment etc.)*
~, fondsbezogene profitability related to production funds
~, unterschiedliche varying profitability
~, volkswirtschaftliche national economic profitability
Rentabilitätsanalyse *f* profitability analysis
Rentabilitätsberechnung *f* profitability calculation [estimate]; cost accounting
Rentabilitätsentwicklung *f* development [growth] of profitability
Rentabilitätsfaktor *m* profitability factor
rentabilitätsfördernd promoting profitability
Rentabilitätsgrad *m s.* **Rentabilitätsniveau**
Rentabilitätsgrenze *f* limit of profitability, break-even point

Rentabilitätsgrundlage *f* basis of profitability
Rentabilitätsindex *m* profitability index
Rentabilitätskennziffer *f* indicator of profitability, profitability indicator
Rentabilitätsmessung *f* measurement of profitability
Rentabilitätsnachweis *m* statement on profitability
Rentabilitätsniveau *n* profitability level, level of profitability
Rentabilitätsprinzip *n* profitability principle, principle of profitability
Rentabilitätsprüfung *f* profitability audit
Rentabilitätsrate *f* rate of return *(on investment etc.)*; rate of profit
~, **fondsbezogene** ratio between gross profit and production funds
~, **selbstkostenbezogene** ratio between gross profit and prime costs
Rentabilitätsrechnung *f* profitability calculation, calculation of profitability
Rentabilitätssatz *m s.* Rentabilitätsrate
Rentabilitätsschwelle *f* margin of profitability, marginal profit, break-even point
Rentabilitätssteigerung *f* profitability increase, increase in profitability
Rentabilitätsunterschied *m* difference in profitability
Rentabilitätsvergleich *m* profitability comparative analysis
Rentabilitätszuwachs *m* profitability increase
Rente *f* (old age) pension, (retirement) pension; annuity; revenue, income; interest (yield) ⋄ ~ **beziehen** to get a(n) (old age) pension
~, **absolute** absolute (ground) rent
~ **auf Lebenszeit** (life) annuity
~ **aus dem Staatshaushalt** government pension
~ **für Arbeitsunfähige** disability pension
~, **erbliche** inheritable pension
~, **ewige** annuity in perpetuity
~, **kapitalisierte** investment of pension fund
~, **lebenslängliche** *s.* ~ **auf Lebenszeit**
~, **nachschüssige** annuity paid at the end of the year
~, **personengebundene** non-inheritable pension
~, **vererbbare** heritable pension
~, **vorschüssige** annuity to be paid at the beginning of the year
Rentenabfindung *f* annuity paid in a lump sum
Rentenalter *n* pension(able) [retirement] age
Rentenanleihe *f* annuity [perpetual] bonds, consols
Rentenanpassung *f* adjustment of pensions *(to growth of prices and wages)*
Rentenanspruch *m* claim to a pension, pension claim
Rentenanweisung *f s.* Rentenbescheid

Rentenbank *f* public mortgage bank; bank granting agricultural credits *(repayable by annuities)*
Rentenbasis *f* basis of annuity payments
Rentenbemessungsgrundlage *f* basis of calculating pensions
Rentenberechtigung *f* pension entitlement, right to a pension
Rentenberichtigung *f s.* Rentenanpassung
Rentenbescheid *m* pension notice
Rentenbezieher *m* recipient of a pension, pensioner
Rentenbezug *m* drawing of a pension
~, **mehrfacher** multiple drawing of pension
Rentenbrief *m* annuity bond
Renteneinkommen *n* pension; unearned income
Rentenempfänger *m* pensioner; annuitant
Rentenerhöhung *f* increase [rise] in (old-age) pension(s)
Rentenfestlegung *f* fixing (the amount) of pension
Rentenfonds *m* (old age) pension fund
Rentengesetz *n* old age pension law
Rentengewährleistung *f* security of payment of pensions
Rentenhöhe *f* amount of pension
Rentenkasse *f* (old age) pension insurance
Rentenkorrektur *f s.* Rentenanpassung
Rentenleistung *f s.* Rentenzahlung
Rentenmarkt *m* bond market
Rentenpapiere *npl* fixed-interest (bearing) securities, bonds
~, **feste** fixed-interest bearing securities
~, **konsolidierte** consolidated securities
Rentenversicherung *f* national [social] pension scheme
~, **private** *s.* ~, **zusätzliche**
~, **zusätzliche** additional (old age) pension insurance
Rentenreform *f* (old age) pension reform, reform of the pension scheme
Rentenschuld *f* annuity charge on land; rent charge
Rententheorie *f* theory of (ground) rent
Rentenumrechnung *f s.* Rentenanpassung
Rentenversorgung *f* provision for old age pension
Rentenwerte *mpl s.* Rentenpapiere
Rentenzahlung *f* payment of pension(s), pension payment; payment of annuity
~, **nachschüssige** payment of annuity at the end of the year
~, **vorschüssige** payment of annuity at the beginning of the year
Rentenzuschlag *m* supplementary pension
Rentier *m* annuitant; person with private means
rentieren, sich to be profitable [economic], to pay, to be worth while

Rentner *m* pensioner, recipient of a pension; annuitant
Reorganisation *f* reorganization, restructuring
reorganisieren to reorganize, to reconstruct, to regroup, to reshape
Reparationen *fpl* reparations ⋄ ~ **leisten** to make reparations
Reparationsabkommen *n* agreement on reparations
Reparationsausschuß *m* reparations committee
Reparationsbeitrag *m* contribution to reparations
Reparationsentnahme *f* taking of reparations
Reparationsforderung *f* reparation(s) claim(s)
Reparationsleistung *f* payment of reparations
Reparationslieferungen *fpl* reparation deliveries
Reparationsschulden *fpl* reparation debts
Reparationszahlung *f* reparation payment
Reparatur *f* repair(s), repair (work) *(machine etc.)*; mending, repairing ⋄ **eine ~ ausführen** to repair, to make repairs *(to s.th.)*; **in ~** under repair
Reparaturabteilung *f* repair department
Reparaturanfall *m* necessary repairs
Reparaturarbeiten *fpl* repairs, repair work
Reparaturauftrag *m* order for repairs, repair order
Reparaturaufwand *m* repair expenses, expenditure on repairs
reparaturbedürftig in need [want] of repair, out of repair
Reparaturbetrieb *m s.* **Reparaturwerkstatt**
Reparaturdienst *m* repair service
Reparatureinheit *f* repair unit *(mean value for planning maintenance and repairs)*
Reparaturen *fpl*:
~, **fremde** outside repairs
~, **laufende** normal repairs
~, **mittlere** medium repairs, partial overhaul
~, **periodische** periodic repairs
~, **planmäßige vorbeugende** planned maintenance (repairs)
~, **vorbeugende** maintenance (repairs)
reparaturfähig repairable
Reparaturfonds *m* fund for repairs
Reparaturintervall *n* interval of repairs
Reparaturkapazitäten *fpl* repair capacities
Reparaturkosten *pl* cost of repair(s)
Reparaturleistungen *fpl* repairs, repair work
~, **hauswirtschaftliche** repairs of household durables
Reparaturmaterial *n* material for repairs
Reparaturnormativ *n* standard mean value for repairs *(standard in terms of money)*
Reparaturnotdienst *m* emergency repair service
Reparaturperiode *f* period of repair
Reparaturplan *m* repair (and maintenance) plan

Reparaturschnelldienst *m* express repair service
Reparaturstützpunkt *m* repair service centre
Reparatursystem *n* system of repairs
Reparaturumlage *f* sharing of repair costs
Reparatur- und Wartungspersonal *n* repair and maintenance personnel
Reparaturverfahren *n* method of repairs
Reparaturvorleistung *f* advance for repairs
Reparaturwerkstatt *f* repair shop; service station, garage *(for cars)*
Reparaturzeit *f* repair time
Reparaturzyklus *m* repair (and maintenance) cycle
reparieren to repair *(machine etc.)*, to mend *(shoes etc.)*
repartieren to apportion *(tax etc.)*; *(st.ex.)* to allot *(shares)*; *(st.ex.)* to scale down *(buying, selling)*
Repartierung *f s.* **Repartition**
Repartition *f* apportionment *(tax etc.)*; *(st.ex.)* allotment *(shares)*; *(st.ex.)* scaling down *(buying, selling)*
Repartitionssteuer *f* apportioned tax
repatriieren to repatriate
Repatriierung *f* repatriation
~ **von Profiten** repatriation of profits
Repatriierungsabkommen *n* repatriation agreement
Report *m* report; *(st.ex.)* contango (rate); *(fin)* premium (in forward transaction)
Reporter *m* reporter
Reporteur *m* *(st.ex.)* taker-in (of stock)
Reportgeschäft *n* *(st.ex.)* continuation business, contango (business), backwardation, carry-over business
Repräsentant *m* representative
Repräsentation *f* representation
Repräsentationsaufwendungen *fpl* expenditure incurred for professional position, representation expenses, (duty) entertainment expenditure [expenses]
Repräsentationsfonds *m* representation [entertainment] fund
Repräsentationsgelder *npl* representation [entertainment] money
Repräsentationskosten *pl* representation [entertainment] costs
repräsentativ representative *(survey etc.)*; in keeping with one's position *(flat, car etc.)*; imposing *(building etc.)*; distinguished *(appearance etc.)*; handsome *(furniture etc.)*
Repräsentativauswahl *f* *(stats)* representative selection
Repräsentativbefragung *f* *(stats)* representative inquiry
Repräsentativumfrage *f s.* **Repräsentativbefragung**

Repräsentativerfassung *f s.* Repräsentativerhebung
Repräsentativerhebung *f (stats)* representative survey [sampling], sample survey
Repräsentativschau *f* representative show
Repräsentativstatistik *f (stats)* representative statistics; representative sampling
Repräsentativverfahren *n (stats)* representative method
reprivatisieren to reprivatise *(factory etc.)*
Reprivatisierung *f* reprivatization *(factory etc.)*
Reproduktion *f* reproduction *(comprises production, distribution, circulation, consumption of goods and creates the social and physical conditions for continuation of production)*
~ der Arbeitskräfte reproduction of manpower
~ der Bevölkerung reproduction of (the) population
~ der Fonds reproduction of funds
~ der Geldfonds reproduction of monetary [financial] funds
~ der Produktionsverhältnisse reproduction of production relations
~ des gesellschaftlichen Gesamtprodukts reproduction of the gross national product
~, einfache simple reproduction *(repetition of production at the same qualitative and quantitative level)*
~, erweiterte extended [expanded] reproduction *(repetition and renovation of the process of production at higher levels, i.e. with an increasing input of productive forces, rising efficiency and increasing quantities and qualities of goods produced)*
~, extensiv erweiterte extensively extended reproduction
~, gebrauchswertmäßige reproduction in use values
~, gesellschaftliche social reproduction
~ in Naturalform reproduction in physical terms
~, intensiv erweiterte intensively extended reproduction
~, wertmäßige reproduction in terms of values
Reproduktionseffekt *m* reproduction effect
Reproduktionsfaktor *m* reproduction factor
Reproduktionsfonds *m* reproduction fund
Reproduktionsform *f* kind of reproduction
Reproduktionskomplex *m* reproduction complex
Reproduktionskosten *pl* reproduction costs, costs of reproduction
Reproduktionskostentheorie *f* theory of reproduction costs
Reproduktionsmodell *n* reproduction model
Reproduktionsoptimierung *f* reproduction optimization, optimization of reproduction

Reproduktionsperiode *f* reproduction period
~ des fixen Kapitals reproduction period of fixed capital
Reproduktionsphase *f* stage of reproduction
Reproduktionspreis *m* reproduction price
Reproduktionsprozeß *m* reproduction process
~, einheitlicher monetärer comprehensive monetary reproduction process
~, gesellschaftlicher social [national] reproduction process
~, menschlicher human reproduction process
~, natürlicher reproduction process in nature *(environment)*
~, pflanzlicher vegetative reproduction process
~, tierischer animal reproduction process
~, volkswirtschaftlicher national economic reproduction process
Reproduktionsrate *f* reproduction rate, rate of reproduction
Reproduktionsschema *n* reproduction scheme
Reproduktionstheorie *f* reproduction theory
Reproduktionswert *m* reproduction value *(of a commodity determined by the expenditure of socially necessary labour for producing it)*
Reproduktionszeit *f* reproduction period
Reproduktionsziffer *f s.* Reproduktionsrate
Reproduktionszyklus *m* reproduction cycle
Reproduzierbarkeit *f* reproducibility
reproduzieren to reproduce
Reservation *f* reservation *(Red Indians)*
Reserve *f* reserve(s); reserve supply [stock] ⋄
etwas in ~ haben to have s.th. in reserve; etwas in ~ halten to keep s.th. in reserve
~, innergebietliche regional resources
Reserveanlage *f* stand-by plant
Reservearmee *f*:
~ an Arbeitskräften army of (unemployed) manpower
~, industrielle army of (unemployed) industrial manpower
Reserveberechnung *f* calculation of reserves *(stocks)*
Reservebestand *m* reserve stock
Reservebildung *f* building up reserves
Reservefonds *m* reserve fund ⋄ zum ~ schlagen to transfer to reserve fund
~, operativer current reserve fund
~, strategischer strategic reserve fund
Reservegrundfonds *m* reserve fixed assets [capital]
Reservegrundmittel *npl* reserve stocks of equipment [machinery]
Reservehaltung *f* stocking of reserves *(materials etc.)*; *(fin)* reserve management
Reservekapazität *f* reserve [standby] capacity
Reservekapital *n* reserve [spare] capital
Reservelager *n* reserve store [warehouse]

Reserven *fpl* reserves ◊ **auf die ~ zurückgreifen** to fall back on one's reserves; **die ~ angreifen** to break into one's reserves
~, **finanzielle** financial reserves
~, **innere** internal reserves
~, **liquide** cash reserves, cash in hand
~, **materielle** material reserves *(stocks of raw materials, goods and semimanufactured goods to ensure continuity of production)*
~, **offene** disclosed [visible] reserves
~, **ökonomische** economic resources
~, **örtliche** local resources
~, **stille** hidden [secret] reserves
~, **strategische** strategic reserves
~, **volkswirtschaftliche** national economic reserves *(material, monetary etc.)*
Reserveteil *n* spare part, spare
Reservevorrat *m* reserve stock
reservieren to reserve, to book (in advance)
reserviert reserved
Reservierung *f* reservation, booking (in advance)
Residualtheorie *f* residual theory
~ **des Lohnes** residual theory of wages
~ **des Profits** residual theory of profit
Resistenz *f* resistance
~, **passive** passive resistance
Resolution *f* resolution ◊ **eine ~ abfassen** to draw up a resolution; **eine ~ ablehnen** to reject [rescind] a resolution; **eine ~ annehmen** to adopt [pass] a resolution; **eine ~ einbringen** to submit [move] a resolution; **eine ~verabschieden** *s.* **eine ~ annehmen**
Resolutionsentwurf *m* draft resolution
Resolutivbedingung *f (jur)* condition subsequent
resozialisieren to rehabilitate *(prisoner etc.)*
Resozialisierung *f* rehabilitation *(prisoner etc.)*
Respektfrist *f (com)* days of grace [respite]
Respekttage *mpl s.* **Respektfrist**
Ressort *n* sphere, field; department *(government, organization etc.)*; portfolio *(minister etc.)*; competence; responsibility
Ressortangelegenheiten *fpl* departmental affairs [matters]
Ressortbesprechung *f* meeting of heads of departments
ressortmäßig departmental
Ressortprinzip *n* principle of budgetary division *(division of budgetary revenues and expenditure according to spheres of responsibility)*
Ressortwirtschaft *f* departmental thinking
Ressourcen *pl* resources
~, **äußere** external resources
~, **biologische** biological resources
~, **demografische** human resources
~, **einheimische** national [domestic, internal] resources

~, **energetische** energy resources
~, **erneuerungsfähige** renewable resources
~, **finanzielle** financial resources
~, **innere** *s.* ~, **einheimische**
~, **limitierte** limited resources
~, **materielle** material resources
~, **natürliche** natural resources
~, **nichterneuerungsfähige** non-renewable resources
~, **nichtreproduzierbare** non-reproducible resources
~, **nichtspeicherbare** non-storable resources
~, **offene** visible resources
~, **örtliche** local resources
~, **reproduzierbare** reproducible resources
~, **speicherbare** storable resources
~, **stille** hidden resources
~, **strategische** strategic resources
~, **territoriale** regional resources
~, **volkswirtschaftliche** national economic resources
~, **wirtschaftliche** economic resources
Ressourcenausgleich *m s.* **Ressourcenbilanzierung**
Ressourcenbedarf *m* requirements in resources; need for resources
Ressourcenbeschränktheit *f* shortage of resources
Ressourcenbilanzierung *f* balancing of resources
Ressourceneinsatz *m* utilization of resources
Ressourcenfreisetzung *f* release of resources
Ressourcenplanung *f* planning of resources
Ressourcenstruktur *f* structure of resources
Ressourcenverteilung *f* distribution of resources; allocation of resources
Rest *m* balance, remainder *(money)*; surplus [remnant] stock *(commodities)*; *(stats)* residual
Restant *m* 1. defaulter, defaulting debtor; 2. unsaleable article; *(acc)* suspense item; *(st.ex.)* drawn [called] bonds that have not been collected
Restanten *mpl* dead stock
Restauration *f* restoration, renovation *(buildings etc.)*
Restaurator *m* restorer *(buildings etc.)*
restaurieren to restore, to renovate *(buildings etc.)*
Restaurierung *f s.* **Restauration**
Restbestand *m* balance, remainder; remaining stock
Restbetrag *m* balance, remainder, remaining amount
~, **geschuldeter** remainder of a debt
~, **unbezahlter** arrears
Restbuchwert *m* residual cost [value], remaining [net] book value

Resteverkauf *m* sale of remnants
Restforderung *f* residual claim, outstanding amount
Restgewinn *m* final profit *(after distribution of gross profit)*
Restgröße *f* *(stats)* residual
Restguthaben *n* remaining (credit) balance
Restitution *f* *(jur)* restitution, restoration; reversal of court decision
Restitutionsklage *f* *(jur)* action for restitution; action for a retrial (of a case)
Restkapital *n* residual [remaining] capital
Restkaufgeld *n* balance of the purchase price [money]
Restkaufgeldhypothek *f* *(jur)* purchase-money mortgage
Restkostenrechnung *f* residual cost accounting
Restkredit *m* remaining credit
Restnachlaß *m* residuary estate
Restnutzungsdauer *f* remaining (working useful) life *(of capital goods)*, remaining life expectancy, unexpired life
Restposten *m* end-of-line items, remaining items, remainders *(goods); (acc)* residual item
Restquadratsumme *f* *(stats)* residual sum of squares
Restriktion *f* restriction; *(maths)* constraint
Restriktionen *fpl:*
   ⋄ jmdm. ~ **auferlegen** to impose restrictions on s.o.
~, **wirtschaftliche** economic restrictions
Restriktionsfestlegung *f* stipulation of restrictions
Restriktionsmaßnahmen *fpl* restrictive measures
Restriktionspolitik *f* restrictive [tight] (economic) policy
restriktiv restrictive
Restsaldo *m* remaining balance
Restschuld *f* remaining [residual] debt(s), unpaid balance (in account) ⋄ **die ~ in Raten bezahlen** to pay the rest in [by] instalments
Reststreuung *f* *(stats)* residual dispersion
Restsumme *f* balance; *(stats)* residual sum
~ **der Abweichungsquadrate** *(stats)* error [residual] sum of squares
Restvarianz *f* *(stats)* error mean-square, residual variance
Restware *f* remnants; remaining stock *(of goods)*
Restwert *m s.* **Restbuchwert**
Restwertabschreibung *f* depreciation of residual cost [value], declining-balance method (of depreciation)
Restwertverfahren *n s.* **Restkostenrechnung**
Restzahlung *f* payment of the balance; final payment
Resultante *f* *(maths)* resultant

Resultat *n* result, outcome
Retouren *fpl (com)* returns, returned goods [sales, merchandise]; *(bank)* dishonoured bills [cheques, *(Am)* checks], bills [cheques, *(Am)* checks] returned unpaid
Retourfracht *f* return [back, homeward] freight [cargo]
retournieren to return *(goods etc.)*
Retourscheck *m* returned cheque [*(Am)* check]
Retourwechsel *m* redraft(ed bill), re-exchange
Retroscheck *s.* **Retourscheck**
retrozedieren to return *(property etc.)*; to cede back *(title etc.)*; *(ins)* to retrocede *(risk etc.)*
Retrozession *f* return *(property etc.); (jur; ins)* retrocession *(title, risk etc.)*
Rettungsaktion *f* rescue operation(s)
Rettungsarbeiten *fpl* rescue work
Rettungsdienst *m* life-saving [rescue] service
Reugeld *n* *(jur)* forfeit (money), penalty *(for withdrawing from a contract); (st.ex.)* option money
Reukauf *m* contract of purchase stipulating payment of a forfeit *(in case of withdrawal from a contract)*
Reuvertrag *m s.* **Reukauf**
revalidieren to revalidate
Revalidierung *f* revalidation
revalieren to recover one's costs; to cover o.s. *(against loss, expense etc.)*
Revalierung *f* cover of one's costs; cover *(against loss, expense etc.)*
Revalierungsklage *f* *(jur)* action for the recovery of expenses *(by the drawee of a bill)*
Revalierungsklausel *f* cover clause
revalorisieren to revalorize (currency); to restore (currency) to its original value
Revalorisierung *f* revalorization
Revalvation *f* revaluation, upvaluation
revalvieren to revalue
Revenue *f* revenue, income *(from estate etc.)*
Revers *m* 1. formal declaration [undertaking] *(in writing)*; document revoking [cancelling] an obligation; 2. reverse (of coin)
Reversale *n* official declaration of intent to observe treaties
Reverssystem *n* *(approx.)* system in which retailers undertake to observe resale price maintenance
Revident *m* *(jur)* party lodging an appeal (on a question of law)
revidieren to revise *(policy etc.)*; to check, to examine, to go over *(invoice etc.)*; to audit *(accounts etc.)*
Revier *n* territory, district, area *(salesman etc.)*; section [district] of a mine, mining district [area]; *(for)* district; (police) district, *(Am)* precinct; beat *(policeman etc.)*; round *(postman)*; station *(waiter)*

Revirement *n* 1. reshuffle *(ministerial, diplomatic posts)*; 2. settling of accounts by transfer and adjustment
Revision *f* revision *(policy etc.)*; check(ing), examination *(invoice etc.)*; audit(ing) *(accounts etc.)*; amendment *(law, treaty etc.)*; *(jur)* appeal
~, **außerordentliche** *(acc)* extraordinary audit(ing)
~, **außerplanmäßige** *(acc)* unscheduled audit(ing)
~, **nichtturnusmäßige** *s.* ~, **außerplanmäßige**
~, **planmäßige** *(acc)* scheduled audit(ing)
~, **stichprobenartige** *(acc)* random audit(ing)
~, **turnusmäßige** *(acc)* regular audit(ing)
~, **vollständige** *(acc)* complete audit(ing)
Revisionsbericht *m* auditor's report
Revisionsfirma *f* auditing firm, firm of auditors
Revisionskommission *f* auditing commission
Revisor *m* auditor; accountant
Revisionismus *m* revisionism
Revisionist *m* revisionist
revisionistisch revisionist
Revokation *f* retraction *(statement etc.)*; *(com)* cancellation *(order etc.)*; *(jur)* revocation *(decision etc.)*
Revolution *f* revolution
~, **bürgerlich-demokratische** bourgeois-democratic revolution
~, **bürgerliche** bourgeois revolution
~, **industrielle** industrial revolution
~, **proletarische** proletarian revolution
~, **technische** technological revolution
~, **wissenschaftlich-technische** scientific and technological [technical] revolution
revolutionär revolutionary
Revolutionär *m* revolutionary
revolutionieren to revolutionize
Revolvingakkreditiv *n* revolving letter of credit
Rezession *f* recession, slump
Rezessionserscheinungen *fpl* symptoms of recession [slump]
Rezessionsperiode *f* period of recession [slump]
reziprok reciprocal
Reziprokwert *m (stats)* reciprocal value
Reziprozität *f* reciprocity
Reziprozitätsgeschäft *n* barter trade [deal]
Reziprozitätsklausel *f* barter clause
Reziprozitätsprinzip *n* principle of reciprocity
Reziprozitätsvertrag *m* barter (trade) agreement
R-Gespräch *n* transferred-charge *(Am)* [collect] call
Richtbetrieb *m* pilot plant
Richtlinie *f* terms of reference; general instruction(s), regulation(s), directive(s), guideline(s), policy outline(s)
Richtpreis *m* guide [guiding, guidance] price; target price
~, **unverbindlicher** recommended [suggested] (retail) price
Richtpreisliste *f* list of guide [guidance, guiding] prices
Richtpreisspanne *f* margin of guide [guidance, guiding] prices
Richtsatz *m* standard [guiding] rate [ratio]
~, **berichtigter** modified standard [guiding] rate
Richtsatzbestände *mpl* standard stocks
richtsatzfrei unlimited
richtsatzgebunden limited by standard rates
Richtsatzkalkulation *f* calculation according to standard [guiding] rates
Richtsatzmethode *f* method of fixing standard [guiding] rates
Richtsatzplan *m (approx.)* plan for financing stocks and working capital
Richtsatzplanbestand *m (approx.)* stocks according to the plan for financing stocks and working capital
Richtsatzplankredit *m (approx.)* planned credit for partially financing stocks
Richtsatzselbstkosten *pl* prime costs according to standard [guiding] rates
Richtsatztage *mpl s.* **Richttage**
Richtsatzverbrauch *m* consumption according to standard [guiding] rates
Richttage *mpl* permitted stock days
Richtwert *m* standard [approximate, recommended] value
Richtwerttabelle *f* table [list] of standard values
Richtzahl *f* guiding figure
Rikambio *m* re-exchange *(draft, process)*; redraft(ed bill)
Rikambiowechsel *m* re-exchange (draft), redraft(ed bill)
Rimesse *f* remittance; *(st.ex.)* drawn bill of exchange
Rinderzucht *f* cattle breeding
Ring *m* ring *(traders etc.)*, pool *(dealers etc.)*, trust *(firms etc.)*
Ringtausch *m* multilateral exchange of flats [*(Am)* apartments]
Risiko *n* risk, danger; *(ins)* risk, hazard; venture *(business)* ◇ **auf eigenes ~** at one's own risk; **das ~ übernehmen** to (under)take the risk; **das ~ verteilen** to spread the risk(s); **ein ~ eingehen** to take [run, incur] a risk; **ein ~ übernehmen** to accept [assume] a risk; **mit einem ~ verbunden sein** to involve a risk; **sich einem ~ aussetzen** to incur a risk
~, **berufliches** risk incident to employment; occupational hazard
~, **finanzielles** financial risk
~, **kalkulatorisches** calculable risk
~, **kalkuliertes** calculated risk
~, **klar erkennbares** obvious risk

~, **versicherbares** insurable risk
~, **wirtschaftliches** commercial risk
~, **wohl abgewogenes** *s.* ~, **kalkuliertes**
Risikoabwälzung *f* passing of risk *(to s.o.)*
Risikoanalyse *f* risk analysis
Risikoaufschlag *m* extra risk charge, risk premium [markup]
Risikoausgleich *m* compensation for risks; *(ins)* balancing of portfolio
Risikoausschluß *m (ins)* exclusion [elimination] of risks
Risikobeitrag *m (ins)* risk premium
risikobereit venturesome, prepared to take a risk
Risikoerhöhung *f (ins)* increase of hazards
Risikofonds *m* risk fund
risikofrei free of [without] risk, riskless, safe
risikofreudig *s.* **risikobereit**
Risikofunktion *f (stats)* risk function
Risikograd *m* degree of risk
Risikoherabsetzung *f (ins)* reduction in hazards
Risikokapital *n* risk [venture] capital
Risikolebensversicherung *f* short-term life assurance [*(Am)* insurance], term assurance [*(Am)* insurance]
risikolos *s.* **risikofrei**
Risikoprämie *f s.* **Risikobeitrag**
Risikostreuung *f* spreading of (the) risk(s), risk spreading, diversification of risks
Risikosumme *f (ins)* amount at risk
Risikoübernahme *f* taking a risk
Risikoversicherung *f* insurance against possible risk
Risikozuschlag *m s.* **Risikoaufschlag**
riskant risky, hazardous
riskieren to risk, to venture, to take a chance *(on s.th.)*
ristornieren *(acc)* to reverse (an entry), to cancel (an entry by making a contra-entry); *(ins)* to revoke, to cancel *(policy)*
Ristorno *n (acc)* reversal [reversing, reverse transfer] of an entry; *(ins)* revocation, cancellation *(policy)*
Ristornogebühr *f (ins)* policy cancellation fee
Ritratte *f* redraft(ed bill), re-exchange
Rittergut *n (hist)* manor; seignorial estate; Junker's estate *(Prussia)*
Rittergutsbesitzer *m (hist)* lord of the manor; Junker *(Prussia)*
Rivale *m* rival; competitor
rivalisieren to rival *(s.o.)*; to compete *(with s.o.)*
Rivalität *f* rivalry; competition
Roboter *m* robot
Robotereinsatz *m* robot application
Robotersteuerung *f* robot control
Robotertechnik *f* robotics
Rodel *m* scroll *(documents)*; *(hist)* document of terms of lease *(between landlord and cottar)*

Rodeland *n (agric)* cleared (wood)land, clearing
roden to clear *(woodland)*; to grub up, to root out *(stump)*; to lift *(potatoes, turnips etc.)*
Rodung *f* 1. clearing *(woodland)*; grubbing up, rooting out *(stumps)*; lifting *(potatoes, turnips etc.)*; 2. cleared woodland
roh gross *(profit etc.)*; raw *(material, food etc.)*; crude *(statistical data, oil etc.)*; rough *(draft, diamond etc.)*; bare, unshaped *(wood etc.)*
Rohanalyse *f* rough analysis
Rohausbeute *f* gross output
Rohbau *m (build)* rough brickwork, shell (construction)
Rohbauarbeiten *fpl* erection of the outer structure of a building
Rohbaumwolle *f* raw cotton
Rohbilanz *f* preliminary [trial, rough, gross] balance (sheet)
Rohdaten *pl (stats)* unprocessed data; *(d.pr.)* raw data
Roheinkommen *n* gross income
Roheinkünfte *pl s.* **Roheinnahmen**
Roheinnahmen *fpl* gross receipts [income]
Rohentwurf *m* rough draft *(report etc.)*; rough sketch *(building, machine etc.)*
Roherlös *m* gross proceeds
Rohertrag *m (ind)* gross output; *(agric)* gross yield
Roherz *n* crude [raw] ore
Roherzeugnis *n s.* **Rohprodukt**
Rohgewicht *n* gross weight
Rohgewinn *m* gross profit(s)
Roh-, Hilfs- und Betriebsstoffe *mpl* raw materials, auxiliaries and fuels, raw materials and supplies
Rohkodierung *f (d.pr.)* skeletal coding
Rohmaterial *n* raw material
Rohmaterialvorräte *mpl* raw material stocks
Rohmetall *n* crude metal
Rohöl *n* crude oil
Rohölverarbeitung *f* crude oil refining
Rohprodukt *n* raw product
Rohproduktenhandel *m* trade in raw products; trade in waste products for industrial re-use
Rohrleger *m* pipe fitter, plumber
Rohrleitung *f* pipe *(for water, gas etc.)*; tube *(for steam, cooling agent etc.)*; pipeline *(over longer distances)*; conduit *(for electrical wires)*
Rohrleitungsnetz *n* network of pipes [tubes]; mains; piping, tubing, plumbing *(building)*
Rohrpost *f* pneumatic (tube) dispatch
Rohrpostanlage *f* system of pneumatic (tube) dispatch
Rohrpostsendung *f* 1. dispatching [conveying, sending] by pneumatic [tube] system *(bills, letters etc.)*; 2. item dispatched [conveyed] by pneumatic tube

Rohschätzung *f* rough estimate
Rohstahl *m* crude [raw] steel
Rohstoff *m* raw material; *(com)* (basic) commodity
~, **agrarischer** agricultural raw material
~, **defizitärer** deficit raw material
~, **einheimischer** domestic [national] raw material
~, **industrieller** industrial raw material
~, **metallischer** metallic raw material
~, **mineralischer** mineral raw material
~, **örtlich vorkommender** locally available raw material
~, **pflanzlicher** vegetable [plant] raw material
~, **sekundärer** secondary raw material
~, **strategischer** strategic raw material
~, **zurückgewonnener** recycled waste material
Rohstoffabkommen *n* raw material [commodity] agreement
rohstoffarm not endowed with raw materials, with few raw material resources
Rohstoffaufkommen *n* raw material output, production of raw material(s)
Rohstoffausbeute *f* raw material yield [output]
Rohstoffausfuhr *f* raw material export
Rohstoffausnutzungsgrad *m* level [degree] of efficiency in utilizing raw materials
Rohstoffausnutzungsnorm *f* efficiency standard [norm] in utilizing raw materials
Rohstoffbasis *f* raw material basis
~, **sekundäre** secondary raw materials available *(scrap iron etc.)*
Rohstoffbedarf *m* raw material requirements
Rohstoffbeschaffung *f* procurement of raw materials
Rohstoffbeschaffungskosten *pl* cost of procuring raw materials
Rohstoffbewirtschaftung *f* raw material controls [rationing]
Rohstoffbilanz *f* balance sheet of raw materials
Rohstoffbilanzierung *f* drawing up a balance sheet of raw materials
Rohstoffeigenproduktion *f* national production of raw materials
Rohstoffeinfuhr *f* raw material import
Rohstoffeinsatz *m* input of raw materials, raw material input
Rohstoffeinsatznorm *f* standard norm [rate] of raw material input *(prescribes quantities of various raw materials to be used in the manufacture of a product)*
Rohstoffeinsparung *f* economies in the use of raw materials
Rohstoffersparnis *f s.* **Rohstoffeinsparung**
Rohstoffexport *m s.* **Rohstoffausfuhr**
Rohstoffgebiet *n* area producing raw materials, raw material area

Rohstoffgewinnungsindustrie *f* raw material [extractive] industry
Rohstoffhortung *f* hoarding [stockpiling] of raw materials
Rohstoffimport *m s.* **Rohstoffeinfuhr**
Rohstoffintensität *f* raw material intensity
Rohstoffkartell *n* commodity cartel
Rohstoffknappheit *f s.* **Rohstoffmangel**
Rohstoffkosten *pl* raw material cost(s)
Rohstoffland *n* raw material producing [primary-producing] country
Rohstofflieferant *m* supplier of raw materials
Rohstofflieferung *f* supply of raw materials
Rohstoffmangel *m* shortage of raw materials, raw material shortage
Rohstoffmarkt *m* raw material [commodity] market
Rohstoffmonopol *n* monopoly in (producing) raw materials
Rohstoffpreis *m* raw material [commodity] price
Rohstoffpreisindex *m* index of raw material prices, commodity price index
Rohstoffquelle *f* raw material source
Rohstoffquellen *fpl:*
~ **des Meeres** sea resources
~ **des Meeresbodens** seabed resources
Rohstoffreserve *f* raw material reserve
Rohstoffressourcen *pl* raw material resources
Rohstoffverbrauch *m* consumption of raw materials, raw material consumption
Rohstoffvereinbarung *f s.* **Rohstoffabkommen**
Rohstoffverknappung *f s.* **Rohstoffmangel**
Rohstoffverteuerung *f* increase in raw material prices
Rohstoffvorkommen *npl s.* **Rohstoffressourcen**
Rohstoffvorräte *mpl s.* **Rohstoffressourcen**
Rohstoffwirtschaft *f* raw material economy
Rohüberschuß *m* gross surplus
Rohumsatz *m* gross sales [turnover]
Rolladen- und Jalosiemacher *m* maker of venetian blinds and roller-type shutters
Rollauftrag *m* collection and delivery order
Rollfuhrdienst *m* cartage department, cartage [haulage] service, collection and delivery service
Rollgeld *n* haulage, cartage, carriage *(charges)*
Rollgut *n* carted goods
Roll-on-roll-off-Verfahren *n* roll-on-roll-off method
Rollverkehr *m* cartage traffic
Röntgenassistent *m* X-ray assistant, radiographer
Rösselsprung-Quadrat *n (stats)* Knut-Wik square
Routentransport *m* liner transport(ation)
Routine *f* routine
Routinearbeit *f* routine work
Routineentscheidung *f* routine decision

routinemäßig routine
Routinesache *f* matter of routine
Rückanspruch *m* counter claim, recourse
Rückantwort *f* reply
Rückauftrag *m* return order
Rückäußerung *s.* **Rückantwort**
Rückbeförderung *f* return transport
Rückbehaltungsrecht *n* right of retention
Rückberufung *f* recall *(diplomat etc.)*
Rückbuchung *f* contra-entry, reverse entry, carry-back
Rückbürge *m* counter-surety
Rückbürgschaft *f* counter-security, counter-surety, counter-guaranty
rückdatieren to antedate, to backdate
Rückdatierung *f* antedating, backdating
Rückdeckungsversicherung *f* insurance to cover a pension fund for employees *(arranged between employer and insurance company)*
Rückeinfuhr *f* reimportation
rückerstatten to refund, to repay, to pay back, to reimburse *(money)*; to return, to restore, to make restitution of *(property)*
Rückerstattung *f* refund(ing), repayment, reimbursement *(money)*; restitution, restoration, return *(property)*
Rückexport *m s.* **Rückeinfuhr**
Rückfahrkarte *f* return ticket, *(Am)* roundtrip ticket
Rückfahrschein *m s.* **Rückfahrkarte**
Rückfahrt *f* return jorney [trip, voyage]
Rückflug *m* return flight, flight back
Rückfluß *m* reflux *(capital etc.)*
~ **der investierten Mittel** reflux of invested capital [funds], return on investment
Rückflußdauer *f* payback [recoupment] period
Rückforderung *f* claim for the return of *(money, article etc.)*, claiming back, reclamation
Rückfracht *f* return [back, homeward] freight [cargo]
Rückfrage *f* (further) question [inquiry, query], counter-question, request for further particulars, checkback
rückfragen to inquire *(of s.o.)*, to check *(with s.o.)*, to ask *(s.o.)* for further particulars
Rückführung *f* return *(goods)*; repatriation *(people, capital etc.)*; *(fin)* repayment; *(d.pr.)* feedback
Rückführungsbetrag *m* agricultural levy
Rückgabe *f* return, restitution, restoration, redelivery
Rückgabebefehl *m (d.pr.)* return statement
Rückgang *m* fall, drop, decrease, decline *(in price etc.)*; fall(ing)-off *(in imports, sales etc.)*; downward movement, retrogression; slump *(trade etc.)*; recession *(economy)*
rückgängig declining, decreasing *(business etc.)*,

falling, dropping, sagging *(prices etc.)* ⋄ ~ **machen** to cancel, to withdraw *(order etc.)*, to annul, to rescind *(contract etc.)*; to call off *(appointment etc.)*; to go back on *(decision etc.)*
Rückgängigmachung *f* cancellation, withdrawal *(order etc.)*, annulment, rescission *(contract etc.)*; calling off *(appointment etc.)*
rückgewinnen to reclaim *(land etc.)*; to recover *(chemical by-product etc.)*; to regenerate *(nutrients in soil etc.)*; to recycle *(waste for industrial re-use)*
Rückgewinnung *f* reclamation *(land etc.)*; recovery *(chemical by-product etc.)*; regeneration *(nutrients in soil etc.)*; recycling *(of waste for industrial re-use)*
~ **von Altstoffen** recycling, salvage [recovery] of waste material and scrap
Rückgewinnungsnorm *f* rate of regeneration; rate of recycling
Rückgriff *m* recourse; resort ⋄ **ohne** ~ without recourse; ~ **gegen** recourse against [to] *(s.o.)*
Rückgriffsanspruch *m* right of recourse
Rückgriffsberechtigter *m* person entitled to recourse
Rückgriffsforderung *f (ins)* reclamation *(from third party)*
Rückgriffsrecht *n* right of recourse
Rückgriffsschuldner *m* person liable to recourse, recourse debtor
Rückindossament *n* re-endorsement, endorsement to a prior endorser
Rückkauf *m* repurchase, buying back; *(fin, ins)* redemption *(securities etc.)*; surrender of policy; *(fin)* callback
Rückkaufagio *n* repurchase premium [agio]
rückkaufen to repurchase, to buy *(s.th.)* back; *(fin, ins)* to redeem
Rückkauffrist *f* period for repurchase
Rückkaufklausel *f* repurchase clause; *(ins)* surrender clause
Rückkaufkurs *m (ins)* rate of surrender value
rückkäuflich repurchasable; *(fin, ins)* redeemable ⋄ **nicht** ~ irredeemable
Rückkaufsrecht *n* right of repurchase; *(fin, ins)* right of redemption
Rückkaufswert *m* repurchase value; *(fin)* redemption value *(bond etc.)*; *(ins)* surrender [cash] value *(of policy)*
Rückkehr *f* return
~ **nach Null** return to zero
Rückkehradresse *f (d.pr.)* return address
Rückkehrbefehl *m (d.pr.)* return instruction
Rückkehrperiode *f (stats)* return period
Rückkehr-zu-Null-Verfahren *n (d.pr.)* return-to-zero recording
rückkoppeln *(d.pr.)* to feed back
Rückkopplung *f (d.pr.)* feedback

Rückkopplungsinformation *f (d.pr.)* feedback information
Rückkopplungssystem *n* feedback system
Rückladung *f* return load [shipment]; return freight [cargo]
Rücklage *f* reserve (fund); reserve(s); savings
Rücklagefonds *m (agric)* reserve fund *(part of the monetary proceeds of a co-operative farm distributed at year-end according to the decision of the membership plenary assembly)*
Rücklagen *fpl*:
~, **freie** available [free, contingency] reserves
~, **gesetzliche** legal [statutory] reserves
~, **offene** declared reserves
~, **stille** hidden [undisclosed, secret] reserves
Rücklagenkonto *n* reserve account
rückläufig declining, decreasing *(business etc.)*, falling, dropping, sagging *(prices etc.)*; downward *(trend etc.)*; retrograde, retrogressive *(development etc.)*
Rückläufigkeit *f* downward movement, decline, decrease *(business etc.)*, fall, drop *(prices etc.)*
Rücklieferung *f* return delivery, redelivery
Rücknahme *f* taking back, repurchase *(goods)*; *(jur)* abandonment, withdrawal *(action)*; revocation *(licence)*
Rücknahmegarantie *f* repurchase guarantee
Rückporto *n* return postage
Rückprämie *f (st.ex.)* premium [money paid] for a put (option), put (option), seller's option
Rückprämiengeschäft *n (st.ex.)* put (business), trading in puts
Rückrechnung *f* 1. *(plan)* recalculation *(method of calculating present requirements and measures on the basis of long-term forecasts of future trends and changes)*; 2. *(fin)* receipt given to endorser *(for payment of a bill of exchange)*
~, **prognostische** long-term recalculation
Rückscheck *m* returned cheque [*(Am)* check]
Rückschlag *m* setback
~, **geschäftlicher** commercial setback, suffering from a business setback
~, **konjunktureller** setback in the business cycle
~, **wirtschaftlicher** economic setback
Rückschluß *m* inference, conclusion
Rückschlußwahrscheinlichkeit *f (stats)* inverse probability
Rückschreiben *n* reply (letter), answer
rückschreitend backward *(trend etc.)*, retrograde, retrogressive *(development etc.)*
Rückschritt *m* step back(wards), retrograde [retrogressive] step, re(tro)gression
rücksenden to send back, to return
Rücksendung *f* sending back, return(ing)
Rücksiedler *m* repatriate, resettler
Rücksiedlung *f* repatriation *(of refugees etc.)*
Rückstand *m* arrears, outstanding debts; backlog *(work, deliveries etc.)* ◊ **einen ~ aufholen** to recover lost ground; to catch up with arrears; to catch up on a backlog; **im ~ sein** to lag behind, to be behind, to be in arrears *(with rent, instalments etc.)*
rückständig outdated, old-fashioned, antiquated, behind the times; backward, underdeveloped; in arrears, behind *(with payment etc.)*; outstanding, overdue *(payment etc.)* ◊ **gesellschaftlich ~** socially backward; **historisch ~** historically backward; **ökonomisch ~** economically backward; **~ sein** to be behind [in arrears] *(with rent, instalments etc.)*; to be backward *(method, economy etc.)*; **sozial-ökonomisch ~** socially and economically backward; **technisch ~** technologically backward
Rückständigkeit *f* backwardness
Rückstandszeit *f* production time lag *(discrepancy between the technologically necessary time and the amount of time currently expended on the manufacture of a product)*
Rückstellung *f* 1. reserve (fund), provision, allowance, sum set aside (for future liabilities and losses); 2. transfer to a reserve (fund)
~ **für Abschreibungen** allowance [provision] for depreciation, depreciation allowance
~ **für Anlageveränderungen** reserve for investment fluctuations
~ **für Ausgleichsforderungen** equalization reserve
~ **für eingegangene Verbindlichkeiten** liability reserve
~ **für Eventualverbindlichkeiten** reserve for contingencies
~ **für Instandhaltungszwecke** maintenance allowance
~ **für Investitionszwecke** resources reserved for (future) investments
~ **für künftige Zahlungen** reserve for future payments
~ **für Mindereinnahmen** deficiency reserve
~ **für Reparaturen und Neuanschaffungen** reserve for deferred repairs and renewals
~ **für Schuldentilgung** reserve for debt redemption
~ **für Unfälle** reserve for accidents
~ **für unvorhergesehene Ausgaben** reserve for contingencies
~ **für zweifelhafte Forderungen** bad debt reserve, reserve [allowance] for bad debts
Rückstellungsbetrag *m* sum reserved, reserved item
Rückstellungsbildung *f* creation of reserves, setting up [establishing, forming] reserves
Rückstellungsfonds *m* reserve fund
Rückstellungskonto *n* reserve (appropriation) account

Rückstellungsposten *m* reserve item
Rückstellungszuweisung *f* reserve allocation
Rückstufung *f* reclassification *(quality etc.)*; downgrading *(job etc.)*; downward adjustment *(salary, tax etc.)*
Rücktritt *m* resignation, retirement *(from office etc.)*; *(jur)* withdrawal from, rescission of
Rücktrittserklärung *f* announcement of (one's) resignation; *(jur)* declaration [notice] of rescission
Rücktrittsgesuch *n* (letter/tender of) resignation
Rücktrittsklausel *f* cancellation clause
Rücktrittsrecht *n* *(jur)* right to withdraw from a contract [to rescind a contract], right of rescission
rückübertragen to retransfer
Rückübertragung *f* retransfer
rückvergüten to refund, to repay *(expenses etc.)*; to reimburse *(s.o.)*
Rückvergütung *f* refund, repayment *(expenses etc.)*; reimbursement; *(railw)* quantity rebate *(granted to consignor)*; *(ins)* surrender value
Rückverkehr *m* returning traffic
Rückversicherer *m* reinsurer
rückversichern to reinsure
rückversichert reinsured
Rückversicherung *f* reinsurance
~, anteilige partial reinsurance
~, proportionale proportionate reinsurance
Rückversicherungsgesellschaft *f* reinsurance company
Rückversicherungsnachweis *m* certificate of reinsurance
Rückversicherungsprämie *f* reinsurance premium
Rückversicherungsvertrag *m* reinsurance contract
Rückwanderer *m* repatriate, returning emigrant
Rückwanderung *f* repatriation; return to one's own country
Rückwaren *fpl* returned goods, goods [merchandise] returned
Rückwechsel *m* redraft(ed bill), re-exchange
Rückweisungsbereich *m* *(stats)* rejection region
Rückweisungslinie *f* *(stats)* rejection line
Rückweisungszahl *f* *(stats)* rejection number
Rückweisungswahrscheinlichkeit *f* *(stats)* probability of rejection
rückwirkend *(jur)* retrospective, retroactive, having retroactive effect
Rückwirkung *f* reaction, repercussion; *(jur)* retroactive [retrospective] effect, retroaction, retrospectiveness
rückzahlbar repayable, returnable, refundable, to be paid back, to be repaid, reimbursable *(money etc.)*; redeemable *(bond etc.)* ⋄ **~ in bar** repayable in cash

Rückzahlbarkeit *f* repayability, refundability, reimbursability *(money etc.)*; redeemability *(bond etc.)*
Rückzahlung *f* repayment, return *(debts etc.)*; reimbursement, refund *(expenses etc.)*; redemption *(bond etc.)*
~ **einer Hypothek** amortization of a mortgage
~ **eines Kredits** redemption of a loan
~ **mit Agio** repayment with [cum] agio
~ **mit Aufschlag** *s.* **~, mit Agio**
~ **zum Nennwert** repayment according to nominal value
Rückzahlungsagio *n* redemption premium, premium payable on redemption *(bond etc.)*
Rückzahlungsanspruch *m* claim to repayment
Rückzahlungsbedingungen *fpl* terms of repayment
Rückzahlungsbetrag *m* amount to be repaid
Rückzahlungsfrist *f* repayment period, period [deadline] of repayment; *(cust)* date of repayment
Rückzahlungsquelle *f* source of repayment
Rückzahlungsrate *f* rate of repayment; instalment
Rückzahlungsschein *m* receipt (of repayment)
Rückzoll *m* (customs) drawback
Ruhegehalt *n* (retirement/old age) pension
Ruhegehaltsempfänger *m* (old age) pensioner
Ruhegeld *n s.* **Ruhegehalt**
Ruhepause *f* break *(from work etc.)*, rest *(from activity etc.)*, rest period *(for pilot etc.)*
Ruhestand *m* retirement ⋄ **im ~** retired; **in den ~ treten** to retire; **in den ~versetzen** to retire, to superannuate, to pension off *(s.o.)*;
Ruhezeit *f* time of rest [repose]; *(d.pr.)* unused time
Ruin *m* ruin, collapse
ruinieren to ruin *(s.o.)*; to spoil *(thing etc.)*
Rumpfbelegschaft *f* skeleton staff
Run *m* run
Runderlaß *m* circular (notice/regulation)
Rundfahrt *f* trip round [tour of] a town [area], sightseeing tour
Rundfahrtproblem *n* *(maths)* route optimization problem
Rundflug *m* sightseeing flight
Rundfrage *f* inquiry (by circular), poll
Rundfunk *m* radio [wireless] broadcasting; radio, wireless
~, privater commercial radio
Rundreise *f* circular tour, round trip
Rundschreiben *n* circular (letter)
Rundung *f* *(maths, stats)* rounding
Rundungsfehler *m* *(maths, stats)* error due to rounding, rounding error
Rüstkosten *pl* change-over [resetting, preparation] cost(s), preproduction cost

Rüstung *f* 1. preparation *(production etc.)*; 2. scaffolding *(building etc.)*; 3. armaments; arms build-up
Rüstungsanleihe *f* arms [armaments] credit
Rüstungsauftrag *m* arms [armaments, defence] contract
Rüstungsausgaben *fpl* arms [armaments] expenditure, expenditure on arms [armaments]
Rüstungsbegrenzung *f* limitation of armaments, arms limitation
Rüstungsbeschränkung *f s.* **Rüstungsbegrenzung**
Rüstungsbetrieb *m* armament [arms] factory
Rüstungsetat *m s.* **Rüstungshaushalt**
Rüstungsexport *m* export of arms
Rüstungsfinanzierung *f* financing of arms
Rüstungsforschung *f* armaments research
Rüstungsgeschäft *n* trade in armaments, arms business
Rüstungsgewinn *m* armaments profit
Rüstungshaushalt *m* arms [defence] budget
Rüstungsimport *m* arms [armaments] import
Rüstungsindustrie *f* arms [armaments, war] industry
Rüstungskapazität *f* armaments capacity
Rüstungskauf *m* purchase of arms [armaments]
Rüstungskontrolle *f* 1. arms [armaments] control; 2. supervision of arms limitation agreement
Rüstungskosten *pl* arms [armaments] costs
Rüstungskredit *m s.* **Rüstungsanleihe**
Rüstungslasten *fpl* burden of armament
Rüstungsmarkt *m* arms [armaments] market
Rüstungsmonopol *n* armament [arms] monopoly
Rüstungspolitik *f* arms [armaments] policy
Rüstungspotential *n* arms [armaments] potential
Rüstungsproduktion *f* arms [armaments] production
Rüstungsprofit *m s.* **Rüstungsgewinn**
Rüstungsprogramm *n* arms [armament] programme
Rüstungsstopp *m* freeze on arms
Rüstungswettlauf *m* arms race
Rüstungswirtschaft *f* war economy
Rüstzeit *f (manuf)* tooling [set-up] time; *(min)* make-ready time *(drilling)*
~ **bei Arbeitsbeginn** start-up [set-up, make--ready] time
~ **nach Arbeitsschluß** shut-down [tear-down] time
Rüstzeug *n* qualifications, know-how, experience

S

Saat *f* 1. growing [standing] crops; 2. seed; 3. sowing; sowing-time, sowing season [period]
Saatbettbereitung *f* preparation of seedbed
Saatfläche *f* seeded field
Saatgut *n* seeds; seedlings
Saatgutaufbereitung *f* seed preparation
Saatgutfonds *m* stock of seeds
Saatgutreservefonds *m* reserve stocks of seeds
Saatgutveredlung *f* improvement of seed grain
Saat- und Pflanzgut *n* seeds and seedlings
Saatzeit *f* sowing-time, sowing season [period]
Saatzucht *f* seed cultivation
Saatzuchtbetrieb *m* seed producing farm, seed nursery
Sabotage *f* sabotage
Saboteur *m* saboteur
sabotieren to sabotage; to torpedo *(plan, scheme etc.)*
Sachanlage *f* real investment
Sachanlagevermögen *n* tangible assets
Sachaufwendungen *fpl s.* **Sachausgaben**
Sachausgaben *fpl* material expenditure(s)
Sachbearbeiter *m* clerk
Sachbeschädigung *f* damage to property, wilful destruction
~, **vorsätzliche** malicious damage
Sachbesitz *m* effects, material property
Sachbeweis *m* objective proof
sachbezogen factual
Sachbezüge *mpl* payment in kind
Sachdepot *n* safe
sachdienlich relevant *(facts etc.)*; suitable, appropriate *(material etc.)*; serviceable, useful
Sache *f* thing, object, article; matter, affair, business, concern; issue; case ◇ **eine ~ vor Gericht verteidigen** to plead a case; **für eine ~ eintreten** to support a cause [an idea, a doctrine]
~, **geschäftliche** business matter
~, **schwebende** pending case
~, **strittige** controversial issue
Sacheinlage *f* 1. valuables in a safe; 2. contribution in kind
Sachen *fpl* things, effects, belongings; clothes; furniture ◇ **in ~ A gegen B** in the matter [case] of A versus [v.s.] B
~, **abhanden gekommene** things lost, lost things
~, **bewegliche** movable things, movables
~, **ersetzbare** replaceable [reparable, recoverable] things
~, **herrenlose** ownerless things
~, **nicht vertretbare** *(jur)* non-fungible things
~, **öffentliche** public affairs

~, **unbewegliche** immovable things, immovables
~, **unersetzbare** irreplaceable things
~, **unvertretbare** s. ~, **nicht vertretbare**
~, **verlorene** s. ~, **abhanden gekommene**
~, **vertretbare** *(jur)* fungible things
Sachenrecht *n (jur)* law of property
Sachentscheidung *f* decision on the merits (of a thing)
Sachfrage *f* factual issue
Sachgebiet *n* field, subject, department of knowledge
sachgemäß appropriate, pertinent
Sachgüter *npl* material goods
Sachkapital *n* capital in kind
Sachkapitalbildung *f* non-money capital formation
Sachkapitalerhöhung *f* non-money capital increase
Sachkenner *m* expert
Sachkenntnis *f* expert [special] knowledge, experience; know-how
Sachkontenrahmen *m* system of budget accounts *(classification of budget accounts)*
Sachkonto *n* (annual) budget account; inventory [property, impersonal] account
Sachkosten *pl* cost of material things
Sachkredit *m* credit in kind
Sachkunde *f s.* **Sachkenntnis**
sachkundig expert(ly), skilled; (well-)versed
Sachkundiger *m s.* **Sachkenner**
Sachlage *f* state of affairs
Sachleistung *f* payment in kind
sachlich real, factual; technical ⋄ ~ **richtig** factually correct
Sachlichkeit *f* objectivity; realism; relevance
~, **neue** functionalism
Sachlohn *m* wage(s) in kind
Sachmangel *m* deficiency, defect, flaw
Sachmängel *mpl* (factual) shortcomings
Sachmängelhaftung *f* warranty of fitness
Sachmängelrüge *f* factual complaints
Sachprämie *f* bonus in kind
Sachregister *n* subject index
Sachschaden *m* damage to property, material damage
Sachschadenersatz *m* indemnity [compensation] for damage to property
Sachschadenhaftpflicht *f* indemnity liability, liability for damage to property
Sachschadenhaftpflichtgesetz *n* indemnity liability act
Sachschadenversicherung *f* property damage liability insurance
Sachspende *f* gift in kind
Sachsteuern *fpl* taxes in kind
Sachurteil *n* expertise
Sachverhalt *m* facts

Sachvermögen *n* material assets, tangible property
Sachversicherung *f* property insurance
Sachverständigenausschuß *m* commission of experts
Sachverständigengutachten *n* expert opinion
Sachverständigenkommission *f s.* **Sachverständigenausschuß**
Sachverständigenurteil *n s.* **Sachverständigengutachten**
Sachverständigenverfahren *n (ins)* procedure for examining damage to goods (by experts)
Sachverständiger *m* expert, specialist, authority ⋄ **einen Sachverständigen zu Rate ziehen** to consult an expert
~ **für Gebrauchsmuster** 1. design examiner; 2. design expert
~ **für Warenzeichenrecht** 1. examiner in charge of trademarks; 2. expert in trademark matters
Sachverzeichnis *n* index; table of contents; inventory
Sachwalter *m* administrator *(of estate etc.)*; trustee; agent
Sachwaltung *f* administration, management *(estate etc.)*
Sachwert *m* real value
Sachwertanleihe *f* loan in kind
Sachwerte *mpl* material assets
Sachwertklausel *f* real value clause
Sachwertlotterie *f* lottery in kind
säen to sow, to seed
Safe *m* safe
Sägemühle *f s.* **Sägewerk**
Sägewerk *n* sawmill
Saison *f* season
saisonabhängig seasonal
saisonal *s.* **saisonabhängig**
Saisonangebot *n* seasonal supply *(goods etc.)*
Saisonarbeit *f* seasonal work
Saisonarbeiter *m* seasonal worker
Saisonarbeitskraft *f s.* **Saisonarbeiter**
Saisonarbeitskräfte *fpl* seasonal labour force [work(ing) force]
Saisonarbeitslosigkeit *f* seasonal unemployment
Saisonartikel *mpl* seasonal goods
Saisonausverkauf *m* clearance [stock-taking] sale, seasonal clearance
Saisonbedarf *m* seasonal needs
saisonbedingt *s.* **saisonabhängig**
Saisonbelieferung *f* seasonal delivery
saisonbereinigt disregarding seasonal fluctuation; *(stats)* seasonally adjusted
Saisonbereinigung *f* disregarding [disregard of] seasonal fluctuations; *(stats)* seasonal adjustment

Saisonbeschäftigung *f* seasonal employment
Saisonbestand *m* seasonal stocks [store]
Saisonbetrieb *m* seasonally-operating factory
Saisoncharakter *m* seasonal character [nature]
Saisonfinanzierungsplan *m* seasonal finance [financing] plan
saisongebunden *s.* **saisonabhängig**
Saisongebundenheit *f* dependence on a season, seasonal dependence [constraint]
saisongemäß according to season
saisongerecht *s.* **saisongemäß**
Saisongeschäft *n* seasonal business
Saisongewerbe *n* seasonal trade
Saisonhandel *m* seasonal trade
Saisonindex *m* seasonal index
Saisonindustrie *f* seasonal industry
Saisonkapazität *f* seasonal capacity
Saisonkarte *f* season ticket
Saisonkoeffizient *m* *(stats)* season coefficient
Saisonkorridor *m* *(stats)* high-low graph
Saisonkräfte *fpl s.* **Saisonarbeitskräfte**
Saisonkredit *m* seasonal credit [loan]
Saisonkrippe *f* seasonal day-nursery [crèche]
Saisonlager *n* 1. seasonal stocks [store] *(goods)*; 2. seasonal storehouse *(storage)*
saisonmäßig *s.* **saisonabhängig**
Saisonpreis *m* seasonal price
Saisonproduktion *f* seasonal production
Saisonschlußverkauf *m* end-of-season sale
Saisonschwankung *f* seasonal fluctuation
~, gleitende *(stats)* moving seasonal variation
Saisontarif *m* seasonal rate
Saisontätigkeit *f s.* **Saisonarbeit**
Saisonverbrauch *m* seasonal consumption
Saisonverkehr *m* seasonal traffic
Saisonvertrag *m* seasonal contract
Saisonvorrat *m* seasonal stock *(goods etc.)*
Saisonwanderung *f* seasonal migration
Saisonware *f* seasonal article
Saisonzahl *f (stats)* season figure
Säkularisation *f* secularization *(of ecclesiastical property)*
säkularisieren to secularize *(ecclesiastical property)*
Säkularisierung *f s.* **Säkularisation**
Saldenausgleich *m* balancing, settlement; clearance
Saldenbilanz *f* final balance sheet
Saldenkonto *n (acc)* balance account
Saldenmethode *f* net financing
Saldenverrechnung *f (bank)* book transfer of balances
Saldenvortrag *m s.* **Saldoübertrag**
saldieren to balance, to settle
Saldiermaschine *f* adding machine
Saldo *m* balance ◊ **einen ~ ausgleichen** to settle [clear] a balance; **einen ~ ausweisen** to show a balance; **einen ~ auszahlen** to pay out a balance; **einen ~ übertragen** to carry forward a balance; **einen ~ überweisen** to remit a balance; **einen ~ vortragen** *s.* **einen ~ übertragen**; **~ zu Ihren Gunsten** your credit balance; **~ zu Ihren Lasten** your debit balance
~, berichtigter adjusted balance
~, effektiver actual balance
~, täglicher daily balance
~, ungedeckter uncovered balance
~, ungenutzter dormant balance
~, verfügbarer available balance
~, vorgetragener balance carried forward
Saldobetrag *m* (amount of) balance
Saldoguthaben *n* credit balance
Saldorechnung *f* invoice for payment of balance
Saldoübertrag *m* carried-forward balance
Saldovortrag *m s.* **Saldoübertrag**
Saldowechsel *m* balance payment by bills
Saldozahlung *f* payment of balance
Salzboden *m* saline soil
Salzsteuer *f* salt-tax
Salzwasser *n* salt-water
Samen- und Pflanzenversand *m* seeds and seedlings dispatching nursery; dispatching of seeds and seedlings
Sammelabschreibung *f* collective depreciation
Sammelaktie *f* collective share [*(Am)* stock]
Sammelaktion *f* fund-raising drive
Sammelanleihe *f* collective loan
Sammelanschluß *m* party-line, collective number
Sammelaufgabe *f (ins)* bordereau
Sammelauftrag *m (com)* collective order; *(bank)* collection order
Sammelavis *m/n* collective advice
Sammelbecken *n* reservoir, storage [collecting] tank
Sammelbeleg *m* collective voucher
Sammelbestellung *f* collective order
Sammelbezeichnung *f* collective name
Sammelbilanz *f (bank)* collecting balance sheet
Sammelbuchung *f* compound entry
Sammeldauerauftrag *m* collective standing order
Sammeldepot *n* general deposit; *(ins)* corporate bonding
Sammelfahrschein *m (railw)* collective [group] ticket
Sammelgebiet *n* catchment area
Sammelgenehmigung *f* collective permit
Sammelgut *n* mixed consignment
Sammelgutspediteur *m* forwarding agent of mixed consignments
Sammelgutverkehr *m* traffic in mixed consignments

Sammelkauf *m* bulk buying
Sammelklausel *f* omnibus clause
Sammelkonossement *n* omnibus bill of lading
Sammelkonto *n* general account
Sammelladung *f* general cargo, *(Am)* carload freight
Sammellager *n* 1. general depot *(goods etc.)*; 2. resettlement camp; assembly centre
Sammellohnschein *m* collective list of wages
sammeln to collect *(money etc.)*; to gather, to pick *(mushrooms etc.)*; to accumulate *(wealth etc.)*; to compile *(lists etc.)*
Sammeln *n* collecting *(money etc.)*; gathering, picking *(mushrooms etc.)*; accumulating *(wealth etc.)*; compiling *(lists etc.)*
Sammelnummer *f* collective number
Sammelpaß *m* collective passport
Sammelplatz *m* meeting-place *(persons etc.)*; depot *(goods etc.)*
Sammelposten *m* miscellaneous item
Sammelpunkt *m s.* **Sammelplatz**
Sammelsendung *f* collected consignment
Sammelstelle *f* collecting point
Sammeltarif *m* group rate
Sammeltransport *m* group transport
Sammelversicherung *f* group insurance
Sammelversicherungsschein *m* group insurance policy
Sammelverwahrung *f* general deposit
Sammelzeichnung *f (d.pr.)* tabulate drawing
Sammler *m* gatherer *(food etc., in primitive society)*; picker *(mushrooms etc.)*; collector *(antique furniture etc.)*
Sammlung *f* collection *(money etc.)*; gathering *(information etc.)*
~, öffentliche public collection *(of money and goods for solidarity purposes)*
Sandboden *m* sandy soil
sanieren to restore, to reconstruct *(flats etc.)*; to stabilize, to reorganize *(economy etc.)*; to redevelop *(urban area etc.)*
Sanierung *f* restoration, reconstruction *(flats etc.)*; stabilization, reorganization *(economy etc.)*; redevelopment *(urban area etc.)*
~ der Finanzen stabilization of finances
~ der Staatsfinanzen stabilization of public finance
~ einer Firma reorganization of a firm [company]
~ eines Kontos improvement in the solvency of an account
~ von Gebäuden restoration [reconstruction] of buildings
~ von Land redevelopment [reclamation] of area
Sanierungsantrag *m* application for reorganization *(company etc.)*

Sanierungsausschuß *m* committee for reorganization
Sanierungsgewinn *m* reconstruction profit
Sanierungskosten *pl* reconstruction costs
Sanierungsmaßnahmen *fpl* reconstruction measures; stabilization [reorganization] measures; redevelopment measures
Sanierungsmittel *npl* finance for reconstruction [stabilization, redevelopment]
Sanierungsplan *m* reconstruction [stabilization, redevelopment] plan
Sanierungsprogramm *n* reconstruction [stabilization, redevelopment] programme
Sanierungsverfahren *n* procedure of reconstruction [reorganization]
Sanierungsvorhaben *n* reconstruction [stabilization, redevelopment] project
Sanktion *f* sanction, approval
sanktionieren to sanction, to approve
Satellitenrechner *m (d.pr.)* satellite computer
Satellitenstadt *f* satellite town
Satellitensystem *n (d.pr.)* satellite system
sättigen to satiate, to satisfy; *(com)* to saturate *(market etc.)*
Sättigung *f* satiaton; *(com)* saturation *(market etc.)*
Sättigungsgrad *m* degree of saturation
Sättigungsgrenze *f* limit [point] of saturation
Sättigungskurve *f* curve of saturation
Sättigungsniveau *n* saturation level
Sättigungsperiode *f* period of saturation
Sättigungsprognose *f* (long-term) forecast of saturation
Sättigungsprozeß *m* process of saturation
Sättigungspunkt *m* saturation point
Sattler *m* saddler
Sattlerhandwerk *n* saddler's trade
Sattlerwaren *fpl* saddlery
Satz *m* proposition; theorem; principle; rate *(charge etc.)*; set *(documents etc.)*; range, assortment *(goods)* ◊ **zu einem bestimmten ~** at a fixed rate; **zu einem ermäßigten ~** at a reduced rate; **zum günstigsten ~** at the most favourable rate
~, fester fixed rate; fixed price
~, höchster maximum rate
~, ortsüblicher local rate
Satzadresse *f (d.pr.)* record address
Satzanzahl *f (d.pr.)* record counting
Satzauswahl *f (d.pr.)* record selection
Satzbestimmung *f (d.pr.)* locating the record
Satzeinteilung *f*:
~ auf dem Magnetband *(d.pr.)* tape layout
Satzerkennungscode *m (d.pr.)* record identifying code
Satzgruppe *f (d.pr.)* grouped record
Satzlängenfeld *n (d.pr.)* record length field

Satzlängen-Steuereinheit *f (d.pr.)* variable record length punching device
Satzlücke *f (d.pr.)* end of record gap, inter-record gap, record gap
Satzspeicher *m (d.pr.)* record storage
~ **eines Druckers** *(d.pr.)* printed record storage
Satzung *f* statute; standing rule, by-law; article; charter
Satzungen *fpl:*
~ **der Vereinten Nationen** Charter of the United Nations
~ **einer Aktiengesellschaft** articles of a company
Satzungsänderung *f* alteration of the statute; changes in the articles *(agreement etc.)*
satzungsgemäß statutory, in accordance with the statute
satzungsmäßig according to the statute [rules]
satzungswidrig unconstitutional
satzweise in sets
Säuglingsfürsorge *f* infant welfare
Säuglingsheim *n* crèche
Säuglingssterblichkeit *f* infant mortality
Säulendiagramm *n (stats)* bar chart; block diagram
~, **mehrfaches** *(stats)* multiple bar chart
~, **unterteiltes** *(stats)* component bar chart
säumig slow, dilatory, tardy *(payments etc.)*; defaulting *(debtor)*
Säumnisgebühr *f* default fee, delay penalty
Säumniszuschlag *m* penalty interest, interest on arrears
Schachbrettabelle *f* latticed table
schachbrettartig chequered
Schachbrettbilanz *f* chess-board balance sheet
schachbrettförmig *s.* **schachbrettartig**
Schacher *m* haggling; *(st.ex.)* jobbery
Schacherei *f s.* **Schacher**
Schacherer *m* haggler
schachern to haggle
schaden to damage; to do damage; to do harm to *(person etc.)*
Schaden *m* damage ❖ **für einen ~ haften** to be liable for damages; **gegen ~ versichern** to insure against damage(s); **~ abschätzen** to assess damage(s); **~ anmelden** to report damage; **~ anrichten** to cause damage; **~ aufnehmen** *s.* **~ abschätzen**; **~ beseitigen** *s.* **~ wiedergutmachen**; **~ decken** *s.* **~ wiedergutmachen**; **~ erleiden** to come to harm *(persons)*; to be damaged; **~ verhüten** to prevent damage; **~ wiedergutmachen** to make good damage; **~ zufügen** to do *(s.o.)* harm, to harm *(s.o.)*; to damage *(s.th.)*; **zu ~ kommen** to suffer [sustain] an injury
~, **absichtlich herbeigeführter** malicious damage
~, **angerichteter** damage done *(to s.th.)*
~, **direkter** direct damage
~, **durch die Versicherung gedeckter** loss covered by insurance
~ **durch höhere Gewalt** damage caused by force majeure
~, **eingetretener** damage incurred
~, **erlittener** damage suffered; loss sustained
~, **festgestellter** ascertained damage, damage found
~, **geringfügiger** nominal damage
~, **geschäftlicher** commercial loss
~, **immaterieller** immaterial damage
~, **körperlicher** bodily harm [injury]
~, **materieller** material damage
~, **mittelbarer** indirect damage
~, **nachgewiesener** proved damage, damage proved
~, **noch nicht eingetretener** damage not yet incurred
~, **regulierter** settled claim (for damages)
~, **tatsächlich entstandener** actual damage
~, **unbedeutender** insignificant [negligible] damage
~, **uneinbringlicher** irretrievable loss
~, **unmittelbarer** direct damage
Schadenabschätzung *f s.* **Schadenfeststellung**
Schadenabwendungspflicht *f* obligation to prevent damages
Schadenanmeldung *f s.* **Schadensmeldung**
Schadenausgleich *m* compensation for damage
Schadenbearbeitung *f* handling of damages
Schadenberechnung *f* calculation of damage
Schadenersatz *m* amends *(for wrong-doing etc.)*; compensation, indemnity *(for damage sustained etc.)*; damages *(expressed in money)* ❖ **Anspruch auf ~ erhalten** to be awarded damages; **auf ~ haften** to be liable for damages; to be responsible for a loss; **auf ~ verklagen** to sue for damages; **für einen Betriebsangehörigen ~ leisten** to compensate a workman for his injuries; **~ aberkennen** to disallow compensation; **~ beanspruchen** to claim damages; **~ erhalten** to recover damages; **~ erlangen** *s.* **~ erhalten**; **~ leisten** to make amends *(for wrong-doing etc.)*; to pay damages; **~ nicht anerkennen** *s.* **~ aberkennen**; **~ verlangen** to lodge a claim for compensation, to claim compensation, to demand damages; **~ zusprechen** to adjudicate damages [compensation]; **zum ~ verpflichtet** liable to pay damages [compensation]
~ **für Berufskrankheiten** compensation for industrial diseases
~, **gesetzlicher** damages regulated by law
~, **vertraglich geregelter** contractually fixed indemnification

Schadenersatzanspruch *m* claim for damages [compensation] ✧ **auf ~ verzichten** to renounce a claim for damages; **~ begründen** to give proof for damages claimed
~, anerkannter recognized claim for damages
~, eingetretener claim for sustained damages
Schadenersatzaufwand *m* costs of compensating damages
Schadenersatzbestimmungen *fpl* compensation provisions
Schadenersatzforderung *f* claim for damages
Schadenersatzklage *f* action [proceedings] for damages ✧ **~ einreichen** to hand in a claim for damages
Schadenersatzklausel *f* loss payable clause
Schadenersatzleistung *f* indemnification, payment of damages [compensation]
Schadenersatzpflicht *f* liability for damages, obligation to pay damages
schadenersatzpflichtig liable for damages
Schadenersatzverpflichtung *f s.* **Schadenersatzpflicht**
Schadenersatzversicherung *f* liability insurance
Schadenfeststellung *f* assessment of damages
Schadengutachter *m (ins)* (damage) adjustor
Schadenrechnung *f* statement of damages
Schadenregulierung *f (ins)* adjustment of damages, settlement of losses
Schadenreserve *f (ins)* policy [claim, loss] reserve
Schadenrückstellung *f s.* **Schadenreserve**
Schadensabfindung *f* indemnification, compensation
Schadensabteilung *f* claims department
Schadensanzeige *f* damage report
Schadensart *f* kind [type] of damage
Schadensaufstellung *f s.* **Schadensanzeige**
Schadensausmaß *n* extent of damage
Schadensberechnung *f s.* **Schadensfeststellung**
Schadensbetrag *m s.* **Schadenssumme**
Schadensbewertung *f* evaluation of loss(es)
Schadensschätzung *f s.* **Schadensfeststellung**
Schadensfall *m* case of damage [loss]
Schadensfestsetzung *f* fixing of damages
Schadensfeststellung *f* assessment of damages
Schadensforderung *f s.* **Schadenersatzforderung**
Schadenshäufigkeit *f* loss frequency
Schadenshöhe *f* amount of losses
Schadensliste *f* list of damage
Schadensmeldung *f* report of damage
Schadensnachweis *m* proof of damage [loss(es)]
Schadensquote *f* amount of damage
Schadensstatistik *f* claim [loss] statistics
Schadensstelle *f* place where damage was incurred

Schadenssumme *f* sum [amount] of damages
Schadensvergütung *f* payment of damages, indemnification for losses
Schadenursache *f* cause of damage
Schadenverhütung *f* prevention of damage
Schadenversicherung *f* indemnity insurance, insurance against damages
Schadenwahrscheinlichkeit *f* probability of damages
schadhaft faulty, defective; damaged
Schadhaftigkeit *f* defectiveness; damaged condition
schädigen to damage, to impair; to harm, to do injury (to); to cause damage; to prejudice *(one's case etc.)*
Schädigung *f* damage; prejudice, detriment *(to one's case etc.)*; impairment *(of one's rights etc.)*
Schädigungsgrad *m* degree of damage; degree of impairment
schädlich harmful, injurious; detrimental; noxious, poisonous *(fumes etc.)*
Schädlichkeit *f* harm, harmfulness; perniciousness; noxiousness *(fumes etc.)*
Schädling *m* pest, destructive insect; destructive weed
Schädlingsbekämpfer *m* insecticide(s) sprayer
Schädlingsbekämpfung *f* pest control
Schädlingsbekämpfungsmittel *n* pesticide; insecticide
schadlos harmless; indemnified
Schadlosbürgschaft *f* collateral guarantee
Schadpark *m* damaged vehicles workshop
Schäfer *m* shepherd
schaffen to make; to create, to set up *(committee etc.)*, to provide *(conditions etc.)*; to procure *(necessities etc.)*; to establish *(order etc.)*
Schaffenskraft *f* creative [productive] power
Schaffner *m* conductor *(bus, tram)*; *(railw)* ticket collector
Schaffung *f* making; creating, creation, setting up *(committee etc.)*, providing, provision *(conditions etc.)*; procurement *(necessities etc.)*; establishing, establishment *(order etc.)*
~ von (mitlaufenden) Basisdaten *(d.pr.)* (on--line) data base industry
Schafhaltung *f* sheep rearing [farming]
Schafzucht *f* sheep rearing [breeding, farming]
Schafzüchter *m* sheep breeder, sheep farmer
Schalldämpfung *f* noise reduction; sound absorption
Schallisolierung *f* sound isolation, sound proofing insulation
Schalter *m* 1. counter, window, desk *(post, bank)*; booking [ticket] office *(railw etc.)*; 2. *(d.pr.)* switch
Schalterdienst *m* counter-service
Schaltergeschäft *n* over-the-counter transaction

Schalterstunden *fpl* banking hours; post-office hours
Schalterverkehr *m s.* **Schaltergeschäft**
Schaltpult *n* control desk
Schaltsystem *n* switching system [circuit]
Schalttafel *f* switchboard
Schandpreis *m* scandalous price
Schankerlaubnis *f* licence for the sale of drinks and beverages
Schankgerechtigkeit *f s.* **Schankerlaubnis**
Schankrecht *n s.* **Schankerlaubnis**
~ **(im Lokal)** on-licence
~ **(über die Straße)** off-licence
Schärfe *f (stats)* power
Schattenhaushalt *m* shadow budget
Schattenpreis *m* shadow price
Schatz *m* treasure
Schatzamt *n* treasury
Schatzanleihe *f* treasury loan
Schatzanweisung *f* exchequer bond, long-term paper; treasury warrant, *(Am)* treasury certificate
~, **unverzinsliche** treasury bill
schätzbar valuable *(services etc.)*, estimable *(values etc.)*
Schatzbildung *f* hoarding
schätzen 1. to estimate *(costs etc.)*; to assess *(taxes etc.)*; to appraise *(damages etc.)*; to value *(houses etc.)*; 2. to reckon, to suppose; 3. to esteem, to appreciate *(the worth of s.o., s.th.)*
Schätzer *m* valuer; *(ins)* appraiser; assessor *(taxes etc.)*
~, **amtlicher** *(ins)* official appraiser
~, **beeidigter** licenced valuer
Schätzfehler *m (stats)* error of estimation
Schatzfunktion *f* treasury function
Schätzfunktion *f (stats)* estimator
~, **absolute nichtverzerrende** *(stats)* absolute unbiassed estimator
~, **asymptotisch effiziente** *(stats)* asymptotically efficient estimator
~, **asymptotisch erwartungstreue** *(stats)* asymptotically unbiassed estimator
~, **asympotisch nicht treffende** *s.* ~, **nichtkonsistente**
~, **asymptotisch nichtverzerrende** *(stats)* asymptotically unbiassed estimator
~, **asymptotisch treffende** *(stats)* consistent estimator
~, **bedingt erwartungstreue** *(stats)* conditionally unbiassed estimator
~, **beste** *(stats)* best estimator
~, **effiziente** *(stats)* efficient estimator
~, **erwartungstreue** *(stats)* unbiassed estimator
~, **höchsteffiziente** *(stats)* most-efficient estimator
~, **höchstleistungsfähige** *s.* ~, **effiziente**

~, **konsistente** *s.* ~, **asymptotisch treffende**
~, **lineare** *(stats)* linear estimator
~ **mit konstantem Risiko, gleichmäßig beste** *(stats)* uniformly best constant risk estimator (U.B.C.R.)
~ **nach der Methode der kleinsten Quadrate** *(stats)* least-squares estimator
~, **nichterwartungstreue** *(stats)* biassed estimator
~, **nichthöchstleistungsfähige** *(stats)* inefficient estimator
~, **nichtkonsistente** *(stats)* inconsistent estimator
~, **nichtreguläre** *(stats)* non-regular estimator
~, **nichtverzerrende** *s.* ~, **erwartungstreue**
~, **quadratische** *(stats)* quadratic estimator
~, **reguläre** *(stats)* regular estimator
~, **stets erwartungstreue** *s.* ~, **absolut nichtverzerrende**
~, **tendenzfreie** *s.* ~, **erwartungstreue**
~, **verzerrende** *s.* ~, **nichterwartungstreue**
Schätzgleichung *f (stats)* estimating equation
~, **nichtverzerrende** *(stats)* unbiassed estimating equation
Schätzpreis *m* estimated price
Schätztheorie *f* theory of estimates
Schätzung *f* estimation, estimate *(costs etc.)*; assessment *(taxes etc.)*; appraisal *(damages etc.)*; valuation *(houses etc.)*
~, **amtliche** official valuation [evaluation]
~, **asymptotisch erwartungstreue** *(stats)* asymptotically unbiassed estimation
~, **effektive** *(fin)* effective assessment
~, **erneute** re-valuation, re-evaluation; re-assessment *(taxes)*
~, **erschöpfende** *(ins)* full appraisal
~, **erwartungstreue** *(stats)* unbiassed estimation
~, **fundierte** *(stats)* well-founded estimation
~, **konsistente** *(stats)* consistent estimation
~, **nichterwartungstreue** *(stats)* biassed estimation
~, **nichtverzerrende** *s.* ~, **erwartungstreue**
~, **optimale** *(stats)* optimum estimation
~, **optimistische** optimistic estimation
~, **passende** proper estimation
~, **pessimistische** pessimistic estimation
~, **sequentielle** *(stats)* sequential estimation
~, **simultane** *(stats)* simultaneous estimation
~, **unverzerrte** *s.* ~, **erwartungstreue**
~, **vorsichtige** conservative estimate
~, **wahrscheinlichste** *(stats)* most probable estimation
~, **wirksame** *s.* ~, **effektive**
Schätzungsbericht *m (ins)* appraisal report
Schätzungsfehler *m s.* **Schätzfehler**
Schätzungslehre *f s.* **Schätzungstheorie**
Schätzungsliste *f (ins)* list of appraisals
Schätzungssumme *f s.* **Schätzwert**

Schätzungstheorie *f (stats)* theory of estimation
Schätzverfahren *n (stats)* method of estimation; *(ins)* method of appraisal
Schatzwechsel *m* treasury bill
Schätzwert *m* estimated value *(cars, houses etc.)*; assessed value *(taxes etc.)*; *(ins)* appraised value
~, **Markoff'scher** *(stats)* Markoff estimate
~ **nach der Methode der kleinsten Quadrate** *(stats)* Markoff estimate
Schau *f* show; exhibition; display; fair
Schaubild *n* diagram; graphic illustration; graph; chart
Schauerprozeß *m (stats)* cascade process
Schaufenster *n* shop-window, show-window ❖ **im ~ ausstellen** to display in the window
Schaufensterauslage *f* window display
Schaufensterausrüstung *f s.* **Schaufensterauslage**
Schaufensterausstattung *f s.* **Schaufensterauslage**
Schaufensterbeleuchtung *f* window illumination
Schaufensterbummel *m* window-shopping ❖ **einen ~ machen** to go window-shopping
Schaufensterdekorateur *m* window-dresser
Schaufensterdekoration *f* window-dressing
Schaufenstergestalter *m s.* **Schaufensterdekorateur**
Schaufenstergestaltung *f s.* **Schaufensterdekoration**
Schaufensterreklame *f* window-display advertising
Schaufensterwerbung *f s.* **Schaufensterreklame**
Schaufensterwettbewerb *m* competition in window-display [window-dressing]
Schaugeschäft *n* show business
Schaupackung *f* dummy package *(for window display etc.)*
Schaustück *n* show-piece; exhibit
Schauware *f* show-goods
Scheck *m* cheque, *(Am)* check ❖ **einen ~ ausschreiben [ausstellen]** to write out [issue, make out] a cheque [*(Am)* check]; **einen ~ einlösen (bei einer Bank)** to get a cheque [*(Am)* check] cashed (at a bank), to cash a cheque [*(Am)* check] (at a bank); **einen ~ fälschen** to forge a cheque [*(Am)* check]; **einen ~ sperren (lassen)** to stop [block] a cheque [*(Am)* check]; to stop payment of a cheque [*(Am)* check] on a check]; **einen ungedeckten ~ ausstellen** to issue a bad cheque [*(Am)* check]; **mit einem ~ bezahlen** to pay by cheque [*(Am)* check]; **zahlbar mit ~** payable by cheque [*(Am)* check]
~, **auf den Namen lautender** non-negotiable cheque [*(Am)* check]

~, **auf den Überbringer lautender** bearer cheque [*(Am)* check]
~, **bestätigter** confirmed cheque [*(Am)* check]
~, **fehlerhafter** defective cheque [*(Am)* check]
~, **gedeckter** covered cheque [*(Am)* check]
~, **gekreuzter** crossed cheque [*(Am)* check]
~, **gesperrter** stopped cheque [*(Am)* check]
~, **girierter** endorsed cheque [*(Am)* check]
~, **nachdatierter** postdated cheque [*(Am)* check]
~, **offener** open [uncrossed] cheque [*(Am)* check]
~, **unausgefüllter** blank cheque [*(Am)* check]
~, **ungedeckter** uncovered cheque [*(Am)* check]
~, **unvollständiger** invalid cheque [*(Am)* check]
~, **verfallener** expired cheque [*(Am)* check]
~, **vordatierter** predated cheque [*(Am)* check]
Scheckabrechnung *f* clearing of cheques [*(Am)* checks]
Scheckabrechnungsstelle *f* clearing house
Scheckabteilung *f* cheque [*(Am)* check] department
Scheckaussteller *m* drawer of a cheque [*(Am)* check]
Scheckbedingungen *fpl* cheque [*(Am)* check] conditions
Scheckbetrag *m* amount on the cheque [*(Am)* check]
Scheckbetrug *m* cheque [*(Am)* check] fraud
Scheckbuch *n* cheque-book, *(Am)* checkbook
Scheckbürgschaft *f* cheque guarantee, *(Am)* check guaranty
Scheckdiskontierung *f* endorsement of cheques [*(Am)* checks]
Scheckempfänger *m* drawee of a cheque [*(Am)* check]
scheckfähig capable of drawing cheques [*(Am)* checks]; capable of being the drawee of cheques [*(Am)* checks]
Scheckfähigkeit *f* capacity to draw cheques [*(Am)* checks]; capacity of being the drawee of cheques [*(Am)* checks]
Scheckfälscher *m* cheque [*(Am)* check] forger
Scheckfälschung *f* forgery of a cheque [*(Am)* check]
Scheckformular *n* cheque [*(Am)* check] form [blank]
Scheckgelder *npl* cheque [*(Am)* check] money
Scheckheft *n s.* **Scheckbuch**
Scheckindossament *n* cheque [*(Am)* check] endorsement
Scheckinhaber *m* bearer of a cheque [*(Am)* check]
Scheckinkasso *n* encashment of cheques [*(Am)* checks]
Scheckinkassospesen *pl* cheque [*(Am)* check] collection charges
Scheckkonto *n* cheque account, *(Am)* checking account

Scheckkurs *m* cheque [*(Am)* check] rate
Scheckregister *n* cheque [*(Am)* check] register
Scheckregreß *m* cheque [*(Am)* check] recourse
Scheckrückgriff *m s.* **Scheckregreß**
Schecksperre *f* stopping of a cheque [*(Am)* check]; cheque [*(Am)* check] blocking; *(Am)* check embargo
Scheck- und Wechselverkehr *m* cheque [*(Am)* check] and bill transactions
Scheckverfahren *n* payment by cheque [*(Am)* check], cheque [*(Am)* check] payment
Scheckverkehr *m* cheque [*(Am)* check] transactions
Scheckverrechnung *f* clearing by cheques [*(Am)* checks]
Scheckverzeichnis *n s.* **Scheckregister**
Scheckvordruck *m s.* **Scheckformular**
Scheckzahlung *f* cheque [*(Am)* check] payment
Scheibenspeicher *m (d.pr.)* disk data storage
Scheideanstalt *f* refinery *(for coins etc.)*
Scheidegeld *n* token coins; small coins
Scheidemünze *f* token coin; small coin
Scheidewert *m (stats)* dividing value
Schein *m* 1. attestation, certificate; receipt; bill; 2. bank note; 3. semblance, appearance; sham
Scheinanweisung *f (d.pr.)* dummy statement
Scheinauktion *f* sham auction
Scheinbefehl *m (d.pr.)* compiler directing statement
Scheinblüte *f* apparent [specious] prosperity, sham boom
Scheinbonität *f* sham solvency
Scheinbuchung *f* fictitious entry
Scheinfaktura *f s.* **Scheinrechnung**
Scheinfirma *f* bogus firm [company]
Scheingeschäft *n* fictitious [dummy] transaction
Scheingesellschaft *f* bogus company
Scheingewinn *m* fictitious profit
Scheingründung *f* fictitious formation (of a company)
Scheinkauf *m* sham [fictitious] purchase
Scheinkonto *n* fictitious account
Scheinkorrelation *f (stats)* illusory [spurious] correlation
Scheinkurs *m* fictitious [sham] rate
Scheinpartner *m* fictitious partner
Scheinprozedur *f (d.pr.)* dummy procedure
Scheinquittung *f* pro forma receipt
Scheinrechnung *f* fictitious invoice
Scheinrentabilität *f* sham profitability [rentability]
Scheinsitz *m* fictitious seat (of a company)
Scheinunternehmen *n* bogus [fictitious, dummy] concern
Scheinverbundenheit *f (stats)* illusory association
Scheinverkauf *m* fictitious sale

Scheinversteigerung *f s.* **Scheinauktion**
Scheinvertrag *m* fictitious contract
Scheinvorgang *m s.* **Scheinbuchung**
Scheinwechsel *m* fictitious [bogus] bill, kite
Scheinwert *m* apparent [imaginary] value
Scheinwiderstand *m (d.pr.)* impedance
Scheinwiderstandsangleichung *f (d.pr.)* impedance matching
Scheinwiderstandsmatrix *f (d.pr.)* impedance matrix
Scheinwohnsitz *m* fictitious domicile
scheitern to fail, to break down *(negotiations etc.)*, to be wrecked *(venture etc.)*
Scheitern *n* failure ◊ **zum ~ bringen** to frustrate, to thwart *(purpose etc.)*; **zum ~ verurteilt** to be doomed to failure
Schelf *m/n* continental shelf
Schema *n* order, arrangement; model, pattern; schedule; diagram ◊ **nach einem ~** on a pattern, schematically
schematisch schematically; routinely; conventional, orthodox
schematisieren to draw up a model; to arrange according to a scheme
Schematisierung *f* drawing up a model; arrangement according to a scheme
schenken to give, to present *(s.th.)*; to donate *(money etc.)*; *(jur)* to acquit; to grant *(s.th.)* gratis
Schenkung *f* gift, present; donation *(money etc.)*; grant
Schenkungsbrief *m* deed of donation [gift]
Schenkungssteuer *f* tax on gifts
Schenkungsurkunde *f* deed of gift
schenkungsweise as a gift; by way of donation
Schicht *f* 1. shift *(work)*; 2. *(stats)* stratum; level *(of society)*
~, geleistete shift worked
~, soziale social stratum, stratum of society
Schichtarbeit *f* shift work
Schichtarbeiter *m* shift worker
Schichtarbeitsplan *m* work plan of a shift
Schichtaufgabe *f s.* **Schichtauftrag**
Schichtauftrag *m* shift order
Schichtausgleich *m* shift differential
Schichtauslastung *f* (full) utilization of shift capacity
~, höhere higher shift efficiency
Schichtauslastungskoeffizient *m s.* **Schichtausnutzungskoeffizient**
Schichtausnutzungskoeffizient *m* shift(-work) coefficient
Schichtbetrieb *m* shift system, working in shifts; enterprise working in shifts
Schichtbrigade *f* team of shift-workers
Schichtdauer *f* shift length
Schichtdienst *m s.* **Schichtarbeit**

Schichtenzuteilung *f (stats)* Neyman allocation
~, bestmögliche *(stats)* optimum allocation
Schichtfaktor *m* shift factor
Schichtkapazität *f* shift capacity
Schichtkoeffizient *m* shift coefficient
Schichtkosten *pl* costs per shift
Schichtleistung *f* shift output, output per shift
Schichtleistungsnorm *f* standard output per shift
Schichtlinienbearbeitung *f* contour [cropping] farming
Schichtlohn *m* shift wage, pay per shift
Schichtnorm *f* shift quota [norm]
Schichtpause *f* shift break
Schichtplan *m* shift plan (of production)
Schichtprämie *f* shift bonus
Schichtregime *n s.* **Schichtsystem**
Schichtsoll *n* (planned) task of a shift
Schichtsystem *n* shift system
~, durchgängiges through-shift system
Schichtübergabe *f s.* **Schichtwechsel**
Schichtung *f (stats)* stratification
~, mehrfache *(stats)* multiple stratification
~ nach erfolgter Auswahl *(stats)* stratification after selection
~, nachträgliche *s.* **~ nach erfolgter Auswahl**
~, soziale social stratification
~, tiefgegliederte *(stats)* deep stratification
Schichtwechsel *m* change of shift, (shift) changeover
~, fliegender through-shift changeover *(machines running non-stop)*
Schichtwechselperiode *f* shift changeover time
schichtweise per shift
Schichtzeit *f s.* **Schichtdauer**
Schichtzeitfonds *m* (total) working time per shift
Schichtzuschlag *m* additional pay for shift work, shift allowance
schicken to send, to dispatch, to forward; to post, to mail *(letters etc.)*; to consign *(parcels, goods etc.)*; to convey *(greetings etc.)*; to remit *(money etc.)*
schieben to profiteer; to sell on the black market, to sell underhand; to smuggle
Schieben *n (st.ex.)* carrying over
Schieber *m* profiteer, black-marketeer; pusher *(drugs)*
Schiebergeschäft *n* profiteering, illegal transaction, shady deal
Schiebertum *n* profiteering
Schiebung *f* profiteering; underhand dealing; manipulation, swindle
Schiedsabkommen *n* arbitration agreement
Schiedsamt *n* board of conciliation
Schiedsgericht *n* court of arbitration ✧ **eine Sache dem ~ unterbreiten** to refer a matter to arbitration; **(sich) einem ~ unterwerfen** to submit to arbitration
~ für Arbeitsstreitigkeiten court of arbitration in labour affairs
schiedsgerichtlich arbitral; by arbitration
Schiedsgerichtsbarkeit *f* arbitral jurisdication
Schiedsgerichtsgebühr *f* arbitration charge
Schiedsgerichtshof *m s.* **Schiedsgericht**
Schiedsgerichtsklausel *f* arbitration clause
Schiedsgerichtsvereinbarung *f s.* **Schiedsabkommen**
Schiedsgerichtsverfahren *n* arbitration proceedings
Schiedsgutachten *n* arbitrator's findings
Schiedskommission *f* arbitration committee
Schiedsparteien *fpl* parties to an arbitration
Schiedsrichter *m* arbitrator, *(Am)* referee; judge
schiedsrichterlich *(com)* by arbitration
Schiedssache *f* arbitral case
Schiedsspruch *m* arbitration [arbitrators'] award ✧ **einen ~ fällen** to make an award; **(sich) einem ~ unterwerfen** to submit to an award
Schiedsstelle *f* arbitration board
Schiedsvereinbarung *f s.* **Schiedsabkommen**
Schiedsverfahren *n* arbitration proceedings
Schiedsvergleich *m* arbitral agreement
Schiedsvertrag *m* contract of arbitration ✧ **einen ~ schließen** to agree [submit] to arbitration
Schiefe *f (stats)* skewness
~, negative *(stats)* negative skewness
~, positive *(stats)* positive skewness
Schienenersatzverkehr *m* relief (commuter) transport service
Schienenfahrzeugschlosser *m (rail)* railway fitter, locomotive fitter; tram(way) fitter
Schienennetz *n* railway network [system]
Schienenparallelverkehr *m* rail and road transport on the same route
Schienenverkehr *m* rail traffic
Schienenweg *m* railway, *(Am)* railroad
Schiene-Straße-Problem *n* rail and road problem
Schiene-Straße-Verkehr *m* rail and road traffic
Schiff *n* ship; vessel; steamer, steamship; boat ✧ **ab ~** ex ship; **per ~** by ship
~, frachtsuchendes vessel seeking freight
~, gechartertes chartered ship
~, regelmäßig fahrendes liner
Schiffahrt *f* navigation, shipping
Schiffahrtsabgabe *f* inland shipping toll [levy] *(levy paid by users of inland waterways)*
Schiffahrtsabkommen *n* shipping agreement
~, Internationales liner conference
Schiffahrtsaktie *f* shipping share [*(Am)* stock]
Schiffahrtsbörse *f s.* **Schifferbörse**
Schiffahrtsgesellschaft *f* shipping company

Schiffahrtskanal *m* canal for shipping, ship canal
Schiffahrtskonferenz *f s.* **Schiffahrtsabkommen**
Schiffahrtslinie *f* shipping route; shipping line
Schiffahrtsperiode *f* shipping season
Schiffahrtsrecht *n* shipping laws
Schiffahrtsstelle *f* shipping branch office
Schiffahrtsstraße *f* (navigable) waterway; shipping route [lane], sea-route
Schiffahrtssubvention *f* shipping subsidy
Schiffahrtstarif *m* shipping rate
Schiffahrtsvertrag *m s.* **Schiffahrtsabkommen**
Schiffahrtsweg *m* sea [shipping] route, waterway
schiffbar navigable
Schiffbarkeit *f* navigability
Schiffbarmachung *f* canalization
Schiffbau *m* shipbuilding
Schiffbauer *m* shipbuilder
Schiffbauschlosser *m* shipbuilding fitter
Schiffer *m* seaman; boatsman
Schifferbetriebsverband *m* shippers' association
Schifferbörse *f* seamen's recruitment office
Schifferentgelt *n* seamen's pay
Schiffsabfertigung *f s.* **Schiffsklarierung**
Schiffsagent *m* shipping agent; shipping agency
Schiffsanteil *m s.* **Schiffsaktie**
Schiffsbank *f s.* **Schiffshypothekenbank**
Schiffsbedarf *m* 1. demand for tonnage [shipping capacity]; demand for ships; 2. ship chandlery, ship catering
Schiffsbefrachter *m* freighter, shipper
Schiffsbefrachtung *f* freighting; charterage, affreightment
Schiffsbefrachtungskontrakt *m s.* **Schiffsbefrachtungsvertrag**
Schiffsbefrachtungsvertrag *m* charterparty
Schiffsbeladung *f* loading of ship
Schiffsbesatzung *f* (ship's) crew
Schiffsbesitzer *m s.* **Schiffseigentümer**
Schiffsbestand *m* tonnage (of a country)
Schiffsbetrieb *m s.* **Schiffsverkehr**
Schiffsbetriebsschlosser *m* ship fitter
Schiffsbrief *m* shipping certificate
Schiffsdarleh(e)n *n* loan with ship serving as security, shipping loan
Schiffseigentümer *m* ship owner
Schiffseigentümervereinigung *f* chamber of shipping
Schiffseigner *m s.* **Schiffseigentümer**
Schiffsfracht *f* (ship's) freight
Schiffsfrachtbrief *m* bill of lading
Schiffsgebühr *f* shipping charge
Schiffsgläubiger *m* bottomry bondholder
Schiffsgut *n* freight
Schiffshaftpflichtversicherung *f* ship's protection and indemnity insurance

Schiffshavarie *f* (ship) collision
Schiffsheuer *f s.* **Schiffsmiete**
Schiffshypothek *f s.* **Schiffsdarleh(e)n**
Schiffshypothekenbank *f* mortgage bank *(mainly dealing with shipping loans)*
Schiffskartell *n* shipping cartel
Schiffsklarierung *f* clearance (of outbound ships)
Schiffsklasse *f* class of ships
Schiffsklasseattest *n* certificate of ship's class
Schiffsklassifizierung *f* classification of ships
Schiffskreditbank *f s.* **Schiffshypothekenbank**
Schiffsladeschein *m* bill of lading
Schiffslade- und Schiffslöschnorm *f* norm for loading and unloading of ships *(expressed in time and weight)*
Schiffsladung *f* shipload; cargo, freight
Schiffslieferant *m* caterer (for ships)
Schiffsliegegeld *n* demurrage
Schiffsliegeplatz *m* (loading) berth
Schiffsliegezeit *f* lay days
Schiffsliste *f* ship's register
Schiffsmakler *m* ship-broker
Schiffsmanifest *n* ship's manifest
Schiffsmeßbrief *m* tonnage certificate, certificate of measurement
Schiffsmiete *f* charter money
Schiffspapiere *npl* ship's [shipping] papers
Schiffspart *m* share in a ship
Schiffspartner *m* part-owner of a ship
Schiffspaß *m* sea-passport
Schiffspatent *n* master's certificate
Schiffspfandbrief *m* bottomry bond
Schiffspfandbriefbank *f s.* **Schiffshypothekenbank**
Schiffspfandrecht *n* maritime lien
Schiffspost *f* sea mail
Schiffsraum *m* shipping space; tonnage
~, **leerer** waste stowage, vacant shipping space
~, **verfügbarer** tonnage; shipping space available
Schiffsreeder *m s.* **Schiffseigentümer**
Schiffsreederei *f* shipping company, shipping line
Schiffsregister *n* ship's register
Schiffsrevision *f* ship inspection
Schiffstagebuch *n* logbook
Schiffstonnage *f* (ship's) tonnage
Schiffsverkehr *m* shipping traffic
Schiffsverpfändung *f* bottomry
Schiffsversicherung *f* hull insurance
Schiffsversorgung *f* supply of ship with provisions; catering (of ships)
Schiffsversteigerung *f* auction of ships
Schiffsverzeichnis *n s.* **Schiffsliste**
Schiffsvorräte *mpl* ship's stores
Schiffswerft *f* shipyard, shipbuilding yard; dockyard

Schiffszertifikat *n* certificate of registry
Schiffszettel *m* shipping order
Schiffszoll *m* tonnage duty
Schlachtausbeute *f* carcass *(expressed in terms of percentage)*
schlachten to slaughter *(animals)*
Schlächter *m* butcher
Schlächterei *f* butcher's shop
Schlachtgewicht *n* dead weight
Schlachthof *m* slaughter-house, abattoir
Schlachtrindproduktion *f* breeding [raising] of slaughter cattle
Schlachttierversicherung *f* fat stock insurance
Schlachtung *f* slaughter(ing) *(animals)*
Schlachtvieh *n* slaughter cattle; fat stock
Schlachtwertklasse *f* class of fattened [fat] cattle *(classification of fat stock)*
Schlafabteil *n* sleeping compartment
Schlafgast *m* night-lodger; overnight guest [visitor]
Schlafgeld *n* lodging money
Schlafgelegenheit *f* sleeping accommodation
Schlafkabine *f* sleeping cabin
Schlafkoje *f* (sleeping) berth
Schlafquartier *n* sleeping quarters
Schlafstelle *f* sleeping-place; lodging house; berth *(ship, train etc.)*
Schlafstellenvermieter *m* lodging-house keeper
Schlafwagen *m* sleeping-car, sleeper
Schlag *m* felling *(timber)*
Schlagbaum *m* toll gate, turnpike
schlagen to fell *(timber)*
Schlager *m* novelty item *(product)*; hit; bestseller
Schlagerpreis *m* record [rock-bottom] price
Schlagerwerbung *f* novelty advertising
Schlagkartei *f (agric)* field card index
Schlagkomplex *m (agric)* complex of fields
Schlagschatz *m* mintage
Schlagvergütung *f (agric)* payment according to area and operations *(in crop production)*
Schlange *f* queue, *(Am)* line ◊ **~ stehen** to queue up, *(Am)* to line up
schlecht bad; base, vile, low, wicked ◊ **finanziell ~ gestellt sein** to be badly situated financially; **~ abgestimmt** badly co-ordinated *(plan etc.)*; ill-timed *(visit to factory etc.)*; **~ begründet** ill-founded *(business venture etc.)*; **~ beraten sein** to be ill-advised *(to launch a product etc.)*; **~ gehen** to be in a bad way *(business etc.)*; **~ verkäuflich** slow of sale; **~ verwalten** to mismanage
Schlechtbereich *m (stats)* rejection region
Schlechterstellung *f* discrimination
schlechtgläubig mala fide, in bad faith
schleichen to creep
Schleichhandel *m* black market; illicit trade, smuggling

Schleichhändler *m* black-marketeer; smuggler
Schleichware *f* smuggled merchandise
Schleifer *m* grinder; polisher; cutter *(precious stones etc.)*
Schleppboot *n* tug(boat)
schleppen 1. to tout *(for customers etc.)*; 2. to tow *(barges etc.)*
Schlepper *m* 1. tout *(for customers etc.)*; 2. breakdown van, *(Am)* recovery vehicle; 3. tug(boat); lighter; 4. tractor
Schleppereinheit *f* tractor unit *(measuring unit in agriculture; one tractor unit equals 15 h.p.)*
Schlepperentgelt *n s.* **Schlepplohn**
Schlepperstunde *f* tractor hour *(service hours of tractors)*
Schleppgebühr *f s.* **Schlepplohn**
Schlepplohn *m* towage
Schleppnetzfischerei *f* trawler fishing
Schleppschiff *n s.* **Schleppboot**
Schleppschiffahrt *f* tug-service; towing
Schleppzug *m* train of barges
Schleuderartikel *m* catchpenny (article)
Schleuderausfuhr *f* dumping
Schleuderexport *m s.* **Schleuderausfuhr**
Schleudergeschäft *n* cutting trade
Schleuderpreis *m* giveaway [throwaway] price; cut price ◊ **zum ~ verkaufen** to sell dirt cheap [very cheaply]
~, monopolistischer monopoly cut price
Schleuderwaren *fpl* dumping goods; cheap goods; cut-price goods
Schleuse *f* sluice, lock
Schleusengeld *n* lock-dues, lock-charges
Schleusenmeister *m s.* **Schleusenwärter**
Schleusentor *n* lock-gate, flood-gate
Schleusenwärter *m* lock-keeper
schlichten to mediate; to arbitrate, to settle by arbitration *(a dispute etc.)*
Schlichter *m* mediator *(as a go-between)*, *(Am)* troubleshooter; arbitrator *(industrial disputes etc.)*
~, amtlicher official mediator, *(Am)* official troubleshooter; official arbitrator, *(Am)* official referee
~, gemeinsamer joint arbiter
~, staatlicher *s.* **~, amtlicher**
Schlichtung *f* mediation; arbitration, settlement by arbitration *(in a dispute etc.)*
Schlichtungsamt *n* arbitration board, board of arbitration, *(Am)* bureau of conciliation
Schlichtungsausschuß *m* arbitration board [committee] ◊ **vor einen ~ kommen** to come before a board [committee] of arbitration, *(Am)* to come before a committee of conciliation
Schlichtungsinstanz *f* court of arbitration
Schlichtungsstelle *f* arbitration board [committee]

Schlichtungsverfahren *n* arbitrational procedure; arbitrational proceedings
Schlichtungsverfügung *f* order to arbitrate
Schlichtungsverhandlungen *fpl* negotiations in settling a dispute
Schlichtungsvertrag *m* agreement in settling a dispute
Schlichtungswesen *n* system of arbitration; arbitral jurisdiction
schließen 1. to close, to wind up, to conclude *(meeting etc.)*; to close, to shut *(shop etc. for the day)*; to close down, to shut down *(factory etc. permanently)*; 2. to make, to enter into *(an alliance etc.)*; 3. to conclude *(agreement etc.)*; 4. *(st.ex.)* to conclude ◊ **fest** ~ *(st.ex.)* to close firm, to finish higher; **flau** ~ *(st.ex.)* to leave off; **schwächer** ~ *(st.ex.)* to finish lower
Schließfach *n* post-office box *(P.O. Box)*; *(bank)* safe deposit box
Schließfachgebühr *f* safe deposit fee; post-office box fee
Schließfachmiete *f s.* **Schließfachgebühr**
Schließfachnummerinserat *n* box number advertisement
Schließfachvermietung *f* renting of safes
Schließung *f* 1. closing, closure, winding up, concluding, conclusion *(meeting etc.)*; closing, shutting *(shop etc. for the day)*; closure, shutting down *(factory etc. permanently)*; 2. making, entering into *(an alliance etc.)*; 3. conclusion *(agreement etc.)*; 4. *(st.ex.)* conclusion, closure
~ **der Aktienumschreibebücher** *(st.ex.)* closing of transfer books
~, **zeitweilige** temporary closure
Schlitz *m* *(d.pr.)* slot
Schlitzkarte *f* *(d.pr.)* slotted card
Schlosser *m* mechanic; fitter; locksmith; metalworker
Schlosserei *f* metalworking shop
Schlotbaron *m* business magnate, tycoon
Schluderarbeit *f* slipshod work
Schlupf *m* reserve *(material etc.)*
Schlupfzeit *f* spare time
~, **bedingt verfügbare** spare time available under special circumstances
~, **bedingte** spare time depending on extraneous circumstances
~, **frei verfügbare** *s.* ~, **freie**
~, **freie** spare time available
~, **gesamte** total spare time
~, **unabhängige** spare time not depending on extraneous circumstances
Schluß *m* 1. conclusion, close, closure; 2. *(st.ex.)* minimum amount allowed for dealing; unit of trade, trading unit, *(Am)* board lot; 3. result ◊ **einen ~ ziehen** to draw a conclusion [an inference] from *(s.th.)*, to conclude [infer] from *(s.th.)*; **einen voreiligen ~ ziehen** to jump to a conclusion; ~ **fest** *(st.ex.)* closing firm; ~ **geordnet** *(st.ex.)* transaction noted; ~ **machen** to call it a day; to put an end to s.th.
~ **der Sitzungsperiode** conclusion of the (parliamentary) session
~, **fester** *(st.ex.)* steady closing
Schlußabrechnung *f* final account [settlement]
Schlußabrechnungstag *m* day of final account; day of final settlement
Schlußabschnitt *m* concluding section *(report etc.)*
Schlußabstimmung *f* final passage *(of bill in parliament etc.)*
Schlußansprache *f* closing speech *(in parliament etc.)*
Schlußantrag *m* motion for closure *(meeting etc.)*
Schlußbemerkung *f* concluding [final] remark, final observation
Schlußbericht *m* final report
Schlußbescheinigung *f* final discharge certificate
Schlußbesprechung *f* final discussion
Schlußbestand *m* closing inventory
Schlußbestimmung *f* final clause
Schlußbestimmungen *fpl* concluding [final] provisions
Schlußbilanz *f* annual [final] balance sheet
Schlußbilanzkonto *n* annual [final] balance sheet account
Schlußbörse *f* *(st.ex.)* terminal market
Schlußbuchung *f* *(acc)* closing entry
Schlußdividende *f* liquidation dividend
Schlüssel *m* 1. key; 2. code, cipher
Schlüsselarbeit *f* key work
Schlüsselberuf *m* key occupation
Schlüsselbetrieb *m* key enterprise
Schlüsselbezeichnung *f* code number
Schlüsselbildung *f* encoding, coding
Schlüsseldienst *m* key service *(at enterprises, institutions etc.)*
Schlüsseleintragung *f* *(d.pr.)* code clause
schlüsselfertig *(build)* ready for immediate occupancy; on a turn-key basis *(project)*
Schlüsselfrage *f* key issue [question]
Schlüsselfunktion *f* key function
Schlüsselgemeinkosten *pl* prorated expenses
Schlüsselgerät *n* *(d.pr.)* ciphering equipment
Schlüsselindustrie *f* key industry
Schlüsselliste *f* economic code register
Schlüssellochung *f* *(d.pr.)* code punching
Schlüsselnummer *f* key number
Schlüsselparameter *m* key parameter
Schlüsselposition *f* key position
Schlüsselstellung *f s.* **Schlüsselposition**
Schlüsselsystematik *f* code nomenclature
Schlüsselsysteme *npl* code systems

Schlüsseltabelle *f s.* **Schlüsselliste**
Schlüsselwort *n (d.pr.)* key word
Schlüsselzahl *f* 1. key figure; 2. code number
Schlüsselzahlprüfeinrichtung *f (d.pr.)* self--checking number device
Schlüsselziffern *fpl* 1. key figures; 2. code numbers
Schlußergebnis *n* final result
schlußfolgern to reason, to conclude
Schlußfolgerung *f* reasoning, conclusion
~, **falsche** fallacy
~, **rechtliche** conclusion of law
~, **tatsächliche** conclusion of fact
Schlußhaltung *f (st.ex.)* final tone
schlüssig conclusive, convincing; logical ◊ **nicht** ~ inconclusive
Schlußimpuls *m (d.pr.)* terminal pulse
Schlußinventur *f* final inventory
Schlußkurs *m (st.ex.)* final quotation, closing price [rate]
Schlußmarkt *m (st.ex.)* terminal market
Schlußnote *f* broker's [contract] note
Schlußnotierung *f (st.ex.)* 1. *s.* **Schlußkurs**; 2. noting the final quotation *(activity)*
~, **gestrige** yesterday's closing rates
Schlußpreis *m s.* **Schlußkurs**
Schlußprotokoll *n* closing record [proceedings, minutes]
Schlußquote *f s.* **Schlußdividende**
Schlußrate *f* final instalment
Schlußrechnung *f* final account; final settlement
Schlußschein *m (st.ex.)* sales note; broker's [contract] note
Schlußsitzung *f* final session
Schlußtermin *m* final [closing] date, deadline
Schlußurteil *n (jur)* final judgement
Schlußverfahren *n* final process
Schlußverfügung *f* final order [decree]
~, **richterliche** *(jur)* final injunction
Schlußverhandlung *f* 1. final negotiations; 2. final hearing
Schlußverkauf *m* clearance sale
~ **im Frühling** spring sale
~ **im Sommer** summer sale [bargain], summer (closing) sale
~ **im Winter** winter clearance sale
Schlußverkaufspreis *m* bargain price
Schlußversammlung *f* annual [final] assembly
Schlußverteilung *f* distribution of assets of a bankrupt estate
Schlußzahlung *f* final [last] payment
Schlußzettel *m s.* **Schlußschein**
schmal narrow *(profit margin etc.)*; poor *(fare etc.)*; small *(income)*
schmälern to lessen, to diminish, to curtail; to impair *(one's rights)*

Schmälerung *f* lessening, diminishing, curtailing, curtailment; impairment *(one's rights)*
Schmalspur *f* narrow gauge
Schmalspurbahn *f* narrow gauge railway
schmarotzen to sponge (on others)
Schmarotzer *m* sponger, parasite
schmarotzerhaft sponging, parasitic(al)
Schmerzensgeld *n* compensation for personal suffering, smart-money
Schmied *m*(black)smith
Schmiede(werkstatt) *f* forge, smith's workshop
schmieren to bribe, to grease s.o.'s palm
Schmiergeld *n* bribe, *(Am)* graft; kickback; slush money
Schmiergelderfonds *m* bribery fund
Schmiergelderunwesen *n* corruption, *(Am)* graft
Schmuggel *m* smuggling
schmuggeln to smuggle, to run contraband
Schmuggelware *f* smuggled goods, contraband
Schmuggler *m* smuggler
Schmutzkonkurrenz *f* sharp practice(s), mean competition
Schmutzzulage *f* extra payment for dirty work
Schmutzzuschlag *m s.* **Schmutzzulage**
Schnappschußprogramm *n (d.pr.)* snapshot program
Schneeballsystem *n* snow-ball system *(in the process of economic growth)*
Schneider *m* tailor; dressmaker
Schneiderarbeit *f* tailor's work; tailoring
Schneiderei *f* tailoring, tailor's business [shop]
Schneidergeselle *m* journeyman tailor
Schneiderhandwerk *n* tailor's trade
Schneiderin *f* tailoress, dressmaker
schneidern to make clothes
Schneiderwerkstatt *f s.* **Schneiderei**
Schnellamt *n* toll exchange, *(Am)* multi-office exchange
Schnellarbeitsmethode *f* rapid working method
Schnellarbeitsverfahren *n s.* **Schnellarbeitsmethode**
Schnellbahn *f* express train, high-speed railway
Schnellbaufließfertigung *f* high-speed construction line method, rapid flow-construction
Schnellbearbeitungsverfahren *n* rapid processing method, rapid method of processing
Schnelldienst *m* express service
Schnelldienstgebühr *f* express charge
Schnelldrucker *m (d.pr.)* automatic [high-speed] printer
Schnelleser *m (d.pr.)* high-speed reader
Schnellfließverfahren *n* rapid flow method
Schnellgaststätte *f* self-service [quick-service] restaurant
Schnellgüterzug *m* express goods [*(Am)* freight] train
Schnellgutverkehr *m* express goods traffic

Schnellimbißstube *f* snack bar
Schnellmast *f (agric)* quick fattening
Schnellocher *m (d.pr.)* high-speed punch
Schnellrecheneinheit *f (d.pr.)* high-speed processor
Schnellrechner *m* high-speed computer
Schnellreparatur *f* express repair
Schnellspeicher *m (d.pr.)* fast register; high-speed memory; high-speed storage
schnellstanzen *(d.pr.)* to gang punch
Schnellstanzer *m (d.pr.)* (automatic) gang punch
schnellverderblich perishable quickly *(vegetables etc.)*
schnellverkäuflich saleable quickly
Schnellverkehr *m* express traffic; no delay service *(telephone)*
schnellverschleißend wearing out at a fast rate
Schnellzug *m* fast [express] train
Schnellzugzuschlag *m* express fare
Schnitt *m* 1. cut, make, style, fashion; pattern; 2. intersection; 3. *(agric)* harvest(ing), reaping, cropping; 4. average; 5. profit
Schnitthandel *m* drapery trade
Schnittwaren *fpl* drapery, *(Am)* dry goods
Schnitzer *m* wood-carver
Schöffe *m (jur)* lay assessor ✧ **einen Schöffen ablehnen** to challenge a lay assessor
Schöffenliste *f* panel of lay assessors
Schonarbeit *f* light work *(for convalescent worker etc.)*
Schonarbeitsplatz *m* light job *(s.* **Schonarbeit***)*
schonen to take care of *(semi-invalids at work etc.)*; to preserve *(woodland etc.)*
Schonfrist *f* period of grace
Schönheitsreparatur *f* interior renovation *(of flat)*
Schönheitssalon *m* beauty parlour
Schonung *f* taking care of *(semi-invalids at work etc.)*; preservation *(woodland etc.)*; (for) plantation of young trees
Schornsteinfeger *m* chimney-sweep(er)
schöpfen to create *(ideas for inventions etc.)*; to derive, to obtain *(experience etc.)*
schöpferisch creative
Schöpferkraft *f* creative power
Schöpfertum *n* creative mind; creativeness, creativity
Schöpfung *f* creation
Schranke *f* barrier; toll-gate; limit
Schranken *fpl*:
✧ **in ~ halten** to restrain *(person etc.)*; to hold in check, to curb *(s.o.'s authority etc.)*; **~ setzen** to set bounds (to) *(s.o.'s authority etc.)*
~, obere upper limits, ceiling
~, ökonomische economic limits
~, soziale social barriers
~, untere lower limits, floor

schrankenlos boundless, unlimited *(authority etc.)*; unrestrained *(behaviour etc.)*
Schrankenwärter *m* gate-keeper
Schreibarbeit *f* deskwork; typing
Schreibautomat *m* typing machine
~, computergesteuerter computer-controlled typing machine
~, lochstreifengesteuerter tape-controlled typing machine
Schreibbüro *n* copying office; typing agency
Schreibdaten *pl (d.pr.)* write data
schreiben to write *(letter etc.)*; to inform *(s.o.)* ✧ **ins reine ~** to make a fair copy; **ins unreine ~** to (make a) draft
Schreiben *n* letter; note; communication ✧ **Ihr geschätztes ~** your esteemed letter
~, amtliches official letter
~, anliegendes attached [enclosed] letter
Schreiber *m* writer
Schreiberei *f* paperwork; writing; typing
Schreibgebühren *fpl* copying [typing] fees
Schreibkraft *f* secretary; typist
Schreibwarenhändler *m* stationer
Schreibwarenhandlung *f* stationer's shop
Schreibzimmer *n* typing office [pool]
Schreiner *m* joiner; carpenter
Schreinerei *f* joiner's workshop
Schrift *f* writing; handwriting; document; publication
Schriftenablage *f* filing
Schriftform *f* writing, written form, proper legal form ✧ **in ~** in writing, written
schriftlich in writing; by letter ✧ **etwas ~ darlegen** to explain s.th. on paper; **~ abfassen** to write; **~ abgefaßt sein** to be in writing; **~ berichten** to report in writing; **~ niederlegen** to set down in writing; **~ vereinbaren** to agree upon in writing, to come to an agreement in writing *(over s.th.)*
Schriftprobe *f* specimen of one's handwriting
Schriftprobenvergleich *m* comparison of handwritings
Schriftsache *f* written matter [document]
Schriftsachverständiger *m* expert in handwriting, handwriting expert, graphologist
Schriftsatz *m* written statement; memorandum; *(jur)* writ; statement of claim
Schriftstück *n* writing, paper; deed, document, instrument
Schriftstücke *npl*:
~, amtliche official documents
Schriftvergleich *m s.* **Schriftprobenvergleich**
Schriftverkehr *m* correspondence
Schriftwechsel *m* correspondence, exchange of letters
Schritt *m* step; pace ✧ **den ersten ~ tun** to make the first move, to take the first [initial]

step; ~ **für** ~ step by step; ~ **halten** to keep pace (with) *(technical developments etc.)*; to keep abreast (with) *(events etc.)*
~, **diplomatischer** demarche
Schritte *mpl* steps ⋄ **gerichtliche** ~ **androhen** to threaten to take legal proceedings; **gerichtliche** ~ **gegen jmdn. unternehmen** to take legal proceedings against s.o.; ~ **unternehmen** to take action
~, **der Gründung vorausgehende** preliminary steps for an establishment
Schrittmacher *m* pace-setter, innovator
Schrittmachertempo *n* pace-setters' tempo
schrittweise *s.* **Schritt für Schritt**
Schrott *m* scrap
Schrotterlös *m* proceeds from scrap sales
Schrotthändler *m* scrap dealer
Schrottlagerplatz *m* scrap yard
Schrottpreis *m* scrap price, price of scrap
Schrottverhüttung *f* scrap smelting
Schrottverkauf *m* scrap sale
Schrottwert *m* residual [recovery] value, scrap value
schrumpfen to dwindle *(exports etc.)*; to depreciate *(currency)*; to shrink *(textiles etc.)*; to contract *(with heat, cold etc.)*
Schrumpfung *f* dwindling *(exports etc.)*; depreciation *(currency)*; shrinkage *(textiles etc.)*; contraction *(with heat, cold etc.)*
Schubschiffahrt *f* pusher navigation
Schubstangenentmistung *f (agric)* handling of pusher manure
Schuhindustrie *f* shoe industry
Schuhmacher *m* shoemaker
Schuhwaren *fpl* footwear
Schuhwarenindustrie *f s.* **Schuhindustrie**
Schulabgänger *m* school leaver
Schulamt *n* board of education
Schulanstalt *f s.* **Schuleinrichtung**
Schulbehörde *f* education(al) authority
Schulbesuch *m* attendance at school
Schulbildung *f* school education
Schulbuchversorgung *f* supply of school books
Schuld *f* 1. debt *(money)*; liability; obligation; 2. *(jur)* fault, responsibility; guilt ⋄ **an einem Unfall** ~ **haben** to be at fault in an accident; **die** ~ **auf jmdn. abwälzen** to shift the blame on to s.o.; **die** ~ **jmdm. zuschieben** *s.* **die** ~ **auf jmdn. abwälzen**; **eine** ~ **abarbeiten** to work off a debt; **eine** ~ **ablösen** to redeem a debt; **eine** ~ **abtragen** to pay off a debt; **eine** ~ **ausbuchen** *s.* **eine** ~ **austragen**; **eine** ~ **austragen** to cancel a debt; **eine** ~ **avalieren** to stand security for a debt; **eine** ~ **begleichen** to settle [pay] a debt; **eine** ~ **bezahlen** *s.* **eine** ~ **begleichen**; **eine** ~ **durch Pfandbestellung absichern** to collaterate; **eine** ~ **einfordern** to claim a debt; **eine** ~ **einklagen** to take legal proceedings to recover a debt; **eine** ~ **einziehen** to collect [recover] a debt; **eine** ~ **entrichten** to discharge a debt; **eine** ~ **fundieren** to fund a debt; **eine** ~ **hypothekarisch absichern** to secure a debt by mortgage; **eine** ~ **konsolidieren** to fund a debt; **eine** ~ **löschen** to cancel a debt; **eine** ~ **regulieren** to settle a debt; **eine** ~ **stunden** to grant a respite for payment of a debt; **eine** ~ **tilgen** *s.* **eine** ~ **begleichen**; **eine** ~ **verjähren lassen** to let a debt expire; **eine** ~ **zahlen** to pay off a debt; **frei von aller** ~ exonerated from all blame; **für eine** ~ **bürgen** to stand as security for a debt; to guarantee a debt; **für eine** ~ **einstehen** to answer for a debt; **in jmds.** ~ **stehen** to be in s.o.'s debt, to be under obligation to s.o.; **jmdm. die** ~ **geben** to ascribe [impute] the fault to s.o.; to blame s.o.; **jmdm. die** ~ **zuschreiben** *s.* **jmdm. die** ~ **geben**; **jmdm. eine** ~ **erlassen** to release s.o. from a debt, to relinquish [waive, cancel] a debt; **jmdn. für die ganze** ~ **haftbar machen** to hold s.o. liable for the whole debt; **keine** ~ **haben** not to be at fault; ~ **geben** to accuse *(s.o.)*; to blame *(s.o.)*; to lay down to *(s.th.)*; ~ **gestehen** to own up; ~ **haben** to be responsible [liable]; to be guilty; **von einer** ~ **befreit werden** to be released from a debt
~, **abgetragene** paid-up debt
~, **ablösbare** redeemable debt
~, **anerkannte** allowed claum
~, **aufgeschobene** deferred liability
~, **ausstehende** outstanding debt
~, **bedenkliche** staggering debt
~, **beitreibbare** recoverable debt
~, **bevorrechtigte** privileged debt
~, **buchmäßige** book debt
~, **einklagbare** debt enforceable at law
~, **fällige** debt due
~, **festgestellte** debt stated [ascertained]
~, **fundierte** funded [consolidated] debt
~, **gestundete** debt given a respite
~, **hypothekarische** mortgage debt
~, **innere** internal debt
~, **konsolidierte** *s.* ~, **fundierte**
~, **nicht einklagbare** debt unenforceable at law
~, **noch nicht fällige** debt not due for payment
~, **öffentliche** public [national] debt
~, **persönliche** individual debt
~, **reine** net debt
~, **rückständige** debt in arrears
~, **schon lange bestehende** debt of old standing
~, **schwankende** *s.* ~, **schwebende**
~, **schwebende** floating debt
~, **staatlich garantierte** debt guaranteed by the government, government-guaranteed debt

~, **tote** dead debt
~, **übrigbleibende** remaining debt
~, **unfundierte** unfunded debt
~, **ungedeckte** unsecured debt
~, **ungewisse** uncertain debt
~, **unsichere** s. ~, **ungewisse**
~, **unverzinsliche** interest-free debt
~, **unzahlbare** insolvable debt
~, **verjährte** *(jur)* prescriptive debt
~, **verzinsliche** interest-bearing debt
~, **zweifelhafte** dubious [doubtful] debt
Schuldabänderung *f* changes in debt
Schuldablösung *f* discharge of a debt
Schuldabtragung *f* writing off [cancelling] of debts
Schuldabtretung *f* transfer [assignment] of debt
Schuldabzahlung *f* liquidation [paying off] of debts
Schuldanerkenntnis *n* acknowledgement of liabilities; acknowledgement of debts ✧ **jmdm. ein ~ schicken** to send s.o. a statement of the amount owing
~, **abstraktes** *(jur)* assumpsit
~, **schriftliches** written evidence of debt
Schuldanerkennung *f s.* **Schuldanerkenntnis**
Schuldauswechslung *f* substitution of debt
Schuldbeitritt *m* participation in liabilities
Schuldbeweis *m (jur)* proof of guilt
schuldbewußt conscious of one's guilt
Schuldbewußtsein *n* consciousness of guilt; guilty conscience
Schuldbrief *m* promissory note, IOU *(abbreviation for: I owe you)*; bond
Schuldbuch *n* journal, ledger, account-book
Schuldbuchforderung *f* book-entry securities
schulden to owe *(s.o. a sum of money)*, to be indebted to *(s.o.)*
Schulden *fpl*:
✧ **alle ~ bezahlen** to pay all that is owing; **faule ~ streichen** to cancel a bad debt; **frei von ~** unemcumbered; **große ~ haben** to be deeply in debt; **in ~ geraten** s. **~ machen**; **in ~ stecken** s. **~ haben**; **in ~ verwickelt sein** to be involved in debts; **mit ~ belasten** to encumber with debts; **mit ~ belastet** debted, encumbered with debts; **nichts als ~ hinterlassen** to leave nothing but debts; **~ abbauen** to reduce debts; **~ abtragen** to write off debts; **~ anerkennen** to acknowledge liabilities; **~ anhäufen** to pile up debts; **~ annullieren** to wipe off [cancel] debts; **~ anwachsen lassen** s. **~ anhäufen**; **~ aufnehmen** to borrow, to contract [incur] debts; **~ einkassieren** to collect debts; **~ eintreiben** to recover [call in] debts; **~ haben** to be in debt; **~ machen** to run into debt, to incur debts; **seine ~ begleichen** to meet [pay, settle] one's debts; **seine ~**

loswerden to clear o.s. of debts; **seine ~ nicht bezahlen** not to pay one's debts; **seine ~ voll bezahlen** to discharge one's debts [liabilities] in full; **sich in ~ stürzen** to run up debts, to plunge into debt; **sich mit ~ belasten** to encumber o.s. with debts; **sich seinen ~ entziehen** to escape payment of one's debts [liabilities]; **sich um die Zahlung seiner ~ herumdrücken** to evade payment of one's debts; **sich von seinen ~ befreien** to pay up one's debts; **sich vor ~ bewahren** to keep o.s. free from debts, to keep o.s. out of debt; **überall ~ haben** to be in debt everywhere
~, **aufgenommene** borrowings, debts incurred
~, **äußere** external [foreign] debts
~ der Gesellschaften corporate debts
~ einer Aktiengesellschaft company's liabilities, liabilities of a company, company's debts, *(Am)* corporation debts
~, **laufende** current debts
~, **riesige** staggering debts
Schuldenabbau *m* reduction of debts
Schuldenabdeckung *f* debt redemption
Schuldenabkommen *n* agreement on debts, debt agreement
Schuldenabtragung *f* cancellation [writing off] of a debt
Schuldenabzahlung *f* payment of debts (by instalments)
Schuldenanerkennung *f s.* **Schuldenanerkenntnis**
Schuldenaufnahme *f* borrowing; contraction of debts
~, **staatliche** government borrowings
Schuldenaufteilung *f* distribution of debts
Schuldenbegleichung *f* debt settlement
Schuldenbezahlung *f* payment of debts
Schuldendienst *m* debt service
Schuldeneinzugsverfahren *n (jur)* proceedings to recover debt
Schuldenentlastung *f s.* **Schuldenerlaß**
Schuldenerhöhung *f* increase in debts
Schuldenerlaß *m* remission [cancellation] of debts
schuldenfrei free from debt, debt-free ✧ **~ sein** to be out of debt; **~ werden** to get rid of debts; **sich ~ halten** to keep out of debt; **sich ~ machen** to free o.s. from debt, to get clear of debt
Schuldenhaftung *f* liability for contracting debts
schuldenhalber owing to debts
Schuldenklage *f (jur)* action for debt
Schuldenkonferenz *f* debt conference
Schuldenkonto *n* debt balance; debt account
Schuldenlast *f* debt burden, burden of debts, indebtedness

Schuldenmasse *f* aggregate liabilities
Schuldennachweis *m* proof of debts
Schuldenposten *m* debt item; sum of money owing
Schuldenregelung *f* settlement of debts, debt settlement; negotiations on debt settlement
Schuldenrückstand *m* debts in arrears
Schuldenrückzahlung *f* repayment of debts
Schuldensaldo *m* debt balance
Schuldenseite *f* debit side (of a balance sheet)
Schuldensenkung *f* reduction of debts, debt reduction
Schuldentilgung *f* debt repayment [redemption], discharge of debts
Schuldentilgungsaufwand *m* debt-service costs
Schuldentilgungsfonds *m* sinking [redemption] fund
Schuldentilgungskasse *f s.* **Schuldentilgungsfonds**
Schuldentilgungsplan *m* debt redemption schedule
Schuldentilgungsreserve *f* (debt) sinking fund reserve
Schuldenverwaltung *f* administration of debts, debt administration
Schulderlaß *m* remission of [release from] a debt, debt cancellation
Schuldforderung *f* debt claim
Schuldforderungen *fpl* debts due [*(Am)* receivable]
Schuldforderungsklage *f s.* **Schuldenklage**
schuldig 1. owing, due *(amount of money)*; 2. liable, responsible, answerable; 3. *(jur)* guilty; culpable ⋄ **für ~ befunden** *(jur)* to be found guilty; **(jmdm. etwas) ~ bleiben** still to owe *(s.th. to s.o.)*; **~ sein** 1. to be under an obligation *(to do s.th.)*; to owe s.o. *(a sum of money)*; 2. to be guilty; **sich ~ bekennen** to acknowledge one's guilt; to plead guilty *(to a charge)*
Schuldiger *m* guilty person [party], culprit; delinquent *(young offender)*
Schuldigkeit *f* duty, obligation
Schuldirektor *m* headmaster, head teacher
Schuldirektorin *f* headmistress
Schuldkapital *n* borrowed capital
Schuldknechtschaft *f* bondage
schuldlos *(jur)* innocent, guiltless; blameless
Schuldlosigkeit *f (jur)* innocence, guiltlessness
Schuldnachweis *m (jur)* proof of guilt
Schuldner *m* debtor ⋄ **einem ~ Zahlungsfrist gewähren** to allow a debtor time to pay; **einen ~ auspfänden** *(jur)* to inquire into the assets of a debtor; **gegen einen ~ zwangsvollstrecken** to distrain upon a debtor
~, flüchtiger absconding debtor
~, gepfändeter attached debtor

~ in laufender Rechnung debtor in current account
~, in Schwierigkeiten befindlicher embarrassed debtor
~, insolventer insolvent debtor
~, in Verzug geratener *s.* **~, säumiger**
~, säumiger defaulting debtor, debtor in arrears
~, schlechter bad debtor
~, unsicherer dubious debtor
~, unzuverlässiger unreliable debtor
~, zahlungsunfähiger *s.* **~, insolventer**
~ zur gesamten Hand *(jur)* joint debtors
Schuldnergesellschaft *f* debtor [obligor] company, *(Am)* debtor corporation
Schuldnerkonto *n* debtor's account
Schuldnerland *n* debtor's country [nation]
Schuldnerstaat *m s.* **Schuldnerland**
Schuldnervermögen *n* debtor's property [assets]
Schuldrecht *n* debt laws
schuldrechtlich contractual
Schuldrest *m* balance due [owing], debt balance
Schuldschein *m* promissory note, IOU *(abbreviation for: I owe you)*; bond
~, bedingter conditional bond
~, (durch Gestellung von Sicherheiten) gedeckter collateral [secured] note
~, erstklassig abgesicherter ironclad promissory note
~, hypothekarisch gesicherter principal note
Schuldscheinaussteller *m* recognizor
Schuldscheinbesitzer *m* warrant creditor
Schuldscheindarleh(e)n *n* open market credit
Schuldscheindarleh(e)nsurkunde *f* open market paper
~, ausstehende warrant payable
Schuldspruch *m* verdict of „guilty"
Schuldtitel *m (jur)* instrument [paper] of indebtedness
Schuldübernahme *f* assumption of debt
~, kumulative cumulative assumption of debts
Schuldübernahmevertrag *m* agreement on assumption of debt
Schuldübertragung *f* transfer of debt
Schuldüberweisung *f s.* **Schuldübertragung**
Schuldumschreibung *f s.* **Schuldumwandlung**; **Schuldübertragung**
Schuldumwandlung *f* conversion of debts; novation; debt-equity swap
Schuldurkunde *f s.* **Schuldschein**
Schuldverhältnis *n* (contractual) obligation
~, persönliches personal obligation
~, ursprüngliches original liability
Schuldverpflichtung *f* liability; contractual obligation
Schuldverschreibung *f* promissory note, (mortgage) bond, debenture (stock/bond)
~, abgestufte classified bond

~ **auf den Inhaber** bearer bond
~ **mit Gewinnbeteiligung** profit-sharing bond, *(Am)* bond; income debenture
Schuldversprechen *n* promissory note
Schuldvertrag *m* debt agreement
Schuldwechsel *m* bill of debt
Schuldzinsen *mpl* credit interest
Schule *f* school
Schuleinrichtung *f* school establishment
schulen to school, to train
Schulentlassungszeugnis *n* school leaving certificate
Schulgeld *n* tuition [school] fees, tuition
Schulgeldfreiheit *f* free tuition [education]
Schulhort *m* after-school care centre
Schulinspektor *m* school inspector, inspector of schools
Schuljahr *n* school year
Schulkenntnisse *fpl* knowledge acquired at school
Schulkollegium *n* staff of teachers, school staff
Schullehrer *m* schoolmaster, teacher
Schullehrerin *f* schoolmistress, teacher
Schulpflicht *f* compulsory education; compulsory attendance at school
schulpflichtig of compulsory school age
Schulsparen *n* saving at school
Schulspeisung *f* school meals
Schulung *f* schooling, training
Schulungskurs *m* training course
Schulwesen *n* system of education
Schund *m s.* **Schundware**
Schundproduktion *f* production of rejects, sub--standard production; rejects
Schundware *f* sub-standard article; reject
Schur *f (agric)* shearing
schürfen to prospect *(for precious metals etc.)*
Schürfen *n* prospecting *(for precious metals etc.)*
Schürfer *m* prospector
Schürfgesellschaft *f* prospecting company
Schürfrecht *n* prospecting rights
Schürfung *f s.* **Schürfen**
Schuster *m* shoemaker; cobbler
Schutt *m* rubble; rubbish, refuse, garbage
Schuttabladeplatz *m* refuse dump
Schüttgewicht *n* bulk weight
Schüttgut *n* bulk [loose] material, bulk goods, bulk freight [cargo], goods in bulk
Schutz *m* protection; shelter, refuge, cover; care
~, **konsularischer** consular protection
~, **rechtlicher** legal protection
~ **von Mutter und Kind** protection of mother and child
schützen to protect, to guard *(s.th.)*, to protect *(car body against rust, children from exploitation etc.)*; to cover *(s.th.)*; to safeguard *(property etc.)*; to shelter *(against inclement weather etc.)*

Schutzgebiet *n* 1. protected area; 2. protectorate
Schutzgüte *f* safety qualities *(of means and methods of labour, i.e. the degree to which they conform to labour safety, hygiene and ease of operation)*
Schutzgütekommission *f* commission for safety qualities
Schutzmarke *f* trademark, brand
Schutzmarkenverband *m* trademark association
Schutzmaßnahme *f* protective measure
Schutzpflanzung *f* protective [anti-erosion] strip of plants; planting of grass, bushes and trees against soil erosion
Schutzrechte *npl* patent rights; trademark rights
Schutzvorrichtung *f* safety guard [device]
Schutzwaldstreifen *m* protective forest belt [strip]
Schutzzoll *m* protective duty
Schutzzollsystem *n* protective system, protectionism
schwach weak; feeble *(excuse etc.)*; low *(performance etc.)*; *(st.ex.)* poor
Schwachstelle *f* weak point
Schwachstellenbekämpfung *f* weak-point control
Schwangere *f* pregnant (woman), expectant mother
Schwangerenberatung *f* 1. maternity advice; 2. maternity advice centre
Schwangerenfürsorge *f* prenatal care, care of expectant mothers
Schwangerschaftsgeld *n* maternity benefit [allowance]
Schwangerschaftsurlaub *m* maternity leave
schwanken to fluctuate *(price etc.)*; to vary *(consumption etc.)*
Schwankung *f* fluctuation *(price etc.)*; variation *(consumption etc.)*
~ **der Chargen** batch variation
~ **der Herstellungslose** *s.* ~ **der Chargen**
~, **jahreszeitliche** seasonal fluctuation; seasonal variations *(fashions etc.)*
~, **konjunkturelle** cyclical fluctuation
~ **zwischen aufeinanderfolgenden Werten** *(stats)* fluctuation
Schwankungsbereich *m* range (of fluctuation)
Schwankungsbreite *f s.* **Schwankungsbereich**
Schwankungsgrenze *f* limit of variation
Schwanzfläche *f*:
~ **einer Verteilung** *(stats)* tail area of a distribution
Schwarzarbeit *f* moonlighting; illicit employment
Schwarzhandel *m* black market(eering), illicit trade ◊ **im** ~ on the black market
Schwarzhandelsgeschäft *n* black market operation [transaction]

Schwarzhändler *m* black marketeer
Schwarzmarkthandel *m s.* **Schwarzhandel**
Schwarzmarktpreis *m* black market price
Schwarzmetallurgie *f* ferrous metal industry
schwebend pending; unresolved, undecided
Schweigegeld *n* hush-money
Schweigepflicht *f* pledge of secrecy; requirement of confidentiality
~, berufliche professional pledge of secrecy, professional discretion
Schweinehaltung *f* pig breeding
Schweinemast *f* pig fattening
Schweinemastanstalt *f* fattening station for pigs
Schweinezucht *f s.* **Schweinehaltung**
Schweißen *n* welding
Schweißer *m* welder
Schweißerei *f* welder's shop
Schwellenwert *m* threshold value
Schwemmland *n* alluvial land
Schwemmlandboden *m (agric)* alluvial soil
Schwerarbeit *f* heavy [hard] work
Schwerarbeiter *m* heavy worker
schwerbehindert disabled
Schwerbehindertenbetreuung *f* care of disabled persons
Schwerbehindertenrente *f* invalid pension
Schwerbehinderter *m* invalid, disabled person
Schwergut *n* heavy goods
Schwergutzuschlag *m* additional charge for heavy goods
Schwerindustrie *f* heavy industry
Schwerlasttransport *m* heavy freight [goods] transport(ation)
Schwermaschinenbau *m* heavy engineering, heavy machine-building industry
Schwermaschinenbauerzeugnis *n* product of heavy engineering [heavy machine-building industry]
Schwerpunktanalyse *f* analysis of crucial points
Schwerpunktbetrieb *m* key [profile-determinant] enterprise
Schwerpunktobjekt *n* key project
Schwerpunktstreik *m* strike at key centres
Schwerpunktversorgung *f* provision of key centres *(with goods etc.)*
Schwerpunktvorhaben *n s.* **Schwerpunktobjekt**
Schwertransport *m* heavy transport
Schwertransporttarif *m* heavy transport rates
schwerverkäuflich difficult to sell
Schwestergesellschaft *f* associate company
Schwierigkeit *f* difficulty
Schwierigkeiten *fpl* difficulties
~, finanzielle financial difficulties
Schwierigkeitsgrad *m* level of difficulties
Schwierigkeitsgruppe *f* class of difficulties

(used in maintenance and repairs in order to classify fixed assets)
Schwindelgeschäft *n* fraud, fraudulent transaction
Schwindelgesellschaft *f s.* **Schwindelunternehmen**
Schwindelunternehmen *n* bogus firm
Schwindler *m* cheat, swindler
Schwingung *f (stats)* oscillation
~, gedämpfte *(stats)* damped oscillation
~, gestörte *(stats)* disturbed oscillation
Schwund *m* loss; shrinkage, loss in weight; leakage
Schwundnorm *f* rate of shrinkage
Schwundprozente *npl* percentage of shrinkage
Schwundverlust *m* loss by shrinkage
schwunghaft lively *(trade etc.)*, prosperous *(business etc.)*
schwungvoll *s.* **schwunghaft**
Sechs-Punkte-Versuch *m (stats)* six-point essay
Sccamt *n* maritime court, Court of Admiralty *(in Great Britain)*
Seearbitragekommission *f* maritime arbitration commission
Seeassekurant *m* maritime insurer
Seeassekuranz *f s.* **Seeversicherung**
Seebeförderung *f* sea transport, *(Am)* ocean transportation
Seebehörde *f s.* **Seeamt**
Seeblockade *f* sea blockade
Seebrief *m* sailing orders; certificate of registry
Seedarleh(e)n *n* bottomry loan
Seefahrer *m* seaman *(merchant fleet)*; sailor *(navy)*
Seefahrt *f* cruise; voyage; navigation, shipping
Seefahrtsamt *n* (merchant) shipping office
Seefahrtsangelegenheiten *fpl* maritime affairs
Seefahrtsbuch *n* seamen's registration book
Seefahrtschule *f* marine school
seefertig ready for sea *(ship)*
Seefisch *m* salt-water fish
Seefischer *m* deep-sea fisher(man)
Seefischerei *f* deep-sea [ocean] fishing
Seefracht *f* cargo, ocean freight
Seefrachtbrief *m* bill of lading
Seefrachtgebühren *fpl* sea [*(Am)* ocean] freight charges
Seefrachtgeschäft *n* sea [*(Am)* ocean] freight business
Seefrachtkosten *pl* sea [*(Am)* ocean] freight costs
Seefrachtordnung *f* sea [*(Am)* ocean] freight regulations
Seefrachtrecht *n* sea [*(Am)* ocean] freight rules and regulations
Seefrachtsatz *m* sea [*(Am)* ocean] freight rate
Seefrachtschiff *n* cargo ship

Seefrachtschiffahrt f cargo shipping, ocean freight service
Seefrachtverkehr m sea [(Am) ocean] freight traffic
Seefrachtversicherung f sea [(Am) ocean] freight insurance
Seefrachtvertrag m contract of affreightment; charter party
Seefunkdienst m maritime [marine] radio service [communication]
Seegebiet n waters
Seegericht n naval court
Seegerichtsbarkeit f maritime jurisdiction
Seegesetz n maritime law
Seegüterversicherung f s. **Seefrachtversicherung**
Seehafen m seaport ⋄ **frei ~ liefern** to deliver free port
Seehafenbetriebsordnung f seaport regulations
Seehafenordnung f port rules and regulations
Seehafenumschlagtarif m (SUT) cargo handling [transshipment] tariff
Seehandel m overseas trade
Seehandelsrecht n sea trade rules and regulations
Seekarte f sea chart
Seekonnossement n sea [(Am) ocean] bill of lading
Seekredit m s. **Seedarleh(e)n**
Seeküste f sea coast, seashore, coastline
Seeladeschein m s. **Seekonnossement**
Seemakler m ship broker
Seemann m seaman
Seemannsgewerkschaft f seamen's union
Seenot f distress at sea
Seenotdienst m salvage service
Seenotrettungsdienst m life-boat [sea rescue] service
Seepolice f marine (insurance) policy
~ auf Namen named marine (insurance) policy
Seeräuber m pirate
Seeräuberei f piracy
Seerecht n maritime law
Seereederei f shipping company
Seereise f voyage, cruise
Seeroute f sea route
Seeschaden m loss suffered at sea, sea-damage average
Seeschadenberechnung f average adjustment
Seeschadenversicherung f s. **Seeversicherung**
Seeschiedsgericht n sea arbitration court
Seeschiffahrt f merchant shipping
Seeschiffahrtskonferenz f shipping conference
Seeschiffahrtsverkehr m maritime traffic
Seespediteur m shipping firm [agent], shipper
Seetransport m sea [ocean] transport, shipment by sea

Seetransportgeschäft n shipping business
Seetransportnetz n sea transport network
seetüchtig seaworthy
Seetüchtigkeit f seaworthiness
Seetüchtigkeitszeugnis n certificate of seaworthiness
Seeverbindung f sea route; shipping line
Seeverkehr m maritime [sea borne] traffic
Seeverkehrswirtschaft f sea [ocean] transport [shipping]
seeverpackt sea-packed, packed for ocean shipment
Seeverpackung f seaproof packing
Seeversicherer m s. **Seeassekurant**
Seeversicherung f marine insurance
Seeversicherungsgesellschaft f marine [maritime] insurance company
Seeversicherungsmakler m marine insurance broker
Seeversicherungspolice f s. **Seepolice**
Seeversicherungsschein m s. **Seepolice**
Seewarte f maritime observation post
Seewechsel m sea bill of exchange
Seeweg m sea route, sea-lane, (Am) ocean-lane
⋄ **auf dem ~ befördert** sea borne; **auf dem ~ schicken** to send by sea
Seezollgrenze f customs sea-boundary
Seezollhafen m customs seaport
Segelliste f sailings (list)
Segelmacher m sails maker
Seilbahn f cable-railway
Seiler m rope-maker
Seilfähre f cable-ferry
Sekretär m secretary
Sekretariat n secretariat, secretary's office
Sektierertum n sectarianism
Sektion f section, department
Sektor m sector
~ der Geldwirtschaft sector of money circulation
~ der Subsistenzwirtschaft subsistence sector
~ der Volkswirtschaft sector of the national economy
~ der Warenwirtschaft sector of commodity production (and exchange)
~, energiewirtschaftlicher energy sector
~, gemischter mixed sector
~, genossenschaftlicher co-operative sector
~, halbstaatlicher semi-state sector
~, industrieller industrial sector
~, kollektivwirtschaftlicher s. **~, genossenschaftlicher**
~, landwirtschaftlicher agricultural sector
~, naturalwirtschaftlicher barter sector; subsistence sector
~, privater private sector
~, staatlicher state [public] sector

Sektorendiagram *n* *(stats)* sectorial diagram
Sektorenintegration *f* integration of economic sectors
Sekundaqualität *f* sub-standard quality
Sekundäraufbereitung *f* secondary processing
Sekundäraufkommen *n* secondary resources
Sekundäreinkommen *n* 1. redistributed income, income in non-productive sectors; 2. secondary income *(from a second job)*
Sekundärenergie *f* secondary energy
Sekundärerfassung *f* collection of secondary data
Sekundärgruppierung *f* *(stats)* secondary grouping
Sekundärinformation *f* secondary information
Sekundärprodukt *n* second-line product *(of enterprise)*
Sekundärrohstoff *m* secondary raw material
Sekundärrohstofferfassung *f* collection of recycling materials
Sekundärverteilung *f* redistribution
Sekundawechsel *m* *(st.ex.)* second of exchange
Selbstabgleich *m* *(d.pr.)* automatic balancing
Selbstabholung *f* collection by the customer
selbständig independent
Selbständiger *m* self-employed person
Selbständigkeit *f* independence
~, politische political independence
~, wirtschaftliche economic independence
~, wirtschaftlich-operative independence in economic management
Selbstanfertigung *f* individually-made product; individual manufacture
Selbstauflösung *f* voluntary dissolution [winding-up] *(company etc.)*
Selbstbedarf *m* personal [own] requirement
Selbstbedienung *f* self-service
Selbstbedienungsgaststätte *f* self-service restaurant
Selbstbedienungsgeschäft *n* self-service shop
Selbstbedienungsladen *m* *s.* Selbstbedienungsgeschäft
Selbstbedienungspostamt *n* self-service post--office
Selbstbedienungsrestaurant *n* *s.* Selbstbedienungsgaststätte
Selbstbedienungstankstelle *f* self-service filling station
Selbstbedienungsverkaufsstelle *f* *s.* Selbstbedienungsgeschäft
Selbstbedienungswäscherei *f* self-service laundry
Selbstbedienungszone *f* self-service area
Selbstbehalt *m* *s.* Selbstbeteiligung
Selbstbehaltsklausel *f* co-insurance clause
Selbstberechnung *f* (one's) own calculation
Selbstbeschränkung *f* voluntary restriction

Selbstbesteuerung *f* (one's) own calculation of taxes (to be paid)
Selbstbestimmung *f* self-determination
Selbstbestimmungsrecht *n* right of self-determination
Selbstbeteiligung *f* *(ins)* net retention; co-insurance *(in the case of reinsurance)*
Selbstbewertung *f* *s.* Selbsteinschätzung
Selbstbewirtschaftung *f* owner-management *(hotels etc.)*; *(agric)* owner-cultivation
Selbsteinschätzung *f* self-assessment *(curriculum vitae)*; *(fin)* self-rating *(for tax purposes etc.)*
Selbstentzündung *f* *(agric)* self-ignition *(inflammable material etc.)*
~ bei der Lagerung *(agric)* self-ignition during storage *(inflammable material etc.)*
Selbsterhaltung *f* self-preservation; self-supporting *(of one's livelihood)*
Selbsterhaltungstrieb *m* instinct of self-preservation
Selbsterhaltungswirtschaft *f* *s.* Selbstversorgungswirtschaft
Selbsterregung *f* *(d.pr.)* self-excitation
Selbsterwirtschaftung *f* self-financing; independent financing
Selbsterzeuger *m* *(agric)* self-producer
Selbstfahrer *m* owner-driver
Selbstfahrvermietung *f* drive-yourself service, rent-a-car service
Selbstfinanzierung *f* self-financing
Selbstfinanzierungsmöglichkeiten *fpl* capacity for self-financing
Selbstgebrauch *m* (one's) own use
selbstgemacht self-made; home-made *(products etc.)*
selbstgenügsam self-sufficient
Selbstgenügsamkeit *f* self-sufficiency
selbstgezogen *(agric)* home-grown *(vegetables etc.)*; home-bred *(poultry etc.)*
selbsthaftend on one's own responsibility
Selbsthaftung *f* self-responsibility
Selbsthilfe *f* self-help
Selbstkontrahent *m* principal
Selbstkontrolle *f* self-control; internal checking *(enterprise affairs etc.)*
selbstkorrigierend *(d.pr.)* self-correcting
Selbstkosten *pl* prime cost *(stemming from labour, materials and other expenditure involved in production)*
~, bereinigte adjusted prime cost
~, betriebliche enterprise prime cost
~, betrieblich notwendige actual prime cost of the enterprise
~, betriebsindividuelle specific enterprise prime cost
~ des Basiszeitraumes prime cost of the period referred to

Selbstkosten

~, **geplante** planned prime cost
~, **gesellschaftliche** social prime cost
~, **gesellschaftlich notwendige** socially necessary prime cost *(the expenditure of living and materialized labour socially necessary for producing a good)*
~, **individuelle** individual prime cost [cost price]
~ **innerhalb eines Industriezweiges** (average) prime cost within an industrial branch
~, **kommerzielle** marketing prime cost
~, **normative** standard prime cost
~, **planmäßige** *s.* ~, **geplante**
~, **reine** net prime cost
Selbstkostenanteil *m* proportion [portion] of prime cost
Selbstkostenberechnung *f* cost accounting, costing
Selbstkostenbereinigung *f* adjustment of prime cost
Selbstkostenbestandteil *m* element [component] of prime cost
selbstkostenbezogen related to prime cost
Selbstkostenentwicklung *f* prime cost development
Selbstkostenerhöhung *f* increase in prime cost
Selbstkostenindex *m* index of prime cost
Selbstkostenkalkulation *f s.* **Selbstkostenberechnung**
Selbstkostenkontrolle *f* control of prime cost
Selbstkostenlimit *n* prime cost limit
Selbstkostenniveau *n* level of prime cost
Selbstkostenplan *m* prime cost plan
Selbstkostenplanung *f* planning of prime cost
Selbstkostenpreis *m* cost price ✧ **unter ~ verkaufen** to sell below (the) cost price; **zum ~** at cost price
Selbstkostenpreistyp *m* kind of cost price
Selbstkostenrechnung *f s.* **Selbstkostenberechnung**
Selbstkostensatz *m* rate of prime cost
Selbstkostensenkung *f* reduction of prime cost
~, **absolute** absolute reduction of prime cost
~, **geplante** planned reduction of prime cost
~, **relative** relative reduction of prime cost
~, **tatsächliche** actual reduction of prime cost
Selbstkostensenkungsauflage *f* given reduction of prime cost
Selbstkostensteigerung *f* increase in prime cost
Selbstkostenstruktur *f* structure of prime cost
Selbstkostenüberschreitung *f* excess over planned prime cost
Selbstkostenveränderung *f* changes in prime cost
Selbstkostenvergleich *m* comparison of prime costs *(of various enterprises or countries)*
Selbstkostenvolumen *n* the amount of prime cost

Selbstkostenwert *m* cost price
Selbstkritik *f* self-criticism
Selbstlauf *m* uncontrolled course
Selbstprogrammierung *f (d.pr.)* automatic programming
selbstprüfend self-checking
Selbstprüfung *f (d.pr.)* built-in check
selbstregulierend self-regulating
Selbstregulierung *f* self-regulation, automatic regulation
Selbstschuldner *m* principal [primary] debtor
selbstschuldnerisch as debtor on one's own account
Selbststeuerung *f* automatic [built-in] control
Selbstveranlagung *f (fin)* self-rating
selbstveranlagungspflichtig obliged to self-rating
Selbstverbrauch *m* domestic consumption; self-consumption, (one's) own consumption
Selbstverladung *f* self-loading *(by customers themselves)*
Selbstverpflichtung *f* personal commitment
Selbstversicherter *m* insured person *(as opposed to co-insured person)*
Selbstversorger *m (agric)* self-provider *(of farm products)*
Selbstversorgung *f* (economic) self-sufficiency, living on one's own produce
Selbstversorgungswirtschaft *f* subsistence economy
Selbstverwaltung *f* self-government, autonomy; self-administration
~, **kommunale** local self-government
Selbstverwertung *f* self-realization *(capital in the production process)*
Selbstwählbetrieb *m* dialling system
Selbstwählfernverkehr *m* subscriber trunk dialling (STD)
Selektion *f* selection
~, **automatische** *(d.pr.)* automatic selection
selektiv selective *(sample surveys etc.)*
Selektivität *f* selectivity
Seltenheitsgüter *npl* scarce goods
Seltenheitswert *m* scarcity value *(precious metals etc.)*
senden to send, to forward, to dispatch; to communicate, to transmit; to broadcast, to telecast
Sendung *f* 1. mission; 2. *(com)* consignment; shipment; 3. transmission *(radio)*; telecast *(TV)*
~, **eingeschriebene** registered letter
~, **fehlgeleitete** misrouted consignment
~, **gemischte** mixed consignment
~, **postlagernde** consignment to be collected
senken to reduce *(costs, materials etc.)*, to lower, to cut *(price etc.)*
Senkung *f* reduction *(costs, material, consumption, price etc.)*, lowering, cut *(price etc.)*

~ **der Ausgaben** reduction of expenditure
~ **der Mindestreserven** reduction of the minimum reserve
~ **des Diskontsatzes** lowering of the bank rate
Separatismus *m* separatism
Separatist *m* separatist
Separatkonto *n* separate account
Separatvertrag *m* separate contract [agreement]
Sequential-Stichprobenverfahren *n* (stats) sequential sample method
sequentiell sequential
Sequenzanalyse *f* (stats) sequential analysis
Sequester *m* sequestrator
Sequestration *f* sequestration; confiscation; compulsory administration (of a debtor's estate etc.); seisin
sequestrieren to sequester, to sequestrate
Serie *f* series; set; issue; range, line (of goods etc.)
Serienanlauf *m* launching of serial [mass] production
Serienanleihe *f* serial bonds
Serienarbeit *f* repetitive work
Serienartikel *m* mass-produced article
Serienausführung *f* standard model
Serienausgabe *f* serial issue (bonds etc.)
Serienbau *m* 1. pre-fabricated house [block of flats]; 2. technique of serial construction
Serienbauweise *f* technique of serial construction
Serienerzeugnis *n* *s.* **Serienartikel**
Serienfabrikat *n* *s.* **Serienartikel**
Serienfabrikation *f* *s.* **Serienfertigung**
Serienfertigung *f* serial production
Seriengröße *f* size of serial production
~, **optimale** optimal [optimum] series
~, **wirtschaftliche** economic series
Serienherstellung *f* *s.* **Serienfertigung**
Serienkalkulation *f* job order cost accounting
serienmäßig *s.* **serienweise**
Serienmodell *n* standard model
Serienproduktion *f* *s.* **Serienfertigung**
Serienrabatt *m* frequency discount, discount for regular purchases
Serienreife *f* readiness for serial production
serienweise in series, in batches
Service *m* (after-sales) service
Sicherheit *f* safety (at work etc.); security (at airport, of pensions, persons etc.); safeguard (against inflation etc.); protection (of investments); certainty (of individuals etc.); surety (for s.o. etc.); reliability (of payment of debts etc.); (collateral) security; (jur) bail ◊ ~ **bieten** to offer security [collateral]; ~ **leisten** to stand security, to furnish security (for a loan), to secure, to guarantee (a loan); (jur) to give [offer] bail

~ **am Arbeitsplatz** job [workplace] safety
~ **des Arbeitsplatzes** job security; security of employment
~, **öffentliche** public security
~, **soziale** social security
~, **statistische** (stats) confidence coefficient
Sicherheiten *fpl* securities, sureties; cover ◊ ~ **bestellen** to furnish collateral
Sicherheitsabstand *m* safe distance (between cars in traffic)
Sicherheitsbestand *m* minimum inventory level; safety level [stock]; (inventory) reserve stock; buffer [reserve, cushion] stock
Sicherheitsbestimmungen *fpl* safety regulations
Sicherheitscode *m* (d.pr.) redundant code
Sicherheitsfaktor *m* safety factor
Sicherheitsfonds *m* safety fund
Sicherheitsgrad *m* degree of safety
Sicherheitsgrenze *f* margin of safety
sicherheitshalber as a precaution
Sicherheitsinspektion *f* (labour) safety inspection
Sicherheitsinspektor *m* (labour) safety inspector
Sicherheitskapital *n* (ins) surplus to policy holders
Sicherheitsklausel *f* safeguard
Sicherheitskoeffizient *m* coefficient of safety
Sicherheitslager *n* safety stock
Sicherheitsleistung *f* 1. security (deposit), surety; cover; (jur) bail; 2. furnishing of (a) security, standing surety ◊ **gegen ~ verkaufen** (st.ex.) to sell on margin
Sicherheitsmaßnahme *f* safety measure, precaution; safeguard
Sicherheitsniveau *n* safety level
Sicherheitsorgan *n* security service
Sicherheitsrücklage *f* contingency reserve, reserve fund
Sicherheitsschranke *f* (stats) confidence level
Sicherheitsspanne *f* margin of error
Sicherheitsstufe *f* (stats) significance level
Sicherheitsstufen *fpl*:
~, **prozentuale** (stats) percentage points
Sicherheitssystem *n* safety system; security system
Sicherheitstechnik *f* safety device
Sicherheitsvorrat *m* safety [reserve] stock
Sicherheitsvorschrift *f* safety rule
Sicherheitswechsel *m* bill (of exchange) deposited as collateral security, collateral bill
Sicherheitszuschlag *m* margin of safety; safety factor (materials, components etc.)
sichern to secure (door etc.); to safeguard (money etc.); to protect (life etc.); to guarantee (quality etc.); to give [provide] security (for) (person etc.); to hedge (against losses etc.); to cover (loan etc.)

sicherstellen to take possession of *(s.th.)*, to seize; to put in safekeeping, to guarantee
Sicherstellung *f* taking possession of *(s.th)*, seizure, seizing; guarantee, garanty
~, geldmäßige monetary guarantee
Sicherung *f* securing *(door etc.)*; safeguarding *(money etc.)*; protection *(life etc.)*; guarantee *(quality etc.)*; hedging *(against losses etc.)*; cover *(loan etc.)*
~ der Geldwertstabilität safeguarding monetary stability; stabilization policy
~ der Realeinkommen safeguarding real incomes
~ des Arbeitsplatzes job protection, safeguarding of jobs
~ gegen Verlust cover against loss
Sicherungsabtretung *f* assignment (of a claim) for security
Sicherungsanlage *f* safety control system
Sicherungseigentum *n* pledged property
Sicherungseigentümer *m* owner of collateral security
Sicherungsfonds *m s.* **Sicherheitsfonds**
Sicherungsformen *fpl* security arrangements
Sicherungsgeber *m* transferor of title to property for purpose of security
Sicherungsgegenstand *m* collateral
Sicherungsgelder *npl* funds pledged as security
Sicherungsgeschäft *n* covering transaction; hedge
Sicherungsgrenze *f s.* **Sicherheitsgrenze**
Sicherungsgrundschuld *f* real estate charge for securing a loan
Sicherungshypothek *f* cautionary [trust] mortgage
Sicherungskäufe *mpl* hedge buying
Sicherungsklausel *f* safeguarding clause
Sicherungsnehmer *m* secured party
Sicherungspatent *n* confirmation patent
Sicherungsprogramm *n (d.pr.)* safeguarding program
Sicherungsreserve *f* deposit security reserve
Sicherungsstufe *f s.* **Sicherheitsstufe**
Sicherungsübereignung *f (jur)* protective conveyance, transfer of ownership as security on a debt
Sicherungsübereignungsvertrag *m (jur)* protective conveyance contract
Sicherungsverfahren *n (jur)* attachment procedure
Sicherungsverkauf *m* hedge selling
Sicherungsvorkehrungen *fpl* protective measures [steps]
Sicherungszession *f s.* **Sicherungsabtretung**
Sicht *f* sight; view ⋄ **auf kurze ~** on a short--term basis, in the short run [term]; over the short term; **auf lange ~** on a long-term basis, in the long run [term, view]; **bei ~** at sight, on presentation; **fällig bei ~** due at sight, due at presentation; **zahlbar bei ~** payable [due] at sight
Sichtanzeige *f (d.pr.)* visual display
Sichtdepositen *npl s.* **Sichteinlagen**
Sichteinlagen *fpl* sight deposits
Sichteinlagenkonto *n* sight deposit account
sichten 1. to sight; 2. to examine; to sift through *(materials, papers etc.)*; to sort out *(letters etc.)*
Sichtgerät *n (d.pr.)* visual display unit
Sichtgeschäft *n* forward transaction
Sichtgeschäfte *npl* futures
Sichtguthaben *n* credit balance payable at call
Sichtkartei *f* reference card-index
Sichtkontrolle *f* visual inspection; *(d.pr.)* visual check [inspection]
Sichtkurs *m* sight [demand] rate
Sichttage *mpl* days of grace [respite]
Sichttratte *f* sight draft, draft at sight
Sichtung *f* 1. sighting; 2. examination; sifting through *(materials, papers etc.)*; sorting out *(letters etc.)*
Sichtverbindlichkeiten *fpl* demand liabilities, liabilities due on presentation
Sichtverkauf *m* display selling
Sichtvermerk *m* 1. endorsement, indorsement; 2. visa
Sichtwechsel *m* sight-bill, sight-draft, bill payable at sight [demand], bill on demand
Sichtwerbung *f* visual advertising
siedeln to settle
Siedler *m* settler
Siedlung *f* settlement, colony; housing estate, suburban colony
Siedlungsgebiet *n* built-up area
Siedlungsgelände *n* development area
Siedlungsnetz *n* network of settlements *(distribution of settlements in an area or region)*
Siedlungspolitik *f* settlement policy
Siedlungsschwerpunkt *m* settlement priority; settlement concentration
~, ländlicher settlement priority in a rural area; concentration of settlement in a rural area
Siedlungsstruktur *f* structure of settlements
Siedlungssystem *n* system of settlements
Siegel *n* seal
Siegelbruch *m* breaking official seals
Siegelordnung *f* seal rules
Sigma-Verfahren *n (stats)* sigma scoring
Signal *n* signal
Signalausfall *m (d.pr.)* drop out
Signalgeber *m (d.pr.)* annunciator
Signalspeicher *m (d.pr.)* latch
Signalwirkung *f* effect of an announcement
Signatarmacht *f s.* **Signatarstaat**
Signatarstaat *m* signatory state [power]

Signatur *f* signature; symbol *(map)*; classification number *(library)*
signieren to sign *(documents etc.)*
Signierung *f* marking *(bill)*; signing *(contract etc.)*
Signifikanz *f (stats)* significance
Signifikanzgrad *m (stats)* significance level
Signifikanzniveau *n s.* **Signifikanzgrad**
Signifikanzschranke *f s.* **Signifikanzgrad**
Signifikanzschwelle *f s.* **Signifikanzgrad**
Signifikanzstufe *f s.* **Signifikanzgrad**
Signum *n* signature; initials; sign, mark
Silber *n* silver
Silberbarren *m* bar [ingot] of silver
Silbergeld *n* silver money [coins]
Silberwährung *f* silver standard
Silo *m/n* silo; grain elevator
Simplexalgorithmus *m (maths)* simplex algorithm
Simplexbetrieb *m (d.pr.)* simplex operation
Simplexkanal *m (d.pr.)* simplex channel
Simplexmethode *f s.* **Simplexverfahren**
Simplexverfahren *n (maths)* simplex method
Simplifikation *f* simplification
Simulation *f* simulation
Simulationsmodell *n* simulation model
Simulationsprogramm *n (d.pr.)* simulator
Simulationsprogrammierung *f (d.pr.)* simulation programming
simulieren to simulate *(process etc.)*, to sham, to feign *(illness etc.)*
simultan simultaneous
Simultanbetrieb *m* simultaneous working *(machinery etc.)*
Simultanhaftung *f* simultaneous [direct and primary] liability
Simultanmoment *m (stats)* joint moment
Simultanplanung *f* simultaneous planning
Simultanrechner *m (d.pr.)* simultaneous [parallel] computer
Simultanverarbeitung *f* parallel [simultaneous] processing [operation]; *(d.pr.)* multiprocessing
Simultanverteilung *f (stats)* joint distribution
sinken to sink, to go down; to fall, to drop *(price, temperature etc.)*; to diminish *(confidence etc.)*; to decline, to wane *(influence etc.)*
Sinn *m* sense, meaning; mind; faculty; inclination, disposition, tendency; feeling, flair; point
Sinus-Grenzwertsatz *m (stats)* sinusoidal limit theorem
Sippe *f* kinship, consanguity; (extended) family; relations; tribe; clan
Sitte *f* custom; usage, practice; habit; tradition
Situation *f* situation; position ⋄ **der ~ gewachsen sein** to rise to [be equal to, master] the occasion; **die ~ retten** to save the situation

Situationsanalyse *f* situation(al) analysis
Sitz *m* seat *(of government, company etc.)*, headquarters, head [main] office, (principal) place of business; statutory [registered] office; site *(industry)*
~ des Käufers buyer's place of business
~ einer Gesellschaft seat of a company, *(Am)* corporate seat [domicile]
Sitzarbeit *f* sedentary work
Sitzland *n* country of incorporation
Sitzordnung *f* seating arrangement(s)
Sitzstreik *m* sit-down [sit-in] strike
Sitzung *f* meeting; conference; session, sitting *(parliament etc.)* ⋄ **bei einer ~ zugegen sein** to attend a meeting; **eine ~ abbrechen** to break off a meeting; **eine ~ abhalten** to hold a meeting; to have a meeting; to be in session; **eine ~ anberaumen** to fix [schedule] a meeting; **eine ~ aufheben** to close [end, terminate] a meeting; **eine ~ einberufen** to call [convene] a meeting; **eine ~ leiten** to chair [preside over] a meeting; **eine ~ schließen** to close a meeting; **eine ~ vertagen** to adjourn a meeting
~, öffentliche public hearing, hearing in public
Sitzungsbericht *m* conference report; report [minutes] of proceedings
Sitzungsperiode *f* session, term
Sitzungsprotokoll *n* minutes of a meeting
Sitzungssaal *m s.* **Sitzungszimmer**
Sitzungszimmer *n* conference room [hall]
Sitzverlegung *f* transfer of place [seat] of business
Skala *f* scale; range; gamut
skalieren to scale
Skalierungsverfahren *n* scale analysis
Sklave *m* slave
Sklavenarbeit *f* slave-labour
Sklavenbefreiung *f* emancipation of slaves
Sklavenhaltergesellschaft *f* slave-owning society
Sklavenhandel *m* slave-trade
Sklavenhändler *m* slave-trader
Sklavenmarkt *m* slave-market
Sklaverei *f* slavery
skontieren to allow discount for
Skonto *m/n* discount ⋄ **ein(en) ~ in Anspruch nehmen** to take a discount
Skontoaufwendungen *fpl* discount paid
Skontoerträge *mpl* discount received
Skontofrist *f* discount period
Skontoprozentsatz *m* percentage of discount
Skontration *f* clearing, settling, balancing *(accounts)*
skontrieren to clear, to settle, to balance *(accounts)*
Skontro *n* auxiliary ledger

S-Kurve *f (stats)* S-curve, Sigmoid curve
Slums *pl* slums
Slutzky-Prozeß *m (stats)* Slutzky process
Sockelbetrag *m* flat cash supplement; extra award to the lowest paid
Sockeltarif *m* basic rate *(wages)*
Sofortabschreibung *f* write-off in full [as incurred], immediate write-off
Soforthilfe *f* immediate aid
Sofort-Liquidität *f* spot cash
Sofortmaßnahme *f* immediate [prompt, urgent] measure
Sofortprogramm *n* crash programme
Sofortreaktion *f* crash reaction *(to changes in the market etc.)*
Sofortverkehr *m (transp)* no-delay service
Sofortzahlung *f* immediate payment
Software *f* software
~, **einheitliche** common software
~, **systemeigene** resident software
~, **übertragbare** portable [transferable] software
Softwareentwicklungskosten *pl* software development cost(s)
Softwarehandel *m* trade in software, software trade
Softwarepaket *n (d.pr.)* software package
Solawechsel *m* promissory note, *(Am)* sole [single] bill
Solidarbürgschaft *f* joint and several guaranty
Solidarhaftung *f* joint and several liability
solidarisieren:
◇ **sich ~ mit** to declare one's solidarity with, to be solidly behind s.o., to identify o.s. with
Solidarität *f* solidarity ◇ **~ bekunden** *s.* **solidarisieren**; **~ üben** *s.* **solidarisieren**
Solidaritätsbeitrag *m* contribution to the solidarity fund
Solidaritätsbewegung *f* solidarity movement
Solidaritätsfonds *m* solidarity fund
Solidaritätsgefühl *n* feeling of solidarity
Solidarschuldner *m* joint [co-principal] debtor
solide sound, reliable *(firm etc.)*; reasonable, fair *(prices)*; sound *(relations)*; solid, sound *(knowledge, work etc.)* solid, robust, durable, wear-resistant *(material, devices etc.)*
Solidität *f* solidity; soundness, trustworthiness
Soll *n* debit, debit-side; target ◇ **im ~ buchen** to enter on the debit side
~ und Haben *n* debit and credit, assets and liabilities
Sollaufkommen *n* planned resources; *(tax)* budgeted revenue
Soll-Ausbringung *f* planned [envisaged] output
Sollbestand *m* nominal balance, calculated assets
Soll-Buchung *f* debit entry
Solleinnahmen *fpl* planned receipts [takings]

Solleistung *f* nominal [rated, standard] output
Soll-Fertigungszeit *f (manuf)* planned direct labour hours
Soll-Ist-Vergleich *m* comparison between planned and actual results *(output, costs etc.)*, target-performance comparison, plan monitoring *(statistical analysis)*
Sollkosten *pl* planned costs
Sollposten *m* debit item [entry]
Soll-Prinzip-Abrechnung *f (home tr)* current accounting of goods turnover
Soll-Saldo *m* debit balance
Sollseite *f s.* **Soll**
Sollstärke *f* authorized strength *(labour force etc.)*
Sollversteuerung *f* calculation of turnover [sales] tax on the basis of pre-arranged receipts
Sollwert *m* 1. nominal [rated] value; 2. *(d.pr.)* set point
Sollzahlen *fpl* target figures
Sollzeit *f* standard time
Sollzinsen *mpl* debtor interest (rates) *(banks)*; debit interest, interest receivable
~ der Banken bank lending rates
Sollzinssatz *m* borrowing rate
solvent solvent, liquid
Solvenz *f* ability [capacity] to pay, debt-paying ability, solvency
Solvenzvorschriften *fpl* statutory solvency regulations
Sommerfahrplan *m* summer timetable
Sommerfrische *f* summer resort
Sommergast *m* summer visitor
Sommergetreide *n* summer grain
Sommerhaus *n* summer-house; weekend cottage
Sommerkleidung *f* summer-wear
Sommerkulturen *fpl* summer crops
Sommerpreis *m* summer price
Sommerschlußverkauf *m* summer sale [bargain], summer (closing) sale
Sommerweizen *m* spring(-sown) wheat
Sommerzeit *f* summer time
Sonderabschreibung *f* special depreciation
Sonderanfertigung *f* special design; custom--made [custom-built] product
Sonderangebot *n* special offer; (special) bargain, bargain sale
Sonderaufgaben *fpl* extra-duty assignments
Sonderauftrag *m* special order *(goods etc.)*; special mission
Sonderausbildung *f* special training
Sonderausführung *f s.* **Sonderanfertigung**
Sonderausgabe *f* 1. special expenditure [expense]; 2. special edition
Sonderausgaben-Pauschalbetrag *m* blanket allowance for special expenses

Sonderausschuß *m* select committee
Sonderausschüttung *f* extra distribution *(dividends etc.)*
Sonderausstattung *f* special equipment
Sonderbeauftragter *m* special representative
Sonderberechnung *f* special accounting ✧ **gegen ~ at** extra cost(s)
Sonderbericht *m* special report
Sonderbestellung *f* special order
Sonderbestimmung *f* special rule, exceptional [special] provision
Sonderbevollmächtigter *m (pol)* plenipotentiary
Sonderbilanz *f* special-purpose balance sheet
Sonderdarleh(e)n *n* special-term loan
Sonderdepot *n* special securities deposit
Sonderdividende *f* extra [special] dividend [bonus]
Sondereigentum *n* estate in severalty
Sondereinnahmen *fpl* extra-ordinary receipts
~ im Staatshaushalt special revenue
Sondereinzelkosten *pl* special direct costs
~ der Fertigung special production costs
~ des Vertriebs special direct sales costs
Sonderermäßigung *f* special price reduction
Sonderfall *m* special [exeptional] case
Sonderfazilitäten *fpl* special facilities
Sonderfertigung *f* special production [manufacture]
Sonderflug *m* extra flight
Sonderfreibetrag *m* special tax-free amount
Sondergebühr *f* extra fee
Sondergefahren *fpl (ins)* extraneous perils
Sondergemeinkosten *pl* special overhead (expenses)
Sondergenehmigung *f* special permit [authorization]
Sondergericht *n* special court
Sondergerichtsbarkeit *f* limited jurisdiction
Sondergesetz *n* special law
Sondergewinn *m* extra profit
Sondergutachten *n* expertise, special expert opinion
Sonderhaushalt *m* extraordinary budget
Sonderinteresse *n* private [special] interest
Sonderkalkulation *f* special-purpose cost estimate
Sonderkonkurs *m* special bankruptcy proceedings
Sonderkontingent *n* special quota
Sonderkonto *n* special account ✧ **auf ~ gutschreiben** to credit to a separate account
Sonderkosten *pl* special expenses
~ der Fertigung special production costs
Sonderkredit *m* special credit
Sonderleistung *f* extra service
Sonderleistungen *fpl*:
~, soziale fringe benefits

Sonderlombard *m* special lombard facility
Sonderlombardkredit *m* special lombard loan
Sonderlombardsystem *n* special lombard system
Sondernachlaß *m* special discount
Sonderorganisationen *fpl* specialized agencies
Sonderposten *m* off-the-line item
Sonderpreis *m* special [preferential, exceptional] price
Sonderprüfer *m* special auditor
Sonderprüfung *f* special audit
Sonderrabatt *m* special discount
Sonderrechte *npl* special (membership) rights
Sonderregelung *f* special treatment; separate settlement; special provision
Sonderrücklage *f* special-purpose reserve, special contingency reserve
Sonderrückstellungen *fpl* special provisions
Sonderschau *f* special display
Sonderschicht *f* extra shift
Sonderschule *f* special school; school for handicapped children
Sondersitzung *f* special session [meeting]
Sondersparte *f* special line (of business)
Sonderstatistiken *fpl (stats)* special purpose statistics
Sonderstellung *f* special position ✧ **eine ~ einnehmen** to occupy a special position
Sondersteuer *f* special tax
Sondertarif *m* special tariff; preferential rate
Sondertyp *m* special type *(machine etc.)*
Sonderumlage *f* special assessment *(costs etc.)*
Sonderurlaub *m* special leave
Sondervergütung *f* extra [premium] pay
Sonderverkauf *m* special sales (at knockdown prices)
Sonderverpackung *f* special packing
Sonderverwahrung *f* individual safe custody of securities
Sondervollmacht *f* special authority [power] *(to negotiate etc.)*
Sondervorteile *mpl* special advantages
Sonderwertberichtigung *f* special valuation adjustment
Sonderziehungsrechte *npl* Special Drawing Rights (SDR)
Sonderzins *m* special interest
Sonderzug *m* special (train)
Sonderzulage *f* special bonus
sondieren to probe, to sound out *(s.o.'s reaction etc.)*, to explore the ground *(for a settlement etc.)*
Sondierungsgespräche *npl* exploratory talks
Sonntagsarbeit *f* Sunday work
Sonntagsfahrkarte *f* week-end ticket
Sorgeberechtigter *m* person having the care and custody *(of child etc.)*

Sorgerecht *n* care and custody *(child etc.)*, right of custody
Sorgfalt *f* care; attention; exactness, accuracy
~, **angemessene** reasonable [ordinary] care
~, **verkehrsübliche** *s.* ~, **angemessene**
Sorgfaltspflicht *f* duty to take care
Sorte *f* sort, kind, species; type; quality, grade *(commodities etc.)*; brand, make *(goods etc.)*; variety
~, **beste** prime quality *(goods etc.)*
~, **minderwertige** low quality *(goods etc.)*
Sorten *fpl* foreign notes and coins
Sortenabteilung *f* foreign currency [money] department
Sortenfertigung *f* continuous batch production
Sortengeschäft *n* dealings in foreign currency [notes and coins]
Sortenhandel *m s.* **Sortengeschäft**
Sortenkalkulation *f* batch-type costing
Sortenkasse *f* foreign currency teller's counter
Sortenkurs *m* exchange rate for foreign notes and coins
Sortenprogramm *n* batch production programme in sequence
Sortenrechnung *f s.* **Sortenkalkulation**
Sortenwechselkosten *pl* batch changeover cost(s)
Sortenzettel *m* bill of specie
sortieren to grade; to sort out, to sift, to arrange
Sortierer *m* sorter
Sortiermaschine *f (d.pr.)* sorting machine
Sortierung *f* assortment; sorting out; sizing; grading; classification
Sortiment *n* range of articles [goods], assortment, collection, set ◊ **das ~ bereinigen** to streamline the product range; **das ~ umstellen** to change the business mix
Sortimentierung *f s.* **Sortierung**
Sortimentsbereinigung *f* streamlining of a product range
Sortimentsbilanz *f* balance sheet of range of articles [goods]
Sortimentsbildung *f* fixing a range of articles [goods] (to be produced)
Sortimentsbreite *f* range [assortment] of goods
Sortimentsbuchhandel *m* retail bookselling
Sortimentsbuchhändler *m* retail bookseller
sortimentsgerecht according to the planned range of articles [goods]; range [assortment] according to order
Sortimentshandel *m* single-line trade
Sortimentskonzeption *f* draft plan of range of articles [goods] (to be produced)
Sortimentsliste *f* list of range [assortment] (of articles)
Sortimentsplan *m* plan of range [assortment] of articles [goods]

Sortimentsplanung *f* planning the range [assortment] of production
Sortimentsprofil *n s.* **Sortimentsstruktur**
Sortimentsstruktur *f* structure of the range [assortment] of articles [goods]
Sortimentstechnologie *f* method of movement of goods in wholesale and retail trade
Sortimentsumschlag *m* turnover of range [assortment] of articles [goods]
sozial social
Sozialabgaben *fpl* contributions for social purposes; social insurance contributions
Sozialamt *n* social welfare office
Sozialarbeit *f* social work
Sozialarbeiter *m* social worker
Sozialaufwand *m* social welfare expenditure
Sozialausgaben *fpl* expenditure for social purposes; social budget expenditure
Sozialbauten *mpl* public buildings *(limited to schools, kindergartens, hospitals etc.)*
Sozialbeihilfe *f* (social) relief payment
Sozialbeitrag *m s.* **Sozialversicherungsbeitrag**
Sozialbericht *m* social policy report
Sozialbudget *n* social welfare budget
Sozialeinkommen *n* income from public sources
Sozialeinrichtungen *fpl* social services; welfare facilities
Sozialfonds *m* social fund
Sozialfürsorge *f* social (welfare) work
Sozialfürsorgeunterstützung *f s.* **Sozialbeihilfe**
Sozialhilfe *f* public assistance, supplementary welfare benefits
sozialisieren to socialize
Sozialisierung *f* socialization
Sozialismus *m* socialism
sozialistisch socialist(ic)
Sozialkapital *n s.* **Sozialfonds**
Sozialkosten *f* social welfare expenditure(s)
Sozialkritik *f* social criticism
sozialkritisch social critical *(report etc.)*
Soziallasten *fpl* social expenditures
Sozialleistung *f* social security benefit
Sozialleistungen *fpl*:
~ **der Unternehmer** employers' social security contributions; employers' provision of facilities
Sozialleistungsrecht *n* laws of social security benefits
Soziallohn *m* socially subsidized wages
sozialökonomisch socio-economic
Sozialplan *m* social plan, plan of social measures *(in enterprises)*
Sozialplanung *f* social planning, planning of social measures *(in enterprises)*
Sozialpolitik *f* social policy *(related to wages, welfare, housing etc.)*

Sozialprodukt *n* (gross) national product
Sozialrente *f* social insurance pension
Sozialrentner *m* social insurance pensioner
Sozialschicht *f* stratum *(of society)*
Sozialstaat *m* welfare state
Sozialstruktur *f* social structure
Sozialunterstützung *f s.* **Sozialbeihilfe**
Sozialversicherung *f* social [national] insurance
Sozialversicherungsbeitrag *m* social insurance contribution
~ **der Berufstätigen** employees' contribution to social insurance
~ **des Betriebes** contribution of the enterprise to social insurance
Sozialversicherungsgrenze *f* maximum (amount) of social insurance contribution
Sozialversicherungshaushalt *m* social insurance budget
Sozialversicherungsleistung *f* social insurance benefits
Sozialversicherungspflicht *f* compulsory enrolment in social [national] insurance
sozialversicherungspflichtig liable to pay social insurance contributions
Sozialversicherungsrente *f s.* **Sozialrente**
Sozialversicherungsträger *m* social insurance institution *(administering the social insurance fund)*
Sozialversicherungszweig *m* social security sector
Sozialvertrag *m* social contract
Sozialwesen *n* social services
Sozialwissenschaft *f* social science
Sozialzulage *f* social allowance, social welfare bonus *(paid by enterprises etc.)*
Soziologie *f* sociology
Sozius *m* partner *(business etc.)*; pillion rider [passenger]
Spalte *f* column
spalten to split *(into factions etc.)*; to divide *(organization etc.)*
Spaltung *f* split, splitting *(into factions etc.)*; division *(organization etc.)*
Spanne *f* span *(period etc.)*; margin
Spannung *f* tension; suspension; stress
Spannweite *f (stats)* range
~, **halbe** *(stats)* semi-range
~, **mittlere** *(stats)* mean range
Spannweitendarstellung *f (stats)* high-low graph
Spannweiten-F-Quotient *m (stats)* substitute F-ratio
Spannweiten-Kontrollkarte *f (stats)* range chart
Spannweitenverlauf *m s.* **Spannweitendarstellung**
Sparanlage *f* savings account
Sparanleihe *f* savings bond
Sparanteil *m* share [proportion] of savings

Sparbank *f s.* **Sparkasse**
Sparbeitrag *m (ins)* savings component *(of a premium)*
Sparbetrag *m* amount of savings
Sparbuch *n* savings-bank book
Sparbüchse *f* savings [money] box
Spardepositen *pl* savings deposits
Spareinlage *f* savings, deposit on a savings account
Spareinlagen *fpl* savings
~, **befristete** time savings deposits
~, **jederzeit rückzahlbare** current account savings
Spareinlagenbestand *m s.* **Spareinlagen**
Spareinlagenentwicklung *f* growth of savings
Spareinlagenkonto *n s.* **Sparkonto**
Spareinlagenzuwachs *m* increase in savings
sparen to save; to practise economy, to economize on *(materials etc.)*
Sparen *n* saving; economizing, economy
Sparentwicklung *f* growth in savings
Sparer *m* saver; depositor; economizer
Sparfonds *m* savings; savings fund *(of the overall economy)*
Sparformen *fpl* kinds of savings
Sparfreudigkeit *f s.* **Sparneigung**
Spargelder *npl s.* **Spareinlagen**
Spargirokonto *n* savings giro account
Spargiroverkehr *m* savings giro transfer business
Sparguthaben *n* savings balance; savings account
Sparhang *m s.* **Sparneigung**
Sparkapital *n* savings capital
Sparkapitalbildung *f* formation of savings capital
Sparkasse *f* savings bank
Sparkassenabteilung *f* savings department
Sparkassenangestellter *m* bank clerk
Sparkassenbetriebswirtschaft *f* savings banking
Sparkassenbuch *n s.* **Sparbuch**
Sparkassendienst *m* savings bank service
Sparkassenfunktion *f* function of a savings bank
Sparkassengeschäft *n* savings business
Sparkassengesetz *n* savings bank act
Sparkassenleiter *m* manager of a savings bank
Sparkassensatzung *f* savings bank regulations
Sparkassen- und Giroverband *m* savings and giro association
Sparkassenwesen *n* system of savings banks
Sparkonto *n* savings account
Sparleistung *f* savings *(activity)*
Sparmaßnahme *f* economy measure
Sparmaßnahmen *fpl* economies
Sparneigung *f* propensity to save

Sparprämie *f* savings premium; *(ins)* initial reserve
Sparprämienlos *n* premium bond
Sparprogramm *n* 1. savings campaign; 2. savings plan
Sparquote *f* national income savings ratio *(ratio between increase in savings and national income)*
Sparrate *f* rate of savings
Sparrentenversicherung *f* old-age pension savings insurance
sparsam economical; thrifty ⋄ **~ leben** to live economically; **~ mit etwas umgehen** to be economical with s.th.; **~ wirtschaften** to economize
Sparsamkeit *f* economy; thriftiness
Sparsamkeitsprinzip *n* economy principle; thriftiness principle
Sparsamkeitsregime *n* regime of economy, economic regime
Spartätigkeit *f* saving
Sparte *f* trade group [section, division]; branch; column, section
Spartheorie *f* savings theory
Spar- und Darleh(e)nskasse *f* savings and loan society
Sparvertrag *m* savings agreement
Sparvolumen *n* volume of savings
Sparzinsen *pl* interest on savings
Sparzwang *m* compulsory saving
Spätkapitalismus *m* late capitalism
spätkapitalistisch late capitalist
Spätverkaufsstelle *f* late-closing store [shop]
spedieren to send, to forward, to dispatch *(goods)*
Spediteur *m* forwarding [shipping] agent, carrier; haulage contractor; furniture remover
~, übernehmender receiving carrier
~, zustellender delivery carrier
Spediteurdokumente *npl* carrier's papers
Spediteur-Durchfrachtkonnossement *n* combined transport bill of lading
Spediteurhaftpflicht *f* forwarding agent's liability
Spediteurhaftpflichtversicherung *f* forwarding agent's liability insurance
Spediteurhaftung *f* carrier liability
Spediteurtransportbescheinigung *f* forwarding agent's certificate of transport (FCT)
Spediteurübernahmebescheinigung *f* forwarding agent's certificate of receipt (FCR)
Spediteurversandbescheinigung *f* forwarding receipt
Spedition *f* 1. forwarding, shipping; 2. forwarding [shipping] agency; haulage contractor; removal firm
Speditionsauftrag *m* dispatch order; haulage order
Speditionsberuf *m* dispatch and forwarding trade; haulage business; furniture removal business
Speditionsfirma *f* dispatching [forwarding] firm; haulage firm; furniture removal firm
Speditionsgebühren *fpl* forwarding charges
Speditionsgeschäft *n* forwarding [dispatching] agency; haulage business; furniture removal business
Speditionsgüter *npl* goods to be forwarded
Speditionshandel *m* carrying trade
Speditionskosten *pl* forwarding [dispatching] costs; haulage costs; removal costs
Speditionsniederlassung *f* carrier branch
Speditionsprovision *f* forwarding commission
Speditionsversicherung *f* delivery [transport] insurance
Speditionsvertrag *m* forwarding [dispatching] contract; haulage contract
Speicher *m* storehouse, warehouse; store-room; reservoir; elevator, silo, granary *(grain)*; *(d.pr.)* storage, memory, store
~, adressierbarer *(d.pr.)* addresses storage
~, aktiver *(d.pr.)* active file
~ mit Auswahlsteuerung *(d.pr.)* selectively addressable memory
~ mit beliebigem Zugriff *(d.pr.)* random access memory [storage] (RAM)
~ mit kurzer Zugriffszeit *(d.pr.)* memory with short access time
~ mit mehreren stabilen Lagen *(d.pr.)* multi-stable memory [storage]
~ mit Wortstruktur *(d.pr.)* word-structured store
~ mit zwei verschiedenen Zugriffszeiten *(d.pr.)* two-level store
Speicherabgabe *f (d.pr.)* storage read-out
Speicherabzug *m (d.pr.)* core storage dump
Speicheradresse *f (d.pr.)* memory address
Speicheradressenregister *n (d.pr.)* memory address register
Speicheradressenzähler *m (d.pr.)* memory address counter
Speicheranordnung *f (d.pr.)* storage arrangement
Speicheranzeige *f (d.pr.)* read-out storage
Speicherarbeiter *m* warehouseman
Speicheraufnahme *f (d.pr.)* storage input
Speicherausdruckprogramm *n (d.pr.)* memory print programme
Speicherausnutzung *f (d.pr.)* storage efficiency [utilization]
Speicherauszug *m (d.pr.)* (memory) dump
Speicherbereich *m (d.pr.)* storage area
Speicherebene *f (d.pr.)* digit plane
Speichereingabe *f (d.pr.)* read-in storage
Speichereinheit *f (d.pr.)* unit of storage, storage unit, memory unit [device]; memory package

Speicherfeld *n (d.pr.)* storage field
Speichergebäude *n* warehouse
Speichergebühren *fpl* warehousing charges
Speichergröße *f (d.pr.)* memory size
Speicherkapazität *f* storing capacity
Speichermarke *f (d.pr.)* storage mark
Speichermiete *f* warehouse rent
speichern to store; to warehouse
Speicheroperation *f (d.pr.)* storage operation
Speicherplatz *m (d.pr.)* memory location
Speicherprotokoll *n (d.pr.)* storage snapshot
Speicherschutz *m (d.pr.)* storage protection
Speichersperre *f (d.pr.)* file interlock
Speicherstelle *f (d.pr.)* storage position
Speichersteuerung *f (d.pr.)* memory control
Speicherstufe *f (d.pr.)* storage level
Speicherung *f* storage; warehousing; accumulation; retention; recording
Speicherungsdichte *f (d.pr.)* storage density
Speicherungszeitraum *m (d.pr.)* storage period
Speicherzeit *f (d.pr.)* storage time; retention time
Speicherzone *f (d.pr.)* storage zone
Speise *f* food; meal; dish
Speisegaststätte *f* restaurant
Speisekarte *f* menu, bill of fare
speisen 1. to eat, to dine; 2. to feed; to power, to energize
Speisenangebot *n* fare offered
Speisenproduktion *f (cat)* preparation of meals [food] *(in restaurants etc.)*; production of prepared foods *(on an industrial scale)*
Speisensortiment *n (cat)* variety of meals [food]
Speisenumsatz *m (cat)* meals sold
Speisenverbrauch *m* food consumption
Speisenvorbereitung *f* preparation of food
Speisewagen *m* restaurant car, dining-car
Speisezettel *m s.* Speisekarte
Spektralbelegungsfunktion *f (stats)* integrated spectrum
Spektraldichte *(stats)* spectral density
Spektraldichtefunktion *f (stats)* power spectrum
Spektralverteilungsfunktion *f (stats)* integrated spectrum
Spektrum *n (stats)* spectrum
Spekulant *m* speculator, speculative dealer
Spekulation *f* speculation ⋄ **die ~ bekämpfen** to curb speculation; **die ~ eindämmen** *s.* **die ~ bekämpfen**
Spekulationscharakter *m* speculative nature
Spekulationsgeschäft *n* speculative transaction
Spekulationsgewinn *m* speculative profit
Spekulationshandel *m* speculative trading; speculating [speculative] trade
Spekulationskauf *m* speculative buying
Spekulationspapiere *npl (st.ex.)* speculative papers

Spekulationspreis *m* speculative price
Spekulationsverkauf *m* speculative selling
Spekulationsverlust *m* losses in speculation, gambling loss
Spekulationswechsel *m* speculative bill of exchange
Spekulationswert *m* speculative value
spekulativ speculative
spekulieren to speculate
Spende *f* gift; donation; contribution
spenden to donate; to contribute *(money etc.)*, to subscribe to *(charity etc.)*
Spender *m* donor, contributor, subscriber; benefactor
Sperrauftrag *m* stop order [payment]
Sperrbereich *m (d.pr.)* off region; cutoff region
Sperrbetrag *m* blocked amount
Sperrdepot *n* stopped deposit
Sperre *f* barrier; ban *(import etc.)*; embargo *(goods etc.)*; stop *(cheque etc.)*; blocking *(account etc.)*; blockade ⋄ **eine ~ aufheben** to lift an embargo; **eine ~ verhängen** to impose an embargo
sperren to stop *(cheque etc.)*; to ban *(import etc.)*; to embargo *(goods etc.)*; to block *(account etc.)*; *(d.pr.)* to inhibit, to lock (out)
Sperrfrist *f (ins)* waiting period
Sperrgebiet *n* prohibited [closed] area
Sperrgut *n* bulky goods
Sperrguthaben *n* blocked account
Sperrkonto *n* blocked account
Sperrliste *f (bank)* stop list
Sperrmajorität *f* vetoing majority; majority vetoing shares [*(Am)* stocks]
Sperrmark *f* blocked mark
Sperrmarkguthaben *n* blocked mark balances
Sperrminorität *f* vetoing minority; minority vetoing shares [*(Am)* stocks]
Sperrung *f* stop, stoppage, stopping; ban; embargo; blocking, prohibition; *(d.pr.)* inhibition, cutoff *(transistor)*
~ von Haushaltsmitteln blocking of budgetary means [resources]
Sperrvermerk *m* non-negotiability notice
Sperrverzeichnis *n s.* Sperrliste
Sperrverzögerungszeit *f (d.pr.)* backward recovery time
Sperrzeit *f* closing hour; *(d.pr.)* off-time
Sperrzoll *m* prohibitive duty [tariff]
Sperrzone *f s.* Sperrgebiet
Spesen *pl* expenses, charges
Spesenabrechnung *f* expense account; accounting of expenses
Spesenaufstellung *f* statement of expenses
Spesenbeleg *m* expense voucher
Spesenberechnung *f* calculation of expenses
spesenfrei without [free of] expenses

Spesenkonto *n* expense account
Spesennachnahme *f s.* **Spesenvergütung**
Spesenrechnung *f* expense account
Spesenvergütung *f* reimbursement of expenses
Spesenvorschuß *m* advance on expenses
Spezialabteilung *f* special department
Spezialanfertigung *f* special production, production on special order; special design
Spezialausbildung *f* special training
Spezialausführung *f s.* **Spezialanfertigung**
Spezialausstellung *f* special exhibition
Spezialbank *f* specialized bank
Spezialbaubetrieb *m* specialized construction enterprise
Spezialbehälter *m s.* **Spezialcontainer**
Spezialbetrieb *m* specialized enterprise; *(agric)* specialized co-operative farm
Spezialbörse *f (st.ex.)* special (commodity) market
Spezialcontainer *m* special container
Spezialdepot *n* special deposits
Spezialfonds *m* special fund
Spezialgeschäft *n* one-line shop
Spezialgroßhandel *m* one-line wholesale trade
Spezialhandel *m* one-line trade
Spezialisierung *f* specialization
~ **der Produktion** specialization of production
~, **erzeugnisgebundene** specialization on the manufacture of a complete product
~, **horizontale** horizontal specialization
~, **innerbetriebliche** specialization in an enterprise
~, **internationale** international specialization
~, **länderweise** country-wise specialization
~, **technologische** specialization in technology
~, **territoriale** regional specialization
~, **überbetriebliche** specialization between enterprises
~, **vertikale** vertical specialization
Spezialisierungsabkommen *n* agreement on specialization
~, **internationales** international agreement on specialization in production
Spezialisierungsempfehlung *f* recommendation on specialization in production
Spezialisierungsgrad *m* degree of specialization
Spezialisierungskoeffizient *m* specialization coefficient
Spezialisierungungsrichtung *f* line of specialization
Spezialisierungsvereinbarung *f* specialization agreement
Spezialisierungsvertrag *m s.* **Spezialisierungsvereinbarung**
Spezialist *m* specialist
Spezialistengruppe *f* group of specialists
Spezialität *f* speciality

Spezialkalkulation *f* special calculation
Spezialkredit *m* special loan
Spezialkreditbrief *m* special letter of credit
Spezialkreditinstitut *n s.* **Spezialbank**
Spezialladen *m s.* **Spezialgeschäft**
Speziallager *n* special warehouse *(for particular line of goods)*
Spezialmärkte *mpl* special markets
Spezialmesse *f* special fair
Spezialproduktion *f* special production
Spezialprojektant *m* special designer
Spezialschau *f* special display
Spezialtarif *m* special tariff; preferential tariff
Spezialverkaufsstelle *f s.* **Spezialgeschäft**
Spezialverpackung *f* special packing
Spezialvollmacht *f* special power of attorney
Spezialzweig *m* special line (of production); special discipline (branch)
Spezieskauf *m* purchase of species
Spezifikation *f s.* **Spezifizierung**
Spezifikationskauf *m* purchase according to specifications
spezifizieren to specify *(amount etc.)*; to give the details of *(s.th.)*; to itemize *(orders etc.)*; to delineate *(policy etc.)*
Spezifizierung *f* specification
Sphäre *f* sphere; sector; domain
~ **der gesellschaftlichen Konsumtion** sector of social consumption
~ **der individuellen Konsumtion** sector of private consumption
~ **der Konsumtion** consumption sector *(non--productive sector)*
~ **der materiellen Produktion** sector [sphere] of material production
~ **der produktiven Konsumtion** sector of productive consumption
~ **der Zirkulation** sphere of circulation *(comprising all stages of the reproduction process where commodities go into productive or unproductive consumption through exchange)*
~ **des persönlichen Verbrauchs** *s.* ~ **der invividuellen Konsumtion**
~, **nichtproduktive** non-productive sector
~, **private** privacy; private sphere; private sector
~, **produzierende** producing sector
Spiel *n* game; play
~, **allgemeineres** more general game
~, **antagonistisches** antagonistic game
~, **erweitertes** extended game
~, **faires** fair play
~, **fiktives** fictitious game
~ **gegen die Natur** game against nature
~, **gerechtes** *(stats)* fair game
~ **in extensiver Form** extensive game
~ **in Normalform** normal game
~, **kontinuierliches** continuous game

Staatsaufbau 465

~, **kooperatives** co-operative game
~, **nichtkooperatives** non-co-operative game
~, **strategisches** strategic game
~, **unendliches** infinite game
~, **unwesentliches** non-essential game
~, **verallgemeinertes** generalized game
~, **wesentliches** essential game
Spielbank *f* gambling establishment; casino
Spieler *m* player
~, **fairer** fair player
~, **fiktiver** fictitious player
Spieleranzahl *f* number of players
Spielgewinn *m* gains
Spielmatrix *f* play matrix
Spielschuld *f* gambling debt
Spieltheorie *f* game theory, theory of games
Spielverlust *m* losses
Spielwaren *fpl* toys
Spielwarenindustrie *f* toy industry
Spielzeugmacher *m* toy-maker
Spinnerei *f* spinning-mill
Spirituosenhandel *m* trade in (wines and) spirits
Spirituosensteuer *f* tax on (wines and) spirits
Spitze *f* 1. top *(performance)*; summit *(conference etc.)*; head, apex *(organization etc.)* ; peak *(period etc.)*; 2. *(ins)* surplus ✧ **an der ~ der Tabelle stehen** to be on top of the scale; to be on top of the table
Spitzen *fpl (st.ex.)* fractions of shares [*(Am)* stocks]
~, **freie** *(agric)* marketable surplus produce (after compulsory deliveries)
Spitzenaktien *fpl* blue-chip shares [*(Am)* stocks]
Spitzenangebot *n* marginal supply
Spitzenausgleich *m* settlement of balance [surplus]
Spitzenbedarf *m* peak demand
Spitzenbelastung *f* peak load
Spitzenbelastungszeit *f* peak hours
Spitzenbetrag *m* residual amount [balance]; *(st.ex.)* fractional amount, *(Am)* odd lot
Spitzenbeträge *mpl* maximum amounts
Spitzenbetrieb *m* top enterprise
Spitzeneinkommen *n* maximum [top] income
Spitzenerzeugnis *n* first-class [top level] product
Spitzengehalt *n* maximum [top] salary
Spitzenindustrie *f* lace industry
Spitzenkräfte *fpl* top management
Spitzenleistung *f* outstanding [top] performance; maximum output; maximum capacity
~, **gestalterische** outstanding creative performance
Spitzenlohn *m* maximum pay
Spitzenpapiere *npl s.* **Spitzenaktien**
Spitzenqualität *f* top quality
Spitzenrate *f* maximum rate *(growth etc.)*

Spitzenstellung *f* top position
Spitzenverkaufszeit *f* rush hours
Spitzenverkehr *m* rush-hour traffic
Spitzenverkehrszeit *f* rush hours
Spitzenwert *m* maximum value
Spontaneität *f* spontaneity
Spontankauf *m* impulsive purchase
Spotgeschäft *n* spot transaction
Spotpreis *m* spot price *(for immediate delivery)*
spottbillig dirt cheap
Spottpreis *m* knockdown price ✧ **zu einem ~** at a knockdown price; **zu einem ~ verkaufen** to sell dirt cheap
Sprechstunde *f* office [business] hours (open to callers); consulting hours *(doctors etc.)*
~, **öffentliche** public consulting hours *(of district councillors etc.)*
Sprechtag *m* day open to public business
Sprung *m* leap, jump
~, **dialektischer** dialectical leap
Sprungkosten *pl (acc)* semi-variable cost
Sprungregreß *m* recourse to prior endorser
Sprungrückgriff *m s.* **Sprungregreß**
Staat *m* state, country; government
Staaten *mpl* states, countries
~, **assoziierte** associated countries
~, **nichtpaktgebundene** non-aligned countries
~, **paktgebundene** allies, allied countries; aligned countries
Staatenbund *m* confederation (of states)
Staatengemeinschaft *f* community of states
staatlich state, government ✧ **~ anerkannt** state registered; **~ gefördert** government [state] sponsored; **~ gelenkt** government [state] controlled
Staatsabgaben *fpl* inland revenue; government taxes [levies]
Staatsabkommen *n* governmental [state] agreement; convention; treaty
Staatsakt *m* act of state; state ceremony
Staatsaktien *fpl* government bonds [securities]
Staatsangehöriger *m* citizen
Staatsangehörigkeit *f* citizenship ✧ **die ~ entziehen** to withdraw citizenship; **jmdm. die ~ aberkennen** to deprive s.o. of his [her] citizenship
Staatsangelegenheit *f* state [government] affair
Staatsangestellter *m* government servant
Staatsanleihe *f* government loan
~, **konsolidierte** consols, consolidated government loan
Staatsanwalt *m* public prosecutor
Staatsanwaltschaft *f* public prosecutor's office
Staatsapparat *m* state authorities; government machinery
Staatsarchiv *n* public record office
Staatsaufbau *m* structure of the state

30 Ök. Wörterb. Deutsch–Englisch

Staatsaufsicht f state control
Staatsausgaben fpl state [public] expenditure(s)
~, **produktive** productive state expenditure(s)
Staatsauszeichnung f state price [award]
Staatsbahn f state railways
Staatsbank f state [central] bank
Staatsbankrott m national bankruptcy [insolvency]
Staatsbeamter m civil servant, government official
Staatsbesitz m state ownership
Staatsbesuch m state visit
Staatsbetrieb m state(-owned) enterprise
Staatsbilanzen fpl 1. state balance sheets; 2. national accounts
Staatsbudget n s. Staatshaushalt
Staatsbürger m s. Staatsangehöriger
Staatsbürgerschaft f s. Staatsangehörigkeit
Staatsdienst m government service ✧ **in den ~ eintreten** to become a civil servant, to enter government service
Staatsdomäne f domain of the state
Staatseffekten pl s. Staatspapiere
staatseigen government-owned, state-owned
Staatseigentum n government [state] property
Staatseinkommen n government revenue(s)
Staatseinkünfte pl s. Staatseinkommen
Staatseinnahmen fpl s. Staatseinkommen
Staatsfinanzen pl state finances
Staatsfinanzierung f state financing
Staatsform f form of government, political system *(of a state)*
Staatsforst m public forest
Staatsgarantie f state [government] guarantee
Staatsgebiet n territory of the state
Staatsgeheimnis n official [state] secret
Staatsgewalt f executive power
Staatsgrenze f frontier, border
Staatsgut n state farm
Staatshaftung f s. Staatsgarantie
Staatshandel m state trading
Staatshaushalt m national budget
~, **außerordentlicher** supplementary budget
~, **ausgeglichener** balanced budget
Staatshaushaltsdefizit n national budget deficit
Staatshaushaltseinnahme f national budget revenue
Staatshaushaltsgesetz m national budget act
Staatshaushaltsordnung f budget regulations
Staatshaushaltsplan m national state budget
Staatshaushaltsüberschuß m budget(ary) surplus
Staatshoheit f sovereignty
Staatsinteresse n interest(s) of the state
Staatsintervention f government [state] intervention
Staatskapitalismus m state capitalism

staatskapitalistisch state capitalist
Staatskasse f treasury, the Exchequer *(UK)*, Federal Treasury *(USA)*
Staatskontrolle f government control
Staatskosten pl public expenses
Staatskredit m public loan, government credit
Staatslasten fpl public burden
Staatsmacht f state power
Staatsmann m statesman
staatsmännisch statesmanlike
Staatsminister m minister
Staatsmonopol n state [government] monopoly
staatsmonopolistisch state monopoly
Staatsnotstand m national emergency
Staatsoberhaupt n head of state
Staatsobligationen fpl government securities; government bonds [*(Am)* stocks, debentures]
~, **festverzinsliche** savings bonds
Staatsordnung f system of government
Staatsorgan n authorities, state organ [body]
Staatsorgane npl:
~, **örtliche** local authorities
~, **zentrale** central authorities
Staatspapiere npl government securities; government bonds
Staatsplan m state plan
Staatsplanaufgabe f state plan task
Staatsplandokument n state plan document
Staatsplannomenklatur f state plan nomenclature
Staatsplanposition f item of the state plan
Staatsplanvorhaben n project of the state plan
Staatsrat m state council
Staatsratserlaß m decree of the state council
Staatsrecht n constitutional law
staatsrechtlich under constitutional law
Staatsreserve f state reserve
Staatsschuld f national [public] debt
~, **aufgeschobene** deferred national [public] debt
~, **äußere** external national [public] debt
~, **innere** internal national [public] debt
~, **konsolidierte** consolidated national [public] debt
~, **schwebende** floating national [public] debt
~, **unkonsolidierte** unconsolidated national [public] debt
Staatsschuldschein m treasury bill, bill of Exchequer *(UK)*
Staatsschuldverschreibung f government bonds
Staatssekretär m under-secretary of state, permanent secretary
Staatssekretariat n state secretariat
Staatssektor m state sector
Staatssicherheitsdienst m state security service
Staatssteuer f government tax
Staatsstreich m coup d'etat

Staatstitel *m s.* **Staatspapiere**
Staatsunternehmen *n* state enterprise
Staatsverfassung *f* constitution *(of a state)*
Staatsvermögen *n* national [public] wealth
Staatsverschuldung *f* national [public] indebtedness; national [public] debt(s)
Staatsvertrag *m* international treaty
Staatsverwaltung *f* state [public] administration
Staatswirtschaft *f* national economy; state sector
Staatswissenschaft *f* political science
Staatswissenschaftler *m* political scientist
Staatszuschuß *m* state subsidy, government grant
Stab *m* staff; panel (of experts)
Stabdiagramm *n (stats)* bar chart; block diagram
stabil stable, steady, solid *(currency etc.)*; sturdy, robust *(furniture etc.)*
stabilisieren to stabilize
Stabilisierung *f* stabilization
~ **der Varianz** *(stats)* stabilization of variance
~, **relative** relative stabilization
Stabilisierungsanleihe *f* stabilization loan
Stabilisierungsfaktor *m* stabilizing factor
Stabilisierungsfonds *m* stabilization fund
Stabilisierungspolitik *f* stabilization policy
~, **ökonomische** policy of economic stabilization
Stabilisierungszoll *m* stabilization duty [tariff]
Stabilität *f* stability
~ **der Reproduktion der Geldfonds** stability of the reproduction of monetary [financial] funds
~ **der Währung** stability of the currency
Stabilitätstest *m (stats)* stability test
Stabsorgan *n* auxiliary [organizing] staff
Stadium *n* stage
Stadt *f* town, city ◊ **in der ~ leben** to live in a town
Stadtabgaben *fpl* municipal taxes, local rates
Stadtanleihe *f* municipal [corporation] loan
Stadtarchiv *n* town [civic] records office
Stadtausschuß *m* city committee; town committee
Stadtbahn *f* city [municipal] railway
Stadtbebauungsplan *m* town plan
Stadtbevölkerung *f* urban population
Stadtbezirk *m* city district; borough *(UK)*
Stadtbezirksausschuß *m* ward committee
Stadtbezirksrat *m* borough councillor *(in large towns and cities)*
Städtebau *m* town [city] planning
Städtebund *m* confederation of towns
Städteplaner *m* planner of towns and cities
Städteplanung *f* town and city planning
Stadtgas *n* (natural) gas; domestic [coal] gas
Stadtgebiet *n* urban area; municipal area
Stadtgemeinde *f* urban community

Stadtgericht *n* city court
Stadtgrenze *f* city boundary
Stadthaushalt *m* city [town] budget
städtisch municipal; urban
Stadtmüll *m* town refuse
Stadtordnung *f* by-laws of a city [town]
Stadtplanung *f* town and city planning
Stadtrandzone *f* suburban area, suburbs; outskirts of the town
Stadtrat *m* municipal [town] councillor
Stadtreinigung *f* street cleaning
Stadtsanierung *f* restoration [reconstruction] of a town
Stadtsparkasse *f* municipal savings bank
Stadtstaat *m* city-state
Stadtteil *m* town district
Stadtverkehr *m* urban [town] traffic
Stadtverordnetenversammlung *f* town [city] assembly
Stadtverordneter *m* member of the town assembly
Stadtverwaltung *f* town [city] administration
Stadtwirtschaft *f* city [town] services *(street cleaning, lighting, removal of refuse etc.)*
Staffel *f* scale *(for calculating interest etc.)*
Staffelanleihe *f* differential loan
Staffelbesteuerung *f* differentiated rate of taxation
Staffellohn *m* differentiated wages
staffeln to scale *(rates etc.)*; to stagger *(working hours etc.)*; to graduate, to grade, to differentiate *(wages, taxes etc.)*
Staffelpreis *m* sliding price
Staffelrechnung *f* 1. calculation of graduated interest; 2. *(d.pr.)* progressive total
Staffelskonto *n* differentiated rate of discount
Staffelspanne *f* differentiated margin
Staffelsteuer *f* differentiated tax
Staffeltarif *m* sliding rate
Staffelung *f* staggering *(working hours etc.)*; graduation, differentiation *(wages, taxes etc.)*
Staffelzins *m* sliding rate of interest
Staffelzinsrechnung *f s.* **Staffelrechnung 1.**
Staffelzoll *m* differentiated [sliding] customs rates
Stagnation *f* stagnation, standstill, inactivity
stagnieren to stagnate
stagnierend stagnating
Stahlbauer *m* steel erector
Stahlindustrie *f* steel industry
Stahlproduktion *f* steel production
Stahlschiffbauer *m* ship construction worker
Stahlwerk *n* steel works
Stamm *m* 1. tribe; 2. regular customers
Stammaktie *f* ordinary share, *(Am)* common stock
Stammbelegschaft *f* permanent employees

Stammbetrieb *m* main enterprise; parent firm [concern]
Stammbevölkerung *f* permanent population
Stammeinlage *f* ordinary share [contribution to capital]
Stammgast *m* regular customer
Stammhaus *n* parent firm [concern]
Stammkapital *n* ordinary share capital, capital stock
~, **verdecktes** hidden [disguised] capital stock
Stammkunde *m s.* Stammgast
Stammkundschaft *f* clientele, regular customers
Stammland *n* country of origin
Stammpersonal *n* permanent staff
Stammunternehmen *n s.* Stammhaus
Stand *m* 1. level *(rates etc.)*; 2. position, standing, rank *(person etc.)*; profession, vocation; 3. class, strata; 4. condition, state *(affairs etc.)*; 5. stand, stall, booth *(fair, market etc.)*
◊ **auf den letzten ~ bringen** to bring s.th. up to date; **einen ~ aufgeben** to vacate a stand [stall, booth]; **einen ~ aufstellen** to erect a stand [stall, booth]; **einen ~ beziehen** to occupy a stand [stall, booth]; **einen ~ kündigen** to give up a stand [stall, booth]; **einen ~ reservieren** to reserve a stand [stall, booth]; **einen ~ verlegen** to move a stand [stall, booth]; **einen ~ wiederbestellen** to rebook a stand [stall, booth]; **vom ~ verkaufen** to sell off-the-stand
~, **bedeckter** (covered) stand
~ **der Aktiva und Passiva** statement of assets and liabilities
~ **der Dinge** state of affairs
~ **der Technik, letzter** latest achievements in engineering [technology]
~ **der Verhandlungen** stage of negotiations
~ **der Vorbereitung** stage of preparation
~, **eigener** individual stand
~, **finanzieller** financial position [situation]
~, **freier** vacant stand [stall, booth]
~, **geschlossener** 1. closed stand [stall, booth]; 2. *s.* ~, **bedeckter**
~, **höchster** top level
~, **leerer** *s.* ~, **freier**
~, **mehrteiliger** sub-divided stand [stall, booth]
~, **montierbarer** mobile stand
~, **niedrigster** lowest level
~, **offener** open stand [stall, booth]
~, **unbesetzter** unoccupied stand [stall, booth]
Standangebot *n* offer of a stand [stall, booth]
Standanmeldung *f* application for a stand [stall, booth]
Standanordnung *f* arrangement of a stand [stall, booth]
Standard *m* standard, norm; pattern
Standardabweichung *f (stats)* standard deviation

Standardartikel *m* standardized product
Standardausführung *f* standard model
Standardbauweise *f* standardized construction
Standardbevölkerung *f (stats)* standard population
Standardelement *n* standardized component; standard unit
Standarderzeugnis *n* standard product
Standardetikett *n* standard label
Standardfehler *m (stats)* standard error
~, **asymptotischer** *(stats)* asymptotic standard error
Standardfehlerprozedur *f (d.pr.)* standard error procedure
Standardform *f s.* Standardausführung
Standardformat *n* standard size
Standardfunktion *f (d.pr.)* standard function
Standardgewicht *n* standard [normal] weight
Standardgröße *f s.* Standardformat
standardisieren to standardize
Standardisierung *f* standardization
~, **komplexe** all-round standardization
Standardisierungsgrad *m* degree of standardization
Standardkennsatz *m (d.pr.)* standard label
Standardklausel *f* standard clause
Standardkollektion *f* standard collection
Standardkosten *pl* standard cost
Standardkostenrechnung *f* standard cost accounting
Standardmaß *n (stats)* standard measure
Standardmaterial *n* 1. standard material; 2. *(d.pr.)* reference material
~, **beglaubigtes** certified reference material
Standardmietvertrag *m* standard rent contract
Standardmodell *n* standard model
Standardmuster *n* standard pattern
Standardnorm *f* standard norm
Standardnote *f (stats)* standard score
Standardpreis *m* standard price
Standardprogramm *n* standard programme; *(d.pr.)* standard program (routine)
Standardpunktwert *m s.* Standardnote
Standardquadrat *n (stats)* standard square
~, **lateinisches** *(stats)* standard latin square
Standardqualität *f* standard quality
Standardreparatur *f* standard repair
Standards *mpl*:
~ **der Rechnungslegung und Berichterstattung, Internationale** international standards of accounting and reporting
~, **internationale** international standards
Standardsoftware *f (d.pr.)* package
Standardsortiment *n* standard assortment
Standardtarif *m* standard rate
Standardtechnologie *f* standard technology
Standardteil *n s.* Standardelement

Standardtyp *m* conventional type
Standardverfahren *n* conventional method
Standardvertrag *m* standard contract
Standardvordruck *m* standard form
Standardware *f s.* **Standardartikel**
Standardwert *m* standard value
Standart *f* kind of stand
Standbeauftragter *m* stand representative
Standbenutzung *f* use of a stand [stall, booth]
Standbesetzung *f* manning of stand [stall, booth]
Standbesichtigung *f* stand [stall, booth] inspection
Standbestätigung *f* confirmation of a stand [stall, booth] applied for *(fair etc.)*
Standbestellung *f* application for space (in the fair/exhibition area)
Standbewachung *f* guarding of stand [stall, booth]
Stand-by-Kredit *m* stand-by credit
Stand-by-Kreditabkommen *n* stand-by agreement
Standfläche *f* stand space [area], area of stand [stall, booth], display area
Standgebühr *f* stand [stall, booth] charges
Standgeld *n* 1. stallage, stall charges; 2. demurrage charges *(railway waggon etc.)*
Standgröße *f* size of stand [stall, booth]
ständig permanent; established *(practice etc.)*; resident *(correspondent etc.)*
Standinhaber *m* standholder, stallholder
Standkosten *pl* costs of stand [stall, booth]
Standmiete *f* stall rent
Standmieter *m* lessee of stand [stall, booth]
Standmieterlös *m* income from leasing stands
Standmietvertrag *m* rent contract for stands
Standort *m* site, location
~, **absatzmarktorientierter** market oriented location
~, **arbeitsorientierter** labour-oriented location
~, **rohstofforientierter** raw-material oriented location
~, **transportkostenorientierter** location with minimum transport costs
Standortanalyse *f* micro-regional analysis
Standortanforderungen *fpl* location requirements
Standortansprüche *mpl* demands made on a location
Standortballung *f* agglomeration
standortbedingt influenced by location
Standortbedingung *f* micro-regional [location] condition
Standortbeeinflussung *f* influence of location on factories; influence of factories on location
Standortbesonderheit *f* particular feature of location

Standortbestimmung *f* fixing the location
Standortfaktor *m* 1. micro-regional factor; 2. *(agric)* habitat factor
Standortgenehmigung *f* permission to locate *(factory etc.)*; location permit
Standortkomplex *m* micro-regional complex *(agglomeration of various projects in a certain area)*
Standortkonzeption *f* micro-regional programme
Standortoptimierung *f* location [micro-regional] optimization *(planning of the most suitable location for an investment project)*
Standortorientierung *f* location policy
Standortplanung *f* planning of the location *(of a project)*, location planning
~, **territoriale** regional location planning
Standortpolitik *f* micro-regional economic policy; location policy
Standortstudie *f* micro-regional study [analysis]
Standortsystem *n* micro-regional system
Standortveränderung *f* change in type of location
Standortverhältnisse *npl* location [site] conditions
Standortverlagerung *f* moving an enterprise to another location
Standortverlegung *f s.* **Standortverlagerung**
Standortverteilung *f*:
~ **der Produktivkräfte** regional distribution of productive forces *(of all enterprises, the labour force etc. over the country)*
Standortwahl *f* choice of location *(for a new project)*
Standortwirkung *f* effect(s) of location; effect(s) on location
Standplatz *m* stand site
Standpunkt *m* point of view; standpoint ◊ **vom gesellschaftlichen** ~ from the social point of view; **vom gestalterischen** ~ from the point of view of design; **vom technischen** ~ from the technical point of view; **vom wirtschaftlichen** ~ from the economic point of view
Standreservierung *f* reservation of stand [stall, booth]
Standvermieter *m* lessor of stands
Standvermietung *f* stand leasing, letting of stands [stalls, booths]
Standzeit *f* 1. idle time; 2. (equipment) life cycle *(machine etc.)*
Stangengold *n* gold in ingots
Stangensilber *n* silver in ingots
Stapelarten *fpl* kinds of stacking
Stapelartikel *mpl* staples
Stapelbetrieb *m (d.pr.)* batch (processing) mode
Stapelfernverarbeitung *f (d.pr.)* remote batch processing

Stapelgut *n* stacked goods
Stapelhandel *m* staple trade
Stapellauf *m* launching *(ship etc.)*
Stapelspeicher *m (d.pr.)* push-down store
Stapelwaren *fpl* staples, staple commodities
Stärke *f* strength *(financial etc.)*; power; heaviness *(traffic etc.)*; severity *(weather etc.)*
~ **der Belegschaft** strength of the labour force
~, **finanzielle** financial strength
~, **zahlenmäßige** numerical strength
stärken to strengthen *(position etc.)*; to boost, to increase *(exports etc.)*
Start *m* start, take-off
Startbedingungen *fpl* starting conditions
starten to start, to take off *(aircraft, economic growth etc.)*
Starthilfe *f* initial aid [help]
Startimpuls *m (d.pr.)* start pulse
Start- und Landegebühren *fpl* starting and landing charges
Startzeit *f* departure [take-off] time *(flight etc.)*; *(d.pr.)* start time
Station *f* 1. station *(railway etc.)*; stop; 2. ward *(hospital)*
stationär stationary
Stationaritätsordnung *f (stats)* order of stationarity
Stationsvorsteher *m* station-master
statisch static
Statistik *f* statistics
~, **amtliche** official statistics
~, **betriebswirtschaftliche** enterprise statistics
~, **landwirtschaftliche** agricultural statistics
~, **mathematische** mathematical statistics
~, **volkswirtschaftliche** macro-economic statistics
Statistiker *m* statistician
Statistikverfahren *n* statistical method
statistisch statistical ⋄ ~ **erfassen** to record statistically
Status *m* status; state of affairs
~, **finanzieller** financial position
~, **rechlicher** legal status
~, **sozialer** social status
Statusanfrage *f (d.pr.)* status request
Statuswort *n (d.pr.)* status word
Statut *n* statute; regulations; articles
~ **der Vereinten Nationen** Charter of the United Nations
statutengemäß statutory, according to regulation; according to articles
statutenwidrig contrary to regulations
Stau *m* traffic congestion; build-up *(flood water etc.)*
Staub- und Abgasgeld *n* penalty for discharging dust and gaseous matter (into the atmosphere) *(in excess of permitted levels)*

stauen to stow *(cargo)*; to dam up *(water)*
Stauen *n* stowing
Stauer *m* stevedore
Stauerei *f* 1. stowage area; 2. stowing enterprise
Stauerlohn *m* stowage, stowage rate
Staukoeffizient *m* stowage factor
Stauleistung *f* stowage, stowing
Stauplan *m* stowage plan
Staurecht *n* right of damming up (water)
Stauung *f* 1. stowage; 2. damming up *(water)*; 3. hold-up *(deliveries etc.)*; congested traffic
stechen 1. to clock in and out *(time clock)*; 2. to cut *(turf, asparagus etc.)*
Stechkarte *f* time card
Stechuhr *f* time clock
Steckbrief *m* warrant of arrest
steigen to increase, to mount, to ascend, to rise
steigend increasing
Steiger *m (min)* pit foreman, *(Am)* overman
steigern to boost *(exports etc.)*, to increase *(output etc.)*, to raise *(prices etc.)*, to force up *(demand etc.)*, to enhance *(quality etc.)*
Steigerung *f* increase *(output etc.)*, rise, raising *(prices etc.)*, forcing up *(demand etc.)*, enhancement, enhancing *(quality etc.)*
~, **jährliche** annual increase *(production etc.)*
Steigerungsbetrag *m* (amount of) increase
Steinbildhauer *m* sculptor
Steindrucker *m* lithographer
Steinmetz *m* stone-mason
Stellage *f s.* Stellagegeschäft
Stellagegeschäft *n (st.ex.)* put and call (PAC), dealing in futures, *(Am)* spread
Stelle *f* 1. place, spot, point; stand, position; 2. job, post; 3. *(maths)* digit, figure ⋄ **an erster** ~ in the first place; **an erster** ~ **stehen** to come first, to take precedence; **an jmds.** ~ **treten** to take the place of s.o.; **an** ~ **von** in place of, instead of; **eine** ~ **antreten** to take up one's duties; **eine** ~ **aufgeben** to leave one's job; **eine** ~ **übernehmen** to take up a post; **sich an die zuständige** ~ **wenden** to apply to the proper agency, to turn to the responsible authorities; **sich um eine freie** ~ **bewerben** to apply for a vacancy [vacant position]; **von der** ~ **kommen** to make progress, to get on
~, **amtliche** agency, office, authorities
~, **ausführende** enforcing agency
~, **entscheidende** decision-making agency [office]
~, **freie** vacancy
~, **führende** leading position
~, **offene** vacancy, opening
~, **örtliche** local authority
~, **schadhafte** defect, flaw
~, **schwache** weak spot [point]

~, **zuständige** responsible [competent] authorities
stellen 1. to put, to place, to set; to display, to arrange; 2. to furnish, to supply, to make available, to provide; 3. *(jur)* to produce *(witness etc.)*
Stellenangebot *n* vacancy *(for a job)*; situation vacant
Stellenangebote *npl* vacancies column *(in newspapers etc.)*
Stellenanzeige *f* vacancy advertisement
Stellengesuch *n* application for a job [post]
stellenlos *s.* stellungslos
Stellenmarkt *m* employment [labour, job] market
Stellennachweis *m* employment agency
Stellenplan *m* employment plan *(of enterprise etc., classifying jobs, salaries, wages etc.)*
Stellenplandisziplin *f* adherence to the employment plan
Stellenplankürzung *f* reduction in the employment plan
Stellenplanüberschreitung *f* overmanning; exceeding the employment plan
Stellensuche *f* looking for a job, job hunting
Stellenvermittlung *f* employment agency; Job Centre *(UK)*; placement [procurement] of jobs
Stellgeld *n* *(st.ex.)* premium for a put and call [*(Am)* spread]
Stellgeschäft *n s.* Stellagegeschäft
Stellmacher *m* cartwright; wheel wright
Stellung *f* 1. position, situation, employment, job, place, post; 2. status, rank; standing; capacity; 3. posture, attitude ◊ **eine beherrschende ~ einnehmen** to occupy a dominating position; **eine führende ~ einnehmen** to occupy a leading position; **~ beziehen** to express an opinion, to comment *(about s.th.)*, to take a clear position *(over s.th.)*
~, **dominierende** dominating position *(market etc.)*
~ **einer Sicherheit** giving security *(for a loan etc.)*
~ **eines Akkreditivs** opening of a credit in favour of s.o.
Stellungnahme *f* opinion expressed, comment, statement
~, **prinzipielle** position [attitude] in principle
stellungslos unemployed
Stellvertreter *m* deputy
Stellvertretung *f* deputyship; representation
Stempel *m* stamp; postmark; brand mark *(animals)*; hallmark *(gold etc.)*
Stempelgebühr *f* stamp fee(s)
Stenotypist(in) *m(f)* stenotypist
Sterbefall *m* (case of) death
Sterbefallversicherung *f* death insurance

Sterbegeld *n* burial allowance
Sterbehäufigkeit *f* mortality frequency
Sterbehilfe *f s.* Sterbegeld
Sterbekasse *f* burial [funeral] fund
Sterbetabelle *f s.* Sterbetafel
Sterbetafel *f (stats)* life table
Sterbeversicherung *f s.* Sterbekasse
Sterbezahl *f s.* Sterbeziffer
Sterbeziffer *f (stats)* death rate
Sterblichkeit *f* mortality
Sterblichkeitsquotient *m (stats)* mortality ratio
~, **standardisierter** *(stats)* standardized mortality ratio
Sterblichkeitsziffer *f* death rate
Stereogramm *n (stats)* stereogram
Sterlingblock *m* sterling block
Sterlingblock-Länder *npl* sterling block countries
Sterlinggebiet *n s.* Sterlingzone
Sterlingguthaben *n* sterling balances
Sterlingkonto *n* sterling account
Sterlingländer *npl s.* Sterlingblock-Länder
Sterlingzone *f* sterling area
Stetigkeit *f (stats)* continuity
~, **stochastische** *(stats)* stochastic continuity
Steuer *f* tax, duty ◊ **der ~ unterliegen** to be liable to tax; **eine ~ aufheben** to abolish [do away with] a tax; **eine ~ eintreiben** to collect a tax; **eine ~ erheben** to levy a tax
Steuerabkommen *n* tax agreement
Steuerabrechnung *f* tax accounting
Steuerabschnitt *m* fiscal period
Steuerabwälzung *f* passing on the taxes *(to sections of people, other production stages etc.)*
Steuerabzug *m* tax deduction
steuerabzugsfähig tax-deductible
Steueramt *n* inland revenue office, tax office
Steueranalyse *f* analysis of state revenues
Steuerangelegenheit *f* tax matter
Steuerangleichung *f* levelling of taxes
Steueranpassung *f* tax adjustment
Steueranpassungsabkommen *n* tax adjustment agreement
Steueranreiz *m* tax incentive
Steueranschlag *m* tax assessment
Steueranspruch *m* claim on taxes
Steueranteil *m* proportion of taxes
Steueranweisung *f (d.pr.)* control record
Steuerart *f* kind of tax
Steueraufkommen *n* tax yield, inland revenue, tax receipts
~ **pro Kopf der Bevölkerung** per capita tax revenue
Steuerauflage *f* imposition of a tax
Steueraufschlag *m* surtax, additional tax
Steuerausfall *m* tax deficit, shortfall in tax revenue

Steuerausgleich *m* tax adjustment
Steueraussetzung *f* postponement of taxes
Steuerbasis *f* tax base; basis of taxation
Steuerbefreiung *f* tax exemption, exemption from taxes [taxation]
steuerbegünstigt enjoying [carrying] tax privileges
Steuerbegünstigung *f* tax privilege
Steuerbehörde *f s.* Steueramt
Steuerbelastung *f* tax contribution *(of the individual)*; incidence of taxation, burden of taxation
Steuerbemessungseinheit *f* unit of tax assessment
Steuerbemessungsgrundlage *f* basis of tax assessment
Steuerberater *m* tax adviser [expert]
Steuerberechnung *f* tax assessment
Steuerbescheid *m* tax assessment; tax demand, notice of tax assessment
Steuerbetrag *m* (amount of) tax
Steuerbetrug *m s.* Steuerhinterziehung
Steuerbilanz *f* tax statement; balance sheet for taxation purposes
Steuerbürde *f s.* Steuerlast
Steuerdaten *pl (d.pr.)* control data
Steuerdelikt *n* fiscal offence
Steuerdruck *m s.* Steuerschraube
Steuereinheit *f (d.pr.)* console [control] unit
Steuereinnahmen *fpl* public revenue, tax yield; tax receipts
Steuereinnehmer *m* tax collector
Steuereintreibung *f s.* Steuereinziehung
Steuereinziehung *f* tax collection
Steuereinzugsverfahren *n* method of tax collection
Steuerentrichtung *f* payment of taxes
Steuererhebung *f* tax collection
Steuererhöhung *f* increase in taxes
Steuererklärung *f* (income) tax return ✧ eine ~ abgeben to make a tax return
~, getrennte separate (income) tax return
Steuererlaß *m* tax exemption, remission of taxes
Steuererleichterung *f* tax relief [abatement], relief from taxation
Steuerermäßigung *f* tax relief
Steuerermittlung *f* tax assessment
Steuerermittlungsverfahren *n* method of tax assessment
Steuerersparnis *f* saving of taxes, tax saving
Steuererstattung *f* refund(ing) [repayment] of taxes
Steuererstattungsverfahren *n* method of refunding taxes
Steuerertrag *m* tax yield
Steueretat *m* tax component of the budget

Steuerfahnder *m* bailiff for collecting overdue taxes
Steuerfahndung *f* tracing tax evasion
Steuerfestsetzung *f* tax assessment
Steuerflucht *f* flight from taxation, transfer of funds to avoid taxation
Steuerforderung *f* tax claim
Steuerform *f* kind of tax
Steuerformular *n* tax form; (blank) tax return
Steuerfrage *f* tax issue
steuerfrei tax-free, tax-exempt *(income etc.)*
Steuerfreibetrag *m* tax-free allowance
Steuerfreigrenze *f* tax-free [tax exemption] limit
Steuerfreiheit *f s.* Steuerbefreiung
Steuergefüge *n* structure of taxes
Steuergeheimnis *n* tax secret
Steuergelder *npl* tax money
Steuergerät *n (d.pr.)* controller
Steuergerechtigkeit *f* equitable distribution of taxes
Steuergeschenk *n* tax gift
Steuergesetz *n* fiscal [tax] law
Steuergesetzgebung *f* tax laws [legislation]
Steuergewinn *m* taxable profit
Steuergleichheit *f s.* Steuergerechtigkeit
Steuergrundlage *f* tax base
Steuergrundsätze *mpl* tax principles
Steuergruppe *f s.* Steuerklasse
Steuerguthaben *n* (sum of) overpaid taxes
Steuergutschein *m* tax reserve certificate, *(Am)* tax bond
Steuerharmonisierung *f s.* Steuerangleichung
Steuerhebeliste *f* tax book [roll]
Steuerhelfer *m* tax adviser [expert]
Steuerherabsetzung *f* reduction [lowering] of taxes
Steuerhinterzieher *m* tax dodger
Steuerhinterziehung *f* tax evasion [avoidance, dodging]
Steuerhöchstgrenze *f* tax limit [ceiling]
Steuerhöchstsatz *m* maximum tax rate
Steuerhoheit *f* right of taxation
Steuerinspektor *m* tax inspector
Steuerjahr *n* fiscal [taxable, financial] year
Steuerkalender *m* list of deadlines for paying taxes
Steuerkarte *f* tax card; *(d.pr.)* control card
Steuerkasse *f* revenue [tax] office
Steuerklasse *f* income tax bracket, scale of taxation
Steuerkompetenz *f s.* Steuerhoheit
Steuerkraft *f* tax-paying capacity *(of social strata etc.)*
Steuerkürzung *f* tax cut [reduction]
Steuerlast *f* tax burden, burden of taxation
Steuerleistung *f* tax payment
steuerlich fiscal, taxable ✧ ~ absetzbar deduct-

Steuersenkung 473

ible from tax; ~ **belastet** tax-ridden; ~ **berechtigt** adjusted for taxation; **~benachteiligt** discriminated in taxation
Steuerliste *f s.* **Steuerhebeliste**
Steuermahnschreiben *n* tax reminder
Steuermarke *f* inland revenue stamp
Steuermaßnahmen *fpl* tax [taxation] measures
Steuermaßzahl *f s.* **Steuersatz**
Steuermeßbetrag *m s.* **Steuersatz**
Steuermethode *f* taxation method
Steuerminderung *f s.* **Steuerherabsetzung**
Steuermindestsatz *m* minimum rate of taxation
Steuermittel *npl* tax money, revenue from taxation
Steuermodus *m (d.pr.)* control mode
Steuermonopol *n* tax monopoly *(of the state)*
Steuern *fpl* taxes, duties ⋄ ~ **auferlegen** to impose taxes; ~ **bezahlen** to pay taxes; ~ **einziehen** to collect taxes; ~ **entrichten** *s.* ~ **zahlen**; ~ **erheben** to raise taxes; ~ **erhöhen** to increase taxes; ~ **erlassen** to remit taxes; ~ **ermäßigen** to afford relief in tax payment, to give tax relief *(to s.o.)*; ~ **erstatten** to repay [refund] taxes; ~ **festsetzen** to assess taxes; ~ **hinterziehen** to evade tax payment [payment of taxes]; ~ **kassieren** *s.* ~ **einziehen**; ~ **senken** to reduce taxes; ~ **zahlen** *s.* ~ **bezahlen**
~, **degressive** degressive taxes
~, **direkte** direct taxes
~, **einheitliche** uniform taxes
~, **einkommensbezogene** earnings-related taxes
~, **ergänzende** supplementary taxes
~, **fällige** taxes payable
~, **gestaffelte** graduated taxes
~, **gestundete** deferred taxes
~, **grenzausgleichsfähige** countervailing duty
~, **indirekte** indirect taxes
~, **kommunale** municipal taxes
~, **nichtabzugsfähige** non-deductible taxes
~, **örtliche** local taxes
~, **progressive** progressive taxes
~, **proportional erhobene** proportional taxes
~, **rückständige** tax arrears
~, **überzahlte** overpaid taxes
~ **und Abgaben** taxes and levies
~ **und Abgaben, inländische** internal revenue taxes
~, **versteckte** hidden taxes
~, **zentrale** central taxes
~, **zusätzliche** additional taxes
~, **zweckgebundene** taxes appropriated for special purposes
Steuernachlaß *m* remission of taxes; tax reduction
Steuernachveranlagung *f* tax reassessment
Steuernachzahlung *f* payment of tax arrears

Steuernovelle *f* revenue bill
Steueroase *f* tax haven
Steuerobjekt *n s.* **Steuergrundlage**
Steuerordnung *f s.* **Steuergesetz**
Steuerparadies *n s.* **Steueroase**
Steuerpauschale *f* lump sum payment of taxes
Steuerperiode *f* fiscal period
Steuerpfandrecht *n* tax lien
Steuerpfändung *f* attachment on property for nonpayment of taxes
Steuerpflicht *f* tax liability
steuerpflichtig liable to taxation
Steuerpflichtiger *m* tax payer
Steuerpolitik *f* taxation [tax, fiscal] policy
Steuerprinzipien *npl s.* **Steuergrundsätze**
Steuerprivileg *n* tax privilege
Steuerprogramm *n* 1. taxation programme; 2. *(d.pr.)* control program; monitor program; driver (handling) routine; scheduler
Steuerprogression *f* graduation of taxes, tax graduation
Steuerprozentsatz *m s.* **Steuersatz**
Steuerprüfer *m s.* **Steuerinspektor**
Steuerprüfung *f* tax examination [auditing]
Steuerpult *n (d.pr.)* console
Steuerquelle *f* source of taxation
Steuerquittung *f* tax receipt
Steuerquote *f* income-tax ratio
Steuerrate *f* tax instalment
Steuerratenzahlung *f* tax payment in instalments
Steuerrecht *n* taxation law
~, **formelles** formal taxation law
Steuerreform *f* tax reform
Steuerrefugium *n s.* **Steueroase**
Steuerregression *f* tax regression
Steuerreserve *f* reserve fund for paying taxes
Steuerrevision *f s.* **Steuerprüfung**
Steuerrevisor *m s.* **Steuerinspektor**
Steuerrolle *f s.* **Steuerhebeliste**
Steuerrückerstattung *f* refunding of overpaid taxes
Steuerrückerstattungsanspruch *m* claim for tax refund
Steuerrückstände *mpl* tax arrears
Steuerrückstellungen *fpl s.* **Steuerreserve**
Steuerrückvergütung *f s.* **Steuerrückerstattung**
Steuersachen *fpl* tax matters
Steuersachverständiger *m* tax expert
Steuersatz *m* tax rate, rate of taxation [tax assessment]
Steuerschraube *f* pressure of taxation
Steuerschuld *f* accrued taxes
Steuerschuldner *m* tax payer in arrears
Steuersenkung *f* lowering of taxation
~, **gestaffelte** graduated lowering of taxation
~, **lineare** flat-rate lowering of taxation

Steuersoll *n* assessed taxes
Steuerspeicher *m (d.pr.)* program counter
Steuerstufe *f (d.pr.)* control stage
Steuerstundung *f* deferment in tax payment
Steuersymbol *n (d.pr.)* control code
Steuersystem *n* tax system, system of taxation
Steuersystematik *f* classification of taxes
Steuertabelle *f* tax table
Steuertarif *m* tax table, scale of taxation
Steuertermine *mpl* deadlines for tax payment
Steuertheorie *f* theory of taxation
Steuerträger *m s.* Steuerzahler
Steuerüberschuß *m* surplus of tax revenue(s)
Steuerumgehung *f s.* Steuerhinterziehung
Steuerumlage *f* tax levy
Steuerumverteilung *f* redistribution of taxes
Steuer- und Gebühreneinnahmen *fpl* inland [internal] revenue
Steuer- und Speichereinheit *f (d.pr.)* control and storage unit
Steuerung *f* steering, control, controlling
~, **finanzpolitische** fiscal [finance] policy steering
~, **ökonomische** economic control [steering]
Steuerungsbefehl *m (d.pr.)* procedure branching statement
Steuerungsdaten *pl (d.pr.)* controlling data
Steuerungsgröße *f (d.pr.)* control quantity
Steuerungskontrolle *f (d.pr.)* control check
Steuerungssystem *n* system of steering; *(d.pr.)* control system
Steuerungs- und Regulierungsinstrument *n* steering and regulating tool [instrument]
Steuerunterlagen *fpl* tax returns and other related papers
Steuerunterschied *m* different rates of taxation
Steuerveranlagung *f* tax assessment
Steuerverbindlichkeiten *fpl* tax liabilities
Steuervergünstigung *f* tax allowance
Steuervergütung *f* tax refund
Steuerverjährung *f* waiving of taxes after expiration of deadline
Steuervermeidung *f* tax avoidance
Steuervorausschätzung *f* tax revenue estimate
Steuervorauszahlung *f* pre-payment of taxes
Steuerwert *m* taxable value
Steuerwesen *n* system of taxation
Steuerzahler *m* tax payer
Steuerzahlung *f* tax payment, payment of taxes
Steuerzuschlag *m* additional tax, surtax
Stichbahn *f (railw)* branch line
Stichjahr *n* fixed year
Stichprobe *f (stats)* sample, random test
~, **angepaßte** *(stats)* balanced sample
~, **bewußt gewählte** *(stats)* purposive sample
~, **diskordante (nach Pitman)** *(stats)* discordant sample
~, **doppelt erhobene** *(stats)* duplicate sample
~, **einmalige** *(stats)* first and final sample
~, **einseitig betonte** *(stats)* biassed sample
~, **feste** *(stats)* fixed sample
~, **festgehaltene** *s.* ~, **feste**
~, **geordnete** *(stats)* ordered sample
~, **geschichtete** *(stats)* stratified sample
~, **kleine** *(stats)* small sample
~, **mehrstufige** *(stats)* multi-stage sample
~ **mit bewußter Auswahl** *(stats)* purposive sample
~ **mit fester Wahrscheinlichkeit, einfache** *(stats)* simple sample
~ **mit Selbstgewichtung** *(stats)* self-weighting sample
~, **nichtzufällige** *(stats)* non-random sample
~, **nicht zufallsgemäße** *s.* ~, **nichtzufällige**
~, **repräsentative** *(stats)* representative sample
~, **sequentielle** *(stats)* sequential sample
~, **unabhängige** *(stats)* independent sample
~, **unverzerrte** *(stats)* defective sample
~, **wiederholte** *(stats)* iterative sample
~, **zufällige** *(stats)* random sample
Stichproben *fpl (stats)* samples
~, **durchdringende** *(stats)* interpenetrating samples
~, **ineinandergreifende** *s.* ~, **durchdringende**
~, **konkordante (nach Pitman)** *(stats)* concordant samples
~, **mehrfache** *(stats)* multiple samples
~ **mit Parallelfällen** *(stats)* matched samples
~, **überlagerte** *s.* ~, **durchdringende**
~, **verbundene** *(stats)* related samples
~ **von ausgewählten Vergleichsfällen** *(stats)* matched samples
Stichprobenanalyse *f (stats)* sample analysis
Stichprobenaufteilung *f*:
~, **optimale (nach Neyman)** *(stats)* optimum allocation
Stichprobenauswahl *f (stats)* selection of samples
Stichprobenbeobachtung *f (stats)* observation of samples
Stichprobendurchschnitt *m* sample average
Stichprobeneinheit *f (stats)* sample unit
Stichprobenentnahme *f (stats)* sampling
~ **aus der Masse** *(stats)* bulk sampling
~, **direkte** *(stats)* direct sampling
~, **einfache** *(stats)* single sampling
~ **für qualitative Merkmale** *(stats)* sampling for attribute
~ **im Gittermuster** *(stats)* lattice sampling
~, **indirekte** *(stats)* indirect sampling
~ **mit Zurücklegen** *(stats)* sampling with replacement
~ **ohne Zurücklegen** *(stats)* sampling without replacement

Stillhaltekredit 475

~, **planlose** *(stats)* chunk sampling
~, **ungleichartige** *(stats)* mixed sampling
~, **unmittelbare** *(stats)* unitary sampling
~ **vom Weg aus** *(stats)* root sampling
~, **zweifache** *(stats)* double sampling
Stichprobenergebnis *n (stats)* sampling result
Stichprobenerhebung *f (stats)* sample survey
Stichprobenfehler *m (stats)* sampling error
Stichprobenfunktion *f (stats)* sample function
Stichprobenkarte *f (stats)* sampling card
Stichprobenkontrolle *f (stats)* sample checking
Stichprobenkovarianzmatrix *f (stats)* sampling covariance matrix
Stichprobenmethode *f (stats)* sampling method
Stichprobenmittel *n (stats)* mean sample
Stichprobenmoment *m (stats)* sample-moment
Stichprobennetz *n (stats)* network of samples
Stichprobenplan *m (stats)* sample design; sampling design *(covering the entire planning of a sample survey)*; sampling plan *(covering steps taken in selecting the sample)*; survey design *(covering choice and training of interviewers etc.)*
Stichprobenprüfung *f s.* **Stichprobenkontrolle**
Stichprobenpunkt *m (stats)* sample point
Stichprobenqualitätskontrolle *f (stats)* sample quality checking
Stichprobenquantil *n (stats)* sample quantile
Stichprobenraum *m (stats)* sample space
Stichprobenregressionskoeffizient *m (stats)* sample correlation coefficient
Stichprobenschema *n (stats)* sampling scheme
~, **zusammengesetztes** *(stats)* composite sampling scheme
Stichprobenstreuung *f (stats)* sample dispersion
Stichprobenstruktur *f (stats)* sampling structure
Stichprobensystem *n (stats)* sample system
~, **doppeltes** *(stats)* duplicate sample system
~, **einfaches** *(stats)* simple sample system
~, **kontinuierliches** *(stats)* sustained sample system
~, **mehrfaches** *(stats)* multiple sample system
Stichprobentechnik *f (stats)* sampling method [technique]
Stichprobentheorie *f (stats)* sampling theory
Stichprobentyp *m (stats)* specified survey design
Stichprobenumfang *m (stats)* sample size
~ **relativer** *(stats)* sampling fraction
Stichprobenuntersuchung *f s.* **Stichprobenanalyse**
Stichprobenverfahren *n (stats)* sampling
~, **doppeltes** *(stats)* duplicate sampling
~, **einfaches** *(stats)* simple sampling
~, **einstufiges** *(stats)* unitary sampling
~, **gemischtes** *(stats)* mixed sampling
~, **mehrfaches** *(stats)* multiple sampling
~ **mit Klumpenauswahl** *(stats)* cluster [nested] sampling

~ **mit Mehrfacherfassung derselben Einheiten** *(stats)* sampling on successive occasions
~ **mit Unterauswahl** *(stats)* subsampling
~, **zufallsähnliches** *(stats)* quasi-random sampling
~, **zweiphasiges** *(stats)* two-phase sampling
~, **zweistufiges** *(stats)* two-stage sampling
Stichprobenverteilung *f (stats)* sampling distribution
Stichprobenverteilungsfunktion *f (stats)* sampling distribution function
stichprobenweise *(stats)* by means of samples
Stichprobenwert *m (stats)* sample value
Stichtag *m* deadline, fixed day, key date; *(st.ex.)* settling day
Stichtagsbestand *m* stock at a fixed date
stichtagsbezogen on a fixed day
Stichtagsinventur *f* stock-taking on a fixed day
Stichtagskontrolle *f* checking on a fixed day
Stichtagspreis *m* price on a fixed day
Stichwahl *f* second ballot
stiften to found, to institute, to establish *(foundation etc.)*; to give, to endow *(scholarship etc.)*; to donate *(money for a specific purpose etc.)*
Stifter *m* founder; donor
Stiftung *f* foundation; trust ⋄ **eine ~ errichten** to create a foundation; to create a trust
~, **freiwillige** voluntary trust
~, **kirchliche** church trust
~, **kündbare** revocable trust
~, **öffentlich-rechtliche** public trust
~, **private** private foundation; private trust
~, **unwiderrufliche** irrevocable trust
~, **widerrufliche** *s.* ~, **kündbare**
~, **wohltätige** charitable institution [establishment]
Stiftungsfonds *m* endowment [trust] fund
Stiftungsgelder *npl* trust money
Stiftungsvermögen *n* trust property; endowment fund
Stiftungsvertrag *m* trust settlement
stillegen to shut down, to close *(enterprises etc.)*; to immobilize, to neutralize *(money etc.)*; to stop, to paralyse *(traffic etc.)*; to put out of commission *(ship)*
Stillegung *f* shut-down, closure *(traffic, enterprise etc.)*; immobilization, neutralization *(money etc.)*; traffic jam, snarl-up, paralysis *(traffic)*; putting out of commission *(ship)*
Stillgeld *n* nursing allowance
stillgelegt shut down, closed *(enterprises etc.)*; neutralized *(money etc.)*; stopped, paralysed *(traffic etc.)*; put out of commission *(ship)*
Stillhalteabkommen *n* standstill agreement
Stillhaltegläubiger *m* standstill creditor
Stillhaltekredit *m* frozen credit

Stillpause *f* break for breast-feeding mothers
Stillstand *m* standstill, stoppage; stagnation; deadlock *(negotiations etc.)* ◊ **zum ~ bringen** to bring to a standstill *(traffic, production line etc.)*; to bring to a deadlock *(negotiations etc.)*; **zum ~ kommen** to come to a standstill *(traffic, production line etc.)*; to come to a deadlock *(negotiations etc.)*
~ der Anlage stoppage of the (whole) plant
~, ganzschichtiger standstill during the whole shift; whole-shift stoppage
~, ganztägiger whole-day stoppage
~, technisch bedingter technically necessary stoppage
~, vollschichtiger *s.* **~, ganzschichtiger**
Stillstandsdauer *f* duration of stoppage
Stillstandskosten *pl* costs of stoppage
Stillstandsreparatur *f (tech)* shut-down maintenance
Stillstands- und Wartezeit *f s.* **Stillstandszeit**
Stillstandszeit *f* downtime, (machine) idle time
~, arbeitsablaufbedingte downtime [(machine) idle time] as part of the work process
~, durch den Arbeiter bedingte downtime [(machine) idle time] caused by (machine) operator
~, pausenbedingte downtime [(machine) idle time] during break
~, störungsbedingte downtime [(machine) idle time] due to machine trouble
Stillzeit *f* lactation period
Stimmabgabe *f* vote, voting
~, freie freedom of election
stimmberechtigt qualified [entitled] to vote
Stimmberechtigter *m* voter
Stimmberechtigung *f s.* **Stimmrecht**
Stimme *f* 1. voice; 2. vote *(election)*
~, ausschlaggebende casting vote
~, beratende having a say without a right to vote
~, beschließende decisive vote
stimmen 1. to vote; 2. to be all right, to be correct
Stimmen *fpl* votes ◊ **~ sammeln** to canvass votes
~, abgegebene votes cast
Stimmenauszählung *f* counting of votes
Stimmenfang *m s.* **Stimmenwerbung**
Stimmengleichheit *f* same number of votes
Stimmenmehrheit *f* majority of votes
Stimmenminderheit *f* minority of votes
Stimmenprüfung *f* scrutiny of votes
Stimmenthaltung *f* abstention from voting
Stimmenwerbung *f* canvassing for votes
Stimmenzahl *f* number of votes
Stimmenzählung *f* counting [scrutiny] of votes
Stimmkarte *f* voting [ballot] paper

Stimmrecht *n* right to vote, suffrage, franchise
~, eingeschränktes restricted right to vote
Stimmrechtsaktie *f* voting share [*(Am)* stock]
Stimmrechtsübertragung *f* transfer of voting right
Stimmrechtsvertretung *f* proxy
Stimmrechtsvollmacht *f s.* **Stimmrechtsvertretung**
Stimmzettel *m* ballot-paper
Stimulanzpreis *m* incentive price
stimulieren to stimulate, to give an incentive; to foster, to promote
stimulierend stimulating, giving an incentive; fostering, promoting
Stimulierung *f* stimulation, incentives; fostering, promotion
~, materielle material incentives
~, moralische moral incentives
~, ökonomische economic incentives
Stimulierungsfonds *m* incentive fund
Stimulierungsmaßnahme *f* incentive measure
Stimulus *m* incentive, stimulus
~, ideeller moral incentive
~, materieller material stimulus [incentive]
~, moralischer *s.* **~, ideeller**
Stipendium *n* scholarship
stochastisch *(stats)* stochastic ◊ **~ größer oder kleiner** *(stats)* stochastically larger or smaller
Stochastisierung *f (stats)* randomisation
stocken to delay, to hold up; *(com)* to stagnate, to slacken *(markets etc.)*; to congest, to snarl up, to jam *(traffic etc.)*
Stockung *f* interruption, delay, hold-up; *(com)* stagnation, slackness, dullness *(market etc.)*; congestion of traffic, traffic jam, standstill *(traffic etc.)*; breakdown *(negotiations etc.)*
Stoff *m* 1. matter, substance; 2. stuff, fabric, material; 3. theme, topic, subject
Stoffluß *m* flow of material
~, volkswirtschaftlicher national economic flow(s) of materials
Stoffflußbild *n* flow chart, chart showing interlocking relations of material flows
Stopppreis *m* fixed price
stören to disrupt *(talks etc.)*, to disturb *(s.o. etc.)*; to dislocate *(traffic etc.)*; to interfere with; to bother *(s.o)*; to disarrange *(s.th.)*
stornieren to cancel *(order etc.)*; *(acc)* to reverse *(an entry)*
Stornierung *f* cancellation, countermanding *(order)*; *(acc)* reversal *(entry)*
~ eines Zahlungsauftrages cancellation of payment
Storno *n* cancellation *(order etc.)*; *(acc)* reversal, counter-entry
Stornobuchung *f (acc)* counter-entry
Störung *f* disruption *(talks etc.)*, disturbance; dis-

location *(traffic etc.)*; interference; disarrangement
~, **stochastische** *(stats)* stochastic disturbance
Störungskoeffizient *m (stats)* coefficient of disturbancy
Störziffer *f (d.pr.)* noisy digit
Strafe *f* penalty; punishment
Strafgebühr *f* surcharge (for non-regular payment)
Strafgeld *n* fine
Strafmaßnahme *f* sanction, penalty
Strafrecht *n* criminal law
Strandgut *n* stranded goods
Strandung *f* stranding, shipwreck
Straße *f* road; street *(in towns and villages)*; highway, highroad
Straßenabgabe *f s.* **Straßenbenutzungsgebühr**
Straßenanliegerbeitrag *m* (financial) contribution by estate owners to road construction
Straßenarbeiten *fpl* road works
Straßenbahn *f* tram(way) ✧ **die ~ benutzen** to take the tram
Straßenbahnverkehr *m* tramway traffic
Straßenbau *m* road building [construction]
Straßenbaubetrieb *m* road construction enterprise
Straßenbauer *m* road builder, roadbuilding worker
Straßenbenutzung *f* use of roads
Straßenbenutzungsgebühr *f* road tax *(for foreign vehicles)*
Straßenfahrzeug *n (road)* vehicle
Straßengewerbe *n* street trading
Straßengüterverkehr *m* road goods transportation
Straßenhandel *m* itinerary trade
Straßenhändler *m* street trader
Straßenkiosk *m* roadside stand; roadside kiosk *(newspaper, magazines etc.)*
Straßennetz *n* network of roads, highway system
Straßenreinigung *f* street cleaning
Straßentransport *m* road transport, haulage
Straßenverkauf *m* hawking
Straßenverkehr *m* road traffic
Straßenverkehrsordnung *f* road traffic regulations
Straßenzoll *m* toll
Straßenzustand *m* road conditions
Strategie *f* strategy
~ des Verhaltens strategy of action *(theory of games)*
~, **gemischte** mixed strategy *(theory of games)*
~, **individuelle** individual strategy *(theory of games)*
~, **maximale** maximum strategy *(theory of games)*
~, **minimale** minimum strategy *(theory of games)*
~, **optimale** optimum strategy *(theory of games)*

~, **reine** pure strategy *(theory of games)*
Strategiewahl *f* choice of strategy *(theory of games)*
Streckenbelastung *f* volume of traffic; *(railw)* load on section
Streckenfracht *f* haulage *(transport rate times distance times weight)*
Streckengeschäft *n* commodity transaction on order of a third person
Streckenlänge *f* mileage, distance
Streckensatz *m* haulage rate
Streckentarif *m s.* **Streckensatz**
streichen to cancel, to delete; *(d.pr.)* to discard
Streichinstrumentenmacher *m* string(ed) instruments maker
Streichung *f* cancellation, deletion
Streifenstichprobenverfahren *n (stats)* zonal sampling
Streik *m* strike ✧ **einen ~ abbrechen** to call off a strike; **einen ~ ausrufen** to call a strike, to call out on strike; **einen ~ beschließen** to resolve to strike; **einen ~ brechen** to break a strike; **sich im ~ befinden** to be on strike
~, **örtlich begrenzter** local strike
~, **wilder** wild-cat strike
~, **zeitlich begrenzter** strike of duration, strike for a fixed period
Streikabstimmung *f* call for a strike vote
Streikaktion *f* strike (action)
Streikandrohung *f* threat of a strike
Streikankündigung *f* strike notice
Streikausschuß *m* strike committee
Streikbewegung *f* strike movement
Streikbrecher *m* strike-breaker, scab
Streikbruch *m* strike-breaking
Streikdauer *f* duration of strike
streiken to strike, to go on strike
Streikender *m* striker
Streikfonds *m* strike fund
Streikfreiheit *f* freedom to strike
Streikgeld *n* strike money [pay]
Streikkasse *f s.* **Streikfonds**
Streiklohn *m s.* **Streikgeld**
Streikposten *m* picket
Streikposten *mpl*:
~, **reisende** flying pickets
Streikrecht *n* right to strike
Streit *m* dispute; controversy; ✧ **einen ~ schlichten** to settle a dispute
Streitfall *m* (a case of) dispute; point of controversy
Streitgegenstand *m* matter in dispute
Streitfrage *f* issue in dispute; controversial point
Streitigkeit *f* dispute, controversy
~, **vermögensrechtliche** dispute over property
Streitobjekt *n s.* **Streitgegenstand**

streng stringent *(measures etc.)*, severe *(penalty etc.)*, strict *(rules etc.)*, rigorous *(demands etc.)*
Strenge *f* strength
~ **eines Tests** *(stats)* strength of a test
Streubesitz *m* scattered property
Streubild *n* *(stats)* scatter diagram
streuen to strew; to scatter; to spread *(manure etc.)*; to disperse
Streuung *f* dispersion; *(stats)* variance
⋄ **ungleich in der** ~ *(stats)* heteroscedastic
~, **binomiale** *(stats)* binomial [Bernoulli] variation
~ **der Werte** spread of values
~, **Lexissche** *(stats)* Lexis variation
~, **mittlere** *(stats)* mean scatter
~, **seitliche** *(d.pr.)* lateral scattering, sideways scatter
~ **von Datenpunkten** *(d.pr.)* scatter of data points
Streuungsdiagramm *n* *(stats)* dispersion diagram
Streuungsfeld *n* *(stats)* dispersion area
Streuungskoeffizient *m* **(von Frisch)** *(stats)* scatter coefficient
Streuungsmaß *n* *(stats)* measure of dispersion
Streuungsmatrix *f* *(stats)* covariance [dispersion] matrix
Streuungsparameter *mpl* *(stats)* dispersion parameters
Streuungstest *m* *(stats)* dispersion test
Streuungszerlegung *f* *(stats)* analysis of variance
Strich *m* dash; line; stroke ⋄ **unter dem** ~ *(acc)* below the line
Strohmann *m* fictitious operator
Strom *m* river; stream; 2. current, power; 3. flow *(traffic etc.)* ⋄ **den** ~ **abschalten** to switch off [stop] the supply of electricity
~, **elektrischer** electric current
~, **schiffbarer** navigable river
Stromabgabe *f* supply of electricity, power supply
Stromabnehmer *m* consumer of electricity
Stromabschaltung *f* power-out; cut-off of power supply
Stromausfall *m* power [mains, electricity] failure
Strombedarf *m* demand for electricity, power requirements
Strombilanz *f* balance sheet of power supply and consumption
Stromentnahme *f* consumption of electricity; use of electricity
Stromerzeugung *f* generation of electric current [power, electricity]
Stromkontingent *n* quota of power supply
Stromlieferung *f* supply of current [electricity, power], power supply
Stromnetz *n* mains

Strompreis *m* electricity rates, charges for electricity
Stromsperre *f* blackout
Stromspitze *f* maximum load of power supply, peak power load
Stromtarif *m* electricity rate(s)
Stromunterbrechung *f* cutting-off of electricity
Stromverbrauch *m* consumption of electricity, electricity consumption
Stromversorgung *f s.* **Stromlieferung**
Stromverteilungsnetz *n* network of power distribution
Stromverteilungssystem *n s.* **Stromverteilungsnetz**
Stromzähler *m* current meter
Struktur *f* 1. structure; 2. *(stats)* configuration; 3. texture *(fabric etc.)*
~, **einfache** *(stats)* simple structure
~, **gesellschaftliche** social structure
~, **latente** *(stats)* latent structure
~, **nichtbeobachtbare** *s.* ~, **latente**
~, **produktionstechnologische** technological structure
~, **regionale** regional structure
~, **soziale** social structure
~, **sozialökonomische** socio-economic structure
~, **technologische** technological structure
~, **wirtschaftliche** economic structure [set-up]
Strukturanalyse *f* structural analysis, analysis of the structure
Strukturänderung *f* structural change(s), change(s) in the structure
Strukturanpassung *f* structural adjustment
strukturbestimmend profile-determinant *(projects, measures, products, sectors etc.)*
Strukturdiagramm *n* *(stats)* structural diagram
Struktureffekt *m* structural effect
Struktureinheit *f* basic unit *(of an enterprise or institution)*
strukturentscheidend *s.* **strukturbestimmend**
Strukturentscheidung *f* decision on structural changes
Strukturentwicklung *f* structural development [growth]
Strukturforschung *f* research on structural problems
~, **territoriale** research on regional structural problems
Strukturgestaltung *f* organization of the structure
strukturieren to pattern, to delineate
Strukturkoeffizient *m* structural coefficient
~, **technologischer** technological structural coefficient
Strukturkonzeption *f* *(plan)* policy outline for structural changes *(in the economy relating to top priority projects or sectors)*

Strukturmodell *n* structural model
Strukturplan *m* structural plan
Strukturplanung *f* structural planning
Strukturpolitik *f* policy for structural changes
Strukturprognose *f* forecast for structural changes *(of the economy)*
strukturverändernd structure-changing
Strukturveränderungen *fpl* structural changes
Strukturverschiebung *f* structural shift(s) *(industry etc.)*; *(d.pr.)* pattern shift
Strukturwandel *m s.* **Strukturveränderungen**
Strukturwechsel *m s.* **Strukturveränderungen**
Stück *n* piece, part; unit; stretch *(road etc.)*
~, **fehlerfreies** *(stats)* effective unit
~, **fehlerhaftes** defective unit
Stückarbeit *f* piecework
Stücke *npl (st.ex.)* stocks and shares
Stückekonto *n* stock account
stückeln to divide into *(currency, shares etc.)*
Stück(e)lung *f* denomination *(currency, shares etc.)*
Stückeverzeichnis *n* inventory; bill of specie
Stückezuteilung *f* distribution of specie
Stückfracht *f s.* **Stückgut**
Stückgut *n* piece goods, mixed cargo ◊ **als ~ zum Versand bringen** to dispatch in carloads; to ship in carloads
Stückgutlieferung *f* delivery of mixed cargo
Stückgutsendung *f* small-lot consignment; parcel
Stückgutspediteur *m* general freight carrier
Stückguttarif *m* mixed cargo rate
Stückgutverkehr *m* mixed cargo transport
Stückgutzustellung *f s.* **Stückgutlieferung**
Stückkosten *pl* unit cost
Stückkostenkalkulation *f* unit cost calculation
Stückleistung *f* output; capacity *(engine etc.)*
Stückliste *f* piece list *(shares etc.)*, parts list *(components etc.)*; specification; inventory
Stücklohn *m* piecerate wages
~, **einfacher** direct piecerate wages
~, **indirekter** indirect piecerate wages
~, **kollektiver** collective piecerate wages
~, **progressiver** graduated [progressive] piecerate wages
Stücklohnarbeit *f* piecework
Stücklohnsatz *m* piece wage rate
Stücklohnsystem *n* system of piecerate wages
Stücknorm *f* norm for piecework
Stücknormzeit *f* standard (working) time per unit
Stücknotierung *f (st.ex.)* quotation *(shares etc.)*
Stückprämie *f* bonus for piecework
Stückpreis *m* price per unit, unit price
Stückpreissystem *n* system of unit prices
Stückrechnung *f* unit calculation
Stückspanne *f* trade margin per unit

Stücktarif *m* piecerate
Stückware *f s.* **Stückgut**
stückweise piece by piece
Stückzahl *f* number of pieces
Stückzahlnorm *f s.* **Stücknorm**
Stückzeit *f* (working) time per unit
Stückzeitnorm *f* standard time per unit
Stückzinsen *mpl* accrued interest (on shares)
Student *m* student, undergraduate
Studentenaustausch *m* exchange of students
Studentisierung *f (stats)* studentisation
Studie *f* study, analysis
~, **technologische** technological study
Studienbewerbung *f* application for enrolment at a university
Studienentwurf *m* draft, draft project
Studienplatz *m* admission *(at colleges etc.)*
studieren to study
Studium *n* study; university education
~, **postgraduales** post-graduate studies
Stufe *f* stage, step, degree, grade, level, standard; rank
Stufenfolge *f* graduation, succession, sequence of stages
Stufenmodell *n* step-wise model
Stufenproduktion *f* production in stages
Stufenprogramm *n* upgrading system *(in education and training)*
Stufentheorie *f* theory of stages
stufenweise stage by stage, stage-wise
Stukkateur *m* stucco-worker
Stunde *f* 1. hour; 2. lesson
stunden to grant a respite, to allow time to pay
Stundenarbeiter *m* worker on hourly wage rate
Stundenerzeugungsplan *m* hourly production plan
Stundenkapazität *f* (output) capacity per hour
Stundenkostennormativ *n* standard rate of costs per hour
~, **maschinen- und anlagenbezogenes** standard rate of costs of machines and equipment per hour
Stundenleistung *f s.* **Stundenkapazität**
Stundenlohn *m* hourly wages
Stundenlohnsatz *m* hourly wage rate
Stundenplan *m* timetable, *(Am)* schedule
Stundenproduktion *f* output per hour
Stundenproduktivität *f* productivity per hour
Stundentarif *m* rate of remuneration per hour
Stundenverdienst *m s.* **Stundenlohn**
Stundung *f* postponement, respite for [delay of] payment
Stundungsfrist *f* respite
Stundungsgesuch *n* request for respite [rescheduling]
Stundungsvertrag *m* agreement on rescheduling (of debts)

Stundungszinsen *mpl* interest on rescheduled debts
Sturm *m (bank)* run
Sturm(schaden)versicherung *f* insurance against damage caused by storm, *(Am)* tornado insurance
Sturz *m* slump, collapse *(market etc.)*; downfall, ruin *(company etc.)*; overthrow *(regime etc.)*
stürzen to slump, to collapse *(market etc.)*; to ruin *(company etc.)*; to overthrow *(regime etc.)*
Sturzgüter *npl* bulk goods
Stutzen *m*:
~ **(einer Verteilung)** *(stats)* truncation
Stützung *f* subsidy, support, allowance
~, **leistungsgebundene** output-related subsidy
Stützungsaktion *f* banking support
Stützungskauf *m* supporting buying *(currency, share prices etc.)*
Stützungskredit *m* emergency credit
Stützungspreis *m* supported price; *(st.ex.)* pegged price
Submission *f* tender
Subskribent *m* subscriber
subskribieren to subscribe
Subskription *f* subscription
Subskriptionspreis *m* subscription price
substantiieren to substantiate *(claim etc.)*
substituieren to substitute
Substituierung *f s.* **Substitution**
Substitution *f* substitution
~ **lebendiger Arbeit** substitution of living labour *(i.e. substitution of machines for manual work)*
Substitutionsanalyse *f* substitution analysis
Substitutionseffekt *m* efficiency of substitution
Substitutionsmethode *f* substitution method
Substitutionsware *f* substitute article
Subvention *f* subsidy
Suchprogramm *n (d.pr.)* search program; finding routine
Suffizienz *f (stats)* sufficiency
~, **gemeinsame** *(stats)* joint sufficiency
~, **simultane** *s.* ~, **gemeinsame**
~, **verbundene** *s.* ~ **gemeinsame**
Suggestivwirkung *f (stats)* "sympathy" effect
Summation *f* summation
~ **über eine gerade Anzahl von Summanden** *(stats)* even summation
Summationsprozeß *m (stats)* summation process
~, **gleitender** *(stats)* moving-summation process
Summe *f* sum, amount, total ◊ **jmdm. eine ~ kreditieren** to credit s.o.'s account with an amount
~, **aufgelaufene** accumulated amount
~, **ausstehende** outstanding amount
~ **der Abweichungsquadrate** *(stats)* deviance, squariance, sum of squares

~ **der Fehlerquadrate** *(maths)* error sum of squares, residual sum of squares
~, **einmalige** lump sum
~, **faktorielle** *(stats)* factorial sum
~, **feste** fixed amount
~, **geschuldete** amount owing
~, **gleitende** *(stats)* moving total
~, **hinterlegte** deposited amount
~, **kumulative** *s.* ~, **aufgelaufene**
~, **überwiesene** remitted amount
~, **veranschlagte** estimated amount, estimate
~, **verfügbare** available amount, amount at disposal
Summenhäufigkeitsverteilung *f (stats)* cumulative frequency distribution
summieren to sum up, to add
Summierung *f* addition, summing up
Summierungsmethode *f* summation method (of evaluation) *(assets)*
Superdividende *f* super dividend; cash surplus
Superkargo *m* supercargo
Supermarkt *m* supermarket
supranational supranational
Surplus *n* surplus
Surplusbevölkerung *f* surplus population
Surpluskapital *n* surplus capital
Surplusprodukt *n* surplus product
Surplusprofit *m* extra [surplus] profit
Surrogat *n* substitute
Süßwarenindustrie *f* confectionary industry
Swapgeschäft *n* swap
Switchgeschäft *n* switch (business)
Symbolschreibweise *f (d.pr.)* symbolic notation
Symbolsprache *f (d.pr.)* symbolic language
Symmetrie *f* symmetry
Sympathiestreik *m* sympathy strike
Synchronisation *f* synchronization
synchronisieren to synchronize; to dub *(film etc.)*
Synchronisierung *f* synchronization; dubbing *(film etc.)*
Syndikalismus *m* syndicalism
Syndikat *n* syndicate
System *n* system
~, **adaptives** adaptive system
~, **binäres** binomial system
~, **dekadisches** *s.* ~, **metrisches**
~ **der automatisierten wissenschaftlich-technischen Information** automated system of scientific and technical information
~ **der Datenverarbeitung, integriertes** integrated system of data processing
~ **der fehlerfreien Arbeit** system of correct [faultless] work, right first time, *(Am)* zero defects
~ **der Leitung, automatisiertes** automated system of management

~ der Leitung, dreistufiges three-tier system of management
~ der Leitung, zweistufiges two-tier system of management
~ ökonomischer Gesetze system of economic laws
~ der Planberechnungen, automatisiertes computer-aided [automated] system of plan calculation(s)
~ der Planung und Leitung, automatisiertes automated [computer-aided] system of planning and management
~ der staatlichen Statistik, automatisiertes automated [computer-aided] system of central statistics
~ der Vertragspreise system of contractual prices
~, dynamisches dynamic system
~, endliches finite system
~, geschlossenes closed system
~, gesteuertes controlled system
~, kybernetisches cybernetic system
~, metrisches metric system
~, offenes open system
~, rekursives *(stats)* recursive system
~, selbsteinstellendes self-adjusting system
~, selbstoptimierendes self-optimizing system
~, selbstorganisierendes self-organizing system
~, selbststeuerndes self-controlling system
~, stabiles stable system
~, statisches static system
~, steuerndes controlling system
~, stochastisches stochastic system
~, technisch-technologisches technical and technological system
~ technisch-wirtschaftlicher Kennziffern system of technological and economic indicators
~, unendliches infinite system
~ von Rechnungsführung und Statistik, einheitliches integrated system of cost accounting and statistics
Systemanalyse *f* system analysis
Systematik *f* system; structure
~ der Ausbildungsberufe classification [list, nomenclature] of skilled trades
~ der Berufe classification [list, nomenclature, catalogue] of trades [vocations]
~ der Planung classification of planning items, planning classification
~ des Staatshaushaltsplanes classification of budget items *(breakdown of the budget according to administrative, regional and economic aspects)*
~ volkswirtschaftliche classification of the national economy
systematisieren to classify; to systematize

Systematisierung *f* classification; systematization
Systemautomatisierung *f* systems automation
Systemregelung *f* automatic regulation
Systemsoftware *f (d.pr.)* system software
Systemsteuerung *f (d.pr.)* control mode
Systemwirksamkeit *f* system effectiveness
Systemtheorie *f* theory of systems, systems theory
~, kybernetische theory of cybernetic systems

T

Tabakgeschäft *n* tobacco(nist) business; tobacco shop, tobacconist's
Tabakhandel *m* tobacco trade
Tabakhändler *m* tobacconist; tobacco dealer
Tabakhandlung *f s.* Tabakgeschäft
Tabakladen *m* tobacco shop
Tabakmonopol *n* monopoly in tobacco, tobacco monopoly
Tabakregie *f* government monopoly in tobacco trade
Tabakspinner *m* tobacco-dresser
Tabaksteuer *f* tobacco tax, duty on tobacco ◊ ~ einführen to introduce a tax on tobacco
Tabakwaren *fpl* tobacco, cigarettes and cigars
Tabakwarenabgabe *f s.* Tabaksteuer
tabellarisch in tables, tabulated, tabular ◊ ~ angeordnet tabulated; ~ anordnen to tabulate
Tabelle *f* table; schedule; tabulation; chart
◊ eine ~ aufstellen to compile a table
~, chronologische chronological table
~, schachbrettartige chequered table
~, statistische statistical table
~, synoptische synoptic table
~, vergleichende comparative table
~, zusammengefaßte aggregated [summary] table
Tabellen *fpl*:
~ zur Berechnung des Nettobetrages von festverzinslichen Papieren bond value tables
Tabellenangaben *fpl* data in the table
Tabellenauszug *m* extract from a table
Tabellenfeld *n* cell of a table
Tabellenform *f* table, tables ◊ in ~ bringen *s.* tabellieren
tabellenförmig *s.* tabellarisch
Tabellenprogramm *n* system of statistical tables
Tabellenwerte *mpl* figures given in a table
tabellieren to tabulate, to tabularize

Tabelliermaschine *f* tabulating machine
Tabellierung *f* compiling a table
Tadel *m* censure, reprimand; blame
Tadelsantrag *m* motion of censure
Tafel *f* 1. table; chart; 2. plaque; board; *(tech)* control panel, console
~, zwei-mal-zwei *(stats)* fourfold table
tafelfertig ready-to-serve, ready-to-eat *(food)*
Tafelgeschäft *n* over the window business, *(Am)* counter trade
Tag *m* day; date ◊ **~ und Nacht geöffnet** open day and night; **unter Tage** *(min)* underground; **vom gleichen ~** of the same date
~, arbeitsfreier free day; holiday
~ der Aussteller exhibitors' day
~, verkaufsoffener normal trading day
Tage *mpl*:
 ◊ **an festgesetzten Tagen** on fixed [stated] days
Tagebau *m* 1. daylight [strip] mine; 2. opencast [surface, strip, open-cut, open-pit] mining
Tagebuch *n* diary, journal; log *(ship)*
Tagegeld *n* travelling [daily, per diem] allowance, allowance per day
Tagegeldleistung *f* payment of subsistence allowance *(by the insurance company to insured persons in case of illness)*
Tagelohn *m* daily wages, a day's wage, daily pay
Tagelöhner *m* day-labourer
Tagelohnsatz *m* day-rate, daily rate of pay
tagen to meet, to sit *(for the purpose of a conference)*
Tagesablauf *m* daily routine; day schedule
Tagesabrechnung *f* daily cash settlement
Tagesabschluß *m* daily balance
Tagesabschlußbuch *n (bank)* daily balance book
Tagesabstimmung *f (bank)* daily adjustment (of accounts)
Tagesanforderung *f* daily demand *(for materials, money etc.)*
Tagesarbeit *f* day-work
Tagesarbeitsleistung *f* daily performance; daily output *(machine)*
Tagesarbeitsnorm *f* work norm per day
Tagesauflage *f* 1. daily task; 2. daily edition *(newspapers)*
Tagesausbeute *f s.* **Tagesförderung**
Tagesausgabe *f* 1. daily expenditure; 2. daily issue *(paper etc.)*
Tagesausstoß *m s.* **Tagesproduktion**
Tagesausweis *m (bank)* daily return
Tagesauszug *m (bank)* daily statement of account
Tagesbedarf *m* (daily) ration; daily requirement *(for materials, money etc.)*
Tagesbericht *m* daily report
Tagesbetrieb *m (min)* surface mining [working]

Tagesbulletin *n* daily bulletin
Tagesdienst *m* day-duty
Tageseinnahme *f* daily takings [receipts]
Tageserlös *m* daily proceeds
Tagesförderung *f* daily output
Tagesgebühr *f* day-rate; daily charge
Tagesgeld *n (bank)* call [day-to-day] money, money on call
Tagesgeschäft *n* daily transactions
Tageskarte *f* day-ticket
Tageskasse *f* 1. daily takings; 2. box-office
Tageskurs *m* day rate; daily quotation *(shares etc.)*; current exchange rate *(currency etc.)*
Tagesleistung *f* daily output [performance]; daily workload
Tagesmeldung *f* daily return [report]
Tagesnorm *f* daily norm
Tagesordnung *f* agenda ◊ **auf die ~ setzen** to put on the agenda; to raise a point *(at a meeting etc.)*; **zur ~ übergehen** to proceed [pass] to the agenda
Tagespolitik *f* day-to-day [current] policy
Tagespost *f* daily mail
Tagespreis *m* current price ◊ **unter dem ~** *(st.ex.)* below today's quotation
Tagespreisprinzip *n (st.ex.)* principle of day-to-day prices
Tagespresse *f* daily papers
Tagesprodukt *n s.* **Tagesproduktion**
Tagesproduktion *f* daily output
Tagesprogramm *n* daily programme
Tagessaldo *m* daily balance
Tagessatz *m* day-rate (of travel allowance)
Tagesschicht *f* day [first] shift
Tagesschluß *m* daily closing
Tagesschwankung *f* daily fluctuation
Tagessoll *n* daily (plan) task
Tagesspesen *pl* daily travel allowance; daily expenses
Tagesstempel *m* date-stamp
Tagesumsatz *m* daily turnover
Tagesverbrauch *m* daily consumption
Tagesverdienst *m* daily earnings
Tagesversand *m* daily consignment
Tageswert *m* present [current] value, today's value [quotation]
Tageszinsen *mpl* daily interest
Tageszulage *f* extra daily pay
Tagewerk *n* day's work, daily task; man-day
tagfertig *(bank)* daily balancing
Tagfertigkeit *f (bank)* daily balancing
täglich daily, per day
Tag- und Nachtarbeit *f* day and night shift
Tagung *f* meeting; conference; congress; session *(parliament etc.)* ◊ **die ~ eröffnen** to open the meeting; **die ~ leiten** to preside over the meeting

Tagungsbericht *m* conference paper [report]
Tagungsleiter *m* chairman, chairperson
Tagungsort *m* venue of a meeting [conference]
Tagungsperiode *f* period of session
Tagungsraum *m* meeting-room, conference room
Tagungsteilnehmer *m* participant at a meeting [conference], conference participant
Taktfertigung *f* cyclic manufacturing technique, cyclic work
Taktstraße *f* production line, automated transfer [machine] line; assembly line
Taktverfahren *n* cyclic work
Taktzeit *f* cycle time *(machine)*; clock-time *(computer)*
Talon *m* talon, renewal coupon
Tanker *m* tanker
Tankerflotte *f* tanker fleet
Tankstelle *f* filling [servicing, petrol] station
Tankwart *m* filing [*(Am)* gas] station attendant, petrol pump attendant
Tantieme *f* percentage share of profits; bonus royalty *(of authors etc.)*; fee *(for directors etc.)*
~, **nichtproduktionsgebundene** non-production bonus, gratuity not related to production
~, **produktionsgebundene** production-related gratuity, production bonus
Tantiemenabgabe *f s.* **Tantiemensteuer**
Tantiemenabrechnung *f* royalty statement
Tantiemensteuer *f* royalty tax
Tara *f* tare (weight) ◊ ~ **vergüten** to allow for tare
~, **durchschnittliche** average tare
~, **geschätzte** estimated tare
~, **übliche** customary tare
Taratarif *m* tara rates [tariff]
Tarazuschlag *m* addition to the net weight *(expressed as percentage of the net weight)*
tarieren to (state the) tare
Tarierung *f* taring
Tarif *m* rates; scale *(of wages)*; *(railw)* table of fares *(persons)*; *(cust)* tariff ◊ **laut ~** as per rate
~, **anzuwendender** applicable rate, rate applicable
~, **autonomer** *(cust)* single tariff
~, **besonderer** *(ins)* specific rate
~, **erhöhter** increased [advanced] rate
~, **ermäßigter** reduced rate; *(cust)* reduced tariff
~, **geltender** valid rate
~, **gemischter** *(cust)* mixed tariff
~, **gesetzlicher** legal rate
~, **gestaffelter** *(cust)* graduated tariff
~, **gleitender** sliding wage rate
Tarifabbau *m* cut in rates; *(cust)* tariff reduction
Tarifabkommen *n* (com) trade agreement; wage [industrial, *(Am)* collective] agreement; *(cust)* tariff agreement

Tarifabschluß *m* wage [industrial, *(Am)* collective] agreement
Tarifänderung *f* changes in rates *(fares, postage etc.)*
Tarifautonomie *f* free collective bargaining
Tarifbahnhof *m (railw)* goods loading station
Tarifbeitrag *m (ins)* premium
Tarifbestimmungen *fpl* tariff conditions [regulations]
Tarifbildungsweg *m (transp)* chargeable route *(route on which charges are based)*
Tarifbindung *f* obligation to pay according to a fixed rate
Tarifentfernung *f (transp)* chargeable distance, distance charged
Tariferhöhung *f* increase in rates
Tarifermäßigung *f* tariff [rate] reduction [concession]
Tariffaktoren *mpl* rating factors
Tarifformen *fpl* kinds of rates; *(cust)* kinds of tariffs
Tariffragen *fpl* wage matters; *(cust)* tariff issues
Tarifgefüge *n* rate system
Tarifgesetzgebung *f (cust)* tariff legislation
Tarifgrenze *f* fare zone
Tarifgrundlohn *m* standard basic wage(s)
Tarifgruppe *f* wage class; salary group
tarifieren to classify *(wages etc.)*; *(cust)* to rate tariffs
Tarifierung *f* classification *(wages etc.)*; *(cust)* rating of tariffs
Tarifierungsordnung *f (cust)* tariff-setting rules; rules for rate-fixing *(wages)*
Tarifierungsvorschriften *fpl (cust)* rules and regulations for tariff-setting; rules and regulations for fixing wage rates
Tarifkampf *m* wage dispute; *(cust)* tariff dispute
Tarifkilometer *m* standard kilometre
Tarifklasse *f s.* **Tarifgruppe**
Tarifklausel *f* wage clause
Tarifkommission *f* wage negotiating committee; *(cust)* tariff commission
Tarifkoordinierung *f* co-ordination of tariffs; co-ordination of wage scales
Tarifkürzung *f* wage reduction, cut in rates
Tariflohn *m* standard [basic] wage(s)
Tariflohnsatz *m* standard wage rate
tarifmäßig according to tariff
Tarifniveau *n* tariff level
Tarifordnung *f* 1. guidelines for wage negotiations; 2. wage structure
Tarifpartner *m* negotiation party to a wage agreement
Tarifpolitik *f* wage policy; rate policy; *(cust)* tariff policy
Tarifprogression *f* differentials in wage rates; differentials in customs duties

Tarifrunde *f* round of wage negotiations
Tarifsatz *m* tariff rate; rate of scale *(wages)*
Tarifschema *n (cust)* list of tariffs
Tarifsenkung *f s.* **Tarifkürzung**
Tarifspanne *f* range of wage rates; range of salaries
Tarifstaffelung *f* graduation of wage rates; graduation of customs duties
Tarifstreitigkeiten *fpl s.* **Tarifkampf**
Tarifsystem *n* system of wage rates; system of rates *(fares, postage etc.)*; *(cust)* system of tariffs
Tariftabelle *f* list of wage rates; *(cust)* list of tariffs
Tariftonne *f* weight in tons chargeable
Tariftonnenkilometer *m* transport rate per ton times kilometres
Tarifunterschied *m* wage differential
Tarifunterschiede *mpl* wage differentials
~, örtlich bedingte regional wage differentials
Tarifurlaub *m* paid leave
Tarifvereinbarung *f s.* **Tarifvertrag**
Tarifverhandlungen *fpl* wage negotiations ◊ **~ führen** to conduct wage negotiations
Tarifvertrag *m* agreed wage rate, wage rate contract, wage [industrial, *(Am)* collective] agreement; *(cust)* tariff agreement
Tarifvertragsbestimmungen *fpl* provisions of the wage agreement
Tarifvorschriften *fpl (cust)* tariff regulations
Tarifvorteil *m (cust)* tariff advantages
Tarifwert *m (cust)* dutiable value *(of goods)*
Tarifwesen *n* rates and tariffs
Tarifzoll *m (cust)* tariff duty ·
Tarifzone *f* area covered by a rate *(transport, telephone etc.)*
Tarifzugeständnisse *npl (cust)* tariff concessions
Tasche *f* pocket; pouch, bag; handbag ◊ **aus eigener ~** out of one's own pocket; **jmdn. aus eigener ~ bezahlen** to pay s.o. from one's own pocket
Taschenausgabe *f* pocketbook, pocket edition
Taschenbuch *n s.* **Taschenausgabe**
~, statistisches statistical pocketbook
Taschenformat *n* pocket size
Taschengeld *n* pocket money, allowance
~, wöchentliches weekly allowance
Tat *f* deed; act; action; achievement, feat ◊ **auf frischer ~ ergriffen werden** to be caught red-handed; **die ~ leugnen** to deny the charge; **in die ~ umsetzen** to put into practice
Tatbericht *m* charge report
Tatbestand *m* fact(s), factual findings; state of affairs ◊ **einen strafbaren ~ erfüllen** to constitute an offence
~, objektiver actual facts

Tatbestandsaufnahme *f* factual statement
Tatbestandsmerkmal *n* characteristic feature
Täter *m* perpetrator; culprit
~, unbekannter some unknown person
Täterschaft *f (jur)* guilt; perpetration of crime
Tatfrage *f* matter [issue, question] of fact
tätig busy, active ◊ **ehrenamtlich ~ sein** to work in an honorary capacity; **freiberuflich ~** working on a freelance basis; **für jmdn. ~ sein** to work for s.o.; **nicht mehr geschäftlich ~ sein** to be no longer in business; **~ sein** to work; to act for *(s.o.)*
tätigen to carry out *(s.th.)*; to effect, to execute *(sales etc.)*, to transact *(business)*
Tätiger *m*:
~, freiberuflich freelance
~, hauptamtlich employee in main occupation
~, schöpferisch creative person
~, wissenschaftlich scientific worker
Tätigkeit *f* activity; action; work, job, occupation; profession ◊ **eine ~ ausüben** to do one's work [duties]; to practice a profession; **eine ~ wieder aufnehmen** to resume an activity; **keine bestimmte ~ ausüben** to have no regular work [job]; **seine ~ beenden** to give up one's work, to relinquish one's position; **~ entfalten** to be active
~, auswärtige outside work; field work; activities abroad
~, beratende advisory activity
~, berufliche professional employment; vocation
~, bisherige previous employment [job, work]
~, dienstliche official duties
~, ehrenamtliche honorary work [position]
~, geistige intellectual work
~, geschäftliche business (activity)
~, gesellschaftlich nützliche socially useful activity [work]
~, gesellschaftliche social activity
~, gewerbliche (private) commercial activity *(tradesmen, craftsmen, shopkeepers etc.)*
~, gewerkschaftliche trade union activity
~, industrielle industrial work
~, intellektuelle intellectual activity
~, kaufmännische commercial work; clerical work
~, leitende executive position [capacity]
~, mechanische routine work
~, praktische practical work
~, produktive productive activity
~, schöpferische creative activity [work]
~, treuhänderische fiduciary activity
~, ununterbrochene period of employment without a break
~, wirtschaftliche economic activity
~, wissenschaftliche scientific work
~, verstärkte increased activity

Tätigkeitsbereich *m* sphere of activity [work]; field of work; scope of activity
Tätigkeitsbericht *m* progress report; business report
Tätigkeitsbeschreibung *f* description of vocation [trade]
Tätigkeitsdauer *f* period of employment
Tätigkeitsfeld *n* sphere of activity [work]; field of work; scope of activity ⋄ **sein ~ ausdehnen** to extend the scope of one's activities
Tätigkeitsgebiet *n* field of activity
Tätigkeitskreis *m s.* Tätigkeitsbereich
Tätigkeitsmerkmal *n* job characteristic, characteristics of a job
Tätigkeitssphäre *f s.* Tätigkeitsbereich
Tätigkeitsvergütung *f* remuneration for a job
Tätigkeitszeit *f* period of employment
Tatsache *f* (matter of) fact
~, **feststehende** matter of fact
~, **vollendete** accomplished fact, fait accompli
Tatsachen *fpl*: ⋄ **auf ~ beruhen** to be founded on facts; **falsche ~ vorspiegeln** to make false pretences; **sich auf den Boden der ~ stellen** to face the facts; **~ bestätigen** *(jur)* to testify to a fact; **~ verkennen** to misapprehend the facts
~, **aktenmäßig feststehende** matter of record
~, **beweiserhebliche** facts used as evidence
~, **festgestellte** facts established
~, **grundlegende** basic facts
~, **klagebegründende** *(jur)* facts constituting the cause of action
~, **neue klagebegründende** *(jur)* new cause of action
~, **unwesentliche** *(jur)* immaterial facts; unessential facts
~, **urkundlich nachweisbare** *(jur)* matter in deed
~, **vorgebrachte** *(jur)* material allegations
~, **wesentliche** *(jur)* material facts; essential facts
tatsächlich real, actual; factual, based on facts
~ und rechtlich *(jur)* in fact and in law
Tatumstände *mpl (jur)* facts of the case
taugen to be fit for, to be suitable for *(work etc.)*
tauglich fit, able; serviceable; sea-worthy *(ship)*
Tauglichkeit *f* fitness, suitability *(for a job etc.)*; validity
Tauglichkeitsprüfung *f* test of fitness [suitability] *(for a job etc.)*
Tauglichkeitszeugnis *n* qualifying certificate
Tausch *m* exchange; swap; barter, trading, *(Am)* truck ⋄ **einen ~ vornehmen** to make an exchange; **im ~ weggeben** to barter away; **in ~ geben** to give in exchange; **in ~ nehmen** to take in exchange; to trade in
Tauschabkommen *n s.* Tauschvertrag

Tauschakt *m* exchange, interchange
Tauschartikel *m s.* Tauschgegenstand
Tauschbefugnis *f* authority to barter; authority to change *(money)*
Tauschberechtigung *f s.* Tauschbefugnis
Tauschbeziehungen *fpl* exchange relations [relationships]
Tauscheinheit *f* barter unit
tauschen to exchange *(marks for yen etc.)*; to change *(money etc.)*; to barter; to swap *(flats etc.)*
Tauschform *f* form of exchange; form of barter
Tauschgegenstand *m* barter goods
Tauschgemeinschaft *f* barter community
Tauschgeschäft *n* exchange (transaction); barter (transaction); *(st.ex.)* swap
Tauschhandel *m* barter trade
Tauschkredit *m* barter credit
Tauschmittel *npl* means of exchange
Tauschobjekt *n s.* Tauschgegenstand
Tauschprodukt *n s.* Tauschgegenstand
Tauschrelation *f* rate of exchange
Täuschung *f* deception, deceit; fraud
Tauschverhältnis *n s.* Tauschrelation
Tauschverkehr *m* currency exchange and barter transactions
Tauschvertrag *m* barter contract [agreement]
tauschweise in [as] exchange; as barter
Tauschwert *m* exchange value; exchangeable value
Tauschwirtschaft *f* barter economy
Tauschzentrale *f* barter shop
Taxation *f s.* Taxierung
Taxationsgebühr *f* valuer's fees, appraiser's fees
Taxator *m* valuer, appraiser *(second-hand cars etc.)*
Taxe *f* 1. valuation, appraisal; estimate; *(tax)* assessment; 2. levy; charge, fee; rate, tariff; 3. taxi ⋄ **nach der ~** after valuation [*(Am)* appraisal]; **~ aufstellen** to draw up a valuation; *(ins)* to make an appraisal; **unter der ~ verkaufen** to sell below the valuer's price
~ über den Wert overvaluation
~ unter dem Wert undervaluation
taxieren to assess, to rate, to value *(real estate, car etc.)*; *(ins)* to appraise *(damages)* ⋄ **zu hoch ~** to overvalue; **zu niedrig ~** to undervalue
Taxieren *n* assessment, valuation *(real estate, car etc.)*; *(ins)* appraisal *(damages)*
taxiert:
⋄ **~ auf** valued at
Taxierung *f* evaluation, assessment *(property)*
Taxifahrer *m* cab [taxi] driver
Taxpreis *m* assessed [estimated] price ⋄ **zu einem ~ von** at an assessed price of
Taxwert *m* estimated [*(Am)* appraised] value
Teamwork *n* teamwork

Technik *f* 1. engineering *(1. as a specific science like refrigeration engineering etc.; 2. as a specific branch of production like refrigeration engineering etc.)*; technology; 2. technique *(like the right choice of technique)*; method, process *(like contact process, tower method etc.)*
Techniker *m* technician
technisch technical; technological; engineering
◊ ~ **begründet** technologically based
technisch-ökonomisch technical and economic
technisch-organisatorisch technical and organizational
technisch-wirtschaftlich *s.* **technisch-ökonomisch**
technisieren to mechanize
Technisierung *f* mechanization
Technisierungsgrad *m* level of mechanization
~ **der Arbeit** level of mechanization of labour
Technisierungskennziffer *f* indicator of mechanization
Technisierungskoeffizient *m* coefficient of mechanization, mechanization coefficient
Technokrat *m* technocrat
Technokratie *f* technocracy
technokratisch technocratic
Technologe *m* technologist
Technologie *f* technology
~, **adaptierte** adapted technology
~, **allgemeine** general technology
~, **ausgereifte** fully developed [full-fledged] technology
~, **einfache** simple technology
~, **entmaterialisierte** disembodied technology
~, **fortgeschrittene** advanced technology
~, **geeignete** appropriate technology
~, **moderne** modern technology
~, **neue** new technology
~, **neueste** up-to-date technology
~, **spezielle** special technology
~, **veraltete** outdated [old] technology
~, **vergegenständlichte** embodied technology
~, **vergleichbare** comparable technology
~, **vergleichende** comparative technology
technologisch technological
Teil *m* 1. piece; portion, part; proportion, share *(income etc.)*; section, segment *(population etc.)*; 2. party *(to an agreement etc.)* ◊ **zum ~** in part, partly
~, **größter** major [greater] part
~, **überlebender** *(ins)* surviving party
~, **vertragschließender** contracting party
~, **wesentlicher** essential part
Teil *n* part, element, component *(machine etc.)*; piece
Teilabladung *f* partial unloading
Teillieferung *f* partial delivery
Teilabschnitt *m* section *(report etc.)*

Teilabtretung *f* partial conveyance *(property etc.)*; partial transfer *(debts etc.)*
Teilakkreditiv *n* letter of partial credit
Teilaktie *f* partial share [*(Am)* stock]
Teilakzept *n* partial acceptance
Teilannahme *f s.* **Teilakzept**
Teilarbeitslosigkeit *f* partial unemployment
Teilaufgabe *f* part of a task
Teilauflösung *f* partial dissolution *(company, reserves etc.)*
Teilausführung *f* partial execution *(order etc.)*
Teilautomation *f s.* **Teilautomatisierung**
teilautomatisiert partially automated
Teilautomatisierung *f* partial automation
teilbar divisible
Teilbarkeit *f* divisibility
Teilbefrachtung *f* partial loading *(lorries etc.)*, partial lading *(ships etc.)*
Teilbeschäftigter *m* part-time worker
Teilbeschäftigung *f* part-time employment
Teilbesitzer *m* part-owner
Teilbetrag *m* part of an amount; instalment
Teilbeträge *mpl*:
◊ **in Teilbeträgen** in denominations
Teilbilanz *f* part of a balance sheet
Teilcharter *m* partial charter-party
Teilchartervertrag *m s.* **Teilcharter**
Teile *mpl* pieces; portions, parts; proportions, shares *(income etc.)*; sections, segments *(population etc)* ◊ **zu gleichen Teilen** in equal parts
~, **beide** both sides [parties]
Teile *npl* parts, elements, components *(machine etc.)*; pieces
~, **auswechselbare** interchangeable parts
~, **bezogene** parts delivered; pieces delivered
Teilefertigung *f* production [manufacture] of components [parts]
~, **zentrale** centralized production of components
Teileigentum *n* part-ownership
Teilerfassung *f* partial coverage; *(stats)* partial census [inquiry, survey]
Teilerfolg *m* partial success
Teilergebnis *n* partial result
Teilerhebung *f (stats)* partial [incomplete] census [inquiry, survey]
Teilerlaß *m* partial exemption [remission] *(debts, penalty etc.)*
Teilersatz *m* partial replacement
Teilerzeugnis *n* component, part of a product
Teilfabrikat *n s.* **Teilerzeugnis**
Teilfertigung *f* partial production [manufacture]
Teilfestpreis *m* partially fixed price
Teilfinanzierungskredit *m* partial financing of loan *(for development project etc.)*
Teilforderung *f* partial claim

Teilfracht *f* partial freight; partial shipment
Teilgebiet *n* section, branch; field *(work etc.)*
Teilgültigkeitsklausel *f* separability clause
Teilhaber *m* joint proprietor; partner, associate ⋄ **als ~ aufgenommen werden** to be admitted as a partner, to join as a partner; **als ~ aufnehmen** to take in as a partner, to admit as a partner, to take *(s.o.)* into partnership; **als ~ ausscheiden** to leave [withdraw from] a partnership; **als ~ eintreten** to become a partner, to go into partnership with *(s.o.)*
~, älterer senior partner
~, abwickelnder liquidating partner
~, aktiver *s.* **~, tätiger**
~, beschränkt haftender limited partner
~, geschäftsführender managing partner
~, jüngerer junior partner
~, persönlich haftender responsible partner
~, stiller sleeping [*(Am)* silent] partner
~, tätiger active [working] partner
~, überlebender surviving partner
~, unbeschränkt haftender associated partner
~, verbleibender continuing partner
~, verstorbener deceased partner
~, zahlungsfähiger solvent partner
~, zahlungsunfähiger partner in default
Teilhaberschaft *f* partnership, co-partnership ⋄ **~ begründen** to organize a partnership
~, auf mündlicher Vereinbarung beruhende oral partnership
~, jederzeit kündbare partnership at will
~, stille sleeping [*(Am)* silent] partnership
Teilhaberspedition *f* participating carrier
Teilhaberverhältnisse *npl* partnership relations [relationship]
Teilhafter *m* partner with limited liability
Teilhaftung *f* limited liability
Teilindossament *n* partial endorsement
Teilinvalidenrente *f* partial disability pension
Teilinvalidität *f* partial disability [incapacity]
~, dauernde permanent partial disability [incapacity]
Teilinventur *f* partial stocktaking
Teilkalkulation *f* calculation of components
Teilkapazität *f* partial capacity *(maximum capacity of one of several production departments)*
Teilkaskoversicherung *f* partial comprehensive insurance
Teilkonvertibilität *f s.* **Teilkonvertierbarkeit**
teilkonvertierbar partially convertible
Teilkonvertierbarkeit *f* partial convertibility
Teilkorrelationskoeffizient *m* coefficient of part-correlation
Teilkostendeckung *f* partial coverage of cost(s)
Teilkrise *f* partial recession
Teilladung *f* partial load
Teilladungen *fpl*:

⋄ **in ~ zum Versand bringen** to dispatch goods in lots; to ship goods in lots
Teilleistung *f* part-performance
Teillieferung *f* part-delivery; instalment
teilmechanisiert partially mechanized
Teilmechanisierung *f* partial mechanization
Teilmonopol *n* partial monopoly
Teilmontage *f* 1. sub-assembly; 2. sub-assembling
Teilnahme *f* participation, co-operation; attendance *(at a meeting)* ⋄ **von der ~ ausgeschlossen** to be excluded from participation
Teilnahmebedingungen *fpl* terms [conditions] of participation
Teilnahmebescheinigung *f* certificate of participation *(fairs etc.)*
Teilnahmegebühren *fpl* fees, charges
Teilnahmekosten *pl s.* **Teilnahmegebühren**
teilnehmen to participate [take part] in
Teilnehmer *m* 1. participant, participator; 2. subscriber *(telephone)*
Teilnehmerbetrieb *m (d.pr.)* time-sharing environment
Teilnehmer-Fernschreibverkehr *m* subscribers' teleprinter [teletype] communication
Teilnehmerfirma *f* participating firm *(fairs etc.)*
Teilnehmergebühr *f* subscriber's charge *(telephone)*
Teilnehmerkreis *m* circle of participants *(fairs etc.)*
Teilnehmerland *n* participating country
Teilnehmerliste *f s.* **Teilnehmerverzeichnis**
Teilnehmerstaat *m s.* **Teilnehmerland**
Teilnehmerverzeichnis *n* list of participants *(conference etc.)*, attendance list *(meeting etc.)*; (telephone) directory
Teilnorm *f* partial norm
Teilobligation *f* partial obligation
Teiloperation *f* partial operation
~, manuelle partial manual operation
~, maschinelle partial mechanical operation
Teiloptimierung *f* partial optimization
Teiloptimierungsmodell *n* partial optimization model
Teilpacht *f* share tenancy
Teilpächter *m* subtenant; sharecropper
Teilpension *f* partial board
Teilpreis *m* part of the price
Teilprognose *f* partial forecast; partial forecasting
Teilprojekt *n* partial project
Teilprüfung *f (stats)* sampling inspection
Teilrationalisierung *f* partial rationalization
Teilraumverfrachtung *f* partial charter *(of a ship)*
Teilrente *f* partial pension
Teilreparatur *f* partial repairs

Teilrevision *f* partial audit
Teilrückzahlung *f* partial repayment
Teilschaden *m* partial damage
Teilschuldner *mpl* co-debtors
Teilschuldverschreibung *f* fractional bond
Teilselbstbedienung *f* partial self-service
Teilstück *n* 1. stretch *(of a road, railway etc.)*; 2. *(stats)* plot
Teiltaktstraße *f* partial transfer line
Teilverflechtungsbilanz *f* partial input-output table
Teilverflechtungsmodell *n* partial input-output model
Teilvorhaben *n s.* **Teilprojekt**
Teilwert *m* part of the value *(goods etc.)*
Teilwertabschreibung *f* component value depreciation
Teilzahlung *f* part-payment, payment by instalments
Teilzahlungsbetrag *m* instalment
Teilzahlungskauf *m* hire-purchase
Teilzahlungskredit *m* hire-purchase credit, instalment (sales) credit
Teilzahlungsverkauf *m* (sale on) hire-purchase
Telefon *n* telephone
Telefonanschluß *m* subscriber's telephone connection ⋄ **mit ~ connected** by telephone
~, gemeinsamer party line
Telefonbesitzer *m* (telephone) subscriber
Telefongebühren *fpl* telephone charges
Telefongespräch *n* telephone call, conversation by telephone ⋄ **ein ~ anmelden** to place a call; **ein ~ brieflich bestätigen** to confirm a telephone message by letter; **ein ~ entgegennehmen** to answer [take] a call
telegrafieren to telegraph, to send a telegram, to wire; to cable
telegrafisch telegraphic, by telegram, per wire; by cable
Telegramm *n* telegram, wire; cable ⋄ **ein ~ aufgeben** to send off a telegram: **ein ~ befördern** to dispatch a telegram
~, dringendes urgent telegram
~ mit bezahlter Antwort reply-paid telegram
~ mit bezahlter Rückantwort pre-paid telegram
Telegrammanschrift *f* telegraphic address
Tempo *n* rate, pace *(of development etc.)*; speed ⋄ **das ~ beschleunigen** to hasten [force] the pace; **in langsamem ~** at a slow rate; **in schnellem ~** at a great [good] speed
Tendenz *f* tendency, trend, inclination, propensity
~, abschwächende *s.* **~, fallende**
~, abwärts gerichtete *s.* **~, fallende**
~, anziehende *s.* **~, steigende**
~, aufwärts gerichtete *s.* **~, steigende**

~, ausgleichende *s.* **~, nivellierende**
~, einheitliche general tendency
~, fallende declining [downward] tendency, *(st.ex.)* bearish tendency
~, heutige present-day tendency
~, kurserholende *(st.ex.)* rallying tendency
~, langfristige long-term tendency [trend], tendency in the long run
~, nivellierende levelling-off tendency
~, preisabschwächende tendency towards falling prices
~, preissteigernde tendency towards increasing prices, upward surge of prices
~, protektionistische protectionist tendency, tendency towards protectionism
~, rückläufige *s.* **~, fallende**
~, saisonbedingte seasonal trend
~, sichere consistent tendency
~, sinkende *s.* **~, fallende**
~, steigende rising tendency, upward trend; *(st.ex.)* bullish tendency, buoyancy *(market etc.)*
~, vorherrschende prevailing tendency
~, zurückhaltende *(st.ex.)* tone of restraint
tendenziös tendentious, prejudiced, biased *(report etc.)*
Tendenzprognose *f* 1. trend forecast; 2. trend forecasting
Tendenzumkehr *f* reversal of trend
Tender *m* tender
tendieren to tend to, to incline to, to show a tendency
Terme-Fixe-Versicherung *f* life insurance
Termin *m* appointed time [day]; fixed date; fixed term; closing date, deadline; date of completion *(job)*; term, time-limit *(duration)*; *(jur)* date of trial, hearing ⋄ **auf ~ kaufen** *(st.ex.)* to purchase forward; **auf ~ verkaufen** *(st.ex.)* to sell forward [on future delivery]; **den ~ einhalten** to keep to the time-limit; **einen ~ anberaumen** to set a date; *(jur)* to fix a date for hearing; **einen ~ ansetzen** *s.* **~ anberaumen; einen ~ auferlegen** to give a final date, to fix a deadline; **einen ~ festsetzen** *s.* **~ anberaumen; einen ~ verlegen** to postpone an appointment; to postpone a hearing; **einen ~ versäumen** to fail to pay in time *(payment etc.)*; to fail to keep an appointment; *(jur)* to fail to appear in court; to (make a) default; **einen ~ zur mündlichen Verhandlung anberaumen** to assign a date for hearing in court
~, abgelaufener expired deadline
~, angemessener suitable date
~, äußerster final date, deadline *(for completing a job etc.)*
~, fester fixed date
~, frühester earliest date

~, **harter** very short deadline; tight programme
~, **kurzer** short deadline
~, **letzter** final date
~, **nächstfolgender** succeeding date
~, **spätester** latest (possible) date
Terminablauf *m* 1. time-schedule; programme; 2. expiry of deadline
Terminabschluß *m s.* **Termingeschäft**
Terminalentscheidung *f (stats)* terminal decision
Terminankaufskurs *m* forward rate of exchange
Terminarbeit *f* assignment with a deadline
Terminauftrag *m* forward order
Terminbestimmung *f s.* **Terminfestsetzung**
Terminbörse *f s.* **Terminmarkt**
Termindevisen *pl* forward currencies
Termindruck *m* pressure of time, under pressure
Termine *mpl*:
◊ **an feste ~ gebunden sein** to be tied to fixed dates
~, **laufende** present [current] engagements
Termineinhaltung *f* adhering [keeping] to the due date
Termineinlage *f (bank)* time-deposit
Terminfestlegung *f s.* **Terminfestsetzung**
Terminfestsetzung *f* fixing a date
Terminfixversicherung *f s.* **Terme-Fixe-Versicherung**
Termingelder *npl s.* **Termineinlage**
termingemäß according to schedule, in due time ◊ ~ **bezahlt** paid in due time, paid at maturity *(debts)*
termingerecht *s.* **termingemäß**
Termingeschäft *n* forward business [contract, operation, transaction, deal], *(Am)* trading in futures, future dealing contract
~, **bedingtes** conditional forward business
~, **festes** forward business on fixed terms
Terminhandel *m s.* **Termingeschäft**
terminieren to fix a deadline
Terminierung *f* fixing of deadlines
Terminkalender *m* (desk) diary, appointments calendar
Terminkäufer *m* forward [*(Am)* futures] buyer
Terminkontrolle *f* control of time-schedule
Terminkurse *mpl* forward [*(Am)* futures] rates
Terminlieferung *f* forward [*(Am)* future] delivery
Terminlieferungsauftrag *m* forward order, *(Am)* order for futures
Terminmarkt *m (st.ex.)* forward exchange market
terminmäßig *s.* **termingemäß**
Terminnot *f s.* **Termindruck**
Terminnotierung *f* forward quotations, *(Am)* quotations for futures
Terminpapiere *npl* securities dealt in for account [*(Am)* future delivery]

Terminplan *m* schedule, timetable
Terminplanung *f* time scheduling
Terminpreis *m* price for forward [*(Am)* future] delivery
Terminsätze *mpl* forward rates of exchange, *(Am)* rates of exchange for future delivery
Terminschluß *m* time bargain
Terminspekulation *f* speculation in forward dealings [*(Am)* futures]
Terminstellung *f s.* **Terminfestsetzung**
Terminüberschneidung *f* clashing of dates
Terminüberschreitung *f* expiry of deadline
Terminverkauf *m* forward selling, sale for forward [*(Am)* future] delivery
Terminverlängerung *f* extension of time *(for payment to complete a job etc.)*
Terminversäumnis *n* default, defaulting *(payment etc.)*, non-observance of deadline
Terminverstoß *m s.* **Terminüberschreitung**
Terminvertrag *m* forward [*(Am)* future] contract
Terminverzögerung *f* lagging behind schedule [deadline]
Terminvorverkauf *m* sale for future demand *(by wholesale trade to retailers)*
Terminwerte *mpl* forward securities, *(Am)* futures
Terminzahlung *f* payment on a fixed date
territorial regional; territorial
Territorialanalyse *f* regional analysis
Territorialebene *f* regional level
Territorialgewässer *npl* territorial waters
Territorialitätsprinzip *n s.* **Territorialprinzip**
Territorialkomplex *m* regional complex
Territorialmodell *n* regional model
Territorialorgan *n* regional organ [authorities]
Territorialplanung *f* regional planning
Territorialökonomie *f* regional economy [economics]
Territorialprinzip *n* regional principle
Territorialprognose *f* regional forecast
Territorialprogramm *n* regional programme
Territorialstruktur *f* regional structure
Territorialverband *m* regional union
Territorialwirtschaft *f s.* **Territorialökonomie**
Territorium *n* territory, region
Tertiawechsel *m (st.ex.)* third of exchange triplicate
Test *m* test, testing; trial
~, **als zulässig erklärter** *(stats)* admissible test
~, **approximativer** *(maths)* approximate test
~, **asymmetrischer** *(stats)* asymmetrical test
~ **auf Größe und Folge von Abweichungen** fitness [aptitude] test; *(stats)* smooth test
~ **auf Normalverteilung** *(stats)* test of normality
~ **auf Stabilität einer Häufigkeit** *(stats)* stability test

~, **Barnard's** *(stats)* C.S.M. test
~, **bedingter** *(stats)* conditional test
~, **Behrens-Fisher** *(stats)* Behrens-Fisher test
~, **bestmöglicher** *(stats)* optimum test
~, **Cochran'scher** *(stats)* Cochran's test
~, **einseitiger** *(stats)* one-sided [single-tail] test
~, **einstufiger** *(stats)* one-stage test
~, **gleichschwänziger** *(stats)* equal tails test
~, **invarianter** *(maths)* invariant test
~, **Kolmogoroff-Smirnoff'scher** *(stats)* Kolmogoroff-Smirnoff test
~, **kombinatorischer** *(stats)* combinatorial test
~, **konsistenter** *(stats)* consistent test
~, **medialer** *(stats)* medial test
~, **mehrstufiger** *(stats)* multi-stage test
~ **mit minimaximalem Schärfeverlust** *(stats)* most stringent test
~ **mit Nebenbedingung** *(stats)* conditional test
~, **nicht überall wirksamer** *(stats)* biased test
~, **orthogonaler** *(stats)* orthogonal test
~, **Pitman'scher** *(stats)* Pitman's test
~, **sequentieller** *(stats)* sequential test
~, **stärkster** *(stats)* most powerful [stringent] test
~, **statistischer** statistical test
~, **symmetrischer** *(stats)* symmetrical test
~, **symmetrisch-zweiseitiger** *(stats)* equal-tails test
~, **trennschärfster** *s.* ~, **stärkster**
~, **unabhängiger** independent test
~, **unzulässiger** *s.* ~, **nicht überall wirksamer**
~, **zweiseitiger** *(stats)* double-tailed [two-sided] test
Testament *n* will, testament ✧ **ein ~ anfechten** to oppose a will; **ein ~ aufheben** to revoke a will; **ein ~ aufsetzen** to make a will; **ein ~ eröffnen** to read out a will; **ein ~ errichten** *s.* **ein ~ aufsetzen**; **ein ~ für ungültig erklären** to set a will aside; **ein ~ machen** to make a testament; **ein ~ umstoßen** *s.* **ein ~ aufheben**; **ein ~ unterschlagen** to suppress a will; **ein ~ vollstrecken** to execute a will
~, **anfechtbares** flawed will
~, **bedingtes** conditional will
~, **eigenhändiges** holographic will [testament]
~, **formloses** informal will
~, **gefälschtes** forged will
~, **gegenseitiges** mutual will [testament]
~, **gemeinschaftliches** joint will
~, **gemeinschaftliches und gegenseitiges** joint and mutual will
~, **handschriftliches** *s.* ~, **eigenhändiges**
~, **jüngeres** later will
~, **schriftliches** written will
~, **ungültiges** invalid will
testamentarisch by will, testamentary ✧ ~ **verfügen** to dispose by will; ~ **vermachen** to bequeath, to devise by will

Testamentseröffnung *f* opening of a will
Testamentsvollstrecker *m* executor of a will
Testamentsvollstreckung *f* execution of a will
Testamentsvorlage *f* presentation [submission] of a will
Testbatterie *f* battery of tests
testen to test
Testhypothese *f* statistical hypothesis
Testmethode *f* experimental method; *(stats)* test method
Testniveau *n* *(stats)* size of a test
Testprogramm *n* test programme
Testtheorie *f* trial theory
Testversuch *m* trial
Testwert *m* *(stats)* test criterion
teuer dear, costly, expensive, high-price
Teuerung *f* dearness, high price, high cost of living
Teuerungsrate *f* rate of increase in prices
Teuerungswelle *f* general rise in prices
Teuerungszulage *f* dearness allowance
Text *m* text; wording
~, **erläuternder** explanatory comment
Textaufbereitungsprogramm *n* *(d.pr.)* text editor
Textbearbeitung *f* text editing
Textilarbeiter *m* textile worker
Textilchemie *f* textile processing
Textilien *pl* textiles
~ **und Bekleidung** *f s.* **Textilwaren und Bekleidung**
Textilindustrie *f* textile industry
Textilmaler *m* textile painter
Textilmaschinen *fpl* textile machinery
Textilmesse *f* textiles fair
Textilwaren *fpl* textiles
~ **und Bekleidung** *f* textiles and clothing
Textilzeichner *m* textile designer
Theorem *n* theorem
~, **Campbell'sches** *(stats)* Campbell's theorem
~, **Craig'sches** *(stats)* Craig's theorem
Theorie *f* theory
~ **der Abhängigkeit** dependence theory
~ **der Entscheidungen** decision theory
~ **der Produktionsfaktoren** theory of production factors
~ **der Spiele** game theory, theory of games
~ **des abnehmenden Bodenertrages** theory of diminishing returns in agriculture
thesaurieren to hoard
Thesaurierung *f* hoarding
Thesaurus *m* thesaurus, vocabulary
Tiefbauer *m* worker in road and underground construction
tiefgekühlt deep-freeze
Tiefstpreis *m* lowest [bottom] price
Tiefststand *m* lowest level *(rate of exchange etc.)*

Tier *n* animal
Tierarzt *m* veterinary surgeon
Tierbestand *m* livestock
Tierhaltung *f* animal husbandry
Tierproduktion *f* livestock farming
~, **industrielle** large-scale livestock farming
Tierschaden *m* damage [caused] by animals
Tierschadenhaftung *f* liability for damage [caused] by animals
Tierschadenverhütung *f* protection against [prevention of] damage by animals
Tierseuche *f* epidemic animal disease
Tierseuchenentschädigung *f (ins)* damage due to epidemic animal disease
Tierversicherung *f* livestock insurance
Tierzucht *f* animal breeding
Tiffanyglaser *m (approx.)* coloured glass-maker
tilgbar repayable, redeemable ⋄ **nicht** ~ irredeemable
Tilgbarkeit *f* redemption
tilgen to reverse, to cancel *(entry etc.)*; to repay, to pay off *(debt etc.)*; to delete, to erase *(misprint etc.)*
Tilgung *f* reversal, cancellation *(entry etc.)*; repayment, paying off *(debt etc.)*; deletion, erasing *(misprint etc.)*
~, **teilweise** partial repayment [settlement] *(of debt)*
~, **vorzeitige** repayment before maturity
Tilgungsabkommen *n* redemption agreement
Tilgungsanleihe *f* redemption [amortization] loan
Tilgungsbetrag *m* redemption money
Tilgungsdarleh(e)n *n s.* **Tilgungsanleihe**
Tilgungsdauer *f* period of repayment, redemption period
Tilgungsfonds *m* sinking [redemption] fund
Tilgungsfrist *f* repayment time; deadline for repayment
Tilgungshypothek *f* redemption mortgage
Tilgungsklausel *f* redemption clause
Tilgungsmodus *m* method [modus operandi] of payment
Tilgungsperiode *f* period of repayment
Tilgungsplan *m* repayment schedule
Tilgungsquote *f* debt instalment; redemption rate
Tilgungsrate *f* rate of repayment, redemption rate
Tilgungsreserve *f s.* **Tilgungsrücklage**
Tilgungsrücklage *f* sinking fund (reserve)
Tilgungsstock *m s.* **Tilgungsfonds**
Tilgungssumme *f s.* **Tilgungsbetrag**
Tilgungstermin *m* deadline for repayment
Tilgungsverpflichtung *f* commitment to repay debt
Tilgungswert *m* amount of redemption

Tilgungszahlung *f* redeption instalment
Tilgungszeit *f* repayment time
Tilgungszeitraum *m s.* **Tilgungsperiode**
Tischler *m* joiner, carpenter, cabinet-maker
Tischlerei *f* joiner's workshop, carpenter's shop
Titel *m* 1. title *(person, book, etc.)*; 2. *(jur)* title (to); title deed; 3. *(com)* securities
Titelkampf *m* competition for an award; finals
Titelliste *f* list of investment indicators
Titelschutz *m* title protection
Tochterbetrieb *m* subsidiary enterprise
Tochterfirma *f* subsidiary (firm)
Tochtergesellschaft *f* subsidiary company
Tochterunternehmen *n s.* **Tochtergesellschaft**
Tod *m* death
~ **durch Unfall** accidental death, death by (an) accident
~, **gewaltsamer** violent death
~, **natürlicher** natural death
~, **nicht natürlicher** unnatural death
Todeserklärung *f* declaration of death
Todesfall *m* death ⋄ **im** ~ in case of death
Todesfallversicherung *f* whole life insurance
~, **reine** whole life assurance
Todesnachweis *m* death certificate
Todesursache *f* cause of death
Toleranz *f* tolerance; remedy *(coins)*
Toleranzbereich *m* tolerance band, range of tolerance
Toleranzfaktor *m* tolerance factor
Toleranzgrenze *f (stats)* tolerance limit, margin of tolerance
~, **obere** upper tolerance limit
~, **untere** lower tolerance limit
Toleranzgrenzen *fpl:*
~, **parameterfreie** *(stats)* non-parametric tolerance limits
Toleranzlinie *f* tolerance curve
Toleranzverteilung *f (stats)* tolerance distribution
Tonnage *f* tonnage
~, **aufgelegte** idle shipping
~ **für Reisecharter** tonnage for passenger charter
~ **für Zeitcharter** time-charter tonnage
~, **seegängige** shipping capacity
~, **stillgelegte** *s.* ~, **aufgelegte**
Tonnageanforderung *f* demand for shipping capacity
Tonnagebedarf *m s.* **Tonnageanforderung**
Tonnagenachfrage *f s.* **Tonnageanforderung**
Tonnageverlust *m* loss of tonnage
Tonne *f* 1. cask, barrel, vat; 2. (metric) ton *(1000 kilograms or 2204.62 English pounds)*
Tonnenfracht *f* freight by the ton
Tonnenideologie *f* tonnage mentality, quantitative approach *(to production problems etc.)*

Tonnenkilometer *m/n* **(tkm)** ton kilometre *(basic unit of transport performance; tons times distance)*
tonnenweise by the ton
Tonnenzoll *m* tonnage duty
Töpfer *m* potter
Torf *m* peat
Torfboden *m* (agric) peat-soil
total total
Totalausverkauf *m* clearance sale
Totalerfassung *f s.* **Totalerhebung**
Totalerhebung *f* complete survey [census, inquiry]
Totalgewicht *n* total weight
Totalprognose *f* complete forecast
Totalschaden *m* total damage
Totalverlust *m* total loss
Totalwert *m* total value
Totgeburt *f* stillbirth, dead birth
Totgeburtenrate *f* stillbirth rate
Toto *n* football pools
Tour *f* tour, excursion, trip; route
Tourenplan *m* route plan
Tourismus *m* tourism
Tourist *m* tourist
Touristenkurs *m* (special) rate of exchange for tourists
Touristik *f* tourism
Trabantenstadt *f* satellite town
Tradition *f* tradition
Traditionalismus *m* traditionalism
Traditionspapier *n* document of title
tragen 1. to take, to carry *(load etc.)*; 2. to bear *(responsibility, interest etc.)*; to defray *(costs)*; 3. to yield, to produce *(fruit etc.)*
Trägerbetrieb *m* responsible enterprise
tragfähig 1. distinct *(majority etc.)*; 2. able to take a load [weight]
Tragfähigkeit *f* 1. carrying [load] capacity; load-limit *(bridge etc.)*; 2. tonnage *(ship)*
Trägheit *f* sluggishness, dullness *(market etc.)*
Tragkraft *f* tonnage, capacity *(ships)*
Trajektschiff *n* ferry, ferry-boat; train ferry
Trajektverkehr *m* ferry traffic
Traktoreinheit *f* tractor unit *(measurement)*
Traktorenbesatz *m* unit of tractors per hectare
Traktorenstunde *f* tractor hour *(measurement)*
Traktoristenbrigade *f* team of tractor drivers
Tramprate *f* tramp rate
Trampschiffahrt *f* tramp shipping
Tramptonnage *f* tramp tonnage
Tranche *f* tranche *(of a loan)*
~, fällige tranche due *(of a loan)*
Transaktion *f* transaction, operation
~ am offenen Markt open market credit transaction
~, banktechnische banking transaction

~, finanzielle financial transaction
~ gegen sofortige Kasse cash transaction
~, geschäftliche business transaction
~, illegale illegal transcation
~, legale legal transaction
~, unerlaubte *s.* **~, illegale**
Transfer *m* transfer
transferabel transferable
Transferabkommen *n* transfer agreement
transferfähig *s.* **transferabel**
Transfergarantie *f* transfer guarantee [warrant]
Transfergebühr *f* transfer charges
transferierbar *s.* **transferabel**
transferieren to transfer
Transferierung *f* transfer
Transferleistung *f* transfer
Transferproblem *n* transfer problem
Transferrisiko *n* transfer risks
Transferspesen *pl* transfer costs
Transformation *f* transformation
~ einer Zufallsveränderlichen *(stats)* variate transformation
~ von Zufallsvariablen, orthogonale *(stats)* orthogonal variate transformation
Transformationstheorien *fpl* transformation theories
Transit *m* transit
Transitabgabe *f s.* **Transitzoll**
Transitausfuhr *f s.* **Transitexport**
Transitbeförderung *f* transit transport(ation)
Transiteinfuhr *f s.* **Transitimport**
Transiterklärung *f* transit declaration
Transiterlaubnis *f* transit permission; transit permit
Transitexport *m* transit export; reexport
Transitfracht *f* transit freight
Transitgebühr *f* transit charges
Transitgeschäft *n* transit business [transactions]
Transitgut *n* transit goods
Transitgutbeförderung *f* transport(ation) of transit goods
Transithafen *m* port of transit
Transithandel *m* transit trade
Transitimport *m* transit import
Transitklausel *f* transit clause
Transitkonnossement *n* through bill of lading
Transitkosten *pl* transit costs
Transitlager *n* bonded warehouse, transit storehouse
Transitland *n* country of transit
transitorisch transitional, transitory; *(acc)* suspense *(account)*
Transitsendung *f* transit consignment
Transitspesen *pl s.* **Transitkosten**
Transittarif *m* rate of transit charges
~, einheitlicher (ETT) uniform rate of transit charges

Transitumschlag *m* turnover of transit goods
Transitverbot *n* ban on transit
Transitverkehr *m* transit [through] traffic
Transitversicherung *f* transit insurance
Transitvisum *n* transit visa
Transitwaren *fpl s.* **Transitgut**
Transitzoll *m* transit duty
Transport *m* transport(ation), conveyance ⋄ **auf dem ~** on the way, in transit
~, innerbetrieblicher intra-enterprise transport
~ per Bahn railway transport
~ per Flugzeug air transport
~ per Kraftfahrzeug road transport
~ per Schiff sea transport
~, schienengebundener *s.* **~ per Bahn**
~, zwischenbetrieblicher inter-enterprise transport(ation)
transportabel portable; transportable
Transportabteilung *f* transport department
Transportagentur *f* transport agency
Transportalgorithmus *m* transport algorithm
Transportanalyse *f* transport analysis
Transportanweisungen *fpl* forwarding instructions
Transportarbeiter *m* transport worker
Transportart *f* mode of transport
Transportaufkommen *n* total transport capacity
Transportauftrag *m* transport order
Transportaufwand *m* transport expenditure *(labour, time, money etc.)*
Transportaufwendungen *fpl s.* **Transportaufwand**
Transportausgaben *fpl* transport costs
Transportausgleichskasse *f* transport cost equalization office
Transportausrüstungen *fpl* transport equipment
Transportausschuß *m* transport commission [committee]
Transportbedarf *m* transport needs
Transportbedarfsanmeldung *f* application for transport capacity
Transportbedarfsermittlung *f* deriving demand for transport capacity
Transportbedingungen *fpl* transport conditions; terms of transport
Transportbehälter *m* container
Transportbescheinigung *f* transport certificate
Transportbetrieb *m* transport enterprise
Transportbilanz *f* transport balance sheet
Transportbrigade *f* transport work team
Transporteinheit *f* transport unit
Transportentfernung *f* transport distance
transportfähig transportable, ready [fit] for transport
Transportfähigkeit *f* capacity to transport
Transportfaktor *m* transport factor
transportfertig ready for transport
transportfest *s.* **transportfähig**
Transportflugzeug *n* transport plane
Transportfunktion *f* transport function
Transportgebühren *fpl* transport charges
Transportgefahr *f* transport risks
Transportgefährdung *f* endangering transport
Transportgelegenheit *f* transport facilities
Transportgemeinschaft *f* transport pool
Transportgenehmigung *f* transport authorization; transport permit
Transportgeschäft *n* transport business; transport firm
Transportgesellschaft *f* transport company
Transportgewerbe *n* transport business
Transporthaftung *f* carrier's liability
transportierbar *s.* **transportfähig**
transportieren to transport, to convey
Transportkapazität *f* transport capacity
Transportkaskoversicherung *f* transport insurance on hull
Transportkette *f* transport chain *(from production enterprise to retail shop)*
Transportkooperation *f* co-operation in transport
Transportkoordinierung *f* co-ordination in transport
Transportkosten *pl s.* **Transportausgaben**
Transportkostenklausel *f* cost clause in transport
Transportleistung *f* transport performance *(in terms of load or persons and distance)*
Transportleistungsbilanz *f* transport balance sheet
Transportleistungsvertrag *m* transport contract
Transportlinie *f* freight route
Transportmakler *m* forwarding agent; transport(ation) agency
Transportmenge *f* load transported *(commodities)*; passengers transported
Transportmittel *npl* means of transport
~, öffentliche public means of transport [conveyance]
Transportmittelabgabe *f* transport levy
Transportmittelversicherung *f* insurance of means of transport
Transportmöglichkeiten *fpl* transport facilities
Transportnorm *f* transport norm *(weight, passengers, distance and time)*
Transportobjekte *npl* passengers and goods transported
Transportökonomik *f* transport economics
Transportoptimierung *f* transport optimization
Transportorganisation *f* organization of transport; transport agency
Transportpapiere *npl* transport documents [papers]
Transportpark *m* fleet of (transport) vehicles

Transportplan *m* transport plan
Transportplanung *f* transport planning
Transportpreis *m s.* **Transportgebühren**
Transportpreisbildung *f* fixing of transport charges
Transportpreispolitik *f* policy in fixing transport charges
Transportpreisstellung *f* quotation of transport charges
Transportproblem *n* transport problem
Transportprodukt *n* transport (performance)
Transportprognose *f* forecast of transport
Transportprozeß *m* transport
Transportraum *m* carrying space; shipping space
Transportraumbilanz *f* balance sheet of transport space
Transportrisiko *n* passenger transport risks; goods transport risks
Transportschaden *m* damage in transit
Transportschadensforderung *f* loss and damage claim in transport
Transportschein *m* transport document
Transportschiff *n* transport ship
Transportschwierigkeiten *fpl* transport difficulties
Transportselbstkosten *pl* prime costs in transport
Transportsoll *n* plan tasks in transport
Transportspesen *pl s.* **Transportausgaben**
Transportstruktur *f* transport structure
Transportsystem *n* system of transport(ation)
~, **fließbandartiges** *(d.pr.)* inline type transfer system
Transporttarif *m* transport rates
Transport-, Umschlags- und Lagerprozesse (TUL-Prozesse) *mpl* transport, handling and storage
Transportunternehmen *n* transport business [company], carriers
Transportverlust *m* loss in transit
Transportversicherung *f* insurance against damage in transit
Transportvertrag *m* transport contract
Transportverzögerung *f* delay in transit; delay in transport *(goods etc.)*
Transportvolumen *n* total goods and passengers (to be) transported
Transportvorschriften *fpl* transport rules and regulations
Transportweg *m* transport route
Transportweite *f* distance
Transportwesen *n* transport(ation) (system)
Transportzweig *m* means of transport *(road, railway, water, and air)*
Trassat *m* drawee *(money, bill etc.)*
Trassant *m* drawer *(money, bill etc.)*

trassieren to draw *(money, bill etc.)*
Tratte *f* bill [letter] of exchange ⋄ **eine ~ akzeptieren** to accept a bill of exchange; **eine ~ ausstellen** to make out a draft; **eine ~ einlösen** to discharge a bill
Trattenavis *m/n* advice of draft
Travellerscheck *m* traveller's cheque [*(Am)* check]
Treffgenauigkeit *f (stats)* accuracy
Treibgut *n* flotsam and jetsam
Treibhaus *n* hot-house
Treibhauswirtschaft *f* hot-house horticulture
Trend *m* trend
~, **analytischer** *(stats)* analytic trend
~, **ansteigender** growing trend
~, **dominierender** dominant trend
~, **nicht linearer** *(stats)* curvilinear [non-linear] trend
~, **parabolischer** *(stats)* parabolic trend
~, **parametrischer** parametric trend
~, **polynomischer** *(stats)* polynomial trend
~, **säkularer** *(stats)* secular trend
~, **sinkender** declining trend
~, **vorherrschender** prevailing trend
Trendanalyse *f* trend analysis
Trendausschaltung *f* elimination of trends
Trendermittlung *f* finding out the trend
Trendextrapolation *f* extrapolation of trends
Trendfunktion *f (stats)* trend function
Trendgleichung *f* trend equation
Trendlinie *f* trend
Trendprognose *f* trend forecast
Trendprojektion *f* projection of a trend *(in a graph etc.)*
Trennanalyse *f (stats)* discriminatory analysis
Trennfunktion *f (stats)* discriminant function, discriminator
~, **lineare** *(stats)* linear discriminant function
Trennschärfe *f* **(eines Tests)** *(stats)* power
Trennschärfefunktion *f (stats)* power function
~, **bedingte** *(stats)* conditional power function
Trennungsentschädigung *f* separation allowance
Trennverfahren *n s.* **Trennanalyse**
Treppendiagramm *n* block diagram, histogram
Tresor *m* safe; strong-room
Tresorabteilung *f* safe-deposit department
Tresorfach *n* safe-deposit box
Tresormiete *f* safe-deposit charge
Treuegelder *npl s.* **Treueprämie**
Treueprämie *f* long-service bonus
Treuerabatt *m* discount for long-standing customers
Treueurlaub *m* long-service leave
Treuhand *f* trust
Treuhandbank *f* trust-bank
Treuhandeigentum *n* trust property

Treuhänder *m* trustee
treuhänderisch in trust
Treuhänderschaft *f* trusteeship
Treuhandgelder *npl* trust money
Treuhandgesellschaft *f* trust company
Treuhandgut *n* trust property
Treuhandverwaltung *f* 1. administration of trust property; 2. *(hist)* administration of trust territory
Triebkraft *f* motive force
Triebkräfte *fpl* motive [driving] forces
~, **gesellschaftliche** social motive forces, driving forces of society
~, **ökonomische** economic motive forces
~, **soziale** social motive forces
Trinkgeld *n* tip
Tripel *npl*:
~, **zirkulare** *(stats)* circular triads
Trockenboden *m* drying-loft
Trockenfracht *f* dry freight
Trockengewicht *n* net weight
Trockentonnage *f* dry freight [goods]
Trockenverlust *m* loss due to drying
Trockenzeit *f* 1. drought; dry season; 2. drying time *(goods etc.)*
Trödler *m* junk-dealer
tropenfest tropic-proof, withstanding tropical conditions
Tropenfestigkeit *f* tropic-proof quality
Troygewicht *n* troy weight
Trust *m* trust
T-Test *m* *(stats)* T-test
TUL-Prozesse *mpl s.* **Transport-, Umschlags- und Lagerprozesse**
Turnus *m* turn, rotation ◊ **im jährlichen** ~ every year, annually; **in regelmäßigem** ~ periodically; **in** ~ **zweijährigem** biennially, every two years
turnusmäßig on a rotating basis, alternating in rotation
t-Verteilung *f* *(stats)* t-distribution
~, **nicht zentrale** *(stats)* non-central t-distribution
T-Wert *m* *(stats)* T-score
Typ *m* type; kind
Typenausführung *f* standard type *(building, construction etc.)*
Typenbau *m* standardized construction
Typenbereinigung *f* product standardization *(reduction of models manufactured)*
Typenmodell *n* prototype model
Typenmuster *n* prototype
Typenprojekt *n* standard project
Typenreihe *f* standardized products *(of the same type)*, standard series
Typentechnologie *f* standard technology
typisieren to standardize
Typisierung *f* standardization
Typung *f s.* **Typisierung**

U

Überakkumulation *f* excess accumulation
überaltert obsolete *(machine etc.)*; out-of-date, out-dated *(model etc.)*; too old *(building etc.)*; overaged *(society etc.)*
Überalterung *f* obsolescence; over-aging *(of population)*
Überangebot *n* excessive supply, oversupply, surplus
Überarbeit *f* overtime
überarbeiten to revise *(text etc.)*; to rework, to reprocess *(used material for further use)*; **sich** ~ to overwork
Überarbeitung *f* 1. revision *(text etc.)*; reworking *(product etc.)*; 2. overwork
Überbau *m* superstructure
überbeanspruchen to make too many demands on *(people etc.)*; to overtax, to overstrain *(machine etc.)*; to overload *(means of transport etc.)*
Überbeanspruchung *f* making too many demands on *(people etc.)*; overtaxing, overstraining *(machine etc.)*; overloading *(means of transport etc.)*
überbelasten to put too great a strain on *(person etc.)*; to overtax *(telephone network etc.)*; to overload *(with goods etc.)*
Überbelastung *f* putting too great a strain on *(person etc.)*; stress; overtaxing *(telephone network etc.)*; overloading *(with goods etc.)*
überbelegt overcrowded
Überbeschäftigung *f* overemployment
Überbesiedlung *f* overpopulation
Überbestand *m* excess stock
Überbesteuerung *f* overtaxation
Überbestimmtheit *f* *(stats)* overidentification
überbetrieblich applicable to all enterprises concerned; higher echelon *(management etc.)*
Überbevölkerung *f* overpopulation, surplus population
~, **absolute** absolute overpopulation
~, **fließende** floating overpopulation
~, **fluktuierende** fluctuating overpopulation
~, **flüssige** *s.* **fließende**
~, **konstante** constant overpopulation
~, **latente** disguised [hidden] overpopulation
~, **relative** relative overpopulation
~, **stagnierende** *s.* ~, **stockende**
~, **stationäre** stationary overpopulation
~, **stockende** stagnant overpopulation
überbewerten to overvalue *(s.th.)*, to overestimate *(person's capacity etc.)*
Überbewertung *f* overvaluation *(of s.th.)*, overestimation *(person's capacity etc.)*
überbezahlen to overpay

Überbezahlung *f* overpay; overpayment
überbieten to outbid, to overbid; to surpass, to outdo ◊ **jmdn. ~** to bid against s.o., to outbid s.o.
Überbietender *m* outbidder
Überbleibsel *n* remainder, remnant; survival, relic, hangover *(custom etc.)*
Überblick *m* survey, overview, general view; summary, review ◊ **einen eindrucksvollen ~ vermitteln** to give an impressive picture *(of s.th.)*; **einen ~ geben** to present [provide] a survey, to give an idea *(of s.th.)*; **einen ~ gewinnen** to gain an overall impression [picture]
Überbordwerfen *n* jettison
überbringen to bring, to deliver, to hand over
Überbringer *m* bearer, conveyor ◊ **auf den ~** in bearer form
Überbringerklausel *f* bearer clause *(in a cheque)*
Überbringerscheck *m* bearer cheque [*(Am)* check]
Überbringung *f* delivery
überbrücken to bridge *(gap etc.)*; to reconcile *(differences etc.)*
Überbrückung *f* bridging *(gap etc.)*; reconciling *(differences etc.)*
Überbrückungsdarleh(e)n *n* stop-gap [stand-by] loan, interim credit
Überbrückungsfinanzierung *f* stop-gap [interim] financing
Überbrückungsgeld *n* stop-gap money
Überbrückungshilfe *f* stop-gap aid
Überbrückungskredit *m s.* **Überbrückungsdarleh(e)n**
Überdeckung *f* excess cover
überdurchschnittlich above average
übereignen to assign, to convey, to transfer *(s.th. to s.o.)*
Übereignung *f* assignment, conveyance, transfer ◊ **eine ~ vornehmen** to make a conveyance
~, bedingte conditional conveyance
~, fiduziarische trust receipt
~, unentgeltliche voluntary conveyance
übereinkommen to agree, to come to terms [an understanding]
Übereinkommen *n* agreement; understanding ◊ **ein ~ treffen** to come to an agreement, to enter into an arrangement; **laut ~** as agreed upon
~, stillschweigendes silent agreement
Übereinkunft *f s.* **Übereinkommen**
~, gegenseitige mutual understanding
übereinstimmen to concur, to agree *(with s.o. on s.th.)*, to share s.o.'s opinion; to correspond, to tally *(data etc.)*; to match *(colour etc.)*
Übereinstimmung *f* harmony; agreement; correspondence, coincidence, congruity; consistency ◊ **in ~ bringen** to harmonize; to make s.th. tally with s.th., to make s.th. agree *(accounts etc.)*; **in ~ mit** in agreement with; in accordance with
~, materielle und finanzielle physical and financial consistency
Übereinstimmungskoeffizient *m (stats)* coefficient of concordance
Überemission *f* overissue
übererfüllen to overfulfil *(production plan etc.)*; to exceed *(norm etc.)*
Übererfüllung *f* overfulfilment *(production plan etc.)*
überetatmäßig exceeding the budget
überfahren 1. to pass over, to cross, to ferry over *(channel etc.)*; 2. to run over *(person)*; to overrun *(signal)*
Überfahrt *f* passage; crossing; ferrying over ◊ **seine ~ abarbeiten** to work one's passage; **seine ~ bezahlen** to pay for one's passage
~, freie free passage
Überfahrtsgeld *n* passage (money)
überfällig overdue *(claim, bill, payment etc.)* ◊ **längst ~** long overdue
Überfinanzierung *f* excess financing
Überfischungsabkommen *n* agreement on overfishing
überfliegen 1. to fly over; 2. to glance over, to skim through *(report etc.)*
überfließen to overflow *(river bank etc.)*
Überflugrecht *n* right of overflight
Überfluß *m* abundance, overabundance, plenty *(food etc.)*; glut, overstock *(goods etc.)*; profusion *(ideas etc.)* ◊ **im ~ leben** to live in affluence; **~ an etwas haben** to have a surplus of s.th.
~ an Bevölkerung overpopulation, surplus population
~ an Kapital excess capital
~, reichlicher plentiful supply
überflüssig abundant, plentiful *(supply of s.th.)*; superfluous, unnecessary; redundant, excess *(workforce etc.)*; surplus, left over *(goods etc.)*
Überflußproduktion *f* surplus production; superfluous production
überfluten to inundate, to flood *(fields etc.)*
überfordern to overcharge; to overtax
Überforderung *f* overcharge; overstrain, overwork
Überfracht *f* excess freight; overweight, excess luggage *(air transport)*
überfremden to bring under foreign control
Überfremdung *f* foreign control, control by foreign capital
überführen 1. to convey, to transport *(goods)*; to transfer *(money etc.)*; 2. to convict *(person of a crime)*; 3. to convince *(s.o.)*

Überführung *f* conveyance, transport *(goods)*; transfer *(money etc.)*
~ **in die Praxis** putting into practice
~ **in die Produktion** transfer into production, application in production *(innovations etc.)*
~ **in Privathand** transfer into private hands
~ **von Forschungsergebnissen in die Produktion** transfer of research results into production, introduction of scientific findings in production
Überfülle *f* superabundance, glut
überfüllen to overfill
überfüllt overcrowded *(bus, tram)*, overfilled *(room, stock)*, glutted *(market)*
Überfüllung *f* complete filling to capacity; cramming *(coach etc.)*; glut *(on a market etc.)*
Übergabe *f* delivery, handing-over *(of s.th.)*; opening *(new housing estate etc.)*
~, **effektive** actual delivery [handing-over]
~, **fiktive** fictitious delivery
~, **schlüsselfertige** *(build)* handing over ready for occupancy [use] *(flat etc.)*
~, **symbolische** symbolic delivery [handing-over]
Übergabeakt *m* act of handing-over
Übergabebescheinigung *f* delivery receipt
Übergabeklausel *f* delivery clause
Übergabepflicht *f*:
~ **des Verkäufers** seller's obligation to hand over *(goods sold)*
Übergabeprotokoll *n* handing-over protocol
Übrgabetermin *m* date of delivery [handing-over]
Übergabeverrechnungspreis *m* clearing delivery price
Übergabeverweigerung *f* refusal to make delivery
Übergangsbahnhof *m* transit station
Übergangsbestände *mpl* temporary stocks
Übergangsbestimmungen *fpl* provisional regulations, temporary provisions
Übergangsgeld *n* stop-gap money
Übergangskonto *n* suspense account
Übergangslösung *f* interim [temporary] solution
Übergangsmaßnahme *f* interim [temporary] measure
Übergangsnorm *f* temporary norm
Übergangsperiode *f* transition period
Übergangsregelung *f* temporary arrangement
Übergangsrente *f* temporary pension
Übergangsstadium *n* transitional stage
Übergangsstufe *f* transition stage
Übergangstarif *m* provisional rate
Übergangswahrscheinlichkeit *f (stats)* transition probability
Übergangswirtschaft *f* economy in (the) transition (period)
Übergangszeit *f* transition period

übergeben to deliver (up), to give (up); to hand over, to present; *(jur)* to take (a matter) to court
Übergebot *n* higher bid
Übergepäck *n* excess luggage
Übergewicht *n* overweight, excess weight
Übergewinn *m* excess profit
Übergewinnsteuer *f* excess profit tax
übergreifen to encroach on, to infringe *(rights etc.)*; to overlap *(production relations etc.)*; to spread *(fire etc.)*
Übergröße *f* outsize
Überhang *m* surplus, excess
~ **an Aufträgen** backlog of orders
~ **an Investitionen** excess of investments
~ **auf dem Geldmarkt** glut of money
~ **der Aktiva** excess of assets
~ **der Ausgaben gegenüber den Einnahmen** excess of expenditure over revenues
~ **zirkulierenden Geldes** surplus [excessive supply of] money
überhitzen to overtax *(boom etc.)*, to overheat *(economy etc.)*
Überhitzung *f* overtaxing *(boom etc.)*, overheating
überhöhen to increase [raise] excessively *(prices etc.)*
Überhöhung *f* excessive increase *(in prices etc.)*
überholen 1. to overhaul *(machines, cars etc.)*; 2. to overtake *(s.o. in s.th.)*; to pass, to overtake *(car etc.)*
Überholung *f* 1. overhaul, reconditioning *(machine etc.)*; 2. passing, overtaking *(car etc.)*
~, **umfassende** general [major] overhaul
Überholungsarbeiten *fpl* restoration work
Überinvestition *f* over-investment
Überkapazität *f* surplus capacity, overcapacity
Überkapitalisierung *f* over-capitalization
überkapitalisiert over-capitalized
Über-Kreuz-Wiederholungsplan *m (stats)* changeover trial, cross-over [switch-back] design
überladen to overload *(lorries etc.)*; to overcharge
Überladung *f* overloading; overcharging, overcharge
Überlandtarif *m* haulage [*(Am)* truck rate]
Überlandtransport *m* long-distance (road) haulage
Überlandverkehr *m* long-distance (road) traffic
Überlappung *f (stats)* transvariation
überlassen to let *(flats etc.)*; to abandon, to relinquish *(right etc.)*; ⋄ **jmdm. etwas überlassen** to let s.o. have s.th.; to leave s.th. to s.o.
Überlassung *f* leaving *(s.th. to s.o.)*; letting *(flat etc.)*; abandonment, cession, relinquishment *(rights etc.)*
Überlassungsvertrag *m* transfer contract

Überlastbarkeit *f* overload capacity
überlasten to overburden *(with taxes, work etc.)*; to overcharge
überlastet overburdened *(work etc.)*; overcharged *(taxes etc.)*
Überlastung *f* overload *(work etc.)*, stress; overcharge
~ **des Energienetzes** overloading the main
überleben to survive
Überleben *n* survival
überlebend surviving
Überlebender *m* survivor
Überlebensfall *m* case of survival
Überlebensversicherung *f* survivor's insurance
Überlebenswahrscheinlichkeit *f* probability of survival
überlebt out-dated, obsolete ⋄ **sich ~ haben** to be antiquated
überlegen to think over, to reconsider ⋄ **~ sein** to be superior to
Überlegenheit *f* superiority
~, **zahlenmäßige** numerical superiority, superiority in numbers
Überlegung *f* consideration, reconsideration ⋄ **mit ~** deliberately; **nach gründlicher ~** after due consideration; **ohne ~** inconsiderately, blindly, on the spur of the moment
Überlegungen *fpl*:
⋄ **aus rein wirtschaftlichen ~** for economic reasons; **aus steuerlichen ~** for tax reasons
überleiten to transfer, to pass on *(research results etc.)*
Überleitung *f* transfer *(research results)*
~ **neuer Erzeugnisse in die Produktion** starting production of new products
Überleitungsauftrag *m* transfer order *(postal cheque operations)*
Überleitungsbestimmungen *fpl* provisional rules [regulations]
Überleitungsfrist *f* period of transfer *(research results into production etc.)*
Überleitungsphase *f* stage of transfer *(results of research into production)*
Überleitungsvertrag *m* (research) transfer agreement *(contract stipulating the application of innovations, new technologies etc. in production)*
überliefern to deliver, to hand over; to hand down to, to pass to *(survivors etc.)*
Überlieferung *f* tradition
Überliegegebühren *fpl s.* **Überliegegeld**
Überliegegeld *n* demurrage
Überliegetage *mpl* (days of) demurrage
Überliegezeit *f* demurrage (time)
Überlimitvorhaben *n* (investment) project requiring approval *(by higher echelons)*
Überliquidität *f* super-liquidity
Übermacht *f* superiority, supremacy

~, **wirtschaftliche** superior economic strength
Übermaß *n* excess ⋄ **im ~** to excess, excessively
übermäßig excessive, exorbitant *(prices etc.)*
übermitteln to convey *(news etc.)*; to transmit *(telephone call etc.)*
Übermittlung *f* conveyance *(news etc.)*; transmission *(telephone call etc.)*
~, **telegrafische** telegraphic transfer *(money etc.)*
Übermittlungsgebühr *f* transmission charge
übernachten to stay overnight, to put up at *(hotel etc.)*
Übernachtung *f* overnight accommodation
Übernachtungsgeld *n* lodging expenses, overnight accommodation costs
Übernachtungsmöglichkeiten *fpl* overnight accommodation facilities
Übernahme *f* taking over, take-over, acceptance; entering upon, succession to *(office etc.)*
~ **einer Arbeit** undertaking a job
~ **einer Hypothek** taking over (of) a mortgage
~ **eines Geschäftes** taking over a business [firm]; taking over a shop
~ **von Papieren gegen Bezahlung** taking over of documents against payment
Übernahmeabkommen *n* purchase and sale agreement; *(st.ex.)* underwriting contract
Übernahmebedingung *f* condition of acceptance
Übernahmebescheinigung *f* receipt
Übernahmebetrag *m (st.ex.)* subscription quota
Übernahmebilanz *f* balance sheet of assets and liabilities *(presented during takeover of an enterprise)*
Übernahmeklausel *f* acceptance clause
Übernahmekonnossement *n* acceptance bill of lading
Übernahmekonsortium *n* underwriting syndicate, underwriters
Übernahmekurs *m (st.ex.)* transfer price [rate]
Übernahmepreis *m* buying price *(goods etc.)*; takeover price *(firm etc.)*
Übernahmeprotokoll *n* statement of transfer *(firm etc.)*
Übernahmeschein *m* receipt
Übernahmetermin *m* date of takeover
Übernahmeverrechnungspreis *m* clearing purchase price
Übernahmeverweigerung *f* non-acceptance, rejection (of acceptance) *(goods, bill)*; refusal to accept *(delivery of letter etc.)*
Übernahmewert *m* purchase value *(second-hand goods etc.)*
übernational supranational, transnational
übernehmen to take over *(responsibility etc.)*; to undertake, to take on *(task etc.)*; to take possession of *(s.th.)*; to take over *(leadership etc.)*
überparteilich non-partisan

Überparteilichkeit *f* non-partisanship
Überplanbestand *m* stock above planned level
Überplangewinn *m* profit above planned level
überplanmäßig exceeding the plan
Überproduktion *f* over-production
~, konjunkturelle cyclical over-production
Überproduktionskrise *f* crisis of over-production
überprüfen to check; to inspect; to scrutinize; to test *(quality etc.)*; to audit *(account etc.)*; to screen *(person)*; to revise *(text etc.)*; to reconsider, to review, to examine *(case etc.)*
Überprüfung *f* checking, inspection; scrutiny, test *(quality etc.)*; auditing *(account etc.)*; screening *(person)*; revision *(text etc.)*; reconsideration, reviewing, examination *(case etc.)*
~ der Bestände overhauling of stock
~, laufende routine inspection
~, periodische periodic inspection
überrechnen *s*. überschlagen
überregional going beyond a region; supranational; nationwide
überreichen to present, to hand in, to submit
Überreichung *f* presentation, handing over
übersättigen to glut, to oversaturate *(market etc.)*
übersättigt glutted, oversaturated *(market etc.)* ⋄
~ sein von to be sated with *(luxuries etc.)*
Übersättigung *f* glut, oversaturation *(market etc.)*
überschätzen to overvalue; to overrate, to overestimate, to overassess *(taxes etc.)*
Überschätzung *f* overvaluation; overrating, overestimate, overassessment *(taxes etc.)*
überschaubar enabling a general view [track] of *(building work etc.)*; easily comprehensible
Überschlag *m* rough calculation, estimate to calculate roughly, to make an estimate *(costs etc.)*
Überschlagsrechnung *f* rough calculation, estimate to transfer *(debt etc.)*
Überschreibung *f* transfer *(debt etc.)*
~ auf ein Konto transfer to an account
überschreiten to exceed *(term of office etc.)*; to transgress, to overstep *(rights etc.)*; to infringe *(law)*
Überschreitung *f* exceeding *(term of office etc.)*; overstepping, transgression *(rights etc.)*; infringement *(law)*
~ des Liefertermins passing [having passed] the delivery deadline
~ des Zahlungstermins having passed the deadline for payment
~ von Vollmachten exceeding one's authority; *(jur)* ultra vires
überschulden to pile on debts
überschuldet deeply in debt, heavily encumbered *(real estate)*
Überschuldung *f* excessive indebtedness; excessive amount of debts

Überschuß *m* surplus, excess; balance ⋄ ~ abwerfen to make a profit [surplus]; ~ überweisen to transfer [remit] the balance
~, buchmäßiger book surplus
~, landwirtschaftlicher agricultural surplus; farm surplus
~, materieller *s*. ~, sachlicher
~, sachlicher physical surplus
~ von Kapital surplus of capital
~, wertmäßiger surplus in terms of value
Überschußangebot *n* excess supply
überschüssig surplus, excess
Überschußland *n* surplus country
überschwemmen to flood, to glut *(market with goods)*
Überschwemmung *f* flooding, glut *(market with goods)*
Überseebank *f* overseas bank
Überseebedarf *m* overseas demand, demand overseas
Überseegeschäft *n s*. Überseehandel
Überseehandel *m* overseas trade
überseeisch overseas, ocean
Überseekunde *m* overseas customer [buyer]
Überseemarkt *m* overseas market
Überseepreis *m* overseas price
Überseetransport *m* overseas shipment [transport]
Überseeverkehr *m* overseas traffic
Überseeverpackung *f* export packing, packing for ocean transport
übersenden to send, to forward, to convey, to consign; to remit *(money)*
Übersender *m* sender, forwarder, forwarding agent, consignor; remitter *(money)*
Übersendung *f* sending, forwarding, dispatch, conveyance, consignment; remittance *(money)*
Übersendungskosten *pl* transport charges
übersetzen 1. to translate; 2. *(d.pr.)* to compile; 3. to ferry across *(over a river etc.)*
Übersetzer *m* 1. translator; 2. *(d.pr.)* compiler
Übersetzerprogramm *n (d.pr.)* translating [compiling] program
Übersetzung *f* 1. translation; 2. ferrying across [over]
~, autorisierte authorized version
~, falsche mistranslation, wrong translation
~, freie free translation
~, ungenaue loose [inaccurate] translation
~, wortgetreue close translation
~, wörtliche literal translation
~, wortwörtliche word-for-word translation
Übersetzungsrechte *npl* translation rights
Übersicht *f* 1. view; 2. review; survey; summary, synopsis; 3. control ⋄ die ~ verlieren to lose control *(over s.th.)*; eine ~ bekommen to obtain a general view *(of s.th.)*

~, **komplexe** general view; comprehensive survey
~, **kurze** short summary *(report etc.)*
~, **statistische** survey, statistical statement
~, **tabellarische** table; schedule
übersiedeln to emigrate
Übersiedler *m* emigrant
Übersiedlung *f* emigration
überstaatlich supranational; multinational
übersteigern to outbid, to overbid; to force up *(prices etc.)*; to push too far *(demands etc.)*
Übersteigerung *f* outbidding; forcing up *(prices etc.)*; pushing too far *(demands etc.)*
übersteuern to overtax
Überstimmen *n* outvoting
~ **eines Antrages** defeat of a motion
überstimmen to outvote, to vote down (motion)
Überstimmung *f s.* **Überstimmen**
Überstunde *f* overtime ◊ **eine ~** one hour of overtime
Überstunden *fpl* overtime ◊ **~ machen** to work overtime, to do overtime work
Überstundenarbeit *f* overtime (work)
Überstundenbezahlung *f* payment for overtime; overtime pay
Überstundenzulage *f s.* **Überstundenzuschlag**
Überstundenzuschlag *m* overtime rate
übertage *(min)* on the surface
Übertagearbeiter *m (min)* surface man [worker, miner]
Übertara *f* excess of tare
übertariflich non-fixed rates *(payment etc.)*; excess charge *(service etc.)*; over and beyond the fixed rate *(of payment etc.)*
überteuern to overcharge; to inflate, to force up *(prices)*
Überteuerung *f* overcharge
Übertrag *m* amount [balance] brought [carried] forward, carry-over; transfer entry
übertragbar transferable, negotiable *(bill, cheque)*, alienable *(documents)* ◊ **nicht ~** non-transferable, non-negotiable *(cheque, bill of exchange etc.)*; inalienable *(personal documents, permits etc.)*
Übertragbarkeit *f* transferability *(of budgetary funds)*, negotiability, alienability
übertragen to transfer *(s.th. to s.o.)*; to assign *(rights, patents etc.)*; to delegate *(powers)*; to apply *(method etc.)*; to copy (out), to transcribe *(text etc.)*; to record *(s.th. on tape)*; to tape *(record)*; to broadcast, to transmit *(s.th.)*; to televise *(s.th.)*
Übertragung *f* transfer *(of s.th. to s.o.)*; assignment *(rights, patents etc.)*; delegation *(powers)*; conveyance *(real estate)*; application *(method etc.)*; copying (out), transcription *(text etc.)*; recording *(of s.th. on tape)*; taping *(record)*; broadcasting, transmission; television transmission ◊ **~ auf andere Tonträger verboten** recording forbidden in any form
~ **eines Grundstückes** conveyance of real estate
Übertragungsurkunde *f* deed of transfer; deed of conveyance *(rights over property etc.)*
Übertragungsvermerk *m* transfer entry; transfer note
Übertragungswagen *m* outside broadcast unit; outside television transmission unit
übertreffen to exceed, to overfulfil *(targets etc.)*
übertreten 1. to overstep, to transgress, to violate *(law etc.)*; 2. to go over to, to change *(party etc.)*
Übertretung *f* transgression, violation *(law etc.)*
Übertritt *m* going over *(to another party etc.)*
überversichern to overinsure
überversichert overinsured
Überversicherung *f* overinsurance
übervölkert overpopulated
Übervölkerung *f* overpopulation
übervorteilen to overcharge, to defraud; to make undue advantage of *(person)*
Übervorteilung *f* overcharge, taking undue advantage of *(person)*
überwachen to keep a watch on *(machine etc.)*; to supervise *(election etc.)*; to monitor *(events, traffic by radar etc.)*
Überwachung *f* keeping a watch on *(machine etc.)*; supervising, supervision *(election etc.)*; monitoring *(events, traffic by radar etc.)*
~, **gesundheitliche** medical care *(prophylactic measures etc.)*; hygiene control *(food preparation, kitchen etc.)*; sanitary inspection
~, **laufende** current inspection
~, **technische** technological supervision
Überwachungsdienst *m* watch; inspection; supervision; monitoring
Überwachungseinrichtung *f* security establishment *(in factories etc.)*
Überwachungsfunktion *f* control function
Überwachungs- und Wegezeit *f* patrol time *(in multiple machine work)*
überweisen to transfer, to remit *(money)*; to refer *(patient to a clinic etc.)*
Überweisung *f* transfer, remittance *(money)*; referral *(of a patient to a clinic etc.)*
~ **durch die Bank** transfer (of money) through the bank, bank transfer
~, **durch die Post** money-order, remittance
~, **telegrafische** telegraphic money-order
Überweisungsauftrag *m* money-order *(by post)*; transfer order *(by bank)*
Überweisungsformular *n* money transfer form
Überweisungsgebühr *f* (money) transfer charge
Überweisungsprovision *f* money transfer charge
Überweisungssammelauftrag *m (bank)* collective transfer order

Überweisungsscheck *m* draft
Überweisungsverfahren *n* money transfer
Überweisungsverkehr *m* money transfer transactions
überwinden to overcome, to surmount
Überwindung *f* overcoming, surmounting
~ der wirtschaftlichen Rückständigkeit overcoming economic backwardness
überzahlen to overpay
Überzahlung *f* overpayment; overpay
überzeichnen to oversubscribe *(shares etc.)*
überzeichnet oversubscribed *(shares etc.)*
Überzeichnung *f* oversubscription *(shares etc.)*
überziehen to overdraw, to make overdrafts
Überziehung *f* overdraft
~, des Lohnfonds exceeding the planned wage fund
~ eines Kontos overdrawing an account
Überziehungskredit *m* overdraft
Überziehungsmöglichkeit *f* overdraft facilities
Überziehungsprovision *f* interest of overdraft
überzogen overdrawn
Uferanlieger *m* riparian
Uferanliegerrechte *npl* riparian rights
Uhrenfabrik *f* watch factory
Uhrengeschäft *n* watchmaker's shop; dealing(s) in watches and clocks
Uhrenindustrie *f* clock and watch industry
Uhrenmechaniker *m* watch repairer
Uhrmacher *m* watchmaker
Ultimo *m* ultimo, last day of the month ❖ **bis ~ gültig** *(st.ex.)* good this month; **per ~** for the monthly settlement
Ultimoabrechnung *f* monthly settlement
Ultimoabschluß *m* monthly settlement; monthly balance sheet
Ultimofälligkeiten *fpl* monthly accruals
Ultimogeld *n* monthly loans
Ultimogeschäft *n* business done for the monthly clearance
Ultimopapiere *npl (st.ex.)* forward securities
umadressieren to readdress, to redirect *(letters etc.)*
Umadressieren *n* readdressing *(letters etc.)*
Umadressierung *f s.* **Umadressieren**
umarbeiten to redesign; to modify; to revise *(text etc.)*
Umarbeitung *f* redesigning; modification; revision *(text etc.)*
Umbau *m* reconstruction *(houses etc.)*; renovation *(flat etc.)*; reorganization *(administration etc.)*; conversion *(of a building to another purpose)*
umbauen to reconstruct *(houses etc.)*; to renovate *(flat etc.)*; to reorganize *(administration etc.)*; to convert *(a building to another purpose)*
umbewerten to revalue, to revaluate

Umbewerten *n s.* **Umbewertung**
Umbewertung *f* revaluation; re-evaluation
~ der Grundmittel re-evaluation of fixed assets
~ der Umlaufmittel re-evaluation of working funds [capital]
umbilden to reorganize *(s.th.)*; to reshuffle
umbuchen to transfer from one account to another
Umbuchung *f (acc)* transfer
umdisponieren 1. to change one's intention, to make new arrangements; 2. to redirect *(goods to another place)*
Umdisponieren *n* 1. changing one's intention, making new arrangements; 2. redirection *(goods from one place to another)*
Umfang *m* extent *(damage etc.)*; range, scope *(operations etc.)*; amount *(luggage etc.)*; area; dimension *(changes etc.)*; volume *(traffic etc.)*; size *(crowd etc.)*; *(maths)* circumference, circuit
~, mengenmäßiger quantity
~, wertmäßiger quantity in value terms
umfirmieren to rename a firm
Umfirmierung *f* renaming of a firm
umformen to reorganize *(company etc.)*; to remodel, to recast, to redesign; to transform
Umformung *f* reorganization *(company etc.)*; remodelling, recast, redesign; transformation
Umfrage *f* enquiry; *(stats)* poll, survey
Umgebung *f* surroundings, environs; environment
umgehen to circumvent, to by-pass *(law, difficulties etc.)*; to evade *(subject etc.)*; to avoid *(answering question etc.)*
umgehend immediately
Umgehung *f* circumvention, by-passing *(law, difficulties etc.)*; evasion *(subject etc.)*; avoidance *(of answering question etc.)*
umgestalten to alter, to reorganize; to transform *(society etc.)*; to recast, to redesign, to remodel
Umgestaltung *f* alteration, reorganization; transformation *(society etc.)*; recast, redesign, remodelling
umgruppieren to regroup
Umgruppierung *f* regrouping
Umkehrmatrix *f* inverse matrix
Umkehrprobe *f (stats)* test
~ bei Indexzahlen *(stats)* reversal test
~ für Indexbasen *(stats)* base reversal test
Umkehrpunkt *m* turning point
Umkehrung *f (stats)* inversion
Umladegebühren *fpl* reloading charges
Umladegut *n* transhipment cargo
Umladehafen *m* entrepôt, transhipment [reloading] port
Umladeklausel *f* transhipment clause
Umladekonnossement *n* transhipment bill of lading

Umladekosten *pl* reloading costs
Umladekran *m* cargo-handling crane
umladen to reload, to tranship
Umladung *f* reloading
Umladungsgebühren *fpl s.* **Umladegebühren**
Umladungskosten *pl s.* **Umladekosten**
Umlage *f* contribution *(to a fund etc.)*; apportionment [apportioning] of costs [charges, premium]; amount of shared costs [charges]; local rates ◊ **eine ~ erheben** to raise a contribution; to impose payment
Umlagebefreiung *f* derating
Umlagenerhebung *f* rating, rate assessment
umlagepflichtig rateable
Umlagepflichtiger *m* rate-payer
umlagern to restore
Umlagerung *f* restorage, restoring
Umlageverfahren *n* method of apportioning costs
Umland *n* surroundings
Umlauf *m* 1. circulation; 2. circular (letter) ◊ **aus dem ~ ziehen** to withdraw from circulation; **im ~** circulating, in circulation; **in ~ bringen** to bring into circulation; **in ~ sein** to be in circulation; **in ~ setzen** to put into circulation, to emit, to issue; to float *(securities etc.)*
umlaufen to circulate
umlaufend circulating; floating *(securities etc.)*
umlauffähig marketable, negotiable
Umlauffähigkeit *f* marketability, negiotability
Umlauffonds *m* working [circulating] capital
~ der nichtproduktiven Sphäre circulating capital in the non-productive sector
~, nichtproduktiver non-productive circulating capital
~, produktiver working capital
Umlauffondsbeanspruchung *f* utilization of working capital
Umlaufgeschwindigkeit *f* circulating rate *(of money)*
Umlaufkredit *m* revolving credit
Umlaufmittel *npl* working capital
~, betriebliche working capital of an enterprise, enterprise-owned working capital *(as opposed to borrowed capital)*
~, fremde borrowed working capital, credits
~, richtsatzplanfreie working capital not bound to the plan
Umlaufmittelabführung *f* transfer of working capital
Umlaufmittelaufwand *m* expenditure of working capital
Umlaufmittelausstattung *f* working capital; provision with working capital
Umlaufmittelbedarf *m* working capital required
Umlaufmittelbestand *m* stock of working capital; working capital in stock

~, materieller stock of physical working capital; physical working capital in stock
Umlaufmittelbestandteil *m* component of working capital
Umlaufmittelbewertung *f* evaluation of working capital
Umlaufmittelbilanzierung *f* balancing of working capital
Umlaufmittelbindung *f* tying up working capital *(to plans and purposes)*
Umlaufmitteldisposition *f* planning the use of working capital
Umlaufmitteleinsparung *f* economies in working capital
Umlaufmittelelement *n s.* **Umlaufmittelbestandteil**
Umlaufmittelerhöhung *f* increase in working capital
Umlaufmittelfinanzierung *f* financing of working capital
Umlaufmittelfonds *m* self-financed working capital
Umlaufmittelintensität *f* working capital intensity *(per unit of output)*
Umlaufmittelkredit *m* loan for financing working capital
Umlaufmittelnorm *f* standard stock of working capital
Umlaufmittelplan *m* plan of working capital
Umlaufmittelplanung *f* planning of working capital
Umlaufmittelrichtsatz *m* standard norm of working capital
Umlaufmittelzuführung *f* provision with working capital
Umlaufvermögen *n* circulating assets
Umlaufwert *m* circulating value *(shares, money etc.)*
Umlaufzeit *f* period of circulation
Umlaufzettel *m* circular
umlegen *(fin)* to rate, to assess; *(ins)* to contribute *(to an amount)*
Umlegung *f (fin)* rating, assessment; *(ins)* contribution *(to an amount)*
~ von Kosten apportionment of costs
Umlegungsbestimmung *f (ins)* contribution clause
umleiten to divert *(traffic)*, to redirect *(letters etc.)*
Umleitung *f* diversion *(traffic)*, redirection *(letters etc.)*
Ummarkierung *f* remarking; relabelling
ummünzen to recoin, to remint
umorganisieren to reorganize
Umorganisierung *f* reorganization
umpacken to repack, to pack up again
umprägen *s.* **ummünzen**
Umprägung *f* recoinage

umprofilieren to restructure *(production etc.)*; to retrain *(workers etc.)*
Umprofilierung *f* restructuring *(production etc.)*; retraining *(workers etc.)*
Umprogrammierung *f (d.pr.)* reprogramming
umqualifizieren to retrain *(workers etc.)*
Umqualifizierung *f* retraining *(of workers etc.)*
umrechnen to convert *(currency etc.)*
Umrechnung *f* conversion
Umrechnungsfaktor *m s.* **Umrechnungskoeffizient**
Umrechnungsformel *f* conversion formula
Umrechnungskoeffizient *m* conversion factor
Umrechnungskurs *m* rate of exchange, exchange rate; parity ⋄ **zum ~ von** at the parity of
~, amtlicher official rate of exchange
Umrechnungssatz *m* exchange rate
Umrechnungsschlüssel *m s.* **Umrechnungsformel**
Umrechnungstabelle *f* table of exchange, conversion table
Umrechnungstafel *f s.* **Umrechnungstabelle**
Umrechnungsverhältnis *n* exchange ratio
Umrechnungswert *m* exchange value
umrüsten to retool *(for new line of production)*; to reequip *(for arms production)*
Umrüstkosten *pl* cost of retooling; cost of reequipment
Umrüstung *f* retooling *(for new line of production)*; reequipment *(for arms production)*
Umrüstzeit *f* changeover time
Umsatz *m* turnover; sales; *(st.ex.)* transactions
~ auf den Außenmärkten foreign trade turnover, sales on foreign markets
~, bankmäßiger bank turnover
~, fakturierter invoiced sale
~, fingierter fictitious turnover [sales]
~, innerbetrieblicher intra-enterprise turnover
~, mengenmäßiger physical turnover, turnover in physical terms
~, steuerpflichtiger taxable turnover [sales]
~, wertmäßiger turnover in terms of value
Umsatzabgabe *f* turnover tax
Umsatzanalyse *f* analysis of sales
Umsatzausfall *m* losses in turnover
Umsatzbelebung *f* increasing turnover
Umsatzbesteuerung *f* taxation of turnover
Umsatzbeteiligung *f* commission; additional pay according to sales
Umsatzbetrag *m s.* **Umsatzgröße**
Umsatzbilanz *f* statement of sales
Umsatzbilanzen *fpl* turnover balance sheets
Umsatzbonus *m s.* **Umsatzprämie**
Umsätze *mpl* sales; transactions
Umsatzentwicklung *f* growth [change] in sales [turnover]

Umsatzerlös *m* gross profit on sales
Umsatzgröße *f* total amount of sales
Umsatzgrößenklasse *f* turnover group *(statistical classification of trade enterprises according to size of turnover)*
Umsatzhöhe *f s.* **Umsatzgröße**
umsatzintensiv with high volume of sales
Umsatzkapital *n* working capital
Umsatzkennzahl *f s.* **Umsatzkennziffer**
Umsatzkennziffer *f* turnover indicator
Umsatzkurve *f* sales curve
Umsatzpacht *f* lease according to sales, percentage lease
Umsatzplan *m* turnover plan
Umsatzplanerfüllung *f* implementation [fulfilment] of the turnover plan
Umsatzplanung *f* turnover planning
Umsatzprämie *f* sales bonus
Umsatzprinzip *n* principle of paying wages according to turnover
Umsatzprovision *f* turnover commission, commission on turnover
Umsatzrückgang *m* decrease [recession falling-off] in sales
Umsatzrückvergütung *f* dividend sharing *(in consumer co-operatives)*
Umsatzschwankungen *fpl* fluctuations in turnover
Umsatzsoll *n* (plan) target in turnover
Umsatzstatistik *f* statistics of sales
Umsatzsteigerung *f* increase in sales
Umsatzsteuer *f* turnover tax
Umsatzsteuererklärung *f* turnover tax return
umsatzsteuerfrei without turnover tax
Umsatzsteuerfreiheit *f* exemption from turnover tax
Umsatzsteuerrecht *n* law of turnover tax
Umsatzsteuerrückvergütung *f* turnover tax refund(ing)
Umsatzsteuersatz *m* turnover tax rate, rate of turnover tax
Umsatzsteuervergütung *f s.* **Umsatzsteuerrückvergütung**
Umsatzstruktur *f* sales structure, structure of sales
Umsatzsumme *f s.* **Umsatzgröße**
Umsatztantieme *f* bonus *(according to sales)*
Umsatzvermögen *n* circulating [current] assets
Umsatzvolumen *n* volume of sales
Umsatzzahlen *fpl* figures on sales, volume of sales
Umsatzziffern *fpl s.* **Umsatzzahlen**
umschichten 1. to regroup, to restructure *(social class)*; 2. to restack *(boxes, tins etc.)*
umschichtig in shifts, in turn
Umschichtung *f* 1. social regrouping [restructuring]; 2. restacking *(boxes, tins etc.)*

Umschlag *m* 1. turnover, circulation *(of capital, funds etc.)*; 2. reloading, transhipment; 3. envelope *(letter)*; cover *(book)*
~ **der Fonds** turnover of funds
~ **der Produktionsgrundfonds** turnover of fixed assets
~ **des Kapitals** capital turnover
~, **innerbetrieblicher** *s.* **Umsatz, innerbetrieblicher**
Umschlagbetrieb *m* reloading enterprise [firm]
Umschlagmittel *npl* reloading equipment
Umschlagplatz *m* place of transhipment [reshipment], reloading point
Umschlagsarbeiten *fpl* reloading
Umschlagsbestand *m* reserve stock for one turnover
Umschlagsfinanzierung *f* financing of turnover *(by loans)*
Umschlagsgeschwindigkeit *f* rate of turnover
Umschlagshafen *m* entrepôt (port), transhipment [reloading] port
Umschlagshäufigkeit *f* capital turnover ratio
Umschlagskapazität *f* capacity for handling cargoes
Umschlagskoeffizient *m* coefficient of turnover
Umschlagskosten *pl* reloading costs
Umschlagskreditierung *f* crediting according to turnover
Umschlagslager *n* warehouse
Umschlagsleistungen *fpl s.* **Umschlagsarbeiten**
Umschlagsnorm *f* standard rate of turnover
Umschlagsperiode *f* period of turnover, turnover period
Umschlagsphase *f* period [stage] of turnover *(comprising purchase, manufacturing and selling of goods)*
Umschlagsprozeß *m* process of turnover
Umschlagsvermögen *n* circulating [current] assets
Umschlagsvertrag *m* loading and reloading contract
Umschlagszahl *f* number of turnovers *(1. frequency of turnover of capital or funds; 2. number of turnovers of money in circulation)*
Umschlagszeit *f* period of turnover *(time needed by advanced capital or funds for going through the stages of manufacturing and circulation)*
Umschlagtarif *m* reloading rates
umschreiben to transcribe; to transfer *(shares etc.)*; to convey *(real estate)*
Umschreibung *f* transcription; transfer *(shares etc.)*; conveyance *(real estate)*
Umschreibungsgebühr *f* registration fee
umschulden to convert debts *(from short-term to long-term debts etc.)*; to (re)fund *(unfunded debts)*; to reschedule debts [debt repayment]
Umschuldung *f* conversion of debts *(from short--term to long-term debts etc.)*; funding *(unfunded debts)*; rescheduling debts
Umschuldungsabkommen *n* agreement on converting [rescheduling] debts
Umschuldungsbestimmungen *fpl* provisions on debt conversion [rescheduling]
Umschuldungsguthaben *n* balance of debt conversion
Umschuldungsklausel *f* debt conversion clause
Umschuldungsplan *m* debt rescheduling plan
Umschuldungssatz *m* rate of debt rescheduling
umschulen to retrain *(workers etc.)*; to move from one school to another, to (re)move [transfer] to another school
Umschulung *f* retraining *(workers etc.)*; moving from one school to another, removal [transfer] to another school
Umschwung *m* (drastic) change
~, **gesellschaftlicher** social changes
umsetzbar realizable; saleable, marketable
Umsetzbarkeit *f* realizability; saleability, marketability
umsetzen . to sell, to dispose of, to realize *(goods etc.)*; 2. to transfer *(manpower etc.)*; 3. to put into practice *(policy etc.)*
Umsetzprogramm *n (d.pr.)* conversion program
Umsetzung *f* 1. sale, disposal, realization *(goods etc.)*; 2. transfer *(manpower etc.)*; 3. putting into practice *(policy etc.)*
~ **von Grundmitteln** relocation of fixed assets
~ **von Haushaltsmitteln** reallocation of budgetary means
umsiedeln to resettle
Umsiedlung *f* resettlement
Umsiedlungsmaßnahmen *fpl* resettlement measures
Umsiedlungspolitik *f* resettlement policy
umsortieren to reassort, to rearrange
Umsortierung *f* reassortment, rearrangement
Umstand *m* circumstance
Umstände *mpl:*
 ⋄ **unvorhergesehener ~ halber** due to unforeseen circumstances
~, **beeinflußbare** circumstances that can be influenced
~, **unbeeinflußbare** circumstances beyond one's control
umstauen to restow
umstellen to put into a different place, to rearrange; to change position; to transpose; to invert; to convert *(currency etc.)*; to assume a different attitude; to adapt *(to new conditions)*; to switch over *(production etc.)*; **sich ~** to adapt o.s. *(to circumstances etc.)*
Umstellung *f* putting into a different place, rearrangement; changing of position; inversion; conversion *(currency etc.)* ; assumption of a

different attitude; adapting *(to new conditions)*; switching over *(production etc.)*
~ **auf neue Erzeugnisse** switching over to new products
~ **der Produktion** switching over to a new line of production
Umstellungskosten *pl* reorganization costs *(for changing production technology and organization of production)*
Umstellungsschwierigkeiten *fpl* difficulties in adapting o.s. *(to new conditions)*
umstrukturieren to restructure *(economy etc.)*
Umstrukturierung *f* restructuring *(economy etc.)*
Umsturz *m* overthrow; revolution
Umtausch *m* exchange; conversion
Umtauschanweisung *f* exchange order
umtauschbar convertible
Umtauschbarkeit *f* convertibility *(currency etc.)*
Umtauschbescheinigung *f* receipt of currency exchange
umtauschen to exchange; to convert *(commodities into commodities etc.)*; to change *(money)*; to exchange *(currency)*
Umtauschformular *n* exchange form
Umtauschkosten *pl* commission for changing money
Umtauschstelle *f* (currency) exchange (office)
Umtauschtransaktion *f* money exchange, exchange operations
Umtauschverhältnis *n* rate of exchange
umverteilen to redistribute
Umverteilung *f* redistribution
~ **von Haushaltsmitteln** redistribution [reallocation] of budgetary means
Umverteilungsfunktion *f* redistribution function
~ **der Staatsfinanzen** redistributing [redistribution, reallocation] function of state finance
Umverteilungsposten *m* item of reallocation [redistribution]
umwälzen to revolutionize
Umwälzung *f* revolution
~, **ökonomische** economic changes
umwandelbar convertible; *(jur)* commutable
Umwandelbarkeit *f* convertibility *(currency etc.)*
umwandeln to transform *(society etc.)*; to rearrange *(debt payments etc.)*; to convert *(securities etc.)*; *(jur)* to commute
Umwandlung *f* transformation *(society etc.)*; rearrangement *(debt payments etc.)*; conversion *(securities etc.)*; *(jur)* commutation
~ **von Schulden in Aktienkapital** conversion of debts into equity, debt-to-equity [debt--equity] swap
Umwandlungsprogramm *n (d.pr.)* assembler
umwechseln to change *(money)*; to exchange for *(s.th.)*; to convert *(securities)*

Umwelt *f* environment
~, **natürliche** nature
~, **soziale** social environment
umweltbedingt caused by the environment
Umweltbedingungen *fpl* environmental conditions
~, **gesellschaftliche** social environmental conditions
~, **natürliche** ecological conditions
umweltbelastend damaging ecologically
umweltbelastet polluted to a dangerous level for the environment
Umweltbelastung *f* ecological damage, damage to the environment
umweltbewußt (to be) aware of the environment [ecology]
Umweltbewußtsein *n* awareness of ecological issues
Umwelteinfluß *m* environmental influence
Umwelterhaltung *f* conservation of nature, environment preservation
Umwelterziehung *f* education in environmental problems [ecological issues]
Umweltfaktoren *mpl* environmental factors
~, **materielle** physical environmental factors
umweltfeindlich ecologically harmful [noxious]; polluting
Umweltforschung *f* environmental research
umweltfreundlich ecologically beneficial, environmental friendly [benign]; nonpolluting
umweltgeschädigt damaged by environmental pollution; ecologically damaged
Umweltgestaltung *f* creation of environmental conditions
Umweltkatastrophe *f* environmental [ecological] disaster
Umweltkontrolle *f* control of environmental conditions
Umweltkrankheiten *fpl* diseases caused by pollution
Umweltkrise *f* ecological crisis
Umweltplanung *f* ecological planning
Umweltpolitik *f* ecological policy
Umweltqualität *f* quality of the environment
Umweltsanierung *f s.* **Umweltverbesserungen**
umweltschädlich ecologically harmful, harmful to the environment
Umweltschutz *m* (nature) conservation, environmental protection, protection of the ecology
Umweltschützer *m* conservationist, environmentalist
Umweltschutzmaßnahmen *fpl* environmental protection measures; (nature) conservation measures
Umweltschutzprogramm *n* environmental protection programme, programme for the conservation of nature

Umweltsünder *m* pollutionist *(person)*; polluter *(factory etc.)*
Umweltverbesserungen *fpl* environmental improvements
Umweltverschmutzung *f* pollution of the environment
Umweltverseuchung *f* contamination of the environment
Umweltwirkungen *fpl* environmental effects
Umwertung *f* revaluation
Umzug *m* (flat/house) move [removal], moving to another flat [house]
Umzugsgeld *n* allowance for house-moving
Umzugsgutversicherung *f* moving insurance
Umzugskosten *pl* removal costs
Umzugsurlaub *m* additional leave for house--moving
unabänderlich unalterable *(situation etc.)*; irreversible, irrevocable *(decision etc.)*
unabdingbar inalienable *(rights etc.)*; indispensable *(condition etc.)*; final *(demand etc.)*
Unabdingbarkeit *f* inalienability *(rights etc.)*
unabhängig independent
Unabhängigkeit *f* independence
unabkömmlich indispensable, irreplaceable
unablösbar *s.* **uneinbringlich**
unablöslich *s.* **uneinbringlich**
unabsehbar immeasurable; incalculable, unbounded, immense; not to be foreseen
unabweisbar unavoidable *(claim etc.)*; pressing, imperative
unabweislich *s.* **unabweisbar**
unabwendbar inevitable *(claim etc.)*
unähnlich unlike, dissimilar
Unähnlichkeit *f (stats)* dissimilarity
Unähnlichkeitsindex *m (stats)* index of dissimilarity
unakzeptierbar *s.* **unannehmbar**
unakzeptiert unaccepted *(bill etc.)*
unanfechtbar unchallengeable, incontestible, indisputable *(claim, decision etc.)*; unassailable *(argument etc.)*; irrefutable *(proof etc.)*; unimpeachable *(person etc.)*; *(jur)* nonappealable
unangemeldet unadvised *(payment etc.)*; without previous notice *(meeting, arrival etc.)*; without previous appointment
unangemessen unsuitable, inappropriate; inadequate
Unangemessenheit *f* unsuitableness; incongruence
unangreifbar unassailable *(claim etc.)*, impregnable *(case etc.)*
unannehmbar unacceptable
unantastbar inviolable, unassailable *(right etc.)*
Unantastbarkeit *f* inviolability *(rights etc.)*
unauffindbar not to be found, untraceable *(person, papers etc.)*; undiscoverable

unaufgefordert without being asked; unsolicited *(contribution etc.)*
unaufgeklärt unexplained *(case etc.)*
unaufgeschlossen *s.* **unerschlossen**
unaufhebbar not to be cancelled
unauflösbar indissoluble *(contract etc.)*; insoluble *(problem etc.)*
Unauflösbarkeit *f* indissolubility *(contract etc.)*; insolubleness
unauflöslich *s.* **unauflösbar**
unaufschiebbar pressing, urgent, not to be postponed
unausführbar impracticable, not feasible *(project etc.)*
Unausführbarkeit *f* impracticability, unfeasibility *(project etc.)*
unausgebaut incomplete, unfinished *(flat etc.)*
unausgebildet untrained, unskilled *(worker etc.)*; undeveloped, under-developed *(abilities etc.)*
unausgefertigt blank *(form etc.)*
unausgeführt unexecuted *(order etc.)*; undone *(work)*
unausgefüllt *s.* **unausgefertigt**
unausgeglichen unbalanced *(budget etc.)*; unequal *(distribution of s.th.)*; unstable *(person)*
Unausgeglichenheit *f* maladjustment *(account etc.)*
unausgestattet without fittings *(flat etc.)*; unequipped *(workshop etc.)*
unbar non-cash
unbeanstandet unopposed; not objected to, without objections
unbeantwortet unanswered ◊ ~ **bleiben** to remain unanswered; to meet with no response *(call, appeal etc.)*
unbearbeitet unprocessed, not dealt with *(application etc.)*; *(ind)* crude, raw; unprocessed, unmachined; *(jur)* pending
unbeaufsichtigt unattended to, not looked after; uncontrolled
unbebaubar unsuitable for construction; *(agric)* uncultivable, unfit for cultivation
unbebaut vacant *(area)*; *(agric)* uncultivated
unbedenklich without hesitation; quite safe, completely harmless
Unbedenklichkeitsbescheinigung *f* clearance certificate *(person)*; import certificate
unbeeidigt unsworn
unbefahrbar impassable; unnavigable *(river etc.)*
unbefrachtet unloaded, empty
unbefristet unlimited; for an unlimited period
unbefugt unauthorized; without permission
unbegeben undisposed, unsold, still in hand *(securities etc.)*
unbeglaubigt unattested, uncertified
unbeglichen unsettled, unpaid *(bill etc.)*
unbegrenzt unlimited *(opportunities, loans etc.)*

unbegründet unfounded, ill-founded *(claims etc.)*
unbegütert not well-propertied; without means
unbehoben unclaimed *(dividend etc.)*
unbeladen empty, unloaded, unladen, without cargo
unbelastet 1. unmortgaged *(building etc.)*; unencumbered *(with debts etc.)*; not in financial straits *(person)*; non-incriminated; 2. *s.* **unbeladen**
unbelebt slack, dull *(market)*; sparse *(traffic etc.)*
Unbelebtheit *f* slackness, dullness *(market)*
unbemittelt *s.* **unbegütert**
Unbemitteltheit *f* lack of means
unbenutzt unused
unberechenbar incalculable, incomputable
Unberechenbarkeit *f* incalculability, incomputability
unberechnet free of charge
unberechtigt unauthorized, not entitled; unlawful; unjustified *(claim etc.)*
Unberechtigter *m* unauthorized person, person not entitled to *(s.th.)*
unberichtigt 1. uncorrected *(text etc.)*; 2. unpaid, unsettled *(bill etc.)*
unbeschädigt undamaged; in good condition; in mint condition *(coins etc.)*
unbeschäftigt unemployed; unoccupied, idle; not engaged
unbeschränkt unlimited, unrestricted *(credit etc.)* ◊ ~ **haften** to be liable without limitation
unbeschrieben blank
unbesetzt unoccupied, vacant *(flat etc.)*; not engaged *(telephone etc.)*
unbesoldet unpaid, in an honorary capacity, honorary *(work)*
unbeständig unsteady *(market)*; unstable *(situation etc.)*; fluctuating *(prices etc.)*
Unbeständigkeit *f* unsteadiness *(market etc.)*; instability *(situation etc.)*
unbestätigt unconfirmed *(letter of credit etc.)*
unbestechlich incorruptible, not open to bribery [bribes]
Unbestechlichkeit *f* incorruptibility
unbestellbar 1. cannot be delivered *(letter etc.)*; 2. cannot be ordered *(goods etc.)*; 3. *(agric)* uncultivable
unbestellt not ordered *(goods etc.)*
unbesteuert untaxed
Unbestimmtheitsmaß *n (stats)* coefficient of non-determination
unbestraft unpunished
unbeweglich rigid *(attitude etc.)*; immovable, real *(property)*
Unbeweglichkeit *f* rigidity *(attitude etc.)*; immobility *(manpower etc.)*
unbewegt unmoved; dormant *(account, capital etc.)*

unbewertet unvalued *(goods etc.)*; unassessed *(taxes etc.)*
unbewirtschaftet 1. not rationed *(food etc.)*; uncontrolled *(market etc.)*; 2. not run *(restaurant etc.)*; 3. *(agric)* not farmed; uncultivated
unbewohnbar uninhabitable *(area etc.)*; unfit for accomodation
unbewohnt unoccupied, vacant *(flat etc.)*; uninhabited *(area etc.)*
Unbewohntheit *f* vacancy *(flat etc.)*
unbezahlbar priceless, invaluable
unbezahlt unpaid, unsettled *(bill etc.)*, outstanding *(debts)*
unbrauchbar useless, unusable ◊ ~ **werden** to become unusable
Unbrauchbarkeit *f* uselessness
undatiert undated, without date *(cheques etc.)*
undekleriert *(cust)* undeclared *(goods etc.)*
undurchführbar impracticable, unfeasible
unecht fictitious, bogus *(business etc.)*; counterfeit *(money)*; artificial, fake *(gems etc.)*
unehelich illegitimate
Unehelichkeit *f* illegitimacy
unehrlich dishonest
Unehrlichkeit *f* dishonesty
Uneigennutz *m* unselfishness
uneigennützig unselfish, selfless, disinterested; nonprofit *(enterprise etc.)*
uneinbringlich irredeemable, unredeemable *(bonds etc.)*; bad *(debts)*
uneingelöst uncollected *(coupon etc.)*; unpaid *(bill etc.)*, unredeemed, dishonoured *(bill of exchange)*
uneingeschränkt unlimited, unrestricted *(power etc.)*; *(com)* unqualified *(acceptance etc.)*
uneinheitlich non-uniform *(prices etc.)*; *(st.ex.)* irregular *(rates)*
Uneinheitlichkeit *f* non-uniformity *(prices etc.)*; *(st.ex.)* irregularity *(rates)*
uneinlösbar inconvertible *(bank notes)*; (promise) which cannot be kept
uneinlöslich *s.* **uneinlösbar**
uneinträglich unprofitable *(deal etc.)*
uneintreibbar irrecoverable *(debts etc.)*
uneinziehbar uncollectable *(taxes etc.)*
unelastisch inelastic *(demand etc.)*
Unelastizität *f* inelasticity *(demand etc.)*
unentgeltlich free *(of charge)*, gratuitous
unentschädigt uncompensated
unerfüllbar unrealizable
unerhoben unraised, not raised *(taxes etc.)*
unerledigt unfinished, incomplete *(piece of job etc.)*; unsettled *(problem etc.)*
unermeßlich immeasurable; incalculable, unbounded, immense *(damage etc.)*; boundless, infinite, vast
unerschlossen undeveloped *(region etc.)*

Unfall

Unfall *m* accident ✧ **aus einem ~ herrühren** to result from an accident; **einen ~ verhüten** to prevent an accident; **einen ~ verschuldet haben** to have caused an accident, to be at fault in an accident; **einen ~ verursachen** to cause an accident; to bring about an accident; **~ ausgenommen** barring accidents; **~ eingeschlossen** accidents included
~, außerdienstlicher off-the-job accident
~, meldepflichtiger accident requiring reporting
~, mittelbarer *(ins)* accident to third party
~, nichtmeldepflichtiger accident not requiring reporting
~, tödlicher *(ins)* fatal accident
~, unvermeidbarer unavoidable accident
Unfallanalyse *f* reconstruction of an accident
unfallanfällig accident-prone
Unfallanzeige *f* notice of an accident
Unfallbegrenzung *f* limiting the damage caused in an accident
Unfallbericht *m* accident report
Unfallbeteiligter *m* person involved in an accident
Unfallentschädigung *f* compensation for accident, accident indemnity
Unfallfolgen *fpl* damage resulting from an accident
Unfallforschung *f* accident research, research on causes of accidents
unfallfrei accident-free
Unfallfürsorge *f* welfare for the victims of accidents
unfallgefährdet *s.* **unfallanfällig**
Unfallgründe *mpl* causes of an accident
Unfallhaftpflicht *f (ins)* employers' liability
Unfallhaftpflichtgesetz *n* employers' accident liability act
Unfallhaftpflichtversicherung *f* employers' liability insurance
Unfallhäufigkeit *f* frequency of accidents
Unfallhinterbliebenenrente *f* accident pension for (surviving) dependants
Unfallkrankengeld *n* sickness benefit in case of accident
Unfallort *m* place of accident
Unfallquelle *f* underlying cause of accident
Unfallquote *f* rate of accidents, accident rate
Unfallrente *f* accident pension
Unfallrisiko *n* risk(s) of accident
Unfallrückstellung *f* (money) reserve for accidents
Unfallschaden *m* damage due to an accident
Unfallschadensmeldung *f* reporting damage caused by an accident; report on damage caused by an accident
Unfallschuldiger *m* party at fault in an accident
Unfallschutz *m* protection against accidents

unfallsicher accident-proof
Unfallstation *f* first-aid post
Unfallstatistik *f* accident statistics
Unfalltod *m* death by accident
Unfallumlage *f* additional premium against accidents
Unfallunterstützung *f* accident relief
Unfalluntersuchung *f* accident investigation, investigation of accidents
Unfallursache *f* cause of accident
Unfallvergütung *f s.* **Unfallunterstützung**
Unfallverhütung *f* accident prevention
Unfallverhütungsmaßnahmen *fpl* measures to prevent accidents
Unfallversicherung *f* accident insurance
~, gewerbliche workmen's compensation insurance
~, landwirtschaftliche agricultural accident insurance
~, private private accident insurance
~, soziale national [social] accident insurance
Unfallversicherungsleistung *f* accident insurance payment
Unfallversicherungspolice *f* accident (insurance) policy
Unfallwahrscheinlichkeit *f* probability of accidents
Unfallzahl *f* number of accidents
Unfallzeit *f* time of accident
Unfallzusatzversicherung *f* supplementary accident insurance *(in addition to life insurance)*
unfertig unfinished
unfrankiert unstamped, (postage) unpaid
unfrei 1. unstamped, postage unpaid; 2. unfree, not free
Unfreier *m* serf *(under feudalism)*
unfundiert unfunded, floating, consolidated
ungangbar 1. impassable *(road etc.)*; 2. not current *(money etc.)*; 3. unsaleable
ungebildet uneducated
Ungebildete *pl* uneducated [unlettered] (people)
Ungebildeter *m* uneducated person
ungebunden free, untied *(financial resources etc.)*
ungedeckt uncovered, without cover *(cheques etc.)*
ungeeignet insuitable, unfit
ungefähr approximate, roughly
ungefährdet not endangered, safe
ungefragt not asked for, unasked, without being asked
ungeklärt *s.* **unaufgeklärt**
ungekündigt without having notice, not under notice
ungekürzt in full *(amount etc.)*; unabridged *(version etc.)*
ungelernt unskilled
ungemünzt uncoined

ungenannt unnamed, anonymous
ungenau inexact, inaccurate
Ungenauigkeit *f* inexactitude, inaccuracy
ungenutzt unused, unutilized, idle, unemployed
ungeschmälert undiminished, whole, in full
ungesichert unsecured *(loan etc.)*, uncovered *(currency etc.)*
ungeteilt undivided *(opinion, loyalty etc.)*
ungetilgt unredeemed *(debt etc.)*
ungewichtet unweighed *(goods etc.)*; *(stats)* unweighted
ungezählt unnumbered; not counted
ungezeichnet unmarked; *(fin)* unsubscribed
ungiriert unendorsed *(cheques etc.)*
ungleich unequal *(treaty etc.)*; unlike
ungleichartig different, heterogeneous
Ungleichartigkeit *f* heterogeneity
Ungleichgewicht *n* disequilibrium, imbalance
Ungleichheit *f* inequality; disparity *(rates etc.)*
ungleichmäßig uneven *(growth etc.)*, disproportionate
Ungleichung *f* unequation
~, **Camp-Meidell'sche** *(stats)* Camp-Meidell inequality
~, **Markoff'sche** *(stats)* Markoff inequality
~, **Tchebycheff-Bienaymé'sche** *(stats)* Bienaymé-Tchebycheff inequality
ungültig invalid, cancelled *(contract etc.)*; not current *(money etc.)*; *(jur)* inoperative ◊ **für ~ erklären** to invalidate, to rescind, to annul, to declare null and void *(contract, agreement etc.)*; **~ machen** to void, to nullify; *(jur)* to quash; **~ werden** to become invalid
Ungültigkeit *f* invalidity *(contract etc.)*; voidness; *(jur)* nullity
Ungültigkeitserklärung *f* invalidation, nullification, notice of legal extinction; cancellation
Universalausrüstung *f* standard equipment
Universalbehälter *m* standard container
Universalerbe *m* sole heir, residuary legatee
Universallager *n* general warehouse [store]
Universalmaschine *f* all-round machine
Universalpolice *f (ins)* comprehensive policy
Universalsortiment *n* whole [complete] range of goods
Universalsukzession *f* sole legacy
Universalvermächtnis *n* residuary legacy
Universalversicherung *f* comprehensive [all-in] insurance
unkalkuliert uncalculated *(prices etc.)*
unkonsolidiert unconsolidated
unkonvertierbar inconvertible
Unkonvertierbarkeit *f* inconvertibility
Unkosten *pl* expenses; cost(s), charges ◊ **abzüglich der ~** deducting the costs, all charges deducted, less out-of-pocket expenses; **~ aufschlüsseln** to break down costs

~, **abzugsfähige** deductible expenses
~, **allgemeine** overhead operating costs
~, **außerordentliche** extra charges
~, **effektive** actual expenses
~, **entstandene** accrued expenses
~, **feststehende** fixed charges
~, **laufende** current expenses
~, **personelle** labour costs
~, **verschiedene** sundry expenses
~, **zusätzliche** additional expenses; additional charges
Unkostenanteil *m* share of expenses, cost rate
Unkostenaufgliederung *f* classification of costs, cost analysis; division of costs
Unkostenaufstellung *f* statement of expenses
Unkostenaufteilung *f* distribution [allocation] of costs; cost distribution
Unkostenbeitrag *m* contribution to costs
Unkostenbelastung *f (ins)* expense charge
Unkostenbeleg *m* receipt
Unkostenberechnung *f* costing, cost calculation
Unkostenbetrag *m* amount of expenses
Unkostendeckung *f* covering of costs
Unkosteneinsparung *f* saving of costs
Unkostenfaktor *m* expense factor
Unkostenposten *m* s. **Unkostenposition**
Unkostenposition *f* cost item
Unkostensenkung *f* reduction of cost
Unkostenverteilung *f* allocation of expenses
unkündbar irrevocable *(decision etc.)*; irredeemable *(loan etc.)*; holding office for life
Unland *n* uncultivable land
unlauter unfair *(competition)*, illicit *(trade)*
unmöbliert unfurnished
unmodern unfashionable, old-fashioned, out of fashion
unmotiviert without motivation; *(jur)* without motive
unmündig under age
Unmündiger *m* minor
Unmündigkeit *f* minority
unnotiert *(st.ex.)* not quoted, *(Am)* unlisted
unnumeriert unnumbered
unökonomisch uneconomic(al)
unparteiisch non-partisan, impartial
Unparteiischer *m* umpire, referee
Unparteilichkeit *f* impartiality
unpassend unsuitable, inopportune
unpassierbar impassable
unpatentiert not patented
unpfändbar unseizable
Unpfändbarkeit *f* indistrainability
unplanmäßig unplanned, not according to plan
Unplanmäßigkeit *f* spontaneity
unplazierbar *(st.ex.)* unmarketable
unpolitisch non-political, unpolitical
unpraktisch impractical

unproduktiv unproductive
Unproduktivität *f* unproductivity
unprofitabel *s.* **unrentabel**
unproportioniert disproportionate
unpünktlich unpunctual
Unpünktlichkeit *f* unpunctuality
unqualifizierbar undefinable
unqualifiziert 1. unskilled *(worker etc.)*, unqualified *(staff member etc.)*; 2. unsuitable
unquittiert without receipt, unreceipted
Unrat *m* rubbish, filth
unrationell wasteful, inefficient
unrealisierbar unrealizable
Unrealisierbarkeit *f* unrealizability
unrecht not right, wrong; unjust, unfair; inopportune *(time etc.)*
Unrecht *n* wrong; injustice
unrechtmäßig unlawful, illegal
Unrechtmäßigkeit *f* unlawfulness, illegality
unredlich dishonest, unfair
Unredlichkeit *f* dishonesty, unfairness
unreell dishonest, unfair; unreliable
unregelmäßig irregular *(delivery etc.)*; erratic *(person etc.)*; anomalous
Unregelmäßigkeit *f* 1. irregularity *(delivery etc.)*; 2. lapse, mistake
unreif immature; unripe *(fruit etc.)*
Unreife *f* immaturity; unripeness *(fruit etc.)*
unrentabel unprofitable
unrichtig incorrect, wrong
Unrichtigkeit *f* incorrectness, inaccuracy
unsachgemäß improper; inexpertly *(execution of an order etc.)*; careless *(storing etc.)*
unschädlich harmless, innocuous; innoxious *(plants etc.)* ⋄ **~ machen** to render harmless
Unschädlichkeit *f* harmlessness
Unschuld *f* innocence
unschuldig innocent
unselbständig dependent
Unselbständiger *m* dependant
Unselbständigkeit *f* dependence
unsicher unsafe, insecure; uncertain, doubtful
Unsicherheit *f* insecurity, uncertainty
unsichtbar invisible
unsolide unreliable, untrustworthy; unsafe *(securities etc.)*
Unsolidität *f* unreliability
unsortiert unsorted
unsozial anti-social
unstatthaft inadmissible
Unstimmigkeit *f* discrepancy; inconsistency
untätig inactive, idle
Untätigkeit *f* inactivity
untauglich unfit
Untauglichkeit *f* unfitness
untaxiert unvalued *(car etc.)*; unassessed *(real estate etc.)*

unteilbar indivisible *(funds etc.)*
Unteilbarkeit *f* indivisibility *(funds etc.)*
Unterabteilung *f* subdivision, branch
Unterangebot *n* shortage *(in the supply of goods etc.)*
Unterausschuß *m* sub-committee
unterbefrachten to underload, to underfreight; to sub-charter
unterbelasten to work below capacity, to underutilize *(capacity)*
Unterbelastung *f* working below capacity, underutilization
unterbelegt undermanned *(crew etc.)*; not fully occupied *(hotel rooms etc.)*
Unterbelegung *f* understaffing; undermanning
unterbeschäftigt underemployed
Unterbeschäftigung *f* underemployment
unterbesetzt understaffed, undermanned
unterbevölkert underpopulated
unterbewerten to undervalue; to underestimate
Unterbewertung *f* undervaluation; underestimation
unterbezahlen to underpay
Unterbezahlung *f* underpayment
unterbieten to undercut, to dump, to undersell, to underbid
Unterbietung *f* undercutting, dumping
Unterbilanz *f* adverse [short] balance, deficit
unterbrechen to interrupt, to cut off *(main etc.)*; to make a break *(meeting etc.)*
Unterbrechung *f* interruption, cutting off *(main etc.)*; break *(meeting etc.)*; *(d.pr.)* interrupt
~ **der Beziehungen** breaking off (of) relations
~ **des Verkehrs** traffic hold-up
~ **einer Sitzung** adjournment of a meeting
~ **eines Gerichtsverfahrens** adjournment of a trial
~, eines Verfahrens suspension of proceedings
Unterbrechungssystem *n (d.pr.)* interrupt system
unterbreiten to submit to, to lay before, to present
Unterbreitung *f* submission, presentation
~ **eines Anspruchs** submission of a claim
~ **eines Antrags** presentation of an application
~ **eines Vorschlages** submission of a proposal
unterbringen 1. to accommodate; 2. to sell *(goods etc.)*; to invest *(capital)*; to place *(securities etc.)*
Unterbringung *f* 1. accommodation; 2. investment *(capital)*; placement *(securities etc.)*
Unterdeckung *f* non-sufficient covering *(of loans etc.)*
unterentwickelt underdeveloped
Unterentwicklung *f* underdevelopment
untererfüllen to underfulfil
untererfüllt underfulfilled

Untererfüllung *f* underfulfilment
unterernähren to underfeed
unterernährt undernourished
Unterernährung *f* undernourishment
unterfakturieren to underrate
Unterfakturierung *f* underrating
Untergang *m* sinking, decline; destruction, fall, ruin; foundering, going down *(ship)*
Untergewicht *n* underweight
Untergrund *m* underground; subsoil
Untergruppe *f (stats)* sub-class
~ **innerhalb der Blöcke** *(stats)* intrablock subgroup
Untergruppen *fpl*:
~, **vermengte** *(stats)* subgroups confounded
Untergruppenzahlen *fpl*:
~, **proportionale** *(stats)* proportional sub-class numbers
Unterhalt *m* 1. maintenance, upkeep *(of a building etc.)*; 2. subsistence, livelihood, living; 3. alimony
unterhalten to maintain *(car etc.)*; to support *(dependants etc.)*; to keep running *(business etc.)*
Unterhaltsanspruch *m* right to financial support; claim to alimony
unterhaltsbedürftig to be in need of financial support
Unterhaltsbeihilfe *f* supplementary maintenance allowance
Unterhaltsbeitrag *m* allowance; alimony
unterhaltsberechtigt entitled to maintenance; entitled to alimony
Unterhaltsberechtigter *m* dependant
Unterhaltsbeschluß *m (jur)* maintenance order
Unterhaltsbetrag *m* (amount of) allowance; (amount of) alimony
Unterhaltsempfänger *m* dependant getting financial support
Unterhaltsentzug *m* withholding of financial support
unterhaltsfähig able to make a living
Unterhaltsforderung *f* claim for financial support
Unterhaltsklage *f (jur)* action for financial support
Unterhaltskosten *pl* costs of maintaining *(s.th.)*; maintenance costs; running costs *(car etc.)*
Unterhaltskostenbeitrag *m* maintenance contribution *(repayment of a part of maintenance costs of and by persons living in convalescent or nursing homes)*
Unterhaltsmittel *npl* means of subsistence, maintenance
Unterhaltspflicht *f* obligation to give financial support
unterhaltspflichtig obliged to give financial support

Unterhaltsrückstände *mpl* arrears in maintenance
Unterhaltsurteil *n s.* **Unterhaltsbeschluß**
Unterhaltsverfahren *n* maintenance proceedings
Unterhaltsverpflichtung *f s.* **Unterhaltspflicht**
Unterhaltszahlung *f* payment of maintenance; payment of alimony
Unterhaltszuschuß *m* maintenance allowance
Unterhaltung *f* 1. maintenance, upkeep; 2. entertainment
~, **laufende** current maintenance
Unterhaltungsarbeiten *fpl* maintenance (work)
Unterhaltungsindustrie *f* entertainment industry
unterhandeln to negotiate, to parley
Unterhändler *m* negotiator, agent, mediator, go-between
Unterhandlung *f* negotiation, parley
Unterhandlungen *fpl* negotiations; talks ◊ **in ~ eintreten** to enter into negotiations [talks]; **in ~ stehen** to negotiate; **~ abbrechen** to call off [break off] negotiations [talks]
unterkapitalisiert under-capitalized
Unterkapitalisierung *f* under-capitalization
Unterklasse *f (stats)* sub-class
Unterklassen *fpl*:
~, **ungleiche** *(stats)* unequal sub-classes
Unterklassenbesetzung *f*:
~, **nichtproportionale** *(stats)* disproportionate sub-class number
Unterkonsumtion *f* under-consumption
Unterkonto *n* sub-account
Unterkunft *f* accommodation, lodging ◊ **~ und Verpflegung frei** free board and lodging
~, **menschliche** accommodation fit to live in
~, **und Verpflegung** *f* board and lodging
Unterlage *f* record, document
Unterlagen *fpl* papers, records, documents; data; sources
~, **buchungstechnische** bookkeeping records
~, **finanzielle** financial records
~, **geschäftliche** commercial documents
~, **statistische** statistical data
~, **technische** technical data
Unterlagenprüfung *f* examining records [documents], checking of data
Unterlagenverzeichnis *n* register of records
unterlassen to omit, to neglect; to cease to do
Unterlassung *f* omission, neglect; *(jur)* default *(duty etc.)*
Unterlieferant *m* sub-contractor
Unterlizenz *f* sub-licence
Untermakler *m* sub-agent, intermediate broker
Untermasse *f s.* **Untergewicht**
Untermatrix *f* sub-matrix
Untermiete *f* sub-tenancy; sublease

Untermieter *m* sub-tenant
Untermietpreis *m* rent
Untermietverhältnis *n* relationship of sub-tenancy
Untermietvertrag *m* agreement of sub-tenancy
unternehmen to undertake *(s.th.)*, to make *(trip etc.)*
Unternehmen *n* enterprise, firm, company; undertaking; venture ◊ **ein ~ sanieren** to reorganize a company
~, **abhängiges** controlled company
~, **aufgesogenes** subsidiary
~, **einverleibendes** takeover firm [company]
~, **gemeinnütziges** public utility company
~, **gemeinsames** joint venture
~, **gemeinwirtschaftliches** public enterprise
~, **gemischtes** mixed company; joint venture
~, **gewerkschaftseigenes** trade-union company
~, **gewinnbringendes** profitable enterprise
~, **marktbeherrschendes** enterprise [concern] dominating the market, monopoly, oligopoly
~, **mittelgroßes** medium-sized company
~, **öffentliches** *s.* ~, **gemeinwirtschaftliches**
~, **privates** private company
~, **staatliches** state enterprise
~, **städtisches** municipal enterprise
~, **unrentables** unprofitable enterprise, non-paying business
Unternehmensbezeichnung *f* name of a firm
Unternehmensforschung *f* operations research
Unternehmensleitung *f* management of a company, company management
Unternehmensplanung *f* management planning
Unternehmensstrategie *f* company strategy
Unternehmenszusammenschluß *m* merger of companies, company merger
Unternehmer *m* entrepreneur; employer, industrialist; contractor
~, **privater** entrepreneur
~, **selbständiger** *s.* ~, **privater**
Unternehmerbürgschaft *f* employers' vicarious responsibility
Unternehmereigenschaften *fpl* entrepreneurial qualities
Unternehmereinkommen *n* enterprise [company] proceeds [revenues]
Unternehmerfunktion *f* managerial function
Unternehmergarantie *f s.* **Unternehmerbürgschaft**
Unternehmergeist *m* enterprising [entrepreneurial] spirit
Unternehmergewinn *m s.* **Unternehmerprofit**
Unternehmerhaftpflichtversicherung *f* employer's liability insurance
Unternehmerhaftung *f* employer's liability
unternehmerisch enterprising
Unternehmerkapital *n* business capital

Unternehmerklasse *f* business class, class of employers
Unternehmerpfandrecht *n* entrepreneurial law of liens and pledges
Unternehmerprofit *m* employer's profit
Unternehmerrisiko *n* entrepreneurial risk
Unternehmerschaft *f* entrepreneurs, entrepreneurship; employers
Unternehmertätigkeit *f* entrepreneurial activities [work]
Unternehmerverband *m* employers' [entrepreneurs'] association
Unternehmervereinigung *f s.* **Unternehmerverband**
Unternehmervertretung *f* managerial representation
Unternehmerwagnis *n s.* **Unternehmerrisiko**
Unternehmerwillkür *f* employer's arbitrariness
Unternehmung *f s.* **Unternehmen**
Unternehmungsform *f* type of enterprise
Unternehmungsgeist *m* enterprising spirit
unterordnen to subordinate *(s.o. to s.o.)*; to sub-divide, to sub-group
Unterordnung *f* subordination; *(stats)* sub-group
Unterorganisation *f* sub-organization
Unterpacht *f* sub-lease
Unterpächter *m* sub-lessee
Unterpari-Ausgabe *f* issue below par
Unterpari-Emission *f s.* **Unterpari-Ausgabe**
Unterpfand *n* pledge, security; pawn; lien hypothec
Unterplanbestand *m* stock below planned level
Unterplangewinn *m* profit below planned level
Unterpreis *m* price below the break-even point; dumping price
Unterproduktion *f* underproduction
Unterprogramm *n* *(d.pr.)* subprogram, subroutine
Unterricht *m* instruction; training; lessons
~, **berufspraktischer** training according to future vocation
~, **berufstheoretischer** training according to theoretical aspects of the vocation (concerned)
unterrichten to inform, to advise; to instruct, to teach, to train; to give lessons
Unterrichtsinformation *f* instruction
Unterrichtung *f* instruction; information, notice
unterschätzen to undervalue; to underestimate, to underrate
Unterschätzung *f* undervaluation; underestimation, underrating
unterscheiden to differentiate, to discriminate, to distinguish, to make a distinction
Unterscheidung *f* differentiation, discrimination, distinction
Unterscheidungsanalyse *f (stats)* discriminatory analysis

Unterscheidungsmerkmal *n* distinctive feature
Unterscheidungszölle *mpl* differential customs tariffs
Unterschied *m* difference; distinction; discrimination
~ zwischen Ein- und Verkaufspreis margin, trade-margin
~ zwischen Stadt und Land difference between town and country
unterschlagen to embezzle
Unterschlagung *f* embezzlement
~ von Beweismaterial suppression of evidence
~ von Briefen interception of letters
~ von Geldern fraudulent misuse of money
Unterschlagungsfall *m* case of embezzlement
Unterschleif *m s.* Unterschlagung
unterschreiben to sign, to undersign ◊ blanko ~ to sign a blank document; eigenhändig ~ to sign by o.s.
unterschreiten to remain under, to fall short of
Unterschreitung *f* remaining under, falling short (of)
~ der Plankosten remaining under planned costs
unterschrieben signed ◊ nicht ~ unsigned; ordnungsgemäß ~ duly [properly] signed
~ und besiegelt under hand and seal
Unterschrift *f* signature ◊ eine ~ beglaubigen to attest [confirm] a signature; eine ~ fälschen to forge a signature; ~ fehlt signature missing; ~ ungenau signature differs; ~ unvollständig incompletely signed; zur ~ vorlegen to submit for signature
~, eigenhändige one's own signature, personal signature
~, gefälschte forged signature
~ pro Prokura procuration signature
Unterschriftenliste *f* signature book; signature list
Unterschriftenverzeichnis *n s.* Unterschriftenliste
Unterschriftsbeglaubigung *f* attestation of signature
unterschriftsberechtigt authorized to sign ◊ ~ sein to be entitled [authorized] to sign, to have power to sign
Unterschriftsberechtigter *m* authorized signer
Unterschriftsberechtigung *f* authority [authorization, power] to sign
Unterschriftsvollmacht *f s.* Unterschriftsberechtigung
unterstehen:
◊ jmdm. ~ to be under the control of s.o. [subordinate to s.o.], to be under s.o.
Unterstellung *f* 1. subordination *(administratively)*; control; 2. misrepresentation; insinuation; presumption

~, behördliche administrative control
~, doppelte dual control
Unterstellungsbereich *m* subordinated section
Unterstellungsverhältnis *n* relationship of subordination
Unterstichprobe *f (stats)* sub-sample
Unterstichproben *fpl*:
~, zwei gemeinsame *(stats)* duplicated sub-samples
Unterstichprobenentnahme *f (stats)* sub-sampling
unterstützen to support, to assist; to relieve; to aid
Unterstützung *f* support, assistance; relief; aid; *(ins)* benefit
~, finanzielle financial support [aid]
~, gegenseitige mutual aid [assistance]
~, materielle material support
~, öffentliche public support
~, staatliche state relief *(money paid to persons)*; government aid *(to enterprises, organizations etc.)*; subsidy, subvention
Unterstützungsanspruch *m* right of (financial) support; claim to benefit
Unterstützungsantrag *m* application for relief
Unterstützungsbeihilfe *f* benefit, relief; allowance
unterstützungsberechtigt entitled to (insurance) benefit
Unterstützungsempfänger *m* recipient of (public) relief [*(ins)* benefits]
Unterstützungsfall *m* case of relief; public charge
Unterstützungsfonds *m* relief fund
Unterstützungsgesuch *n s.* Unterstützungsantrag
Unterstützungsleistungen *fpl* benefits, allowances
Unterstützungssatz *m* rate of benefit
Unterstützungssystem *n* welfare system
Unterstützungszahlungen *fpl* relief payments
Unterstützungszeitraum *m* benefit period
untersuchen to study *(project etc.)*; to examine *(validity of document etc.)*; to inspect *(damage to factory etc.)*; to investigate, to inquire into *(case etc.)*
Untersuchung *f* study *(project etc.)*; examination *(validity of document etc.)*; inspection *(damage to factory etc.)*; investigation, inquiry *(case etc.)*
◊ eine ~ vornehmen to carry out an examination *(medical care etc.)*; to make an inspection *(by higher organs etc.)*; to make an inquiry *(court, statistics etc.)*; to make investigations *(police)*; to carry out studies *(in scientific fields)*
~, amtliche official inquiry; inspection
~, ärztliche physical examination, medical check-up

~, **betriebswirtschaftliche** business administration study
~, **einmalige statistische** non-recurring statistical inquiry [survey]
~, **gerichtliche** judicial inquiry
~, **informelle** informal inquiry
~, **ökonometrische** econometric study
~, **periodische** periodic [regular] inquiry
~, **polizeiliche** investigations by the police, police investigations
~, **statistische** (statistical) inquiry [survey]
~, **zollamtliche** examination by the customs (office)
Untersuchungsausschuß *m* committee of inquiry
Untersuchungsbefund *m* report of examination
Untersuchungsbericht *m* report of inquiry
Untersuchungseinheit *f (stats)* unit of inquiry
~, **kleinste** *(stats)* elementary unit
Untersuchungsempfang *m (stats)* amount of inspection
~, **mittlerer** *(stats)* average amount of inspection
Untersuchungsergebnis *n* result of inquiry
Untersuchungsfläche *f (stats)* cell of inquiry
~, **kleinste** *(stats)* basic cell
Untersuchungsperiode *f* period of examination; period of inspection
Untersuchungsrichter *m* investigating judge
Untersuchungszeitraum *m s.* **Untersuchungsperiode**
Untersuchungsziel *n* aim of studies *(heuristic etc.)*
Untertagearbeit *f* underground work
Untertagearbeiter *m* miner; underground worker
Untertagebau *m* (underground) mining
untertariflich below wage rates
unterteilen to subdivide
Unterteilung *f* subdivision
untervermieten to sublet
Untervermieten *n s.* **Untervermietung**
Untervermieter *m* subletter, sublessor
Untervermietung *f* subletting
Untervermietungsrecht *n* right to sublet
unterverpachten to sublease
Unterverpächter *m* sublessor
Unterverpachtung *f* sublease
unterversichern to underinsure
unterversichert underinsured
Unterversicherung *f* underinsurance
Untervertrag *m* subcontract
unterwegs in transit
Unterwegskosten *pl* charges en route
unterweisen to instruct; to train, to teach
Unterweisung *f* instruction; training
unterwertig below (the) value; substandard (goods etc.)

unterzeichnen *s.* **unterschreiben**
Unterzeichner *m* signer; subscriber *(bonds etc.)*; signatory *(treaties etc.)*
Unterzeichneter *m* undersigned
Unterzeichnung *f* signing; subscription *(bonds etc.)*; ratification *(treaties etc.)*
untilgbar irredeemable *(bonds etc.)*; perpetual *(annuity etc.)*
Untilgbarkeit *f* irredeemability *(bonds etc.)*; permanence *(annuity etc.)*
Untreue *f* unfaithfulness; disloyalty; fraudulent conversion
untüchtig 1. unfit, inefficient, incapable; 2. unseaworthy
Untüchtigkeit *f* unfitness, incapacity
unveräußerlich not for sale, inalienable; not transferable, unassignable; non-negotiable
Unveräußerlichkeit *f* inalienability; unsaleableness
unverbindlich not binding, noncommittal; subject to prior sale *(offer)*, subject to change *(price)*
Unverbindlichkeit *f* nonobligation; noncommitment
unverbraucht unused, not (fully) used
unverbrieft unchartered *(without regulation)*; unsecured *(loans etc.)*
unverbürgt unauthenticated; unconfirmed
unverdient unearned
unverdorben unspoilt, fresh
unveredelt unimproved; unprocessed *(raw materials etc.)*
unverehelicht *s.* **unverheiratet**
unvereidigt unsworn
unvereinbar incompatible
Unvereinbarkeit *f* incompatibility
unverfälscht unadulterated *(food etc.)*, pure *(wine etc.)*
unverhältnismäßig disproportionate, out of proportion; excessive *(prices etc.)*
unverheiratet unmarried, single
Unverheirateter *m* single (person)
unverjährbar imprescriptable; not subject to the statute of limitation *(crime etc.)*
Unverjährbarkeit *f* imprescriptibility
unverjährt still valid
unverkäuflich unsaleable, not for sale
Unverkäuflichkeit *f* unsaleability
unverkauft unsold
unverkürzt uncurtailed, unabridged *(text etc.)*
Unverletzbarkeit *f* inviolability *(bank secret etc.)*
unverletzlich inviolable
Unvermögen *n* disability, inability, powerlessness
unvermögend without means; incapable; powerless
unverpachtet unleased

unverpackt unpacked
unverpfändet unpledged
unverschuldet 1. through no fault *(of one's own, of s.o.)*; 2. not in debt; unencumbered *(estate etc.)*
unversehrt undamaged, intact
Unversehrtheit *f* integrity *(person)*; intactness *(parcel etc.)*
unversichert uninsured
unversiegelt unsealed
unversteuert untaxed
unverteilt unallotted
unverwertbar not negotiable *(bonds etc.)*; uncollectable *(debt etc.)*; unsaleable *(goods etc.)*
unverwertet unrealized
unverzinslich interest-free, bearing no interest
unverzollt duty unpaid; in bond
unverzüglich immediate, prompt, without delay
unvollständig incomplete
Unvollständigkeit *f* insufficiency *(documents etc.)*; incompleteness
unvorhergesehen unforeseen
unvorteilhaft unprofitable; unfavourable, disadvantageous
unwiderruflich irrevocable *(letter of credit etc.)*
unwirksam inoperative, ineffective ⋄ **für ~ erklären** to set aside; **~ werden** to get [become] void
unwirtschaftlich uneconomic(al)
Unwirtschaftlichkeit *f* unprofitableness *(of a process etc.)*
unzerbrechlich unbreakable
unzugänglich inaccessible *(area etc.)*; unapproachable *(person)*
unzulänglich insufficient, inadequate
Unzulänglichkeit *f* insufficiency; inadequacy
unzulässig inadmissible *(evidence etc.)*; improper *(behaviour etc.)*; undue, unwarranted *(influence etc.)*; excessive *(weight, speed etc.)*
Unzulässigkeit *f* inadmissibility *(evidence etc.)*; impropriety *(behaviour etc.)*; excess *(weight, speed etc.)*
unzurechnungsfähig of unsound mind, mentally defective
Unzurechnungsfähigkeit *f* irresponsibility, non-responsibility
unzustellbar undeliverable *(letter etc.)*
Unzustellbarkeit *f* nondelivery
unzuverlässig unreliable
Unzuverlässigkeit *f* unreliability
~ bei Schätzfunktionen und Tests *(stats)* bias
Urabstimmung *f* voting by all trade unionists *(for industrial action)*
Urbanisierung *f* urbanization
Urbanisierungsgrad *m* degree of urbanization
urbar arable ⋄ **~ machen** to cultivate; to reclaim *(desert etc.)*

Urbarmachung *f* cultivation; reclamation
Urbevölkerung *f* aborigines
Ureinwohner *m* aboriginal
Urgemeinschaft *f* primitive society
Urgesellschaft *f s.* **Urgemeinschaft**
Urheber *m* author
Urheberrecht *n* copyright
Urheberschutz *m* author's protection
Urheber- und Erfinderrecht *n*:
~, **internationales** international copyright and patent rights
Urkommunismus *m* primitive communism
Urkunde *f* document, deed, legal instrument
~, **amtliche** public document
Urkundenfälscher *m* forger of documents
Urkundenfälschung *f* forgery of documents
Urkundenhinterlegung *f* depositing of documents
Urkundenprüfung *f* examination of documents
Urkundensteuer *f* fee *(for a document)*
urkundlich documentary
Urlaub *m* vacation, holidays; leave ⋄ **seinen ~ antreten** to go on leave; **seinen ~ verlängern** to extend one's leave; **~ beantragen** to ask [apply] for leave
~, **bezahlter** paid holidays [leave]
~, **unbezahlter** leave without pay, unpaid leave
~, **zusätzlich gewährter** additional leave
Urlauber *m* person on leave; holidaymaker, *(Am)* vacationist
Urlauberbetreuung *f* provision of holiday amenities
Urlauberverkehr *m* holiday [*(Am)* vacation] traffic
Urlaubsabgeltung *f* extra pay in lieu of holidays
Urlaubsanspruch *m* claim to holidays
Urlaubsantrag *m* application for leave
urlaubsberechtigt eligible for leave
Urlaubsbestimmungen *fpl* provisions of leave
Urlaubsbezahlung *f* leave pay
Urlaubsentschädigung *f s.* **Urlaubsabgeltung**
Urlaubsgeld *n* holiday [leave] pay
Urlaubsgesuch *n s.* **Urlaubsantrag**
Urlaubsplan *m* leave schedule
Urlaubsplanung *f* planning of holidays
Urlaubssperre *f* stoppage of leave
Urlaubsvereinbarung *f* holiday agreement *(between management and trade union)*
Urlaubsverlängerung *f* extension of one's holidays [leave]
Urlaubswesen *n* holiday system [service]
Urlaubszeit *f* holiday season, vacation period
Urprodukt *n* primary product
Ursache *f* reason; ground; cause
~, **mitwirkende** *(ins)* instrumental cause
~, **unmittelbare** *(ins)* immediate [direct] cause
Ursachenzusammenhang *m* causality

ursächlich

ursächlich causal
Urschrift f original
Ursprung m origin, source; nationality
ursprünglich original, primary
Ursprungsauszeichnung f informative labelling (of origin)
Ursprungsbezeichnung f mark of origin
Ursprungsland n country of origin
Ursprungsvermerk m indication of origin
Ursprungszertifikat n s. **Ursprungszeugnis**
Ursprungszeugnis n certificate of origin
Urteil n judgement, verdict; sentence (of penalty); decision
Urteilsspruch m sentence
Urteilsverkündung f pronouncement [passing] of judgement
Urteilsvollstreckung f judgement execution
Usance f usage, practice, custom
Usancenhandel m trading in foreign exchange
Usowechsel m bill at usance

V

vakant vacant, unoccupied
Vakanz f vacancy
validieren to make valid, to validate
Validierung f validation
Valoren pl shares, (Am) stocks
Valoren- und Wertsachenversicherung f registered mail insurance
Valorisation f valorization
valorisieren to valorize
Valorisierung f 1. validation; 2. valorization
Valuta f foreign exchange [currency]
~, **harte** hard currency
~, **konvertierbare** convertible currency
~, **unbeständige** unstable currency
~, **unveränderliche** currency with a fixed standard
~, **veränderliche** currency with a flexible standard
~, **weiche** soft currency
Valutaabschluß m currency transaction
Valutaakzept n acceptance in foreign exchange
Valutaanleihe f loan (granted) in foreign exchange
Valutaanrecht n eligibility for foreign currency
Valutaaufkommen n foreign exchange receipts, foreign currency earnings
Valutaaufkommensplan m foreign exchange receipts plan, plan of foreign currency earnings

Valutaaufwand m s. **Valutaausgaben**
Valutaaufwertung f revaluation of foreign currency
Valutaausgaben fpl expenditure in foreign currency
Valutabankkredit m bank loan in foreign currency
Valutabedarfsplan m foreign exchange [currency] requirements plan
Valutabescheinigung f foreign exchange certificate
Valutabeschränkungen fpl foreign exchange regulations
Valutabewirtschaftung f control of foreign exchange
Valutabeziehungen fpl foreign exchange relations
Valutadumping n releasing foreign currency holdings on the money market
Valutaeinkaufspreis m import price in foreign exchange
Valutaeinnahmen fpl foreign exchange receipts, receipts in foreign exchange
Valutaentwertung f devaluation of foreign exchange
Valutaerklärung f declaration of foreign currency
Valutaerlös m foreign exchange proceeds [earnings], proceeds in foreign exchange
Valutafonds m (total) foreign exchange fund
Valutaforderung f claim in foreign currency
Valutagegenwert m value in foreign currency
Valutageschäft n foreign currency transaction
Valutagesetzgebung f foreign exchange legislation
Valutaguthaben n foreign exchange holdings
Valutaintervention f intervention in foreign exchange (market)
Valutaklausel f foreign exchange clause
Valutakonto n account in foreign exchange; foreign exchange account
Valutakontrolle f foreign exchange control
Valutakredit m foreign currency loan, loan in foreign currency
Valutakupon m coupon in foreign currency
Valutakurs m (foreign) exchange rate
Valutamangel m shortage [lack] of foreign exchange
Valutamarkt m foreign exchange [currency] market
Valutamittel npl foreign exchange
Valutamonopol n (state) monopoly in foreign exchange
Valutanotierung f quotation of foreign exchange
Valutapapiere npl foreign stock
Valutaparität f exchange rate, rate of exchange

Valutaplan *m* plan of foreign currency
Valutaplanung *f* planning of foreign exchange
Valutapolitik *f* foreign exchange policy
Valutapreis *m* price in foreign exchange
Valutapreisbildung *f* pricing in foreign exchange
Valutapreiskalkulation *f* price calculation in foreign exchange
Valutapreispolitik *f* pricing policy in foreign exchange
Valutapreisveränderung *f* price changes in foreign exchange
Valutapreisverbesserung *f* price improvement in foreign exchange
Valutapreisvereinbarung *f* agreement on prices in foreign currency
Valutapreisverschlechterung *f* price deterioration in foreign exchange
Valutaprobleme *npl* foreign exchange problems
Valutaquittung *f* foreign exchange receipt
Valutaregulierung *f s.* **Valutakontrolle**
Valutareserven *fpl* foreign exchange reserves; foreign exchange resources [stock]
Valutarisiko *n* exchange risk
Valutaschuld *f* foreign exchange liabilities
Valutaschwankung *f* fluctuation in foreign exchange rate(s)
Valutaspekulation *f* speculation in foreign exchange
Valutaverhältnis *n s.* **Valutakurs**
Valutaverkaufspreis *m* delivery price in foreign exchange; rate of exchange
Valutaverlust *m* losses in foreign exchange
Valutaverrechnungspreis *m* accounting price in foreign exchange
Valutaversicherung *f* insurance in foreign currency
Valutawechsel *m* bill of exchange in foreign currency
Valutawerte *mpl* foreign exchange securities, securities in foreign exchange
Valutazone *f* currency area
Valuten *fpl* foreign exchange, (different kinds of) foreign currency
Valutenarbitrage *f* arbitration of foreign exchange
Valutengewinn *m* (foreign) exchange profit
Valutenguthaben *n s.* **Valutaguthaben**
Valutenhändler *m* foreign exchange dealer
Valutenkonto *n s.* **Valutakonto**
Valutenkurs *m s.* **Valutakurs**
Valutenverlust *m s.* **Valutaverlust**
valutieren to value; *(st.ex.)* to state the value date
Valutierung *f* (stating the) value (date) ⋄ **die ~ feststellen** *(st.ex.)* to state the value date

Valvation *f* valuation
variabel variable, variant; *(st.ex.)* fluctuating
Variabilität *f* variability
Variabilitätskoeffizient *m* variability coefficient
Variable *f* variable, variate; variant
~, **abhängige** dependent variable
~, **beobachtbare** *(stats)* observable variable
~, **diskrete** *(stats)* discrete variate
~, **fiktive** *(stats)* dummy variable
~, **integrierende** *(stats)* integrating variate
~, **komplexe** *(stats)* comprehensive variate
~, **kontinuierliche** *(stats)* continuous variate
~, **latente** *(stats)* latent variable
~, **mehrdimensionale** *(stats)* multidimensional variate
~, **prädeterminierte** *s.* ~, **primäre**
~, **primäre** *(stats)* predicated variable, predicator
~, **schädliche** *(stats)* detrimental variable
~, **überflüssige** *(stats)* superfluous variable
~, **ursächliche** *(stats)* cause [explanatory] variable
~, **vorgegebene** *(stats)* predicated variable
~, **vorherbestimmte** *(stats)* predetermined variable
~, **zufällige** *(stats)* random variable
Variablenmerkmal *n s.* **Variationsmerkmal**
Variante *f* variant
~, **technologische** technological variant
Variantenberechnung *f s.* **Variantenrechnung**
Variantenbreite *f* range of variants
Variantenkombination *f* combination of variants
Variantenprognose *f* (long-term) forecast of variants
Variantenrechnung *f* calculation of variants
Variantenvergleich *m* comparison of variants
Varianz *f* variance
~ **der gemeinsamen Faktoren** *(stats)* common--factor variance
~ **der Stichprobenverteilung** *(stats)* sampling variance
~, **gesamte** *(stats)* total variance
~ **innerhalb der Gruppen** *(stats)* within-group variance
~ **innerhalb der Klassen** *(stats)* intra-class variance
~ **innerhalb der Primäreinheiten** *(stats)* internal variance
~ **innerhalb einer Stichprobe** *(stats)* internal variance of a sample
~, **kleinstmögliche** *(stats)* minimum variance
~ **von Stichprobendurchschnitten** *(stats)* variance of average samples
~ **zwischen den Gruppen** *(stats)* between--groups [inter-group] variance
~ **zwischen den Klassen** *(stats)* interclass variance

~ zwischen den Primäreinheiten *(stats)* external variance
Varianzanalyse *f (stats)* analysis of variance
Varianzkomponente *f (stats)* variance component
Varianz-Verhältnis-Test *m (stats)* variance-ratio test
Variation *f* variation
~, überlagerte *(stats)* superimposed variation
Variationsbreite *f* range [amplitude] of variations
Variationsfähigkeit *f* variability
Variationsfeld *n (stats)* variation field
Variationskarte *f (stats)* variation chart
Variationskoeffizient *m* coefficient of variation
Variationskurve *f (stats)* frequency curve
Variationsmerkmal *n (stats)* varietal character
Variationsrechnung *f (stats)* calculus of variation
Variationsreihe *f (stats)* distribution of variations, frequency distribution
Variationsstatistik *f* statistics of variances
Variationsweite *f* extent of variation, *(stats)* range
Variator *m s.* **Variationskoeffizient**
Varietät *f* variety
variieren to vary
Vasallenstaat *m* vassal (state); satellite state
Vater *m* father
Vaterschaft *f* paternity ◇ **die ~ anerkennen** to recognize a natural child; **die ~ feststellen** to establish paternity; to affiliate a child to s.o.
Vaterschaftsfeststellung *f* paternity order; affiliation of a child to s.o.
VdN-Rente *f* pension for victims of fascism
VEG *s.* **Gut, volkseigenes**
Vektor *m* vector
Vektoranalyse *f* vector analysis
Vektordiagramm *n* vector diagram
Vektorfunktion *f* vector function
verabreden to agree upon; to fix an appointment; **sich ~** to make an appointment
verabredet having an appointment ◇ **wie ~** as agreed upon
verabredetermaßen *s.* **verabredungsgemäß**
Verabredung *f* appointment
verabredungsgemäß according to agreement
verabschieden to bid farewell; to discharge; to retire; to take leave of *(s.o.)*
verabschiedet discharged; retired; passed *(law etc.)*; taken leave of *(s.o.)*
Verabschiedung *f* discharge; retirement; taking leave of *(s.o.)*
verallgemeinern to generalize
Verallgemeinerung *f* generalization
veralten to become obsolete [antiquated] *(methods etc.)*, to go out of fashion

Veralten *n* obsolescence
~, moralisches obsolescence
Veränderliche *f* variable, variate; variant
Veränderlichkeit *f* variability
verändern to change; to alter; to modify
verändert changed
Veränderung *f* change; alteration; modification; fluctuation *(rates of exchange etc.)*; variation; shift *(in policy etc.)*
Veränderungen *fpl*:
  ◇ **~ unterliegen** to be subject to changes; **~ vornehmen** to make changes [alterations, modifications]
~, geschäftliche business changes
~, gesellschaftliche social changes; social transformation
~, strukturelle structural changes
veränderungshalber because of changes; for a change
Veränderungsrate *f* rate of changes *(products etc.)*
Veränderungstempo *n* pace of change(s)
veranlagen to assess *(taxes etc.)*, to rate *(local taxes etc.)* ◇ **zu hoch ~** to overassess *(taxes etc.)*, to overrate *(local taxes etc.)*
veranlagt 1. assessed, rated; 2. having a propensity to *(fluctuate etc.)* ◇ **nicht ~** unassessed, unrated
Veranlagter *m* taxpayer; ratepayer
Veranlagung *f* 1. assessment, taxation, rating; 2. propensity
~, anteilmäßige proportional assessment
~ auf Grund von Schätzungen arbitrary assessment
~, besondere 1. separate assessment; 2. special ability, talent
~, fiktive fictitious assessment
~, gemeinsame joint assessment
~, nachträgliche subsequent assessment
~, ordnungsgemäße proper assessment
~, willkürliche *s.* **~ auf Grund von Schätzungen**
~, zusätzliche additional assessment
Veranlagungsbescheid *m* tax assessment note
Veranlagungsgegenstand *m s.* **Veranlagungsobjekt**
Veranlagungsgrundlage *f* base of taxation
Veranlagungsjahr *n* taxable year
Veranlagungsliste *f* assessment list
Veranlagungsmethode *f* taxation method
Veranlagungsobjekt *n* unit of assessment
Veranlagungsperiode *f* taxable period
veranlagungspflichtig assessable; rateable
Veranlagungsrichtlinien *fpl* (tax) assessment guidelines
Veranlagungssatz *m* rate of assessment, tax rate
Veranlagungssteuer *f* tax according to decla-

ration *(income tax calculated according to tax declaration)*
Veranlagungswert *m* assessed [rateable] value
Veranlagungszeitraum *m s.* **Veranlagungsperiode**
veranlassen to arrange *(payment etc.)*; to occasion, to cause, to give rise to, to induce; to instigate; to motivate, to bring about
veranschlagen to estimate, to calculate roughly *(costs etc.)*
veranschlagt valued ◊ ~ **werden** to be calculated
Veranschlagung *f* appropriation *(of funds in the budget)*; valuation, estimate
~, **annähernde** approximate calculation, estimate
veranstalten to arrange, to organize
Veranstalter *m* organizer
Veranstaltung *f* arrangement, organization; event; meeting; entertainment, performance
~, **gesellige** social event
~, **internationale** international event
~, **kommerzielle** business meeting
~, **kulturelle** cultural event [show, performance]
~, **öffentliche** public event [performance]
Veranstaltungskalender *m* calendar of events
Veranstaltungsort *m* venue; place of event
Veranstaltungsplan *m* programme
Veranstaltungsprogramm *n s.* **Veranstaltungsplan**
Veranstaltungsraum *m* assembly room
Veranstaltungstermin *m* date of event [performance]
Veranstaltungsturnus *m* sequence of events
verantworten to answer [account] for, to be responsible for
verantwortlich accountable, responsible ◊ **jmdn.** ~ **machen für** to hold s.b. responsible for; ~ **sein für** to be responsible for
Verantwortlichkeit *f* responsibility
~, **alleinige** undivided [sole] responsibility
~, **disziplinarische** personal [legal] accountability
~, **materielle** physical responsibility *(1. civil law: responsibility for non-contractual behaviour; 2. labour code: responsibility of working people for physical damages caused by them)*
~, **persönliche** personal responsibility
~, **strafrechtliche** responsibility under criminal law
~, **ungeteilte** *s.* **alleinige**
~, **volle** full responsibility
Verantwortung *f* responsibility ◊ **auf eigene** ~ on one's own responsibility; **auf Ihre** ~ at your risk; **auf unsere** ~ at our risk, under our guarantee; **die** ~ **übernehmen für** to assume [take, accept] responsibility for; **gemeinsam die** ~ **übernehmen** to assume joint responsibility; **gerichtlich zur** ~ **ziehen** to sue, to take legal steps; **jmdn. zur** ~ **ziehen** to call s.o. to account, to hold s.o. responsible; **seiner** ~ **gerecht werden** to comply with one's responsibility; ~ **tragen** to bear responsibility; ~ **übernehmen** to assume responsibility;
~, **berufliche** professional responsibility
~, **erhöhte** increased responsibility
~, **gesellschaftliche** social responsibility
~, **persönliche** personal responsibility
Verantwortungsbereich *m* scope of responsibility
verantwortungsbewußt responsible *(behaviour)*
verantwortungsvoll in a responsible way
verarbeiten to process *(raw materials etc.)* ◊ **maschinell** ~ to machine
verarbeitend processing; manufacturing
verarbeitet processed, finished
Verarbeitung *f* processing; manufacture; workmanship
~, **erste** first processing
~, **industrielle** industrial processing
~, **systemabhängige** *(d.pr.)* on-line processing
~, **systemunabhängige** *(d.pr.)* off-line processing
Verarbeitungsbetrieb *m* factory, processing plant
Verarbeitungsgrad *m* degree of processing
Verarbeitungsindustrie *f* processing industry; manufacturing industry
Verarbeitungskosten *pl* manufacturing costs, cost of processing
Verarbeitungsstufe *f* processing stage
Verarbeitungsverbot *n* prohibition on processing
Verarbeitungswerk *n s.* **Verarbeitungsbetrieb**
verarmen to sink into poverty, to become poor; to impoverish
verarmt poverty-stricken ◊ ~ **sein** to be reduced to poverty
Verarmung *f* impoverishment; pauperization
verauktionieren to sell at an auction
Verauktionierung *f* selling at an auction
verausgaben to spend, to expend; **sich** ~ to overspend, to spend beyond one's means
verausgabt spent ◊ **nicht** ~ unspent; **sich** ~ **haben** to have run out of cash
Verausgabung *f* spending, expenditure
Veräußerer *m* seller, disposer
veräußerlich saleable, alienable; transferable, assignable; negotiable ◊ **nicht** ~ not for sale, inalienable; not transferable, unassignable; non-negotiable
veräußern to sell; to transfer, to assign; to alienate *(land, rights, etc.)*
Veräußerung *f* alienation *(of property etc.)*, sale, disposal

Veräußerungsbedingungen *fpl* terms [conditions] of sale
Veräußerungsbefugnis *f s.* **Veräußerungsvollmacht**
Veräußerungsgenehmigung *f* permission to dispose property
Veräußerungsgewinn *m* profit on fixed assets sold; sales profit
Veräußerungsrecht *n* right of disposal, alienation
Veräußerungsverbot *n* restraint on alienation
Veräußerungsvollmacht *f* authority to dispose property, power to alienate (property)
Veräußerungswert *m* selling value
Verbalnote *f* verbal note
Verband *m* association; union, federation; society
~, **gemeinnütziger** public utility association
~, **örtlicher** local association
Verbandskasse *f* treasury (of an association)
Verbandsmitglied *n* member of an association; union member
Verbandsmitgliedschaft *f* membership of an association
Verbandssatzung *f* articles of an association
Verbandswesen *n* system of associations; associations
verbannen to exile, to banish
Verbannter *m* exile, exiled person; outlaw
Verbannung *f* exile, banishment; expulsion
verbauen 1. to use *(materials in construction etc.)*; to use up *(money in construction etc.)*; 2. to build badly [shoddily, cheaply], to jerry-build
verbergen to conceal, to hide
verbessern to improve, to make better; to correct, to rectify *(mistake etc.)*; to revise *(text etc.)*; to amend *(motion, bill etc.)*; *(agric)* to ameliorate *(land etc.)*, to improve *(soil)* ⋄ **sich finanziell ~** to improve one's financial position; to get a rise; **sich materiell ~** to improve one's material conditions; **sich wohnungsmäßig ~** to improve one's living conditions
Verbesserung *f* improvement; correction, rectifying, rectification *(mistake etc.)*; revision *(text etc.)*; amendment *(motion, bill etc.)*; *(agric)* amelioration *(land)*, improvement *(soil)*
~ **der Umweltbedingungen** improvement in environmental conditions
Verbesserungen *fpl*:
~, **technische** technical improvements; technological improvements
Verbesserungsantrag *m* amendment ⋄ **einen ~ ablehnen** to reject an amendment; **einen ~ annehmen** to accept an amendment, to vote in favour of (amendment); **einen ~ stellen** to move an amendment

verbesserungsbedürftig in need of improvement
verbesserungsfähig capable of improvement
Verbesserungsvorschlag *m* suggestion [proposal] for improvements *(at place of work etc.)*
~, **patentfähiger** *s.* **patentierungswürdiger**
~, **patentierungswürdiger** patentable improvement
verbieten to forbid, to prohibit
verbilligen to reduce [lower] the price [cost], to cheapen
verbilligt low-priced *(goods etc.)*
Verbilligung *f* reduction in price, price reduction, cheapening
verbinden to connect, to put through *(phone call etc.)*; to link *(s.th. to s.th.)*; to join *(points etc.)*; to associate *(s.o. with s.o./s.th.)*; to tie *(some concession to a condition etc.)*
verbindlich binding, obligatory; obliging
Verbindlichkeit *f* 1. commitment; obligation; liability; binding force; 2. courtesy; compliment ⋄ **ohne ~** without obligation
~, **bedingte** contingent obligation
Verbindlichkeiten *fpl* obligations; debts, liabilities ⋄ **seinen ~ nachkommen** to meet one's obligations; to discharge one's debts; **seinen ~ nicht nachkommen** not to meet one's obligations; to default in payments; **~ eingehen** to enter into commitments, to assume obligations
~ **aus Akzepten** *s.* **~ aus Wechseln**
~ **aus Einlagekonten** deposit liabilities
~, **ausländische** foreign debts
~ **aus Löhnen** liabilities from unpaid wages
~ **aus Schuldscheinen** *s.* **~ aus Wechseln**
~, **ausstehende** outstanding debts
~ **aus Warenlieferungen und Leistungen** debts contracted [incurred] from supply of goods and services
~ **aus Wechseln** bills payable
~, **befristete** time liabilities
~, **eingegangene** contracted obligations; contracted debts, debts incurred
~, **fällige** liabilities due
~, **feste** fixed liabilities
~ **gegenüber der Bank** bank debts
~ **gegenüber Dritten** liabilities to outsiders
~, **gleichbleibende** *s.* ~, **feste**
~, **gleichrangige** liabilities of equal priority
~, **konsolidierte** *s.* ~, **langfristige**
~, **kurzfristige** short-term credits
~, **langfristige** funded [long-term] liabilities
~, **laufende** current liabilities
~, **offene** *s.* ~, **ausstehende**
~, **reservepflichtige** liabilities subject to reserve requirements
~, **sofort fällige** sight liabilities

~, **sonstige** miscellaneous debts
~, **ungesicherte** unsecured liabilities
~, **vertragliche** contractual obligations
Verbindung *f* connection *(phone call etc.)*; link; association *(of s.o. with s.o./s.th.)*; contact *(with s.o./s.th.)* ⋄ **mit jmdm. in ~ treten** to get in touch with s.o., to enter into relations with s.o., to contact s.o.; **sich mit jmdm. in ~ setzen** to contact s.o.
~, **briefliche** correspondence
~, **direkte** direct communication *(railway etc.)*
~, **durchgehende** through connection
~, **regelmäßige** regular line
~, **telefonische** telephone connection
Verbindungen *fpl* connections, relations
~, **geschäftliche** business relations
~, **langjährige** long-standing relations
Verbindungsbüro *n* liaison office
Verbindungsgebühren *fpl (d.pr.)* connect-time charges
Verbindungsstelle *f* connecting point; channel of communication
Verbot *n* prohibition
verboten forbidden, prohibited; off-limits *(area etc.)*
Verbrauch *m* consumption; use, application
~, **anteiliger** proportionate consumption
~, **aufgeschobener** delayed consumption
~, **direkter** final consumption
~, **externer** (product for) public consumption
~, **genormter** standardized consumption *(fuel etc.)*
~, **gesellschaftlicher** social consumption
~, **gewerblicher** industrial consumption
~, **industrieller** *s.* ~, **gewerblicher**
~, **inländischer** home [internal, domestic] consumption
~, **landwirtschaftlicher** farm consumption
~, **laufender** current consumption
~, **maximaler** maximum consumption
~, **minimaler** minimum consumption
~, **nichtproduktiver** *s.* ~, **unproduktiver**
~, **normaler** normal consumption
~, **örtlicher** local consumption
~, **parasitärer** parasitic consumption
~, **persönlicher** individual consumption
~, **planmäßiger** planned consumption
~, **privater** private consumption
~ **pro Kopf** per capita consumption
~ **produktionsbedingter** *s.* ~, **produktiver**
~, **produktiver** productive consumption
~, **sparsamer** economic use; economy run *(car etc.)*
~, **spezifischer** consumption per unit
~, **überhöhter** excessive consumption
~, **überplanmäßiger** consumption exceeding the plan

~, **übriger** miscellaneous [other] consumption
~, **unproduktiver** unproductive consumption
~, **zurückgestellter** *s.* ~, **aufgeschobener**
~, **zusätzlicher** additional consumption
verbrauchen to consume; to use; to wear out; to spend
Verbraucher *m* consumer; customer; user; *(d.pr.)* load
~, **gewerblicher** industrial user
~, **inländischer** home [domestic] consumer
~, **letzter** ultimate user; final consumer
~, **potentieller** prospective consumer
Verbraucherabzahlungskredit *m* consumer credit
Verbraucheranalyse *f* consumer analysis
Verbraucherbefragung *f* consumer research [survey]
Verbraucherbewegung *f* consumer movement
Verbraucherboykott *m* consumer boycott
Verbrauchereinheit *f* consuming unit
Verbrauchergenossenschaft *f* consumer co-operative (society)
Verbrauchergewohnheiten *fpl* consumer habits
Verbrauchergruppe *f* group of consumers, consumer group
Verbraucherhöchstpreis *m* retail ceiling price
Verbraucherkredit *m s.* **Verbraucherabzahlungskredit**
Verbraucherkreis *m* consumers
Verbraucherland *n* consuming country
Verbrauchermacht *f* consumer power
Verbrauchermarkt *m* consumers' market
Verbrauchernachfrage *f* consumer demand
Verbraucherpreis *m* consumer [retail] price
Verbraucherpreisbildung *f* consumer price formation
Verbraucherpreisindex *m* consumer price index
Verbraucherpreisvorschläge *mpl* price offers, proposed prices
Verbraucherrisiko *n* consumer's risk
Verbraucherschaft *f* consumers
Verbraucherschicht *f* consumer group
Verbraucherschutz *m* consumer protection
Verbraucherschwerpunkt *m* centre of consumption
verbraucherseitig from the point of view of consumers
Verbrauchersortiment *n s.* **Verbrauchssortiment**
Verbrauchersteuer *f s.* **Verbrauchssteuer**
Verbraucherstreik *m* consumers' strike
Verbraucherstruktur *f* consumer structure
Verbrauchertest *m* consumer test *(by a sample of consumers)*
Verbraucher-Test-Organisation *f* organization for testing consumer goods; Consumers' Association *(UK)*

Verbraucherumfrage *f* consumer survey
Verbraucherwerbung *f* consumer advertising
Verbraucherzentrum *n s.* **Verbraucherschwerpunkt**
Verbraucherzweig *m* user [consumer] branch *(of industry etc. of a product)*
Verbrauchsabgabe *f* tax on consumer goods
Verbrauchsabweichung *f* deviation from normal consumption
Verbrauchsanstieg *m* increase in consumption
Verbrauchsartikel *m* (consumer) article, article of consumption
Verbrauchsausgaben *fpl* expenditure on consumption
Verbrauchsbesteuerung *f* 1. taxation of consumer goods; 2. taxation on consumption
Verbrauchseinheit *f* consuming unit; unit of consumption
Verbrauchselastizität *f* elasticity of consumption
Verbrauchsermittlung *f s.* **Verbrauchsforschung**
Verbrauchsforschung *f* consumption research
Verbrauchsfreudigkeit *f s.* **Verbrauchsneigung**
Verbrauchsfunktion *f* consumption function
Verbrauchsgewohnheit *f* consumer habit
Verbrauchsgüter *npl* consumer goods
~, **kurzlebige** perishable goods; goods with short service-life
~, **langlebige** consumer durables
Verbrauchsgüterbereich *m* sector of consumer goods
Verbrauchsgüterindustrie *f* consumer goods industry
Verbrauchsgütermarkt *m* consumer goods market
Verbrauchsgütersektor *m s.* **Verbrauchsgüterbereich**
Verbrauchskapazität *f* consumption capacity
Verbrauchskennziffer *f* consumption indicator *(statistical figure indicating the utilization or consumption of a certain good per capita, per household or social establishment)*
Verbrauchskoeffizient *m* consumption coefficient
Verbrauchskonzeption *f* programme of consumption
Verbrauchsland *n s.* **Verbraucherland**
Verbrauchslenkung *f* consumption control
Verbrauchsmarkt *m s.* **Verbrauchermarkt**
Verbrauchsmenge *f* amount of goods consumed
Verbrauchsneigung *f* propensity to consume
Verbrauchsniveau *n* level of consumption
Verbrauchsnorm *f* consumption norm [standard] *(of material etc.)*
Verbrauchsnormierung *f* fixing the norm [standards] of consumption *(materials etc.)*

Verbrauchsnormung *f s.* **Verbrauchsnormierung**
Verbrauchsplanung *f* consumption planning
Verbrauchsquote *f* rate of consumption
Verbrauchsregelung *f* rationing of goods
Verbrauchsrekord *m* consumption record
Verbrauchsrichtung *f* consumption trend
Verbrauchsrückgang *m* decrease in consumption
Verbrauchssatz *m s.* **Verbrauchsquote**
Verbrauchsskala *f* range of consumption
Verbrauchssortiment *n* assortment [mix] (of consumer goods)
Verbrauchsstatistik *f* consumption statistics
Verbrauchssteigerung *f s.* **Verbrauchsanstieg**
Verbrauchssteuer *f* indirect tax, excise duty
verbrauchssteuerfrei unexcised
verbrauchssteuerpflichtig excisable
Verbrauchsstruktur *f* consumption pattern, structure of consumption
Verbrauchsumschichtungen *fpl* changes [shifts] in the pattern of consumption
Verbrauchswerbung *f s.* **Verbraucherwerbung**
Verbrauchswert *m* use-value
verbrauchswirksam affecting consumption
verbraucht used up; finished ⋄ **nicht** ~ unused, not fully used
verbreiten to spread, to diffuse; to distribute; to disseminate *(ideas, knowledge etc.)*
Verbreitung *f* spreading, diffusion; distribution; dissemination *(ideas, knowledge etc.)*
~ **von Informationen** dissemination of information
Verbreitungsgebiet *n* area of coverage, distribution [circulation] area
verbriefen to confirm by documents; to secure by charter
verbrieft chartered; licensed
verbuchen to book *(order etc.)*; *(acc)* to enter, to make an entry
Verbuchung *f (acc)* entry
~, **nachträgliche** *(acc)* post entry
Verbuchungsdatum *n* date of entry *(item etc.)*
Verbund *m* integration *(power system etc.)*
Verbundenheit *f* bond, tie; connection, relationship; *(stats)* association, colligation, connection
verbunden sein 1. to be obliged; 2. to be tied to *(project etc.)*
verbünden, sich to confederate; to ally, to form an alliance
Verbündeter *m* ally
Verbundnetz *n* integrated grid
Verbundprodukt *n* compound product
Verbundwirtschaft *f* technical and organizational linkage *(of power stations, industrial enterprises etc.)*

verbürgen, sich to warrant, to guarantee, to stand surety, to give security; to bail
verbürgt warranted; confirmed; authentic
Verdacht *m* suspicion
verdächtig suspicious
Verderb *m* decay; waste *(foodstuffs etc.)*; ruin, destruction; deterioration
verderben 1. to spoil; to get spoiled [damaged]; to go bad, to deteriorate; to perish; 2. to ruin; to destroy
verderblich perishable *(goods)* ◊ **leicht ~** perishable
Verderblichkeit *f* perishableness *(of goods)*
verdienen 1. to earn, to gain, to get, to win *(money)*; 2. to deserve, to merit *(appreciation)* ◊ **nebenbei ~** to earn from a secondary occupation; to moonlight; **zusätzlich ~** to earn additionally
Verdiener *m* earner; bread-winner
Verdienst *m* earnings, wages; salary; gain, profit
~, effektiver actual earnings [wages, salary]
~, entgangener lost earnings [wages, salary]
~, zusätzlicher additional earnings [wages, salary]
Verdienst *n* merit *(appreciation)*
Verdienstausfall *m* loss of earnings [wages, salary]
Verdienstspanne *f* profit margin
verdient:
 ◊ **sich um etwas ~ machen** to earn merit for doing s.th.
verdingen to hire out *(s.th.)*; **sich ~** to go into service (with), to hire o.s. out
Verdingung *f* hire, hiring out; *(jur)* adjudication
Verdingungsergebnis *n* *(jur)* adjudication
Verdingungsvertrag *m* hiring-out agreement
verdorben spoilt; tainted *(meat)*
verdrängen to push away; to displace; to price out *(goods from the market etc.)*; to oust *(s.o. from office etc.)*
Verdrängung *f* displacement; ousting *(s.o. from office etc.)*
Vedünnungsreihe *f* *(stats)* dilution series
veredeln to process, to finish, to refine *(raw materials, goods etc.)*; to improve *(soil)*; to upgrade *(product etc.)*
veredelt processed, finished; improved *(soil)*; upgraded *(product etc.)*
Veredelung *f* processing, finishing, refining; upgrading *(product etc.)*; improvement *(soil)*
Veredelungsbetrieb *m* processing enterprise
Veredelungserzeugnis *n* processed [finished] product; upgraded product
Veredelungsindustrie *f* processing industry
Veredelungskosten *pl* costs of product upgrading
Veredelungsland *n* processing country

Veredelungspolice *f* *(ins)* combining policy
Veredelungsprodukt *n* upgraded product
Veredelungsproduktion *f* finishing production
Veredlungsprozeß *m* (product) upgrading process; finishing process
Veredelungsverfahren *n* s. Veredelungsprozeß
Veredelungsverkehr *m* international (commercial) subcontracting, *(Am)* crossborder contracting
~, aktiver re-export (of goods upgraded), export processing
~, passiver (processing for) re-import (of goods upgraded), re-import processing
Veredelungswirtschaft *f* processing (branches)
vereidigen to swear *(s.o.)* in, to put *(s.o.)* under oath
vereidigt sworn *(broker etc.)*
Vereidigung *f* swearing in
vereinbar compatible (with), consistent (with)
vereinbaren to agree upon, to arrange; to stipulate ◊ **im voraus ~** to pre-arrange; **sich nicht ~ lassen** to be inconsistent with; **sich ~ lassen** to be consistent with
vereinbart agreed (upon), stipulated ◊ **wie ~** as agreed (upon), as stipulated
Vereinbarung *f* agreement; arrangement; clause, provision ◊ **eine ~ erzielen** to reach an agreement; **eine ~ nicht einhalten** to break an agreement; **eine ~ treffen** *s.* **eine ~ erzielen**; **nach ~** by appointment; **sich an eine ~ halten** to keep to an agreement
~, internationale international convention
~, mündliche verbal agreement
~, schriftliche written agreement
~, stillschweigende implicit contract [agreement], gentlemen's agreement
~, vertragliche contractual arrangement [agreement]
~, völkerrechtliche (international) convention
~, vorläufige interim agreement
Vereinbarungen *fpl*:
 ◊ **entgegen früheren ~** against previous arrangements
vereinbarungsgemäß as per agreement
Vereinbarungspreis *m* agreed price
vereinfachen to simplify
Vereinfachung *f* simplification
vereinheitlichen to make uniform; to unify; to standardize
Vereinheitlichung *f* unification; standardization
vereinigen to unite *(people etc.)*; to combine, to merge, to fuse *(enterprises etc.)*; **sich ~** to ally o.s. with *(s.o. etc.)*; to join in *(partnership, marriage etc.)*
vereinigt united; joined
Vereinigung *f* 1. association, union; organization, society; 2. amalgamation, merger

~, berufliche professional association
~ der Arbeitgeberverbände association of employers, employers' association
~, gemeinnützige non-profit(-making) organization
~, internationale international union [federation]
~, wirtschaftliche economic union
~, wohltätige welfare [benevolent] organization
Verelendung *f* pauperization; impoverishment; immiserization
~ des Proletariats, absolute absolute pauperization of the proletariat
~ des Proletariats, relative relative pauperization of the proletariat
Verelendungstheorie *f* theory of pauperization
Verfahren *n* 1. process, method, technique; 2. *(jur)* procedure, (legal) proceedings; 3. policy, system *(guide-lines etc.)* ✧ **ein ~ eröffnen** *(jur)* to open (legal) proceedings; **ein ~ gegen jmdn. einleiten** to institute [take] legal proceedings against s.o.
~, abgekürztes *(jur)* summary proceedings
~, abtrennbares *(jur)* separable proceedings
~, einheitliches 1. standard procedure; 2. standard technology
~, gerichtliches court trial; legal proceedings
~, getrenntes *(jur)* separate action
~, industrielles industrial method [technology]
~, konkursrechtliches (legal) proceedings in bankruptcy
~, materialsparendes *(ind)* material-economizing method
~, neues *(ind)* new process [method, technique, technology]
~, ordentliches *(jur)* legal proceedings
~, patentfähiges *(ind)* patentable method [process]
~, privatrechtliches *(jur)* civil proceedings
~, strafrechtliches criminal proceedings
~, verteilungsfreies *(stats)* distribution-free method
~, verteilungsunabhängiges *s.* **~, verteilungsfreies**
Verfahrenseinstellung *f (jur)* stay of proceedings
Verfahrenskosten *pl* legal costs
Verfahrensregeln *fpl* standing rules
Verfahrensträger *m* technologically leading enterprise
Verfahrensvorschriften *fpl* rules of procedure
Verfall *m* decay, ruin; dilapidation *(buildings)*; forfeiture *(claim etc.)*; expiry, expiration *(visa etc.)*; foreclosure *(mortgage etc.)*; maturity *(bill etc.)* ✧ **bei ~** upon expiry; when due, at maturity *(bill etc.)*
Verfalldatum *n* date of expiry; date of maturity

verfallen to (fall into) decay, to go to ruin; to fall into disrepair *(buildings etc.)*; to become forfeited *(claim etc.)*; to expire *(visa etc.)*; to foreclose *(mortgage etc.)*; to become mature, to be due *(bill etc.)*
verfallend decayed, ruinous; dilapidated *(buildings etc.)*; forfeited *(claim etc.)*; expired *(visa etc.)*; foreclosed *(mortgage etc.)*
Verfallklausel *f* expiry clause
Verfallserklärung *f (com)* foreclosure
Verfallserscheinung *f* symptom of decline [decay]
Verfallszeitpunkt *m* day of payment; due date; expiry date
Verfalltag *m s.* **Verfallszeitpunkt**
verfälschen to falsify *(statement etc.)*; to counterfeit *(bank notes etc.)*; to forge *(signature etc.)*; to adulterate *(commodities etc.)*
Verfälschung *f* falsification *(statement etc.)*; counterfeiting *(bank notes etc.)*; forging, forgery *(signature etc.)*; adulteration *(commodities etc.)*; *(stats)* bias
verfassen to draw up, to draft *(document etc.)*, to write *(report etc.)*
Verfasser *m* author, writer
Verfassung *f* 1. state, condition; 2. constitution *(of a state)*; 3. drawing up, drafting *(document etc.)*, writing *(report etc.)* ✧ **in guter ~** in good condition
~, finanzielle financial state [position]
Verfassungsänderung *f* constitutional amendment
Verfassungsbestimmung *f* constitutional provision
Verfassungsbruch *m* violation of the constitution
verfassungsgemäß *s.* **verfassungsmäßig**
Verfassungskrise *f* constitutional crisis
verfassungsmäßig constitutional
Verfassungsrecht *n* constitutional law
Verfassungsrechte *npl* constitutional rights ✧ **~ aufheben** to abrogate constitutional rights
verfassungsrechtlich legal, according to constitutional law
Verfassungsreform *f* constitutional reform
Verfassungsurkunde *f* constitution, constitutional charter
Verfassungsvorschrift *f s.* **Verfassungsbestimmung**
verfassungswidrig unconstitutional
verfaulen to rot *(fruits, vegetables etc.)*, to moulder *(food etc.)*; to decay *(society etc.)*
verfechten to stand up for, to defend; to argue, to advocate, to champion *(idea etc.)*
Verfechter *m* protagonist; advocate; champion
Verfechtung *f* defence; arguing *(ideas etc.)*
verfehlen to miss; to fail

verfehlt wrong; false; misspent; miscarried
Verfehlung *f* mistake; offence
verfeinern to improve; to refine, to process
Verfeinerung *f* improving, improvement; refining, refinement; processing
verfertigen to fabricate, to manufacture, to make
Verfertigung *f* fabrication, manufacture, making
Verflechtung *f* interlocking, interdependence; business concentration; interrelation
~, **statistische** interrelationship of statistical figures
~, **wirtschaftliche** economic interdependence
Verflechtungsanalyse *f* input-output analysis
Verflechtungsbeziehungen *fpl* interlocking relations, relations of interdependence
Verflechtungsbilanz *f* input-output table
~ **der Geldbeziehungen** monetary input-output table, input-output table of monetary relations
~ **der Produktion und Verteilung der Erzeugnisse** input-output table of production and allocation of goods
~ **der Warenzirkulation** input-output table of commodity circulation
~ **des gesellschaftlichen Gesamtprodukts** input-output table of the gross product
~, **dynamische** dynamic input-output table
~, **dynamische zwischengebietliche** dynamic interregional input-output table
~, **finanzielle** financial input-output table
~, **halbdynamische** semi-dynamic input-output table
~, **materielle** input-output table in physical terms
~, **territoriale** regional input-output table
~, **volkswirtschaftliche** national economic input-output table
Verflechtungsbilanzierung *f* balancing by means of input-output table(s)
Verflechtungskoeffizient *m* input-output coefficient
Verflechtungsmethode *f* method of balancing by means of input-output table(s)
~, **materiell-finanzielle** method of balancing by means of input-output table in physical and financial terms
Verflechtungsmodell *n* input-output model
verfolgen to pursue, to follow (up) *(idea etc.)*; to persecute *(person)*; *(jur)* to prosecute
Verfolgung *f* pursuit, following (up) *(idea etc.)*; persecution *(person)*; *(jur)* prosecution
verfrachten to charter *(ship)*; to load, to ship
Verfrachter *m* freighter, forwarding agent, *(Am)* shipper
Verfrachtung *f* freighting, carriage, shipment, shipping; chartering, hiring out

verfügbar available, disposable, in hand ◇ **nicht ~** unavailable, indisposable; **uneingeschränkt ~** fully available
Verfügbarkeit *f* availability
verfügen 1. to decree, to order, to arrange; 2. to dispose of, to be master of, to have at one's disposal; 3. to proceed to
Verfügung *f* 1. decree, order, arrangement; 2. disposal, having at one's disposal ◇ **jmdm. etwas zur ~ stellen** to place s.th. at s.o.'s disposal; **sich zur ~ halten** to stand by; **zur ~ haben** to have at hand; **zur ~ halten** to hold to the order *(money)*; **zur ~ stehen** to be available; to stand by; to be at one's disposal
~, **alleinige** sole use
~, **einstweilige** interim injunction, restraining order
~, **freie** free disposal
~, **letztwillige** testamentary disposition
~, **nachträgliche** retrospective order
Verfügungen *fpl* arrangements; instructions ◇ **~ treffen** to make arrangements, to give orders
Verfügungsbefugnis *f* power of disposal
verfügungsberechtigt entitled to dispose
Verfügungsberechtigung *f s.* **Verfügungsbefugnis**
Verfügungsbeschränkung *f* restraint
Verfügungsgewalt *f* control, disposal
Verfügungsklausel *f* disposal clause
Verfügungsmacht *f s.* **Verfügungsrecht**
Verfügungsrecht *n* right of disposal [disposing]
~, **unbeschränktes** outright disposal
Verfügungsverbot *n (jur)* interdiction, restraining order
Vergabe *f* giving away; *(com)* placing *(orders etc.)*; allocation *(public means etc.)*
~ **von Wohnraum** allocation of flats
vergeben to give away; *(com)* to place *(orders etc.)*; to allocate *(public means etc.)*
vergegenständlichen to materialize
vergehen to pass (away), to elapse, to disappear; to waste away; to perish ◇ **sich ~ gegen** to offend against, to violate, to injure, to assault *(law etc.)*
Vergehen *n* offence
vergelten to repay, to pay back, to return; to reward; to retaliate
Vergeltung *f* return; reward; retaliation, reprisal
Vergeltungszoll *m* retaliatory tariff
vergenossenschaften to form co-operative societies
vergenossenschaftlichen *s.* **vergenossenschaften**
Vergenossenschaft(lich)ung *f* forming co-operative societies
vergesellschaften to nationalize, to socialize
vergesellschaftet nationalized, socialized

Vergesellschaftung *f* socialization
~ **der Arbeit** socialization of labour *(process of heightening the social division of labour)*
~ **der Produktion** socialization of production *(process of heightening the social division of production)*
~ **der Produktionsmittel** socialization of the means of production
vergeuden to waste, to squander *(resources etc.)*
Vergeudung *f* waste, wasting, squandering *(resources etc.)*
Vergleich *m* 1. comparison; comparative analysis; 2. agreement; arrangement; settlement, adjustment, compromise, composition ✧ **einem ~ standhalten mit** to stand a comparison with; **einen ~ abschließen** to come to a compromise, to arrive at a composition *(among a group of creditors and debtors)*; **einen ~ anstellen** to draw a parallel; **einen ~ aufheben** to set aside a composition; **einen ~ herbeiführen** to arrange a settlement; **einen ~ schließen** to compromise *(on s.th.)*
~, **außergerichtlicher** out-of-court settlement
~, **gütlicher** amicable settlement
~, **innerbetrieblicher** intra-enterprise comparative analysis [comparison] *(part of enterprise analysis to compare technical and economic indices of various departments)*
~, **internationaler** international comparison; international statement *(on s.th.)*
~, **multipler** *(maths)* multiple comparison
~, **orthogonaler** *(maths)* orthogonal comparison
~, **paarweise** *(stats)* paired comparison
~, **statistischer** statistical analysis [comparison]
~, **vorgeschlagener** compromise offered
~, **zwischenbetrieblicher** inter-enterprise comparative analysis
vergleichbar comparable ✧ **nicht ~** incommensurate *(salary etc., with one's qualification)*; not comparable
Vergleichbarkeit *f* comparability, comparableness
vergleichen to compare; to collate, to check *(accounts etc.)*; to adjust, to settle *(matters etc.)*
vergleichend comparative
Vergleichsabkommen *n* composition deed
Vergleichsabschluß *m* reaching an agreement
Vergleichsabschnitt *m* base period
Vergleichsanalyse *f* comparative analysis
Vergleichsangaben *fpl* comparative data
Vergleichsangebot *n* offer of a compromise
Vergleichsantrag *m* letter offering a compromise; *(jur)* petition for an arrangement
Vergleichsbedingungen *fpl* terms of settlement
Vergleichsbilanz *f* liquidating balance sheet
Vergleichsdaten *pl s.* **Vergleichsangaben**
Vergleichserzeugnis *n* comparable product

Vergleichsforderung *f* liquidated demand
Vergleichsforschung *f* comparative studies
Vergleichsgegenstand *m* object of comparison
Vergleichsglied *n* *(d.pr.)* device for making a comparison
Vergleichsgrundlagen *fpl* bases of comparison; principles of settlement
Vergleichsgruppen *fpl (stats)* matched samples
Vergleichsjahr *n* base year
Vergleichsmaß *n* criteria of comparison; standard
Vergleichsmaßstab *m* scale of comparison
Vergleichsobjekt *n s.* **Vergleichsgegenstand**
Vergleichsordnung *f* insolvency laws
Vergleichsperiode *f s.* **Vergleichsabschnitt**
Vergleichspreis *m* comparable price; comparative price
Vergleichsquote *f* rate of composition
Vergleichssatz *m s.* **Vergleichsquote**
Vergleichssortiment *n* comparable range of goods
Vergleichsstichproben *fpl (stats)* compared samples
~, **abgestimmte** *(stats)* matched samples
Vergleichssumme *f* (amount of) composition
Vergleichstabelle *f* comparative table
Vergleichstarif *m* comparable rate
Vergleichsunterlagen *fpl* bases of comparison
Vergleichsurkunde *f* deed of settlement, composition deed
Vergleichsverfahren *n* insolvency [settlement] proceedings
Vergleichsversuch *m (stats)* repetition
Vergleichsvertrag *m* composition agreement
Vergleichsverwalter *m* estate manager
Vergleichsvorschlag *m s.* **Vergleichsangebot**
vergleichsweise by way of comparison, comparatively
Vergleichswert *m* relative value; liquidation value
Vergleichszahlen *fpl s.* **Vergleichsangaben**
Vergleichszeitraum *m s.* **Vergleichsabschnitt**
Vergnügungsindustrie *f* entertainment industry
Vergnügungsreise *f* pleasure trip
Vergnügungssteuer *f* entertainment tax
Vergnügungsviertel *n* amusement centre
Vergolder *m* gilder
vergriffen sold out, out of stock *(books etc.)*
vergrößern to enlarge; to increase; to extend; to expand
Vergrößerung *f* enlargement; increase; extension; expansion
vergrößerungsfähig increasable; expandable
Vergünstigung *f* allowance; reduction, deduction *(price)*; concession, privilege, preference
Vergünstigungen *fpl*:
✧ ~ **erhalten** to get preferences; ~ **gewähren**

Verhandlungen 527

to make allowances, to grant preferential treatment
~, **steuerliche** tax privileges
~, **tarifliche** tariff preferences
vergüten 1. to remunerate, to pay *(for work done)*; to reimburse; 2. *(ind)* to refine, to improve *(products etc.)*
Vergütung *f* remuneration, payment *(for work done)*; compensation *(as indemnification)*; fee *(for services rendered etc.)*; reimbursement ◊ **als ~** as payment; **gegen ~** for remuneration; **ohne ~** without compensation
~, **angemessene** fair and reasonable compensation
~ **der Arbeit** remuneration [payment] for work
~, **einmalige** one-time [non-recurring, once-off] payment; lump-sum payment
~, **finanzielle** financial compensation
~ **in Naturalien** compensation in kind; payment [remuneration] in kind
Vergütungsausgleich *m* compensation, indemnification
Vergütungsliste *f* list of wage rates; *(cust)* list of tariffs
Vergütungsordnung *f* salary regulations
Vergütungssatz *m* rate of remuneration, salary rate; rate of compensation
Vergütungsstufe *f* salary level
Vergütungssystem *n* remuneration system
~, **einheitliches** uniform system of remuneration
verhagelt damaged by hail
verhalten to keep back, to stop, to retain; **sich ~** 1. to behave, to act; 2. *(maths)* to be in the ratio of
Verhalten *n* behaviour, conduct; attitude; keeping back, retention
~, **asoziales** anti-social behaviour
~, **induktives** *(stats)* inductive behaviour
~, **ökonomisches** economic behaviour
Verhaltensweise *f* way of acting, behaviour
Verhältnis *n* relation; proportion; rate; ratio ◊ **im umgekehrten ~** in inverse ratio; **im ~ (von)** at the rate (of), in the ratio (of); **in ein richtiges ~ bringen** to proportion; **in keinem ~ stehen** to be out of proportion; **nicht im ~ stehend** disproportionate, out of proportion
~, **besitzähnliches** quasi-possession
~ **der Momente** *(stats)* moment ratio
~, **eheliches** conjugal relation
~, **festes** definitive ratio
~, **intervalutarisches** rate of exchange
~, **nießbrauchähnliches** quasi-usufruct
~, **persönliches** personal relationship
~, **prozentuales** percentage
~, **sachliches** business-like relations
~, **vertragsähnliches** quasi-contractual relationship

~, **verwahrungsähnliches** quasi-deposit
~, **zahlenmäßiges** ratio
Verhältnisanteil *m* proportionate share
verhältnisgleich proportionate
Verhältnisgröße *f* relative figure
Verhältniskennzahl *f* index
Verhältniskennziffer *f s.* **Verhältniskennzahl**
Verhältnisklausel *f* average clause
verhältnismäßig in proportion, proportionate, proportional; relatively, comparatively
Verhältnismaßstab *m (stats)* ratio scale
Verhältnisschätzfunktion *f (stats)* ratio estimator
Verhältnisse *npl* relations; situation, position, conditions; status; circumstances ◊ **in ärmlichen Verhältnissen leben** to live in poverty; **in dürftigen Verhältnissen leben** to be in needy circumstances; **in guten Verhältnissen** to be comfortably off; **in guten Verhältnissen leben** to be in good circumstances, to be well-off; **seinen Verhältnissen entsprechend leben** to live within one's means; **über seine ~ leben** to live beyond one's means
~, **berufliche** professional status
~, **beschränkte** poor circumstances
~, **feudale** feudal relations; feudal conditions
~, **finanzielle** financial conditions [status]
~, **gesellschaftliche** social relations; social conditions [situation, circumstances]
~, **soziale** social conditions
Verhältniswert *m* relative value
verhältniswidrig disproportionate
Verhältniszahl *f (stats)* coefficient, ratio, rate
~, **genetische** *(stats)* genetic coefficient
~, **spezifische** *(stats)* specific rate
~, **synthetische** *(stats)* general coefficient
Verhältnisziffer *f s.* **Verhältniszahl**
verhandeln to negotiate; to discuss, to argue, to debate; *(jur)* to plead, to try *(a case)* ◊ **geheim ~** to negotiate in secret; **mündlich ~** to discuss; *(jur)* to argue *(a case)*; **streitig ~** *(jur)* to settle by legal means; **über etwas ~** to negotiate over s.th.
verhandelt dealt with
Verhandlung *f* negotiation *(agreement, treaty etc.)*; talks, conference; *(jur)* proceeding, hearing; trial *(criminal case)* ◊ **eine ~ verschieben** to postpone [put off] a case; **eine ~ vertagen** to postpone a case
~, **erneute** *(jur)* rehearing, retrial
~, **gerichtliche** trial
~, **nochmalige** *s.* ~, **erneute**
~, **öffentliche** 1. open trial; tribunal; 2. open debate *(parliament etc.)*
Verhandlungen *fpl* negotiations; discussions; *(jur)* hearing ◊ **in ~ eintreten** to enter into negotiations; **~ eröffnen** to open negotiations;

Verhandlungen

~ **in Gang setzen** to set negotiations in train, to start negotiations
Verhandlungsbericht *m* minutes, report of the proceedings
Verhandlungsbevollmächtigter *m* person authorized to negotiate
verhandlungsfähig negotiable
Verhandlungsfähigkeit *f* negotiability
Verhandlungsgegenstand *m* issue, item (on the agenda)
Verhandlungsgrundlage *f* basis of negotiations
Verhandlungsort *m* venue, place of negotiations
Verhandlungspartner *m* party, partner *(in negotiations etc.)*
Verhandlungsposition *f* bargaining position
~, **starke** strong bargaining position
Verhandlungsprotokoll *n s.* **Verhandlungsbericht**
verhandlungsreif ready for negotiation; *(jur)* ready for trial
Verhandlungsstärke *f* bargaining power
Verhandlungstag *m (jur)* day of trial
Verhandlungsvollmacht *f* power [authority] to negotiate
verheiraten to marry; to give in marriage; **sich** ~ to get married
verheiratet married
Verheirateter *m* married person
verhindern to prevent, to hinder
verhindernd prohibitive *(prices, duties etc.)*
Verhinderung *f* prevention; restraint
Verhinderungsfall *m* case of prevention
verhüten to prevent, to ward off
verhütend preventive
Verhütung *f* prevention
~ **von Frostschäden** protection against damage by frost
verjährbar prescriptible
verjähren to become prescriptive; to come under the statute of limitations
verjährt prescriptive; barred by the statute of limitations
Verjährung *f* prescription; statute of limitations
◊ **der** ~ **unterliegen** to be subject to the statute of limitations
Verjährungsfrist *f* period of limitation; period of prescription
~, **gesetzliche** statutory limitation
verkalkulieren, sich to miscalculate
Verkauf *m* sale; selling; realization ◊ **einen** ~ **rückgängig machen** to rescind a sale; **zum** ~ **for sale; zum** ~ **anbieten** to offer for sale; **zum** ~ **kommen** to be sold
~ **auf Kommissionsbasis** sale on commission
~ **auf Kreditbasis** sale on credit
~ **auf offener Straße** street trading [vending]
~ **auf Probe** sale on approval

~ **auf Rechnung** sale on account
~ **auf Teilzahlung** instalment sale
~ **auf Zeit** forward [future] sale
~ **auf Ziel** credit sale
~ **aus zweiter Hand** second-hand sale
~, **betrügerischer** bogus [fraudulent] sale
~ **durch Versandhandel** mail-order sale
~ **en detail** retail trade
~ **en gros** wholesale trade
~ **fingierter** sham sale
~, **freier** free sale
~, **freihändiger** sale by auction
~ **gegen Barzahlung** cash sale, sale over the counter
~ **gegen Nachnahme** cash-on-delivery sale
~, **gerichtlicher** compulsory sale by the court
~, **gewinnbringender** profitable sale
~ **mit Rückgaberecht** sale and return
~ **mit Rückkaufsrecht** sale with privilege of repurchase
~ **nach Muster** sale by sample
~ **nach Probe** *s.* ~ **nach Muster**
~, **öffentlicher** public sale
~ **pro forma** pro forma sale
~, **rationierter** rationed sale
~, **rückgängig gemachter** cancelled [countermanded] sale
~ **über den Ladentisch** over-the-counter sale
~, **unrationierter** *s.* ~, **freier**
~ **unter dem Ladentisch** under-the-counter sale
~ **unter Eigentumsvorbehalt** executory sale
~ **unter Vorbehalt** conditional sale
~ **zu Verlustpreisen** selling at a loss
~, **zwangsweise durchgeführter** compulsory sale
~, **zwangsweiser** *s.* ~, **zwangsweise durchgeführter**
Verkäufe *mpl* sales; transactions
~ **auf Baisse** *(st.ex.)* selling stocks short
~ **auf dem offenen Markt** open market sales
~ **aus dem Portefeuille** sales from the portfolio
~ **in Partien** sales in lots
~ **von Nostroeffekten** *s.* ~ **aus dem Portefeuille**
verkaufen to sell ◊ **bestens** ~ *(st.ex.)* to sell at the best possible rates; **billig** ~ to sell cheap, to sell at a low price; **direkt** ~ to sell direct; **en gros** ~ to sell to wholesale, to sell in the gross; **freihändig** ~ to sell off-hand; **gegen bar** ~ to sell for cash; **indirekt** ~ to sell indirectly; **meistbietend** ~ to sell to the highest bidder; **öffentlich** ~ to sell publicly; **preiswert** ~ to sell at a good price; **sich gut** ~ to be quick of sale; **stückweise** ~ to sell by the piece; **teuer** ~ to sell at a high price; **zu billig** ~ to sell too cheap

Verkäufer *m* shop assistant; seller
Verkäuferin *f* salesgirl
Verkäuferkartell *n* price ring
Verkäuferland *n* seller's country
Verkäufermarkt *m* sellers' market
verkäuflich saleable, marketable; on sale ⋄ **frei** ~ free on sale; **gut** ~ easily saleable, easy to sell; **nicht** ~ not for sale, unsaleable; **schlecht** ~ hard to sell; **schwer** ~ slow of sale; ~ **sein** to be for sale
Verkäuflichkeit *f* marketability
Verkaufsabkommen *n* sales agreement *(among cartels to divide up the market)*
Verkaufsabrechnung *f* sales account
Verkaufsabsichten *fpl* sales intentions
Verkaufsabsprache *f s.* **Verkaufsabkommen**
Verkaufsabteilung *f* sales department
Verkaufsagent *m* sales agent
Verkaufsagentur *f* sales agency; sales agent
Verkaufsakt *m* sale
Verkaufsanalyse *f* sales analysis
Verkaufsangebot *n* sales offer
Verkaufsanreiz *m* selling appeal
Verkaufsanstrengungen *fpl* sales efforts
Verkaufsanzeige *f* sales advertisement
Verkaufsapparat *m* sales machinery
Verkaufsauftrag *m* selling order
Verkaufsaufwendungen *fpl* sales expenditure
Verkaufsauslage *f* sales display
Verkaufsausrüstung *f* sales equipment and fittings
Verkaufsaussichten *fpl* sales prospects
Verkaufsausstellung *f* sales display [show, exhibition]
Verkaufsautomat *m* (automatic) vending machine
Verkaufsbedingungen *fpl* terms [conditions] of sale
~, **Allgemeine** General Terms [Conditions] of Sale
Verkaufsbeleg *m* sales slip
Verkaufsbemühungen *fpl s.* **Verkaufsanstrengungen**
Verkaufsberechtigung *f* authority to sell
Verkaufsbereitschaft *f* readiness for sale
Verkaufsbescheinigung *f* certificate of sale
Verkaufsbeschränkung *f* restriction on sales, selling [sales] restriction
Verkaufsbezirk *m s.* **Verkaufsgebiet**
Verkaufsbüro *n* sales office
Verkaufseinrichtung *f* shop, store
Verkaufserfahrung *f* sales experience
Verkaufserfolg *m* sales success
Verkaufsergebnis *n* sales results
Verkaufserlaubnis *f* licence [authority] to sell
Verkaufserlös *m* proceeds from sales
Verkaufsertrag *m s.* **Verkaufserlös**

Verkaufserwartungen *fpl* sales expectations
verkaufsfähig saleable, marketable
Verkaufsfähigkeit *f* saleability, marketability
Verkaufsfläche *f s.* **Verkaufsraumfläche**
Verkaufsförderung *f* sales promotion
Verkaufsform *f* methods of sales, selling methods
Verkaufsforschung *f* market research
Verkaufsgebiet *n* sales area
Verkaufsgegenstand *m* article of sale
Verkaufsgelegenheit *f* sales opportunity
Verkaufsgemeinschaft *f* joint sales agency
Verkaufsgenehmigung *f s.* **Verkaufserlaubnis**
Verkaufsgenossenschaft *f* sales co-operative (society)
Verkaufsgespräch *n* sales talks
Verkaufsgewicht *n* selling weight
Verkaufsgewinn *m* sales profit
Verkaufshalle *f* market hall
Verkaufshilfe *f* help in selling s.th.; shop assistant
Verkaufskalkulation *f* sales calculation
~, **nachträgliche** post-sales calculation
~, **vorausschauende** prospective sales calculation
Verkaufskampagne *f* sales campaign
Verkaufskapazität *f* sales capacity
Verkaufskartell *n s.* **Verkäuferkartell**
Verkaufskiosk *m* kiosk
Verkaufsklima *n* sales climate, market atmosphere
Verkaufskommission *f* sales committee
Verkaufskontingent *n* sales quota
Verkaufskonto *n* sales account
Verkaufskontor *n* sales agency
Verkaufskontrakt *m* sales contract
Verkaufskontrolle *f* sales control
Verkaufskosten *pl* selling costs
Verkaufskraft *f* shop assistant, salesman, saleswoman, salesgirl
Verkaufskultur *f* standard of sales service, quality of service and personnel (in retail trade)
Verkaufskurs *m (st.ex.)* asked price
Verkaufslager *n* store (room)
Verkaufsland *n s.* **Verkäuferland**
Verkaufsleistung *f* sales
Verkaufsleiter *m* sales manager
Verkaufslimit *n* sales limit
Verkaufslizenz *f s.* **Verkaufserlaubnis**
Verkaufsmarkt *m s.* **Verkäufermarkt**
Verkaufsmesse *f* sales fair
Verkaufsmethode *f* sales method
~, **unlautere** unfair [disreputable] sales method
Verkaufsmöglichkeit *f. s.* **Verkaufsgelegenheit**
Verkaufsmonopol *n* sales monopoly
Verkaufsmuster *n* sales sample

Verkaufsneigung *f* inclination to sell; propensity to sell
Verkaufsnetz *n* sales network
Verkaufsnorm *f* sales norm
Verkaufsofferte *f* sales offer
Verkaufsorder *f* sales order, order to sell
Verkaufsorganisation *f* sales organization
Verkaufsort *m* place of sale
Verkaufspersonal *n* shop assistants; salesmen; saleswomen, salesgirls; sales personnel
Verkaufspolitik *f* sales policy
Verkaufspotential *n* sales capacity
Verkaufspraktiken *fpl* sales practices
Verkaufspreis *m* selling price
Verkaufspreisklausel *f* selling clause
Verkaufsprinzipien *npl* sales principles
Verkaufsprognose *f* sales forecast
Verkaufsprogramm *n* sales programme
Verkaufsprovision *f* sales commission
Verkaufspsychologie *f* selling psychology
Verkaufsquote *f* sales quota
Verkaufsrabatt *m* sales discount
Verkaufsraum *m* sales room
Verkaufsraumfläche *f* shop floorspace
Verkaufsrechnung *f* bill; invoice
Verkaufsrecht *n* licence; selling rights
~, **ausschließliches** exclusive selling rigths
Verkaufssaison *f* selling season
Verkaufsschau *f s.* **Verkaufsausstellung**
Verkaufsschlager *m* hit, best-seller
Verkaufsschulung *f* sales training
Verkaufsspanne *f* sales margin
Verkaufsspesen *pl* sales expenses
Verkaufsstand *m* kiosk, booth, stand, stall
Verkaufsstatistik *f* sales statistics
Verkaufsstelle *f* shop, *(Am)* store ⋄ **eine ~ leiten** to run a shop; **eine ~ schließen** to close (down) a shop; **eine ~ übernehmen** to take over a shop
~ **betriebseigene** factory-owned shop
Verkaufsstellenausschuß *m* advisory board of a shop *(elected members of public to assist in planning and management of a co-operative shop in an honorary capacity)*
Verkaufsstellenbeirat *m* advisory board of a shop
Verkaufsstellenbericht *m* shop [shopkeeper's] report
Verkaufsstellenleiter *m* shop manager
Verkaufsstellennetz *n* network of shops *(in an area)*
Verkaufsstellenplan *m* sales plan of a shop
Verkaufsstellenplanabrechnung *f* sales plan accounting of a shop
Verkaufsstellenübernahme *f* taking over a shop
Verkaufsstellenvertrag *m* delivery contract *(concluded between the manager of a shop, as recipient, and an industrial or agricultural enterprise, as supplier)*
Verkaufssteuer *f* sales tax
Verkaufsstopp *m* sales stop
Verkaufsstützpunkt *m* 1. foreign sales branch *(of exporters)*; 2. local kiosk *(at building sites etc.)*; mobile kiosk *(at camping places etc.)*
Verkaufssyndikat *n* sales syndicate
Verkaufssystem *n* sales system
Verkaufstage *mpl* sales days
Verkaufstätigkeit *f* sales (work); marketing (work)
Verkaufstechnik *f s.* **Verkaufsmethoden**
Verkaufstraining *n* sales training
Verkaufstüchtigkeit *f* salesmanship
Verkaufsumsatz *m* sales turnover
Verkaufs- und Auslieferungszeit *f* period of sale and delivery
Verkaufsunkosten *pl s.* **Verkaufsspesen**
Verkaufsunterlagen *fpl* sales documents
Verkaufsveranstaltung *f* sales promotion
Verkaufsverbot *n* ban on sales
Verkaufsvereinbarung *f s.* **Verkaufsabkommen**
Verkaufsverfahren *n s.* **Verkaufsmethode**
Verkaufsverhandlungen *fpl* sales negotiations
Verkaufsvertrag *m* contract of purchase, sales [purchase] contract; deed of purchase; title deed *(real estate)*; bill of sale *(ships)*
Verkaufsvertreter *m* sales agent
~, **alleiniger** sole agent
Verkaufsvertretung *f* sales agency
Verkaufsvollmacht *f s.* **Verkaufsberechtigung**
Verkaufsvolumen *n* amount of sales
Verkaufsvoraussage *f s.* **Verkaufsprognose**
Verkaufsvorgang *m* sales act
Verkaufswagen *m* mobile shop
Verkaufswerbung *f* sales promotion, consumer advertising
Verkaufswert *m* sales value
Verkaufswettbewerb *m* sales contest
Verkaufswoche *f* sales [market] week
Verkaufszahlen *fpl* market data
Verkaufszeit *f* period of sale
Verkaufszentrale *f* sales centre
Verkaufszentrum *n* shopping centre
Verkaufsziel *n* sales target
Verkaufsziffern *fpl s.* **Verkaufszahlen**
Verkaufszone *f* sales area
Verkaufszusage *f* sales promise
verkauft sold ⋄ **nicht ~** unsold
Verkehr *m* traffic; transportation; commerce, business, trade; service, communication; circulation ⋄ **aus dem ~ ziehen** to withdraw from circulation; **dem ~ übergeben** to open to traffic; **den ~ einstellen** to stop transport; **den ~ regeln** to regulate the traffic; **den ~ umleiten** to divert [reroute] traffic; **in den**

freien ~ geben to release into free circulation; in ~ bringen to put into circulation, to issue, to emit *(money, securities etc.)*
~, **bargeldloser** cashless transaction
~, **direkter** through traffic
~, **fließender** flowing traffic
~, **freier** free commerce, unrestricted trade
~, **gebrochener** transport with changing means of conveyance
~, **geschäftlicher** business relations
~, **grenzüberschreitender** traffic across the frontier(s), cross-border traffic; international border traffic
~, **individueller** private transport
~, **kombinierter** combined transport(ation)
~, **kommerzieller** transport of goods; commercial transactions
~, **ländlicher** rural transport
~, **laufender** 1. flowing traffic; 2. regular contacts
~, **lebhafter** *(st.ex.)* lively dealings
~, **nichtkommerzieller** non-commercial transactions
~, **öffentlicher** public transport
~, **schleichender** crawling traffic
~, **städtischer** urban transport
~, **starker** heavy traffic
~, **stockender** unsteady flow of traffic
~, **telegrafischer** telegraphic communication
~, **ungebrochener** through transport *(without changing the means of transport)*
verkehren 1. to turn the wrong way; to revert (to); to change (to), to transform; 2. *(transp)* to ply [run] (between); 3. to associate (with), to see a good deal *(of s.o.)*
Verkehrsabgaben *fpl* road tax
Verkehrsabkommen *n* transport agreement; traffic agreement
Verkehrsabteilung *f* traffic department; transport department
Verkehrsader *f* arterial road
Verkehrsamt *n s.* **Verkehrsbüro**
Verkehrsanalyse *f* traffic analysis, analysis of traffic flow(s)
Verkehrsanlagen *fpl* transport facilities
Verkehrsausstellung *f* exhibition of transport and communications
Verkehrsbedürfnis *n* need for transportation
Verkehrsbeschränkung *f* traffic restriction
Verkehrsbestimmungen *fpl* traffic rules
Verkehrsbetrieb *m* transport enterprise [firm]
~, **städtischer** municipal [local] transport service(s)
Verkehrsbüro *n* tourist office
Verkehrsdichte *f* density of traffic
~ **im Güterverkehr** freight density, density of goods traffic

~ **im Personenverkehr** density of passenger traffic
Verkehrserleichterungen *fpl* transport facilities
Verkehrsfläche *f (transp)* traffic area; *(home tr)* customers' area
Verkehrsfrequenz *f* frequency of means of transport(ation)
verkehrsgünstig in a favourable position for traffic facilities
Verkehrshindernis *n* traffic barrier [obstruction]
Verkehrshypothek *f* common law mortgage
Verkehrskaufmann *m* commercial clerk (with special skills in transport and tourism)
Verkehrsknotenpunkt *m* junction
Verkehrskoordination *f* co-ordination of transport facilities
Verkehrsleistung *f* performance of the transport(ation) sector
Verkehrsmittel *npl* transport facilities, means of transport
~, **öffentliche** public means of transport
~, **städtische** urban means of transport
Verkehrsnetz *n* communication network
Verkehrsordnung *f* traffic regulations; highway code
Verkehrsplan *m* traffic plan
~, **komplexer** comprehensive traffic plan *(drafted by regional authorities for co-ordination of all forms of transport)*
Verkehrsplanung *f* traffic planning
Verkehrspolitik *f* transport [traffic] policy
Verkehrspolizei *f* traffic police
Verkehrsprobleme *npl* traffic [transport] problems
Verkehrsprognose *f* forecast of transport development
Verkehrsrecht *n* traffic code
~, **internationales** international traffic code
Verkehrsregelung *f* traffic control
Verkehrsrisiko *n* traffic hazard
Verkehrsschwankungen *fpl* traffic variations [fluctuations]
Verkehrssicherheit *f* traffic [road] safety, safety in traffic [on the road]
Verkehrsspitze *f* peak [rush] hours, peak of traffic
Verkehrsstärke *f* traffic load
Verkehrsstatistik *f* transport [traffic] statistics
Verkehrsstau *m* traffic jam
Verkehrssteuer *f* 1. (property) conveyance tax; 2. road tax; tax on freight transport
Verkehrsstörung *f* interruption of traffic; traffic congestion
Verkehrsstockung *f s.* **Verkehrsstau**
Verkehrsstrom *m* flow of traffic, traffic flow(s).
Verkehrsstruktur *f* structure of the communication system

Verkehrssystem *n* system of transport(ation)
Verkehrsteilnehmer *m* road user
Verkehrsteilnehmerschulung *f* schooling of road users
Verkehrsträger *m* 1. transport firm(s); 2. means of transport
Verkehrsträgerwechsel *m* changes in the means of transport *(from one point to another)*
Verkehrs- und Nachrichtenwesen *n* transport and communications
verkehrsunfähig *(st.ex.)* non-negotiable
Verkehrsunfall *m* traffic [road] accident
Verkehrsunfallstatistik *f* statistics of traffic accidents
Verkehrsunfallverhütung *f* prevention of traffic accidents
Verkehrsunternehmen *n* transport enterprise
Verkehrsverbindung *f* transport connection
Verkehrsverhältnisse *npl* traffic conditions
Verkehrsverlagerung *f* restructuring of the means of transport *(e.g. from road to rail)*
Verkehrsweg *m* means of transport *(e.g. road, rail, sea, air)*
Verkehrswerbung *f* tourist publicity [advertising]
Verkehrswert *m* market value
~, echter *(tax)* clear market value
Verkehrswesen *n* transport(ation) (system); traffic
Verkehrswirtschaft *f* 1. *(transp)* transport(ation); 2. market economy
Verkehrswissenschaft *f* science of transport(ation)
Verkehrszählung *f* traffic census
Verkehrsziffern *fpl s.* **Verkehrszählung**
Verkettung *f* linkage
Verkettungsgliedzahl *f (stats)* chain index
Verkettungsziffer *f (stats)* chain-relative, link--relevative
verklagen to accuse; to sue, to bring an action against *(s.o.)*
verklaren to protest, to make a protest
Verklarung *f* ship's protest
Verklarungsakte *f* protest
verklausulieren to arrange in clauses, to stipulate (in a clause)
Verklausulierung *f* stipulation (in a clause)
verkleinern to make smaller, to diminish; to reduce *(business etc.)*
Verkleinerung *f* diminishing; reduction *(business etc.)*
verknappen to run short of *(s.th.)*, to shorten (artificially); **sich ~** to become scarce
Verknappung *f* shortage, scarcity; (artificial) shortage ◇ **infolge zeitweiliger ~** owing to temporary scarcity
Verknappungserscheinung *f s.* **Verknappung**

verknüpfen to connect; to combine
Verknüpfung *f* connection; combination; linkage, linking
Verknüpfungsprogramm *n (d.pr.)* linking routine
verkörpern to embody; to personify; to represent
Verkörperung *f* embodiment; personification; representation
verkosten to test, to try *(food etc.)*
verköstigen to board, to feed
Verköstigung *f* board, boarding, food
Verkostung *f* tasting
verkünden to announce, to make known; to publish, to proclaim; to promulgate *(law etc.)*; *(jur)* to pronounce *(sentence)*
Verkündung *f* announcement; publication, proclamation; promulgation *(law etc.)*; *(jur)* pronouncement *(sentence)*
verkürzen to shorten *(working hours, distance etc.)*; to cut short *(stay etc.)*; to narrow gap *(in income between various groups etc.)*
Verkürzung *f* shortening *(working hours, distance etc.)*; cutting short *(stay etc.)*; narrowing gap *(in income between various groups etc.)*
Verladeanlage *f* loading facilities [equipment, gear]
Verladearbeiten *fpl* loading; shipping *(at port)*
Verladeauftrag *m* loading [shipping] order
Verladebahnhof *m* loading station
verladebereit ready to take cargo; ready to be loaded; ready to be shipped
Verladebestimmungen *fpl* loading regulations
Verladebetrieb *m* loading enterprise
Verladeeinrichtung *f* loading equipment; loading [discharging] hall *(mining)*
Verladegebühr *f* loading charges; shipping charges
Verladegewicht *n* loaded weight; shipped weight
Verladegut *n* goods loaded; freight; cargo, cargoes
Verladehafen *m* port of lading
Verladekai *m* quay, wharf
Verladekosten *pl* loading [shipping] costs
Verladeliste *f* freight list; shipper's manifest
verladen to load; to ship
Verladen *n* loading; shipping
Verladeorder *f* loading [shipping] order
Verladeort *m* loading place
Verladepapiere *npl* loading documents
Verlader *m* shipping agent; consignor
Verladerampe *f* loading platform
Verladeschein *m* certificate of receipt
Verladespesen *pl s.* **Verladegebühr**
Verladestation *f s.* **Verladebahnhof**
Verladestelle *f s.* **Verladeort**
Verladevorschriften *fpl s.* **Verladebestimmungen**

Verladung *f* loading; shipping ◊ **nach ~** when loaded; when shipped; **zur ~ bereit** ready for loading; ready for shipping
Verladungsanzeige *f* loading [shipping] advice
Verladungskosten *pl s.* **Verladekosten**
Verladungspapiere *npl s.* **Verladepapiere**
Verladungsschein *m* bill of lading
Verlag *m* publishing house, publishers
verlagern to shift, to displace; to evacuate, to remove
Verlagerung *f* evacuation, removal *(of an enterprise)*; restructuring of the means of transport *(e.g. road, rail, sea, air)*
Verlagsbuchhändler *m s.* **Verleger**
Verlagshandel *m* publishing business [trade]
Verlagshaus *n s.* **Verlag**
Verlagskosten *pl* publishing costs
Verlagslektor *m* (publishing house) editor
Verlagspreis *m* publishing price
Verlagsrecht *n* publisher's right
Verlagsrechte *npl* publishing rights ◊ **~ ablösen** to commute publishing rights; **~ beantragen** to apply for registration of publishing rights; **~ bei** publishing rights by; **~ besitzen** to own publishing rights; **~ erneuern** to renew publishing rights; **~ verletzen** to infringe publishing rights; **~ wahren** to maintain publishing rights
Verlagswesen *n* publishing business
verlangen to demand; to require; to desire
Verlangen *n* demand; request; desire ◊ **auf ~** by request
verlängern to extend, to prolong *(visa etc.)*, to renew *(licence etc.)*
Verlängerung *f* extension, prolongation *(visa etc.)*, renewal *(licence etc.)*
~ **der Arbeitszeit** extension of working hours
~ **der Gültigkeitsdauer** extension of validity
~ **der Zahlungsfrist** extension of time for payment
~ **eines Abonnements** renewal of a subscription
~, **stillschweigende** implicit renewal *(contract etc.)*
Verlängerungsantrag *m* application for extension (of time)
Verlängerungsklausel *f* renewal clause
Verlängerungspolice *f (ins)* renewal policy
Verlängerungsprämie *f (ins)* renewal premium
Verlängerungsquittung *f (ins)* renewal receipt
Verlängerungswechsel *m (st.ex.)* continuation bill
verlangsamen to slow down, to retard
Verlangsamung *f* retardation
verlangt ◊ **~ werden** to be asked for
verlassen to leave *(working place etc.)*; to disembark *(ship)*, to get off *(train etc.)* ◊ **sich ~ auf** to rely on *(s.o. etc.)*

verläßlich reliable
Verläßlichkeit *f* reliability
Verlauf *m* course; progress, development; trend, tendency ◊ **im weiteren ~** in the sequel of, later on; **nach ~ von** after a lapse of
Verlaufsanalyse *f* trend analysis
Verlaufsrichtung *f* trend, tendency
~, **langfristige** *(stats)* secular trend
verlegen 1. to postpone *(appointment etc.)*, to adjourn *(meeting etc.)*; 2. to evacuate, to remove *(enterprise etc.)*; 3. to publish
Verlegen *n* publishing
Verleger *m* publisher
Verlegung *f* 1. postponement *(appointment etc.)*, adjournment *(meeting etc.)*; 2. evacuation, removal *(enterprise etc.)*
Verlegungskosten *pl* costs of removal
Verleih *m* hire, hiring
verleihbar lendable
Verleiheinnahmen *fpl* rentals
verleihen 1. to lend (out), to loan *(money etc.)*; 2. to grant *(rights etc.)*; to bestow, to confer *(title etc.)*
Verleiher *m* lender
Verleihgebühr *f* lending fee, hire charge
Verleihung *f* 1. lending, loan *(money etc.)*; 2. granting *(rights etc.)*, bestowal, bestowing, conferment *(title etc.)*
~ **eines akademischen Grades** conferment of an academic degree
~ **eines Preises** awarding a prize
~ **von Nutzungsrechten** granting rights of use *(land etc.)*
Verleihungsurkunde *f* diploma *(academic degrees etc.)*; prize certificate *(awards etc.)*; charter *(specific rights etc. granted by the head of state)*
verletzbar vulnerable; susceptible
verletzen to injure, to hurt; to damage; to break, to contravene, to violate *(law etc.)*
verletzt injured
Verletzung *f* injury; damage; breach, violation, transgression *(law etc.)* ◊ **unter ~ von** in contravention of
~ **der Brandschutzvorschriften** breach [neglect] of fire prevention regulations
~ **des Bankgeheimnisses** breach of banker's discretion, breaking the code of bank secrecy
~ **des Berufsgeheimnisses** breach of professional secrecy [descretion], breaking the professional code of secrecy
~ **des Garantieversprechens** breach of warranty
~ **eines Geschäftsgeheimnisses** breaking a business secret
~ **eines Vertrages** infringement of a contract
~ **von Warenzeichen** infringement of trademarks

verlieren to lose
Verlierer *m* loser
verlorengehen to get lost
verlosbar callable [disposable] by lot
verlosen to dispose of by lot
Verlosung *f* lottery; raffle
~, **regelmäßige** regular drawing
Verlust *m* loss; bereavement; waste, wastage; leak, escape *(gas etc.)*; forfeiture *(confiscation etc.)*; shrinkage *(goods etc.)* ✧ **als ~ abschreiben** to charge off as loss; **als ~ buchen** to enter [put] as loss; **aufgeben unter ~** to cut one's losses *(in order to avoid further losses)*; **bei ~** if lost; *(jur)* with forfeiture of; **einen ~ abwenden** to turn off a loss; **einen ~ ausgleichen** to offset a loss; **einen ~ ausweisen** to show a loss; **einen ~ decken** to make good [cover] a loss; **einen ~ erleiden** to sustain a loss; **einen ~ ersetzen** to make good [make up for] a loss; **einen ~ vergüten** *s.* **einen ~ decken**; **einen ~ verursachen** to cause a loss; **mit ~ abschließen** to result in a loss; **mit ~ verkaufen** to sell at a loss
~, **absetzbarer** *s.* ~, **abzugsfähiger**
~, **absoluter** dead loss
~, **abzugsfähiger** deductible loss
~ **an Informationen** loss of information
~, **außerplanmäßiger** unplanned loss
~, **buchmäßiger** accounting loss
~, **direkter** direct loss
~, **eingetretener** incurred loss
~, **erlittener** loss sustained
~, **geplanter** *s.* ~, **planmäßiger**
~, **indirekter** indirect loss
~, **mittelbarer** *s.* ~, **indirekter**
~, **planmäßiger** planned losses
~, **reiner** net loss
~, **tatsächlicher** actual loss
~, **teilweiser** partial loss
~, **unmittelbarer** *s.* ~, **direkter**
Verlustabschluß *m* losing bargain
Verlustanteil *m* proportion of losses
Verlustanzeige *f (ins)* immediate notice (of damages)
Verlustartikel *m* unprofitable article
Verlustaufteilung *f* allocation [distribution] of losses
Verlustausgleich *m* making up [compensating] for losses
Verlustbegrenzung *f* limitation of losses
Verlustberechnung *f* calculation of losses
Verlustbetrieb *m* enterprise working with a deficit
Verlustbilanz *f* deficit balance sheet
verlustbringend detrimental
Verluste *mpl* losses ✧ ~ **gleichmäßig verteilen** to apportion losses evenly

Verlustfaktor *m* loss-producing factor
Verlustfunktion *f (stats)* loss function
Verlustgeschäft *n* losing business, loss bargain
Verlustkalkulation *f s.* **Verlustberechnung**
Verlustkonto *n* loss account; account showing a debit balance
Verlustkurve *f* loss curve
verlustlos without any loss
Verlustmatrix *f (stats)* loss matrix
Verlustminderung *f* reduction of losses
Verlustnachweis *m (ins)* proof of loss
Verlustquelle *f* source of losses
Verlustquote *f* ratio of loss, loss ratio
Verlustrechnung *f* loss account
verlustreich bad, poor *(harvest etc.)*
Verlustsaldo *m* balance showing a loss, debit balance
Verlustspanne *f* loss margin
Verluststützung *f* deficit financing
~, **globale** general financing of deficits
~, **produktgebundene** deficit financing related to specific products
Verlustverteilung *f s.* **Verlustaufteilung**
Verlustvortrag *m* debt balance carried forward
Verlustwahrscheinlichkeit *f* probability of losses
Verlustwirtschaft *f* loss-sustaining economy
Verlustzeit *f* wasted time
vermachen to leave, to bequeath *(s.th. for s.o.)*; *(jur)* to devise
Vermächtnis *n* legacy, bequest ✧ **ein ~ aussetzen** to bequeath *(s.th. to s.o.)*
~, **bedingtes** conditional devise
~ **mit aufschiebender Bedingung** executory devise
~, **unbedingtes** absolute legacy
Vermächtnisnehmer *m* legatee
Vermächtnissteuer *f* death duty, inheritance tax
vermarkten to market *(products etc.)*
Vermarktung *f* marketing
~, **dezentralisierte** decentralized marketing
~, **zentralisierte** centralized marketing
Vermarktungskonzept *n* marketing concept
vermehren to increase, to augment; to propagate, to breed; to add to, to expand *(money circulation)*
Vermehrung *f* increase, augmenting; propagation, breeding; expansion *(money circulation)*
Vermehrungsbetrieb *m (agric)* farm producing seeds and seedlings
Vermehrungsvertrag *m* seeds and seedlings contract *(between agricultural farms and specialized nursery to produce highly improved seeds)*
vermeiden to avoid; to evade
Vermeidung *f* avoidance ✧ **zur ~ weiterer Verluste** cutting one's losses
vermengen to confound; to mix up, to blend

Vermengen *n (stats)* confounding
~, **ausgewogenes** *(stats)* balanced confounding
~ **bei geteilten Parzellen** *(stats)* split-plot confounding
~, **doppeltes** *(stats)* double confounding
~ **in faktoriellen Versuchsplänen** *(stats)* confounding in factorial design
~, **teilweises** *(stats)* partial confounding
Vermerk *m* note; notice; remark; endorsement
vermessen to measure, to make measurements; to survey *(land)*
Vermesser *m* surveyor
Vermessung *f* measuring; measurement; survey *(land)*
Vermessungsamt *n* survey office [department]
Vermessungsfachmann *m* (land) surveyor
Vermessungsgebühren *fpl* surveying fees
Vermessungsingenieur *m s.* **Vermesser**
Vermessungskosten *pl s.* **Vermessungsgebühren**
vermietbar rentable *(flat etc.)*
vermieten to hire out, to let (on hire); to rent *(a car)*
Vermieter *m* lessor; landlord
Vermieterhaftpflichtversicherung *f* lessor's liability insurance
Vermieterin *f* landlady
Vermieterpfandrecht *n* landlord's warrant
vermietet rented, hired ⋄ **nicht** ~ vacant *(flat etc.)*
Vermietung *f* letting; leasing; hiring out
~ **von Kraftwagen** renting a car
Vermietungsfläche *f* area to be let *(fair etc.)*
vermindern to lessen, to diminish *(value of s.th. etc.)*; to reduce, to lower, to decrease *(prices etc.)*; to impair *(quality of s.th.)*; to retrench, to cut back *(staff etc.)*; **sich** ~ to diminish, to lessen *(value of s.th.)*; to impair *(quality of s.th.)*
Verminderung *f* lessening, diminishing *(value of s.th.)*, reduction, lowering, decreasing *(prices etc.)*; impairment *(quality of s.th.)*; retrenchment, cutting back *(staff etc.)*
vermitteln to arrange, to adjust; to settle *(disputes etc.)*; to negotiate *(loan etc.)*; to procure, to obtain, to get *(s.th. for s.o.)*, to supply *(s.o. with s.th.)*; to convey, to offer *(idea etc.)*, to impart *(knowledge etc.)*; to mediate *(deal etc.)*; to put a call through *(telephone)*
Vermittler *m* intermediary, mediator *(between countries for a purpose etc.)*; go-between *(to arrange marriages etc.)*; *(com)* agent, middleman
Vermittlerrolle *f* role of mediator
Vermittlung *f* arrangement, adjustment; settlement *(disputes etc.)*; negotiation *(loan etc.)*; procurement, obtaining, getting *(s.th. for s.o.)*; suppling *(s.o. with s.th.)*; conveying, offering *(idea etc.)*, imparting *(knowledge etc.)*; mediating *(deal etc.)*; exchange *(telephone)*
Vermittlungsgebühr *f (com)* commission
Vermittlungsgeschäft *n* agency business
Vermittlungsgroßhandel *m* agency wholesale trade
Vermögen *n* 1. property, funds, assets; 2. faculty, power, capacity, ability ⋄ ~, **zufällige Fehler zu verringern** *(stats)* error reducing power
~, **abgesondertes** separate property
~, **angelegtes** invested capital
~, **anmeldepflichtiges** property to be declared
~, **ausländisches** foreign assets, alien property
~, **bares** cash assets
~, **belastetes** encumbered estate
~, **beschlagnahmtes** confiscated property
~, **bewegliches** movable property, movables
~, **blockiertes** frozen funds
~, **eigenes** one's own property; independent means
~, **ererbtes** inherited property
~, **ertragbringendes** profitable assets
~, **feindliches** enemy property
~, **flüssiges** liquid assets
~, **gemeinsames** common property
~, **genossenschaftliches** co-operative property
~, **gepfändetes** seized property; impounded livestock
~, **gesperrtes** *s.* ~, **blockiertes**
~, **hinterlegtes** bailed property
~, **landwirtschaftliches** *(tax)* agricultural property *(all property of an agricultural enterprise with the exception of money, monetary claims and bonds or securities, debts and surplus stocks of working capital)*
~, **liquides** *s.* ~„ **flüssiges**
~, **mobiles** *s.* ~, **bewegliches**
~, **öffentliches** public property
~, **persönliches** private property
~, **schuldenfreies** *s.* ~, **unbelastetes**
~, **steuerpflichtiges** property liable for taxation
~, **treuhänderisch verwaltetes** trust estate
~, **unbelastetes** unencumbered estate
~, **unbewegliches** immovable property, immovables
~, **verbleibendes** remaining property
~, **verfallenes** forfeited assets
~, **verwaltetes** administered property
~, **zinstragendes** interest-bearing assets
~, **zweckgebundenes** earmarked assets
vermögend rich, wealthy, well-off, propertied
Vermögensabgabe *f* capital levy
Vermögensabschätzung *f s.* **Vermögensbewertung**
Vermögensabschreibung *f* depreciation of assets

Vermögensabtretung *f* voluntary assignment of property
Vermögensänderungen *fpl* changes in assets
Vermögensangabe *f s.* **Vermögenserklärung**
Vermögensangelegenheiten *fpl* matters relating to property
Vermögensanlage *f* investment of capital
Vermögensanmeldung *f s.* **Vermögenserklärung**
Vermögensanteil *m* share of property
Vermögensarten *fpl* kinds of property *(e.g. agricultural property, real property etc.)*
Vermögensaufnahme *f s.* **Vermögensbewertung**
Vermögensaufstellung *f* list of property, property statement
Vermögensaufteilung *f* distribution of assets
Vermögensauseinandersetzung *f* partition of assets
Vermögensausweis *m* statement of assets and liabilities
Vermögensbelastung *f* encumbrance of estate
Vermögensberater *m* investment adviser
Vermögensberatung *f* investment advice
Vermögensbeschlagnahme *f* seizure [attachment, confiscation] of property, distraint of property
Vermögensbestand *m* assets
Vermögensbestandskonto *n* assets account
Vermögensbestandteil *m* part of the assets [property]
Vermögensbesteuerung *f* taxation of property
Vermögensbetrag *m* amount of assets
Vermögensbewegung *f* capital transactions
Vermögensbewertung *f* valuation of property; *(fin)* tax assessment on property
Vermögensbilanz *f s.* **Vermögensaufstellung**
Vermögensbildung *f* formation of property; capital formation
Vermögensdelikt *n* offence against property
Vermögenseinbeziehung *f s.* **Vermögensbeschlagnahme**
Vermögenseinbuße *f* loss of property
Vermögenseinstufung *f* classification of assets
Vermögenserklärung *f* declaration of property, property declaration
Vermögensertrag *m* returns on assets (invested)
Vermögenserwerb *m* acquisition of property
Vermögensfreigabe *f* release of property
Vermögensgegenstände *mpl* parts of the assets
Vermögensgemeinschaft *f* owners of joint property
Vermögenskonto *n s.* **Vermögensbestandskonto**
Vermögenslage *f* financial situation [standing]
◊ **seine ~ verschleiern** to conceal one's financial condition

vermögenslos not well-propertied; without means
Vermögensmasse *f s.* **Vermögensbestand**
Vermögensmehrung *f* increase in assets [property]
Vermögensnachteil *m* detriment to one's property
Vermögensnachweis *m* property qualification
Vermögensneubewertung *f* reassessment of assets and liabilities
Vermögenspfleger *m s.* **Vermögensverwalter**
vermögensrechtlich under the law of property
Vermögensrückgabe *f* restitution of property, restoration of confiscated property
Vermögensschaden *m* damage to property
Vermögensschaden-Haftpflichtversicherung *f* property damage liability insurance
Vermögensschätzung *f s.* **Vermögensbewertung**
Vermögensschichtung *f* distribution of wealth *(in society)*
Vermögensseite *f (acc)* assets side
Vermögensstand *m s.* **Vermögenslage**
Vermögensstatistik *f* statistics on property ownership
Vermögensstatus *m s.* **Vermögenslage**
Vermögenssteuer *f* property tax
~ **auf bewegliche Sachen** tax on movable property
~ **auf Grundbesitz** real estate tax, tax on real estate
~ **auf Kapitalvermögen** capital tax
Vermögenssteuerbescheinigung *f* property tax receipt
Vermögenssteuererklärung *f* (property) tax return
Vermögenssubstanz *f* total assets
Vermögensteil *m* portion of property
Vermögenstransaktion *f* capital transaction
Vermögensübernahme *f* taking over of property
Vermögensübersicht *f* survey on property
Vermögensübertragung *f* transfer of property
Vermögensverfügung *f* disposal of property
Vermögensvergleich *m* comparison of property
Vermögensverhältnisse *npl s.* **Vermögenslage**
Vermögensverlust *m* loss of property
Vermögensverschiebung *f* 1. shift in property ownership; 2. fraudulent transaction of assets
Vermögensverschleierung *f* concealment of assets
Vermögensversicherung *f* property insurance
Vermögensverteilung *f* distribution of property
Vermögensverwalter *m* trustee
Vermögensverwaltung *f* administration of property; trusteeship
Vermögensvorteil *m* fortune ◊ **sich einen ~ verschaffen** to amass a fortune

Vermögenswert *m* financial worth; value of property
Vermögenswerte *mpl* assets; securities; resources
~, **abschreibungsfähige** depreciable property
~, **angabepflichtige** assets to be declared [reported]
~, **ausgesonderte** assets sorted out
~, **blockierte** frozen assets
~, **effektive** active assets
~, **fiktive** fictitious assets
~, **immaterielle** intangible property
~, **kurzfristig realisierbare** liquid assets
~, **materielle** tangible assets
~, **nichtangabepflichtige** assets not to be declared [reported]
~, **nichtrealisierbare** unrealizable assets
~, **überflüssige** superfluous assets
~, **übertragbare** negotiable kind of property
~, **verfügbare** ready assets
~, **verschleierte** concealed assets
Vermögenszunahme *f* wealth increase, increased wealth
Vermögenszuwachs *m s.* **Vermögenszunahme**
Vermögenszuwachsrechnung *f* account on increase in assets [property]
vernachlässigen to neglect (to do) *(one's duties etc.)*
Vernachlässigung *f* neglecting *(duties etc.)*; negligence
vernünftig reasonable *(offer, prices etc.)*
veröffentlichen to publish; to announce, to make known, to give notice
Veröffentlichung *f* publication; announcement
Veröffentlichungskosten *pl* publishing costs
Veröffentlichungspflicht *f* obligation to publish *(balance sheets of companies etc.)*
verordnen to decree
Verordnung *f* decree, regulation
~, **außer Kraft gesetzte** repealed regulation
~, **einschränkende** restraining order
~, **geltende** regulation in force
~, **ministerielle** ministerial order
~, **polizeiliche** police order
verpachtbar leasable
verpachten to lease
Verpächter *m* lessor, leaser, landlord *(land etc.)*
verpachtet leased
Verpachtung *f* lease, leasing, letting on lease
verpacken to pack *(goods in cases etc.)*, to wrap *(things with paper etc.)*, to package *(in packets etc.)*
Verpacken *n* packing *(goods in cases etc.)*, wrapping *(things with paper etc.)*, packaging *(in packets etc.)*
Verpackung *f* packing; packing material; package ⋄ **einschließlich ~** packing included;

~ **ausgenommen** exclusive of packing, packing excluded; ~ **besonders berechnet** packing extra; ~ **nicht einbegriffen** packing not included; ~ **wird nicht berechnet** no charge for packing
~, **feste** firm [solid] packing
~, **haltbare** solid package
~, **handelsübliche** normal (trade) packing
~, **hochseefeste** *s.* ~, **seetaugliche**
~, **mangelhafte** defective packing
~, **ordnungsgemäße** packing according to instructions [rules]
~, **seetaugliche** seaworthy [sea-proof] packing
~, **seetüchtige** *s.* ~, **seetaugliche**
~, **vorschriftsmäßige** packing according to stipulations
~, **wiederverwendbare** re-use package
Verpackungsart *f* kind [type] of packing
Verpackungsbestimmungen *fpl* packaging regulations [stipulations]
Verpackungserfordernisse *npl* packaging requirements
Verpackungsgewicht *n* tare (weight)
Verpackungsindustrie *f* packaging industry
Verpackungsklausel *f* packing clause
Verpackungskosten *pl* packing charges [cost]
verpackungslos without packing, loose
Verpackungsmasse *f s.* **Verpackungsgewicht**
Verpackungsmaterial *n s.* **Verpackungsmittel**
Verpackungsmesse *f* packaging fair
Verpackungsmittel *n* packing material, package
Verpackungsmittellager *n* storage for packing materials
Verpackungspreis *m* packing price
Verpackungspreisstellung *f* fixing of packing price
Verpackungsprozeß *m* (process of) packing
Verpackungsraum *m* packing room
Verpackungsrichtlinien *fpl* packing instructions
Verpackungsschaden *m* packaging defect
Verpackungsweise *f s.* **Verpackungsart**
Verpackungszettel *m* packing slip [instructions]
verpfändbar pawnable
verpfänden to pledge; to mortgage; to pawn
Verpfänden *n* pledging; mortgaging; pawning, pawn
Verpfänder *m* pledger; pawner
Verpfändung *f* pledging; mortgaging; pawning, pawn
~ **beweglichen Eigentums** pledge of movable property
Verpfändungsurkunde *f* mortgage deed; pawn receipt
Verpfändungswert *m* value of pawned article
verpflegen to board; to cater for
Verpflegung *f* board; food; supply of meals ⋄ **ohne ~** without board

Verpflegung

~, **freie** free board
~, **volle** full board
Verpflegungsgeld n catering allowance
Verpflegungskosten pl board, catering costs
Verpflegungssatz m catering allowance; ration
Verpflegungszulage f catering [maintenance, food] allowance
verpflichten to oblige, to bind; to engage; **sich ~ to bind** [commit] o.s. *(to do s.th.)*
verpflichtet obliged, bound; indebted; engaged; obligatory ◊ **gesetzlich ~** liable by law; **vertraglich ~** liable by contract
Verpflichteter m obligee; debtor
Verpflichtung f duty; obligation; liability; commitment; engagement; responsibility ◊ **eine ~ auf sich nehmen** to assume [take over, shoulder] a responsibility; **eine ~ einhalten** to fulfil an obligation; **eine ~ eingehen** to enter into a commitment; **eine ~ übernehmen** to assume an obligation; **einer ~ nachkommen** to fulfil an obligation; **einer ~ nicht nachkommen** not to fulfil an obligation; **jmdn. aus seiner ~ entlassen** to discharge s.o. from his duty; **jmdm. eine ~ auferlegen** to impose an obligation on s.o.; **jmdn. von einer ~ befreien** to exempt s.o. from a liability; **seine ~ erfüllen** to carry out one's [comply with one's, fulfil an] obligation; **seiner ~ enthoben sein** to be released from one's obligation; **sich einer ~ entledigen** to fulfil one's duty; **sich einer ~ entziehen** to evade one's obligation
~, **allgemeine** general obligation
~, **bedingte** contingent liability
~, **bestehende** existing liability [obligation]
~, **bindende** binding obligation
~, **einklagbare** civil obligation
~, **einseitige** one-sided commitment
~, **entstandene** accrued liability
~, **finanzielle** financial commitment
~, **gesamtschuldnerische** joint liability
~, **gesetzliche** legal obligation
~, **laufende** current commitment
~, **moralische** moral duty
~, **persönliche** personal commitment
~, **schriftliche** commitment in writing
~, **schuldrechtliche** s. ~, **einklagbare**
~, **solidarische** solidarity commitment
~, **stillschweigende** implicit commitment, implied obligation
~, **unmittelbare** direct obligation
~, **vertragliche** contractual obligation
~, **vertragsähnliche** quasi-contractual obligation
Verpflichtungen fpl:
~, **außenpolitische** foreign policy commitments
~, **außenwirtschaftliche** foreign economic [trade] commitments; foreign debts
~, **gegenseitige** mutual obligations

~ **gegenüber Dritten** liabilities to outsiders
~, **geschäftliche** business commitments
~, **gesellschaftliche** social engagements
~, **kurzfristige** short-term liabilities
~, **langfristige** long-term liabilities
~, **laufende** current engagements
~, **sonstige** other liabilities; other engagements
~, **steuerliche** tax liabilities
Verpflichtungserklärung f pledge; bond
Verpflichtungsschein m surety bond
verplanen 1. to budget for; to plan; 2. to miscalculate
verplant 1. budgeted for; planned; 2. miscalculated
verproviantieren to supply with food
verquicken to confound, to amalgamate, to mix up
Verquicken n s. **Verquickung**
Verquickung f confounding, amalgamation
Verrat m betrayal; treason *(country)*; treachery; disclosure *(secret etc.)*
verraten to betray *(country etc.)*; to disclose, to divulge *(secret etc.)*
verrechnen 1. to settle (an account), to set off against, to compensate, to clear; 2. to charge to account; 3. to make an error *(in accounting)*
Verrechnung f settling, settlement, clearing, offset ◊ **nur zur ~** not negotiable
~, **bargeldlose** (cashless) clearing
~, **gegenseitige** (mutual) clearing
~, **zwischenstaatliche** inter-state clearing
Verrechnungen fpl clearing
~, **innere** internal clearing
~, **mehrseitige** multilateral clearing
Verrechnungsabkommen n clearing agreement
Verrechnungsauftrag m clearing order
Verrechnungsbank f clearing bank; clearing house
Verrechnungsbasis f clearing base
Verrechnungsbedingungen fpl terms of clearing
Verrechnungsbeleg m bank slip [receipt]
Verrechnungsbeziehungen fpl clearing relations
Verrechnungsbilanz f clearing balance
Verrechnungsdokument n clearing document
Verrechnungsdollar m accounting dollar
Verrechnungseinheit f accounting [clearing] unit
Verrechnungsfonds m settlement fund
Verrechnungsform f clearing method [form]
Verrechnungsgeschäft n clearing operation
Verrechnungsgewinn m profit on clearing
Verrechnungsguthaben n balance on offset account
Verrechnungskonto n clearing [offset] account
Verrechnungskredit m clearing [offset] credit
Verrechnungskurs m exchange rate; making-up price

Verrechnungsland *n* clearing country
Verrechnungsmethode *f* method of clearing, clearing method
Verrechnungsnetz *n* clearing network
Verrechnungsposten *m* clearing item
Verrechnungspreis *m* accounting price
~, **innerbetrieblicher** internal accounting price
~, **zweiginterner** accounting price within a branch (of industry)
Verrechnungsrate *f* cost accounting rate *(planned amount added monthly to the prime cost for equalizing irregular costs)*
Verrechnungsrubel *m* accounting rouble
Verrechnungssaldo *m s.* **Verrechnungsspitze**
Verrechnungssatz *m* specified rate of exchange
Verrechnungsscheck *m* crossed cheque
Verrechnungsschuld *f* clearing debt
Verrechnungsspitze *f* clearing balance
Verrechnungsstelle *f* clearing house [office]
Verrechnungssystem *n* clearing system
Verrechnungsverfahren *n* clearing method
Verrechnungsverkehr *m* clearing transactions
~, **bargeldloser** (cashless) clearing transactions
~, **mehrseitiger** multilateral clearing transactions
~, **zweiseitiger** bilateral clearing transactions
Verrechnungsvermerk *m* crossing
Verrechnungswährung *f* clearing [accounting, agreement] currency
Verrechnungsweg *m* clearing channel
Verrechnungswesen *n s.* **Verrechnungssystem**
Verrechnungszahlungen *fpl* transferable payments
Verrechnungszeitraum *m* clearing period
verriegeln to lock, to block; *(d.pr.)* to latch *(chip enables etc.)*
Verriegelung *f* locking, blocking; *(d.pr.)* latching *(chip enables etc.)*
verringern to reduce *(share of capital etc.)*, to decrease *(prices etc.)*, to lessen *(value etc.)*; **sich** ~ to deteriorate *(performance of machine etc.)*
Verringerung *f* reduction *(share of capital etc.)*, decrease *(prices etc.)*, lessening *(value etc.)*
versachlichen to realize, to materialize *(relations etc.)*
Versachlichung *f* realization, materialization *(relations etc.)*
~ **der gesellschaftlichen Beziehungen** realization [materialization] of social relation(ship)s
versammeln to meet, to assemble, to gather *(people etc.)*; to convene *(meeting)*, to convoke *(assembly by summons)*; to rally *(political supporters)*
Versammlung *f* meeting, assembling, gathering *(people etc.)*; assembly; convening, convention; convoking *(assembly by summons)*; convocation; rally *(political supporters)* ◊ **eine** ~

abhalten to hold a meeting; **eine** ~ **auflösen** to dissolve a meeting; to break up a meeting [rally] *(by force)*; **eine** ~ **einberufen** to call a meeting, to convene an assembly; **eine** ~ **eröffnen** to open a meeting; **eine** ~ **leiten** to chair a meeting; **eine** ~ **schließen** to close a meeting; **eine** ~ **verbieten** to ban a meeting
~, **außerordentliche** extraordinary [special] meeting
~, **beratende** advisory council
~, **öffentliche** public meeting
Versammlungsfreiheit *f* freedom of meeting [assembly]
Versammlungsleiter *m* chairperson, chairman, chairwoman
Versammlungsort *m* meeting place
Versammlungsrecht *n* right of assembly
Versammlungsverbot *n* ban on a (public) meeting
Versand *m* dispatch, forwarding; conveyance; shipment, shipping; posting, mailing; delivery ◊ **den** ~ **durchführen** *s.* **versenden; zum** ~ **bringen** to consign, to send, to forward; to ship; to post, to mail
~ **auf dem Landwege** land transport
~ **auf eigene Rechnung** dispatch on one's own account
~ **auf gemeinsame Rechnung** dispatch on joint account; shipment on joint account
~, **binnenstaatlicher** domestic dispatch [*(Am)* shipment]
~ **gegen Nachnahme** charges forward, cash on delivery (c.o.d.)
~ **per Bahn** dispatch [delivery, transport] by rail
~, **sofortiger** prompt dispatch *(of goods)*
~, **zwischenstaatlicher** international dispatch
Versandabteilung *f* dispatch [forwarding] department
Versandangestellter *m* forwarding clerk
Versandanmeldung *f (cust)* transit declaration
Versandanschrift *f* address of consignee
Versandanweisungen *fpl* instructions for dispatch, forwarding [shipping] instructions
Versandanzeige *f* dispatch [consignment, receiving] note, shipping [forwarding] advice [announcement], letter of advice; way-bill
Versandauftrag *m* dispatch order; shipping order
Versandbahnhof *m* forwarding [sending, starting] station ◊ **frei** ~ free to dispatch station
Versandbedingungen *fpl* forwarding terms; shipping terms
Versandbehälter *m* package conveyer; shipping container
Versandbenachrichtigung *f* dispatch [consignment, receiving] note

versandbereit ready for dispatch; ready for shipment
Versandbereitstellungskredit *m* stand-by credit (for dispatch)
Versandbescheinigung *f* dispatch certificate; shipping certificate
Versandbestellung *f* mail-order buying, postal shopping
Versandbuch *n* forwarding book; book of shipments
Versandbuchhandel *m* mail-order book trade
Versandbüro *n* forwarding agency
Versanddokument *n* transport document
Versandentfernung *f* distance of forwarding
versandfähig transportable
Versandfähigkeit *f* transportability
versandfertig *s.* **versandbereit**
Versandform *f* kind of dispatch
Versandformalitäten *fpl* forwarding formalities
Versandgebiet *n* forwarding area
Versandgebühren *fpl* forwarding charges; mailing expenses
Versandgeschäft *n* catalogue [mail-order] sale, mail-order business ⋄ **durch** ~ by mail order
Versandhandel *m* mail-order trade [business]
Versandgroßhandel *m* mail-order wholesale trade
Versandgroßhändler *m* mail-order wholesaler
Versandhafen *m* port of lading [loading]
Versandhaus *n* mail-order house
Versandhauskatalog *m s.* **Versandkatalog**
Versandhausreklame *f* mail-order advertising
Versandkatalog *m* trade [mail-order] catalogue
Versandklausel *f* forwarding clause [stipulation]
Versandkonto *n* dispatch account; shipment account
Versandkosten *pl* forwarding costs [charges]; shipping costs; costs [charges] of delivery; freight expenses *(railway)*
Versandleiter *m* head of dispatch department; shipping supervisor
Versandleitung *f* dispatch [shipping] management
Versandliste *f* packing [freight] list; shipping bill
Versandmeister *m* foreman of dispatch department [shipping department]
Versandmeldung *f* ready-for-dispatch note; ready-for-shipment note
Versandmöglichkeiten *fpl* forwarding facilities; shipping facilities
Versandnorm *f* forwarding standard [norm] *(quantity fixed according to the most economical use of means of transport etc.)*
Versandort *m* dispatch [forwarding, shipping] point, point of shipment
Versandpapiere *npl* dispatch documents [papers]; shipping documents; document bills; movement documents *(customs)* ⋄ **bar gegen** ~ cash against document(s)
Versandprobe *f* sample
Versandrechnung *f* invoice, shipping invoice
Versandscheck *m (bank)* out-of-town cheque [*(Am)* check]
Versandschein *m* advice note
Versandspesen *pl* forwarding expenses
Versandstation *f s.* **Versandbahnhof**
Versandtag *m* date of dispatch; date of shipment
Versandtermin *m* date of dispatch; date of shipment, shipping time; mailing date
Versandvereinigung *f* (transport) pool
Versandverfahren *n* transit procedure *(customs)*
Versandvorschriften *fpl s.* **Versandanweisungen**
Versandwaren *fpl* forwarded [dispatched] goods; shipped goods
Versandwechsel *m* out-of-town bill; out-of--country [foreign] bill
Versandweg *m* dispatch [shipping] route
Versandweise *f* method of dispatch; method of shipment
Versandwerbung *f* mail advertising
Versandwert *m* value of dispatch; value of shipments
Versandzeichen *n* dispatch mark; shipping mark
Versandzeit *f* mailing time; time of shipment
Versatzgeschäft *n* pawnbroking
versäumen to neglect *(duty etc.)*; to fail *(to make payment etc.)*, to omit *(to do s.th.)* ⋄ ~ **zu zahlen** to fail to pay
Versäumnis *n* neglect; omission, failure; default *(term)*
~ **der rechtzeitigen Geltendmachung einer Forderung** *(jur)* laches
Versäumnisgebühr *f* penalty; fine; default fee
Versäumnisurteil *n* default judgement, judgement by default
verschachern to barter away
verschachteln 1. to interlock; 2. *(d.pr.)* to interleave *(input-output operations etc.)*; to interlace, to nest *(subroutines etc.)*
Verschachtelung *f* 1. interlocking *(enterprises)*; 2. *(d.pr.)* interleaving, nesting *(subroutines etc.)*
~ **des Aktienkapitals** interlocking stock ownership
verschaffen to supply, to procure, to provide, to furnish
verschärfen to intensify; to aggravate *(situation etc.)*; to tighten *(credit policy etc.)*; to stiffen *(competition etc.)*
Verschärfung *f* intensification; aggravation *(situation etc.)*; tightening *(credit policy etc.)*; stiffening *(competition etc.)*
verschicken to send off, to dispatch, to forward; to ship; to post, to mail

Verschiebebahnhof *m* shunting [marshalling] yard, *(Am)* switch yard
verschieben 1. to shift, to (re)move; to put off, to defer, to postpone *(meeting, fair, decision etc.)*; to procrastinate; to adjourn *(session etc.)*; to delay *(payment etc.)*; 2. to disarrange, to displace; 3. to sell underhand, to sell under the counter *(goods on the black market)* ◇ **etwas auf später ~** to defer s.th. to a later date
Verschiebung *f* 1. shift(ing); deferment, deferral, postponement *(meeting, fair, decision etc.)*; adjournment *(session etc.)*; delaying *(payment etc.)*; 2. disarrangement, displacement; 3. selling goods on the black market
~, arithmetische *(d.pr.)* arithmetic shift
~ der Angebotskurve shift in supply, shifting the supply curve
~ der Einkommensverteilung shift in distribution of income, income distributional shift
~ der Nachfragekurve shift in demand, shifting the demand curve
~, logische *(d.pr.)* logical shift
~, schrittweise *(d.pr.)* mechanical stepping; incremental shift
~, vertikale *(d.pr.)* vertical translation
~, zeitliche (time) lag
~, zirkulare *(d.pr.)* circular [cycle] shift
Verschiebungsparameter *m (stats)* translation parameter
Verschiebungsprogramm *n (d.pr.)* relocation program
Verschiebungstest *m (stats)* slippage test
verschieden different, distinct (from); dissimilar, unlike; various, several, diverse; miscellaneous
verschiedenartig of a different kind, different, dissimilar, heterogenous; varied, diversified
Verschiedenartigkeit *f* difference, heterogeneity; variety
Verschiedenes sundries, miscellaneous items; Any Other Business (AOB) *(meeting)*
Verschiedenheit *f* difference; dissimilarity; variety, diversity; disparity
verschiffen to ship, to freight, to send by sea, to transport by ship
Verschiffer *m* shipper
Verschiffung *f* shipping, shipment, water carriage, transport by ship ◇ **zur ~ empfangen** received for shipment
Verschiffungsauftrag *m* shipping order
Verschiffungsbescheinigung *f* certificate of shipment
Verschiffungsdokumente *npl s.* **Verschiffungspapiere**
Verschiffungsgewicht *n* shipping weight
Verschiffungshafen *m* port of shipment
Verschiffungskonnossement *n* ocean bill of lading

Verschiffungskosten *pl* shipping charges
Verschiffungskredit *m* shipping loan
Verschiffungsland *n* country of shipment
Verschiffungsorder *f* shipping order
Verschiffungsort *m* point [port] of shipment
Verschiffungspapiere *npl* shipping documents
◇ **durch ~ gedeckt** covered by shipping documents
Verschiffungsspesen *pl* shipping costs
verschlechtern to deteriorate, to impair; to make worse, to worsen; to depreciate; to set back; to debase *(coin etc.)*
Verschlechterung *f* deterioration, worsening; depreciation; setback
~ der Gewinnsituation worsening of profits [earnings]
~ der Kaufkraft worsening [deterioration] of purchasing power
~ der Zahlungsbilanz deterioration of the balance of payments
verschleiern to veil, to disguise, to conceal; to cook, to doctor, to fake *(balance sheet etc.)*
Verschleierung *f* veiling, disguising, concealment; tampering with, cooking, doctoring, faking *(balance sheet etc.)*; window-dressing *(negative facts)*
~ von Vermögenswerten concealment of assets
Verschleierungsmaßnahmen *fpl* camouflage measures
Verschleiß *m* wear and tear
~ der Produktionsanlagen wear and tear of fixed assets
~, moralischer obsolescence
~, normaler normal wear and tear
~, physischer physical wear and tear
~, technischer *s.* **~, physischer**
verschleißen to wear out
Verschleißfestigkeit *f* resistance to wear
Verschleißgrad *m* degree [extent] of wear and tear
Verschleißkoeffizient *m* coefficient of wear and tear
Verschleißnorm *f* standard rate of wear and tear
Verschleißquote *f* extent of wear and tear *(in terms of percentage)*
verschleppen to delay; to practise obstruction
Verschleppung *f* delay; obstruction
Verschleppungsmethoden *fpl* delaying methods
Verschleppungstaktik *f* delaying tactics
verschleudern to undersell, to sell at a loss, to sell under value; to sell at ruinous prices, to sell off dirt cheap; to dump; to dissipate *(energy, efforts etc.)*, to squander *(property)*
Verschleuderung *f* underselling, selling under value; dumping; selling at dumping [ruinous] prices; dissipation *(energy, efforts etc.)*; squandering *(property)*

~ **lebendiger Arbeit** waste of labour
~ **vergegenständlichter Arbeit** waste of dead labour *(machinery, materials etc.)*
~ **von Beständen** selling of stocks under value
~ **von Vermögen** squandering (of) property
Verschluß *m* 1. lock; 2. *(cust)* seal; bond ⋄ **aus dem zollamtlichen ~ nehmen** to take out of bond; **unter ~** under seal; **unter ~ halten** to keep under lock and key; **unter ~ legen** *(cust)* to bond; **unter zollamtlichem ~** bonded, in bond
Verschlußanerkenntnis *f* seal acknowledgement
verschlüsseln to code, to encode ⋄ **digital ~** *(d.pr.)* to digitize
verschlüsselt coded ⋄ **numerisch ~** *(d.pr.)* numerically coded
Verschlüsselung *f* coding, encoding
Verschlußmarke *f* seal
Verschlußsache *f* classified matter
verschmelzen to amalgamate, to fuse, to merge, to consolidate
Verschmelzung *f* amalgamation, fusion, merger, consolidation
~ **durch Aufnahme** merger
~ **durch Neubildung** consolidation
Verschmelzungsvertrag *m* merger, amalgamation
verschmutzen to pollute *(water, air etc.)*; to soil, to dirty *(textiles etc.)*
Verschmutzung *f* pollution *(water, air etc.)*; soiling *(textiles etc.)*
Verschnitt *m* blend *(tobacco etc.)*
verschnitten blended
verschreiben to assign, to make over *(property etc. to s.o.)*; to prescribe *(medicine etc.)*; to write incorrectly, to misspell
Verschreibung *f* assignment *(of property etc. to s.o.)*; bond, deed *(document etc.)*; prescription *(medicine etc.)*
verschrotten to scrap *(machinery etc.)*; to break up *(ships etc.)*
Verschrottung *f* scrapping *(machinery etc.)*; breaking up *(ships etc.)*
verschulden to encumber with debts; to be guilty of, to be to blame for *(accident etc.)*; to be the cause of, to cause *(break-down etc.)*; **sich ~** to encumber o.s. with debts, to run into debt(s), to incur debts
Verschulden *n* fault; guilt *(accident etc.)*; cause *(break-down etc.)* ⋄ **frei von ~ sein** to be free from blame; **keinerlei ~** no fault; **ohne ~** without fault; not to blame
~ **bei Vertragsabschluß** culpa in contrahendo
~, **beiderseitiges** mutual contributory fault, both-to-blame
~, **mitwirkendes** contributory negligence
~, **strafbares** criminal negligence

~, **zum Schadenersatz verpflichtendes** actionable negligence
Verschuldensbilanz *f* statement of affairs
Verschuldenshaftung *f* liability for default, liability based on (proof of) fault
Verschuldensneigung *f* propensity to incur debts [liabilities]
verschuldet indebted, in debt ⋄ **hoch ~ sein** to be deeply involved in debt; **nicht ~** without debts; **~ sein** to be in debt, to stand in debt; **völlig ~ sein** to be completely in debt(s), immersed [encumbered, plunged] in debt
Verschuldung *f* indebtedness; (amount of) debts
~ **bei Banken** bank indebtedness
~, **erhebliche** heavy [excessive] indebtedness; excessive amount of debts
~, **kommunale** indebtedness [amount of debts] of local authorities
~, **kurzfristige** short-term indebtedness; amount of short-term debts
~, **langfristige** long-term indebtedness; amount of long-term debts
~, **staatliche** state [government, public] indebtedness; amount of state [government, public] debts
~, **zugelassene** legal debt limit [ceiling] *(of counties, towns etc.)*
Verschuldungsgrad *m* debt-equity ratio *(total liabilities to total equity)*; level of debts
Verschuldungsgrenze *f* debt limit [ceiling]
Verschuldungskoeffizient *m s.* **Verschuldungsgrad**
Verschuldungsneigung *f* propensity to get into debt(s)
Verschuldungspotential *n* borrowing capacity
Verschuldungsspielraum *m* debt margin
verschweigen to conceal; to keep secret, to withhold, to hold back, to hide (from)
Verschweigen *n* concealment
~ **rechtlicher Tatsachen** failure to disclose material facts, suppression of material facts
~ **rechtserheblicher Umstände** *(jur)* material concealment
verschwenden to squander, to waste
verschwenderisch wasteful
Verschwendung *f* waste, wastage *(materials etc.)*, dissipation *(efforts, energy etc.)*
~ **von Ressourcen** wasting of resources
verschwiegen discrete, close, reticent ⋄ **~ sein** to keep a secret
Verschwiegenheit *f* discretion, secrecy ⋄ **zur ~ verpflichtet sein** to be sworn to secrecy
versehen 1. to provide, to furnish, to supply, to afford with *(goods, money etc.)*; 2. to perform, to discharge *(duties)*; to hold, to administer *(office)*; to fill *(position)*; 3. to make a mistake
Versehrter *m* invalid, disabled person

Versehrtenrente *f* disability allowance
Versehrtenstufe *f* degree of disablement
Versehrtenunterstützung *f* benefit for invalidity [disability]
versenden to send (off), to dispatch, to forward; to convey, to transport; to consign, to ship; to freight *(rail etc.)*; to post, to mail, to deliver
Versender *m* sender, forwarder; consignor, shipper
Versendung *f* sending (off), dispatch, forwarding; conveyance, transport, transportation, consignment, shipment; posting, mailing
 ⋄ **während der ~** in transit
– **mit der Bahn** consignment of goods by train
Versendungskauf *m* sale to destination according to buyer's instructions
Versendungskosten *pl* transport charges [costs]; shipping charges [costs]
Versendungsort *m* place of consignment; shipping point
versetzen 1. to shift, to displace, to remove; to move, to transfer *(employees)*; 2. to (put in) pawn, to pledge
Versetzung *f* 1. shift(ing), displacement; removal, transfer, relocation *(employees)*; 2. pawning, pledging
~, aus Betriebsgründen erfolgende transfer for management reasons
– **in den Ruhestand** retirement, retiring, superannuation, pensioning (off)
– **von Arbeitskräften in andere Schichten** transfer of labour from one shift to another
Versetzungen *fpl*:
~, innerbetriebliche inter-enterprise [inter-plant] transfer
– **innerhalb des Betriebes** transfer within an enterprise [a firm]
– **innerhalb einer Abteilung** transfer within a department
– **von einer Abteilung in eine andere** transfer between departments
versicherbar insurable, assurable
Versicherer *m* insurer, assurer; underwriter *(ship's etc.)*
versichern 1. to assure, to certify; 2. to insure, to underwrite *(property etc.)*, to assure *(life)*
 ⋄ **sich ~ lassen** to take out an insurance (policy); **zu hoch ~** to insure above value, to overinsure; **zu niedrig ~** to insure below value, to underinsure
versichert insured ⋄ **voll ~** fully insured
Versichertendividende *f* bonus
Versicherter *m s.* Versicherungsnehmer
Versicherung *f* 1. assurance, affirmation *(declaration etc.)*; 2. insurance, underwriting *(property etc.)*; assurance *(life)*, life insurance ⋄ **durch ~ gedeckt** covered by insurance; **eine ~ abschließen** to take out an insurance policy, to effect an insurance; **eine ~ unterhalten** to be insured; **eine ~ vermitteln** to arrange an insurance; **eine ~ wiederaufnehmen** to reinstate an insurance; **eine ~ zurückkaufen** to surrender an insurance policy
~, abgelaufene expired insurance
– **anomaler Risiken** insurance of abnormal risks
– **auf den Erlebensfall** endowment insurance
– **auf den Todesfall** insurance payable at death, whole life insurance
– **auf den Todes- und Erlebensfall** endowment life insurance
– **auf erstes Risiko** insurance against first risk
~, aufgestockte extended insurance
~, aufrechterhaltene insurance carried
– **auf Zeit** time insurance
– **auf zweites Risiko** insurance against second risk
~, beitragsfreie paid-up insurance
– **der Ladung** cargo insurance
– **des technischen Risikos** insurance against technological risks
~, fällige matured insurance
~, freiwillige voluntary [optional] insurance
– **für eigene Rechnung** insurance for own account
– **für fremde Rechnung** insurance for third party account
– **für Rechnung „Wen es angeht"** insurance for account "to whom it may concern"
– **gegen alle Risiken** all-risk insurance; comprehensive insurance
– **gegen außergewöhnliche Risiken** contingency (risk) insurance
– **gegen Blitzschlag** lightning insurance
– **gegen Ernteschäden** insurance of crops
~, gegenseitige mutual insurance
~, gewinnbeteiligte participating insurance
~, kurzfristige (short-)term insurance
– **mit festem Auszahlungstermin** insurance with fixed pay date, endowment insurance
~, nicht gewinnbeteiligte non-participating insurance
~, noch laufende (insurance) policy still in force
~, noch nicht abgelaufene unexpired insurance
~, obligatorische compulsory insurance
~, prämienfreie *s.* **~, beitragsfreie**
~, prolongierte extended insurance
~, staatliche state insurance
~, vorausbezahlte prepaid insurance
~, zu hohe overinsurance
~, zu niedrige underinsurance
~, zusätzliche additional [collateral] insurance
Versicherungsablauf *m* expiry [expiration] of policy

Versicherungsabschätzung *f* insurance appraisal
Versicherungsabschluß *m* taking out of an insurance; contract of insurance; issuance of a policy
Versicherungsabschlüsse *mpl* transactions at the insurance office
Versicherungsabteilung *f* insurance department
Versicherungsagent *m* insurance agent
Versicherungsagentur *f* insurance office
Versicherungsaktien *fpl* insurance shares [(Am) stocks]
Versicherungsalter *n* insured's age
Versicherungsangestellter *m* insurance clerk
Versicherungsanspruch *m* insurance claim
  ⋄ **einen ~ verpfänden** to pledge an insurance
  ~ des Begünstigten claim by the beneficiary
  ~ noch nicht entschiedener open claim in insurance
Versicherungsansprüche *mpl*:
~, anerkannte acknowledged insurance claims
Versicherungsanstalt *f* insurance company
Versicherungsantrag *m* application for insurance ⋄ **einen ~ entgegennehmen** to secure an application for insurance
Versicherungsanwalt *m* lawyer (dealing with insurance matters)
Versicherungsaufnahmeantrag *m s.* **Versicherungsantrag**
Versicherungsausmaß *n* range of policies in insurance
Versicherungsaußendienst *m* insurance field service
Versicherungsbearbeiter *m s.* **Versicherungsangestellter**
Versicherungsbedingungen *fpl* terms of (insurance) policy, insurance (policy) conditions, policy provisions
~, Allgemeine General Terms [Conditions] of Insurance
Versicherungsbedürfnis *n* need for an insurance
Versicherungsbeginn *m* commencement of insurance cover
Versicherungsbegrenzung *f* limitation for insurance policy
Versicherungsbeirat *m* insurance advisory board
Versicherungsbeitrag *m* insurance premium
~, im voraus bezahlter insurance premium paid in advance
Versicherungsberater *m* actuarial consultant
Versicherungsberatung *f* actuarial consultation
Versicherungsberechtigter *m* beneficiary of insurance
Versicherungsbescheinigung *f s.* **Versicherungspolice**

Versicherungsbestand *m* number of insured persons
Versicherungsbesteuerung *f* insurance taxation
Versicherungsbestimmungen *fpl s.* **Versicherungsbedingungen**
Versicherungsbetrag *m* amount insured (by the policy)
Versicherungsbetrieb *m s.* **Versicherungsanstalt**
Versicherungsbetrug *m* insurance fraud
Versicherungsbilanz *f* insurance balance sheet
Versicherungsbüro *n* insurance office
Versicherungsdarleh(e)n *n* insurance loan
Versicherungsdauer *f* period insured, period of coverage, term [period] of insurance
~, noch nicht abgelaufene years to run for period insured
Versicherungsdeckung *f* insurance cover [coverage]
Versicherungsdichte *f* proportion of policy-holders
Versicherungsende *n* date of expiry of insurance policy
versicherungsfähig insurable, assurable ⋄ **nicht ~** uninsurable
Versicherungsfähigkeit *f* insurability
Versicherungsfall *m* insurance case; insured event
Versicherungsfonds *m* insurance fund
Versicherungsform *f* kind of insurance policy
Versicherungsformular *n* insurance form
Versicherungsgeber *m s.* **Versicherer**
Versicherungsgebühr *f* insurance premium
Versicherungsgegenstand *m* object insured
Versicherungsgeschäft *n* insurance business; insurance transaction
Versicherungsgesellschaft *f* insurance company
  ⋄ **bei einer ~ versichern** to insure in an insurance office
~ auf Gegenseitigkeit mutual insurance company
~, universelle multiple line insurance company
~, zugelassene admitted insurance company
Versicherungsgewerbe *n s.* **Versicherungswesen**
Versicherungsgewinn *m* insurance profit; underwriting profit
~, vertragsmäßiger convenanted benefit
Versicherungshöhe *f s.* **Versicherungsbetrag**
Versicherungsinspektor *m* insurance inspector
Versicherungsjahr *n* insurance policy year
Versicherungsjahre *npl* years of insurance coverage
Versicherungskalkulation *f* actuarial calculation
Versicherungskapital *n* insurance capital; insurance stock
Versicherungskarte *f* social insurance card
Versicherungsklausel *f* insurance clause

Versicherungskosten *pl* insurance charges [costs]
Versicherungslasten *fpl s.* **Versicherungskosten**
Versicherungsleistung *f* (national) insurance benefit
Versicherungsmakler *m s.* **Versicherungsagent**
Versicherungsmarke *f* policy stamp
Versicherungsmarkt *m* insurance market
Versicherungsmathematik *f* actuarial theory
Versicherungsmathematiker *m* actuary
versicherungsmathematisch actuarial
Versicherungsmöglichkeit *f* insurance facility; underwriting capacity
Versicherungsmonopol *n* insurance monopoly
Versicherungsnachtrag *m* endorsement on insurance policy
Versicherungsnehmer *m* insured [assured] person, (insurance) policy-holder; beneficiary of insurance policy; person taking out insurance
Versicherungsperiode *f* insured period
Versicherungspflicht *f* compulsory insurance; obligation to insure
versicherungspflichtig liable to pay national insurance premium; subject to compulsory insurance
Versicherungspolice *f* (insurance) policy ⋄ **eine ~ aufrechterhalten** to keep a(n) (insurance) policy alive; **eine ~ ausstellen** to issue a(n) (insurance) policy; **eine ~ einlösen** to pay the first insurance premium; **eine ~ erlangen** to obtain a(n) (insurance) policy; **eine ~ erwerben** to take out an insurance policy; **seine ~ bezahlen** to pay one's insurance premium
– **für ein besonderes Risiko, kurzfristige** special risk (insurance) policy
– **für einen bestimmten Zeitraum** time (insurance) policy
–, **für mehr als ein Jahr ausgestellte** long rate (insurance) policy
–, **laufende** current (insurance) policy
– **mit Gewinnberechtigung** participating (insurance) policy
–, **offene** open (insurance) policy
– **ohne Gewinnbeteiligung** non-participating (insurance) policy
–, **prämienfreie** non-contributory social insurance
–, **prolongierte** extended term (insurance) policy
–, **Selbstbehalt ausschließende** fixed amount (insurance) policy
–, **taxierte** valued (insurance) policy
–, **ungültige** lapsed (insurance) policy
–, **unkündbare** non-cancellable (insurance) policy

Versicherungspolitik *f* insurance policy
Versicherungsprämie *f* insurance premium
–, **verauslagte** advanced (insurance) premium
Versicherungsprämien *fpl*:
⋄ **~ fortzahlen** to pay (insurance) premiums to date
Versicherungsprovision *f* insurance commission
Versicherungsprüfer *m* insurance auditor; actuary
Versicherungsrate *f s.* **Versicherungsbeitrag**
Versicherungsrecht *n* insurance law
Versicherungsrevisor *m s.* **Versicherungsprüfer**
Versicherungsrisiko *n* insurance [insurable] risk, insured risk
Versicherungsrückkauf *m* surrender of insurance policy
Versicherungsrückkaufwert *m* surrender value of insurance policy
Versicherungssachverständiger *m* valuer [*(Am)* appraiser] of damages covered by (insurance) policy
Versicherungssatz *m* insurance rate
Versicherungsschaden *m* amount of damages covered by (insurance) policy
Versicherungsschein *m s.* **Versicherungspolice**
Versicherungsschutz *m* insurance protection, cover(age) ⋄ **kein ~ bei Beschlagnahme** free of capture and seizure
–, **sofortiger** immediate national insurance cover
–, **zusätzlicher** extended insurance cover(age)
Versicherungssparen *n* saving through insurance companies
Versicherungssparte *f* line of insurance business; insurance class
Versicherungsstatistiker *m* actuary
versicherungsstatistisch actuarial
Versicherungssteuer *f* insurance tax
Versicherungsstreitigkeiten *fpl* insurance policy claims
Versicherungssumme *f s.* **Versicherungsbetrag**
Versicherungssyndikat *n* underwriting syndicate *(shipping)*
Versicherungssystem *n* insurance system
Versicherungstabelle *f* table of insurance premiums
Versicherungstarif *m* rate of insurance premium
Versicherungstätigkeit *f* insurance transactions
Versicherungstechnik *f* actuarial system
versicherungstechnisch actuarial ⋄ **~ einwandfrei** actuarially sound
Versicherungstermin *m* date of policy
Versicherungsträger *m s.* **Versicherer**
Versicherungsumfang *m s.* **Versicherungsbetrag**

Versicherungsunkosten *pl* incidental costs of insurance
Versicherungsunterlagen *fpl* insurance papers [records]
Versicherungsunternehmen *n s.* Versicherungsanstalt
Versicherungsurkunde *f s.* Versicherungspolice
Versicherungsvereinbarungen *fpl*:
~, **besondere** additional clause to an insurance policy
Versicherungsverhältnis *n* insurance relationship
Versicherungsverlängerung *f* extension of (insurance) policy
Versicherungsverlust *m* insurer's loss; underwriter's loss
Versicherungsvertrag *m* contract between insurer and policy-holder ◊ **einen ~ abschließen** to take out a(n) (insurance) policy
Versicherungsvertreter *m s.* Versicherungsagent
Versicherungsvertretung *f s.* Versicherungsagentur
Versicherungsvorauszahlung *f* insurance premium paid in advance
Versicherungsvorauszahlungskonto *n* prepaid insurance account
Versicherungswechsel *m* insurance draft
Versicherungswert *m* value insured, policy [insurance] value, insurable value
Versicherungswerte *mpl* insurance stocks
Versicherungswesen *n* insurance business
Versicherungswirtschaft *f s.* Versicherungswesen
Versicherungswissenschaft *f* (science of) insurance *(branch of economic science)*
Versicherungszeit *f* term of insurance
Versicherungszertifikat *n s.* Versicherungspolice
Versicherungszwang *m* obligation to insure; compulsory insurance
Versicherungszweig *m* insurance line [branch]
versiegeln to seal
versiegelt sealed
versiegen to dry up; to be exhausted *(resources)*; to be cut off *(funds)*
versiert experienced, versed
Version *f* version, variant of a type
versorgen to provide *(food etc.)*, to supply *(goods etc.)*, to furnish with *(equipment etc.)*; to maintain, to support *(family etc.)*; to care for, to look after, to nurse *(child etc.)* ◊ **jmdn. ~ to** provide for s.o.
Versorger *m* provider, mainstay, bread-winner *(family)*
versorgt stocked; provided for ◊ **~ sein** to be provided for

Versorgung *f* provision *(food etc.)*, supply *(goods etc.)*, furnishing with *(equipment etc.)*; maintenance, support *(family etc.)*; care of, looking after, nursing *(child etc.)*
~ **der Bevölkerung** supply of consumer goods and services to consumers
~, **materiell-technische** supply of materials and equipment
~, **mengengerechte** supply according to quantity required
~, **qualitätsgerechte** supply according to quality required
~, **termingerechte** supply according to (time) schedule
Versorgungsalter *m* pensionable age
Versorgungsanlagen *fpl* public utilities
Versorgungsanspruch *m* claim to maintenance; pensions claim
Versorgungsbasis *f* base of supplies, supply base *(for provisions etc.)*
versorgungsberechtigt entitled to maintenance; eligible for a pension
Versorgungsbereich *m* supply area
Versorgungsbetrieb *m* public utility; catering enterprise [firm]
~, **kommunaler** public utility run by local authorities, municipally owned utility
Versorgungsbetriebe *mpl* service centres and utilities
Versorgungsbezüge *mpl* pension
Versorgungsbilanz *f* sources and uses balance sheet of consumer goods and services
Versorgungseffekt *m* supply effect
Versorgungseinrichtung *f* institution for the supply of consumer goods and services
Versorgungsengpaß *m* bottleneck in the supply of s.th.
~ **an Konsumgütern und Dienstleistungen** bottleneck in the supply of consumer goods and services
~ **an Material** bottleneck in the supply of materials
Versorgungsfonds *m* funds earmarked for s.th. *(pensions etc.)*
Versorgungsgebiet *n* supply area
Versorgungsgrad *m* level of provision with s.th. *(consumer goods, medical care etc.)*
Versorgungsgroßhandel *m* wholesale suppliers
~ **der Landwirtschaft** wholesale suppliers in agricultural equipment
Versorgungsgüter *npl* supplies
Versorgungsinspektion *f* supply inspection office
Versorgungskontor *n* industrial supply office
Versorgungskonzeption *f* supplies programme
Versorgungslage *f* supply situation [position]; food situation

~, **angespannte** tight supply situation
Versorgungslager *n* supply store
Versorgungsleistung *f* (total) supply of consumer goods and/or services
Versorgungslücke *f* supply gap
Versorgungsnetz *n* network of shops and service centres; supply network
Versorgungsniveau *n* quality and quantity of supplies (of consumer goods and services)
Versorgungsperiode *f* rationing period *(foodstuffs etc.)*; supply period *(of coal for the winter)*
Versorgungsplan *m* supplies plan (of consumer goods and services)
Versorgungsplanung *f* planning of supplies (of consumer goods and services)
Versorgungspolitik *f* supplies policy (of consumer goods and services)
Versorgungsproblem *n* supply problem
Versorgungsprogramm *n* supplies programme
Versorgungsquelle *f* source of supply
Versorgungsschiff *n* supply ship
Versorgungsschwierigkeiten *fpl* difficulties of supply
Versorgungsstelle *f* supply centre
Versorgungssystem *n* supply system; system of retail trade and services
Versorgungsunternehmen *n* 1. public utilities; 2. catering firm
Versorgungsverpflichtung *f* obligation to provide a pension
Versorgungswesen *n* public assistance, poor-relief
Versorgungswirtschaft *f* public services [utilities], service sector and utilities
verspäten, sich to be late, to be overdue, to be behind time *(ship, train etc.)*
verspätet late; overdue; behind schedule ⋄ **~ zahlen** to pay behind schedule
Verspätung *f* delay, lateness; tardiness ⋄ **~ haben** to be late [overdue]; to be behind schedule *(train etc.)*
Verspätungsschaden *m* damage due to delayed performance of contract
Verspätungszinsen *mpl* penalty interest
Verspätungszuschläge *mpl* extra [additional] payments due to delayed performance of a contract
verspekulieren, sich to make a bad speculation
versprechen to promise
Versprechen *n* promise ⋄ **ein ~ erfüllen** to carry out [fulfil] a promise; **sein ~ halten** to keep one's promise; **sich nicht an sein ~ halten** not to keep one's promise
~, **schriftliches** promise in writing
Versprechensgeber *m* promisor
verstaatlichen to nationalize, to transfer to state ownership

Verstaatlichung *f* nationalization
~ **der Industrie** nationalization of industry
~ **von Grund und Boden** nationalization of land
verstädtern to urbanize
Verstädterung *f* urbanization
verständigen to inform, to notify, to advise ⋄ **sich mit jmdm. ~** to come to [reach] an agreement with s.o.
Verständigung *f* information, notification; understanding, agreement, arrangement, settlement ⋄ **zu einer ~ gelangen** to come to an agreement [arrangement]
~, **briefliche** written communication
~, **telefonische** telephone message
~, **telegrafische** telegraphic advice
Verständigungsverkehr *m* (d.pr.) handshake *(between microprocessor and memory)*
verstärken to strengthen, to reinforce *(efforts etc.)*; to intensify *(work etc.)*; to increase, to add to *(capital etc.)*
Verstärkung *f* strengthening; intensification
verstauen to stow *(ship)*
Verstauung *f* stowage *(ship)*
Verstauungskosten *pl* costs of stowage
versteifen, sich to stiffen, to harden *(attitudes etc.)*; to insist on *(opinion etc.)*
Versteifung *f* tightening
~ **des Geldmarktes** tightening of the money market
Versteigerer *m* auctioneer
versteigern to sell by [at] auction, to sell by public sale, to auction, to put up at auction [for public sale] ⋄ **~ lassen** to put up at auction
versteigert sold by public auction ⋄ **~ werden** to be sold by public auction; to come under the hammer
Versteigerung *f* auction (sales), selling [sale] by auction, public sale ⋄ **zur ~ bringen** to put up at [by] auction; **zur ~ kommen** to be sold at [by] auction
~, **öffentliche** public auction
Versteigerungsankündigung *f* notice of sale by auction
Versteigerungsbedingungen *fpl* terms of auction
Versteigerungserlös *m* proceeds of an auction
Versteigerungsfirma *f* auction company
Versteigerungsgebühren *fpl* auction fees, lot money
Versteigerungskosten *pl s.* Versteigerungsgebühren
Versteigerungslimit *n* limit for bidding, bidding limit
Versteigerungsliste *f* auction bill, catalogue of sale

Versteigerungslokal *n* sales room
Versteigerungsort *m* place of auction
Versteigerungspreis *m* auction price
Versteigerungstermin *m* auction day
versteuerbar taxable, dutiable
versteuern to pay taxes [duty] on
versteuert duty [taxes] paid, net of tax
Versteuerung *f* taxation, payment of taxes
Versteuerungswert *m* taxable [rateable] value
Verstoß *m* offence; contravention *(agreement etc.)*; infraction, infringement *(rules etc.)*; violation *(law etc.)*
~ **gegen das Gesetz** violation [breach] of the law
~ **gegen die Betriebsordnung** infraction of factory rules
~ **gegen die Vertragsbestimmungen** infringement of the stipulations of a contract
verstoßen:
 ⋄ ~ **gegen** to offend (against); to contravene *(agreement etc.)*; to infringe *(rules etc.)*, to violate *(law etc.)*
verstreichen to expire *(time limit etc.)*; to pass *(time)*
Versuch *m* trial, attempt; experiment; test
 ⋄ **einen** ~ **durchführen** to conduct a test
~, **faktorieller** *(stats)* factorial experiment
~, **kurzfristiger** short-term test
~, **zusammengesetzter** *(stats)* complex experiment
Versuche *mpl*:
~ **mit ungleichen Stufenzahlen, faktorielle** *(stats)* mixed factorial experiments
~, **unabhängige** *(stats)* independent trials
versuchen to try, to attempt; to test
Versuchsabteilung *f* research [experimental] department
Versuchsanlage *f* testing plant; pilot plant; *(d.pr.)* experimental system
Versuchsanordnung *f* experimental layout
Versuchsanstalt *f* research institute [centre]
Versuchsauftrag *m* experimental order
Versuchsaufwand *m* research expenditure(s), experimental expenses
Versuchsbericht *m* research report
Versuchsbetrieb *m* trial operation; pilot plant, scale production
Versuchsergebnis *n* test result
Versuchsfarm *f s.* **Versuchsgut**
Versuchsfehler *m (stats)* experimental error
Versuchsfeld *n* 1. field of experiment; 2. proving ground; 3. crop experimental area
Versuchsglied *n (stats)* treatment
Versuchsgut *n* experimental farm
Versuchsingenieur *m* research [test] engineer
Versuchslaboratorium *n* research [test] laboratory

Versuchsmarkt *m* test market
Versuchsmodell *n* test model
Versuchsmuster *n* pilot model
Versuchsordnung *f s.* **Versuchsplan**
Versuchsplan *m (stats)* design
~, **asymmetrischer faktorieller** *(stats)* asymmetrical factorial design
~ **einfach verketteter Blöcke** *(stats)* singly--linked block design
~ **im Dreiecksystem** *(stats)* triangular design
~, **in gleichgroße Gruppen teilbarer** *(stats)* group divisible design
~, **mehrfaktorieller** *(stats)* multi-factorial design
~ **mit einfachem Gitter** *(stats)* simple lattice design
~ **mit geteilten Parzellen** *(stats)* split-plot design
~ **mit Gittern** *(stats)* lattice design
~ **mit Gruppenwechsel** *(stats)* change-over [cross-over, switch-back] design
~ **mit halber Wiederholung** *(stats)* half-replicate design
~ **mit Quadergitter** *(stats)* cuboidal lattice design
~ **mit teilweise ausgewogenen unvollständigen Blöcken** *(stats)* partially balanced incomplete block design
~ **mit vollständig zufälliger Zuteilung** *(stats)* completely randomised design
~, **orthogonaler** *(stats)* orthogonal design
~, **quasi-faktorieller** *(stats)* quasi-factorial design
~, **systematischer** *(stats)* systematic design
~, **zyklischer** *(stats)* cyclic design
Versuchsproduktion *f* pilot production
Versuchsprojekt *n* pilot scheme
Versuchsprozeß *m* test case
Versuchsreihe *f* test series; series of experiments
Versuchsserie *f s.* **Versuchsreihe**
Versuchsstadium *n* experimental stage
Versuchsstand *m* test stand; *(agric)* experimental bed
Versuchsstation *f* experimental research plant; *(agric)* experimental cattle breeding centre
Versuchsstrecke *f* test track
Versuchs- und Entwicklungskosten *pl* cost(s) of experiments and development
versuchsweise by way of trial, by way of an experiment
Versuchswerbung *f* test marketing
Versuchszwecke *mpl*:
 ⋄ **zu Versuchszwecken** for experimental purposes
Versuch-und-Irrtum-Methode *f* trial and error method
vertagen to adjourn, to postpone *(meeting etc.)*;

to defer, to put off *(decision etc.)*; to prorogue *(parliament)*
Vertagung *f* adjournment, postponement *(meeting etc.)*; deferment *(decision etc.)* ◊ **~ beantragen** to move an adjournment of a case
Vertagungsantrag *m* motion to adjourn
vertauschbar exchangeable, interchangeable
Vertauschbarkeit *f* exchangeability, interchangeability
vertauschen to exchange, to barter; to substitute
verteidigen, sich to defend o.s.; to plead one's cause *(before court)*
Verteidigung *f* defence
Verteidigungsausgaben *fpl* defence expenditure
Verteidigungsbeitrag *m* defence contribution
verteilbar distributable
verteilen to distribute *(s.th.)*; to hand out *(leaflets)*; to divide; to allocate, to allot, to apportion *(resources etc.)*; to settle up, to appropriate *(assets of a bankrupt etc.)*; to spread (over) *(investments etc.)* ◊ **neu ~** to re-allocate, to redistribute
Verteiler *m* 1. distributor; 2. mailing [distribution] list
Verteilerkette *f* distribution chain
Verteilerliste *f* mailing [distribution] list
Verteilernetz *n* distribution network
Verteilerorganisation *f* distributing organization
Verteilerpostamt *n* general post office
Verteilerschlüssel *m* distribution list
Verteilung *f* distribution *(income etc.)*; dealing out; allocation, allotment, apportionment *(resources etc.)*; disposition, arrangement ◊ **zur ~ bringen** to distribute
~, **abgeschnittene** *(stats)* truncated distribution
~ **abhängiger Ereignisse** *(stats)* contagious distribution
~, **anteilmäßige** pro rata distribution
~, **asymmetrische** *(stats)* asymmetrical [skew] distribution
~, **asymptotische** *(stats)* asymptotic distribution
~, **Bernoulli'sche** *(stats)* Bernoulli [binomial] distribution
~, **binomische** s. ~, **Bernoulli'sche**
~, **Charlier'sche** *(stats)* Charlier distribution
~ **der Bevölkerung** distribution of population
~ **der Konkursmasse** distribution of assets
~ **der Kosten** distribution of costs
~ **der Steuerbelastung** distribution of taxation; distribution of tax burden
~ **der Unkosten** allocation [distribution] of expenses [expenditures]
~ **des Einkommens** income distribution
~ **des Gewinns** distribution of profit
~ **des Reingewinns** distribution of net profit
~ **des Risikos** spread of risk

~ **des Varianz-Verhältnisses** *(stats)* variance-ratio distribution
~ **einer Dividende** paying out (of) a dividend
~ **eines Nachlasses** distribution of an estate
~, **gemeinsame** *(stats)* joint distribution
~, **geometrische** *(stats)* geometric [continuous] distribution
~, **gestutzte** s. ~, **abgeschnittene**
~, **hypergeometrische** *(stats)* hypergeometric distribution
~ **in Stichproben** *(stats)* sampling distribution
~, **J-förmige** *(stats)* J-shaped distribution
~, **kreisperiodische** *(stats)* circular distribution
~, **log-normale** *(stats)* lognormal [Galton-Mc-Allister] distribution
~, **mangelhafte** maldistribution
~, **mehrdimensionale** *(stats)* multivariate distribution
~, **mehrgipflige** *(stats)* multi-modal distribution
~ **mit bekannter Fehlmenge, abgeschnittene** *(stats)* censored distribution
~, **multinominale** *(stats)* multinomial distribution
~ **nach den Bedürfnissen** distribution (of income) according to needs
~ **nach der Arbeitsleistung** distribution (of income) according to work
~ **nach einer logarithmischen Reihe** *(stats)* logarithmic series distribution
~, **nichtsinguläre** *(stats)* non-singular distribution
~, **polynomiale** s. ~, **polynomische**
~, **polynomische** *(stats)* multinomial distribution
~, **prozentuale** percentage distribution
~, **rechteckige** *(stats)* rectangular distribution
~, **schiefe** s. ~, **asymmetrische**
~, **singuläre** *(stats)* singular distribution
~, **stationäre** *(stats)* stationary distribution
~, **stetige** *(stats)* continuous distribution
~, **Student'sche** *(stats)* "student's" distribution, t-distribution
~, **verbundene** s. ~, **gemeinsame**
~ **von Arbeitskräften** allocation of manpower
~ **von Reaktionsschwellenwerten** *(stats)* tolerance distribution
~, **zweidimensionale** *(stats)* bivariate distribution
~, **zweidimensionale diskrete** *(stats)* point bivariate distribution
~, **zweigipflige** *(stats)* bimodal distribution
~, **zweiseitig exponentielle** *(stats)* double exponential distribution
~, **zyklische** s. ~, **kreisperiodische**
Verteilungsamt *n* s. **Verteilerpostamt**
Verteilungsdichte *f (stats)* frequency of distribution
verteilungsfrei *(stats)* non-parametric

Verteilungsfunktion *f (stats)* distribution function
~, **kumulative** *(stats)* cumulative distribution function
Verteilungskosten *pl* cost(s) of distribution
Verteilungskurve *f (stats)* distribution curve
Verteilungsmodus *m* distribution formula
Verteilungsschlüssel *m* distribution ratio [coefficient], allocation base [formula]
Verteilungsverhältnis *n*:
~, **festes** fixed ratio
verteuern to raise [increase] the price
Verteuerung *f* increase [advance] in price(s)
Vertikalkonzern *m* vertical group (of affiliated companies)
Vertikalregistratur *f* vertical filing
Vertikalverflechtung *f* vertical interlocking
Vertrag *m* contract; covenant, compact, agreement *(business etc.)*; *(pol)* treaty, pact, convention, agreement; deed, instrument *(document)*
◊ **an einem ~ beteiligt sein** to be a party to an agreement; **auf Grund eines Vertrages** on the basis of a contract; pursuant to a contract; **durch ~ gebunden sein** to be bound by contract, to be liable under a contract; **einem ~ beitreten** to become party to an agreement; **einen schriftlichen ~ abschließen** to enter into a written agreement; **einen ~ abändern** to modify a contract; **einen ~ abfassen** to draw up a contract; **einen ~ abschließen** to conclude a contract; **einen ~ anfechten** to void [rescind] a contract; **einen ~ annehmen** to adopt a contract; **einen ~ annullieren** to annul [cancel] a contract; **einen ~ aufheben** *s.* **einen ~ annullieren**; **einen ~ aufkündigen** to renounce a treaty; to renounce a contract [an agreement]; **einen ~ auflösen** to annul [cancel] a contract [an agreement]; **einen ~ aufrechterhalten** to go on [continue] with a contract [an agreement]; **einen ~ aufsetzen** to draw up [draft] a contract [an agreement]; **einen ~ ausarbeiten** *s.* **einen ~ aufsetzen**; **einen ~ ausfertigen** *s.* **einen ~ aufsetzen**; **einen ~ beenden** to terminate [end] a contract [an agreement]; **einen ~ bestätigen** to ratify a treaty; to confirm a contract [an agreement]; **einen ~ brechen** to breach a contract [an agreement]; **einen ~ entwerfen** *s.* **einen ~ aufsetzen**; **einen ~ erfüllen** to fulfil a contract [an agreement]; **einen ~ erneuern** to renew a contract [an agreement]; **einen ~ für ungültig [nichtig] erklären** to declare a contract [an agreement] null and void; **einen ~ im gegenseitigen Einvernehmen aufheben** to rescind a contract [an agreement] by mutual consent; **einen ~ kündigen** to revoke a contract [an agreement]; **einen ~ lösen** to dissolve an agreement [a contract]; **einen ~ nicht anerkennen** to repudiate a contract, to deny an agreement; **einen ~ nicht bestätigen** not to confirm a contract [an agreement]; **einen ~ ratifizieren** to ratify a treaty [an agreement]; **einen ~ registrieren lassen** to enter a deed; **einen ~ schließen** to come to [enter into, conclude] an agreement; **einen ~ unterzeichnen** to sign a contract; **einen ~ verlängern** to prolong a contract; **einen ~ verletzen** to violate a treaty; to violate a contract [an agreement]; **laut ~** by agreement; **sich an einen ~ halten** to abide by an agreement; **von einem ~ zurücktreten** to withdraw from an agreement [a contract]; **während der Dauer des Vertrages** during the life of the contract; **zu einem ~ gelangen** to come to an agreement
~, **amtlich registrierter** contract of record
~, **anfechtbarer** voidable contract
~ **auf Gegenseitigkeit** mutual agreement
~, **ausdrücklich geschlossener** express contract
~, **bedingter** conditional contract, executory agreement [contract]
~, **belastender** onerous contract
~, **bestehender** existing contract
~, **beurkundeter** instrument in writing
~, **erfüllter** executed contract [covenant]
~, **fehlerhafter** invalid [defective] contract
~, **fester** firm contract
~, **fingierter** sham contract
~, **formbedürftiger** specialty contract
~, **formfreier** *s.* ~, **formloser**
~, **formgebundener** *s.* ~, **formbedürftiger**
~, **förmlicher** solemn agreement; sealed instrument
~, **formloser** parol [simple] contract, agreement under hand
~, **gegenseitiger** reciprocal contract
~, **gemeinschaftlicher** joint contract
~, **gültiger** valid contract
~, **innerbetrieblicher** *(agric)* inner-co-operative contract
~, **internationaler** international agreement; international convention; international treaty
~, **kündbarer** terminable contract
~, **langfristiger** long-term contract
~, **mehrseitiger** multilateral agreement
~, **mündlicher** oral [simple] contract
~, **nicht erfüllter** unfulfilled contract
~, **nichtiger** void contract
~, **nicht notarieller** unsealed contract
~, **noch nicht erfüllter** executory (open) contract
~, **notarieller** contract under seal, specialty (sealed) contract
~, **ordnungsgemäß errichteter** contract drawn up in due form

~, **ordnungsgemäßer** contract in due form
~, **rechtsverbindlicher** legally binding contract
~, **schriftlicher** written contract
~, **schuldrechtlicher** obligatory (personal) covenant
~, **stillschweigend geschlossener** implied contract, tacit agreement
~ **über ein Entwicklungsvorhaben** development project contract
~ **über mehrere Lieferungen** multiple delivery contract
~, **verbindlicher** firm [binding] contract
~, **vorläufiger** provisional contract [agreement]
~, **wechselseitig bindender** mutually binding contract
~, **wechselseitiger** mutual contract
~ **zugunsten Dritter** third party beneficiary contract
~, **zweiseitiger** s. ~, **wechselseitiger**
vertraglich by [under] treaty; contractual, by [under] contract [agreement] ◊ **sich ~ binden** to bind o.s. by treaty; to bind o.s. by contract [agreement]; **~ festlegen** to stipulate in a treaty; to stipulate in a contract [an agreement]; **~ gebunden** bound by a treaty; bound by contract; **~ nicht vereinbart** not stipulated by treaty; not stipulated by contract; **~ regeln** to settle by agreement; **~ vereinbaren** to stipulate [provide] by treaty; to stipulate [provide] by contract; **~ vereinbart** by treaty; by contract, conventional, stipulated, (as) contracted; **~ verpflichtet** bound by treaty; bound by contract, convenanted, under articles; **~ vorgesehen** provided by the articles of a treaty; provided by the articles (of a contract); **wie ~ vereinbart** as provided in the treaty; as provided in the contract
Vertragsablauf *m* expiration of a treaty; expiration of a contract [an agreement]
Vertragsabmachungen *fpl*:
~, **schriftliche** articles of a contract
Vertragsabschluß *m* conclusion of a treaty; conclusion of a contract ◊ **bei ~** at the making of a treaty; at the making of a contract; **einen ~ verschleppen** to delay the conclusion of a contract [an agreement]
~, **nicht zustande gekommener** loss of a treaty; loss of a contract
Vertragsabschlußpflicht *f*:
~, **gesetzliche** legal obligations to conclude contracts
vertragsähnlich quasi contract(ual)
Vertragsänderung *f* alteration of a treaty; alteration of a contract [an agreement]
Vertragsanfechtung *f* challenge of a contract
Vertragsangebot *n* tender
Vertragsannahme *f* acceptance of a tender

Vertragsanspruch *m* contractual claim
Vertragsartikel *m* clause of a contract
Vertragsaufhebung *f* cancellation [rescission] of a contract
Vertragsaufkündigung *f* notice of termination of a contract
Vertragsauflösung *f* annulment [cancellation] of a contract
Vertragsauslegung *f* interpretation of the terms of a contract
Vertragsbedingungen *fpl* terms [provisions] of a treaty; terms [conditions, provisions, stipulations] of a contract [an agreement]
Vertragsbeendigung *f* termination of a treaty; termination of a contract [an agreement]
Vertragsbeginn *m* commencement of a treaty; commencement of a contract [an agreement]
Vertragsbeitritt *m* accession to a treaty; accession to an agreement
Vertragsbereitschaft *f* willingness to enter into a treaty; willingness to enter into a contract [an agreement]
Vertragsbestand *m (ins)* total policies outstanding
Vertragsbestandteil *m* (integral) part of a treaty; (integral) part of a contract [an agreement]
Vertragsbestimmungen *fpl* terms [provisions] of a treaty; terms [conditions, provisions, stipulations] of a contract [an agreement] ◊ **nach den ~** under [in accordance with] the articles of treaty; under [in accordance with] the articles [provisions] of a contract; **sich an die ~ halten** to comply with the terms of a treaty; to comply with the terms of a contract; **~ festlegen** to set forth terms in a treaty; to set forth terms in a contract; **~ verletzen** to violate the terms of a treaty; to violate the terms of a contract
~, **allgemeine** general terms of a contract
~, **besondere** special terms of a treaty; special terms of a contract
Vertragsbeteiligter *m* party to a treaty; party to a contract [an agreement]
Vertragsbrecher *m* party breaching the contract [agreement]
Vertragsbruch *m* breach of a contract
vertragsbrüchig breaching the terms of a contract ◊ **~ werden** to break a contract
Vertragsdatum *n* date of a contract
Vertragsdauer *f* life [term] of a treaty; life [term] of a contract [an agreement], contractual period
Vertragsdisziplin *f* adherence to the terms of a contract
Vertragsentwurf *m* draft treaty; draft contract [agreement]

Vertragserfüllung *f* fulfilment of a contract
~, mangelnde failure to fulfil the terms of a contract
Vertragserneuerung *f* renewal of a treaty; renewal of a contract
vertragsfähig (legally) competent [capable] to contract, having contractual capacity
Vertragsfähigkeit *f* competency [capability] to contract, contractual capacity
Vertragsformeln *fpl* (printed) general terms of a contract
Vertragsformen *fpl* 1. kinds [forms] of contract; 2. *(ins)* types of cover
Vertragsforschung *f* contract(ed) research
Vertragsfreiheit *f* freedom of contract
Vertragsgebiet *n* contractual territory
Vertragsgegenstand *m* subject matter of a contract
vertragsgemäß according to [in accordance with] (the terms of) the contract, as per agreement, conformable to the contract, contractual ◇ **nicht ~** not according to [in accordance with] (the terms of) the contract
Vertragsgesetz *n* law of contract
Vertragsgrundlage *f* basis of contract [agreement]
Vertragsgültigkeit *f* force [validity] of a contract
Vertragshafen *m* treaty port
Vertragshaftung *f* contractual liability
Vertragshändler *m* contract dealer
Vertragshilfe *f* contract rescission *(court ruling freeing person from onerous burden)*
Vertragsinhalt *m* contents of the contract
Vertragsklauseln *fpl* clauses in a contract
Vertragskündigung *f* revocation of a contract
Vertragsland *n* treaty country; contracting country
Vertragsleistung *f* contractual obligation ◇ **mit der ~ in Verzug kommen** to get behind with the performance of a contract, to fail to complete within the contract time
Vertragslücke *f* loophole in a contract [an agreement]
Vertragspartei *f* party to a treaty; party to a contract
Vertragspartner *m s.* **Vertragspartei**
Vertragsperiode *f* contractual period
Vertragspflicht *f* contractual obligation [duty], duty [obligation] under a contract, contractual commitment
Vertragspreis *m* contract price
Vertragsrecht *n* law of contract
Vertragsrechte *npl* contractual rights, rights under a contract
Vertragsschluß *m* making a contract, conclusion of an agreement
Vertragsschuld *f* contract(ual) debt

Vertragssparen *n* saving linked to a scheme
Vertragsstaat *m* contracting state; member country
Vertragsstrafe *f* penal obligation [clause]; penalty for breach of contract; contract(ual) penalty, penalty for non-performance of contract
Vertragssystem *n* contract system
Vertragstarif *m* conventional tariff *(customs)*
Vertragstermin *m* contract date [deadline]
Vertragstext *m* wording of a treaty; wording of a contract
vertragstreu true to the contract ◇ **~ sein** to abide by an agreement
Vertragstreue *f* observance of contracts, contractual fidelity
Vertragstyp *m* type of contract
Vertrags- und Lieferbedingungen *fpl*:
~, Allgemeine General Terms [Conditions] of Contract and Delivery
Vertrags- und Lieferstatistik *f* statistical report of supplies and services according to contract *(for checking the fulfilment of contracts according to range of articles, quality and time-limit)*
vertragsunfähig incompetent to contract
Vertragsunfähigkeit *f* incapacity to contract
Vertragsungültigkeit *f* voidance of a contract
Vertragsunterzeichnung *f* signature of a treaty; signature of a contract
Vertragsurkunde *f* contract, contractual document
Vertragsverbindlichkeit *f* contractual obligation, liability of a contract
Vertragsverhältnis *n* contractual relationship ◇ **ein ~ beenden** to terminate a contract; **ein ~ herstellen** to establish privity of a contract
Vertragsverhandlungen *fpl* negotiations for a treaty [an agreement], contract negotiations
Vertragsverlängerung *f* extension of a treaty; extension of a contract
Vertragsverletzung *f* breach [violation] of contract ◇ **sich einer ~ schuldig machen** to become liable to a summons
Vertragsverpflichtung *f* contractual obligation
Vertragsversicherung *f* contract insurance
Vertragsvollmacht *f* power to contract
Vertragsvorbehalt *m* proviso, reservation
Vertragsvorlauf *m* forward contracts *(contracts in supplies and deliveries for forthcoming plan periods)*
Vertragswährung *f* currency of contract
Vertragswerk *n* set of agreements
Vertragswerkstatt *f* (specialized) repair shop *(working under contract with a particular production enterprise and doing all necessary repairs of articles etc. sold by this enterprise)*
Vertragswert *m* expectation value
vertragswidrig contrary to (the terms of) an

agreement, contrary to a contract, not conforming [conformable] to a contract
Vertragswidrigkeit *f* contractual defect, lack of conformity with the contract
Vertragszeitraum *m* duration of a contract, contractual period
Vertragszinsen *mpl* stipulated interest
vertrauen to trust, to rely (upon), to have confidence (in)
Vertrauen *n* trust, reliance, confidence; faith
⋄ **im ~** confidentially, in confidence, between ourselves; **im ~ auf** trusting to, relying on; **sein ~ setzen auf** to put one's trust in; **~ erlangen** to get [obtain] confidence; **~ rechtfertigen** to deserve confidence; **~ wiederherstellen** to restore confidence
Vertrauensarzt *m* doctor [physician] acting as medical referee under social insurance legislation; company doctor
Vertrauensbereich *m* (*stats*) confidence region [belt, interval]
~, engster (*stats*) shortest confidence interval
Vertrauensbereiche *mpl*:
~, trennschärfste (*stats*) most selective confidence intervals
Vertrauensbruch *m* breach of trust [faith]
Vertrauensgrenzen *fpl* (*stats*) confidence limits
Vertrauensintervall *n s.* **Vertrauensbereich**
Vertrauenskredit *m* loan on trust
Vertrauensleute *pl* union shop stewards [organizers]
Vertrauensmann *m* union shop steward [organizer]; reliable [trustworthy] person
Vertrauensmißbrauch *m* abuse of trust [confidence]
Vertrauensperson *f* reliable [trustworthy] person
Vertrauensposten *m* position of trust
Vertrauenssache *f* confidential matter
Vertrauensstellung *f s.* **Vertrauensposten**
Vertrauensverhältnis *n* personal confidence
Vertrauensverlust *m* loss of confidence [trust]
Vertrauensvotum *n* vote of confidence
Vertrauenswert *m*:
~ einer Marke brand preference
vertrauenswürdig trustworthy, reliable, credible
Vertrauenswürdigkeit *f* trustworthiness, reliability
vertraulich confidential ⋄ **streng ~** strictly confidential; **streng ~ behandeln** to treat strictly confidentially
Vertraulichkeit *f* confidence; intimacy
vertraut:
⋄ **sich mit etwas ~ machen** to make o.s. familiar with s.th., to familiarize [acquaint] o.s. with s.th.
vertreiben 1. to drive away, to expel (*s.o.*); 2. to sell, to distribute (*goods*)

Vertreibung *f* 1. expulsion; 2. selling, distribution (*goods*)
vertretbar justifiable, warrantable; defensible; reasonable; fungible
Vertretbarkeit *f* defensibility; substitution
vertreten to represent (*firm etc.*); to deputize for (*s.o.*); to act as substitute; to defend, to answer for; to advocate (*cause etc.*); to appear for, to act for, to act on behalf of (*s.o. etc.*)
⋄ **jmdn. ~** to represent s.o., to act for [on behalf of] s.o., to appear for s.o.; to deputize for s.o.
Vertreter *m* representative, deputy; (*com*) agent; commercial traveller, travelling salesman
⋄ **als ~** as a representative, in a representative capacity; as an agent; as a deputy; **als ~ handeln** to act as a representative; to act as an agent; **jmdn. zu seinem ~ bestimmen** to appoint s.o. as one's deputy
~, alleiniger sole agent
~, amtlicher official representative
~, bestellter appointed representative
~, bevollmächtigter accredited [authorized] representative
~, gemeinsamer joint agent
~, gesetzlicher legal representative
~, persönlicher personal representative
~, ständiger permanent representative
Vertreterbefugnisse *fpl* power of an agent
Vertreterbericht *m* agent's report
Vertreterbezirk *m* agent's territory
Vertreterkosten *pl* agency costs
Vertreterprovision *f* agent's [agency] commission
Vertretervertrag *m* agency contract
Vertretervollmacht *f* power of attorney, power of an agent
Vertretung *f* representation; agency ⋄ **die ~ einer Firma übernehmen** to take over the agency of a firm; **mit der ~ beauftragt sein** to be appointed as a representative [an agent]
~, ausschließliche sole agency
~ durch einen Anwalt (*jur*) representation by a lawyer
Vertretungsbefugnis *f s.* **Vertretungsvollmacht**
vertretungsberechtigt authorized to act (as)
Vertretungsberechtigter *m* authorized representative, person acting for [on behalf of]
Vertretungsvollmacht *f* power of attorney
vertretungsweise as a representative [proxy]
Vertrieb *m* sale, marketing; distribution
~, direkter direct selling [sales] (*without wholesale dealer*)
Vertriebsabkommen *n* sales agreement
Vertriebsabteilung *f* sales department, marketing division
Vertriebsagentur *f* marketing agency

Vertriebsanstrengungen *fpl* sales efforts
Vertriebsapparat *m* marketing organization *(of an enterprise)*
Vertriebsaufwand *m* marketing [selling, distribution] costs, costs of marketing
Vertriebsbedingungen *fpl* terms [conditions] of sale
Vertriebsberater *m* marketing adviser
Vertriebsbeschränkungen *fpl* restrictions on sales, selling [sales] restrictions
Vertriebsbüro *n* sales office
Vertriebseinrichtungen *fpl* marketing facilities
Vertriebsförderung *f* promotion of sale(s), sales promotion
Vertriebsgebiet *n* market, marketing [trading] area, outlet
Vertriebsgemeinkosten *pl* sales overhead costs
Vertriebsgemeinschaft *f* joint marketing organization
Vertriebsgenossenschaft *f* marketing association
Vertriebsgeschäft *n* marketing
Vertriebsgesellschaft *f* marketing company
Vertriebskalkulation *f* calculation of cost(s) of sales
Vertriebskanäle *mpl* channels of distribution [marketing], channels for trade
Vertriebskosten *pl s.* **Vertriebsaufwand**
Vertriebskostenanalyse *f* analysis of distribution cost(s)
Vertriebskostenrechnung *f* distributive cost accounting
Vertriebslager *n* warehouse, store
Vertriebsleiter *m* head of the sales department, sales manager
Vertriebsleitung *f* sales [marketing] management
Vertriebsmethoden *fpl* marketing [selling, distribution] methods
Vertriebsmonopol *n* market [sales] monopoly
Vertriebsnetz *n* trading network
Vertriebsorganisation *f* 1. marketing organization; 2. organization of marketing *(as part of the sphere of circulation including the institutional set-up and marketing methods)*
Vertriebspersonal *n* sales [marketing] personnel
Vertriebsplan *m* marketing [sales] plan
Vertriebspolitik *f* marketing [sales] policy
Vertriebsprogramm *n* marketing [sales] programme
Vertriebsrecht *n* selling rights
Vertriebsrisiko *n* sales risk
Vertriebsschulung *f* training in marketing
Vertriebsspanne *f* trade margin
Vertriebsstrategie *f* marketing [sales] strategy
Vertriebsstruktur *f* distribution structure
Vertriebssystem *n* marketing [sales] system

Vertriebsunkosten *pl s.* **Vertriebsaufwand**
Vertriebsunternehmen *n* distributing enterprise, sales agency
Vertriebsvereinbarung *f* sales agreement
Vertriebsvertrag *m s.* **Vertriebsvereinbarung**
Vertriebswege *mpl s.* **Vertriebskanäle**
Vertriebswesen *n s.* **Vertriebssystem**
veruntreuen to embezzle
Veruntreuung *f* embezzlement
~ **öffentlicher Gelder** misappropriation of public funds
Veruntreuungsversicherung *f* fidelity insurance
verursachen to cause, to give rise to
Verursachung *f* cause
Verursachungsprinzip *n (ins)* causing principle
verurteilen to condemn; to sentence, to convict
Verurteilung *f* condemnation; sentence, conviction
vervielfältigen to duplicate, to reproduce, to mimeograph
Vervielfältigung *f* duplicate; duplication, reproduction, mimeographing
Vervielfältigungszeit *f (d.pr.)* step-and-repeat time
vervollkommnen to complete; to improve *(planning etc.)*
Vervollkommnung *f* completion; improvement *(planning etc.)*
vervollständigen to complete; to replenish *(stock etc.)*
Vervollständigung *f* completion; replenishing, replenishment *(stocks etc.)*
verwahren to keep, to guard from *(article for safekeeping etc.)*, to have in safekeeping *(money etc.)*; to preserve; **sich ~ gegen** to protest against
Verwahrer *m* keeper, safekeeper; custodian
Verwahrkonto *n* safekeeping account
verwahrlosen to become demoralized; to become ruined by neglect; to overrun with weeds *(garden etc.)*
verwahrlost demoralized; uncared for, neglected
Verwahrstück *n* article for safekeeping
Verwahrung *f* 1. keeping, safekeeping *(money etc.)*; custody; 2. protest, protesting ⋄ **etwas in ~ nehmen** to take care of s.th.; **gegen etwas ~ einlegen** to (enter a) protest against s.th.; **jmdn. in ~ nehmen** to put s.o. into custody
~, gerichtliche *(jur)* custodianship
Verwahrungsgebühr *f* charges for safekeeping
Verwahrungsort *m* place of safekeeping, depository, repository
Verwahrungsvertrag *m* contract on safekeeping
verwalten to administer, to manage, to conduct; to control, to supervise ⋄ **schlecht ~** to mismanage

Verwalter *m* administrator; curator
Verwaltung *f* 1. administration; management;
  2. administrative authority; office
  ~ **der Sozialversicherung** social [national] insurance office
  ~ **der Staatsfinanzen** administration of public revenue
  ~ **eines Amtes** exercise of an office
  ~, **kommunale** local [municipal] government
  ~, **öffentliche** local government service
  ~, **öffentlicher Gelder** administration of public funds
  ~, **staatliche** government, state administration
  ~, **treuhänderische** trusteeship, trust administration
  ~ **von Effekten** safekeeping of securities
Verwaltungsabteilung *f* administrative branch
Verwaltungsakt *m* administrative act
Verwaltungsangelegenheit *f* administrative matter(s)
Verwaltungsangestellter *m* (administrative) official, clerk
Verwaltungsanordnung *f* administrative instructions
Verwaltungsapparat *m* administration
Verwaltungsarbeit *f* administrative work
Verwaltungsaufgaben *fpl* administrative [management] duties
Verwaltungsaufwand *m* administrative costs [expenditures] *(time, money etc.)*
Verwaltungsaufwendungen *fpl s.* **Verwaltungsausgaben**
Verwaltungsausgaben *fpl* administrative expenditure(s) [expenses]
Verwaltungsausschuß *m* committee of management, administrative body
Verwaltungsbehörde *f* administration, government office, board of management
Verwaltungsbereich *m* administrative department; administrative competence
Verwaltungsbezirk *m* administrative area [region, county]
Verwaltungsbuchführung *f* administration accounting
Verwaltungsbüro *n* office
Verwaltungschef *m* head of administration
Verwaltungsdienst *m* administrative service
Verwaltungsdirektor *m* administrative manager
Verwaltungsdistrikt *m s.* **Verwaltungsbezirk**
Verwaltungseinheit *f* administrative unit
Verwaltungseinteilung *f s.* **Verwaltungsstruktur**
Verwaltungsfachleute *pl* administrative experts
Verwaltungsfonds *m* administrative fund
Verwaltungsfunktion *f* administrative function
Verwaltungsgebäude *n* administrative [office] building, administration

Verwaltungsgebiet *n s.* **Verwaltungsbezirk**
Verwaltungsgebühr *f* fee, charge(s)
Verwaltungsgemeinkosten *pl* general management costs
Verwaltungsgericht *n* administrative court
Verwaltungsgliederung *f s.* **Verwaltungsstruktur**
Verwaltungskosten *pl* administrative costs
Verwaltungskostenanteil *m (ins)* loading costs
Verwaltungskostenstellen *fpl* administrative cost centre
Verwaltungskostenumlage *f* portion of administrative costs
verwaltungsmäßig administrative, government(al), ministerial, managerial
Verwaltungsmaßnahme *f* administrative [governmental, ministerial, managerial] act [measure]
Verwaltungsmethode *f* administrative method
Verwaltungsmitglied *n* member of an administration
Verwaltungsoperation *f (d.pr.)* housekeeping operation
Verwaltungsorgan *n* administrative body
Verwaltungsorganisation *f* administrative organization
Verwaltungspersonal *n* administrative staff
Verwaltungsprogramm *n (d.pr.)* management program
Verwaltungsrat *m* administrative board, board of directors, committee of management
Verwaltungsrecht *n* administrative law
Verwaltungsreform *f* administrative reform
Verwaltungsstelle *f* administration, administrative office
Verwaltungsstruktur *f* administrative structure
Verwaltungstechnik *f s.* **Verwaltungsmethode**
verwaltungstechnisch administrative
Verwaltungsträger *m s.* **Verwaltungsorgan**
Verwaltungsverfügung *f s.* **Verwaltungsanordnung**
Verwaltungsvorgang *m* administrative matter
Verwaltungsweg *m* administrative channels
  ◇ **auf dem** ~ through administrative channels
Verwaltungswesen *n* (public) administration
Verwaltungswirtschaft *f* planned economy
  ~, **zentrale** centrally planned economy
verwandt related; similar, kindred; allied
Verwandte *pl* relatives, relations
  ~, **nächste** next of kin
Verwandter *m* relative
  ~ **ersten Grades** immediate relative, relative in the first degree
Verwandtschaft *f s.* **Verwandte**
verwandtschaftlich kindred; as relatives [relations]
Verwandtschaftsgrad *m* degree of relationship

verwarnen to warn, to caution; to admonish
Verwarnung *f* warning, caution; admonishment
~, **gebührenpflichtige** on-the-spot fine *(traffic etc.)*
~, **gerichtliche** *(jur)* warning from the judge *(during a hearing)*; injunction *(restraining person from doing s.th. etc.)*
verwässern to water down, to dilute *(wine etc.)*
verweigern to deny *(s.o. s.th.)*; to refuse *(s.th.)*; to withhold *(permission etc.)*
verweigert refused
Verweigerung *f* denial; refusal
~ **der Annahme** non-acceptance *(letter etc.)*
Verweigerungsquote *f (stats)* refusal rate
Verweis *m* 1. reproof, admonition, reprimand; 2. reference
verweisen 1. to reprove, to admonish, to reprimand; 2. to refer to, to indicate; 3. to remove, to expel *(s.o. from an institution etc.)*
verwendbar suitable; applicable; to be employed [utilized] as
verwenden to use, to utilize, to employ; to apply; to spend, to expend ◊ **sich ~ für jmdn.** to intercede with a person on behalf of s.o.; to use one's influence on behalf of s.o.
Verwendung *f* use, utilization, employment; application ◊ **keine ~ haben für** to have no use for, not to be in need of
~, **ausschließliche** exclusive use
~ **des Nationaleinkommens** use [utilization, appropriation] of the national income
~ **des Prämienfonds** use [appropriation] of the bonus fund
~, **gemeinwirtschaftliche** use on a collective basis, collective use
~, **interne** international use
~, **nichtverbrauchswirksame** utilization (which is) not earmarked for consumption
~, **rationelle** rational use [employment] *(resources etc.)*
~, **sinnvolle** appropriate use [utilization]
~, **unrechtmäßige** s. ~, **widerrechtliche**
~, **vielseitige** versatility, many-sided use
~ **von Haushaltsmitteln** appropriation of budgetary means
~, **widerrechtliche** conversion *(of trust property for personal use etc.)*, unlawful use *(of s.th.)*
Verwendungsbereich *m* scope of utilization
Verwendungsfonds *mpl* funds earmarked for certain purposes
Verwendungsnachweis *m* statement on utilization (of funds)
Verwendungsposition *f* item of utilization *(budgetary resources etc.)*
Verwendungsstruktur *f* earmarking of use
Verwendungszweck *m* use, purpose of use, intended use *(of s.th.)*

verwertbar usable, utilizable; realizable, saleable, marketable; negotiable
Verwertbarkeit *f* realizability, negotiability
verwerten to make use of *(s.th.)*, to use, to utilize; to realize, to sell *(shares etc.)*; ◊ **sich gut ~ lassen** to fetch a good price, to find a ready market; **sich schwer ~ lassen** to find no sale [market]; difficult to find a use *(for s.th.)*
Verwertung *f* utilization; employment, use; realization, sale; salvage, recovery, recycling
~ **des Kapitals** utilization of capital
~, **geschäftliche** commercialization
~, **gewerbliche** industrial use
Verwertungsbedingungen *fpl* conditions of utilization *(capital etc.)*
Verwertungsklausel *f* realization clause
Verwertungskosten *pl* mining [extraction] costs *(mineral resources etc.)*; recycling costs *(second-hand materials etc.)*; costs of realization *(commodities etc.)*
Verwertungsprozeß *m* process of utilization
~ **des Kapitals** process of capital utilization
Verwertungsrate *f* rate of exploitation
Verwertungsrechte *npl* exploitation rights
verwirkbar forfeitable *(rights etc.)*
Verwirkbarkeit *f* forfeitableness *(rights etc.)*
verwirken to forfeit, to lose *(right etc.)*; to incur, to merit *(punishment etc.)*
verwirklichen to realize; to implement *(plan etc.)*; **sich ~** to materialize, to realize *(an idea etc.)*
Verwirklichung *f* realization, materialization; implementation *(plan etc.)*
verwirkt forfeited
Verwirkung *f* forfeiture, loss *(right etc.)*
Verwirkungsklausel *f* defeasance clause
verwirtschaften to squander (away), to dissipate
verwissenschaftlichen to introduce science *(in s.th.)*
Verwissenschaftlichung *f* introduction of science *(in s.th.)*
~ **der Produktion** introduction of science in production
verwüsten to devastate; to lay waste
Verwüstung *f* devastation
verzählen, sich to miscount, to make a mistake (in counting)
verzehren to consume, to eat (up)
verzeichnen to note [write] down; to record, to register; to list; to score *(success etc.)*; *(st.ex.)* to quote
verzeichnet written down; registered
Verzeichnis *n* list, catalogue; register; specification; index; inventory
~, **alphabetisches** alphabetic(al) list [index]
~ **der Nachlaßgegenstände** inventory of the estate

~, **tabellarisches** table
Verzerrung *f (stats)* bias
~ **durch Gewichtung** *(stats)* weight bias
~ **durch Mittelwertzahl** *(stats)* type bias
~, **innewohnende** *(stats)* inherent bias
~ **nach oben** *(stats)* upward bias
~ **nach unten** *(stats)* downward bias
Verzicht *m* renunciation *(of a claim to s.th.)*; waiver *(duty, levy, right etc.)*; *(jur)* abandonment *(property)* ◊ ~ **leisten** *s.* **verzichten**
verzichten to do without, to forego *(s.th.)*; to give up, to renounce *(a claim to s.th.)*; to waive *(duty, levy, right etc.)*; to dispense with *(action etc.)*; *(jur)* to abandon *(property)*
Verzichterklärung *f* waiver, disclaimer ◊ **eine ~ abgeben** to sign a waiver
Verzichtleistung *f* renunciation, *(jur)* abandonment
Verzichtleistungsklausel *f* waiver clause
Verzichtschreiben *n (jur)* letter of renunciation
Verzichturkunde *f* deed of renunciation
verziehen to (re)move *(from one place to another)*
verzinsen to yield [bear] interest
verzinslich bearing interest ◊ ~ **anlegen** to put out at interest, to invest; ~ **vom** ... interest payable from ...
Verzinsung *f* interest; payment of interest; rate of interest; interest return
~, **durchschnittliche** average yield (of interest)
~, **effektive** net return (of interest)
~, **gesetzliche** legal rate of interest
~, **laufende** flat yield (of interest)
Verzinsungsfaktor *m* rate of interest
Verzinsungsperiode *f* interest period, period of interest
verzogen:
◊ **falls ~** if moved, in case of change of address
verzögern to delay *(delivery, payment etc.)*, to retard *(effect etc.)*
Verzögerung *f* delay *(delivery, payment etc.)*, retardation *(effect etc.)* ◊ **keine ~ zulassen** to permit of no delay
~, **zeitliche** time lag
Verzögerungseffekt *m* retarding effect
Verzögerungstaktik *f* delaying tactics
verzollbar dutiable, subject to duty
verzollen to impose duty *(on s.th.)*
verzollt duty-paid, declared
Verzollung *f* payment of duty; (customs) clearance
Verzollungskosten *pl* (customs) clearance charges
Verzollungspapiere *npl* (customs) clearance papers
Verzug *m* delay, postponement ◊ **bei ~ der Zahlung** in the case of arrears of payment; **in** ~ **in arrears**; **ohne** ~ without delay, immediately
Verzugsaktie *f* deferred share [*(Am)* stock]
Verzugsklausel *f* clause relating to default
Verzugsobligation *f* preference bonds
Verzugsstrafe *f s.* **Verzugszinsen**
Verzugstage *mpl* days of grace
Verzugszinsen *mpl* penalty interest, interest on arrears
Verzugszuschläge *mpl* additional payment on arrears
Verzweigungsprozeß *m (stats)* branching [multiplicative] process
Viehausstellung *f* cattle show
Viehbesatz *m* stocking, livestock density
Viehbestand *m* livestock
Viehbestandsplanung *f* livestock planning
Viehfutter *n* fodder
Viehhaltung *f* animal farming [husbandry]
Viehhandel *m* cattle trade
Viehhändler *m* cattle trader, livestock dealer
Viehhof *m* slaughter-house, abattoir
Viehmarkt *m* cattle market
Viehmast *f* fattening of cattle
Viehtransport *m* cattle transport
Viehversicherung *f* livestock insurance
Viehweide *f* pasture, pasturage
Viehwirtschaft *f* stock-farming, animal husbandry
Viehwirtschaftsbetrieb *m* livestock [stock, cattle] farm, *(Am)* ranch
Viehzählung *f* livestock census
Viehzucht *f* livestock [animal] breeding
Viehzüchter *m* stockbreeder, cattle farmer, *(Am)* rancher
Vielfachcomputersystem *n* multiple computer system
Vielfacheinteilung *f s.* **Vielfachklassifizierung**
Vielfachklassifizierung *f (stats)* manifold classification
Vielfeldersystem *n* system of rotational cropping
Vielfelderwirtschaft *f* rotational cropping
Vierfachtafel *f (stats)* fourfold [two-by-two frequency) table
Vierfeldertafel *f s.* **Vierfachtafel**
Vierjahresplan *m* four-year plan
Viermächteabkommen *n* quadripartite treaty
Vierschichtarbeit *f* four-shift work; round-the--clock shifts
Vierteljahresabrechnung *f* quarterly account; *(st.ex.)* term settlement
Vierteljahresausweis *m (bank)* quarterly return
Vierteljahresbericht *m* quarterly statement
vierteljährlich quarterly
Viertelswert *m (stats)* quartile
Visagebühr *f* visa fee

Visum *n* visa ◊ **ein ~ beantragen** to apply for a visa; **ein ~ erhalten** to get a visa; **ein ~ erteilen** to give [issue] a visa; **ein ~ verweigern** to refuse a visa
Visumantrag *m* visa application
Visumerteilung *f* issue of a visa
~, kostenlose issue of a visa free of charge, issue of a free visa
Visumformalitäten *fpl* visa formalities
Visumverlängerung *f* extension of a visa
Vizekanzler *m* vice-chancellor
Vizekonsul *m* vice-consul
Vizepräsident *m* vice-president
Volk *n* people
Völkerbund *m* League of Nations
Völkergemeinschaft *f* commonwealth of nations
Völkerrecht *n* international law
völkerrechtlich under international law
Volksabstimmung *f* plebiscite
Volksaktie *f* low par-value [baby] share
Volksaufstand *m* popular (up)rising; revolution
Volksbefragung *f* referendum *(by the government)*; public opinion poll *(by institutions etc.)*
Volksbegehren *n* demand for a plebiscite [referendum]
Volksbildung *f* education
Volksdemokratie *f* people's democracy
volkseigen nationally-owned
Volkseigentum *n* national [people's] property
Volkseinkommen *n* national income
Volksfront *f* people's front
Volksgemeinschaft *f* community
Volkshochschule *f* adult education classes, evening school
Volkskapitalismus *m* people's capitalism
Volkskontrollausschuß *m* committee of popular control
Volkskontrolle *f* popular control *(by citizens acting in an honorary capacity)*
Volksmassen *fpl* the broad masses
Volksschichten *fpl* social strata
Volksschulbildung *f* primary (school) education
Volksschule *f* primary school
Volksschulwesen *n* primary education
Volks- und Berufszählung *f* population and vocation census
Volksverbrauch *m* national consumption
Volksvermögen *n* national wealth
Volksvertreter *m* deputy, elected [people's] representative
Volksvertretung *f* representation of the people, people's representation
Volkswirt *m* economist
Volkswirtschaft *f* national economy
volkswirtschaftlich national economic
Volkswirtschaftsbereich *m* sector of the national economy

Volkswirtschaftsbilanz *f* balance sheet of the national economy
Volkswirtschaftslehre *f* economics
Volkswirtschaftsmethode *f* finished products method *(method for calculating the value of the total production of a national economy as opposed to method of enterprise classification)*
Volkswirtschaftsplan *m* national economic plan
Volkswirtschaftsplanung *f* national economic planning
Volkswirtschaftstheorie *f s.* **Volkswirtschaftslehre**
Volkswirtschaftszweig *m* national economic branch
Volkswohlfahrt *f* public [national] welfare
Volkszählung *f* (population) census
voll full, complete, whole, entire
Vollautomation *f* full automation
vollautomatisch fully automatic
vollautomatisiert fully automated
Vollbelegung *f* full booking
vollberechtigt fully qualified *(member of an organization etc.)*
vollbeschäftigt fully employed
Vollbeschäftigteneinheit *f (stats)* unit of fully employed labour force
Vollbeschäftigter *m* full-time worker
Vollbeschäftigung *f* full employment
Vollbeschäftigungsgrad *m* level of full employment
Vollbeschäftigungspolitik *f* policy of full employment
Volleigentümer *m* sole owner
vollenden to finish, to terminate; to accomplish, to complete
vollendet accomplished
Vollendung *f* finishing, termination; completion
Vollendungsfrist *f* (specified) time for completion *(job etc.)*
Vollerhebung *f* 1. imposition *(tax etc.)*; 2. *(stats)* complete survey [inquiry]; complete census
Vollgehalt *m* full value *(coins etc.)*
Vollgewicht *n* full weight
Vollgiro *n* full [direct] endorsement
vollgültig valid
Vollindossament *n s.* **Vollgiro**
Vollinvalide *m* invalid, permanently disabled person
Vollinvalidität *f* permanent disability, total incapacity
volljährig major, of age, adult
Volljährigkeit *f* majority, full age, adulthood
Volljährigkeitserklärung *f* declaration of majority
Vollkasko *n (ins)* comprehensive coverage
Vollkaskoversicherung *f* comprehensive motorcar and property damage insurance

Vollmacht *f* full power(s), authority, power of attorney ◊ **eine rechtsgültige ~ besitzen** to have legal power [authenticated power of attorney]; **jmdn. mit ~ versehen** to invest s.o. with power
Vollmachtsurkunde *f* letter of attorney
Vollmachtswiderruf *m* revocation of power
Vollmatrose *m* able-bodied seaman
Vollmatrose *m* **der Hochseefischerei** able--bodied seaman in ocean fishing fleet
vollmechanisiert fully mechanized, automated
Vollmechanisierung *f* full [complete] mechanization, automation
Vollpension *f* full board
Vollrente *f* full pension
vollständig complete, entire
Vollständigkeit *f* completeness, entirety
Vollständigkeitserklärung *f* liability certificate
Vollständigkeitsklausel *f* perfect attestation clause
vollstreckbar executory, enforceable ◊ **nicht ~** unenforceable
Vollstreckbarkeit *f* enforceability
vollstrecken to carry out (a sentence)
Vollstreckung *f* carrying out (a sentence)
Vollstreckungsbefehl *m* court order (to seal property)
Vollverlust *m* complete loss
Vollversammlung *f* general assembly
Vollversicherung *f* comprehensive insurance
vollwertig up to standard ◊ **nicht ~** below (the) standard
vollzählig complete
Volumen *n* volume; size; capacity, content
~ des Außenhandelsumsatzes, physisches phyiscal volume of foreign trade turnover
~, physisches physical volume, capacity
Von-bis-Preis *m* price ranging from ... to ...
Von-bis-Spanne *f* margin ranging from ... to ...
Vorankündigung *f* advance notice, announcement
Voranmeldung *f* prior application; registration, reservation; previous appointment *(at the dentist etc.)*
Voranschlag *m* estimate
Voranzeige *f s.* **Vorankündigung**
Vorarbeit *f* preparatory [ground] work, preparation
vorarbeiten 1. to prepare in advance; 2. to work in advance
Vorarbeiter *m* foreman
voraus ahead ◊ **im ~** in advance, beforehand
vorausbedingen to stipulate beforehand
Vorausbedingung *f* condition, precondition, stipulation
vorausberechnen to calculate beforehand, to estimate

Vorausberechnung *f* estimate
~, statistische (statistical) projection
vorausbestellen to order in advance
Vorausbestellung *f* advance order
vorausbezahlen to pay in advance, to prepay
Vorausbezahlung *f* payment in advance, prepayment
vorausdatieren to ante-date
vorausdatiert ante-dated
Vorausdatierung *f* ante-dating
Vorausleistung *f* work to be done before payment; fulfilment of prior condition
Vorausprämie *f (ins)* advance premium
Vorausrechnung *f* invoice sent in advance
Voraussage *f* prediction *(development trend etc.)*; forecast *(market situation, weather etc.)*
voraussagen to predict *(development trend etc.)*; to forecast *(market situation, weather etc.)*; to foretell *(events etc.)*
Voraussagespanne *f* 1. *s.* **Vorhersagezeitraum**; 2. *(stats)* prediction interval
Vorausschätzung *f s.* **Vorausberechnung**
Vorausschau *f* forecast, forecasting
voraussetzen to presuppose, to assume, to presume; to require
Voraussetzung *f* prerequisite, precondition; supposition, assumption
Voraussicht *f* foresight
voraussichtlich probably, very likely
Vorauswahl *f* (pre)selection
Vorauswahlprozeß *m* process of (pre)selection
Vorauswechsel *m* advance bill
vorauszahlbar payable in advance
Vorauszahlung *f* payment in advance
Vorauszahlungsprämie *f (ins)* advance premium
Vorbehalt *m* reservation; proviso ◊ **ohne ~** without reservation; **unter ~** with reservation; under the proviso
~, geheimer (mental) reservation
vorbehaltlich with a proviso, on (the) condition that
vorbehaltlos without reservation
Vorbehaltsgut *n* separate estate
Vorbehaltsklausel *f* proviso clause
Vorbeitrag *m (ins)* initial premium
vorbelastet already pledged; already mortgaged
Vorbelastung *f* prior encumbrance(s)
Vorbenutzung *f* prior use *(patent)*
vorbereiten to prepare, to arrange *(s.th.)*; *(d.pr.)* to initialize
vorbereitend preparatory
Vorbereitung *f* preparation, arrangement
~, konstruktive designing *(as part of preplanning and preorganisation of production)*
~, technische technical preparation
Vorbereitungsarbeiten *fpl* preparatory [preliminary] work

Vorbereitungsaufwand *m* preparation expenditure(s)
Vorbereitungskosten *pl* preparation costs
Vorbereitungsprogramm *n* preparatory programme; *(d.pr.)* initializer
Vorbereitungs- und Abschlußarbeiten *fpl* preparatory and finishing work
Vorbereitungs- und Abschlußkosten *pl* preparatory and finishing costs
Vorbereitungs- und Abschlußzeit *f* preparatory and finishing time
Vorbereitungszeit *f* preparation time
Vorbescheid *m* interim order
vorbestellen to order in advance
Vorbestellpreis *m* subscription price
Vorbestellung *f* advance order, reservation
vorbestraft previously convicted
vorbeugen to hinder, to prevent
vorbeugend preventive
Vorbeugungsmaßnahme *f* preventive measure
Vorbilanz *f* preliminary balance sheet
vorbilanzieren to draw up [make] a preliminary balance sheet
Vorbilanzierung *f* drawing up [making] a preliminary balance sheet
Vorbildung *f* educational background; qualification required *(for a job)*
vordatieren *s.* **vorausdatieren**
vordatiert *s.* **vorausdatiert**
Vordatierung *f s.* **Vorausdatierung**
Vordergrund-Hintergrund-Arbeitsweise *f (d.pr.)* foreground-background mode
Vordergrund-Hintergrund-Technik *f (d.pr.)* foreground-background philosophy
Vordergrundprogramm *n (d.pr.)* foreground program
Vorerhebung *f (stats)* pilot [exploratory] survey
Vorerzeugnis *n* primary product
Vorfabrikation *f* prefabrication
vorfabriziert prefabricated
Vorfahrt *f* right of way
vorfahrtsberechtigt main *(road)*
Vorfall *m* occurrence; event, incident; case; *(acc)* item
vorfinanzieren to prefinance
Vorfinanzierung *f* prefinancing
vorfristig ahead of time [schedule]
vorführen to demonstrate *(car etc.)*; to present
Vorführung *f* demonstration *(car etc.)*; presentation
Vorgabe *f* standard *(norm)*; given data
~, staatliche plan tasks given by the state
Vorgabezeiten *fpl* time standards
Vorgang *m* 1. proceedings *(at a meeting, court etc.)*; procedure; process occurrence; event, incident; 2. *(acc)* item; 3. case
~, arbeitsintensiver labour-intensive process

Vorgänger *m* predecessor
vorgeben 1. to give *(s.th.)* as target; 2. to profess, to pretend *(s.th.)*; 3. *(d.pr.)* to preset
Vorgesetzter *m* superior, chief
vorgreifen to anticipate *(one's income)*; to forestall
Vorgriff *m* 1. anticipation *(of one's income)*; 2. *(d.pr.)* look-ahead
Vorgrundverarbeitung *f (d.pr.)* foreground processing
Vorhaben *n* project; plan
Vorhaltekosten *pl* costs of utilization and repairs *(of construction machinery etc.)*
Vorherrschaft *f* predominance
vorherrschen to prevail
Vorhersage *f s.* **Voraussage**
vorhersagen *s.* **voraussagen**
Vorhersagezeitraum *m* period of forecast [prediction]
Vorjahr *n* previous [last, preceding] year
vorjährig of last year
vorkalkulieren to precalculate
Vorkalkulation *f* preliminary calculation
Vorkapitalismus *m* precapitalism; precapitalist formation
vorkapitalistisch precapitalist
Vorkasse *f s.* **Vorausbezahlung**
Vorkauf *m* preemption
vorkaufsberechtigt having preemptive right
Vorkaufsberechtigter *m* preemptor
Vorkaufsberechtigung *f* preemptive right
Vorkaufsklausel *f* preemptive clause
Vorkaufspreis *m* preemption price
Vorkaufsrecht *n* right of preemption ⋄ **das ~ haben** to have the first refusal; **sich das ~ vorbehalten** to reserve an option to acquire *(s.th.)*
Vorkaufsvertrag *m* preemption contract
vorkommen to take place, to happen, to occur; to be found
Vorkommen *n* deposits *(minerals etc.)*; occurrence *(events etc.)*
Vorkommnis *n* occurrence, event, incident
Vorkonnossement *n* through bill of lading
Vorkreditierung *f s.* **Vorfinanzierung**
Vorkriegsausfuhr *f* prewar exports
Vorkriegsbeteiligung *f* prewar holdings
Vorkriegsleistung *f* prewar preformance *(economy etc.)*
Vorkriegsniveau *n* prewar level *(production etc.)*
Vorkriegsproduktion *f* prewar production
Vorkriegsstand *m s.* **Vorkriegsniveau**
vorladen 1. to summon *(witness)*; 2. *(d.pr.)* to precharge
Vorladen *n (d.pr.)* precharging
Vorladung *f* summons, writ of summons; citation

Vorlage *f* 1. model, pattern, copy; 2. bill *(parliamentary)*; 3. submission *(documents etc.)* ⋄ **bei ~ on demand; eine ~ einbringen** to bring in a bill; **gegen ~** on presentation; **nach ~** matching the sample; **zahlbar bei ~** payable on presentation; **zur ~ bei** for submission to
Vorlauf *m* lead; work ahead of schedule
~ in der Produktion work ahead of schedule in production
~, wissenschaftlich-technischer lead in science and technology
Vorlaufabschnitt *m* period of lead
Vorlaufforschung *f* research in advance
Vorlaufkoeffizient *m* lead coefficient
vorlegen to lay [put] before, to present, to submit *(documents etc.)*; to exhibit, to show
Vorlegung *f* presentation, submission *(documents etc.)*
Vorlegungsfrist *f* (final) date of presentation *(documents etc.)*
vorleisten to pay in advance, to do s.th. in advance
Vorleistung *f* payment in advance, prepayment; performance
Vormaterial *n* raw material; semifinished product
Vormonat *m* previous month
Vormund *m* guardian; custodian
~, gerichtlich bestellter guardian by appointment of the court
~, gesetzlicher natural guardian
vormundschaftlich custodial
Vorort *m* suburb
Vorortbahn *f* suburban railway
Vorortverkehr *m* suburban traffic
Vorpfändung *f* seizure under a prior claim
Vorprodukt *n* semifinished product; primary product
Vorprüfung *f* preliminary examination; preliminary audit
Vorrang *m* precedence, priority; pre-eminence
~, zeitlicher priority of date
Vorranggläubiger *m* prior creditor
Vorranghypothek *f* first [senior] mortgage
vorrangig of prior rank
Vorrangigkeit *f* priority
Vorrangprogramm *n* *(d.pr.)* priority routine
Vorrangverarbeitung *f* *(d.pr.)* priority processing
Vorrat *m* store, stock; provision, supply (stores); reserve
~, laufender current stock
~, produktionsbedingter productive stock
~, richtsatzplangebundener planned stock
~, zweckgebundener stock reserved (for some purpose)
Vorräte *mpl* stocks; inventories
~, ausreichende adequate supply

~, berechnete stocks taken into account
~, bestätigte confirmed stocks
~, erschöpfte depleted stocks
~, geschätzte estimated stocks
~, prognostische forecasted stocks, stocks in the long run
~, prognostizierte forecasted stocks
~, vorhandene available stocks, supply on hand
vorrätig in stock, on hand ⋄ **nicht mehr ~** no longer in stock, sold out; **nicht ~** not in [on] stock [available], out of stock
Vorratsaktie *f* reserved share [*(Am)* stock]
Vorratsanfertigung *f s.* **Vorratsproduktion**
Vorratsbilanzen *fpl* balance sheets of stocks
Vorratsbildung *f* stocking, building up reserve stock
Vorratseinkäufe *mpl* stockpiling purchases *(commodities on the international market etc.)*; purchases for reserve stock *(shops, enterprises, families etc.)*
Vorratshaltung *f* stock-keeping
~, ökonomisch begründete economically substantiated stocking of goods, stocking for sound economic reasons
Vorratsintensität *f* level of stocks required
Vorratsniveau *n* level of stocks
Vorratskonto *n* stock account
Vorratskredit *m* credit for stockpiling; credit for reserve stock
Vorratslager *n* warehouse
Vorratsnorm *f* (standard) norm for keeping stocks
Vorratsnormativ *n* standard norm for keeping stocks
Vorratsnormierung *f* fixing of norms for keeping stocks
Vorratsnormung *f s.* **Vorratsnormierung**
Vorratsproduktion *f* production for stocks
Vorrats- und Lagerwirtschaft *f* stockpiling and stock-keeping
Vorratswirtschaft *f* stockpiling; stock-keeping
Vorratszugang *m* incoming goods for stock--keeping
Vorratszuwachs *m* growth [increase] in stocks
Vorrechner *m* *(d.pr.)* satellite [back-up] computer, front-end processor
Vorrecht *n* privilege, prerogative; priority; preference ⋄ **ein ~ aufheben** to withdraw a privilege; **ein ~ beanspruchen** to claim a privilege; **ein ~ einräumen** to grant a privilege; **ein ~ haben** to be privileged; **mit einem ~ ausgestattet sein** to be preferred
~, persönliches personal privilege
Vorrechtsaktien *fpl* preference shares [*(Am)* stocks]
Vorrechtsanleihe *f* preference loan
Vorrechtsforderung *f* preferential claim

Vorrechtsgläubiger *m* privileged creditor
Vorrichtung *f* device, contrivance, mechanism
Vorrichtungen *fpl* facilities
Vorsaison *f* preseason, early season
Vorsaisongeschäft *n* business in the early season
Vorsatz *m* purpose, intention; malice
vorsätzlich intentional; *(jur)* with malice aforethought
Vorschau *f s.* **Vorausschau**
vorschießen to advance (money)
Vorschlag *m* proposal, suggestion, proposition; recommendation; nomination; motion *(parliament etc.)* ⋄ **auf ~** on request; **auf ~ von** at the suggestion of, on the proposal of; **einem ~ zustimmen** to agree to a proposal [suggestion]; **einen ~ ablehnen** to reject [turn down] a proposal; **einen ~ annehmen** to adopt [accept] a proposal; **einen ~ machen** to make a proposition, to suggest; **einen ~ unterstützen** to give support to a proposal
vorschlagen to propose, to suggest; to recommend; to nominate; to move a motion *(parliament etc.)*
Vorschlagsrecht *n* right of nomination
Vorschlags- und Erfindungswesen *n* system of suggestions for improvements and inventions
vorschreiben to prescribe; to order, to dictate to
Vorschrift *f* instruction(s), direction(s); regulation(s), rule(s), provision(s) ⋄ **nach geltender ~** according to regulations in force; **nach ~** according to instructions *(use of device etc.)*; **nach ~ arbeiten** to work to rule
~, gesetzliche official instructions
Vorschriften *fpl*:
⋄ **den ~ entsprechend** complying with the rules; **den ~ zuwiderhandeln** to contravene rules and regulations, to disregard instructions; **~ erlassen** to give instructions; to pass rules and regulations
vorschriftsgemäß correct; according to instructions, in accordance with rules and regulations; in due form, in a proper way; as ordered
vorschriftsmäßig *s.* **vorschriftsgemäß**
Vorschub *m* 1. aid, assistance; 2. *(tech)* feed ⋄ **~ leisten** to support *(s.o.)*; to render assistance (in the furtherance of a cause); *(jur)* to aid and abet
Vorschule *f* preschool class
Vorschuß *m* advance(d money); loan ⋄ **einen ~ erhalten** to receive an advance *(from salary etc.)*; **einen ~ geben** to give an advance *(from salary etc.)*; **einen ~ leisten auf** to advance money on; **einen ~ nehmen** to take an advance *(from salary etc.)*; **einen ~ verlangen** to ask for an advance *(from salary etc.)*

Vorschüsse *mpl (acc)* payments in advance, advances
~ auf Warenlieferungen und Leistungen *(acc)* advances in anticipation of goods and services
~, geleistete *(acc)* advances granted [given]
~, kurzfristige *(acc)* day-to-day advances
vorschußweise as an advance
Vorschußzahlung *f* advance payment
Vorsicht *f* caution, prudence, care; beware!, look out!, take care!
vorsichtig cautious
Vorsichtsmaßnahme *f* precautionary measure
Vorsichtsmaßregel *f* precaution, precautionary measure
Vorsitz *m* chairpersonship; chairmanship; presidency ⋄ **den ~ führen** to be in the chair, to preside; **den ~ übernehmen** to take the chair; **unter ~ von** under the chairmanship of
vorsitzen to be in the chair, to preside
Vorsitzende *f* chairwoman
Vorsitzender *m* chairperson; chairman; president
~, stellvertretender deputy chairperson [chairman, chairwoman], vice-president
Vorsorge *f* provision ⋄ **~ treffen** to take precautions; to make provisions for *(future etc.)*, to provide against *(old age)*
vorsorgen to take care of *(s.th.)*; to provide for
Vorsorgepflicht *f* obligation to ensure safety *(traffic etc.)*
Vorsorgeversicherung *f* provident insurance
vorsorglich careful
Vorstadium *n* preliminary stage
Vorstadt *f* suburb
Vorstadtbevölkerung *f* suburban population, suburbans
Vorstadtbewohner *m* resident of the suburb, suburban
Vorstadtgebiet *n* suburban area
Vorstadtverkehr *m s.* **Vorortverkehr**
Vorstand *m* executive committee *(association etc.)*; board of directors *(company etc.)*; board of trustees *(foundation etc.)*; management committee *(co-operative society etc.)*
Vorstandsmitglied *n* member of the executive committee *(association etc.)*; director, member of the board *(company etc.)*; governor of the board of trustees; member of the management committee *(co-operative society etc.)*
Vorstandssitzung *f* meeting of the executive committee; meeting of the board of directors; meeting of the board of trustees; meeting of the management committee *(co-operative society etc.)*
Vorstandsvorsitzender *m* chairman of the board, president; chairman of the management committee *(co-operative society etc.)*

Vorstandswahl *f* election to the executive committee; election to the board; election to the management committee
vorstehen to head *(department etc.)*
Vorsteher *m* head, chief
vorstellen to present, to introduce *(s.o. to s.o.)*
Vorstellung *f* 1. presentation, introduction; 2. performance *(theatre etc.)*; 3. conception, idea, notion
Vorsteuerabzug *m* prepayment of taxes
Vorstrafe *f* previous conviction
vorstrecken *s.* **vorschießen**
Vorstudien *fpl* preliminary studies *(for project etc.)*
Vorstudienanstalt *f* pre-university college
Vorstufe *f s.* **Vorstadium**
Vorstufenprodukt *n* product of the previous stage (of production); semi-finished product
Vorteil *m* advantage, profit, benefit ⋄ **sich einen ~ verschaffen** to gain an advantage; **von ~ sein** to be of advantage; **zu Ihrem ~** to your advantage, in your favour; **zu unserem ~** to our advantage, in our favour
~, absoluter absolute advantage
~, beiderseitiger *s.* **~, gegenseitiger**
~, gegenseitiger mutual advantage [benefit]
~, komparativer comparative advantage
~, wirtschaftlicher economic advantage
vorteilhaft advantageous
Vortrag *m* 1. lecture; report; 2. *(acc)* balance, amount carried forward
vortragen 1. to deliver a lecture; to give a report, to report; 2. *(acc)* to carry forward
vor- und nachgelagert backward and forward linked *(stages of production)*
Voruntersuchung *f* preliminary hearing [investigation]; preliminary examination
Vorverarbeitungsberechnung *f (d.pr.)* preprocessing computing
Vorvergütung *f* remuneration in advance
Vorverhandlungen *fpl* 1. preliminary negotiations [discussions] *(preparing contract etc.)*; 2. *(jur)* preliminary hearing
Vorverkauf *m* advance booking ⋄ **im ~** bookable at *(office etc.)*; bookable in advance
Vorverkaufsgebühr *f* booking charge
Vorverkaufskasse *f* booking office
Vorverkaufsstelle *f s.* **Vorverkaufskasse**
Vorvertrag *m* preliminary agreement
Vorwahl *f* 1. preliminary election, *(Am)* primary; 2. *(post)* code number *(for dialling a telephone call)*; 3. (pre)selection
Vorwegleistung *f s.* **Vorauszahlung**
vorzählen to count in s.o.'s presence
Vorzeichentest *m (stats)* sign test
Vorzeichenwechseltest *m (stats)* reversal test
vorzeigen to present *(bill etc.)*

vorzeitig premature
Vorzug *m* 1. priority, preference; advantage; 2. *(railw)* relief train
Vorzugsaktien *fpl* preference shares [*(Am)* stocks]
Vorzugsbedingungen *fpl* preferential terms
Vorzugsbehandlung *f* preference, preferential treatment
Vorzugsdividende *f* preferential dividend
Vorzugsfracht *f* preference freight
Vorzugsfrachtsätze *mpl* commodity rates; preferential freight rates
Vorzugsgläubiger *m* preferential [prior] creditor
Vorzugsobligationen *fpl* preferential [participating, senior] bonds
Vorzugspfandrecht *n* prior lien
Vorzugspreis *m* special discount price; *(st.ex.)* special rate *(securities etc.)*
Vorzugsrabatt *m* preferential [special] discount
Vorzugsrecht *n* preferential right; preferential claim; preference
Vorzugssatz *m* preferential rate
Vorzugsstimmrecht *n* preferential voting rights
Vorzugstarif *m* preferential tariff
Vorzugsumrechnungskurs *m* preferential rate of exchange
vorzugsweise by preference
Vorzugswert *m (d.pr.)* preferred value
Vorzugszahlungen *fpl* preferential payments *(in bankruptcy)*
Vorzugszoll *m* preferential tariff [duty]
Votum *n* vote
~, einstimmiges unanimous vote

W

Waage *f* weighing machine; balance *(pharmacy etc.)*; scales, weighbridge *(vehicles)*
Waagenbauer *m* worker in building weighing machines
wachsen to grow; to thrive; to increase, to extend; to mount *(tension etc.)*
Wachstum *n* growth; increase
~, differenziertes differential growth
~, exponentielles exponential growth [increase]
~, gleichgewichtiges balanced growth
~, selbsttragendes self-sustaining growth
~, vorrangiges foremost growth; priority in growth
Wachstumsangleichung *f* levelling of (economic) growth
Wachstumsaussichten *fpl* prospects of (economic) growth, growth prospects

Wachstumsdynamik *f* dynamics of growth
Wachstumseffekt *m* (economic) growth effect
Wachstumsfaktor *m* factor of (economic) growth, growth factor
wachstumsfördernd growth-promoting
Wachstumsforschung *f* research in (economic) growth, (economic) growth research
Wachstumsfunktion *f* growth function
Wachstumsgeschwindigkeit *f s.* **Wachstumstempo**
Wachstumsgesetz *n* law of growth
Wachstumsgrenze *f* limit to growth
wachstumshemmend growth-inhibiting
Wachstumsintensität *f* (economic) growth intensity
Wachstumskomponente *f* component [factor] of (economic) growth, growth component [factor]
Wachstumskonzeption *f* conception [policy outline] of (economic) growth, growth conception
Wachstumskriterium *n* criterion of growth
Wachstumskurve *f* growth curve
Wachstumsmodell *n* growth model, model of (economic) growth
Wachstumsoptimum *n* (economic) growth optimum
Wachstumsplanung *f* (economic) growth planning, planning of (economic) growth
Wachstumspolitik *f* (economic) growth policy
Wachstumsprognose *f* (economic) growth forecast
Wachstumsproportionalität *f* (economic) growth proportionality, proportionality in (economic) growth
Wachstumsrate *f* (economic) growth rate, rate of (economic) growth
Wachstumsrelationen *fpl* proportions in (economic) growth
Wachstumstempo *n* (economic) growth tempo, pace of (economic) growth
Wachstumstendenz *f* tendency [trend] of (economic) growth
Wachstumstheorie *f* theory of (economic) growth
Wachstumstrend *m s.* **Wachstumstendenz**
Wachstumsunterschied *m* differences in (economic) growth
Waffen *fpl* weapons, arms
Waffenausfuhr *f* arms export, export of arms
Waffenausfuhrverbot *n* ban on export of arms
Waffenfabrikation *f* manufacture of weapons [arms]
Waffenhandel *m* trade in arms
Waffenschmuggel *m* smuggling of arms, gun--running
Waffenstillstand *m* armistice
Wägegebühr *f s.* **Wägegeld**

Wägegeld *n* weighing cost, weighage
wagen to venture, to risk
Wagen *m* vehicle; car; truck, lorry; van; *(railw)* carriage, waggon, *(Am)* truck, coach *(passengers)*
Wagenachskilometer *m/n (railw)* waggon-axle kilometre *(s.* **Wagenkilometer***)*
Wagenauslastung *f* load factor, utilization of loading capacity *(in a truck, wagon etc.)*
Wagenbestand *m (railw)* rolling stock
Wagenkilometer *m/n (railw)* waggon kilometre *(distance covered by rail waggon in a given time)*
Wagenladung *f* waggon [truck] load
Wagenpark *m* vehicle fleet; *(railw)* rolling stock
Wagenstandsgeld *n (railw)* loading delay penalty, fine [penalty] for exceeding loading time; demurrage
Wagenumlauf *m s.* **Wagenumschlag**
Wagenumschlag *m (railw)* loading turnover of a waggon
Wäger *m* weigher
~, **amtlicher** official weigher
Wäge- und Meßvorrichtung *f* weighing and measuring device
Waggon *m (railw)* goods waggon [van], *(Am)* freight car; railway carriage, *(Am)* railroad car *(for passengers)*
Waggonbau *m* railway waggon construction
Waggonladung *f (railw)* waggon [truck] load
Waggonlieferung *f (railw)* delivery by waggon
Waggonsendung *f s.* **Waggonlieferung**
waggonweise by the carload [truck load, waggon load]
Wagnis *n* venture, risk
~, **kalkulatorisches** calculated risk
Wagnisdeckung *f (ins)* risk coverage
Wagnisprüfung *f (ins)* examining risks
Wagnisverluste *mpl* losses caused by risks
Wahl *f* choice; selection; quality; *(pol)* election
⋄ **die ~ haben** to have the choice; **keine ~ haben** to have no choice [alternative]; **nach jmds. ~** according to s.o.'s choice; **zur ~ zugelassen sein** to be qualified to vote
~ **der Technologie** choice of technology
~, **erste** first choice; first-class *(goods etc.)*
~, **zweite** second choice; second-class *(goods etc.)*
Wahlakt *m* polling
Wahlalter *n* voting age
wählbar eligible ⋄ **nicht ~** not eligible, ineligible
Wählbarkeit *f* eligibility
wahlberechtigt entitled to vote
Wahlbeteiligung *f* percentage poll
Wahlbezirk *m* constituency; ward *(local elections)*
wählen to choose; to select; *(pol)* to elect, to vote ⋄ **einstimmig ~** to elect unanimously
Wähler *m* voter

Wahlergebnis n election result
Wählerliste f voters' list, electoral register
Wahlkabine f polling booth
Wahlkreis m s. **Wahlbezirk**
Wahllokal n polling station
wahllos indiscriminately
Wahlrecht n right to vote, franchise
Wahlresultat n election result ⋄ **das ~ bekanntmachen** to announce the election results
Wahlsortiment n optional range of goods
Wahltag m election [polling] day
wahlunfähig not entitled to vote
wahlunwürdig disqualified from voting
Wahlurne f ballot box
Wahlversammlung f election meeting
wahlweise by choice, alternatively
Wahlzettel m voting [ballot] paper
wahren to safeguard, to protect *(interests)*; to preserve *(reputation)*; to keep *(secret etc.)*; to observe *(proprieties etc.)*
Wahrheit f truth; reality
~ einer Prognose veracity of a forecast
~, objektive objective [real] truth
~, relative relative truth
Wahrheitstreue f reliability; authenticity
~ einer Information reliability [authenticity] of information
wahrnehmen to be aware of *(changes etc.)*; to observe *(deadline etc.)*; to take *(opportunity etc.)*; to look after *(affairs, rights etc.)*
wahrscheinlich probably
Wahrscheinlichkeit f probability
~ a posteriori s. **~, statistische**
~, aposteriorische s. **~, statistische**
~ a priori *(stats)* prior probability
~, apriorische s. **~ a priori**
~, bedingte *(stats)* conditional probability
~, direkte *(stats)* direct probability
~, empirische *(stats)* empirical probability
~, fiduziäre *(stats)* fiducial probability
~, komplementäre *(stats)* complementary probability
~, statistische posterior probability
~, totale *(stats)* total probability
~, unbedingte *(stats)* unconditional probability
Wahrscheinlichkeitsaussage f probability prediction
Wahrscheinlichkeitsbelegung f *(stats)* probability mass
Wahrscheinlichkeitsbeweis m *(stats)* probability proof
Wahrscheinlichkeitsdichte f *(stats)* probability density
Wahrscheinlichkeitsdichtefunktion f *(stats)* probability density function
Wahrscheinlichkeitseinschränkung f *(stats)* restriction of probability, probability restriction

Wahrscheinlichkeitselement n *(stats)* probability element
Wahrscheinlichkeitsfehler m *(stats)* probability error
Wahrscheinlichkeitsfläche f *(stats)* probability surface
Wahrscheinlichkeitsfunktion f probability function
~, kumulative *(stats)* cumulative probability function
Wahrscheinlichkeitsgrad m *(stats)* degree of probability
Wahrscheinlichkeitsgrenze f *(stats)* probability limit
Wahrscheinlichkeitsintegral n *(stats)* probability integral
Wahrscheinlichkeitsintegraltransformation f *(stats)* probability integral transformation
Wahrscheinlichkeitsintensität f *(stats)* density function
Wahrscheinlichkeitskurve f *(stats)* probability curve
Wahrscheinlichkeitslehre f s. **Wahrscheinlichkeitstheorie**
Wahrscheinlichkeitspapier n *(stats)* probability paper
~, binomiales *(stats)* binomial probability paper
~, normales *(stats)* normal probability paper
Wahrscheinlichkeitsrechnung f probability calculus
Wahrscheinlichkeitsschluß m *(stats)* probability conclusion
Wahrscheinlichkeitssystem n *(stats)* probability system
wahrscheinlichkeitstheoretisch *(stats)* from the aspect of probability theory
Wahrscheinlichkeitstheorie f probability theory
Wahrscheinlichkeitsstichprobe f *(stats)* probability sample
Wahrscheinlichkeitsverhältnis n *(stats)* probability ratio
Wahrscheinlichkeitsverhältnistest m *(stats)* probability-ratio test
~, sequentieller *(stats)* sequential probability-ratio test
Wahrscheinlichkeitsverteilung f *(stats)* probability distribution
Wahrscheinlichkeitsverteilungsfunktion f *(stats)* probability distribution function
Wahrung f safeguarding, protection ⋄ **unter ~ des beiderseitigen Nutzens** with due observance of mutual benefit [advantage]
Währung f currency; standard ⋄ **zahlbar in ausländischer~** payable in foreign currency
~, ausländische foreign currency [exchange]
~, beschränkt konvertierbare partially convertible currency

~, **entwertete** depreciated currency
~, **feste** s ~, **harte**
~, **frei konvertierbare** freely convertible currency
~, **freie** s. ~, **frei konvertierbare**
~, **gemeinsame** common currency
~, **gesetzlich anerkannte** legal tender, (Am) lawful money
~, **gesteuerte** managed currency
~, **harte** hard currency
~, **hinkende** limping standard
~, **inländische** domestic [local] currency
~, **kollektive** s. ~, **gemeinsame**
~, **konvertierbare** convertible currency
~, **nicht konvertierbare** non-convertible [blocked] currency
~, **stabile** stable currency
~, **teilkonvertierbare** s. ~, **beschränkt konvertierbare**
~, **überbewertete** over-valued currency
~, **vereinbarte** agreed currency
~, **weiche** soft currency
~, **zerrüttete** disorganized currency
Währungsabkommen n monetary [currency] agreement
Währungsabwertung f devaluation, depreciation of currency, currency depreciation
Währungsangleichung f adjustment of exchange rates
Währungsanleihe f monetary loan
Währungsaufwertung f currency upgrading [revaluation] (as opposed to devaluation)
Währungsausgleichsfonds m exchange equalization fund
Währungsbasis f standard
Währungsbeschränkungen fpl currency restrictions
Währungsbeziehungen fpl currency relations
Währungsblock m currency block
Währungsdeckung f gold and convertible currency reserves, currency cover
Währungsdisparität f disparity of exchange
Währungseinheit f currency unit
Währungsfaktura f currency [foreign exchange] invoice
Währungsfonds m monetary fund
~, **Internationaler (IWF)** International Monetary Fund (IMF)
Währungsforderung f claim (to payment) in foreign currency; (amount of) claim to be paid in foreign currency
Währungsfragen fpl monetary issues
Währungsgebiet n currency area
Währungsgesetz n currency act
Währungsgewinnabgabe f levy on profits resulting from monetary reform
Währungsgrundlage f s. **Währungsbasis**

Währungsguthaben n foreign exchange holdings [balance]
Währungshoheit f right to issue money
Währungsklausel f currency clause
Währungskonto n foreign exchange account
Währungskonvertibilität f currency convertibility
Währungskredit m loan in foreign currency
Währungskrise f monetary crisis
Währungskurs m rate of exchange, exchange rate
Währungsmanipulation f currency manipulation
Währungsmechanismus m currency mechanism
Währungsmetall n standard metal (gold and silver)
Währungsparität f par of exchange
Währungspolitik f monetary policy
währungspolitisch from the point of view of monetary policy
Währungspreis m foreign exchange quotation
Währungsprobleme npl currency problems; monetary problems
Währungsraum m s. **Währungsgebiet**
Währungsreform f monetary [currency] reform
Währungsrelation f s. **Währungsparität**
Währungsrembours m reimbursement in foreign currency
Währungsreserven fpl monetary [currency] reserve(s)
Währungsrisiko n exchange risk
Währungsschwankungen fpl currency fluctuations
Währungsspekulation f currency speculation
Währungsstabilisierung f currency stabilization, stabilization of the rate of exchange
Währungsstabilität f currency stability
Währungssystem n currency [monetary] system
~, **bimetallisches** bimetallic system of currency, bimetallic standard
~, **internationales** international monetary system
Währungstabelle f exchange rate table
Währungsübersicht f s. **Währungstabelle**
Währungsumstellung f currency conversion; monetary reform
Währungsumtausch m currency exchange
Währungs- und Finanzmechanismus m monetary and fiscal mechanism
Währungs- und Geldpolitik f currency and monetary policy
Währungsunion f monetary union
Währungsverfall m rapid depreciation of currency
Währungsverhältnisse npl proportion of money in circulation (to effective demand in an

economy); currency conditions *(for rate of exchange)*
Währungsvorräte *mpl s.* **Währungsreserven**
Währungsvorteile *mpl* advantages in the rate of exchange
Währungszone *f s.* **Währungsgebiet**
Währungszusammenbruch *m* collapse of currency
Waise *f* orphan
Waisenhaus *n* orphanage, orphan's home
Waisenrente *f* survivor benefit
waldarm sparsely wooded
Waldbestand *m* forest stand
Waldfläche *f* wooded area
Waldland *n* woodland
waldreich rich in forests, well-wooded
Waldwirtschaft *f* forestry, forest culture
Walzwerker *m* rolling steel worker
Wandel *m* change
Wandelanleihe *f* convertible loan
wandelbar convertible; changeable; variable
Wandelobligationen *fpl* convertible bonds
Wandelschuldverschreibungen *fpl s.* **Wandelobligationen**
Wanderarbeiter *m* seasonal [migrant] worker; itinerant worker
Wanderausstellung *f* mobile [travelling, touring] exhibition
Wandergewerbe *n* itinerant trade
Wanderhandwerk *n s.* **Wandergewerbe**
Wanderung *f* migration
~, **saisonbedingte** seasonal migration
Wanderungsbilanz *f* balance sheet of migration
Wanderungsstatistik *f* statistics of migration, migration statistics
Wanderwirtschaft *f* nomadic economy
Wandlung *f* conversion; change; *(jur)* redhibition *(purchase)*
Wandlungsfehler *m* redhibitory defect
Wandlungsklage *f* redhibitory action
Wandlungsverfahren *n* redhibitory suit
Ware *f* commodity, article (of commerce); product; merchandise; goods; *(st.ex.)* stock, supply
✧ (~) **unterliegt der Bruttoverzollung** (commodity) is dutiable on gross weight
~, **abgelagerte** matured article *(wine etc.);* seasoned goods *(wood etc.);* well-seasoned article *(cigar etc.)*
~, **abgepackte** prepacked goods
~, **absatzfähige** *s.* ~, **absetzbare**
~, **absetzbare** marketable [saleable] article
~, **allgemeine** universal commodity
~, **angekündigte** goods advised
~, **ausgestellte** goods displayed
~, **ausgesuchte** high-quality goods, goods of very good quality; choice [selected] fruit
~, **aussortierte** goods sorted out

~, **austauschbare** exchangeable commodity; replaceable goods
~, **beschädigte** damaged article
~, **bestellte** ordered goods
~, **besteuerbare** taxable goods
~, **börsengängige** goods quoted on exchange
~, **deklarierte** declared goods *(at the customs office)*
~, **einheimische** home-made [local] goods, domestic product
~, **eintreffende** incoming goods
~, **erstklassige** first-class article
~, **fehlerfreie** faultless goods, goods in perfect condition
~, **fehlerhafte** faulty goods
~, **flüssige** liquids
~, **gängige** fast-moving [fast-selling] goods
~, **gebrauchsfertige** goods ready for use
~, **gepackte** goods packed
~, **geringwertige** goods of inferior [poor] quality
~, **harte** essential goods; goods in steady demand
~, **hochwertige** high-quality goods
~, **im Stück verkaufte** piece goods
~, **inländische** domestic [inland] product
~, **knappe** goods in short supply
~, **lagerungsfähige** storable goods
~, **langlebige** durables, durable goods
~, **lebensnotwendige** necessary article; necessities of life
~, **lebenswichtige** *s.* ~, **lebensnotwendige**
~, **leicht verderbliche** highly perishable goods
~, **lose** loose goods
~, **mangelhafte** defective article; low-quality goods
~, **marktfähige** *s.* ~, **absetzbare**
~, **marktgängige** marketable goods
~, **nicht deklarierte** undeclared goods *(at the customs office)*
~, **preisgebundene** fixed-price article, price-controlled merchandize
~, **preisgestützte** subsidized [price-supported] article
~, **preisgünstige** low-priced article [commodity]
~, **preiswerte** *s.* ~, **preisgünstige**
~, **prima** first-class article; first-class goods
~, **reexportierte** re-exported goods
~, **retournierte** *s.* ~, **zurückgesandte**
~, **rollende** goods in transit by rail
~, **schwer absetzbare** slow-selling goods
~, **schwer verkäufliche** *s.* ~, **schwer absetzbare**
~, **schwimmende** goods in transit by ship
~, **sicherungsübereignete** pledged goods [merchandise]
~, **sofort lieferbare** spot goods, spots
~, **sortierte** graded goods

~, **überlagerte** old stock
~, **unterwegs befindliche** goods in transit *(between consignor and consignee)*
~, **unverkäufliche** dead commodity (stock)
~, **unverzollte** unbonded goods
~, **verderbliche** perishable goods, perishables
~, **verknappte** scarce commodity [goods]
~, **verpfändete** pledged goods, goods lying in pledge; pawned articles
~, **verschiffte** goods shipped, shipped goods
~, **versicherte** insured goods
~, **verzollte** cleared goods, goods out of bond
~, **weiche** non-essential goods
~, **wertgeminderte** substandard goods
~, **zurückgesandte** returned goods
Ware-Empfänger-Plan *m* plan of goods and consignees
Ware-Geld-Austausch *m* commodity transactions by means of money
Ware-Geld-Beziehungen *fpl* commodity-money relations
Ware-Land-Plan *m* country-wise commodity plan, commodity plan according to country
Waren *fpl*:
◊ **rückzahlbar in** ~ repayable in kind; **~ an jmdn. zum Versand bringen** to dispatch goods to the consignation of s.o.; **~ auf Kommissionsbasis verkaufen** to sell goods on a commission basis [on commission]; **~ beanstanden** to register [make] complaints about goods; to reject goods delivered; **~ beleihen** to lend money on goods; **~ in den Verkehr bringen** to put commodities on the market; **~ mit Zoll belasten [belegen]** to impose a tariff on goods; **~ prompt zahlen** to pay for goods before delivery; **~ zum Verkauf bringen** to sell goods
~, **auf Kredit gekaufte** goods bought on credit
~, **auf Rechnung versandte** goods consigned on account
~, **bewirtschaftete** rationed goods
~ **der aperiodischen Nachfrage** consumer durables
~ **der häufigen Nachfrage** commodities [goods, items] in continual demand
~ **der gehobenen Preislage** consumer goods in the higher price range, high-priced consumer goods
~ **der mittleren Preislage** consumer goods in the middle price range, medium-priced consumer goods
~ **der oberen Preislage** *s.* ~ **der gehobenen Preislage**
~ **der periodischen Nachfrage** commodities [goods, items] in recurrent demand
~ **der unteren Preislage** consumer goods in the lower price range, low-priced consumer goods

~ **des aperiodischen Bedarfs** *s.* ~ **der aperiodischen Nachfrage**
~ **des dezentralisierten Warenfonds** commodities not planned centrally
~ **des Grundbedarfs** essential consumer goods
~ **des Massenbedarfs** *s.* ~ **des täglichen Bedarfs**
~ **des periodischen Bedarfs** *s.* ~ **der periodischen Nachfrage**
~ **des täglichen Bedarfs** necessary articles; necessities of life
~ **des zentralisierten Fonds** centrally planned goods
~, **disponible** stock on hand
~, **eingebürgerte** well-introduced articles
~, **eingeführte** imports, imported goods
~, **eingelagerte** stored goods, goods in storage
~, **exportauftragsgebundene** goods required for fulfilling export orders
~, **exportierte** exports, exported goods
~, **fakturierte** goods invoiced
~, **freigegebene** articles taken out of control; *(cust)* released goods
~, **für den Export bestimmte** goods intended for export
~, **gelagerte** stored goods
~, **gelieferte** goods sold and delivered
~, **genormte** standardized articles [goods]
~, **im Preis herabgesetzte** price-reduced articles, marked-down commodities [merchandise]
~, **in Kommission gegebene** goods on commission
~, **industriell hergestellte** manufactured [machine-made] goods
~, **käufliche** goods for sale
~, **kontingentierte** quota goods, rationed commodities
~, **kriegswichtige** strategic goods
~, **leicht realisierbare** easily marketable [saleable] goods
~, **markenfreie** *s.* ~, **nicht bewirtschaftete**
~, **markenlose** unbranded articles [goods]
~, **markenpflichtige** *s.* ~, **bewirtschaftete**
~, **minderwertige** low-quality goods
~, **modische** fashionable articles
~, **nicht bewirtschaftete** nonrationed goods, commodities not under control
~, **nicht kriegswichtige** nonstrategic goods
~, **sperrige** bulky goods
~, **unbestellte** unordered goods, goods not ordered
~, **unbezahlte** unpaid goods
~ **unter Zollverschluß** bonded goods
~ **unter Zollverschluß liegende** bonded goods, goods in bond
~, **unverderbliche** nonperishable goods, nonperishables

~, **unverzollt eingeführte** s. ~, **zollfrei eingeführte**
~, **verfügbare** available goods, stock on hand
~ **(von) hoher Qualität** high-quality goods
~, **zollfrei eingeführte** duty-free imported goods
~, **zollfreie** duty-free articles [goods]
~, **zollpflichtige** dutiable goods
Warenabkommen n commodity agreement
~, **internationales** international commodity agreement
Warenabsatz m marketing [sale] of goods
Warenabsatzorganisation f marketing and sales organization
Warenabsender m consignor
Warenakkreditiv n (commercial) letter of credit
Warenakzept n trade acceptance
Warenanalyse f product analysis
Warenangebot n goods offered *(for sale)*, supply of goods
Warenannahme f 1. acceptance of goods, receiving of goods; 2. receiving department
Warenanordnung f arrangement of goods (displayed)
Warenäquivalent n commodity equivalent
Warenart f kind of commodity
Warenaufkommen n output of goods
Warenaufnahme f inventory taking, stocktaking
Warenaufstellung f list of goods (delivered), specification of goods
Warenauftrag m buyer's order
Warenausfuhr f commodity export; export(ation) of goods
Warenausfuhrgenehmigung f export permit [licence]
Warenausgabe f delivery of goods; goods counter *(in departmental stores etc.)*
Warenausgang m outgoing goods
Warenausgangsbuch n goods outward book
Warenausgangsjournal n s. **Warenausgangsbuch**
Warenausgangskonto n sales account
Warenauslage f display of goods
Warenauslieferung f delivery of goods
Warenauslieferungsanweisung f order sheet [note] *(to warehouse)*
Warenausstellung f trade fair; exhibition (of goods); display of goods
Warenaustausch m exchange of goods
~, **wertungleicher** non-equivalent exchange of goods
~, **zwischenstaatlicher** international bartering
Warenaustauschabkommen n barter agreement
Warenaustauschfonds m stock of goods for exchange
Warenaustauschgeschäft n exchange of commodities; barter trade

Warenaustauschoperation f barter transaction
Warenauswahl f range of goods [merchandise]
Warenautomat m automatic selling machine, vending machine
Warenbedarf m demand for goods
Warenbegleitpapiere npl documents [papers] accompanying goods
Warenbegleitschein m waybill; shipping note
Warenbehälter m container
Warenbeleihung f s. **Warenlombard**
Warenbelieferung f supply of goods
Warenbereitstellung f provision of consumer goods
Warenbeschädigung f damage to goods
Warenbeschaffung f procurement of goods
Warenbeschaffungskosten pl costs of procurement, procurement cost
Warenbestand m stock, stock-in-hand, stock-in-trade
Warenbestände mpl stocked goods, inventories
Warenbestandskonto n inventory [stock] account
Warenbestellbuch n order book
Warenbestellung f indent, order; ordering of goods, placing an order for goods ◊ **eine ~ aufgeben** to place an order for goods, to put goods on order
Warenbevorschussung f commodity advance, advance payment for future deliveries
Warenbewegung f movement of goods
~, **innerbetriebliche** intra-enterprise movement of goods
Warenbewertung f evaluation of goods
Warenbewirtschaftung f rationing (of goods)
Warenbezeichnung f trade description, description of commodities
~, **falsche** false trade description
Warenbezieher m consignee, recipient; importer
Warenbeziehungen fpl commodity relations
Warenbezug m purchase of goods
Warenbezugskosten pl miscellaneous purchasing charges
Warenbilanz f commodity balance sheet
Warenbörse f commodity [produce] exchange
Warencharakter m commodity nature
~ **der Arbeitskraft** commodity nature of labour power
~ **der Arbeitsprodukte** commodity nature of labour products
Warendecke f goods available *(in a national economy)*
Warendeckung f commodity cover(age)
Warendefizit n s. **Warenmanko**
Warendeklaration f specification (of goods)
Warendepot n warehouse
Warendiskont m trade discount *(among wholesalers)*; discount *(to customers)*

Warendokumente *npl* trade documents
Wareneinfuhr *f* import(ation) of goods
Wareneingang *m* goods received, incoming goods
Wareneingangsbuch *n* goods inward book
Wareneingangsjournal *n s.* **Wareneingangsbuch**
Wareneingangskonto *n* (goods) purchase account
Wareneingangskontrolle *f* check on incoming goods
Wareneingangsschein *m* goods delivery receipt
Wareneinheit *f* unit of goods
Wareneinkauf *m* purchase of goods; purchasing department
Wareneinkaufsbuch *n s.* **Wareneingangsbuch**
Wareneinkaufskonto *n s.* **Wareneingangskonto**
Wareneinsatz *m* commodity input
Wareneinstandspreis *m* cost price (of goods)
Wareneinstufung *f* classification of commodities [goods]
Warenempfänger *m* consignee
Warenempfangsbestätigung *f* receipt for goods, delivery receipt
Warenempfangsschein *m s.* **Warenempfangsbestätigung**
Warenexport *m* commodity [goods] export, export of goods
Warenfetischismus *m* commodity fetishism
Warenfluß *m* flow of goods
Warenfonds *m* total commodities available
Warenfondsbilanzierung *f* balancing of total commodities available
Warenfondsentwicklung *f* growth in the amount of commodities
Warenforderungen *fpl* claims arising from commodity deliveries and services
Warenform *f* commodity, merchandise
Warenfunktion *f* commodity function
Warengattung *f* kind [line] of goods
Warengeschäft *n* commodity transaction(s)
Warengruppe *f* group of commodities *(classification etc.)*
Warenhandbuch *n* catalogue of goods
Warenhandel *m* trade in goods
Warenhandelsbilanz *f* balance of trade, trade balance
Warenhandlungskapital *n* trading [commercial] capital; stock in trade
Warenhaus *n* department(al) store
Warenhausdieb *m* shop-lifter
Warenhausdiebstahl *m* shop-lifting
Warenhausprogramm *n* uneconomic range of goods *(produced by an enterprise)*, uneconomic output mix
Warenhortung *f* hoarding of goods

Warenhunger *m* extremely high demand for goods
Warenimport *m* commodity [goods] import, import of goods
Wareninventar *n* inventory of goods
Warenkapital *n* commodity capital
Warenkatalog *m* catalogue of goods [merchandise]
Warenkauf *m* purchase of goods
Warenklasse *f* class of goods
Warenklassifikation *f* classification of commodities [goods]
Warenknappheit *f* shortage of goods [commodities]
Warenkonto *n* goods account
Warenkontrolle *f* commodity inspection, merchandise control
Warenkorb *m* shopping basket; *(stats)* basket of goods *(to measure cost of living etc.)*
Warenkredit *m* commercial loan; credit in kind [goods]
Warenkreditabkommen *n* commercial loan agreement
Warenkreditbrief *m* commercial letter of credit
Warenkreditbürgschaft *f* commercial guarantee credit
Warenkunde *f* commodity studies
Warenlager *n* 1. warehouse, store, depot; 2. stock(-in-trade)
Warenlagerung *f* storage, warehousing
Warenlieferung *f* delivery of goods
Warenliste *f* list of goods [commodities]
Warenlombard *m* collateral loan (on commodities), advances against commodities
Warenmakler *m* commodity broker
Warenmangel *m* scarcity [shortage] of goods
Warenmanko *n* deficit of goods
Warenmarkt *m* commodity market
Warenmenge *f* amount of goods
Warenmesse *f* fair, trade fair
Warenmuster *n* sample
~ **ohne Handelswert** sample without commercial value
Warennachfrage *f* demand for goods
Warenneubewertung *f* re-evaluation of goods
Warennomenklatur *f* classification [nomenclature] of goods
~ **des Außenhandels, einheitliche** uniform classification [nomenclature] of export and import commodities [international trade]
Warennummer *f* commodity index number
Warenpartie *f* lot of goods, goods lot
Warenposition *f* commodity item
Warenposten *m* commodity item, lot
Warenprämie *f* bonus in kind
Warenpreis *m* commodity price
Warenpreisklausel *f* commodity price clause

Warenpreissumme *f* total (amount) of commodity prices
Warenprobe *f* sample
~, **kostenlose** free sample
Warenproduktion *f* commodity production
~, **abgesetzte** commodity production sold
~, **einfache** simple [small] commodity production
~, **finanzgeplante** financially planned commodity production
~, **industrielle** industrial commodity production
~, **kleine** *s.* ~, **einfache**
~, **nichtindustrielle** non-industrial commodity production
~, **nicht vergleichbare** non-comparable commodity production
~, **private** private commodity production
~, **prüf- und klassifizierungspflichtige** commodity production subject to checking and classification
~, **prüf- und überwachungszeichenpflichtige** commodity production subject to checking and control stamp
~, **realisierte** *s.* ~, **abgesetzte**
~, **vergleichbare** comparable commodity production
Warenproduzent *m* commodity producer
~, **einfacher** simple [small] commodity producer
~, **kleiner** *s.* ~, **einfacher**
Warenprüfer *m* quality inspector
Warenprüfung *f* quality control [inspection]
Warenprüfungsamt *n* quality inspection office
Warenqualität *f* quality of goods
Warenrabatt *m s.* **Warendiskont**
Warenrechnung *f* invoice
~, **spezifizierte** detailed invoice [account]
Warenrechnungspreis *m* billed (commodity) price
Warenreserve *f* stock reserve
Warenreste *mpl* remnants; odds and ends
Warenretouren *fpl* returned goods
Warenrisiko *n* sales risk
Warenrückgabe *f* goods returned by the customer
Warenrücksendung *f* return of goods *(by shop to wholesaler etc.)*
Warenrückvergütung *f* refund, repayment *(expenses etc.)*; reimbursement; *(railw)* quantity rebate *(granted to consignor)*; *(ins)* surrender value
Warensaldo *m* commodity balance
Warenschau *f* goods display
Warenschwund *m* shrinkage of perishables
Warensendung *f* consignment (of goods)
Warenskonto *n s.* **Warendiskont**
Warensortiment *n* range [line] of goods
Warenspeicher *m* warehouse, depot

Warenspezifikation *f* specification [*(Am)* itemization] of goods
Warenstatistik *f* commodity statistics
Warensteuer *f* duty, excise, tax on commodities
Warenstrom *m* flow of goods
Warenströme *mpl* trade flows, flows of trade
Warenstruktur *f* kinds of goods
Warensystematik *f* classification of commodities
Warentausch *m* barter (trade)
Warentermingeschäft *n* trade in commodity futures
Warentest *m* testing of goods
Warentransaktion *f* commodity transaction
Warentransit *m* transit of goods
Warentransport *m* transport(ation) of goods
Warentransportversicherung *f* goods [merchandise] transport insurance
Warenübereignung *f* transfer of ownership of goods
Warenüberfluß *m* abundance [surplus] of goods
Warenübergabe *f* delivery [handing over] of goods
Warenumsatz *m* goods [commodity] turnover
Warenumsatzplan *m* plan of goods [commodity] turnover
Warenumsatzplanung *f* planning of goods [commodity] turnover
Warenumsatzsteuer *f* goods [commodity] turnover tax
Warenumsatz- und Bereitstellungsbilanzen *fpl* balance sheets of commodity turnover and supply of consumer goods
Warenumschlag *m* movement of goods; turnover
Warenumschlagsfinanzierung *f* financing of movement of goods
Warenumschlagskreditierung *f* crediting according to the movement of goods, financing of the movement of goods by credits
Warenumtausch *m* exchanging one article for another
Waren- und Leistungsbilanz *f* balance of trade and payments
Warenverbindlichkeiten *fpl* debts contracted [incurred] from supply of goods and services
Warenverbrauch *m* consumption of goods
Warenverkauf *m* sale of goods
Warenverkaufsbuch *n* sales book
Warenverkaufskonto *n* sales account
Warenverkehr *m* goods trade
Warenverknappung *f* scarcity of goods
Warenverlust *m* ullage; shrinkage
Warenverpackung *f* package; packaging; wrapping
Warenversand *m* consignment; shipping
Warenversandkosten *pl* consignment [shipping] costs

Warenversicherung *f* goods [merchandise] insurance
Warenversorgung *f* supply of goods
Warenverteilung *f* distribution of goods
Warenvertreter *m* travelling agent
Warenvertrieb *m s.* **Warenabsatz**
Warenvertriebskosten *pl* cost(s) of marketing and sales
Warenvertriebsorganisation *f* marketing and sales organization; organization of marketing and sales
Warenverzeichnis *n* inventory [list] of goods
Warenvolumen *n* amount of goods
Warenvorrat *m* stock-in-trade
Warenvorräte *mpl* stocked goods
Warenvorschüsse *mpl s.* **Warenkredit**
Warenwährung *f* commodity standard
Warenwechsel *m* commercial bill [paper], *(Am)* business paper
Warenweg *m* route of goods (transported)
Warenwert *m* value of goods
Warenwirtschaft *f s.* **Warenproduktion**
~, **einfache** *s.* **Warenproduktion, einfache**
~, **kleine** *s.* **Warenproduktion, einfache**
Warenzeichen *n* trademark ⋄ **als ~ eintragen** to trademark; **als ~ eintragen lassen** *s.* **ein ~ anmelden; ein ~ anmelden** to register a trademark; **ein ~ benutzen** to use a trademark; **ein ~ verletzen** to infringe on a trademark
~, **eingetragenes** registered trademark
Warenzeichen *npl:*
~, **verbundene** associated trademarks
Warenzeichenbenutzung *f* use of registered trademark
Warenzeicheneintragung *f* registering [registration] of trademark
Warenzeichenrecht *n* trademark law
Warenzeichenrechte *npl* trademark rights
Warenzeichenregister *n* register of trademarks
Warenzeichenschutz *m* trademark protection
Warenzeichenverband *m* trademark association
Warenzeichenverletzung *f* infringement of trademarks
Warenzirkulation *f* commodity circulation
Warenzoll *m* customs duty
Warenzufuhr *f s.* **Warenversorgung**
Warenzugang *m* receipt of goods, goods received
Wärmeausnutzung *f* heat utilization
Wärmebedarf *m* heat requirement
wärmebeständig heat-resistant
Wärmebilanz *f* heat balance (sheet)
Wärmeenergie *f* thermal energy, thermo-energy
Wärmeenergietarif *m* thermal energy rate, thermo-energy rate; thermal energy rating, thermo-energy rating

Wärmemenge *f* quantity of heat
warnen to warn
Warnstreik *m* token strike
Warnung *f* warning; admonition
Warrant *m* warrant
Wartegeld *n* half-pay *(officials etc.);* demurrage *(ship etc.)*
Warteliste *f* waiting list
warten 1. to wait (for); 2. to nurse; to service, to maintain *(machinery etc.)* ⋄ **jmdn. ~ lassen** to keep s.o. waiting
Warteraum *m* waiting room
Warteschlange *f (stats)* queue, *(Am)* line(-up)
Warteschlangenproblem *n (stats)* queuing [*(Am)* line(-up)] problem
Warteschlangentheorie *f (stats)* queuing theory
Warte- und Stillstandszeiten *fpl* down time
Wartezeit *f* 1. waiting time [period]; 2. down time *(machinery etc.)*
~, **arbeitsablaufbedingte** waiting time conditioned by work process
Wartezeitprobleme *npl* congestion problems *(traffic etc.)*
Wartung *f* maintenance, *(Am)* upkeep
~, **laufende** current repairs; regular maintenance
~, **periodische** periodic overhaul
~, **technische** maintenance
~, **vorbeugende** preventive maintenance [repair]
Wartungsabkommen *n* maintenance contract
Wartungsarbeiten *fpl* maintenance (work)
~, **festgelegte** scheduled maintenance work
Wartungsdienst *m* maintenance service
wartungsfrei maintenance-free
Wartungskosten *pl* maintenance costs
Wartungsmechaniker *m* **für Datenverarbeitungs- und Büromaschinen** maintenance mechanic for computers and office equipment
Wartungspersonal *n* service personnel
Wartungsreparatur *f* maintenance repair
Wartungs- und Reparaturaufwand *m* expenditures on maintenance and repair
Wartungszeit *f* maintenance time; down time *(machinery etc.)*
Wäscherei *f* laundry
Wasserbedarf *m* water requirements [needs]
Wasserbilanz *f* balance sheet of water supply
wasserdicht waterproof, watertight
wasserdurchlässig non-watertight
Wasserhaltung *f* utilization of water
Wasserhaushaltsbilanz *f s.* **Wasserbilanz**
Wasserkosten *pl* water cost(s)
Wassernutzung *f* water utilization
Wassernutzungsentgelt *n* water utilization charges
Wassernutzungsrecht *n* right of water utilization
Wasserpreis *m* water rate

Wasserrecht *n* water law
Wasserschutz *m* water protection
Wasserstraße *f* inland waterway; strait
Wasserstraßenbenutzungsgebühr *f* toll, fee *(for use of waterway)*
Wasserstraßennetz *n* system [network] of waterways
Wasserstraßenordnung *f* waterway regulations
Wasserstraßenverkehr *m* inland waterway traffic
wasserundurchlässig *s.* **wasserdicht**
Wasserundurchlässigkeit *f* watertightness
Wasserverbrauch *m* water consumption
Wasserverdrängung *f* (water) displacement
Wasserversorgung *f* water supply
Wasserversorgungsbilanz *f s.* **Wasserbilanz**
Wasserwirtschaft *f s.* **Wasserversorgung**
Wasserwirtschaftsbilanz *f s.* **Wasserbilanz**
Wechsel *m* 1. change *(money etc.)*; exchange *(goods, currency etc.)*; fluctuation *(capital, demand etc.)*; rotation *(of crops)*; *(d.pr.)* changeover; 2. bill *(of exchange)*, draft ◊ **einen ~ ausstellen** to draw up [issue] a bill; **einen ~ diskontieren** to discount a bill; **einen ~ einlösen** to pay [meet, discharge] a bill; **einen ~ indossieren** to endorse a bill; **einen ~ mit Sicht(vermerk) versehen** to sight (a bill); **einen ~ präsentieren** to present a bill *(for payment)*; **einen ~ prolongieren** to prolong [extend, renew] a bill; **einen ~ reiten** to job a bill, to fly a kite; **einen ~ ziehen** to draw up [issue] a bill; **einen ~ zu Protest gehen lassen** to have a bill protested; **einen ~ zur Einlösung vorlegen** to present a bill *(for payment)*
~, **abgelaufener** bill overdue
~, **akzeptierter** accepted bill
~, **angekaufter** investment bill
~ **auf lange Sicht** long(-dated) bill
~, **ausgestellter** drawn [issued] bill, draft
~, **ausländischer** foreign bill, bill in foreign currency
~, **aval(is)ierter** guaranteed bill
~, **bankfähiger** bankable bill
~, **befristeter** time bill
~, **börsenfähiger** negotiable bill
~ **der Arbeitsstelle** change of employment
~, **diskontfähiger** bankable bill
~, **diskontierter** discounted bill
~, **eigener** promissory note, bill drawn on o.s.
~, **eingelöster** honoured bill
~, **fälliger** expired bill
~, **falscher** forged bill
~, **gefälschter** *s.* ~, **falscher**
~, **gezogener** *s.* ~, **ausgestellter**
~, **girierter** endorsed bill
~, **laufender** bill in circulation

~, **monatlicher** monthly allowance
~, **notleidender** bill held over, dishonoured bill
~, **protestierter** dishonoured bill, bill noted for protest
~, **trassierter** *s.* ~, **ausgestellter**
~, **überfälliger** bill overdue
~, **unbegebbarer** non-negotiable bill
~, **unbezahlter** dishonoured bill
~, **ungedeckter** uncovered bill, kite
~, **verfallener** matured bill
Wechselabrechnung *f* liquidation of bills
Wechselabteilung *f (bank)* bill department
Wechselagio *n* discount (on bills)
Wechselakzept *n s.* **Wechselannahme**
Wechselakzeptant *m* acceptor of a bill
Wechselannahme *f* acceptance of a bill, letter of acceptance ◊ **eine ~ verweigern** to dishonour a bill
Wechselarbitrage *f* arbitration of exchange
Wechselausstellung *f* issuance of a bill
Wechselbank *f* exchange bank
Wechselbestand *m* bills in [on] hand
Wechselbeziehung *f* correlation, interrelation
Wechselbuch *n* bill book [ledger]
Wechselbürge *m* guarantor for a bill
Wechselbürgschaft *f* guarantee of a bill ◊ **eine ~ leisten** to back a bill
Wechseldebitorenkonto *n* bills receivable account
Wechseldeckung *f* cover(age) of a bill
Wechseldiskont *m* discount on a bill, bill discount
Wechseldiskontgeschäft *n* bill discounting
Wechseldiskontkredit *m* acceptance credit
Wechseldiskontsatz *m* bill discount rate
Wechselfälscher *m* bill forger
Wechselfälschung *f* bill forgery
Wechselforderung *f* claim arising from a bill
Wechselformular *n* blank bill
Wechselfrist *f* usance *(of a bill)*
Wechselgeld *n* change
Wechselgeschäft *n* exchange business; (exchange) discounting transaction; bill--broker's business
Wechselgeschäfte *npl* discount transactions
Wechselgesetz *n* bill of exchange act
Wechselgiro *n* special endorsement
Wechselhandel *m* bill [note] brokerage
Wechselinhaber *m* holder of a bill
Wechselinkasso *n* draft [note] collection
Wechselinkassogeschäft *n s.* **Wechseldiskontgeschäft**
Wechselklage *f* action against drawer of a bill
Wechselkommission *f* bill brokerage
Wechselkonto *n* liability ledger; bills account
Wechselkredit *m* acceptance credit, loan on bills [a bill]

Wechselkreditoren *mpl* bills payable
Wechselkreditorenkonto *n* bills payable account
Wechselkurs *m* rate of exchange
~, **einheitlicher** uniform rate of exchange
~, **fester** fixed rate of exchange
~, **frei schwankender** floating rate of exchange
~, **multipler** multiple rate of exchange
~, **starrer** *s.* ~, **fester**
Wechselkursnotierung *f* foreign exchange rates
Wechselkurszettel *m* list of foreign exchange rates
Wechsellaufzeit *f* currency of a bill
Wechsellombard *m* loan on bills
Wechsellombardierung *f* lending money with bill pledged as security
Wechselmakler *m* bill (and note) broker
wechseln to change; to exchange *(currency etc.)*
Wechseln *n* changing; exchange *(currency)*
Wechselnehmer *m* buyer of a bill, payee
Wechselnotierungen *fpl* quotation of bills
Wechselobligationen *fpl* convertible bonds
Wechselordnung *f* (codified) law of bills (of exchange)
Wechselportefeuille *n* bills in hand, bill holdings
Wechselprotest *m* protest (of a bill) ⋄ **einen ~ erheben** to protest a bill
Wechselprovision *f* commission (on bills), bill brokerage
Wechselprozeß *m* proceedings against a bill
Wechselrecht *n* exchange law
Wechselrediskont *m* rediscount of bills
Wechselregreß *m* exchange recourse
Wechselreiterei *f* drawing and redrawing of bills, jobbing in bills, bill-jobbing ⋄ **~ betreiben** to fly a kite
Wechselremittierung *f* remittance of bills
Wechselrückgriff *m s.* **Wechselregreß**
Wechselschicht *f* rotating shift
Wechselschulden *fpl* bills [notes] payable
Wechselschuldner *m* bill debtor
wechselseitig reciprocal, mutual; alternate
Wechselskonto *n s.* **Wechseldiskont**
Wechselspekulant *m* bill jobber
Wechselspekulation *f* jobbing in [speculation on] bills
Wechselstelle *f* exchange office [counter]
Wechselstube *f* exchange office
Wechselumlauf *m* circulation of bills
Wechselverbindlichkeiten *fpl s.* **Wechselschulden**
Wechselverkehr *m* exchange dealings
Wechselverpflichtungen *fpl s.* **Wechselschulden**
Wechselwirkung *f* reciprocal (larger) action, interaction

Wechselwirkungskomponente *f (stats)* component of interaction
Wechselwirkungsordnung *f (stats)* order of interaction
Wechselwirtschaft *f (agric)* rotation of crops, crop rotation
Wechselzins *m* discount (on bills)
Weg *m* 1. way, path; road, street; route, course; 2. manner, means ⋄ **auf dem ~ durch die Instanzen** through (official) channels; **auf diplomatischem ~** through diplomatic channels; **auf gerichtlichem ~** by legal steps
~, **kritischer** *(stats)* critical path
~, **nichtkritischer** *(stats)* non-critical path
~, **öffentlicher** public road [path]
~, **subkritischer** *(stats)* sub-critical path
Wegebau *m* road construction [making, building]
Wegegeld *n* 1. toll; 2. travelling allowance
Wegegerechtigkeit *f* right of way
Wegekosten *pl* 1. maintenance costs of transport routes *(excluding public roads and waterways)*; 2. travel costs, travelling allowance *(of craftsmen etc.)*
Wegerecht *n s.* **Wegegerechtigkeit**
Wegesteuer *f* toll
Wegeunfall *m* accident on the way *(from or to place of work)*
Wegeunterhaltungspflicht *f* obligation to maintain roads
Wegezoll *m s.* **Wegegeld**
Wegstichprobenverfahren *n (stats)* route sampling
Wehrsold *m* soldier's pay
Wehrwirtschaft *f* war economy; economy geared to war preparation
weiblich female
Weichwährung *f* soft currency
Weichwährungsland *n* soft currency country
Weidebesatz *m* grazing density, pasturage
Weidegerechtigkeit *f* commonage, common of pasture
Weiderecht *n s.* **Weidegerechtigkeit**
Weideversicherung *f* pasture insurance
Weidewirtschaft *f* pasture farming
Weigerung *f* refusal
Weigerungsgrund *m* reason for refusal
Weihnachtsgratifikation *f* Christmas bonus
Weihnachtsmarkt *m* Christmas bazaar
Weinküfer *m* cooper
Weinsteuer *f* wine tax, tax on wine
Weisung *f* order, instruction, direction; *(jur)* ruling ⋄ **auf ~** by order; **auf ~ und für Rechnung von** by order and on account of; **laut ~** according to instructions
Weisungsbefugnis *f* authorization [power] to give orders

weisungsberechtigt entitled (with the power/ right) to issue orders [give instructions]
weisungsgebunden subject to instructions [directions]
weisungsgemäß s. laut Weisung
Weisungsinformation f s. Weisung
Weisungsrecht n right [power] to issue orders [give instructions]
Weiterausfuhr f re-export(ation)
weiterbefördern to reforward, to redirect *(letters etc.)*; to provide further transport(ation) *(goods, passengers)*
Weiterbeförderung f reforwarding, redirecting *(letters etc.)*; further transport(ation) *(goods, passengers)*
Weiterbildung f further [adult] education; post-graduate studies; in-service training
~, **berufliche** further vocational training
Weiterentwicklung f further development
~, **technologische** further technological development
~ **von Erzeugnissen** further development of products
Weitergabe f passing-on, transmission
~ **von Erfahrungen** passing on of experiences *(to s.o.)*
weitergeben to pass on, to transmit
weiterleiten s. weitergeben
Weiterleitung f s. Weitergabe
weiterschicken s. weitersenden
weitersenden to send on
weiterverarbeiten to process further; to finish
Weiterverarbeitung f further processing, subsequent treatment
weiterveräußern to resell
Weiterveräußerung f reselling, resale
Weiterveräußerungsbedingungen fpl terms [conditions] of resale
Weitervergabe f subletting, underletting
weitervergeben to sublet, to underlet
Weiterverkauf m s. Weiterveräußerung
weiterverkaufen s. weiterveräußern
weitervermieten to sublet
Weitervermietung f subletting
weiterverpachten to sublease
Weiterverpachtung f subleasing
weiterverpfänden to subpledge
Weiterverpfändung f subpledging
weiterzahlen to pay on
Weiterzahlung f paying further ✧ **bei ~ des Gehalts** paying the salary further
Weitstreckenverkehr m long-distance traffic
Weitwohner m long-distance commuter
Weizenabkommen n:
~, **Internationales** International Wheat Agreement
Weizenproduktion f wheat crop [production]

Welt f world
Weltagrarmarkt m international market of agricultural produce
weltanschaulich from the philosophical point of view, ideological(ly)
Weltanschauung f view [philosophy] of life; world outlook; ideology
Weltarbeitskonferenz f International Labour Conference
Weltarbeitsrecht n International Labour Code
Weltausbeute f world output
Weltausfuhr f world exports
Weltausstellung f international exhibition, world's fair
Weltbedarf m international requirements
weltbekannt world-renowned, world-famous
Weltbevölkerung f world population
Welteinfuhr f world imports
Welterdölreserven fpl world (crude) oil resources
Welterzeugung f world production [output]
Weltfördermenge f world output
Weltgeld n universal money
Welthandel m international [world] trade
Welthandelsflotte f world merchant fleet
Welthandelskonferenz f world trade conference
Welthandelspreis m s. Weltmarktpreis
Welthandelszentrum n international trade centre
Weltherrschaft f world domination
Welthöchststand m highest world standard
Welthungerhilfe f international food aid
Weltmacht f world power
Weltmachtpolitik f power policy
Weltmarke f world-famous make
Weltmarkt m world market
~, **einheitlicher** unified world market
weltmarktfähig fit for the world market, competitive on the world [international] market
Weltmarktfähigkeit f competitive capacity *(of s.th.)* on the world market
weltmarktgerecht meeting the requirements of the world market
Weltmarktpreis m world market [international] price
Weltmarktpreisindex m index of world market [international] prices
Weltmonopol n global monopoly
Weltnahrungsmittelhandel m world trade in food
Weltnahrungsmittelknappheit f world food shortage
Weltnahrungsmittelversorgung f world food supply
Weltnahrungsmittelvorräte mpl world food reserves
Weltniveau n world [international] standard

Weltorganisation f world organization
Weltpolitik f international [world] politics
Weltproduktion f s. **Welterzeugung**
Weltspitze f world class
Weltspitzenerzeugnis n top-quality product
Weltstand m s. **Weltniveau**
Weltstandsvergleich m comparison with the world standard
Weltsystem n world system
Weltverbrauch m world consumption
Weltverkehr m international traffic
Weltvertriebsrecht n global right to sell
Weltwährung f universal currency
Weltwährungsfonds m International Monetary Fund (IMF)
weltweit world-wide, global
Weltwirtschaft f international [world] economy
Weltwirtschaftsgipfel m economic summit (meeting)
Weltwirtschaftskonferenz f World Economic Conference
Weltwirtschaftskrise f international economic crisis, world depression
Weltwirtschaftslehre f international economics
Weltwirtschaftssystem n world economic system
Werbeabteilung f advertising [publicity] department
Werbeagentur f advertising agency
Werbeaktion f advertising campaign
Werbeanalyse f advertisement analysis
Werbeanzeige f advertisement
Werbeatelier n commercial studio
Werbeauftrag m advertisement order
Werbeaufwand m s. **Werbeausgaben**
Werbeausgaben fpl advertising expenditure(s)
Werbeausstellung f advertising exhibition
Werbebeilage f advertising enclosure [handbill]
Werbeberater m advertising consultant
Werbebrief m publicity [sales] letter
Werbebudget n advertising fund [budget]
Werbebüro n advertising agency [contractors]; (labour) recruiting office
Werbedrucksache f (printed) advertising matter
Werbedurchsage f radio spot
~, **eingeblendete** straight commercial
Werbeerfolg m advertising result
Werbeetat m s. **Werbebudget**
Werbefachmann m advertising expert
Werbefachschule f school of advertising
Werbefeldzug m publicity [advertising] campaign
Werbefernsehen n commercial television
Werbefilm m advertising [publicity] film
Werbefirma f advertising contractor [firm]
Werbefläche f advertising space
Werbeflug m advertising flight

Werbeforschung f advertising research
Werbefunk m radio advertising
Werbegebühren fpl advertising rates
Werbegeschenk n advertising gift
Werbegespräch n advertising talk
Werbegraphik f commercial art
Werbegraphiker m commercial designer [artist]
Werbegrundsätze mpl principles of advertising
Werbekampagne f s. **Werbefeldzug**
Werbekonzeption f advertising programme [concept]
Werbekosten pl advertising costs
Werbekraft f advertising appeal
werbekräftig having advertising appeal
Werbeleiter m advertising manager
Werbematerial n advertising material
Werbemethode f advertising method
Werbemittel n advertising medium
Werbemittel npl advertising media, means of publicity
Werbemuster n trial sample
werben to advertise, to make publicity (for); to recruit (labour force etc.), to canvass (customers etc.)
Werben n s. **Werbung**
Werbeplan m advertising plan
Werbepolitik f advertising policy
Werbeprospekt m advertising pamphlet [leaflet, folder]
Werbeschrift f prospectus, brochure; advertising pamphlet [leaflet, folder]
Werbesendung f 1. advertising mail; 2. commercial (by radio and television)
Werbespruch m advertising slogan
Werbetätigkeit f advertising, publicity
Werbetechnik f advertising technique
Werbeträger m s. **Werbemittel**
Werbeunkosten pl s. **Werbekosten**
Werbeunterlagen fpl s. **Werbematerial**
Werbeunternehmen n s. **Werbefirma**
Werbeveranstaltung f advertising [publicity] show [exhibition]
Werbewesen n s. **Werbewirtschaft**
werbewirksam having advertising appeal
Werbewirksamkeit f advertising appeal
Werbewirkung f publicity [advertising] effect
Werbewirtschaft f advertising
Werbezettel m handbill, folder
Werbezweck m advertising purpose
Werbung f publicity, advertising, sales promotion; canvassing (votes etc.)
~, **direkte** direct [straight] advertising
~, **indirekte** advertising through reputation
Werbungsaufwand m s. **Werbeausgaben**
Werbungskosten pl s. **Werbekosten**
Werdegang m career; curriculum vitae
~, **beruflicher** employment history

~, **politischer** political background
Werft *f* shipyard
Werftanlage *f* wharf; shipyard; dockyard
Werftarbeiter *m* docker, dock-worker
Werk *n* 1. work; deed, action; 2. works, undertaking, enterprise, (industrial) plant, factory ✧ **ab ~** ex factory; **frei ab ~** free ex factory
Werkanlage *f* (industrial) plant
Werkbank *f* workbench
Werkdirektor *m s.* **Werkleiter**
Werkleiter *m* works manager
Werken *n s.* **Werkunterricht**
Werkfahrgemeinschaft *f* inter-enterprise transport pool
Werkgelände *n* factory area
Werkhalle *f* production [workshop] floor
Werkkantine *f s.* **Werkküche**
Werkküche *f* factory canteen
Werkküchenessen *n* canteen meals
Werklieferungsvertrag *m* job order contract
Werkmeister *m* foreman
Werkrestaurant *n s.* **Werkküche**
Werksangehöriger *m* factory [works] employee
Werkschutz *m* factory security service; factory security officer
werkseigen company-owned; enterprise-owned
Werkserprobung *f* factory test
Werkskantine *f s.* **Werkküche**
Werksnorm *f s.* **Werkstandard**
Werkspionage *f* industrial espionage
Werkstandard *m* work standard (specification)
Werkstatt *f* workshop
Werkstattarbeit *f* workshop production *(as opposed to flow production)*
Werkstattauftrag *m* work order; job order
Werkstätte *f* workshop; factory, works; place of work
Werkstattfertigung *f s.* **Werkstattarbeit**
Werkstattkosten *pl* workshop costs
Werkstattleiter *m* production department manager
Werkstattmontage *f* shop assembly
Werkstattprinzip *n* workshop principle
Werkstattschreiber *m* time recorder
Werkstoff *m* material, stock; raw material
Werkstoffeinsatz *m* use of material
Werkstoffermüdung *f* material fatigue
Werkstoffersparnis *f* economy in the use [saving] of material
Werkstoffkosten *pl* cost(s) of material(s)
Werkstoffprüfer *m* tester of materials, materials tester
Werkstoffprüfung *f* material testing
Werkstoffverbrauch *m* consumption of material, material consumption
Werkstoffverlust *m* loss of material
Werkstück *n* workpiece, working part

Werkstudent *m* working student
Werksverkaufspreis *m* industry delivery price
Werksvorfertigung *f (build)* prefabrication
Werkswohnung *f* factory-owned flat
Werkszeitung *f* factory [works, enterprise] newspaper [journal]
Werktag *m* workday, weekday
werktags on working days
werktätig working
Werktätige *pl* working people [population]
Werktätiger *m* working person
Werktisch *m s.* **Werkbank**
Werkunterricht *m* handicrafts; arts and crafts
Werkverkehr *m* intra-works transport; works [enterprise] transport service *(for commuting)*
Werkvertrag *m* work contract, contract of manufacture
Werkzeug *n* tool, instrument, implement
Werkzeugausrüstung *f* tool-kit
Werkzeugbau *m* tool production
Werkzeugfertigung *f s.* **Werkzeugbau**
Werkzeuggeld *n* tool allowance
Werkzeugkasten *m* tool-box
Werkzeugkosten *pl* tool costs
Werkzeugmacher *m* tool maker
Werkzeugmaschinenbau *m* machine-tool engineering industry
Werkzeugschuppen *m* tool shed
Werkzeugsortiment *n* range of tools
Werkzeugverbrauch *m* consumption of tools, tool consumption
Werkzeugverschleiß *m* wear and tear of tools
wert worth; worthy; esteemed, valued; valuable
Wert *m* value; equivalent; standard *(of a coin)*; price *(goods etc.)* ✧ **an ~ gewinnen** to rise in value; **an ~ zunehmen** to improve in value; **dem ~ nach** *(cust)* ad valorem, due to its [according to the] value; **großen ~ legen (auf)** to attach great importance (to); **im ~ sinken** to fall in value; **im ~ steigen** to rise in value; **mit ~ s.** **per ~**; **per ~** *(st.ex.)* value as on; **unter ~ verkaufen** to sell below value [cost price]; **von geringem ~** of small value; **~ per** value per *(unit etc.)*
~, **aktuell angezeigter** *(d.pr.)* currently displayed value
~, **gesellschaftlicher** social value
~, **hinzugefügter** value added
~, **kritischer** *(stats)* critical value
~, **neuer** 1. newly created value *(s.* **Neuwert)**; 2. *(ins)* original value
~, **seltenster** *(stats)* antimode
~, **stationärer** *(d.pr.)* steady-state value
~, **stofflicher** material value
~, **subjektiver** subjective [personal] value; use--value
~, **tatsächlicher** real value

578 Wert

~, **übertragener** transferred value
~, **veranschlagter** estimated value
~, **versicherbarer** insurable value
~, **voller** total value
~, **vorgegebener** given value
~, **vorgeschossener** advanced value
~, **wahrer** s. ~, **tatsächlicher**
~, **wahrscheinlichster** (stats) most probable value
~, **zu versteuernder** taxable value
~, **zufälliger** accidental value
~, **zulässiger** permissible value
Wertanalyse f value analysis
Wertänderung f change(s) in value
Wertangabe f declaration [statement] of value
Wertansatz m value estimate, valuation, appraisal
Wertarbeit f high-class workmanship, first-class work; quality product
Wertausdruck m expression of value (of commodities)
Wertaustausch m exchange of values
Wertbegriff m value concept
Wertberechnung f valuation, evaluation; value calculation
Wertberichtigung f value adjustment
Wertberichtigungsbuchung f (acc) reversing entry
Wertberichtigungskonto n (acc) contra account
Wertberichtigungsposten m (acc) adjustment item
wertbeständig of stable value
Wertbeständigkeit f stability (of value), stable value
Wertbestandteil m value component
Wertbestimmung f valuation; computation; (tax) assessment
Wertbewegung f s. **Wertänderung**
Wertbeziehungen fpl value relations
Wertbilanz f balance sheet in terms of value
Wertbildung f creation of value(s), value formation
Wertbildungsprozeß m process of value creation; production process
Wertbildungs- und Verteilungsprozeß m process of value production and distribution
Wertbrief m insured letter
Wertdaten pl value indicators; figures in value terms
Wertdeklaration f declaration of value; declared value
Werte mpl 1. (system of) values; 2. goods; capital assets; 3. (st.ex.) securities, stocks
~, **amtlich notierte** quoted [listed] securities
~, **ausländische** foreign stocks
~, **äußerste** (stats) extreme values
~, **empirische** empirical figures
~, **errechnete** calculated figures
~, **festverzinsliche** fixed interest bearing securities
~, **gangbare** (st.ex.) saleable stocks
~, **gegebene** figures given
~, **gehandelte** (st.ex.) negotiated stocks
~, **immaterielle** intangible assets
~, **internationale** international securities
~, **marktgängige** s. ~, **gangbare**
~, **materielle** tangible assets
~, **mündelsichere** trustee securities [(Am) stocks]
~, **nicht notierte** unquoted [unlisted] securities
~, **rechnerisch ermittelte** s. ~, **errechnete**
~, **repräsentative** representative figures
~, **rückzahlbare** redeemable securities
~, **spekulative** speculative investments
~, **unkündbare** irredeemable securities
~, **verschiedene** miscellaneous [sundry] securities
~, **wirtschaftliche** capital assets
Werteinheit f unit [standard] of value
Wertelement n s. **Wertbestandteil**
werten to value; to appraise; to judge, to consider
Wertentwicklung f growth of value; increase in value
Werterhaltung f maintenance of fixed assets
Werterhaltungsarbeiten fpl maintenance (work)
Werterhaltungskosten pl maintenance expenditures; expenditures for replacement and maintenance; maintenance expenditures for fixed assets
Werterhöhung f rise in value
Wertermittlung f appraisal; appraisement; (assessed) valuation
Werterneuerung f renewal of fixed assets
Werterneuerungsfonds m fund of renewal of fixed assets
Werterneuerungskonto n account concerning [for] renewal of fixed assets
Wertersatz m compensation, indemnification
Werterstattung f s. **Wertersatz**
werteschaffend productive
Wertfaktor m factor of value
Wertform f form of value
~, **allgemeine** general form of value
~, **einfache** elementary form of value
~, **entfaltete** expanded form of value
~, **totale** total form of value
Wertfortschreibung f adjusted basis (taxation of estates)
wertfrei value-free; unbiassed; objective
Wertgegenstand m article of value
Wertgegenstände mpl valuables
wertgemindert deteriorated [reduced] in value
Wertgesetz n law of value
wertgleich of equal value
Wertgrenze f value limit

~, obere maximum limit [value]
~, untere minimum limit [value]
Wertgröße *f* magnitude of value
Wertigkeit *f* importance
~ **der Ware** importance of a commodity *(distinguishing essential and non-essential goods in trade policy)*
Wertkategorie *f* category of value
Wertkennziffer *f* value index [indicator]
Wertlehre *f s.* **Werttheorie**
wertlos of no value, worthless
Wertmaß *n* measure of value
Wertmaßfunktion *f* function of measure of value
wertmäßig in value, in terms of value; ad valorem
Wertmessung *f* value measurement, measurement of value
Wertminderung *f* depreciation, deterioration in value ⋄ **eine ~ erfahren** to lose in value
Wertmodifikation *f* modification of value
Wertpaket *n* insured parcel
Wertpapierabsatz *m* sale of securities
Wertpapierabteilung *f (bank)* securities department
Wertpapieranlage *f* investment (in securities)
Wertpapierbereinigung *f* validation of securities
Wertpapierbestand *m* security holdings
Wertpapierbörse *f* stock exchange [market]
Wertpapiere *npl* securities ⋄ **~ zur Börse zulassen** to qualify securities for sale to the public
~, **abhandengekommene** lost [missing] securities
~, **an der Börse gehandelte** securities dealt in on the stock exchange
Wertpapieremission *f* issue of securities
Wertpapiergeschäfte *npl* transactions in securities
Wertpapiergesetz *n* securities act
Wertpapierhandel *m* trading in securities
Wertpapierinhaber *m* holder [owner, depositor] of securities
Wertpapierkonto *n* deposit account
Wertpapiermarkt *m* securities market
Wertpapiersteuer *f* stamp duty (on securities)
Wertpapierverkauf *m s.* **Wertpapierabsatz**
Wertpapierverkehr *m s.* **Wertpapierhandel**
Wertpapierversicherung *f* securities insurance
Wertpapierverzeichnis *n* statement of securities (deposited)
Wert-Preis-Abweichung *f* value-price deviation
Wertprodukt *n* value added *(in a product)*
Wertproduktion *f* production of value
Wertquantum *n* quantity of value
Wertrealisierung *f* realization of value

Wertrechnung *f* value calculation
Wertsachen *fpl* valuables
wertschaffend productive, creative
Wertschöpfung *f* production [creation] of value, value production
Wertschätzung *f* esteem (for), appreciation (of)
Wertschwankung *f* value fluctuation
Wertsendung *f* consignment of valuables; remittance *(money)*
Wertsicherung *f* guarantee against devaluation
Wertsicherungsklausel *f* devaluation guarantee clause
Wertsteigerung *f* increase in value
Wertstruktur *f* composition of value
Wertsubstanz *f* substance of value
Wertsumme *f* total [sum of] value
Werttarif *m* ad valorem tariff
Werttheorie *f* value theory
Wertübertragung *f* transfer of value
Wertung *f* valuation; appraisal, estimate; rating; judging; evaluation
Wertverpflechtungsbilanz *f* input-output table in terms of value
Wertvergleich *m* comparison of value
Wertverhältnis *n* value relation(ship); ratio of value
Wertverlust *m* depreciation in value
Wertverringerung *f s.* **Wertverlust**
Wertverzehr *m* consumption of value
wertvoll valuable; precious
Wertvorteil *m* cost advantage
Wertzoll *m* ad valorem duty
Wertzuwachs *m* increment (in value); betterment *(estates etc.)*
Wertzuwachsmessung *f* measurement of increment in value
Wertzuwachssteuer *f* 1. value-added tax; 2. capital gains tax
Wesen *n* 1. being, creature; 2. essence; reality, substance, nature; character, disposition
Wettbewerb *m* competition, contest; emulation ⋄ **in ~ treten mit** to enter into competition with; to emulate
~, **freier** free competition
~, **unlauterer** unfair competition
Wettbewerbsbeschränkung *f* restraint of trade
Wettbewerbsbewegung *f* emulation movement
Wettbewerbsergebnisse *npl* results of emulation
wettbewerbsfähig competitive
Wettbewerbskommission *f* emulation affairs committee
Wettbewerbsverbot *n* total restraint of competition; competition clause
Wettbewerbswirtschaft *f* competitive economy
Whittaker-Periodogramm *n (stats)* Whittaker periodogram

wichten *(stats)* to weight
Wichtung *f (stats)* weighting
Widerruf *m* disavowal; revocation; *(com)* countermand
widerrufen to disavow; to revoke; *(com)* to countermand
Widerrufklausel *f* revocable clause
widerruflich revocable *(letter of credit etc.)*
Widerspruch *m* contradiction; inconsistency; opposition, conflict *(views etc.)*
~, antagonistischer antagonistic contradiction
~, innerer inconsistency
~, nichtantagonistischer non-antagonistic contradiction
Widerspruchstriaden *fpl (stats)* circular triads
widerstandsfähig resistant
Widerstandsfähigkeit *f* resistance
Wiederanlage *f* reinvestment
wiederanlegen to reinvest
wiederanschaffen s. wiederbeschaffen
Wiederanschaffung *f* s. Wiederbeschaffung
Wiederanschaffungskosten *pl* s. Wiederbeschaffungskosten
Wiederanschaffungswert *m* s. Wiederbeschaffungskosten
wiederanstellen s, wiedereinstellen
Wiederanstellung *f* s. Wiedereinstellung
wiederanwenden to reuse; to reapply
Wiederanwendung *f* reuse; reapplication
wiederanziehen *(st.ex.)* to recover *(rates etc.)*
Wiederaufbau *m* reconstruction
Wiederaufbauanleihe *f* reconstruction loan
Wiederaufbauarbeiten *fpl* reconstruction work
wiederaufbauen to reconstruct
Wiederaufbaukosten *pl* costs of reconstruction
Wiederaufbaukredit *m* reconstruction loan [credit]
Wiederaufbaumaßnahmen *fpl* reconstruction measures
Wiederaufbaumittel *npl* reconstruction fund
Wiederaufbauplan *m* plan of reconstruction, reconstruction plan
Wiederaufbauprogramm *n* reconstruction programme
wiederaufforsten to reforest
Wiederaufforstung *f* reforestation
wiederauffüllen to replenish *(stocks etc.)*; to refill *(cask etc.)*
wiederaufleben to revive, to reactivate; to recover
Wiederaufleben *n* revival, reactivation; recovery
Wiederaufnahme *f* reopening *(business etc.)*; resumption *(diplomatic relations etc.)*
wiederaufnehmen to reopen *(business etc.)*, to resume *(diplomatic relations etc.)*
wiederaufrüsten to rearm
Wiederaufrüstung *f* rearmament

Wiederaufschwung *m* recovery
wiederaufwerten to revalue
Wiederaufwertung *f* revaluation
Wiederausfuhr *f* re-export(ation)
wiederausführen to re-export
wiederbeladen to reload
Wiederbeladung *f* reload; reloading
wiederbeleben to revive; to resurrect; to reactivate
Wiederbelebung *f* revival; resurrection
~, konjunkturelle business [trade] revival
wiederbeschaffen to replace; to repurchase
Wiederbeschaffung *f* replacement; repurchase
Wiederbeschaffungskosten *pl* replacement costs *(fixed assets)*
Wiederbeschaffungspreis *m* s. Wiederbeschaffungskosten
Wiederbeschaffungswert *m* s. Wiederbeschaffungskosten
wiederbeschäftigen to re-employ
Wiederbeschäftigung *f* re-employment
wiederbesiedeln to resettle
Wiederbesiedlung *f* resettlement
Wiederbeteiligung *f* renewed participation
wiedereinberufen to resummon; to reconvene
Wiedereinberufung *f* resummons
wiedereinbringen to bring back, to restore; to recoup
Wiedereinbringung *f* restoration; recoupment
Wiedereinfuhr *f* re-import(ation)
wiedereinführen to re-import; to re-introduce *(securities to the market etc.)*
Wiedereinführung *f* reintroduction *(of securities to the market etc.)*
wiedereingeben *(d.pr.)* to re-input
wiedereingliedern to resettle; to rehabilitate
Wiedereingliederung *f* resettlement; rehabilitation
~, berufliche vocational rehabilitation
wiedereinlagern to rewarehouse
wiedereinlösen to redeem *(pledge etc.)*
Wiedereinlösung *f* redemption *(pledge etc.)*
Wiedereinreiseerlaubnis *f* re-entry permit
Wiedereinsatz *m* 1. re-utilization *(material)*; 2. *(agric)* farm-produced inputs *(feed grains, menure etc.)*
wiedereinschiffen to re-embark *(passengers)*
Wiedereinschiffung *f* re-embarkation
wiedereinsetzen 1. to restore, reinstate; 2. to reuse *(material etc.)*; 3. *(agric)* to use internally
wiedereinstellen to re-employ, to rehire, to re-engage
Wiedereinstellung *f* re-employment, re-engagement
wiedereintreten to rejoin *(company etc.)*
wiedererhalten to get back, to repossess *(property etc.)*

wiedererlangen s. **wiedererhalten**
Wiedererlangung f repossession (*property etc.*)
wiederernennen to reappoint
Wiederernennung f reappointment
wiedereröffnen to reopen (*shop etc.*)
Wiedereröffnung f reopening (*shop etc.*); resumption (*talks etc.*)
wiedererstatten to restore; to reimburse (*money etc.*); to refund (*excess taxes etc.*)
Wiedererstattung f reimbursement (*money etc.*); refund, refunding (*excess taxes etc.*)
Wiederfangstichprobenverfahren n (*stats*) capture release sampling
wiedergeben to give back, to return, to restore, to restitute
Wiedergesundung f recovery
wiedergewinnen to reclaim; to recover, to retrieve; to recycle (*scrap etc.*)
Wiedergewinnung f reclamation; recovery, retrieval; recycling (*scrap etc.*), salvage (*ship etc.*)
~ **von Grundstoffen aus Abfallstoffen** recycling
wiedergutbringen (*acc*) to recredit
wiedergutmachen to make amends for; to compensate
Wiedergutmachung f restitution, restoration; compensation; reparation
Wiedergutmachungsabkommen n reparation agreement
Wiedergutmachungsanspruch m claim to compensation; claim to reparation
wiederherstellen to restore; to re-establish (*connections*); (*jur*) to restitute
Wiederherstellprogramm n (*d.pr.*) recovery program
Wiederherstellung f restoration, repair; re-establishment; (*jur*) restitution
Wiederherstellungspreis m s. **Wiederbeschaffungskosten**
Wiederherstellungsreparatur f overhaul
Wiederholung f repetition; replication
~, **teilweise** (*stats*) fractional replication
Wiederholungsbefehl m (*d.pr.*) repetition instruction
Wiederholungsbesuch m (*stats*) call-back
Wiederholungsfehler m (*d.pr.*) repetitive error
Wiederholungsgenauigkeit f (*stats*) precision
Wiederholungsprogramm n (*d.pr.*) rerun program
Wiederholungsreihe f (*stats*) set of trials
~, **einheitliche** (*stats*) uniformity trial
Wiederinbesitznahme f getting back
wiederinstandsetzen to repair
Wiederinstandsetzung f repair
Wiederinstandsetzungskosten pl repairs, repair costs, costs of repair

Wiederkauf m repurchase
wiederkaufen to repurchase, to buy back
Wiederkäufer m repurchaser
Wiederkaufsrecht n right to repurchase
Wiederkehrperiode f (*stats*) return period
wiederprogrammierbar (*d.pr.*) reprogrammable
Wiederprogrammierung f (*d.pr.*) reprogramming
wiedervereinigen to reunite
Wiedervereinigung f reunification, reunion
Wiederverkauf m resale
wiederverkaufen to resell
Wiederverkäufer m retail trader; middleman ◊ **an ~ verkaufen** to sell to the trade
wiederverkäuflich resaleable
Wiederverkaufspreis m resale [reselling] price
Wiederverkaufsrecht n right to resell
Wiederverkaufswert m s. **Wiederverkaufspreis**
wiederverwenden to reuse (*package etc.*)
Wiederverwendung f reuse (*package etc.*)
Wiederverwendungsaufwand m recycling cost(s)
Wiederverwendungsprojekte npl reusable designs
Wiederverwendungsverpackung f two-way package
wiederverwerten to reutilize (*waste material etc.*)
Wiederverwertung f reutilization (*waste material etc.*)
Wiederwahl f reelection
wiederwählbar eligible for reelection
wiederwählen to reelect
wiederzulassen to readmit
Wiederzulassung f readmission
Wiegegeld n weighage, weighing charges
Wiegemeister m weigher
wiegen to weigh
Wiegeschein m weigh-note
Wiese f meadow(land)
Wild n game
Wildbestand m stock of game
Wilddieb m poacher
Wilddieberei f poaching
Wildhüter m gamekeeper
Wildpark m (natural) reservation; deer park
Wildschaden m damage done by game
Wild- und Geflügelhandlung f game and poultry shop
Willenserklärung f declaration of intention ◊ **eine ~ abgeben** to express one's intention
Willkür f arbitrary act(ion), arbitrariness; capriciousness
Willkürakt m arbitrary act(ion)
willkürlich arbitrary
Windbruch m (*for*) damage caused by storm
Winkeltransformation f (*stats*) angular transformation

Winterbetrieb *m* winter operation
Winterfahrplan *m* winter timetable
winterfest winter-proof ⋄ ~ **machen** to adopt measures before the onset of winter, *(Am)* to adopt measures to winterize
Winterfestmachung *f* measures to withstand winter, *(Am)* winterization
Winterfrucht *f* winter crop
Wintergetreide *n* winter corn
Winterkleidung *f* winter clothes [wear]
Wintermode *f* winter fashion
Winterpreis *m* winter price
Wintersaat *f s.* **Wintergetreide**
Wintersaison *f* winter season
Winterschlußverkauf *m* winter clearance sale
Wintervorrat *m* winter stocks
Winterzuschlag *m* 1. winter surcharge *(lignite etc.)*; winter transport [freight] rate; 2. additional winter pay
Winterzwischenfrucht *f* winter intercrop
Winzer *m* vine dresser [grower]
wirken 1. to act, to do, to work, to effect, to produce; to bring about; to be active; 2. to weave ⋄ ~ **auf** to have an effect [impact] on; to influence, to impress
wirklich real, actual; true, genuine
Wirklichkeit *f* reality
wirksam active; effective, efficient
Wirksamkeit *f* activity; effectiveness, efficiency, efficacy; effect
Wirkung *f* action, working, operation; efficiency, efficacy; effect; impact; impression; influence; response ⋄ **mit sofortiger** ~ with immediate effect; **mit** ~ **vom** with effect from
~, **auflösende** suspensory effect
~, **beschränkte** limited operation; limited effect
~, **bindende** binding effect
~, **gesetzliche** (with) legal force
~, **quadratische** *(stats)* quadratic response
~, **quantitative** *(stats)* quantitative response
~, **rechtliche** legal effect
~, **unabhängige** *(stats)* independent action
Wirkungsbereich *m* range, radius of action
Wirkungsdauer *f* duration
Wirkungsfläche *f (stats)* response surface
Wirkungsgrad *m* (degree of) efficiency; (degree of) impact
~ **der Arbeit** degree of efficiency of labour
~, **wirtschaftlicher** degree of economic efficiency
Wirkungsgröße *f*:
~, **transformierte** *(stats)* response metameter
Wirkungskreis *m* sphere of activity; sphere of influence
wirkungslos ineffectual, inefficient
Wirkungsveränderliche *f (stats)* effect variable
wirkungsvoll effective, striking

Wirt *m* innkeeper, publican, *(Am)* saloonkeeper; proprietor *(hotel etc.)*; landlord *(houses)*
Wirtschaft *f* 1. housekeeping, domestic economy; household; 2. economy, economic system; 3. *(agric)* farm, holding; husbandry; 4. inn, public house
~, **bezirksgeleitete** enterprises managed by the county [regional] authorities
~, **dienstleistende** (domestic) service sector
~, **extensive** expanding [extensively growing] economy; *(agric)* extensive agriculture
~, **freie** free [uncontrolled] economy
~, **gelenkte** controlled economy
~, **gemischte** mixed economy
~, **geplante** planned economy
~, **geschlossene** closed economic system [economy]
~, **gewerbliche** industry and trade
~, **individuelle** individual farm; individual farming
~, **intensive** intensively growing economy
~, **kreisgeleitete** enterprises managed by the district authorities
~, **monopolistische** monopoly economy
~, **nicht geplante** unplanned economy
~, **oligopolistische** oligopolistic economy
~, **örtlichgeleitete** locally managed enterprises
~, **private** 1. economy based on private ownership in the means of production; 2. *(agric)* private holding
~, **stadtnahe** suburban enterprises
~, **stationäre** settled economy
~, **vergesellschaftete** socialized enterprises
~, **volkseigene** nationally-owned enterprises
~, **zentralgeleitete** centrally managed [run] enterprises
wirtschaften to keep house, to run the household; to manage; to economize ⋄ **gut** ~ to economize, to operate economically; **schlecht** ~ to mismanage
Wirtschafter *m* economist
wirtschaftlich economic, economical, efficient; profitable, paying ⋄ ~ **schwach entwickelt** economically less developed
Wirtschaftlichkeit *f* efficiency; profitability; good management, economy *(saving)*
Wirtschaftlichkeitsberechnung *f* calculation of profitability [efficiency]
Wirtschaftlichkeitsgrenze *f* limits to economic efficiency; break-even point
Wirtschaftlichkeitskennziffer *f* indicator of efficiency, efficiency indicator
Wirtschaftlichkeitsprinzip *n* principle of efficiency [profitability, good management]; profitability criterion
Wirschaftlichkeitsrechnung *f s.* **Wirtschaftlichkeitsberechnung**

Wirtschaftlichkeitsuntersuchung *f* investigation of economic efficiency
wirtschaftlich-organisatorisch economic and organizational *(measures etc.)*
Wirtschaftsabkommen *n* economic [commercial] agreement
Wirtschaftsablauf *m* economic development, economic process; business cycle
Wirtschaftsabteilung *f* economic department
Wirtschaftsanalyse *f* economic analysis; business analysis
Wirtschaftsanalytiker *m* economic analyst
Wirtschaftsanstieg *m s.* **Wirtschaftsaufschwung**
Wirtschaftsartikel *m* household article
Wirtschaftsaufbau *m* structure of economy, economic structure; reconstruction of economy
Wirtschaftsaufschwung *m* economic upturn [revival, upswing]
Wirtschaftsauftrag *m* (commercial) order
Wirtschaftsausgaben *fpl* household expenditure
Wirtschaftsausschuß *m* economic committee; economic commission
Wirtschaftsaussichten *fpl* business prospects
Wirtschaftsautarkie *f* autarchy
Wirtschaftsbarometer *n* business barometer
Wirtschaftsbeihilfe *f* cost-of-living bonus
Wirtschaftsbelange *mpl* economic matters [affairs]
Wirtschaftsbelebung *f* business revival
Wirtschaftsberater *m* economic adviser; business consultant
Wirtschaftsbereich *m* sector of the economy, economic sector
Wirtschaftsbericht *m* economic report
Wirtschaftsberichterstatter *m* economic correspondent [reporter]
Wirtschaftsbeschränkungen *fpl* economic restrictions
Wirtschaftsbesprechungen *fpl* economic talks [discussions]
Wirtschaftsbetrachtung *f* economic survey
Wirtschaftsbetrieb *m* catering (department)
Wirtschaftsbeziehungen *fpl* economic [business] relations ◊ ~ **abbrechen** to break off economic relations; ~ **aufnehmen** *s.* ~ **herstellen**; ~ **herstellen** to establish economic relations; ~ **intensivieren** to intensify economic relations
Wirtschaftsbezirk *m* economic region
Wirtschaftsblock *m* economic block
Wirtschaftsblockade *f* economic blockade [embargo]
Wirtschaftsblüte *f* prosperity; (cyclical) boom
Wirtschaftsboykott *m* economic boycott
Wirtschaftschaos *n* economic chaos

Wirtschaftsdepression *f* economic [business] depression [crisis]
Wirtschaftsdrucksache *f* economic printed matter
Wirtschaftseinheit *f* (basic) economic unit
Wirtschaftsentwicklung *f* economic development
Wirtschaftserfolg *m* economic success; business success
Wirtschaftsethik *f* business ethics
Wirtschaftsexpansion *f* economic expansion
Wirtschaftsexperte *m s.* **Wirtschaftsfachmann**
Wirtschaftsfachmann *m* economist, expert in economic matters
Wirtschaftsfaktoren *mpl* economic factors
wirtschaftsfeindlich anti-commercial *(measures etc.)*
Wirtschaftsfläche *f* economically-used area *(of a country, district, farm etc.)*
Wirtschaftsflaute *f* recession
Wirtschaftsflug *m* aerial work *(crop spraying etc.)*
Wirtschaftsform *f* economic system
Wirtschaftsforschung *f* economic [business] research
Wirtschaftsfragen *fpl* economic issues
Wirtschaftsführung *f* management of the economy, economic management
Wirtschaftsgebäude *n* farm building(s)
Wirtschaftsgebiet *n* economic area [region]
~, **einheitliches** co-ordinated economic area *(for economic development etc.)*
Wirtschaftsgefüge *n* economic structure [system]
Wirtschaftsgeld *n* housekeeping money
Wirtschaftsgemeinschaft *f* economic community
Wirtschaftsgeographie *f* economic geography
Wirtschaftsgeschichte *f* economic history
Wirtschaftsgesetz *n* commercial law
Wirtschaftsgesetzgebung *f* legislation on economic matters
Wirtschaftsgruppe *f* economic group; trust
Wirtschaftsgüter *npl* goods, articles
~, **kurzlebige** consumer non-durables
~, **langlebige** consumer durables
Wirtschaftshilfe *f* economic aid
Wirtschaftsintegration *f* economic integration
Wirtschaftsinteressen *npl* economic [commercial, business] interests
Wirtschaftsisolationismus *m* (theory of) economic isolation
Wirtschaftsjahr *n* financial [fiscal] year
Wirtschaftsjournalist *m* journalist specializing in economic matters, business reporter, financial journalist
Wirtschaftskampf *m* economic competition
Wirtschaftskartell *n* cartel, ring, *(Am)* trust

Wirtschaftskaufmann *m* commercial clerk
Wirtschaftskommission *f* economic commission
Wirtschaftskonferenz *f* economic conference
Wirtschaftskontrolle *f* economic control; business control
~, **komplexe** comprehensive economic control
Wirtschaftskooperation *f* economic co-operation
Wirtschaftskredit *m* commercial credit
Wirtschaftskorrespondent *m s.* **Wirtschaftsberichterstatter**
Wirtschaftskraft *f* economic power [capacity, potential(ity)]
Wirtschaftskreise *mpl* business circles; industrialists
Wirtschaftskreislauf *m* economic cycle; business cycle
Wirtschaftskrieg *m* trade war
Wirtschaftskrise *f* economic crisis
Wirtschaftslage *f* economic situation; business conditions
Wirtschaftsleben *n* economic life; economy
Wirtschaftslehre *f* economics; political economy
Wirtschaftslenkung *f* state economic control
Wirtschaftsliberalismus *m* economic liberalism
Wirtschaftsmacht *f* economic power
Wirtschaftsmaßnahmen *fpl* economic measures
Wirtschaftsmathematik *f* economic mathematics
Wirtschaftsmoral *f s.* **Wirtschaftsethik**
Wirtschaftsnachrichten *fpl* business reports
Wirtschaftsnormen *fpl* economic [trade] standards
Wirtschaftsordnung *f* economic system [order]
Wirtschaftsorganisation *f* 1. economic [business] organization; 2. economic unit *(e.g. trading organization)*
Wirtschaftspatent *n* special patent *(where the government has the right to determine its use)*
Wirtschaftspfleger *m* social worker specializing in domestic duties [housekeeping]
Wirtschaftsplan *m* (national) economic plan
Wirtschaftsplanung *f* economic planning
Wirtschaftspolitik *f* economic policy
wirtschaftspolitisch economic (policy) *(measures etc.)*
Wirtschaftspotential *n* economic potential(ities)
Wirtschaftspraxis *f* economic practice, economic [business] life
Wirtschaftspresse *f* economic (periodicals and) papers
Wirtschaftsprognose *f* economic forecast [prognosis]
Wirtschaftsprogramm *n* economic programme
Wirtschaftsprojekt *n* industrial project

Wirtschaftsprozeß *m* economic process
Wirtschaftsprüfer *m* chartered accountant
Wirtschaftsprüfung *f* auditing
Wirtschaftsprüfungsbericht *m* auditor's report
Wirtschaftspsychologie *f* industrial psychology
Wirtschaftsrat *m* economic council
Wirtschaftsraum *m* trading area
Wirtschaftsrechnung *f* household budgeting
Wirtschaftsrecht *n* commercial law and economic regulations
Wirtschaftsredakteur *m* editor for economic affairs
Wirtschaftsreform *f* economic reform(s)
Wirtschaftsrisiko *n* economic risk
Wirtschaftssabotage *f* industrial sabotage
Wirtschaftssachverständiger *m* industrial [economic] expert
Wirtschaftssanktion *f* 1. penalty for neglect of duties [breach of contract]; 2. economic sanction
Wirtschaftsschädigung *f* damage to the economy
Wirtschaftssektor *m* sector of the economy
Wirtschaftssituation *f s.* **Wirtschaftslage**
Wirtschaftsspionage *f* industrial espionage
Wirtschaftsstabilität *f* economic stability
Wirtschaftsstatistik *f* (economic) statistics
Wirtschaftsstraftaten *fpl* crimes (in commercial dealings)
Wirtschaftsstruktur *f* structure of the economy, economic structure
Wirtschaftsstufentheorie *f* theory of the stages of economic growth (and development)
Wirtschaftssystem *n* economic system
Wirtschaftstagung *f s.* **Wirtschaftskonferenz**
Wirtschaftstendenz *f* business trend
Wirtschaftstheorie *f* economic theory
Wirtschafts- und Sozialausschuß *m* economic and social committee
Wirtschafts- und Sozialrat *m* economic and social council
Wirtschafts- und Währungsunion *f* economic and monetary union
Wirtschaftsunternehmen *n* commercial enterprise [establishment]
~, **kommunales** public utility
Wirtschaftsverband *m* trade association
Wirtschaftsverbindungen *fpl* economic links [relations]
Wirtschaftsvereinbarung *f* economic agreement; commercial contract
Wirtschaftsvereinigung *f* economic organization
~, **internationale** international economic organization
Wirtschaftsverhandlungen *fpl* economic negotiations

Wirtschaftsvertrag m commercial contract
Wirtschaftsverträge mpl:
~, **zwei- und mehrseitige** bilateral and multilateral commercial contracts
Wirtschaftswachstum n economic growth
~, **extensives** extensive economic growth
Wirtschaftswelt f business world
Wirtschaftswerbung f commercial advertising; business publicity
Wirtschaftswissenschaften fpl economics, economic science(s)
Wirtschaftswissenschaftler m economist
Wirtschaftszentrum n business [industrial, trade] centre
Wirtschaftsziele npl economic aims [objectives]
Wirtschaftszweig m sector [branch] of the economy
Wirtshaus n restaurant (in the broadest sense of the word including cafe, public-house, teashop, inn etc.)
Wissenschaft f science
~, **angewandte** applied science
~, **angrenzende** (branch of) science bordering another
~, **interdisziplinäre** inter-disciplinary science
~, **reine** pure science
~ **von der Wissenschaft** science of science
Wissenschaften fpl sciences
~, **technische** engineering (sciences)
Wissenschaftler m scientist (usually in natural sciences)
Wissenschaftsausgaben fpl expenditures for scientific purposes
Wissenschaftsbeziehungen fpl scientific relations
Wissenschaftseinrichtung f scientific institution [institute]
Wissenschaftsfinanzierung f financing of research [science]
Wissenschaftsförderung f promotion of sciences
Wissenschaftsintegration f integration of sciences
Wissenschaftskonzeption f programme for scientific development
Wissenschaftskooperation f scientific co-operation
Wissenschaftskoordinierung f co-ordination of scientific activities [research]
Wissenschaftsplanung f planning of scientific activities [sciences]
Wissenschaftspolitik f science policy
Wissenschaftsprognose f forecast [prognosis] (of trends) in science
Wissenschafts- und Technologieplanung f planning of science and technology
Woche f week

Wochenabschluß m (acc) weekly return
Wochenarbeitszeit f working hours per week
Wochenausweis m (com) weekly statement
Wochenbeihilfe f s. **Wochengeld**
Wochengeld n maternity benefit
Wochenhilfe f s. **Wochengeld**
Wochenkarte f weekly season ticket
Wochenlohn m weekly wage
Wochenmarkt m weekly market
Wochenproduktion f weekly output [production]
Wochenrate f weekly instalment
Wochentag m weekday
wochentags on weekdays
wöchentlich weekly
wochenweise s. **wöchentlich**
Wohl n prosperity; welfare
Wohlfahrt f welfare
Wohlfahrtsamt n relief [welfare] office
Wohlfahrtsempfänger m recipient of public relief
Wohlfahrtspflege f care, solicitude; welfare, welfare work [service(s)]
Wohlfahrtsstaat m welfare state
Wohlfahrtsunterstützung f public relief
wohlhabend wealthy, well-off, prosperous
Wohlstand m prosperity; wealth ⋄ **im ~ leben** to be prosperous [well-off], to be in affluent circumstances
~, **gesellschaftlicher** social welfare
Wohlstandsindex m cost-of-living index
wohltätig benevolent, charitable
Wohltätigkeit f charity
Wohltätigkeitsbasar m charity bazaar
Wohltätigkeitseinrichtung f charity institution
Wohltätigkeitsfonds m charity fund
Wohltätigkeitsorganisation f charity organization
Wohltätigkeitsveranstaltung f charity performance
Wohltätigkeitsverein m charity society
Wohnbauten pl dwelling houses, residential buildings
Wohnbedarf m s. **Wohnungsbedarf**
Wohnbedingungen fpl housing conditions
Wohnberechtigung f residential permit
Wohnbevölkerung f residents
Wohndichte f density of population
wohnen to live, to reside
Wohnfläche f floor space
Wohngebiet n residential area [quarter]
Wohngegend f s. **Wohngebiet**
~, „**billige**" low-rent residential area
Wohngeld n rent allowance
Wohngeldzuschuß m s. **Wohngeld**
Wohngemeinschaft f community living together (in a house or flat)

wohnhaft residing, living
Wohnheim *n* hostel
Wohnlage *f s.* **Wohngebiet**
Wohnmietrecht *n* tenancy law
Wohnort *m* residence, domicile
Wohnraum *m* residential [living] space
Wohnraumbeschaffung *f* provision of housing
Wohnraumbewirtschaftung *f* housing control
Wohnraumbilanzen *fpl* balance sheet of housing units (flats)
Wohnraumentfremdung *f* conversion of flats [houses] *(into offices etc.)*
Wohnraumfonds *m s.* **Wohnungsfonds**
Wohnraumlenkung *f* housing control; housing office
Wohnraumpolitik *f* housing policy
Wohnraumzählung *f* housing census
Wohnrecht *n* right to reside
Wohnsiedlung *f* (residential) settlement
Wohnsitz *m* (place of) residence
~, **fester** fixed address, settled place of residence
~, **ständiger** permanent place of residence
Wohnstandard *m* housing standard
Wohn- und Lebensverhältnisse *npl* living conditions
Wohnung *f* flat; house; residence; dwelling
~, **abgeschlossene** self-contained flat
~, **betriebsnahe** home close to (place of) work
~, **leerstehende** empty flat [house]
~, **möblierte** furnished flat [house]
~, **überbelegte** overcrowded dwelling
Wohnungen *fpl*:
~, **zu modernisierende, um- und auszubauende** flats to be modernised and renovated
Wohnungsamt *n* housing office
Wohnungsbau *m* housing construction
~, **individueller** private housing construction
~, **komplexer** comprehensive housing programme *(including social infrastructure)*
~, **sozialer** government assisted house-building
Wohnungsbaudarleh(e)n *n s.* **Wohnungsbaukredit**
Wohnungsbaufinanzierung *f* financing of housing
Wohnungsbaugenossenschaft *f* co-operative housing society
Wohnungsbaukosten *pl* housing construction costs
Wohnungsbaukredit *m* housing loan, *(Am)* home financing
Wohnungsbauprogramm *n* housing programme
Wohnungsbedarf *m* flats required, housing requirement
Wohnungsbedingungen *fpl s.* **Wohnbedingungen**
Wohnbestand *m* total number of flats and houses

Wohnungsbestandsaufnahme *f s.* **Wohnraumzählung**
Wohnungsdefizit *n* housing shortage *(expressed in numbers)*
Wohnungseigentum *n* ownership of flat [house]
Wohnungseigentümer *m* owner of flat [house]
Wohnungseinheit *f* housing unit
Wohnungsfonds *m* housing fund
Wohnungsfrage *f* housing issue
Wohnungsgröße *f* size of flat
Wohnungsinhaber *m* tenant; householder
Wohnungsknappheit *f s.* **Wohnungsmangel**
wohnungslos homeless
Wohnungsmangel *m* housing shortage
Wohnungsmiete *f* rent (of flat)
Wohnungsmietrecht *n s.* **Wohnmietrecht**
Wohnungsmietvertrag *m* lease contract, contract of tenancy, tenancy agreement
Wohnungsnachweis *m* house-agency; housing registry
Wohnungsneubau *m* new housing
Wohnungsnot *f* housing shortage; dire need of housing
Wohnungspolitik *f s.* **Wohnraumpolitik**
Wohnungsproblem *n* housing problem
Wohnungsprogramm *n s.* **Wohnungsbauprogramm**
Wohnungsstandard *m s.* **Wohnstandard**
Wohnungsstatistik *f* housing statistics
Wohnungssuche *f* flat-hunting
Wohnungstausch *m* exchange of flats, flat swapping
Wohnungstauschzentrale *f* central office for exchange of flats
Wohnungswechsel *m* change of residence
Wohnungswirtschaft *f* provision and organization of housing; housing business
Wohnverhältnisse *npl* housing conditions
Wohnviertel *n* residental quarter [district]
Wohnwagen *m* caravan
Wölbung *f (stats)* kurtosis
~, **normale** *(stats)* mesokurtosis
~, **überhohe** *(stats)* leptokurtosis
Wortsymbol *n (d.pr.)* label
Wortübertragungszeit *f (d.pr.)* word period
Wucher *m* usury
Wucherer *m* usurer
Wuchergeschäft *n* usury, usury trade
Wuchergewinn *m* usurious [inordinate] profit
wucherisch usurious
Wucherkapital *n* usurer's capital
Wucherkredit *m* usurer's credit [loan]
wuchern to practise usury
Wucherpreis *m* usurious price
Wucherprofit *m s.* **Wuchergewinn**
Wucherzinsen *mpl* usurious [excessive] interest
Würfelgitter *n (stats)* cubic lattice

Z

Zahl *f* number; figure; digit; cipher
~, durchschnittliche average figure
~, endliche finite number
~ fehlerhafter Stücke, zugelassene *(stats)* allowable defects
~, ganze integral number
~, gebrochene fractional number
~, maximale maximum number
~, reelle real number
zahlbar payable
zählbar countable
Zahlbarkeit *f* maturity
Zählbereich *m (d.pr.)* count range
zahlen to pay, to settle, to meet *(bill)* ⋄ **im voraus ~** to pay in advance; **in bar ~** to pay in cash [cash down]; **jährlich ~** to pay yearly [annually]; **monatlich ~** to pay monthly; **postnumerando ~** to pay on receipt; **prompt ~** to pay immediately; to pay promptly; **pünktlich ~** to pay in [on] time; to pay promptly; **sofort ~** to pay immediately; **wöchentlich ~** to pay weekly
Zahlen *fpl* numbers; figures ⋄ **aus den roten ~ kommen** to get out of the red; **aus den roten ~ sein** to be out of the red; **in den roten ~ stehen** to be in the red; **in die roten ~ kommen** to get into the red; **in runden ~** in round figures
~, unendliche nonfinite [infinite] numbers
~, vorläufige preliminary figures
~, zulässige *(stats)* admissible numbers
zählen to count
Zählen *n* counting, reckoning
Zahlenangaben *fpl* (numerical) data, figures
Zahlenbeispiel *n* numerical example
Zahlenbereich *m* number range
Zahlenfolge *f* numerical order
Zahlengröße *f* numerical quantity
Zahlenlotterie *f s.* **Zahlenlotto**
Zahlenlotto *n* lottery by numbers
zahlenmäßig numerical
Zahlenordnung *f s.* **Zahlenfolge**
Zahlenreihe *f* numerical series
Zahlensymbol *n* numerical symbol
Zahlensystem *n* numerical system
Zahlentafel *f* table of figures; multiplication table
Zahlentheorie *f* theory of numbers
Zahlenverhältnis *n* numerical proportion
Zahlenwert *m* numerical value
Zahler *m* payer
Zähler *m* 1. census taker; 2. meter *(gas etc.)*; 3. counter; 4. *(maths)* numerator; 5. teller *(parliament etc.)*

Zählerstand *m* meter reading *(gas etc.)*; *(d.pr.)* counter reading, result of count
Zahlkarte *f* money-order form; giro transfer form
Zählkarte *f* census-paper
zahllos countless, numberless, innumerable
zahlreich numerous
Zahlstelle *f* pay-office, cashier's office
Zahltag *m* payday; *(st.ex.)* settling day
Zahlung *f* payment; settlement, clearance *(of a debt)* ⋄ **an Zahlungs Statt** in lieu of cash [payment]; **auf sofortige ~ bestehen** to demand [insist] on immediate payment; **auf ~ bestehen** to insist on payment; **die ~ anmahnen** to claim [demand] payment, to call on s.o. to pay; **die ~ aufschieben** to defer [delay, postpone] payment; **die ~ aussetzen** to suspend payment; **die ~ einstellen** to stop [suspend] payment; to declare oneself insolvent; **die ~ erfolgt in ...** payment shall be effected in ... *(currency)*; **die ~ erleichtern** to grant favourable terms of payment, to grant payment facilities; **die ~ gerichtlich eintreiben** to enforce payment by legal proceedings; **die ~ leisten** to effect [make] payment, to pay (a debt); **die ~ sicherstellen** to secure payment; **die ~ stunden** to grant a respite in payment, to extend the period of payment; **die ~ verweigern** to refuse payment; **die ~ wieder aufnehmen** to resume payment; **gegen ~ der Gebühren** (up)on payment of the charges [fees]; **in ~ geben** to trade in; **in ~ nehmen** to take in payment; **jmdm. die ~ erlassen** to release s.o. from payment; **jmdn. zur ~ auffordern** to call on s.o. to pay; **mit der ~ im Rückstand bleiben** to be in arrears in one's payment, to default on one's payment; **mit der ~ im Rückstand sein** to be in arrears [behind] with payment; **zur ~ auffordern** to demand payment; **zur ~ der Kosten verurteilt** to be ordered to pay the costs
~, anteilige prorata payment
~, aufgeschobene deferred payment
~ auf Verlangen payment on request
~, außerordentliche extra payment
~, ausstehende outstanding debt
~, avisierte amount advised
~, bare cash payment
~, bargeldlose payment by transfer, cashless payment
~ bei Auftragserteilung cash with order
~ bei Eingang der Waren payable on delivery [at time of delivery]; *(post)* cash on delivery (COD)
~ durch Akkreditiv payment by letter of credit
~, einmalige lumpsum payment
~, effektive real payment

Zahlung

~, **eingegangene** payment received
~, **endgültige** final payment
~, **erste** initial payment
~, **fällige** payment due
~, **fingierte** fictitious payment
~, **freiwillige** voluntary payment
~, **fristgemäße** payment in due time
~ **gegen Dokumente** payment against documents
~ **gegen Kasse** *s.* ~ **in bar**
~, **geleistete** payment made
~ **in bar** payment in cash
~ **in Teilbeträgen** payment by instalments
~, **nachträgliche** subsequent payment; additional payment
~, **prompte** prompt payment
~, **pünktliche** payment in [on] time
~, **säumige** defaulting [slow] payment
~, **sofortige** immediate payment, spot cash
~, **überfällige** overdue payment
~, **unbare** cashless payment
~ **unter Vorbehalt** payment with reservation
~, **verspätete** delayed payment
~, **verweigerte** payment refused
~, **vollständige** payment in full
~ **vor Fälligkeit** payment in advance [anticipation]
~ **zu Gunsten eines Dritten** payment on behalf of a third person
Zählung *f* count(ing); *(stats)* census
Zahlungen *fpl* payments
~, **laufend anfallende** periodic payments
~, **monatliche** monthly payments
~, **rückständige** arrears, arrears in payment
~, **vierteljährliche** quarterly payments
~, **wiederkehrende** recurring payments
~ **zum Parikurs** *(st.ex.)* parity payments
Zahlungsabkommen *n* payment(s) agreement
~ **auf Clearingbasis** payments agreement on a clearing basis
~ **auf Regierungsebene** payments agreement on a governmental basis, governmental payments agreement
Zahlungsabwicklung *f* payment transaction [settlement]
Zahlungsanweisung *f* payment order; *(post)* money-order, postal order; giro transfer order
Zahlungsanzeige *f* advice of payment
Zahlungsart *f* method [way] of payment
Zahlungsaufforderung *f* request [demand] for payment
Zahlungsaufschub *m* extension of time for payment, respite; moratorium ◊ ~ **gewähren** to grant an extension of time for payment, to grant a respite
~, **befristeter** limited respite [extension of time] for payment

Zahlungsauftrag *m* payment order, order for payment
Zahlungsausgang *m* out-payment
Zahlungsausgleich *m* settlement of payments, clearing, settlements
~, **unbarer** clearance
Zahlungsbedingungen *fpl* terms [conditions] of payment
~, **günstige** favourable terms of payment, easy payment
~, **übliche** usual terms of payment
~, **ungünstige** unfavourable terms of payment
Zahlungsbefehl *m* writ of execution of payment; **einen ~ bewirken** to take out a writ of execution (for payment)
Zahlungsbefugnis *f* authority to make payments
Zahlungsbeleg *m* voucher
Zahlungsbereitschaft *f* readiness to pay; liquidity, solvency
Zahlungsbescheinigung *f* receipt
Zahlungsbilanz *f* balance of payments
~, **aktive** credit balance of payments
~, **ausgeglichene** equilibrium in the balance of payments
~, **laufende** current balance of payments
~ **nach Ländern** country-wise balance of payments
~ **nach Währungsgebieten** balance of payments according to currency areas
~, **passive** debit balance of payments
~, **unausgeglichene** disequilibrium in the balance of payments
Zahlungsbilanzausgleich *m* equilibrium in balance of payments
~, **bilateraler** bilateral balancing of the balance of payments
~, **multilateraler** multilateral balancing of the balance of payments
Zahlungsbilanzdefizit *n* deficit in balance of payments, payments deficit
Zahlungsbilanzkredit *m* loan for the balance of payments *(for balancing current account)*
Zahlungsbilanzkrise *f* crisis in the balance of payments, balance-of-payments crisis
Zahlungsbilanzposition *f* item in the balance of payments
Zahlungsbilanzreserve *f* payments balance reserve
Zahlungsbilanzsaldo *m* balance of/on (the) payments (balance)
Zahlungsbilanzschwierigkeiten *fpl* difficulties with the balance of payments
Zahlungsbilanzüberschuß *m* surplus; in balance of payments, balance-of-payments surplus; surplus on current account
Zahlungsdisziplin *f* paying promptly *(debts etc.)*
Zahlungsdokument *n s.* **Zahlungsbeleg**

Zahlungseingang *m* in-payment; payments received
Zahlungseingangsdatum *n* date of receipt of payment *(in ledger)*
Zahlungseinstellung *f* suspension of payment
Zahlungsempfänger *m* payee
Zahlungserleichterung *f* facilities for payment
Zahlungsermächtigung *f s.* **Zahlungsbefugnis**
zahlungsfähig solvent; able to pay; sound *(firm)*
Zahlungsfähigkeit *f* solvency; ability to pay
Zahlungsform *f* method of payment
Zahlungsfrist *f* term [date] of payment ⋄ **die ~ einhalten** to keep to the term of payment; **die ~ verlängern** to extend the time for payment
Zahlungsfristenkontrolle *f* checking payments due
Zahlungsgepflogenheiten *fpl* normal practice of making payments; usual terms of payment
Zahlungsklausel *f* payments clause
zahlungskräftig solvent
Zahlungskredit *m* payments credit
Zahlungsleistung *f* payment
Zahlungsmittel *n* means *(sg or pl)* of payment
~, allgemeines universal means of payment
~, ausländisches foreign currency
~, gesetzliches legal tender
~, inländisches domestic means of payment
~, internationales international means of payment
Zahlungsmittelumlauf *m* money circulation
Zahlungsmodalitäten *fpl s.* **Zahlungsbedingungen**
Zahlungsmodus *m s.* **Zahlungsform**
Zahlungsnachlaß *m* discount; rebate, deduction
Zahlungsnachweis *m s.* **Zahlungsbeleg**
Zahlungsorder *f* payment order
Zahlungsort *m* place of payment
Zahlungsperiode *f s.* **Zahlungszeit**
Zahlungspflicht *f* liability to pay
zahlungspflichtig liable to pay; responsible for payment
Zahlungspflichtiger *m* person [institution] liable to pay
Zahlungsreserve *f* payment reserve (for payments to be made)
Zahlungsrückstand *m* arrears in payments
Zahlungssaldo *m* balance to be paid [settled]
Zahlungsschreiben *n* dunning, request for payment, reminder; warning
Zahlungsschwierigkeiten *fpl* difficulties to pay [in paying] ⋄ **in ~ befindlich** to be financially embarrassed; **in ~ geraten** to run into financial difficulties
Zahlungssperre *f* blocking of payments
Zahlungsstop *m s.* **Zahlungseinstellung**
Zahlungsstundung *f* delay in payment, respite granted for payment

Zahlungssurrogat *n* substitute for money
Zahlungstag *m* payment day; *(st.ex.)* settling day
Zahlungstermin *m* date of payment
~, äußerster final date of payment
~, mittlerer average due date of payment
~, vereinbarter contractual due date of payment
Zahlungstitel *mpl* bonds; obligations; securities
Zahlungsübereinkommen *n* payment(s) agreement
Zahlungsüberhang *m* rest of payment; excess of payment
zahlungsunfähig insolvent; unable to pay
Zahlungsunfähigkeit *f* insolvency; inability to pay
Zahlungsunion *f* payments union
Zahlungsunterbrechung *f* interruption of regular payments
Zahlungsverbindlichkeit *f* liability to pay
Zahlungsverbot *n* stoppage of payments
Zahlungsvereinbarung *f s.* **Zahlungsübereinkommen**
Zahlungsverkehr *m* payment transfers [transactions]
~, barer cash payments
~, bargeldloser cashless transfers, clearance
~, inländischer domestic payment transactions
~, internationaler international payment transactions
~, nichtkommerzieller noncommercial payments
~, unbarer cashless payments
Zahlungsvermögen *n s.* **Zahlungsfähigkeit**
Zahlungsverpflichtung *f* financial responsibility [commitment]
Zahlungsverpflichtungen *fpl* financial commitments
~, auswärtige foreign (financial) commitments
Zahlungsverschreibung *f* promissory note; (mortgage) bond, debenture (stock/bond)
Zahlungsversprechen *n* promise to pay
~, gesamtschuldnerisches joint obligation [promise] to pay
Zahlungsverweigerung *f* refusal to pay, repudiation of payments
Zahlungsverzögerung *f* delay in payment
Zahlungsverzug *m* default in payment
Zahlungsvollmacht *f* authorization to pay
Zahlungsvorgang *m s.* **Zahlung**
Zahlungsweise *f* mode of payment
Zahlungszeit *f* time of payment
Zahlungszeitpunkt *m s.* **Zahlungstag**
Zahlungsziel *n* grace period, period allowed for payment ⋄ **ein ~ einräumen** to grant a respite
~, offenes open terms
Zählwert *m (d.pr.)* count number

Zahnarzt *m* dentist, dental surgeon
Zeche *f* 1. mine; coal pit; mining company; 2. bill
Zechenbesitzer *m* mine owner
Zedent *m* transferor, assigner; endorser
zedierbar transferable, assignable; to be endorsed
zedieren to transfer, to assign; to endorse
Zedierung *f* transfer
Zehntelstelle *f (stats)* decile
Zehntelwert *m s.* Zehntelstelle
Zeichen *n* sign, mark; brand, trademark *(goods)*; symbol *(map etc.)*; signal identification; character ⋄ **Ihr ~** your reference; **unser ~** our reference
Zeichenbüro *n* drawing office
Zeichendauer *f (d.pr.)* character duration; digit period [time]
Zeichendichte *f (d.pr.)* character density
Zeichenelement *n (d.pr.)* format character; signal element
Zeichenerklärung *f* signs and symbols, explanation of signs and symbols used
Zeichenfolge *f (d.pr.)* character string
Zeichenfolgenfunktion *f (d.pr.)* string function
Zeichengruppe *f (d.pr.)* burst
Zeichenkontrolle *f (d.pr.)* character check
Zeichenschutz *m* trademark and design protection
Zeichensystem *m* code
Zeichenteilmenge *f (d.pr.)* character subset
zeichnen 1. to draw; to design; to mark; to brand; 2. to sign *(documents etc.)*; 3. to subscribe for *(bonds etc.)*, to subscribe to *(loans etc.)*
Zeichner *m* 1. drawer; designer; 2. subscriber
~, technischer industrial designer; draughtsman
zeichnerisch by (means of) a graph
Zeichnung *f* 1. drawing, design; diagram; 2. subscription *(loan etc.)*
~ einer Anleihe subscription to a loan
~, maßstabsgerechte scale drawing
Zeichnungsbedingungen *fpl* terms of subscription
Zeichnungsbefugnis *f* authorization to sign
zeichnungsberechtigt authorized to sign; entitled to subscribe
Zeichnungsberechtigter *m* allotee *(shares etc.)*
Zeichnungsberechtigung *f* authorization to sign; right to subscribe *(loan etc.)*
Zeichnungsbetrag *m* amount subscribed
Zeichnungsbogen *m* subscription list
Zeichnungsfrist *f* subscription period
Zeichnungskurs *m* issue price
Zeichnungsliste *f s.* Zeichnungsbogen
Zeichnungsvollmacht *f s.* Zeichnungsberechtigung

Zeit *f* time, space of time; term; duration; period, epoch, era, age; season; days, times ⋄ **auf einige ~** for a certain time; **auf ~ on** credit, on account; forward *(purchase etc.)*; for a fixed period; **auf ~ kaufen** to buy forward [on credit]; **auf ~ verkaufen** to sell on credit; **im Laufe der ~** in the course of time; **in absehbarer ~** in the foreseeable future, within a reasonable period of time; **in früherer ~** formerly, in early times; **in jüngster ~** quite recently; **mit der ~** with time; **nach einiger ~** after some time; **über seine ~ (frei) bestimmen** to dispose of one's time (freely); **um diese ~** about that time; **vor kurzer ~** a short time ago; **zu einer bestimmten ~** at a given time; **zur festgesetzten ~** at a [the] fixed time, at the time fixed; **zur ~** at present; at the time
~, angemessene reasonable time
~, arbeitsfreie free [spare] time
~, beobachtete observed time
~, bestimmende governing time
~, festgesetzte stated [fixed] time
~, flaue slack period
~, freie leisure (time)
~ für auftragsfremde Tätigkeit time allotted for jobbing work
~ für Fehlleistungen nonproductive time
~ für natürliche Bedürfnisse und arbeitsbedingte Erholungspausen (work) break, interval (for refreshment)
~ für persönlich bedingte vermeidbare Untätigkeit avoidable idle time
~ für Vorbereitungs- und Abschlußarbeiten (machine) setting and job dismantling time
~ für vorgeschriebene Pausen prescribed break
~ je Arbeitsvorgang cycle time
~, Mitteleuropäische (MEZ) Central European Time (CET)
~, nicht berücksichtigte unaccounted time
~, Osteuropäische (OEZ) East European Time
~, vorgegebene allowed time
~, Westeuropäische (WEZ) Greenwich Mean Time (GMT)
Zeitablauf *m* lapse of time
Zeitablaufplan *m* time schedule; timetable
Zeitabschnitt *m* epoch, period
Zeitabstand *m* time interval
Zeitalter *n* era; generation; epoch
Zeitangabe *f* date; exact date and hour
Zeitanteil *m* portion of time
~ des Arbeitsvorganges, vom Arbeitsablauf abhängiger process-controlled time
~ des Arbeitsvorganges, von der Maschine abhängiger machine controlled time
Zeitaufnahme *f* timing

Zeitaufwand *m* time spent
Zeitbasis *f* time base
~ einer Prognose base period of a forecast
Zeitbegriff *m* concept(ion) of time
Zeitbudget *n* time budget
~ der Bevölkerung time budget of the population
Zeitdauer *f* (length of) time; period; term; duration
Zeitdruck *m* pressure of time, under pressure
Zeiteffekt *m* time effect *(impact of the dynamics of the reproduction process on all its elements, its structure and its results within a certain - past or future - period of time)*
Zeiteinheit *f* unit of time
Zeiteinsparung *f* economizing [saving] of time
Zeiteinteilung *f* schedule, timing
Zeiten *fpl* times ⋄ in ~ der Not in times of need
Zeitermittlung *f s.* Zeitaufnahme
zeitersparend timesaving
Zeitersparnis *f* saving of time, timesaving
Zeitfaktor *m* time factor [element]; *(d.pr.)* time-contributing factor
Zeitfolge *f* chronological order
Zeitfonds *m* total (working) time available
zeitgemäß timely; seasonable, up-to-date
Zeitgeschäft *n* time purchase [bargain], *(Am)* forward transaction
Zeitgeschmack *m* prevailing taste
Zeitgliederung *f* time scheduling
~ der Produktion production time scheduling, break-down of operating time
Zeithorizont *m* time horizon
Zeitkarte *f* season ticket
Zeitkauf *m* forward purchase
Zeitkennziffer *f* time indicator
Zeitkonstante *f* time constant
Zeitlauf *m* period [course] of time
Zeitlohn *m* time wages
Zeitmangel *m* lack of time
Zeitmaß *n* measure of time; time scale
Zeitmaßstab *m* time scale
Zeitmessung *f* measurement of time, timing
Zeitmittelwert *m* time average, mean time value
Zeitmittelwertbildung *f* time averaging
Zeitnorm *f* working-time standard
Zeitnormativ *n* time standard [norm] *(time needed for producing s.th.)*
Zeitnormativkatalog *m* catalogue of time standards [norms]
Zeitökonomie *f* economy of time
Zeitpacht *f* limited lease
Zeitplan *m* timetable
Zeitplanung *f* drawing up a timetable, time scheduling
Zeitpreis *m* present [current] price

Zeitpunkt *m* point of time, moment, instant
Zeitquantum *n* time quantum
Zeitrafferaufnahme *f* memomotion photography
zeitraubend time-consuming
Zeitraum *m* period, space of time
Zeitrechnung *f* chronology
Zeitreihe *f* time series
Zeitrente *f* annuity
Zeitreserven *fpl* time resources
Zeitrichtwerte *mpl* work norms
Zeitsichtwechsel *m* after-sight bill
Zeitskala *f* time scale
Zeitspanne *f* space [length] of time
zeitsparend time-saving
Zeitstaffelung *f (d.pr.)* time sharing
Zeitstempel *m* (automatic) time stamp
Zeitsteuerung *f* timing
Zeitstrukturkoeffizient *m* coefficient of time structure
Zeitstudie *f* time study
Zeitstudien *fpl* work measurement, time studies
Zeitstudium *n* time analysis [study]
Zeitsummenmethode *f* method of measuring labour productivity *(by comparing goods produced with living labour expended)*
Zeittafel *f* chronological table
Zeitteilverfahren *n (d.pr.)* time sharing
Zeitüberwachungsdauer *f (d.pr.)* time-out period
Zeit-Umkehr-Probe *f (stats)* time-reversal test
Zeitungsabonnement *n* subscription to a paper
Zeitungsanzeige *f* newspaper [press] advertisement; announcement in the press
Zeitungsinserat *n s.* Zeitungsanzeige
Zeitungskiosk *m* news-stall, newspaper stall, *(Am)* newsstand
Zeitungsreklame *f* newspaper [press] advertisement
Zeitungsverkäufer *m* newsvendor, newspaper seller
Zeitungsvertriebsamt *n* central office for the sale [distribution] of newspapers (and periodicals)
Zeitungswerbung *f* newspaper [press] advertising
Zeitungswesen *n* journalism; the daily press
Zeitvergeudung *f* waste of time
Zeitverhältnis *n* time relation
Zeitverlust *m* loss of time
Zeitverzögerungskoeffizient *m* coefficient of delay
Zeitvorgabe *f* prescribed time *(for producing a component)*
zeitweilig temporary, for the time being
zeitweise temporarily, from time to time, occasionally

Zeitwert *m* 1. present [current] value, time value; 2. time spent *(in determining* **Zeitnormativ)**
~, **gewählter** selected time value
Zeitwertquotient *m* time-value quotient
Zeitwertversicherung *f* insurance according to time value
Zeit-Wirkungs-Verteilung *f (stats)* response-time distribution
Zeitzuschlag *m* additional time, time allowance
~ **bei Wechsel der Serie** batch changeover allowance
~ **bei Wechsel des Arbeitsauftrages** job changeover allowance
~, **betrieblich vereinbarter** policy allowance
~ **für arbeitsablaufbedingte Wartezeit** unoccupied time allowance
~ **für Ausschuß** reject allowance
~ **für Erholung und persönliche Bedürfnisse** relaxation allowance
~, **für zusätzliche Arbeiten** excess work allowance
zensieren to examine; to give marks; to censor *(news etc.)*
Zensor *m* censor
Zensur *f* marks; censorship *(news etc.)*
Zensus *m* census
zentral central ✧ ~ **gelegen** centrally situated
Zentralarchiv *n* central record office
Zentralbank *f* central bank, Federal [Reserve] Bank, *(Am)* Federal Reserve Bank
zentralbankfähig eligible for rediscount by the central bank *(bills etc.)*
Zentralbankgeld *n* central bank money, Federal [Reserve] Bank money, *(Am)* Federal Reserve Bank money
Zentralbankpolitik *f* central bank credit policy
Zentralbankrat *m* board of governors of the central bank, *(Am)* Board of Governors of the Federal Reserve System
Zentralbanksystem *n* reserve bank system
Zentralbehörde *f* central authority
Zentrale *f* main [head, central] office; central telephone exchange
Zentraleinheit *f (d.pr.)* central processing unit (CPU)
Zentralelement *n (d.pr.)* central processing element (CPE)
Zentralentscheidung *f (plan)* central decision, decision at the central level
Zentralentscheidungsfindung *f* central decision-making, decision-making at the central level
Zentralinstitut *n* central institute
Zentralisation *f* centralization
zentralisieren to centralize
zentralisiert centralized

Zentralisierung *f* centralization
Zentralisierungsfunktion *f* centralizing function *(of state finance etc.)*
Zentralisierungstendenzen *fpl* centralizing tendencies
Zentralismus *m* centralism
Zentralmarkt *m* central market
Zentralnotenbank *f* central [federal reserve] bank
Zentralorganisation *f* central organization
Zentralregierung *f* central government
Zentralregistratur *f* central registry office
Zentralspeicher *m (d.pr.)* main memory
Zentralstelle *f* central [co-ordinating] office
Zentralsteuerung *f* central control; *(d.pr.)* centralized (common) control
Zentralverwaltung *f* central administration [office]
Zentralverwaltungswirtschaft *f* centrally planned economy
Zentralwert *m (stats)* median
Zentrierfehler *m (d.pr.)* centring error
Zentroid-Verfahren *n (stats)* centroid method
Zentrum *n* centre; middle
~, **agrochemisches (ACZ)** agro-chemical centre
~ **der Lage** *(stats)* centre of location
~, **wissenschaftlich-technisches (WTZ)** scientific and technological centre
zerbrechen to break, to shatter, to smash
zerbrechlich fragile *(glass etc.)*; brittle *(metal etc.)*
Zerfall *m* ruin, decay; decadence; disintegration
zerfallen to fall to pieces; to decay
zerlegbar collapsible *(boat etc.)*, demountable *(machine etc.)*; detachable *(furniture etc.)*; *(maths)* divisible
zerlegen to part, to divide, to separate; to cut up; to carve *(meat etc.)*; to split up; to dismantle *(machine etc.)*; to strip *(s.th. down)*
Zerlegung *f* splitting up; dismantling *(machine etc.)*; *(stats)* partition; decomposition
~ **von Mischverteilungen** *(stats)* dissection of heterogeneous distributions
~ **von χ^2** *(stats)* partition of chi-squared [χ^2]
zerrütten to ruin *(economy etc.)*; to disorganize *(currency etc.)*; to wreck *(scheme etc.)*
Zerrüttung *f* ruin *(economy etc.)*; disorganization *(currency etc.)*; wrecking *(scheme etc.)*
zersplittern to disperse; to splinter *(wood etc.)*; to dissipate *(resources, forces etc.)*
Zersplitterung *f* dispersal *(manufacturing, investments etc.)*; dissipation
Zertifikat *n* certificate
Zession *f* assignment, transfer; conveyance *(real estate etc.)*
zessionsfähig assignable
Zessionskredit *m* credit on abandonment of claims

Zettel *m* slip; label; note
Zeug *n* stuff, material; clothes; textiles; things; tools
Zeuge *m* witness
zeugen 1. to bear witness, to testify; 2. to procreate
Zeugenaussage *f* evidence
~, **belastende** incriminating evidence
~, **falsche** false evidence
~, **mündliche** oral evidence
~, **schriftliche** written evidence
Zeugenaussagen *fpl*:
~, **(einander) widersprechende** conflicting evidence
Zeugenbeeinflussung *f* tampering with witnesses; interference with witnesses
Zeugenbestechung *f* subornation of a witness
Zeugeneinvernahme *f* oral evidence; interrogation
Zeugengeld *n* compensation money for witness
Zeugenvernehmung *f* hearing of witness
Zeugnis *n* certificate, attestation; *(jur)* testimony, evidence; testimonial *(jobs etc.)*; report *(school etc.)*
Zeugnisabschrift *f* copy of a testimonial [a certificate, an evidence, a report]
Zeugnisverweigerung *f* refusal to give evidence
ziehen 1. to pull; to draw *(shares etc.)*; to tow *(boats etc.)*; 2. *(agric)* to grow
Ziehung *f* drawing *(shares etc.)*
Ziehungsrechte *npl* drawing rights
Ziehungstag *m* drawing day
Ziel *n* 1. aim, target, goal, object, objective; 2. destination; 3. *(fin)* date of payment ⋄ **auf** ~ on credit, forward; **auf** ~ **kaufen** to buy on terms
Zieladresse *f (d.pr.)* destination address
Zielausdruck *m (d.pr.)* designational expression
Zielbahnhof *m* station of destination; terminal station
Zielbaummethode *f (plan)* target-tree method
Zielertrag *m (d.pr.)* designational proceeds
Zielertragsmatrix *f (d.pr.)* matrix of designational proceeds
Zielfunktion *f (plan)* target function
Zielgeschäft *n* time [forward] purchase
Zielgröße *f* objective
Zielhierarchie *f* target hierarchy
Zielkauf *m s.* **Zielgeschäft**
Zielkette *f* target chain, chain of targets
Zielkredit *m* time credit
Zielmärkte *mpl* target markets
Zielmethode *f* target method
Zielort *m* point [place] of destination
Zielprämie *f* incentive bonus
Zielpreis *m* basing rate
Zielprognose *f* target forecast [prognosis]

Zielprogramm *n* target programme; object programme
~, **langfristiges** long-term target programme
Zielprogrammethode *f* target programming method
Zielsetzung *f s.* **Zielstellung**
Zielstellung *f* fixing an aim; objective, target
~, **technisch-ökonomische** technical and economic objective [goal]
Zielsystem *n* system of targets
Zielverkauf *m* forward selling
Zielwert *m (d.pr.)* target value
Zierkeramiker *m* ornamental ceramics worker
Ziffer *f* number, figure; cipher; digit
Ziffern *fpl*:
~, **amtliche** official figures; official return
Ziffernmaterial *n* data
Ziffernrechenmaschine *f* digital computer
Ziffernübertragungszeit *f (d.pr.)* digit period
Zigarettensteuer *f* tobacco tax, duty on tobacco
Zimmer *n* room ⋄ **ein** ~ **belegen** to occupy a room; **ein** ~ **bestellen** to book a room; **ein** ~ **mieten** to rent a room; **ein** ~ **reservieren** to reserve a room; **ein** ~ **vermieten** to let a room; ~ **frei** room to let
~, **möbliertes** furnished room
~, **nichtmöbliertes** unfurnished room
Zimmerer *m* carpenter
Zimmergröße *f* size of a room
Zimmerkellner *m* floor waiter
Zimmermädchen *n* chambermaid
Zimmermann *m* carpenter
Zimmernachweis *m* accommodation bureau
Zimmerpreis *m* room rent; cost of a room *(hotel)*
Zimmerreservierung *f* room reservation
Zimmervermieter *m* landlord
Zimmervermietung *f* letting of rooms; accommodation bureau
Zinngießer *m* tinsmith, tinner, pewterer
Zins *m* 1. interest; 2. tribute ⋄ **auf** ~ to interest
~, **einfacher** (simple) interest
Zinsabbau *m* reduction of interest
Zinsabkommen *n* agreement on interest rates
Zinsabschnitt *m* coupon
Zinsabzug *m* interest discount [reduction]
Zinsanleihe *f* interest bearing loan
Zinsarbitrage *f* interest arbitrage
Zinsauflauf *m* accrual of interest
Zinsaufstellung *f* statement on interest
Zinsaufwand *m s.* **Zinsaufwendungen**
Zinsaufwendungen *fpl* amount of interest to be paid
Zinsausfall *m* loss of interest
Zinsausgleich *m* adjustment of interest
zinsbar *s.* **zinstragend**
Zinsbedingungen *fpl* terms of interest

Zinsbelastung f interest charge
Zinsberechnung f interest computation, calculation of interest
Zinsbogen m coupon-sheet
zinsbringend s. zinstragend
Zinsdarleh(e)n n s. **Zinsanleihe**
Zinsdivisor m interest denominator
Zinseingang m interest received
Zinseingänge mpl accrued interest
Zinseinkommen n income from interest
Zinsen mpl interest; (acc) interest charges ✧ **auf**
~ s. **auf Zins**; **die ~ kapitalisieren** to capitalize interest; **die ~ zum Kapital schlagen** to capitalize interest; **mit ~** with interest; **mit ~ belasten** to charge interest; **ohne ~** without interest; **~ abwerfen** to draw interest; to earn interest; **~ ausrechnen** to calculate interest; **~ berechnen** s. **~ ausrechnen**; **~ bringen** s. **~ tragen**; **~ tragen** to bear [earn] interest
~ aus Kapitalanlagen interest on capital investments
~ aus Kontokorrenten (bank) interest on current accounts
~, fällige interest due [payable]
~, gestundete deferred interest
~ gutgeschriebene credited interest
~, halbjährliche semi-annual interest
~, jährliche annual interest
~, kalkulatorische imputed interest
~, laufende current interest
~, reine true interest
~, rückständige interest in arrears, arrears in interest
~, überfällige overdue interest
~, übliche usual interest
~, vereinbarte contractual interest, interest agreed upon
Zinsendienst m payment [servicing] of interest
Zinsenkonto n s. **Zinskonto**
Zinsenlast f s. **Zinslast**
Zinsensammelkonto n collectible interest account
Zinserhöhung f raising the rate of interest
Zinsermäßigung f reduction of the rate of interest
Zinserneuerungsschein m renewal coupon
Zinsertrag m yield in interest
Zinserträge mpl proceeds in interest, interest income
Zinsertragssteuer f tax on interest
Zinseszins m compound interest ✧ **auf ~ at** compound interest
Zinseszinsbetrag m compound amount
Zinseszinsformel f formula for compound interest
Zinseszinsrechnung f calculation of compound interest

Zinsforderung f interest claim
Zinsformel f interest formula
zinsfrei interest-free
Zinsfuß m s. **Zinssatz**
Zinsgarantie f guaranteed interest
Zinsgefälle n interest differential [margin]
Zinsgewinn m interest income; (st.ex.) profit from differential rates of interest
Zinsgut n leasehold
Zinsgutschrift f crediting of interest; amount of interest credited
Zinshöhe f amount of interest
Zinsklausel f interest clause
Zinskonditionen fpl terms of credits [interest payment]
Zinskonto n interest account
Zinskosten pl interest
Zinslast f interest charge
Zinsliste f 1. sheet of coupons, (Am) talon; 2. list of accrued interest
zinslos without interest, free of interest, interest-free, non-interest bearing
Zinsmarge f interest margin
Zinsmehraufwand m (acc) net interest paid [payable]
Zinsmehrertrag m (acc) net interest earnings [earned]
Zinsnachlaß m s. **Zinsermäßigung**
Zinspapier n security on interest
Zinsperiode f interest-paying period
zinspflichtig interest-bearing; subject to rent
Zinspolitik f interest policy
Zinsrate f s. **Zinssatz**
Zinsrechnung f calculation of interest
Zinsrückerstattung f refunding of interest
Zinsrückstände mpl s. **Zinsen, rückständige**
Zinssaldo m balance of interest
Zinssammelkonto n s. **Zinsensammelkonto**
Zinssatz m rate of interest
~, amtlicher official rate of interest
~, ermäßigter reduced rate of interest
~, gesetzlicher legal rate of interest
~, gleitender sliding rate of interest
Zinsschein m coupon; dividend warrant
Zinsscheinbogen m coupon sheet
Zinssenkung f s. **Zinsermäßigung**
Zinsspanne f (bank) margin of bank profit
Zinstabelle f table of interest rates
zinstragend interest-bearing
Zinsumwandlung f conversion of interest
Zinsunterschied m interest differential
Zinsverbindlichkeiten fpl interest to be paid, accrued interest payable
Zinsvergünstigung f deduction of the rate of interest, preferential rates of interest
Zinsvergütung f rebate on interest
Zinsverlust m loss of interest

Zinsversprechen *n s.* **Zinsklausel**
Zinszahlung *f* payment of interest
zirka about, approximately, circa
Zirkaklausel *f* circa clause
Zirkapreis *m* approximate price
Zirkular *n* circular
Zirkulärformel *f (stats)* circular formula
Zirkularkreditbrief *m* 1. letter of credit; 2. credentials *(of representative)*
Zirkularreihenformel *f s.* **Zirkulärformel**
Zirkularscheck *m* travel(l)er's cheque [(Am) check]
Zirkulartest *m (stats)* circular test
Zirkulation *f* circulation
Zirkulationsakt *m s.* **Zirkulation**
Zirkulationsart *f* kind of circulation
Zirkulationsbeziehungen *fpl* relationships in circulation *(money, commodities etc.)*
zirkulationsfähig marketable, saleable *(goods etc.)*; fungible *(as money)*
Zirkulationsfonds *m* circulation funds
Zirkulationsform *f s.* **Zirkulationsart**
Zirkulationsfunktion *f* circulation function
Zirkulationsgeschwindigkeit *f* velocity of circulation *(velocity of commodity and money turnover)*
Zirkulationskanal *m* channel of circulation
Zirkulationskapital *n* working [circulation] capital
Zirkulationskosten *pl* circulation costs
~, **allgemeine** general costs of circulation
~ **des Außenhandels** costs in conducting foreign trade
~, **direkte** *s.* ~, **reine**
~, **echte** *s.* ~, **reine**
~, **heterogene** *s.* ~, **unechte**
~, **indirekte** indirect circulation costs *(advertisement etc.)*
~, **reine** pure costs of circulation *(directly connected with the transformation of money into commodities and vice-versa)*
~, **unechte** finishing, packing, storing and transport costs *(in the sphere of circulation)*
~, **unreine** *s.* ~, **unechte**
Zirkulationskredit *m* commercial credit
Zirkulationsmasse *f* 1. amount of money in circulation; 2. (amount of) commodities in circulation
Zirkulationsmittel *npl* means of circulation
Zirkulationsperiode *f* period of circulation
Zirkulationsphase *f* stage of circulation
Zirkulationsprozeß *m* circulation process
Zirkulationsreserve *f s.* **Zirkulationsvorrat**
Zirkulationssphäre *f* sphere of circulation
Zirkulationsstadium *n s.* **Zirkulationsphase**
Zirkulationsstockung *f* interruption of circulation

Zirkulationstätigkeit *f* circulation activities
Zirkulationsverflechtungsbilanz *f* circulation input-output table *(for planning, balancing, and analysing economic relations in the sphere of circulation as well as between circulation and other processes)*
Zirkulationsvorgang *m* (process of) circulation
Zirkulationsvorrat *m* stocks of commodities and money *(for circulation)*
Zirkulationsweg *m s.* **Zirkulationskanal**
Zirkulationswert *m* price *(of goods, shares etc.)*
Zirkulationszeit *f* circulation time
zirkulieren to circulate
zirkulierend circulating, current
Ziseleur *m* ornamental setter
Zivilangestellter *m* civil employee
Zivilbevölkerung *f* civilian population
Zivilgesetzbuch *n* civil code
Zivilgesetzgebung *f* legislation on civil matters
Zivilisation *f* civilization
Zivilluftfahrt *f* civil aviation
Zivilluftfahrtabkommen *n* civil aviation agreement
Zivilprozeß *m* civil action
Zivilprozeßordnung *f* Code of Civil Procedure, *(Am)* Civil Practice Act
Zivilrecht *n* civil law
zivilrechtlich under [according to] civil law
Zivilverwaltung *f* civil administration
Z-Karte *f (stats)* Z-chart
Z-Methode *f (stats)* Lidstone-method
Zoll *m* 1. inch; 2. *(cust)* (customs) duty; tariff; toll; 3. customs house [clearance] ◊ **aus dem ~ freigeben** to remove the seal from *(sth.)*; **den ~ aufheben** to abolish customs duties; **den ~ erhöhen** to increase duties; **den ~ passieren** to go through the customs; **den ~ senken** to lower [reduce] the rate of duty; **~ auferlegen** to impose duties (on); **~ bezahlen** *s.* **~ entrichten**; **~ einnehmen** to take customs duties; **~ entrichten** to pay customs duties; **~ erheben** to levy customs duties; **~ rückerstatten** to refund customs duties
~, **gleitender** flexible tariff
~, **kombinierter** compound duty
Zollabfertigung *f* customs clearance [clearing]
Zollabfertigungsgebühren *fpl* (customs) clearance charges [fees]
Zollabfertigungskosten *pl* costs of customs clearance
Zollabfertigungspapiere *npl* customs clearance papers
Zollabfertigungsschein *m* customs permit; bill of sufferance *(ship)*
Zollabfertigungsstelle *f* customs office
Zollabgabe *f* customs duty
Zollabkommen *n* customs agreement

Zollabteilung *f* customs department
Zollager *n* bonded [in-bond] warehouse
Zollamt *n* customs-office, customs
zollamtlich customs, by the customs
Zollangabe *f* customs declaration
Zollangelegenheiten *fpl* tariff matters
Zollangestellter *m* customs official [officer]
Zollanmeldung *f* customs declaration
~ **für zollfreie Waren** (customs) declaration for duty-free goods
Zollaufschlag *m* additional duty
Zollaufsicht *f* customs inspection
Zollaufsichtsstelle *f* customs house
Zollausfuhrerklärung *f* customs declaration outwards
Zollauskunft *f* tariff information
Zollausland *n* nondomestic [foreign] territory (for customs purposes)
Zollautonomie *f* customs tariff autonomy
Zollbahnhof *m* customs station
Zollbanderole *f* customs revenue stamp
Zollbeamter *m* customs officer
Zollbearbeitung *f s.* **Zollabfertigung**
Zollbefreiung *f* exemption from (customs) duty
Zollbefund *m* customs findings, findings of customs inspection
Zollbegleitpapiere *npl* customs documents *(accompanying goods)*
Zollbegleitschein *m* customs document *(accompanying goods)*
Zollbegünstigung *f* preferential treatment in customs tariffs
Zollbehandlung *f s.* **Zollabfertigung**
Zollbehörde *f* customs authorities
Zollbelastung *f s.* **Zoll 2.**
Zollbemessung *f* assessment of customs duties
Zollbemessungsgrundlage *f* basis of customs duties
Zollberechnung *f* calculation of duty
Zollbeschau *f s.* **Zollkontrolle**
Zollbescheid *m* customs notice
Zollbescheinigung *f* customs certificate; clearance certificate *(ship)*
Zollbeschlagnahme *f* customs seizure
Zollbestimmungen *fpl* customs regulations
Zollbewertung *f* customs valuation
Zollbüro *n s.* **Zollabfertigungsstelle**
Zolldeklaration *f s.* **Zollerklärung**
Zolldepot *n* (customs) bonded warehouse
Zolldienst *m* customs service
Zolldienststelle *f s.* **Zollabfertigungsstelle**
Zolldifferenzierung *f* variable (customs) duty rates
Zolldiskriminierung *f* tariff discrimination
Zolldokument *n* customs document
Zolldurchfuhrschein *m* transhipment bond note
Zolldurchlaßschein *m s.* **Zolldurchfuhrschein**

Zolldurchsuchung *f s.* **Zollkontrolle**
Zolleinfuhrerklärung *f s.* **Zolleinfuhrschein**
Zolleinfuhrschein *m* bill of entry
Zolleingangsdeklaration *f s.* **Zolleinfuhrschein**
Zolleingangsschein *m s.* **Zolleinfuhrschein**
Zolleinlagerung *f* bonding
Zolleinnahmen *fpl* customs revenue
Zollempfangsbescheinigung *f s.* **Zollquittung**
Zollentrichtung *f* payment of duty
Zollerhebung *f* levying of customs duties
Zollerhöhung *f* increase of tariffs
Zollerklärung *f* customs declaration
Zollerlaß *m* exemption from customs duties
Zollerledigung *f* customs clearance
Zollerleichterungen *fpl* customs facilities
Zollermäßigung *f* reduction of tariffs
Zollerstattung *f s.* **Zollrückvergütung**
Zollfahndung *f* prevention of smuggling; tracing smuggled goods [smugglers]
Zollfahndungsdienst *m* customs intelligence service
Zollfaktura *f* legalized invoice *(for the customs office)*
Zollformalitäten *fpl* customs formalities
Zollfragen *fpl s.* **Zollangelegenheiten**
zollfrei duty-free
Zollfreigabe *f* (customs) release from bond
Zollfreigabeschein *m* customs permit
Zollfreihafen *m* free port
Zollfreiheit *f* exemption from duty
Zollfreischein *m s.* **Zollfreigabeschein**
Zollfreischreibung *f* clearance of nondutiable goods
Zollfreizone *f* duty-free zone
Zollgebiet *n* customs district [territory]
Zollgebühren *fpl* customs duties
Zollgebührenrechnung *f* bill of customs
zollgeschützt tariff-protected
Zollgesetz *n* customs and tariff act
Zollgesetzgebung *f* tariff [customs] legislation
Zollgrenze *f* customs frontier [border]
Zollgut *n* bonded goods
Zollhafen *m* (bonded) port
Zollhaus *n s.* **Zollamt**
Zollherabsetzung *f* (general) reduction of customs duties
Zollhinterzieher *m* customs defrauder; smuggler
Zollhinterziehung *f* evasion of customs duty
Zollhoheit *f* customs autonomy; right to collect customs duties
Zollinhaltserklärung *f s.* **Zollerklärung**
Zollinland *n* domestic territory (for customs purposes), customs area
Zollinspektor *m* customs inspector
Zollkai *m/n* customs quay [wharf]
Zollkasse *f* customs collection office
Zollklarierung *f s.* **Zollerklärung**

Zollkontrolle *f* customs examination [check(ing)]
Zollkonvention *f* (international) customs convention
Zollmauer *f* tariff wall
Zollnacherhebung *f* additional levy of customs duties
Zollnachweis *m s.* **Zollbescheinigung**
Zöllner *m* customs collector; customs official
Zollniederlage *f s.* **Zollager**
Zollnomenklatur *f* classification of customs rates of traded goods
Zollpapiere *npl* customs papers; clearance papers *(ship)*
zollpflichtig dutiable, liable to customs duties
Zollplombe *f s.* **Zollsiegel**
Zollpolitik *f* tariff policy
Zollprüfung *f s.* **Zollkontrolle**
Zollquittung *f* customs receipt; certificate of clearance *(ships)*
Zollrechnung *f* bill of duties *(paid or to be paid)*; amount of customs duties
Zollrecht *n* customs laws; tariff legislation
Zollreform *f* tariff reform
Zollregister *n* customs tariffs
Zollrevision *f s.* **Zollkontrolle**
Zollrückgabeschein *m* customs debenture, debenture certificate
Zollrückvergütung *f* duty drawback, *(Am)* customs rebate
Zollsachverständiger *m* customs expert; tariffs expert
Zollsatz *m* rate of duty
Zollschein *m s.* **Zollquittung**
Zollschranke *f* customs [tariff] barrier
Zollschuppen *m s.* **Zollager**
Zollschutz *m* tariff protection
Zollschutzschranken *fpl* tariff barriers
Zollsenkung *f* tariff reduction
~, **individuelle** reduction of import duties for certain goods
Zollsiegel *n* customs seal
Zollskala *f* scale of customs rates
Zollspeicher *m s.* **Zollager**
Zollstation *f s.* **Zollbahnhof**
Zollstelle *f s.* **Zollabfertigungsstelle**
Zollstempel *m* customs stamp
Zollstreitigkeit *f* tariff dispute
Zollsystem *n* tariff system
Zolltarif *m* tariff; customs (rate of duties); tariff information catalogue
~, **gemischter** compound tariff
Zolltarifänderung *f* revision of tariff rates
Zolltarifschema *n* customs tariff table
Zollüberwachung *f* customs watch
Zoll- und Devisenerklärung *f* declaration of goods and currency, customs declaration

Zollunion *f* customs union
Zolluntersuchung *f s.* **Zollkontrolle**
Zollverein *m s.* **Zollunion**
Zollvereinbarung *f* tariff agreement
Zollvergehen *n* customs offence
Zollvergünstigung *f* tariff preference(s)
Zollvergütung *f s.* **Zollrückvergütung**
Zollverhandlungen *fpl* tariff negotiations
Zollvermerk *m* customs remarks *(with a stamp)*
Zollverordnungen *fpl s.* **Zollgesetz**
Zollverschluß *m* bond, customs seal ◊ **unter ~** in bond; **unter ~ lassen** to leave in bond
Zollverschlußvorschriften *fpl* bonding requirements
Zollverschlußwaren *fpl* bonded [in-bond] goods
Zollvertrag *m* tariff treaty
Zollverwaltung *f* customs authorities
Zollverzeichnis *n* tariff information catalogue
Zollvormerkschein *m* excise bond, bond note
Zollvorschriften *fpl* customs rules
Zollvorzugssatz *m* preferential rate of duty
Zollwert *m* dutiable value
Zollwesen *n s.* **Zollsystem**
Zone *f* zone; territory; area
Zonenabgrenzung *f* zoning
Zonenpreis *m* zonal price
Zonentarif *m* zonal transport rate
Zoologe *m* zoologist
Z-Punktwerte *mpl (stats)* z-scores
~, **standardisierte** *(stats)* standardized scores
Z-Test *m (stats)* z-test
Z-Transformation *f (stats)* z-transformation
Zubehör *n* accessories; fittings; equipment
Zubehörliste *f* list of accessories
Zubehörteile *npl s.* **Zubehör**
Zubereitung *f* preparation; dressing
zubilligen to concede, to grant, to allow *(privileges etc.)*
Zubilligung *f* concession, grant *(privileges etc.)*
Zubringer *m* access road
Zubringerdienst *m* 1. feeder (transport) service; 2. *(d.pr.)* access
~, **mitlaufender** *(d.pr.)* on-line access
Zubringerverkehr *m* feeder traffic
~, **örtlicher** local haulage
Zucht *f* 1. breeding, rearing, farming *(animals)*; cultivation, growing *(plants)*; 2. breed, race, stock
Zuchtbuch *n* stud-bock
züchten to breed *(animals etc.)*; to grow, to cultivate *(plants etc.)*; to culture *(in artificial medium etc.)*
Züchter *m* breeder *(animals etc.)*, keeper *(bees etc.)*; grower *(plants etc.)*
Zuchttier *n* breeding animal
Züchtung *f* breeding farming *(animals etc.)*; growing, cultivation *(plants etc.)*; culture

Zuchtvieh *n* breeding cattle
Zuckerbäcker *m* confectioner
Zuckerbörse *f* sugar exchange
Zuckerfabrik *f* sugar factory
Zuckerindustrie *f* sugar industry
Zuckerraffinerie *f* sugar refinery
zuerkennen to award *(prizes etc.)*; *(jur)* to adjudicate
Zuerkennung *f* award *(prizes etc.)*; *(jur)* adjudication
Zufahrt *f* entrance; approach (road)
Zufall *m* chance, accident; coincidence; occurrence; *(stats)* random ⋄ **durch ~** by chance, accidentally, by accident; **etwas dem ~ überlassen** to leave s.th. to chance
zufällig chance, accidental
zufälligerweise by chance, incidentally, accidentally
Zufälligkeit *f* chance; contingency
Zufälligkeitsgrad *m* *(stats)* degree of randomness
Zufallsabweichung *f* *(stats)* random variable
Zufallsanfangszahl *f* *(stats)* random start
Zufallsanordnung *f* *(stats)* random order
Zufallsauswahl *f* *(stats)* random selection
Zufallsereignis *f* *(stats)* random event
Zufallsfehler *m* *(stats)* random error
~, reiner *(stats)* unbiassed error
Zufallsfolge *f* *(stats)* random series
Zufallsgesetz *n* law of probability
Zufallshandlung *f* inadvertent action
Zufallskomponente *f* *(stats)* random component
Zufallskurve *f* *(stats)* probability curve
Zufallsmoment *n* chance factor
Zufallsprozeß *n* *(stats)* random process
~, additiver *(stats)* additive [random walk] process
~, reiner *(stats)* pure random process
Zufallsstart *f s.* **Zufallsanfangszahl**
Zufallsstichprobe *f* *(stats)* random sample; *(stats)* probability sample
~, nichteingeschränkte *(stats)* unrestricted random sample
~, uneingeschränkte *s.* **~, nichteingeschränkte**
Zufallsstichprobenfehler *m* *(stats)* random sampling error
Zufallsstreuung *f* chance variation
Zufallsvariable *f* *(stats)* random variable
~, kanonische *(stats)* canonical variate
~, normale *(stats)* normal deviate
~, standardisierte *(stats)* unit normal variate
~, teilweise konsistente *(stats)* partially consistent observations
Zufallsveränderliche *f* *(stats)* random variable
~, diskrete *(stats)* discrete variate
~, endogene *(stats)* endogenous variate
~, exogene *(stats)* exogenous variate

~, kontinuierliche *(stats)* continuous variate
~, standardisierte *(stats)* standardized variate
Zufallsverteilung *f* *(stats)* random distribution
Zufallsweg *m* *(stats)* random walk
Zufallszahl *f* random number
Zufallszahlen *fpl* *(stats)* random sampling numbers
Zufallszuteilung *f* *(stats)* randomization
~, eingeschränkte *(stats)* restricted randomization
zufließen to accrue to *(profit etc. to s.o.)*
Zufluß *m* inflow, influx *(capital etc.)*; supply *(goods etc.)*
zufügen to add to; to do, to cause *(damage etc.)*
Zufuhr *f* supply; provisions; bringing up of supplies
zuführen to bring to; to procure, to supply; to convey, to feed, to conduct
Zuführung *f* supply; provision; feed; payment; allocation; addition
Zug *m* 1. train; 2. feature, trait; characteristic; 3. pull, tug; 4. migration *(birds etc.)*; 5. draught
~, direkter direct train
~, durchgehender through train
~, fahrplanmäßiger ordinary train
Zugabe *f* addition; extra; makeweight; *(com)* free gift
Zugang *m* 1. entrance, door; access; approach; 2. increase; accrual; in-payment; incoming stocks
~ von Arbeitskräften inflow [increase] of labour force [manpower]
Zugänge *mpl* additions *(to staff members etc.)*; *(acc)* accruals, receipts
zugänglich accessible; approachable; open to *(public etc.)* ⋄ **leicht ~** easily accessible [approachable]; **~ machen** to render accessible
Zugangsprozeß *m* birth process
~, reiner *(stats)* pure birth process
Zugangs- und Abgangsprozeß *m* *(stats)* birth-and-death process
Zugangs- und Abgangsrate *f* *(stats)* birth-and-death rate
Zugankunft *m* arrival of a train
zugeben 1. to admit, to give in; to confess; 2. to give [throw] into the bargain
zugegen present *(at meeting etc.)*
zugehen 1. to come to hand, to reach *(goods etc.)*; 2. to close
zugehören to belong to
zugehörig belonging to, appertaining to; accompanying
Zugehörigkeit *f* forming part of; membership *(institution etc.)*; relationship; attachment to a system
~ zu einer Gewerkschaft union membership

zugelassen allowed, permitted, authorized; admitted; licensed; *(st.ex.)* quoted, *(Am)* listed ◊ **nicht ~** unauthorized; not admitted; unlicensed; *(st.ex.)* not quoted, *(Am)* unlisted
zugesellen to associate with
zugestanden conceded, acknowledged; admitted
Zugeständnis *n* concession; compromise; admission *(wrong-doing etc.)* ◊ **ein ~ aussetzen** to withold a concession; **ein ~ machen** to make a concession, to stretch a point
~, steuerliches tax concession
Zugeständnisse *npl* concessions ◊ **preisliche ~ machen** to make price concessions; **~ zurücknehmen** to withdraw concessions
zugestehen to concede; to admit, to confess *(wrong-doing etc.)*, to own up *(mistake etc.)*
zugestellt delivered
zugeteilt allotted, allocated
Zugewanderter *m* newcomer; immigrant
Zugezogener *m* incomer
Zugfähre *f* train ferry
Zugfolge *f* train service [schedule] ◊ **die ~ ändern** to alter the running of trains
Zugfolgeverkürzung *f* increasing the number of trains
Zugkraft *f* attraction *(customers etc.)*; *(tech)* tractive force, power of traction
zugkräftig attractive, popular
zugrunde:
◊ **~ gehen** to perish; **~ gerichtet sein** to be ruined; **~ legen** to take as a basis (for); **~ liegen** to be the basis (of); **~ richten** to ruin, to go rack and ruin
Zug-um-Zug-Geschäft *n* (transaction on the basis of) cash on delivery
Zug-um-Zug-Zahlung *f s.* **Zug-um-Zug-Geschäft**
zugunsten to the advantage of; in favour of; for the benefit of ◊ **~ von** to the account of
zugute:
◊ **~ halten** to allow for, to take into consideration; **~ kommen lassen** to give (a person) the benefit of
Zugverbindung *f* train [rail] connection
Zugverkehr *m* train service; rail traffic ◊ **den ~ einschränken** to curtail [cut] the train service; **~ zwischen zwei Plätzen einrichten** to run a train service between two places
Zuhörer *m* listener, hearer, (member of the) audience
Zuhörerschaft *f* audience, listeners
~, anspruchsvolle critical audience
Zukauf *m* additional purchase
zukaufen to buy in addition
Zukunft *f* future, time to come; prospects ◊ **die ~ sicherstellen** to make provision for the future; **eine große ~ haben** to have great [fine, good] prospects (before one); **für die ~ vorsorgen** to save in anticipation of the future; **in ~** in future; hereafter, hereinafter *(in agreement etc.)*
~ eines Unternehmens business future
zukünftig future
Zukunftsaussichten *fpl* (future) prospects
Zukunftsplanung *f* forward planning
zuladen to put in additional load
Zuladung *f* additional load(ing)
Zulage *f* increase (in salary/wages); extra pay; allowance; addition ◊ **eine ~ bekommen** to get a rise in wages [salary]; **eine ~ geben** to give a rise in wages [salary]
~, produktionsunabhängige non-production bonus
zulassen to admit *(to an examination etc.)*; to permit *(use of s.th. etc.)*; to authorize *(trading etc.)*; to grant licence *(vehicles etc.)*; to register *(doctors etc.)*; to call to the bar *(barristers)* ◊ **wieder ~** to readmit
zulässig admissible, permissible, allowable
Zulässigkeit *f* admissibility
Zulassung *f* 1. admission, admittance *(to an examination etc.)*; permission *(of use of s.th. etc.)*; authorization *(trading etc.)*; granting licence; 2. licence *(vehicles etc.)*; registration *(doctors etc.)* ◊ **eine ~ beantragen** to apply for a licence [concession]; **eine ~ erwerben** to take out a licence; **eine ~ gewähren** to grant a concession; **eine ~ widerrufen** to revoke a licence; **sich eine ~ erschleichen** to obtain a licence under false pretences; **sich eine ~ geben lassen** *s.* **eine ~ erwerben**
~ zur zollfreien Wiedereinfuhr licence for duty-free reimport
Zulassungsanspruch *m* right of admission *(examination etc.)*
Zulassungsantrag *m* application for admission
zulassungsberechtigt admissible; qualified, eligible
Zulassungsberechtigung *f* qualification *(lawyer etc.)*
Zulassungsbescheinigung *f* licence, permit
~ eines Flugzeuges certificate of airworthiness
~ eines Schiffes certificate of seaworthiness
~ für Landfahrzeuge certificate of roadworthiness
Zulassungserfordernisse *npl* qualification requirements
Zulassungsgebühr *f* entrance [admission] fee *(examination etc.)*; entrance [admission] charge *(places of entertainment etc.)*
Zulassungsgesuch *n s.* **Zulassungsantrag**
Zulassungskarte *f* admission ticket [certificate]
Zulassungsnummer *f* licence number *(car etc.)*, permit number *(carriage of goods etc.)*

Zulassungsort *m* place (of issue)
Zulassungspapiere *npl* registration papers
Zulassungsprüfung *f* entrance examination; driving test *(car etc.)*
Zulassungsstelle *f* licensing office; *(st.ex.)* admission board
Zulassungsverfahren *n* licensing procedure
Zulassungsvoraussetzung *f* requirements for admission, qualification requirements; requirements to pass test *(driving licence etc.)*; membership qualification *(association etc.)*
Zulassungswettbewerb *m* competitive examination
Zulauf *m* crowd, rush, run ⋄ **~ haben** to be popular, to draw crowds
zulegen to put more to, to add to, to increase ⋄ **sich etwas ~** to get [buy, procure] s.th.
Zulieferant *m* subcontractor; supplier
Zulieferbetrieb *m* auxiliary enterprise, supplier, subcontractor [subcontracting firm]
Zuliefergarantie *f* guarantee of supply *(components etc.)*
Zulieferindustriezweig *m* supplier, subcontractor; complementary sector [branch]
zuliefern to supply *(raw material, components etc.)*
Zulieferung *f* supply *(raw material, components etc.)*
zumachen to close, to shut *(window, shop etc.)*; to close down (permanently) *(shop)*; to seal *(letters)*
zumessen to measure out; to allot, to assign *(task)*; to apportion *(share)*
Zunahme *f* increase (in), increment, rise *(prices etc.)*; growth (of) *(population etc.)*
Zunahmefaktor *m* growth factor
Zunahmerate *f* growth rate, rate of growth
zunehmen to increase, to rise *(prices etc.)*; to grow *(population etc.)*
zunehmend increasing; growing
Zunft *f* guild; corporation
zunutze:
⋄ **sich etwas ~ machen** to utilize s.th., to exploit s.th. for one's own purpose
zuordnen to attach to, to appoint to
Zuordnung *f* co-ordination; assignment
Zuordnungszahl *f (stats)* classification statistic
Zupfinstrumentenmacher *m* plucked instruments maker
zuraten to advise, to recommend
zurechnen to add; to attribute, to ascribe to, to impute; to include, to class
Zurechnung *f* addition; attribution, imputation; inclusion
zurechnungsfähig competent, responsible, of sound mind, accountable
Zurechnungsfähigkeit *f* responsibility, competence, accountability

zurechtweisen to reprimand, to rebuke
Zurechtweisung *f* reprimand, reproof, rebuke
zurück back; in arrears, behind; returned
zurückbegeben to return, to go back
zurückbehalten to detain; to keep back, to hold; to retain, to withhold
Zurückbehaltung *f* detention; retention, withholding
zurückbekommen to get back, to recover
zurückbelasten *(acc)* to charge back
zurückberufen to recall, to call back
zurückbezahlen to pay back, to repay, to refund, to discharge, to clear, to wipe off *(debt)*
zurückbringen to bring back, to recall
zurückdatieren to antedate
zurückerhalten to recover, to get back
zurückerlangen to recover, to get back, to regain
zurückerstatten to return, to restitute; to refund, to pay back *(money)*
zurückfließen to flow back
zurückfordern to claim back, to reclaim
zurückgeben to give back, to return; to restore, to restitute
zurückgehen to go down *(orders etc.)*, to fall off *(receipts etc.)*, to decline, to drop *(prices etc.)*, to deteriorate *(in value etc.)*, to recede *(flood etc.)*
zurückhalten to keep back; *(jur)* to restrain
zurückhaltend reserved; cautious, reluctant *(customer etc.)*; *(st.ex.)* flat, dead, dull, stagnant
Zurückhaltungsrecht *n* right of detention; retainer, lien on goods
Zurückkauf *m* 1. repurchase, buying back; 2. *(fin, ins)* redemption *(securities etc.)*; surrender of policy; *(fin)* callback
zurückkaufen to repurchase, to rebuy; to redeem; *(st.ex.)* to buy in
zurücklegen 1. to lay aside; to save, to put by; to earmark for; 2. to traverse; to complete, to attain *(age)*; to go through course
Zurücklegen *n (stats)* replacement
~, teilweises *(stats)* partial replacement
Zurücknahme *f* 1. taking back; 2. *(jur)* withdrawal *(action)*; revocation *(licence)*
zurücknehmen to take back, to withdraw, to retract; to revoke
zurückrufen to recall; to call back *(telephone)*; to withdraw
zurückschicken to send back, to return
zurücksetzen to lower, to reduce *(prices etc.)*
zurückstehen:
⋄ **hinter etwas/jmdm. ~** to be inferior to s.th./s.o.
zurückstellen to put back; to reserve; to set aside (as reserve); to lay [set] aside *(goods etc.)*; to postpone, to adjourn *(meeting etc.)*

zurückströmen s. zurückfließen
zurücktreten to retire; to resign
zurückvergüten to reimburse, to repay
zurückverkaufen to sell back
zurückverladen to reload; to reship
zurückverlangen to reclaim, to claim back
zurückweisen to reject, to refuse; *(st.ex.)* to dishonour
Zurückweisung *f* refusal, rejection
Zurückweisungslinie *f (stats)* rejection line
zurückziehen to withdraw; to cancel *(order etc.)*
Zusammenarbeit *f* co-operation
~, industrielle industrial co-operation
~, technisch-wissenschaftliche technological and scientific co-operation
zusammenarbeiten to co-operate; to work together
zusammenballen to concentrate; to aggregate
Zusammenballung *f* concentration; aggregation; pooling
zusammenfassen to summarize *(report etc.)*, to sum up *(narrative)*
Zusammenfassung *f* summary *(report etc.)*, résumé; synopsis
~ der Summen der Fehlerquadrate *(stats)* pooling of errors
~ von Klassen *(stats)* pooling of classes
~ von Prüfverfahren *(stats)* combination of tests
~ von Quadratsummen *(stats)* pooling of sums of squares
Zusammenhang *m* connection
zusammenhängen to be connected [linked] *(with s.th.)*
Zusammenhangsindex *m (stats)* index of connection
zusammenkaufen to buy up
zusammenlegen 1. to fold up *(papers etc.)*; 2. to merge *(enterprises etc.)*; to amalgamate, to consolidate *(shares etc.)*; to join *(plots of land etc.)*; to hold together *(meeting etc.)*; to club together, to pool one's money *(for a purpose)*
Zusammenlegung *f* merging, merger *(enterprises etc.)*; amalgamation, consolidation *(shares etc.)*; joining *(plots of land etc.)*; holding together *(meeting etc.)*
zusammenschalten to interconnect; *(d.pr.)* to patch *(software)*
Zusammenschaltung *f* interconnection
zusammensetzen to put together; to compose, to make up
Zusammensetzen *n* construction, formation
Zusammensetzung *f* composition; combination; structure
~, organische organic composition *(capital)*
Zusammensetzverfahren *n* synthesis
zusammenstellen to put together; to arrange *(s.th. according to a pattern)*; to compile *(data, report etc.)*; to draw up *(timetable etc.)*; to make up *(list)*; to draft *(speech etc.)*; to assemble *(group)*
Zusammenstellung *f* putting together; arranging *(s.th. according to a pattern)*; compiling, compilation *(data, report etc.)*; drawing up *(timetable etc.)*; making up *(list)*; drafting *(speech etc.)*; assembling *(group)*
zusammentreffen to meet, to meet each other; to coincide; to adjoin
Zusammentreffen *n* encounter; coincidence, concurrence; *(stats)* matching
Zusatzabkommen *n* supplementary agreement
Zusatzbedingungen *fpl* additional conditions; supplementary clause(s)
Zusatzbesteuerung *f* surtax
Zusatzgewinn *m* extra [additional] profit
Zusatzkosten *pl* additional [extra] cost(s)
Zusatzkredit *m* supplementary credit
~, planmäßiger planned supplementary credit
~, planwidriger unplanned supplementary credit
Zusatzlohn *m* wage supplement, extra wages
Zusatzprotokoll *n* supplementary protocol
Zusatzprovision *f* additional commission
Zusatzrente *f* supplementary [additional] pension
Zusatzspeicher *m (d.pr.)* backing (auxiliary) store, extension memory; extra data storage
Zusatzsteuer *f* supplementary tax, surtax
Zusatztarif *m* additional [extra] rate of transport *(goods)*, extra fare *(passengers)*
Zusatzurlaub *m* extra holiday
Zusatzvergütung *f* additional [extra] remuneration
Zusatzversicherung *f* additional [supplementary] insurance
Zusatzvertrag *m* additional [supplementary] contract [agreement]
Zuschlag *m* surcharge, additional [extra] charge ⋄ einen ~ zahlen to pay extra charges
Zuschlagsgröße *f* amount of additional charge
Zuschlagskalkulation *f (acc)* accounting by items, indirect calculation
Zuschlagszoll *m* additional duty
Zuschuß *m* subsidy; grant; extra allowance *(paid to individuals)*
~, staatlicher government [state] subsidy
Zuschußbedarf *m* central budget allocation *(to close the gap in local budgets)*
Zuschußfinanzierung *f* subsidy financing
Zustand *m* condition, state; circumstances, state of affairs; position, situation; status *(legal, political etc.)* ⋄ in unbeschädigtem ~ in an undamaged condition [state]
~, ordnungsgemäßer proper [perfect] condition, good order

~, **technischer** technical condition
~, **vertragsloser** situation [state of affairs] in the absence of contracts
Zuständigkeit *f* competence; responsibility; powers; *(jur)* jurisdiction
zustellen to deliver *(mail, newspapers etc.)*
Zustellgebühr *f* delivery charge
Zustellung *f* delivery, handing over; *(jur)* writ
Zustellungsurkunde *f (jur)* writ of summons
Zustellungsvermerk *m* delivery note *(confirming delivery of post)*
zustimmen to agree to, to consent, to assent to
Zustimmung *f* agreement, consent
~, **schriftliche** written consent
Zustrom *m* influx *(people)*; stream *(visitors)*; inflow *(money etc.)*
Zuteilbarkeit *f (stats)* stratification
zuteilen to allot, to allocate, to apportion; to ration
Zuteilung *f* allocation, apportioning; quota; ration
~ **der Unterschichten** *(stats)* control of substrata
zuverlässig reliable, dependable; authentic *(information etc.)*
Zuverlässigkeit *f* reliability, dependability; authenticity *(information etc.)*
Zuverlässigkeitskoeffizient *m (stats)* reliability coefficient
Zuverlässigkeitsprüfung *f* verification, reliability test
Zuwachs *m* growth; increment, increase, accretion
Zuwachsdaten *pl (d.pr.)* incremental data
Zuwachsrate *f* rate of increase
zuwandern to immigrate
Zuwanderung *f* immigration
zuweisen to assign; to allot, to allocate, to apportion; to grant, to allow
Zuweisung *f* allocation, assignment *(budgetary means etc.)*
Zuweisungsanweisung *f (d.pr.)* assignment statement
zuwenden to turn to [towards]; to switch over to; to devote to
Zuwendung *f* allowance, benefit; allocation; grant; donation
~, **soziale** social benefit(s)
Z-Verteilung *f (stats)* z-distribution
Zwang *m* compulsion, coercion; force; constraint; (moral) obligation; pressure
~, **außerökonomischer** non-economic pressure
~, **ökonomischer** economic pressure [necessity]
zwangsbewirtschaftet rationed *(goods, food)*
Zwangsbewirtschaftung *f* rationing *(goods, food etc.)*
Zwangsverkauf *m* compulsory sale

Zwanzig-Prozent-Werte *mpl (stats)* quintiles
zweckbestimmt appropriated, earmarked for
Zweckbestimmung *f* appropriation; earmarking *(funds etc.)*
Zweckbindung *f* earmarking *(funds etc.)*
zweckentfremden to use *(s.th.)* for a purpose other than originally intended ⋄ **ein Zimmer** ~ to convert a room (to office use)
zweckgebunden appropriated; earmarked
Zweckgebundenheit *f s.* **Zweckbestimmung**
Zwecksparen *n* special-purpose saving
Zweideutigkeitsmaß *n (stats)* coefficient of alienation
Zweidritteldeckung *f* two-thirds cover [security]
Zwei-Ebenen-Planung *f* two-level planning
Zweiersystem *n (d.pr.)* binary scale of notation
Zwei-Faktor-Theorie *f (stats)* two-factor theory
Zweig *m* branch *(national economy etc.)*
~, **führender** leading [key] branch
Zweigbetrieb *m* branch enterprise, subsidiary
Zweigbilanz *f* branch balance sheet
Zweigfonds *m* branch fund
Zweiggruppe *f* group of branches *(industry etc.)*
Zweiggruppierung *f* grouping of branches *(industry etc.)*
Zweigklassifikation *f* classification of branches *(industry etc.)*
Zweigklassifizierung *f s.* **Zweigklassifikation**
Zweigleitung *f* branch management
Zweigmethodik *f* specific regulations in a branch *(for planning etc.)*
Zweigmodell *n* branch model
Zweigniederlassung *f s.* **Zweigbetrieb**
Zweigordnung *f s.* **Zweigmethodik**
Zweigperspektivplan *m* branch perspective plan
Zweigprinzip *n* branch principle of managing industries
Zweigprognose *f* forecast [prognosis] of branch development
Zweigprogramm *n* branch development programme
Zweigrentabilität *f* (industrial) branch profitability
Zweigressourcen *fpl* (industrial) branch resources
zweigspezifisch specific (with respect to a branch)
Zweigstelle *f* branch (office)
Zweigstruktur *f* branch structure *(economy, industry etc.)*
Zweigverflechtungsbilanz *f* branch input--output table
Zweigverflechtungsmodell *n* branch input--output model
Zweikreissystem *n (d.pr.)* two-circuit system
Zwei-mal-zwei-Einteilung *f (stats)* double dichotomy

Zwei-Produkten-Modell *n* two-product model
Zweiphasenplanung *f* two-phase [two-stage] planning
Zweireihenkorrelation *f (stats)* biserial correlation
Zweischichtensystem *n* two-shift system
Zweiteilung *f (stats)* dichotomy
Zweitlieferant *m* subcontractor; subsupplier; *(d.pr.)* second source
Zweitschrift *f* copy, duplicate
Zweitspeicher *m (d.pr.)* secondary store [memory]
Zwischenabschluß *m* interim balance sheet
zwischenbetrieblich inter-plant, inter-enterprise; inter-farm
Zwischenbilanz *f* interim result; interim (financial) statement
Zwischenfruchtanbau *m* intercrop
zwischengenossenschaftlich inter-co-operative
Zwischengruppenvarianz *f (stats)* between--groups variance
Zwischenhafen *m* intermediate port
Zwischenhandel *m* intermediate trade, commission business; wholesale trade
Zwischenhändler *m* middleman; agent; wholesale trader; intermediary ⋄ **ohne ~ verkaufen** to sell direct
Zwischenkalkulation *f* interim calculation
Zwischenklassenvarianz *f (stats)* interclass variance
Zwischenkontrolle *f* interim checking [follow-up]
Zwischenkredit *m* interim credit
Zwischenlager *n* intermediate store [warehouse]
Zwischenlagerung *f* intermediate storage
Zwischenlösung *f* interim solution

Zwischenprodukt *n* semi-finished [intermediate] product
Zwischenprogramm *n (d.pr.)* interlude
Zwischenspeicher *m (d.pr.)* temporary (information) store [storage]
zwischenspeichern *(d.pr.)* to store temporarily, to buffer, to latch; to dump
Zwischenspeicherung *f (d.pr.)* intermediate (memory) storage, temporary storage
zwischenstaatlich inter-government(al), international
Zwischensumme *f* subtotal; *(d.pr.)* batch total
Zwischenträgermontage *f (d.pr.)* beam tape assembly
Zwischenverarbeitung *f (d.pr.)* intermediate processing
Zwischenverbrauch *m* intermediate consumption
Zwischenverbraucher *m* intermediate consumer
Zwischenverkauf *m* prior [intermediate] sale
zwischenzweiglich inter-branch
Zwischenzyklus *m (d.pr.)* intermediate cycle
Zyklendauer *f* duration of a cycle
~, minimale minimum duration of a cycle
Zyklendiagramm *n* cycle diagram
Zyklus *m* cycle
~, dreiteiliger *(d.pr.)* three-part cycle
Zyklusarbeit *f* cyclical work
Zyklusverfügbarkeit *f (d.pr.)* cycle availability
Zykluszählung *f (d.pr.)* cycle counting
Zykluszeit *f* cycle time [period]
~ des Speichers *(d.pr.)* cycle time of the memory *(from the beginning of one access cycle to the next)*
Zylinderadresse *f (d.pr.)* cylinder address

Abkürzungen
Abbreviations

abbr	abbreviation	
	Abkürzung	
acc	accounting	
	Rechnungswesen	
agric	agriculture	
	Landwirtschaft	
Am	American English	
	amerikanisches Englisch	
a.p.	a person	
	jemand	
approx.	approximately	
	in etwa, ungefähr	
bank	banking	
	Bankwesen	
build	building	
	Bauwesen	
cat	catering	
	Gaststättenwesen, Hotelwesen	
coll	colloquial	
	umgangssprachlich	
com	commerce	
	Handel	
cust	customs	
	Zollwesen	
d.pr.	data processing	
	Datenverarbeitung	
e.g.	for example	
	zum Beispiel	
esp.	especially	
	besonders	
etc.	etcetera	
	und so weiter	
f	feminine	
	Femininum	
fin	finance	
	Finanzwesen	
for	forestry	
	Forstwirtschaft	
for tr	foreign trade	
	Außenhandel	
hist	history, historical	
	Geschichte, geschichtlich	
home tr	home trade	
	Binnenhandel	